P9-CAM-166

Fodor's 2011

IRELAND

Fodor's Travel Publications · New York, Toronto, London, Sydney, Auckland
www.fodors.com

Be a Fodor's Correspondent

Share your trip with Fodor's

Our latest guidebook to Ireland—now in full color—owes its success to travelers like you. Throughout, you'll find photographs submitted by members of Fodors.com to our "Show Us Your Ireland" photo contest. On page 627 you'll find the grand prize-winning photograph by Fodors.com member "Traveling." It shows the famous Carrick-a-Rede rope bridge, a sight found on the Giant's Causeway coast of Northern Ireland. The tiny bridge spans a 60-foot gap between the Antrim mainland and the Carrick-a-Rede islet, offering a thrilling walk over the sea that, to quote the winner, was "not for the faint of heart, but so worth the journey."

We are especially proud of this color edition. No other guide to Ireland is as up to date or has as much practical planning information, along with hundreds of color photographs and illustrated maps. We've also included "Word of Mouth" quotes from travelers who shared their experiences with others on our forums. If you're inspired and can plan a better trip because of this guide, we've done our job.

We invite you to join the travel conversation: Your opinion matters to us and to your fellow travelers. Come to Fodors.com to plan your trip, share an experience, ask a question, submit a photograph, post a review, or write a trip report. Tell our editors about your trip. They want to know what went well and how we can make this guide even better. Share your opinions at our feedback center at fodors.com/feedback, or email us at editors@fodors.com with the subject line "Ireland Editor." You might find your comments published in a future Fodor's guide. We look forward to hearing from you.

Happy traveling!

Tim Jarrell, Publisher

FODOR'S IRELAND 2011
Editor: Robert I. C. Fisher

Editorial Contributors: Paul Clements, Andrew Collins, Alannah Hopkin, Anto Howard

Production Editor: Evangelos Vasilakis
Maps & Illustrations: David Lindroth, Mark Stroud, *cartographers;* Bob Blake, Rebecca Baer, *map editors;* William Wu, *information graphics*
Design: Fabrizio La Rocca, *creative director;* Guido Caroti, Siobhan O'Hare, *art directors;* Tina Malaney, Nora Rosansky, Chie Ushio, Jessica Walsh, Ann McBride, *designers;* Melanie Marin, *senior picture editor*
Cover Photo: (Dunguaire Castle, Kinvara, Galway): SIME/eStock Photo
Production Manager: Amanda Bullock

ISBN 978-1-4000-0490-4

ISSN 0071-6464

SPECIAL SALES
This book is available at special discounts for bulk purchases for sales promotions or premiums. Special editions, including personalized covers, excerpts of existing books, and corporate imprints, can be created in large quantities for special needs. For more information, write to Special Markets/Premium Sales, 1745 Broadway, MD 6-2, New York, New York 10019, or e-mail specialmarkets@randomhouse.com.

AN IMPORTANT TIP & AN INVITATION
Although all prices, opening times, and other details in this book are based on information supplied to us at press time, changes occur all the time in the travel world, and Fodor's cannot accept responsibility for facts that become outdated or for inadvertent errors or omissions. So **always confirm information when it matters,** especially if you're making a detour to visit a specific place. Your experiences—positive and negative— matter to us. If we have missed or misstated something, **please write to us.** We follow up on all suggestions. Contact the Ireland editor at editors@fodors.com or c/o Fodor's at 1745 Broadway, New York, NY 10019.

PRINTED IN CHINA

10 9 8 7 6 5 4 3 2 1

CONTENTS

Fodor's Features

6 < **Contents**

ABOUT
THIS BOOK

Our Ratings

Sometimes you find terrific travel experiences and sometimes they just find you. But usually the burden is on you to select the right combination of experiences. That's where our ratings come in.

As travelers we've all discovered a place so wonderful that its worthiness is obvious. And sometimes that place is so experiential that superlatives don't do it justice: you just have to be there to know. These sights, properties, and experiences get our highest rating, **Fodor's Choice,** indicated by orange stars throughout this book.

Black stars highlight sights and properties we deem **Highly Recommended,** places that our writers, editors, and readers praise again and again for consistency and excellence.

By default, there's another category: any place we include in this book is by definition worth your time, unless we say otherwise. And we will.

Disagree with any of our choices? Care to nominate a place or suggest that we rate one more highly? Visit our feedback center at www.fodors.com/feedback.

Budget Well

Hotel and restaurant price categories from ¢ to $$$$ are defined in the opening pages of each chapter. For attractions, we always give standard adult admission fees; reductions are usually available for children, students, and senior citizens. Want to pay with plastic? **AE, D, DC, MC, V** following restaurant and hotel listings indicate if American Express, Discover, Diners Club, MasterCard, and Visa are accepted.

Restaurants

Unless we state otherwise, restaurants are open for lunch and dinner daily. We mention dress only when there's a specific requirement and reservations only when they're essential or not accepted—it's always best to book ahead.

Hotels

Hotels have private bath, phone, TV, and air-conditioning, unless stated otherwise, and operate on the European Plan (aka EP, meaning without meals), unless we specify that they use the Continental Plan (CP, with a Continental breakfast), Breakfast Plan (BP, with a full breakfast), or Modified American Plan (MAP, with breakfast and dinner). We always list facilities but not whether

you'll be charged an extra fee to use them, so when pricing accommodations, find out what's included.

Listings
★	Fodor's Choice
★	Highly recommended
✉	Physical address
✛	Directions or Map coordinates
⌂	Mailing address
☎	Telephone
🖷	Fax
⊕	On the Web
✍	E-mail
🎫	Admission fee
⊙	Open/closed times
Ⓜ	Metro stations
▭	Credit cards

Hotels & Restaurants
🏨	Hotel
⇤	Number of rooms
⚴	Facilities
ⵙⵓ	Meal plans
✗	Restaurant
⌂	Reservations
🛆	Dress code
⌇	Smoking
⌁	BYOB

Outdoors
🏌	Golf
⛺	Camping

Other
☺	Family-friendly
⇨	See also
✉	Branch address
☞	Take note

Experience
Ireland

WHAT'S NEW

From Boom to . . . ?

After a decade of riding the back of the explosive "Celtic Tiger" economic boom, the party (some called it an orgy) is officially over. Not so long ago, a two-bedroom terrace house in Dublin was selling for $600,000 and the capital city was buying more BMWs than Bavaria. By 2008, the hung-over country was waking up as if from a drunken dream from an era where house-selling was the ponzi scheme of choice and a consumerist ethos of spend, spend, spend had replaced the discredited church as the national religion. The ongoing negative fallout is familiar the world over: property prices have nearly halved, unemployment has trebled, and "the recession" has replaced "the boom" as the most boring thing to bring up in the midst of a good pub conservation. But even though it all ended in tears, the decade-long period of rapid growth and expansion changed the face of timeless Ireland forever. The paw print of the "Tiger" is everywhere: brash modern buildings; state-of-the-art highways; well-educated, confident (some might say cocky) young people; a slew of new immigrants from all corners of the globe; and the highest mobile phone usage in Europe—the Ireland of idyllic postcard simplicity (if it ever existed) is truly gone forever, and with it, all those images of red-haired colleens leading turf-laden donkeys to thatched cottages.

Happily, beneath all the innovations, credit card bills, and high-speed text messaging, that ageless, magical, Irish thing endures. Ireland's landscape is still ancient, empty, and breathtakingly beautiful. History, drama, and passion ooze out of every ruined castle wall and old Irish poem. Like the Janus stones and sheelana-gigs of its pre-Christian past, the real

Ireland is two-faced, embracing the past while focusing on the future. In fact there is an undercurrent of opinion in the country that the end of the "Tiger" might, in the long term, help to save a lot of what is best about Ireland. Greed is no longer good, and there is a movement back towards some of the simpler things in life. There has been an explosion in vegetable gardens, with community allotments springing up on abandoned development sites. The curse of hastily built, ugly holiday bungalows blighting Ireland's most pristine natural wilderness sites has been banished and Dublin's fragile cityscape won't be assaulted by yet another block of Lego-like, overpriced apartments.

But it is not only the landscape that's rediscovering itself after years of abuse. The essence of what makes Ireland a special place to live and visit is the warmth of its people and their ability to find time for each other and strangers. These ideas of time and friendliness were half-buried under the 24/7 commuter rush and euro-fuelled mania that swept across the country in the boom years. Even the famed Irish sense of humor seemed to get lost in too much boorish money-talk. It's dangerous to romanticize about any benefits of a deep recession, but when the recovery comes perhaps the country will make sure it doesn't lose its head again, remembering to value the less-ephemeral, more solid wonders of the old, green island on the edge of Europe.

Are We Too Dear, Dear?

In tandem with easier comparison to other European countries through common usage of the euro comes the harsh reality of just how expensive Ireland became in recent years. While the economic downturn has put a stop to the

worst price gouging, some Irish businesses have been slower than others to re-adjust prices. Okay, so the average house has halved in price, but what about a cup of coffee? Well, a double espresso still runs three euros in some Dublin bars, but just one euro in Milan. Hotels have been the quickest to react to the slump, with massive discounts across the board along with the opportunity to haggle over quoted prices. Swanky, high-end Dublin accommodations are up to 30% cheaper. Restaurants and cafés, on the other hand, have been tardy in taking the eraser to their often exorbitant price lists, but are slowly starting to get the message.

How about dinner for two in a restaurant with a bottle of house wine? What costs $60 in Paris can cost up to $90 in the Emerald Isle. Pub owners, always suspected of greediness by the local imbibers, have deemed it good enough to merely freeze the price of a pint of Guinness at around $4.50. Wanna talk DVDs, clothes, shoes? Prices are falling, but not fast enough to make them bargains. But keep your eyes peeled for the endless series of sales and closing-down offers springing up all over the shops with posh addresses. Overall Ireland is not cheap by any standards, and that includes Tokyo, London, and New York, but prices are falling and in a couple of years they should be competitive with the rest of Europe.

A Hundred Thousand Chinese Welcomes

Does part of your Irish itinerary include discourse with a genuine local barman full of wit and wisdom regarding his native land? You may have to search far and wide to find this endangered species in 2010 as most pubs now have at least two or three recently arrived immigrants

dispensing tipples. Even with the recent economic crash, over 300,000 immigrants call Ireland home with Chinese, Poles, Lithuanians, Hungarians, Latvians, and Nigerians being among the most common. The hospitality industry tapped this new immigrant wave—perhaps just as well, since most Irish people have little interest in the unsocial hours of the bar and hotel business anymore.

The new emigrants are efficient, courteous, and good humored—but they've got a long way to go to match the caustic, all-knowing info you'll get from an Irish barman. There are still quite a few left, though: catch 'em while you can.

Mary (Cough), I Think I Love You (Cough, Cough)

Though famous for their rebelliousness through the centuries, the Irish took to the pub smoking ban with a meekness that prompted many acres of newsprint. Now everybody's getting on board the "no butts" bandwagon—France, the United Kingdom, and Italy are presently looking to enforce similar bans. But maybe the acceptance of the smoking ban is not entirely about the health concerns and clean air—it's also brought a whole new angle to the boy-meets-girl romance dance.

Faced with die-hard smokers who threatened to stay home, pub owners rushed to fill every inch of sidewalk with special open-air sections devoted to consumers of the demon weed. Warming heaters, outdoor seating, and overhead plasma TV screens followed. Soon all the action moved outdoors—a whole new ballgame for Irish folk. Frequently, pub bands play to 50 people indoors, while 150 gaze in from the sidewalk. Around the office water cooler next morning can be heard:

"I don't even like smoking, but it's where all the cute guys are." Masters of making the best of a bad situation, the Irish have turned the smoking debate into a dating agency where dubious intentions make perfect bedfellows with bad habits.

The Not So Long and Not So Winding Road

One concrete—and that's literally concrete—Celtic Tiger monument you'll celebrate on a visit to Ireland is the vastly improved road network. In the last year alone a bunch of top-quality motorways have finally opened in their entirety and immediately hacked a large chunk off driving times between Dublin and all the major cities. Cork is suddenly almost an hour nearer, Waterford 45 minutes, Galway 40 minutes, and you can now get to Belfast in less than two hours. "M" is the magic letter signifying these new motorways, and they are all connected up to each other and to the smaller, but also revamped, national roads (distinguished by the letter "N"). A real pleasure in Ireland is driving on the small, winding country roads, but they were no way to get from one urban center to another. You can still enjoy these smaller roads with the fecund hedgerows and beautiful views on day trips from the cities or when you are in no hurry to get where you're going.

Knead Me, Mould Me . . . Slowly

Up to the 1990s, Ireland took a simple line on food preparation—fry it, boil it, or roast it, within an inch of its life. As cheap fares on Ryanair shuttled Irish travelers to France and Italy for weekends, a different attitude began to prevail about food and how best to prepare it. So long spuds and gravy, *Benevento* pasta carbonara. More recently, Ireland has joined the Slow Food Movement (⊕ *www.slowfoodireland.com*), an international network of people interested in the promotion, production, and consumption of good food. Begun in Italy, the movement has strong links all over the world with a well-established presence in Ireland supporting food artisans, their handmade produce, and the skills they embody. Many of the weekend food markets springing up in Irish country towns are directly connected to this epicurean phenomenon. *Slow Dublin*, written by Anto Howard, the author of the Dublin chapter, is a great introduction to all things Slow in Dublin.

Getting It Right, Eco-Style

Irish engineering and its relationship with the fragile earth has come in for a fair amount of shtick in recent years—new suburbs with zero green spaces, exploding cities precariously balanced on 100-year-old sewage systems, and roads with the worst traffic chaos in Europe. If you're ever stuck for a pub opener, ask about the state of the roads then move quickly out of range from the bile that will inevitably pour forth.

How pleasant then that the Atlantic Edge visitor center at the Cliffs of Moher (⊕ *www.cliffsofmoher.com*) opened to universal applause a few years ago. The building is sunk into the contours of the land and covered by a grass hillside. The center uses renewable energy sources such as solar energy and a ground source heat pump. Visitors enter via a viewing ramp that provides access to the central floor and its themed areas exploring different elements of the cliffs: Ocean, Rock, Nature, and Man. The tour continues from the central dome via a winding tunnel that evokes the many caves of the area to a theater housing a virtual reality cliff-face adventure called, "The Ledge."

WHEN TO GO

In summer the weather is pleasant, the days are long (daylight lasts until after 10 in late June and July), and the countryside is green. But there are crowds in popular holiday spots, and prices for accommodations are at their peak. As British and Irish school vacations overlap from late June to mid-September, vacationers descend on popular coastal resorts in the south, west, and east. Unless you're determined to enjoy the short (July and August) swimming season, it's best to visit Ireland outside peak travel months. Fall and spring are good times to travel (late September can be dry and warm, although the weather can be unpredictable). Seasonal hotels and restaurants close from early or mid-November until mid-March or Easter. During this off-season, prices are lower than in summer, but your selection is limited, and many minor attractions close. St. Patrick's Week gives a focal point to a spring visit, but some Americans may find the saint's-day celebrations a little less enthusiastic than the ones back home. Dublin, however, has a weekend-long series of activities, including a parade and the Lord Mayor's Ball. If you're planning an Easter visit, don't forget that most theaters close from Thursday to Sunday of Holy Week (the week preceding Easter), and all bars and restaurants, except those serving hotel residents, close on Good Friday. Many hotels arrange Christmas packages. Mid-November to mid-February is either too cold or too wet for all but the keenest golfers, although some of the coastal links courses are playable.

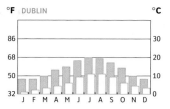

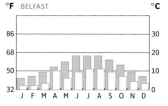

WHAT'S WHERE

Numbers correspond to chapters.

2 Dublin. A transformed city since the days of O'Casey and Joyce, Ireland's capital may have replaced its legendary tenements with modern high-rises but its essential spirit remains intact. One of Europe's most popular city-break destinations, it has art, culture, Georgian architecture, and, of course, hundreds of pubs where conversation and vocal dexterity continue to flourish within an increasingly multicultural mix. Get spirited (pun intended) at the Guinness Brewery, "Rock 'n Stroll" your way through hip Temple Bar, and be illuminated by the *Book of Kells* at Trinity College's great library.

3 Dublin Environs. The counties outside the Pale are a treasure trove of history, monastic settlements, ancient tombs, battlefields, and peaceful valleys only an hour from the hubbub of the capital's center. From the lush greenery of Kildare and Wicklow, to the mythology and traditions of Meath and Louth, the historic timeline encompasses many of the pivotal pre-Christian and early Church locales of Ireland's past. Listen for ancient echoes at the Hill of Tara, hike into prehistory at Newgrange, and opt for opulence at Castletown House.

4 The Midlands. Overlooked by many visitors due to the region's relative absence of 'Wow!' factor attractions, this verdant oasis of bog and lake harks back to the simpler, and slower, life of Ireland 40 years ago. Friendly, almost shy natives, old-style pubs, unspoiled vistas and walks, plus a wealth of historic ruins make for a relaxing adventure into the way we were. Tree-hug one of the great yews at Tullynally Gardens, lift your spirits at Clonmacnoise, and take a river cruise down the Shannon.

5 The Southeast. Ireland's sunniest corner (with almost double the national average), the coastal counties have long been the favored hideaway of Dublin folk on vacation. Quiet seaside villages, country houses, and some of the nation's best land make for easy access en route to Cork or Kerry. Inland, counties like Kilkenny and Tipperary offer a lion's share of history and important monuments in the main towns, Wexford and Waterford. Follow in the footsteps of St. Patrick at the Rock of Cashel, dig the ducal lifestyle at Lismore, and romp in the brisk waters of the pristine beaches around the fishing village of Ardmore.

6 The Southwest. The counties of Kerry and Limerick have sights that top every tourist's must-see list. The most brazenly scenic coastal drive in the land, the Ring of Kerry, will use up your entire flash card in a jiffy! While there, take a wet and wonderful ride out to the sea-wrapped Skellig islands, whose twin peaks rise out of the sea. The Gap of Dunloe lets you walk through the heart of Killarney's purple mountains and cross the glittering blue lake of Killarney. And don't forget to have your Nikon handy for Ireland's prettiest village, Adare. Everywhere, the glories of Ireland's coastline combine to paint a canvas that still casts a potent spell upon the stranger.

MAYO

Achill Island

Clare Island

Clew Bay

Inishturk

Inishbofin

Lough Corrib

Oileáin Árainn (Aran Islands)

Galway B

Kilrush

Mouth of the Shannon

Listowel

Tralee

Corca Dhuibne (Dingle Peninsula)

Blasket Islands

Dingle Bay

Killarney

Skellig Rocks

Iveragh Peninsula

KERRY

6

Kenmare Bay

Beara Peninsula

Bantry Bay

Mizen Head

Malin Head

Toraigh
(Tory Island)

Rathlin Island

Ariann Mhor
(Aranmore Island)

Gweebarra
Bay

Portrush

Coleraine

SCOTLAND
(United Kingdom)

North Channel

Derry City
DERRY

ANTRIM

Ballymena

Larne

Letterkenny

DONEGAL

Strabane

Island Magee

Belfast Lough

Donegal
Town

Omagh

Cookstown

Lough
Neagh

BELFAST

Newtownards

Donegal
Bay

Ballyshannon

Lower
Lough Erne

TYRONE

Dungannon

DOWN

Killala
Bay

Sligo
Bay

LEITRIM

FERMANACH

Upper
Lough Erne

Monaghan
City

Armagh City

ARMAGH

Newry

Newcastle

Ballina

Sligo Town

SLIGO

MONAGHAN

Cavan

Dundalk

Lough
Conn

Castlebar

ROSCOMMON

CAVAN

LOUTH

Dundalk Bay

Lough
Mask

Knock

River Shannon

Longford

Drogheda

LONGFORD

MEATH

Galway
Bay

GALWAY

Ballinasloe

WESTMEATH

Mullingar

4

Athlone

3

DUBLIN

2

DUBLIN

Galway City

OFFALY

Naas

Dún Laoghaire

Birr

KILDARE

Bray *Irish Sea*

REPUBLIC OF IRELAND

Portlaoise

WICKLOW

Wicklow

LAOIS

Athy

Ennis

Nenagh

Roscrea

CLARE

Shannon

TIPPERARY

Kilkenny
City

Arklow

Limerick

Thurles

CARLOW

Gorey

LIMERICK City

KILKENNY

Newcastle
West

Tipperary
Town

Cashel

5

WEXFORD

Mallow

Farahy

Clonmel

Carrick-on-Suir

Wexford Town

WATERFORD

Waterford

CORK

Midleton

Youghal

St. George's Channel

Cork City

Cobh

Kinsale

Skibbereen

0   50 mi

0   50 km

WHAT'S WHERE

7 **County Cork.** After exploring the delights of Cork City—museums, lively pubs, quirky cafés, and lots of good music, trad and otherwise—use it as a base to explore Ireland's largest county, as nearby everyone heads to get the gift of gab by kissing the famous Blarney Stone. Get your fill of five-star scenery by traveling east to Shanagarry—teach yourself good taste at Ballymaloe House, pioneer of the new Irish cuisine. Due south is the "Irish St-Tropez," fashionable Kinsale, while westward lies Bantry, one of Ireland's finest stately homes which sits atop a breathtaking bluff over Bantry Bay. From here a cliff-top road with stunning views leads to ruggedly beautiful Glengarriff.

8 **County Clare, Galway, and the Aran Islands.** Set with postcard-perfect villages like Doolin, the lunar landscape of the Burren, and the towering Cliffs of Moher (they'll give you a new understanding of the word "awesome"), County Clare is pure tourist gold. For a complete change of pace, head to nearby Galway City: one of Ireland's liveliest, it has a compact historic center bursting with artistic energy and a lively pub culture. This is also the place to organize your trip to the Oileáin Árainn (Aran Islands), three outposts of Gaelic civilization, which still have a strong whiff of the "old ways"—and not just the whiff of turf smoke.

9 **Connemara and County Mayo.** With the most westerly seaboard in Europe, this region remains a place apart—the most Irish part of Ireland. Connemara is an almost uninhabited landscape of misty bogland, studded with deep blue lakes under huge Atlantic skies, and distant purple hills: painters and photographers have strived for generations to capture the ever-changing light. Nearby is the delightful village of Cong, setting for *The Quiet Man*, where fetching ivy-covered thatched cottages contrast with the baronial splendor of Ashford Castle. For bright lights, head to Clifden and Westport, both lively small towns of great charm.

10 **The Northwest.** Sligo, Leitrim, and Donegal are homelands of rugged, self-sufficient people and roads where wandering sheep and cows are still the norm. Weatherwise, the area gets more than its fair share of the elements—a condition more than compensated for in its warm welcomes. Take a poetry break beside Yeats's grave near Ben Bulben, discover hidden Glencolumbkille, and immerse yourself in Irish in Sligo town.

11 **Northern Ireland.** This region has positively bloomed since the peace dividend of recent times, which finally nailed the coffin lid upon "the Troubles." From the beauty of Antrim's coastline to the vibrant cultural renaissance of Derry and Belfast, Northern Ireland has finally emerged from the yoke of its sectarian past into a present full of promise and possibility. Cross the Giant's Causeway, slide into a cozy snug in a pub on Belfast's Golden Mile, and trail after Eire's "wee folk" in the shimmery Glens of Antrim.

MAYO

9

Achill Island
Clare Island
Clew Bay
Inishturk
Inishbofin

Lough Corrib

Oileáin Árainn
(Aran Islands)
Galway

Kilrush

Mouth of the Shannon
Listowel
Tralee
Corca Dhuibne
(Dingle Peninsula)
Blasket Islands
Dingle Bay
Killarney
Iveragh KERRY
Peninsula
Skellig Rocks
Beara Peninsula
Kenmare Bay
Bantry Bay
Mizen Head

Malin Head

Rathlin Island

Toraigh
(Tory Island)

Portrush

SCOTLAND
(United Kingdom)

Coleraine

Derry City

ANTRIM

Ballymena

Larne

Island Magee

Ariann Mhor
(Aranmore Island)

Letterkenny

DERRY

NORTHERN
IRELAND
(United Kingdom)

11

Belfast Lough

Gweebarra
Bay

DONEGAL

Strabane

Omagh

Cookstown

Lough
Neagh

BELFAST

Newtownards

Donegal
Town

TYRONE

Dungannon

DOWN

Donegal
Bay

Ballyshannon

Lower
Lough Erne

10

FERMANAGH

Armagh City

Killala
Bay

Sligo
Bay

LEITRIM

Upper
Lough Erne

Monaghan
City

ARMAGH

Newcastle

Ballina

Sligo Town

SLIGO

MONAGHAN

Newry

ough
Conn

Cavan

Dundalk

Castlebar

ROSCOMMON

CAVAN

Dundalk Bay

Lough
Mask

Knock

Longford

LOUTH

Drogheda

LONGFORD

MEATH

River Shannon

GALWAY

WESTMEATH

Mullingar

DUBLIN

Ballinasloe

Athlone

DUBLIN

Bay

Galway City

8

OFFALY

Naas

Dún Laoghaire

Birr

Portlaoise

Bray

Irish Sea

REPUBLIC OF IRELAND

KILDARE

Ennis

Roscrea

LAOIS

Athy

WICKLOW

Wicklow

CLARE

Nenagh

Kilkenny
City

Arklow

Shannon

TIPPERARY

CARLOW

Gorey

Limerick
City

Thurles

KILKENNY

LIMERICK

Cashel

WEXFORD

Newcastle
West

Tipperary
Town

Clonmel

Carrick-on-Suir

Wexford Town

Mallow

Farahy

WATERFORD

Waterford

CORK

7

Midleton

Youghal

St. George's Channel

Cork City

Cobh

Kinsale

Skibbereen

North Channel

North Channel

Lough Foyle

0   50 mi

0   50 km

IRELAND PLANNER

Getting Around

There was a time not so long ago when Ireland's bus and rail network left much to be desired.

While still slightly antiquated in reaching some areas (Sligo and Donegal, for example), the system has improved greatly over the past decade.

All urban centers and towns are now interconnected by bus and rail, and you shouldn't have great difficulty crisscrossing the country in any direction you desire.

But if you can, opt for a car—its greater flexibility combined with the possibility of meandering down byways and country lanes opens up a great many more vistas than any train will do.

The ability to change your itinerary midstream due to unpredictable weather or other circumstances also makes a rental the most flexible option.

Rental rates are on par with most EU countries, and offices are located at all airports, ferry terminals, and town centers.

During the summer months, it's wise to book in advance.

Finding a Place to Stay

Determining your budget is the key here—are you content with B&Bs and small hotels, or do you want to splurge on castles and grand country houses? It's best when planning your trip to Ireland to set aside a few hours of Web browsing to familiarize yourself with costs and standards. Certainly prices have fallen in the last year, and value is there to be had with careful planning. As well as our own site—⊕ Fodors.com—which should be your first stop, try ⊕ www.goireland.com and ⊕ www.visitdublin.ie. The Irish Tourist Board's Web site—⊕ www.discoverireland.com—is a mine of information and a good overview of the whole country. For a week's stay in Ireland, consider small city-center hotels in Dublin, Cork, and Galway; use B&Bs in the country as a means of getting up-close and personal with the locals. For at least one night, consider staying in a castle or country house—it'll be costly, but very memorable. Ashford or Dromoland would be top of the castles list, with Mount Juliet, Hilton Park, and Tinakilly the leaders in the country-house stakes. Check out ⊕ www.irelandsbluebook.com for a select listing.

Feeling Festive?

If you plan to visit the biggest festivals and events in Ireland, book well in advance. In March, Ireland's major St. Patrick's event is the **Dublin Festival and Parade** (⊕ www.stpatricksday.ie), which inclues fireworks and bands from the United States. In April, see the spectacular **World Irish Dancing Championships** (⊕ www.clrg.ie/oireachtas.htm). In May, the **Fleadh Nua,** the annual festival of traditional Irish music, song, and dance, takes place in Ennis, County Clare. August brings a highlight of the traditional-music calendar, the **Fleadh Cheoil na hEireann** (⊕ www.clonmel-fleadh.com), held during the last weekend of August or the first weekend in September, an extravaganza across the country. In October, the **Dublin Theatre Festival** (⊕ www.dublintheatrefestival.com) puts on 10 international productions, 10 Irish plays, and a fringe of 60-plus plays. In October, the **Wexford Opera Festival** (⊕ www.wexfordopera.com) is high glamour.

Meeting the Locals

The pub remains the center of all Irish social life, in spite of the smoking ban that many gloomy commentators predicted would be the death knell of the trade.

In any village or town, your local pub counter remains the best place to hear decent music, local gossip, and an overview of the world at large that's uniquely Irish.

Given Ireland's more hurried pace in recent times, the pub is no longer much of a daytime haunt (except for a good lunch on the road).

For really getting into the vibe, saunter along to the nearest hostelry anytime after 9 PM and buy a round for the few patrons nearest you at the bar—it may cost you $20, but you'll have a front-row seat for true Irish theater for the next two hours.

Meeting the locals is an opportunity that's available anywhere, really—at the post office, the local shop, at a crossroads, on a sleepy Main Street.

It all comes down to gently breaking the ice with tried-and-tested topics like: the weather (obviously), the state of the economy (it's "brutal"), the price of the pint (still too high), and pretty much any sporting event you feel like mentioning—the Irish are crazy about most of them.

Safety Tips

Ireland is still essentially a safe country, but you do need to observe some basic precautions.

Don't leave valuables in a rental car: this is advice countless visitors neglect with sad consequences. Most car theft is opportunistic—if there's nothing visible like a pocketbook, a bag, a camera, even maps or guides within the car, most likely your petty criminal will amble past toward more available pickings.

Likewise, when parking in urban areas, use a car park—this also guards against auto clampers (a recent scourge of Irish towns, where fines to release your car cost up to €130).

Carry only the minimal amount of cash with perhaps one credit card when strolling around the streets and shops—while handbag snatching is minimal, there's no point in making yourself a possible target.

Stretching Your Dollar

At this writing, the dollar is stronger than usual against the euro—($1.35 to €1)—but the situation is pretty fluid. While nobody wants to penny-pinch on vacation, a few changes can yield savings without upsetting your holiday.

For starters, take a bus from the airport—it'll be one-quarter the cost of a cab and will get you into town twice as fast on dedicated bus corridors now operating in all cities.

Opt for B&Bs. They're well located and they'll have comfy bedrooms, good food, and an all-knowing landlady to answer all your questions. Listen carefully to her advice on bargain shopping, as she's got an inside line you'll not find on any Web site. In restaurants, opt for the house wine—people have become serious wine-drinkers in recent years and the house stuff is no longer just "plonk" for unsophisticated palates.

At lunchtime, why not try a picnic? After all, you're here to see scenery, and given that the changeable weather does allow for some dazzling sunshine most days, why not pack a few sandwiches and some drinks or coffee? Ireland is full of wonderful road pull-ins where you can park, walk a few minutes, and dine in glorious isolation to the sound of gurgling streams, lowing cows, or wind echoing across an open plain.

IRELAND TODAY

Politics

There's nothing like the worse economic crisis in living memory to shake up the political waters. A "steady as she goes" attitude that prevailed among voters for the past 10 years has been turned on its head, with the center-right Fianna Fáil government and its current leader, Brian Cowen seriously unpopular. But they have a slim coalition majority in Parliament and will try to hang on until some sort of recovery in the country's finances prevents their annihilation at the next general election. The handshake between Bertie Ahern and Northern Ireland leader, Ian Paisley, at the Battle of the Boyne site in 2007 marked the absolute end of violence in the North and a new dawn upon a political divide that has lasted centuries. At any bar counter, however, talk of politics will lead directly to the ailing economy or the Irish health service and its poor state—everybody will tell you a story of taking their kid to the local emergency room and waiting five hours for someone to look at a broken finger. One recent government minister described the health portfolio as "Angola," a concise definition that spoke volumes. Ireland's a great country with wonderful people, goes the common view—just don't get sick.

Economics

Even before the global financial calamities of the last year, the average Irish person would traditionally lean toward a "glass half-empty" position after any initial probing. "Can it last?" was a mantra that played across a thousand pub counters up and down the land when talk of the famous Celtic Tiger economy unfolded. Well with wages falling the building boom bust and those IT multinationals closing up shop it turns out those stout-supping doomsayers were right all along. So now the pub economists have all changed tack—"It's bottomed out" is the new mantra, as they optimistically toast the elusive "green shoots." And at least the price of the pint has been frozen!

Media

As the Church confessional is no longer the purge-zone of choice for the majority of Irish people, radio and TV talk shows have stepped in to fill the void. Every topic under the sun is squeezed and caressed over the airwaves on a daily basis—lesbian nuns, love on the Web, cheap retirement in Bulgaria, mothers and daughters double-date rules, not to mention one beer-tasting show where brands from around the world are digested in an ever-downward spiral of hilarious drunkenness. Not quite Howard Stern, you understand, but eons beyond Vatican II, all the same. Newspapers include the major three dailies: the *Irish Times,* the *Irish Independent,* and the *Irish Examiner.* A host of U.K. tabloids have also entered the market in recent years, with the *Mail,* the *Sun,* and the *Mirror* being the leading lights. So-called "freesheets"—morning commuter giveaway papers containing a condensed version of the day's news plus heaps of advertising—are similarly flexing their literary muscles.

People

For all their dangerous propensity to whack up the biggest credit card debt in Europe on BMW's, boob jobs, and second homes on Capri, most Irish were, at heart, as confused by life in Celtic Tiger Ireland as the tourist might have been. It all came to us too fast and to flashy, how could we say no? The Irish, when they have a job, still work the longest hours on average in Europe, but despite their breezy, world-weary air, they remain

largely as enthusiastic and comic about life as they ever were. One caller to a radio show summed up his ideal life: "a two-car garage, sex with my wife twice a week, a 12 handicap, and kids who won't call me a loser to my face." The average Joe is in there somewhere.

Religion

Priests and bishops (and even the Pope) continue to hit the headlines through sex scandals and revelations of criminal pedophilia cover-ups that have rocked Ireland for over a decade. The church has fallen a long way in the estimation of most of the population and suddenly the media is not afraid to ask some searing questions about the Church's past and future. Older people are struggling to come to terms with this national loss of trust in their hallowed institution while increasing numbers of younger folks are turning their backs on regular mass-going. Irish-born men entering the priesthood is down to a handful each year and African priests are often shipped in to fill the breach. A majority of the population will still go to Church for births, marriages, and funerals but there is a noted decrease in involvement of priests in the social fabric of Irish life. The Catholic Church in Ireland, it seems, will have to quickly redefine and rebrand itself if it is not to go the way of the Church of England in the U.K. and become a minority sideshow.

Sports

That enduring love affair between the Irish and their sports continues unabated regardless of any other cultural changes. Football and hurling are still enshrined as the national pastimes—but only just ahead of rugby, soccer, and horse racing. For a small nation, Ireland has consistently punched above its weight in the global arena, as exemplified by the recent domination of Rugby's Six Nations tournament by the men in green. Every second pub has a satellite dish pulling down anything from badminton in Bhutan to sumo wrestling in Tokyo. It's no surprise that images of winning football teams reside in pride of place on many pub walls.

Culture

Neither the World Wide Web, cellular texting, nor Internet gaming will dent the nation's fondness for the written word. Although there have been few to match the talent of Shaw, Wilde, and Joyce, the huge-selling works of Frank McCourt, Joe O'Connor, Roddy Doyle, and Pat McCabe underline the country as one of the biggest book-buying populations in Europe. In the movies, time and tide have taken us a long way from John Wayne in *The Quiet Man* to writer-directors like Neil Jordan, Jim Sheridan, and Noel Pearson and their warts-and-all visions of modern Ireland.

The Sexes

Equality in the bedroom happened 10 years ago—much more problematic has been the more recent balancing of the scales in the boardroom. Irish women have moved right up the corporate ladder since the late '90s and now challenge and frequently best their male counterparts for the big jobs. Sure, there are many glass ceilings still to shatter, but an unstoppable momentum has begun and God knows where it will all lead. Stay at home Dads? Check. What happens in Macau stays in Macau bachelorette weekends? Check. Fortysomething divorcees with teen boy toys in tow? Check. Most traditional males are hoping it's a horrible nightmare they'll soon wake from. Only time will tell.

IRELAND'S TOP ATTRACTIONS

The Rock of Cashel

(A) The center of tribal and religious power for more than a thousand years, it became the seat of the Munster Kings in the 5th century. Handed over to the early Christian Church in 1101, the medieval abbey perched on a limestone mount in Tipperary contains rare Romanesque sculpture and carvings celebrating St. Patrick's visit there in 450.

Newgrange

(B) Stonehenge and the pyramids at Giza are spring chickens compared to Newgrange, one of the most fascinating sites near Dublin. Built around 5,200 years ago, Newgrange is a passage tomb—a huge mound of earth with a stone passageway leading to a burial chamber constructed entirely of dry stone (mortar wasn't invented yet). Steeped in Celtic myth and lore, these graves were built for the Kings of Tara. Untouched for centuries, the main chamber was excavated in the 1960s and

revealed itself as the world's oldest solar observatory, where the sun's rays light up the interior on December 21 each year.

The Giant's Causeway

(C) Irish mythology claims that the warrior Finn MacCool laid the Antrim causeway himself to enable easy crossing to his lover on Staffa Island off the Scottish coast, where similar basalt columns are found. Formed by volcanic eruptions more than 60 million years ago, the area is a magical mix of looming cliffs and thundering surf—and an awesome reminder of nature's power.

Book of Kells

(D) If you visit only one attraction in Dublin, let it be this extraordinary creation housed in Trinity College. Often called "the most beautiful book in the world," the manuscript dates to the 8th or 9th century and remains a marvel of intricacy and creativity. Fashioned by monks probably based on the Hebridean island of Iona,

and worked with reed pens and iron-gall ink on a folded section of vellum, the manuscript demonstrates a sense of sublime balance and beauty in elaborate interlaces, abstractions, and "carpet-pages."

The Blarney Stone

(E) One of the country's most enduring myths, wherein kissing a stone high upon the battlements of a ruined Cork castle bestows a magical eloquence on the visitor, may also be one of its most ludicrous. Grasped by the ankles and hanging perilously upside down to pucker upon ancient rock, you'll certainly have a tall tale to tell the folks back home. Despite the difficulty, there's generally a long line waiting to scale the skeletal remains of Blarney Castle, a strangely derelict edifice in the other neatly groomed estate; try to visit in the very early morning.

Ring of Kerry

(F) Ireland's most popular scenic route, the Ring of Kerry is one of Europe's grandest drives, combining mountainous splendor with a spectacularly varied coastline. It's best to escape the tour buses that choke its main road by taking to the hills on foot, by horseback, or by bike.

Aran Islands

(G) Famed for their haunting beauty, these three islands set in Galway Bay have lured artists, writers, and multitudes of curious visitors for decades. On Inishmore, Inishmaan, and Inisheer you'll find a mode of life that reflects man's struggle against nature. Topped with the stone forts and crisscrossed by ancient "garden" walls, they epitomize solitude—one reason Irish bards like playwright J. M. Synge visited them many times.

TOP EXPERIENCES

Sonatas in Ancient Grandeur
Among the architectural grandeur that is Bantry House in Cork, the annual music festival (⊕ *www.westcorkmusic.ie*) allows for languid sunsets, picnics on the lawns, and sublime sounds from some of Europe's top classical musicians. The notes may be highbrow, but the vibe is indelibly Irish-mellow.

The Write Stuff
Fancy getting up close and personal with Lawrence Block, Roddy Doyle, Joe O'Connor, Neil Jordan, Pat Conroy, and a host of other literary greats? **Listowel Writer's Week** (⊕ *www.writersweek.ie*) is a chaotic and seriously democratic gathering devoted to all things literary—including numerous workshops by the greats where info on writing your own masterpiece is there for the asking. This being Kerry, expect discussions to last well toward dawn.

Making "Long Bullets"
On the back roads of West Cork and Armagh, the ancient art of road bowling continues to thrive—the only places in Ireland where the game is still played. Two men, two 28-ounce balls of iron, and a 3-mi stretch of quiet country lane are the ingredients; the man with the least throws wins. Join the massive crowds that follow this slice of ancient Ireland called "long bullets" or "score" by locals—and place a bet to add to the excitement.

Acting the Goat
Puck Fair in Kerry (⊕ *www.puckfair.ie*) is the oldest festival in Ireland, dating back to pagan times, where a goat is made king for three days of drinking, dancing, and general abandon. Pubs stay open all night, traveler folk sell horses and cows on Main Street, and up to 100,000 people crowd this tiny town of 58 pubs for a mad three-day weekend. All in all, truly one of Ireland's most unusual festivals.

A Night on the Cobblestones
The Trinity Ball (⊕ *www.trinityball.ie*) happens in May just before students face end-of-year exams. The biggest enclosed party in Europe, it takes place around the ancient confines of this gorgeous Dublin city center seat of learning and offers everything from Strauss waltzes to punk, hip-hop, and good old rock 'n' roll. Tuxedos and ball gowns are the order of the day. The party officially ends at dawn—and then everybody heads to Grafton Street for breakfast.

Make Like a Bird
Happening on the May Bank Holiday Weekend, the **Kinvara Cuckoo Fleadh** (⊕ *www.kinvara.com*) is perfectly timed to welcome in the warmer evenings of early summer. A well-established and richly deserved reputation has ensured that the fleadh has become a showcase for the best in traditional music, attracting musicians from all over the country and beyond. An added bonus is having it in one of the country's prettiest towns.

Gather Those Boats
Cruínniu na mBád (⊕ *www.cruinniunambad.com*), or the Gathering of the Boats, is basically a big booze-up and regatta to celebrate the unique and beautiful boat that is the Galway Hooker—a sleek, dark little sailing vessel with rusty red sails originally used to transport turf and other necessities along the harsh Atlantic coast of Ireland. The event takes place around the second week in August around southern County Galway, with traditional boat races the excuse for a "hooley," or party of trad music and late nights.

Food, Glorious Food

Long noted for its cuisine innovations, the **Kinsale Gourmet Festival** (⊕ *www.kinsale-restaurants.com*) is all about the happy pursuit of great food and wine plus the excitable bravado of this infectious coastal town. Buy a weekend ticket, have breakfast on a boat, lunch at a pierside pub, and dinner at any of the dozens of great eateries in this amazingly friendly town.

Have a Flutter on the Nags

Galway Race Week (⊕ *www.galway races.com*) is one of the country's biggest events with most of Dublin, Cork, and Limerick decamping to the City of the Tribes for a July week of celebration centered half around equine excellence and half around pub sessions. Every politician worth his salt hits the races to press the flesh, followed by legions of supporters and onlookers out for the "craic"—of which there is an endless supply.

Lark in the Park

Every June, Cork city struts its artistic stuff with the **Midsummer Festival** (⊕ *www.cork festival.com*), a mix of music, film, and theater. Be sure to get tickets for whatever the Corcadorca Theatre Company is doing—in the past they've taken Shakespeare to the local courthouse, the city morgue, and the expansive green spaces of Fitzgerald's Park: a very different experience from a company constantly pushing the envelope.

Good for the Sole

On the last Sunday in July, join the thousands of pilgrims/adventurers who climb Mayo's **Croagh Patrick** (⊕ *www.croagh-patrick.com*)—and in your bare feet for the full purging of your misdeeds. A ghostly hill, tricky loose stones underfoot, and a Mass overlooking Clew Bay: it all adds up to an experience that is difficult but hugely rewarding.

Blooming Forth

Even though it is now reckoned that more Americans and Japanese attend the events surrounding **Bloomsday** (⊕ *www.james-joyce.ie*) than Irish people, it hasn't taken away a jot from an event that continues to grow regardless. Most Irish, if they're being honest, will probably admit to "never having actually finished *Ulysses*," but are still happy to discourse at length over devilled kidneys and other Joycean delights on the hidden meanings within this legendary work.

Clash of the Ash

Usually happening on the first Sunday in September, the **All-Ireland Hurling Final** (⊕ *www.gaa.ie*), at Dublin's Croke Park, is a uniquely Irish sporting spectacle. Thirty highly amped players clutching ash hurleys whack a heavy leather ball, or sliothar, at warp speeds around the pitch as they slug it out for the sport's highest prize. Raw emotions, brilliant color, and Harry Potter–ish skills like you won't see back home make it memorable.

What a Wonderful World

For jazz lovers, the **Cork Jazz Festival** (⊕ *www.corkjazzfestival.com*) in October is a perfect antidote to the approaching dark evenings of winter. George Melly, one of the music legends who visits regularly, puts it thus: "I forget where I've parked, where I'm meant to be playing, and, sometimes, even who I am—but it all works out in the end." A fair description of a festival with heart and soul.

QUINTESSENTIAL IRELAND

The Pub: Pillar of Irish Social Life

It's been said that the pub is the poor man's university. If this is true, Ireland has more than 10,000 opportunities for higher education. Even if you only order an Evian, a visit to a pub (if not two or three) is a must.

The Irish public house is a national institution—down to the spectacle, at some pubs, of patrons standing at closing time for the playing of Ireland's national anthem. Samuel Beckett would often repair to a pub, believing a glass of Guinness stout was the best way to ward off depression.

Pubs remain pillars of Irish social life—places to chat, listen, learn, gossip, and, of course, enjoy a throaty sing-along.

Impromptu concerts often break out, and if you're really enjoying the craic—quintessentially Irish friendly chat and lively conversation—it's good form to buy a pint for the performers.

Wherever you go, remember that when you order a Guinness, the barman first pours it three-quarters of the way, then lets it settle, then tops it off and brings it over to the bar.

The customer should then wait again until the top-up has settled, at which point the brew turns a deep black.

The mark of a perfect pint? As you drink the liquid down, the brew will leave thin rings on the glass to mark each mouthful.

"Fleadhs" and Festivals

From bouncing-baby competitions to traditional-music festivals, the tradition of the fleadh (festival, pronounced "flah") is alive and well in Ireland year-round.

Before you leave home, check on regional Irish tourist Web sites or, upon arrival, discuss the local happenings with local tourist boards or your hotel concierge.

If you want to get a sense of Irish culture and indulge in some of its pleasures, start by familiarizing yourself with the rituals of daily life. These
are a few highlights—things you can take part in with relative ease.

Music festivals rule the roost—Kinvara's
Cuckoo Fleadh, Galway's Festival of Irish
Popular Music, the giant Fleadh Cheoil
na hÉireann, and the World Irish Danc-
ing Championships (held every April in
Ennis) are some major events.

But there are also village festivals dedicated to hill-walking, fishing, poetry, art,
and food; the Mullaghmore Lobster Festival in August always proves mighty tasty.

Keep A'Clappin' and A'Tappin'

Ceol agus craic, loosely translated as
"music and merriment," are not simply
recreations in Ireland. They are part of the
very fabric of the national identity.

Ask most Irish men or women in exile
what they miss most about home and,
more than likely, those words "the craic"
will be uttered.

And the beat and rhythm that accompany
Irish fun are the "4/4" of the reel and the
jig. Wherever you go you'll find that every

town buzzes with its own blend of styles
and sounds.

In its most exciting form, "trad" music is
an impromptu affair, with a single guitar
or fiddle player belting out a few tunes
until other musicians—flute, whistle, uilleann pipes, concertina, and bodhrán
drum—seem to arrive out of the pub's
dark corners and are quickly drawn into
the unstoppable force of the session.

A check of local event guides will turn up
a wealth of live entertainment—if you're
lucky you'll find a world-class artist in
performance whose talents are unsung
outside a small circle of friends and fans.

On some nights, Dublin itself—with more
than 120 different clubs and music pubs to
choose from—almost becomes one giant
traditional-music jam session. Where to
head first? Just take a walk down Grafton
Street and keep your ears open.

IF YOU LIKE

The Most Beautiful Villages

Nearly everyone has a mind's-eye view of the perfect Irish village. Cozy huddles filled with charming calendar cottages, mossy churchyards, and oozing with thatched-roof-pewter-and-china-dog atmosphere, these spots have a sense of once-upon-a-timefied tranquility that not even tour buses can ruin. Should you be after medicine for overtired nerves—a gentle peace in beautiful surroundings with a people so warm you'll be on first-name terms in five minutes—these will be your Arcadias. Many are so nestled away they remain the despair of motorists, but then no penciled itinerary is half as fun as stumbling upon these four-leaf clovers. Here are four of the most famous—but why not summon up courage, venture out on the lesser roads, and throw away the map?

Kinvara, Co. Galway. This village is picture-perfect, thanks to its gorgeous bayside locale, great walks, and numerous pubs. North of the town is spectacularly sited Dunguaire Castle, noted for its medieval-banquet evenings.

Cong, Co. Mayo. John Ford's *The Quiet Man* introduced this charmer to the world and the singular beauty of its whitewashed single-story cottages with tied-on thatched roofs.

Adare, Co. Limerick. Right out of a storybook, this celebrated village of low-slung Tudor cottages is adorned with ivied churches and a moated castle from the days when knighthood was in flower.

Lismore, Co. Tipperary. Set within some of Ireland's lushest pasturelands and lorded over by the Duke of Devonshire's castle, dreamy Lismore is popular with both romantic folk and anglers (the sparkling Blackwater here teems with salmon).

New Irish Cuisine

To the astonishment—and delight—of many visitors, Ireland has undergone of a food revolution. Not far out of Dublin you begin to see some of the reasons all about you: livestock grazing in impossibly green fields, clear waters to spawn the freshest fish, and acres of produce thriving in the temperate climate. But it is Ireland's chefs who are the stars of the rapidly changing food scene. Having traveled the world, they're now producing a Pan-European, postmodern cuisine. This New Irish cuisine—sometimes referred to as *cuisine Irelandaise*—marries simple treatments of traditional dishes, such as Clonakilty black pudding, Clare nettle soup, Galway oysters, and Cong wild salmon, with exotic influences from Europe, North America, and the Pacific Rim. That noted, the Irish are a feisty lot not about to let newfangled food get the better of them. Food in Ireland has become more international in flavor, but there has also been a renaissance of authentically Irish cuisine based on regional cooking, thanks to the teachings and cookbooks of Myrtle Allen.

Thornton's, Dublin. Newer-than-now-nouvelle and grand-ol'-Irish ingredients collide in the kitchen of culinary wizard Kevin Thornton. Don't miss his moonshine sauce.

Ballymaloe House, Shanagarry. Presided over by Myrtle Allen, this famed outpost of Irish country-house cuisine uses marvelously fresh local produce, including seafood from the picturesque port of Ballycotton.

The Tannery, Dungarvan. Sir Andrew Lloyd Webber is just one foodie who raves over culinary wizard Paul Flynn's breast of wood pigeon on toasted brioche with truffle oil.

Celtic Sites

From rush hour on busy O'Connell Street in Dublin it's a long way to Tipperary's Cashel of the Kings, a group of ancient church relics—the largest in all Ireland—perched high above the plain on its famous rock. The journey is worth it, since it takes you back in time to the legendary days when Celtic Christianity conquered the isle of Eire. Beginning in the 5th century AD, hallowed shrines and monasteries sprung up across the land, often dotted with treasures sacred—the famous High Crosses, inscribed with biblical symbols and stories—and profane, such as the lofty Round Towers, lookouts for Viking raids. Just north of Dublin, around the Boyne Valley, you'll find two great sites: Tara, where "The Harp That Once Through Tara's Halls" played, and also Newgrange, once seat of the High Kings of Ireland.

Clonmacnoise, Co. Offaly. The isolated monastery at the confluence of two rivers was famous throughout Europe as a center of learning. It's also a royal burial ground.

Glendalough, Co. Wicklow. A monastery founded by a hermit in the 6th century, attacked by Vikings in the 10th century, and plundered by the English in the 12th century—your typical Irish ruins.

Rock of Cashel, Co. Tipperary. A cluster of ruins—cathedral, chapel, round tower—crowning a circular, mist-shrouded rock that rises from a plain.

Tara, Co. Meath. Fabled home of one of Ireland's titular High Kings, the ageless Hill of Tara has fired up people's imaginations from early Christians to Scarlett O'Hara.

The Most Stately Houses

Ireland's stately homes are either proud reminders of a shared history with Britain or symbols of an oppressive colonial past. If you're interested in luxurious pomp and reliving the decadence of yesteryear, there's no denying the magnificence of these country estates and lavish mansions, erected by the Anglo-Irish Protestant Ascendancy in the 17th, 18th, and 19th centuries. The wealthy settlers constructed ornate houses in various architectural styles, with Palladian designs popular in the first half of the 18th century, before the Neoclassical and neo-Gothic influences took over. In the last century, several majestic piles—notably Ashford Castle in Cong and Dromoland Castle in Newmarket-on-Fergus—became hotels, so anyone can now enjoy a queen-for-a-stay fantasy.

Castle Ward, Co. Down. An architectural curiosity, in that it was built inside and out in two distinct styles, Classical and Gothic—perhaps because Viscount Bangor and his wife never could agree on anything.

Bantry House, Bantry, Co. Cork. Set in Italianate gardens and perched over one of Ireland's most spectacular bays, this manor has a Continental air, thanks to its extensive art collection, tapestries, and fine French furniture.

Castletown House, Co. Kildare. Renaissance architect Andrea Palladio would surely have approved of this exceedingly large and grand Palladian country house.

Florence Court, Co. Down. With magnificent Georgian-period stuccoed salons, this shimmering white mansion is strikingly set against the Cuilcagh Mountains where, legend has it, you can hear the "song of the little people."

Retail Therapy

Once you get past all the traditional Irish leprechauns with MADE IN CHINA stickers on their bottoms, you'll find that Ireland has some of Europe's finest-quality goods. Objects like a Donegal tweed hat or a hand-knit Aran sweater, a Belfast linen tablecloth, or a piece of Waterford or Cavan crystal can be pricey but will last a lifetime. In Dublin look for antiques, vintage books, or au courant European and Irish fashions, many showcased at cool shops like Costume and Platform. Galway has its share of galleries and offbeat boutiques and is a great spot for book shopping. Keep an eye open for signs indicating crafts workshops, where independent craftspeople sell directly from their studios. The best of the North's traditional products, many made according to time-honored methods, include exquisite linen, laces, and superior handmade woolen garments. Traditional music CDs and the unadorned blackthorn walking stick are two good choices at the other end of the price scale.

John Molloy, Ardara. One of many shops in town where you can stake your claim to an heirloom Aran sweater or dream-woven Donegal tweed scarf.

O'Sullivan Antiques, Dublin. Mia Farrow and Liam Neeson are just two fans of this purveyor of 19th-century delights.

Ardmore Pottery and Craft Gallery, Ardmore, Co. Waterford. Home to potter Mary Lincoln, this is one of the most beloved, creative, and cleverly stocked craft shops in the country.

Belleek Pottery, Co. Fermanagh. Any bride would be honored to receive a "Blessing Plate" of Parian china from this famed maker.

Natural Wonders

It's not always easy to conjure up leprechauns and druids in today's Ireland, but head to any of its famously brooding landscapes and those legendary times will seem like yesterday. With its romantic coastlines, wild bogs, and rugged seascapes, the Emerald Isle is especially rich in rugged, wildly gorgeous spectacle. Around its natural splendors, the countryside is dotted with villages where sheep outnumber residents by 100 to 1. Unfortunately, sheep don't also outnumber tourists.

The Aran Islands, Galway Bay. The islands battle dramatically with sea and storm and now welcome droves of visitors who fall under the spell of their brooding beauty.

The Skelligs, Ring of Kerry. Be warned: these spectacular pinnacles of rock soaring out of the sea will haunt you for days.

The Burren, Co. Clare. A 300-square-km (116-square-mi) expanse that is one of Ireland's strangest landscapes, the Burren stretches off as far as the eye can see in a gray, rocky, lunar landscape that becomes a wild rock garden in spring.

Cliffs of Moher, Co. Clare. One of Ireland's most breathtaking natural sights, these majestic cliffs stretch for 8 km (5 mi). At some points, the only thing separating you from the sea, 700 feet below, is a patch of slippery heather.

Giant's Causeway, Co. Antrim, Northern Ireland. There are equal measures of legend and science surrounding this rock formation—a cluster of 37,000-odd volcanic basalt pillars.

The Perfect Links

What makes Irish golf so great—and increasingly popular—is the natural architecture. The wild, wonderful coastline seems to be made for links golf; unlike many international courses, these courses have few forests, ponds, or short roughs. Most famous of these links courses is the celebrated Ballybunion. Fortunately, the courses can be played year-round—an asset in rainy Ireland. Pack plenty of sweaters and rain gear, and make sure you're in good shape: electric carts are available only at the most expensive courses. Golf clubs and bags can be rented almost anywhere. With the exception of the ancient Royal Belfast, all golf clubs in Ireland are happy to have visitors (and charge well for the privilege), and several tour operators have made golf excursions an art, so it's easy to have the golf trip of a lifetime.

Ballybunion Golf Club, Co. Kerry. On the Old Course, one of the country's classics, each and every hole is a pleasure.

The K Club, Co. Kildare. You'd have to be a nongolfer and a hermit not to have heard of this course, one of the country's most prestigious and demanding.

Portmarnock Golf Club, Co. Dublin. One of the nation's "Big Four" golf clubs (along with Ballybunion, Royal County Down, and Royal Portrush), Portmarnock is a links course near Dublin.

Royal County Down, Northern Ireland. A lunar landscape makes this course as beautiful as it is difficult.

Literary Haunts

Irish literature developed its distinctive traits largely because of Ireland's physical and political isolation. Yet the nation has produced a disproportionately large number of internationally famous authors for a country of her size, including four Nobel Prize winners—George Bernard Shaw, W. B. Yeats, Samuel Beckett, and Seamus Heaney. The list of literary notables is a whole lot longer and includes James Joyce, Oscar Wilde, Sean O'Casey, Sean O'Faolain, Brian Friel, and Edna O'Brien. Indeed, the country's literary heritage is evident everywhere you go. In Dublin you'll find Joyce's Liffey; Dean Swift's cathedral; and the Abbey Theatre, a potent symbol of Ireland's great playwrights. Yeats opens up the county of Sligo; the Aran Islands were the inspiration of J. M. Synge; and Cork inspired the works of Frank O'Connor. Wherever you are in Ireland, its literary heritage is never far away.

Trinity College, Dublin. Founded by Queen Elizabeth I, this university provided the greats—Beckett, Wilde, Stoker—with 30 acres of stomping grounds.

Limerick City, Co. Limerick. Frank McCourt's *Angela's Ashes* had thousands heading here to tour Angela's city and partake of the tearfulness of it all.

Sligo Town, Co. Sligo. Take in the town where William Butler Yeats grew up, then visit his grave in Drumcliff to view his beloved mountain, Ben Bulben.

GREAT ITINERARIES

THE EAST AND THE SOUTH

5 to 10 days

Dublin's literary charm and Georgian riches, and rugged County Wicklow and the historic Meath plains are all just a few hours' drive from each other. Here you'll find the Boyne Valley, the cradle of native Irish civilization—no one will want to miss sacred Tara, Kells, Newgrange, and Glendalough, all time-burnished sites that guard the roots of Irishness. More idyllic pleasures can be found at Powerscourt, the grandest gardens in the land. In the south you'll find fishing towns and bustling markets, coastal panoramas, and—just outside of crazy Killarney (oh, and it is crazy, an emerald-green Orlando)—stunning mountain-and-lake scenery.

Dublin

1 to 3 days. Dublin's pleasures are uncontainable. James Joyce's Dublin holds treasures for all sorts. Literary types: explore Trinity College, Beckett's stomping grounds, and its legendary *Book of Kells*. Visit key Joyce sites and the Dublin Writers Museum, and indulge in the Dublin Literary Pub Crawl. Joyce fanatics: arrive a week before Bloomsday (June 16) for Bloomstime celebrations. Literary or not, stroll around the city center and take in the elegant Georgian architecture around St. Stephen's Green, austere Dublin Castle, and the national treasures in the museums around Merrion Square and pedestrianized Grafton Street. Check out Temple Bar, Dublin's party zone, and join locals in this city-of-1,000-pubs for a foamy pint in the late afternoon. Pubs are the center of Dublin activity, and the locals never lose their natural curiosity about "strangers."

You will frequently be asked, "Are you enjoying your holiday?" "Yes" is not good enough: What they're really after is your life story, and if you haven't got a good one you might want to make one up. Pay your respects by taking a tour of the ever-popular Guinness Brewery and Storehouse. Night options: catch a show at W. B. Yeats's old haunt, the Abbey Theatre; see some Victorian music hall shows at the Olympia Theatre; or listen to traditional or alternative music at a pub or other venue. Last call arrives early at pubs, even here, so if you're still revved, go to Lesson Street and hit the nightclubs. For a dose of unmitigated Irish enthusiasm, join the roaring crowds at Croke Park and see some traditional Gaelic football and hurling.

Boyne Valley and County Wicklow

2 days. Walt Disney couldn't have planned it better. The small counties immediately to the north, south, and west of Dublin—historically known as the Pale—seem expressly designed for the sightseer. The entire region is like an open-air museum, layered with legendary Celtic sites, spectacular gardens, and elegant Palladian country estates. First head to the Boyne Valley, a short trip north of the capital. Spend the morning walking among the Iron Age ruins of the rolling Hill of Tara. After a picnic lunch on top of the hill, drive through ancient Kells—one of the centers of early Christianity in Ireland—and then to Newgrange, famous for its ancient passage graves. One thousand years older than Stonehenge, the great white-quartz structure merits two or three hours. Spend the rest of your day driving through the low hills and valleys of County Meath and to Georgian-era Slane, a manorial town planned by the Conynghams. Dominating the town are

elegant Slane Castle and 500-foot Slane Hill. Backtrack to Kells or continue to Drogheda and spend the night. The following day, head south of Dublin through the County Wicklow mountains. You might want to stop in one of the small, quiet towns along the Wicklow Way hiking trail and go for a short hike. Drive on to stately Powerscourt House, whose gardens epitomize the glory and grandeur of the Anglo-Irish aristocracy. From the profane to the sacred, head next to the "monastic city" of Glendalough and the medieval monastery of the hermit St. Kevin. Repair to Ireland's highest village, Roundwood, for lunch at the town's 17th-century inn.

West Cork and Kerry

4 days. Head about 250 km (155 mi) southwest to Cork City, filled with tall Georgian houses and old quays and perfect for a half day of walking. The place has few don't-miss attractions, but that's not the point: unlike many other towns, Cork is very much alive. As Europe's 2005 City of Culture, it has a progressive university, art galleries, offbeat cafés, a formidable pub scene, and some of the country's best traditional music. Drive south to Kinsale, once heralded as the gourmet capital of Ireland, an old fishing town turned resort, with many good restaurants. A slow three- or four-hour drive along the coast and up through the small towns of West Cork takes you through the kind of landscape that inspired Ireland's nickname, the Emerald Isle. Spend the night in the market town of Skibbereen. Next morning, cross into County Kerry and head straight for Killarney, at the center of a scattering of azure lakes and heather-clad mountains. Although it has been almost transformed into a Celtic theme park by a flood of tourists, it's a good base for exploring your pick of two great Atlantic-pounded peninsulas: the strikingly scenic Ring of Kerry and the beloved Dingle Peninsula. Both offer stunning ocean views, hilly landscapes (like the Macgillycuddy's Reeks mountains), and welcoming towns with good B&Bs. To do justice to the fabulous views of the Ring, you need a minimum of two days, especially if traveling by bus. The five-hour drive back to Dublin takes you through Limerick City and the lakes of the Midlands.

THE WEST AND THE NORTH

6 to 7 days

"To hell or to Connaught" was the choice given the native population by Cromwell, and indeed the harsh, barren landscape of parts of the west and north might appear cursed to the eye of an uprooted farmer. But there's an appeal in the very wildness of counties Clare, Galway, Mayo, Sligo, and Donegal, with their stunning, steep coastlines hammered and shaped for aeons by the Atlantic. Here, in isolated communities, you'll hear locals speaking Irish as they go about their business. The arrival of peace has opened the lush pastures of long-suffering Northern Ireland to travelers.

Galway and Clare

2 days. A three-hour drive west from Dublin leads straight to the 710-foot-high Cliffs of Moher, perhaps the single most impressive sight in Ireland. Using the waterside village of Ballyvaughan as your base, spend a day exploring the lunar landscape of the harsh, limestone Burren. In spring it becomes a mighty rock garden of exotic colors. The next morning, head north out of Ballyvaughan toward Galway City. On the way you'll pass 2-million-year-old Ailwee Cave and the picture-perfect village of Kinvara. Galway City, spectacularly overlooking Galway Bay, is rapidly growing, vibrant, and packed with culture and history. If time allows, drive west to Ros an Mhil (Rossaveal) and take a boat to the fabled Aran Islands. Spend the night in Galway City.

North and West to Donegal

2 days. Northwest of Galway City is tiny Clifden, with some of the country's best Atlantic views. From here, head east through one of the most beautiful stretches of road in Connemara—through Kylemore Valley, home of Kylemore Abbey, a huge Gothic Revival castle. After seeing the castle and its grounds, head north through tiny Leenane (the setting of the hit Broadway play, The Beauty Queen of Leenane) and on to the most attractive town in County Mayo, Westport. It's the perfect spot to spend the night: the 18th-century planned town is on an inlet of Clew Bay, and some of the west coast's finest beaches are nearby. Your drive north leads through the heart of Yeats Country in Sligo. Just north of cozy Sligo Town is the stark outline of a great hill, Ben Bulben, in whose shadow poet Yeats wanted to be buried. South of town, follow the signposted Yeats Trail around woody, gorgeously scenic Lough Gill. Continuing north, you pass Yeats's simple grave in unassuming Drumcliff, a 3000 BC tomb in Creevykeel, and small Donegal Town. Head north through Letterkenny on the tight, meandering roads, into the windswept mountains and along the jagged coastline of northern Donegal. A trip on a fishing boat to one of the many islands off the coast is a must, as is a slow drive along the coast from the Gweedore Headland, covered with heather and gorse, to the former plantation village of Dunfanaghy (Dun Fionnachaid), heart of Donegal's Irish-speaking Gaeltacht region and a friendly place to spend the night.

Northern Ireland

2 days. Begin exploring the province in historic, divided Derry City (called Londonderry by Unionists), Northern Ireland's second city. A few hours are sufficient to take in the views from the old city walls and the fascinating murals of the Catholic Bogside district. Continue

on to two of the region's main attractions, the 13th-century Norman fortress of Dunluce Castle and the Giant's Causeway, shaped from volcanic rock some 60 million years ago. Heading south, sticking to coastal roads for the best scenery, you'll soon pass through the Glens of Antrim, whose green hills roll down into the sea. Tucked in the glens are a number of small, unpretentious towns with great hotels. Early in the morning, head straight to Northern Ireland's capital, Belfast. The old port city, gray and often wet, is a fascinating place, recovering from years of strife. A morning of driving through its streets will have to suffice before you head west through the rustic, pretty countryside to Lough Neagh, the largest lake in the British Isles. It's time to head back to Dublin, but if you're ahead of schedule, take the longer route that passes through the glorious Mountains of Mourne and around icy-blue Carlingford Lough.

BY CAR: SOME TIPS

Road signs are generally in both Irish and English, although in Gaeltacht (Irish speaking) areas new laws now mandate signs in Irish *only* (most such regions are located in the counties along the Western coast of the country, Donegal and Connemara in particular). Thus, if traveling in these areas, invest in a good, detailed map with both Irish and English names.

Another new law has mandated that all speed limit signs now need to be posted in kilometers—not miles—per hour (a bit of a nuisance, as most cars have speedometers in miles). Signage is currently being changed throughout Ireland.

Remember to slow down on smaller, countryside lanes and roads: traffic jams can sometimes be caused by flocks of sheep and herds of cattle, not cars.

Brand-new divided highways are the fastest way to get from one point to another, but use caution: highways sometimes end as abruptly as they begin.

GREAT OUTDOORS

TOP BOATING TRIPS

Imagine the scene: gentle waves lap at the edges as your boat heads for open water drawing a perfect silver line across the tranquil mirror-flat surface. Every sound is crystal clear: a dog barks, a kingfisher whirrs past flying low across the water, and fellow-sailors shout a hearty welcome. This magical moment can easily be yours in Ireland, thanks to the wealth of possibilities for either guided tours or private hires.

Coast or Inland?

Ireland's indented western seaboard from Donegal to Cork has many first-class sailing opportunities. The main towns have sailing clubs in scenic areas. The best option is to choose an area such as West Cork and spend a week sailing from port to port. If you want to enjoy the very heart of Ireland, the River Shannon offers an unequalled choice of boating trips from the north Midlands down to Limerick. Cruisers can be hired at Carrick-on-Shannon, Banagher, and Portumna. Crossing the Irish border, the Shannon-Erne Waterway has opened up a little-known area of untamed beauty. And the renaissance of Ireland's canals is a recent regeneration success.

The Five Best Boating Trips?

River Barrow: hire a traditional steel canal boat at Rathangan in Co. Kildare for a 120 km (70 mi) trip along the idyllic Barrow—Ireland's oldest navigation—passing through a Chaucerian landscape and dropping anchor at Graiguenamanagh (known as Graig); en route sign up for a canalways pub crawl.

West Cork Sailing: the harbors of the ports-of-call along this coast, such as Kinsale, Glandore, Baltimore, and Bantry, offer delightful overnight stays.

River Shannon Cruising: one of the best places to hire from is the delightful boating town of Carrick-on-Shannon—putter your leisurely way down to Lough Ree or as far as the Lower Shannon.

Fermanagh Lakes: with 700 km (430 mi) of rivers, lakes, and canals, Fermanagh is tops. Upper and Lower Lough Erne are dotted with islands topped with castles or Round Towers ideal for exploring.

Royal Canal: with its reconstructed locks and bridges, the 145 km (90 mi) canal is perfect for those on narrow boats, and in 2010 it became fully navigable from Dublin to Richmond Harbor in Co. Longford. Towpaths run from the Liffey all the way to the Shannon.

Guided Tours or Private Hire?

A first-time boatie? Get some courses under your belt by contacting the International Sailing Schools Association. Of course, if you want to sit back and have it all done for you, book half-day or full-day guided pleasure cruises. For more info, see "Cruising on the Shannon" in the Midlands chapter.

Information, Please?

⊕ www.sailing.ie; ⊕ www.sailingschools. org; ⊕ www.discoverireland.ie/lakelands; ⊕ www.waterwaysireland.org; ⊕ www. iwai.ie; Emerald Star Cruisers: ⊕ www. emeraldstar.ie; Riversdale Barge Holidays: ⊕ www.riversdalebargeholidays. com; Canalways Ireland: ⊕ www.canalways.ie; Royal Canal Cruisers: ⊕ www. royalcanalcruisers.com

BEST WALKS AND HIKES

Catch the right day and an Irish hilltop can seem like a slice of heaven. The country is laced with 33 well-marked walking trails. If you're not feeling adventurous, a stroll through a forest park or a lakeside dander are wonderful options. Whether you want a two-hour afternoon ramble or a week-long trek, every taste is catered for by numerous companies that offer organized walking holidays (there's also a plethora of weekend walking festivals—see "Hiking the West" in the Connemara chapter).

The Top Hiking Regions?

The Reeks of Kerry: Munster, in the Southwest of the country, has Ireland's biggest mountains with the MacGillicuddy's Reeks in Kerry (1,039 m, 3,414 ft) leading the way in the hierarchy of height. They attract serious hill walkers and serious gongoozlers (those who like to gaze up at the peaks).

West is Best: Many of Ireland's West Coast walking routes are framed by spectacular Atlantic scenery: Connemara, Sligo, and Donegal are renowned for the allure of their hills with thrilling views.

Ulster Way: Relaunched in 2009, the 1,000 km (625 mi) circular Ulster Way crosses the most stunning upland areas of Northern Ireland including the impressive Mountains of Mourne.

The Four Top Walks?

Burren, Co. Clare: an unforgettable trip into an otherworldly place, this lunar-like landscape is threaded with looped walks, rare flowers, and ancient ruins, many with a backdrop of unbeatable views across Galway Bay. The entire Burren Way is a 15 km (21 mi), five-hour pleasure-filled walk.

Silent Valley, Co. Down: catch a bus from Newcastle and, after a two-hour (undemanding) walk around this idyllic place, you will realize why it was so named.

Glendalough, Co. Wicklow: the gentle, three-hour circular Spink Walk takes you across a wooden bridge, along a boardwalk, through conifer woodland and alongside the Upper Lake with sweeping views over the valley.

Slievenamon, Co. Tipperary: an unmistakable landmark famed in song, there is an easy track to the top where a burial cairn reputedly contains the entrance to the Celtic underworld.

Weather or Not?

Irish weather is fickle, mist comes down quickly, and it's easy to get lost. Check the forecast and leave word with someone at your hotel about where you are going. Layers of waterproof gear and fleeces are a good bet so you can strip off when the sun comes out (don't worry, it will appear if you wait long enough!). Even though signposting is generally good in hill areas bring a map: free walking guides are available from regional tourism offices but invest in Ordnance Survey Discovery maps available at newsagents for €8. Wear comfy boots and bring fruit or chocolate and a warm or hydrating drink.

Information, Please?

The two best web sites are: ⊕ www.discoverireland.ie/walking and ⊕ www.walkni.com.

IRISH FAMILY NAMES

Antrim

Lynch
McDonnell
McNeill
O'Hara
O'Neill
Quinn

Armagh

Hanlon
McCann

Carlow

Kinsella
Nolan
O'Neill

Cavan

Boylan
Lynch
McCabe
McGovern
McGowan
McNally
O'Reilly
Sheridan

Clare

Aherne
Boland
Clancy
Daly
Lynch
McGrath
McInerney
McMahon
McNamara
Molon(e)y
O'Brien
O'Dea
O'Grady
O'Halloran
O'Loughlin

Cork

Barry
Callaghan
Cullinane
Donovan
Driscoll
Flynn
Hennessey
Hogan
Lynch
McCarthy
McSweeney
Murphy
Nugent
O'Casey

O'Cullane
(Collins)
O'Keefe
O'Leary
O'Mahony
O'Riordan
Roche
Scanlon
Sheridan

Derry

Cahan
Hegarty
Kelly
McLaughlin

Donegal

Boyle
Clery
Doherty
Friel
Gallagher
Gormley
McGrath
McLoughlin
McSweeney
Mooney
O'Donnell

Down

Lynch
McGuinness
O'Neil
White

Dublin

Hennessey
O'Casey
Plunkett

Fermanagh

Cassidy
Connolly
Corrigan
Flanagan
Maguire
McManus

Galway

Blake
Burke
Clery
Fah(e)y
French
Jennings
Joyce
Kelly
Kenny
Kirwan
Lynch

Madden
Moran
O'Flaherty
O'Halloran

Kerry

Connor
Fitzgerald
Galvin
McCarthy
Moriarty
O'Connell
O'Donoghue
O'Shea
O'Sullivan

Kildare

Cullen
Fitzgerald
O'Byrne
White

Kilkenny

Butler
Fitzpatrick
O'Carroll
Tobin

Laois

Dempsey
Doran
Dunn(e)
Kelly
Moore

Leitrim

Clancy
O'Rourke

Limerick

Fitzgerald
Fitzgibbon
McKeough
O'Brien
O'Cullane
(Collins)
O'Grady
Woulfe

Longford

O'Farrell
Quinn

Louth

O'Carroll
Plunkett

Mayo

Burke
Costello
Dugan

Gormley
Horan
Jennings
Jordan
Kelly
Madden
O'Malley

Meath

Coffey
Connolly
Cusack
Dillon
Hayes
Hennessey
Plunkett
Quinlan

Monaghan

Boylan
Connolly
Hanratty
McKenna
McMahon
McNally

Offaly

Coghlan
Dempsey
Fallon
Malone
Meagher
(Maher)
Molloy
O'Carroll
Sheridan

Roscommon

Fallon
Flanagan
Flynn
Hanley
McDermot
McKeogh
McManus
Molloy
Murphy

Sligo

Boland
Higgins
McDonagh
O'Dowd
O'Hara
Rafferty

Tipperary

Butler
Fogarty
Kennedy

Lynch
Meagher
(Maher)
O'Carroll
O'Dwyer
O'Meara
Purcell
Ryan

Tyrone

Cahan
Donnelly
Gormley
Hagan
Murphy
O'Neill
Quinn

Waterford

Keane
McGrath
O'Brien
Phelan
Power

Westmeath

Coffey
Dalton
Daly
Dillon
Sheridan

Wexford

Doran
Doyle
Hartley
Kavanagh
Keating
Kinsella
McKeogh
Redmond
Walsh

Wicklow

Cullen
Kelly
McKeogh
O'Byrne
O'Toole

ANCESTOR-HUNTING

Over 46 million Americans claim Irish ancestry, and the desire to trace those long-lost roots back in the "auld sod" can run deep. Here are some pointers for how you can make your trip to Ireland a journey into your past.

Before You Go

The more you can learn about your ancestors, the more fruitful your search is going to be once you're on Irish soil. Crucial facts include:

■ The name of your ancestor

■ Names of that ancestor's parents/spouse

■ His or her date of birth, marriage, or death

■ County and parish of origin in Ireland

■ Religious denomination

The first place to seek information is directly from members of your family. A grandparent or a great aunt with a story to tell can be the source of important clues. And relatives who don't know any family history may have documents stored away that can help with your sleuthing—old letters, wills, diaries, birth certificates, photos.

If family resources aren't leading you anywhere, try turning to the Mormon Church. They've made it their mission to collect mountains of genealogical information, much of which it makes available free of charge at ⊕ *familyresearch. org*; plug in the name a relative, and you may find records that include parents' names and places of origin. You can also visit one of hundreds of research centers throughout the United States (addresses for which are available on the Web site).

On the Ground in Ireland

Ancestor hunters have long traveled throughout Ireland to comb parish church records, but most of these records are now available on microfilm in Dublin at the **National Library** (⊠ *Kildare St.* ☎ *01/603–0200* ⊕ *www.nil.ie*). The library is a great place to begin your hunting; you can consult a research adviser there free of charge.

Civil records—dating back to 1865—are available at the **General Register Office** (⊠ *8–11 Lombard St. E, Dublin* ☎ *01/635–4423* ⊕ *www.groireland.ie*). Records for Anglican marriages date from 1845. The **National Archives** (⊠ *Bishop St., Dublin* ⊕ *www.nationalarchives.ie*) has census records and, like the National Library, provides free genealogy consultations.

For Northern Ireland, you can find information at the **Centre for Migration Studies** (⊠ *Mellon Rd., Castletown, Omagh* ☎ *028/8225–6315* ⊕ *www.qub.ac.uk/cms/*) at the Ulster American Folk Park and the **Public Records Office** (⊠ *Balmoral Ave., Belfast* ☎ *028/9025–5905* ⊕ *www.proni. gov.uk*)

None of these places has actual records available online, but their Web sites provide information about genealogical research. If you'd rather not spend your vacation in a record hall, you can hire a professional to do your spadework. The **Association of Professional Genealogists** in Ireland (⊕ *www. irishgenealogy.ie*) will present you with a "package of discovery" upon your arrival. The *Irish Times* newspaper also has ancestor-hunting resources (⊕ *www.ireland. com/ancestor*). And the National Library provides references for professionals.

Dublin

WORD OF MOUTH

"I loved Dublin. It is not a huge city, which is its charm and it has tons to do. I believe Dublin is on the 'sunny' side of the country. Someone help me with this, but isn't the weather a bit better there than on the west coast? We were there at the end of July and the weather was perfect. And why do people never comment on how beautiful Dublin is?"

—kelliebellie

WELCOME TO DUBLIN

TOP REASONS TO GO

★ **Georgian Elegance:** Dublin's signature architectural style makes its most triumphant showing in Merrion, Fitzwilliam, Mountjoy, and Parnell squares.

★ **The Guinness Brewery and Storehouse:** A high-tech museum tells the story of Guinness, Dublin's black blood. At the top, the Gravity Bar has the city's best views.

★ **Toe-Tapping "Trad":** If your your head is still throbbing from last night's sing-along at the pub, head to other music-mad venues like the Olympia Theatre for the best in Irish folk music.

★ **Magnificent Museums:** From the Renoirs at the Hugh Lane to the Tara Brooch at the National Museum and the first editions of Joyce at the Dublin Writers Museum, Dublin is one big treasure chest.

★ **Trinity College:** An oasis of books, granite, and grass sits at the heart of the city. Highlights are the exquisitely illustrated *Book of Kells* and the ornate Long Room.

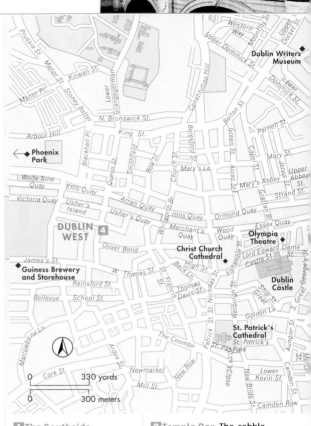

1 The Southside. Between Christ Church Cathedral and Trinity College lies a concentration of famous sights. Merrion Square is the heart of the Georgian district; to its west, four major museums sit side by side. Southwest from here is quaint St. Stephen's Green, which connects to Trinity via stylish, pedestrian-only Grafton Street.

2 Temple Bar. The cobblestone streets and small lanes bounded by Wellington Quay and Dame Street have been transformed into Dublin's trendiest neighborhood. The nightlife doesn't stop at "last call," and on weekends the streets are packed with young people from all over Europe.

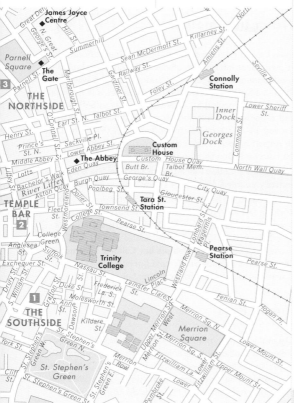

2

GETTING ORIENTED

Despite the seismic changes of the decade-long, and now defunct, Celtic Tiger economy, Dublin happily remains an intimate capital that mixes elegant Georgian buildings, wrought-iron bridges, a battalion of booksellers, and more than 1,000 pubs. The heart of the city is the River Liffey, which runs east to west, splitting Dublin neatly in two. The more affluent Southside has a greater concentration of sights, and it can seem a world apart from the more working-class Northside. North or south, Dublin is compact and easily navigated, making it a great walking city.

3 The Northside.

Less affluent but more eloquent than the Southside, this neighborhood was once home to James Joyce; today it's the site of the Dublin Writers Museum and the James Joyce Centre. Other highlights are the grand Custom House, historic O'Connell Street, and Dublin's two great theaters, the Abbey and the Gate.

4 Dublin West. This former

industrial district stretches from Christ Church west to that other Dublin shrine, the Guinness Brewery. Imposing Dublin Castle houses the Chester Beatty Library—arguably the most impressive museum in Ireland. Phoenix Park, Europe's largest public city park, hugs the north bank of the Liffey.

DUBLIN PLANNER

Transportation Basics

Central Dublin is compact, so walking is the first choice for getting around. Main thoroughfares can become crowded with pedestrians, especially at rush hour, so plan routes along side streets for less bustle.

When your feet need a break, turn to public transit. There's an extensive network of buses, and the pleasant LUAS tram system has two lines running through the city center. You can hail a taxi, get one at a stand, or phone a taxi company. Because they're allowed to use bus lanes, taxis get through traffic faster than private vehicles do. Navigating the city on your own in a rental car is an expensive headache. *For the details about getting around, see the Getting Around section.*

Day-Tripping on the DART

The DART (Dublin Area Rapid Transit) train line runs from the fishing village of Howth, at the northern tip of Dublin Bay, south to the seaside resort of Bray in Wicklow. The route hugs the coastline, providing one spectacular view after another. And with tickets running a little under €4, the price is right.

Visitor Information

Fáilte Ireland (aka Bord Fáilte), the Irish Tourist Board, has its own visitor information offices in the entrance hall of its headquarters at Baggot Street Bridge; it's open weekdays 9:15–5:15. The main Dublin Tourism center is in the former (and still spectacular) St. Andrew's Church on Suffolk Street and is open July–September, Monday–Saturday 8:30–6, Sunday 11–5:30, and October–June, daily 9–6. The Dublin Airport branch is open daily 8 AM–10 PM; the branch at the Ferryport, Dun Laoghaire, is open daily 10–9.

The Temple Bar Information Centre produces the easy-to-use, annually updated *Temple Bar Guide,* with complete listings.

Fáilte Ireland (✉ *Baggot St. Bridge, Southside* ☎ *01/602–4000 in Dublin; 1850/230330 in rest of Ireland* ⊕ *www.discoverireland.com*). **Dublin Tourism** (✉ *Suffolk St. off Grafton St., Southside* ☎ *1850/230330* ⊕ *www.visitdublin.com*). **Temple Bar Cultural Information Centre** (✉ *18 Eustace St., Temple Bar* ☎ *01/677–2255* ⊕ *www.templebar.ie/informationcentre*).

Dublin Pass

Like many tourist capitals around the world, Dublin now features a special pass to help travelers save on admission prices. In conjunction with Dublin Tourism, the Dublin Pass is issued for one, two, three, or six days, and allows free (or, rather, reduced, since the cards do cost something) admission to 30 sights, including the Guinness Brewery, the Dublin Zoo, the Dublin Writers Museum, and Christ Church Cathedral. Prices are €35 for one day; €55 for two days; €65 for three days; and €95 for six days; children's prices are much lower. You can buy your card online and have it waiting for you at one of Dublin's tourist information offices when you arrive. Another plus: you can jump to the head of any line at participating museums and sights.

Information Dublin Tourism (✉ *Suffolk St. off Grafton St., Southside* ☎ *01/605–7700 in Dublin; 1850/230330 in rest of Ireland* ⊕ *www.dublinpass.ie*).

Meeting the Dubs

The most appealing thing about Dublin isn't the sights, or even the great pubs and restaurants. It's the people—the citizens, the Dubs. They're fun, funny, and irreverent, and most of them love nothing better than talking to strangers. So, to get the most out of your visit, make a point of rubbing elbows with the locals. The pub is a natural spot to do this *(⇨ see "Trip to the Pub" later in this chapter)*, but almost any place will do. Ask for directions on a street corner (even if you don't need them), and you might be on your way to a brilliant conversation.

Mind the Slag

"Slagging" is the Dubliner's favorite type of humor. It consists of mildly—or not so mildly—insulting a friend or a soon-to-be-friend in sharp but jovial fashion. It's best employed to deflate vanity or hubris, but clearly marks out the victim as well-liked and worthy. Packed buses and late-night chip shops are classic slagging venues.

Dublin with a Guiding Hand

Dublin is a walker's city, and it's a city full of storytellers. Put two and two together, and it's little surprise that Dublin is a particularly good place for guided walking tours. There are scores of informative, jovial guides eager to reveal the mysteries of "dirty, darling Dublin"—*specific recommendations are found in the Close-Up box "Dublin Sightseeing Tours" below.* Tours usually have a theme that falls into one of three categories: history, culture, or music. While you're learning about the city and getting to know a garrulous local, you can also swap stories and recommendations with other visitors along for the walk.

When to Go

When is it best—and worst—to pay a call on the Irish capital? The summer offers a real lift, as the natives spill out of the pubs into the slew of sidewalk cafés and open-air restaurants. The week around St. Patrick's Day (March 17) is, naturally, a nonstop festival of parades, cultural happenings, and "hooleys" (long nights of partying) throughout the city.

Christmas in Dublin seems to last a month, and the city's old-style illuminations match the genteel, warm mood of the locals. The downside quickly follows, however, for January and February are damp hangover months.

A warm sweater is a must all year round, as even summer nights can occasionally get chilly. Dublin gets its share of rain (though a lot less than other parts of Ireland), so an umbrella is a good investment—and best to make it a strong one, as the winds show no mercy to cheaper models.

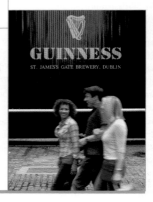

GETTING AROUND

Fares and Schedules

DART service starts at 6:30 AM and runs until 11:30 PM; at peak periods—8 to 9:30 AM and 5 to 7 PM—trains arrive every five minutes. At other times of the day, the intervals between trains are 15 to 25 minutes. Individual fares begin at €1.65 and range up to €3.30 one way. You'll pay a heavy penalty for traveling the DART without a ticket. LUAS trams run from 5:30 AM until 12:30 AM Monday to Saturday and 7 AM until 11:30 PM on Sunday. They come every 7 to 10 minutes at peak times and every 15 to 20 minutes after that. Fares begin at €1.50 and increase up to €2.50 one way according to the number of zones travelled.

Train Information

Connolly Station (✉ *Amiens St., Northside*). **DART** (☎ *01/836–6222* ⊕ *www.irishrail.ie/dart*). **Heuston Station** (✉ *End of Victoria Quay, Dublin West*). **Irish Rail–Iarnod Éireann** (⊕ *www.irishrail.ie*). **Irish Rail Travel Centre** (✉ *35 Lower Abbey St., Northside* ☎ *01/836–6222* ⊕ *www.irishrail.ie*). **LUAS** (☎ *800/300–604* ⊕ *www.luas. ie*). **Pearse Station** (✉ *Westland Row, Southside*).

Train and Tram Travel

As a delightfully compact city, Dublin does not have—or need—a subway system. But its LUAS trams and DART electric railway are a great way to get around the city center and beyond.

The DART (Dublin Area Rapid Transit) connects Dublin with Howth to the north and Bray to the south on a fast, efficient, super scenic train line that hugs the coastline.

But this line also runs through the center city with three convenient stations. Useful for tourists and travelers interested in training around the city center, these are Tara Street (near O'Connell Bridge) and Pearse Street (near Trinity College and Grafton Street) on the Southside, and Connolly Station on the Northside. Then this rail line continues on to such seaside destinations as Dun Laoghaire, Dalkey, and Bray.

As for the LUAS tram service, it runs two lines right into the heart of the city.

The Red Line carries the super-sleek silver trams from Tallaght in the southwest suburbs all the way to Connolly Station in the Northside city center.

This line also takes you to Hueston Station in the southwest of the city center, right by the Guinness Storehouse (James Street Stop), and near to the Royal Hospital Kilmainham (Rialto Stop). It then carries you across the Liffey and through the Smithfield district.

The Northside Abbey Street stop is a minute from O'Connell Street, itself just a short hop across the river from Temple Bar.

The Green Line runs from the Sandyford residential suburb south of the city right into St. Stephen's Green; this line is useful for ferrying visitors between the district of Ballsbridge, with all its hotels, to St. Stephen's Green, Grafton Street, and the heart of the Georgian city center on the Southside.

Together, these lines cross the city center north and south, and so the LUAS is ideal for short hops across those areas.

Tickets can be bought at stations, but it's also possible to buy weekly rail tickets, as well as weekly or monthly rail-and-bus tickets, from the Irish Rail Travel Centre.

Bus Travel

Busaras, just behind the Custom House on the Northside, is Dublin's main station for buses to and from the city.

Dublin Bus runs the city's regular buses. Bus Éireann is the main intercity bus company, with service throughout the country. Aircoach has direct bus connections to Cork and Belfast, and is usually a bit cheaper than Bus Éireann.

In town, there's an extensive network of buses, most of which are green double-deckers.

Some bus services run on cross-city routes, including the smaller "Imp" buses, but most buses start in the city center.

Buses to the north of the city begin in the Lower Abbey Street–Parnell Street area, while those to the west begin in Middle Abbey Street and in the Aston Quay area.

Routes to the southern suburbs begin at Eden Quay and in the College Street area.

Several buses link the DART stations, and another regular bus route connects the two main provincial railway stations, Connolly and Heuston.

If the destination board indicates AN LÁR, that means that the bus is going to the city center.

Museumlink is a shuttle service that links up the National Museum of Natural History, National Museum of Archaeology and History, and the National Museum of Decorative Arts and History. You can catch it outside any of the three museums.

FARES AND SCHEDULES

In the city, fares begin at €1.15 and are paid to the driver, who will accept inexact fares, but you'll have to go to the central office in Dublin to pick up your change as marked on your ticket.

Change transactions and the city's heavy traffic can slow service considerably.

Most bus lines run until 11:30 at night, but some late-night buses run Friday to Saturday until 4:30 AM on some major routes; the fare is €5.

Bus Information Aircoach (☎ 01/844-7118 ⊕ www.aircoach.ie). **Busaras** (⊠ Store St., Northside ☎ 01/830-2222). **Bus Éireann** (☎ 01/873-4222 ⊕ www.buseireann.ie). **Dublin Bus** (⊠ 59 Upper O'Connell St., Northside ☎ 01/873-4222 ⊕ www.dublinbus.ie).

Boat and Ferry Travel

Irish Ferries runs a regular high-speed car and passenger service into Dublin port from Holyhead in Wales. The crossing takes 1 hour and 50 minutes on the faster *Dublin Swift* and 3 hours and 15 minutes on the huge *Ulysses*.

Stena Line has services to both Dublin and nearby Dun Laoghaire port from Holyhead (3½ hours). They also run a high-speed service, known as HSS, which takes about 1 hour and 40 minutes.

Prices and departure times vary according to season, so call to confirm.

Norfolk Line sails from Dublin to Liverpool but travel time is a fairly slow 7 hours.

In summer, reservations are strongly recommended; book online or through a travel agent.

Dozens of taxis wait to take you into town from both ports, or you can take DART or a bus to the city center.

Irish Ferries (⊠ Merrion Row, Southside ☎ 01/661-0511 ⊕ www.irishferries.co.uk).

Norfolk Line (⊠ Southside ☎ 01/819-2999 ⊕ www.norfolkline.com).

Stena Line (⊠ Ferryport, Dun Laoghaire, South County Dublin ☎ 01/204-7777 ⊕ www.stenaline.ie).

GETTING AROUND

Trains to and from Dublin

Irish Rail (Iarnród Éireann) runs intercity trains connecting Dublin with the rest of Ireland.

Connolly Station provides train service to and from the east coast, Belfast, the north (with stops in Malahide, Skerries, and Drogheda), the Northwest, and some destinations to the south, such as Wicklow.

Heuston Station is the place for trains to and from the South and West including Galway, Limerick, and Cork. Trains also run from here to Kildare Town, Newbridge, and other west of Dublin stops.

Taxi Information

NRC Taxies (☎ 01/677–2222).
City Cabs (☎ 01/668–3333).
SCR Taxis (☎ 01/473–1166).

Main Airlines

Aer Arann (☎ 01/814–5240 ⊕ www.aerarann.com).
Aer Lingus (☎ 01/844–4747 ⊕ www.aerlingus.com).
Continental (☎ 1890/925–252 ⊕ www.continental.com).
Delta (☎ 01/844–4166 or 01/676–8080 ⊕ www.delta.com). Ryanair (☎ 01/844–4411 ⊕ www.ryanair.com).

Air Travel

Dublin Airport, 10 km (6 mi) north of the city center, serves international and domestic flights. Three airlines have regularly scheduled flights from the United States to Dublin. Aer Lingus flies direct from New York, Boston, Los Angeles, San Francisco, Orlando, Baltimore, Washington, and Chicago to Dublin. Continental flies from New York (Newark Liberty International Airport) to Dublin. Delta flies from Atlanta to Dublin via New York. There are daily services to Dublin from all major London airports. Flights to Dublin also leave from Birmingham, Bristol, East Midlands, Liverpool, Luton, Manchester, Leeds/Bradford, Newcastle, Edinburgh, and Glasgow.

Within Ireland, Aer Lingus operates flights from Dublin to Belfast, Cork, Derry, Kerry, Shannon, Galway, Knock in County Mayo, Donegal, Waterford, and Sligo. Ryanair flies to Belfast, and Aer Arann flies to Cork, Sligo, Knock, Galway, and Donegal.

Airport Buses and Taxis

Dublin Bus operates the Airlink shuttle service between Dublin Airport and the city center, with departures outside the arrivals gateway. Service runs from 5:45 AM to 11:30 PM, at intervals of about 10 minutes (after 8 PM buses run every 20 minutes), to as far as O'Connell Street and then Dublin's main bus station (Busaras), behind the Custom House on the Northside. Journey time from the airport to the city center is normally 30 minutes, but it may be longer in heavy traffic. The single fare is €6 and round-trip is €10; pay the driver inside the bus or purchase a one-day bus pass for the same price. If you have time, you can save money by taking a regular bus for €2. Aircoach's comfortable coaches run from the airport to the city center 24 hours a day for €7 one way and €12 round-trip. The service stops at the major hotels. A taxi is a quicker alternative than the bus to get from the airport to Dublin center. A line of taxis waits by the arrivals gateway; the fare for the 30-minute journey to any of the main city-center hotels is about €19 to €22 plus tip (tips don't have to be large). Ask about the fare before leaving the airport.

Car Travel

Renting a car in Dublin is very expensive, with high rates and a 12.5% local tax. Gasoline is also expensive by U.S. standards, at around €1.22 a liter. Peak-period car-rental rates begin at around €260 a week for the smallest stick models, like a Ford Fiesta. Dublin has many car-rental companies, and it pays to shop around and to avoid "cowboy" outfits without proper licenses. A dozen car-rental companies have desks at Dublin Airport; all the main national and international firms also have branches in the city center.

Traffic in Ireland has increased exponentially in the last few years, and nowhere has the impact been felt more than in Dublin, where the city's complicated one-way streets are congested not only during the morning and evening rush hours but often during much of the day. If possible, avoid driving a car except to get in and out of the city (and be sure to ask your hotel or guesthouse for clear directions to get you out of town).

Taxi Travel

There are taxi stands beside the central bus station, and at train stations, O'Connell Bridge, St. Stephen's Green, College Green, and near major hotels; the Dublin telephone directory has a complete list. The initial charge is €4.10, with an additional charge of about €1 per kilometer thereafter. The fare is displayed on a meter (make sure it's on). You may, instead, want to phone a taxi company and ask for a cab to meet you at your hotel, but this may cost up to €2 extra. Each extra passenger costs €1, but there is no charge for luggage.

Many taxis run all night, but the demand, especially on weekends (and particularly near clubs on the Leeson Street strip and elsewhere, which stay open until 4 AM or later), can make for long lines at taxi stands. Hackney cabs, which also operate in the city, have neither roof signs nor meters and will sometimes respond to hotels' requests for a cab.

Although the taxi fleet in Dublin is large, the cabs are non-standard and some cars are neither spacious nor in pristine condition. NRC Taxis has a reliable track record. City Cabs is one of the city's biggest but also the busiest. SCR Taxis has some of the friendliest drivers.

Dublin's Must-Dos

Raise a glass to James Joyce on a **Literary Pub Crawl.**

Be illuminated by the medieval Book of Kells at the **Long Gallery of Trinity College.**

"Rock n' Stroll" your way through hip a **Temple Bar** guided tour.

Go gloriously Georgian on 18th-century **Merrion Square.**

Get spirited (pun intended) on a tour of the **Guinness Brewery and Storehouse.**

Pluck a lucky four-leaf clover on **St. Stephen's Green.**

Snack on Spatchcock Quail at Bono's **Tea Room** celeb spot.

Recapture Rococo times in the time-burnished salons of **Newman House.**

Imagine yourself the squire of a Palace Row town house at the **Dublin City Gallery, The Hugh Lane.**

"Become" a Dubliner with a cup of coffee at **Bewley's Oriental Café** on Grafton Street.

Airport Information

Dublin Airport
(📞 *01/844–4900*
⊕ *www.dublin-airport.com*).

DUBLIN'S SEAFOOD BOUNTY

Clarenbridge oysters, Carlingford Lough mussels, Ballina wild smoked salmon, Donegal crab—the menus of the top restaurants in Dublin are now full of some of the most flavorsome seafood on the planet. Surprisingly, Ireland has only recently fallen in love with its own array of briny treasures, and thereby hangs a fish tale.

(above) The Irish treasure of the deep—smoked salmon; (right, top) When it comes to fish and chips, some say the greasier the better; (right, bottom) Seaweed is a chic new condiment.

A somewhat apocryphal story about Ireland joining the EEC (European Economic Community) in 1973 has the government given a stark choice: you can farm or you can fish but you can't do both. They chose to protect farming and the result was the massive overfishing of giant Spanish factory ships of Irish waters. This fact may, in part, explain why Ireland—a relative pollution-free, sea-surrounded nation—is not one of the first places gourmands think of for great seafood. Historically, there was also a certain snobbery about eating fish, as it was seen as peasant food only suitable for fasting Fridays. Well, things have certainly changed in the last two decades as a new breed of home-grown chefs has pushed the importance of locally sourced seafood on their menus.

TOP FISHY JOINTS

Some stand-out joints in Dublin go that extra mile. The oyster stall at the Temple Bar Farmer's Market every Saturday is something of a Dublin institution, where affordable Atlantic oysters and white wine are downed alfresco. Les Fréres Jacques delivers true Gallic panache to its lobsters. The no-frills Kingfisher is noted for its whole rainbow trout.

2

SMOKED SALMON

From all corners of Ireland small producers are now making some of Europe's finest smoked salmon. Obviously, and perhaps unfortunately, the wild Atlantic salmon still has a richer, more piquant taste than its farmed cousin.

The word "Wild" in the description will tell you the fish isn't farmed. The traditional smoking method uses only Irish oak, which gives it a very distinctive, subtle flavor, and deep orange color.

The best time to enjoy smoked salmon is over some toasted Dublin brown bread with a simple squeeze of lemon and some coarse black pepper to add that little extra tang.

IRISH CHOWDER

It's the pint of heavy cream and density of mussels tossed into the mix that makes Irish seafood chowder such a great snack on the run.

It's also a dish that even the most humble of eateries doesn't usually mess up, although the general rule still applies: the nearer to the coast the eaterie is located, the better its chowder. Regular fish stock is often used but clam juice—an Irish speciality—also adds to the unique flavor.

FISH AND CHIPS

Every Dubliner will argue about the best place to get their favorite fast-food dish of fish and chips, but few will quarrel

with the fact that cod, ray, and haddock are the top three battered delights to go for.

Interestingly, the descendants of 1950s Italian immigrants—with names like Macari and Borza—are the recognized masters of the battering art, and you'll find one of their eponymously named shops in almost every neighborhood. Tip: a single portion is usually enough to feed two!

SEAWEED

Yes, the Irish are slowly discovering the delights of farming native seaweed for use in the kitchen and elsewhere. Irish seaweed is usually gathered along the Western seaboard, dried, and then sold in small packets, a bit like herbs.

Look closely at restaurant menus and you'll find dulse, carrageen moss, and various kelps and wracks all turning up to add spice to risottos, salads, soups, breads, and even ice cream.

The local spa industry has cottoned on, developing "algotherapies," including wraps, aging creams, and even full-on seaweed baths. Enjoy chowders at Ireland's great seafood festivals: the Galway Oyster Festival, the event in Baltimore in West Cork, and the Killybegs festival.

Updated by
Anto Howard

Ask any Dubliner what's happening and you may hear echoes of one of W. B. Yeats's most-quoted lines: "All changed, changed utterly." While you can no longer hear the roar of the Celtic Tiger, a decade of a white-hot economy transformed Dublin into one of Western Europe's most popular urban destinations. Whether or not you're out to enjoy the old or new Dublin, you'll find it a colossally entertaining city, all the more astonishing considering its intimate size.

It is ironic and telling that James Joyce chose Dublin as the setting for his famous *Ulysses, Dubliners,* and *A Portrait of the Artist as a Young Man* because it was a "center of paralysis" where nothing much ever changed. Which only proves that even the greats get it wrong sometimes. Indeed, if Joyce were to return to his once genteel hometown today—disappointed with the city's provincial outlook, he left it in 1902 at the age of 20—and take a quasi-Homeric odyssey through the city (as he so famously does in *Ulysses*), would he even recognize Dublin as his "Dear Dirty Dumpling, foosterfather of fingalls and dottergills"?

For instance, what would he make of Temple Bar—the city's erstwhile down-at-the-heels neighborhood, now crammed with restaurants and trendy hotels and suffused with a nonstop, international-party atmosphere? Or the simple sophistication of the open-air restaurants of the tiny Italian Quarter (named Ouartie Bloom after his own creation), complete with sultry tango lessons? Or of the hot/cool Irishness, where every aspect of Celtic culture results in sold-out theaters, from Conor McPherson's Broadway hit, *The Seafarer,* to *Riverdance,* the old Irish mass-jig recast as a Las Vegas extravaganza? Plus, the resurrected Joyce might be stirred by the songs of U2, fired up by the sultry acting of Colin Farrell, and moved by the poems of Nobel laureate Seamus Heaney. As for Ireland's capital, even after the Celtic Tiger party has faded, elegant shops and hotels, galleries, art-house cinemas, coffeehouses, and a stunning variety of restaurants can be found on almost every street in Dublin, transforming the provincial city that suffocated Joyce into a place almost as cosmopolitan as the Paris to which he fled.

The recent economic downturn has provoked a few Dublin citizens to protest that the boomtown transformation of their heretofore tranquil city has permanently affected its spirit and character. These skeptics (skepticism long being a favorite pastime in the capital city) await the outcome of "Dublin: The Sequel," and their greatest fear is the possibility that the tattered old lady on the Liffey has become a little less unique, a little more like everywhere else.

Oh ye of little faith: the rare aul' gem that is Dublin is far from buried. The fundamentals—the Georgian elegance of Merrion Square, the Norman drama of Christ Church Cathedral, the foamy pint at an atmospheric pub—are still on hand to gratify. Most of all, there are the locals themselves: the nod and grin when you catch their eye on the street, the eagerness to hear half your life story before they tell you all of theirs, and their paradoxically dark but warm sense of humor.

EXPLORING DUBLIN

"In Dublin's fair city, where the girls are so pretty"—so went the centuries-old ditty. Today, there are parts of the city that may not be fair or pretty, but although you may not be conscious of it while you're in the center city, Dublin *does* boast a beautiful setting: it loops around the edge of Dublin Bay and on a plain at the edge of the gorgeous, green Dublin and Wicklow mountains, which rise softly just to the south. From the glass-wall top of the Guinness Storehouse in the heart of town, the sight of the city, the bay, and the mountains will take your breath away. From the city's noted vantage points, such as the South Wall, which stretches far out into Dublin Bay, you can nearly get a full measure of the city. From north to south, Dublin stretches 16 km (10 mi); in total, it covers 28,000 acres—but Dublin's heart is far more compact than these numbers indicate. Like Paris, London, and Florence, a river runs right through it. The River Liffey divides the capital into the Northside and the Southside, as everyone calls the two principal center-city areas, and virtually all the major sights are well within less than an hour's walk of one another.

Our coverage is organized into six sections exploring the main neighborhoods of Dublin city (plus one excursion into the northern suburbs of County Dublin). The first two sections—The Southside and Southeast Dublin—focus on many of the city center's major sights: Trinity College, St. Stephen's Green, Merrion Square, and Grafton Street. The third section, Temple Bar, takes you through this revived neighborhood, still the hippest zone in the capital. The Northside section covers major cultural sights north of the Liffey and east of Capel Street, including the James Joyce Centre, Gate Theatre, Dublin Writers Museum, and the Hugh Lane municipal art gallery. It also includes the majestic Custom House and the rapidly developed, high-rise Docklands area near the mouth of the river. The next section, Dublin West, picks up across Dame Street

CLOSE UP

Dublin Past and Present

Until 500 AD, Dublin was little more than a crossroads—albeit a critical one—for four of the main thoroughfares that traversed the country. It had two names: Baile Atha Cliath, meaning City of the Hurdles, bestowed by Celtic traders in the 2nd century AD; and Dubhlinn, or "dark pool," after a body of water believed to have been where Dublin Castle now stands.

In 837, Norsemen carried out the first invasion of Dublin, to be followed by new waves of warriors staking their claim to the city—from the 12th-century Anglo-Normans to Oliver Cromwell in 1651.

Not until the 18th century did Dublin reach a golden age, when the patronage of wealthy nobles turned the city into one of Europe's most prepossessing capitals. But the era of "the glorious eighteenth" was short-lived; in 1800, the Act of Union brought Ireland and Britain together into the United Kingdom, and power moved to London.

The 19th century proved to be a time of political turmoil, although Daniel O'Connell, the first Catholic lord mayor of Dublin, won early success with the introduction of Catholic Emancipation in 1829. During the late 1840s, Dublin escaped the worst effects of the famine that ravaged much of southern and western Ireland.

The city entered another period of upheaval in the first decades of the 20th century, marked by the Easter Uprising of 1916. A war for independence from Britain began in 1919, followed by establishment of the Irish Free State in December 1921 and subsequent civil war. In its aftermath Dublin entered an era of political and cultural conservatism, which continued until the late 1970s. A major turning point occurred in 1972, when Ireland joined the European Economic Community.

In the 1980s, while the economy remained in recession, Irish musicians stormed the American and British barricades of rock-and-roll music, with U2 climbing to the topmost heights.

The 1990s and first years of the 21st century have truly been Ireland's boom time, set in motion to a great extent by the country's participation in the European Union. When Ireland approved the new EU treaty in 1992, it was one of the poorest member nations, qualifying it for grants of all kinds.

Ireland quickly transformed itself into the economic envy of the world, propelled by massive investment from multinational corporations, particularly in the telecommunications, software, and service industries. In 2000 the government announced that Ireland was the world's largest exporter of software. But the later years of the Tiger were fueled by a crazy property bubble and Dublin, like most of the world, suddenly woke up with one doozy of an economic hangover.

Today, roughly a third of the Irish Republic's 4.1 million people live in Dublin and its suburbs. It's a city of young people—astonishingly so (students from all over Ireland attend Trinity College and the city's dozen other universities). Many of them have their eyes feverishly focused on the future.

Reflected in the waters of the Liffey, the Custom House is just one of the many famed Dublin landmarks spectacularly illuminated at night.

from Temple Bar and continues west through the historic, working-class Liberties neighborhood to the Guinness Brewery and Storehouse, the city's most popular attraction. In addition, it includes the two main cathedrals and the cobblestone old-market district of Smithfield. Finally, the Phoenix Park and Environs section covers the most western fringe of the Northside and the great public park itself. If you're planning to take in all the sights, you may wish to invest in the city's special tourist ticket, the **Dublin Pass**; *for more information, see the section in our Dublin Planner pages.*

If you're visiting Dublin for more than two or three days, you'll have time to explore farther afield. There's plenty to see and do a short distance from the city center—in the suburbs of County Dublin. *Worthwhile destinations in these parts of the county are covered in the Side Trips section at the end of this chapter.*

DUBLIN'S SOUTHSIDE: TRINITY COLLEGE TO ST. STEPHEN'S GREEN

The River Liffey provides a useful aid of orientation, flowing as it does through the direct middle of Dublin. If you ask a native Dubliner for directions—from under an umbrella, as it will probably be raining in the approved Irish manner—he or she will most likely reply in terms of "up" or "down," up meaning away from the river, and down toward it. Until recently, Dublin's center of gravity was O'Connell Bridge, a diplomatic landmark in that it avoided locating the center either north or south of the river—strong local loyalties still prevailed among "Northsiders" and "Southsiders," and neither group would ever accept that the city's center lay elsewhere than on their own side. The 20th century, however, saw diplomacy fall by the wayside—Dublin's heart now beats loudest southward across the Liffey, due in part to a large-scale refurbishment and pedestrianization of Grafton Street, which made this already upscale shopping address the main street on which to shop, stop, and be seen. At the foot of Grafton Street is the city's most famous and recognizable landmark, Trinity College; at the top of it is Dublin's most popular strolling retreat, St. Stephen's Green, a 27-acre landscaped park with flowers, lakes, bridges, and Dubliners enjoying their time-outs.

Numbers in the margin correspond to numbers on the Dublin South-side map.

TOP ATTRACTIONS

2 **Bank of Ireland.** Across the street from the west facade of Trinity College stands one of Dublin's most striking buildings, formerly the original home of Irish Parliament. Sir Edward Lovett Pearce designed the central section in 1729; three other architects would ultimately be involved in the remainder of the building's construction. A pedimented portico fronted by six massive Corinthian columns dominates the grand facade, which follows the curve of Westmoreland Street as it meets College Green, once a Viking meeting place and burial ground. Two years after Parliament was abolished in 1801 under the Act of Union, which brought Ireland under the direct rule of Britain, the building was bought for the equivalent of €50,790 by the Bank of Ireland. Inside, stucco rosettes adorn the coffered ceiling in the pastel-hue, colonnaded, clerestoried main banking hall, at one time the Court of Requests, where citizens' petitions were heard. Just down the hall is the original House of Lords, with an oak-panel nave, a 1,233-drop Waterford glass chandelier, and tapestries depicting the Battle of the Boyne and the Siege of Derry; ask a guard to show you in. Visitors are welcome during normal banking hours; the Dublin historian and author Éamonn Mac Thomáis conducts brief guided tours every Tuesday at 10:30, 11:30, and 1:45. ✉ *2 College Green, Southside* ☎ *01/661–5933* ⊕ *www.visitdublin.com* ☞ *Free* ☉ *Mon.–Wed. and Fri. 10–4, Thurs. 10–5.*

3 **Grafton Street.** It's no more than 200 yards long and about 20 feet wide, but brick-lined Grafton Street, open only to pedestrians, can claim to be the most humming street in the city, if not in all of Ireland. It's one of Dublin's vital spines: the most direct route between the front door of Trinity College and St. Stephen's Green, and the city's premier shopping street, with Dublin's most distinguished department store, Brown Thomas, as well as tried and trusted Marks & Spencer. Grafton Street and the smaller alleyways that radiate off it offer dozens of independent stores, a dozen or so colorful flower sellers, and some of the Southside's most popular watering holes. In summer, buskers from all over the world line both sides of the street, pouring out the sounds of drum, whistle, pipe, and string.

NEED A BREAK?

The granddaddy of the capital's cafés, Bewley's Oriental Café (✉ *78 Grafton St., Southside* ☎ *01/672–7700*), came within a heartbeat of extinction a few years back, after having served coffee and sticky buns

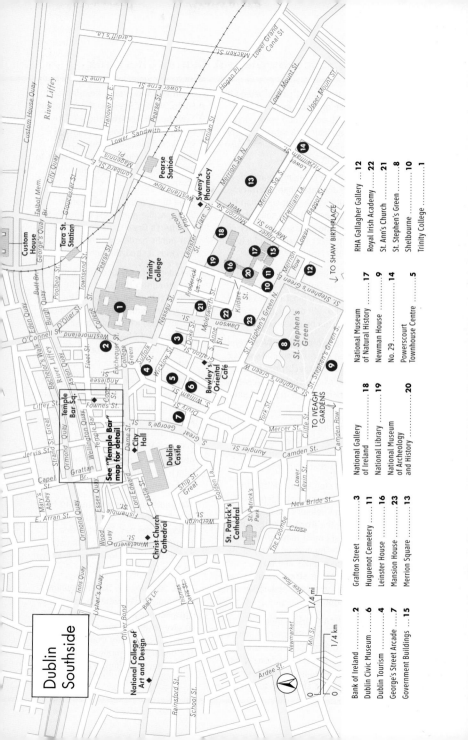

Dublin Southside

Bank of Ireland **2**
Dublin Civic Museum **6**
Dublin Tourism **4**
George's Street Arcade ... **7**
Government Buildings ... **15**

Grafton Street **3**
Huguenot Cemetery **11**
Leinster House **16**
Mansion House **23**
Merrion Square **13**

National Gallery
of Ireland **17**
National Library **19**
National Museum
of Archeology
and History **20**

National Museum
of Natural History **12**
Newman House **9**
No. 29 .... **14**
Powerscourt
Townhouse Centre **5**

RHA Gallagher Gallery ... **12**
Royal Irish Academy **22**
St. Ann's Church **21**
St. Stephen's Green **8**
Shelbourne **10**
Trinity College **1**

Dublin Step-by-Step: A Center City Walk

Touring the largest city in Ireland in the space of a day sounds like an impossible goal, but if you're determined you can do a large chunk of it in a single sunrise-to-sunset span. Think Dublin 101.

South of the Liffey are graceful squares and fashionable terraces from Dublin's elegant Georgian heyday; interspersed with some of the city's leading sights, this center-city area is perfect for an introductory tour of the city.

You might begin at **O'Connell Bridge**—as Dublin has no central focal point, most natives have regarded the bridge as the city's Piccadilly Circus or Times Square.

Then head south down Westmoreland Street on your way to view one of Dublin's most spectacular buildings, James Gandon's 18th-century **Parliament House,** now the Bank of Ireland building.

After you drink in the grand colonnades, cross the street to the genteel, elegant campus of **Trinity College**—the oldest seat of Irish learning.

Your first stop should be the Old Library, to see the staggering Long Room and Ireland's greatest art treasure, the **Book of Kells,** one of the world's most famous—and most beautiful—illuminated manuscripts. Leave the campus and take a stroll along **Grafton Street,** Dublin's busiest shopping street the pedestrian spine of the Southside.

The **Dublin Tourism** office, in a spectacular medieval former church, is just off Grafton Street, on the corner of Suffolk Street. If Grafton Street's shops whet your appetite for more browsing and shopping, turn right down Wicklow Street, then left onto South William Street to **Powerscourt Townhouse Centre,** where a faux-Georgian atrium houses high-end shops and pleasant eateries. The **Dublin Civic Museum** is next door to Powerscourt, across the alley on its south flank.

Head back to the end of Grafton Street, at the northwest corner of **St. Stephen's Green,** Dublin's most popular public garden, which absolutely demands a stroll-through.

The magnificently Georgian 18th-century **Newman House** is on the south side of the green. Amble back across the green, exiting onto the northeast corner, at which stands the pillared and corniced **Shelbourne** hotel, a grand place for tea or lunch (you've earned it!).

At this corner of the Green in olden days was the "Beaux Walk," a favorite 18th-century gathering place for fashionable Dubliners. Chances are you won't bump into a duke on his way to a Handel concert but then neither will you have to dodge pigs, which were a feature of the cityscape back then.

Walk north on Merrion Street to **Merrion Square**—one of Dublin's most attractive squares. The east side of Merrion Square and its continuation, Fitzwilliam Street, form what is known as **"the Georgian Mile."**

On a clear day the Dublin Mountains are visible in the distance and the prospect has almost been preserved to give an impression of the spacious feel of 18th-century Dublin (excepting the unattractive, modern office block of the Electricity Supply Board).

2

Walk down the south side of the square to one of Dublin's most fascinating historic house renovations found on **Lower Fitzwilliam Street, No. 29** to be precise.

Then cut back through the square to the head to **Dublin's museum quarter**, which has an array of amazing museum, starting out with the charmingly 19th-century **National Museum of Natural History** and the moderate-size **National Gallery of Ireland**, where you can feast your eyes on masterworks by Rubens, Caravaggio, Uccello, and Goya (don't forget its top-rated restaurant).

The last leg—hopefully not literally—of this walk begins up Kildare Street to the **National Library.** If you want to take a peek at the famously domed Reading Room, get a visitor's pass; or just be content to study the entrance hall's display of library treasures.

Many visitors will bypass the library and go instead behind the back of Leinster House toward the looming domed rotunda entrance of the **National Museum of Archaeology and History.** Here, fabled Celtic treasures, including the Cross of Cong and the Gleninsheen Gorget, await you.

A short walk west along Molesworth Street takes you to Dawson Street. St. Ann's Church, the reticent Royal Irish Academy, and private Mansion House—the mayor's residence—are all on the left side as you walk toward St. Stephen's Green.

If you're interested in George Bernard Shaw, you may want to take a 15-minute walk from the Green to the **Shaw Birthplace**—from the bottom of Dawson Street make a right and then a left around the green until you arrive at Harcourt Street.

After a short walk south, make a right onto Harrington Street and a right again onto Synge Street and the Shaw house.

From here, it is only appropriate to hop on a tram and head north of the Liffey to the famous **Dublin Writers Museum,** set in a gorgeous 18th-century mansion.

Perhaps end the day with a performance at the nearby **Gate Theatre,** another Georgian eye-pleaser, or spend the evening exploring the cobbled streets, many cafés, and shops of Dublin's boho quarter, the compact **Temple Bar area,** back on the south bank of the Liffey.

Walk through Merchant's Arch, the symbolic entry into the district (see if you can spot the surveillance cameras up on the walls), which leads you onto the area's long spine, named Temple Bar here but also called Fleet Street (to the east) and Essex Street (to the west). You're right at Temple Bar Square, one of the two largest plazas in the neighborhood.

You can easily breeze through Temple Bar in an hour or so, but if you've got the time, plan to chill out here by drifting in and out of the dozens of stores and galleries, relaxing at a café over a cup of coffee or at a pub over a pint, or, if you're looking for a change from sightseeing, maybe even catching a film at one of the art cinemas.

And because you couldn't fit in a stop at the Guinness Brewery and Storehouse, top the evening off with a pint at the Stag's Head pub just across Dame Street.

to Dubliners since its founding by the Quakers in 1842. Fortunately, the old dame was saved and turned into a combination café, pizza, and pasta joint. Best of all, a revamp brought back some of the old grandeur associated with Bewley's, including the exotic picture wallpaper and trademark stained-glass windows, designed by the distinguished early-20th-century artist Harry Clarke. The place is worth a visit if only to sit in the super-comfortable velvet seats over a cup of quality coffee, and people-watch just like Dubliners have for well over 150 years. There's even a cute little theater upstairs with lunchtime shows. The ticket price (€15) includes homemade soup and brown bread.

❾ Newman House. One of the greatest glories of Georgian Dublin, Newman House is actually two imposing town houses joined together. The earlier of the two, No. 85 St. Stephen's Green (1738), was originally known as Clanwilliam House. Designed by Richard Castle, favored architect of Dublin's rich and famous, it features a winged Palladian window on the Wicklow granite facade. It has two landmarks of Irish Georgian style: the Apollo Room, decorated with stuccowork depicting the sun god and his muses; and the magnificent Saloon, "the supreme example of Dublin Baroque," according to scholars Jacqueline O'Brien and Desmond Guinness. The Saloon is crowned with an exuberant ceiling aswirl with cupids and gods, created by the Brothers Lafranchini, the finest *stuccadores* (plaster-workers) of 18th-century Dublin. Next door at No. 86 (1765), the staircase, set against pastel swags, is one of the city's most beautiful Rococo examples—with floral swags and musical instruments picked out in cake-frosting white. Catholic University (described by James Joyce in *A Portrait of the Artist as a Young Man*) was established in this building in 1850, with Cardinal John Henry Newman as its first rector. To explore the houses you must join a guided tour. At the back of Newman House hides Iveagh Gardens *(see below).* ✉ *85–86 St. Stephen's Green, Southside* ☎ *01/716–7422* ⊕ *www.visitdublin.com* ✉ *House and garden €5* ☼ *Tours June–Aug., Tues.–Fri. at 2, 3, and 4.*

❺ Powerscourt Townhouse Centre. Lucky man, the Viscount Powerscourt. In the mid-18th century, not only did he build Ireland's most spectacular country house, in Enniskerry, County Wicklow (which bears the family name), but he also decided to rival that structure's grandeur with one of Dublin's largest stone mansions. Staffed with 22 servants and built of granite from the viscount's quarry in the Wicklow Hills, Powerscourt House was a major statement in the Palladian style. Designed by Robert Mack in 1771, it's a massive edifice that towers over the little street it sits on (note the top story, framed by large volutes, which was intended as an observatory). Inside, there are Rococo salons designed by James McCullagh, splendid examples of plasterwork in the Adamesque style and—surprise!—a shopping atrium, installed in and around the covered courtyard. The stores here include high-quality Irish crafts shops and numerous food stalls. The mall exit leads to the St. Teresa's Carmelite Church and Johnson's Court. Beside the church, a pedestrian lane leads onto Grafton Street. ✉ *59 S. William St., Southside* ☎ *01/679–7000*

⊕ *www.powerscourtcentre.com*
⊗ *Mon.–Wed. and Fri. 10–6,*
Thurs. 10–8, Sat. 9–9, Sun. noon–
6; limited shops open Sun.

8 St. Stephen's Green. Dubliners call it
simply Stephen's Green, and green it
is (year-round)—a verdant, 27-acre
Southside square that was used for
the public punishment of criminals
until 1664. After a long period of

WORD OF MOUTH

"We meandered around St. Stephen's Green for a bit. Reminded
me of Central Park but with
more of a garden feel to it. Very,
very nice."

—Ocnmeg

---

decline, it became a private park in 1814—the first time in its history
that it was closed to the public. Its fortunes changed again in 1880,
when Sir Arthur Guinness (a member of the Guinness brewery family
who was later known as Lord Ardiluan), paid for it to be laid out anew.
Flower gardens, formal lawns, a Victorian bandstand, and an ornamental lake with lots of waterfowl are all within the park's borders, connected by paths guaranteeing that strolling here or just passing through
will offer up unexpected delights (such as palm trees). Among the park's
many statues are a memorial to W. B. Yeats and another to Joyce by
Henry Moore, and the *Three Fates,* a dramatic group of bronze female
figures watching over human destiny. In the 18th century the walk on
the north side of the green was referred to as the Beaux Walk because
most of Dublin's gentlemen's clubs were in town houses here. Today
it's dominated by the legendary Shelbourne hotel. On the south side is
the alluring Georgian-gorgeous Newman House. ⊠ *Southside* 🖃 *Free*
⊗ *Daily sunrise–sunset.*

10 Shelbourne. The iconic, redbrick, white-wood-trim Shelbourne hotel
commands "the best address in Dublin" from the north side of St. Stephen's Green, where it has stood since 1865. The new restaurant and
lounge, and the completely redesigned guest rooms and public spaces
constitute a major face-lift for Dublin's most iconic hotel. Afternoon
tea in the very opulent Lord Mayor's Lounge is a true Dublin treat to
be enjoyed by all. In 1921 the Irish Free State's constitution was drafted
here, in a first-floor suite. Elizabeth Bowen wrote her novel *The Hotel*
about this very place. ⊠ *27 St. Stephen's Green, Southside* ☎ *01/676–*
6471 ⊕ *www.marriott.co.uk.*

1 Trinity College. Founded in 1592 by Queen Elizabeth I to "civilize" (Her
Majesty's word) Dublin, Trinity is Ireland's oldest and most famous
college. The memorably atmospheric campus is a must; here you can
track the shadows of some of the noted alumni, such as Jonathan Swift
(1667–1745), Oscar Wilde (1854–1900), Bram Stoker (1847–1912),
and Samuel Beckett (1906–89). Trinity College, Dublin (familiarly
known as TCD), was founded on the site of the confiscated Priory of
All Hallows. For centuries Trinity was the preserve of the Protestant
Church; a free education was offered to Catholics—provided that they
accepted the Protestant faith. As a legacy of this condition, until 1966
Catholics who wished to study at Trinity had to obtain a dispensation
from their bishop or face excommunication.

Continued on page 70

LITERARY DUBLIN

A PLAYWRIGHT ON EVERY CORNER

As any visit to the Dublin Writers Museum will prove, this city packs more literary punch per square foot than practically any other spot on the planet. While the Irish capital may be relatively small in geographic terms, it looms huge as a country of the imagination. Dubliners wrote some of the greatest works of Western literature, including these immortal titles: *Ulysses*, *Gulliver's Travels*, *Dracula*, *The Importance of Being Earnest*, and *Waiting for Godot*. Today Dublin is a veritable literary theme park: within a few minutes' walk you can visit the birthplace of George Bernard Shaw, see where Sean O'Casey wrote *Juno and the Paycock*, and pop into the pub where Brendan Behan loved to get marinated.

Above, Long Gallery library at Trinity College; Left and right, first editions of Joyce, Swift, Behan, and O'Casey

Dubliners

by JAMES JOYCE

THE ALBATROSS

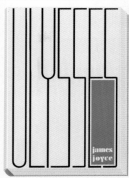

Ulysses, First American Edition

Dublin Writers Museum, Gallery of Writers

A WAY WITH WORDS
As tellers of the tallest tales, speakers of Gaelic (reputedly the world's most perfect medium for prayers, curses, and seduction), and the finest practitioners of the art of blarney, it's little surprise that the Hibernian race produced no fewer than four Nobel prize winners: Shaw, W. B. Yeats, Samuel Beckett, and Seamus Heaney. But what is surprising is that this tiny, long-colonized island on the outskirts of Europe somehow managed to maneuver itself to the very heart of literature in the language of the invader itself, English. And at that heart's core lies Dublin.

A ramble through literary Dublin is a crash course in Irish soul.

FOR BETTER OR VERSE
By the 18th century, the Gaelic tradition was trumped by the boom of literature written in English, often by second- or third-generation descendants of English settlers, such as William Congreve, Richard Brinsley Sheridan, and Oliver Goldsmith. With the Easter Uprising of 1916, so many Irish writers found themselves censored that "being banned" became a matter of prestige (it also did wonders for book sales abroad, with a smuggled copy of *Ulysses* becoming the ultimate status symbol). Sadly, many writers became exiles; most famously, Joyce was joined in Paris by Beckett in 1932.

DUBLIN B(U)Y THE BOOK
Book lovers know that a guidebook to this city is an anthology of Irish literature in itself. Dublin's Northside is studded with landmarks immortalized in James Joyce's novels. A stone's throw from the Liffey is the Abbey Theater, a potent symbol of Ireland's great playwrights. To the south lies Trinity College, alma mater of Jonathan Swift, Bram Stoker, Oscar Wilde, and Samuel Beckett. And scattered around the city are thousands of pubs where storytelling evolved as the incurable Irish "disease." They are the perfect places to take a time-out while touring Dublin's leading literary shrines and sites.

THE TRAIL OF TALES

 Allowing you to turn the pages of the city, as it were, with your feet, a literary ramble through Dublin is a magical mystery tour through more than 400 years of Irish history.

The view from Parliament Square, Trinity College

DUBLIN WRITERS MUSEUM. The best place to start any literary tour of the city, this gloriously restored 18th-century mansion was once the home of the Jameson Whiskey family (booze and writers are never too far apart in Dublin). Its Edwardian rooms are filled with inky treasures like the 1804 edition of Swift's *Gulliver's Travels* and the 1899 first edition of Stoker's *Dracula*. ⊠ 18 Parnell Sq. N ☎ 01/872–2077 ⊕ www.-writersmuseum.com.

GATE THEATER. Landmarked by its noble Palladian portico, this magnificent Georgian theater (built 1784) today sees the premieres of some of Ireland's most talked-about plays. Orson Welles and James Mason got their starts here. ⊠ Cavendish Row ☎ 01/874–4045 ⊕ www.-gate-theater.ie.

JAMES JOYCE CENTRE. Now an extensive library dedicated to arguably the greatest novelist of the 20th century,

this sumptuously decorated 18th-century town house was featured in *Ulysses* as a dancing academy. Letters from Beckett, Joyce's guitar and cane, and a Joyce edition illustrated by Matisse are collection highlights. ⊠ 35 N. Great George's St. ☎ 01/878–8547 ⊕ www.jamesjoyce.ie.

SEAN O'CASEY HOUSE. A one-time construction laborer, O'Casey became Ireland's greatest modern playwright and this is the house where he wrote all his famous Abbey plays, including *Juno and the Paycock* and *The Plough and the Stars*. ⊠ 422 N. Circular Rd.

ABBEY THEATRE. Hard to believe this 1950s modernist eyesore is the fabled home of Ireland's national theater company, established on a wave of nationalist passion by Yeats and his patron, Lady Gregory, in 1904. Here premiered J. M. Synge's scandalous *Playboy of the Western World* and the working-class plays of Sean O'Casey. The foyer

and bar display mementos of the theater's fabled "Abbeyists." ⊠ Lower Abbey St. ☎ 01/878–7222 ⊕ www.-abbeytheater.ie.

TRINITY COLLEGE DUBLIN. This 400-year-old college has an incredible record for turning out literary giants like Swift, Goldsmith, Wilde, Synge, Stoker, and Beckett. Majestically presiding over its famous library is the 9th-century Book of Kells, mother of all Irish tomes. ⊠ Front Sq. ☎ 01/896–2320 ⊕ www.tcd.ie/library.

NATIONAL LIBRARY. Joyce used the 1890 Main Reading Room, with its dramatic domed ceiling, as the scene of the great literary debate in *Ulysses*. At No. 30 Kildare Street a plaque marks a former residence of *Dracula*'s creator, Bram Stoker. ⊠ Kildare St. ☎ 01/603–0200 ⊕ www.nli.ie.

MERRION SQUARE. An elegant mansion, which can be toured, No. 1 Merrion Square is the former Oscar Wilde family residence. A

Neary's Pub

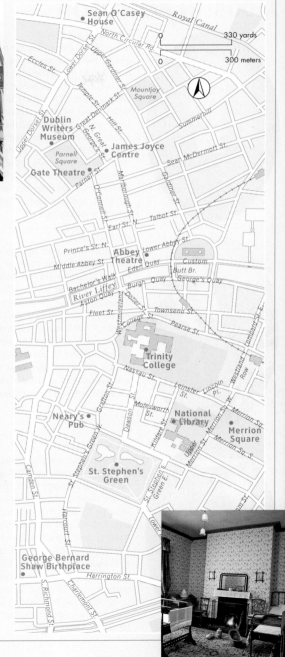

statue of Oscar reclines in the park opposite. Around the square, note the plaques that indicate former residents, including W. B. Yeats and Sheridan le Fanu, Dublin's most famous ghost-story teller.

ST. STEPHEN'S GREEN. This pretty, flower-filled little park is home to a wonderful statue of Joyce.

GEORGE BERNARD SHAW BIRTHPLACE. Shaw lived in this modest, Victorian terrace house until he was 10 and the painstaking restoration of the little rooms highlights a cramped, claustrophobic atmosphere Eliza Doolittle would have felt at home in. ⊠ 33 Synge St. ☎ 01/475–0854 ⊕ www.-visitdublin.com.

NEARY'S PUB. The Victorian-style interiors here were once haunted by Dublin's literary set, most notably the raconteur Brendan Behan. ⊠ 1 Chatham St. ☎ 01/677–7371.

See main Exploring for full texts on these landmarks.

Shaw Birthplace

A DUBLIN PANTHEON

JONATHAN SWIFT

"Where fierce indignation can no longer tear his heart": Swift, one of the great satirists in the English language, willed these words be carved on his tomb at Dublin's St. Patrick's Cathedral. Swift was born on November 30, 1667, in the Liberties area of Dublin. Life would deal him many misfortunes, but he gave as good as he got, venting his great anger with a pen sharper than any sword. His rage at the British government's mistreatment of the Irish was turned into the brilliant satire *A Modest Proposal* where he politely recommends a solution to the dual problems of hunger and overpopulation: breed babies for meat. Best remembered for the brilliant moral fable *Gulliver's Travels*, he died on October 19, 1745, and is buried in Dublin's St. Patrick's Cathedral, where he was dean.

OSCAR WILDE

The greatest wit of his age and arguably any other, Wilde was born on October 16, 1834, at 21 Westland Row in Dublin, the son of an eminent eye doctor. He was educated at Trinity College, where he was a promising boxer and was quoted as saying his greatest challenge was learning to live up to the blue china he had installed in his rooms. Wilde moved to London in 1879, where he married, had children, and became celebrated for the plays *The Importance of Being Earnest* and *Salome* and his titillating novel *The Picture of Dorian Gray*. But his life was always more famous than his work and a scandalous affair with the aristocratic Alfred Douglas finally led to his ruin and imprisonment.

W. B. YEATS

Poet, dramatist, and prose writer, Yeats—winner of the Nobel Prize for Literature in 1923—stands as one of the greatest English-language poets of the 20th century. And yet in Ireland itself he is best remembered for his key role in the struggle for Irish freedom and the revival of Irish culture, including his part in forming the Abbey Theatre (National Theatre). Born in the seaside suburb of Sandymount in Dublin in 1865, his fascination with Celtic folklore and the stories of Cuchulainn can be seen throughout his early poems and plays. But many of his greatest poems are haunted by the dashing figure of Maud Gonne, actress, revolutionary, and unrequited love. He died in 1939 in Paris but his body was buried in Drucliffe, at the foot of Ben Bulben mountain in his beloved County Sligo.

GEORGE BERNARD SHAW

G. Bernard Shaw—he hated George, and never used it either personally or professionally—was born in Dublin in 1856. His father was a boozing corn merchant and his mother a professional singer. When Shaw was a boy his mother ran away with her voice coach, and it may be no coincidence that his plays are dotted with problem child/parent relationships. In 1886 he went to London where plays such as *Pygmalion* and *Saint Joan* helped propel him to international stardom. Pacifist, socialist, and feminist, Shaw was a true original, a radical in the real sense of the word, his work always challenging the norms of his day. He lived to the ripe old age of 94 and died in 1950 after falling off a ladder while trimming trees outside his house.

SEAN O'CASEY

The first working-class Irish literary great, dramatist O'Casey was born at 85 Upper Dorset Street in the inner-city Dublin slums in 1880. Problems with his eyes as a child kept him indoors where he gleaned a love of reading. An early advocate of Yeats's Celtic Revival, he later found his true faith in the socialism of union leader Jim Larkin. His trilogy of great tragicomedies—*Shadow of a Gunman, Juno and the Paycock,* and *The Plough and the Stars*—all deal with ordinary families caught up in the maelstrom of Irish politics and were performed at Yeats's Abbey in the 1920s. Their playful language and riotous action have made them classics ever since. He spent his later life in England and died in Devon in 1964.

BRENDAN BEHAN

Writer, fighter, drinker, and wit, Brendan Francis Behan was born in Dublin's Holles Street Hospital in 1923 into an educated, political working-class family. Urged on by his fiercely patriotic grandmother, he joined Fiánna Eireann, the youth wing of the IRA and, in 1939, was jailed for three years for possessing explosives. In prison he began to write but it wasn't until the 1950s that he hit it big with *The Quare Fellow*, a play based on his prison experiences, and later works *The Hostage* and *Borstal Boy*. But it was in the bars of Dublin that the "demon drinker" Behan delivered many of his greatest lines—alas, lost now forever. A self-proclaimed "drinker with a writing problem," he died in 1964 at the age of only 41.

REJOICE!: The Darlin' Dublin of James Joyce

If Joyce fans make one pilgrimage in their lives, let it be to Dublin on June 16th for Bloomsday. June 16th, of course, is the day Leopold Bloom toured Dublin in *Ulysses*, and commemorative events take place all week long leading up to the big day (and night).

Grown men and women stroll the streets attired in black suits and carrying fresh bars of lemon soap in their pockets, imitating the unsassuming hero of what is arguably the 20th century's greatest novel. Denounced as obscene, blasphemous, and unreadable when it was first published in 1922 (and then banned in the U.S. until 1933), this 1,000-page riff on Homer's *Odyssey* portrays three characters—Leopold Bloom, a Jewish ad salesman, his wife, Molly, and friend Stephen Daedelus—as they wander through Dublin during the span of one day, June 16th, 1904. Dedicated Joyceans flock to the weeklong event, now called "Bloomstime," for Bloomsday breakfasts (where they can enjoy, like Bloom himself, "grilled mutton kidneys . . . which gave to his palate a fine tang of faintly scented urine"), readings, performances, and general merriment.

But don't despair if you miss Bloomsday, because you can experience the Dublin that inspired the author's novels year-round. James Joyce (1882-1941) set all his major works—*Dubliners*, *A Portrait of the Artist as a Young Man*, *Ulysses*, and *Finnegan's Wake*—in the city where he was born and spent the first 22 years of his life. Joyce knew and remembered Dublin in such detail that he bragged (and that's the word) that, if the city were destroyed, it could be rebuilt in its entirety from his written works.

Left, Joyce Statue, Earl Street;
Top left, a portrait of James Joyce, 1915
Top right, Bloomsday celebrations

IN THE FOOTSTEPS OF A POET: A James Joyce Walk

Begin in the heart of the Northside, on Prince's Street, next to the GPO (General Post Office), where the office of the old and popular *Freeman's Journal* newspaper (published 1763–1924) was once located and where Bloom once worked.

Head north up O'Connell Street down Parnell Square before turning right onto Dorset Street and then left onto Eccles Street. Leopold and Molly Bloom's fictional home stood at 7 Eccles Street, north of Parnell Square.

Head back to Dorset Street and go east. Take a right onto Gardiner Street and then a left onto Great Denmark Street and Belvedere College. Between 1893 and 1898, Joyce studied at Belvedere College (☎ 01/874–3974) under the Jesuits; it's housed in a splendid 18th-century mansion. The **James Joyce Centre** (☎ 01/878-8547 ⊕ www.jamesjoyce.ie), a few steps from Belvedere College on North Great George's Street, is the hub of Bloomsday celebrations.

Go back to Gardiner Street and then south until you come to Railway Street on your left. The site of **Bella Cohen's Brothel** (⊠ 82 Railway St.) is in an area

that in Joyce's day contained many houses of ill repute. A long walk back down O'Connell Street to the bridge and then a right will take you to Ormond Quay. On the western edge of the Northside, the **Ormond Quay Hotel** (⊠ Upper Ormond Quay ☎ 01/872–

1811) was an afternoon rendezvous spot for Bloom.

Across the Liffey, walk up Grafton Street to **Davy Byrne's Pub** (⊠ 21 Duke St., ☎ 01/671–1298). Here, Bloom comes to settle down for a glass of Burgundy and a Gorgonzola cheese sandwich, and meets his friend Nosey Flynn. Today, the pub has gone very upscale from its pre-World War II days, but even Joyce would have cracked a smile at the sight of the shamrock-painted ceiling and the murals of Joycean Dublin by Liam Proud.

After a stop at Davy Byrne's, proceed via Molesworth Street to the **National Library**— where Bloom has a near meeting with Blazes Boylan, his wife's lover. Walk up Molesworth Street until you hit Trinity. Take a right and walk to Lincoln Place. No establishment mentioned by Joyce has changed less since his time than **Sweny's Pharmacy** (⊠ Lincoln Pl.), which still has its black-and-white exterior and an interior crammed with potions and vials.

As seen here on Parliament Square, memorial statues stand as tribute to Trinity College's famed alumni, including Oliver Goldsmith and Samuel Beckett.

Trinity's grounds cover 40 acres. Most of its buildings were constructed in the 18th and early 19th centuries. The extensive **West Front,** with a classical pedimented portico in the Corinthian style, faces College Green and is directly across from the Bank of Ireland; it was built between 1755 and 1759, and is possibly the work of Theodore Jacobsen, architect of London's Foundling Hospital. The design is repeated on the interior, so the view is the same from outside the gates and from the quadrangle inside. On the lawn in front of the inner facade stand statues of two alumni, orator Edmund Burke (1729–97) and dramatist Oliver Goldsmith (1730–74). Like the West Front, **Parliament Square** (commonly known as Front Square), the cobblestone quadrangle that lies just beyond this first patch of lawn, dates from the 18th century. On the right side of the square is Sir William Chambers's theater, or Examination Hall, dating from the mid-1780s, which contains the college's most splendid Adamesque interior, designed by Michael Stapleton. The hall houses an impressive organ retrieved from an 18th-century Spanish ship and a gilded oak chandelier from the old House of Commons; concerts are sometimes held here. The chapel, left of the quadrangle, has stucco ceilings and fine woodwork. The theater and the chapel were designed by Scotsman William Chambers in the late 18th century. The looming campanile, or bell tower, is the symbolic heart of the college; erected in 1853, it dominates the center of the square. To the left of the campanile is the Graduates Memorial Building, or GMB. Built in 1892, the slightly Gothic building now contains the offices of the Philosophical and Historical societies, Trinity's ancient and fiercely competitive debating groups. At the back of the square stands old redbrick Rubrics, looking rather ordinary and out of place among the gray granite and cobblestones. Rubrics, now used as housing for students and faculty, dates from 1690, making it the oldest campus building still standing.

The **Old Library** houses Ireland's largest collection of books and manu-scripts; its principal treasure is the *Book of Kells*, generally considered to be the most striking manuscript ever produced in the Anglo-Saxon world and one of the great masterpieces of early Christian art. The book, which dates to the 9th century, is a splendidly illuminated version of the Gospels. It was once thought to be lost—the Vikings looted the book in 1007 for its jeweled cover but ultimately left the manuscript behind. In the 12th century, Guardius Cambensis declared that the book was made by an angel's hand in answer to a prayer of St. Bridget's; in the 20th century, scholars decided instead that the book originated on the island of Iona off Scotland's coast, where followers of St. Columba lived until the island came under siege in the early to mid-9th century. They fled to Kells, County Meath, taking the book with them. The 680-page work was re-bound in four volumes in 1953, two of which are usually displayed at a time, so you typically see no more than four original pages. (Some wags have taken to calling it the "Page of Kells.") However, such is the incredible workmanship of the *Book of Kells* that one folio alone is worth the entirety of many other painted manuscripts. On some pages, it has been determined that within a quarter inch, no fewer than 158 interlacements of a ribbon pattern of white lines on a black background can be discerned—little wonder some historians feel this book contains all the designs to be found in Celtic art. Note, too, the extraordinary colors, some of which were derived from shellfish, beetles' wings, and crushed pearls. The most famous page shows the "XPI" monogram (symbol of Christ), but if this page is not on dis-play, you can still see a replica of it, and many of the other lavishly illustrated pages, in the adjacent exhibition—dedicated to the history, artistry, and conservation of the book—through which you must pass to see the originals.

Because of the fame and beauty of the *Book of Kells*—now the center-piece of an exhibition called "Turning Darkness into Light" and with a brand-new fan base due to the 2009 Oscar contender animated film, *The Secret of Kells*—it's all too easy to overlook the other treasures in the library. They include a beautiful early Irish harp; the *Book of Armagh,* a 9th-century copy of the New Testament that also contains St. Patrick's Confession; and the legendary *Book of Durrow,* a 7th-century Gospel book from County Offaly. You may have to wait in line to enter the library if you don't get here early in the day.

The main library room, also known as the **Long Room,** is one of Dub-lin's most staggering sights. At 213 feet long and 42 feet wide, it con-tains in its 21 alcoves approximately 200,000 of the 3 million volumes in Trinity's collection. Originally the room had a flat plaster ceiling, but in 1859–60 the need for more shelving resulted in a decision to raise the level of the roof and add the barrel-vault ceiling and the gallery bookcases. Since the 1801 Copyright Act, the college has received a copy of every book published in Britain and Ireland, and a great num-ber of these publications must be stored in other parts of the campus and beyond. Of note are the carved Royal Arms of Queen Elizabeth

I above the library entrance—the only surviving relic of the original college buildings—and, lining the Long Room, a grand series of marble busts, of which the most famous is Roubiliac's depiction of Jonathan Swift. The Trinity College Library Shop sells books, clothing, jewelry, and postcards. ⊠ *Front Sq., Southside* ☏ *01/896–2320* ⊕ *www.tcd.ie/library* ⊡ *€9* ☉ *May–Sept., Mon.–Sat. 9:30–5, Sun. 9:30–4:30; Oct.–Apr., Mon.–Sat. 9:30–5, Sun. noon–4:30.*

WORD OF MOUTH

"At first, the *Book of Kells* doesn't sound fantastic—as my husband told me, we're paying 9 euros to go look at a book?—but this is more than a book. It is a work of art done in the most painstaking fashion."

—akila

Trinity College's starkly modern Arts and Social Sciences Building, with an entrance on Nassau Street, houses the **Douglas Hyde Gallery of Modern Art,** which concentrates on contemporary art exhibitions and has its own bookstore. Also in the building, down some steps from the gallery, is a snack bar serving coffee, tea, and sandwiches, where students willing to chat about life in the old college frequently gather. ⊠ *Nassau St., Southside* ☏ *01/896–1116* ⊕ *www.douglashydegallery.com* ⊡ *Free* ☉ *Mon.–Wed. and Fri. 11–6, Thurs. 11–7, Sat. 11–4:45.*

The **Berkeley Library,** the main student library at Trinity, was built in 1967 and is named after the philosopher and alumnus George Berkeley (pronounced "Barkley," like the basketball player). The small open space in front of the library contains a spherical brass sculpture designed by Arnaldo Pomodoro. A very modern, sleek extension dominates the Nassau Street side of the campus. The library is not open to the public. ⊠ *Nassau St., Southside* ☏ *01/896–1661* ⊕ *www.tcd.ie* ☉ *Grounds daily 8* AM–*10* PM.

☾ The kid-friendly **Science Gallery** occupies a funky building at the rear of the college. Its constantly changing exhibitions aim to allow art and science to meet—or collide, as the case may be, with an emphasis on fun and joining in off-the-wall experiments. ⊠ *Pearse St., Southside* ☏ *01/896–4091* ⊕ *ww.sciencegallery.org* ⊡ *Free* ☉ *Hrs vary with each exhibition.*

WORTH NOTING

❻ **Dublin Civic Museum.** Built between 1765 and 1771 as an exhibition hall for the Society of Artists, this building later was used as the City Assembly House, precursor of City Hall. The museum's esoteric collection includes Stone Age flints, Viking coins, old maps and prints of the city, and the sculpted head of British admiral Horatio Nelson, which used to top Nelson's Pillar, beside the General Post Office on O'Connell Street; the column was toppled by an IRA explosion in 1966 on the 50th anniversary of the Easter Uprising. The museum also holds temporary exhibitions relating to the city. ⊠ *58 S. William St., Southside* ☏ *01/679–4260* ⊕ *www.dublincity.ie* ⊡ *Free* ☉ *Tues.–Sat. 10–6, Sun. 11–2.*

❹ **Dublin Tourism.** Medieval St. Andrew's Church, deconsecrated and fallen into ruin, has been resurrected as the home of Dublin Tourism, a private organization that provides the most complete information on Dublin's sights, restaurants, and hotels; you can even rent a car and book theater tickets here. The office has reservations facilities for all Dublin hotels, as well as guided tours, a plethora of brochures, and a gift shop. A pleasant café upstairs serves sandwiches and drinks. ⊠ *St. Andrew's Church, Suffolk St., Southside* ☎ *01/605–7700; 1850/230330 in Ireland* ⊕ *www.visitdublin.com* ☼ *July–Sept., Mon.–Sat. 8:30–6, Sun. 11–5:30; Oct.–June, daily 9–6.*

❼ George's Street Arcade. This Victorian covered market fills the block between Drury Street and South Great George's Street. Two dozen or so stalls sell books, prints, clothing (new and secondhand), exotic foodstuffs, and trinkets. ⊠ *S. Great George's St., Southside* ☼ *Mon.– Sat. 9–6.*

NEED A BREAK?

With its mahogany bar, mirrors, and plasterwork ceilings, the **Long Hall Pub** (⊠ *51 S. Great George's St., Southside* ☎ *01/475–1590*) is one of Dublin's most ornate traditional taverns. It's a good place to take a break for a cup of tea or a cheeky daytime pint of Guinness.

⓫ Huguenot Cemetery. One of the last such burial grounds in Dublin, this cemetery was used in the late 17th century by French Protestants who had fled persecution in their native land. The cemetery gates are rarely open, but you can view the grounds from the street—it's on the northeast corner across from the square. ⊠ *27 St. Stephen's Green N, Southside.*

⓬ RHA Gallagher Gallery. The Royal Hibernian Academy, an old Dublin institution, is housed in a well-lighted building, one of the largest exhibition spaces in the city. The gallery holds adventurous exhibitions of the best in contemporary art, both from Ireland and abroad. ⊠ *15 Ely Pl., off St. Stephen's Green, Southside* ☎ *01/661–2558* ⊕ *www. royalhibernianacademy.ie* 🎟 *Free* ☼ *Wed.–Sat. 11–7, Sun. 2–5.*

OFF THE BEATEN PATH

Fodor's Choice ★ **Iveagh Gardens.** Dublin's best-kept secret has to be this 1865 Ninian Niven–designed "English Landscape" walled garden that shockingly few natives seem to even know about. The architect showed off his dramatic flair in the rustic grotto and cascade, the sunken panels of lawn with their fountains, the blooming rosarium, and wonderful little wooded areas. This public park has no playground, but kids really love the "secret garden" feel to the place and the fact that the waterfall has rocks from every one of Ireland's 32 counties. Restoration of the gardens began in 1995 and has left the city with a Victorian treasure complete with a perfect box hedge and a working sundial. Access is from Hatch Street. ⊠ *Clonmel St., Southside* 🎟 *Free* ☼ *Daily 8–sunset.*

GEORGIAN DUBLIN: MUSEUMS AND MARVELS

If there's one travel poster that signifies "Dublin" more than any other, it's the one that depicts 50 or so Georgian doorways—door after colorful door, all graced with lovely fanlights upheld by columns. A building boom began in Dublin in the early 18th century as the Protestant

Ascendancy constructed terraced town houses for themselves, and civic structures for their city, in the style that came to be known as Georgian, after the four successive British Georges who ruled from 1714 through 1830. The Georgian architectural rage owed much to architects such as James Gandon and Richard Castle. They and others were influenced by the great Italian Andrea Palladio (1508–80), whose *Four Books of Architecture* were published in the 1720s in London and helped to pre-cipitate the revival of his style, which swept through England and its colonies. Never again would Dublin be so "smart," its visitors' book so full of aristocratic names, its Southside streets so filled with decorum and style. "Serene red and pink houses showed beautifully designed doorways, the one spot of variation in the uniformity of facade," as architectural historian James Reynolds puts it. Today, Dublin's South-side remains a veritable shop window of the Georgian style, though there are many period sights on the Northside as well (for instance, the august interiors of the Dublin Writers Museum and Belvedere College, or James Gandon's great civic structures, the Custom House and the Four Courts, found quayside).

But Georgian splendor is just the icing on the cake of this neighborhood. For there are also four of the most fascinating and glamorous museums in Ireland, conveniently sitting cheek by jowl: the National Gallery of Ireland, the National Library, the National Museum of Natural History, and the National Museum of Archaeology and History. Priceless old master paintings, legendary Celtic treasures, mythic prehistoric "Irish elks," and George Bernard Shaw manuscripts—there is enough here to keep you occupied for days.

Numbers in the margin correspond to numbers on the Dublin South-side map.

TOP ATTRACTIONS

16 **Leinster House.** Commissioned by the Duke of Leinster and built in 1745, this residence—Dublin's Versailles—almost single-handedly ignited the Georgian style that dominated Dublin for 100 years. It was not only the largest private home in the city but Richard Castle's first structure in Ireland (Castle—or Casells, to use his original German spelling—was a follower of the 16th-century Italian architect Palladio and designed some of the country's most important 18th-century country houses). Inside, the grand salons were ornamented with coffered ceilings, Rem-brandts, and Van Dycks—fitting settings for the parties often given by the duke's wife (and celebrated beauty), Lady Emily Lennox. The building has two facades: the one facing Merrion Square is designed in the style of a country house; the other, on Kildare Street, resembles that of a town house. The latter facade—ignoring the ground floor—was a major inspiration for Irishman James Hoban's designs for the White House in Washington, D. C. Built in hard Ardbracan limestone, the exterior of the house makes a cold impression, and, in fact, the duke's heirs pronounced the house "melancholy" and fled. Today, the house is the seat of Dáil Éireann (the House of Representatives, pronounced dawl *e*-rin) and Seanad Éireann (the Senate, pronounced sha-*nad e*-rin), which together constitute the Irish Parliament. When the Dáil is not in session, tours can be arranged weekdays; when the Dáil is in session, tours are available only on Monday and Friday. The Dáil visitor gallery is included in the tour, but it can also be accessed on days when the Dáil is in session and tours are not available. To arrange a visit, contact the public relations office. ⊠ *Kildare St., Southeast Dublin* ☎ *01/618–3781* ⊕ *www.oireachtas.ie* ✆ *Free.*

⑬ Merrion Square. Created between 1762 and 1764, this tranquil square a few blocks east of St. Stephen's Green is lined on three sides by some of Dublin's best-preserved Georgian town houses, many of which have brightly painted front doors crowned by intricate fanlights. Leinster House, the National Museum of Natural History, and the National Gallery line the west side of the square. It's on the other sides, however, that the Georgian terrace streetscape comes into its own—the finest houses are on the north border. Even when the flower gardens here are not in bloom, the vibrant, mostly evergreen grounds, dotted with sculpture and threaded with meandering paths, are worth strolling through. Several distinguished Dubliners have lived on the square, including Oscar Wilde's parents, Sir William and "Speranza" Wilde (No. 1); Irish national leader Daniel O'Connell (No. 58); and authors W. B. Yeats (Nos. 52 and 82) and Sheridan LeFanu (No. 70). As you walk past the houses, read the plaques on the house facades, which identify former inhabitants. Until 50 years ago the square was a fashionable residential area, but today most of the houses serve as offices. At the south end of Merrion Square, on Upper Mount Street, stands the Church of Ireland St. Stephen's Church. Known locally as the "pepper canister" church because of its cupola, the structure was inspired in part by Wren's churches in London. ⊠ *Southeast Dublin* ☉ *Daily sunrise–sunset.*

Fodor'sChoice
★

⑱ National Gallery of Ireland. Caravaggio's *The Taking of Christ* (1602), Van Gogh's *Rooftops of Paris* (1886), Vermeer's *Lady Writing a Letter with Her Maid* (circa 1670) . . . you get the picture. The National Gallery of Ireland—the first in a series of major civic buildings on the west side of Merrion Square—is one of Europe's finest smaller art museums, with "smaller" being a relative term: the collection holds more than 2,500 paintings and some 10,000 other works. But unlike Europe's largest art museums, the National Gallery can be thoroughly covered in a morning or afternoon without inducing exhaustion. An 1854 Act of Parliament provided for the establishment of the museum, which was helped along by William Dargan (1799–1867), who was responsible for building much of Ireland's rail network (he is honored by a statue on the front

Fodor'sChoice
★

WHAT A CHARACTER!

If you want to size up a real Irish character, check out one of the National Gallery's most eye-knocking paintings, Sir Joshua Reynolds's *First Earl of Bellamont* (1773). Depicted in pink silks and ostrich plumes, Charles Coote was a notorious womanizer (leading to his nickname, the "Hibernian Seducer") and was shot in the groin for his troubles by rival Lord Townshend. Famously, Coote gave his inaugural speech as quartermaster-general of Ireland in *French*, continually referred to his County Cavan neighbors as "Hottentots," and wound up marrying the daughter of the super-rich Duke of Leinster.

CLOSE UP

Dublin's Gorgeous Georgians

"Extraordinary Dublin!" sigh art lovers and connoisseurs of the 18th century. It was during the "Gorgeous Eighteenth" that this duckling of a city was transformed into a preening swan, largely by the Georgian style of art and architecture that flowered between 1714 and 1820 during the reigns of the four English Georges.

Today Dublin remains in good part a sublimely Georgian city, thanks to enduring grace notes: the commodious and uniformly laid-out streets, the genteel town squares, the redbrick mansions accented with demilune (half-moon) fan windows. The great 18th-century showpieces are **Merrion, Fitzwilliam, Mountjoy,** and **Parnell squares. Merrion Square East,** the longest Georgian street in town, reveals scenes of decorum, elegance, polish, and charm, all woven into a "tapestry of rosy brick and white enamel," to quote the 18th-century connoisseur Horace Walpole.

Setting off the facades are fanlighted doors (often lacquered in black, green, yellow, or red) and the celebrated "patent reveal" window trims— thin plaster linings painted white to catch the light. These half-moon fanlights—as iconic of the city as clock towers are of Zurich—are often in the Neoclassical style known as the Adamesque (which was inspired by the designs of the great English architect Robert Adam).

Many facades appear severely plain, but don't be fooled: just behind their stately front doors are entry rooms and stairways aswirl with tinted Rococo plasterwork, often the work of *stuccadores* (plaster-workers) from Italy (including the talented Lafranchini brothers). Magnificent **Newman**

House, one of the finest of Georgian houses, is open to the public. **Belvedere College** (⊠ *6 Great Denmark St., Northside* ☎ *01/874–3974* ⊕ *www.belvederecollege.ie*) is open by appointment only.

The Palladian style—as the Georgian style was then called—began to reign supreme in domestic architecture in 1745, when the Croesus-rich Earl of Kildare returned from an Italian grand tour and built a gigantic Palladian palace called **Leinster House** in the seedy section of town.

"Where I go, fashion will follow," he declared, and indeed it did. By then, the Anglo-Irish elite had given the city London airs by building the **Parliament House** (now the Bank of Ireland), the **Royal Exchange** (now City Hall), the **Custom House,** and the **Four Courts** in the new style.

But this phase of high fashion came to an end with the Act of Union: according to historian Maurice Craig, "On the last stroke of midnight, December 31, 1800, the gaily caparisoned horses turned into mice, the coaches into pumpkins, the silks and brocades into rags, and Ireland was once again the Cinderella among the nations."

It was nearly 150 years before the spotlight shone once again on 18th-century Dublin. In recent decades, the conservation efforts of the **Irish Georgian Society** (⊠ *74 Merrion Sq., Southside* ☎ *01/676–7053* ⊕ *www.igs. ie*) have done much to restore Dublin to its Georgian splendor. Thanks to its founders, the Hon. Desmond Guinness and his late wife, Mariga, many historic houses, including that of George Bernard Shaw on Synge Street, have been saved and preserved.

Topped by half-moon fanlights, the brightly hued doorways of Merrion Square are icons of Dublin's 18th-century Georgian style.

lawn). The 1864 building was designed by Francis Fowke, who was also responsible for London's Victoria & Albert Museum.

A highlight of the museum is the major collection of paintings by Irish artists from the 17th through 20th centuries, including works by Roderic O'Conor (1860–1940), Sir William Orpen (1878–1931), and William Leech (1881–1968). The Yeats Museum section contains works by members of the Yeats family. Jack B. Yeats (1871–1957), the brother of writer W. B. Yeats, is by far the best-known Irish painter of the 20th century. He painted portraits and landscapes in an abstract Expressionist style not unlike that of the Bay Area Figurative painters of the 1950s and '60s. His *The Liffey Swim* (1923) is particularly worth seeing for its Dublin subject matter (the annual swim is still held, usually on the first weekend in September).

The collection also claims exceptional paintings from the 17th-century French, Dutch, Italian, and Spanish schools. Among the highlights are those mentioned above and Rembrandt's *Rest on the Flight into Egypt* (1647), Poussin's *The Holy Family* (1649) and *Lamentation over the Dead Christ* (circa 1655–60), and Goya's *Portrait of Doña Antonia Zárate* (circa 1810). Don't miss the portrait of the *First Earl of Bellamont* (1773) by Sir Joshua Reynolds; the earl was among the first to introduce the Georgian fashion to Ireland, and this portrait flaunts the extraordinary style of the man himself. The French Impressionists are represented with paintings by Monet, Sisley, and Renoir. The British collection and the Irish National Portrait collection are displayed in the north wing of the gallery, while the Millennium Wing, a standout of postmodern architecture in Dublin, houses part of the permanent collection and also stages major international traveling exhibits. The amply stocked gift shop is a good place to pick up books on Irish artists. Free guided tours are available on Saturday at 2 and on Sunday at 1 and 2. ⊠ *Merrion Sq. W, Southeast Dublin* ☎ *01/661–5133* ⊕ *www. nationalgallery.ie* ⊠ *Free; special exhibits €10* ⊙ *Mon.–Wed., Fri., and Sat. 9:30–5:30, Thurs. 9:30–8:30, Sun. noon–5:30.*

NEED A BREAK?

Joly Café (⊠ *Kildare St., Southside* ☎ *01/603–0257*), **the National Library's light-filled tearoom, is usually one of the city's more serene lunchtime spots. There's a light, French country influence to the fare, with top specials including crumbly quiches and a hearty chicken bake. Their organic sandwiches and coffees are also top quality. It's open Monday–Wednesday 9:30–7, Thursday–Friday 9:30–4:45, Saturday 9:30–4:30.**

⑲ National Library. Ireland is one of the few countries in the world where you can happily admit to being a writer. And few countries as geographically diminutive as Ireland have garnered as many recipients of the Nobel Prize for Literature. Along with works by W. B. Yeats (1923), George Bernard Shaw (1925), Samuel Beckett (1969), and Seamus Heaney (1995), the National Library contains first editions of every major Irish writer, including books by Jonathan Swift, Oliver Goldsmith, and James Joyce (who used the library as the scene of the great literary debate in *Ulysses*). In addition, almost every book ever published in Ireland is kept here, along with an unequaled selection of old maps and an extensive collection of Irish newspapers and magazines— more than 5 million items in all.

The library is housed in a rather stiff Neoclassical building with colonnaded porticoes and an excess of ornamentation—it's not one of Dublin's architectural showpieces. But inside, the main Reading Room, opened in 1890 to house the collections of the Royal Dublin Society, has a dramatic dome ceiling, beneath which countless authors have researched and written. The personal papers of greats such as W. B. Yeats are also on display. The library also has a free genealogical consultancy service that can advise you on how to trace your Irish ancestors. ⊠ *Kildare St., Southeast Dublin* ☎ *01/603–0200* ⊕ *www.nli.ie* ⊠ *Free* ⊙ *Mon.–Wed. 9:30–9, Thurs. and Fri. 9:30–5, Sat. 9:30–4:30.*

⑳ National Museum of Archaeology and History. Just south of Leinster House ★ is Ireland's National Museum of Archaeology and History, which has a fabled collection of Irish artifacts dating from 7000 BC to the present. Organized around a grand rotunda, the museum is elaborately decorated, with mosaic floors, marble columns, balustrades, and fancy ironwork. It has the largest collection of Celtic antiquities in the world, including gold jewelry, carved stones, bronze tools, and weapons.

The Treasury collection, including some of the museum's most renowned pieces, is open on a permanent basis. Among the priceless relics on display are the 8th-century Ardagh Chalice, a two-handled silver cup with gold filigree ornamentation; the bronze-coated iron St. Patrick's Bell, the oldest surviving example (5th–8th century) of Irish metalwork; the 8th-century Tara Brooch, an intricately decorated piece made of white bronze, amber, and glass; and the 12th-century bejeweled oak Cross of Cong, covered with silver and bronze panels.

The "*Or*: Ireland's Gold" exhibition gathers together the most impressive pieces of surprisingly delicate and intricate prehistoric goldwork—including sun disks and the late Bronze Age gold collar known as the Gleninsheen Gorget—that range in dates from 2200 to 500 BC. Upstairs, Viking Ireland is a permanent exhibit on the Norsemen, featuring a full-size Viking skeleton, swords, leather works recovered in Dublin and surrounding areas, and a replica of a small Viking boat. The newest attraction is an exhibition entitled "Kinship and Sacrifice," centering on a number of Iron Age "bog bodies" found along with other objects in Ireland's peat bogs.

MANSIONS AND MOONSHINE

"We passed row after row of identical Georgian houses, all with different brightly painted doors and rounded window arches. The story is that men were too drunk after a night at the pub to know which door was the right one unless it was painted a bright, strong color (red, blue, etc.). I don't know if the story is true, but it certainly makes sense!"

—Green Dragon

In contrast to the ebullient late-Victorian architecture of the main museum building, the design of the National Museum Annex is purely functional; it hosts temporary shows of Irish antiquities. The 18th-century Collins Barracks, near Phoenix Park *(see below)*, houses the National Museum of Decorative Arts and History, a collection of glass, silver, furniture, and other decorative arts. ⊠ *Kildare St. Annex, 7–9 Merrion Row, Southeast Dublin* ☎ *01/677–7444* ⊕ *www.museum.ie* ▣ *Free* ⊙ *Tues.–Sat. 10–5, Sun. 2–5.*

WORTH NOTING

🕒 **Government Buildings.** The swan song of British architecture in the capital, this enormous complex, a landmark of Edwardian Baroque, was the last Neoclassical edifice to be erected by the British government. It was designed by Sir Aston Webb, who did many of the similarly grand buildings in London's Piccadilly Circus, to serve as the College of Science in the early 1900s. Following a major restoration, these buildings became the offices of the Department of the *taoiseach* (the prime minister, pronounced *tea*-shuck) and the *tánaiste* (the deputy prime minister, pronounced tawn-*ish*-ta). Fine examples of contemporary Irish furniture and carpets populate the offices. A stained-glass window, known as "My Four Green Fields," was made by Evie Hone for the 1939 New York World's Fair. It depicts the four ancient provinces of Ireland: Munster, Ulster, Leinster, and Connacht. The government offices are accessible only via 35-minute guided tours on Saturday. They are dramatically illuminated every night. ⊠ *Upper Merrion St., Southeast Dublin* ☎ *01/662–4888* ⊕ *www.taoiseach.gov.ie* ▣ *Free; pick up tickets from National Gallery on day of tour* ⊙ *Tours Sat. 10:30–3:30.*

🕒 **Mansion House.** The mayor of Dublin resides at the Mansion House, which dates from 1710. It was built for Joshua Dawson, who later sold the property to the government on the condition that "one loaf of

Dating from 1123, the bejeweled oak Cross of Cong is among the greatest treasures on view at the National Museum of Archaeology and History.

double refined sugar of six pounds weight" be delivered to him every Christmas. In 1919 the Declaration of Irish Independence was adopted here. The house is not open to the public. ⊠ *Dawson St., Southeast Dublin*.

⓱ National Museum of Natural History. The famed explorer of the African interior, Dr. Stanley Livingstone (of "Dr. Livingstone, I presume?" fame), inaugurated this museum when it opened in 1857. It's little changed from Victorian times and remains a fascinating repository of mounted mammals, birds, and other flora and fauna. The Irish Room houses the most famous exhibits: skeletons of the extinct, prehistoric, giant "Irish elk." The International Animals Collection includes a 65-foot whale skeleton suspended from the roof. Another highlight is the very beautiful Blaschka Collection, finely detailed glass models of marine creatures, the zoological accuracy of which has never been achieved again in glass. At this writing, the museum is undergoing renovations following a roof cave-in—it's possible the building will not reopen until 2012, though the facade is still worth a walk-by. Built in 1856 to hold the Royal Dublin Society's rapidly expanding collection, it was designed by Frederick Clarendon to sit in harmony with the National Gallery on the other side of Leinster Lawn. When it was completed, it formed an annex to Leinster House and was connected to it by a curved, closed Corinthian colonnade. In 1909 a new entrance was constructed at the east end of the building on Merrion Street. ⊠ *Merrion St., Southeast Dublin* ☎ *01/677–7444* ⊕ *www.museum.ie* ☜ *Free* ◷ *Closed to public until 2012*.

14 **No. 29.** Everything in this carefully refurbished 1794 home, known simply as Number Twenty-Nine, is in keeping with the elegant lifestyle of the Dublin middle class between 1790 and 1820, the height of the Georgian period, when the house was owned by a wine merchant's widow. From the basement to the attic—in the kitchen, nursery, servants' quarters, and the formal living areas—the National Museum has re-created the period's style with authentic furniture, paintings, carpets, curtains, paint, wallpapers, and even bell pulls. ⊠ *29 Lower Fitzwilliam St., Southeast Dublin* ☎ *01/702–6165* ⊕ *www.esb.ie/numbertwentynine* ⊡ *€6* ☉ *Tues.–Sat. 10–5, Sun. noon–5.*

22 **Royal Irish Academy.** The country's leading learned society houses important documents in its 18th-century library, including a large collection of ancient Irish manuscripts, such as the 11th- to 12th-century *Book of the Dun Cow,* and the library of the 18th-century poet Thomas Moore. ⊠ *19 Dawson St., Southeast Dublin* ☎ *01/676–2570* ⊕ *www. ria.ie* ⊡ *Free* ☉ *Mon.–Thurs. 9:30–5:30, Fri. 9:30–5.*

21 **St. Ann's Church.** St. Ann's plain, neo-Romanesque granite exterior, built in 1868, belies the rich Georgian interior of the church, which Isaac Wills designed in 1720. Highlights of the interior include polished-wood balconies, ornate plasterwork, and shelving in the chancel dating from 1723—and still in use for organizing the distribution of bread to the parish's poor. ⊠ *Dawson St., Southeast Dublin* ☎ *01/676–7727* ⊕ *www. stannschurch.ie* ⊡ *Free* ☉ *Weekdays 10–4, Sun. for services.*

OFF THE BEATEN PATH

Shaw Birthplace. "Author of many plays" is the simple accolade to George Bernard Shaw (1856–1950) on the plaque outside his birthplace. The Nobel laureate was born here to a once prosperous family fallen on hard times. Shaw lived in this modest, Victorian terrace house until he was 10 and remembered it as having a "loveless" feel. The painstaking restoration of the little rooms highlights the cramped, claustrophobic atmosphere. All the details of a family home—wallpaper, paint, fittings, curtains, furniture, utensils, pictures, rugs—remain, and it appears as if the family has just gone out for the afternoon. You can almost hear one of Mrs. Shaw's musical recitals in the tiny front parlor. The children's bedrooms are filled with photographs and original documents and letters that throw light on Shaw's career. ⊠ *33 Synge St., Southeast Dublin* ☎ *01/475–0854* ⊕ *www.visitdublin.com* ⊡ *€6* ☉ *June–Aug., Tues.–Fri., 10–1 and 2–5, Sat. 2–5.*

TEMPLE BAR: THE CHANGING FACE

Locals complain about the late-night noise, and visitors sometimes say the place has the feel of a Dublin theme park, but a visit to modern Dublin wouldn't be complete without spending some time in the city's most famously vibrant area. More than any other neighborhood in the city, Temple Bar represents the dramatic changes (good and bad) and ascending fortunes of Dublin that came about in the last decade of the 20th century. The area, which takes its name from one of the streets of its central spine, was targeted for redevelopment in 1991–92 after a long period of neglect, having survived widely rumored plans to turn it into a massive bus depot and/or a giant parking lot. Temple Bar took off as Dublin's version of New York's SoHo, Paris's Bastille, or London's Notting Hill—a thriving mix of high and alternative culture distinct from what you'll find in any other part of the city. Dotting the area's narrow cobblestone streets and pedestrian alleyways are new apartment buildings (inside they tend to be small and uninspired), vintage-clothing stores, postage-stamp-size boutiques selling €250 sunglasses and other expensive gewgaws, art galleries, a hotel resuscitated by U2, hip restaurants, pubs, clubs, European-style cafés, and a smattering of cultural venues.

Temple Bar's regeneration was no doubt abetted by that one surefire real-estate asset that appealed to the Viking founders of the area: location. The area is bordered by Dame Street to the south, the Liffey to the north, Fishamble Street to the west, and Westmoreland Street to the east. In fact, Temple Bar is situated so perfectly between everywhere else in Dublin that it's difficult to believe this neighborhood was once largely forsaken. It's now sometimes called the "playing ground of young Dublin," and for good reason: on weekend evenings and daily in summer it teems with young people—not only from Dublin but from all over Europe—drawn by its pubs, clubs, and lively *craic* (good conversation and fun).

Some who have witnessed Temple Bar's rapid gentrification and commercialization complain that it's lost its artistic soul—*Harper's Bazaar* said it was in danger of becoming "a sort of pseudoplace," like London's Covent Garden Piazza or Paris's Les Halles. In the afternoon the area is more family friendly and the ice-cream parlors and coffee shops are busy, but there's no denying that after dark this is the place to go if you want to party like a spring breaker—in the rain.

Numbers in the margin correspond to numbers on the Temple Bar map.

TOP ATTRACTIONS

29 **Gallery of Photography.** Dublin's premier photography gallery has a permanent collection of early-20th-century Irish photography and also puts on monthly exhibitions of work by contemporary Irish and international photographers. The gallery is an invaluable social record of Ireland. The bookstore is the best place in town to browse for photography books and to pick up arty postcards. ⊠ *Meeting House Sq. S, Temple Bar* ☎ *01/671–4654* ⊕ *www.galleryofphotography.ie* ☜ *Free* ☾ *Tues.–Sat. 11–6, Sun. 1–6.*

24 **Ha'penny Bridge.** Every Dubliner has a story about meeting someone on this cast-iron Victorian bridge, a heavily trafficked footbridge that crosses the Liffey at a prime spot—Temple Bar is on the south side, and the bridge provides the fastest route to the thriving Mary and Henry streets shopping areas to the north. Until early in the 20th century, a halfpenny toll was charged to cross it. Congestion on the Ha'penny has been relieved with the opening of the Millennium Footbridge a few hundred yards up the river. A refurbishment, including new railings, a return to the original white color, and tasteful lighting at night, has given the bridge a new lease on life.

26 **Irish Film Institute (IFI).** The opening of the IFI in a former Quaker meeting-house helped to launch the revitalization of Temple Bar. It has two comfortable art-house cinemas showing revivals and new independent films, the Irish Film Archive, a bookstore for cineastes, and a popular bar and restaurant-café, all of which make this one of the neighborhood's most vital cultural institutions and *the* place to be seen. On Saturday nights in summer, the center screens films outdoors on Meeting House Square. ⊠ *6 Eustace St., Temple Bar* ☎ *01/679–5744* ⊕ *www.ifi.ie* 🎟 *Free* ☉ *Weekdays 9:30* AM*–midnight, weekends 11* AM*–midnight.*

NEED A BREAK?

The buzzing **Irish Film Institute Café** (⊠ *6 Eustace St., Temple Bar* ☎ *01/679–5744*) is a pleasant place for a lunchtime break. Sandwiches are large and healthful, with plenty of vegetarian choices, and the people-watching is unmatched.

27 **Meeting House Square.** The square, which is behind the Ark and accessed via Curved Street, takes its name from a nearby Quaker meetinghouse. Today it's something of a gathering place for Dublin's youth and artists. Numerous summer events—classic movies (Saturday night), theater, games, and family programs—take place here. (Thankfully, seats are installed.) The square is also a favorite site for the continuously changing street sculpture that pops up all over Temple Bar (artists commissioned by the city sometimes create oddball pieces, such as half of a Volkswagen protruding from a wall). Year-round, the square is a great spot to sit, people-watch, and take in the sounds of the performing buskers who swarm to the place. There's also an organic food market here every Saturday morning.

32 ★ **Olympia Theatre.** One of the most atmospheric places in Europe to see musical acts, the Olympia is Dublin's second-oldest theater, and one of its busiest. This classic Victorian music hall, built in 1879, has a gorgeous red wrought-iron facade. The Olympia's long-standing Friday and Saturday series, "Midnight at the Olympia," has brought numerous musical performers to Dublin, and the theater has also seen many notable actors strut across its stage, including Alec Guinness, Peggy Ashcroft, Noël Coward, and even the old-time Hollywood team of Laurel and Hardy. Big-name performers like Van Morrison often choose the intimacy of the Olympia over larger venues. It's really a hot place to see some fine performances, so if you have a chance, by all means, go. Conveniently, there are two pubs here—through doors directly off the back of the theater's orchestra section. ⊠ *72 Dame St., Temple Bar* ☎ *01/677–7744* ⊕ *www.mcd.ie/olympia.*

31 ★ **Wall of Fame.** If you're strolling through Temple Bar and suddenly come upon a group of slack-jawed young people staring wide-eyed at a large wall, then you've probably stumbled upon the Wall of Fame. The whole front wall of the Button Factory music venue has become a giant tribute to the giants of Irish rock music. Twelve huge photos adorn the wall, including a very young and innocent U2, a very beautiful Sinead O'Connor, and a very drunk Shane McGowan. ⊠ *Curved St, Temple Bar* ☎ *01/607–9202.*

Continued on page 92

A TRIP TO THE PUB

For any visitor to Ireland who wants to see the natives in their bare element—to witness them at full pace, no-holds-barred—a trip to a busy pub is a must. Luckily for you, a pub is above all a welcoming place, where a visitor is seen as a source of new, exotic stories and, more importantly, as an unsullied audience for the locals and their tall tales.

The term "pub" is shorthand for "public house," which is an apt name for one of Ireland's great institutions. Stepping into a pub (and there seems to be one on every corner) is the easiest way to transport yourself into the thick of Irish life. A pub, of course, is a drinking establishment, and for better or worse the Irish have a deep, abiding relationship with drink—particularly their beloved black stout.

The point, however, isn't what you drink, but where: in the warmth of the public house, in company. It's the place to tell stories, most of them true, and to hear music. It's where locals go to mark the key stages of their lives: to wet a new baby's head; to celebrate a graduation; to announce an engagement; and finally to wake a corpse.

Top, Temple Bar district;
Opposite, Dublin pub

HOW TO CHOOSE A PUB

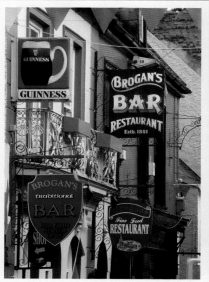

Not all pubs are created equal. Throughout this book we recommend some of the finest, but here are a few ways to distinguish the real gold from the sparkling pyrite:

■ Qualified, experienced bar staff—not grubby students dreaming of the round-the-world trip they are working to save up for. A uniform of white shirt and black trousers is often a good sign.

■ At least one man over sixty (preferably with a cap of some description) drinking at the bar (not at a table). He should know the good bars by now, right?

■ No TV. Or, if there is a TV it should be hidden away in a corner, only to be used for horse racing and other major sporting events.

■ No recorded music. A pub is a place to talk and listen. Occasional live music is okay, especially a traditional session.

■ Bathrooms are clean but not *too* clean. They are purely functional, not polished chambers for hanging out and chatting with friends about your new Blackberry.

THE QUEST FOR THE CRAIC

Pub-going at its best has a touch of magic to it: conversation flows, spirits rise, and inhibitions evaporate. There's a word in Gaelic for this happy condition: the craic, which roughly translates as "lively talk and good times." The craic is the sort of thing that's difficult to find only when you're looking too hard for it. Large crowds, loud music, and one pint too many can also make the craic elusive. When your companions all seem clever and handsome, and you can't imagine better company in the world, that's when you know you've found it.

Top left, pub signs in O'Connell Street, Ennis, County Clare; Right, the Long Hall Pub, Dublin

PUB ETIQUETTE

■ First, if you want to meet people and get into the craic, belly up to the bar counter and pass up a seat at a table.

■ Always place your drink order at the bar and don't heckle the barkeepers to get their attention. They're professionals—they'll see you soon enough.

■ If you do take a table, bring your dirty glasses back to the bar before you leave, or when you order another round.

■ In present-day Ireland, male and female pubgoers usually get equal treatment. At the most traditional places, though, it's still customary in mixed company for the man to order drinks at the bar while the woman takes a table seat.

■ Don't tip the barkeepers, except at Christmas, when you can offer to buy them a drink.

■ Never sip from your Guinness until it has fully settled. You'll know this from the deep black color and perfectly defined white head.

■ Don't smoke in the bar; it's against the law. But feel free to gather outside in the rain and chat with the other unfortunates. It's a great spot to start a romance.

■ You have to be at least 18 years old to *drink* in a pub, but kids are welcome during the day, and nondrinking minors as young as 14 are often tolerated at night.

MAKING THE ROUNDS

You may get caught up in the "rounds" system, in which each pub mate takes turns to "shout" an order. Your new friends may forget to tell you when it's your round, but any failure to "put your hand in your pocket" may lead to a reputation that will follow you to the grave. To miss your "shout" is to become known for "short arms and long pockets" and to be shunned by decent people.

LAST CALL

Technically, pubs have to stop serving at 11:30 Mon.–Thurs., 12:30 Fri.–Sat., and 11 Sun. At the end of the night, ignore the first five calls of "Time please, ladies and gentle-men!" from the barman. You'll know he's getting serious by the roar of his voice.

THE "BLACK STUFF"

— Rich, creamy head.

— Nearly black in color, with a very slight coffee-like aftertaste.

— As you drink, the head will leave "rings of pleasure" down the side of the glass.

THE POUR

The storage and pouring of a pint of stout is almost as important as the brewing. The best quality is usually found in older bars that sell a lot of pints—meaning the beer you get hasn't been sitting in the keg too long and the pipes are well coated.

Pouring a pint consists of two stages: The glass is filled three-quarters full, then allowed to sit. After the head settles, the glass is filled to the top (stage two).

Why the painstaking ritual? Because the barkeeper knows you don't want your first sip to be a mouthful of foam. And because the flavor's that much sweeter for the waiting.

Stout, a dark beer made using roasted malts or barley, originated in Ireland, and it's the country's national drink, consumed in pubs with unflagging allegiance.

GUINNESS. For most Irish, the name Guinness is synonymous with stout. With massive breweries in Africa and the Americas, it really is a world brand, but the "true" pint still flows from the original brewery at St. James Gate in Dublin. While some old-timers still drink the more malty bottled version, draught Guinness is now the standard. A deep, creamy texture and slightly bitter first taste is followed by a milder, more "toasty" aftertaste.

MURPHY'S. The Murphy Brewery was founded by James Murphy in 1856 in Cork City. Murphy's is very much a Cork drink, and often suffers from "second city" complex in relation to its giant rival Guinness. Corkonians say Murphy's has a less bitter, more nutty flavor than the "Dublin stout."

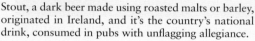

BEAMISH. Another Cork drink, a little sweeter and less dry than either Guinness or Murphy's, and so a little easier on the novice palate. Beamish and Crawford Brewery began making beer in 1792.

WELCOME TO IRELAND'S LIVING ROOM . . .

Pub food is a lunchtime thing; the prices are reasonable, and the quality can be quite good. Ask for a menu at the bar. If you're near a coast, look for sea-food specialties, from oysters and mussels to smoked salmon. With beef-and-Guinness stew, you can drink your stout and eat it too.

Although the majority of your companions will be drinking stout, you do have other options.

A lager is always available—Heineken and Carlsberg are the most popular brands.

If you're thirsting for something stronger, take a nip of Irish whiskey, which tends to be less smoky and intensely flavored than its Scotch cousin. Jameson and Bushmills, both smooth blends, are the standard varieties, and you can usually find a single-malt as well.

On the other hand, if the booze isn't your thing, you can always choose tea, soda, or a bottle of water. (Ballygowan is the Irish Evian.) It's fine to order nonalcoholic drinks—many people who drive do so.

"TRAD" MUSIC IN ITS NATURAL DOMAIN

The pub is an ideal place to hear traditional Irish music. Performances can have a spontaneous air to them, but they don't start up just anywhere. Pubs that accommodate live sessions have signs saying so; and they're more common outside Dublin than in the city. To learn more about Irish music, see "Gael Force" in chapter 8.

Top, musicians performing at Gus O'Connor's pub in Doolin, County Clare; Right, oysters and a (half) pint, Galway

Dublin Sightseeing Tours

Having a guide enrich your sightseeing hours proves to be very worth the investment, as attests this contributor to the Fodors.com forum on Ireland:

"The top three things that we saw/did in Dublin were: 1) Traditional Musical Pub Crawl, 2) Kilmainham Gaol, and 3) Historical Walking Tour of Dublin. All of these activities had a guide and they were all EXCELLENT! They were not only informative, but very entertaining as well. We found this to be the case wherever we went that had a guided tour."

With this in mind, here are some top recommendations for touring the city.

BUS TOURS
Dublin Bus has three- and four-hour tours of the North and South coastlines, taking in sights like the James Joyce Tower and the Casino at Marino. The one-hour City Tour takes in the city center sights like Trinity College, the Royal Hospital Kilmainham, and Phoenix Park.

The one-hour City Tour, with hourly departures, allows you to hop on and off at any of the main sights.

Tickets are available from the driver or Dublin Bus.

There's also a continuous guided open-top bus tour (€15), run by Dublin Bus, which allows you to hop on and off the bus as often as you wish and visit some 23 sights along its route.

The company also conducts a north-city coastal tour, going to Howth, and a south-city tour, traveling as far as Enniskerry.

Gray Line Tours runs city-center tours that cover the same sights as the Dublin Bus itineraries.

Bus Éireann organizes day tours out of Busaras, the main bus station, to country destinations such as Glendalough.

Bus Éireann (☎ 01/836–6111 ⊕ www.buseireann.ie). **Dublin Bus** (☎ 01/873–4222 ⊕ www.dublinbus. ie). **Gray Line Tours** (☎ 01/670–8822 ⊕ www.grayline.com).

PUB AND MUSICAL TOURS
Dublin Tourism has a booklet on its self-guided Rock n' Stroll trail, which covers 16 sights with associations to such performers as Bob Geldof, Christy Moore, Sinéad O'Connor, and U2.

Most of the sights are in the city center and Temple Bar.

The Traditional Musical Pub Crawl begins at Oliver St. John Gogarty and moves on to other famous Temple Bar pubs. Led by two professional musicians who perform songs and tell the story of Irish music, the tour is given April–October, daily at 7:30 PM, and from Thursday to Saturday, at 7:30 PM, the rest of the year; the cost is €12.

The Viking Splash Tour is a big hit with kids. The amphibious ex–U.S. military vehicle tours the city center before launching onto the water by the IFSC (International Financial Service Center, near the Custom House). Kids get a helmet to wear and love terrifying native pedestrians with the "Viking roar." An adult ticket is €20.

Colm Quilligan arranges highly enjoyable evening tours of the literary pubs of Dublin, where "brain cells are replaced as quickly as they are drowned."

The *Dublin Literary Pub Crawl* is a 122-page guide to those Dublin pubs with the greatest literary associations; it's widely available in the city's bookstores.

TOUR CONTACTS
Colm Quilligan (☎ *01/454–0228* ⊕ *www.dublinpubcrawl.com*). **Traditional Musical Pub Crawl** (✉ *20 Lower Stephens St., Southside* ☎ *01/478–0191* ⊕ *www.discoverdublin.ie*). **Viking Splash** (☎ *01/707–6000* ⊕ *www.vikingsplash.ie*).

WALKING TOURS
Dublin Tourism has a new iWalk tour with a podcast audio guide narrated by well-known historian and artist Pat Liddy.

Historical Walking Tours of Dublin, run by Trinity College history graduate students, are excellent two-hour introductions to the city. The Bord Fáilte–approved tours take place from May to September, starting at the front gate of Trinity College, daily at 11 AM and 3 PM, with an extra tour on weekends at noon. These tours are also available October and April daily at 11 AM and November to March, Friday–Sunday at 11 AM. The cost is €12.

Dublin Footsteps conducts a Georgian/Literary Walking Tour that leaves from the Grafton Street branch of Bewley's Oriental Café June–September, Monday, Wednesday, Friday, and Saturday at 11; each tour lasts approximately two hours and costs €10.

Trinity Tours organizes walks of the Trinity College campus on weekends from March 17 (St. Patrick's Day) through mid-May and daily from mid-May to September. The half-hour tour costs €10 and includes the *Book of*

Kells exhibit; tours start at the college's main gate every 40 minutes from 10:15 AM. There are generally nine tours a day.

The 1916 Rebellion Tour is an exciting walk that outlines the key areas and events of the violent Dublin rebellion that began Ireland's march to independence.

The guides are passionately political and the two-hour tour never flags.

They meet at the International Bar on Wicklow Street and operate February through October, Monday to Saturday at 11:30 AM and Sunday at 1 PM. The cost is €12.

Information Dublin Footsteps (☎ *01/496–0641* ⊕ *www.visitdublin.com*). **Historical Walking Tours of Dublin** (☎ *01/878–0227* ⊕ *www.historicalinsights.ie*). **Trinity Tours** (☎ *01/608–2320* ⊕ *www.tcd.ie/Library/old-library/tour-attractions*). **1916 Rebellion Tour** (☎ *086/858–3847* ⊕ *www.1916rising.com*).

CARRIAGE TOURS
Horse-drawn-carriage tours are available around Dublin and in Phoenix Park.

For tours of the park, contact the Department of the Arts, Culture and the Gaeltacht.

Carriages can be hired at the Grafton Street corner of St. Stephen's Green, without prior reservations.

Information Department of the Arts, Culture and the Gaeltacht (☎ *01/661–3111*).

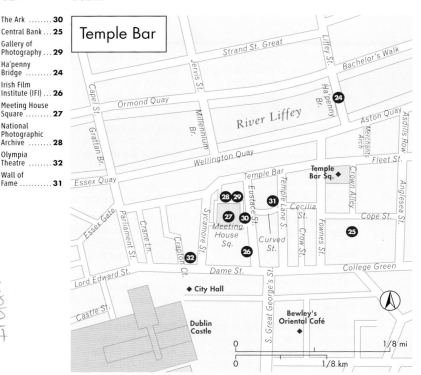

Ireland

NEED A BREAK? The creamiest, frothiest coffees in all of Temple Bar can be had at the **Joy of Coffee/Image Gallery Café** (⊠ *25 E. Essex St., Temple Bar* ☎ *01/679–3393*) ; the wall of windows floods light onto the small gallery, where original photographs adorn the walls.

WORTH NOTING

30 **The Ark.** If you're traveling with children and looking for something fun to do, stop by the Ark, Ireland's cultural center for children, housed in a former Presbyterian church. Its theater opens onto Meeting House Square for outdoor performances in summer. A gallery and workshop space host ongoing activities. ⊠ *11a Eustace St., Temple Bar* ☎ *01/670–7788* ⊕ *www.ark.ie* ☞ *Free* ☉ *Weekdays 10–5, weekends only if there's a show.*

25 **Central Bank.** Everyone in Dublin seems to have an opinion on the Central Bank. Designed by Sam Stephenson in 1978, the controversial, ultramodern glass-and-concrete building suspends huge concrete slabs around a central axis. It was originally one story higher, but the top floor had to be lopped off, as it was hazardous to low-flying planes. Watch out for—or just watch—the skateboarders and in-line skaters who have taken over the little plaza in front of the building. ⊠ *Dame*

St., Temple Bar ☎ *01/671–6666* ⊕ *www.centralbank.ie* ⊙ *Week-days 10–6.*

②⑧ National Photographic Archive. Formerly housed in the National Library's main building, the National Photographic Archive now has a stylish home in Temple Bar. The collection comprises approximately 600,000 photographs, most of which are Irish, making up a priceless visual history of the nation. Although most of the photographs are historical, dating as far back as the mid-19th century, there's also a large number of contemporary pictures. Subject matter ranges from topographical views to studio portraits, from political events to early tourist photographs. You can also buy a print of your favorite photo. ✉ *Meeting House Sq., Temple Bar* ☎ *01/603–0374* ⊕ *www.nli.ie/en/national-photographic-archive.aspx* 🎫 *Free* ⊙ *Weekdays 10–5, Sat. 10–2.*

> **TOO GREAT A TOLL**
>
> William Butler Yeats was one of many Dubliners who found the halfpenny toll of Ha'penny Bridge too steep. He detoured to O'Connell Bridge instead.

2

ACROSS THE LIFFEY: THE NORTHSIDE

"What do you call a Northsider in a suit? The accused." So went the old joke. But faded stereotypes about the Northside being Dublin's poorer and more deprived half were partly washed away beneath the wave of Celtic Tiger development. Locals and visitors alike are discovering the no-nonsense, laid-back charm of the Northside's revamped Georgian wonders, understated cultural gems, high-quality restaurants, and buzzing ethnic diversity.

If you stand on O'Connell Bridge or the pedestrian-only Ha'penny span, you'll get excellent views up and down the River Liffey, known in Gaelic as the *abha na life,* transcribed phonetically as Anna Livia by James Joyce in *Finnegan's Wake.* Here, framed with embankments like those along Paris's Seine, the river nears the end of its 128-km (80-mi) journey from the Wicklow Mountains to the Irish Sea. And near the bridges, you begin a pilgrimage into James Joyce country—north of the Liffey, in the center of town—and the captivating sights of Dublin's Northside, a mix of densely thronged shopping streets and genteelly refurbished homes.

For much of the 18th century, the upper echelons of Dublin society lived in the Georgian houses in the Northside—around Mountjoy Square—and shopped along Capel Street, which was lined with stores selling fine furniture and silver. But development of the Southside—the Georgian Leinster House in 1745, Merrion Square in 1764, and Fitzwilliam Square in 1825—changed the Northside's fortunes. The city's fashionable social center crossed the Liffey, and although some of the Northside's illustrious inhabitants stuck it out, the area gradually became run-down. The Northside's fortunes have now changed back, however. Once-derelict swaths of houses, especially on and near the Liffey, have been rehabilitated, and large shopping centers have opened on Mary and Jervis streets. The high-rise Docklands area, east of the Custom

House, is pocked with modern high-rise apartments. More importantly, the new Daniel Libeskind–designed, 2,000-seat, Grand Canal Theatre has shifted the cultural tectonic plates of Dublin towards this area. In addition, the beginnings of a little Chinatown are forming on Parnell Street, while a swing bridge has been added between City Quay and the Northside. O'Connell Street itself has been partially pedestrianized, and most impressive of all is the Spire, the street's 395-foot-high stainless-steel monument.

Numbers in the margin correspond to numbers on the Dublin Northside map.

TOP ATTRACTIONS

47 Custom House. Seen at its best when reflected in the waters of the Liffey during the short interval when the high tide is on the turn, the Custom House is the city's most spectacular Georgian building. Extending 375 feet on the north side of the river, this is the work of James Gandon, an English architect who arrived in Ireland in 1781, when the building's construction commenced (it continued for 10 years). Crafted from gleaming Portland stone, the central portico is linked by arcades to pavilions at either end. A statue of Commerce tops the copper dome, whose puny circumference, unfortunately, is out of proportion to the rest of the building. Statues on the main facade are based on allegorical themes. Note the exquisitely carved lions and unicorns supporting the arms of Ireland at the far ends of the facade. After Republicans set fire to the building in 1921, it was completely restored and reconstructed to house government offices. A visitor center traces the building's history and significance, and the life of Gandon. ⊠ *Custom House Quay, Northside* ☎ *01/888–2538* ⊕ *www.visitdublin.com* 🖃 *Free* 🕑 *Mid-Mar.–Oct., weekdays 10–12:30, weekends 2–5; Nov.–mid-Mar., Wed.–Fri. 10–12:30, Sun. 2–5.*

39 Dublin City Gallery, The Hugh Lane. Built as a town house for the Earl of
★ Charlemont in 1762, this residence was so grand that the Parnell Square street on which it sits was nicknamed "Palace Row" in its honor. Sir William Chambers, who also built the Marino Casino for Charlemont, designed the structure in the best Palladian manner. Its delicate and rigidly correct facade, extended by two demilune (half-moon) arcades, was fashioned from the "new" white Ardmulcan stone (now seasoned to gray). Charlemont was one of the cultural locomotives of 18th-century Dublin—his walls were hung with Titians and Hogarths, and he frequently dined with Oliver Goldsmith and Sir Joshua Reynolds—so he would undoubtedly be delighted that his home is now a gallery, named after Sir Hugh Lane, a nephew of Lady Gregory (W. B. Yeats's aristocratic patron). Lane collected both Impressionist paintings and 19th-century Irish and Anglo-Irish works. A complicated agreement with the National Gallery in London (reached after heated diplomatic dispute) stipulates that a portion of the 39 French paintings amassed by Lane shuttle between London and here. Time it right and you'll be able to see Pissarro's *Printemps*, Manet's *Eva Gonzales*, Morisot's *Jour d'Été*, and, the jewel of the collection, Renoir's *Les Parapluies*.

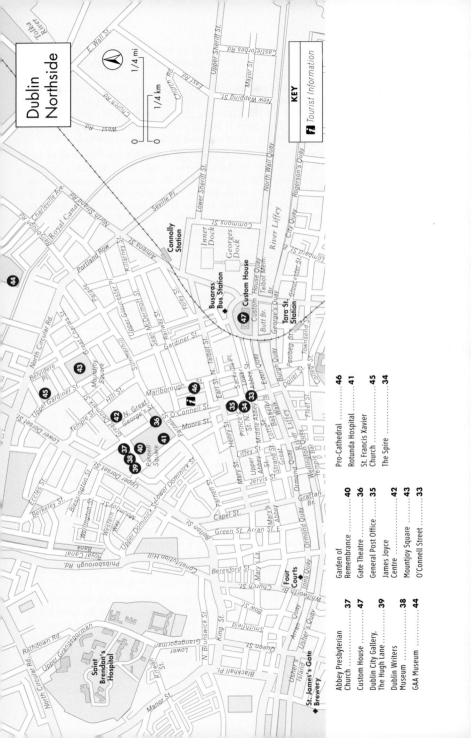

Dublin Northside

N

1/4 mi

1/4 km

KEY

Tourist Information

In something of a snub to the British art establishment, the late Francis Bacon's partner donated the entire contents of the artist's studio to the gallery. The studio of arguably Britain's premier 20th-century artist has been reconstructed here in all its gaudy glory as a permanent display. It gives you a unique opportunity to observe the bravura technique of the artist responsible for such masterpieces as *Study After Velázquez* and the tragic splash-and-crash *Triptych*. Also on display are Bacon's diary, books, and apparently everything else picked up off his floor.

Between the collection of Irish paintings in the National Gallery of Ireland and the superlative works on display here, you can quickly become familiar with Irish 20th-century art. Irish artists represented include Roderic O'Conor, well known for his views of the west of Ireland; William Leech, including his *Girl with a Tinsel Scarf* and *The Cigarette*; and the most famous of the group, Jack B. Yeats (W. B.'s brother). The museum has a dozen of his paintings, including *Ball Alley* and *There Is No Night*. The mystically serene Sean Scully Gallery displays seven giant canvasses by Ireland's renowned abstract modernist. ⊠ *Parnell Sq. N, Northside* ☎ *01/222–5550* ⊕ *www.hughlane.ie* 🖾 *Free* ☉ *Tues.–Thurs. 10–6, Fri. and Sat. 10–5, Sun. 11–5.*

❸❽ ★ Dublin Writers Museum. "If you would know Ireland—body and soul—you must read its poems and stories," wrote W. B. Yeats in 1891. Further investigation into the Irish way with words can be found at this unique museum, in a magnificently restored 18th-century town house on the north side of Parnell Square. The mansion, once the home of John Jameson, of the Irish whiskey family, centers on the Gallery of Writers, an enormous drawing room gorgeously decorated with paintings, Adamesque plasterwork, and a deep Edwardian lincrusta frieze. Rare manuscripts, diaries, posters, letters, limited and first editions, photographs, and other mementos commemorate the lives and works of the nation's greatest writers—and there are many of them, so leave plenty of time—including Joyce, Shaw, J. M. Synge, Lady Gregory, W. B. Yeats, Beckett, and others. On display are an 1804 edition of Swift's *Gulliver's Travels,* an 1899 first edition of Bram Stoker's *Dracula,* and an 1899 edition of Wilde's *Ballad of Reading Gaol.* There's a "Teller of Tales" exhibit showcasing Behan, O'Flaherty, and O'Faoláin. Readings are periodically held, and there's a room dedicated to children's literature. The bookshop and café make this an ideal place to spend a rainy afternoon. If you lose track of time and stay until the closing hour, you might want to dine at Chapter One, a highly regarded restaurant in the basement, which would have had Joyce ecstatic over its currant-sprinkled scones. ⊠ *18 Parnell Sq. N, Northside* ☎ *01/872–2077* ⊕ *www.writersmuseum.com* 🖾 *€7.50* ☉ *Mon.–Sat. 10–5, Sun. 11–5.*

❸❻ Gate Theatre. The show begins here as soon as you walk into the auditorium, a gorgeously Georgian masterwork designed by Richard Johnston in 1784 as an assembly room for the Rotunda Hospital complex. The Gate has been one of Dublin's most important theaters since its founding in 1929 by Mícheál MacLiammóir and Hilton Edwards, who also founded Galway City's An Taibhdhearc as the national Irish-language theater. The Gate stages many established productions by Irish as well as foreign playwrights—and plenty of foreign actors have performed here, including Orson Welles (his first paid performance) and James Mason (early in his career). ✉ *Cavendish Row, Northside* ☎ *01/874–4045* ⊕ *www.gate-theatre.ie* ☼ *Shows Mon.–Sat.*

㉟ General Post Office. One of the great civic buildings of Dublin's Georgian era, the GPO's fame is based on the role it played in the Easter Uprising. The building, with its impressive Neoclassical facade, was designed by Francis Johnston and built by the British between 1814 and 1818 as a center of communications. This gave it great strategic importance—and was one of the reasons it was chosen by the insurgent forces in 1916 as a headquarters. Here, on Easter Monday, 1916, the Republican forces, about 2,000 in number and under the guidance of Pádrig Pearse and James Connolly, stormed the building and issued the Proclamation of the Irish Republic. After a week of shelling, the GPO lay in ruins; 13 rebels were ultimately executed, including Connolly, who was dying of gangrene from a wound in a leg shattered in the fighting and had to be propped up in a chair in front of the firing squad. Most of the original building was destroyed, though the facade survived, albeit with the scars of bullets on its pillars. Rebuilt and reopened in 1929, it became a working post office with an attractive two-story main concourse. A bronze sculpture depicting the dying Cuchulainn, a leader of the Red Branch Knights in Celtic mythology, sits in the front window. The 1916 Proclamation and the names of its signatories are inscribed on the green marble plinth. There are plans to turn the GPO into a permanent 1916 museum or possibly to rehouse the Abbey Theatre here. ✉ *O'Connell St., Northside* ☎ *01/872–8888* ⊕ *www.anpost.ie* ✉ *Free* ☼ *Mon.–Sat. 8–8, Sun. 10:30–6.*

NEED A BREAK? For a classic Dublin pub with a cozy, warm atmosphere, stop in at **The Sackville Lounge** (✉ *Sackville Pl., Northside* ☎ *01/874–5222*). It's popular with theater folk and old flat-cap Dublin men and pours a smooth pint of the black stuff.

㊷ James Joyce Centre. Few may have read him, but everyone in Ireland has at least heard of James Joyce (1882–1941)—especially since owning a copy of his censored and suppressed *Ulysses* was one of the top status symbols of the early 20th century. Joyce is of course now acknowledged as one of the greatest modern authors, and his *Dubliners, Finnegan's Wake,* and *A Portrait of the Artist as a Young Man* can even be read as quirky "travel guides" to Dublin. Open to the public, this restored 18th-century Georgian town house, once the dancing academy of Professor Denis J. Maginni (which many will recognize from a reading of *Ulysses*), is a center for Joycean studies and events related to the author. It has an extensive library and archives, exhibition rooms, a bookstore, and a café. The collection includes letters from Beckett, Joyce's guitar and cane, and a celebrated edition of *Ulysses* illustrated by Matisse. The interactive "James Joyce and Ulysses" exhibition allows you to delve into the mysteries and controversies of the novel. The center is the main organizer of "Bloomstime," which marks the week leading up to the Bloomsday celebrations. (Bloomsday, June 16, is the single day *Ulysses* chronicles, as Leopold Bloom winds his way around Dublin in 1904.) ⊠ *35 N. Great George's St., Northside* ☎ *01/878–8547* ⊕ *www.jamesjoyce.ie* 🖃 *€5, guided tour €10* ⊙ *Tues.–Sat. 10–5, Sun. noon–5.*

㉝ O'Connell Street. Dublin's most famous thoroughfare, which is 150 feet wide, was previously known as Sackville Street, but its name was changed in 1924, two years after the founding of the Irish Free State. After the devastation of the 1916 Easter Uprising, the Northside street had to be almost entirely reconstructed, a task that took until the end of the 1920s. At one time the main attraction of the street was Nelson's Pillar, a Doric column towering over the city center and a marvelous vantage point, but it was blown up in 1966, on the 50th anniversary of the Easter Uprising. A major cleanup and repaving have returned the street to some of its old glory. The large monument at the south end of the street is dedicated to Daniel O'Connell (1775–1847), "The Liberator," and was erected in 1854 as a tribute to the orator's achievement in securing Catholic Emancipation in 1829. Seated winged figures represent the four Victories—Courage, Eloquence, Fidelity, and Patriotism—all exemplified by O'Connell. Ireland's four ancient provinces—Munster, Leinster, Ulster, and Connacht—are identified by their respective coats of arms. Look closely and you'll notice that O'Connell is wearing a glove on one hand, as he did for much of his adult life, a self-imposed penance for shooting a man in a duel. But even the great man himself is dwarfed by the newest addition to O'Connell Street: the 395-foot-high Spire was built in Nelson's Pillar's place in 2003, and today this gigantic, stainless-steel monument dominates the street.

㊻ Pro-Cathedral. Dublin's principal Catholic cathedral (also known as St. Mary's) is a great place to hear the best Irish male voices: a Palestrina choir, in which the great Irish tenor John McCormack began his career, sings in Latin here every Sunday morning at 11. The cathedral, built between 1816 and 1825, has a classical church design—on a suitably epic scale. The church's facade, with a six-Doric-pillared portico, is based on the Temple of Theseus in Athens; the interior is modeled after the Grecian-Doric style of St. Philippe du Roule in Paris. But the building was never granted full cathedral status, nor has the identity of its architect ever been discovered; the only clue to its creation is in the church ledger, which lists a "Mr. P." as the builder. ⊠ *83 Marlborough St., Northside* ☎ *01/874–5441* ⊕ *www.procathedral.ie* 🖃 *Free* ⊙ *Weekdays 7:30–6:45, Sat. 7:30–7:15, Sun. 9–1:45 and 5:30–7:45.*

㉞ The Spire. Christened the "Stiletto in the Ghetto" by local smart alecks, this needlelike monument is the most exciting thing to happen to Dublin's skyline in decades. The Spire, also known as the Monument of Light, was originally planned as part of the city's millennium celebrations. But Ian Ritchie's spectacular 395-foot-high monument wasn't erected until the beginning of 2003. Seven times taller than the nearby General Post Office, the stainless-steel structure rises from the spot where Nelson's Pillar once stood. Approximately 10 feet in diameter at its base, the softly lighted monument narrows to only 1 foot at its apex—the upper part of the Spire sways gently when the wind blows. The monument's creators envisioned it serving as a beacon for the whole of the city, and it will certainly be the first thing you see as you drive into Dublin from the airport. ⊠ *O'Connell St., Northside.*

WORTH NOTING

37 Abbey Presbyterian Church. Built on the profits of sin—well, by a generous wine merchant actually—and topped with a soaring Gothic spire, this church anchors the northeast corner of Parnell Square, an area that was the city's most fashionable address during the gilded days of the 18th-century Ascendancy. Popularly known as Findlater's Church, after the merchant Alex Findlater, the church was completed in 1864 with an interior that has a stark Presbyterian mood despite stained-glass windows and ornate pews. For a bird's-eye view of the area, climb the small staircase that leads to the balcony. ⊠ *Parnell Sq., Northside* ☎ *01/837–8600* ⬧ *Free* ☉ *Hrs vary.*

44 GAA Museum. The Irish are sports crazy and reserve their fiercest pride for their native games. In the bowels of Croke Park, the main stadium and headquarters of the GAA (Gaelic Athletic Association), this museum gives you a great introduction to native Irish sport. The four Gaelic games (football, hurling, camogie, and handball) are explained in detail, and if you're brave enough you can have a go yourself. High-tech displays take you through the history and highlights of the games. *National Awakening* is a really smart, interesting short film reflecting the key impact of the GAA on the emergence of the Irish nation and the forging of a new Irish identity. The exhilarating *A Day in September* captures the thrill and passion of All Ireland finals day—the annual denouement of the inter-county hurling and Gaelic football seasons—which is every bit as important to the locals as the Super Bowl is to sports fans in the United States. Tours of the stadium, the fourth largest in Europe, are available. ⊠ *New Stand, Croke Park, North County Dublin* ☎ *01/855–8176* ⬧ *museum.gaa.ie* ⬧ *Museum €6, museum and stadium tour €11* ☉ *July and Aug., daily 9:30–6; Sept.–June, Mon.–Sat. 9:30–5, Sun. noon–5.*

40 Garden of Remembrance. Opened 50 years after the Easter Uprising of 1916, the garden in Parnell Square commemorates those who died fighting for Ireland's freedom. At the garden's entrance is a large plaza; steps lead down to the fountain area, graced with a sculpture by contemporary Irish artist Oisín Kelly, based on the mythological Children of Lír, who were turned into swans. The garden serves as an oasis of tranquility in the middle of the busy city. ⊠ *Parnell Sq., Northside* ⬧ *Free* ☉ *Daily 9–5.*

43 Mountjoy Square. Built over the course of the two decades leading up to 1818, this Northside square was once surrounded by elegant terraced houses. Today only the northern side remains intact. The houses on the once derelict southern side have been converted into apartments. Irishman Brian Boru, who led his soldiers to victory against the Vikings in the Battle of Clontarf in 1014, was said to have pitched camp before the confrontation on the site of Mountjoy Square. Playwright Sean

O'Casey lived here, at No. 35, and used the square as a setting for *The Shadow of a Gunman.*

㊶ Rotunda Hospital. The Rotunda, founded in 1745 as the first maternity hospital in Ireland and Britain, was designed on a grand scale by architect Richard Castle (1690–1751), with a three-story tower and a copper cupola. It's now mostly worth a visit for its chapel, which has elaborate plasterwork and, appropriately, honors motherhood; it was built by Bartholomew Cramillion between 1757 and 1758. The Gate Theatre, in a lavish Georgian assembly room, is on the O'Connell Street side of this large complex. ⊠ *Parnell St., Northside* ☎ *01/873–0700.*

㊺ St. Francis Xavier Church. One of the city's finest churches in the classical style, the Jesuit St. Francis Xavier's was begun in 1829, the year of Catholic Emancipation, and was completed three years later. The building is designed in the shape of a Latin cross, with a distinctive Ionic portico and an unusual coffered ceiling. The striking, faux-marble high altarpiece, decorated with lapis lazuli, came from Italy. The church appears in James Joyce's story "Grace." ⊠ *Upper Gardiner St., Northside* ☎ *01/836–3411* 💲 *Free* ⏱ *Daily 7 AM–8:30 PM.*

DUBLIN WEST: CATHEDRALS AND GUINNESS

A cornucopia of things quintessentially Dublin, this area is studded with treasures and pleasures ranging from the opulent 18th-century salons of Dublin Castle to time-burnished St. Patrick's Cathedral, and from the Liberties neighborhood—redoubt of the city's best antiques stores—to the Irish Museum of Modern Art (housed at the strikingly renovated Royal Hospital Kilmainham). You can time-travel from the 10th-century crypt at Christ Church Cathedral—the city's oldest surviving structure—to the modern plant of the Guinness Brewery and its storehouse museum.

You can also cross the Liffey for a visit to Smithfield. Bordered on the east by Church Street, on the west by Blackhall Place, to the north by King Street, and to the south by the Liffey, Smithfield is Dublin's old market area where flowers, fruit, vegetables, and even horses have been sold for generations. Chosen as a flagship for north inner-city renovation, the area saw a major face-lift in the last few years—with mixed reactions from the locals. The beautiful cobblestones of its streets have been taken up, refinished, and replaced, and giant masts topped with gaslights send 6-foot-high flames over Smithfield Square—now the venue for a winter ice-skating rink. Early morning is a special time in Smithfield, as the wholesale fruit and vegetable sellers still ply their trade in the wonderful 19th-century covered market. Traditional music bars like the Cobblestone, a favorite of the market traders, now sit side by side with modern hotels like the Park Inn, and the Old Jameson Distillery museum.

Keep in mind that Dublin is compact. The following sights aren't far from those in the other city-center neighborhoods. In fact, City Hall is just across the street from Temple Bar, and Christ Church Cathedral is a short walk farther west. The westernmost sights covered here—notably the Royal Hospital and Kilmainham Gaol—are, however, at some distance, so if you're not an enthusiastic walker, you may want to drive or catch a cab, bus, or LUAS tram to them.

Numbers in the margin correspond to numbers on the Dublin West and Phoenix Park map.

TOP ATTRACTIONS

(50) Fodor's Choice ★ **Chester Beatty Library.** A connoisseur's delight, this "library" is considered by many to be the most impressive museum in Ireland. After Sir Alfred Chester Beatty (1875–1968), a Canadian mining millionaire and a collector with a flawless eye, assembled one of the most significant collections of Islamic and Far Eastern art in the Western world, he donated it to Ireland. Housed in the gorgeous clock-tower building of Dublin Castle, and voted European Museum of the Year in 2002, the library is one of Dublin's real gems. Among the exhibits are clay tablets from Babylon dating from 2700 BC, Japanese wood-block prints, Chinese jade books, and Turkish and Persian paintings. The second floor, dedicated to the major religions, houses 250 manuscripts of the Koran from across the Muslim world, as well as one of the earliest Gospels. The first-floor "Arts of the Book" exhibition looks at the different origins and finest examples of books throughout the world. Life-size Buddhas from Burma and rhino cups from China are among the other curios on show. Guided tours of the library are available on Tuesday and Saturday at 2:30 PM. On sunny days the garden is one of the most tranquil places in central Dublin. The shop is full of unique and exotic souvenirs relating to the collection. ✉ *Castle St., Dublin West* ☎ *01/407–0750* 🌐 *www.cbl.ie* 🎟 *Free* 🕒 *May–Sept., weekdays 10–5, Sat. 11–5, Sun. 1–5; Oct.–Apr., Tues.–Fri. 10–5, Sat. 11–5, Sun. 1–5.*

NEED A BREAK?

Silk Road Café (✉ *Chester Beatty Library, Castle St., Dublin West* ☎ *01/407–0770* 🌐 *www.silkroadcafe.ie*) is a great-value, Middle Eastern delight hidden away in the Chester Beatty Library. The buffet-style menu is always full of exotic surprises and the light-filled room and serene atmosphere make you want to linger longer than you should. It's open Tuesday–Friday 10–4:30, Saturday 11–4:30, and Sunday 1–4:30.

(51) ★ **Christ Church Cathedral.** You'd never know from the outside that the first Christianized Danish king built a wooden church at this site in 1038; because of the extensive 19th-century renovation of its stonework and trim, the cathedral looks more Victorian than Anglo-Norman. Construction on the present Christ Church—the flagship of the Church of Ireland and one of two Protestant cathedrals in Dublin (the other is St. Patrick's just to the south)—was begun in 1172 by Strongbow, a Norman baron and conqueror of Dublin for the English Crown, and continued for 50 years. By 1875 the cathedral had deteriorated badly; a major renovation gave it much of the look it has today, including the addition of one of Dublin's most charming structures: a Bridge of Sighs–like affair that connects the cathedral to the old Synod Hall, which now holds the Viking multimedia exhibition, Dublinia. Remains from the 12th-century building include the north wall of the nave, the west bay of the choir, and the fine stonework of the transepts, with their pointed arches and supporting columns. Strongbow himself is

buried in the cathedral, beneath an impressive effigy. The vast, sturdy **crypt**, with its 12th- and 13th-century vaults, is Dublin's oldest surviving structure and the building's most notable feature. The Treasures of Christ Church exhibition includes manuscripts, various historic artifacts, and the tabernacle used when James II worshipped here. But the real marvel are the mortified bodies of a cat and rat—they were trapped in an organ pipe in the 1860s—who seem caught in a cartoon chase for all eternity. At 6 PM on Wednesday and Thursday you can enjoy the glories of a choral evensong and the bell ringers usually practice on Fridays at 7 PM. ⊠ *Christ Church Pl. and Winetavern St., Dublin West* ☎ *01/677–8099* ⊕ *www.cccdub.ie* 💶 *€6 CJune–Aug., weekdays 9:45–6:15, Sat. 9:45–4:15, Sun. 12:30–2:30 and 4:30–6:15; Sept.–May, Mon.–Sat. 9:45–4:15, Sun. 12:30–2:30.*

❹❽ City Hall. Facing the Liffey from Cork Hill at the top of Parliament Street, this grand Georgian municipal building (1769–79), once the Royal Exchange, marks the southwest corner of Temple Bar. Today it's the seat of the Dublin Corporation, the elected body that governs the city. Thomas Cooley designed the building with 12 columns that encircle the domed central rotunda, which has a fine mosaic floor and 12 frescoes depicting Dublin legends and ancient Irish historical scenes. The 20-foot-high sculpture to the right is of Daniel O'Connell, "The Liberator." He looks like he's about to begin the famous speech he gave here in 1800. The building houses a multimedia exhibition—with artifacts, kiosks, graphics, and audiovisual presentations—tracing the evolution of Ireland's 1,000-year-old capital. ⊠ *Dame St., Dublin West* ☎ *01/222–2204* ⊕ *www.dublincity.ie/recreationandculture* 💶 *€4* 🕑 *Mon.–Sat. 10–5:15.*

❹❾ Dublin Castle. Neil Jordan's film *Michael Collins* captured Dublin Castle's near indomitable status well: seat and symbol of the British rule of Ireland for more than seven centuries, the castle figured largely in Ireland's turbulent history early in the 20th century. It's now mainly used for Irish and EU governmental purposes. The sprawling Great Courtyard is the reputed site of the Black Pool (Dubh Linn, pronounced *dove*-lin) from which Dublin got its name. In the Lower Castle Yard, the Record Tower, the earliest of several towers on the site, is the largest remaining relic of the original Norman buildings, built by King John between 1208 and 1220. The clock-tower building now houses the Chester Beatty Library. Guided tours are available of the principal State Apartments (on the southern side of the Upper Castle Yard), formerly the residence of the English viceroys and now used by the president of Ireland to host visiting heads of state and EU ministers. The State Apartments are lavishly furnished with rich Donegal carpets and illuminated by Waterford glass chandeliers. The largest and most impressive of these chambers, St. Patrick's Hall, with its gilt pillars and painted ceiling, is used for the inauguration of Irish presidents. The Round Drawing Room, in Bermingham Tower, dates from 1411 and was rebuilt in 1777; numerous Irish leaders were imprisoned in the tower from the 16th century to the early 20th century. The blue oval Wedgwood Room contains Chippendale chairs and a marble fireplace. The Castle Vaults now hold an elegant little patisserie and bistro.

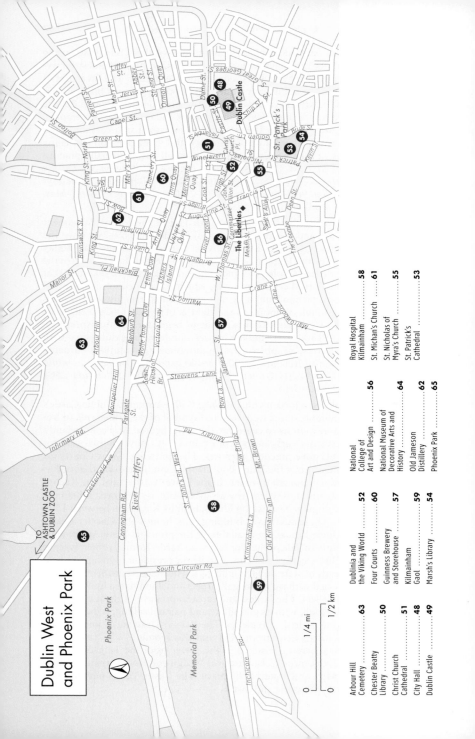

Dublin West and Phoenix Park

0 ——— 1/4 mi
0 ——— 1/2 km

TO
ASHTOWN CASTLE
& DUBLIN ZOO

Dublin Castle

The Liberties

Phoenix Park

Memorial Park

Carved oak panels and stained glass depicting viceroys' coats of arms grace the interior of the Church of the Holy Trinity (formerly called Chapel Royal), on the castle grounds. The church was designed in 1814 by Francis Johnston, who also designed the original General Post Office building on O'Connell Street. Once you're inside, look up—you'll see an elaborate array of fan vaults on the ceiling. More than 100 carved heads adorn the walls outside: among them, St. Peter and Jonathan Swift preside over the north door, St. Patrick and Brian Boru over the east.

One-hour guided tours of the castle are available every half hour, but the rooms are closed when in official use, so call ahead. The easiest way into the castle is through the Cork Hill Gate, just west of City Hall. ⊠ *Castle St., Dublin West* ☎ *01/645–8813* ⊕ *www.dublincastle.ie* ▨ *State Apartments €4.50 including tour* ⊘ *Mon.–Sat. 10–4:45, Sun. 2–4:45.*

60 **Four Courts.** The stately Corinthian portico and the circular central hall warrant a visit here, to the seat of the High Court of Justice of Ireland. The distinctive copper-cover dome topping a colonnaded rotunda makes this one of Dublin's most instantly recognizable buildings. The view from the rotunda is terrific. Built between 1786 and 1802, the Four Courts are James Gandon's second Dublin masterpiece—close on the heels of his Custom House, located downstream on the same side of the River Liffey. In 1922, during the Irish Civil War, the Four Courts was almost totally destroyed by shelling—the adjoining Public Records Office was gutted, and many priceless legal documents, including innumerable family records, were destroyed. Restoration took 10 years. Tours of the building are not given, but you're welcome to sit in while the courts are in session. ⊠ *Inns Quay, Dublin West* ☎ *01/872–5555* ⊕ *www.courts.ie* ⊘ *Daily 10–1 and 2:15–4.*

57 Fodor's Choice ★ **Guinness Brewery and Storehouse.** Ireland's all-dominating brewery—founded by Arthur Guinness in 1759 and at one time the largest stout-producing brewery in the world—spans a 60-acre spread west of Christ Church Cathedral. Not surprisingly, it's the most popular tourist destination in town—after all, the Irish national drink is Guinness stout, a dark brew made with roasted malt. The brewery itself is closed to the public, but the Guinness Storehouse is a spectacular attraction, designed to woo you with the wonders of the "dark stuff." In a 1904 cast-iron-and-brick warehouse, the museum display covers six floors built around a huge, central glass atrium. Beneath the glass floor of the lobby you can see Arthur Guinness's original lease on the site, for a whopping 9,000 years. The exhibition elucidates the brewing process and its history, with antique presses and vats, a look at bottle and can design through the ages, a history of the Guinness family, and a fascinating archive of Guinness advertisements. You might think it's all a bit much (it's only a drink, after all), and parts of the exhibit do feel a little over the top—readers complain about the numerous ads and promos for the brew at nearly every turn. The star attraction is undoubtedly the top-floor **Gravity Bar,** with 360-degree floor-to-ceiling glass walls that offer a nonpareil view out over the city at sunset while you sip your free pint. One of the bar's first clients was one William Jefferson Clinton. The Guinness Shop on the ground floor is full of funky lifestyle merchandise. They run a St. Patrick's Festival every year with music, dance, and, of course, the drinking of many pints. ✉ *St. James' Gate, Dublin West* ☎ *01/408–4800* ⊕ *www.guinness-storehouse.com* 💰*€15* ⊙ *July and Aug., daily 9:30–7; Sept.–June, daily 9:30–5.*

59 ★ **Kilmainham Gaol.** Leaders of many failed Irish rebellions spent their last days in this grim, forbidding structure, and it holds a special place in the myth and memory of the country. The 1916 commanders Pádrig Pearse and James Connolly were held here before being executed in the prison yard. Other famous inmates included the revolutionary Robert Emmet and Charles Stewart Parnell, a leading politician. You can visit the prison only as part of a very moving and exciting guided tour, which leaves every hour on the hour. The cells are a chilling sight, and the guided tour and a 30-minute audiovisual presentation relate a graphic account of Ireland's political history over the past 200 years—from an Irish Nationalist viewpoint. A new exhibition explores the history of the prison and its restoration. A small tearoom is on the premises. ✉ *Inchicore Rd., Dublin West* ☎ *01/453–5984* ⊕ *www.heritageireland. ie* 💰*€6* ⊙ *Apr.–Sept., daily 9:30–5; Oct.–Mar., Mon.–Sat. 9:30–4, Sun. 10–5.*

58 ★ **Royal Hospital Kilmainham.** This replica of Les Invalides in Paris is regarded as the most important 17th-century building in Ireland. Commissioned as a hospice for disabled and veteran soldiers by James Butler—the Duke of Ormonde and viceroy to King Charles II—it was completed in 1684, making it the first building erected in Dublin's golden age. It survived into the 1920s as a hospital, but after the founding of the Irish Free State in 1922, the building fell into disrepair. The entire edifice has since been restored to what it once was.

The structure's four galleries are arranged around a courtyard; there's also a grand dining hall—100 feet long by 50 feet wide. The architectural highlight is the hospital's Baroque chapel, distinguished by its extraordinary plasterwork ceiling and fine wood carvings. "There is nothing in Ireland from the 17th century that can come near this masterpiece," raved cultural historian John FitzMaurice Mills. The Royal Hospital also houses the **Irish Museum of Modern Art,** which concentrates on the work of contemporary Irish artists such as Richard Deacon, Richard Gorman, Dorothy Cross, Sean Scully, Matt Mullican, Louis Le Brocquy, and James Coleman. The museum also displays works by some non-Irish 20th-century greats, including Picasso and Miró, plus recent hotshots like Damien Hirst, and regularly hosts touring shows from major European museums. The Grass Roots Café serves light fare such as soups and sandwiches. The hospital is a short ride by taxi or bus from the city center. ✉ *Kilmainham La., Dublin West* ☎ *01/612–9900* ⊕ *www.imma.ie* 💰 *Free* ⊙ *Royal Hospital Tues.–Sat. 10–5:30, Sun. noon–5:30. Museum Tues. and Thurs.–Sat. 10–5:30, Wed. 10:30–5:30, Sun. noon–5:30; tours Wed. and Fri. at 2:30, Sat. at 11:30.*

53 Fodor'sChoice ★ **St. Patrick's Cathedral.** The largest cathedral in Dublin and also the national cathedral of the Church of Ireland, St. Patrick's is the second of the capital's two Protestant cathedrals. (The other is Christ Church, and the reason Dublin has two cathedrals is because St. Patrick's originally stood outside the walls of Dublin, while its close neighbor was within the walls and belonged to the see of Dublin.) Legend has it that in the 5th century St. Patrick baptized many converts at a well on the site of the cathedral. The original building, dedicated in 1192 and early English Gothic in style, was an unsuccessful attempt to assert supremacy over Christ Church

FROM PEW TO VIEW

While in the shadow of St. Patrick's Cathedral, head from Patrick Close to Patrick Street; look down the street toward the Liffey for a fine view of Christ Church.

Cathedral. At 305 feet, this is the longest church in the country, a fact Oliver Cromwell's troops—no friends to the Irish—found useful as they made the church's nave into their stable in the 17th century. They left the building in a terrible state; its current condition is largely due to the benevolence of Sir Benjamin Guinness—of the brewing family—who started financing major restoration work in 1860.

Make sure you see the gloriously heraldic Choir of St. Patrick's, hung with colorful medieval banners, and find the tomb of the most famous of St. Patrick's many illustrious deans, Jonathan Swift, immortal author of *Gulliver's Travels,* who held office from 1713 to 1745. Swift's tomb is in the south aisle, not far from that of his beloved "Stella," Mrs. Esther Johnson. Swift's epitaph is inscribed over the robing-room door. W. B. Yeats—who translated it thus: "Swift has sailed into his rest; Savage indignation there cannot lacerate his breast"—declared it the greatest epitaph of all time. Other memorials include the 17th-century Boyle Monument, with its numerous painted figures of family members, and the monument to Turlough O'Carolan, the last of the Irish bards and one of the country's finest harp players. Immediately north of the cathedral is a small park, with statues of many of Dublin's literary figures and St. Patrick's Well. "Living Stones" is the cathedral's permanent exhibition celebrating St. Patrick's place in the life of the city. If you're a music lover, you're in for a treat; matins (9:40 AM) and evensong (5:45 PM) are still sung on many days. ⊠ *Patrick St., Dublin West* ☎ *01/453–9472* ⊕ *www.stpatrickscathedral.ie* ⊒ *€5.50* ☉ *Mar.– Oct., Mon.–Sat. 9–5, Sun. 9–11, 12:45–3, and 4:15–5:30; Nov.–Feb. Mon.–Sat. 9–5, Sun. 9–4:30.*

WORTH NOTING

❷ Dublinia and the Viking World. Ever wanted a chance to put your head in the stocks? Dublin's Medieval Trust has set up an entertaining and informative reconstruction of everyday life in medieval Dublin. The recently updated main exhibits use high-tech audiovisual and computer displays; you can also see a scale model of what Dublin was like around 1500, a medieval maze, a life-size reconstruction based on the 13th-century dockside at Wood Quay, and a fine view from the tower. For a more modern take on the city, check out the James Malton series of prints of 18th-century Dublin, hanging on the walls of the coffee shop. Dublinia is in the old Synod Hall (formerly a meeting place for bishops of the Church of Ireland), joined via a covered stonework Victorian bridge to Christ Church Cathedral. An exhibition on "The Viking World" consists of a similar reconstruction of life in even earlier Viking Dublin, including a Viking burial. An exhibition called "Historical Hunters" puts you in the role of archaeologist with interactive digs and a lab to test your newfound knowledge. There's a guided tour at 2:30 PM every day. ⊠ *St. Michael's Hill, Dublin West* ☎ *01/679–4611* ⊕ *www. dublinia.ie* ▭ *Exhibit €6.25* ⊙ *Apr.–Sept., daily 10–4:15; Oct.–Mar., daily 10–4.*

🔢 **Marsh's Library.** When Ireland's first public library was founded and endowed in 1701 by Narcissus Marsh, the Archbishop of Dublin, it was made open to "All Graduates and Gentlemen." The two-story brick Georgian building has remained virtually the same since then. It houses a priceless collection of 250 manuscripts and 25,000 15th- to 18th-century books. Many of these rare volumes were locked inside cages, as were the readers who wished to peruse them. The cages were to discourage the often impecunious students, who may have been tempted to make the books their own. The library has been restored with great attention to its original architectural details, especially in the book stacks. It's a short walk west from St. Stephen's Green and is accessed through a charming little cottage garden. ⊠ *St. Patrick's Close off Patrick St., Dublin West* ☎ *01/454–3511* ⊕ *www.marshlibrary.ie* ▭ *€2.50* ⊙ *Mon. and Wed.–Fri. 10–1 and 2–5, Sat. 10:30–1.*

🔢 **National College of Art and Design.** The delicate welding of glass and iron onto the redbrick Victorian facade of this onetime factory makes this school worth a visit. A walk around the cobblestone central courtyard often gives the added bonus of viewing students working away in glass, clay, metal, and stone. The glass-fronted new gallery combines work by local, national, and international avant-garde artists. ⊠ *Thomas St., Dublin West* ☎ *01/671–1377* ⊕ *www.ncad.ie* ▭ *Free* ⊙ *Weekdays 9–7.*

🔢 **Old Jameson Distillery.** Founded in 1791, this distillery produced one of Ireland's most famous whiskeys for nearly 200 years, until 1966, when local distilleries merged to form Irish Distillers and moved to a purpose-built, ultramodern distillery in Middleton, County Cork. Part of the complex was converted into the group's head office, and the distillery itself became a museum. There's a short audiovisual history of the industry, which had its origins 1,500 years ago in Middle Eastern perfume making. You can also tour the old distillery, and learn about the distilling of whiskey from grain to bottle, or view a reconstruction of a former warehouse, where the colorful nicknames of former barrel makers are recorded. The 40-minute tour includes a complimentary tasting (remember: Irish whiskey is best drunk without a mixer—try it straight or with water); four attendees are invited to taste different brands of Irish whiskey and compare them against bourbon and Scotch. If you have a large group and everyone wants to do this, phone in advance to arrange it. You can also get tutored in whiskey tasting. ⊠ *Bow St., Dublin West* ☎ *01/807–2355* ⊕ *www.jamesonwhiskey.com/ heritage* ▭ *€13.50* ⊙ *Daily 9–6:30; tours every ½ hr up to 5:30.*

🔢 **St. Michan's Church.** However macabre, St. Michan's main claim to fame is down in the vaults, where the totally dry atmosphere has preserved several corpses in a remarkable state of mummification. They lie in open caskets. Most of the resident deceased are thought to have been

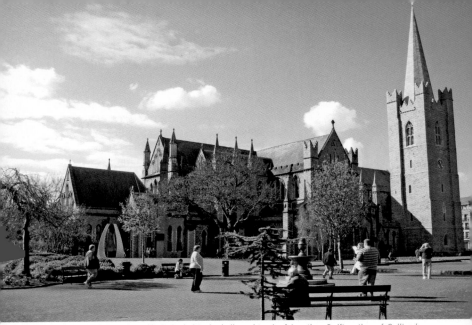

Inside gloriously heraldic St. Patrick's Cathedral is the hallowed tomb of Jonathan Swift, author of *Gulliver's Travels* and former cathedral dean.

Dublin tradespeople (one was, they say, a religious crusader). Except for its 120-foot-high bell tower, this Anglican church is architecturally undistinguished. The church was built in 1685 on the site of an 11th-century Danish church (Michan was a Danish saint). Another reason to come is to see the 18th-century organ, which Handel supposedly played for the first performance of *Messiah*. Don't forget to check out the Stool of Repentance—the only one still in existence in the city. Parishioners judged to be "open and notoriously naughty livers" used it to do public penance. ⌧ *Lower Church St., Dublin West* ☎ *01/872–4154* 💶 *€4* 🕐 *Mid-Mar.–Oct., weekdays 10–12:45 and 2–4:30, Sat. 10–12:45, Sun. service at 10 AM; Nov.–mid-Mar., weekdays 12:30–3:30, Sat. 10–12:45, Sun. service at 10 AM.*

⑤⑤ St. Nicholas of Myra's Church. A grand Neoclassical style characterizes this church, completed in 1834. The highly ornate chapel inside includes ceiling panels of the 12 apostles, and a pietà raised 20 feet above the marble altar, guarded on each side by angels sculpted by John Hogan while he was in Florence. The tiny nuptial chapel to the right has a small Harry Clarke stained-glass window. ⌧ *St. Nicholas St., Dublin West* ☎ *01/454–2172* 💶 *Free* 🕐 *Hrs vary.*

"TAKE IT AISY": PHOENIX PARK AND ENVIRONS

Far and away Dublin's largest park, Phoenix Park (the name is an anglicization of the Irish *Fionn Uisce*, meaning "clear water") is a vast, green, arrowhead-shaped oasis north of the Liffey, about a 20-minute walk from the city center. It's the city's main escape valve and sports center (cricket, soccer, Gaelic games, and polo), and the home of the

Home to the city zoo and plenty of cricket fields, Phoenix Park—the largest urban park in Europe—is a favorite escape for stressed-out Dubliners.

noble creatures of the Dublin Zoo. A handful of other cultural sights near the park also merit a visit.

Numbers in the margin correspond to numbers on the Dublin West and Phoenix Park map.

TOP ATTRACTIONS

⑥④ ★ National Museum of Decorative Arts and History. Connoisseurs of the decorative arts have always had a special fondness for Irish style, whose glories range from Bronze Age Celtic jewels to the 20th-century Moderne furniture of Eileen Gray. Here, in one gigantic treasure chest, is the full panoply of the National Museum's collection of glass, silver, furniture, and other decorative arts. The setting is spectacular: the huge Collins Barracks, named for the assassinated Irish Republican leader Michael Collins (1890–1922). Built in the early 18th century, and designed by Captain Thomas Burgh, these erstwhile "Royal Barracks" were stylishly renovated to become a showcase for the museum, which opened in September 1997. The displays are far ranging, covering everything from one of the greatest collections of Irish silver in the world to Irish period furniture—you'll see that the country's take on Chippendale was far earthier than the English mode. "The Way We Wore: 250 Years of Irish Clothing and Jewelry" and a thousand years of Irish coins are other highlights. Headlining the collections are some extraordinary objects, including the Fonthill Vase, the William Smith O'Brien Gold Cup, and the Lord Chancellor's Mace. ⊠ *Benburb St., Dublin West* ☎ *01/677-7444* ⊕ *www.museum.ie* ☒ *Free* ⊙ *Tues.–Sat. 10–5, Sun. 2–5.*

⑥⑤ Phoenix Park. Europe's largest public park, which extends about 5 km (3 mi) along the Liffey's north bank, encompasses 1,752 acres of verdant green lawns, woods, lakes, and playing fields. Sunday is the best time to visit: games of cricket, football (soccer), polo, baseball, hurling (a combination of lacrosse, baseball, and field hockey), and Irish football are likely to be in progress. Old-fashioned gas lamps line both sides of Chesterfield Avenue, the main road that bisects the park for 4 km (2½ mi), which was named for Lord Chesterfield, a lord lieutenant of Ireland, who laid out the road in the 1740s. To the right as you enter the park is the People's Garden, a colorful flower garden designed in 1864.

You're guaranteed to see wildlife at the **Dublin Zoo** (✉ *Dublin West* ☎ *01/677–1425* ⊕ *www.dublinzoo.ie*), the third-oldest public zoo in the world, founded in 1830, and just a short walk beyond the People's Garden. A major renovation completed in 2007 has now given new life and luster to the old place. Animals from tropical climes are kept in unbarred enclosures, and Arctic species swim in the lakes close to the reptile house. Some 700 lions have been bred here since the 1850s, one of whom became familiar to movie fans the world over when MGM used him for its trademark. (As they will tell you at the zoo, he is in fact yawning in that familiar shot: an American lion had to be hired to roar and the "voice" was dubbed.) The African Plains section houses the zoo's larger species; the Nakuru Safari is a new 25-minute tour of this area. World of Primates is a gathering of the usual suspects from tiny colobus monkeys to big gorillas. In summer the Lakeside Café serves ice cream and drinks. Admission to the Dublin Zoo is €15. Hours are March through September, daily 9:30–6; October, daily 9:30–5:30; November through December, daily 9:30–4; January, daily 9:30–4; February, daily 9:30–5.

A real genteel, family treat is a trip to elegant **Farmleigh House** (✉ *Phoenix Park, Dublin West* ☎ *01/677–1425* ⊕ *www.farmleigh.ie*), a 78-acre Edwardian estate situated to the northwest of the park with a working farm, walled and sunken gardens, wonderful picnic-friendly grounds, a regular organic food market, and a house full of antique furnishings and historic art. Admission is free. Hours are mid-March through December, Tuesday–Wednesday 10–4, Thursday–Sunday 10–4:45.

Also within the park is a **visitor center** (✉ *Dublin West* ☎ *01/677–0095* ⊕ *www.heritageireland.ie*), in the 17th-century fortified Ashtown Castle; it has information about the park's history, flora, and fauna. Admission to the center is free. Hours are mid-March to October, daily 10–5:45; November to mid-March, Wednesday–Sunday 9:30–5:30.

NEED A BREAK?

Ryan's Pub (✉ *28 Parkgate St., Dublin West* ☎ 01/677–6097), one of Dublin's last remaining genuine late-Victorian-era pubs, has changed little since its last remodeling—in 1896. It's right near the entrance to Phoenix Park.

WORTH NOTING

Arbour Hill Cemetery. All 14 Irishmen executed by the British following the 1916 Easter Uprising are buried here, including Pádrig Pearse, who led the rebellion; his younger brother Willie, who played a minor role in the uprising; and James Connolly, a socialist and labor leader wounded in the battle. Too weak from his wounds to stand, Connolly was tied to a chair and then shot. The burial ground is a simple but formal area, with the names of the dead leaders carved in stone beside an inscription of the proclamation they issued during the uprising. ⊠ *Arbour Hill, Dublin West* ☎ *01/605–7700* ⊕ *www.heritageireland.ie* ⊠ *Free* ⊘ *Weekdays 8–4, Sat. 11–4, Sun. 9:30–4.*

WHERE TO EAT

THE SCENE

By Anto Howard

Heard the joke about Irish food? One week after your dinner and you're hungry again. That, in fact, was in the old days when critics bemoaned the *pot*luck of the Irish—but those times are long and thankfully gone. Today, if you arrive thinking you're going to eat potatoes, potatoes, and more potatoes, be prepared to have your preconceptions overturned—and to be enthralled and very happily sated in the process. Why? Because Ireland has undergone a food revolution, and some of Dublin's chefs are leading the charge.

No longer does a pub crawl turn up a better meal than one in a fancy restaurant. Dubliners who can afford it forgo heading to the "local" to down a pint after work because they've now made reservations at the newest eateries and hippest showplaces (of course, the pubs and the pints come later in the evening).

At these hotspots, euro-toques continue to come up with new and glorious ways to abuse your waistline. Roast scallop with spiced pork belly and au gratin cauliflower, all in a daring caper-and-raisin sauce? Sautéed rabbit loin with Clonakilty black pudding? As these dishes reveal, Dublin's top cooks are determined to take advantage of the fact that Ireland has some of the best "raw materials" in the world. Given that it is a small island on which one is never farther than an hour-and-a-half drive from the coast, it is not only its seaside restaurants that can claim to serve fish on the same day it's caught. In addition, the freshest Limerick hams, tastiest Cork *crubins* (pigs' trotters), and most succulent Galway Bay oysters arrive in the city every day.

But since Dublin was a magnet for immigrants during the Celtic Tiger prosperity, the city was suddenly hot with Indian curries, Thai chilies, and Pan-Asian fireworks. Ethnic restaurants now have a firm foothold in the city's foodie culture—you can indulge your passion for superb French or Italian food one day, then enjoy Korean barbecue the next. This interest in far-flung food has heralded a new wave of internationally trained professionals who have stamped their own *blás* (Irish for "gloss") on traditional ingredients.

The current economic turnaround has focused the locals' minds on one drawback of the new Dublin dining scene—a lot of restaurants were getting away with overpricing during the boom years. Change has been slower than in the hotel sector and a lot of à la carte menus are still too expensive, but many top eateries are reducing their prices and also now offer affordable fixed-price lunch menus, which can be considered bargains for the cash-conscious epicurean.

Another welcome phenomenon has been the arrival of little, family-run Italian joints with great food, no fuss, and real coffee, all at a good price. Enoteca delle Langhe on the northside of the quays and the fantastically bustling Dunne and Crescenzi near Trinity are two of the best. The twin wonders of L'Gueuleton and Gruel have introduced Dublin to the joys of affordable, casual, but always classy French cuisine. Fallon and Byrne has introduced the deli/restaurant/wine bar, all-under-one-roof idea to great acclaim—and with quality, organic ingredients to boot.

KNOW-HOW

The Irish dine later than Americans. They stay up later, too, and reservations are usually not booked before 6:30 or 7 PM and up to around 10 PM. Lunch is generally served from 12:30 to 2:30. Pubs often serve food through the day—until 8:30 or 9 PM. Most pubs are family-friendly and welcome children until 7 PM. The Irish are an informal bunch, so smart-casual dress is typical. A few of the more formal restaurants, however, do expect you to wear a jacket and tie (noted below). And remember: shorts and sneakers are out except at the "eat-and-run" end of the spectrum.

Of course, and alas, Starbucks has long ago planted its ubiquitous flag in Dublin, but there are scores of independent cafés serving excellent coffee, and often good sandwiches. Other eateries, borrowing trends from all around the world, serve inexpensive pizzas, focaccia, pitas, tacos, and wraps (which are fast gaining in popularity over the sandwich). It's worthwhile to see if the restaurant of your choice offers an early-bird or pre- or post-theater menu, with significantly lower set prices at specific times, usually up to 7:30 PM and after the show. Value Added Tax (V.A.T.)—a 13.5% tax on food and a government excise tax on drinks—will automatically be added to your bill. Before paying, check to see whether a service charge has been included on your bill, which is often the case for groups of five or more. If so, you can pay the entire bill with a credit card; if not, it's customary to leave a tip in cash (10% to 15%) even if you're paying the main bill by credit card.

WORD OF MOUTH

"Here's a cool marketing fact we never knew before: Do you know the Guinness Book of World Records? Of course you do. Well, it was originally created as an advertising tool. One of the execs back in the 1950s wanted to settle a bar room bet he made with someone, and didn't have a way of finding an answer—so he came up with the idea to publish a book containing every record imaginable. That way, they could sell them for use in bars around the world, so that the Guinness name would always be there to settle bets. Who knew?"
—Erin74

WHAT IT COSTS IN EUROS				
	¢	$	$$	$$$	$$$$
AT DINNER	under €12	€12–€18	€19–€24	€25–€32	over €32

Restaurant prices are per person for a main course at dinner.

BEST BETS FOR DUBLIN DINING

With hundreds of restaurants to choose from, how will you decide where to eat? Fodor's writers and editors have selected their favorite restaurants by price, cuisine, and experience *in the lists below*. You can also search by neighborhood for excellent eating experiences—just peruse the following pages. Or find specific details about a restaurant in the full reviews, which are listed alphabetically.

Fodor'sChoice ★

Busyfeet & Coco Café, ¢, p. 115
Cake Café, $, p. 115
Chapter One, $$$$, p. 129
Dunne and Crescenzi, $, p. 115
Enoteca delle Langhe, ¢, p. 129
L'Gueuleton, $$, p. 117
Oliver's, $$, p. 123
Patrick Guilbaud, $$$$, p. 124
The Winding Stair, $$, p. 131

By Price

¢

Enoteca delle Langhe, p. 129
Kingfisher, p. 130
Soup Dragon, p. 130
Wagamama, p. 119

$

Cake Café, p. 115
Dunne and Crescenzi, p. 115
French Paradox, p. 131
Gruel, p. 127
The Good World, p. 116

$$

Eden, p. 125
L'Gueuleton, p. 117
Oliver's, p. 123
The Winding Stair, p. 131

$$$

Dax, p. 122
One Pico, p. 124
Unicorn, p. 125

$$$$

Chapter One, p. 129
Les Frères Jacques, p. 127

Patrick Guilbaud, p. 124
Thornton's, p. 119

By Type

CHILD-FRIENDLY

Bad Ass Café, $, p. 125
Cake Café, $, p. 115
Dunne and Crescenzi, $, p. 115
Enoteca delle Langhe, ¢, p. 129
The Steps of Rome, $, p. 118

EXPENSE ACCOUNT

Chapter One, $$$$, p. 129
Patrick Guilbaud, $$$$, p. 124
Shanahan's on the Green, $$$$, p. 118
Town Bar and Grill, $$, p. 124

GREAT VIEWS

Cake Café, $, p. 115
Eden, $$, p. 125
The Winding Stair, $$, p. 131

HOT SPOT

Cake Café, $, p. 115
Hop House, $, p. 129
La Maison, $, p. 117
Oliver's, $$, p. 123

LOTS OF LOCALS

Busyfeet & Coco Café, ¢, p. 115
The Good World, $, p. 116
Gruel, $, p. 127
L'Gueuleton, $$, p. 117
Mermaid Café, $$, p. 127

MOST ROMANTIC

Chapter One, $$$$, p. 129
L'Gueuleton, $$, p. 117
One Pico, $$$, p. 124

DELICIOUS DECOR

Balzac, $$, p. 119
Cake Café, $, p. 115
Chapter One, $$$$, p. 129
Patrick Guilbaud, $$$$, p. 124
The Tea Room, $$–$$$, p. 127

CITY CENTER: THE SOUTHSIDE

Use the coordinate (✛ 1:B2) at the end of each listing to locate a site on the corresponding Where to Eat in Dublin map.

¢

CAFÉ

Fodor's Choice

★

✕ **Busyfeet & Coco Café.** This bustling, quirky bohemian café emphasizes good, wholesome food. Organic ingredients play a prominent role on a menu that's laden with delicious salads and sandwiches. Try the grilled goat-cheese salad served with walnut-and-raisin toast and sun-dried-tomato tapenade on a bed of arugula. The delicious Mediterranean quesadilla wrap—with roasted vegetables, napolitana sauce, and mature cheddar—is a must. It's also one of the city center's best-situated spots for a bit of people-watching, as Dublin's young and hip stroll by all day long. ⊠ *41–42 S. William St., Southside* ☎ *01/671–9514* ▭ *No credit cards* ✛ *1:C4.*

$

CAFÉ

Fodor's Choice

★

✕ **Cake Café.** When the head of the Slow Food Dublin movement opens a café, expectations are going to be high. Michille Darmody's dreamy little Cake Café fulfills every one of them. As it is in a plant-filled courtyard at the back of the restored Daintree building, try to snag an outside table if the weather is decent. Then chill out and chow down on simple savory and sweet delights, all made with a loving, homey touch. Local, organic, and seasonal are the words to live by here and the terrine of Cashel Blue cheese with hazelnut is a typically delicious lunch dish. Save room for the delicate tarts and moist chocolate-chocolate brownie. This is also the perfect summer spot for a cheeky daytime glass of prosecco with a few nibbles in the courtyard. And don't forget their fun cookery classes: they are the talk of the town. ⊠ *Daintree Bldg., Pleasants Pl., Southside* ☎ *01/478–9394* ⊕ *www.thecakecafe.ie* ▭ *MC, V* ☾ *Closed Sun. No dinner Mon. and Sat.* ✛ *1:B5.*

$

ITALIAN

Fodor's Choice

★

✕ **Dunne and Crescenzi.** Nothing succeeds like success. So popular is this classy little Italian joint just off Nassau Street that they've expanded into the premises two doors down. Pity the poor little coffee shop in between trying to compete with the unpretentious brilliance of this brother-and-sister restaurant and deli. The menu is extensive but simple: panini (sandwiches), a horde of antipasti choices, a few choice pasta specials, and some evening meat dishes and desserts. The all-Italian kitchen staff work wonders with high-quality imported ingredients. The tagliere della casa—a selection of typical Italian salumi and farmhouse cheeses garnished with preserves and served on warm bread—makes a great light lunch. A couple of long tables make it perfect for a group, and the hundreds of bottles of wine on shelves cover every inch of the walls. ⊠ *14 S. Fredrick St., Southside* ☎ *01/677–3815* ⊕ *www.dunneandcrescenzi.com* ▭ *AE, MC, V* ✛ *1:D4.*

$$

FRENCH

★

✕ **Fallon and Byrne.** The fresh, new one-stop-shop for everything organic and delicious in Dublin, Fallon and Byrne combines a huge deli with a cozy cellar wine bar and expansive second-floor French brasserie. Located on the top floor of a beautiful old telephone exchange building, the high-ceiling, light-filled dining room has a bustling, city-center atmosphere. The menu covers everything from burgers to loin of rabbit, but the panfried halibut with herb bnocchi, baby fennel, and salsa verde and the veal liver with onion relish, pancetta, grape seed, and mustard dressing are typical treats. Leave room for the lemon-ricotta cheesecake

EATING WELL IN DUBLIN

The abundant high-quality produce the country is famous for is now receiving the care and attention of world-class chefs in the capital city's restaurants. Salmon is mixed with smoked haddock for fish cakes served with anchovy and parsley butter; black pudding is butter-fried and covered in an apple compote; and Irish beef is spiced and topped with a tangy avocado salsa.

Even the humble potato is being shaped and transformed into potato cakes and boxty (potato-and-flour pancake), and colcannon—a traditional Irish dish with bacon and cabbage—is getting a nouvelle spin.

Being an agricultural country with a maritime industry, Ireland benefits from a copious supply of freshly grown and readily available produce and seafood. Excellent Irish beef, pork, ham, and lamb appear on almost every menu.

Keep an eye out, too, for seasonal specials, such as wild or farmed quail and pheasant. Rich seafood harvests mean you can find fresh and smoked salmon, oysters, mussels, and shellfish in many guises— all vying with tender cuts of meat and an appetizing selection of quality vegetables.

Excellent dairy products are also essential to Irish cuisine. Dollops of fresh cream with home-baked desserts promise some exciting conclusions to these feasts—though you could also opt to finish a meal with a selection of native cheeses.

Leave room for the mature cheddars and luscious blue cheeses, the slightly sweet Dubliner, St. Tola goat's cheese from Clare, and Carrigburne Brie from Wexford—only a few of the many fine artisanal cheeses produced around the country.

While you're in Dublin, do indulge at least once in the traditional Irish breakfast, which is often served all day. It includes rashers (bacon), sausages, black-and-white pudding (types of sausage), mushrooms, tomatoes, and a fried egg—with lots of traditional homemade brown and soda breads and the famous Irish creamery butter. You'll need a pot or two of tea to wash this down. Known as an "Ulster Fry" in Northern Ireland, this breakfast is often the biggest—and best—meal of the day.

with ginger ice cream. You can pick up a bottle of wine in the wine cellar and enjoy it for a small corkage fee. ⊠ *11–17 Exchequer St., Southside* ☎ *01/472–1010* ⊕ *www.fallonandbyrne.com* ▭ *MC, V* ✢ *1:C3.*

$ ✕ **The Good World.** When Dublin's growing Chinese population wants
CHINESE   a big, uptown night out they come here. The surroundings are modest,
★   with large round tables—ideal for groups—in a somewhat dark but comfortable room. But the food is authentic and inspired—ask for the black-cover Chinese menu, not the standard, dumbed-down one. The dim sum selection is nonpareil in Ireland, with the mixed-meat dumplings a standout, and the chili-salt squid melts in the mouth. It's the perfect spot to order a load of dishes to be shared by an adventurous group. As is often the case with Chinese restaurants in Ireland, the desserts are not really worth trying. ⊠ *18 S. Great George's St., Southside* ☎ *01/677–5373* ▭ *AE, MC, V* ✢ *1:B3.*

2

$$ ╳ **Il Primo.** Ex-employees often make great owners, and John Farrell and
ITALIAN Anita Thoma like to run this little two-story Italian restaurant like an
intimate dinner party. A little quote board outside offers a daily pearl
of wisdom, and old wooden tables and chairs give the two small dining
rooms a casual feel. The friendly, if cramped, surroundings attract a
devoted clientele and John's collection of contemporary art adds a dash
of flair to the walls. The slow-cooked beef cheek with duck-fat roasted
potatoes and root vegetables is a standout evening dish. For something
a little lighter, the risotto with smoked salmon, dill, and horseradish
is a must. The wine list—heavy with Italian influences—is, to quote a
local phrase, as long as your arm. ⊠ *16 Montague St., off Harcourt St.,
Southside* ☎ *01/478–3373* ⊕ *www.ilprimo.ie* ▭ *AE, MC, V* ☽ *Closed
Sun. No lunch Sat.* ✛ *1:C3.*

$ ╳ **Jaipur.** Call to mind all the stereotypes of bad, production-line Indian
INDIAN restaurants. Then consign them to the flames, for Jaipur is something
different altogether. A spacious room with a sweeping staircase and con-
temporary furnishings reflects Jaipur's modern, cutting-edge approach
to Indian cuisine. Mixed with traditional dishes, such as chicken tikka
masala, are more unusual preparations, such as *duck vindaloo* (Barbary
duck simmered in chili, cinnamon, conconut vinegar, and palm sugar).
The delightful *karwari* is a sweet-and-sour butterfish in a tamarind-
flavor broth redolent of coastal-south-Indian spices. Try the Jaipur
Jugalbandi, a selection of five appetizers. Dishes can be toned down
or spiced up to suit your palate, and service is courteous and prompt.
Another plus: the wine list is well thought out. ⊠ *41 S. Great George's
St., Southside* ☎ *01/677–0999* ⊕ *www.jaipur.ie* ⌂ *Reservations essential*
▭ *AE, MC, V* ✛ *1:B4.*

$$ ╳ **L'Gueuleton.** Dubliners don't do waiting, but you'll see hungry crowds
FRENCH doing just that outside this no-reservations-accepted, exceptional new
Fodor'sChoice eatery just off George's Street. L'Gueuleton's has lost a little of its inti-
★ macy since it expanded, but the crowds still come for authentic French
food at a fair price. Start with the *duck egg mayonnaise with celery
salt and watercress.* For a main course, the Toulouse sausages with
choucroute and Lyonnaise potatoes somehow manages to be hearty and
adventurous at the same time. Desserts have a devilishly childish touch
to them—passion-fruit cake with white chocolate sauce is a typical
example. Although you can't phone in a reservation, you can go there
early in the evening and put your name down for a table along with
your cell-phone number. They will give you a call 20 minutes before
your table is ready. People also gather outside hoping to be fitted in
during the evening. ⊠ *1 Fade St., Southside* ☎ *01/675–3708* ⊕ *www.
lgueuleton.com* ▭ *MC, V* ✛ *1:B4.*

$ ╳ **La Maison.** Closing one of the city's favorite little bakery/cafés would
FRENCH have been a crime if it hadn't been replaced by such an intimate, classy
★ little eatery. La Maison des Gourmets became simply La Maison and,
although the delicious pastries were lost forever, this bustling, unpretentious bistro now boasts one of the most inviting and good value menus
in the city. The look is very much casual bistro, a satisfying backdrop
for starters like the potted crab with cucumber, chili, and coriander and
mouthwatering mains including rabbit casserole with smoked bacon

and mashed potatoes. The chocolate fondant is a dessert to die for. ⊠ *15 Castle Market, Southside* ☎ *01/672–7258* ⊕ *www.lamaisonrestaurant. ie* ⊟ *MC, V* ⊗ *Closed Sun.* ✢ *1:C4.*

$ ✕ **Mao.** Everything is Asian fusion at this bustling café—which has
ASIAN quickly blossomed into a mini-franchise across the city—from the little Andy Warhol pastiche of Chairman Mao on the washroom door to the eclectic mix of dishes on the menu, which combine Thai, Vietnamese, and other Southeast Asian elements. Top choices include the Chicken lemongrass salad, chili squid, crispy whole sea bass with scallops, and the *nasi goreng* (Indonesian fried rice with chicken and shrimp). ⊠ *2 Chatham Row, Southside* ☎ *01/670–4899* ⊕ *www.cafemao.com* ⟀ *Reservations not accepted* ⊟ *MC, V* ✢ *1:B5.*

¢ ✕ **Nude.** One-word names for restaurants and cafés were all the rage in
VEGETARIAN Dublin about 10 years ago. Many of them have fallen by the wayside, but Nude, a sleek, eco-friendly fast-food café, has been such a success that owner Norman Hewson—brother of U2's Bono—has opened another branch for takeout only on Upper Leeson Street. The canteen-style tables set the extremely casual atmosphere—don't be surprised if your neighbor strikes up a conversation. You order at the counter and someone delivers to your table in double-quick time. The menu is mostly vegetarian, and everything on it is made with organic and free-range ingredients. Choose from homemade soups and vegetable wraps (chicken satay is a classic), smoothies, and fresh-squeezed juices. On weekend nights DJs spin while you dine. ⊠ *21 Suffolk St., Southside* ☎ *01/677–4804* ⊟ *MC, V* ✢ *1:C3.*

$$$$ ✕ **Shanahan's on the Green.** Big, bad (meaning good, of course) steaks
AMERICAN are the guilty-pleasure draw at this American-style steak house. Happily, quantity doesn't necessarily diminish quality and Shanahan's arguably serves the best beef in the country, all certified Irish Angus, of course. The building itself is an Irish Georgian glory, designed by Richard Cassels, Dublin's leading 18th-century architect. Glowing with gilded chandeliers and graced with a few marble fireplaces, this restored town house offers a sleekly elegant setting in which to chow down on some of the tenderest beef this side of Kobe (they cook it in a special high-temperature oven, searing the outside to keep the inside good and juicy). If steak doesn't float your boat, they also do a mean panfried wild seabass with wild garlic, Morteau sausage, and morel mushrooms. Oreo-cookie-crust cheesecake is the perfect way to finish off the feast, but many will consider the decor—think sash windows, gilt mirrors, and plush carpets—rich enough. ⊠ *119 St. Stephen's Green, Southside* ☎ *01/407–0939* ⊕ *www.shanahans.ie* ⟀ *Reservations essential* ⊟ *AE, DC, MC, V* ⊗ *No lunch Sat.–Thurs.* ✢ *1:C4.*

$ ✕ **The Steps of Rome.** Discerning natives flock to this place for a cheap
ITALIAN lunch, or a good takeout. Just a few steps from Grafton Street, this Italian eatery is also popular for a late-night bite. Slices of delicious, thin-crust pizza, with all the traditional toppings, are the main attraction. The *funghi* (mushroom) pizza is particularly good. The few tables are usually full, but it's worth waiting around for the classic Italian pasta dishes like the cannelloni. Some diners just opt for the fresh salads with focaccia. Follow it all with cheesecake or tiramisu, and good

strong espresso. ✉ *1 Chatham Ct., Southside* ☎ *01/670–5630* ▭ *No credit cards* ⊹ *1:C4.*

$$$$ ✗ **Thornton's.** Forget the stretched metaphors: if you're passionate about
FRENCH food, this place is a must. Thornton's cooking style is light, and his
★ dishes are small masterpieces of structural engineering, piled almost
dangerously high in towers of food. Dinner is a set, three-course menu
and a highlight is the loin of wild venison with roasted parsnip cones,
potato gnocchi, and Valrhona chocolate sauce. Desserts range from
apple tart tatin to prune and Armagnac soufflé. Sheridans of Dublin
supplies the enormous selection of cheeses. The dining room is simple
and elegant—there's little to distract you from the exquisite food—and
the Canapé Bar is the perfect spot for a pre- or post-theater snack with
a glass of champagne. ✉ *Fitzwilliam Hotel, St. Stephen's Green, Southside* ☎ *01/478–7008* ⊕ *www.thorntonsrestaurant.com* ⌂ *Reservations
essential* ▭ *AE, DC, MC, V* ⊘ *Closed Sun. and Mon. No lunch Wed.*
⊹ *1:C4.*

$ ✗ **Wagamama.** Canteen food wasn't like this at your school. Modeled
JAPANESE on a Japanese canteen, Wagamama, with its long wooden tables and
benches and high ceilings with exposed metal piping, ensures a unique
communal dining experience. It attracts a young, loud crowd and is
constantly busy. Formal courses aren't acknowledged—food is served
as soon as it's ready, and appetizers and main courses arrive together.
Edamame—steamed and salted green soybeans in the pod—are a delicious starter and great fun to pop open and eat. Choose from filling
bowls of *ginger chicken udon* (teppan-fried udon noodles with chicken,
egg, beansprouts, spring onion, and chili) or chili beef ramen, and wash
it down with fresh fruit or vegetable juice. There's also a fine selection
of beers and sakes for the less abstemious. ✉ *S. King St., Southside*
☎ *01/478–2152* ⊕ *www.wagamama.ie* ▭ *AE, MC, V* ⊹ *1:C4.*

$$ ✗ **Yamamori.** Dublin's young and mobile folk went noodle-mad a few
JAPANESE years ago and Yamamori jumped to the top of the list for these ramen
addicts. The open plan and family-style tables have kept it popular with
the hip crowd. The meals-in-a-bowl are a splendid slurping experience,
and although you'll be supplied with a small Chinese-style soupspoon,
the best approach is with chopsticks. The *yasai yaki soba*, Chinese-style
noodles with Asian vegetables and egg, garnished with *menma* (dried
bamboo) and spring onions, is a favorite example. You can also get
sushi and sashimi, plus delicious chicken teriyaki, but the bento box
combo meal is always the best value. ✉ *71–72 S. Great George's St.,
Southside* ☎ *01/475–5001* ⊕ *www.yamamorinoodles.ie* ▭ *AE, MC, V*
⊹ *1:B3.*

SOUTHEAST DUBLIN

*Use the coordinate (⊹ 1:B2) at the end of each listing to locate a site
on the corresponding Where to Eat in Dublin map.*

$$ ✗ **Balzac.** A recently arrived player on the Dublin dining stage, Balzac
FRENCH aims to re-create the glamour of the best Parisian brasseries. The spar-
klingly handsome dining room, with its giant wall mirrors, high windows, stained-glass ceiling, and glitzy candelabra, is one of the most
impressive in the city. But the atmosphere is still casual, and the menu

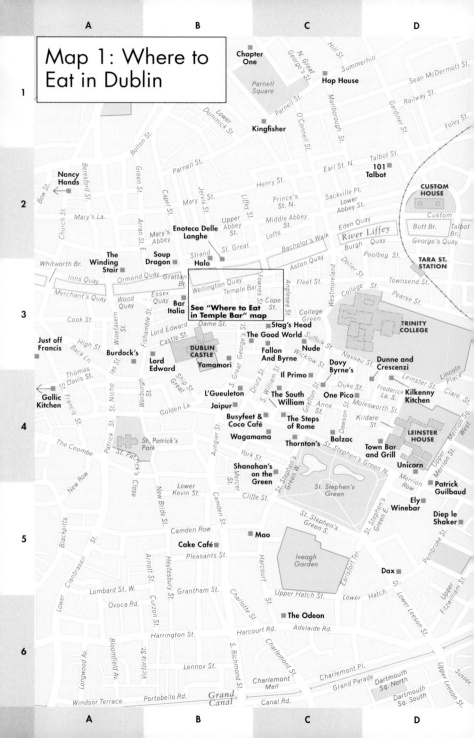

Map 1: Where to Eat in Dublin

A   **B**   **C**   **D**

Chapter One

Parnell Square

Hop House

Kingfisher

Nancy Hands

101 Talbot

CUSTOM HOUSE

Enoteca Delle Langhe

The Winding Stair

Soup Dragon

Halo

River Liffey

TARA ST. STATION

Bar Italia

See "Where to Eat in Temple Bar" map

Just off Francis

Burdock's

Stag's Head

The Good World

Nude

DUBLIN CASTLE

Fallon And Byrne

TRINITY COLLEGE

Gallic Kitchen

Lord Edward

Yamamori

Il Primo

Davy Byrne's

Dunne and Crescenzi

Kilkenny Kitchen

L'Gueuleton

One Pico

Jaipur

The South William

LEINSTER HOUSE

Busyfeet & Coco Café

The Steps of Rome

Wagamama

Thornton's

Balzac

Town Bar and Grill

St. Patrick's Park

Shanahan's on the Green

Unicorn

St. Stephen's Green

Patrick Guilbaud

Ely Winebar

Diep le Shaker

Mao

Cake Café

Iveagh Garden

Dax

The Odeon

Grand Canal

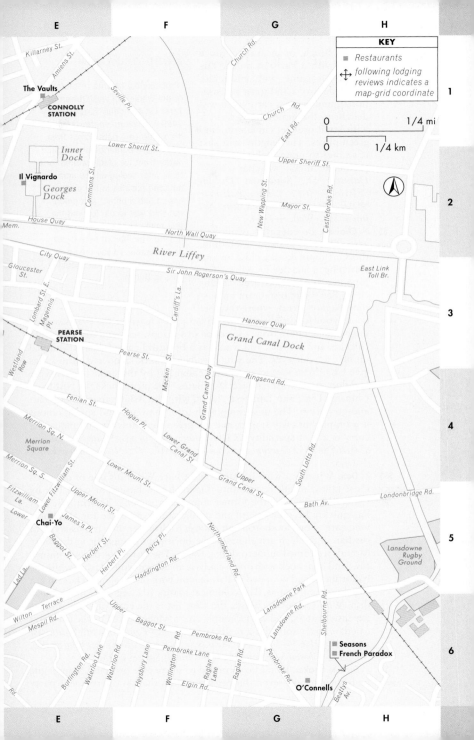

KEY

■ *Restaurants*

↔ *following lodging reviews indicates a map-grid coordinate*

0   1/4 mi

0   1/4 km

Killarney St.

Amiens St.

The Vaults ■

CONNOLLY STATION

Seville Pl.

Church Rd.

Church Rd.

East Rd.

Lower Sheriff St.

Upper Sheriff St.

Inner Dock

Commons St.

New Wapping St.

Mayor St.

Castleforbes Rd.

Il Vignardo ■

Georges Dock

House Quay

Mem.

North Wall Quay

River Liffey

City Quay

Gloucester St.

Sir John Rogerson's Quay

East Link Toll Br.

Lombard St. E.

Magennis Pl.

PEARSE STATION

Cardiff's La.

Hanover Quay

Grand Canal Dock

Westland Row

Pearse St.

Macken St.

Grand Canal Quay

Ringsend Rd.

Fenian St.

Hogan Pl.

Lower Grand Canal St.

South Lotts Rd.

Merrion Sq. N.

Merrion Square

Merrion Sq. S.

Lower Mount St.

Upper Grand Canal St.

Londonbridge Rd.

Fitzwilliam La.

Lower Fitzwilliam St.

Upper Mount St.

Bath Av.

Lower

James's Pl.

Chai-Yo ■

Herbert St.

Percy Pl.

Northumberland Rd.

Lansdowne Rugby Ground

Baggot St.

Herbert Pl.

Haddington Rd.

Lad La.

Wilton Terrace

Mespil Rd.

Upper

Baggot St.

Rd.

Pembroke Rd.

Lansdowne Park

Lansdowne Rd.

Shelbourne Rd.

Burlington Rd.

Waterloo Lane

Waterloo Rd.

Heysbury Lane

Pembroke Lane

Wellington Rd.

Raglan Lane

Raglan Rd.

Pembroke Rd.

Seasons ■

French Paradox ■

Elgin Rd.

O'Connells ■

Beatys Av.

Rd.

1

2

3

4

5

6

has a touch of peasant France mixed with a Parisian finish. The terrine of game with pistachio, spiced damsons and toast is sensational, and serious carnivores will delight in the honey braised duck with sevill orange, cinnamon, and green olives. The lengthy wine list is second to none. Balzac offers a pretheater menu weekdays. ⊠ *35 Dawson St., Southeast Dublin* ☎ *01/677–8611* ⊕ *www.balzac.ie* ⊟ *AE, MC, V* ⊗ *Closed Sun. No lunch Sat.–Wed.* ✢ *1:C4.*

$$ ✕ **Chai-Yo.** Be educated while you
ASIAN eat. There's always something thrilling about getting close up and watching a master at work. The Japanese teppanyaki area at this classy Pan Asian restaurant on bustling Baggot Street, where the chef cooks your food right on your tabletop, is a feast for the eye as well as the palate. Choose from a selection of scallops, sea bass, steak, teriyaki chicken, and prawns, and watch as a beautiful grilled dish is whipped up before your eyes. The white walls and dark lacquered furnishings give Chai-Yo a serene ambience, enhanced by the delicate glassware and fine, green-washed-porcelain plates. The menu picks the best from Chinese, Thai, and Japanese dishes, with the Asian tapas a good eat-and-go option. The miso soup with tofu, seaweed, and spring onions is a simple but tasty starter, and the green shell mussels and pineapple curry is a chef speciality. ⊠ *100 Lower Baggot St., Southeast Dublin* ☎ *01/676–7652* ⊕ *www.chaiyo.ie* ⊟ *AE, MC, V* ⊗ *No lunch weekends* ✢ *1:E5.*

$$$ ✕ **Dax.** When is a wine bar not a wine bar? When it's one of the city's
FRENCH most talked-about restaurants. Opened as a basement wine bar by
★ Olivier Meisonnave, the former sommelier at stellar Thornton's, Dax has quickly become one of the dining spots of choice for Dubliners who care about food. You can choose to drink or dine (tapas-style) at the bar, in the lush armchairs of the open-plan lounge, or in the more formal, restrained-modern dining room. The terrine of pressed guinea fowl and ham hock with apple coulis is an adventurous starter, while the ballottine of cod wrapped in Parma ham with olive oil mash potato is a standout main course. The cold meat platter is a finger-lickin' little bar dish. With Olivier in charge, the wine list is the envy of many a more expensive eatery, and with a couple dozen wines poured by the glass you can dare to try something really special. ⊠ *23 Pembroke St., Southeast Dublin* ☎ *01/676–1494* ⊕ *www.dax.ie* ⊛ *Reservations essential* ⊟ *AE, MC, V* ⊗ *Closed Sun. and Mon. No lunch Sat.* ✢ *1:D5.*

$$ ✕ **Diep le Shaker.** Don't be surprised to see people ordering champagne
ASIAN with their meals—even during a recession there's a permanent party

Does beautiful décor make delicious food taste even more delicious? Dine at Balzac—one of Dublin's leading scene-arenas—and find out.

vibe at this flamboyant Thai restaurant, which attracts Ireland's wealthy in droves. Comfortable high-back armchairs, quality art on the walls, and elegant stemware make this a stylish place to dine. But only half the reason for going is to see and be seen. Try the great red curry with coconut milk, bamboo shoots, Thai aubergines, chili, and sweet basil. It's slightly off the beaten track, on a narrow lane off Pembroke Street. ✉ *55 Pembroke La., Southeast Dublin* ☎ *01/661–1829* ⊕ *www.diep. net* ⏴ *Reservations essential* ☰ *AE, MC, V* ☾ *Closed Sun. and Mon. No lunch Sat.* ✛ *1:D5.*

$$
IRISH

✕ **Ely Winebar.** Almost equidistant from the twin dames of Dublin hotel elegance, the Shelbourne and the Merrion, Ely started out as a mere wine bar—and oh, what a selection of wines they have, many of them by the glass. But it has quickly grown into a wonderful little eatery with organic meat and vegetables from the owner's family farm in County Clare, guaranteeing a tasty mouthful in every bite. Dishes tend to be simple—bangers and mash, a scrumptious panfried monkfish, Killaha oysters with brown bread—but incredibly fresh and succulent. The plate of mature Irish and Continental cheeses is the perfect finish—with a glass of wine, of course. ✉ *22 Ely Pl., Southeast Dublin* ☎ *01/676– 8986* ⊕ *www.elywinebar.ie* ☰ *AE, MC, V* ☾ *Closed Sun. No lunch Sat.* ✛ *1:D5.*

$$
FRENCH
Fodor's Choice
★

✕ **Oliver's.** O'Brien's of Lesson Street is an old-school, pint-drinking Dublin pub and probably the last place you'd expect to find hosting a much talked-about new restaurant upstairs. Head up to the cozy second floor, however, to experience some Gallic magic. The decor is simple to a fault, you might even end up on a pub stool, but the menu is proof positive that the eponymous chef-owner Olivier Quenet once worked at the nonpareil Patrick Guilbaud. Black pudding with caramelized apple is one sumptuous starter; for main courses, check out the rabbit and pigeon pie with a snowflake light crust or the skate with brown butter and chard. The wine list is a parade of French stars in all price ranges. ⊠ *8–9 Sussex Terrace, Upper Lesson St., Southside* ☎ *01/668–2594* ⊟ *MC, V* ✛ *1:D6.*

$$$

MODERN IRISH

★

✕ **One Pico.** Grown women have been known to swoon when chef-owner Eamonn O'Reilly walks into the dining room of his little restaurant tucked away in a quiet lane only a few minutes from Stephen's Green. Eamonn cuts quite a dash, but it's his sophisticated, daring, contemporary cuisine that tends to seduce visitors to One Pico. Try the incredible langoustine risotto to start. Dishes such as roast rump of veal with fricassee of girolles, pearl onion, and truffle, and *pomme sarladaise* (a southern France version of mashed potatoes) demonstrate a savvy use of native ingredients. Follow this with the banana parfait with date and toffee ice cream and sticky toffee doughnuts. As is usual with Dublin's luxe eateries, the fixed-price lunch and pretheater menus offer great value. ⊠ *5–6 Molesworth Pl., off Schoolhouse La., Southeast Dublin* ☎ *01/676–0300* ⊕ *www.onepico.com* ⌸ *Reservations essential* ⊟ *AE, MC, V* ✛ *1:C4.*

$$$$

FRENCH

Fodor'sChoice

★

✕ **Patrick Guilbaud.** The words "Dublin's finest restaurant" often share the same breath as the name of this do-be-impressed place on the ground floor of the Merrion Hotel. The menu is described as French, but chef Guillaume Lebrun's genius lies in his occasional daring use of traditional Irish ingredients—so often abused and taken for granted—to create the unexpected. The best dishes are flawless: Clogher Head lobster ravioli, veal sweetbreads and licorice, or the spiced pigeon with buttery cabbage are among the best options. Follow that, if you can, with the *assiette au chocolat* (a tray of five hot and cold chocolate desserts). The ambience is just as delicious—if you're into lofty, minimalist dining rooms and Irish modern art (the Roderick O'Connors and Louis LeBrocquys are all from the owner's private collection). Nearly as impressive is the 70-page wine list, the view of the Merrion's manicured gardens, and the two-course lunch special for €38. Soaring white vaults and white walls won't make you feel warm and cozy, but you can always go somewhere else for that. ⊠ *21 Upper Merrion St., Southeast Dublin* ☎ *01/676–4192* ⊕ *www.restaurantpatrickguilbaud.ie* ⌸ *Reservations essential* ⊟ *AE, DC, MC, V* ☻ *Closed Sun. and Mon.* ✛ *1:D5*

$$

ITALIAN

✕ **Town Bar and Grill.** Even basements can surprise, and an old wine merchant's cellar on Kildare Street has been transformed into this cozy, modern-Italian trattoria. The elegant, New York–vibe dining room has a definite buzz, with live music some nights and numerous Irish celebrities have already made this a regular haunt. Chef Philip likes to take traditional Italian classics and give them a little—just a little—twist. The roast breast of wood pigeon with chestnut lasagne and Cumberland sauce is one of the most exciting starters. For mains try the roast Italian seafood casserole with clams, fish, chorizo, and red peppers. Baked cherry cheesecake with vanilla ice cream is a nice guilty way to finish. ⊠ *21 Kildare St., Southeast Dublin* ☎ *01/662–4724* ⊕ *www. townbarandgrill.com* ⊟ *AE, MC, V* ✛ *1:D4.*

$$$
MEDITERRANEAN
★

✕ **Unicorn.** If there is an art to finding the perfect place when you want to get slightly sozzled over some quality eats, then the Unicorn is a Southside masterwork. Posher locals love to head here when they want to let their hair down in some wine-fuelled, late-evening craic. The atmosphere is loose and relaxed, especially on the little terrace overlooking Merrion Court. Even better,

A TASTY TIP

Patrick Guilbaud, Chapter One, One Pico, and other high-end places prove the simple adage: great chefs make great restaurants. Many have fixed-price lunch menus that are excellent bargains for the cash-conscious epicurean.

2

the menu is scrumptious Italian. Hot antipasti include chicken livers Marsala and calamari fritti, and tempting but guilty main courses include veal cutlets on the bone with Gorgonzola dolce and marsala jus or the Linguine with Dublin bay prawns, courgettes, garlic, chili, and white wine. To dine here, you must turn your mobile phone to silent—how cool is that? ⊠ *12B Merrion Ct., Southeast Dublin* ☎*01/676–2182* ⊕ *www.unicornrestaurant.com* ⌂ *Reservations essential* ▭ *AE, MC, V* ☾ *Closed Sun.* ✛ *1:D4.*

TEMPLE BAR

Use the coordinate (✛ 2:B2) at the end of each listing to locate a site on the corresponding Where to Eat in Temple Bar map.

$
AMERICAN

✕ **Bad Ass Café.** If you want to make a Dublin native wince, mention with excitement that Sinéad O'Connor used to wait tables at this lively café in a converted warehouse between the Central Bank and Ha'penny Bridge. (A Rock n' Stroll tour plaque notes O'Connor's past here.) Old-fashioned cash shuttles whiz around the ceiling of the barnlike space, which has bare floors and primary colors inside and out. You can indulge in some great people-watching behind the wall of glass here. The food—mainly pizzas, pastas, and burgers—is unexceptional, but the Bad Ass can be a lot of fun and appetites of all ages love it. ⊠ *9–11 Crown Alley, Temple Bar* ☎*01/671–2596* ⊕ *www.badasscafe. com* ▭ *AE, MC, V* ✛ *2:C2.*

$$
MODERN IRISH
★

✕ **Eden.** Eden is where arty and media types are likely to gather to talk about, well, themselves. It has an open kitchen and a high wall of glass through which you can observe one of Temple Bar's main squares. Patio-style doors lead to an outdoor eating area—a major plus in a city with relatively few alfresco dining spots. On weekend nights in summer you can enjoy an outdoor movie in Meeting House Square while you eat. Seasonal menus are in vogue here, but standout dishes include marinated black mission fig tart, and Castletownebere scallops with minted pea risotto, sugar snap peas, and crispy pancetta. Desserts include a tempting pear and cinnamon crumble cheesecake. ⊠ *Meeting House Sq., Temple Bar* ☎*01/670–5372* ⊕ *www.edenrestaurant.ie* ⌂ *Reservations essential* ▭ *AE, MC, V* ✛ *2:B2.*

$
AMERICAN

✕ **Elephant & Castle.** The Elephant was long established in Temple Bar before the Tiger (Celtic, that is) changed the neighborhood forever. Large windows are great for people-watching in the city's trendiest

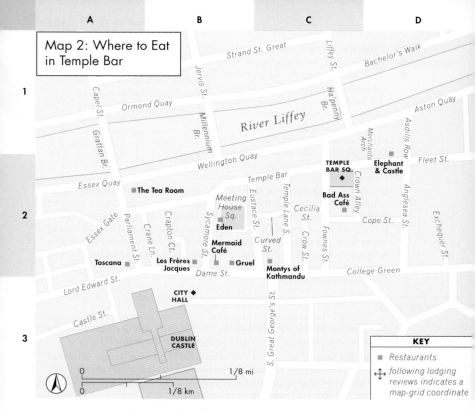

Map 2: Where to Eat in Temple Bar

A   B   C   D

Strand St. Great

Liffey St.

Bachelor's Walk

1

Capel St.

Jervis St.

Ormond Quay

Ha'penny Br.

Aston Quay

Grattan Br.

Millennium Br.

River Liffey

Merchants Arch

Asdills Row

Fleet St.

Wellington Quay

TEMPLE BAR SQ. ◆

Elephant & Castle ■

Essex Quay

Temple Bar

■ The Tea Room

Eustace St.

Temple Lane S.

Crown Alley

Anglesea St.

2

Essex Gate

Parliament St.

Crane Ln.

Crapton Ct.

Sycamore St.

Meeting House Sq.

Eden ■

Cecilia St.

Bad Ass Café ■

Cope St.

Exchequer St.

Mermaid Café ■

Curved St.

Crow St.

Fownes St.

Toscana ■

Les Frères Jacques ■

■ Gruel

Dame St.

Montys of Kathmandu ■

College Green

Lord Edward St.

CITY ◆ HALL

S. Great George's St.

Castle St.

3

DUBLIN CASTLE

0   1/8 mi
0   1/8 km

KEY

■ Restaurants

⬩ following lodging reviews indicates a map-grid coordinate

area, but "nothing fancy" would be a good motto for the traditional American food. Charcoal-grilled burgers, salads, omelets, sandwiches, and pasta make up the much-thumbed menu. Sunday brunch is always packed. The portions are some of the most generous in Dublin. When the service is good, the turnover tends to be quick, although you may be inclined to linger. New Yorkers, take note: yes, this is a cousin of the restaurant of the same name in Greenwich Village. ⊠ *18 Temple Bar, Temple Bar* 🕾 *01/679–3121* ⊕ *www.elephantandcastle.ie* 🖘 *Reservations not accepted* 🚍 *AE, MC, V* ⬩ *2:D1.*

$ ✕ **Gruel.** Too many people know about this little joint to call it a secret
ECLECTIC anymore. The brash, lively staff are masters of knowing when you need them and when you don't. The atmosphere is chatty and crowded and the no-nonsense quality grub focuses on a few reliable classics done to the highest quality—porridge with plum jam for breakfast, bangers and mash, Thai fish cakes—along with a couple of new dishes every week (how about risotto with roast sweet potato, basil, and chili?). They make their own soup stocks from scratch, and the daily "roast on a role" sandwich is a real filler-upper at lunch. ⊠ *67 Dame St., Temple Bar* 🕾 *01/670–7119* ⊕ *www.gruel.ie* 🖘 *Reservations not accepted* 🚍 *MC, V* ⬩ *2:B2.*

$$$$ ✕**Les Frères Jacques.** Many restaurants call themselves French, but this
FRENCH elegant eatery next to the Olympia Theatre positively reeks of Gallic
★ panache. Old prints of Paris and Deauville hang on the green-paper
walls, and the French waiters, dressed in white Irish linen and black
bow ties, exude a European charm without being excessively formal.
Expect traditional French cooking that nods to the seasons. Seafood is a
major attraction, and lobster (fished right from the tank—a "plus" that
people with delicate sensibilities will find a definite minus) is typically
roasted and flambéed with Irish whiskey. Others prefer the seared lamp
with grilled polenta and buttered mint juices. Also recommended are the
seasonal game specialties. A piano player performs Friday and Saturday
evenings and on the occasional weeknight. ⊠ *74 Dame St., Temple Bar*
☎ *01/679–4555* ⊕ *www.lesfreresjacques.com* ⤴ *Reservations essential*
⊟ *AE, MC, V* ☺ *Closed Sun. No lunch Sat.* ✢ *2:B2.*

$$ ✕**Mermaid Café.** Hope you don't mind sharing your dinner conversation
ECLECTIC with the people next to you. The Mermaid has the simple, crowded
feel of a very upmarket canteen, with large tables set close together
and casual, but classy, service. One of the chef-owners dabbles in fine
art, and his tastes in this area are reflected in his artistic and decorative
style of bistro cooking. It's not cheap, but the food is reliable. Lunch is
an exceptional value—crispy mackerel, huge hearty seafood casseroles,
panfried lamb's liver with horseradish mash and beetroot jus, or char-
grilled rib eye with sage and mustard mash, fine beans, and roast garlic,
and herb butter. Attention to detail and a thoughtful wine list make this
modest restaurant with tall windows looking onto busy Dame Street
one of the most popular eateries in Temple Bar. ⊠ *69 Dame St., Temple*
Bar ☎ *01/670–8236* ⊕ *www.mermaid.ie* ⊟ *MC, V* ✢ *2:B2.*

$$ ✕**Montys of Kathmandu.** Montys proudly declares itself the "only Nepal-
ASIAN ese restaurant in Dublin." Was there ever any doubt? The bland decor
is nothing to write home about, but the food at this little eatery in
the middle of hypermodern Temple Bar is as authentic as it is unique.
Poleko squid (lightly spiced and barbecued in a tandoori oven and
served in a sizzler) or lamb *Choila* (with fresh chilis, ginger, garlic, herbs,
and a dash of red wine) are the more adventurous starters. For a main
course try *Mo Mo,* dumplings served with Mo Mo chutney, a favorite
street dish in Kathmandu. The wine cellar is surprisingly varied. ⊠ *28*
Eustace St., Temple Bar ☎ *01/670–4911* ⊕ *www.montys.ie* ⊟ *AE, MC,*
V ☺ *No lunch* ✢ *2:C2.*

$$–$$$ ✕**The Tea Room.** In the Clarence Hotel, you can sit around all day and
MODERN IRISH hope that Bono and the boys of U2—they own the joint, after all—
might turn up for a quick snack. Other stars of stage and screen often
stay at the hotel and stop in at the Tea Room. Minimalistically hued in
golden oak, eggshell white, and light yellows, the high-ceiling room is a
perfect stage for off-duty celebs. The contrast between this high-vaulted
cocoon and busy Essex Street—whose madding crowds can be glimpsed
through the double-height windows—could not be more dramatic. The
menu has been slimmed down in recent times with a focus on a smaller
number of dramatic dishes like gingerbread crusted sea bass with cassoulet of coco bean or the soya glazed pork belly with wilted samphire
and hazelnut. ⊠ *Clarence Hotel, 6–8 Wellington Quay, Temple Bar*

Cuisine Irelandaise mixes new French cuisine with old Irish ingredients and results—such as this squab in Irish Whiskey sauce at Les Frères Jacques—are *très delicieux.*

☎ *01/407–0813* ⊕ *www.theclarence.ie* 🍴 *Reservations essential* ▭ *AE, MC, V* ☺ *No lunch Sat.* ✛ *2:A2.*

$$ ✕ **Toscana.** A genuine trattoria in the heart of crazy Temple Bar, Toscana
ITALIAN buzzes with chatter all evening long and offers a popular pretheater menu. A Mediterranean slant to the simple dining room includes plenty of Italian landscapes, cream tones, and wood. A typical starter is the panfried crab claws in garlic. The *penne entrecote* is strips of Irish beef panfried with onions, garlic, and olive oil and tossed in a plum tomato and cream sauce. The meat and pizza dishes are also always reliable and the Bailey's cheesecake with chocolate sauce is a dessert that will have your taste buds tap dancing. ✉ *3 Cork Hill, Dame St., Temple Bar* ☎ *01/670–9785* ⊕ *www.toscana.ie* ▭ *AE, DC, MC, V* ✛ *2:A2.*

THE NORTHSIDE

Use the coordinate (✛ 1:B2) at the end of each listing to locate a site on the corresponding Where to Eat in Dublin map.

$ ✕ **101 Talbot.** Sardi's it's not, but the 101 has that certain buzz that
MEDITERRANEAN comes only from restaurants popular with the artistic and literary set. Close to the Abbey and Gate theaters, so there's no danger of missing a curtain call, this slightly frantic upstairs restaurant showcases an ever-changing exhibition of local artists' work. The creative contemporary food—with eclectic Mediterranean and Eastern influences—uses fresh local ingredients. Try the slow roasted pork belly with red wine gravy and sautéed cabbage. The roast red peppers stuffed with spicy curried lentils also impresses. Healthful options and several vegetarian choices

make this a highly versatile restaurant. ✉ *101 Talbot St., Northside* ☎ *01/874–5011* ⊕ *www.101talbot.ie* ⟁ *Reservations essential* ▭ *AE, MC, V* ☉ *Closed Sun. and Mon.* ✦ *1:D2*

$$$$
MODERN IRISH
Fodor'sChoice
★

✕ **Chapter One.** This wonderful, culture-vulture favorite gets its name from its location, downstairs in the vaulted, stone-wall basement of the Dublin Writers Museum; the natural stone-and-wood setting makes it cozily cavelike. The contemporary French eatery is currently the culinary king of the Northside, thanks to chef-proprietor Ross Lewis's way with such dishes as breast of guinea fowl, with creamed spinach, Perigord truffle, and cheesed macaroni. W. B. Yeats himself would have loved the John Dory overflowing with crushed Jerusalem artichoke, Morteau sausage, and poached shellfish, while Synge probably would have fancied the Dublin version of Proust's madeleine: rich bread-and-butter pudding, a favorite of working-class Irish mothers for generations, here turned into an outrageously filling work of art. ✉ *18–19 Parnell Sq., Northside* ☎ *01/873–2266* ⊕ *www.chapteronerestaurant. com* ⟁ *Reservations essential* ▭ *AE, DC, MC, V* ☉ *Closed Sun. and Mon. No lunch Sat.* ✦ *1:B1*

¢
ITALIAN
Fodor'sChoice
★

✕ **Enoteca delle Langhe.** Officially called Quartier Bloom in tribute to Joyce's most famous character, a charming little (very little) Italian quarter has sprung up just off Ormond Quay, bringing a chorus of approval from Dubliners long starved of quality, down-to-earth Italian food. It consists of a communal plaza area, a fabulous mural that's a modern take on Leonardo da Vinci's *The Last Supper,* and a couple of places to eat, including Enoteca delle Langhe. Italian-owned and -operated, Langhe serves up the full enoteca experience: quality, affordable Italian wines (more than 75% are sourced from the Langhe district); a limited but enticing selection of appetizers—try the perfect bruschetta with scrumptious toppings like sun-dried-tomato pesto and sautéed zucchini—warm, friendly, family-style service; and a constant buzz in the air. In summer tango dancers perform outside. ✉ *Blooms La., Northside* ☎ *01/888–0834* ▭ *AE, MC, V* ✦ *1:B2.*

$$$
MODERN IRISH

✕ **Halo.** Judges from the nearby Four Courts rest their wigs on empty seats while the fashion crowd chats over multicolor drinks at this chic restaurant in the even chicer Morrison Hotel. A restyling has slightly softened the severity of the soaring ceiling and minimalism of the dramatic two-story dining room, devised by fashion designer John Rocha. It looks its best at night: moody and mysterious. European fusion is the tag new chef Richie Wilson gives his menu. Seafood is the focus of his star dishes; the fillet of turbot with Iberian ham, truffle sauce, and a lentil stew is a rich and warm favorite. For a starter try the seared scallops with confit of suckling pig with apple puree. As a fitting finale, desserts are miniature works of art on enormous china platters. ✉ *Morrison Hotel, Ormond Quay, Northside* ☎ *01/887–2400* ⊕ *www. morrisonhotel.ie* ▭ *AE, DC, MC, V* ☉ *No lunch* ✦ *1:B2.*

$
KOREAN

✕ **Hop House.** A unique Korean standout in the slew of cheap and cheerful Chinese eateries that have opened on Parnell Street (some local wags are already calling it Chinatown), Hop House is a restaurant and a pub in one. Part of the old Shakespeare pub has been transformed into the friendliest, best-value new restaurant in the city. The dining room is bright and busy, with little table buzzers for service and the sounds of music spilling over from the bar next door. Traditional Korean specialties like kimchi are augmented with a large selection of sushi rolls, including the mouthwatering Black Tiger Roll with avocado, crab meat, eel, and teriyaki sauce. Hot dishes include spicy pork and squid. ⊠ *160 Parnell St., Northside* ☎ *01/872–8318* ☰ *MC, V* ✛ *1:C1.*

$ ✕ **Il Vignardo.** Sometimes when it comes to dining, the where is more

ITALIAN important than the what. Il Vignardo serves some of Dublin's tasti-

★ est cheap and cheerful pizzas and pasta, but it's the unique decor that elevates this place a little above the rest. The dramatically vaulted ceilings, painted with creeping vines and branches, burst into bloom as they rise from Tuscan columns and evoke thoughts of Italian vineyards and sunshine. Outside, the sheltered courtyard garden, a real oasis in a city-center setting, is perfect for summer dining or just a little aperitif. If you want to spend a little extra, try the bread-crumbed chicken fillet topped with tomato and mozzarella. But who can resist the lasagna, served up with minced Irish beef? ⊠ *Hotel Isaccs, Store St., Northside* ☎ *01/855–3099* ⊕ *www.ilvignardo.com* ☰ *AE, MC, V* ⊘ *No lunch weekends* ✛ *1:E2.*

¢ ✕ **Kingfisher.** Don't let the down-at-heel canteen decor put you off—this

IRISH place has been around for a long time and is a master of the art of fish-and-chips. But there's so much more to a mammoth value menu full of seafood surprises like such Dublin favorites as cod and ray (or more unusual choices like halibut). They even serve up a whole sea bass and rainbow trout. Their huge Irish breakfasts have won awards and all the meats come fresh from the owners' own farm. The Northside locals love this place and give it a lively, community atmosphere. ⊠ *166–168 Parnell St., Northside* ☎ *01/872–8732* ☰ *MC, V* ✛ *1:C4.*

¢ ✕ **Soup Dragon.** This tiny café and take-out soup shop serves an aston-

IRISH ishing array of fresh soups daily. Soups come in three sizes, and you

★ can get vegetarian soup or soups with meat- or fish-based broth. Best bets include red pepper, tomato, and goat cheese soup; fragrant Thai chicken soup; beef chili; and hearty mussel, potato, and leek soup. The friendly staff make fine coffee and delicious smoothies. The cost of soup includes bread and a piece of fruit for dessert—an excellent value—and they also do a decent grab-and-go breakfast. A second Soup Dragon has just opened around the corner on Ormond Quay. ⊠ *168 Capel St., Northside* ☎ *01/872–3277* ⊕ *www.soupdragon.com* ☰ *No credit cards* ⊘ *Closed Sun. No dinner* ✛ *1:B3.*

$ ✕ **The Vaults.** Come eat under the train station. Not exactly the best

ITALIAN sales pitch you've ever heard, but this wonderful, long-neglected space beneath Connolly Station was imaginatively revamped to create one of the city's most fashionable dining spots. Cavernous arches, smooth Portland stone floors, striking furniture, and dramatic lighting create the background for a mostly young business set. Each of the vaults is decorated in its own style, ranging from hypermodern to turn-of-the-20th-century elegant. Cocktails are a specialty, although it's worth a visit for the food alone. The Italian chef makes everything from scratch, including the pizza dough. A wide-ranging menu covers light snack options alongside more substantial dishes like the house pizza, a blend

2

of tomato, mozzarella, prawns, red onion, and herbs. Be sure to leave room for the excellent bread-and-butter pudding. Note that dinner is served only until 8. ⊠ *Harbourmaster Pl., Northside* ☎ *01/605–4700* ⊕ *www.thevaults.ie* ⊟ *AE, MC, V* ⊘ *Closed weekends* ✢ *1:E1.*

$$
The Winding Stair. A dark cloud hung over Dublin when one of its
IRISH
Fodor'sChoice
★
favorite secondhand bookshop-cafés, The Winding Stair, was set to close. But the silver lining appeared in the form of this atmospheric, buzzing little restaurant, which reemerged in the old space, replete with a downstairs bookshop and the well-worn name. Upstairs, former habitués will enjoy seeing the old bookcases around the walls (some of which are now stacked with wine). To get the real feel for the place try to get a table looking out over the Ha'penny Bridge and the slow-flowing river beneath. Traditional Irish food re-created with an adventurous twist best describes the terrific menu, which is greatly helped by organic credentials, as nearly everything on the menu is locally sourced. The corned beef and crispy cabbage with mustard sauce is a standout, as is the roasted Jerusalem artichoke and cauliflower crumble with vintage Irish cheddar sauce and baby spinach salad. An inventive wine list and a wonderful Irish farmhouse cheese selection are two more treats on offer. If your sweet tooth is acting up try the mind-blowing bread-and-butter pudding for dessert. ⊠ *40 Lower Ormond Quay, Northside* ☎ *01/872–7320* ⊕ *www.winding-stair.com* ⊟ *AE, MC, V* ✢ *1:A3.*

SOUTH DUBLIN: THE GRAND CANAL AND BALLSBRIDGE

Use the coordinate (✢ 1:B2) at the end of each listing to locate a site on the corresponding Where to Eat in Dublin map.

$
French Paradox. Like the people of the south of France who inspired
FRENCH
★
the place, relaxed but stylish would best describe the decor and dining at this little restaurant above a wineshop. French Paradox has found a real niche in the Dublin scene. Wine buffs, Francophiles, and gourmets flock here for the hearty traditional fare and Mediterranean environment. Share the *assiette le fond de barrique,* a selection of charcuterie, pâté, and cheese, or perhaps indulge in a selection of cured Irish fish or a choice from the foie gras menu. Select a nice bottle from the ground-floor wineshop (mostly French labels) and sip it in situ for a mere €8 corkage fee along with a few "French tapas." Seating is limited. ⊠ *53 Shelbourne Rd., Ballsbridge* ☎ *01/660–4068* ⊕ *www.thefrenchparadox.com* ⌂ *Reservations essential* ⊟ *AE, MC, V* ⊘ *Closed Sun.* ✢ *1:H6.*

$$$
O'Connells. When it comes to cooking, pedigree counts. Owner Tom
MODERN IRISH
★
O'Connell is a brother to Ireland's favorite celebrity chef, Darina Allen, famed for her "slow food" Ballymaloe Cookery School in Cork. Tom, now located in a brand-new dining room at the Ballsbridge Court hotel, follows the family blueprint by showcasing locally produced meats and game that can be traced to their source (in many cases, an individual farm). Add to this a focus on fresh Irish produce and you have the makings of a feast that is deliriously, quintessentially Irish. Spiced beef is prepared according to an old Cork recipe, salmon fillet is "hot smoked" by the restaurant itself, while Ashe's Annascaul Black Pudding is handmade on the Dingle peninsula. You can also try the spit-roasted duck (carved

at your table) or the breaded free-range Irish pork schnitzel—or an omelet made from organic eggs from free-range chickens, with peppers, zucchini, and a sweet chili sauce. A tremendous selection of fresh breads is on display in the open kitchen, which turns into a buffet for breakfast and lunch. The cheese board is a who's who of Irish farmhouse cheeses, including the Ferguson family's tangy Gubbeen. ⊠ *Ballsbridge Court Hotel, Lansdowne Rd., Ballsbridge* ☎ *01/665–5940* ⊕ *www. oconnellsballsbridge.com* ⊟ *AE, DC, MC, V* ⊹ *1:G6.*

$$$$ ✕ **Seasons.** Although the restaurant at the Dublin branch of the vaunted
MODERN IRISH   Four Seasons hotel took a little time to find its feet in and out of the kitchen, it has finally staked its claim in Dublin's dining scene—Sunday brunch has become a ritual for many well-to-do Dublin Southsiders. Highly dramatic dishes, served in the large and slightly overwhelming silver-service dining room, creatively incorporate local (and often organic) ingredients. A starter of Dublin Bay prawns with fresh mint, mango, and cashew salad might be followed by twice-cooked duck breast with poached mango, stir-fired Asian greens, and chili caramel. Sommelier Simon Keegan is one of the best in the country. ⊠ *Four Seasons Hotel, Simmonscourt Rd., Ballsbridge* ☎ *01/665–4642* ⊕ *www. fourseasons.com/dublin* ⌗ *Reservations essential* ⊟ *AE, DC, MC, V* ⊹ *1:H6.*

DUBLIN WEST

Use the coordinate (⊹ 1:B2) at the end of each listing to locate a site on the corresponding Where to Eat in Dublin map.

¢   ✕ **Burdock's.** Old man Burdock has moved on and the place hasn't been
IRISH   the same since. But the hordes still join the inevitable queue at Dublin's famous take-out fish-and-chips shop, right next door to the Lord Edward pub. You can eat in the gardens of St. Patrick's Cathedral, a five-minute walk away. Fresh cod is a classic, and the battered sausage a particular Dublin favorite, but the real stars here are the long, thick, freshly cut chips, which have a slightly smoky aftertaste. ⊠ *2 Werburgh St., Dublin West* ☎ *01/454–0306* ⊟ *No credit cards* ⊹ *1:A3.*

¢   ✕ **Gallic Kitchen.** Canny Dubliners make regular pilgrimages to Sarah
CAFÉ   Webb's bakery, where some of the best pastries in town are available daily. There's no seating in this powerhouse patisserie, but long counters allow space for perching your coffee and tucking into the finest sweet and savory treats. Pop in for a morning coffee and a pear tart; try the quiche or salmon roulade with homemade salsa for lunch; or simply take afternoon tea with a scrumptious scone. Expect queues at lunchtime, and be sure to buy in bulk for the tastiest take-out picnic in town. ⊠ *49 Francis St., Liberties* ☎ *01/454–4912* ⊕ *www.gallickitchen. com* ⊟ *MC, V* ⊙ *Closed Sun. No dinner* ⊹ *1:A4.*

¢   ✕ **Just Off Francis.** If there is a gastronomic silver lining from the economic
CONTINENTAL   downturn it may be the great-value, quality little eateries springing up in a new, lower-rent environment like the Liberties. Started by two enterprising local lads, this tiny Italian-inspired spot keeps the choices simple—salads, pastas, plus a few select mains and starters—and the prices low. But that doesn't prevent satisfying appetizers or "smalls"

like the creamy seafood chowder or the always-changing bread-and-dips combo. From the "bigs" list try the Italian sausage and cream mash with cider gravy. 'Tis a great place for a salad or sandwich lunch. ⊠ *78 Thomas St., Liberties* ☎ *01/473–8807* ⊕ *www.justofffrancis.ie* ⊟ *MC, V* ☺ *Closed Sun.* ✚ *1:A3*

$$ **Lord Edward.** Culinary trends and fashions may come and go but
SEAFOOD Dublin's oldest seafood restaurant remains resolutely traditional. On the cozy top floor above a lovely old bar of the same name, the Lord Edward looks out on the front entrance of Christ Church Cathedral. They do a mean Irish stew but the stars here are definitely the seafood dishes, usually smothered in a totally unhip but delicious, calorie-packed creamy sauce. The salmon and the cod are two favorites, and the lobster Mornay is also special. ⊠ *23 Christ Church Pl., Dublin West* ☎ *01/454–2420* ⊕ *www.lordedward.ie* ⊟ *AE, MC, V* ☺ *Closed Sun. No lunch Sat.* ✚ *1:B2.*

PHOENIX PARK AND ENVIRONS

Use the coordinate (✚ 1:B2) at the end of each listing to locate a site on the corresponding Where to Eat in Dublin map.

$$ **Nancy Hands.** It's a fine line to walk: to re-create tradition without
ECLECTIC coming across like a theme bar. Happily, Nancy Hands just about pulls it off. A galleylike room juxtaposes old wood, raw brick, and antiques with contemporary art to create a convivial, cozy dining area. The bar food is good, but the upstairs restaurant operates on a more serious level. Hearty specialties include scallops of turkey panfried with wild mushrooms and served with a creamy penne pasta and the leg of rabbit with steamed dumplings. Numerous wines are served by the glass, and the selection of spirits is one of the most impressive in the country. ⊠ *30–32 Parkgate St., Dublin West* ☎ *01/677–0149* ⊕ *www.nancyhands.ie* ⋍ *Reservations essential* ⊟ *MC, V* ✚ *1:A2.*

WHERE TO STAY

THE SCENE

The economic slowdown has abruptly halted the "absolute avalanche of new hotels" as the *Irish Times* characterized Dublin's accommodation boom. But visitors still have an impressive choice of elegant lodgings all over the city, including the classy and intimate La Stampa on Dawson Street, the totally revamped landmarks of the Shelbourne and the Wesbury, and some tempting choices found in Ballsbridge, an inner "suburb" that's a 20-minute walk from the city center. For something uniquely Dublin, you can always stay at one of the elegant guesthouses that occupy former Georgian town houses found on both sides of the Liffey.

The current recession means prices are falling rapidly, especially at the high and medium end, and Dublin now has a good selection of quality affordable accommodations, including many moderately priced hotels with basic but agreeable rooms. Most guesthouses, long the mainstay of the economy end of the market, have thankfully upgraded their facilities

BEST BETS FOR DUBLIN LODGING

Fodor's offers a selective listing of high-quality lodging experiences at every price range, from the city's best budget options to its most sophisticated luxury hotel. Here, we've compiled our top recommendations by price and experience. The very best properties—those that provide a particularly remarkable experience—are designated with a Fodor's Choice symbol.

and now provide rooms with private bathrooms or showers, as well as cable color televisions, direct-dial telephones, and Internet connections. The bigger hotels are all equipped with in-room data ports or Wi-Fi. If you've rented a car and you're not staying at a hotel with parking, it's worth considering a location out of the city center, such as Dalkey or Killiney, where the surroundings are more pleasant and you won't have to worry about parking on city streets.

WHAT IT COSTS IN EUROS					
	¢	$	$$	$$$	$$$$
FOR TWO PEOPLE	under €80	€80–€120	€121–€170	€171–€210	over €210

Prices are for a standard double room in high season, including V.A.T. and a service charge (often applied in larger hotels). Most hotels operate on the European Plan (EP), with no meals included in the basic room rate, or, if indicated, with Breakfast Plan (BP).

PRICES

A reduction in demand for rooms means that Dublin's high rates have fallen somewhat but are still in line with the best hotels of any major European or North American city (and factoring in the exchange rate means a hotel room can take a substantial bite out of your budget). Service charges range from 15% in expensive hotels to zero in moderate and inexpensive ones. Be sure to inquire when you make reservations.

As a general rule of thumb, lodgings on the north side of the River Liffey tend to be more affordable than those on the south. Bed-and-breakfasts charge as little as €46 a night per person, but they tend to be in suburban areas—generally a 15-minute bus ride from the center of the city. This is not in itself a great drawback, and savings can be significant. Many hotels have a weekend, or "B&B," rate that's often 30% to 40% cheaper than the ordinary rate; some hotels also have a midweek special that provides discounts of up to 35%. These rates are available throughout the year but are harder to get in high season. Ask about them when booking a room (they are available only on a prebooked basis), especially if you plan a brief or weekend stay. Finally, don't be afraid to haggle, especially in the off-season.

CITY CENTER: THE SOUTHSIDE

Use the coordinate (✢ B2) at the end of each listing to locate a site on the corresponding Where to Stay in Dublin map.

$$$–$$$$ **Brooks.** Even though it has nearly 100 rooms, the Brooks likes to describe itself as a boutique property, and it does manage to convey the classy, personal touch of a much smaller establishment. A two-minute walk from Grafton Street, it is the perfect place to sit and recover if the Irish rain plays havoc with your plans: public spaces and the bar are warm and full of leather chairs, high-veneer oak paneling, and decorative bookcases. The rooms are bright if a little functional, with cream and beige tones. The beds are so big you could get lost in them, and each comes with a five-choice "pillow menu." Situated so near to the

Gaiety Theatre, the hotel's Jasmin Bar is the ideal spot for a pre- or post-theater drink. **Pros:** next to Grafton Street; live piano music in bar; rooms refurbished every six years. **Cons:** ugly, office-block exterior; business clientele makes for slightly flat atmosphere; standard rooms on small side. ⊠ *Drury St., Southside* ☎ *01/670–4000* ⊕ *www.brookshotel. ie* ⤴ *98 rooms* ♿ *In-room: a/c, DVD, Wi-Fi. In-hotel: restaurant, bar, gym, parking (paid)* ⊟ *AE, DC, MC, V* ✛ *C3.*

$$–$$$

Fodor'sChoice

★

🏨 **Central Hotel.** Every modern city needs its little oasis, and the Central's book-and-armchair-filled Library Bar—warmed by a Victorian fireplace—nicely fits the bill. Established in 1887, this grand, old-style redbrick spot is in the heart of the city center, steps from Grafton Street and Temple Bar. Guest rooms are snug and pretty simple, with flocked bedspreads, racing paintings, and 19th-century bric-a-brac. The stately hotel dining room beguiles with its pastel-green walls, bookcases, and gilt-frame pictures. **Pros:** delightful Library Bar; original 1887 facade; old-fashioned feel. **Cons:** rooms a bit snug; street noise in some rooms; bad form—you have to prepay up front! ⊠ *1–5 Exchequer St., Southside* ☎ *01/679–7302* ⊕ *www.centralhotel.ie* ⤴ *67 rooms, 3 suites* ♿ *In-room: a/c, Wi-Fi. In-hotel: restaurant, bar* ⊟ *AE, MC, V* ⦿ *BP* ✛ *C3.*

$–$$

🏨 **Grafton House.** A stone's throw from the famous shopping street that gave it its name, this Victorian Gothic–style building has been tastefully transformed into one of central Dublin's best bargains. The guest rooms are a little cramped, but they're brightly decorated with cheerful pine furnishings, and the small size of the place ensures warm, friendly service. The rooms vary in size, but not price, so be bold and ask for a bigger one. They are simply decorated, with original wood floors, and occasional quirky, individual touches like exposed beams. **Pros:** best value in city center; warm, unfussy service; simple but cool design. **Cons:** some rooms are cramped; can suffer from street noise; no elevator. ⊠ *26–27 S. Great George's St., Southside* ☎ *01/679–2041* ⊕ *www. graftonguesthouse.com* ⤴ *16 rooms* ♿ *In-room: no a/c, Wi-Fi. In-hotel: Wi-Fi hotspot* ⊟ *AE, MC, V* ⦿ *BP* ✛ *C3.*

$

Fodor'sChoice

★

🏨 **Kelly's Hotel.** With buzzing Hogan's bar and the classy L'Gueuleton restaurant right downstairs, this cool little hotel is already at the epicenter of trendy Dublin living. Situated in an original Victorian redbrick, the standard rooms are small and quirky, but devoid of clutter with an all white and no-fuss design broken up with a few colorful lamps and candleholders; there's a real cozy, authentic Dublin feel to each one of them. If you feel like splurging just a little, the penthouse suite has two roomier bedrooms and great views down the busy street. **Pros:** killer city-center location; one of the city's best restaurants downstairs; great spot to bump into interesting Dubliners. **Cons:** some rooms are cramped; can suffer from street noise; no elevator. ⊠ *36 S. Great George's St., Southside* ☎ *01/648–0010* ⊕ *www.kellysdublin.com* ⤴ *15 rooms, 2 suites* ♿ *In-room: no a/c, Wi-Fi. In-hotel: Wi-Fi hotspot* ⊟ *MC, V* ⦿ *BP* ✛ *C3.*

$$$$

Fodor'sChoice

★

🏨 **Shelbourne.** Paris has the Ritz, New York has the Pierre, and Dublin has the Shelbourne. Resplendent in its broad, ornamented, pink-and-white, mid-Victorian facade, this grande dame of Stephen's Green has reopened after a no-expense-spared, head-to-toe, two-year renovation.

Few other hotels enjoy such beloved and landmark status as the Shelbourne.

One of the new breed of boutique hotels, La Stampa delivers European high style.

Long famed as the Dublin home of the nation's literati, the hotel has been immortalized by authors running from Thackeray to Elizabeth Bowen. The Constitution of the Irish Free State was framed within its venerable walls, and almost as venerable a tradition was to take tea in the Lord Mayor's Lounge, just off the towering, marble-floor, cream-and-crystal lobby with its gilded pillars and brass candelabras. Having grown a little long in the tooth, however, the Shelbourne transformed its public spaces with original, daring furniture, textiles, and colors. Today, the most sumptuous place in town has just gotten more so—too bad most of the patina is gone. The shock of the new begins in the lobby, where the Irish Chippendale chairs have given way to contempo Irish art. Happily, the guest rooms are almost as luxurious as the lobby, with the marble bathrooms a real tactile pleasure. Rooms in front overlook the Green (one of Dublin's squares more blighted than most by modern development); those in the back, without a view, are quieter. **Pros:** afternoon tea in Lord Mayor's Lounge; Irish art worth gazing at; all-around luxury. **Cons:** some noise in front rooms; pricey; feels a little stuffy at times. ⊠ *27 St. Stephen's Green, Southside* ☎ *01/663–4500; 800/543–4300 in U.S.* ⊕ *www.marriott.co.uk* ⟳ *246 rooms, 19 suites* ♤ *In-room: a/c, refrigerator, Wi-Fi. In-hotel: restaurant, bars* ⊟ *AE, DC, MC, V* ✛ *D4.*

$$$$ ⊡ **Westbury.** Glowing after a major face-lift and a favorite with the platinum credit-card set, this luxurious, chandelier-filled, modern hotel is just off Grafton Street, the shopping mecca of Dublin. You can join elegantly dressed Dubliners for afternoon tea in The Gallery, the spacious mezzanine-level main lobby, furnished with a grand piano and a great view out onto the busy streets. Newly refurbished rooms boast handmade Irish furniture and carpets, plus duck-down duvets. Most inviting are the suites, which combine four-poster bed opulence with a very understated, sleek look. The strangely titled Wilde–The Restaurant serves lunches and dinners; while the street-level bar and brasserie Café Novo goes for a more relaxed menu and feel. **Pros:** prime people-watching from The Gallery; great shopping location just off Grafton Street; the Art Deco glamour of the Marble bar. **Cons:** tries a little too hard to be posh; right in the center of the city's bustle. ⊠ *Grafton St., Southside* ☎ *01/679–1122* ⊕ *www.doylecollection.com* ⟳ *187 rooms, 18 suites* ♤ *In-room: a/c, refrigerator, Internet. In-hotel: 2 restaurants, bar, gym, Wi-Fi hotspot, parking (paid)* ⊟ *AE, DC, MC, V* ✛ *D4.*

$$$$ ⊡ **Westin Dublin.** If you've ever dreamed of spending the night in a bank,
★ here's your chance. Reconstructed from three 19th-century landmark buildings (including a former bank) across the road from Trinity College, the Westin is all about location. The public spaces re-create a little of the splendor of yesteryear: marble pillars, tall mahogany doorways, blazing fireplaces, and period detailing on the walls and ceilings. The bedrooms, on the other hand, are functional and small, with crisp, white Indian linen and custom-made beds the only luxurious touches. The rooms that overlook Trinity College are a little more expensive, but the chance to watch the students in a leisurely game of cricket on a summer weekend makes all the difference. The Exchange restaurant and Mint Bar are in the original vaults of the bank. **Pros:** beside Temple Bar but

not in Temple Bar; overlooks Trinity College; in-room spa treatments. **Cons:** on a busy traffic corner; windowless, uninviting bar; mediocre restaurants. ⊠ *College Green, Southside* ☎ *01/645–1000* ⊕ *www. thewestindublin.com* ⊲ *141 rooms, 22 suites* ♻ *In-room: a/c, refrigerator, Wi-Fi. In-hotel: restaurant, bars, gym, parking (paid)* ☰ *AE, DC, MC, V* ⊹ *D4.*

2

SOUTHEAST DUBLIN: AROUND MERRION SQUARE

Use the coordinate (⊹ B2) at the end of each listing to locate a site on the corresponding Where to Stay in Dublin map.

$$$$ ⊡ **Conrad Dublin International.** Ask for—no, insist on—a room on one of the top three floors. The best thing about the ugly-on-the-outside, seven-story, redbrick and smoked-glass Conrad is the spectacular views out over the city. Just off St. Stephen's Green, the Conrad firmly aims for international business travelers. Gleaming light-color marble graces the large formal lobby. Rooms are rather cramped but are nicely outfitted with natural-wood furnishings, painted in sand colors and pastel greens, and have Spanish marble in the bathrooms. A note to light sleepers: the air-conditioning/heating system can be noisy. The Alex restaurant specializes in seafood and Alfie Byrne's is a slightly fake "Dublin pub." **Pros:** Gary the concierge; great views on higher floors; marble bathrooms. **Cons:** drab, 1970s-style corridors; slightly cramped standard rooms; poor views on lower floors. ⊠ *Earlsfort Terr., Southeast Dublin* ☎ *01/676–5555* ⊕ *www.conradhotels.com* ⊲ *182 rooms, 10 suites* ♻ *In-room: a/c, refrigerator, Internet. In-hotel: restaurant, bars, gym, Wi-Fi hotspot, parking (paid)* ☰ *AE, DC, MC, V* ⊹ *D5.*

$–$$ ⊡ **Kilronan House.** A good guesthouse should cheer you up when you come home at the end of a long day's touring. This large, mid-19th-century terraced house with a glorious, elegant white facade will bring a smile to your face every time. The ground-floor sitting room is a real cozy winter treat when a big fire is on. Some of the rooms are quite basic, in cream and beige, but they are all airy and bright, and the richly patterned wallpaper and carpets and orthopedic beds (rather rare in Dublin guesthouses) give them a touch of class. The guesthouse is a five-minute walk from St. Stephen's Green. **Pros:** great price for location; beautiful, calming facade; cozy sitting room. **Cons:** public areas a bit worn; uncreative room furnishings; no Internet in rooms; no elevator. ⊠ *70 Adelaide Rd., Southeast Dublin* ☎ *01/475–5266* ⊕ *www. kilronanhousehotel.com* ⊲ *12 rooms* ♻ *In-room: no a/c. In-hotel: Wi-Fi hotspot, parking (free)* ☰ *MC, V* ⊹ *D5.*

$$–$$$
Fodor'sChoice
★
⊡ **La Stampa.** Definitely a good thing in a small and very pretty package, this intimate town-house hotel, above the ever-popular and spectacular Balzac restaurant and 50 yards from Trinity College, is one of the classiest recent arrivals on the Dublin scene. Each suite is individually decorated with an Asian theme—lots of wood, simple color schemes, and velvet bedspreads imported from Paris add to the luxury. Balzac is a vast and soigné brasserie; even more eye-catching is Samsara, a Moroccan-theme bar that is a fantasia of tin chandeliers, multihued stained glass, and oh-so-sexy ambience. There is even a little luxury

spa with Eastern treatments. For the price, there are few better spots in town. **Pros:** great luxury for the price; choice of three quality restaurants; spa oasis in the city. **Cons:** small hotel fills up quickly; no parking; one could overdose on the Asian theme. ⊠ *35 Dawson St., Southeast Dublin* ☎ *01/677–4444* ⊕ *www.lastampa.ie* ⤵ *23 rooms, 5 suites* ⚹ *In-room: a/c, refrigerator, DVD, Wi-Fi. In-hotel: 3 restaurants, spa* ⊟ *AE, DC, MC, V* ✛ *D4.*

$$$$
Fodor's Choice
★

Merrion. Arthur Wellesley, the Duke of Wellington and hero of Waterloo, once famously commented when queried about his Irish birth: "Just because a man is born in a stable doesn't make him a horse." His "stable," directly across from Government Buildings between Stephen's Green and Merrion Square, is one of the four exactingly restored Georgian town houses that make up this luxurious hotel. Some of the stately guest rooms are appointed in classic Georgian style—from the crisp linen sheets to the Carrara-marble bathrooms. Some are vaulted with delicate Adamesque plasterwork ceilings, and others are graced with magnificent, original marble fireplaces. Still, the decor is almost too spiffy—if this is the 18th century, it has been buffed to a shiny 21st-century gloss—so, to fully enjoy the historic patina, opt for one of the more authentic rooms in the Main House at the front. The staff are obviously accustomed to dealing with heads of state and royalty, so ladies shouldn't be surprised if they are addressed as "Madame." And all will enjoy the hotel's little spa, a perfect place to unwind. Clearly, this place must be very special, since leading Dublin restaurateur Patrick Guilbaud has moved his eponymous and fabulous restaurant here. **Pros:** Patrick Guilbaud restaurant; infinity pool; city-center location; attentive staff. **Cons:** you'll pay extra for a room in the original house; rooms are over-decorated; overly attentive staff. ⊠ *Upper Merrion St., Southeast Dublin* ☎ *01/603–0600* ⊕ *www.merrionhotel.com* ⤵ *123 rooms, 19 suites* ⚹ *In-room: a/c, safe, DVD, Internet, Wi-Fi* ⊟ *AE, DC, MC, V* ✛ *E4.*

$$$$
Fodor's Choice
★

Number 31. Arguably the most unique and authentic Georgian accommodation Dublin has to offer is in the old home of Sam Stephenson, Dublin's most famous and highly controversial modernist architect. He strikingly renovated two Georgian mews in the early 1960s as a private home. They are now connected via a small but beautiful garden to the grand house they once served. Together they form a one-in-a-million guesthouse a short walk from St. Stephen's Green, which gives you a choice of bedroom styles: sublime Georgian elegance or serene cool modern. Exhausted but exuberant after a grand renovation, owners Deirdre and Noel Comer are gracious hosts who serve made-to-order breakfasts at refectory tables in the balcony dining room (try the homemade cranberry bread). The white-tile sunken living room, with its black leather sectional sofa and modern artwork that includes a David Hockney print, may make you think you're in California. If that essay in *Wallpaper* doesn't send you, you'll be happy enough ensconced in one of the period-style guest rooms, one of which—No. 21—has a ceiling so lofty and corniced even a royal would feel at home. **Pros:** the king and queen of guesthouse hosts; serene decor and art; best breakfast in the city. **Cons:** a few rooms can be a little noisy; no elevator; a little pricey in the current market. ⊠ *31 Leeson Close, Southeast Dublin* ☎ *01/676–5011* ⊕ *www.number31.ie* ⤴ *21 rooms* ♿ *In-room: no a/c, DVD, Wi-Fi. In-hotel: parking (free)* ▤ *AE, MC, V* ⊹ *E5.*

$$–$$$ 🏨 **Premier Suites Dublin.** Get a top-floor suite at this modernized Georgian town house just off St. Stephen's Green and lord it over the whole Southside. The suites, considerably larger than the average hotel room, include one or two bedrooms, a separate sitting room, a fully equipped kitchen, washing machine, and bath. You can request two single beds in one of the rooms, so this place is great for families. **Pros:** top-floor suites have spectacular city views; ground-floor suites have private entrances. **Cons:** decor is modern, motel-functional. ⊠ *14–17 Lower Leeson St., Southeast Dublin* ☎ *01/638–1111* ⊕ *www.premiersuitesdublin.com* ⤴ *30 suites* ♿ *In-room: a/c, kitchen, Wi-Fi. In-hotel: parking (paid)* ▤ *AE, MC, V.*

TEMPLE BAR

Use the coordinate (⊹ B2) at the end of each listing to locate a site on the corresponding Where to Stay in Dublin map.

$–$$ 🏨 **Arlington Temple Bar.** As with many Dublin hotels, the interior of the Arlington doesn't quite live up to the fabulous facade of one of Dublin's finest Edwardian buildings. Inside, the atmosphere is very much functional and appeals primarily to a business clientele—drawn by the location near the Central Bank and Trinity College. But rooms are a good size, with a simple, slightly monotonous beige and off-white color scheme. The Forum bar keeps up the democratic theme with a reliable selection of bar food. **Pros:** beautiful Edwardian facade; good price for Temple Bar; near a few good music bars. **Cons:** rooms purely functional; public spaces slightly worn; mainly business clientele. ⊠ *Lord Edward St., Temple Bar* ☎ *01/670–8777* ⊕ *www.arlingtonhoteltemplebar.com* ⤴ *63 rooms* ♿ *In-room: no a/c. In-hotel: bar, Wi-Fi hotspot* ▤ *AE, MC, V* ⊹ *C3.*

$$$$ 🏨 **The Clarence.** If coolness is contagious you might want a room at Temple Bar's most prestigious hotel. You might well bump into celebrity friends of co-owners Bono and the Edge of U2. Dating to 1852, the grand old hotel was given a total, no-expense-spared overhaul by its new owners in the early 1990s. The unique shapes and Arts-and-Crafts style of the old hotel were maintained in the Octagon Bar and the elegant Tea Room restaurant. Guest rooms, with Shaker-style furniture, are a bit disappointing, decorated in a mishmash of earth tones accented with deep purple, gold, cardinal red, and royal blue. With the exception of those in the penthouse suite, rooms are small. The laissez-faire service seems to take its cue from the minimalist style, so if you like to be pampered, stay elsewhere. **Pros:** stylish Octagon Bar; the owners might be on-premises; Tea Room restaurant. **Cons:** rooms a bit small; some rooms suffer from street noise; paying a premium for "cool." ⊠ *6–8 Wellington Quay, Temple Bar* ☎ *01/407–0800* ⊕ *www. theclarence.ie* ⤴ *44 rooms, 5 suites* ♿ *In-room: a/c, refrigerator, DVD, Internet, Wi-Fi. In-hotel: restaurant, bar, gym, Wi-Fi hotspot, parking (paid)* ▤ *AE, DC, MC, V* ⊹ *C3.*

$$–$$$ ⊞ **The Morgan.** A sparkling gem among a lot of very drab hotels in Temple Bar, the Morgan boasts about its chic design and decor, and the individually designed bedrooms and luxurious, colorful bathrooms are indeed pleasing to the eye. It is the hotel's extended-stay suites, however, that really set it apart from the crowd. With a fully equipped kitchen and a spacious, gadget-filled living room, you can hunker down and make yourself comfortable for a week or two. The generously heated outside courtyard is perfect for cocktails. **Pros:** individually, excitingly designed bathrooms; great cocktail bar; extended-stay apartments are good value. **Cons:** a little over-designed in places; no parking; no restaurant. ⊠ *10 Fleet St., Temple Bar* ☎ *01/643–7000* ⊕ *www.themorgan. com* ⬈ *107 rooms, 14 suites* ⚘ *In-room: no a/c (some), refrigerator, Wi-Fi. In-hotel: bar* ⊟ *AE, DC, MC, V* ✛ *D3.*

$$–$$$ ⊞ **Paramount.** Classic 1930s American movies seem to have been the inspiration for the look of this medium-size hotel in the heart of Temple Bar. They opted to maintain its classy Victorian facade, but the flashy wooden entrance looks more New York than London. The foyer continues this theme of Empire elegance with incredibly comfortable leather couches, bleached-blond-oak floors, and burgundy curtains. Dark woods and subtle colors decorate the bedrooms—again, very 1930s (if not Bogie and Bacall). If you're fond of a tipple, try the hotel's Art Deco Turks Head Bar and Chop House. **Pros:** stylish, integrated design; right in the heart of Temple Bar's action; good value during the week. **Cons:** street noise can be a problem; no a/c; fills up on weekends. ⊠ *Parliament St. and Essex Gate, Temple Bar* ☎ *01/417–9900* ⊕ *www. paramounthotel.ie* ⬈ *64 rooms* ⚘ *In-room: no a/c, Wi-Fi. In-hotel: restaurant, bar* ⊟ *AE, MC, V* ✛ *C3.*

THE NORTHSIDE

Use the coordinate (✛ B2) at the end of each listing to locate a site on the corresponding Where to Stay in Dublin map.

$–$$ ⊞ **Academy Plaza Hotel.** This modern, architecturally uninspiring hotel has been getting rave reviews since a major revamp trebled its size and seriously upgraded its rooms and services. Being just off O'Connell Street in a slightly unfashionable neighborhood means you get lots comfort at less than the Southside price. Rooms have a finished, contemporary feel with extra-large beds and rich rust and beige color schemes. Little touches like free newspapers and perfectly sound-insulated windows make you feel like you're being take care of. The main restaurant offers an Asian menu and Sir Harry's bar has a warm, relaxed vibe. **Pros:** great sound proofing; newly renovated; choice of restaurants. **Cons:** unfashionable location; rooms are not huge; bland exterior. ⊠ *10–14 Findlater Pl., Northside* ☎ *01/878–0666* ⊕ *www.academyplazahotel.ie* ⬈ *273 rooms, 12 suites* ⚘ *In-room: a/c, refrigerator, Wi-Fi. In-hotel: 2 restaurants, bar, gym, parking (paid)* ⊟ *AE, MC, V* ✛ *D2.*

$–$$ ⊞ **Castle Hotel.** Staying in a good-value Georgian house on the Northside
Fodor'sChoice can be a hit-and-miss affair quality-wise, but the Castle has just under-
★ gone a major renovation, which makes the most of the lovely Georgian setting by maintaining the period staircases, original plasterwork,

2

antique mirrors, and open fires in the winter. Some guest rooms are quite small but simply and smartly turned out. Try to get one in the original Georgian house, with a fireplace if possible and at the back to eliminate any street noise. Note that the Castle gets busy (and more expensive) when there are big games or concerts at Croke Park, but it is a great value the rest of the year. **Pros:** owner managed; great Georgian original features; newly renovated public areas. **Cons:** small rooms; some street noise; fee for parking. ⊠ *Gardiner Row, Northside* ☎ *01/874–6949* ⊕ *www.thecastlehotelgroup.com* ⇆ *133 rooms* ⌂ *In-room: a/c, Wi-Fi. In-hotel: Wi-Fi hotspot, parking (paid)* ⊟ *MC, V* ⊹ *D2.*

$ 🖼 **Charleville Lodge.** If Dublin's city center is a Georgian wonder, a short
Fodor's Choice   commute out to the historic Phibsborough area of Dublin's Northside
★   will transport you to the elegantly Victorian 19th century. Here, in a row of beautifully restored terraced houses you can enjoy quality time in Charleville Lodge's dramatically lighted residents' lounge, complete with twinkling chandeliers, plush wing chairs, and a working fireplace. An antiquarian's delight, this grand salon is a great spot to chat with other travelers who have dared to stray off the beaten path. Upstairs, guest rooms are simple but brightly colored, wide, and have refreshingly high ceilings. As for the commute, the No. 10 bus takes but five minutes and it's even a great walk in good weather. All in all, this hostelry offers a touch of luxury at great value. **Pros:** outside the city-center hustle; antiquarian's delight; near Phoenix Park. **Cons:** outside the city center; two-night minimum on some rooms in summer weekends; no elevator. ⊠ *268–272 N. Circular Rd., Northside, Phibsborough* ☎ *01/838–6633* ⊕ *www.charlevillelodge.ie* ⇆ *30 rooms* ⌂ *In-room: no a/c, Wi-Fi. In-hotel: Internet terminal, parking (free)* ⊟ *MC, V* ⊙*I BP* ⊹ *C1.*

$$–$$$ 🖼 **Clarion Hotel IFSC.** Built with business guests in mind, this high-rise hotel has been a surprise hit with tourists. Smack in the middle of the International Financial Services Centre, the Clarion, with its office-block-like exterior, is indistinguishable from many of the financial institutions that surround it. The public spaces, however, are bright and cheery, if a little uninspired. The bedrooms—big by Dublin standards—are all straight lines and contemporary light-oak furnishings. Shades of blue and taupe do create a calm environment (the hotel claims its environment is guided by Eastern philosophy, no less), but for true serenity try to get a room at the front with great views out over the Liffey. Because the hotel mainly caters to business travelers, weekend bargains are a definite possibility—make sure you ask. **Pros:** weekend bargains available; room to swing a couple of cats in big rooms; area super-quiet at night. **Cons:** room design pretty functional; business clientele; area super-quiet (aka dead) at night. ⊠ *IFSC, Northside* ☎ *01/433–8800* ⊕ *www.clarionhotelifsc.com* ⇆ *145 rooms, 17 suites* ⌂ *In-room: a/c, refrigerator, Wi-Fi. In-hotel: restaurant, bar, pool, gym, parking (paid)* ⊟ *AE, DC, MC, V* ⊹ *E2.*

$ 🖼 **Gresham.** It originally opened in 1817 and it's been ages since this O'Connell Street landmark was an up-market place to stay north of the river. Now, however, renovations and a drop in price have suddenly made the Gresham a solid city center option once again. Big beds are a major plus in the muted if unexciting room designs, and the bathrooms

The Merrion began life as the residence of the first Duke of Wellington.

The Pembroke Townhouse gives Georgian style a delightful 21st-century spin.

2

are roomy for price range. There's an old-school touch about the ample facilities in each room and the laid-back but attentive service. Public spaces have a nice buzz about them and the bar is popular with locals out for the night. Try to get a room overlooking iconic O'Connell Street, though it may cost you a little extra. **Pros:** great value for city center; great views down O'Connell Street. **Cons:** bar and public areas can get busy; room design unexciting; extra charge for room with a view. ⊠ *23 Upper O'Connell St., Northside* 🕾 *01/874–6881* ⊕ *www. gresham-hotels.com* 🔊 *279 rooms, 9 suites* ⌂ *In-room: a/c, refrigerator, Wi-Fi. In-hotel: restaurant, bar, gym, parking (paid)* ▭ *AE, DC, MC, V* ✢ *D2.*

¢–$ ⬚ **Globetrotters Tourist Hostel.** Globetrotters is a reliable Dublin hostel, with a pleasant outdoor courtyard; reasonably clean, locking dorm rooms with en-suite showers; a turf (that is, not wood) fire; comfortable bunk beds (with lamps for late-night reading); and a delicious all-you-can-eat breakfast. Plus, you're within walking distance of the city center, one block from the bus station, and two blocks from the train station. The owners also run Town House, a relaxed B&B in the same building, with double rooms and all the basic amenities. **Pros:** "cheap as chips" as the locals say; all-you-can-eat breakfast; attached to a B&B if you need more comfort. **Cons:** located in a slightly run-down part of the city; attracts a young, boisterous crowd; dorm living not for everyone. ⊠ *47–48 Lower Gardiner St., Northside* 🕾 *01/878–8808* ⊕ *www. globetrottersdublin.com* 🔊 *94 dorm beds with shared bath, 38 double rooms* ⌂ *In-room: no a/c, no TV (some). In-hotel: restaurant, Wi-Fi hotspot* ▭ *MC, V* ⦿| *BP* ✢ *E2.*

¢–$ ⬚ **Marian Guest House.** A veritable Everest of fine Irish meats, the Marian's mighty full Irish breakfast, with black pudding and smoked bacon, is reason enough to stay at this family-run redbrick guesthouse just off beautiful Mountjoy Square (the whole family can speak Irish, by the way). The place has a real old-school Irish hospitality feel with only six rooms, so you get lots of attention and pampering. Rooms are fairly basic, but clean, bright, and pleasant. **Pros:** heart-stoppingly good breakfast; family-owned and -run; small. **Cons:** located in a slightly run-down part of the city; gets some street noise; fairly basic rooms. ⊠ *21 Upper Gardiner St., Northside* 🕾 *01/874–4129* ⊕ *www.marianguesthouse.ie* 🔊 *6 rooms* ⌂ *In-room: no a/c* ▭ *MC, V* ⦿| *BP* ✢ *D1.*

$$–$$$ ⬚ **The Morrison.** How do you make a Dublin hotel instantly trendy? Simple: get the country's top fashion guru to design the interiors. John Rocha had the last word on everything at this über-modern trendsetting hotel, down to the toiletries and staff uniforms. Past the 18th-century Georgian facade, a new feng shui–inspired refurbishment adds a touch of Japanese elegance to the existing unfussy, almost Scandinavian style. The Georgian Suites have a warmer feel, thanks to wooden floors and large windows over the Liffey. Some visitors complain that the place leaves them a little cold, though others claim that in trying to be too cool the Morrison is as good as a London boutique hotel, though many times the size. Halo, the hotel's nouvelle Irish restaurant, has a newly restyled, more relaxed feel with antique tables and velvet chairs, plus one of the most ambitiously delicious menus in town. Halfway between

the Ha'penny and Capel Street bridges, the Morrison is no more than a 10-minute walk from Trinity College. **Pros:** people-watching-worthy cocktail bar; seriously designed rooms; experimental cuisine at Halo restaurant. **Cons:** tries a little too hard to be cool; located on busy road. ⊠ *Ormond Quay, Northside* ☎ *01/887–2400* ⊕ *www.morrisonhotel.ie* ↴ *120 rooms, 18 suites* ♿ *In-room: a/c, refrigerator, Internet. In-hotel: restaurant, bars, parking (paid)* ☐ *AE, DC, MC, V* ✛ *C3.*

SOUTH DUBLIN: THE GRAND CANAL AND BALLSBRIDGE

Use the coordinate (✛ B2) at the end of each listing to locate a site on the corresponding Where to Stay in Dublin map.

$–$$
★
🏠 **Ariel Guest House.** The homemade preserves and oven-warm scones are reason enough to stay at this redbrick 1850 Victorian guesthouse in one of Dublin's poshest tree-lined suburbs. It's a few steps from a DART stop and a 15-minute walk from St. Stephen's Green. Restored rooms in the main house are lovingly decorated with Georgian antiques, Victoriana, and period wallpaper and drapes. The 13 rooms at the back of the house are more spartan, but all are immaculate. A Waterford-crystal chandelier hangs over the comfortable leather and mahogany furniture in the gracious, fireplace-warmed drawing room where afternoon tea is served. **Pros:** four-poster beds in larger rooms; fantastic collection of Victoriana throughout the house; good price for smaller rooms. **Cons:** no longer run by owner; no elevator; a good walk to the city center. ⊠ *52 Lansdowne Rd., Ballsbridge* ☎ *01/668–5512* ⊕ *www.ariel-house. net* ↴ *37 rooms* ♿ *In-room: no a/c, Wi-Fi. In-hotel: Wi-Fi hotspot, parking (free)* ☐ *MC, V* � *BP* ✛ *G5.*

$$$–$$$$
🏠 **Burlington.** Another genuine institution saved by a failed property deal, Ireland's largest hotel is one of those landmarks where nearly every Irish person seems to have spent at least one night (or so they claim). The hotel's impersonal, 1972 glass-and-concrete facade is not very inviting, but newly refurbished public spaces use wooden floors and trimmings to take the edge off the uninspired building. The generous-size rooms, furnished in modern minimalist style, with neutral tones, have large picture windows. The Bellini Bar goes for a very chic cocktail-lounge look. **Pros:** a Dublin institution; large, light-filled rooms; part of a small, Irish-owned group. **Cons:** looks a little bit like a parking garage; staff not as experienced as they used to be; very big. ⊠ *Upper Leeson St., Ballsbridge* ☎ *01/660–5222* ⊕ *www.burlingtonhotel. ie* ↴ *500 rooms, 6 suites* ♿ *In-room: a/c, refrigerator (some), Internet. In-hotel: 2 restaurants, bar, Wi-Fi hotspot, parking (free)* ☐ *AE, DC, MC, V* ✛ *E6.*

$–$$
🏠 **D4 Berkeley.** A collapsed property deal has seen the rebirth of this much-mourned Dublin favorite previously known as the Berkley Court. Old-school luxury has been replaced with a more modest, contemporary hotel experience, but the great value prices reflect this simpler outlook. The guest rooms are big and comfortable, if aesthetically uninspired in muted tones and soft fabrics. The ghosts of the great and the good who once stayed here stroll through the wood-panel lobby which retains a little of its old opulence. O'Connells restaurant is a top Dublin

2

eatery and the Berkeley Bar is a twinkling piano joint with an open fire. **Pros:** great price for the upmarket location; facilities of nearby sister hotels available to guests; huge suites are good value for families. **Cons:** attracts a lot of conferences; service not as strong as it used to be. ⊠ *Pembroke Rd., Ballsbridge* ☎ *01/668–4468* ⊕ *www.d4hotels.ie* ⤵ *173 rooms, 15 suites* ⌂ *In-room: a/c, refrigerator, Internet. In-hotel: restaurant, bar, Wi-Fi hotspot, parking (paid)* ▭ *AE, MC, V* ✛ *F5.*

$$$$ 🛏 **Dylan.** "Sensual" is a word this luxury boutique hotel in an old Victorian building uses to describe itself, and it does have the feel of a place you might go for a naughty night with that someone special. The mysteriously lighted exterior looks beautiful at dusk. Inside, individually designed bedrooms feature leather padded walls, textured wallpaper, hypermodern furnishings, and seriously sexy beds (one room even has a mirror on the ceiling). It might be a little too much, but there's no denying the place is unique and an interesting addition to the sometimes staid Dublin scene. The restaurant continues the over-the-top decor with a lavish 1940s glam look, but the food is a little hit or miss. **Pros:** great spot for a romantic weekend; individually designed rooms; property is big enough to ensure privacy, small enough to still feel intimate. **Cons:** trying a little too hard to be cool; hit-or-miss restaurant; hasn't really adjusted prices in downturn. ⊠ *Eastmoreland Pl., Ballsbridge* ☎ *01/660–3000* ⊕ *www.dylan.ie* ⤵ *38 rooms, 6 suites* ⌂ *In-room: a/c, refrigerator, Wi-Fi. In-hotel: restaurant, bar* ▭ *AE, DC, MC, V* ✛ *F5.*

$$$–$$$$ 🛏 **Four Seasons.** Much controversy surrounds the brash, postmodern—critics would say faux Victorian-Georgian hybrid—architecture of this hotel. The six-floor building mixes pre-20th-century design with modern glass and concrete. The impressive landscaping—it has 4 acres of gardens—aims to make the hotel seem like an oasis; a big effort has been made to ensure that a bit of greenery can be seen from most rooms. Guest rooms are spacious, with large windows that allow light to flood in. A selection of landscapes on the hotel walls lends the place a warm touch. The lower-level spa is one of the finest in the country, with a naturally lighted lap pool. The Lobby Lounge is a popular afternoon tea spot. **Pros:** one of the country's top spas; prices have dropped considerably; Lobby Lounge great for afternoon tea. **Cons:** a bit of an architectural mishmash; room design not the most inventive; pricey year-round. ⊠ *Simmonscourt Rd., Ballsbridge* ☎ *01/665–4000* ⊕ *www.fourseasons. com/dublin* ⤵ *157 rooms, 40 suites* ⌂ *In-room: a/c, refrigerator, DVD, Internet, Wi-Fi. In-hotel: 2 restaurants, bars, pool, gym, spa, parking (free)* ▭ *AE, DC, MC, V* ✛ *G6.*

$$–$$$ 🛏 **Herbert Park Hotel.** For maximum pleasure secure a room overlooking the park of the same name adjacent to this independently owned hotel, which is also beside the Dodder River. Two of the expensive suites even have large balconies with views of the park or the leafy suburbs. Relaxing shades of cream and white predominate in the spacious rooms, along with splashes of red. The hotel's large, light-filled lobby has floor-to-ceiling windows and a slanted glass roof. The spacious bar, terrace lounge, and restaurant are Japanese-inspired minimalist in style. You can dine on the restaurant terrace in warm weather. **Pros:** independently owned hotel; terrace dining in summer; Sunday jazz buffet is a treat.

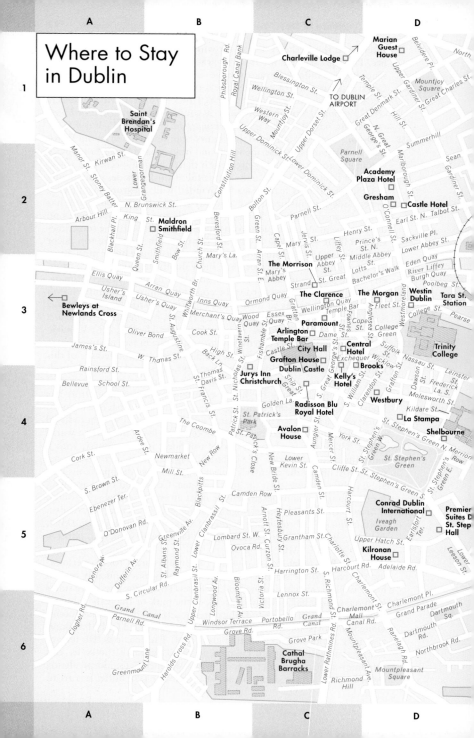

Where to Stay in Dublin

A B C D

1

Phibsborough Rd.
Royal Canal Bank

Marian Guest House

Belvidere Pl.

North

Charleville Lodge

Blessington St.

Temple St.

Upper Gardiner St.

Great Charles St.

Mountjoy Square

Wellington St.

TO DUBLIN AIRPORT

Great Denmark St.

N. Great George's St.

Hill St.

Summerhill

Sean

Western Way

Mountjoy St.

Upper Dorsett St.

Lower Dominick St.

Parnell Square

Academy Plaza Hotel

Marlborough St.

Gardiner St.

Saint Brendan's Hospital

Manor St.

Stoney Batter

Lower Grangegorman

Kirwan St.

Constitution Hill

Upper Dominick St.

Bolton St.

Gresham

O'Connell St.

Earl St. N. Talbot St.

Castle Hotel

2

N. Brunswick St.

Arbour Hill

Blackhall Pl.

King St.

Maldron Smithfield

Beresford St.

Green St.

Parnell St.

Henry St.

Prince's St. N.

Sackville Pl.

Lower Abbey St.

Bow St.

Church St.

Mary's La.

Capel St.

Jervis St.

Mary St.

Upper Abbey St.

Middle Abbey St.

Eden Quay

River Liffey
Burgh Quay

Arran St. E.

Lotts

The Morrison

Mary's Abbey

St. Great

Strand

Bachelor's Walk

Poolbeg St.

Westin Dublin

Tara St. Station

Ellis Quay

Usher's Island

Usher's Quay

Arran Quay

Whitworth Br.

Inns Quay

Ormond Quay

The Clarence

Wellington Quay

Temple Bar

Fleet St.

The Morgan

College St.

Pearse

3

Bewleys at Newlands Cross

Merchant's Quay

St. Augustine

Wood Quay

Essex Quay

Grattan Br.

Ship St.

Paramount

Temple Bar

Copeland St.

Central Hotel

Suffolk St.

Nassau St.

Trinity College

Oliver Bond

Cook St.

High St.

Back Ln.

Arlington Temple Bar

Dame St.

Exchequer St.

Brooks

Wicklow St.

St. Frederick La. S.

James's St.

W. Thomas St.

City Hall

Grafton House

Dublin Castle

S. Great George's St.

S. William St.

Dawson St.

Molesworth St.

Rainsford St.

Fishamble St.

Castle St.

Jurys Inn Christchurch

Kelly's Hotel

Clarendon St.

Grafton St.

Kildare St.

Leinster

Bellevue

School St.

St. Nicholas St.

Winetavern St.

Thomas Davis St.

Westbury

La Stampa

4

Cork St.

The Coombe

Francis St.

Patrick St.

St. Patrick's Park

Golden La.

Radisson Blu Royal Hotel

Aungier St.

Mercer St.

Shelbourne

St. Stephen's Green N.

Merrion Row

Newmarket

New Row

New Bride St.

Avalon House

York St.

St. Stephen's Green

St. Stephen's Green E.

Mill St.

Blackpitts

St. Patrick's Close

Lower Kevin St.

Camden St.

Cliffe St.

St. Stephen's Green S.

S. Brown St.

Greenville Av.

Camden Row

St. Stephen's Green

5

Ebenezer Ter.

St. Albans Rd.

Raymond St.

Lower Clanbrassil St.

Pleasants St.

Heytesbury St.

Charlotte St.

Conrad Dublin International

Iveagh Garden

Premier Suites D St. Step Hall

O'Donovan Rd.

Lombard St. W.

Ovoca Rd.

Grantham St.

Upper Hatch St.

Earlsfort Ter.

Lower Leeson St.

Dufferin Av.

Upper Clanbrasil St.

Longwood Av.

Victoria St.

Harrington St.

Harcourt Rd.

Adelaide Rd.

Kilronan House

Denoren Rd.

S. Circular Rd.

Bloomfield Av.

Lennox St.

S. Richmond St.

Harcourt St.

Charlemont St.

Charlemont Pl.

Dartmouth Sq.

6

Clogher Rd.

Grand Canal
Parnell Rd.

Windsor Terrace

Portobello Rd.

Grand Canal

Charlemont Mall

Canal Rd.

Grand Parade

Dartmouth Rd.

Harolds Cross Rd.

Grove Rd.

Grove Park

Lower Rathmines Rd.

Mountpleasant Ave.

Northbrook Rd.

Greenmount Lane

Cathal Brugha Barracks

Richmond Hill

Mountpleasant Square

A B C D

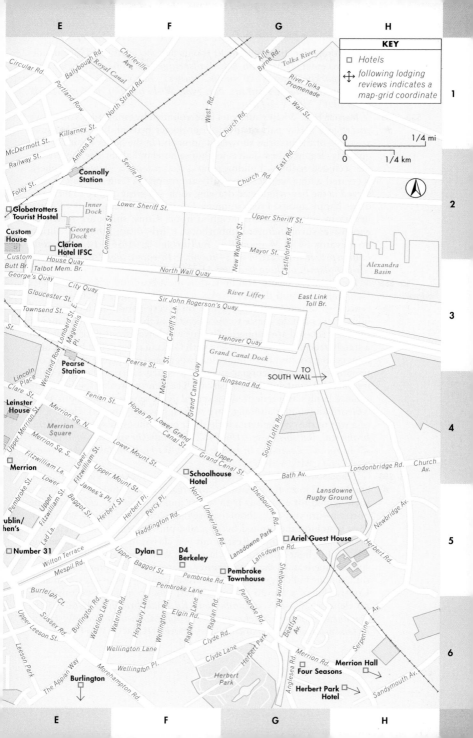

Cons: looks like an office block; rooms not too exciting; a bit outside the city center. ✉ *Merrion Rd., Ballsbridge* ☎ *01/667–2200* ⊕ *www. herbertparkhotel.ie* ⤴ *150 rooms, 3 suites* ⚓ *In-room: a/c, refrigerator, Internet. In-hotel: restaurant, bar, gym, Wi-Fi hotspot, parking (paid)* ⊟ *AE, DC, MC, V* ⊹ *H6.*

$$$–$$$$
★
🖼 **Merrion Hall.** When your hotel is surrounded by embassies, you know you're in a classy part of town. Four-poster beds and whirlpool spas are some of the luxuries showered upon you in the better rooms at this quaintly elegant Edwardian town-house hotel in Ballsbridge. Ivy covers the secluded redbrick building, and a *Room with a View* atmosphere is created with a wonderfully stuffy afternoon tea (and also fine wines) served in the bay-windowed drawing room—a great chance to meet the other happy guests. **Pros:** stunning Edwardian building; lots of extra luxury in suites; beautiful neighborhood. **Cons:** suites are relatively expensive; surrounding neighborhood a little dead; limited facilities; no elevator. ✉ *54 Merrion Rd., Ballsbridge* ☎ *01/668–1426* ⊕ *www. halpinsprivatehotels.com* ⤴ *34 rooms* ⚓ *In-room: a/c, Wi-Fi. In-hotel: Wi-Fi hotspot, parking (free)* ⊟ *AE, MC, V* ⊹ *H6.*

$$–$$$
Fodor's Choice
★
🖼 **Pembroke Townhouse.** Dublin is at its most beautiful when it wears its Georgian face, and the Pembroke, a superb example of classic 18th-century grandeur, captures the city on a very good hair day. "Townhouse" does not do justice to the splendor of the place, but does hint at the cozy, relaxed atmosphere. The fan-windowed front door leads into a stately reception area, complete with Grecian pillars. The bright, airy, high-ceiling rooms are all individually designed in a gentle clash of contemporary chic and Georgian symmetry. Nearly every wall bears a striking piece of contemporary Irish art. The hearty breakfast—including sautéed lamb's liver if desired—is served in the serene dining room. **Pros:** a Georgian wonderland; big, airy rooms; privately owned. **Cons:** a bit of a trip to the city center; a little short on facilities; no a/c. ✉ *90 Pembroke Rd., Ballsbridge* ☎ *01/660–0277* ⊕ *www.pembroketownhouse.ie* ⤴ *41 rooms, 7 suites* ⚓ *In-room: no a/c, Wi-Fi. In-hotel: parking (free)* ⊟ *AE, DC, MC, V* ⊹ *G5.*

$$–$$$
★
🖼 **Schoolhouse Hotel.** Excuse the pun, but this converted Victorian parochial school just off the Grand Canal really is an A-plus. The rooms—each named for a famous Irish writer and hung with a corresponding portrait—are very old-school (excuse the second pun) luxury, with thick rugs matching the quilted bedspreads, plus beautiful oak chairs and desks. The Schoolhouse Restaurant is a classy, modern-Irish eatery in a beautiful, light-filled former classroom with a barrel ceiling. In-room spa treatments take the edge off after a hard day's shopping. **Pros:** beautiful, unique building; top-class Irish restaurant; in-room spa treatments. **Cons:** a bit of a trip to the city center; fills up quickly; no minibars; no elevator. ✉ *2–8 Northumberland Rd., Ballsbridge* ☎ *01/667–5014* ⊕ *www.schoolhousehotel.com* ⤴ *31 rooms* ⚓ *In-room: a/c Wi-Fi. In-hotel: restaurant, bar, parking (free)* ⊟ *AE, DC, MC, V* ⊹ *F4.*

DUBLIN WEST

2

Use the coordinate (✛ B2) at the end of each listing to locate a site on the corresponding Where to Stay in Dublin map.

¢–$ ★ 🏨 **Avalon House.** Many young, independent travelers rate this cleverly restored redbrick Victorian medical school, a five-minute walk southwest from Grafton Street and 5 to 10 minutes from some of the city's best music venues, the most appealing of Dublin's hostels. Avalon House has a mix of dormitories, rooms without bath, and rooms with bath. The dorm rooms and en-suite quads all have loft areas that offer more privacy than you'd typically find in a multi-bed room. The public spaces have pine floors, high ceilings, and even an open fire. Their Bald Barista café has one of the best espressos in the city. **Pros:** beautiful, historic building; communal kitchen for cooking; cheapest city-center spot. **Cons:** you need to like sharing with students; street noise can be an issue on weekends; in-room facilities limited. ⊠ *55 Aungier St., Dublin West* 🕾 *01/475–0001* ⊕ *www.avalon-house.ie* ⤳ *40 4-bed rooms, 35 with bath; 26 twin rooms, 4 with bath; 4 single rooms with shared bath; 5 12-bed dorms, 1 10-bed dorm and 1 26-bed dorm, all with shared bath* ♿ *In-room: no a/c, no TV. In-hotel: restaurant, Wi-Fi hotspot* ☰ *AE, MC, V* ✛ *C4.*

¢ 🏨 **Bewleys at Newlands Cross.** Cheap and cheerful would best sum up this four-story franchise hotel on the southwest outskirts of the city. It's ideal if you're planning to head out of the city early (especially to points in the southwest and west) and don't want to deal with morning traffic. The hotel is emulating the formula popularized by Jurys Inns, in which rooms—here each has a double bed, a single bed, and a sofa bed—are a flat rate for up to three adults or two adults and two children. **Pros:** great value for families; good location if you're heading south next day; Bewleys' delicious coffee in the morning. **Cons:** mainly business clientele; well outside the city center; overlooks the expressway. ⊠ *Newlands Cross at Naas Rd., Dublin West* 🕾 *01/464–0140* ⊕ *www.bewleyshotels.com* ⤳ *2,59 rooms* ♿ *In-room: no a/c, Wi-Fi. In-hotel: restaurant, parking (free)* ☰ *AE, MC, V* ✛ *A3.*

$$ 🏨 **Jurys Inn Christchurch.** Expect few frills at this functional budget hotel, part of a Jurys mini-chain that offers a low, fixed room rate for up to three adults or two adults and two children. (The branch at Custom House Quay operates according to the same plan.) The biggest plus is the pleasant location, on a hill facing Christ Church Cathedral and within walking distance of most city-center attractions. The big but somewhat spartan rooms are decorated in primary colors and have utilitarian furniture. The restaurant and bar are equally functional. **Pros:** good value for families; views of Christ Church; near Temple Bar. **Cons:** ugly building; basic, functional rooms; tends to be popular with bachelor(ette) parties. ⊠ *Christ Church Pl., Dublin West* 🕾 *01/454–0000* ⊕ *www.jurysinn.com* ⤳ *182 rooms* ♿ *In-room: a/c, Internet. In-hotel: restaurant, bar, Wi-Fi hotspot, parking (paid)* ☰ *AE, DC, MC, V* ✛ *B3.*

$–$$ 🏨 **Maldron Smithfield.** On Smithfield Plaza, this snazzy, good-value hotel is at the heart of Dublin's refurbished old-market district area. The look, outside and in, is definitely functional-modern, but the beige and brown tones do soften things a bit and the public spaces are bright and cheerful. Bedrooms are big for the price and most include large floor-to-ceiling windows allowing for great light, plus under-floor heating in the bathrooms. Try to get a room at the front on a higher floor, as they have some stunning views looking out onto the plaza and to the city beyond. **Pros:** located on an open plaza; great views from rooms in front on higher floors; under-floor heating in bathrooms. **Cons:** no proper restaurant. ⊠ *Smithfield Village, Dublin West* ☎ *01/485–0900* ⊕ *www.maldronhotels.com* ➷ *85 rooms, 7 suites* ⟑ *In-room: a/c, Internet. In-hotel: bar, parking (paid)* ⊟ *AE, DC, MC, V* ✛ *B2.*

$$–$$$ 🏨 **Radisson Blu Royal Hotel, Dublin.** Is it possible to be elegant and functional at the same time? The new sleek glass-and-concrete Radisson, just off South Great George's Street, offers to-the-point business accommodations with a real dash of cool and understated Scandinavian style. Public spaces are painted in very daring (for Ireland) dark browns and warm reds, with subtle lighting creating a soothing atmosphere. Each room at the front—more clean lines and minimal fuss—has one wall that is basically a huge window, and a bathroom with earthy wood and stone finishes. The cocktail bar Sure is a hit with the locals, and the open-plan restaurant looks great. **Pros:** right in the heart of "real Dublin"; stylish, understated decor; luxurious bathrooms. **Cons:** looks out over a block of flats; restaurant is getting mixed reviews; mostly business clientele. ⊠ *Golden La., Dublin West* ☎ *01/898–2900* ⊕ *www.radissonblu.com* ➷ *138 rooms, 12 suites* ⟑ *In-room: a/c, safe, Wi-Fi. In-hotel: restaurant, room service, bar, Wi-Fi hotspot, parking (paid)* ⊟ *AE, DC, MC, V* ✛ *C4.*

NIGHTLIFE AND THE ARTS

Long before Stephen Dedalus's excursions into "nighttown" in James Joyce's *Ulysses,* Dublin was proud of its lively after-hours scene, particularly its thriving pubs. But the now tamed Celtic Tiger economy, the envy of all Europe, turned Dublin into one of the most happening destinations on the whole continent. Some of the old watering holes were replaced with huge, London-style "superbars," which, with the ubiquitous DJ in the corner, walk the fine line between pub and club. Most nights, the city's nightspots overflow with young cell-phone-toting Dubliners and Europeans, who descend on the capital for weekend getaways (though the recent downturn has seen a slowdown in weekend visitors). The city's 900-plus pubs are its main source of entertainment; many public houses in the city center have live music—from rock to jazz to traditional Irish.

Theater is an essential element of life in the city that was home to O'Casey, Synge, W. B. Yeats, and Beckett. Today Dublin has seven major theaters that reproduce the Irish "classics," and also present newer fare from the likes of Martin McDonagh and Conor McPherson. Opera, long overlooked, now has a home in the restored old Gaiety Theatre. The big new player on the Dublin stage is the the massive Libeskind-designed Grand Canal Theatre, which boasts over 2,000 seats for opera, ballet, rock, and theater lovers.

Check the following newspapers for informative listings: the *Irish Times* publishes a daily guide to what's happening in Dublin and the rest of the country, and has complete film and theater schedules. The *Evening Herald* lists theaters, cinemas, and pubs with live entertainment. The *Big Issue* is a weekly guide to film, theater, and musical events around the city. The *Event Guide,* a weekly free paper that lists music, cinema, theater, art shows, and dance clubs, is available in pubs and cafés around the city. In peak season, consult the free Bord Fáilte (Irish Tourist Board) leaflet "Events of the Week." The **Temple Bar Web site** (⊕ *www.templebar. ie*) provides information about events in the Temple Bar area.

NIGHTLIFE

Dubliners have always enjoyed a night out, but during the Celtic Tiger years they turned nocturnal pleasures into a high-octane works of art. Things have slowed down a little with the economic downturn but the clubs still draw regular party crowds on weekends. In Dublin's clubs the dominant sound is still hip-hop and house music, and the crowd that flocks to them every night of the week is of the trendy, under-30 generation. Leeson Street—just off St. Stephen's Green, south of the Liffey, and known as "the strip"—is a slightly frayed and uncool nightclub area aimed at the over-30 crowd that revs up at pub closing time and stays active until 4 AM. The dress code at Leeson Street's dance clubs is informal, but jeans and sneakers are not welcome. Most of these clubs are licensed only to sell wine, and the prices can be exorbitant (up to €30 for a mediocre bottle); the upside is that most don't charge to get in.

Some of Dublin's classic pubs—arguably some of the finest watering holes in the world—were unfortunately remodeled in the boom years with modern interiors and designer drinks, to attract a younger, upwardly mobile crowd. Beware Dublin Tourism's "Official Dublin Pub Guide," which has a tendency to recommend many of these bland spots. Despite the changes, however, the traditional pub has steadfastly clung to its role as the primary center of Dublin's social life. The city has nearly 1,000 pubs ("licensed tabernacles," writer Flann O'Brien calls them). And although the vision of elderly men enjoying a chinwag over a creamy pint of stout has become something of a rarity, there are still plenty of places where you can enjoy a quiet (or not so quiet) drink and a chat. Last drinks are called at 11:30 PM Monday to Thursday, 12:30 AM Friday and Saturday, and 11 PM on Sunday. Some city-center pubs have extended opening hours and don't serve last drinks until 1:45 AM.

A word of warning: although most pubs and clubs are perfectly safe, the lads can get lively and public drunkenness is very much a part of Dublin's nightlife, especially around Temple Bar and South Great George's Street. If you will need late-night transportation, try to arrange it with your hotel before you go out.

IRISH CABARET, MUSIC, AND DANCING

★ **Bewley's Café Theatre** (⊠ *Grafton St., Southside* ☎ *086/878–4001*), with its "Live at The Oriental Room" nights, has become the atmospheric cabaret hot spot in Dublin.

The Sugar Club (✉ *8 Lower Leeson St., Southside* ☎ *01/678–7188*) is a landmark venue with tables that has regular performance (some touted as "burlesque") nights.

JAZZ

International (✉ *Wicklow St., Southside* ☎ *01/677–9250*) hosts the Dirty Jazz Club upstairs on Tuesday night.

JJ Smyth's (✉ *12 Aungier St., Southside* ☎ *01/475–2565*) is an old-time jazz venue where the Pendulum Club on Sunday is a popular hangout for all the "jazz heads."

The Mint Bar (✉ *Westin Hotel, College Green, Southside* ☎ *01/645–1000*), a basement venue, presents Velvet Lounge bands and guests every Saturday night.

NIGHTCLUBS

NORTHSIDE **The Academy** (✉ *57 Middle Abbey St., Northside* ☎ *01/877–9999*) is a music mecca with four floors of entertainment of every kind anchored by big-name local and international DJs. It attracts a young, dance-crazy crowd who like to party until the wee hours.

Andrew's Lane (✉ *Andrews La., Southside* ☎ *01/478–0766*), once a bastion of experimental theatre, now hosts a cozy club and regular live indie gigs.

SOUTHSIDE **The Gaiety** (✉ *S. King St., Southside* ☎ *01/677–1921*) is an eclectic, live music and club mix located on the various floors of the beautiful, Victorian-era Gaiety Theatre after hours.

Lillie's Bordello (✉ *Grafton St., Southside* ☎ *01/679–9204*) was once the hot spot for celebs but is now more for regular Joes: a popular hangout for a young late-night crowd.

The Pod (✉ *Harcourt St., Southside* ☎ *01/478–0166*), also known as the "Place of Dance," qualifies as Dublin's most renowned dance club, especially among the younger set. Whether you get in depends as much on what you're wearing as on your age.

Rí Ra (✉ *Dame Ct., Southside* ☎ *01/677–4835*), part of the hugely popular Globe bar, has lost some of its shine in recent years. The name means "uproar" in Irish, and on most nights the place does go a little wild. Upstairs is more low-key.

★ **Tripod** (✉ *Old Harcourt St. Station, Harcourt St., Southside* ☎ *01/478–0166*), adjacent to the Pod and the Crawdaddy music venue, can pack in more than 1,300 people and surround them with state-of-the-art sound and light. It regularly hosts Irish and international rock acts, and celebrity DJs from Europe and the United States. It has full bar facilities.

Underground@Kennedy's (✉ *31–32 Westland Row, Southside* ☎ *01/661–1124*) is a real dive of a basement club that attracts cutting-edge European DJs and a serious dance and hip-hop crowd.

TEMPLE BAR **Button Factory** (✉ *Curved St., Temple Bar* ☎ *01/670–9202*), a happening music venue, mixes top DJs and up-and-coming live acts.

Club M (✉ *Cope St., Temple Bar* ☎ *01/671–5274*) is an old school disco-type venue that's popular with the suburban crowd in town for the night. Their theme nights—like "school disco"—tend to be popular.

PUBS

Use the coordinate (✛ B2) at the end of each listing to locate a site on the corresponding Dublin Pubs map.

"When I die I want to decompose in a barrel of porter and have it served in all the pubs in Dublin." Author J. P. Donleavy realized that it's impossible to think of Dublin without also thinking of its 1,000 or so "public houses." These are what give Dublin so much of its character, and they're largely to blame for the fierce loyalty Dublin inspires among locals and visitors. Some wag once asked if it was possible to cross Dublin without passing a single pub along the way. The answer was "Yes, but only if you go into every one." As a general rule, the area between Grafton and Great George's streets is a gold mine for classy pubs. Another good bet is the Temple Bar district (though some of the newer ones are all plastic and mirrors). And if it's real spit-on-the-floor hideaways you're after, head across the Liffey to the areas around Parnell Square or Smithfield. But beware the tourist-trap faux traditional pubs where you can hardly hear the music for the roar of the seven flat-screen TVs blaring out soccer games.

NORTHSIDE **The Flowing Tide** (✉ *Lower Abbey St., Northside* ☎ *01/874–0842*), directly across from the Abbey Theatre, draws a lively pre- and post-theater crowd. No TVs, quality pub talk, and a great pint of Guinness make it a worthwhile visit. ✛ *E2*

Morrison Bar (✉ *Morrison Hotel, Upper Ormond Quay, Northside* ☎ *01/878–2999*) is a modern, stylish bar in one of Dublin's most designer-friendly hotels. The loungy bar overlooks the river it's named after and attracts a crowd that likes to dress up and talk about it. ✛ *C3*

Pantibar (✉ *Capel St., Northside* ☎ *01/874–0710*) is a new, amusingly named gay bar fronted by the infamous Dublin drag queen Panti. The place has loud music at night but is pretty chilled-out during the day. ✛ *C2*

SOUTHSIDE AND SOUTH-EAST DUBLIN **Cassidy's** (✉ *42 Lower Camden St., Southside* ☎ *01/475–1429*), once a quality neighborhood pub with a tasty pint of stout, has morphed into an often overcrowded but very popular spot with young revelers. ✛ *D5*

Cellar Bar (✉ *24 Upper Merrion St., Southeast Dublin* ☎ *01/603–0600*), at the Merrion Hotel, is in a stylish 18th-century wine vault with bare brick walls and vaulted ceilings. It tends to draw a well-heeled crowd. ✛ *E4*

Davy Byrne's (✉ *21 Duke St., Southside* ☎ *01/671–1298*) is a pilgrimage stop for Joyceans. In *Ulysses,* Leopold Bloom stops in here for a glass of Burgundy and a Gorgonzola-cheese sandwich. He then leaves the pub and walks to Dawson Street, where he helps a blind man cross the road. Unfortunately, the decor is greatly changed from Joyce's day, but it still serves some fine pub grub. ✛ *D4*

Doheny & Nesbitt (✉ *5 Lower Baggot St., Southeast Dublin* ☎ *01/676–2945*), a traditional spot with snugs, dark wooden furnishings, and smoke-darkened ceilings, has hardly changed over the decades. ✛ *E4*

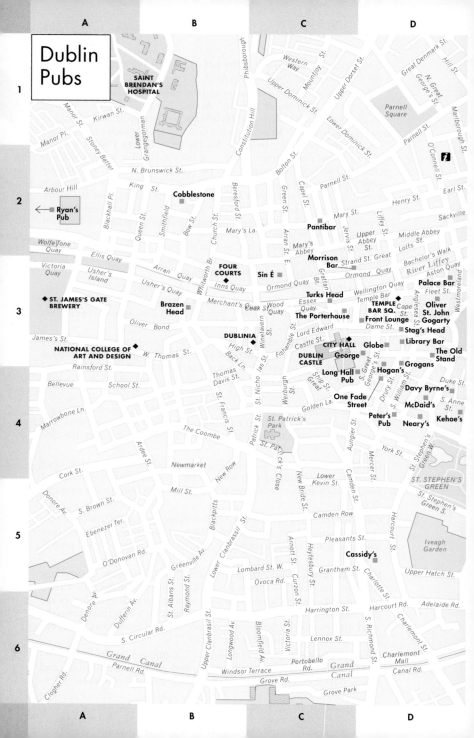

Dublin Pubs

A
B
C
D

1

SAINT BRENDAN'S HOSPITAL
Western Way
St.
Mountjoy
Upper Dorset St.
Phibsborough
Upper Dominick St.
Lower Dominick St.
Parnell Square
Great Denmark St.
Hill St.
N. Great George's St.
Parnell St.
Marlborough St.
O'Connell St.

Manor St.
Kirwan St.
Lower Grangegorman
Constitution Hill
Parnell St.
Henry St.
Earl St.

2
Arbour Hill
← Ryan's Pub
King St.
Cobblestone
Beresford St.
Green St.
Mary St.
Liffey St.
Upper Abbey St.
Jervis St.
Sackville

Manor Pl.
Blackhall Pl.
Queen St.
Smithfield
Bow St.
Church St.
Mary's La.
Arran St. E.
Mary's Abbey
Strand St. Great
Middle Abbey St.
Lotts
Bachelor's Walk

Wolfe Tone Quay
Ellis Quay
Pantibar
Morrison Bar
Ormond Quay
River Liffey
Aston Quay
Westmoreland

Victoria Quay
Usher's Island
Usher's Quay
Arran Quay
Whitworth Br.
FOUR COURTS
Inns Quay
Sin É
Grattan Br.
Wellington Quay
Temple Bar
Palace Bar
Fleet St.

3
♦ ST. JAMES'S GATE BREWERY
Brazen Head
Merchant's Quay
Wood Quay
Essex Quay
Turks Head
The Porterhouse
TEMPLE BAR SQ.
Front Lounge
♦
Oliver St. John Gogarty
Stag's Head

James's St.
Oliver Bond
DUBLINIA
Winetavern St.
Lord Edward St.
Dame St.
Library Bar

♦ NATIONAL COLLEGE OF ART AND DESIGN
High St.
Castle St.
CITY HALL ♦
Globe
The Old Stand

Rainsford St.
W. Thomas St.
Back La.
St. Nicholas St.
Fishamble St.
DUBLIN CASTLE
George
Grogans
Duke St.

Bellevue
School St.
Thomas Davis St.
Ship St. Great
Hogan's
Davy Byrne's
S. Anne St.

4
Marrowbone Ln.
The Coombe
St. Francis St.
Werburgh St.
Golden La.
Long Hall Pub
George's St. Great
Dury St.
S. William St.
One Fade Street
McDaid's
Kehoe's

Cork St.
Ardee St.
Newmarket
New Row
Patrick St.
St. Patrick's Park
St. Patrick's Close
Peter's Pub
Neary's
York St.
St. Stephen's Green W.

5
Donore Av.
S. Brown St.
Mill St.
Blackpitts
New Bride St.
Lower Kevin St.
Camden St.
Mercer St.
Cassidy's
ST. STEPHEN'S GREEN
Iveagh Garden
Upper Hatch St.

O'Donovan Rd.
Greenville Av.
Lower Clanbrassil St.
Lombard St. W.
Ovoca Rd.
Curzon St.
Arnott St.
Heytesbury St.
Grantham St.
Pleasants St.
Camden Row
St. Stephen's Green S.
Harcourt St.

Ebenezer Ter.
Dufferin Av.
St. Albans St.
Raymond St.
Harrington St.
Harcourt Rd.
Adelaide Rd.

6
S. Circular Rd.
Grand Canal
Parnell Rd.
Clogher Rd.
Upper Clanbrassil St.
Longwood Av.
Bloomfield Av.
Victoria St.
Windsor Terrace
Portobello Rd.
Grand Canal
Grove Rd.
Grove Park
Charlemont St.
Charlemont Mall
Canal Rd.
Lennox St.
S. Richmond St.

A
B
C
D

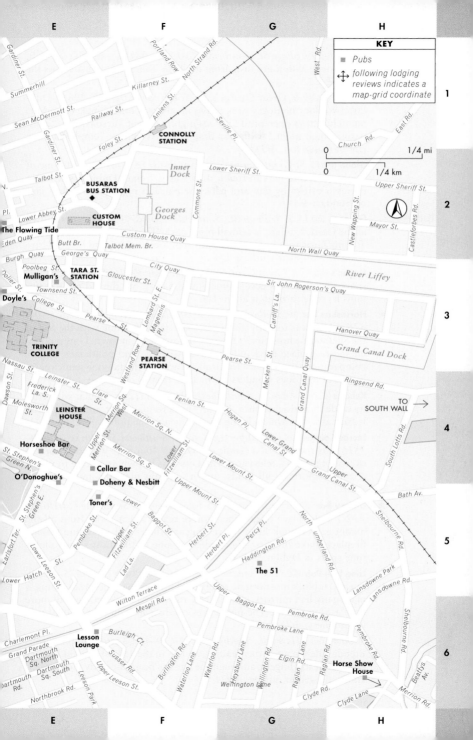

Doyle's (✉ *9 College St., Southside* ☎ *01/671–0616*), a small, cozy pub, is a favorite with journalists from the *Irish Times* office, just across the street. ✛ *E3*

George (✉ *89 S. Great George's St., Southside* ☎ *01/478–2983*), Dublin's two-floor main gay pub, draws an almost entirely male crowd; its nightclub stays open until 2:30 AM nightly except Tuesday. The "alternative bingo night," with star drag act Miss Shirley Temple Bar, is a riot of risqué fun. ✛ *D3*

Globe (✉ *11 S. Great George's St., Southside* ☎ *01/671–1220*), one of the hippest café-bars in town, draws arty, trendy Dubliners who sip espresso drinks by day and pack the place at night. There's live jazz on Sunday. ✛ *D3*

Fodor's Choice
★   **Grogans** (✉ *15 S. William St., Southside* ☎ *01/677–9320*), also known as the Castle Lounge, is a small place packed with creative folk. Owner Tommy Grogan is known as a patron of local artists, and his walls are covered with their work. ✛ *D3*

Hogan's (✉ *35 S. Great George's St., Southside* ☎ *01/677–5904*), a huge space on two levels, gets jammed most nights, but the old place maintains its style through it all. ✛ *D4*

★   **Horseshoe Bar** (✉ *Shelbourne, 27 St. Stephen's Green, Southside* ☎ *01/ 676–6471*) was recently given a massive face-lift along with the rest of the Shelbourne hotel and is now the hottest ticket in town. Long a popular meeting place for Dublin's businesspeople and politicians, there's comparatively little space for drinkers around the famous semicircular bar—but this does wonders for making friends quickly. ✛ *E4*

Kehoe's (✉ *9 S. Anne St., Southside* ☎ *01/677–8312*) is popular with Trinity students and academics. The tiny back room is cozy, and the upstairs is basically the owner's living room, open to the public. ✛ *D4*

Lesson Lounge (✉ *148 Upper Lesson St., Southeast Dublin* ☎ *01/660– 3816*) has the look of a classic old Dublin "boozer," with one notable exception: it has a television. The Lesson is known as a place to watch televised sports of all kinds, and it's always pleasant and inclusive. ✛ *E6*

★   **Library Bar** (✉ *Central Hotel, 1–5 Exchequer St., Southside* ☎ *01/679– 7302*) is the place to go when you're ready to get away from all the madness. The book-lined shelves, big armchairs and sofas, and blazing fireplace make this first-floor hideaway one of the most serene nighttime spots in Dublin. ✛ *D3*

Long Hall Pub (✉ *51 S. Great George's St., Southside* ☎ *01/475–1590*), one of Dublin's most ornate traditional taverns, has Victorian lamps, a mahogany bar, mirrors, chandeliers, and plasterwork ceilings, all more than 100 years old. The pub serves sandwiches and an excellent pint of Guinness. ✛ *D4*

McDaid's (✉ *3 Harry St., Southside* ☎ *01/679–4395*) attracted boisterous Brendan Behan and other leading writers in the 1950s; its wild literary reputation still lingers, although the bar has been discreetly modernized and is altogether quieter. ✛ *D4*

Some say Dubliners now give the Temple Bar district the brush-off; others still find it the pulsing aorta of the city's nightlife.

Mulligan's (⊠ *8 Poolbeg St., Southside* ☎ *01/677–5582*) is synonymous in Dublin with a truly inspirational pint of Guinness. Until a few years ago no women were admitted. Today journalists, locals, and students of both sexes flock here for the perfect pint. ✢ *E3*

Neary's (⊠ *1 Chatham St., Southside* ☎ *01/677–7371*), with an exotic, Victorian-style interior, was once the haunt of music-hall artists and a certain literary set, including Brendan Behan. Join the actors from the adjacent Gaiety Theatre for a good pub lunch. ✢ *D4*

Fodor's Choice
★
One Fade Street (⊠ *1 Fade St., Southside* ☎ *01/675–3708*) is not actually the name of this very cool new bar, but it's the best available because the place considers itself too hip to even have a name. Above the wonderful L'Gueuleton restaurant this open-plan, buzzing bar even has a cute little covered patio. ✢ *D4*

O'Donoghue's (⊠ *15 Merrion Row, Southside* ☎ *01/676–2807*), a cheerful hangout, has impromptu musical performances that often spill out onto the street. ✢ *E4*

The Old Stand (⊠ *37 Exchequer St., Southside* ☎ *01/677–7220*), one of the oldest pubs in the city, is named after the Old Stand stadium at Lansdowne Road, home to Irish rugby and football. The pub is renowned for great pints and fine steaks. ✢ *D3*

Peter's Pub (⊠ *Johnson Place, Southside* ☎ *01/677–8588*), the epitome of the cozy little boozer, hugs a busy corner where people-watching becomes an art at the outside tables in summer. ✢ *D4*

Fodor's Choice
★
Stag's Head (⊠ *1 Dame Ct., Southside* ☎ *01/679–3701*) dates from 1770 and was rebuilt in 1895. Theater people from the nearby Olympia,

journalists, and Trinity students gather around the unusual Connemara red-marble bar. The interior is a Victorian beaut. ✛ *D3*

Toner's (✉ *139 Lower Baggot St., Southside* ☎ *01/676–3090*), though billed as a Victorian bar, actually goes back 200 years, with an original flagstone floor to prove its antiquity, as well as wooden drawers running up to the ceiling—a relic of the days when bars doubled as grocery shops. Oliver St. John Gogarty, who was the model for Buck Mulligan in James Joyce's *Ulysses,* accompanied W. B. Yeats here, in what was purportedly the latter's only visit to a pub. ✛ *E5*

TEMPLE BAR **Front Lounge** (✉ *33 Parliament St., Temple Bar* ☎ *01/679–3988*), a modern pub, caters to a mixed crowd of young professionals, both gay and straight. ✛ *D3*

Oliver St. John Gogarty (✉ *57 Fleet St., Temple Bar* ☎ *01/671–1822*) is a lively bar that attracts all ages and nationalities; it overflows with patrons in summer. On most nights there's traditional Irish music upstairs. ✛ *D3*

Palace Bar (✉ *21 Fleet St., Temple Bar* ☎ *01/677–9290*), scarcely changed since the 1940s, is tiled and rather barren looking, but is popular with journalists and writers (the *Irish Times* is nearby). The walls are lined with cartoons drawn by newspaper illustrators. ✛ *D3*

The Porterhouse (✉ *16–18 Parliament St., Temple Bar* ☎ *01/679–8847*) is one of the few bars in Ireland to brew its own beer. The Plain Porter has won the best stout award at the "Brewing Oscars," beating out the mighty Guinness. The tasteful interior is all dark woods and soft lighting. ✛ *C3*

Turks Head (✉ *Parliament St., Temple Bar* ☎ *01/679–2606*), a very nontraditional Irish bar, is known for its extravagant mosaics and vibrant, late-night DJ-driven sounds. ✛ *C3*

BALLSBRIDGE **The 51** (✉ *Haddington Rd., Ballsbridge* ☎ *01/660–0150*) is famous for its collection of whiskies from around the world. Its Beer Garden is always buzzing with activity in fine weather. ✛ *G5*

The Horse Show House (✉ *32 Merrion Rd., Ballsbridge* ☎ *01/668–9424*), a Ballsbridge institution, is a favorite of the boisterous but welcoming rugby and show-jumping set. Great spot to watch sports of any kind. ✛ *H6*

DUBLIN WEST **Brazen Head** (✉ *Bridge St., Dublin West* ☎ *01/677–9549*), Dublin's oldest pub (the site has been licensed since 1198), has stone walls and open fireplaces—it has hardly changed over the years. The pub is renowned for traditional-music performances and lively sing-along sessions on Sunday evenings. On the south side of the Liffey quays, it's a little difficult to find—turn down Lower Bridge Street and make a right onto the old lane. ✛ *B3*

Cobblestone (✉ *N. King St., Dublin West* ☎ *01/872–1799*) is a glorious house of ale in the best Dublin tradition, popular with Smithfield Market workers. Its chatty imbibers and live traditional music are attracting a more varied, younger crowd from all over town. ✛ *B2*

★ **Ryan's Pub** (⊠ *28 Parkgate St., Dublin West* ☎ *01/677–6097*) is one of Dublin's last genuine, late-Victorian-era pubs, and has changed little since its last (1896) remodeling. ✛ *A2*

Sin É (⊠ *14–15 Ormond Quay, Dublin West* ☎ *01/878–7009*) is a no-frills (but somehow very cool) hangout for students and lovers of reggae, soul, and R&B. ✛ *C3*

THE ARTS

CLASSICAL MUSIC AND OPERA

SOUTHSIDE **Dublin City Gallery, The Hugh Lane** (⊠ *Parnell Sq. N, Northside* ☎ *01/222–5550*) is a serene home to Sundays@Noon, a series of free Sunday concerts featuring some top Irish and international talent.

SOUTHEAST DUBLIN **National Concert Hall** (⊠ *Earlsfort Terr., Southeast Dublin* ☎ *01/475–1666* ⊕ *www.nch.ie*), just off St. Stephen's Green, is Dublin's main theater for classical music of all kinds, from symphonies to chamber groups. The slightly austere Neoclassical building was transformed in 1981 into one of Europe's finest medium-size concert halls. It houses the cream of Irish classical musicians, the National Symphony Orchestra of Ireland. A host of guest international conductors and performers— Maxim Vengerov, Radu Lupu, and Pinchas Zukerman are just a few of the soloists who have appeared—keep the standard very high, and performances continue throughout the year. The concert year picks up speed in mid-September and sails through to June; July and August also get many dazzling troupes. The smaller, more intimate John Field and Carolan rooms are perfect for chamber music.

Grand Canal Theatre (⊠ *Grand Canal Sq., Southeast Dublin* ☎ *01/677–7999* ⊕ *www.grandcanaltheatre.ie*) is housed in a spanking new, brash Daniel Liebskind–designed building in the growing docklands area of the city. With a 2,000-plus capacity it's Ireland's biggest theater space and will house the best of international ballet, classical music, pop gigs, and even Broadway musicals.

St. Stephen's Church (⊠ *Merrion Sq., Southeast Dublin* ☎ *01/288–0663*) stages a regular program of choral and orchestral events under its glorious "pepper canister" cupola.

DUBLIN WEST **Opera Ireland** (⊠ *West Wing 3, Adelaide Chambers, Peter St., Dublin West* ☎ *01/478–6041* ⊕ *www.operaireland.com*) performs at the Gaiety Theatre; call to find out what's on.

TEMPLE BAR **Opera Theatre Company** (⊠ *Temple Bar Music Centre, Curved St., Temple Bar* ☎ *01/679–4962* ⊕ *www.opera.ie*) is Ireland's only touring opera company. It performs at venues in Dublin and throughout the country.

DUBLIN WEST **Royal Hospital Kilmainham** (⊠ *Military Rd., Dublin West* ☎ *01/671–8666* ⊕ *www.rhk.ie*) presents frequent classical concerts in its magnificent 17th-century interior.

Don't forget that U2 hail from Dublin. You'll find a calendar packed with rock, techno, and break-beat in the city's many clubs and concert halls.

FILM

NORTHSIDE **Cineworld** (✉ *Parnell Center, Parnell St., Northside* ☎ *01/872–8400*), a 17-screen theater just off O'Connell Street, is the city center's only multiplex movie house; it shows the latest commercial features.

Savoy Cinema (✉ *O'Connell St., Northside* ☎ *01/874–6000*), just across from the General Post Office, is a four-screen theater with the largest screen in the country.

TEMPLE BAR **Irish Film Institute** (✉ *6 Eustace St., Temple Bar* ☎ *01/677–8788*) shows classic and new independent films.

ROCK AND CONTEMPORARY MUSIC

NORTHSIDE **The O2 Arena** (✉ *Northwall Quay, Northside* ☎ *01/836–3633* ⊕ *www. theo2.ie*) is a high-tech, 14,500-capacity big-gig venue that replaced the cold and unloved Point Depot.

★ **Andrew's Lane Theatre** (✉ *9–11 Andrew's La., Southside* ☎ *01/679–5720*),
SOUTHSIDE an intimate old theater, has been transformed into Dublin's newest live-music venue.

Crawdaddy (✉ *Old Harcourt Station, Harcourt St., Southside* ☎ *01/476– 3374*) is an intimate venue at the center of the hot Pod nightclub complex. A predecessor to *Rolling Stone, Crawdaddy* was the very first rock magazine in the United States. The place is an homage to that bygone era of sweat, three chords, and the truth.

International Bar (✉ *Wicklow St., Southside* ☎ *01/677–9250*) has a long-established, tiny, get-close-to-the-band venue upstairs. It hosts theater in the afternoon.

The Village (✉ 26 Wexford St., Southside ☎ 01/475–8555), set in a striking, glass-front building, isn't too fussy about the kind of bands it hosts, so long as their amps are turned up full and the lead singer knows how to scream.

Whelan's (✉ 25 Wexford St., Southside ☎ 01/478–0766), just off the southeastern corner of St. Stephen's Green, is one of the city's best—and most popular—music venues. Well-known performers play everything from rock to folk to traditional music. The same owners run the Village bar and venue next door.

★ TEMPLE BAR **Button Factory** (✉ Curved St., Temple Bar ☎ 01/670–0533) is a new music venue and club rolled into one. It buzzes with activity every day of the week. Live acts range from rock bands to world music to singer-songwriters.

Olympia Theatre (✉ 72 Dame St., Temple Bar ☎ 01/677–7744) puts on "Midnight from the Olympia" shows every Friday and Saturday from midnight to 2 AM, with everything from rock to country.

DUBLIN WEST **Vicar Street** (✉ 58–59 Thomas St., Dublin West ☎ 01/454–5533), just across from Christ Church Cathedral, is a venue for intimate concerts. It often plays host to folk music, jazz, and comedy, as well as rock performances.

THEATER

NORTHSIDE **Abbey Theatre** (✉ Lower Abbey St., Northside ☎ 01/878–7222 ⊕ www.abbeytheatre.ie) is the fabled home of Ireland's national theater company. In 1904 W. B. Yeats and his patron, Lady Gregory, opened the theater, which became a major center for the Irish literary renaissance—the place that first staged works by J. M. Synge and Sean O'Casey, among many others. Plays by recent Irish drama heavyweights like Brian Friel, Tom Murphy, Hugh Leonard, and John B. Keane have all premiered here, and memorable productions of international greats like Mamet, Ibsen, and Shakespeare have also been performed. You should not, however, arrive expecting 19th-century grandeur: the original structure burned down in 1951. Unfortunately, an ugly concrete boxlike auditorium was built in its place—but what it may lack in esthetics it makes up for in space and acoustics, especially after a new internal renovation. Some say the repertoire is overly reverential and mainstream, but such chestnuts as Dion Boucicault's *The Shaughran* wind up being applauded by many. Happily, the Abbey's sister theater at the same address, the Peacock, offers more experimental drama. But the Abbey will always be relevant since much of the theatergoing public still looks to it as a barometer of Irish culture.

Gate Theatre (⊠ *Cavendish Row, Parnell Sq., Northside* ☎ *01/874–4045* ⊕ *www.gate-theatre.ie*), an intimate 371-seat theater in a jewel-like Georgian assembly hall, produces the classics and contemporary plays by leading Irish writers, including Beckett, Wilde (the production of *Salome* was a worldwide hit), Shaw, and the younger generation of dramatists, such as Conor McPherson.

SOUTHSIDE **Gaiety Theatre** (⊠ *S. King St., Southside* ☎ *01/677–1717*) is the home of Opera Ireland when it's not showing musical comedy, drama, and revues. On weekends this elegant theater is taken over by a nightclub with live music and cabaret.

Samuel Beckett Centre (⊠ *Trinity College, Southside* ☎ *01/608–2266*) is home to Trinity's drama department, as well as visiting European groups. Dance is often performed here by visiting troupes.

TEMPLE BAR **New Project Arts Centre** (⊠ *39 E. Essex St., Temple Bar* ☎ *01/671–2321*) is a theater and performance space in an ugly modern building at the center of Temple Bar. Fringe and mainstream theater, contemporary music, and experimental art have all found a home here.

The New Theatre (⊠ *43 E. Essex St., Temple Bar* ☎ *01/670–3361*) is a troupe with a political agenda, so you'll often find this newly renovated space favors Irish working-class writers like Sean O'Casey and Brendan Behan.

Olympia Theatre (⊠ *72 Dame St., Temple Bar* ☎ *01/677–7744*) is Dublin's oldest and premier multipurpose theatrical venue. In addition to its high-profile musical performances, it has seasons of comedy, vaudeville, and ballet.

Smock Alley (⊠ *Lower Exchange St., Temple Bar* ☎ *01/679–9277*) is a wonderfully atmospheric theater space tucked down a little lane. It is the historic site of a famous 17th-century Dublin theater.

SPORTS

FOOTBALL

Soccer—called football in Europe—is very popular in Ireland, largely due to the euphoria resulting from the national team's successes since the late 1980s. However, the places where you can watch it aren't ideal—they tend to be small and out-of-date. **Aviva Stadium** (⊠ *62 Lansdowne Rd., Ballsbridge* ☎ *01/238–2300*), a vast rugby stadium, is the main center for international matches. The old stadium was demolished and has been replaced by a state-of-the-art arena. In the soccer and rugby games were played at Croke Park—the first time in history that so-called foreign games were be allowed on the Gaelic Athletic Association's hallowed turf.

League of Ireland matches take place throughout the city on Friday evening or Sunday afternoon from March to November. For details, contact the **Football Association of Ireland** (⊠ *80 Merrion Sq. S, Southeast Dublin* ☎ *01/676–6864*).

GAELIC GAMES

The traditional games of Ireland, Gaelic football and hurling, attract a huge following, with roaring crowds cheering on their county teams. Games are held at Croke Park, the stunning, high-tech national stadium for Gaelic games, just north of the city center. For details of matches, contact the **Gaelic Athletic Association** (*GAA ⊠ Croke Park, North County Dublin* ☎ *01/836–3222* ⊕ *www.gaa.ie*).

HORSE RACING

Horse racing—from flat to hurdle to steeplechase—is one of the great sporting loves of the Irish. The sport is closely followed and betting is popular, but the social side of attending races is equally important to Dubliners. The main course in Dublin is **Leopardstown** (⊠ *Leopardstown Rd., South County Dublin* ☎ *01/289–3607* ⊕ *www.leopardstown.com*), an ultramodern course that in February hosts the Hennessey Gold Cup, Ireland's most prestigious steeplechase. Summertime is devoted to flat racing, and the rest of the year to racing over fences. You can also nip in for a quick meal at the restaurant.

The **Curragh** (⊠ *Off Exit 12 of M7 between Newbridge and Kildare Town, County Kildare* ☎ *045/441–205* ⊕ *www.curragh.ie*), southwest of Dublin off M7, hosts the five Classics, the most important flat races of the season, from May to September. There are numerous bars here and two restaurants. **Fairyhouse** (⊠ *Ratoath, County Meath* ☎ *01/825–6167* ⊕ *www.fairyhouseracecourse.ie*) hosts the Grand National, the most popular steeplechase of the season, every Easter Monday.

SHOPPING

The only known specimens of leprechauns or shillelaghs in Ireland are those in souvenir-shop windows, and shamrocks mainly bloom around the borders of Irish linen handkerchiefs and tablecloths. But in Dublin's shops you can find much more than kitschy designs. There's a tremendous variety of stores here, many of which are quite sophisticated—as a walk through Dublin's central shopping area, from O'Connell to Grafton Street, will prove. Department stores stock internationally known fashion-designer goods and housewares, and small (and often pricey) boutiques sell Irish crafts and other merchandise. Don't expect too many bargains here. And be prepared, if you're shopping in central Dublin, to push through crowds—especially in the afternoons and on weekends. Most large shops and department stores are open Monday to Saturday 9 to 6, with late hours on Thursday until 9. Although nearly all department stores are closed on Sunday, some smaller specialty shops stay open. *Those with later closing hours are noted below.* You're particularly likely to find sales in January, February, July, and August.

SHOPPING STREETS

NORTHSIDE

Henry Street, where cash-conscious Dubliners shop, runs westward from O'Connell Street. Arnotts department store is the anchor here; smaller, specialty stores sell CDs, footwear, and clothing. Henry Street's continuation, Mary Street, has a branch of Marks & Spencer and the Jervis Shopping Centre.

O'Connell Street, the city's main thoroughfare, is more downscale than Southside city streets (such as Grafton Street), but it is still worth a walk. One of Dublin's largest department stores, Clery's, is here, across from the GPO. On the same side of the street as the post office is Eason's, a large book, magazine, and stationery store.

SOUTHSIDE

Dawson Street, just east of Grafton Street between Nassau Street to the north and St. Stephen's Green to the south, is the city's primary bookstore avenue. Waterstone's and Hodges Figgis face each other from opposite sides of the street.

Francis Street and surrounding areas, such as the Coombe, have plenty of shops where you can browse. It's all part of the Liberties, the oldest part of the city and the hub of Dublin's antiques trade. If you're looking for something in particular, dealers will gladly recommend the appropriate store to you. It's also home to a couple of hot new galleries.

Grafton Street, Dublin's bustling pedestrian-only main shopping street, has two department stores: down-to-earth Marks & Spencer and *trés* chic Brown Thomas. The rest of the street is taken up by shops, many of them branches of international chains, such as the Body Shop and Bally, and many British chains. This is also the spot to buy fresh flowers, available at reasonable prices from outdoor stands. On the smaller streets off Grafton Street—especially Duke Street, South Anne Street, and Chatham Street—are worthwhile crafts, clothing, and designer housewares shops.

Nassau Street, Dublin's main tourist-oriented thoroughfare, has some of the best-known stores selling Irish goods, but you won't find many locals shopping here. Still, if you're looking for classic Irish gifts to take home, you should be sure at least to browse along here.

Temple Bar, Dublin's hippest neighborhood, is dotted with small, precious boutiques—mainly intimate, quirky shops that traffic in a small selection of trendy goods, from vintage clothes to some of the most avant-garde Irish garb anywhere in the city.

SHOPPING CENTERS

NORTHSIDE

The chq Building (✉ *IFSC, Docklands, Northside*) is the glittering, beating heart of shopping in the Docklands area. Stores include Henry Jermyn shirts, Environment Furniture, and The Pink Room shoe boutique.

Ilac Centre (✉ *Henry St., Northside*) was Dublin's first large, modern shopping center, with two department stores, hundreds of specialty shops, and several restaurants. The stores are not as exclusive as those at some of the other centers, but there's plenty of free parking.

Jervis Shopping Centre (✉ *Jervis and Mary Sts., Northside* ☎ *01/878-1323*) is a slightly high-end center housing some of the major British chain stores. It has a compact design and plenty of parking.

Shop-till-you-droppers love Grafton Street, a store-lined address custom-made for serious retail therapy.

SOUTHSIDE

Powerscourt Townhouse Centre (✉ *59 S. William St., Southside*), the former town home of Lord Powerscourt, built in 1771, has an interior court-yard that has been refurbished and roofed over; a pianist often plays on the dais at ground-floor level. Coffee shops and restaurants share space with a mix of stores selling antiques and crafts. You can also buy original Irish fashions by young designers here.

Royal Hibernian Way (✉ *Off Dawson St., between S. Anne and Duke Sts., Southside* ☎ *01/679–5919*) is on the former site of the two-century-old Royal Hibernian Hotel, a coaching inn that was demolished in 1983. The pricey, stylish shops—about 20 or 30, many selling fashionable clothes—are small in scale and include a branch of Leonidas, the Bel-gian chocolate firm.

St. Stephen's Green Centre (✉ *Northwest corner of St. Stephen's Green, Southside* ☎ *01/478–0888*), Dublin's largest and most ambitious shop-ping complex, resembles a giant greenhouse, with Victorian-style iron-work. On three floors overlooked by a giant clock, the 100 mostly small shops sell crafts, fashions, and household goods.

Westbury Mall (✉ *Westbury Hotel, off Grafton St., Southside*) is an upmarket shopping mall where you can buy designer jewelry, antique rugs, and decorative goods.

CLOSE UP

Dublin à la Mode

The success of shops like Costume and Platform has given young Irish designers the confidence to produce more original and impressive work. One of Costume's most popular designers, **Helen James,** graduated from NCAD in textile design in 1992. She went straight to New York, where she worked for Donna Karan, Club Monaco, and Victoria's Secret, among others. She returned to Ireland in 2002 and developed her line of unique, hand-printed textile accessories. Many people say there is a delicate Japanese feel to her work.

Footwear has long been an area overlooked by Irish designers, but Irishwoman **Eileen Shields** has been living and working in New York since 1988; for almost 10 years she designed footwear for Donna Karan. Her own premiere collection is all about clean, bold lines. Materials include antique kid, fine suede, python, and soft patent leather. Textures are often strongly contrasting, while colors are sensual and sophisticated. You can get the shoes online at ⊕ www.eileenshields.com, or in her store on Scarlett Row in Temple Bar.

The Tucker family has been a key player in Irish fashion since the 1960s, and new-generation **Leigh Tucker** has quickly established herself as one of Dublin's classiest young designers. Fine tailoring is her trademark—the finish on her eveningwear is nonpareil—and beaded French lace and draped jersey are her favorite materials. Her line can be found in boutiques across Ireland and at Costume in Dublin, and she's now making wedding dresses as well.

DEPARTMENT STORES

Arnotts (⊠ *Henry St., Northside* ☎ *01/805–0400*), on three floors, stocks a wide selection of clothing, household accessories, and sporting goods. It is known for matching quality with value. There is a Gap section downstairs.

★ **Brown Thomas** (⊠ *Grafton St., Southside* ☎ *01/605–6666*), Dublin's most exclusive department store, stocks the leading designer names (including some Irish designers) in clothing and cosmetics, plus lots of stylish accessories. There's also a good selection of crystal.

Clery's (⊠ *O'Connell St., Northside* ☎ *01/878–6000*), once the city's most fashionable department store, is still worth a visit. You'll find all kinds of merchandise—from clothing to home appliances—on its four floors. Note that goods sold here reflect a distinctly modest, traditional sense of style.

Debenhams (⊠ *Henry St., Northside* ☎ *01/814–7200*), the U.K. chain store, has opened in the city center and includes a Zara section along with its own clothing and homeware lines.

Dunnes Stores (⊠ *St. Stephen's Green Centre, Southside* ☎ *01/478–0188* ⊠ *Henry St., Northside* ☎ *01/872–6833* ⊠ *Ilac Center, Mary St., Northside* ☎ *01/873–0211*) is Ireland's largest chain of department stores. All of the branches stock fashion (including the exciting Savida range), household, and grocery items, and have a reputation for value and variety.

Eason's (⌧ *O'Connell St., Northside* ☏ *01/873–3811* ⌧ *Ilac Center, Mary St., Northside* ☏ *01/872–1322*) is known primarily for its large selection of books, magazines, and stationery; the larger O'Connell Street branch sells tapes, CDs, records, videos, and other audiovisual goodies.

Marks & Spencer (⌧ *Grafton St., Southside* ☏ *01/679–7855* ⌧ *Henry St., Northside* ☏ *01/872–8833*), perennial competitor to Brown Thomas, stocks everything from fashion (including lingerie) to tasty, unusual groceries. The Grafton Street branch even has its own currency exchange, which doesn't charge commission.

OUTDOOR MARKETS

Blackrock Market, held on weekends, is one of the oldest markets in the country and is a classic, eclectic assortment of bric-a-brac with rare objects, furniture, books, and just about everything else.

Cows Lane Market, held on weekends in summer at the west edge of Temple Bar, is home to some of the most innovative young fashion and accessory designers in the country.

Docklands Market, held every Thursday from 10 to 3 in the area beside the IFSC, has an eclectic selection of food, fashion, and design. It's a nice place to hang out if you want to be near the water on a sunny day.

Dublin Food Co-op is a breath of eco-friendly fresh air on the Dublin food-shopping scene. The members-run co-op has a quality food market in a wonderful old space in Newmarket at the heart of the Liberties district every Thursday and Saturday. They even encourage the use of a few words of Irish among the locals as they shop for organic veggies, flowers, cheeses, and wines. They have also just started a flea market on the last Sunday of the month.

Loft Market is a collective of some of Dublin's most progressive design talent and includes jewelry, lifestyle products, clothing, and art. It's on the top floor of Powerscourt Townhouse every Friday, Saturday, and Sunday.

Meeting House Square Market, held Saturday morning in the heart of Temple Bar, is a good place to buy homemade foodstuffs: breads, chocolate, and organic veggies.

SPECIALTY SHOPS

ANTIQUES

Dublin is one of Europe's best cities in which to buy antiques, largely due to a long and proud tradition of restoration and high-quality craftsmanship. The Liberties, Dublin's oldest district, is, fittingly, the hub of the antiques trade, and is chockablock with shops and traders. Bachelor's Walk, along the quays, also has some decent shops. It's quite a seller's market, but bargains are still possible.

Antiques Fairs Ireland (⊕ *www.antiquesfairsireland.com*) takes place monthly, in a number of Dublin hotels.

Christy Bird (⊠ *32 S. Richmond St., Dublin West* ☎ *01/475–4049*) is Dublin's oldest furniture shop and was recycling household items before anyone else dreamed of it. Besides quality Irish antiques they have a local craftsman who makes great classic reproductions to order.

O'Sullivan Antiques (⊠ *43–44 Francis St., Dublin West* ☎ *01/454–1143 or 01/453–9659*) specializes in 18th- and 19th-century furniture and has a high-profile clientele, including Mia Farrow and Liam Neeson. It even has a sister shop in New York.

BOOKS

You won't have any difficulty weighing down your suitcase with books. Ireland, after all, produced four Nobel literature laureates in just under 75 years. If you're at all interested in modern and contemporary literature, be sure to leave yourself time to browse through the bookstores, as you're likely to find books available here you can't find back home. Best of all, thanks to an enlightened national social policy, there's no tax on books, so if you buy only books, you don't have to worry about getting V.A.T. slips.

Books Upstairs (⊠ *36 College Green, Southside* ☎ *01/679–6687*) carries an excellent selection of special-interest books, including gay and feminist literature, psychology, and self-help books.

Cathach Books (⊠ *10 Duke St., Southside* ☎ *01/671–8676*) sells first editions of Irish literature and many other books of Irish interest, plus old maps of Dublin and Ireland.

Eason's/Hanna's (⊠ *29 Nassau St., Southside* ☎ *01/677–1255*) sells secondhand and mass-market paperbacks and hardcovers, and has a good selection of works on travel and Ireland.

Hodges Figgis (⊠ *56–58 Dawson St., Southeast Dublin* ☎ *01/677–4754*), Dublin's leading independent bookstore, stocks 1½ million books on three floors. There's a pleasant café on the first floor.

Hughes & Hughes (⊠ *St. Stephen's Green Centre, Southside* ☎ *01/478–3060*) has strong travel and Irish-interest sections. There's also a store at Dublin Airport.

Reads (⊠ *24–25 Nassau St., Southside* ☎ *01/679–6011*) somehow manages to sell best sellers cheaper than any of its rivals. Also, it has a decent Irish section.

Stokes (⊠ *George's Street Arcade, Southside* ☎ *01/671–3584*) is a gem of an antique bookstore with a great used-book section.

Waterstone's (⊠ *7 Dawson St., Southeast Dublin* ☎ *01/679–1415*), a large two-story branch of the British chain, features a fine selection of Irish and international books.

CHINA, CRYSTAL, CERAMICS, AND JEWELRY

Ireland is *the* place to buy Waterford crystal, which is available in a wide selection of products, including relatively inexpensive items. Other lines are now gaining recognition, such as Cavan, Galway, and Tipperary crystal.

Appleby's (✉ *Johnson's Ct., Southside* ☎ *01/679–9572*) is the best known of the several classy, old-style jewelry shops that line tiny Johnson's Court, a delightful little lane off busy Grafton Street.

Barry Doyle Design (✉ *George's Street Arcade, Southside* ☎ *01/671–2838*) is a true original with his Celtic modern jewelry. You can even watch him at work in his adjoining studio.

Blarney Woollen Mills (✉ *21–23 Nassau St., Southside* ☎ *01/671–0068*) is one of the best places for Belleek china, Waterford and Galway crystal, and Irish linen.

House of Ireland (✉ *37–38 Nassau St., Southside* ☎ *01/671–1111*) has an extensive selection of crystal, jewelry, tweeds, sweaters, and other upscale goods.

Kilkenny Shop (✉ *5–6 Nassau St., Southside* ☎ *01/677–7066*) specializes in contemporary Irish-made ceramics, pottery, and silver jewelry, and regularly holds exhibits of exciting new work by Irish craftspeople.

McDowells (✉ *3 Upper O'Connell St., Northside* ☎ *01/874–4961*), a jewelry shop popular with Dubliners, has been in business for more than 100 years.

Trinity Crafts (✉ *27 Nassau St., Southside* ☎ *01/672–5663*) is your one-stop shop for everything cheesy Irish, including "The leprechauns make me do it" mugs and Guinness-logo underwear.

Weir & Sons (✉ *96 Grafton St., Southside* ☎ *01/677–9678*), Dublin's most prestigious jeweler, sells not only jewelry and watches, but also china, glass, lamps, silver, and leather.

CLOTHING STORES

A-Wear (✉ *Grafton St., Southside* ☎ *01/872–4644*) has become something of a fashion institution for both men and women. Leading Irish designers, including John Rocha, supply A-Wear with a steady stream of exciting new looks.

BT2 (✉ *Grafton St., Southside* ☎ *01/605–6666*) is swanky Brown Thomas's impressive attempt to woo a younger crowd. Most of the major labels are present, including DKNY and Paul Smith.

Costume (✉ *10 Castel Market, Southside* ☎ *01/679–4188*) is a classy boutique where Dubliners with fashion sense and money like to shop for colorful, stylish clothes. Local designers include Leigh, Helen James, and Antonia Campbell-Hughes; Temperley and Preen are among the international designers featured.

Dolls (✉ *32 Clarendon St., Southside* ☎ *01/672–9004*), an independent boutique, likes to boast of its unusual designer pieces. Featured international designers include Karen Walker and Future Classics.

H&M (✉ *Ilac Centre, Northside* ☎ *01/872–7206*), the trendy Scandinavian clothes and accessory store, has opened in the Ilac Centre. They even do their own cosmetics line.

No. 6 (✉ *6 Castle Market, Southside* ☎ *01/670–8846*) stocks clothes, handbags, and furniture by Irish designers, including Conor Holden and Helen McAliden, along with fabrics from Foxford.

Potrero Hill (⊠ *Royal Hiberian Way, Dawson St., Southside* ☎ *01/872–7206*) pompously calls itself a "lifestyle concept" store but their stable of cool, lesser-known international designers make it a must-stop for hip shoppers.

Smock (⊠ *31 Drury St., Southside* ☎ *01/613–9000*) is a tiny designer shop with great, left-field taste. International labels include Pearson, Veronique, and A. F. Vandevoft. They also carry a beautiful line in fine jewelry.

MUSIC

Celtic Note (⊠ *12 Nassau St., Southside* ☎ *01/670–4157*) is aimed at the tourist market, with lots of compilations and greatest-hits formats.

Claddagh Records (⊠ *2 Cecilia St., Temple Bar* ☎ *01/679–3664*) has a good selection of traditional and folk music.

Gael Linn (⊠ *26 Merrion Sq., Southside* ☎ *01/676–7283*) specializes in traditional Irish music and Irish-language recordings; it's where the aficionados go.

HMV (⊠ *65 Grafton St., Southside* ☎ *01/679–5334* ⊠ *18 Henry St., Northside* ☎ *01/872–2095*) is one of the largest record shops in town.

McCullogh Piggott (⊠ *25 Suffolk St., Southside* ☎ *01/671–2410*) is the best place in town to buy instruments, sheet music, scores, and books about music.

SWEATERS AND TWEEDS

Don't think Irish woolens are limited to Aran sweaters and tweed jackets. You can choose souvenirs from a wide selection of hats, gloves, scarves, blankets, and other goods here. If you're traveling outside of Dublin, you may want to wait to make purchases elsewhere, but if Dublin is it, you still have plenty of good shops from which to choose. The tweed sold in Dublin comes from two main sources: Donegal and Connemara. Labels inside the garments guarantee their authenticity. Kilkenny Shop and House of Ireland *listed under China, Crystal, Ceramics, and Jewelry, above,* are also great places for all things woolen. The following are the other largest retailers of traditional Irish woolen goods in the city.

Avoca Handweavers (⊠ *11–13 Suffolk St., Southside* ☎ *01/677–4215*) is a beautiful store with an eclectic collection of knitwear from contemporary Irish designers. The children's wear section on the second floor is a real joy. They also stock original ceramics.

Blarney Woollen Mills (⊠ *21–23 Nassau St., Southside* ☎ *01/451–6111*) stocks a good selection of tweed, linen, and wool sweaters from their mills in County Cork, in all price ranges.

Cleo (⊠ *18 Kildare St., Southeast Dublin* ☎ *01/676–1421*) sells hand-knit sweaters and accessories made only from natural fibers; it also carries its own designs.

Kevin and Howlin (⊠ *31 Nassau St., Southside* ☎ *01/677–0257*) specializes in handwoven tweed men's jackets, suits, and hats, and also sells tweed fabric.

Monaghan's (✉ *Royal Hibernian Way, 15–17 Grafton St., Southside* ☎ *01/677–0823*) is a quality men's store that specializes in cashmere.

SIDE TRIPS: NORTH COUNTY DUBLIN

Dublin's northern suburbs remain largely residential, but there are a few places worth the trip, such as the architectural gem Marino Casino. As with most suburban areas, walking may not be the best way to get around. It's good, but not essential, to have a car. Buses and trains serve most of these areas.

MARINO CASINO

Take Malahide Rd. from Dublin's north city center for 4 km (2½ mi). Or take Bus 20A or Bus 24 to Casino from Cathal Brugha St. in north city center.

Fodor's Choice ★ One of Dublin's most exquisite, yet also most underrated, architectural landmarks, the Marino Casino (the name means "little house by the sea," and the building overlooks Dublin Harbour) is a small-scale, Palladian-style Greek temple, built between 1762 and 1771 from a plan by Sir William Chambers. Often compared to the Petit Trianon at Versailles, it was commissioned by the great Irish grandee Lord Charlemont as a summerhouse. Inside, highlights are the china-closet boudoir, the huge golden sunset in the ceiling of the main drawing room, and the signs of the zodiac in the ceiling of the bijou library. When you realize that the structure has, in fact, 16 rooms—there are bedrooms upstairs—Sir William's sleight-of-hand is readily apparent: from its exterior, the structure seems to contain only one room. It makes a good stop on the way to Malahide, Howth, or North Bull Island. ✉ *Malahide Rd., Marino, North County Dublin* ☎ *01/833–1618* ⊕ *www.heritageireland. ie* 🎫 *€3* ☙ *May–Oct., daily 10–5.*

MALAHIDE

By car, drive from north city center on R107 for 14½ km (9 mi). Or catch hourly train from Connolly Station. Or board Bus 42 to Malahide, which leaves every 15 minutes from Beresford Pl. behind Custom House.

↻ Fodor's Choice ★ Malahide is chiefly known for its glorious **Malahide Castle,** a picture-book castle occupied by the Talbot family from 1185 until 1976, when it was sold to the Dublin County Council. The great expanse of parkland around the castle has more than 5,000 different species of trees and shrubs, all clearly labeled. The castle itself combines styles and crosses centuries; the earliest section, the three-story tower house, dates from the 12th century. Hung with many family portraits, the medieval great hall is the only one in Ireland that is preserved in its original form. Authentic 18th-century pieces furnish the other rooms. Within the castle, the **Fry Model Railway Museum** houses rare, handmade models of the Irish railway and one of the world's largest miniature railway displays, which covers an area of 2,500 square feet. Tara's Palace, a dollhouse that was made to raise funds for children's charities, is also here; it has 25 rooms, all fully furnished in miniature. ✉ *10 km (6 mi) north of Howth on Coast Rd., North County Dublin* ☎ *01/846–2184* ⊕ *www.*

malahidecastle.com ✉ *Castle €7.50, castle and railway museum €11.50* ☉ *Apr.–Sept., Mon.–Sat. 10–5, Sun. 11–6; Oct.–Mar., Mon.–Sat. 10–5, Sun. 11–5.*

☾
★ One of the greatest stately homes of Ireland, **Newbridge House,** in nearby Donabate, was built between 1740 and 1760 for Charles Cobbe, Archbishop of Dublin. A showpiece in the Georgian and Regency styles, the house is less a museum than a home because the Cobbe family still resides here, part of a novel scheme the municipal government allowed when they took over the house in 1985. The sober exterior and even more sober entrance hall—all Portland stone and Welsh slate—don't prepare you for the splendor of Newbridge's Red Drawing Room, perhaps Ireland's most sumptuous 18th-century salon. Cobbe's son, Thomas, and his wife, Lady Betty Beresford, sister of the marquess of Waterford, had amassed a great collection of paintings and needed a hall in which to show them off, so they built a back wing of the house to incorporate an enormous room built for entertaining and impressing others. That it does, thanks to its crimson walls, fluted Corinthian columns, dozens of Old Masters, and glamorous Rococo-style plaster ceiling designed by the Dublin stuccadore Richard Williams. Elsewhere in the house are fascinating family heirlooms: the kitchens still have their original utensils; crafts workshops and some examples of old-style transportation, such as coaches, are in the courtyard; and there is even a Museum of Curiosities, complete with the mummified ear of an Egyptian bull and relics of Lady Betty's medical practice (her chilblain plaster became famous). Some fine paintings are left, but the greatest were sold centuries ago in order to build proper houses for the estate servants. Beyond the house's walled garden are 366 acres of parkland and a restored 18th-century animal farm. The coffee shop is renowned for the quality and selection of its homemade goods. You can travel from Malahide to Donabate by train, which takes about 10 minutes. From the Donabate train station, it's a 15-minute walk to the Newbridge House grounds. ✉ *Donabate, 8 km (5 mi) north of Malahide, signposted from N1, North County Dublin* ☎ *01/843–6534* ⊕ *www. fingalcoco.ie* ✉ *€7* ☉ *Apr.–Sept., Tues.–Sat. 10–1 and 2–5, Sun. noon–6; Oct.–Mar., weekends noon–5.*

Dublin Environs

INCLUDING COUNTIES CAVAN, DUBLIN,
KILDARE, LOUTH, MEATH, AND WICKLOW

WORD OF MOUTH

"Newgrange is a very special place. Go in the morning as there
may be no space for you later in the day. When they were
building it about 4,000 years ago they obviously knew nothing
about tourism!"

—sandylan

WELCOME TO DUBLIN ENVIRONS

TOP REASONS TO GO

★ **Newgrange in Winter:** Just standing amid these 5,000-year-old tombs (which predate the pyramids), you'll wonder: how did they build them?

★ **A Day at the Races:** The Irish may like a drink, but they really love to gamble, as you'll discover in Kildare, center of the Irish bloodstock world.

★ **Spectacular Georgian Country Houses:** Modesty never struck the rich Anglo-Irishman, whose propensity to flaunt his riches led to such over-the-top stately homes as Castletown, Russborough, and Powerscourt.

★ **Wicklow Is for Walkers:** There's no better way to meet the locals and see the land than trekking out on the 132-km-long (82-mi-long) Wicklow Way, Ireland's most popular trail.

★ **Early Morning at Glendalough:** Before the tour buses arrive, channel the spirit of the 6th-century, isolation-seeking St. Kevin.

1 The Boyne Valley. Set 48 km (30 mi) north of Dublin, this entire area is redolent with prehistoric and pagan sites. You don't have to be an Indiana Jones to be awed by the Hill of Tara or Newgrange, a Neolithic burial ground and solar observatory still evocative of the mysteries of pre-Celtic civilization.

2 County Wicklow. Set with dense woods and idyllic lakes, "the garden of Ireland" is a favorite day out for Dubliners, thanks to sylvan estates like Powerscourt and Glendalough, a 6th-century monastic site so serene you may be tempted to renounce the profane world.

3 County Kildare and West Wicklow. After visiting stately Castletown and Russborough—two monuments to Ireland's Georgian age of elegance—check out Derby Day at the Curragh racecourse. The grinning bookmakers are just waiting to take your money.

3

GETTING ORIENTED

The Dublin environs includes three main regions: County Wicklow's coast and mountains, the Boyne Valley, and County Kildare. The Boyne Valley includes much of counties Meath and Louth to the north and east of Dublin. Kildare and Wicklow are to the southeast and south of the capital. Tour this small region, or opt for day trips from Dublin, especially to the Wicklow Mountains, which rise up suddenly at the fringes of the city.

DUBLIN ENVIRONS PLANNER

Finding a Place to Stay

A lot of people opt to stay in Dublin and take day trips to the environs. If that's the case, a hotel on the south side of the city or in South County Dublin might be a good idea if you're planning to spend time in Wicklow or East Kildare. For Meath and Louth, a hotel on the north side or to the west of the city might work better. If you don't want to "commute" from the city, the noted country-house hotels around Kildare and Wicklow are a great option. They are surprisingly good value for the unique, luxurious experience they offer. Bed-and-breakfasts are another good option, and though the ones in this region tend to be a little more expensive than in other parts of Ireland, they also are a little classier and more stylish.

Transportation Basics

Driving distances to the nether reaches of this chapter from Dublin are less than two hours (in decent traffic), so the best option might be to base yourself in the city and make a couple of day trips into this region.

For example, a trip to Newgrange, Tara, and the National Stud might take up one day. Then you can head into the Wicklow Mountains to Powerscourt House and then to Glendalough on another day.

Country-house buffs can easily knock off Castletown and Russborough—two of the grandest in the land—in one afternoon.

A car is handy, of course, and gives you flexibility to get off the beaten track and explore the numerous small towns and villages of Wicklow and west Kildare.

But if you don't fancy driving on small country roads, then there are many one-day and half-day bus tours from the city that take in the major sights.

Visitor Information

For information on travel in the Dublin environs, contact one of the following Tourist Information Offices (TIOs) year-round: Dublin Tourism/Bord Fáilte, Dundalk, or Wicklow Town. In summer, temporary TIOs are open throughout the environs, in towns such as Drogheda and Dundalk in County Louth and Kildare Town in County Kildare.

This region is a puzzle quilt of many county agencies so below is a list of the main Web sites for the various counties found in this chapter. East Coast Midlands Tourism is the department of Bord Fáilte directly responsible for the Dublin environs area, and its Web site is also very useful.

Under n the town listings in the chapter, we list separate Web tourism sites for the bigger towns.

Tourism Information County Louth Tourism (⊕ www. louthholidays.com, www.countylouth.com). **County Louth Tourism** (⊕ www.louthholidays.com, www.countylouth. com). **County Kildare Tourism** (⊕ www.kildare.ie/tourism). **County Wicklow Tourism** (⊕ www.visitwicklow.ie). **East Coast Midlands Tourism** (⊕ www.eastcoastmidlands.ie).

3

Guided Tours

Bus Éireann runs guided bus tours to many of the historic and scenic locations throughout the Dublin environs daily in summer. Visits include trips to Glendalough in Wicklow; Boyne Valley and Newgrange in County Louth; and the Hill of Tara, Trim, and Navan in County Meath. All tours depart from Busaras Station, Dublin; information is available by phone Monday–Saturday 8:30–7, Sunday 10–7. Gray Line Tours, a privately owned touring company, also runs many guided bus tours throughout the Dublin environs between May and September. Their Grand Wicklow Tour lasts seven hours, as does their day trip to Newgrange and Mellifont Abbey. Prices start at €38. Wild Wicklow Tours uses minibuses that can handle smaller groups and take you off the beaten track. Their full-day trips to Glendalough also take in Avoca Handweavers and a Dublin coastal drive. Prices start at €28. Railtours Ireland has a half-day rail tour into the Wicklow Mountains. The train stops at Arklow and then a bus takes you through Avoca and on to Glendalough. The cost is €39.

Tour Information Bus Éireann (☎ 01/836–6111 ⊕ www.buseireann.ie). **Gray Line Tours** (☎ 01/670–8822 ⊕ www.grayline.com). **Wild Wicklow Tours** (☎ 01/280–1899 ⊕ www.wildwicklow.ie). **Railtours Ireland** (☎ 01/856–0045 ⊕ www.railtoursireland.com).

It's All About the Serenity

Glendalough and Newgrange really are unique places, historically and indeed spiritually. They are not sights to be rushed through with a checklist of things to see. It's all about the atmosphere, the serenity, and the silence. So, in both places give yourself plenty of time. They are also best enjoyed in relative tranquility, so try to go as early in the morning as you can and beat the crowds. Many visitors find that both places may be at their best outside the summer months.

The Great Outdoors

Wicklow is Ireland's premier walking county, with the Wicklow Way trail the central attraction. Many of Ireland's best golf courses are also in the region, with the majestic K Club in Kildare topping the list as home of the 2006 Ryder Cup. Sailing and water sports are popular all along the coast north and south of the city, with Brittas Bay north of Arklow a favorite beach and Carlingford Loch east of Dundalk a center for water sports. Lessons and equipment are usually available at each location, for a price, of course. The Boyne, Liffey, and many smaller rivers and lakes make the area perfect for coarse and salmon fishing. Tackle and boats are usually rentable nearby.

When to Go

While certainly not the wettest part of Ireland (the West gets that dubious distinction), the counties around Dublin do get their fair share of rain. June, July, August, and September tend to be the driest months, and the good news is that the rain in the region in summer is usually light and short-lived. Wicklow, with all its hills and valleys, seems to have an obscure microclimate of its own, so don't rely too much on the weatherman to get it right.

DINING AND LODGING PRICE CATEGORIES (IN EUROS)

	¢	$	$$	$$$	$$$$
Restaurants	under €12	€12–€18	€19–€24	€25–€32	over €32
Hotels	under €80	€80–€120	€121–€170	€171–€210	over €210

Restaurant prices are for a main course at dinner. Hotel prices are for a standard double room in high season.

GETTING AROUND

Train Travel

Irish Rail (Iarnród Éireann) trains run the length of the east coast. Their lines extend from Dundalk to the north in County Louth to Arklow along the coast in County Wicklow.

Trains make many stops along the way. Top stations along the coastal route include Drogheda, Dublin (the main stations are Connolly Station and Pearse Station), Bray, Greystones, Wicklow, and Rathdrum.

From Heuston Station, the Arrow, a commuter train service, runs westward to Celbridge, Naas, Newbridge, and Kildare Town.

Contact Irish Rail for schedule and fare information.

Stations in Dublin include Connolly Station (on Amiens St.), Heuston Station (Victoria Quay and St. John's Rd. W), and Pearse Station (Westland Row).

Train Information **Irish Rail–Iarnod Éireann** (☏ 01/836–6222 in Dublin, 041/983–8749 in Drogheda ⊕ www.irishrail.ie).

Bus Travel

Bus services link Dublin with the main and smaller towns in the area. All buses for the region depart from Dublin's Busaras, the central bus station, at Store Street. For bus inquiries, contact Bus Éireann. You can reach Enniskerry and the Powerscourt Estate by taking Dublin Bus No. 44 from the Dublin quays area. The No. 45 and No. 45a head to Bray and the No. 84 goes to Greystones from near Merrion Square. St. Kevin's, a private bus service, runs daily from Dublin (outside the Royal College of Surgeons on St. Stephen's Green) to Glendalough, stopping off at Bray, Kilmacanogue, Roundwood, and Laragh en route. Buses leave Dublin daily at 11:30 AM and 6 PM (7 PM on weekends from March to September); buses leave Glendalough weekdays at 7:15 AM and 4:30 PM (9:45 AM and 5:40 PM on weekends from March to September). One-way fare is €13; a round-trip ticket costs €20.

Bus Information **Bus Éireann** (☏ 01/836–6111 ⊕ www.buseireann.ie). **Dublin Bus** (☏ 01/873–4222 ⊕ www.dublinbus.ie). **St. Kevin's** (☏ 01/281–8119 ⊕ www.glendaloughbus.com).

Car Travel

The easiest and best way to tour Dublin's environs is by car, because many sights are not served by public transportation, and what service there is, especially to outlying areas, is infrequent. To visit destinations in the Boyne Valley, follow N3, along the east side of Phoenix Park, out of the city and make Trim and Tara your first stops. Alternatively, leave Dublin via N1/M1 toward Belfast. To reach destinations in County Kildare, follow the quays along the south side of the River Liffey (they are one-way westbound) to St. John's Road West (N7/M7); in a matter of minutes, you're heading for open countryside. Avoid traveling this route during the evening peak rush hours, especially on Friday, when Dubliners are themselves making their weekend getaways. To reach destinations in County Wicklow, N11/M11 is the fastest and most clearly marked route. The two more scenic routes to Glendalough are R115 to R759 to R755, or R177 to R755.

3

Updated by
Anto Howard

Walt Disney himself couldn't have planned it better. The small counties immediately north, south, and west of Dublin—historically known as the Pale—seem expressly designed to entertain and enchant the sightseer. The entire region is layer-cake rich with legendary Celtic sites, gorgeous gardens, and the most elegant Palladian country estates in Ireland.

Due to its location on the Irish Sea, facing Europe, the region was the first to attract the earliest "tourists"—conquerors and rulers—and the first over which they exercised the greatest influence. Traces of each new wave remain: the Celts chose Tara as the center of their kingdom; the Danes sailed the rivers Boyne and Liffey to establish many of today's towns; and the region's great Protestant-built houses of the 18th century remind us that the Pale (originally the Pale referred to the area of eastern Ireland ruled directly by the Normans) was the starting point and administrative center for the long, violent English colonization of the whole island.

The Dublin environs include three basic geographical regions: County Wicklow's coast and mountains, the Boyne Valley, and County Kildare. Lying tantalizingly close to the south of Dublin is the mountainous county of Wicklow, which contains some of the most *et-in-Arcadia-ego* scenery in the Emerald Isle. Here, the gently rounded Wicklow Mountains—to some, they are Ireland's finest—contain the evocative monastic settlement at Glendalough, many later abbeys and churches, and scores of the most beguiling attractions for the art lover: the great 18th-century estates of the Anglo-Irish aristocracy, whose reigning lords and ladies, prone to a certain sense of inferiority, were determined not to be outdone by the extravagant efforts of their English compatriots. The result was a string of spectacular stately home extravaganzas, such as Castletown, Powerscourt, and Russborough.

IRELAND'S HISTORIC HEART

Stone Age, Celtic, Early Christian, and Norman: the country is scattered with sites that act as signposts in the long and twisting story called "Ireland." But by circumstance of geography and mystical significance many of the great stone ghosts to ancient Ireland are concentrated in the counties immediately surrounding Dublin.

(top) Newgrange is a spectacular passage tomb; (right, top) The Stone of Destiny is a powerful spiritual center found on the Hill of Tara; (right, bottom) Graves and High Crosses hallow the grounds of Glendalough

Here, often so closely thrown together as to make an almost Disneyesque mockery of the vastness of time and history, stand the man-made wonders that are impressive but slightly melancholic reminders of more heroic and more savage ages. In fact, a tour down the valley of the River Boyne is a trip into the past, back beyond history, to the Neolithic tombs of Newgrange, the druidic holy place of the Hill of Tara, the monasteries of Early Christianity, and the Norman castles of the chain-mailed invader who brought a bloody end to so much of Celtic Ireland. Not far from Dublin, chart the rise and fall of Irish culture at their glorious monuments.

THE HIGH CROSS

The Celtic High Cross is an endearing symbol of Ireland, and Monasterboice—a former monastic settlement—has more of them than anywhere in Ireland. Dating to AD 923, the twenty-foot-high Muireadach Cross is the best preserved, as its panels depicting the slaying of Abel, David and Goliath, and the Last Judgement prove. The nearby 110-foot round tower gives you a view of the once-glorious monastic site.

NEWGRANGE

Built in the fourth millennium BC, a thousand years before Stonehenge, Newgrange is not only one of the world's pristine surviving passage tombs but also a great granite reminder of the ingenuity, spirituality, and perseverance of modern Ireland's Neolithic ancestors.

How did they move 250,000 tons of stone? How did they align it to perfectly capture the first rays of the dawn sun on the winter solstice? The thrill of visiting and entering the somber tomb at Newgrange lies not only in what you discover but in the awesome mysteries that can only be answered by the imagination.

GLENDALOUGH

A single early morning hour spent in the isolated and serene Glendalough valley—green jewel set admidst the Wicklow Mountains—should be enough to convince you St. Kevin the monk made the perfect choice when he was searching for sixth century solitude and peace.

The simplicity, separation, and sparsness that were at the heart of Early Christianity in Ireland is sublimely apparent in the hermit's cave called St. Kevin's Bed and the ruins of the tiny Church of the Oratory.

HILL OF TARA

Visitors are sometimes disappointed when they finally see the mythical Hill of

Tara, spiritual and regal heart of Celtic and druidic Ireland. It is now just a hill after all—300-feet-high with awesome views out over the flat central plains of Ireland and all the way to Galway in the west. But with a little reading at the interpretive center and a lot of imagination you can stand here and picture the Iron Age fort that once stood here and the huge *feis* or national assembly where Celtic Ireland passed its laws and settled its tribal disputes. It is a place that is both beyond history and made of it.

MELLIFONT ABBEY

As well as war, the Normans brought great stone church building to Ireland and one of their greatest religious monuments is Mellifont Abbey. Founded in 1142 Celtic-Ireland by St. Malachy, the main parts of the abbey were built a little later in the Norman style, including the two story chapter house and the octagonal Lavabo, where the monks used to wash.

Although much of the abbey is in ruins, it still manages to illustrate the medieval church's rise to wealth and power in Ireland. Incidentally, the term "Celtic" is derived from the tribes that arrived on Irish shores around 700 BC, first called Galli by the Romans and then named Gaels in Ireland.

North of Dublin lies the Boyne Valley, with its abundant ruins of Celtic Ireland extending from counties Meath to Louth. Some of the country's most evocative Neolithic ruins—including the famous passage graves at Newgrange—are nestled into this landscape, where layer upon layer of history reach back into earlier, unknowable ages. It was west of Drogheda—a fascinating town settled by the Vikings in the early 10th century—that the Tuatha De Danann, onetime residents of Ireland, went underground when defeated by invading Milesians and became, it's said, "the good people" (or fairies) of Irish legend. In pagan times this area was the home of Ireland's high kings, and the center of religious life. All roads led to Tara, the fabled Hill of Kings, the royal seat, and the place where the national assembly was held. Today, time seems to stand still—and you should, too, for it's almost sacrilegious to introduce a note of urgency here.

Southwest of Dublin are the flat pastoral plains of County Kildare; the plains stretch between the western Midlands and the foothills of the Dublin and Wicklow mountains—both names actually refer to the same mountain range, but each marks its county's claim to the land. Kildare is the flattest part of Ireland, a natural playing field for breeding, training, and racing some of the world's premier Thoroughbreds.

Rapid, omnivorous expansion of the capital city in the decade of the Celtic Tiger saw its suburban limits spread deep into the once bucolic areas of Meath and Kildare, and the natives of these areas feared that their more rural way of life was under threat. Don't be surprised to hear Dublin accents starting to dominate in towns like Navan and Naas. But the new prosperity also meant the local young men and women no longer had to head off up to "the big smoke" of Dublin or even farther afield to find work, and the counties of the Pale saw their populations rise for the first time in decades. These days, however, the recent economic slowdown and a slump in property values have disproportionately hit these satellite towns and areas so dependent on the economy of Dublin.

THE BOYNE VALLEY

For every wistful schoolboy in Ireland the River Boyne is a name that resonates with history and adventure. It was on the banks of that river in 1014 that the Celtic chieftain Brian Boru defeated the Danish in a decisive battle that returned the east of Ireland to native rule. It was also by this river that Protestant William of Orange defeated the Catholic armies of exiled James II of England, in 1690. In fact, this whole area, only 48 km (30 mi) north of cosmopolitan Dublin, is soaked in stories and legends that predate the pyramids. You can't throw a stick anywhere in the valley without hitting some trace of Irish history. The great prehistoric, pagan, and Celtic monuments of the wide arc of fertile land known as the Boyne Valley invariably evoke a sense of wonder. You don't have to be an archaeologist to be awed by Newgrange and Knowth—set beside the River Boyne—or the Hill of Tara, Mellifont Abbey, or the High Cross of Monasterboice. One way to approach exploring this area is to start at the town of Trim, the locale closest to Dublin, and work your way

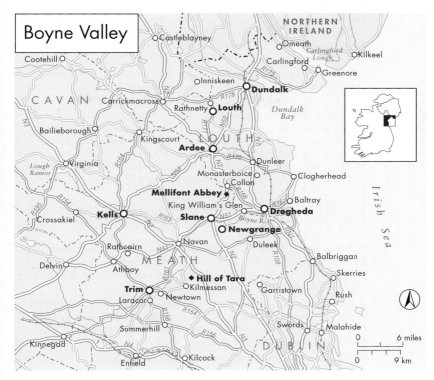

Boyne Valley

north. Keep in mind that Omeath and the scenic Cooley Peninsula at the end of this section are on the border of Northern Ireland.

TRIM

51 km (32 mi) northwest of Dublin via N3 to R154.

The heritage town of Trim, on the River Boyne, contains some of the finest medieval ruins in Ireland. In 1359, on the instructions of King Edward III, the town was walled and its fortifications were strengthened. In the 15th century several parliaments were held here. Oliver Cromwell massacred most of its inhabitants when he captured the town in 1649.

Visitor Information Trim Tourist Office (✉ *Old Town Hall, Castle St.* ☎ *046/943-7227* ⊕ *www.meath.ie*).

EXPLORING

Trim Castle, the largest Anglo-Norman fortress in Ireland, dominates present-day Trim from its 2½-acre site, which slopes down to the river's placid waters. Built by Hugh de Lacy in 1173, the castle was soon destroyed, and then rebuilt from 1190 to 1220. The ruins include an enormous keep with 70-foot-high turrets flanked by rectangular towers. The outer castle wall is almost 500 yards long, and five D-shaped towers survive. So impressive is the castle that it was used as a medieval backdrop in Mel

Gibson's movie *Braveheart*. The admission price includes a house tour. ✉ *Trim* ☎ *046/943–8619* ⊕ *www.heritageireland.ie* 🖾 *Keep and grounds €4, grounds only €3* ☉ *Easter–Sept., daily 10–6; Oct. daily 9:30–5:30; Nov.–Jan. weekends 9–5; Feb.–Easter, weekends 9:30–5:30.*

Facing the river is the **Royal Mint**, a ruin that illustrates Trim's political importance in the Middle Ages. It produced coins with colorful names like "Irelands" and "Patricks" right up into the 15th century.

The **Yellow Steeple** overlooks Trim from a ridge situated opposite the castle. The structure was built in 1368 and is a remnant of the Augustinian abbey of St. Mary's, founded in the 13th century, which itself was the site of a great medieval pilgrimage to a statue of the Blessed Virgin. Much of the tower was deliberately destroyed in 1649 to prevent its falling into Cromwell's hands, and today only the striking, 125-foot-high east wall remains.

The Church of Ireland **St. Patrick's Cathedral** (✉ *Loman St.*) dates from early in the 19th century, but the square tower is from an earlier structure built in 1449.

In the old town hall, the **Visitor Center**'s audiovisual display, "The Power and the Glory," tells the story of the arrival of the Normans and of medieval Trim. ✉ *Castle St.* ☎ *046/943–7227* ⊕ *www.meathtourism.ie* 🖾 *€3.20 for audiovisual show* ☉ *Mon.–Sat. 9:30–5:30, Sun. noon–5:30.*

If your ancestors are from County Meath, take advantage of the family-history tracing service at the **Meath Heritage and Genealogy Center.** ✉ *Castle St.* ☎ *046/943–6633* ⊕ *www.meathroots.com* 🖾 *Free* ☉ *Mon.–Thurs. 9–1 and 1:30–5, Fri. 9–2.*

At **Newtown**, 1¼ km (¾ mi) east of Trim on the banks of the River Boyne, are the ruins of what was once the largest cathedral in Ireland, built beginning in 1210 by Simon de Rochfort, the first Anglo-Norman bishop of Meath.

At **Laracor**, 3 km (2 mi) south of Trim on R158, a wall to the left of the rectory is where Jonathan Swift (1667–1745), the satirical writer, poet, and author of *Gulliver's Travels*, was rector from 1699 until 1713, when he was made dean of St. Patrick's Cathedral in Dublin. Nearby are the walls of the cottage where Esther Johnson, the "Stella" who inspired much of Swift's writings, once lived.

One of the most pleasant villages of south County Meath, **Summerhill**, 8 km (5 mi) southeast of Laracor along R158, has a large square and a village green with a 15th-century cross.

Cnoc an Linsigh, an attractive area south of Summerhill with forest walks and picnic sites, is ideal for a half day of meandering. Many of the lanes that crisscross this part of County Meath provide delightful driving between high hedgerows, and afford occasional views of the lush, pastoral countryside.

WHERE TO STAY

¢–$ 🏠 **Tigh Catháin.** The "House of O'Catháin" is a Tudor-style country cottage about 1 km (½ mi) outside of town on the Longwood road. Owner Marie Keane has artfully decorated the four large bedrooms in different color schemes echoing the natural colors of the region. But the real wonders here are the lovely gardens out back and in front, perfect for lounging around in the sun. Family rooms include a double and two single beds. **Pros:** family-owned and -run; big, hearty breakfast; glorious gardens. **Cons:** small and often booked up; half a mile to nearest town; few facilities. ⊠ *High St., Co. Meath* ☎ *046/943–1996* ⊕ *www.tighcathaintrim.com* ⇨ *4 rooms* ⌂ *In-room: a/c, Wi-Fi. In-hotel: Wi-Fi hotspot, parking (free)* ❰❑❱ *BP.*

HILL OF TARA

8 km (5 mi) northeast of Trim, 40 km (25 mi) northwest off N3.

In the legends and the popular imagination of the Irish this ancient site has taken on mythic proportions. As with much of the idealization of the Celtic past, it was the 19th-century revival led by W. B. Yeats and Lady Gregory that was responsible for the near-religious veneration of this Celtic site, set at the junction of the five ancient roads of Ireland, and known in popular folklore as the seat of the High Kings of Ireland. The 19th-century ballad by Thomas Moore, "The Harp That Once Through Tara's Halls," was also a major factor in the long over-romanticized view of Tara. Today, its ancestral banqueting hall and great buildings (one was the former palace of the Ard Rí, or High King) have all vanished but for a few columns. Still, the site is awe-inspiring.

GETTING HERE

BUS TRAVEL Bus Éireann has regular service linking Dublin and Navan that passes within 1 km (2 mi) of the site (€10.30 one-way, €13.70 round-trip; 40 minutes; departures every hour Monday to Saturday and a day on Sunday). Ask the driver to drop you at the Tara Cross and follow the signs. Alternatively you can take the bus all the way to Navan and get a taxi the 7 mi back to Tara for about €15. Mary Gibbons Tours has buses leaving weekdays at 10:30 AM and Saturdays at 8:30 AM from outside the Dublin Tourism office on Suffolk Street as well as from some of the major hotels. They charge €35, which includes a round-trip ticket and admission to the Hill of Tara and Newgrange.

ESSENTIALS

Transportation Contacts Mary Gibbons Tours (☎ *086/335–1355* ⊕ *www.newgrangetours.com*).

EXPLORING

From the top of the Hill of Tara—it rises more than 300 feet above sea level—you can see across the flat central plain of Ireland, with the mountains of east Galway visible from nearly 160 km (100 mi) away. In the mid-19th century, the nationalist leader Daniel O'Connell staged a mass rally here that supposedly drew more than a million people—which would be nearly a third of Ireland's current population. On-site, first pay a call on the Interpretative Center housed in an old Church of Ireland church on the hillside. Here, you can learn the story of Tara and its legends. Without this background it will be difficult to identify many of the earthworks at Tara. Or just call upon your imagination to evoke the millennia-old spirit of the place and picture it in its prime, with the tribes congregating for some great pagan ceremony.

Systematic excavation by 20th-century archaeologists has led to the conclusion that the largest remains are those of an Iron Age fort that had multiple ring forts, some of which were ruined in the 19th century by religious zealots from England searching for the Ark of the Covenant here. The "Mound of the Hostages," a Neolithic passage grave, most likely gave the place its sacred air. During the hill's reign as a royal seat, which lasted to the 11th century, a great *feis* (national assembly) was held here every third year, during which laws were passed and tribal disputes settled. Tara's influence waned with the arrival of Christianity; the last king to live here was Malachy II, who died in 1022. But as with so many other prominent sites of the Irish pre-Christian era, Christianity remade Tara in its own image. Today a modern statue of St. Patrick stands here, as does a pillar stone that may have been the coronation stone (it was reputed to call out in approval when a king was crowned). In the graveyard of the adjacent Anglican church is a pillar with the worn image of a pagan god, and a Bronze Age stone standing on end. By car, the Hill of Tara is just off the N3, the main road between Dublin and Cavan, 47 km (29 mi), or about 40 minutes, north of the capital. From Belfast take the M1 and connect with the N51 at Drogheda. The trip is 158 km (98 mi) and takes about an hour and thirty minutes. ⊠ *Hill of Tara* ☎ *046/902–5903* ⊕ *www. heritageireland.ie* ◻ *€3* ☉ *May 28—Sept. 16, daily 10–6.*

> **FIRES OF FAITH**
>
> The Hill of Tara's decline was predicted one Easter Eve in the 5th century when, in accordance with the Druid religion, the lighting of fires was forbidden. Suddenly, on a hillside some miles away, flames were spotted. "If that fire is not quenched now," said a Druid leader, "it will burn forever and will consume Tara." The fire had been lighted by St. Patrick at Slane, to celebrate the Christian rites of the Paschal.

WHERE TO EAT AND STAY

$$

MODERN IRISH

✕ **Eden.** One of Dublin's endearingly favorite, chic restaurants has set up a second home in the vaulted cellar of Bellinter House. The restaurant sticks to its seasonal ethos with menus based on produce sourced locally. Boxty (potato-cake) salad is an interesting twist on a traditional starter, and the oven-baked whole sea bream filled with lemongrass on bok choy is an exciting main. ⊠ *Bellinter House, Navan (4 km [2 mi] northwest of Hill of Tara and 7 km [5 mi] south of Navan)* ☎ *046/903–0909* ⊕ *www.bellinterhouse.com* ◿ *Reservations essential* ▭ *AE, MC, V.*

$$$–$$$$

Fodor'sChoice

★

▥ **Bellinter House.** Surrounded by 12 acres on the banks of the Boyne, this splendid 1750 country house was once the home of the infamously wild, party-loving Briscoe clan (their high jinks once included a crazy dig for the Ark of the Covenant on the nearby Hill of Tara). The new owners have brought back the old glories of the place, and added a few modern twists: an infinity pool now graces the landscape, and contemporary lighting, handmade ash-wood furniture, and futuristic art installations mix easily with the drawing room's 18th-century decorative plasterwork. While new rooms have been constructed in the old pavilion wings and the stables have been turned into cute, compact modern apartments, the four original massive bedrooms in the main house are the real Georgian gems of Bellinter. Their huge windows allow light to play across the wood-panel walls and deep yellow rugs. Beautiful indoor and outdoor pools plus a large on-site spa with numerous treatments ensure maximum luxury. **Pros:** stunningly authentic four original rooms; serene infinity pool; great value since prices dropped. **Cons:** newer rooms not quite up to old house standard; staff can be a little inexperienced. ⊠ *Navan (7 km [4½ mi] south of Navan and 4 km [2½ mi] northwest of Hill of Tara), Co. Meath* ☎ *046/903–0900* ⊕ *www.bellinterhouse.com* ⇱ *34 rooms* ⌂ *In-room: a/c, safe, refrigerator, Wi-Fi. In-hotel: restaurant, bar, pools, spa, Wi-Fi hotspot* ▭ *AE, MC, V* ⦶ *BP.*

3

KELLS

24 km (15 mi) northwest of Navan on N3.

In the 9th century, a group of monks from Iona in Scotland took refuge at Kells (Ceanannus Mór) after being expelled by the Danes. St. Columba had founded a monastery here 300 years earlier, and although some historians think it was indigenous monks who wrote and illustrated the *Book of Kells*—the Latin version of the four Gospels, and one of Ireland's greatest medieval treasures—most scholars now believe that the Scottish monks brought it with them. Reputed to have been fished out of a watery bog at Kells, the legendary manuscript was removed for safekeeping during the Cromwellian wars to Trinity College, Dublin, where it remains. A large exhibit is now devoted to it in the college's Old Library, where a few of the original pages at a time are on view.

A copy of the *Book of Kells* is on display in the Church of Ireland **St. Columba's** in Kells; it's open until 5 on weekdays and until 1 on Saturday and is a more pleasant, less rushed way to see the book compared with the madness of Trinity College in high season. Four elaborately carved High Crosses stand in the church graveyard; you'll find the stump of a fifth in the marketplace—during the 1798 uprising against British rule it was used as a gallows.

Similar in appearance to St. Kevin's Church at Glendalough and Cormac's Chapel at Cashel, **St. Colmcille's House** is a small, two-story, 7th-century church measuring about 24 feet square and nearly 40 feet high, with a steeply pitched stone roof.

The nearly 100-foot-high **round tower,** adjacent to St. Colmcille's House, dates to before 1076 and is in almost perfect condition. Its top story has five windows, each facing an ancient entrance into the medieval town. For further information about Kells, see the sponsored Web site: ⊕ *www.meath.ie.*

NEWGRANGE

Fodor'sChoice
★

21 km (13 mi) east of Kells off N51, 28 km (17 mi) northwest of Dublin off N2.

GETTING HERE

BUS TRAVEL   Bus Éireann Route 163 from Dublin to Drogheda stops at Newgrange (€12 round-trip from Dublin, €4.80 from Drogheda; departures on the hour from 10 AM to 6 PM daily. Mary Gibbons Tours has buses leaving weekdays at 10:30 AM and Saturdays at 8:30 AM from outside the Dublin Tourism office on Suffolk Street as well as some of the major hotels. They charge €35 which includes a round trip ticket and admission to the Hill of Tara and Newgrange. Over The Top Tours runs a daily shuttle bus from Dublin to Newgrange from the Gresham Hotel on O'Connell Street daily at 8:45 and 11:15 AM. It's €17 round-trip.

> **LET THERE BE A LIGHT SHOW**
>
> A visit to Newgrange's passage grave during the winter solstice is considered to be a memorable experience. You'll have to get on the nine-year waiting list to reserve one of the 24 places available on each of the five mornings (December 19–23). And then pray that no clouds obscure the sun and ruin the light show the Bronze Age builders intended.

ESSENTIALS

Transportation Contacts Mary Gibbons Tours (☎ 086/335–1355 ⊕ www.newgrangetours.com). **Over the Top Tours** (☎ 01/860–0404 ⊕ www.overthetoptours.com).

Visitor Information Brú na Bóinne Visitor Centre (✉ *Near Donore village, Co. Meath [21 km/ 13 mi east of Kells off the N51 and 28 km/17 mi northwest of Dublin on the N2]* ⊕ www.heritageireland.ie/en/MidlandsEastCoast). The Brú na Bóinne Visitor Centre is near the village of Donore, County Meath, and is the starting point for all visits to and tours of Newgrange and Knowth.

EXPLORING

How the people who built the Newgrange tumulus transported the stones to the spot remains a mystery. The mound above the tomb measures more than 330 feet across and reaches a height of 36 feet at the front. White quartz stone was used for the retaining wall, and egg-shaped gray stones were studded at intervals. The passage grave may have been the world's earliest solar observatory. It was so carefully constructed that, for five days on and around the winter solstice, the rays of the rising sun still hit a roof box above the lintel at the entrance to the grave. The rays then shine for about 20 minutes down the main interior passageway to illuminate the burial chamber. The site was restored in 1962 after years of neglect and quarrying. The geometric designs on some stones at the center of the burial chamber continue to baffle experts.

The prehistoric sites of nearby Dowth and Knowth have been under excavation since 1962, and although Dowth is still closed to the public, **Knowth** is now open. The great tumulus at Knowth is comparable in size and shape to Newgrange, standing at 40 feet and having a diameter of approximately 214 feet. Some 150 giant stones, many of them beautifully decorated, surrounded the mound. More than 1,600 boulders,

Built between 3100 and 2900 BC, Newgrange is strikingly adorned with boulders carved with Neolithic triple spirals and diamonds.

each weighing from one to several tons, were used in the construction. The earliest tombs and carved stones date from the Stone Age (3000 BC), although the site was in use until the early 14th century. In the early Christian era (4th–8th century AD) it was the seat of the High Kings of Ireland. Much of the site is still under excavation, and you can often watch archaeologists at work here. Access to Newgrange and Knowth is solely via **Brú na Bóinne** (Palace of the Boyne), the Boyne Valley visitor center. Arrive early if possible, because you can't book ahead of time and Newgrange often sells out in high season. The last tour leaves the visitor center 1 hour and 45 minutes before closing. ⊠ *Off N2, signposted from Slane, Donore* ☎ *041/988–0300* ⊕ *www.heritageireland. ie* ⊠ *Newgrange and interpretive center €6, Knowth and interpretive center €5* ☾ *Newgrange and Knowth Nov.–Jan., daily 9–5; Feb.–Apr. and Oct., daily 9:30–5:30; May, daily 9–6:30; June–mid-Sept., daily 9–7; mid- to late Sept., daily 9–6:30.*

SLANE

2½ km (1½ mi) north of Newgrange, 46 km (29 mi) northwest of Dublin on N2.

Slane Castle is the draw at this small, Georgian village, built in the 18th century around a crossroads on the north side of the River Boyne. For further information about Slane, see the sponsored Web site: ⊕ *www. slanetourism.ie.*

The 16th-century building known as the **Hermitage** was constructed on the site where St. Erc, a local man converted to Christianity by St.

Patrick himself, led a hermit's existence. All that remains of his original monastery is the faint trace of the circular ditch, but the ruins of the later church include a nave and a chancel with a tower in between.

The stately 18th-century **Slane Castle** is beautifully situated overlooking a natural amphitheater. In 1981 the castle's owner, Anglo-Irish Lord Henry Mountcharles, staged the first of what have been some of Ire-

land's largest outdoor rock concerts; REM's show holds the record for attendance, with 70,000. In 2001, after a decade of renovation following a devastating fire, the castle reopened to the public. The tour includes the main hall, with its delicate plasterwork and beautiful stained glass, the dazzling red, neo-Gothic ballroom completed in 1821 for the visit of King George IV, and other rooms. The stunning parklands were laid out by Capability Brown, the famous 18th-century landscape gardener. ☎ 041/988–4400 ⊕ www.slanecastle.ie 🖾 €7 ⊗ Mid-May–June 10 and June 20–Aug. 31, Sun.–Thurs. noon–5.

North of Slane town is the 500-foot-high **Slane Hill,** where St. Patrick proclaimed the arrival of Christianity in 433 by lighting the Paschal Fire. From the top, you have sweeping views of the Boyne Valley. On a clear day, the panorama stretches from Trim to Drogheda, a vista extending 40 km (25 mi).

☺ A two-hour tour of farmer Willie Redhouse's fully functioning arable and livestock **Newgrange Farm** includes feeding the ducks, bottle-feeding the lambs, a tour of the aviaries with their exotic birds, and a straw maze for the kids. A blacksmith gives demonstrations of his ancient art, and there is a nice tractor-trailer ride around the farm. Every Sunday at 3 PM the Sheep Derby takes place, with teddy bears tied astride the animals in the place of jockeys. Visiting children are made "owners" of individual sheep for the duration of the race. The farm lies 3 km (2 mi) east of Slane on N51. ☎ 041/982–4119 ⊕ www.newgrangefarm. com 🖾 €8 ⊗ Easter–Aug., daily 10–5.

WHERE TO STAY

$$$–$$$$
Fodor's Choice
★

🔆 **Tankardstown House.** Voted the best private house hotel in Ireland in a national newspaper, Tankardstown is a sumptuous historic manor house 3 km (2 mi) from Slane. A squat, two-story manor, Tankardstown sits on 80 acres of breathtaking parkland, sheltered by a forested hill, and surrounded by a classic walled garden. Owners Trish and Brian Conroy spent four years lovingly restoring this Georgian delight from a state of absolute disrepair. No expense was spared on the six guest rooms nor the seven courtyard cottages, to create a tasteful homage to the age of cascading drapes, delicate plasterwork ceilings, and Sheraton-style antiques. On site is the Brabazon restaurant; located in the old cowshed, it offers great outdoor dining options in summer and an intimate, romantic dining room for the chillier times of year. **Pros:**

authentic Georgian exterior and interiors; idyllic natural setting; cottages a great option for families. **Cons:** not cheap in the current climate; limited facilities for the price. ⊠ *Slane (2.5 km [1 mi] from the gates of Slane Castle), Co. Meath* ☎ *041/982–4621* ⊕ *www.tankardstown.ie* ⏎ *6 rooms, 1 suite, 7 cottages* △ *In-room: no a/c, Wi-Fi (cottages only). In-hotel: restaurant, Wi-Fi hotspot* ▤ *AE, MC, V* ⦿| *BP.*

DROGHEDA

3

15½ km (9 mi) east of Slane on N51, 45 km (28 mi) north of Dublin on N1.

Drogheda (pronounced draw-*hee*-da) is one of the most enjoyable and historic towns on the east coast of Ireland—and a setting for one of the most tragic events in Irish history, the seige and massacre wrought by Oliver Cromwell's English army. It was colonized in 911 by the Danish Vikings; two centuries later, the town was taken over by Hugh de Lacy, the Anglo-Norman lord of Trim, who was responsible for fortifying the towns along the River Boyne. At first, two separate towns existed, one on the northern bank, the other on the southern bank. In 1412, already heavily walled and fortified, Drogheda was unified, making it the largest English town in Ireland. Today, large 18th-century warehouses line the northern bank of the Boyne. The center of town, around West Street, is the historic heart of Drogheda.

GETTING HERE

BUS TRAVEL Drogheda's bus station is just south of the river on the corner of John Street and Donore Road. Bus Éireann operates Expressway and regular services connecting Drogheda to Dublin (€5.40 one-way, €9 round-trip; 40 minutes; buses daily every hour); to Belfast (€14 one-way, €20 round-trip; 1 hour 30 minutes; 12 buses daily); to Dundalk (€4.50 one-way, €9 round-trip; 30 minutes; 12 buses daily); and to Navan (€6.20 one-way, €10.20 round-trip; 40 minutes; 7 buses daily). The train station is just south of the river and east of the town center on the Dublin Road. Five express trains and 10 slower trains a day arrive from Hueston Station in Dublin (€18 round-trip, 51 minutes [express], 15 trains a day). Drogheda is connected to Belfast (€10 single, €20 round-trip; 1 hour 40 minutes; 7 trains a day) and Dundalk (20 minutes, 13 trains daily) on the same line.

TRAIN TRAVEL Serviced by Irish Rail, Drogheda's train station is just south of the river and east of the town center on the Dublin Road. Five express trains and 10 slower trains a day arrive from Hueston Station in Dublin (€18 round-trip, 51 minutes [express], 15 trains a day). Drogheda is connected to Belfast (€10 single, €20 round-trip; 1 hour 40 minutes; 7 trains a day) and Dundalk (20 minutes, 13 trains daily) on the same line.

Visitor Information Drogheda Tourist Office. (⊠ *Bus Éireann Depot* ☎ *041/983–7070* ⊕ *www.drogheda.ie*).

EXPLORING

The center of town, around West Street, is the historic heart of Drogheda. Among the town's leading landmarks is the long **railway viaduct**, which towers over the river. Built around 1850 as part of the railway line from Dublin to Belfast, it's still used and is a splendid example of Victorian engineering. Its height above the river makes the viaduct Drogheda's most prominent landmark.

The bank building on the corner of West and Shop streets, called the **Tholsel,** is an 18th-century square granite edifice with a cupola.

The 13th-century **St. Laurence's Gate,** one of the two surviving entrances from Drogheda's original 11 gates in its town walls, has two four-story drum towers and is one of the most perfect examples in Ireland of a medieval town gate. **Butler's Gate,** near the Millmount Museum, predates St. Laurence's Gate by 50 years or more.

The Gothic-Revival Roman Catholic **St. Peter's Church** (⊠ *West St.*) houses the preserved head of St. Oliver Plunkett. Primate of all Ireland, he was martyred in 1681 at Tyburn in London; his head was pulled from the execution flames.

A severe, 18th-century church within an enclosed courtyard, the Anglican **St. Peter's** (⊠ *Fair St.*) is rarely open except for Sunday services. It's worth a peek for its setting and the fine views over the town from the churchyard.

Perhaps the main attraction in Drogheda lies across the river from the town center. The **Millmount Museum and Martello Tower,** off the Dublin road (N1) south of Drogheda, shares space in a renovated British Army barracks with crafts workshops, including a pottery- and picture-gallery and studio. It was on the hill at Millmount that the townsfolk made their last stand against the bloodthirsty Roundheads of Cromwell. Perhaps in defiance of Cromwell's attempt to obliterate the town from the map, the museum contains relics of eight centuries of Drogheda's commercial and industrial past, including painted banners of the old trade guilds, a circular willow-and-leather coracle (the traditional fishing boat on the River Boyne), and many instruments and utensils from domestic and factory use. Most moving are the mementos of the infamous 1649 massacre of 3,000 people by Cromwell. There are also geological and archaeological displays. The exhibit inside the Martello Tower adjacent to the museum focuses on the military history of Drogheda. ⊠ *Millmount* ☎ *041/983–3097* ⊕ *www.millmount.net* 🖼 *Museum €3.50, tower €3* ⊗ *Mon.–Sat. 9:30–5:30, Sun. 2–5.*

WHERE TO STAY

$$$ 🏨 **Boyne Valley Hotel and Country Club.** A 1-km (½-mi) drive leads to this 19th-century mansion on 16 acres that was once owned by a Drogheda brewing family. The newer wing of this hotel has double rooms, all with contemporary (if slightly uninspired) furnishings and bright color schemes full of flower prints and pastels. The public spaces have been restored in period fashion, with Neoclassical pillars, intricate plasterwork, and crystal chandeliers. A large conservatory houses a bar and overlooks the grounds, while a spacious hall is decorated with antiques and comfy chairs. Cellars Bistro specializes in fresh fish and big steaks. **Pros:** great activity facilities; lovely grounds; recent steep price reduction. **Cons:** uninspired decor; newer building a touch functional; restaurant only open weekends. ⊠ *Dublin Rd., Co. Louth* ☎ *041/983–7737* ⊕ *www.boyne-valley-hotel.ie* 🛏 *71 rooms* ♿ *In-room: a/c, Wi-Fi. In-hotel: restaurant, bar, golf course, tennis courts, pool, gym, spa* ⊟ *AE, DC, MC, V* ⎮⊗⎮*BP.*

$ **D Hotel.** A dramatic location right on the south bank of the Boyne easily makes up for the slightly functional exterior of this trendy new hotel smack in the center of medieval Drogheda. To take full advantage, bag a room on a higher floor with a vista out over the water and the town to the Boyne Valley beyond. Guest rooms are very Swedish Modern in feel, thanks to light woods and muted colors, with a touch of luxury in the goose-down duvets and elegant bathrooms. The riverside bar and white-linen restaurant have already become favorite hang-out spots for locals and visitors alike. The menu isn't particularly original but braised pork belly with savoy cabbage or panfried fillet of sea bream are rich and hearty. **Pros:** dramatic riverside location; extra comfy big beds; great terrace for drinks and people-watching. **Cons:** only some rooms have great views; uninspired exterior design; restaurant open weekends only. ⊠ *Scotch Hall, Co. Louth* ☎ *041/987–7700* ⊕ *www.thedhotel.com* ⤴ *102 rooms* ⌂ *In-room: a/c, Wi-Fi. In-hotel: restaurant, bar, gym* ☰ *AE, MC, V* ⦿⧠*BP.*

MELLIFONT ABBEY

10 km (8 mi) northwest of Drogheda off R168.

On the eastern bank of the River Mattock, which creates a natural border between counties Meath and Louth, lie the remains of Mellifont Abbey, the first Cistercian monastery in Ireland. Founded in 1142 by St. Malachy, archbishop of Armagh, it was inspired by the formal structure surrounding a courtyard of St. Bernard of Clairvaux's monastery, which St. Malachy had visited. Among the substantial ruins are the two-story chapter house, built in 12th-century English-Norman style and once a daily meeting place for the monks; it now houses a collection of medieval glazed tiles. Four walls of the 13th-century octagonal lavabo, or washing place, still stand, as do some arches from the Romanesque cloister. At its peak Mellifont presided over almost 40 other Cistercian monasteries throughout Ireland, but all were suppressed by Henry VIII in 1539 after his break with the Catholic Church. Adjacent to the parking lot is a small **architectural museum** depicting the history of the abbey and the craftsmanship that went into its construction. ⊠ *Near Collon* ☎ *041/982–6459* ⊕ *www.heritageireland.ie* ⛁ *€3* ⊙ *Late May–Sept., daily 10–5:15.*

WHERE TO EAT

$$$$

IRISH

✕ **Forge Gallery Restaurant.** For generations the local forge was the burning heart of any rural Irish community, and this well-established restaurant is still something of a beacon to locals and visitors for miles around. Warm rose and plum tones and antique furnishings decorate this two-story eatery in a converted forge, and an old fireplace fills the place with a comforting warmth and light. The cuisine mixes French Provençal with a strong hint of traditional Irish cooking. Two popular specialties are roast duckling served on a bed of greens, with spring onion, soy, and ginger sauce, and turbot baked in lemon and thyme and served with red pepper sauce. Make sure you try one of the seasonal homemade soups. Paintings by local artists hang in the reception area and are for sale. Reservations are essential on weekends. ⊠ *North of Slane on N2, Collon* ☎ *041/982–6272* ⊕ *www.forgegalleryrestaurant. ie* ☰ *AE, DC, MC, V* ⊙ *Closed Sun. and Mon. No lunch.*

ARDEE

14½ km (9 mi) northwest of Mellifont Abbey on N2.

The road from Mellifont Abbey to Ardee passes through Monasterboice, home to some of Ireland's finest medieval High Crosses. Near the village's Round Tower, you'll find the famed Muireadach Cross and, nearby, the West Cross, the tallest in all the country. Once you take in these noted medieval sculptures, continue on to the market town of Ardee, found at the northern edge of the Pale. Here stand two 13th-century castles: Ardee Castle and Hatch's Castle. The town of Ardee (Baile Átha Fhirdia or Ferdia's Ford), interestingly, was named after the ford where the mythical folk hero Cuchulainn fought his foster brother Ferdia. There's a statue depicting this battle at the start of the riverside walk.

Ardee Castle (the one with square corners) was founded by Roger de Peppard in 1207, but much of the present building dates to the 15th century and later. The castle faces north—its objective to protect the Anglo-Irish Pale from the untamed Celtic tribes of Ulster. It was converted into a courthouse in the 19th century.

Hatch's Castle (with rounded corners) is a private residence and not open to the public. Built in the 13th century, it was given by Cromwell as a gift to the loyal Hatch family. If you look closely you can see it still flaunts two 18th-century cannons at its entrance.

St. Mary's Church of Ireland on Main Street incorporates part of a 13th-century Carmelite church burned by Edward the Bruce in 1316, including the holy water font. The current building was constructed in the 19th century.

WHERE TO EAT

$$
SEAFOOD

✕ **The Glyde Inn.** Sitting right on the edge of Dundalk Bay and overlooking the Cooley and Mourne mountains, this stolid little guesthouse ("inn" is pushing it) and pub now also features a quality surf-and-turf restaurant. You'd never know the Glyde was established way back in 1700, as it is now such a casual, no-fuss place. Happily, the hospitality matches the locally sourced, delicious food, and great vistas. The menu ranges from fish-and-chips—comfort food at its best—to lobster (the poor critters are housed in a tank tiny enough to make some people lose their appetite). The owners also have a few B&B rooms. ✉ *Annagassan, 12 km (7 mi) east of Ardee* ☎ *042/937–2350* ⊕ *www.theglydeinn.ie* ⊟ *MC, V.*

LOUTH

11½ km (7 mi) north of Ardee on R171.

Louth warrants a visit, if only for the splendidly preserved oratory here. St. Patrick, Ireland's patron saint, was reputed to have built his first church (which is no longer here) in this hilltop village in the 5th century. He also made St. Mochta (d. 534) the first bishop of Louth.

Standing at the center of the village is the excellently preserved **St. Mochta's House,** an oratory dating from the 11th century, whose steeply pitched stone roof can be reached by a stairway. The house is freely accessible—but watch out for cattle (and their droppings) in the surrounding field.

Nearby **Knockabbey Castle and Gardens** are perfect for a relaxing after-noon when the weather's good. Originally built in 1399, the castle was expanded by the Bellew family in 1650 and again in 1754, before suffer-ing major damage in an IRA raid in 1923. But the real treat here is the recently restored historical water gardens, which originally date from as far as the 11th century. A stroll will take you through wildflower mead-ows, herbaceous borders, a Victorian flower garden, and a restored glasshouse. ⊠ *Louth Village* ☎ *01/677–8816* ⊕ *www.knockabbeycastle. com* 🚮 *House €6, gardens €6* ☉ *May and Sept., weekends 10:30–5:30; June–Aug., Tues.–Sun. 10:30–5:30.*

DUNDALK

14½ km (9 mi) east of Inniskeen, 80 km (50 mi) north of Dublin on N1.

Perfectly positioned as a hub to explore the region north and south of the border, Dundalk—only 9½ km (6 mi) from Northern Ireland—is the main town of County Louth (Ireland's smallest county). Its earliest settlement dates from the early Christian period, around the 7th century. In May the town hosts an avant-garde "fringe" drama and visual arts festival (with a nice schedule of children's events).

GETTING HERE

BUS TRAVEL Dundalk's bus station is on Long Walk near the main shopping cen-ter. Bus Éireann runs regular buses to Dublin (€7.20 one-way, €10.80 round-trip; 1 hour 30 minutes; 12 buses daily) and Belfast and Drogheda (€4.50 one-way, €9 round-trip; 30 minutes; 12 buses daily).

TRAIN TRAVEL Serviced by Irish Rail, Clarke Train Station is on Carrickmacross Road. There are daily trains to Dublin (€10 one-way, €20 round-trip; 1 hour 20 minutes; 10 trains daily); Belfast (€10 one-way, €20 round-trip; 1 hour 20 minutes; 10 trains daily); and Drogheda (€9.50 one-way, €17.50 round-trip; 20 minutes; 13 trains daily).

Visitor Information Dundalk Tourist Office (⊠ *Jocelyn St.* ☎ *042/933–5484* ⊕ *www.dundalkonline.com*).

EXPLORING

Dundalk is an uninspiring, frontier town but has some fine, notable his-toric buildings. On Mill Street, the **bell tower** of a Franciscan monastery with Gothic windows dates from the 13th century.

St. Patrick's Cathedral was built between 1835 and 1847, when the Gothic Revival was at its height. With its buttresses and mosaics lining the chancel and the side chapel walls, the cathedral was modeled on the 15th-century King's College Chapel at Cambridge, England. The fine exterior was built in Newry granite, and the high altar and pulpit are of carved Caen stone. ⊠ *Town center* ☉ *Daily 8–6.*

The Market House, the Town Hall, and the Courthouse are examples of the town's 19th-century heritage; the **Courthouse** is the most impres-sive of the three, built in the 1820s in a severe Greek Revival style, with Doric columns supporting the portico. It stands north of St. Patrick's Cathedral.

The **Dundalk County Museum**, in a beautifully restored 18th-century warehouse, is dedicated to preserving the history of the dying local industries, such as beer brewing, cigarette manufacturing, shoe and boot making, and railway engineering. Other exhibits deal with the history of Louth from 7500 BC to the present. ⊠ *Joycelyn St.* ☎ *042/932–7056* ⊕ *www.dundalkmuseum.ie* 🎫 *€3.80* ☽ *Tues.–Sat. 10:30–5.*

WHERE TO STAY

$$$ 🍴 **Ballymascanlon House Hotel.** This Victorian mansion with a slightly severe but elegant modern addition sits on 130 acres on the scenic Cooley Peninsula just north of Dundalk. The place has a reputation for comfort and good cuisine. Reproduction period pieces fill the extra-large guest rooms, which overlook either the spacious gardens or old stable yard. The restaurant serves a set menu of Irish and French cuisine; it specializes in fresh seafood, such as lobster in season. Vegetarian plates are also available. **Pros:** guest rooms big enough to get lost in; cheap golf for residents; good weekend, all-inclusive deals. **Cons:** a little pricey for the area; in-room facilities sparse; popular for weddings. ⊠ *Dundalk, Co. Louth* ☎ *042/935–8200* ⊕ *www.ballymascanlon.com* 🛏 *90 rooms* ♿ *In-room: a/c, Wi-Fi. In-hotel: restaurant, bars, golf course, tennis courts, pool, gym, Wi-Fi hotspot* ⊟ *AE, DC, MC, V* ⊙⊩ *BP.*

¢ 🍴 **Innisfree House.** An early-20th-century, redbrick gem in the heart of Dundalk, Innisfree House is shockingly good value considering the genteel, stylish atmosphere created by the beautiful Edwardian furniture and antiques throughout. All nine bedrooms are carefully decorated in a lovingly cluttered style—try to get one with one of the grander metal or wooden framed old-school beds. The breakfast is hearty and fresh, but a real treat is afternoon tea in the cute tearoom. Dinner can be booked in the "days of yore" dining room. **Pros:** genuine afternoon tea served; option of evening dining; authentic Edwardian furnishings. **Cons:** not in the most picturesque area; maybe a little over-decorated; short on facilities. ⊠ *Carrick Rd., Dundalk, Co. Louth* ☎ *042/933–4912* ⊕ *www.innisfreehouse.ie* 🛏 *9 rooms* ♿ *In-room: no a/c. In-hotel: parking (paid)* ⊟ *MC, V* ⊙⊩ *BP.*

UNWELCOME WAGON

The area around Dundalk is closely connected with Cuchulainn (pronounced *coo*-chu-lain)—"a greater hero than Hercules or Achilles," as Frank McCourt, in *Angela's Ashes,* quotes his father. Cuchulainn, the warrior of the Irish epic *Táin Bó Cuailnge* (Cattle Raid of Cooley), heroically defended this area of ancient Ulster against invaders.

COUNTY WICKLOW

Make your way to the fourth or fifth story of almost any building in Dublin that faces south and you can see off in the distance—amazingly, not *that* far off in the distance—the green, smooth hills of the Dublin and Wicklow mountains. On a clear day the mountains are even visible from some streets in and around the city center. If your idea of solace is green hills, and your visit to Ireland is otherwise limited to Dublin, County Wicklow—or Cill Mhantain (pronounced kill *wan*-tan), as it's known in Irish—should be on your itinerary. Not that the secret isn't out; rugged and mountainous with dark, wooded forests, central Wicklow, known as the "garden of Ireland," is a popular picnic area among Dubliners. It has some of Ireland's grandest 18th-century mansions, and cradles one of the country's earliest Christian retreats: Glendalough. Nestled in a valley of dense woods and placid lakes, Glendalough and environs can seem (at least during the off-season) practically untouched since their heyday 1,000 years ago. The granite mountains that have protected Glendalough all these years run into the sea along the east coast, which has several popular sandy beaches. Journey from Dublin down to Arklow, sticking to the east side of the Wicklow Mountains. A quick note about getting here: it takes stamina to extract yourself from the unmarked maze of the Dublin exurbs (your best bet is to take N11, which becomes M11, and then again N11). Once you've accomplished that feat, this gorgeous, mysterious terrain awaits.

BRAY

22 km (14 mi) south of Dublin on N11, 8 km (5 mi) east of Enniskerry on R755.

One of Ireland's oldest seaside resorts, Bray is a trim, growing village known for its summer cottages and sand-and-shingle beach, which stretches for 2 km (1 mi). When the trains first arrived from Dublin in 1854, Bray became the number-one spot for urban vacationers and subsequently took on the appearance of an English oceanfront town. Some Dubliners still flock to the faded glory of Bray's boardwalk to push baby carriages and soak up the sun. It's the terminus of the DART train from Dublin, so it's easy to get here without a car. Uncrowded trails for hiking and mountain biking crisscross the mountains bordering Bray to the south. One of the best is a well-marked path leading from the beach to the 10-foot-tall cross that crowns the spiny peak of Bray Head, a rocky outcrop that rises 791 feet from the sea. The semi-difficult, one-hour climb affords stunning views of Wicklow Town and Dublin Bay.

The **Heritage Centre,** opposite the Royal Hotel, in the old courthouse, houses on its lower level a re-created castle dungeon with a 1,000-years-of-Bray exhibition. Upstairs is a huge model railway and a display about modern Bray. ☒ *Lower Main St.* ☎ *01/286–6796* ⊕ *www. braytowncouncil.ie* 🗐 €2 ☺ *June–Aug., weekdays 9–1 and 2–5, Sat. 10–3; Sept.–May, weekdays 9:30–1 and 2–4:30, Sat. 10–3.*

One Martello Terrace (☎ *01/286–8407*), at the harbor, is Bray's most famous address. James Joyce (1882–1941) lived here between 1887 and 1891 and used the house as the setting for the Christmas dinner in *A Portrait of the Artist as a Young Man.* Today the house is owned by an Irish Teachta Dála (member of Parliament, informally known as a "TD"). The phone number listed above rings at her constituency office; someone there should be able to help scholars and devotees arrange a visit. (Call on Thursday between 10 AM and 1 PM.) Although the residence has been renovated, the dining room portrayed in Joyce's novel maintains the spirit of his time.

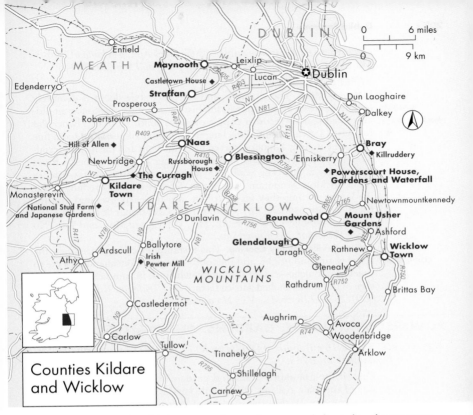

Counties Kildare and Wicklow

National Sealife is an aquarium and museum dedicated to the creatures of the sea, with an emphasis on those that occupy the waters around Ireland. Besides massive sea tanks that contain all manner of swimming things, there's a major conservation project with captive breeding of sea horses. **FinZone** is an undersea adventure trail perfect for kids, including puzzles to solve, and Nemo's Kingdom is a coral reef tank with all the fish portrayed in the Disney movie. Touch-screen computers and video games give the whole thing a high-tech feel. In winter, call to confirm opening times before visiting. ⊠ *Strand Rd.* ☎ *01/286–6939* ⊕ *www.sealifeeurope.com* ☛ *€12* ⊗ *Mar.–Oct., daily 10–5; Nov.–Feb. weekdays 11–4, weekends 10–5.*

The 17th-century formal gardens at **Killruddery House** are precisely arranged, with fine beech hedges, Victorian statuary, and a parterre of lavender and roses. The Brabazon family, the earls of Meath, have lived here since 1618. In 1820 they hired William Morris to remodel the house as a revival Elizabethan mansion. The estate also has a Crystal Palace conservatory modeled on those at the botanic gardens in Dublin. Killruddery Arts organizes year-round arts events including the kid-friendly Enchanted Garden in late June and a silent film festival in mid-March. ⊠ *Off Bray–Greystones Rd., 3 km (2 mi) south of Bray, Killruddery* ☎ *01/286–3405* ⊕ *www.killruddery.com* ☛ *House*

*and gardens €10, gardens only €6 ☉ Gardens Apr., weekends 12:30–5;
May–Sept., daily 12:30–5; house May, June, and Sept., daily 1–5.*

WHERE TO EAT

$$
SEAFOOD
Fodor's Choice
★

× **Hungry Monk.** The cloisters- and refectory-style decor is definitely
tongue-in-cheek at this upbeat, fun bistro in sleepy Greystones, an old-
fashioned seaside resort a couple of miles south of Bray. Owner Pat
Keown is a great host and his laughter and love of good food and fine
wine are catching. Dinner is served by candlelight and the menu special-
izes in uncluttered seafood dishes in summer and wild game on those
cold winter nights. The Seafood Symphony is a particular favorite, as
is the Wicklow Mountain lamb shank. Sunday lunches are famous for
the length of time they go on (often into the early evening) and for
the lively atmosphere. ⊠ *1 Church Rd., Greystones* ☎ *01/287–5759*
⊕ *www.thehungrymonk.ie* ⊟ *AE, MC, V* ☉ *Closed Mon. and Tues. No
lunch Wed.–Sat. No dinner Sun.*

¢
CONTINENTAL

× **Summerville Country Cooking.** This restaurant's ceilings are high, the
space is airy and bright, and the food—ranging from shepherd's pie to
vegetarian quiche—tastes absolutely delicious. In summer take advan-
tage of the sun-drenched garden terrace. ⊠ *1 Trafalgar Rd., Greystones*
☎ *01/287–4228* ⊟ *MC, V* ☉ *No dinner.*

POWERSCOURT HOUSE, GARDENS, AND WATERFALL

Fodor's Choice
★

*25 km (16 mi) south of Dublin on R117, 22 km (14 mi) north of Glen-
dalough on R755.*

One of the grandest estates and gardens in Ireland, Powerscourt is
one of the main reasons why people head to Enniskerry, but just one
among many. Within the shadow of famous Sugar Loaf Mountain,
Enniskerry remains one of the prettiest villages in Ireland. It's built
around a sloping central triangular square with a backdrop of the
wooded Wicklow Mountains. That noted, Enniskerry is the gateway
to get to Powerscourt.

GETTING HERE

BUS TRAVEL

Dublin Bus No. 44 goes from Townsend Street (near the Tara Street
DART station on the south side of Dubin's quays) to Enniskerry. The
fare is €1.85 each way and you'll need to walk the mile to Powerscourt
from the bus stop in Enniskerry. Alternatively, you can take the Irish
Rail's DART train line from Dublin city center to Bray and then take
Dublin bus No. 185 (€1.35) from outside the DART station in Bray
all the way to Powerscourt. Be careful, as not all No. 185 buses go to
Powerscourt, only the 185c buses. Check the bus timetable or ask the
driver before you get on to make sure you have the right bus.

EXPLORING

They really had the life, those old aristocrats. At more than 14,000
acres, including stunning formal gardens and a 400-foot waterfall,
Powerscourt must have been some place to call home. The grounds
were originally granted to Sir Richard Wingfield, the first viscount
of Powerscourt, by King James I of England in 1609. Richard Castle
(1690–1751), the architect of Russborough House, was hired to design

the great house. His was an age not known for modesty, and he chose the grand Palladian style. The house took nine years to complete and was ready to move into in 1740. It was truly one of the great houses of Ireland and, indeed, all of Britain.

Unfortunately, you won't be able to see much of it. A terrible fire almost completely destroyed the house in 1974, cruelly on the eve of a huge party to celebrate the completion of a lengthy restoration by the Slazenger family of golfing manufacturing fame. A second period of renovation is currently under way and the original ballroom on the first floor—once "the grandest room in any Irish house," according to historian Desmond Guinness—is the only room that gives a sense of the place's former glory. It was based on Palladio's version of the "Egyptian Hall" designed by Vitruvius, architect to Augustus, emperor of Rome.

Powerscourt Gardens, considered among the finest in Europe, were laid out from 1745 to 1767 following the completion of the house—and were radically redesigned in the Victorian style, from 1843 to 1875, by Daniel Robertson. The Villa Butera in Sicily inspired him to set these gardens with sweeping terraces, antique sculptures, and a circular pond and fountain flanked by winged horses. There's a celebrated view of the Italianate patterned ramps, lawns, and pond across the beautiful, heavily wooded Dargle Valley, which stair-steps to the horizon and the noble profile of Sugar Loaf Mountain. The grounds include many specimen trees (plants grown for exhibition), an avenue of monkey puzzle trees, a parterre of brightly colored summer flowers, and a Japanese garden. The kitchen gardens, with their modest rows of flowers, are a striking antidote to the classical formality of the main sections. A cute café, crafts and interior design shops, a garden center, and a children's play area are also in the house and on the grounds. ⊠ *Enniskerry* ☎ *01/204–6000* ⊕ *www.powerscourt.ie* 🏷 *€8* ⊙ *Daily 9:30–5:30.*

One of the most inspiring sights to the writers and artists of the Romantic generation, the 400-foot **Powerscourt Waterfall,** 5 km (3 mi) south of the gardens, is the highest in the British Isles. ⊠ *Enniskerry* 🏷 *€5* ⊙ *Mar., Apr., Sept., and Oct., daily 10:30–5:30; May–Aug., daily 9:30–7; Nov.–Feb., daily 10:30–4.*

WHERE TO EAT AND STAY

$$$$ ✕ **Gordon Ramsay at Powerscourt.** Star of the bleep-ridden *Hell's Kitchen* TV
FRENCH show, Scottish superchef, and bad boy of English cuisine Gordon Ramsey has now set up shop in Ireland at the spectacular Ritz-Carlton hotel.
★ Having already amassed a string of restaurants worldwide, including London's only Michelin three-star, it's not surprising that the eponymous chef doesn't actually cook here but, happily, his inventive stamp can be seen all over the menu. Low ceilings give the very formal dining room a slightly overbearing feel, but large windows open onto a big terrace that is ideal for summer dining. The food is constantly exciting and innovative and the six-course tasting menu is a great value. Starters include the stunning ravioli of lobster and Clare Island salmon with a lemongrass sauce. Top mains include the Wexford rosé veal with pickled artichokes, broad beans, and girolle mushrooms. ⊠ *Ritz-Carlton Powerscourt, Enniskerry* ☎ *01/274–9377* 🍷 *Reservations essential* ⊟ *AE, MC, V.*

3

¢ ✕ **Poppies Country Cooking.** This cozy
IRISH café—with a pine-panel ceiling,
farmhouse furniture, and paintings
of poppies on the walls—is a great
place for breakfast, lunch, or late-
afternoon tea. Expect potato cakes,
shepherd's pie, lasagna, vegetarian
quiche, house salads, and soup. But
the most popular dishes are Poppies
chicken (a casserole-like concoc-
tion) and homity pie (potpie with

potatoes, onion, garlic, and cream cheese). For dessert try the apple
pie or the rhubarb crumble, which is so good that the Irish rugby team
stops by for it after practice. ⊠ *The Square, Enniskerry* ☎ *01/282–8869*
⊕ *www.poppies.ie* ⊟ *MC, V* ⊘ *No dinner.*

$$$$ 🏨 **Ritz-Carlton Powerscourt.** Set on the Powerscourt estate, the gargan-
★   tuan Palladian-style exterior of this Xanadu may seem out of place,
but luxury always makes itself at home. The lobby is so cavernous it
conjures up Las Vegas but the Georgian cast of its decor strikes the
right glamorous note. Certainly, no one can carp about the views of
the fabled Sugar Loaf peak outside the soaring windows. Guest rooms
with the same view cost a bit more, but even the standard rooms—in
relaxing beiges and robin's-egg blues with modern versions of 18th-
century furnishings—are large and have marble bathrooms warmed
by under-floor heating. Conversation-worthy are the TV sets recessed
into bathroom mirrors, the mammoth crystal-lighted indoor pool, and
the "lifestyle" showers at the spa, one of the most luxurious in Ireland.
Taste buds are mightily indulged, too, thanks to Gordon Ramsay's
restaurant, where such entrées as roast fillet of pork with Champagne
sauerkraut go for 40-odd euros; cheaper fare is available at McGills'
pub (Supreme of Chicken for €19; hotdogs for €5), while the Sugar
Loaf Lounge is just the place to sit on an emerald-green settee, savor a
Pistachio Financier pastry, and count your blessings at being here, and
here. **Pros:** sumptuous pool and spa; top restaurant; beautiful setting in
Powerscourt grounds. **Cons:** some people have called the exterior over-
the-top; garden rooms don't have a great view; can feel very busy at
times. ⊠ *Powerscourt Estate, Enniskerry, Co. Wicklow* ☎ *01/274–8888*
⊕ *www.ritzcarlton.com* ➥ *76 rooms, 124 suites* ⚲ *In-room: a/c, safe,
refrigerator, Wi-Fi. In-hotel: 2 restaurants, bars, golf course, pool, gym,
spa, Wi-Fi hotspot, parking (paid)* ⊟ *AE, DC, MC, V.*

ROUNDWOOD

★   *18 km (11 mi) south of Enniskerry on R755.*

At 800 feet above sea level, Roundwood is the highest village in Ireland.
It's also surrounded by spectacular mountain scenery. The Sunday afternoon market in the village hall, where cakes, jams, and other homemade
goods are sold, livens up what is otherwise a sleepy place. From the
broad main street, by the Roundwood Inn, a minor road leads west

for 8 km (5 mi) to two lakes, Lough Dan and Lough Tay, lying deep between forested mountains like Norwegian fjords.

WHERE TO EAT

$ ✕ **Roundwood Inn.** Travel back to the 17th century at this inn evocatively
IRISH   furnished in a traditional style, with wooden floors, dark furniture, and
★   diamond-shaped windows. Though there's bar food available daily for lunch and dinner, the restaurant area opens only for Friday and Saturday dinner and Sunday lunch and offers a combination of Continental and Irish cuisines, reflecting the traditions of the German proprietor, Jurgen Schwalm, and his Irish wife, Aine. The place is best known for its wonderful, hearty, reasonably priced bar food (served in a nook of the bar)—try the glorious cream of seafood soup. They also serve an excellent succulent seafood platter of salmon, oysters, lobster, and shrimp along with a very gamey pheasant casserole. ⊠ *Main St.* ☎ *01/281–8107* ☝ *Reservations essential* 🗖 *AE, MC, V.*

GLENDALOUGH

Fodor's Choice   *9 km (6 mi) southeast of Roundwood via R755 and R756.*
★   Nestled in a lush, quiet valley deep in the rugged Wicklow Mountains, among two lakes, evergreen and deciduous trees, and acres of windswept heather, Gleann dá Loch ("glen of two lakes") is one of Ireland's premier monastic sites. The hermit monks of early Christian Ireland were drawn to the Edenlike quality of some of the valleys in this area, and this evocative settlement remains to this day a sight to calm a troubled soul. Stand here in the early morning (before the crowds and the hordes of school-trippers arrive), and you can appreciate what drew the solitude-seeking St. Kevin to this spot. St. Kevin—or Coemghein, "fair begotten" in Irish (d. 618)—was a descendant of the royal house of Leinster who renounced the world and came here to live as a hermit before opening the monastery in 550. Glendalough then flourished as a monastic center until 1398, when English soldiers plundered the site, leaving the ruins that you see today.

GETTING HERE

BUS TRAVEL   St. Kevin's Bus departs from Dublin outside the Mansion House on Dawson Street (€13 one-way, €20 round-trip; 1½ hours) March to September, weekdays at 11:30 AM and 6 PM, weekends at 11:30 AM and 7 PM; October to February, daily at 11:30 AM and 6 PM. It also stops at the town hall in Bray. Departures from Glendalough are March to September, weekdays 7:15 AM and 4:30 PM, weekends 9:45 AM and 5:40 PM; October to February daily at 7:15 AM and 4:30 PM. In July and August there is an extra bus at 9:45 AM weekdays.

TRAIN TRAVEL   There is no direct train to Glendalough but you can take the Irish Rail train from Dublin's Connolly Station as far as Rathdrum (€20 round trip; 1 hour 20 minutes) and then take a taxi (approximately €10) the 11 km (7 mi) from there to Glendalough.

ESSENTIALS

Transportation Contacts St. Kevin's Bus (☎ *01/281–8119*
🌐 *www.glendaloughbus.com*).

3

EXPLORING

Glendalough's visitor center is a good place to orient yourself and pick up a useful pamphlet. Many of the ruins are clumped together beyond the visitor center, but some of the oldest surround the Upper Lake, where signed paths direct you through spectacular scenery devoid of crowds. Most ruins are open all day and are freely accessible.

Probably the oldest building on the site, presumed to date from St. Kevin's time, is the **Teampaill na Skellig** (Church of the Oratory), on the south shore of the Upper Lake. A little to the east is **St. Kevin's Bed,** a tiny cave in the rock face, about 30 feet above the level of the lake, where St. Kevin lived his hermit's existence. It's not easily accessible; you approach the cave by boat, but climbing the cliff to the cave can be dangerous. At the southeast corner of the Upper Lake is the 11th-century **Reefert Church,** with the ruins of a nave and a chancel. The saint also lived in the adjoining, ruined beehive hut with five crosses, which marked the original boundary of the monastery. You get a superb view of the valley from here.

The ruins by the edge of the Lower Lake are the most important of those at Glendalough. The **gateway,** beside the Glendalough Hotel, is the only surviving entrance to an ancient monastic site anywhere in Ireland. An extensive **graveyard** lies within, with hundreds of elaborately decorated crosses, as well as a perfectly preserved six-story **round tower.** Built in the 11th or 12th century, it stands 100 feet high, with an entrance 25 feet above ground level.

The largest building at Glendalough is the substantially intact 7th- to 9th-century **cathedral,** where you can find the nave (small for a large church, only 30 feet wide by 50 feet long), chancel, and ornamental oolite limestone window, which may have been imported from England. South of the cathedral is the 11-foot-high Celtic **St. Kevin's Cross.** Made of granite, it's the best-preserved such cross on the site. **St. Kevin's Church** is an early barrel-vaulted oratory with a high-pitched stone roof. ☎ 0404/45325 ⊕ *www.heritageireland.ie* 🖼 *Ruins free, visitor center €3* ☉ *Ruins daily 24 hrs. Visitor center mid-Mar.–mid-Oct., daily 9:30–6; mid-Oct.–mid-Mar., daily 9:30–5; last admission 45 mins before closing.*

WHERE TO STAY

$ 🏠 **Derrymore House.** On 6 acres of woodland above the Lower Lake in Glendalough Valley, Derrymore is one of the most serene B&Bs in Wicklow. Wild goats, foxes, and rabbits inhabit the nearby woods. The Kelleher family are avid traditional musicians and music can be heard regularly in their home. The bedrooms are big and comfortable, with Victorian beds and en-suite bathrooms. The full Irish breakfast is the perfect way to start the day; they can also provide a packed lunch for walkers. **Pros:** family-owned and -run; music played in the house by family; Victorian beds. **Cons:** room decor is basic; gets fully booked easily; family lives in house. ⊠ *Co. Wicklow* ☎ *0404/45493* ⊕ *www. glendaloughaccommodation.com* 🛏 *5 rooms* ⚿ *In-room: no a/c, Wi-Fi* ⊟ *No credit cards* ◎| *BP.*

Even though destroyed by Viking raids and then disbanded as a monastery by the Reformation, medieval Glendalough remains magical and magnificent.

MOUNT USHER GARDENS

★ *18 km (11 mi) east of Glendalough via R755 and R763.*

Covering more than 20 acres on the banks of the River Vartry, the gardens here were first laid out in 1868 by textile magnate Edward Walpole. Succeeding generations of the Walpole family further planted and maintained the grounds, which today have more than 5,000 species. The "Robinsonian" (that is, informal) gardener has made the most of the riverside locale by planting eucalypti, azaleas, camellias, and rhododendrons. The river is visible from nearly every place in the gardens; miniature suspension bridges bounce and sway underfoot as you cross the river. Near the entrance, you'll find a cluster of crafts shops (including a pottery workshop) as well as a bookstore and self-service tearoom. The twin villages of Ashford and Rathnew are to the south and east, and Newtownmountkennedy is to the north. ⊠ *Ashford* ☎ *0404/40205* ⊕ *www.mountushergardens.ie* 🎟 *€7.50* ☉ *Mar.–Oct., daily 10:30–5:20.*

WHERE TO STAY

$$$ ⌂ **Hunter's Hotel.** The oldest coaching inn in Ireland, Hunter's has been
★ owned and operated by the same family since 1820. On 2 acres of flower gardens (the Knot Garden is an award winner) beside the Vartry River, the beautiful white building wraps snugly around a courtyard. Nothing inside—from the taxidermied animals on the walls to the tiny, cozy little bar—feels like it's there for show, but instead seems to have been placed in that spot by time itself. The guest rooms are simple, bright, and neat with lovely period furnishings. Try to get one that overlooks

the gardens so the sound of the river can lull you to sleep. The restaurant prepares good, hearty food, with local game a regular feature. **Pros:** family-owned and -run for nearly 200 years; enchanting gardens; fine restaurant. **Cons:** books up easily; bedrooms aren't huge. ⊠ *Newrath Bridge, Rathnew, Co. Wicklow* ☎ *0404/40106* ⊕ *www. hunters.ie* ⇆ *16 rooms* ⚼ *In-room: a/c. In-hotel: restaurant, bar, parking* ▭ *MC, V* ¶◎¶ *BP.*

CURVES AHEAD

Getting to hallowed Glendalough from Dublin is easy, thanks to the St. Kevin's bus service. If you're driving, consider taking the scenic route along R115, but be prepared for awesome, austere mountain-top passes. Don't take this route if you're in a hurry, and don't expect a lot of signage—just concentrate on the nifty views.

$$$$ 🖭 **Tinakilly House.** All aboard who's going aboard! William and Bee Power have beautifully restored this Victorian-Italianate mansion, built in the 1870s by seafaring Captain Robert Halpin. The lobby has mementos of his nautical exploits, including paintings and ship models; Victorian antiques fill the house. Some bedrooms have four-poster beds, sitting areas, and views of the Wicklow landscape, the Irish Sea, or the lovely gardens on the 7-acre grounds. In the dining room, expect to be served French-influenced Irish cuisine, with fresh vegetables from the garden. Brown and fruit breads are baked daily. **Pros:** authentic Victorian old house; great strolling garden. **Cons:** newer rooms not as unique as older ones; large number of guest rooms make for less intimacy; a little pricey in high season. ⊠ *Rathnew, Co. Wicklow* ☎ *0404/69274* ⊕ *www.tinakilly.ie* ⇆ *52 rooms, 5 suites* ⚼ *In-room: no a/c, Wi-Fi. In-hotel: restaurant, bar, tennis court, Wi-Fi hotspot* ▭ *AE, DC, MC, V* ¶◎¶ *BP.*

WICKLOW TOWN

26 km (16 mi) east of Glendalough on R763, 51 km (32 mi) south of Dublin on N11.

At the entrance to the attractive, tree-lined Main Street of Wicklow Town sprawl the extensive ruins of a 13th-century Franciscan friary. Wicklow, from the Danish *wyking alo,* means "Viking meadow," testifying to the very ancient roots of this region.

Visitor Information Wicklow Town Tourist Office (⊠ *Rialto House, Fitzwilliam Sq.* ☎ *0404/69117* ⊕ *www.visitwicklow.ie*).

EXPLORING

The **friary** was closed down during the 16th-century dissolution of the monasteries, but its ruins are a reminder of Wicklow's stormy past, which began with the unwelcome reception given to St. Patrick on his arrival in AD 432. Inquire at the nearby **priest's house** (⊠ *Main St.* ☎ *0404/67196*) to see the ruins. The streets of Wicklow ran with blood during the 1798 rebellion when Billy Byrne, member of a wealthy local Catholic family, led rebels from south and central Wicklow against the forces of the Crown. Byrne was eventually captured and executed at Gallow's Hill just outside town. There is a memorial to him in the middle of Market Square.

The old **Wicklow's Historic Gaol,** just above Market Square, has been converted into a museum and heritage center, where it's possible to trace your genealogical roots in the area. Computer displays and life-size models tell the gruesome history of the jail, from the 1798 rebellion to the late 19th century. ⊠ *Market Sq.* ☎ *0404/61599* ⊕ *www. wicklowshistoricgaol.com* ⊠ *€7.30* ☉ *Feb.–Dec., Mon.–Sat. 10:30–4:30, Sun. 11–4:30; Jan. daily noon–3.*

The **harbor** is Wicklow Town's most appealing area. Take Harbour Road down to the pier; a bridge across the River Vartry leads to a second, smaller pier, at the northern end of the harbor. From this end, follow the shingle beach, which stretches for 5 km (3 mi); behind the beach is the broad lough, a lagoon noted for its wildfowl.

Immediately south of the harbor, perched on a promontory that has good views of the Wicklow coastline, is the ruin of the **Black Castle.** This structure was built in 1169 by Maurice Fitzgerald, an Anglo-Norman lord who arrived with the English invasion of Ireland. The ruins (freely accessible) extend over a large area; with some difficulty, you can climb down to the water's edge.

Between one bank of the River Vartry and the road to Dublin stands the **Protestant Church,** which incorporates various unusual details: a Romanesque door, 12th-century stonework, fine pews, and an atmospheric graveyard. The church is topped off by a copper, onion-shaped cupola, added as an afterthought in 1771. ⊠ *Free* ☉ *Daily 10–6.*

WHERE TO EAT AND STAY

$$$$
SEAFOOD
★
✕ **The Strawberry Tree.** Claiming to be Ireland's only "certified organic restaurant," this spot has been getting top reviews for its serious approach to all-natural but always stylish cuisine. Idyllically located at the heart of the vast new BrookLodge Spa hotel, the mod/trad complex is tucked away in a rural Wicklow valley. The glossy decor—midnight-blue walls, mirrored ceiling, and gleaming mahogany furniture—consequently comes as a dramatic contrast but cues you into the classy service and creative menu. Wild woodpigeon terrine, purple sprouting broccoli soup, and steamed wild pollock with green beans and beurre blanc comprise part of the feast, one that can be enjoyed at the Big Table, which seats up to 40. After dessert, check out the spectacular wine cellar. ⊠ *Brooklodge, Macreddin Village* ☎ *0402/36444* ⊕ *www.brooklodge.com* ▭ *MC, V.*

$$$$
▦ **Wicklow Head Lighthouse.** This 95-foot-high stone tower—first built in 1781—once supported an eight-sided lantern, and has been renovated by the Irish Landmark Trust as a lodging. It sleeps four to six people in two delightfully quirky octagonal bedrooms and one double sofa bed in the sitting room. The kitchen–dining room at the top has stunning views out over the coast. Don't forget anything in the car; it's a long way down. You rent the entire lighthouse, and you must book for at least two nights. The old lighthouse is just south of town on Wicklow Head, right next to the new, automated one. **Pros:** unique lodging experience; stunning views; inexpensive if you have a group of people. **Cons:** a lot of stairs; books out easily. ⊠ *Wicklow Head* ☎ *01/670–4733* ⊕ *www.irishlandmark.com* ⬐ *2 rooms* ⚒ *In-room: no a/c, kitchen, no TV* ▭ *MC, V.*

COUNTY KILDARE TO WEST WICKLOW

Of all the artistic delights that beckon both north and south of Dublin, few impress as much as the imposing country estates of County Wicklow. Here, during the "glorious eighteenth," great Anglo-Irish estates were built by English "princes of Elegance and Prodigality." Only an hour or two from Dublin, these estates—Russborough, Powerscourt, and Castletown are but three of the most famous—were profoundly influenced by the country villas of the great Italian architect Andrea Palladio, who erected the estates of the Venetian aristocracy along the Brenta Canal, only a short distance from the city on the lagoon. As in other parts of Ireland, the ancestral homes of the dwindling members of the Anglo-Irish ascendancy dot the landscape in the Pale.

Horse racing is a passion in Ireland—just about every little town has at least one betting shop—and County Kildare is the country's horse capital. Nestled between the basins of the River Liffey to the north and the River Barrow to the east, its gently sloping hills and grass-filled plains are perfect for breeding and racing Thoroughbreds. For some visitors, the fabled National Stud Farm just outside Kildare Town provides a fascinating glimpse into the world of horse breeding. And don't forget the fabled Japanese Gardens, adjacent to the National Stud, which are among Europe's finest. You may want to pick up this leg from Glendalough—the spectacular drive across the Wicklow Gap, from Glendalough to Hollywood, makes for a glorious entrance into Kildare. *One last note: consult the Southeast chapter, if you make it as far south as Castledermot, because Carlow and environs are only 10 km (6 mi) farther south.*

MAYNOOTH

21 km (13 mi) southwest of Dublin.

A few minutes south of the tiny Georgian town of Maynooth is the hamlet of Celbridge, official address to Ireland's largest country house, **Castletown** *(see "Treasure Hunt: The Anglo-Irish Georgian House," in this chapter)*. After touring Castletown, head slightly to the west to find Maynooth's **St. Patrick's College.** What was once a center for the training of Catholic priests is now one of Ireland's most important lay universities. The visitor center chronicles the college's history and that of the Catholic Church in Ireland. Stroll through the university gardens—the Path of Saints or the Path of Sinners. At the entrance to St. Patrick's College are the ruins of Maynooth Castle, the ancient seat of the Fitzgerald family. The Fitzgeralds' fortunes changed for the worse when they led the rebellion of 1536 (it failed). The castle keep, which dates from the 13th century, and the great hall are still in decent condition. Mrs. Saults at 9 Parson Street has the key. Pick up a leaflet at reception for a self-guided tour. ☎ *01/628–5222* ⊕ *www.nuim.ie* ✉ *Free.*

STRAFFAN

5 km (3 mi) southwest of Castletown House on R403, 25½ km (16 mi) southwest of Dublin.

Its attractive location on the banks of the River Liffey, its unique butterfly farm, and the Kildare Hotel and Country Club—where Arnold Palmer designed the K Club, one of Ireland's most renowned 18-hole golf courses—are what make Straffan so appealing.

The only one of its kind in Ireland, the **Straffan Butterfly Farm** has a tropical house with exotic plants, butterflies, and moths. Mounted and framed butterflies are for sale. ☎ *01/627–1109* ⊕ *www.straffanbutterflyfarm. com* ☞ *€7* ⊙ *June–Aug., daily noon–5:30.*

The **Steam Museum** covers the history of Irish steam engines, handsome machines used both in industry and agriculture—for churning butter or threshing corn, for example. There's also a fun collection of model locomotives. Engineers are present on "live steam days" every Sunday and bank holiday. The adjoining Lodge Park Walled Garden is included in the price and is perfect for a leisurely summer stroll. ✉ *Lodge Park* ☎ *01/627–3155* ⊕ *www.steam-museum.com* ☞ *€7.50* ⊙ *June–Aug., Wed.–Sun. 2–6; May and Sept., by appointment only.*

WHERE TO STAY

$$$$
Fodor's Choice
★

🖭 Barberstown Castle. With a 13th-century castle keep at one end, an Elizabethan section in the middle, a large Georgian country house at the other end, and a whole new modern wing, Barberstown represents 750 years of Irish history. Ask for a room in one of the old sections where turf fires blaze in ornate fireplaces in the three sumptuously decorated lounges. Reproduction pieces fill the bedrooms, some of which have four-poster beds. The Georgian-style restaurant serves creatively prepared French food, also on tap for special parties in the banqueting room of the castle keep. **Pros:** 20 acres of serene gardens; privately run; real fires in public spaces. **Cons:** prices still a little Celtic Tiger like; newer wings not as special as old house. ✉ *Co. Kildare* ☎ *01/628–8157* ⊕ *www.barberstowncastle.ie* ⬐ *59 rooms* ⚲ *In-room: some a/c, Wi-Fi. In-hotel: restaurant, bar* ▭ *AE, MC, V* ⍾ *BP, MAP.*

$$$$
🖭 Kildare Hotel and Country Club. Manicured gardens and the renowned Arnold Palmer–designed K Club golf course surround this mansard-roof country mansion. The spacious, comfortable guest rooms are each uniquely decorated with antiques, and all have large windows that overlook either the Liffey or the golf course. (The rooms in the old house are best.) The hotel also has a leasing agreement with several privately owned cottages on the property. Chef Michel Flamme serves an unashamedly French menu—albeit with the hint of an Irish flavor—at the Byerly Turk Restaurant (named after a famous racehorse). The K Club had the honor of hosting the biennial Ryder Cup golf tournament in 2006. **Pros:** all-around luxury; great service; championship golf course on doorstep. **Cons:** very expensive year-round. ✉ *K Club, Co. Kildare* ☎ *01/601–7200* ⊕ *www.kclub.ie* ⬐ *60 rooms, 9 suites, 23 apartments* ⚲ *In-room: a/c, safe, refrigerator, Wi-Fi. In-hotel: 3 restaurants, bars, golf course, pool, spa, Wi-Fi hotspot, parking (paid)* ▭ *AE, DC, MC, V* ⍾ *BP, MAP.*

NAAS

13 km (8 mi) south of Straffan on R407, 30 km (19 mi) southwest of Dublin on N7.

The seat of County Kildare and a thriving market town in the heartland of Irish Thoroughbred country, Naas (pronounced nace) is full of pubs with high stools where short men (trainee jockeys) discuss the merits of their various stables.

Naas has its own small racecourse, but **Punchestown Racecourse** (✉ *3 km [2 mi] south of Naas on R411* ☎ *045/897–704*) has a wonderful setting amid rolling plains, with the Wicklow Mountains a spectacular backdrop. Horse races are held regularly here, but the most popular event is the Punchestown National Hunt Festival in April.

BLESSINGTON

10 km (6 mi) southeast of Naas on R410, 23 km (14 mi) southwest of Dublin on N181.

Just outside the small village of Blessington are two of the marvels of Ireland: fabulous, art-filled, 18th-century **Russborough House** *(see "Treasure Hunt: The Anglo-Irish Georgian House" in this chapter)* and its adjacent **Poulaphouca Reservoir.** Known locally as the Blessington Lakes, Poulaphouca (pronounced pool-a-*fook*-a) is a large, meandering, artificial lake minutes from Russborough House that provides Dublin's water supply. You can drive around the entire perimeter of the reservoir on minor roads; on its southern end lies Hollywood Glen, a particularly beautiful natural spot.

On the western shore of the lakes, the small market town of **Blessington,** with its wide main street lined on both sides by tall trees and Georgian buildings, is one of the most charming villages in the area. It was founded in the late 17th century, and was a stop on the Dublin–Waterford mail-coach service in the mid-19th century. Until 1932, a steam train ran from here to Dublin.

Beyond the southern tip of the Poulaphouca Reservoir, 13 km (8 mi) south of Blessington on N81, look for a small sign for the **Piper's Stones,** a Bronze Age stone circle that was probably used in a ritual connected with worship of the sun. It's just a short walk from the road.

You can take in splendid views of the Blessington Lakes from the top of **Church Mountain,** which you reach via a vigorous walk through Woodenboley Wood, at the southern tip of Hollywood Glen. Follow the main forest track for about 20 minutes and then take the narrow path that heads up the side of the forest to the mountaintop for about another half hour.

WHERE TO STAY

$$$$
IRISH
Fodor's Choice
★

Rathsallagh House. At the end of a long drive that winds through a golf course, and set in 530 acres of parkland, is Rathsallagh House, which came into being when low-slung, ivy-covered Queen Anne stables were converted into a farmhouse in 1798. Enveloping couches and chairs, fresh flower arrangements, large windows, fireplaces, and lots of lamps furnish the two drawing rooms. Large rooms have enchanting, pastoral

Continued on page 220

TREASURE HUNT

THE ANGLO-IRISH GEORGIAN HOUSE

For an upclose look at the Lifestyles of the Rich and Famous, 18th-century style, nothing beats a visit to the great treasure houses of Castletown and Russborough. Set just a half-hour south of Dublin and located only 20 miles apart, they offer a unique peek through the keyhole into the extravagant world of Ireland's "Princes of Elegance and Prodigality."

Castletown House and its impressive grounds.

When the Palladian architectural craze swept across England, the Anglo-Irish—determined not to be outdone—set about building palaces in their own domain that would be the equal of anything in the mother country. Both Castletown House and Russborough House set new benchmarks in symmetry, elegance, and harmony for the Georgian style, which reigned supreme from 1714 to 1830, and was named after the four Georges who successively sat on the English throne.

This style was greatly influenced by the villa designs of the 16th-century Italian architect Andrea Palladio.

Although Castletown remains the largest private house in Ireland, and Russborough has the longest façade of any domicile in the country, Georgian groupies know that the real treasures lie inside: ceilings lavishly worked in Italianate stuccowork, priceless Old Master paintings, and an intimate look at the glory and grandeur of the Anglo-Irish lords.

CASTLETOWN: A GEORGIAN VERSAILLES

★ Fodor's Choice

Reputedly the inspiration for a certain building at 1600 Pennsylvania Avenue, Castletown remains the finest example of an Irish Palladian–style house.

In 1722, William Conolly (1662–1729) decided to build himself a house befitting his new status as the speaker of the Irish House of Commons and Ireland's wealthiest man. On an estate 20 km (12 mi) southwest of Dublin, he began work on Castletown, designed in the latest Neoclassical fashion by the Florentine architect Alessandro Galilei. As it turns out, a young Irish designer and Palladian aficionado by the name of Sir Edward Lovett Pearce (1699–1733) was traveling in Italy, met Galilei, and soon signed on to oversee the completion of the house. Inspired by the use of outlying wings to frame a main building—the "winged device" used in Palladio's Venetian villas—Lovett Pearce added Castletown's striking colonnades and side pavillons in 1724. It is said that between them a staggering total of 365 windows were built into the overall design of the house—legend has it that a team of four servants were kept busy year-round keeping them all clean.

Conolly died before the interior of the house was completed, and work resumed in 1758 when his great nephew Thomas, and more importantly, his 15-year-old wife, Lady Louisa Lennox, took up residence there. Luckily, Louisa's passion for interior decoration led to the creation of some of Ireland's most stunning salons, including the Print Room and the Long Gallery. Little of the original furnishings remain today, but there is plenty of evidence of the ingenuity of Louisa and her artisans, chief among whom were the Lafranchini brothers, master crafstmen who created the famous wall plasterwork, considered masterpieces of their kind. Rescued in 1967 by Desmond Guinness of the brewing family, Castletown was deeded to the Irish state and remains the headquarters for the Irish Georgian Society.

Above left: Castletown House facade
Above right: The family crest of William Conolly.

CASTLETOWN HOUSE

✉ Celbridge

☎ 01/628–8252

🌐 www.castletownhouse.ie

💶 € 4.50

🕐 Open Mar. 17—mid-Nov., Wed.–Sat. 10–5, Sun. 10–6.

THE ENTRANCE HALL

Studded with 17th-century hunting scenes painted by Paul de Vos, this soaring white-on-white entryway showcases one of Ireland's greatest staircases. Also extraordinary are the walls festooned with plasterwork sculpted by the Brothers Lafranchini, famous for their stuccoed swags, flora, and portraits.

THE LONG GALLERY

Upstairs at the rear of the house, this massive room—almost 80 feet by 23 feet—is the most notable of the public rooms. Hued in a vibrant cobalt blue and topped by a coved ceiling covered with Italianate stuccowork and graced by three Venetian Murano glass chandeliers, it is a striking exercise in the antique Pompeian style.

THE PRINT ROOM

Smaller but even more memorable is the Print Room, the only example in Ireland of this elegant fad. Fashionable young women loved to glue black-and-white prints—here, looking like oversize postage stamps in a giant album—onto salon walls. This was the 18th-century forerunner of today's teens covering their walls with posters of rock-star icons.

Above left: The Grand Staircase. Upper right: 18th-century Italian engravings decorate the Print Room. Bottom right: A marble statue within the Long Gallery. Far right: Mahogony bureau made for Lady Louisa, circa 1760.

WHAT A WAY TO GO

"I do not get any idea of the beauty of my house if I live in it…only if I can gaze upon the house from far off," proclaimed Lady Louisa in 1821 of her beloved Castletown. In her late seventies, she had a tent built on the front lawn so she could study the house at her leisure. After one evening on the lawn she promptly caught a chill and died.

5 OTHER GREAT GEORGIAN HOUSES

Newbridge, County Dublin

Emo Court, County Laois

Westport House, County Mayo

Florence Court, County Fermanagh

Castle Coole, County Fermanagh

RUSSBOROUGH: A TEMPLE TO ART

An Irish Xanadu, Russborough House pulls out all the stops to achieve Palladian perfection.

Another conspicuously grand house rising seemingly in the middle of nowhere—actually the western part of County Wicklow—Russborough was an extravagance paid for by the wages of beer. In 1741, a year after inheriting a vast fortune from his brewer father, Joseph Leeson commissioned architect Richard Castle to build him a home of palatial stature, and was rewarded with this slightly over-the-top house, whose monumental 700-foot-long façade one-upped every other great house in Ireland. Following Castle's death, the project was taken over and completed by his associate, Francis Bindon. Today, the house serves as a showcase for the celebrated collection of Old Master paintings of Sir Alfred Beit, a descendant of the De Beers diamond family, who had bought and majestically restored the property in 1952.

PRINCELY MAGNIFICENCE

The first sight of Russborough draws gasps from visitors: a mile-long, beech-lined avenue leads to a distant embankment on which sits the longest house frontage in Ireland. Constructed of silver-gray Wicklow granite, the façade encompasses a seven-bay central block, from either end of which radiate semicircular loggias connecting the flanking wings—the finest example in Ireland of Palladio's "winged device."

The interiors are full of grand period rooms that were elegantly refurbished in the 1950s by their new, moneyed owner under the eye of the legendary 20th-century decorator, Lady Colefax. The Hall is centered around a massive black Kilkenny marble chimneypiece and has a ceiling modeled after one in the Irish Parliament. Four 18th-century Joseph Vernet marine landscapes—once missing

Top left: A look at the 700–foot façade of Russborough House. Bottom left: The grand Saloon. Above right: The Hall. Opposite, top: Drawing Room. Opposite: Vermeer's *Lady Writing a Letter*.

RUSSBOROUGH HOUSE

✉ Off N81, Blessington

☎ 045/865-239

🌐 www.russborough.ie

🎫 € 10

🕐 Open May–Sept., daily 10–6; Apr. and Oct., Sun. 10–5.

but found by Sir Alfred—once again grace the glorious stucco moldings created to frame them in the Drawing Room. The grandest room, the Saloon, is famed for its 18th-century stucco ceiling by the Lafranchini brothers; fine Old Masters hang on walls covered in 19th-century Genoese velvet. The views out the windows take in the foothills of the Wicklow Mountains and the famous Poulaphouca reservoir in front of the house.

VERMEER, DIAMONDS, AND GANGSTERS

If it can be said that beer paid for the house, then diamonds paid for the paintings. Russborough House is today as famed for its art collection—and the numerous attempts, some successful, to steal it—as for its architecture. Credit for this must go to Sir Alfred Beit (1903—1994), nephew of the cofounder of De Beers Diamonds. One evening in 1974 while Alfred was enjoying a quiet dinner with his wife, the door burst open and in marched Rose Dugdale, an English millionaire's daughter turned IRA stalwart. Her gang "liberated" 19 of the Beit masterpieces, including Vermeer's fabled *Lady Writing a Letter*, hopefully to bargain for the release of two IRA members jailed in London. Once the paintings were recovered a week later, Sir Alfred decided to donate 17 works to the National Gallery of Ireland. Alas, a week before the handing-over ceremony in 1986, Sir Alfred and his wife were again settling down to dine when in marched Martin Cahill, a.k.a. "The General," Dublin's most notorious underworld boss (and subject of three major movies). He made off with the Vermeer and 16 other paintings. They were returned and now sit safely (we hope) in the National Gallery.

STUCCADORES

Sounds better than plaster-workers, no? Baroque exuberance reigns in the house's lavishly ornamented plasterwork ceilings executed by the celebrated stuccadores, the Brothers Lafranchini, who originally hailed from Switzerland and worked in other great houses in Ireland, including Castletown. Their decorative flair adorns the Music Room and Library, but even these pale compared to the plasterwork done by an unknown artisan in the Staircase Hall—an extravaganza of whipped-cream moldings, cornucopias, and Rococo scrolls: "the ravings of a maniac," according to one 19th-century critic, who guessed that only an Irishman would have had the blarney to pull it off.

names like Buttercup, Over Arch, and the Yellow Room, with its claw-foot bath set in an alcove. Try to get a room overlooking the walled garden, where the scent of wildflowers wafts in through the beautiful French doors. The outstanding haute-Irish dinner menu changes daily. Specialties include organic Wicklow lamb chops with sweet-and-sour garden turnip and thyme-scented jus. **Pros:** 530 acres of parkland; luxury bathrooms; superb dining room. **Cons:** books up easily; some variance in room quality; expensive food. ⊠ *Dunlavin, Co. Wicklow* ☎ *045/403–112* ⊕ *www.rathsallagh.com* ↩ *31 rooms* 🛏 *In-room: a/c, Wi-Fi. In-hotel: restaurant, bar, golf course, tennis court* ⊟ *AE, DC, MC, V* ⊚ *BP, MAP.*

THE CURRAGH

8 km (5 mi) southwest of Naas on M7, 25½ km (16 mi) west of Pou-laphouca Reservoir.

The broad plain of the Curragh, bisected by the main N7 road, is the biggest area of common land in Ireland, encompassing about 31 square km (12 square mi) and devoted mainly to grazing.

This is Ireland's major racing center, home of the **Curragh Racecourse** (⊠ *N7* ☎ *045/441–205* ⊕ *www.curragh.ie*) ; the Irish Derby and other international horse races are run here.

KILDARE TOWN

5 km (3 mi) west of the Curragh on M7, 51 km (32 mi) southwest of Dublin via N7 and M7.

Horse breeding is the cornerstone of County Kildare's thriving economy, and Kildare Town is the place to come if you're crazy about horses. But, in addition to all things equine, Kildare boasts such stellar attractions, including the famous Japanese Gardens.

GETTING HERE

BUS TRAVEL   Bus Éireann runs a regular daily bus to the center of town from Dublin (€10.30 one-way, €13.70 round-trip; 1 hour; 14 buses daily).

TRAIN TRAVEL   Kildare Town train station is just outside town but a free bus service meets the trains and drops you into the center of town. Kildare Town is a major rail junction serviced by Irish Rail and has trains to Dublin (€11 one-way, €22 round-trip; 45 minutes; about 10 trains a day); Galway (€18 one-way, €35 round-trip; 2 hours; 4 trains daily); Limerick (€20 one-way, €39 round-trip; 1 hour 45 minutes; 4 trains daily); and Cork (€28 one-way, €56 round-trip; 2 hours 25 minutes; 2 to 4 trains daily).

Visitor Information Kildare Tourist Office (⊠ *Market House* ☎ *045/521–240* ⊕ *www.kildare.ie/tourism*).

EXPLORING

Right off Kildare's main market square, the **Silken Thomas** (☎ *045/522–232*) pub re-creates an old-world atmosphere with open fireplaces, dark wood, and leaded lights; it's a good place to stop for lunch before exploring the sights here.

The Church of Ireland **St. Brigid's Cathedral** is where the eponymous saint founded a religious settlement in the 5th century. The present cathedral, with its stocky tower, is a restored 13th-century structure. It was partially rebuilt around 1686, but restoration work wasn't completed for another 200 years. The stained-glass west window of the cathedral depicts three of Ireland's greatest saints: Brigid, Patrick, and Columba. In pre-Christian times Druids gathered around a sacred oak that stood on the grounds and from which Kildare (*Cill Dara*), or the "church of the oak," gets its name. Also on the grounds is a restored fire pit reclaimed from the time of Brigid, when a fire was kept burning—by a chaste woman—in a female-only fire temple. Interestingly, Brigid started the place for women, but it was she who asked monks to move here as well. ☒ *Off Market Sq.* ☎ *No phone* 💷 *€2* ☉ *May–Sept., Mon.–Sat. 10–1 and 2–5, Sun. 2–5.*

The 108-foot-high **round tower,** in the graveyard of St. Brigid's Cathedral, is the second highest in Ireland (the highest is in Kilmacduagh in County Galway). It dates from the 12th century. Extraordinary views across much of the Midlands await you if you're energetic enough to climb the stairs to the top. ☎ *045/521–229* 💷 *€4* ☉ *May–Sept., Mon.–Sat. 10–1 and 2–5, Sun. 2–5.*

If you're a horse aficionado, or even just curious, check out the **National Stud Farm,** a main center of Ireland's racing industry. The Stud was founded in 1900 by brewing heir Colonel William Hall-Walker, and transferred to the Irish state in 1945. It's here that breeding stallions are groomed, exercised, tested, and bred. Spring and early summer, when mares have foals, are the best times to visit. The **National Stud Horse Museum,** also on the grounds, recounts the history of horses in Ireland. Its most outstanding exhibit is the skeleton of Arkle, the Irish racehorse that won major victories in Ireland and England during the late 1960s. The museum also contains medieval evidence of horses, such as bones from 13th-century Dublin, and some early examples of equestrian equipment. ☒ *1½ km (1 mi) south of Kildare Town* ☎ *045/521–617* ⊕ *www.irish-national-stud.ie* 💷 *€11, includes entry to Japanese Gardens* ☉ *Mid-Feb.–mid-Nov., daily 9:30–5:30, mid-Nov.–Dec. daily 9:30–5.*

★ Adjacent to the National Stud Farm, the **Japanese Gardens** were created between 1906 and 1910 by the Stud's founder, Colonel Hall-Walker, and laid out by a Japanese gardener, Tassa Eida, and his son Minoru. The gardens are recognized as among the finest Asian gardens in the world, although they're more of an East–West hybrid than authentically Japanese. The Scots pine trees, for instance, are an appropriate stand-in for traditional Japanese pines, which signify long life and happiness. The gardens symbolically chart the human progression from birth to death, although the focus is on the male journey. A series of landmarks runs along a meandering path: the Tunnel of Ignorance (No. 3) represents a child's lack of understanding; the Engagement and Marriage bridges (Nos. 8 and 9) span a small stream; and from the Hill of Ambition (No. 13), you can look back over your joys and sorrows. It ends with the Gateway to Eternity (No. 20), beyond which lies a Zen Buddhist meditation sand garden. This is a worthwhile destination any time of the year, though it's particularly glorious in spring and fall. ⊠ *About 2½ km (1½ mi) south of Kildare Town, clearly signposted off Market Sq.* ☎ *045/521–617* ⊕ *www.irish-national-stud.ie* ⊠ *€11, includes entry to National Stud Farm* ⊗ *Mid-Feb.–mid-Nov., daily 9:30–5:30; mid-Nov.–Dec., daily 9:30–5.*

WHERE TO EAT AND STAY

$$$$
CONTINENTAL
Fodor's Choice
★

✕ **La Serre.** Stunningly beautiful, this restaurant now crowns the baronial estate surroundings of the Lyons Demense. Choosing between a table in the sheltered courtyard or

> **HORSEFEATHERS!**
>
> National Stud Farm founder Colonel Hall-Walker may just have been more than a little eccentric—a believer in astrology, he had charts drawn up for his foals. Those with unfavorable predictions were sold right away. He even built the stallion stalls with lantern roofs to allow the moon and stars to work their magic on the equine occupants.

the splendid Turner-designed conservatory is the hardest thing about dining here—nearly everything on chef Paul Carroll's menu is a winner. He masterfully mixes Mediterranean moods in such stellar choices as the roast scallops with oxtail–Jerusalem artichoke purée or his signature pork loin with pearl onions and apple sage sauce. Others will pounce on the classic fish pie. But the tastiest thing here may be the conservatory: one of the most gorgeous dining rooms in all Europe, it gloriously mixes hard-rock walls, Victorian glasshouse windows, and fanciful farm-utensil "bouquets" (on either side of the soaring fireplace) to create a swooningly delicious ambience. If you can tear yourself away, it will be for the barbecues that are hosted in the courtyard every Sunday in summer. La Serre is part of the impressively restored Village at Lyons complex that is built up around an historic canal stop and manor estate. Adjacent to the restaurant is the Shackleton House, with 12 guest rooms (starting at €175) all done in a flawless mix of Chesterfield sofas, modern luxury, and Irish Palladian decoration. ⊠ *Celbridge* ☎ *01/630–3500* ⊕ *www.villageatlyons.com* ⊟ *AE, DC, MC, V* ⊗ *Closed Mon. and Tues. No dinner Sun.*

$$$–$$$$ 🛏 **Keadeen Hotel.** The luxurious spa and health center are the big attractions at this family-owned hotel on 10 acres of flower-filled gardens. Light is a constant theme in the spacious bedrooms with pastel-color finishings and big windows overlooking the lawns below. Giant wall murals in the Derby Room restaurant are dedicated to the true heroes of Kildare, those famous racehorses. Don't miss the chance to take a dip in the ancient-Roman-style pool; it's a real miniature sea of tranquility. **Pros:** good spa and pool; light-filled rooms. **Cons:** uninspired architecture; popular for weddings; can feel very busy at times. ⊠ *Newbridge, Co. Kildare* ☎ *045/431–666* ⊕ *www.keadeenhotel.ie* ⊷ *75 rooms* ♿ *In-room: a/c, Wi-Fi. In-hotel: restaurant, bar, pool, gym, spa, parking (free)* ⊟ *AE, MC, V* ⦿ *BP, MAP.*

The Midlands

INCLUDING COUNTIES CAVAN, LAOIS,
LEITRIM, LONGFORD, MONAGHAN, OFFALY,
ROSCOMMON, AND WESTMEATH

WORD OF MOUTH

"Clonmacnoise is literally at the very heart of Ireland. The view is
awesome, over the wide Shannon, with swans and herons always
there, and boats creaming slowly along. The pictures don't do
it justice. For me the most moving thing was seeing that High
Cross . . . you can touch it. Immense spiritual power there. The
peace that this holy place exudes is awesome."

—anchoress

WELCOME TO THE MIDLANDS

TOP REASONS TO GO

★ **Stately Clonmacnoise:** Atmospheric and still spirit-warm, this great early Christian monastery survived Viking, Norman, and English invaders over the centuries.

★ **Green Mansions:** "The biggest farm in the world," the Midlands is also home to stately homes and gardens, including fairy-tale Tullynally Castle and Birr Castle.

★ **Hiking the Slieve Bloom Mountains:** Dip in and out of the 20-mi Slieve Bloom Trail, ideal hiking country for those with a yen to rise above their surroundings.

★ **Athlone:** The newly restored 13th-century castle along with the quirky shops and Europe's oldest pub on the left bank are worth taking time to visit.

★ **The Treasure House of Emo:** A quintessential landmark of 18th-century Palladian elegance, Emo—the former home of the Earl of Portarlington—has a spectacular rotunda inspired by Rome's Pantheon.

1 The Eastern Midlands. Just an hour from Dublin, this region is essentially rich farmland but is studded with even richer sights: grand homes like Emo Court, Belvedere House, and Tullynally Castle; once-upon-a-time villages such as Abbeyleix; and the historic treats of Fore Abbey and Locke's Distillery. Leaving the ancient kingdom of Leinster, you come to two counties of Ulster: Cavan and Monaghan. Beyond Cavan Town you enter the heart of the Northern Lakelands, dotted with hundreds of beautiful lakes.

2 The Western Midlands. One of the corners of "hidden Ireland," this region is unblighted by crowds. While some of the country's most distinctive boglands are here, cultural treasures also beckon: stately Birr Castle and Strokestown House, and the great early Christian monastery of Clonmacnoise, burial place of the Kings of Tara.

GETTING ORIENTED

Perfect for the relaxed visitor who values the subtle over the spectacular, the flat, fertile plain at the center of Ireland is full of relatively undiscovered historic towns, abbey ruins, and grand houses. Though just two hours from the chaotic rush of Dublin, Cork, or Galway, the region is carpeted with countryside perfect for bicycling: no wonder stressed-out Dubliners love to head here to chill out.

THE MIDLANDS PLANNER

Transportation Basics

The roads of the Midlands offer an easier intro to Irish driving than the hairpin bends of West Cork and Connemara. Because the area has a decent network of main arteries and off-the-beaten-track byroads, a car may deliver the best option for covering the widest itinerary. Happily, bus and train routes in the region have improved greatly over the past two decades. Public transport services are regular through the main towns—Athlone, Portarlington, Abbeyleix, Nenagh, Cavan, and Longford. Of course, you may have to transfer—give time and attention to the appropriate timetables when planning your jaunts.

However, the freedom of your own wheels will bring ample rewards in transporting you to the area's many hidden lakes and villages. Don't be surprised to round a bend only to confront a herd of sheep idly grazing with little hurry about them—do what the locals do, slow to a stop and wait for an opening in the woolly mass to occur. The same goes for cows. Refrain from honking your horn on these occasions—it will only confirm your status as an impatient tourist, and, besides, the cows won't take a bit of notice.

Finding a Place to Stay

The Irish bed-and-breakfast offers great value in the Midlands—farmhouses and homes geared to paying guests provide direct contact with local families and the lore of their area. Time was when these kinds of accommodations veered toward the spartan—not anymore. Good beds, decent heating, en-suite bathrooms, and the legendary Irish breakfast are now the norm; broadband, flat-screen TVs, and computer games courtesy of the landlady's kids are often part of the bargain.

Although B&Bs may not offer the same kind of privacy as hotels, they still work delightfully well as the ultimate way to meet genuine Irish folk—a bird's-eye view into working families and the organized chaos of a country household.

As commercial progress has blossomed in the Midlands, so, too, have the options in hotels, country houses, and cottage rentals increased. Pretty much every town now has more than one decent hotel—most with health centers and spa facilities.

From June to early September, tourism gets into serious stride, bolstered by the many Irish families using their holiday homes and getaway cottages in the region.

Finding accommodation is never a major problem—except for those weekends when a town is holding an annual music festival.

Tourist offices generally cope bravely with these seasonal influxes and if you arrive without local knowledge or reservations, there's rarely a problem that can't be solved with a few phone calls.

At a rock concert in Abbeyleix a few years ago, we heard that four travelers found temporary lodgings in a convent, but that's another story altogether.

A Blaze of Festivals

The first decade of the 21st century has produced a blaze of festivals celebrating music, drama, literature, and small-town fairs throughout the Midlands. Music dominates at some, such as **Castle Palooza Festival** (⊕ www.castlepalooza.com), held at Charleville Castle in Tullamore over the August holiday weekend. The **Festival of Fires** (⊕ www.festivalofthefires.com), at Westmeath's Hill of Uisneach (the historic residence of the High Kings of Ireland and a gathering place for tribes and clans), features theater and music and is Europe's oldest festival. In mid-July, one of Ireland's best-loved songwriters, Percy French, is celebrated in Roscommon town and at **Castlecoote House** (⊕ www.percyfrench.ie) with a summer school, complete with concerts and lectures. French was born at Cloonyquinn House near Elphin, and his best-known songs include "Are Ye Right There Michael?," and "Phil the Fluther's Ball."

South Ulster gets in on the act when Virginia in Cavan hosts the annual **Pumpkin Festival** (⊕ www.virginia.ie) on the October holiday weekend with some of Europe's largest pumpkins. Next door, County Monaghan holds its **Flat Lake Festival** (⊕ www.theflatlakefestival.com) in Clones in mid-August. The event focuses on arts, books, films, and music with numerous literary readings in tents and straw-filled barns—there's even sheep karaoke. Can a sheep dance?

Many other towns have rural shows or arts festivals. The **Terryglass Arts Festival** (⊕ www.terryglassartsfestival.ie) in North Tipperary, for example, presents music, dance, and street theater for five days in the third week of August. Ireland's biggest agricultural gathering—the **Tullamore Show** (⊕ www.tullamoreshow.com)—attracts 60,000 annually in early August to its new site on the Butterfield estate near Blueball on the road to Birr. An international visitor center opened in 2009 caters to the huge crowds of overseas visitors who flock to see the largest assembly of cattle anywhere in Ireland competing in 1,000 classes for 42 national titles.

When to Go

C'mon, this is Ireland, after all—a rain mac or windbreaker should never be far from your side when you visit the Midlands. Though, in fairness, it must be said that the legendary "soft" weather has become noticeably more clement; since 2000, Ireland has been recording more hours of sunshine.

The incremental increase in the number of sunny days each year has prompted many philosophical discussions in Irish pubs on whether that itty-bitty hole in the ozone is really such a bad thing. The best time to visit the Midlands is the spring and summer when there's at least a better chance of some sunshine, although bring a rain mac just in case.

Midlands Musts

With historical monuments such as Clonmacnoise, Fore Abbey, and the Rock of Dunamase, as well as many fine ancient architectural gems such as Emo Court and Carrig Glas Manor, you'll never be more than 16 km (10 mi) from ancient history.

If you just want to wander where your nose takes you for a few days, the relatively quiet roads, unpopulated countryside, and tucked-away vistas around the Slieve Blooms will deliver many peaceful rewards.

DINING AND LODGING PRICE CATEGORIES (IN EUROS)					
	¢	$	$$	$$$	$$$$
Restaurants	under €12	€12–€18	€19–€24	€25–€32	over €32
Hotels	under €80	€80–€120	€121–€170	€171–€210	over €210

Restaurant prices are for a main course at dinner. Hotel prices are for a standard double room in high season.

GETTING AROUND

Air Travel

Dublin Airport is the principal international airport that serves the Midlands; car-rental facilities are available here.

Sligo Airport has daily flights from Dublin on Aer Lingus.

Airport Information Aer Lingus (☎ 0818/365–000 ⊕ www.aerlingus.com). **Dublin Airport** (☎ 01/814–1111 ⊕ www.dublinairport.com). **Sligo Airport** (☎ 071/916–8280 ⊕ www.sligoairport.com).

Visitor Information

Four Midlands Tourist Information Offices (TIOs) are open all year: Cavan, Monaghan, Mullingar, and Portlaoise.

The Mullingar TIO has information on Counties Westmeath, Offaly, Monaghan, Cavan, and Laois.

Another five Midlands TIOs are open seasonally: Athlone (April–October), Birr (May–September), Clonmacnoise (April–October), Longford (June–September), and Tullamore (mid-June–mid-September).

Find tourist office addresses, phone numbers, and Web sites listed under the main town headings *throughout this chapter*.

Bus Travel

With a much more extensive network than trains, buses are a better bet for exploring much of the Midlands. Most small towns and villages are serviced by at least one bus per day, while trains are generally limited to towns on main lines linking cities.

Bus Éireann runs an express bus from Dublin to Mullingar in 1½ hours, with a round-trip fare of €29. Buses depart three times daily.

A regular-speed bus, leaving twice daily, makes the trip in two hours. Express buses also make stops at Longford (2¼ hours), Boyle (3¼ hours), and Sligo (4¼ hours).

There's also a daily bus from Mullingar to Athlone and an express service connecting Galway, Athlone, Longford, Cavan, Clones, Monaghan, and Sligo.

Details of all bus services are available from the Bus Éireann depots *listed below*. In addition, the train stations for the following larger towns also act as their bus depots: Athlone, Cavan, and Longford.

Bus Information Bus Éireann (☎ 01/836–6111 in Dublin ⊕ www.buseireann.ie). **Cavan Bus Office** (☎ 049/433–1709). **Monaghan Bus Office** (☎ 047/82377). **Ulsterbus** (☎ 004/4289–066–6630 ⊕ www.translink.co.uk).

Car Travel

For optimum touring, a car is sometimes necessary to really explore the region.

Mullingar, Longford, and Boyle are on the main N4 route between Dublin and Sligo.

It takes one hour to drive the 55 km (34 mi) from Dublin to Mullingar and two hours from Mullingar to Sligo (150 km [93 mi]).

If you are coming to Mullingar from southwestern Ireland, take N52 to Nenagh, where it meets N7, and follow that into Limerick.

R390 from Mullingar leads you west to the new Athlone bypass, where it connects with N6 to Galway. The 120-km (75-mi) drive takes about 2½ hours.

Train Travel

All trains are run by Irish Rail. A direct-rail service links Longford (via Mullingar) to Dublin (Connolly Station); on average, eight trains per day make the 1¾-hour journey. This excursion costs €20.50 one-way and €22.50 round-trip. Contact Irish Rail for information.

Trains from Mullingar to Dublin run regularly (i.e., every 2 hours) Monday through Friday, with a restricted service on weekends; stops include Longford (35 minutes), Boyle (1¼ hours), and Sligo (2 hours).

Portlaoise is served by a good commuter service and many of the intercity Dublin–Cork trains stop here.

The intercity service to Galway City from Dublin Heuston serves Portarlington, Tullamore, and Athlone.

Roscrea and Nenagh are served by a twice-daily train to Limerick City.

Train Information Athlone Railway Station (☎ 090/648–4406). **Cavan Bus Office** (☎ 049/433–1709). **Irish Rail** (☎ 01/836–6222 ⊕ www.irishrail.ie). **Longford Railway Station** (☎ 043/3345208). **Sligo Railway Station** (☎ 071/916–0066).

Tour Options

To plan a trip within any particular county or area, you're best off starting with the local tourist office (see listings under town name). They will have a thorough list of the must-see attractions in their areas. Several of the region's larger travel agencies (listed below) also organize tours.

Tour Companies Airboran Travel (✉ 4 Lismard Ct., Portlaoise ☎ 057/862–1226). **Grenham Travel** (✉ 1 Connaught St., Athlone ☎ 090/649–2028). **O'Hanrahan Travel** (✉ 59 Dublin St., Monaghan ☎ 047/81133). **Trikon Travel** (✉ Castle St., Roscommon ☎ 090/662–6243).

Road Conditions

Most of the winding roads in the Midlands are uncrowded, although you may encounter an occasional animal or agricultural machine crossing the road.

In Mullingar, the cattle-trading town, roads can become badly congested.

Local Car Rental Agencies Gerry Mullin (✉ North Rd., Monaghan ☎ 047/81396).

A Cyclist's Paradise

One of the best ways to immerse yourself in the Midlands is to meander through the region on a bike.

Although the area may not offer the spectacular scenery of the more hilly coastal regions, its level, Netherlands-like terrain means a less strenuous ride.

The twisting roads are generally in good (well, good enough) condition.

Happily, there are picnic spots galore in the many state-owned forests just off the main roads.

Fáilte Ireland recommends two tours: one of the Athlone-Mullingar-Roscommon area, and another of the Cavan-Monaghan-Mullingar region.

The more rural regions of Laois allow you to spend days exploring beautiful glens, waterfalls, nature trails, and wooded regions around the Slieve Bloom Mountains.

Try to avoid the major trunk roads that bisect the region. After all, this is an area that deserves thorough and leisurely exploration!

Contact the regional and township tourist offices for all the details.

4

CRUISING ON THE SHANNON

Whether you opt for a one-hour or one-week journey—and choose between a guided boat tour or private boat hire—cruising on the River Shannon is a never-to-be-forgotten experience, giving a new perspective on 'oul Ireland.

(top) A great vacation along the Shannon river; (right, top) Many travelers opt to boat n' bike down river to the boating hub of Athlone; (right, bottom) Ireland's "inland sea," Lough Derg

Think of blissful relaxing times on the river, mooring for lunch at a quayside inn, or sampling traditional culture with gregarious lock-keepers. Along the Shannon's 334-km (207-mi) length you can head to major boating hubs like Athlone, or to historic stretches where it meanders past ancient settlements (such as Clonmacnoise), or to lakes aplenty. The biggest is Ireland's "inland sea," Lough Derg, bordered by easygoing villages like Terryglass and Mountshannon that offer appealingly quiet streets, stone-built cottage restaurants, and rustic harborside bars with picnic tables (many with evening music or Irish dancing sessions). Remember the motto of Shannon cruising is: "There's no hurry"—the boats travel at only 11 kph (7 mph), so a river journey is a slow affair with time to drink in the history, wildlife, and inland gems of an older Ireland many thought had disappeared.

BEST TIME TO GO

Good times to cruise are in May through early June. Rentals are cheaper, the waterways are less crowded, the weather is generally favorable, and daylight stretches well into late evening. Whenever you go, get the scoop on permits, moorings, and river by-laws from Waterways Ireland (⊕ *www. waterwaysireland.org*)

A WONDERFUL DAY ON THE WATER

On the map, the scale of the Shannon may look daunting—it *is* the longest river in Ireland or Britain—but that's one reason why many people opt for an idyllic day-long exploration. If you've time only for a short guided journey then one of the best is up river from Athlone to Lough Ree on a three-hour trip on board the *Viking* boat, costing €10–€20. Or opt to go down river to magnificent Clonmacnois. You can also board pleasure cruisers at Killaloe and Dromineer. If you're feeling romantic, try an evening cruise with the Moon River company which operates a luxurious 100-seater from Carrick-on-Shannon. A detailed commentary is provided on these cruises.

Guided Cruises Moon River ✉ *Carrick-on-Shannon, Co. Leitrim* ☎ *071/962–1777* ⊕ *www.moonriver.ie.*

The Viking ✉ *Athlone, Co. Westmeath* ☎ *090/647–3383* ⊕ *www.vikingtoursireland.ie.*

Silver Line Cruisers (The River Queen) ✉ *Banagher, Co. Offaly* ☎ *057/915–1112* ⊕ *www.silverlinecruisers.com.*

The Spirit of Killaloe ✉ *Killaloe, Co. Clare* ☎ *086/814–0559* ⊕ *www.killaloe.ie/ thespiritofkillaloe.*

GOING WITH THE SHANNON FLOW

As the Shannon has its own slow-paced signature—a place where you are alive to the layers of history along the riverside and sequestered villages, which are a joy to explore—why not consider your own boat hire? The beauty of a personal cruise is that you can concoct your own itinerary, moving at your own speed and stopping off where the notion, and the motion, takes you.

There are four main boating towns for hiring cruisers: Carrick-on-Shannon, Portumna, Banagher, and Williamstown. From luxury cabin cruisers to barges or smaller boats, a glittering array of vessels is available for rent. Prices range from €650 for a two- to four-berth cruiser for one week in the quieter off-season, and from €1,750 in the more expensive summer months. With most companies, you can also rent for three-night/four-day short breaks. Rates start from €450 for the fall and early spring periods, rising to €1,600 in summer.

Boat Hires Carrick Craft ✉ *Carrick-on-Shannon, Co. Leitrim* ☎ *071/962–1777* ⊕ *www.carrickcraft.com.*

Emerald Star ✉ *Portumna, Co. Galway* ☎ *071/962–7633* ⊕ *www.emeraldstar.ie.*

Silver Line Cruisers ✉ *Banagher, Co. Offaly* ☎ *057/915–1112* ⊕ *www. silverlinecruisers.com.*

Shannon Castle Line ✉ *Williamstown Harbor, Whitegate, Co. Clare* ☎ *061/927–042* ⊕ *www.shannoncruisers.com.*

Updated by
Paul Clements

Irish schoolchildren were once taught to think of their country as a saucer, with mountains edging the rim and a dip in the middle. The dip is the Midlands—or the Lakelands, as it's sometimes referred to—and this often-overlooked region comprises nine counties: Cavan, Laois (pronounced leash), Westmeath, Longford, Offaly, Roscommon, Monaghan, Leitrim, and Tipperary. Ask people from other parts of Ireland what the purpose of the Midlands is and they will jest that the region exists simply to hold the rest of the country together.

Indeed, the Midlands is sometimes looked upon with disdain by the Irish people, a few of whom consider the area dull and mundane (the worst of offenses in Ireland). The perception is a bit true: the flat plains of the Midlands are the kind of terrain you rush through on the way to someplace else, and with no major city in the region (Dublin lies to the east, Galway and Limerick to the west, and Cork to the south), it remains a quiet and geographically unspectacular place. Night owls should probably keep going—the wildest thing in these parts is the wind.

But that is precisely why many travelers consider the Midlands a gem in the making. For when it comes to studying how Ireland gets on with its daily life, there are few better places. Here, a town's main hotel is usually one of its prime social centers and can be a good place from which to partake of local life. If you miss out witnessing a wedding reception, First Communion supper, or meeting of the Lions Club, you can still get to know the locals simply by walking along a village's main street. Happily so, since there are plenty of folks who have nothing to do but be pleasant. Here, the pace of life is slower, every neighbor's face is familiar, and there are plenty of minor roads linking the more scenic areas—and if you're in no particular hurry, these are the ones to take. Spend enough time in the region and you might even get to recognize the difference between a Cavan twang and a Tipperary brogue.

The tourist sun also shines brightly on the region because of its notable cultural highlights. Among them are Clonmacnoise, Ireland's most important monastic ruins; historic towns with age-old industries, such as lace making and crystal making; the gorgeous gardens of Birr Castle; and some of Ireland's finest Anglo-Irish houses, including Strokestown Park House, Emo Court, and some of Ireland's most historically delightful hotels. As for scenic pleasures, this region of the country has its fair share of Ireland's 800 bodies of water. Speckling this lush countryside, many of these lakes were formed by glacial action some 10,000 years ago. Because of all the water, much of the landscape is blanket bog, a unique ecosystem that's worth exploring. The River Shannon, one of the longest rivers in Europe and the longest in Britain or Ireland, bisects the Midlands from north to south, piercing a series of loughs (lakes): Lough Allen, Lough Ree, and Lough Derg. The Royal Canal and the Grand Canal cross the Midlands from east to west, ending in the Shannon north and south of Lough Ree.

4

This chapter is organized into two Midlands sections: eastern and western. The first can be easily covered in an extended visit to the Midlands region, as it starts in Abbeyleix, County Laois, and charts a course almost due north to Northern Ireland. But not quite: the tour makes a loop to head back southward, linking up with the second tour. This includes sights west, which means they can be easily visited if you fly into Shannon and begin your explorations in the western half of the country. No matter which region of the Midlands you explore, you'll discover that some towns and villages are hives of activity as young Dublin families make their weekend homes in this pastoral, and infinitely more affordable, region beyond the Pale. They reckon if Charlotte Brontë spent her honeymoon here and Anthony Trollope settled in one of the region's villages to write two of his novels, it's good enough for them.

THE EASTERN MIDLANDS

The eastern fringe of the Midlands is about an hour's drive from Dublin, and a visit to the area could easily be grafted onto a trip to the Dublin environs. In spite of its proximity to the capital, or perhaps because of it, this area is a bit removed from the regular tourist trail and is a source of constant surprises. Unspoiled Georgian villages, ruined castles, and quaint "towns-that-time-forgot" dot the landscape. There are also plenty of opportunities for hill walking, horseback riding, and other outdoor pursuits. Fans of stately homes are in for a treat, as Emo Court and Gardens, Charleville Forest Castle, Belvedere House Gardens, and Tullynally Castle await them.

The Eastern Midlands fan out from the central point of Mullingar. With richer farmland than is found in the northern area of the Midlands, the eastern region tends toward agriculture. But the Dublin commuter culture means that you're as likely to be delayed on a back road by a badly parked BMW as by a slow-moving tractor on its way home from the dairy.

The Midlands

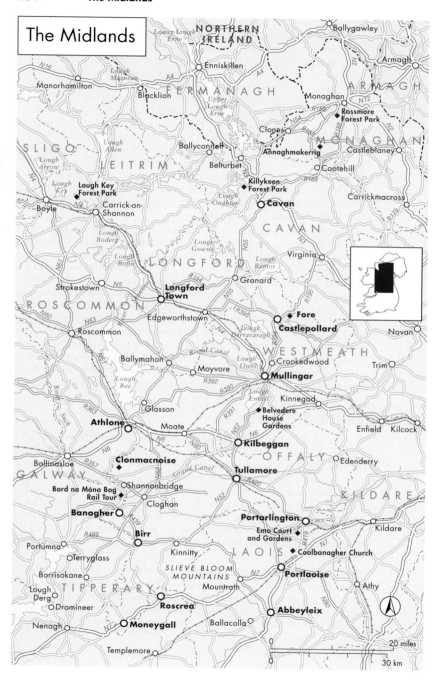

ABBEYLEIX

99 km (61 mi) southwest of Dublin.

"One of the most pleasing villages in Leinster, with each cottage having a useful garden!" Thus spoke noted 19th-century writer J. M. Brewer of Abbeyleix in 1826. Today it happily remains one of the most elegant small towns in Ireland, having retained its charming Georgian ambience and its broad main street, which is lined with well-appointed, stone-cut buildings and original shop fronts in the traditionally ornate Irish style. The entire tree-lined village was built in the 18th century, on the orders of the Viscount de Vesci, to house servants and tradesmen working on his nearby estate. Many town houses and vernacular buildings date from the 1850s, but more recent buildings, including the Market House, erected in 1906, and the Hibernian Bank, from 1900, contribute greatly to the town's tranquil and refined character.

GETTING HERE

BUS TRAVEL   From Dublin or Cork, you can catch one of the six daily Bus Éireann Expressway coaches. Journey time is just under two hours from Dublin and 2¾ hours from Cork. Round-trip tickets to either cost €22.

EXPLORING

★   Don't miss **Morrissey's Pub and Grocery Store,** which has been a working public house since 1775. One of Ireland's best-loved drinking emporiums, it has a dark, wood-panel interior furnished with antique bar fittings. Customers can warm themselves by an ancient potbelly stove. Until 2005 this establishment still functioned as a shop, and while it retains its stocks of groceries, they are no longer for sale. An evocative time capsule, it serves as a reminder of times when you could purchase a pound of butter, the newspaper, and cattle feed while enjoying the obligatory pint of Guinness. In 2008 the owners extended the bar into a 60-seat lounge called No. 10. Thankfully, the pub's prevailing genius loci remains unchanged. Food, including an all-day breakfast with bacon, sausage, black-and-white pudding, and eggs, is served 10:30–9 and you can dine alfresco at picnic tables at the front of the bar. ⊠ *Main St.* ☎ *057/873–1281.*

The **Heritage House,** the former North Boys School, has fascinating informative displays on the de Vesci family and the history of Abbeyleix. The school was originally constructed for the education of Catholics (at the other end of the town you'll find the South School, built for Protestants). Also accessible through the Heritage House is the original Sexton's House (no extra charge), which boasts a stylish interior from the turn of the 19th century. The center also has a crafts shop and coffee parlor. ⊠ *Top of town* ☎ *057/873–1653* ⊕ *www.heritagehousemuseum.com* 🖃€3 ☉ *Apr.–Sept., weekdays 9–5, weekends 1–5; Oct.–Mar. weekdays 9–5.*

Ballinakill, a pretty Georgian village about 5 km (3 mi) south of Abbeyleix, contains the **Heywood Gardens,** designed by the English architect Sir Edwin Lutyens in the early 20th century within an existing 18th-century park. The Lutyenses' house burned down, but the gardens, with landscaping most likely attributable to the famed Gertrude Jekyll, are worth a detour. Guided tours are available through this gardener's paradise,

4

where a formal lawn flanked by traditional herbaceous borders leads to a sunken Italian garden. ✉ *Ballinakill* ☎ *057/873–3563* ⊕ *www.heritageireland.ie* ✉ *Free* ⊗ *Daily 9–dusk.*

WHERE TO STAY

$ 🔁 **Foxrock Inn.** A friendly red setter by the name of Shannon and a terrier called Marley greet new arrivals at this modest guesthouse in the heart of the County Laois countryside. The main attraction of this inn, set in the tiny village of Clough, is the genuinely warm welcome extended by its owners, Sean and Marian Hyland. The enthusiastic couple can bring you up to date on the 200-year history of the inn and adjacent pub, advise you on hiking in the Slieve Bloom Mountains, and organize golf and angling packages. Traditional music on Tuesday night in summer is a big local draw. Rooms are plain but clean and comfortable. Simple, home-cooked dinners and packed lunches are available by advance booking. Clough is 12 km (8 mi) west of Abbeyleix (signposted off the R434 road to Borris-in-Ossory). **Pros:** well off the tourist track but plenty of activities in surrounding area; friendly owners who are knowledgeable about the area. **Cons:** no frills; rooms don't come with any extras. ✉ *Clough, Ballacolla, Co. Laois* ☎ *057/873–8637* ⊕ *www.foxrockinn.com* ⇗ *5 rooms* ♿ *In-room: no a/c, no phone, no TV. In-hotel: restaurant, Internet terminal* ⊟ *AE, V* ⦿ *BP.*

> ### WRECKED RUGS
>
> The carpets for the ill-fated *Titanic* were woven at a now-defunct carpet factory in Abbeyleix.

PORTLAOISE

14 km (9 mi) north of Abbeyleix.

Near the heart of County Laois, the rich farmland south and west of Portlaoise, an hour by train, bus or car from Dublin, is one of Ireland's undiscovered gems. Golf, fishing, hiking, and horseback riding are traditional sports hereabouts, and the development of the Grand Canal for recreational purposes is adding to the area's attractions. Explore the pretty villages and romantic, ivy-covered ruins by car, or follow one of the many hiking trails.

GETTING HERE

BUS TRAVEL   Bus routes leading to Ireland's three main cities—Dublin, Cork, and Limerick—converge at Portlaoise. Bus Éireann operates frequent daily services on the three-hour journey to Cork via Cashel and Cahir with Dublin a one-hour bus ride away via Monasterevin and Kildare; tickets cost €25 round-trip, while Limerick is a three-hour journey via Mountrath, Roscrea, Moneygall, and Nenagh. An independent operator, JJ Kavanagh & Sons, runs two buses daily except Sunday to Carlow and Kilkenny (€12 round-trip), and Dublin Coach offers a €10 fare to Dublin Airport.

TRAIN TRAVEL   Just 70 minutes from Dublin, Portlaoise has 14 daily Irish Rail trains to the capital and is on the main line linking it with Cork, Limerick, and Tralee. The round-trip journey from Portlaoise's small station, five minutes from the town center, to Dublin's Heuston station costs €28.50.

Portarlington can be reached by train as it's a stop on the Dublin–Athlone line; you can also take a southbound train from here to Limerick or continue your journey as far southwest as Killarney (change at Thurles) and Tralee. The fare to Killarney is €54.50 €62 round-trip.

Visitor Information Portlaoise Tourist Office. (✉ *James Fintan Lawlor Ave., Co. Laois* ☎ *057/862–1178* ⊕ *www.discoverireland.ie/eastcoast*).

ESSENTIALS

Transportation Contacts Dublin Coach (☎ *018/627–566* ⊕ *www.dublincoach. ie*). **JJ Kavanagh** (☎ *056/883–1106*).

EXPLORING

Portlaoise's name is derived from the Irish for "Fort of Laois" and refers to the town's strife-filled history. In terms of its architecture, it's rather eclectic—it feels as if bits of other towns were picked up and dropped randomly onto the site. Once best known for having Ireland's highest-security prison, which housed the IRA's most notorious members during the 1970s and '80s and still looms over the town, Portlaoise is undergoing a renaissance. The main street, which once formed part of the main Dublin–Cork road, is now largely given over to pedestrians; pubs and restaurants are flourishing; and the thriving Dunamaise Arts Centre adds an extra dash of culture.

At the Tourist Information Office in Portlaoise you can pick up a map of the **Laois Heritage Trail** (⊕ *www.laoistourism.ie*), a signposted, daylong drive on quiet back roads that takes in 13 heritage sites, ranging from Abbeyleix to Emo Court. The circular trail starts in Borris-in-Ossory on N7.

A dramatic 150-foot-high limestone outcrop, the famous **Rock of Dunamase** dominates the landscape east of Portlaoise. For this reason, it was used as a military stronghold. As far back as AD 140 its occupants kept watch against marauders, and it was fought over in turn by the Vikings, Normans, Irish, and English. Today it's crowned by the ruins of a 12th-century castle, once home to Diarmuid MacMurrough, king of Leinster, who precipitated the Norman invasion when he invited the famed and feared Norman leader Strongbow to Ireland to marry his daughter, whose dowry included the Rock. Some of the castle's thick walls still stand. The main reason for visiting the Rock today is to take the short walk to its summit to enjoy the view of the Slieve Bloom Mountains to the north and the Wicklow Mountains to the south. ✉ *5 km (3 mi) east of Portlaoise on N80 (Stradbally Rd.).*

WHERE TO EAT AND STAY

$ ✕ **Kingfisher.** In the town center, this is a particularly lively and stylish spot.
INDIAN The high-ceiling room was once a banking hall, but now its softly lighted
★ walls glow with warm terra-cotta tones, the perfect complement to the slightly spicy Punjabi cuisine. *Pappadams* (crunchy lentil-flour breads) and condiments appear on the table before you order, and the friendly staff in traditional dress can guide you expertly through the long menu. Dishes vary from mild and creamy meat kormas to fresh cod with a mild blend of spices and lemon juice to chicken "cooked with angry green chilies." Last orders for dinner are taken as late as 10:45 PM, so this is definitely the place to go when your tummy rumbles late on a summer's eve. ✉ *Old AIB Bank,*

Main St. ☎ *057/866–2500* ⊕ *www. kingfisherrestaurant.com* ▭ *AE, MC, V* ⊗ *No lunch Sat.–Tues.*

$$
CONTINENTAL
Fodor's Choice
★

✗ **The Lemon Tree.** Although on Portlaoise's main street, this spot is its best-kept culinary secret. It combines an informal atmosphere with modern-but-cozy surroundings. Starters might include duck confit with hoisin sauce; many enjoy the prime Irish Angus sirloin for the main course or loin of Slaney valley lamb roasted in bacon. The popular fresh fish dishes that tantalize the taste buds include scallops, and fillet of sea bass grilled with black olive tapenade. Lunch is available only to groups, by advance reservation. The restaurant is on the first floor of the premises; downstairs, Delaney's pub serves bar food during the day. ✉ *67 Main St.* ☎ *057/866–2200* ⊕ *www.grellandelaney. com/lemontree* ▭ *AE, MC, V* ⊗ *No dinner Mon. No lunch.*

$$$–$$$$
Fodor's Choice
★

🏨 **Heritage Golf & Spa Resort.** Step into this hotel's spacious, light-filled atrium with its touches of marble, cherrywood, and mahogany and you quickly realize you have entered another world. This sprawling complex opened its doors in 2006 and has proved a hugely popular Midlands draw. The rooms—all elegantly appointed with classical furniture and artwork—look out over an 18-hole course and across to the Slieve Bloom Mountains. The Arlington restaurant offers an Irish twist to cooking with such delights as grilled black sole on the bone with nutty butter. More informal options are found in the Sol Oriens Italian restaurant, or opt for the blow-out Pink Afternoon Tea (at €55 for two with a glass of Taittinger rosé Champagne). A tunnel links the hotel to the spa, where the tyranny of endless choices stretches to more than 70 treatments. The parkland championship course (home to a golf school) was codesigned by Seve Ballesteros and features challenging doglegs, as well as lakes (stocked with brown trout). **Pros:** a haven of peace, calm, and elegance; the smoked haddock at breakfast is a winner. **Cons:** the grass-cutters start early so prepare for a lawnmower wake-up around 6:30; isolated from any nearby towns. ✉ *Killenard* ☎ *057/864–5500* ⊕ *www.theheritage.com* ⤳ *98 rooms, 13 suites* ☆ *In-room: a/c, Wi-Fi. In-hotel: 3 restaurants, bars, golf course, tennis court, gym, Internet terminal* ▭ *AE, MC, V* ⏺️*BP.*

$$
★

🏨 **Ivyleigh House.** Owners Dinah and Jerry Campion say they like to give their guests "the best of everything," and that maxim is certainly in evidence the minute you step inside this elegant Georgian town house next to the Portlaoise railway station. Open fires, antiques, and sumptuously cozy sofas await you in the beige-on-brown, wood-accented sitting room. Upstairs, luxurious drapes grace the sash windows of the spacious bedrooms, most of which are done in dramatic hues like pink and emerald. A virtual avalanche of plump cushions scattered on your antique bed reinforces the tone of rest and relaxation. Guests find it hard to choose from all the goodies on the scrumptious breakfast menu, but few can resist the Cashel Blue cheese cakes. Room TVs are available by request. **Pros:** breakfasts are lavish, filling, and imaginative;

luxury linens. **Cons:** no baths, so it's a power shower only; the town lacks much in the way of evening activities. ⊠ *Bank Pl., Portlaoise, Co. Laois* ☎ *057/862–2081* ⊕ *www.ivyleigh.com* ↩ *6 rooms* ☼ *In-room: no a/c, no TV (some), Internet* ⊟ *MC, V* ⓞ *BP.*

NIGHTLIFE AND THE ARTS

★ Also known as Turley's Bar, the canal-side **Anchor Inn** (⊠ *Grand Canal near Stradbally, Vicarstown* ☎ *No phone*), 10 km (6 mi) east of Portlaoise on N80, is popular for its lively Monday-night traditional-music sessions, which start around 10. Sessions take place more frequently in spring and summer. Fishing, boating, and canal-bank walks are all accessible from this location.

The lively **Dunamaise Arts Centre** (⊠ *Main St.* ☎ *057/866–3355* ⊕ *www. dunamaise.ie*) has a 240-seat theater, an art gallery, and a friendly coffeehouse (open daily 8:30–5:30). You may catch a professional production on tour or a local amateur show. The exhibition space displays the work, usually of a surprisingly high standard, of contemporary Irish artists. It's built into the back of the 18th-century stone courthouse on Church Street in a space that used to be the town jail.

PORTARLINGTON

13 km (8 mi) northeast of Portlaoise.

Built on the River Barrow in the late 17th century, Portarlington was originally an English settlement. Later, a Huguenot colony developed here, and French surnames are still common in the area. Some good examples of Georgian architecture can be seen in the town.

★ A quintessential landmark of Irish Palladian elegance lies just 7 km (4½ mi) south of Portarlington. **Emo Court and Gardens** is one of the finest large-scale country houses near Dublin that is open to the public. Even if you elect to skip over much of the Midlands, try to tack on a visit to Emo, especially if you're in Kildare or Wicklow counties. To come upon the house from the main drive, an avenue lined with magisterial Wellingtonia trees, is to experience one of Ireland's great treasure-house views. Begun in 1790 by James Gandon, architect of the Custom House and the Four Courts in Dublin, Emo (the name derives from the Italian version of the original Irish name Imoe) is thought to be Gandon's only domestic work matching the grand scale of his Dublin civic buildings. Construction continued on and off for 70 years, as family money troubles followed the untimely death of Emo's original patron and owner, the first earl of Portarlington.

In 1996 Emo's English-born owner donated the house to the Irish nation. The ground-floor rooms have been beautifully restored and decorated and are prime examples of life on the grand scale. Among the highlights are the entrance hall, with trompe l'oeil paintings in the apses on each side, and the library, which has a carved Italian-marble mantel with putti frolicking among grapevines. But the showstopper, and one of the finest rooms in Ireland, is the dome rotunda—the work of one of Gandon's successors, the Irish architect William Caldbeck—inspired by the Roman Pantheon. Marble pilasters with gilded Corinthian capitals

In the spring, the gardens at Emo Court rival the splendor of its Neoclassical-style salons—here, a section of parkland abloom with bluebells.

support the rotunda's blue-and-white coffered dome. Emo's 55 acres of grounds include a 20-acre lake, lawns planted with yew trees, a small garden (the Clocker) with Japanese maples, and a larger one (the Grapery) with rare trees and shrubs. There's also a tearoom on the premises. ✉ *Emo* ☎ *057/862–6573* 🌐 *www.heritageireland.ie* ✉ *Gardens free, house €3* 🕐 *Gardens daily 9–dusk, house mid-June–mid-Sept., daily 10–6; last tour at 5.*

★ **Coolbanagher Church,** the familiar name for the exquisite Church of St. John the Evangelist, was, like Emo Court and Gardens, designed by James Gandon. On view inside are Gandon's original 1795 plans and an elaborately sculpted 15th-century font from an earlier church that stood nearby. Adjacent to the church is Gandon's mausoleum for Lord Portarlington, his patron at Emo. The church is open daily spring through autumn; at other times, ask around in the tiny village for a key, or at the rectory, a 10-minute drive away. ✉ *8½ km (5 mi) south of Portarlington on R419* ☎ *057/864–6538* ✉ *Free* 🕐 *May–Oct., daily 9–6.*

WHERE TO STAY

¢–$ 🍴 **Eskermore House.** In summer, a delightful display of rambling roses adorns the doorway of this charming farmhouse. The old-world quirks of these lovely lodgings also include a chiming grandfather clock and an organ in the sitting room for musically gifted guests (those without a talent for tickling the ivory are gently urged to refrain). Located 9 km (6 mi) west of Edenderry on R402, this is a good base for hiking in the Slieve Bloom Mountains. The guest rooms are simply but comfortably furnished and face south over a beech-tree-lined avenue and semi-wild gardens. The sitting room has an open turf fire, a piano, and cable TV;

room TVs are available on request. Host Ann Mooney will prepare a wholesome dinner with advance notice. **Pros:** great-value accommodation in peaceful surroundings; the open fire is a pure delight. **Cons:** few frills on offer; rooms are basic. ⊠ *Mount Lucas, Edenderry, Co. Offaly* ☎ *057/935–3079* ⊕ *www.eskermore.com* ⤴ *3 rooms* ⌂ *In-room: no a/c, no phone. In-hotel: Internet terminal, some pets allowed* ▭ *MC, V* ⦿⧘ *BP.*

\$\$ 🖼 **Roundwood House.** There's a dreamlike beauty to this place. As you **Fodor's Choice** arrive, a dark tree-lined avenue suddenly opens up to reveal a dramati-**★** cally gorgeous Palladian villa. A flock of white geese and a friendly dog called Sheridan form the welcoming party to this chateau-esque mansion on the slopes of the Slieve Bloom Mountains. Antique family portraits of the builders—the Sharps, a prominent Quaker family whose wealth derived from the mid-1600s woolen industry—adorn the walls of the curio-filled drawing room. The bedrooms in the main house are elegant and airy, or opt for cozier chambers in the adjacent 17th-century Old House. Tiniest of all is the Cottage, a stone charmer whose original tenants may have been Hansel and Gretel. Affable hosts Hannah and Paddy Flynn often share your table at dinner. Attractive deals make this retreat an affordable and unforgettable experience. The house is 5 km (3 mi) from Mountrath on the scenic road to Kinnitty. **Pros:** friendly hosts; mature woodland is ideal for walks. **Cons:** dinner is served at a communal table; renovations are occasionally under way so check if builders are at work. ⊠ *Mountrath, Co. Laois* ☎ *057/873–2120* ⊕ *www.roundwoodhouse.com* ⤴ *10 rooms, plus 3 self-catering cottages* ⌂ *In-room: no a/c, no phone, no TV. In-hotel: restaurant, Internet terminal* ▭ *AE, DC, MC, V* ⦿⧘ *BP.*

TULLAMORE

27 km (17 mi) northwest of Portarlington.

The county seat of Offaly, Tullamore is a bustling market town that has thrived since Ireland's "Celtic Tiger" boom in the mid-1990s and continues to prosper. Its most famous native is Ireland's Taoiseach and former finance minister Brian Cowen, and the people here share his down-to-earth approach to life. The town's historical success was based on its location on the Grand Canal, one of Ireland's most important trading links during the 18th and 19th centuries.

GETTING HERE

BUS TRAVEL Tullamore's central location means travelers are reasonably well served by Bus Éireann buses. An enjoyable cross-country Midlands jaunt (weekdays only) links Tullamore with Dublin (two hours east) at one end and Portumna in south Galway at the other. From Dublin, stops include Propserous, Clane, and Celbridge. In the other direction you can travel west from Tullamore to Birr, Banagher, and Portumna. Kilkenny (2¼ hours) and Waterford (3¼ hours) lie in a direct route south with twice-daily services, while a short hop northwest will take you to the neighboring towns of Clara, Moate, or Athlone. Mullingar is served by the Galway–Dundalk Bus Éireann Expressway and the Longford–Dublin service.

4

Train and bus services coalesce at Cormac Street in Tullamore. Daily from early morning, 10 fast trains leave for Dublin (€27.50 round-trip), 70 minutes away, and six head west to Galway (€17.50 round-trip), a 90-minute trip. The main Sligo–Dublin route has three daily trains to Mullingar, about 32 km (26 mi) north of Tullamore. Dublin is an hour away (€20.30 round-trip); Sligo is a two-hour journey (€34.50 round-trip).

Visitor Information Tullamore Tourist Office (✉ *Bury Quay, Co. Offaly* ☎ *057/935–2617* ⊕ *www.tullamore.org* ⊙ *Mid-June–mid-Sept. only*).

EXPLORING

One relic of Tullamore's former splendor is found on the southwestern edge of town, where, if you take the road heading to Birr from the center of Tullamore, you'll find a storybook vision in splendid Tin Soldier Fortress style: **Charleville Forest Castle.** Perhaps the finest Neo-Gothic, British-style 19th-century castle in Ireland, its Flag Tower and turrets rise above its domain of 30 acres of woodland walks and gardens. The Georgian–Gothic Revival house was built as a symbol of English might triumphing over French force (the French revolutionary forces, to be exact, who had become a little too cozy with the Irish locals). In fact, the floor plan is even modeled on the Union Jack. Commissioned by Baron Tullamore and dating from 1812, the castle is a rural example of the work of architect Francis Johnston, who was responsible for many of Dublin's stately Georgian buildings. The interiors are somewhat the worse for wear—most are gigantic chambers with a few sticks of furniture—but the William Morris–designed dining room still has its original stenciled wallpaper. Guided tours of the interior are available. Descended through the Bury family, who eventually lost their fortune and left no heirs, the castle became an orphan in the 1960s but has been slowly restored. The surrounding forest is said to be haunted by the spirits of the ancient Druids. ✉ *1½ km (1 mi) outside Tullamore on N52 to Birr* ☎ *057/932–3040* ⊕ *www.charlevillecastle.ie* ⊠ *€16 for one adult or couple. Additional members of same party €6* ⊙ *May, weekends 2–5; June–Sept., Wed.–Sun. 2–5; Oct.–Apr., by appointment.*

Tullamore Dew Irish Whiskey can trace its roots to 1829, when the Tullamore Distillery was founded. It was greatly expanded under the aegis of Daniel E. Williams, whose family became joint shareholders, and his own initials, D-E-W, were added to the whiskey's name, inspiring the slogan "Give every man his Dew" (which appeared on the bottles for many years). You can visit the **Tullamore Dew Heritage Center,** a restored 19th-century warehouse once used for storing and maturing the whiskey, where guided tours take place weekdays at 11:30 and 2:30 and include a complimentary tipple of Tullamore Dew Whiskey or the even more famous Irish Mist Liqueur. Sip it slowly and it may reveal the secrets of its Irish Midlands character. Guided tours are available, and there are also self-guided booklets in English. There's also a tourist kiosk inside. ✉ *Bury Quay* ☎ *057/932–5015* ⊕ *www.tullamore-dew. org* ⊠ *€6 self-guided, €8 guided* ⊙ *May–Sept., Mon.–Sat. 9–6, Sun. noon–5; Oct.–Apr., Mon.–Sat. 10–5, Sun. noon–5.*

WHERE TO STAY

¢–$ 🏡 **Annaharvey Farm.** A loving conversion of an old-world grain barn into an elegant accommodation has marked the past several years for innkeepers Lynda and Henry Deverell. Just 6 km (4 mi) outside of Tullamore town on the Portarlington road, this family farmhouse dedicated to all things equestrian contains pitch-pine floors, massive roof beams, and open fireplaces. Guest rooms are cozy and comfy

and decorated with equestrian prints. It matters not a bit, however, if your interest doesn't run to things horsey—the area has all manner of walking, cycling, and golfing opportunities, and Clonmacnoise and Birr Castle are just a short drive away. Horses, though, are a big interest, as the inn hosts many owners giving their treasured Connemara ponies a spin Meals (available to guests only) are served in the kitchen. **Pros:** well away from the main road, secluded location; the clear Offaly night skies are filled with thousands of stars. **Cons:** no dinner choice; bathrooms are small; noisy neighing horses may disturb your slumber. ✉ *Tullamore, Co. Offaly* ☎ *057/934–3544* ⊕ *www.annaharveyfarm.ie* ⇆ *7 rooms* ⌂ *In-room: no a/c, Internet* ▬ *MC, V* ☯ *Closed Dec. and Jan.*

SPORTS AND THE OUTDOORS

GOLF **Esker Hills Golf & Country Club** (✉ *5 km [3 mi] north of Tullamore on N80* ☎ *057/935–5999* ⊕ *www.eskerhillsgolf.com*) is a challenging 18-hole championship course with natural lakes and woodlands.

KILBEGGAN

11 km (7 mi) north of Tullamore.

It's the whiskey (the Irish spell their traditional tipple with an "e") that brings most people to the unassuming little town of Kilbeggan. The town is the home of **Locke's Distillery,** which is the oldest pot-still distillery in the world and the last of its type in Ireland. This whiskey-lover's mecca was established in 1757 but was closed down as a functioning distillery in 1954. It has found new life as a museum of industrial archaeology illustrating the process of Irish pot-whiskey distillation and the social history of the workers. Homemade food is available in Locke's pantry restaurant. ☎ *057/933–2134* ⊕ *www.lockesdistillerymuseum.ie* 💶 *€7* ☯ *Apr.–Oct., daily 9–6; Nov.–Mar., daily 10–4.*

MULLINGAR

24 km (15 mi) northeast of Kilbeggan.

The Irish are great ones for wrapping an insult up in a lyrical turn of phrase. Rather than describe a woman as overweight they'll say with a wink she's "beef to the ankle, like a Mullingar heifer." Of course, the phrase also illustrates Mullingar's role as Ireland's beef capital, a town surrounded by rich countryside where cattle trading has historically been one of the chief occupations. It's also County Westmeath's major town—a busy commercial and cattle-trading center on the Royal Canal, midway between two large, attractive lakes, Lough Owel and Lough Ennel. Buildings here date mostly from the 19th century. Although best used as a base to tour the surrounding countryside, Mullingar has some sights worthy of your time.

Visitor Information Mullingar Discover Ireland Centre (⊠ *Market Sq., Co. Westmeath* ☎ *044/934–8650* ⊕ *www.discoverireland.ie/lakelands*).

EXPLORING

The town's largest structure is the Renaissance-style Catholic **Cathedral of Christ the King,** completed in 1939. Note the facade's finely carved stonework, and the mosaics of St. Patrick and St. Anne by the Russian artist Boris Anrep in the spacious interior. There's a museum in the cathedral, and tours are available. ⊠ *Mary St.* ☎ *044/934–8338* ⊕ *www. mullingarparish.com* ⊘ *Daily 8–8.*

Genesis Gift Gallery sells crystal, jewelry, fine art, and furnishings. You can purchase everything from whiskey measures to baby gifts in both pewter and bronze. There's a coffee shop on the premises. ⊠ *Great Down, the Downs* ☎ *044/934–3078* ⊕ *www.westmeathdesigners.com* ⊘ *Weekdays 9:30–6, Sat. 10–6.*

☾ **Belvedere House Gardens** occupies a beautiful spot on the northeast shore
★ of Lough Ennel. Access to this stately mid-18th-century hunting lodge with extensive gardens is through the servants' entrance—so you can see what life behind the scenes was like back then. Cries and whispers haunt this estate. Built in 1740 by architect Richard Cassels for Robert Rochfort, first earl of Belvedere, it became a byword for debauchery and dissipation, thanks to the high jinks of Rochfort's wife, the "very handsome" Mary Molesworth. After falling passionately in love with Rochfort's younger brother (and bearing him a child), she was locked up in another family house for decades. Robert regaled guests with the "scandal" while offering sumptuous dinners at this house under its great 18th-century plasterwork ceilings. He spent much of his family fortune dotting the gardens of the estate with "follies," including the Jealous Wall, a gigantic mock-castle ruin that served to cover up a view of the adjoining estate, owned by another brother, also hated. Today, the interiors are a quirky mix of Georgian stateliness and Victorian charm. The noted bow and Palladian windows have great parkland views sloping down to the lake and its islands. You can tour the 160 acres of the estate and woodland trails on the Belvedere tram. Also on the estate are a restaurant, a coffee shop, an animal sanctuary, and a children's play area. ⊠ *4 km (2½ mi) south of Mullingar on N52* ☎ *044/934–9060* ⊕ *www.belvedere-house.ie* ✉ *House and parkland €8.75, tram €2* ⊘ *Mar., Apr., Sept., and Oct., daily 10–7; May–Aug., daily 10–9; Nov.–Feb., daily 10:30–4:30.*

WHERE TO STAY

$$$$ 🛏 **Temple Country Retreat and Spa.** If you're hoping to recharge your bat-
★ teries, this is just the place. This modern retreat is surrounded by 100 acres of parkland, and boasts all you could want in terms of relaxation

therapy. One of the 80 available restorative spa therapies is a version of the traditional mudpack, using bog peat (in a country where peat is normally cut from the bog and burned for fuel, this new use for turf has been raising Irish eyebrows). Special bed-and-breakfast rates are available along with pricier spa packages. The menu offers such winners as seared sea bass with caramelized apple with hints of basil, mint, and cream. The owner, Bernadette Fagan, likes to quote Virginia Woolf to guests: "One cannot think well, love well, or sleep well if one has not dined well." Temple Country Retreat and Spa is along N6, almost equidistant from Mullingar, Tullamore, and Athlone. **Pros:** serene and peaceful, the perfect escape; top-class food in comfortable surroundings. **Cons:** no TVs; having to leave. ⊠ *Horseleap, Moate, Co. Westmeath* ☎ *057/933–5118* ⊕ *www.templespa.ie* ⤳ *23 rooms, 2 suites* ⌂ *In-room: no a/c, no TV, Internet. In-hotel: spa, bicycles, no kids under 16* ⊟ *AE, MC, V* ⊗ *Closed Christmas wk* ❘⊙❘ *FAP.*

SPORTS AND THE OUTDOORS

GOLF **Delvin Castle Golf Club** (⊠ *Delvin* ☎ *044/966–4315*) is an 18-hole course in a mature parkland setting. It has beautiful views across north Westmeath.

CASTLEPOLLARD

Fodor's Choice *21 km (13 mi) north of Mullingar.*
★

A pretty village of multihue 18th- and 19th-century houses laid out around a large, triangular green, Castlepollard is also home to **Tullynally Castle and Gardens,** the largest castle in Ireland that still functions as a family home. This is not just any family: the Pakenhams are the famous Irish tribe that has given us Elizabeth Longford (whose biography of Queen Victoria is in most libraries) and Antonia Fraser, wife of the late playwright Harold Pinter and best-selling biographer of Mary, Queen of Scots, among others. In fact, Tullynally—the name, literally translated, means "Hill of the Swans"—has been the home of 10 generations of this family, which also married into the earldom of Longford. Lady Fraser's brother Thomas, a historian, is the current earl but does not use the title. As a result of an 18th-century "Gothicization," the former Georgian house was transformed into a faux castle by architect Francis Johnston; the resulting 600 feet of battlements were not just for bluff, as the earls were foes of Catholic emancipation. Inside, the family has struggled to make the vast salons warm and cozy—a bit of a losing battle. The house really comes into its own as a stage set for the surrounding park—the gray-stone structure is so long and has so many towers it looks like a miniature town from a distance. The total circumference of the building's masonry adds up to nearly ½ km (¼ mi) and includes a motley agglomeration of towers, turrets, and crenellations that date from the first early fortified building (circa 1655) up through the mid-19th century, when additions in the Gothic Revival style went up one after another.

Today, more attention is given to the beautiful parkland, in part because Thomas Pakenham is a tree-hugger extraordinaire. He is the author of several books, his most famous being *Meetings with Remarkable Trees* (1996), an exceptional art book that includes many of his magnificent photographs. The estate's rolling parkland was laid out in 1760, much along the lines you see today, with fine rhododendrons, numerous trees, and two ornamental lakes. A garden walk through the grounds in front of the castle leads to a spacious flower garden, a pond, a grotto, and walled gardens. The kitchen garden here is one of the largest in Ireland, with a row of old Irish yew trees. Don't miss the forest path, which takes you around the perimeter of the parkland and affords excellent views of the romantic castle. ✉ *1½ km (1 mi) west of Castlepollard on the R395 road to Granard* ☎ *044/966–1159* ⊕ *www.tullynallycastle.com* ✆ *€6* ⊘ *May and June, weekends 2–6, July–mid-Aug., daily 2–6.*

FORE

5 km (3 mi) east of Castlepollard.

You've heard of the seven wonders of the ancient world, but here in the heart of the Irish Midlands is a tiny village with seven wonders all to itself! According to Irish myth, this is the place where water runs uphill, where there's a tree that will not burn and water that will not boil, among other fantastical occurrences. The village is known not only for its legend, but also for its medieval church and the remains (supposedly the largest in Ireland) of a Benedictine abbey.

The spectacular remains of **Fore Abbey** dominate the simple village—its structure is massive and its imposing square towers and loophole windows make it resemble a castle rather than an abbey. Elsewhere in town, St. Fechin's Church, dating from the 10th century, has a massive, cross-inscribed lintel stone.

CAVAN

36 km (22 mi) north of Fore, 114 km (71 mi) northwest of Dublin.

Like all the larger towns of the region, Cavan is growing and prosperous. It is perhaps best known for its crystal factory. But as one of the main transporation hubs of the Midlands, Cavan has also attracted an impressive array of restaurant and hotels, so this is a fine base for exploring this region, which lies near the border to Northern Ireland. There are two central streets: with its pubs and shops, Main Street is like many other streets in similar Irish towns; Farnham Street has Georgian houses, churches, a courthouse, and a bus station.

GETTING HERE

BUS TRAVEL Cavan—the town and surrounding south Ulster area including neighboring Monaghan—relies on an extensive bus network for public transport. The town is on the Bus Éireann Galway–Belfast, Athlone–Belfast, and Dublin–Donegal Expressway routes. Frequent buses run daily to Dublin (€22 round-trip). This service also goes to the northwest Donegal highlands. Twice daily, the cross-border Belfast-bound buses on their way from Galway or Athlone stop in Cavan. The town is equidistant from Belfast and Galway with journey time to both cities about three hours. Services to small towns throughout Cavan and Monaghan operate weekdays. A 90-minute cross-country local service links Dundalk with Cavan calling at Carrickmacross, Kingscourt, Shercock, and Bailieboro.

Tullynally Castle—the largest in Ireland (just a small portion is shown here)—is surrounded by spectacular parkland, forest paths, and kitchen gardens.

Visitor Information Cavan Tourist Office (✉ *Farnham St., Co. Cavan* ☎ *049/433–1942* ⊕ *www.cavantourism.com*).

EXPLORING

For a quirky Cavan diversion head for the **Bear Essentials Ireland & Silver Bear Centre** (☎ *049/952–3461* ⊕ *www.bearessentials.ie*), where you can view the largest collection of teddy bears in Ireland. Each bear is handcrafted in the workshop from the finest mohair. The Bear Essentials Showroom is next door. The center, run by Anke Morgenroth, originally from Hamburg, is at Tirnawannagh, Bawnboy, and is open daily.

WHERE TO EAT

$$$$
IRISH
Fodor'sChoice
★

✕ **MacNean's Restaurant.** Quality doesn't come cheap but every bite in Neven Maguire's restaurant is a sublime taste sensation. No surprise—this is one of the best restaurants in Ireland. The five-course dinner menu, priced at €70, is an unhurried affair—it even comes with pre-starters and pre-desserts. Winning appetizers include an artistically presented study of shellfish, and the confit of Thornhill duck leg served with balsamic jelly. Top mains include rare breed of caramelized pork belly and pan-seared turbot. The Menu Prestige, at €125, delivers a staggering nine courses: your taste buds may never again experience such an explosion of epicurean delights as quail with seared foie gras terrine, poached sea oyster, and glazed fillet of venison oozing with truffle butter. The five-course Sunday lunch at €39 is a great value. Given the remoteness of the town of Blacklion, mattresses may be as important as menus, so why not book an upstairs guest room when reserving a table to avoid a post-dinner, late-night drive? ✉ *Blacklion, Co. Cavan*

☎ *071/985–3022* ⊕ *www.macneanrestaurant.com* ▭ *MC, V* ☺ *Closed Jan., Mon. and Tues., and Wed. Feb.–Apr.* ⦿ *BP.*

$$$
IRISH
Fodor's Choice
★

✕ **The Olde Post Inn.** The magic formula of a genuine Irish welcome and immaculate food inspired with a culinary flourish is what draws people to the restaurant in the Olde Post Inn. In a restored stone former post office nestled within an elegantly landscaped garden, the restaurant has won a clutch of awards and, as a result, is often booked solid. Chef-owner Gearóid Lynch gives a dramatic modern twist to some Irish classics, including loin of Finnebrogue venison, monkfish with bacon-and-cabbage terrine, and the positively mouthwatering suckling pig with *poitín* liquor sauce. A Lynch specialty is Chicken Le Coq Hardi, which comes stuffed with potato, apple, bacon, and herbs served with a whiskey sauce. The five-course dinner menu costs €56. Ingredients are sourced with care and the owner respects local and regional food. To get here, take the N53 to Cloverhill from Cavan Town. ⊠ *Cloverhill* ☎ *047/55555* ⊕ *www.theoldepostinn.com* ☺ *Closed Mon.* ▭ *MC, V.*

$$
IRISH
Fodor's Choice
★

✕ **Pol O'D Restaurant.** Consisting of two rooms spread over two floors, this characterful restaurant of stripped pine and exposed stonework is a busy dinner place much favored by locals. Chef-owner Paul O'Dowd opts for contemporary Irish fare with a little adventure in dishes such as smoked duck salad, quails' egg salad, and a seafood medley with prawns and lemon sauce. Standard dishes reflecting traditional rural tastes include steak, lamb, and duck. Pristine starched tablecloths, simple candlelight, and local staff make Pol O'D an unexpected pleasure in an area not generally blessed with multiple options come dinnertime. Children are welcome, as is traditional music, which happens on a spontaneous basis. ⊠ *Main St., Ballyconnell* ☎ *049/952–6228* ▭ *AE, MC, V* ☺ *Closed Sun.–Tues.*

WHERE TO STAY

$$–$$$
★

⬚ **Cabra Castle.** A spectacular collection of mock-Gothic towers, turrets, and crenellations, this hotel-castle stands sentinel amid charming parkland with mature trees and pristine lawns. Cabra boasts rooms of all shapes and sizes, from cozy attic rooms to elaborate, supersize suites. Rooms in the castle are recommended, but many of the bedrooms are in the adjoining courtyard area, in a carefully restored stone outbuilding overlooking a walled garden. The Victorian-Gothic theme of the main castle is carried through in the bar and the restaurant (reservations are a must for lunch or dinner) with varying degrees of success. Don't miss the castle gallery, which has hand-painted ceilings and leaded-glass windows. **Pros:** stunning views of the surrounding countryside; a romantic retreat with attentive personal service. **Cons:** emphasis appears to be on weddings. ⊠ *65 km (40 mi) south of Cavan, on R 179 Carrickmacross Rd., Kingscourt, Co. Cavan* ☎ *042/966–7030* ⊕ *www.cabracastle.com* ⇱ *80 rooms, 6 suites, 6 self-catering lodges* ⬚ *In-room: no a/c. In-hotel: restaurant, bar, golf course, tennis courts* ▭ *AE, MC, V* ⦿ *BP.*

$$
Fodor's Choice
★

⬚ **MacNean House & Restaurant.** With his famous restaurant set in an isolated location, it wasn't long before chef Neven Maguire decided to add on some cosseting guest rooms to his establishment. Now diners who work their way through his nine-course tasting menu can simply repair to the 10 accommodations, done up in a traditional but cool Irish style. As many diners have learned, the 65-km (40-mi) detour makes a lot more sense if you are heading from Dublin northwest to Sligo or Donegal and also take in an overnight. But be warned: this place is perpetually busy, and there's a long waiting list for weekends; Maguire has a simple epigram summing up his dining and accommodation: "We don't sleep five-star but we eat five-star." In 2010, he extended his Blacklion "empire" to cater to the overnight crowds by opening new overspill rooms in two properties on the outskirts of the village: the Rectory (four rooms) and the Courtyard (two rooms). There is a pick-up and drop-off service to and from the restaurant. **Pros:** a classy and exceptionally comfortable house with flawless service; freshly made cookies are delivered to your room each day. **Cons:** rooms feel more like B&B standard; little else to do in the area apart from feasting. ✉ *Blacklion, Co. Cavan* ☎ *071/985–3022* ⊕ *www.macneanrestaurant. com* ☴ *MC, V* ☾ *Closed Jan. and Mon.–Wed. Feb.–Dec.* ⊠|*BP.*

$ ▥ **The Olde Post Inn.** In the village of Cloverhill, this lovingly restored
Fodor'sChoice former post office (if you hadn't guessed from the name) has won a
★ clutch of awards and, as a result, is often booked solid. Having a top-rated restaurant doesn't hurt. Big open turf fires and cut-stone walls provide the key to the warm feeling you get when you step inside. Dark beams and simple wooden furniture help create a rustic feel; if you're in an energetic frame of mind there are some easy walking routes in this largely flat part of Ulster. The six guest bedrooms, all in the original part of the postmaster's residence, have been modernized with contemporary bathrooms and plasma-TV screens. There's also a conservatory. To get here, take the N53 to Cloverhill from Cavan Town. **Pros:** guests are assured of a friendly and hospitable south Ulster welcome; an old-world place with a modern feel. **Cons:** some bathrooms are on the small side; little nighttime activity in the immediate area. ✉ *Cloverhill, Co. Cavan* ☎ *047/55555* ⊕ *www.theoldepostinn.com* ⤴ *6 rooms* ♿ *In-room: no a/c. In-hotel: restaurant* ☴ *MC, V* ⊠|*BP.*

LONGFORD TOWN

37 km (23 mi) southwest of Cavan, 124 km (77 mi) northwest of Dublin.

Longford, the seat of County Longford and a typical small market-town community, is rich in literary associations, though after Oliver Goldsmith, the names in the county's pantheon of writers may draw a blank from all but the most dedicated Irish literature enthusiasts. Longford Town provides a good base for exploring the largely untouristed countryside surrounding it. A day trip to the pretty heritage village of Ardagh (10 km [7 mi] southeast of Longford Town), with its quaint houses and village green, is a popular option. The **Genealogy Centre** (✉ *17 Dublin St.* ☎ *043/337–1235*) is worth visiting to search of your roots.

GETTING HERE
BUS TRAVEL Convenient for making Midlands connections, Longford buses stop outside Longford train station. Bus Éireann routes fan out in all directions. Nine buses ply the Longford–Dublin airport and city route (2¼–2½ hours, €29 return), and buses run west to Galway and Ballina, south

to Athlone, Kilkenny, and as far as Waterford on the south coast, a 4¾-hour trek. Buses also run to Belfast from Longford (travel time is four hours, €39 round-trip). You can catch a bus to nearby towns, such as Cavan, Boyle, Carrick-on-Shannon, Roscommon, and Mullingar. There are six buses serving Sligo; there's also a cross-border bus from Longford to Derry operated in conjunction with Ulsterbus; journey time is four hours.

TRAIN TRAVEL   Unlike many Midlands towns, Longford is doubly blessed with both train and bus links. The town is on the main Irish Rail Dublin–Sligo railway line and eight trains call here. Dublin is 1¾ hours (€22.50 round-trip), and Sligo is 1¼ hours (€20.30 round-trip). You can take trains west along this route to Dromod, Carrick-on-Shannon, and Boyle or east to Edgeworthstown, Mullingar, and Maynooth.

Visitor Information Longford Town Tourist Office (✉ *Market Sq., Co. Longford* ☎ *043/334–2577* ⊙ *June–Sept. only*).

EXPLORING

A lovely spot near Longford Town is Newtowncashel, on the banks of Lough Ree, where you can visit **Bogwood Sculptures,** a fascinating work-shop run by sculptors Michael and Kevin Casey. The center displays sculptures and keepsakes made from bogwood, which is hewn from the 5,000-year-old trees submerged and ultimately preserved by the area's ancient peatlands. To get there from Longford drive 14 km (9 mi) on the N63 to Lanesborough, then take the R392 for 2 km (1 mi) and follow signs for Turreen–Newtowncashel. ✉ *Barley Harbour, Newtowncashel* ☎ *043/332–5297* ⊕ *www.bogwood.net* 🖃 *Free* ⊙ *Mon.–Sat. 10–6.*

WHERE TO EAT AND STAY

$ ✕ **The Purple Onion.** A perfect resting place for tired and hungry travel-
IRISH   ers on the road to the west of Longford Town, this pub and restaurant
Fodor'sChoice   is on the main street of a tiny Shannon-side village. This place was
★   originally a standard public house with the obligatory low ceilings, nooks, crannies, and snugs, but under the patronage of Pauline Roe and Paul Dempsey it has been transformed into a gourmet's delight— a special "gastro pub," now abustle with locals, cruise-boat tourists, and food lovers from all over. Specialties include baked guinea fowl on chanterelle mushroom risotto with sherry gravy, and roast rump of lamb on colcannon with mint gravy and tomato chutney. Potatoes and vegetables are abundant and even served (atypically, for an Irish pub) al dente. After all that, it's worth leaving space for the Toblerone cheese-cake, which has become the sweet talk of Longford. An upstairs gallery has work by some of the finest and best-known Irish artists, including Jack B. Yeats and Paul Henry, among 100 others. To get here from Longford Town drive 10 km (6 mi) west on the N5. ✉ *Tarmonbarry* ☎ *043/335–9919* ⊕ *www.purpleonion.ie* 🖃 *AE, MC, V.*

$–$$ 🍴 **Keenan's Hotel.** Initially known as a pub, Keenan's has evolved into a first-rate restaurant perfectly capable of challenging the Purple Onion next door for culinary polish and panache. Meanwhile, the B&B on the west side of the pub and the hotel accommodations overlooking the Shannon make Keenan's a virtual village within a village at this East Midlands junction. **Pros:** friendly and helpful family-run operation.

Cons: Tarmonberry is best as a one-night stand on your way east or west. ✉ *Rte. N5, Longford–Tarmonberry, Co. Roscommon* ☎ *043/332–6052* ⊕ *www.keenans.ie* ⚓ *20 rooms* ⚐ *In-room: a/c. In-hotel: restaurant, bar, Wi-Fi hotspot, parking (free)* ⊟ *AE, DC, MC, V.*

$–$$ 🏨 **Viewmount House.** An exquisite Georgian home once owned by the ★ Earl of Longford, Viewmount has been restored to its former charm by James and Beryl Kearney. The bedrooms are full of character and have impressive period wallpapers and antique mahogany wardrobes and beds. Breakfast is served in a vaulted room cheerily painted in Wedgwood blue. The 4 acres of grounds that surround the house are a gardener's paradise with an old orchard, a formal garden, and a Japanese garden complete with full-size pagoda. In 2008 the owners converted a stable block, retaining the stone walls, and turning it into the VM Restaurant with seating for 60. It serves flavor-filled delights, like pan-roasted saddle of rabbit with sweet-potato puree, cooked by head chef Gary O'Hanlon, and at €53 the five-course dinner menu is great value. The house is 2 km (1 mi) outside Longford Town, just off the old Dublin road (R393). **Pros:** a wonderfully restored house; comfort and hospitality are the order of your stay. **Cons:** 20-minute walk into town; limited amount to do in Longford. ✉ *Dublin Rd., Co. Longford* ☎ *043/334–1919* ⊕ *www.viewmounthouse.com* ⚓ *12 rooms, 7 suites* ⚐ *In-room: no a/c, Internet. In-hotel: restaurant* ⊟ *AE, MC, V* ⏏ *BP.*

NIGHTLIFE AND THE ARTS

The center of a thriving local arts scene is the **Backstage Theatre** (✉ *Farneyhoogan, Longford* ☎ *043/334–7888* ⊕ *www.backstage.ie*). In a country where many patriotic souls see the indigenous sports of Gaelic football and hurling as art forms, it's perhaps appropriate that the venue is on the grounds of the local Gaelic Athletic Association club, whose team has the intimidating title of the "Longford Slashers." Catch a local match before heading into the theater for a dose of drama, dance, classical music, or opera. The theater and club are located a mile outside Longford on the road to Athlone.

THE WESTERN MIDLANDS

This section of the Midlands covers the area's western fringe, making its way from the heart of the region, the town of Longford, and skirting the hilly landscape of County Leitrim, dappled with lakes and beloved of anglers for its fish-filled waters. The area is the country's most sparsely populated, though it has a light sprinkling of villages and, until his death in 2006, was the home of one of Ireland's leading writers, John McGahern; at the end of July, the John McGahern International Seminar and Summer School—a series of lectures, workshops, and tours—is held in Carrick-on-Shannon in his honor. Moving south through Roscommon, western Offaly, and the northern part of Tipperary, the scenery is generally low on spectacle but high on unspoiled, lush, and undulating countryside. The towns are small and undistinguished, except Birr and Strokestown, both designed to complement the "big houses" that share their names. This is one of the parts of the country where you're most likely to encounter the "hidden Ireland"—a place unblighted by the plastic leprechaun syndrome of the more touristy areas to the south and west. The historic highlight of this region is the ancient site of Clonmacnoise, an important monastery of early Christian Ireland. The route then takes you southward, to northern County Tipperary.

In 2008 the Irish President, Mary McAleese, launched a trail to honor the celebrated English Victorian novelist Anthony Trollope (1815–82), who lived in the village of Drumsna in County Leitrim. The **Anthony Trollope Trail** takes in 27 locations throughout Leitrim and incorporates many fascinating topographical locations including an area along the River Shannon known as Flaggy Bottoms. Trollope, a senior civil servant, was sent to Drumsna in 1843 to investigate the financial affairs of the postmaster. While living there he wrote his first novel *The Macdermots of Ballycloran,* drawing inspiration from the nearby ruin of Headford House. A leaflet and information on the trail is available from the **tourist office** (☎ 071/962–0170) in Carrick-on-Shannon,

ATHLONE

34 km (21 mi) southeast of Longford Town, 127 km (79 mi) west of Dublin, 121 km (75 mi) east of Limerick.

The mighty Shannon flows majestically through the heart of Athlone, yet for years it seemed as if the town was happy to turn its back on one of Europe's great waterways. That trend has been well and truly reversed and with it has come a real buzz of regeneration. The area around Athlone Castle has transformed into a veritable "Left Bank," and on both sides of the Shannon, new restaurants and stylishly modern architecture have sprung up along streets lined with 200-year-old buildings that have been given some imaginative repurposing alongside one of Ireland's most architecturally dazzling churches. Once upon a time, tourists were few and far between in what was cuttingly termed the "dead center" of Ireland—but the renaissance has made Athlone an increasingly attractive destination.

GETTING HERE

BUS TRAVEL   With its central location, Athlone is an important Bus Éireann hub with connecting Expressway services to more than 20 principal towns and cities as well as dozens of smaller destinations across Ireland. Major routes embrace roads west to Galway, east to Dublin, south to Limerick, Killarney, Cork, Waterford, and Kilkenny. Northwards, some routes are operated in conjunction with Ulsterbus; choose from Westport, Sligo, and Derry; Longford, Cavan, and Belfast; or direct to Dundalk. Typical fares are €23.50 round-trip to Dublin, €15.50 round-trip to Galway, and €33.50 round-trip to Kilkenny.

TRAIN TRAVEL   Trains branch out in three main directions from Athlone: southwest to Galway, west to Westport, and east to Dublin. Regular daily trains link the capital of the Midlands with a network of towns. From Athlone, the east–west intercity Irish Rail Galway-Dublin service takes 1¾ hours to reach Dublin.

Visitor Information Athlone Tourist Office. (✉ *Athlone Castle, Co. Westmeath* ☎ *090/649–4630* ⊕ *www.discoverathlone.ie* ☉ *Apr.–Oct. only).*

An entry in Fodor's "Show Us Your Ireland" contest, this entry submitted by Bartholomew shows a young lass at the 2009 Birr Arts Festival.

EXPLORING

Beside the River Shannon, at the southern end of Lough Ree, stands **Athlone Castle,** a Norman stronghold built in the 13th century. After their defeat at the Battle of the Boyne in 1691, the Irish retreated to Athlone and made the river their first line of defense. To celebrate its 800th anniversary in 2010, the castle underwent a program of modernization and upgrading that included repairing the courtyard and ramp with cobblestones. The castle, a fine example of a Norman stronghold with a strategic role in Irish history, houses a small museum of artifacts relating to Athlone's eventful past. The castle gatehouse serves as the town's tourist office. Admission includes access to the newly remodeled interpretive center depicting a re-enactment of the siege of Athlone in 1691, and the life of the tenor John McCormack (1884–1945), an Athlone native and a global phenomenon of his day. ⊠ *Town Bridge* ☎ *090/649–2912* ⊕ *www.athlone.ie* 🎫 *€6* ⊙ *May–Sept., daily 10–5; Oct.–Apr., by appointment.*

Revitalized and gleaming after an ambitious makeover completed in 2010, **St. Peter and St. Paul Catholic Church** sparkles with its newly restored granite walls—a striking ecclesiastical and architectural Baroque landmark that many come to see. Built in a completely different style from that generally adopted in Ireland, the church opened on June 29, 1937—the feast day of the patron saints of St. Peter and St. Paul. Repair work on the impressive interior included re-decoration of the vaulted ceiling, walls, floors, and pews. Dominating the skyline for many miles around, the twin campanili symbolize the saints, while the squat copper dome adds to the overall grace of this much-loved building. Look out too for the six fine stained-glass windows from the famed Harry Clarke Studios in Dublin. The tribute window to St. Patrick is a riot of glorious color. ⊠ *Market Sq.* ☎ *090/649–2171* ⊕ *www.drum.ie/parish* ☉ *Daily 8–6.*

WHERE TO EAT AND STAY

\$\$ ✕ **Kin Khao Thai Restaurant.** You can't miss (and you'd be foolish to pass by) the distinctive yellow-and-red insignia of what is widely regarded as the leading Thai restaurant in the Midlands, if not in all of Ireland. Adam Lyons runs a slick first-floor operation in a 650-year-old building on the west bank. The extensive menu features dishes rarely available outside Thailand, including the Crying Tiger (grilled fillet of beef on a sizzling hot platter with a hot chili sauce) and Jungle Curry (an extremely hot curry made with mixed vegetables and chicken, beef, or prawns). Ceiling fans and balloon bamboo lights help create the perfect gastronomic scene—it's not hard to imagine yourself in Chiang Mai. Just keep the water jug handy (or a glass of Curim Gold Celtic wheat beer), as the smooth richness of coconut milk doesn't offset this fiery food. ⊠ *Abbey La.* ☎ *090/649–8805* ⊕ *www.kinkhaothai.ie* ⊟ *MC, V.*

\$\$\$ ✕ **The Left Bank Bistro.** One of Athlone's culinary gems, this bistro is noted
ECLECTIC for its early-bird menu which now runs through the evening, filled with
Fodor'sChoice such delights as roast salmon fillet, beef Stroganoff, or South Indian
★ vegetable curry with rice and yogurt. The main dinner menu favors Asian fusion with steaks, fish, and duck dominating. For lunch the most popular dish is tandoori chicken breast on focaccia bread with sautéed potatoes. Irresistible desserts include Mississippi mud pie, pavlova roulade, and lemon-and-lime cheesecake. Ask Annie McNamara, one of the joint owners, about the Left Bank dressing, a specially bottled vinaigrette that people come from all across Ireland and farther afield to buy. ⊠ *Fry Pl.* ☎ *090/649–4446* ⊕ *www.leftbankbistro.com* ⊟ *AE, MC, V* ☉ *Closed Sun. and Mon.*

¢–\$ 🛏 **Bastion B&B.** An inviting glow hits you as you step into the long narrow corridor of this unconventional B&B, all nooks and little staircases, and with a high funky and fun quotient. Run by two brothers, Anthony and Vinny McCay, the Bastion occupies a former drapery shop. Simply and tastefully furnished with crisp white linens and comfy beds, this is an easygoing place to chill for a few days. You're spoiled for dining options, surrounded by Italian, Indian, Thai, Lebanese, and modern Irish restaurants as well as several pubs within a few minutes' walk on Athlone's left bank. **Pros:** healthy buffet breakfasts offer up cereal, fresh breads, fruit and cheese; minimalist chic and no clutter; historic character of neighborhood. **Cons:** bathrooms are small; no phones, TVs, or elevators. ⊠ *2 Bastion St., Co. Westmeath* ☎ *090/649–4954* ⊕ *www.thebastion.net* ↬ *7 rooms* ⚒ *In-room: a/c, Wi-Fi. In-hotel: Wi-Fi hotspot* ⊟ *MC, V.*

\$\$\$–\$\$\$\$ 🛏 **Glasson Hotel and Golf Club.** Stand on the third green on a sunny day
Fodor'sChoice and you can appreciate just why golfers love this idyllically sited, 18-hole
★ championship course. With views extending out to Hare Island and beyond to Lough Ree, this hotel has seen its popularity rise with golfers every year since 1993, when the welcoming hosts Tom and Breda Reid turned a 70-acre field into a challenging course (designed by Christy O'Connor Jr.). To their 1780 stone manor house, they added wings

that wed traditional architecture with plate-glass and steel frames. Guest rooms are decorated in buffs and creams with beds with pocket-sprung mattresses and fluffy duvets. The restaurant offers winning dishes like honey-roast duck with bacon champ. Non-golfing visitors can avail themselves of free boat service into Athlone for shopping—the courtesy cabin cruiser transports shoppers for hour trip. **Pros:** family-run; an enthralling place to de-stress with woodland walks and boat trips all nearby. **Cons:** strong winds can whip in off the lake on breezy days—bring a sweater; bunker discussions dominate the conversation at breakfast, so be prepared. ✉ *Glasson, Co. Westmeath* ☎ *090/648–5120* ⊕ *www.glassongolfhotel.ie* ⤢ *65 rooms, 9 suites* ♿ *In-room: a/c, Wi-Fi. In-hotel: restaurant, bar, golf course, gym* ⊟ *AE, DC, MC, V* ⦿ *BP.*

> **A GREAT IRISH TENOR**
>
> Count John McCormack (1884–1945), whose story is told in Athone Castle's interpretative center, was perhaps the finest lyric tenor Ireland has produced. Born in Athlone, he recorded 600 records from 1914 to 1918 and made the Hollywood film *Song of My Heart.* A memorial bust stands on Grace Road by the Shannon.

4

$$-$$$ ⌸ **Radisson Blu Hotel.** In a prime location on the banks of the Shannon, this 127-room property has a distinctive water theme. More than half the units have superb views of the meandering river and look across to the Sts. Peter and Paul's church. Guest rooms are clean, comfortable, and modern, decorated in two styles: urban or ocean. Swans preen around the bridge and cruisers are berthed beside the hotel. The Elements Restaurant presents lunch and dinner, and you can snack on lighter fare at the Quayside Bar. Everything you need to see and do in Athlone is a short walk away. Between May and September, Friday Fever barbecues light up the terrace. **Pros:** stunning views; top-notch location for exploring the town, castle, and left bank; free parking. **Cons:** precooked breakfasts are mediocre; good pool but no spa. ✉ *Northgate St., Co. Westmeath* ☎ *090/644–2600* ⊕ *www.radissonblu.ie/hotel-athlone* ⤢ *127 rooms, 10 suites* ♿ *In-room: Wi-Fi. In-hotel: restaurant, bar, pool* ⊟ *AE, DC, MC, V.*

$$$–$$$$ ⌸ **Wineport Lodge.** Once a wooden boathouse, this lakeside restaurant-★ with-rooms is billed as Ireland's first "wine hotel." Stylishly modern—all orange cedarwood and plate-glass windows—and set against parkland groves of trees, the striking light-filled wood-and-glass building seems like it was airlifted from Sweden. Inside, guests make a beeline to the restaurant, where chef Feargal O'Donnell draws praise for his imaginative cooking and the way he matches food to the extensive wine menu. Mouthwatering offerings such as smoked Ardrahan rarebit or pan-roasted breast of duckling with goat cheese and spiced pear risotto are standard fare. The guest rooms are minimalist but stylishly adorned with leopard-skin prints and goose-down duvets. All face the setting sun and look out over the placid waters of Killinure Lough. Glasson lies 5 km (3 mi) north of Athlone. **Pros:** catch the right sunset, and this is one of the most enchanting hideaways in Ireland; the under-floor bathroom heating is luxurious. **Cons:** the serenity is occasionally broken by jet-skiers on the lough; restaurant service can be slow. ✉ *Glasson, Co. Westmeath*

Goldsmith Country

All that glitters may not be Goldsmith but that hasn't prevented the Irish tourist board from promoting the Northern Lakelands to the burgeoning literary tourism market as "Goldsmith Country."

Yes, this is the region that gave birth to the writer Oliver Goldsmith (1730–74), celebrated for his farcical drama *She Stoops to Conquer* and his classic novel *The Vicar of Wakefield.* Goldsmith left his homeland as a teenager and returned rarely. However, he is thought to have drawn on memories of his native Longford for his most renowned poem, "The Deserted Village." At Goldsmith's childhood home in Lissoy in County Longford, only the bare walls of the family house remain standing. At Pallas, near Ballymahon in County Longford, his birthplace, there's a statue in his memory but little else. The plot of *She Stoops to Conquer* involves a misunderstanding in which a traveler mistakes a private house for an inn. This actually happened to Goldsmith at Ardagh House, now a college, in the center of the village of Ardagh (just off N55) in County Longford. In the same play the character Tony Lumpkin sings a song about a pub called the Three Jolly Pigeons; today the pub of the same name, on the Ballymahon road (N55) north of Athlone, is the headquarters of the Oliver Goldsmith Summer School.

Every year on the first weekend in June, leading academics from around the world speak on Goldsmith at this pub and other venues, and there are readings by the best of Ireland's contemporary poets and evening traditional-music sessions in the tiny, atmospheric, traditional country pub. Call the **Athlone Tourist Office** (🕾 *090/649–4630*) for more information.

🕾 *090/643–9010* ⊕ *www.wineport.ie* ⤵ *29 rooms, 14 suites* ♨ *In-room: a/c, Wi-Fi. In-hotel: restaurant, bar* ⊟ *AE, DC, MC, V* ⊧◯⊨ *BP.*

NIGHTLIFE

In Athlone's buzzing Left Bank sector, **Sean's Bar** (⊠ *13 Main St.* 🕾 *090/649–2358* ⊕ *www.seansbar.ie*) styles itself as the world's oldest pub (a claim some cynics dispute although a framed certificate from the *Guinness Book of Records* says otherwise), dating to 900 AD. Sawdust on the floor of this dimly lighted, low-ceiling, long narrow bar helps give it a rustic look and soaks up spillages. Framed pictures and prints line the walls alongside maps of the Shannon navigation system, and the beer garden stretches almost down to the water. There's traditional music most nights.

SHOPPING

The Left Bank district is a jumble of lanes and small streets lined with pubs, antiques shops, bookstores, and one of the few surviving Irish bookbinders. The funky **Bastion Gallery** (⊠ *6 Bastion St.* 🕾 *090/649–4948*) sells quirky gifts, books, and toys and is an Aladdin's cave of a place in which to browse. Michael Jackson, on a recording trip to the Irish Midlands, spent two hours in the shop one evening in 2006.

John's Bookshop (⊠ *9 Main St.* 🕾 *090/649–4151*), owned and run since 1997 by the affable John Donohue, is exactly the way a secondhand bookstore should be: cluttered, disorganized, and heaving with rare and signed Irish-related, and general books. Make time for a stop at the **Ballinahown Irish Designer Craft Village** (✉ *N62, south from Athlone to Limerick* ☎ *090/643–0222* ⊕ *www.irishdesignercraftvillage.com*). Two separate and distinctive stores—Core Crafted Design and Celtic Roots Studio—sell distinctive local crafts, ranging from bog-oak sculpture to honey as well as an outstanding choice of ceramics, jewelry, glasswork, and textiles. It's the last village in Westmeath as you travel to Clonmacnoise. Core is based in the Old Schoolhouse, and Celtic Roots Studio is next door.

SPORTS AND THE OUTDOORS

BICYCLING A combination of unfrequented back roads and lakeside scenery makes this attractive biking country. Rent bikes from **Buckleys Cycles** (✉ *Kenna Centre, Dublin Rd.* ☎ *090/647–8989* ⊕ *www.buckleycycles.ie*).

BOATING A boat trip reveals the importance of Athlone's strategic location on the River Shannon as well as the beauty of the region. For the complete scoop on getting out on the water, see our special section on "Cruising on the Shannon" in this chapter. **The Viking** (✉ *The Strand* ☎ *090/647–3383* ⊕ *www.vikingtours.ie*) is a replica of a Viking longboat that travels up the Shannon to nearby Lough Ree. Originally built in 1923, it's the longest-serving timber passenger boat in Ireland or the United Kingdom. The cost is €15; sailings take place daily March through October. Check the Web site for exact times. River cruisers can be rented from **Athlone Cruisers Ltd.** (✉ *Jolly Mariner Marina* ☎ *090/647–2892*). *Also see "Cruising on the Shannon" in this chapter.*

GOLF **Athlone Golf Club** (✉ *Hodson Bay* ☎ *090/649–2073* ⊕ *www.athlonegolfclub. ie*) is a lakeside 18-hole parkland course.

CLONMACNOISE

20 km (12 mi) south of Athlone, 93 km (58 mi) east of Galway.

Many ancient sites dot the River Shannon, but Clonmacnoise is early Christian Ireland's foremost monastic settlement and, like Chartres, a royal site. The monastery was founded by St. Ciaran between 543 and 549 at a location that was not as remote as it now appears to be: near the intersection of what were then two of Ireland's most vital routes—the Shannon River, running north–south, and the Eiscir Riada, running east–west. Like Glendalough, Celtic Ireland's other great monastic site, Clonmacnoise benefited from its isolation; surrounded by bog, it's accessible only via one road or via the Shannon.

GETTING HERE

BUS AND BOAT TRAVEL It takes dedication to get here. Clonmacnoise is well-nigh impossible to reach by public transport, with no trains and the nearest Bus Éireann in Ballinahown, a request stop on the Limerick–Athlone route. Even then you need a taxi at a cost of up to €40 to complete the 15-minute journey to the site. If you haven't a car, it's best to book a trip with companies such as CIE Tours, Paddywagon, Shamrocker, or Midland Tours. Or opt to board a boat in Athlone for 90-minute journey to the jetty beside Clonmacnoise visitor center. Trips are run on the *Viking* and advance booking is necessary. The round-trip journey is €15.

One of Ireland's greatest monastic settlements, Clonmacnoise was nearly leveled in places—including the Norman Castle seen above—but has other ruins that still inspire awe.

Visitor Information Clonmacnoise Tourist Office (✉ *Shannonbridge, Co. Offaly* ☎ *090/967–4134* ⊘ *Apr.–Oct. only*).

EXPLORING

★ Thanks to its location, Clonmacnoise survived almost everything thrown at it, including raids by feuding Irish tribes, Vikings, and Normans. But when the English garrison arrived from Athlone in 1552, they ruthlessly reduced the site to ruin. Still, with a little imagination, you can picture life here in medieval times, when the nobles of Europe sent their sons to be educated by the local monks.

The monastery was founded on an esker (natural gravel ridge) overlooking the Shannon and a marshy area known as the Callows, which today is protected habitat for the corncrake, a wading bird. Numerous buildings and ruins remain. The small **cathedral** dates to as far as the 10th century but has additions from the 15th century. It was the burial place of kings of Connaught and of Tara, and of Rory O'Conor, the last high king of Ireland, who was buried here in 1198. The two round towers include **O'Rourke's Tower,** which was struck by lightning and subsequently rebuilt in the 12th century. There are eight **smaller churches,** the littlest of which is thought to be the burial place of St. Ciaran. The High Crosses have been moved into the visitor center to protect them from the elements (copies stand in their original places); the best preserved of these is the Cross of the Scriptures, also known as Flann's Cross. Some of the treasures and manuscripts originating from Clonmacnoise are now housed in Dublin, most at the National Museum.

Clonmacnoise has always been a prestigious burial place. Among the ancient stones are many other graves dating from the 17th to the mid-20th century. The whole place is time-burnished, though in midsummer it can be difficult to avoid the throngs of tourists. There are tours every hour during the summer season. ⊠ *Near Shannonbridge* ☎ *090/967–4195* ⊕ *www.heritageireland.ie* ⊡ *€6* ⊙ *Nov.–mid-Mar., daily 10–5:15; mid-Mar.–mid-May and mid-Sept.–Oct., daily 10–6; mid-May–mid-Sept., daily 9–7. Last admission 45 mins before closing.*

BANAGHER

31 km (19 mi) south of Clonmacnoise.

"Well, that beats Banagher!" This small Shannon-side town is best known in Ireland because of this common phrase, which dates from the 19th century when the town was the very worst example of a "rotten borough"—a corrupt electoral area controlled by the local landed gentry. In short, if something "beats Banagher" it's either pretty bad or rather extraordinary. Nowadays, Banagher is a lively marina town that is a popular base for water-sports enthusiasts. Charlotte Brontë (1816–55) famously spent her honeymoon here.

Flynn's (⊠ *Main St.* ☎ *057/915–1312*), in the center of town, is worth visiting to appreciate its light and spacious Victorian-style design. The lunch menu includes generously filled sandwiches, salad platters, a roast meat of the day, and chicken, fish, or burgers with chips.

If you happen to be in Banagher in summer, consider taking a **Shannon cruise** on *The River Queen,* an enclosed launch that seats 54 passengers and has a full bar on board. *Silver Line Cruisers Ltd.* ⊠ *The Marina* ☎ *057/915–1112* ⊕ *www.silverlinecruisers.com* ⊡ *€12* ⊙ *Cruises June–mid-Sept., Sun. at 2.*

Paddling a canoe is a nice alternative to a river cruise. **Shannon Adventure Canoeing and Camping Holidays** rents Canadian-class canoes, which allow you to explore the Shannon and other waterways on your own terms. ⊠ *The Marina* ☎ *057/915–1411* ⊕ *www.discoverireland.ie* ⊙ *May–Oct., daily.*

NIGHTLIFE

Travelers love **J. J. Hough's** (⊠ *Main St.* ☎ *No phone*), where on spring and summer nights there's usually a sing-along around the German piano. Note the walls decorated with business cards, testifying to the pub's popularity the world over. Side rooms lead to a beer garden with wooden chairs and tables.

BIRR

12 km (7 mi) southeast of Banagher, 130 km (81 mi) west of Dublin.

Beautifully reminiscent of an English country town with its tree-lined malls and well-preserved houses, the heritage town of Birr has roots that date to the 6th century. Still, it's that mid-18th-century Georgian building boom that sets the tone.

Visitor Information Birr Tourist Office (✉ *Brendan St., Co. Offaly* ☎ *057/912–0110* ⊕ *www.discoverireland.ie/offaly* ⊗ *May–Sept. only*).

EXPLORING

Fodor'sChoice ★ All roads in Birr lead to the gates of **Birr Castle Demesne,** a gorgeous Gothic Revival castle (built around an earlier 17th-century castle that was damaged by fire in 1823) that is still the home of the earls of Rosse. It's not open to the public, but you can visit the surrounding 150 acres of gardens. The present earl and countess of Rosse continue the family tradition of making botanical expeditions all over the world for specimens of rare trees, plants, and shrubs. The formal gardens contain the tallest box hedges in the world (at 32 feet) and vine-sheltered hornbeam allées. In spring, check out the wonderful display of flowering magnolias, cherries, crab apples, and naturalized narcissi; in autumn, the maples, chestnuts, and weeping beeches blaze red and gold. The grounds are laid out around a lake and along the banks of two adjacent rivers, above one of which stands the castle. The grounds also contain **Ireland's Historic Science Centre,** an exhibition on astronomy, photography, botany, and engineering housed in the stable block. The giant (72-inch-long) reflecting telescope, built in 1845, remained the largest in the world for 75 years. Allow at least two hours to see everything. There's a crafts shop, and the Courtyard Café serves soup, salads, sandwiches, and daily lunch specials. ✉ *Rosse Row* ☎ *057/912–0336* ⊕ *www.birrcastle.com* ✈ *Castle grounds €9* ⊗ *Nov.–Mar., daily noon–4; Apr.–Oct., daily 9–6.*

WHERE TO EAT AND STAY

$ ✕ **The Thatch Bar.** It's worth venturing 2 km (1 mi) south of Birr, just off
IRISH the N62 Roscrea road, into this thatched country pub and restaurant, which offers a warm welcome and imaginative food. Inexpensive meals are available at the bar at lunchtime and early evening (until 7:30); in the evening, the restaurant offers a choice of a five-course dinner menu or an à la carte menu. Pigeon and rabbit terrines and sirloin steaks with mushrooms in garlic sauce vie for diners' attention with more exotic dishes like kangaroo and locally farmed ostrich. ✉ *Crinkil* ☎ *057/912–0682* ▭ *DC, MC, V* ⊗ *No dinner Mon.; no dinner Sun. Oct.–Apr.*

$$ 🏨 **Dooly's.** This unpretentious country hotel began life as a coach house some 275 years ago and has retained its old-style charm. Floral patterns, open fires, and a relaxed welcome invite you in. It's in Birr's central square, and a five-minute walk from the castle. The bustling bar and coffee shop are popular with locals. For a more formal dining experience you could try the Emmet Room restaurant, where fish dishes such as medallions of monkfish or grilled salmon fillet with garlic potato are specialties alongside a selection of Italian offerings. All guest rooms were given a makeover in 2008 to add some zest to this old staging post. **Pros:** huge rooms with acres of space for moving around in; a handy Midlands stopover, if you're on your way to the west coast. **Cons:** the weekend disco goes on until the early hours, so bring your earplugs; stairs can be difficult for the disabled or elderly. ✉ *Emmet Sq., Co. Offaly* ☎ *057/912–0032* ⊕ *www.doolyshotel.com* ⤶ *18 rooms* ♿ *In-room: no a/c, Wi-Fi. In-hotel: restaurant, bar* ▭ *AE, DC, MC, V* ‖◎‖ *BP.*

Getting Bogged Down

CLOSE UP

Like the Eskimos with their 100 different words for snow, the natives of the Midlands retain a historic attachment to their vast boglands and will extol its virtues at length if prompted by a stranger.

In rural parts, turf, or peat, still accounts for much of the winter fuel supply and locals can always be counted upon to discuss in great detail the quality and consistency of this uniquely native resource.

"Grand year for the turf" will generally indicate a sunny August—key drying time when the "sods" are cut and allowed to dry along the banks. Conversely, "wicked bad turf" denotes a typically soft Irish summer with poor drying.

Along country lanes, the sight of reeks of cut turf is still commonplace. If you're tired of using the weather as a conversational icebreaker, try turf as an alternative and virtually guaranteed discourse igniter.

No matter that from a distance an Irish peat bog looks like a flat, treeless piece of waterlogged land. A close-up view shows a much more exciting landscape.

Bogs support an extraordinary amount of wildlife, including larks and snipe, pale-blue dragonflies, and Greenland white-fronted geese. Amid the pools and lakes of the peat bog, amazing jewel-like wildflowers thrive, from purple bell heather to yellow bog asphodel, all alongside grasses, lichens, and mosses.

As you pass through the small town of Shannonbridge, 10 km (6 mi) south of Clonmacnoise, on either side of the road are vast stretches of chocolate-brown boglands and isolated industrial plants for processing the area's natural resource.

Bord na Móna, the same government agency that makes commercial use of other boglands, has jurisdiction over the area.

¢ ⌖ **The Maltings.** Sheltered beneath the eaves of Birr Castle on a riverbank, this converted cut-stone storehouse—built to store malt for Guinness in 1810—is a good option for families and offers special rates for children. The spacious rooms have small windows, country pine furniture, and simple matching floral drapes and spreads. **Pros:** idyllic location; attractive rooms; great breakfasts. **Cons:** beginning to show signs of wear and tear; no dinner available, but there are several restaurants in the area. ⊠ *Castle St., Co. Offaly* 🕾 *057/912–1345* ⌖ *10 rooms* ⌕ *In-room: no a/c, Internet* ⊟ *MC, V* ⫶◯⫶ *BP.*

MONEYGALL

18 km (12 mi) south of Birr, 9 km (6 mi) southwest of Roscrea, 38 km (27 mi) northeast of Limerick.

The village of Moneygall (population 298) is an unassuming place on the main N7 Dublin–Limerick road, but it was thrust into the spotlight in November 2008 with President Obama's election. The reason? His great-great-great grandfather came from Moneygall. Records found by historians show that his maternal ancestors lived and worked

DID YOU KNOW?

Still home to the earl of Rosse, Birr Castle is closed to the public but its "demesne"—nearly 100 acres of gardens—is open to showcase the family tradition of undertaking daring expeditions and bringing horticultural treasures back home. Find a secluded place for a picnic and dream an afternoon away.

in the Moneygall area more than 160 years ago and worshipped at Templeharry church, 4 mi from the village. President Obama's late mother Ann Dunham was a descendant of Fulmouth Kearney, who was Obama's great-great-great-grandfather, and who left the village for New York in 1850 to eventually settle in Ohio. Kearney's birthplace was thought to have been demolished, but researchers from Trinity College Dublin have discovered the house—albeit substantially rebuilt—still standing just yards from Ollie Hayes's Bar on the main street. The pub has an "Obama Corner," decorated with press clippings, framed letters and photos, and a tall cardboard cutout. On a Thursday evening you may see the Obama Set Dancers strutting their Cashel and Ballycommon sets and practicing a mix of jigs, reels, polkas, and hornpipes. There are two Hayes' pubs in Moneygall, but Ollie's is easily distinguished as it flies the Stars and Stripes outside.

> **DELIGHTFULLY DIFFERENT**
>
> The tourist board deserves credit for doing its best to promote the Midlands. A sign in Emmet Square in the center of Birr proudly proclaims: "Offaly is an exciting pastiche of contrasting scenery, delightfully different moods, and uniformly hospitable people." Now, if that doesn't inspire you to spend some time here, then nothing will.

ROSCREA

19 km (12 mi) south of Birr.

Every corner you turn in this charming town will offer reminders of its rich and sometimes turbulent past. Ancient castles, towers, and churches dot the skyline, proof of a heritage that dates to the 7th century. Roscrea is on the main N7 road between Dublin and Cork, making it ideal as a stopover en route to the south. The road cuts right through the remains of a monastery founded by St. Cronan. It also passes the west facade of a 12th-century Romanesque church that now forms an entrance gate to a modern Catholic church. Above the structure's rounded doorway is a hoodmold enclosing the figure of a bishop, probably St. Cronan.

GETTING HERE

BUS TRAVEL   The Bus Éireann Expressway from Busaras station in Dublin takes 2½ hours to Roscrea. Thirteen buses a day pass through en route from Dublin to Limerick (€22 round-trip). The Roscrea–Limerick leg of the journey is 70 minutes (€12.50 round-trip). From Roscrea you can also catch a bus south to Cashel (2¼ hours) and Cork (3 hours) as well as north to Athlone (70 minutes) or as far northwest as Sligo, a journey time of nearly 5 hours.

TRAIN TRAVEL   The Irish Rail Dublin–Limerick train stops in Roscrea twice on weekdays. Dublin is a 90-minute journey by train (€42.50 round-trip). In the other direction, Limerick is 90 minutes away (€28.50 round-trip). Nenagh is 30 minutes by train (€12 round-trip).

EXPLORING

In the very center of town is **Roscrea Castle,** a Norman fortress dating from 1314, given by King Richard II to the duke of Ormonde. Inside are vaulted rooms graced with tapestries and 16th-century furniture. A ticket to it also gains entry to the adjacent **Damer House,** a superb example of an early-18th-century town house on the grand scale. It was built in 1725 within the curtain walls of the castle, at a time when homes were often constructed beside or attached to the strongholds they replaced. The house has a plain, symmetrical facade and a magnificent carved-pine staircase inside; on display are exhibits about local history. To get here, start with your back to St. Cronan's monastery, turn left, and then turn right onto Castle Street. ⊠ *Castle St.* ☎ *0505–21850* ⊕ *www.heritageireland.ie* 🖃 *€4* ☉ *May–Sept., daily 9:30–6; Oct.–Apr., weekends 10–5.*

For a real taste of some honest-to-goodness Tipperary home baking, try to catch the **Roscrea Country Market,** held every Friday afternoon. At 1:45 a large queue forms outside the Abbey Hall for wholegrain scones and breads, apple and rhubarb tarts, fruit and sponge cakes, and homemade jams. Potatoes, vegetables, eggs from free-range chickens, and flowers are also on offer. The market has been running since 1962, and is open only for an hour—so get there early.

The Southeast

INCLUDING COUNTIES CARLOW, KILKENNY, TIPPERARY, WATERFORD, AND WEXFORD

WORD OF MOUTH

"After a delicious breakfast we headed to Kilkenny. The sun was shining and the sky was blue. (Am I really in Ireland?) With its medieval roots; narrow, cobblestoned side streets; brightly painted shops; pubs; cathedrals; and the castle, [Kilkenny] encompasses so many of the sights and sounds that tourists come to Ireland for. I could barely stop snapping photos."

—songdoc

WELCOME TO THE SOUTHEAST

TOP REASONS TO GO

★ **Sacred Ardmore:** St. Declan founded Ireland's first Christian settlement near this beautifully situated fishing village on the Waterford coast.

★ **Kilkenny, Ireland's Medieval Capital:** With its famous 14th-century "witch," Petronilla, *Camelot*-worthy Black Abbey, and fairy-tale Kilkenny Castle, the city still conjures up the days of knights and damsels.

★ **Pretty-as-a-postcard Lismore:** Presided over by the neo-Baronial castle of the Dukes of Devonshire, this storybook village has attracted visitors ranging from Sir Walter Raleigh to Fred Astaire.

★ **Cashel of the Kings:** Ireland's "Rock of Ages," this spectacular 200-foot-tall rock bluff was the ancient seat of the Kings of Munster.

★ **Wexford and Waterford:** Big-city lights shine brightest here, thanks to such attractions as the famed Wexford Opera Festival and the 1,000-year-old saga retold at Waterford Treasures.

1 Kilkenny City. Creativity is evident in every aspect of this town, from its medieval stonework to its array of modern and traditional craft and design found in galleries and studios as well as the many festivals and events held here year-round.

2 Southeast Inlands. Redolent of the Middle Ages, this once-upon-a-time-ified region is home to some thrilling medieval sights, including Leighlinbridge's Black Castle, the tiny village of Old Leighlin, and Jerpoint Abbey, the most famous Cistercian ruins in Ireland.

4 Southeast Coast. Combining the best of Ireland's climate with some wonderful sand-and-sea settings, this coastal headland is noted for quaint villages like Kilmore Quay and Ballyhack, the bustling and historic city of Waterford, and beachfront locations that attract Dubliners by the droves.

GETTING ORIENTED

Set around Tipperary— Ireland's largest inland county—the Southeast is a vast region that stretches from the town of Carlow near the border of County Wicklow in the north to Ardmore near the border of County Cork in the south. Although main towns can be packed with camera-wielding tourists, you can easily escape the tour buses thanks to endless expanses of tranquil countryside.

3 Wexford Town. The warm welcome, the ancient Viking streets, and the tiny, atmospheric Theatre Royal add to the cultural pleasures as this proud town puts on its Sunday best for the Wexford Opera Festival, a weeklong binge of arias and charm held every October.

5 In and Around County Tipperary. The greatest group of monastic ruins in Ireland—the Rock of Cashel—lords it over miles of the idyllic region known as the Golden Vale along with some relentlessly romantic sights, like the 19th-century village of Lismore and Cahir's charming Swiss Cottage.

THE SOUTHEAST PLANNER

Transportation Basics

The Southeast is well served with transportation infrastructure. Waterford Airport allows easy access to the United Kingdom, while Rosslare allows the option of ferry crossings to France and beyond. Train and bus services are plentiful, with Waterford, Kilkenny, and Wexford the main hubs for connections to Dublin and Cork. A car is the best option for covering ground quickly and easily. Unlike the Midlands, where the volume of traffic is generally mellow, roads in this Southeast corner can be busy during the summer months.

Finding a Place to Stay

Festivals, the good weather, and commerce make the Southeast popular, so plan way ahead for a stay in any of the main towns (and in many country manors, which usually have fewer than six bedrooms and fill up fast). As always, the local tourist offices can offer assistance if you arrive without reservations. Assume that all hotel rooms reviewed have in-room phones, TVs, and private bathrooms, unless otherwise indicated.

Talk Radio

As you'll no doubt spend a good portion of your time behind the wheel during your travels, tune in to Irish radio for another angle on the country. If you want to feel the true pulse of the nation, check out any of the RTE Radio 1's morning and afternoon programs with well-known jocks like Ryan Tubridy and Joe Duffy allowing the nation to give full vent to their spleens across the airwaves. Smaller local radio stations are another good option and in a country still reeling from the government mismanagement and social damage of the recent economic crash, the radio has become Ireland's modern confessional and a serious insight into what makes the Irish tick.

Eating Well in the Southeast

Other than its fabled strawberries, the Southeast is probably best known for its rich seafood, especially Wexford mussels, crab, and locally caught salmon. Kilmore Quay, noted for lobster and deep-sea fishing, hosts an annual Seafood Festival the second week of July. Many restaurants serve local lamb, beef, and game in season.

Food is usually prepared in a simple, country-house style, but be ready for some pleasant surprises, as there are a number of ambitious Irish chefs at work in the Southeast's restaurants and hotels. The best of the region's cuisine rests on modern interpretations of classic dishes.

One leading light in the area, chef Kevin Dundon at Dunbrody House, expounds a philosophy of understated but delicious food both in his cooking school and in his cookbook, *Full On Irish*. Informed by his culinary experience, dishes such as tea-smoked chicken and tarragon-glazed lamb exemplify Dundon's modern, international take on his Irish roots.

Another of the Southeast's prominent chefs, Paul Flynn of the Tannery is renowned among Irish foodies for his wonderful inventiveness using local ingredients with a French twist; his seafood dishes are often works of art.

Passion on the High "C"s

Held in late October–early November, the two-week-long annual **Wexford Opera Festival** (⊕ www.wexfordopera.com) is the biggest social and artistic event in the entire Southeast.

From mid-September until the final curtain comes down, Wexford becomes home to a colorful cast of international singers, designers, and musicians, as the town prepares for the annual staging of three grand opera productions at the brand new Wexford Opera House.

The festival has a huge international cachet, and the actual productions are expensive, full-dress affairs. The selection of operas runs toward the recherché and the choice is usually the envy of opera maestros around the world.

In 2009 the operas featured were two conversation pieces: *Virginia* by Saverio Mercadante and *The Golden Ticket*, a new opera based on the children's book *Charlie and The Chocolate Factory*.

Prices are around €25–€130 a ticket, but the extensive fringe events and concerts are usually around €20, and sometimes far more fun. The best thing about the festival for non–opera buffs, though, is the excitement in the air: art exhibitions, street music, parades, and window-dressing contests are held every year, and local bars compete in a Singing Pubs competition.

The bad news: nearly every single bed within a large radius of Wexford is booked during the festival weeks, and usually for months before the actual event kicks off.

Feeling Festive?

With practically every hamlet and village across the country glorying in its own festival or excuse for later pub opening, the Southeast delivers some of Ireland's most popular gatherings.

Carlow's Eigse Arts festival is a 10-day celebration of visual arts in June.

In August the Spraoi festival is a display of talented exuberance in Waterford City, using the city's extensive pedestrian areas; and Kilkenny's Arts Festival attracts many global premieres to its weeklong calendar in August.

Check with the tourist boards for listings and dates of all events, big and small.

When to Go

As well as having some of the richest land in the country, the Southeast is the envy of all Ireland for that most elusive element—sunshine.

The region is also one of the driest in Ireland, which is saying something in a country where seldom do more than three days pass without some rain.

Compared with an average of 80 inches on parts of the west coast, the Southeast gets as little as 40 inches of rainfall per year, varying from the finest light drizzle (a soft day, thank goodness!) to full-blown downpours.

DINING AND LODGING PRICE CATEGORIES (IN EUROS)

	¢	$	$$	$$$	$$$$
Restaurants	under €12	€12–€18	€19–€24	€25–€32	over €32
Hotels	under €80	€80–€120	€121–€170	€171–€210	over €210

Restaurant prices are for a main course at dinner. Hotel prices are for a standard double room in high season.

GETTING AROUND

Tour Options

Irish City Tours in Kilkenny operates open-top coach tours from the castle gate Easter through September, daily 10:30–5.

Burtchaell Tours in Waterford City leads a Waterford walk at noon and 2 PM daily from March through September. Tours depart from the Granville Hotel. Walking tours of Kilkenny are arranged by Tynan Tours from the Kilkenny TIO. These tours take place daily April through October, and Tuesday through Saturday, November to March.

Walking tours of historic Wexford Town can be prebooked for groups by contacting Wexford Walking Tours. Book tours through town tourist offices.

Walking Tours Burtchaell Tours of Waterford City (☎ 051/873–711). **Irish City Tours** (☎ 01/458–0054). **Tynan Tours of Kilkenny City** (☎ 087/265–1745).

Boat and Ferry Travel

If you are coming to Ireland from England or the Continent, chances are you'll end up on a ferry bound for Rosslare Harbor, 19 km (12 mi) south of Wexford, one of Ireland's busiest ferry ports.

Happily, right by the main ferry harbor in Rosslare, officially known as Rosslare-Europort, are the town's trail depot and bus station.

There are two main companies that service Rosslare. Irish Ferries connects Rosslare to Pembroke, Wales, and France's Cherbourg and Roscoff. Stena Line sails directly between Rosslare Ferryport and Fishguard, Wales.

They both have small information kiosks in the ultramodern terminal, which also has a tourist office, lockers, and a sprawling waiting room. There's also a mediocre café, where you can get fast food and coffee.

You can purchase ferry tickets at the terminal, but try to reserve a space in advance through the companies' Cork or Dublin office to avoid the frequent sellouts, particularly in summer and any time the Irish soccer team is playing in a major tournament abroad.

Reservations are also a must if you're traveling by car or motorcycle because onboard parking space is at a premium.

The journey from France to Ireland is free for EurailPass holders, last time we checked.

In most months, Irish Ferries makes the nearly four-hour crossing to Pembroke, Wales, twice daily. Departure times vary from season to season; check the Web site for schedules. The journey to Cherbourg and Rosscoff, France, is usually once daily.

Stena Line usually sails twice daily to Fishguard, a voyage that takes approximately three hours.

Boat and Ferry Information Irish Ferries (☎ 053/913–3158 ⊕ www.irishferries.com). **Passage East Car Ferry Company** (☎ 051/382–480 ⊕ www.passageferry.ie). **Stena Line** (☎ 053/916–1590 ⊕ www.stenaline.ie).

Car Travel

Waterford City, the regional capital, is easily accessible from all parts of Ireland.

From Dublin, take N7 southwest, change to N9 in Naas and then to the M9, and continue along this as it bypasses Carlow Town and Thomastown until it terminates in Waterford. N25 travels east–west through Waterford City, connecting it with Cork in the west and Wexford Town in the east. From Limerick and Tipperary Town, N24 stretches southeast until it, too, ends in Waterford City.

For the most part, the main roads in the Southeast are of good quality and are free of congestion. Side roads are generally narrow and twisting, and you should keep an eye out for farm machinery and animals on country roads.

Train Travel

Waterford City is linked by Irish Rail service to Dublin. Trains run from Plunkett Station in Waterford City to Dublin four times daily, making stops at Thomastown, Kilkenny, Bagenalstown, and Carlow Town.

The daily train between Waterford City and Limerick makes stops at Carrick-on-Suir, Clonmel, Cahir, and Tipperary Town. The train between Rosslare and Waterford City runs twice daily.

Train Information **Irish Rail** (☎ 01/836–6222 in Dublin; 051/873–401 in Waterford ⊕ www.irishrail.ie). **MacDonagh Station** (✉ St. John's St., Kilkenny City). **O'Hanrahan Station** (✉ Redmond Pl., Wexford). **Plunkett Station** (✉ Dock Rd., Waterford).

Air Travel

Aer Arann flies five times daily in both directions between Waterford City and London's Luton Airport. There are also flights to Manchester, Birmingham, and Galway.

Waterford Regional Airport is on the Waterford–Ballymacaw road in Killowen. Waterford City is less than 10 km (6 mi) from the airport. A hackney cab from the airport into Waterford City costs approximately €18.

Carrier **Aer Arann** (☎ 1890/462–726 ⊕ www.aerarann.ie). **Airport Information Waterford Regional Airport** (☎ 051/875–589 ⊕ www.waterfordairport.ie).

Visitor Information

Eight Tourist Information Offices (TIOs) in the Southeast are open all year.

They are Carlow Town, Dungarvan, Enniscorthy, Gorey, Kilkenny, Lismore, Waterford City, and Wexford Town.

Another five TIOs are open seasonally: Cahir (May–September); Cashel (April–September); Rosslare (April–September); Tipperary Town (May–October); and Tramore (June–August).

If traveling extensively by public transportation, be sure to load up on information (schedules, the best taxi-for-hire companies, etc.) upon arriving at the train and bus stations in Kilkenny City, Wexford Town, and Waterford City.

Bus Travel

Bus Éireann makes the Waterford–Dublin journey 10 times a day for about €12.20 one-way and €15 round-trip. There are six buses daily between Waterford City and Limerick, and four between Waterford City and Rosslare. The Cork–Waterford bus runs 13 times a day. In Waterford City, the terminal is Waterford Bus Station.

Bus Information Bus Éireann (☎ 01/836–6111 in Dublin; 051/879–000 in Waterford ⊕ www.buseireann.ie). **J.J. Kavanagh & Sons** (☎ 2056/883–1106 ⊕ www.jjkavanagh.ie).

Updated by
Anto Howard

The Irish like to label their regions, and "Ireland's Sunny Southeast" is the tag they've applied to counties Wexford, Carlow, Kilkenny, Tipperary, and Waterford. The moniker is by no means merely fanciful: the weather station on the coast at Rosslare reports that this region receives more hours of sunshine than any other part of the country. Little wonder the outdoors-loving Irish have made the Southeast's coast a popular warm-weather vacation destination.

Receiving almost double the rays found anywhere else, the shore resorts buzz with activity from May to October. Thousands of families take their annual summer holidays here, where picnics and barbecues—often a rain-washed fantasy elsewhere in Ireland—are a golden reality.

The entire Southeast is rich with natural beauty—not the rugged and wild wonders found to the north and west, but a coast that alternates between long, sandy beaches and rocky bays backed by low cliffs, and an inland landscape of fertile river valleys and lush, undulating pastureland. The landscape of the region is diverse, the appeal universal: you'll find seaside fishing villages with thatched cottages, and Tipperary's verdant, picturesque Golden Vale. The region doesn't lack for culture, either. History-rich Ardmore, Carlow Town, the cities of Kilkenny and Waterford, and Wexford Town have retained traces of their successive waves of invaders—Celt, Viking, and Norman.

The most important of these destinations is Kilkenny City, a major ecclesiastic and political center until the 17th century and now a lively market town. Its streets still hold remnants from medieval times—most notably St. Canice's Cathedral—and a magnificent 12th-century castle that received a sumptuous Victorian makeover. Wexford's narrow streets are built on one side of a wide estuary, giving it a delightful maritime air. Waterford, although less immediately attractive than Wexford, is also built at the confluence of two of the region's rivers, the Suir and the Barrow. It offers a rich selection of Viking and Norman remains, some attractive Georgian buildings, and the visitor center and shop at the famed Waterford Glass Factory (which, a few years ago, stopped manufacturing here).

Deeper into the countryside, rustic charms beckon. The road between Rosslare and Ballyhack passes through quiet, atypical, flat countryside dotted with thatched cottages. In the far southwest of County Waterford, near the Cork border, Ardmore presents early Christian ruins on an exposed headland, while, in the wooded splendor of the Blackwater Valley, the tiny cathedral town of Lismore has a hauntingly beautiful fairy-tale castle.

KILKENNY CITY

101 km (63 mi) southwest of Dublin via N9 and N10.

Dubbed "Ireland's Medieval Capital" by its tourist board, and also called "the Oasis of Ireland" for its many pubs and watering holes, Kilkenny is one of the country's most alluring destinations. It demands to be explored by foot or bicycle, thanks to its easily circumnavigated town center, a 900-year-old Norman citadel that is now a lovely place of Georgian streets and Tudor stone houses. The city (population 25,000) is impressively preserved and attractively situated on the River Nore, which forms the moat of the magnificently restored Kilkenny Castle. In the 6th century, St. Canice (aka "the builder of churches") established a large monastic school here. The town's name reflects Canice's central role: Kil Cainneach means "Church of Canice." Kilkenny did not take on its medieval look for another 400 years, when the Anglo-Normans fortified the city with a castle, gates, and a brawny wall. Kilkenny City's central location means that it's not too far from anywhere else in Ireland. It's 101 km (62 mi) southwest of Dublin via the N9, M9, and M10. Major road improvements mean it only takes 1 hour 45 minutes. Cork is 2-hour drive, while Waterford City is only a 40-minute hop.

GETTING HERE

BUS TRAVEL The bus station is a bit down from the train station on St. John's Street and Bus Éireann runs eight buses a day to Dublin for a 2 hour 10 minute trip that costs €10.80 one-way and €13.50 round-trip. Three buses a day go to Cork for a three-hour trip that costs €16.70 one-way and €21.60 round-trip. J.J. Kavanagh & Sons runs five buses a day from the station directly to Dublin airport for a three-hour journey that costs €18 one-way and €28 round-trip.

TRAIN TRAVEL MacDonagh Station, the city train station, is a short walk from the city center at the top of St. John's Street. The station is on the Dublin—Waterford City line, which also serves Athy, Carlow, Bagenalstown, and Thomastown. Irish Rail runs six trains a day in each direction and the trip to Dublin takes about 1 hour 45 minutes and costs €20 each way.

While studded with plenty of historic sights, Kilkenny also welcomes the traveler with traditional and "characterful" pubs.

There is no direct train to Cork, but five trains a day go via Newbridge for a four-hour journey that costs €20.

Visitor Information Kilkenny Tourist Office (✉ *Shee Alms House, Rose Inn St., Co. Kilkenny* ☎ *056/775-1500* ⊕ *www.kilkennytourism.ie*).

EXPLORING

The city center is small, and despite the large number of historic sights and picturesque streets—in particular, Butter Slip and High Street—you can easily cover it in less than three hours. One of the most pleasant cities south of Dublin (and one of its most sports-minded—from July to September practically the only topic of conversation is the fate of the city's team at the All-Ireland Hurling Championship), Kilkenny City has become in recent years something of a haven for artists and craft workers seeking an escape from Dublin. At such venues as the Kilkenny Design Centre, you can find an array of crafts, especially ceramics and sweaters, for sale. The city has more than 60 pubs, many of them on Parliament and High streets, which also support a lively music scene. Many of the town's pubs and shops have old-fashioned, highly individualized, brightly painted facades, created as part of the town's 1980s revival of this Victorian tradition. So after taking in Kilkenny Castle and the Riverfront Canal Walk—an overgrown pathway that meanders along the castle grounds—mosey down High and Kieran streets. These parallel avenues, considered the historic center of Kilkenny, are connected by a series of horse cart–wide lanes and are fronted with some of the city's best-preserved pubs and Victorian flats. Be sure to look up over the existing modern storefronts to catch a glimpse of how the city looked in years past, as many of the buildings still have second-floor facades reflecting historic decorative styles. High and Kieran streets eventually merge into Parliament Street—the main commercial street—which stretches down to Irishtown.

Kilkenny holds a special place in the history of Anglo-Irish relations. The infamous 1366 Statutes of Kilkenny, intended to strengthen English authority in Ireland by keeping the heirs of the Anglo-Norman invaders from assimilating into the Irish way of life, was an attempt at apartheid. Intermarriage became a crime punishable by death. Anglo-Norman settlers could lose their estates for speaking Irish, for giving their children Irish names, or for dressing in Irish clothing. The native Irish were forced to live outside the town walls in shantytowns. Ironically, Irish and Anglo-Norman assimilation was already well under way by the time the statutes went into effect; perhaps if this intermingling had been allowed to evolve naturally, Anglo-Irish relations in the 20th century might have been more harmonious.

By the early 17th century, Irish Catholics began to chafe under such repression; they tried to bring about reforms with the Confederation of Kilkenny, which governed Ireland from 1642 to 1648, with Kilkenny as the capital. Pope Innocent X sent money and arms. Cromwell responded in 1650 by overrunning the town and sacking the cathedral, which he then used as a stable for his horses. This marked the end of Kilkenny's "Golden Age"; however, the succeeding centuries were not uneventful. In 1798 the city was placed under martial law due to a revolt by the United Irishmen; in 1904 King Edward VII paid a visit; and in 1923, at the height of Ireland's civil war, forces opposed to a government peace deal with the British briefly occupied Kilkenny Castle.

TOP ATTRACTIONS

2 Black Abbey. With a stained-glass, carved-stone interior that seems right out of the musical *Camelot*, the 13th-century Black Abbey is one of the most evocative and beautiful Irish medieval structures. Note the famous 1340 five-gabled Rosary Window, an entire wall agleam with ruby and sapphire glass, depicting the life of Christ. Home to a Dominican order of monks since 1225, the abbey was restored as a church by the order, whose black capes gave the abbey its name. Interestingly, it's also one of the few medieval churches still owned by the Roman Catholic Church, as most of the oldest churches in Ireland were built by the Normans and reverted to the Church of Ireland (Anglican) when the English turned to Protestantism. Nearby is the Black Freren Gate (14th century), the last remaining gateway to the medieval city of yore. ✉ *South of St. Canice's Cathedral* ☎ *056/772–1279* ✉ *Free* ☉ *Daily 9–1 and 2–6.*

4 Kyteler's Inn. The oldest inn in town, Kyteler's is notorious as the place where Dame Alice Le Kyteler, a member of a wealthy banking family and an alleged witch and "brothel keeper," was accused in 1324 of poisoning her four husbands. So, at least, said the enemies of this apparently very merry widow. The restaurant retains its medieval aura, thanks to its 14th-century stonework and exposed beams down in the cellar, built up around Kieran's Well, which predates the house itself.

Food and drink in this popular pub are as simple and plentiful as they would have been in Dame Alice's day—but minus her extra ingredients *(see the CloseUp box "From Stake to Steak" for more information).* ✉ *Kieran St.* ☎ *056/772–1064* ⊕ *www.kytelersinn.ie.*

❼ **Kilkenny Castle.** A bewitching marriage of Gothic and Victorian styles,
★ the town "castle" dominates the south end of town. Amid rolling lawns beside the River Nore, the gray-stone castellated mansion bristles with battlements, spire towers, and numerous chimneys, which the Victorians loved to use to conjure up fairy-tale images of knights and damsels. Standing on 50 acres of landscaped parkland (look for the garden shaped in the form of a gigantic Celtic cross), Kilkenny Castle was built in 1172. Kilkenny Castle served for more than 500 years, beginning in 1391, as the seat of one of the more powerful clans in Irish history, the Butler family, members of which were later designated earls and dukes of Ormonde. Around 1820, William Robert, son of the first marquess of Ormonde, overhauled the castle to make it a wonderland in the Victorian Feudal Revival style. In 1859 John Pollen was called in to redo the most impressive part of the interior, the 150-foot-long, aptly named Long Gallery, a refined, airy hall. Its dazzling green walls are hung with a vast collection of family portraits and frayed tapestries, while above hangs a skylighted, marvelously decorated ceiling, replete with oak beams carved with Celtic lacework and brilliantly painted animal heads. The main staircase was also redone in the mid-1800s to become a showpiece of Ruskinian Gothic. In 1967 the sixth marquess of Ormonde handed over the building to the state for the rather pathetic sum of 75. A guided tour visits many of the salons, and the castle's Butler Gallery houses a superb collection of Irish modern art, including examples by Nathaniel Hone, Jack B. Yeats, Sir John Lavery, Louis Le Brocquy, and James Turrell. ✉ *The Parade* ☎ *056/772–1450* ⊕ *www. kilkennycastle.ie* 🎫 *Castle tour €6, grounds and Butler Gallery free* ⊙ *Apr., May, and Sept., daily 9:30–5:30; June–Aug., daily 9:30–5:30; Oct.–Feb., daily 9:30–4:30, Mar. 9:30–5.*

❶ **St. Canice's Cathedral.** The recent discovery that President Obama's great-great-great-Uncle John Kearney was once the bishop of Ossory and is buried on the grounds of St. Canice's Cathedral boosted its public image no end. In spite of Cromwell's defacements this is still one of the finest cathedrals in Ireland; it's the country's second-largest medieval church, after St. Patrick's Cathedral in Dublin. The bulk of the 13th-century structure (restored in 1866) was built in the early English style. Inside the massive walls is an exuberant Gothic interior, given a somber grandeur by the extensive use of a locally quarried black marble. Many of the memorials and tombstone effigies represent distinguished descendants of the Normans, some depicted in full suits of armor. Look for a female effigy in the south aisle wearing the old Irish, or Kinsale, cloak; a 12th-century black-marble font at the southwest end of the nave; and St. Ciaran's Chair in the north transept, also made of black marble, with 13th-century sculptures on the arms. The biggest attraction on the grounds is the 102-foot-high round tower, which was built in 847 by King O'Carroll of Ossory and is all that remains of the monastic development reputedly begun in the 6th century, around which the town developed. If you have

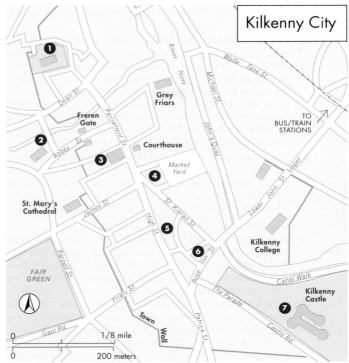

the energy, climb the tower's 167 steps for the tremendous 360-degree view from the top, as well as for the thrill of mounting 102 steps on make-shift wooden stairs. Next door is St. Canice's Library, containing some 3,000 16th- and 17th-century volumes. ⊠ *Dean St.* ☎ *056/776–4971* ⊕ *www.stcanicescathedral.com* ⊠ *Cathedral €4, tower €3* ⊗ *Cathedral June–Aug., Mon.–Sat. 9–6, Sun. 2–6; Apr., May, and Sept., Mon.–Sat. 10–1 and 2–5, Sun. 2–5; Oct.–Mar., Mon.–Sat. 10–1 and 2–4, Sun. 2–4. Tower access depends on weather.*

WORTH NOTING

❸ **Rothe House.** Set with splendidly sturdy stonework, Rothe House is one of the finest examples in Ireland of a Tudor-era merchant's house. There's a feeling of time travel as you step off the busy main street and into this medieval complex with its stone-wall courtyards, one of which houses a medieval well. Built by John Rothe between 1594 and 1610, it's owned by the Kilkenny Archaeological Society and houses a collection of Bronze Age artifacts, ogham stones (carved with early Celtic symbols and messages), and period costumes. The reconstruction of the Burgage Garden was recently completed and recreates, down to the plant types themselves, a typical 17th-century Irish merchant's garden. There's also a genealogical research facility that can help you trace your ancestry. ⊠ *Parliament St.* ☎ *056/772–2893* ⊕ *www.rothehouse.com* ⊠ *€5, garden only*

€2 ⊙ Apr.–Oct., Mon.–Sat. 10:30–5, Sun. 3–5; Nov.–Mar., Mon.–Sat. 10:30–4:30.

❺ Tholsel. Kilkenny's town hall was built in 1761 on Parliament Street and stands near the site of the medieval Market Cross. With its distinctive clock tower and grand entrance portico, this limestone-marble building stands on the site of the execution of poor Petronilla, the "witch" burned at the stake in the 14th century in lieu of her mistress, Dame Alice Le Kyteler. The building itself burned down in 1985, but has since been completely rebuilt and now houses the city's municipal archives. Adjacent to the Tholsel is **Alice's Castle,** a town jail rather grandly fitted out in 18th-century architectural ornamentation.

❻ Tourist Information Office *(TIO). This* is housed in the Shee Alms House (off the east side of High Street). The building was erected in 1582 by Sir Richard Shee as a hospital for the poor and functioned as such until 1895. ⊠ *Rose Inn St.* ☏ *056/775–1500* ⊕ *www.discoverireland.ie/southeast* ⊙ *Apr.–Oct., Mon.–Sat. 9–6; Nov.–Mar., Mon.–Sat. 9:15–5.*

WHERE TO EAT

$$
MEDITERRANEAN
✕ **Café Sol.** There's always a lively buzz about this small eatery, with its tropics-tinted decor and chirpy staff. Chef Liam O'Hanlon gives European flair to the best of local produce, famous Kilkenny beef, and fish bought daily off the quays at Dunmore East. The emphasis is on contemporary Mediterranean-influenced cuisine. The slow roasted pork belly with wholegrain mustard creamed potatoes and roasted root vegetables is one of the more delicious offerings. During the day, light meals and sandwiches are on offer; at night, dining is more formal. ⊠ *William St.* ☏ *056/776–4987* ⊕ *www.cafesolkilkenny.com* ▭ *MC, V.*

$
IRISH
✕ **Langton's.** When it comes to restaurants and pubs, this is Kilkenny Central. A landmark since the 1940s, Langton's is a labyrinth of interconnected bars and eateries. Most of the seating areas, all with open fires, have different personalities—from the leather-upholstered gentlemen's club in the Horseshoe Bar to an attempt at art deco in the spacious dining room. Up front is one of Ireland's most famous "eating pubs," often crammed with punters to the rafters of its low ceiling. For more tranquil environs, head out back, where you can chow down in a neo-Gothic garden framed by a stretch of the old city walls. The main restaurant has a great reputation and offers well-prepared traditional dishes, including (of course) Irish stew. They also have 30 art-deco-style hotel rooms upstairs. ⊠ *69 John St.* ☏ *056/776–5133* ⊕ *www.langtons.ie* ▭ *MC, V.*

$$
ITALIAN
✕ **Ristorante Rinuccini.** A warm glow emanates from this excellent Italian restaurant as you descend the steps into its dining room in the basement of a Georgian town house. Owner-chef Antonio Cavaliere is intensely involved in preparing such luscious pasta dishes as *tortelloni* stuffed with ricotta and spinach and served in a Gorgonzola sauce. Other specialties, such as rack of Irish lamb slow cooked with herbs and rend wine, go particularly well with Antonio's garlic roasted potatoes—highly recommended as a side dish. A splendid all-Italian wine list complements the menu, and there's a host of delicious homemade desserts. This is one of the best Italian options in town. The restaurant accommodates

overnight guests in the town house above. ☒ *1 The Parade, across from Kilkenny Castle* ☎ *056/776–1575* ⊕ *www.rinuccini.com* ⌂ *Reservations essential* ═ *AE, DC, MC, V.*

WHERE TO STAY

$$$
★ ⛫ **Butler House.** The closest you'll get to living in Kilkenny Castle during your stay in the city, the Dowager Duchess of Ormonde's 18th-century former town house is still an integral part of the castle complex. It's a charming piece of Georgian grandeur with an ivy-covered three-bay facade and a walled garden. Inside, the reception salon has a magnificent plaster ceiling and marble fireplaces. Upstairs, any

> **THROW AWAY THE KEY**
>
> Across the road from Rothe House stands the stern limestone facade of Kilkenny Courthouse, below which lies an extremely spooky dungeon. Until the early 19th century, convicts were locked up, four or five to a darkened cell, and literally left to rot. Those who managed to live through the experience emerged in a deranged state. You can visit the prison as part of a walking tour of the city, arranged through the city's tourist information office.

grande dame might look askance—a gradual renovation of the guest rooms is ongoing, so the decor ranges from muted 1970s minimalist to bright modern. The rooms vary in size, with some big as a house and others on the snug side. If you can, treat yourself to one of the huge, high-ceiling bedrooms overlooking the garden and castle. The only slight disadvantage (if you look at things that way) is that breakfast is not served on the premises; for your morning meal you must saunter through the walled rose garden to the adjoining Kilkenny Design Centre. **Pros:** live in a castle for a few days; serene walled garden; breakfast in the old stables of Kilkenny Castle. **Cons:** books up quickly; no restaurant or bar; some rooms a lot smaller than others. ☒ *16 Patrick St., Co. Kilkenny* ☎ *056/776–5707* ⊕ *www.butler.ie* ⟿ *12 rooms, 1 suite* ⌂ *In-room: no a/c, Wi-Fi. In-hotel: parking (free)* ═ *AE, DC, MC, V* ⦿ *BP.*

$–$$ ⛫ **Zuni Townhouse and Restaurant.** This popular, family-owned, city-center hotel boasts the chichi gloss of a big-city boutique lodging but without the icy-cool reception you get in some fashionable joints. The clientele is mainly Dublin weekenders in search of Kilkenny's legendary nightlife, as well as a good cross section of local businesspeople and foreign tourists. Relaxed and welcoming, rooms are minimalist in style, with walls painted in strong, modern colors. Zuni also has a good nouvelle restaurant, where the food, like the decor, is contemporary and light. The new café is a perfect for a light lunch. **Pros:** right in the heart of the city; family owned and run; only 13 rooms. **Cons:** books up quickly; business clientele can stifle atmosphere; can get noisy outside on weekends. ☒ *26 Patrick St., Co. Kilkenny* ☎ *056/772–3999* ⊕ *www.zuni.ie* ⟿ *13 rooms* ⌂ *In-room: no a/c, Wi-Fi. In-hotel: restaurant, bar, Wi-Fi hotspot, parking (free)* ═ *AE, DC, MC, V* ⦿ *BP.*

One of the most famous rooms in Ireland, the Long Gallery transformed Kilkenny Castle into a wonderland of the Victorian Feudal Revival style.

NIGHTLIFE AND THE ARTS

Every August, Kilkenny becomes the focus for Ireland's culture vultures when the **Kilkenny Arts Festival** (☎ 056/776–3663 ⊕ *www.kilkennyarts.ie*) takes over the city for about two weeks. The emphasis in the past was on classical music, but the program has grown increasingly populist. Street theater, elaborate parades, and even a rock concert (staged in the conveniently named Woodstock Desmesne) have lent the festival a more contemporary air and there's even speculation that it might soon eclipse Ireland's premier arts festival in Galway.

If you're craving a pint, you have a choice of pubs along Parliament and High streets. **John Cleere's** (⊠ *22 Parliament St.* ☎ *056/776–2573*) is the best pub in town for a mix of live traditional music, poetry readings, and theatrical plays. The **Pumphouse** (⊠ *26 Parliament St.* ☎ *056/776–3924*) has traditional music during the week and live rock and pop on weekends. **Tynan's Bridge House** (⊠ *2 Horseleap Slip* ☎ *056/21291*) is set on one of Kilkenny's famous "slips," and was first used as an exercise run for dray horses. Inside, you can guess that the pub is more than 200 years old from all the gas lamps, silver tankards, and historic teapots on display. The **Widow McGraths** (⊠ *29 Parliament St.* ☎ *056/775–2520*) celebrates July 4 with a barbecue in its beer garden. It's also a good spot for live music.

The **Watergate Theatre** (⊠ *Parliament St.* ☎ *056/776–1674* ⊕ *www.watergatetheatre.com*) hosts opera, plays, concerts, comedy, and other entertainment at reasonable prices.

SPORTS AND THE OUTDOORS

GAELIC
FOOTBALL

The 1366 Statutes of Kilkenny expressly forbade the ancient Irish game of hurling. No matter: today, Kilkenny is considered one of the great hurling counties. Like its neighbor and archenemy, Wexford, Kilkenny has a long history of success in hurling, and as the annual All-Ireland Hurling Championships draws to its final stages during June and July, interest in the county's team runs to fever pitch. Catch the home team at matches held at **Kilkenny GAA Grounds** (⊠ *Nowlan Park* ☎ *056/777–0008* ⊕ *www.gaa.ie*).

SHOPPING

Kilkenny is a byword for attractive, original crafts that combine traditional arts with modern design elements.

You can see glass being blown at the **Jerpoint Glass Studio** (⊠ *16 km [10 mi] south of Kilkenny in the valley of the River Nore, Stoneyford* ☎ *056/772–4350* ⊕ *www.jerpointglass.com*), where the glass is heavy, modern, uncut, and hand finished. The studio's factory shop is a good place to pick up a bargain. The town's leading outlet, the **Kilkenny Design Centre** (⊠ *Kilkenny Castle* ☎ *056/772–2118* ⊕ *www.kilkennydesign.com*), in the old stable yard opposite the castle, sells ceramics, jewelry, sweaters, and handwoven textiles.

Murphy Jewellers (⊠ *85 High St.* ☎ *056/772–1127* ⊕ *www.murphy-jewellers.com*) specializes in heraldic jewelry.

★ **Nicholas Mosse Pottery** (⊠ *Bennettsbridge* ☎ *056/772–7505* ⊕ *www.nicholasmosse.com*) is the best-known name in Irish ceramics. Nicholas first set up his potter's wheel in an old flour mill in this quiet village (16 km [10 mi] south of Kilkenny) in 1975. Since then, the business has boomed and the rustic floral-pattern pottery created here is instantly recognizable for its "spongeware" designs. A visit here allows you to see the pottery being made, and the adjoining factory shop often has good bargains.

Rudolf Heltzel (⊠ *10 Patrick St.* ☎ *056/772–1497* ⊕ *www.heltzel.ie*) is known for its striking, modern designs in gold and silver jewelry.

Stoneware Jackson Pottery (⊠ *Bennettsbridge* ☎ *056/772–7175* ⊕ *www.stonewarejackson.com*) makes distinctive, hand-thrown tableware and lamps.

The **Sweater Shop** (⊠ *81 High St.* ☎ *056/776–3405* ⊕ *www.sweatershop.ie*) carries a great selection of Irish-weave sweaters.

SOUTHEAST INLANDS

North of Kilkenny City is a region notably rich in historical sights. Travel through the farmlands of the Barrow Valley to the small county seat of Carlow Town, with scenic detours to Leighlinbridge's picturesque castle and Old Leighlin's time-stained cathedral.

LEIGHLINBRIDGE

★ *14 km (9 mi) northeast of Kilkenny City on N10.*

Sure, Ireland 'tis a land of sweet vistas, and one of the most romantic is found here on the east bank of Leighlinbridge: romantic, Norman-era **Black Castle,** poetically mirrored in the waters of the River Barrow and framed by the bulk of a grandly medieval bridge. With five stone arches spanning the river since 1320, this is reputed to be one of the oldest functioning bridges in Europe and makes a magnificent repoussoir for the castle. Built in 1181 as one of the earliest Norman fortresses in Ireland, it has been the scene of countless battles and sieges. Its hulking, 400-year-old main tower still stands, all but daring you to set up your easel and canvas on the adjoining ageless towpath.

WHERE TO EAT AND STAY

$$–$$$ ⬚ **Lord Bagenal Inn.** Old and new spectacularly collide at this noted hostelry. Its historic heart, a famous 19th-century pub, still nestles on the banks of the River Barrow in the center of Leighlinbridge. Built in the early 1800s, its maze of nooks and fireplaces gives away its age in spite of renovations. A quaint walled garden complete with water accents adds to the charm. These days, his Lordship also offers a stopover for weary travelers, thanks to a hypermodern wing built in the past few years. The showpiece is a vast, contempo-vibe restaurant, where prices run upwards of the $$ category: The Waterfront (reservations essential), where signature dishes include *crubeen* (pickled pigs' feet) braised in port and stuffed with truffles; baked monkfish fillet wrapped in Serrano ham with a mango salsa; or fresh turbot with asparagus in beurre blanc. As for the nearly 40 guest rooms, they shimmer in modern style and the lobby and hallways are fetchingly adorned with new Irish artworks. Niceties include an award-winning wine cellar and a pungent array of fine cigars on stock—although with Ireland's smoking ban now in full effect, you will be asked to enjoy your Cohiba outside. **Pros:** winning mix of ancient and modern. **Cons:** miserably unhelpful Web site; uncommunicative staff. ✉ *Main St., Co. Carlow* ☎ *059/972–1668* ⊕ *www.lordbagenal.com* ↝ *40 rooms* ᗧ *In-room: Wi-Fi. In-hotel: a/c, restaurant, Wi-Fi hotspot* ⊟ *AE, MC, V.*

OLD LEIGHLIN

5¾ km (3 mi) west of Leighlinbridge, signposted to right off N9.

Home to one of Ireland's undiscovered gems of late-medieval architecture, the tiny village of Old Leighlin first found fame as the site of a monastery, founded in the 7th century by St. Laserian, that once accommodated 1,500 monks. It hosted the church synod in 630 at which the Celtic Church first accepted the Roman date for the celebration of Easter (the date was officially accepted at the Synod of Whitby in 664); this decision marked the beginning of a move away from old Brehon Law and the deliberalization of the Church. The old monastery was rebuilt in the 12th century as **St. Laserian's Cathedral.** Sitting among green fields, with a castellated tower and Irish-Gothic windows, it evokes a stirring sense of Wordsworthian forlornness. Enlarged in the 16th century, its interior is noted for its 11th-century font, a 200-year-

CLOSE UP

Hurling: Fast and Furious

Hurling: a Limerick versus Tipperary match

Get chatting with the locals in almost any pub across the Southeast, mention the sport of hurling, and an enthusiastic and often passionate conversation is bound to ensue. The region is the heartland of this ancient sport, whose followers have an almost religious obsession with the game.

Hurling is a kind of aerial field hockey with players wielding curved sticks. Its history comes from Ireland's Celtic ancestors, but it bears about the same relation to field hockey as ice hockey does to roller-skating. It's no accident that prowess on the hurling field is regarded as a supreme qualification for election to public office. A man who succeeds at hurling is eminently capable of dealing with anything that fate and the spite of other politicians can throw at him. Hurling is also an extremely skillful sport. A player must have excellent hand-eye coordination combined with an ability to run at high speeds while balancing a small golf-ball-size ball on his *camán* (hurling stick). Fans will proudly tell you it's also the world's fastest team sport.

Ireland's other chief sporting pastimes, including soccer and hurling's cousin, Gaelic football, take a backseat in this part of the country. Stars like Kilkenny's Henry Shefflin, rather than professional soccer players, are sporting icons for local kids. Counties Tipperary, Wexford, and Waterford are among the top teams in the region, but Kilkenny (nicknamed "The Cats") is currently the undisputed top team in the country. It has won the last three All-Ireland hurling championships and is considered one of the best teams in history.

There's an intense rivalry between the counties, especially between old foes Tipperary and Kilkenny. When it gets down to club level, passions run even higher. Almost every parish in the region has a hurling club, and a quick inquiry with locals will usually be enough to find out when the next game is on. Even for the uninitiated, hurling is a great spectator sport. Sporty types wishing to give it a go, be warned; it's fast, furious, and entails more than a hint of danger, as players flail the air to capture the bullet-fast *sliotar* (hurling ball).

old grand wind organ, and a fine wood vaulted ceiling. Guided tours are available. General admission is free but a donation of €1 is suggested. ☎ *059/972–1411* ⊕ *www. cashel.anglican.org* ⊠ *Free* ☉ *Mid-June–Aug., weekdays 10–4.*

THOMASTOWN

14½ km (9 mi) south of Kilkenny on R700 and N9.

Thomastown, originally the seat of the kings of Ossory (an ancient Irish kingdom), is a pretty, stone-built village on the River Nore. It takes its name from Thomas FitzAnthony of Leinster, who encircled the town with a wall in the 13th century. Fragments of this medieval wall remain, as do the partly ruined 13th-century church of St. Mary, and Mullins Castle, adjacent to the town bridge.

Fodor'sChoice
★   Landmarked by its rearing and massive 15th-century tower, **Jerpoint Abbey,** near Thomastown, is one of the most notable Cistercian ruins in Ireland, dating from about 1160. The church, tombs, and the restored cloisters are must-sees for lovers of the Irish Romanesque. The vast cloister is decorated with affecting carvings of human figures and fantastical mythical creatures, including knights and knaves (one with a stomachache) and the assorted dragon or two. Dissolved in 1540, Jerpoint was taken over, as was so much around these parts, by the earls of Ormonde. The one part of the abbey that remains alive, so to speak, is its hallowed cemetery—the natives are still buried here. Guided tours of the impressive complex are available from mid-June to mid-September (last admission is 45 minutes before closing). ⊠ *2 km (1 mi) south of Thomastown on N9* ☎ *056/24623* ⊕ *www.heritageireland.ie* ⊠ *€3* ☉ *Mar.–May and mid-Sept.–Oct., daily 10–5; June–mid-Sept., daily 10–6; Nov.–Feb., daily 10–4.*

WHERE TO EAT AND STAY

$ ▫ **Ballyduff House.** This wonderfully picturesque house was used as a
★   location in the nostalgic movie adaptation of Maeve Binchy's *Circle of Friends.* As the clematis-clad mansion comes into view at the top of a gently curving driveway you can understand why. Relaxation, long walks, and a warm welcome are the order of the day here. Four large, period bedrooms (one is a heavenly, super-stylish vision in multiple hues of green) are decorated with Georgian furniture and ornate wallpaper and afford wonderful views of the river. You are welcome to walk around the gardens and participate in trout and salmon fishing. Mount Juliet Golf Course is less than a five-minute drive away. **Pros:** family-owned and -run; stunningly authentic mansion; guests can use kitchen to prepare a picnic. **Cons:** only four rooms, so often full; few modern facilities; breakfast so good you'll want seconds. ⊠ *Co. Kilkenny* ☎ *056/775–8488* ⊕ *www.ballyduffhouse.com* ⊅ *4 rooms* ⚲ *In-room: no a/c, Internet. In-hotel: Internet terminal* ⊟ *No credit cards* ☉ *Closed Dec.–Feb.* ⦿ *BP.*

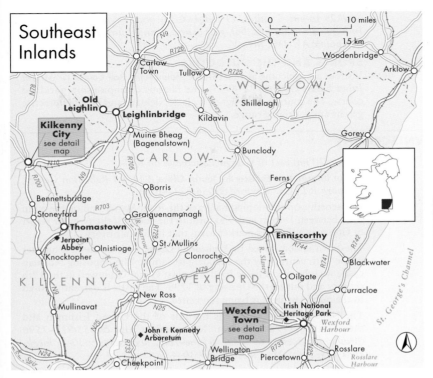

Southeast Inlands

$$$$ Mount Juliet. Once part of the nearby medieval Jerpoint Abbey estate and then famous as the seat of a horse-racing stud, Mount Juliet has long been an address of note in County Kilkenny. Today, this 1,500-acre kingdom is still lorded over by its three-story Georgian mansion, which the second earl of Carrick built along the banks of the River Nore and named in honor of his wife, Lady Juliana. Now a Conrad hotel, this estate proffers the full princely treatment, thanks to a spa, a famous golf course, and an array of restaurants that tempt one never to leave the grounds (from casual bistro to the haute Lady Helen's Restaurant). The imposing mansion, whose elegant sash windows and mansard roof are creeper-covered in the best stately house manner, was subjected to full-blast renovation treatment in 1968. Begone, creaky floors and time-stained walls (and yesteryear's charm?); hello, large accommodations decorated with vibrant hues and fine fabrics, and suites with super-king-size beds and original fireplaces. Rooms are also available in a separate building, the Hunters Yard, plus there are modern and very luxe two-room lodges. For many, the Jack Nicklaus–designed golf course—which has hosted the Irish Open on three occasions—is *the* reason to head here. **Pros:** great golf on your doorstep; pampering spa; aside beautiful River Nore. **Cons:** rooms outside main house a little inferior; some authentic charm sacrificed for modern comfort. ✉ *Thomastown, Co. Kilkenny* ☎ *056/777–3000* ⊕ *www.mountjuliet.*

ie ↪*29 rooms, 2 suites, 11 lodges* ⚙ *In-room: no a/c, Wi-Fi (some). In-hotel: 2 restaurants, bar, golf course, tennis court, pool, spa, Wi-Fi hotspot* ☰ *AE, DC, MC, V.*

SPORTS AND THE OUTDOORS

GOLF   Visitors are welcome at the 18-hole **Mount Juliet Golf Course** (✉ *Mount Juliet Estate* ☎ *056/772–4455*), the famous championship parkland course. The course was designed by Jack Nicklaus and includes practice greens and a driving range.

ENNISCORTHY

32 km (20 mi) east of Graiguenamanagh on R744.

Visitor Information Enniscorthy Tourist Office (✉ *1798 Rebellion Centre, Millpark Rd., Co. Wexford* ☎ *054/923–4699*).

Enniscorthy, on the sloping banks of the River Slaney and on the main road between Dublin and Wexford, to the south of the popular resort of Gorey, is a thriving market town that is rich in history.

The town is dominated by **Enniscorthy Castle,** built in the first quarter of the 13th century by the Prendergast family. The imposing Norman castle was the site of fierce battles against Oliver Cromwell in the 17th century and during the Uprising of 1798. The castle is currently closed to the public while it is being renovated.

The **National 1798 Centre** tells the tale of the United Irishmen and the ill-fated 1798 rebellion. ✉ *Arnold's Cross* ☎ *053/923–7596* ⊕ *www.1798centre.ie* 🎟 *€6* ⊙ *June–Aug., weekdays 9:30–5, weekends 1–5; Sept.–May, weekdays 9:30–4.*

St. Aidan's Cathedral stands on a commanding site overlooking the Slaney. This Gothic Revival structure was built in the mid-19th century under the direction of Augustus Welby Pugin, architect of the Houses of Parliament in London. ✉ *Cathedral St.* ☎ *053/923–5777* 🎟 *Free* ⊙ *Daily 10–6.*

WHERE TO EAT AND STAY

$$$–$$$$ 🔲 **Kilmokea Country House.** A former Georgian rectory dating to 1794,
Fodor'sChoice   Kilmokea presides over 7 acres of gardens blooming by the River Barrow.
★   It recently earned an Irish Heritage Garden certificate—a justifiable reward for 52 years of horticultural creation and dedication. The formal walled gardens were originally started in 1947 and contain over 130 different species to delight green-thumbers. Presiding over this domain are Mark and Emma Hewlett, who have managed to gild this lily with all manner of delights. Guest bedrooms are lavish with four-poster beds and great window views. For dinner, a grand, maroon-hue salon offers ambitious and expensive prix-fixe meals; for lunches and teas repair to the Georgian Tea Rooms conservatory. Kilmokea is located on the R733 south from New Ross to Ballyhack—look out for the signpost to Kilmokea Gardens. **Pros:** family-owned and -run; incredible gardens; four-poster beds. **Cons:** no Internet in rooms; some rooms are expensive for this region; books up quickly. ✉ *Great Island, Campile, Co. Wexford* ☎ *051/388–109* ⊕ *www. kilmokea.com* ↪ *6 rooms* ⚙ *In-room: no a/c, Wi-Fi. In-hotel: restaurant, tennis court, pool, spa, Wi-Fi hotspot* ☰ *MC, V.*

$ 🏠 **Salville House.** Local legend has it that this fine Victorian farmhouse was once the home of a couple of "disreputable" ladies who danced at the Folies Bergère in Paris. Things are much more respectable nowadays: Gordon and Jane Parker have created a hilltop haven where food and relaxation are the order of the day. Gordon's inspired contemporary cuisine has a growing group of fans. Guests dine around a mahogany table and are invited to bring their own wine. The bedrooms are spacious, with plenty of books on the shelves and a great view of the River Slaney. In summer a grass tennis court in front of the house adds to its charm. To get here, look for the signpost, 2 km (1 mi) out of Enniscorthy on the Wexford road. **Pros:** family-owned and -run; wonderful home-style food; great views. **Cons:** only five rooms; no air-conditioning; can be a little tricky to find. ✉ *Wexford Rd., Co. Wexford* ☎ *053/923–5252* ⊕ *www.salvillehouse.com* 🛏 *5 rooms* ⚷ *In-room: no a/c, no phone, no TV, Wi-Fi (some). In-hotel: tennis court, Wi-Fi hotspot* 🚫 *No credit cards* ⏏ *BP.*

SHOPPING

Kiltrea Bridge Pottery (✉ *Kiltrea, Caime* ☎ *053/923–5107* ⊕ *www. kiltreapottery.com*) stocks garden pots, plant pots, and country kitchen crocks.

WEXFORD TOWN

19 km (12 mi) south of Enniscorthy, 62 km (39 mi) northeast of Waterford City, 115 km (72 mi) southwest of Dublin.

Wexford's history goes back to prehistoric times, though you'll find scant traces of them now. Much more obvious are the Viking and Norman associations, evident in alleys as well as in the town walls, some of which are still standing. Today, this coastal town is most famed for the Wexford Opera Festival, usually held in October, which has been seducing the world with wonderful productions of rare opera for over 50 years. The warm and vivacious welcome, the narrow and ancient Viking streets, and the tiny, atmospheric Theatre Royal add to the pleasure of this event and of any visit to Wexford Town. Wexford is reached by car using the N11/M11 and the N25. The drive to Dublin on improved roads takes about two hours.

GETTING HERE

BUS TRAVEL Inter-city buses leave from O'Hanrahan train station on Redmond Place. Bus Éireann has nine buses a day going to Dublin (three hours; €14.90 one-way, €17.60 round-trip), nine a day going to Rosslare (30 minutes; €4.50 one-way, €7.50 round-trip), and six a day Monday–Saturday, three on Sunday, going to Waterford City (three hours; €7.50 one-way, €17.60 round-trip).

TRAIN TRAVEL O'Hanrahan Station serves Irish Rail trains at the northern end of town on Redmond Place. Wexford is on the Dublin–Roslare line and three trains a day go to and from Dublin; the 2½-hour trip costs €22.50 one-way or same-day return and €28.50 open return. The short hop to Rosslare costs €4 and takes 25 minutes. There are no direct trains to Cork or Waterford.

Visitor Information Wexford Tourist Office (✉ *Crescent Quay, Co. Wexford* ☎ *053/912–3111* ⊕ *www.wexfordtourism.com*).

EXPLORING

From its appearance today, you would barely realize that Wexford is an ancient place, but in fact it was defined on maps by the Greek cartographer Ptolemy as long ago as the 2nd century AD. Its Irish name is Loch Garman, but the Vikings called it Waesfjord—the harbor of the mudflats—which became Wexford in English. Wexford became an English garrison town after it was taken by Oliver Cromwell in 1649.

The River Slaney empties into the sea at Wexford Town. The harbor has silted up since the days when Viking longboats docked here; nowadays only a few small trawlers fish from here. Wexford Town's compact center is on the south bank of the Slaney. Running parallel to the quays on the riverfront is the main street (the name changes several times), the major shopping street of the town, with a pleasant mix of old-fashioned bakeries, butcher shops, stylish boutiques, and a share of Wexford's many pubs. It can be explored on foot in an hour or two. Allow at least half a day in the area if you also intend to visit the Heritage Park at nearby Ferrycarrig, and a full day if you want to take in Johnstown Castle Gardens and its agricultural museum, or walk in the nature reserve at nearby Curracloe Beach. The town is at its best in late October and early November, when the presence of the Wexford Opera Festival creates a carnival atmosphere.

Rising above the town's rooftops are the graceful spires of two elegant examples of 19th-century Gothic architecture. These **twin churches** have identical exteriors, their foundation stones were laid on the same day, and their spires each reach a height of 230 feet. The **Church of the Assumption** is on Bride Street. The **Church of the Immaculate Conception** is on Rowe Street.

TOP ATTRACTIONS

❽ **Irish National Heritage Park.** A 35-acre, open-air living history museum ☾ beside the River Slaney, this is one of Ireland's most successful and ★ enjoyable family attractions. In about 1½ hours, a guide takes you through 9,000 years of Irish history—from the first evidence of humans on this island, at around 7000 BC, to the Norman settlements of the mid-12th century. Full-scale replicas of typical dwelling places illustrate the changes in beliefs and lifestyles. Highlights of the tour include a prehistoric homestead, a *crannóg* (lake dwelling), an early Christian *rath* (fortified farmstead), a Christian monastery, a horizontal water mill, a Viking longhouse, and a Norman castle. There are also examples of pre-Christian burial sites and a stone circle. Most of the exhibits are "inhabited" by students in appropriate historic dress who will answer questions. The riverside site includes several nature trails. ✉ *5 km (3 mi) north of Wexford Town on N11, Ferrycarrig* ☎ *053/910–733* ⊕ *www.inhp.com* 🖭 *€8* ☉ *May–Aug., daily 9:30–6:30; Sept.–Apr., daily 9:30–5:30.*

Viking longboasts once docked where fishing trawlers now berth in Wexford's busy harbor.

Fodor's Choice **Johnstown Castle Gardens.** Only Walt Disney might have bettered the
★ storybook look of the massive, Victorian Gothic, gray-stone castle set at
the heart of this beautiful garden estate. Located 5 km (3 mi) southwest
of Wexford following the N25 (direction Rosslare), these magnificent
parklands—with splendid towering trees, lakes, and ornamental gardens—offer a grand frame to the castle. A Gothic Revival extravaganza,
this turreted, battlemented, and machicolated edifice, which bristles in
silver-gray ashlar, was built for the Grogan-Morgan family between
1810 and 1855. Unfortunately, you can't tour the building (it houses a
national agricultural college) other than its entrance hall, but the well-
maintained grounds are open to the public. The centerpiece is the 5-acre
lake, one side of which has a terrace, lined with statues, from which
to take in the panorama of the mirrored castle. Because there's such a
variety of trees framing the view—Japanese cedars, Atlantic blue cedars,
golden Lawson cypresses—there's color through much of the calendar.
Nearby are the Devil's Gate walled garden—a woodland garden set
around the ruins of the medieval castle of Rathlannon—and the **Irish
Agricultural Museum.** The latter, housed in the quadrangular stable
yards, shows what life was once like in rural Ireland. It also contains
a 5,000-square-foot exhibition on the potato and the Great Famine
(1845–49). ⊠ *Signposted just off N25, 6 km (4 mi) southwest of Wexford Town* ☎ *053/914–2888* ⊕ *www.irishagrimuseum.ie* ⊠ *Gardens
May–Sept. €2 (€6 for a car), Oct.–Apr. free. Museum €6* ☉ *Gardens
daily 9–5:30. Museum Apr.–mid-Nov., weekdays 9–5, weekends 11–5;
mid-Nov.–Mar. weekdays 9–12:30 and 1:30–5.*

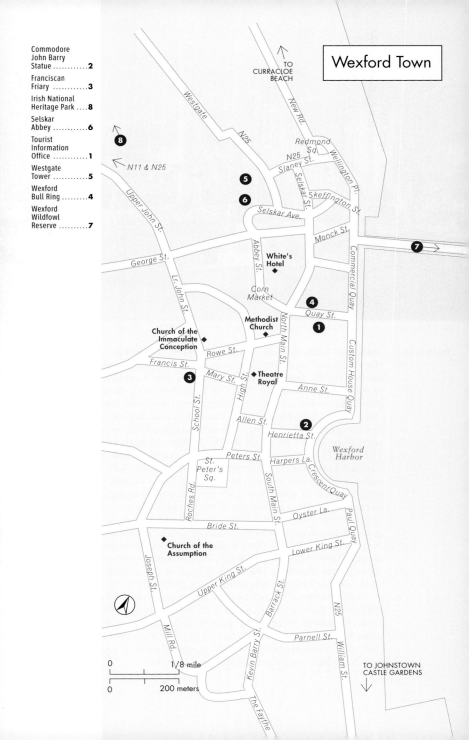

Wexford Town

TO CURRACLOE BEACH

N11 & N25

Westgate

N25

New Rd.

Redmond Sq.

N25

Slaney St.

Wellington Pl.

5

6

Selskar St.

Skeffington St.

Selskar Ave.

Monck St.

Upper John St.

George St.

Abbey St.

White's Hotel

Commercial Quay

7

Corn Market

Lr. John St.

4

Quay St.

1

North Main St.

Custom House Quay

Methodist Church

Church of the Immaculate Conception

Rowe St.

Francis St.

3

Mary St.

High St.

◆ **Theatre Royal**

Anne St.

School St.

Allen St.

2

Henrietta St.

Peters St.

Harpers La.

Wexford Harbor

St. Peter's Sq.

South Main St.

Crescent Quay

Roches Rd.

Bride St.

Oyster La.

Paul Quay

◆ **Church of the Assumption**

Lower King St.

Joseph St.

Upper King St.

Barrack St.

N25

Mill Rd.

Parnell St.

William St.

Kevin Barry St.

The Faythe

TO JOHNSTOWN CASTLE GARDENS

0   1/8 mile

0   200 meters

5 **Westgate Tower.** The largest of five fortified gateways in the Norman and Viking town walls, Westgate is the only one remaining. The early-13th-century tower has been sensitively restored. Keep an eye out as you wander this part of town for other preserved segments of the old town walls. ⊠ *Westgate.*

4 **Wexford Bull Ring.** Once the scene of bull baiting, a cruel medieval sport that was popular among the Norman nobility, this arena was sad witness to other bloody crimes. Notoriously, in 1649, Cromwell's soldiers massacred 300 panic-stricken townspeople who had gathered here to pray as the army stormed their town. The memory of this heartless leader has remained a dark folk legacy for centuries and is only now beginning to fade. A housing development at the old Cromwell's Fort is one of the ritzier addresses in town. ⊠ *Quay St., back toward quays.*

7 **Wexford Wildfowl Reserve.** A nature lover's paradise, this is found just a short walk across the bridge from the main part of town. Today, it shelters one-third of the world's Greenland white-fronted geese. As many as 10,000 of them spend their winters on the mudflats, known locally as slobs, which also draw ducks, swans, and other waterfowl. Observation hides are provided for bird-watchers, and an audiovisual show and exhibitions are available at the visitor center. Lectures on the teeming birdlife of the reserve can be arranged on request. ⊠ *North Slob, Wexford Harbor* ☎ *053/912–3129* ⊕ *www.heritageireland.ie* ⊠ *Free* ⊙ *Daily 9–5.*

WORTH NOTING

2 **Commodore John Barry Statue.** Standing in the center of Crescent Quay, this large bronze commemorates the man who came to be known as the father of the American Navy. Born in 1745 in nearby Ballysampson, Barry (1745–1803) settled in Philadelphia at age 15, became a brilliant naval fighter during the War of Independence (thus avenging his Irish ancestors), and trained many young naval officers who went on to achieve fame.

3 **Franciscan Friary.** This town landmark has a ceiling worth noting for its fine, locally crafted stuccowork. ⊠ *School St.* ☎ *053/912–2758* ⊠ *Free* ⊙ *Daily 8:30–6:30.*

6 **Selskar Abbey.** This 12th-century abbey witnessed the first treaty between the Irish and the Normans signed in 1169. Today only ruins remain. ⊠ *Selskar St., south of Westgate Tower.*

1 **Tourist Information Office.** A good place from which to start exploring Wexford Town on foot, this also is a font of information with leads about guided walking tours organized by local historians. ⊠ *Quay Front* ☎ *053/912–3111.*

THE SOUTHEAST THROUGH THE AGES

The Southeast's coastal and inland areas have long, interesting histories. The Kings of Munster had their ceremonial center on the Rock of Cashel, a vast, cathedral-top rock rising above the plain.

Legend has it that St. Patrick converted the High King of Ireland to Christianity here. In the 7th century, Cashel became an important monastic settlement and bishopric, and there were also thriving early Christian monasteries at Kilkenny, Ardmore, and Lismore.

But the quiet life of Christian Ireland was disrupted from the 9th century onward by a series of Viking invasions.

Liking what they found here—a pleasant climate, rich, easily cultivated land, and a series of sheltered harbors—the Vikings stayed on, founding the towns of Wexford and Waterford. (Waterford's name comes from the Norse Vadrefjord, Wexford's from Waesfjord.)

But less than two centuries later, the Southeast was the location of the most significant turning point in Ireland's recorded history.

In 1169 the Normans (who had conquered England a hundred years before) landed at Bannow Bay in County Wexford. It was the beginning of what Irish patriots commonly describe as "800 years of English oppression."

The English were invited into Ireland by the former king of Leinster, Dermot MacMurrough, who hoped to regain his crown with the help of the Norman earl, Richard FitzGilbert de Clare, famously known as "Strong-

bow." To seal their pact, Dermot's daughter Aoife married Strongbow.

It was symbolic of the way that the Normans, once they had conquered the country, integrated into Irish life. It wasn't long before the Normans were described as being "more Irish than the Irish themselves."

To this day, reminders of the Norman influence on Ireland remain strongest in the Southeast.

Norman surnames are the most obvious indicator of the region's history, as names like Butler, Fitzgerald, Roche, and Fitzmaurice are all commonplace hereabouts. The architectural legacy of the Normans is also easy to spot in this part of Ireland.

The streetscapes of Kilkenny, Wexford, and Waterford cities owe their origins to the Normans. Travel the rural side roads of the region and it won't be long before you come across the ruins of a Norman castle, or "keep."

Some are used to house animals or hay, while the best preserved are those that were integrated into later medieval or Georgian structures.

The Anglo-Normans and the Irish chieftains soon started to intermarry, but the process of integration came to a halt in 1366 with the Statutes of Kilkenny, based on English fears that if such intermingling continued they would lose whatever control over Ireland they had.

Oliver Cromwell's Irish campaign of 1650, attempted to crush Catholic opposition to the English parliament, brought widespread woe, as did the failed, bloody rebellion of 1798, which centered on Wicklow and Wexford.

WHERE TO EAT

¢ ✕ **La Dolce Vita.** You might have to queue behind a few locals to get
ITALIAN seated in this little Italian deli-eatery in a surprisingly serene spot just off
the busy shopping area. Hearty food, high standards, people's prices: it's
the perfect place to break up a day sightseeing with one of their classy
salads or genuinely fresh pasta dishes. They also do a soup and risotto
of the day and an imaginative fish and meat dish for hungrier folk. ✉ *6
Trimmers La.* ☎ *053/917–0806* ▭ *MC, V* ☺ *Closed Sun. No dinner.*

$$ ✕ **Reed Restaurant.** Local seafood is the big draw at this independent res-
IRISH taurant located at the family-popular Ferrycarrig hotel. Fresh-off-the-
boat fish from Kilmore Quay is a favorite, but the Killurin lamb is just
as local and tasty while more exotic dishes like ostrich fillet are also on
offer. Check out the wine menu, one of the better ones in the Southeast.
While the tables are formally appointed with crisp white linen, the light-
filled dining room has a friendly, relaxed vibe. Try to grab a table that
allows you to enjoy the romantically serene riverfront view. ✉ *Ferrycar-
rig Hotel, Ferrycarrig Bridge* ☎ *053/912–0999* ▭ *AE, DC, MC, V.*

WHERE TO STAY

$$$–$$$$ ⊡ **Ferrycarrig.** A real favorite with families, this spot, 4 km (2½ mi)
MEDITERRANEAN outside town, offers plenty of peace and tranquility for parents thanks
☺ to its pleasant riverside location. They have special "family rooms," but
the spacious bedrooms have wonderful views of the river, and some also
have balconies. The Reed restaurant overlooks its pleasant waterside
location with a menu concentrating on seafood. For the kids they have
a day-care facility and a swimming pool. There's also a well-equipped
health center. **Pros:** family-friendly; good restaurant; riverside location.
Cons: can get a bit hectic in summer; a little overpriced; some rooms bet-
ter than others. ✉ *Ferrycarrig Bridge (3 km/2 mi from Wexford Town
on the N11), Co. Wexford* ☎ *053/912–0999* ⊕ *www.ferrycarrighotel.
ie* ☞ *98 rooms, 4 suites* ⚐ *In-room: no a/c, Wi-Fi. In-hotel: restaurant,
bar, pool, gym, Wi-Fi hotspot* ▭ *AE, DC, MC, V* ⧉ *BP.*

$ ⊡ **McMenamin's Townhouse.** From opera divas to Hollywood stars,
they've all stayed at this cozy Victorian town house. It's become one
of the lodgings of choice for the annual opera festival held in the town
each autumn and is also popular as a last stopover for travelers heading
for the Rosslare ferry to France. The bedrooms are spacious, warm, and
immaculate, with large pieces of highly polished Victorian furniture and
antique beds, including a mahogany half-tester. There are about eight
choices at breakfast, including fresh fish of the day and hot porridge.
Make sure you taste Kay and Seamus McMenamin's homemade whis-
key marmalade. **Pros:** family-owned and -run; great breakfast; beautiful
antique beds in rooms. **Cons:** only four rooms so it books up quickly;
no Internet in rooms; no TVs in rooms. ✉ *6 Glena Terr., Spawell Rd.,
Co. Wexford* ☎ *053/914–6442* ⊕ *www.wexford-bedandbreakfast.
com* ☞ *4 rooms* ⚐ *In-room: no a/c, no phone, no TV. In-hotel: Wi-Fi
hotspot* ▭ *MC, V* ☺ *Closed last 2 wks of Dec.* ⧉ *BP.*

5

NIGHTLIFE AND THE ARTS

Wexford's grand and hoary landmark, the Theatre Royal has been entirely rebuilt to serve as the Wexford Opera Theatre for the world-famous **Wexford Opera Festival** (✉ *27 High St.* ☎ *053/912–2144 box office* ⊕ *www.wexfordopera.com*), held in this new house during the last two weeks of October and the beginning of November. The town's leading cultural event, the festival has been going strong since 1951 and features seldom-performed operas sung by top talent from all over the world. The strikingly modern, Keith Williams-designed building is custom built for opera and offers fabulous views out over Mount Lenister to the northwest and Tuskar Rock lighthouse to the southeast. The surprisingly large main auditorium seats 749 with a smaller second space for 172. Along with an ever-expanding offering of more populist fare performed in small venues and pubs, the festival supplies a feast of concerts and recitals that start at 11 AM and continue until midnight. *For the full aria, see "Passion on the High 'C's" in the Planner at the front of this chapter.* Year-round, touring companies and local productions are also seen at these venues.

As the saying goes, if you can find a street without at least one bar on it, you've left Wexford. **Centenary Stores** (✉ *Charlotte St.* ☎ *053/912–4424*) is a Victorian-style pub. The adjoining nightclub makes it a popular place for the young crowd. Lunch is Monday through Saturday, and there's traditional music every Sunday morning. **The Sky and the Ground** (✉ *112 S. Main St.* ☎ *053/912–1273*) is one of the best pubs in town and is a mecca for Irish music sessions, which pack in the crowds from Monday through Thursday. Dating to the 13th century, the **Thomas Moore Tavern** (✉ *Cornmarket* ☎ *053/912–4348*) is Wexford's oldest pub, named after the renowned Irish poet whose parents lived here. The pub has its original medieval walls and fine old beams along the ceiling. It's the perfect place for a quiet drink by the fire. Light lunches and snacks are served on weekdays between noon and 3.

SPORTS

GAELIC FOOTBALL You can watch Gaelic football and hurling at the **Wexford Park GAA** (✉ *Clonard Rd.* ☎ *053/9144808* ⊕ *www.wexford.gaa.ie*).

SHOPPING

Barker's (✉ *36 S. Main St.* ☎ *053/912–3159*) stocks Waterford crystal, local pottery, and crafts. **Martins Jewellers** (✉ *Lower Rowe St.* ☎ *053/912–2635*) specializes in handmade Celtic jewelry. **Westgate Design** (✉ *22 N. Main St.* ☎ *053/912–3787*) carries a good selection of Irish crafts, clothing, pottery, candles, and jewelry; there's also a restaurant here.

WATERFORD AND THE SOUTHEAST COAST

This journey takes you along mainly minor roads through the prettiest parts of the coast in Counties Wexford and Waterford, pausing midway to explore Waterford City—home of the dazzling cut glass—on foot. Along the way expect to see long golden beaches, quaint fishing villages like Kilmore Quay and Ballyhack, some of the country's best nature reserves, and Tramore, Ireland's most unredeemable family waterside resort. If you're coming from the Continent or England, chances are you'll end up on a ferry bound for Rosslare Harbour, one of Ireland's busiest ferry ports.

ROSSLARE

16 km (10 mi) southeast of Wexford Town on R470.

Sometimes called Ireland's sunniest spot, the village of Rosslare is a seaside getaway with an attractive beach. Many vacationers head here to hike, golf, sun, and swim. But the truth is that most visitors are only here to take the ferry from the Rosslare-Europort terminal, the only reason (some point out) you should find yourself in this otherwise dull little town. As Rosslare is so well connected to the ferry port the roads to major cities to and from here are very good: N81, N11, and N25. The car trip from Dublin takes around 2 hours 12 minutes. Cork is 179 km (111 mi) northwest or 2 hours 45 minutes away via the N25. Rosslare is only 16 km (9 mi) southeast of Wexford Town on the R470.

GETTING HERE

BOAT TRAVEL Stena Line Express sails May to September between Rosslare Harbor and Fishguard in Wales (adult €30, car and driver €117–€222; 2 hours; 2 sailings per day). Stena Line also runs its Superferry (adult €30, car and driver €72–€182; 3½ hours; 2 sailings per day) year-round. Irish Ferries sails to Pembroke in Wales (3¾ hours, twice daily). Single fares start at €30 for a foot passenger, €69 for a car and driver. Between April and December there are ferries to Cherbourg, France (19½ hours, up to three a week).

BUS TRAVEL Bus Éireann has services from Rosslare-Europort to many cities and towns in Ireland including Dublin (€16.70 one-way, €23 round-trip; 3 hours; 13 daily Monday–Saturday, 11 on Sunday) and Cork (€21.20 one-way, €30.20 round-trip; 4 hours; five daily Monday–Saturday, 3 on Sunday) that goes via Waterford City (€14.90 one-way, €20.70 round-trip; 1½ hours).

TRAIN TRAVEL Irish Rail runs three trains daily on the Dublin–Rosslare Europort line via Wexford Town. The trip to Dublin takes three hours (€22.50 one-way, €28.50 round-trip) and to Wexford Town only 25 minutes (€5.90 one-way, €8.20 round-trip). Trains on the Rosslare Europort–Limerick route stop in Waterford City (€17 one-way, €28 round-trip; 1¼ hours) twice a day from Monday to Saturday.

EXPLORING

Rosslare Harbour, 8 km (5 mi) south of the village, is the terminus for car ferries from Fishguard and Pembroke in Wales (a four-hour trip) and from Cherbourg and Roscoff in France (a 22-hour trip). The two ferry companies, Irish Ferries and Stena Sealink serving Rosslare Harbour have small information kiosks in the ultramodern terminal, which also has lockers, a sprawling waiting room, and a café. You can purchase ferry tickets at the terminal. Reservations are also a must if you're traveling by car because onboard parking space is at a premium. The **Rosslare Harbour rail depot** (☎ *053/915–7937* ⊕ *www.irishrail.ie*), adjacent to the ferry terminal, is served by frequent trains to Dublin's Connolly Station and Cork (change at Limerick Junction). Bus Éireann's Rosslare Harbour depot also adjoins the rail station.

WHERE TO STAY

$$$–$$$$ ☎ **Kelly's.** Somewhat of a legend
CONTINENTAL   with Irish vacationers, the Kelly
★   family started this place in 1895 and it has become exceedingly popular. The reasons are numerous—a stunning beachfront location, second-to-none entertainment and leisure facilities, a child-friendly approach, and a reputation for good food being just a few. The guest rooms are comfort-laden havens decked out with rustic furnishings—try to get one with views of Rosslare Strand. The SeaSpa incorporates a Seawater Vitality Pool, Bio Sauna, Mud Rooms, and seaweed baths among its many eco-friendly pleasures. Note that in July and August the hotel insists on a one-week minimum stay at full-board prices. **Pros:** great value for families; lots of activities; quality spa on-site. **Cons:** lots of kids can make it hectic in summer; fairly basic facilities in rooms; quite pricey in current climate. ⊠ *Co. Wexford* ☎ *053/913–2114* ⊕ *www. kellys.ie* ➲ *114 rooms, 4 suites* ☖ *In-room: refrigerator. In-hotel: a/c, 2 restaurants, golf course, tennis courts, pools, gym, spa, bicycles, Wi-Fi hotspot* ⊟ *AE, MC, V* ☉ *Closed Dec.–mid-Feb.* ⦿⣿ *BP, MAP.*

NIGHTLIFE AND THE ARTS

The Porthole Bar (⊠ *Rosslare Harbor* ☎ *053/913–3110*), at the Hotel Rosslare, is a trendy spot with designer decor featuring stonework and fish tanks. It's popular for live music on weekends.

SPORTS

Rosslare Golf Club (⊠ *Rosslare Strand* ☎ *053/913–2203* ⊕ *www. rosslaregolf.com*) is a 27-hole championship links. A mixture of links and parkland can be found at the 27-hole **St. Helen's Bay** (⊠ *Kilrane* ☎ *053/913–3234* ⊕ *www.sthelensbay.com*).

BALLYHACK

Fodor's Choice   *54 km (24 mi) west of Kilmore Quay.*
★

On the upper reaches of Waterford Harbor, this pretty village with a square castle keep, wooden buildings, thatch cottages, and a green, hilly background is admired by painters and photographers. A small car ferry makes the five-minute crossing to Passage East and Waterford.

The gray-stone keep of **Ballyhack Castle** dates from the 16th century. It was once owned by the Knights Templars of St. John of Jerusalem, who held the ferry rights by royal charter. The first two floors have been renovated and house local-history exhibits. Guided tours are available by appointment, and the last admission is 45 minutes before closing. ☎ *051/389–468* ⊕ *www.4heritageireland.ie* ⛴ *Free* ☉ *Mid-June–mid-*

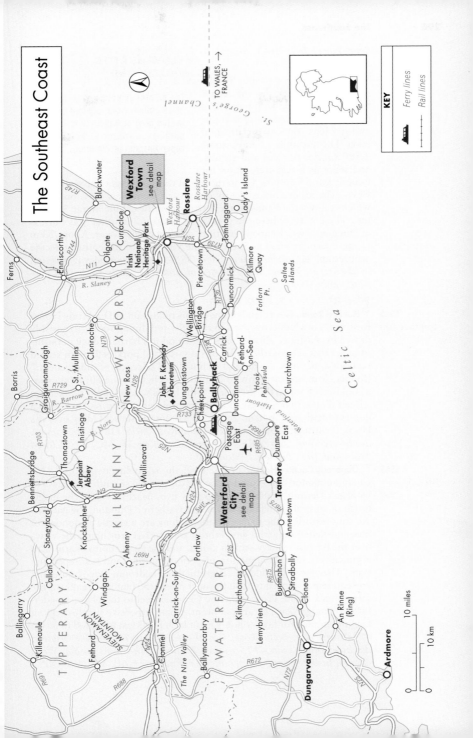

The Southeast Coast

KEY
Ferry lines
Rail lines

St. George's Channel

TO WALES, FRANCE →

Celtic Sea

Wexford Town see detail map

Waterford City see detail map

Irish National Heritage Park

John F. Kennedy Arboretum

Jerpoint Abbey

Rosslare

Rosslare Harbour

Wexford Harbour

Lady's Island

Tomhaggard

Kilmore Quay

Salltee Islands

Forlorn Pt.

Duncormick

Piercetown

Wellington Bridge

Carrick

Fethard-on-Sea

Churchtown

Hook Peninsula

Duncannon

Waterford Harbour

Dunmore East

Tramore

Passage East

Ballyhack

Checkpoint

Dungulstown

New Ross

Clonroche

Ferns

Enniscorthy

Blackwater

Curracloe

Oilgate

R. Slaney

WEXFORD

St. Mullins

Graiguenamanagh

Borris

R. Barrow

Inistioge

Thomastown

Bennettsbridge

R. Nore

Mullinavat

KILKENNY

Knocktopher

Ahenny

Carrick-on-Suir

Portlaw

Stoneyford

Callan

Ballingarry

Killenaule

Fethard

Windgap

TIPPERARY

SLIEVENAMON MOUNTAIN

Clonmel

The Nire Valley

Ballymacarbry

WATERFORD

Kilmacthomas

Lemybrien

Burmahon

Stradbally

Clonea

Annestown

An Rinne (Ring)

Dungarvan

Ardmore

R. Suir

10 miles

10 km

Sept., weekdays 10–1 and 2–6, weekends 10–6.

Twelve kilometers (8 mi) to the north of Ballyhack lies the **John F. Kennedy Arboretum,** with more than 600 acres of forest, nature trails, and gardens, plus an ornamental lake. The grounds contain some 4,500 species of trees and shrubs, and serve as a resource center for

SLOW BOAT TO WATERFORD

The Knights Templars of St. John of Jerusalem were required to keep a boat at Ballyhack to transport injured knights to the King's Leper Hospital at Waterford.

botanists and foresters. Go to the top of the park to get fine panoramic views. The arboretum is clearly signposted from New Ross on R733, which follows the banks of the Barrow southward for about 5 km (3 mi). The cottage where the president's great-grandfather was born is in Dunganstown; Kennedy relatives still live in the house. About 2 km (1 mi) down the road at Slieve Coillte you can see the entrance to the arboretum. ⊠ *Dunganstown* ☎ *051/388–171* ⊕ *www.heritageireland. ie* ⊡ *€3* ☉ *May–Aug., daily 10–8; Apr. and Sept., daily 10–6:30; Oct.– Mar., daily 10–5.*

WHERE TO EAT AND STAY

$$$$
CONTEMPORARY

✕ **Harvest Room.** Gourmands come to this restaurant at Dunbrody House to stuff themselves cross-eyed in the ruby-red dining room, irresistibly drawn by master celebrity chef Kevin Dundon's Barbary duck in burnt-orange sauce, char-grilled fillet of slow-roasted pork belly with seared scallops and a lime confit, and a chocolate "selection of indulgences." (In fact, you can learn how to cook these delights yourself; Kevin runs a cooking school on the premises, with classes scheduled for weekends.) After a dinner that is likely to be memorable sip-to-sup, sit back with a goblet of Irish mist in hand and catch a dramatic sunset fading over the Hook Peninsula. ⊠ *Arthurstown, New Ross* ☎ *051/389–600* ⊕ *www. dunbrodyhouse.com* ⚭ *Reservations essential* ▭ *AE, MC, V* ☉ *Closed Mon. and Tues. No lunch Mon.–Sat.*

$$$$
Fodor'sChoice
★

📺 **Dunbrody Country House.** A rural jewel, this sprawling two-story 1830s Georgian manor house used to be the digs of the seventh marquess of Donegal, Dermot Chichester (who now lives nearby). Under the magic touch of current chatelains, Kevin and Catherine Dundon, the gardens are soul-restoring, the manse's public salons are a soigné symphony of mix-and-match tangerine-hue fabrics and stuffed armchairs, the views over the Barrow estuary remain grand, and the guest rooms charm with a judiciously luxe combination of period antiques and fine reproductions. They recently added a delightful three-bedroom lodge house that you can rent. No need to rush the next morn: the famous breakfasts are served until 11:30. **Pros:** authentic Georgian feel to the place; wonderful strolling gardens; great restaurant. **Cons:** expensive for this region; facilities limited for luxury hotel; giant Irish breakfast too good to resist. ⊠ *Arthurstown, New Ross, Co. Wexford* ☎ *051/389–600* ⊕ *www. dunbrodyhouse.com* ⮑ *15 rooms, 7 suites* ☆ *In-room: no a/c, Wi-Fi (some). In-hotel: restaurant, bar, Wi-Fi hotspot* ▭ *AE, MC, V* ⧖|BP.

WATERFORD CITY

10 km (6 mi) west of Ballyhack by ferry and road (R683), 62 km (39 mi) southwest of Wexford Town, 158 km (98 mi) southwest of Dublin.

The largest town in the Southeast and Ireland's oldest city, Waterford was founded by the Vikings in the 9th century and was taken over by Strongbow, the Norman invader,

> ### WATERFORD CITY LIMITS
>
> Off Colbeck Street along Spring Garden Alley, you can see one of the remaining portions of the old city wall; there are sections all around the town center.

with much bloodshed in 1170. The city resisted Cromwell's 1649 attacks, but fell the following year. It did not prosper again until 1783, when George and William Penrose set out to create "plain and cut flint glass, useful and ornamental," and thereby set in motion a glass-manufacturing industry long without equal but, beginning in 2008, sadly hit by the global economic slump.

GETTING HERE AND AROUND

BOAT TRAVEL It can be a long drive around the coast from Wexford to Waterford and the Passage East Car Ferry Company operates year-round from Passage East in Wexford to Ballyhack near Waterford City. The five-minute crossing are continuous from from 7 AM until 10 PM April through September and until 8 PM the rest of the year (with first sailing on Sundays at 9:30 AM). The cost is €8 one-way and €12 round-trip for a car and passengers and €2 one-way, €3 round-trip for a foot passenger.

BUS TRAVEL Bus Éireann has a station on the waterfront at Merchant's Quay and runs regular buses to cities and towns all over the country including Dublin (€12.20 one-way, €14.40 round-trip; 3 hours); Tramore (€2.50 one-way, €5 round-trip; 30 minutes); Wexford (€7.20 one-way, €17.60 round trip; 1½ hours); Dungarvan (€10.30 one-way, €13.70 round-trip; 50 minutes); and Cork (€17.10 one-way, €23.40 round-trip; 2¼ hours). Bus Éireann also runs a local city bus service in Waterford city, with five routes (Nos. 601, 602, 605, 609, 610) that cover the city center.

TRAIN TRAVEL Plunkett Station is on the north side of the river in Waterford's city center. Irish Rail runs trains to Dublin (€10 one-way, €20 round-trip; 2¾ hours; four to six daily); Kilkenny (€10 one-way, €20 round-trip; 45 minutes; four to six daily); and Limerick (€17 one-way, €34 round-trip; 2¾ hours; three daily Monday–Saturday).

Visitor Information Waterford City Tourist Office (✉ *41 The Quay, Co. Waterford* ☎ *051/875–823* ⊕ *www.waterfordtourism.org*).

EXPLORING

Waterford has better-preserved city walls than anywhere else in Ireland but Derry. Initially, the slightly run-down commercial center doesn't look promising. You need to park your car and proceed on foot to discover the heritage that the city has made admirable efforts since the mid-1990s to preserve, in particular the grand 18th-century Georgian buildings that Waterford architect John Roberts (1714–96) built, including the town's Protestant and Catholic cathedrals.

If arriving by car, Waterford City is a little isolated in the southwest corner of Ireland but it is now only a 2-hour 12-minute drive from Dublin on the vastly improved N9/M9. Cork is 125 km (77 mi) west on the N25 and N27 with the drive taking nearly 2 hours. It's only 52 km (32 mi) and 45 minutes to Kilkenny on the N9 and N10.

Waterford's compact town center can be visited in a couple of hours. Do note, unhappily, that the famous Waterford Glass Visitor Centre is no longer in existence, but plans are in the offing to unveil a new Waterford attraction or museum sometime in the near future. For now, happily, the town still offers an impressive Waterford Treasures exhibition.

The **city quays**—at the corner of Custom House Parade and Peter Street—are a good place to begin a tour of Waterford City. (The TIO is also down here, at the Granary on Merchant's Quay.) The city quays stretch for nearly 2 km (1 mi) along the River Suir and were described in the 18th century as the best in Europe.

If the weather is favorable, consider taking a **cruise** along Waterford's harbor and the wide, picturesque estuary of the River Suir. You can enjoy lunch, afternoon tea, or dinner aboard a luxury river cruiser or simply take in the sights. The boat departs from the quay opposite the TIO, where you can purchase tickets. ⊠ *Merchant's Quay* ☎ *051/421–723 Galley Cruises* ⊕ *www.rivercruises.ie* ⊗ *Cruises Apr.–Oct., daily at 12:30, 3, and 7, weather permitting.*

TOP ATTRACTIONS

❷ **City Hall.** One of Waterford's finer Georgian buildings, the City Hall on the Mall, dates from 1783 and was designed by John Roberts, a native of the city. Nearby are some good examples of domestic Georgian architecture—tall, well-proportioned houses with typically Irish semicircular fanlights above the doors. The arms of Waterford hang over City Hall's own entrance, which leads into a spacious foyer that originally was a town meeting place and merchants' exchange. The building contains two lovely theaters, an old Waterford dinner service, and an enormous 1802 Waterford glass chandelier, which hangs in the Council Chamber (a copy of the chandelier hangs in Independence Hall in Philadelphia). The Victorian horseshoe-shaped Theatre Royal is the venue for the annual Festival of Light Opera in September. ⊠ *The Mall* ☎ *051/309–900* 🎫 *Free* ⊗ *Weekdays 9–5.*

❹ **Christ Church Cathedral.** Lovers of Georgian decorative arts will want
★ to visit this late-18th-century Church of Ireland cathedral designed by local architect John Roberts and the only Neoclassical Georgian cathedral in Ireland. Inside, all is cup-of-tea elegance—yellow walls, white-stucco trim in designs of florets and laurels, grand Corinthian columns—and you can see why architectural historian Mark Girouard called this "the finest 18th-century ecclesiastical building in Ireland." It stands on the site of a great Norman Gothic cathedral. The then Bishop Cheneix, it's oft told, wouldn't consider knocking that great edifice down—never, that is, until it was arranged for a little stone vaulting to fall in his path. Medievalists will be sad, but those who prize Age of Enlightenment high style will rejoice. Try catch one of the regular choral concerts held here (see Web site for details) to get the full atmospheric

Waterford City

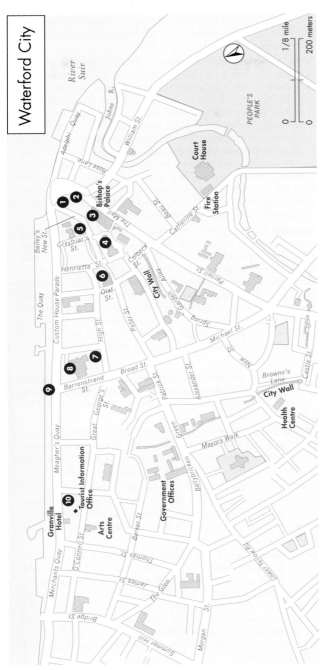

River Suir

Adelphi Quay

Johns R.

Rose Lane

William St.

Bailey's New St.

Greyfriar's St.

Henrietta St.

The Quay

Custom House Parade

Olaf St.

High St.

Peter St.

Colbeck St.

City Wall

Gratton

Spring

Beau St.

Catherine St.

Parnell St.

Michael St.

New St.

Browne's Lane

City Wall

Castle St.

Health Centre

Court House

Fire Station

PEOPLE'S PARK

Broad St.

Barronstrand St.

Patrick St.

Alexander St.

Green

Mayors Walk

Ballybricken

Government Offices

Great George's St.

Meagher's Quay

Tourist Information Office

Granville Hotel

Arts Centre

Barker St.

Merchants Quay

O'Connell St.

Thomas St.

James St.

The Glen

Bridge St.

Summer Hill

Morgan St.

Lower Yellow Rd.

0   1/8 mile

0   200 meters

5

Bishop's Palace **3**

Blackfriars Abbey **7**

Christ Church Cathedral ... **4**

City Hall **2**

French Church **5**

Holy Trinity Cathedral **8**

Reginald's Tower **1**

St. Olaf's Church **6**

Victorian Clock Tower **9**

Waterford Treasures **10**

reward. ⊠ *Henrietta St.* ☎ *051/858–958* ⊕ *www.christchurchwaterford. com* ▣ *€3* ⊗ *Weekdays 10–1 and 2–5, Sat. 2–4 (rest of year by appointment only for tours).*

❶ Reginald's Tower. A waterside circular tower on the east end of Waterford's quays, this marks the apex of a triangle containing the old walled city of Waterford. Built by the Vikings for the city's defense in 1003, it has 80-foot-high, 10-foot-thick walls; an interior stairway leads to the top. The tower served in turn as the residence for a succession of Anglo-Norman kings (including Henry II, John, and Richard II), a mint for silver coins, a prison, and an arsenal. It's said that Strongbow's marriage to Eva, the daughter of Dermot MacMurrough, took place here in the late 12th century, thus uniting the Norman invaders with the native Irish. It has been restored to its original medieval appearance and furnished with appropriate 11th- to 15th-century artifacts. ⊠ *The Quay* ☎ *051/304– 220* ⊕ *www.heritageireland.ie* ▣ *€3* ⊗ *June–Sept., daily 10–6; Easter–May and Oct., daily 10–5; Nov.–Easter, Wed.–Sun. 10–5.*

❿ Waterford Treasures. Located above the Southeast's main TIO, Waterford

Fodor'sChoice
★

Treasures uses interactive audiovisual technology to guide you through 1,000 years in the history of Waterford. Entertaining and educational, the exhibition displays Waterford's rich inheritance of rare and beautiful artifacts—from the Charter Roll of 1372, a list of all charters granted to Waterford up to that time, written in Latin on vellum, to the sword of King Edward IV, to 18th-century crystal. A restaurant and a shop are also on the premises. ⊠ *The Granary, Merchant's Quay* ☎ *051/304–500* ⊕ *www.waterfordtreasures.com* ▣ *€7* ⊗ *Sept.–May, Mon.–Sat. 9–5, Sun. 11–5; June–Aug., Mon.–Sat. 9:30–6, Sun. 11–6.*

WORTH NOTING

❸ Bishop's Palace. Among the most imposing of the remaining Georgian town houses, the Bishop's Palace is now used by the local council but the foyer is open to the public. ⊠ *Alongside City Hall on the Mall* ▣ *Free* ⊗ *Weekdays 9–5.*

❼ Blackfriars Abbey. The ruined tower of Blackfriars belonged to a Dominican abbey founded in 1226 and returned to the Crown in 1541 after the dissolution of the monasteries. It was used as a courthouse until Cromwellian forces destroyed it in the 17th century. ⊠ *High St.*

❺ French Church. Roofless ruins are all that remain of French Church, a 13th-century Franciscan abbey. The church, also known as Greyfriars, was given to a group of Huguenot refugees (hence the "French") in 1695. A splendid east window remains amid the ruins. The key is available at Reginald's Tower. ⊠ *Greyfriars St.*

❽ Holy Trinity Cathedral. This Roman Catholic cathedral has a simple facade and a richly (some would say garishly) decorated interior with high, vaulted ceilings and ornate Corinthian pillars. It was designed in Neoclassical style by John Roberts, who also designed Christ Church Cathedral and City Hall. Surprisingly, it was built in the late 18th century—when Catholicism was barely tolerated—on land granted by the Protestant city fathers. ⊠ *Barronstrand St., between High St. and clock tower on quays* ☎ *051/875–166* ⊕ *www.waterford-cathedral.com* ▣ *Free* ⊗ *Daily 8:30–5:30.*

Since the 1990s, Waterford has made successful efforts to restore its historic streets and sights, including the town's Catholic and Protestant cathedrals.

⑥ St. Olaf's Church. Built, as the name implies, by the Vikings in the mid-11th century, this church has one sole extant remnant: its original door, which has been incorporated into the wall of the existing building (a meeting hall). ⊠ *St. Olaf's St.*

⑨ Victorian Clock Tower. Built in 1864 with public donations, this landmark has little great architectural merit but does serves as a reminder of the days when Waterford was a thriving, bustling port. ⊠ *Merchant's Quay.*

WHERE TO EAT

$$ ✕ **Bodega.** All the county newspapers comment on this as the fun place
MEDITERRANEAN to eat in Waterford and this casual Mediterranean eatery does like to put on a bit of a party. Bright colors and comfortable couches are festive. The extensive and inventive wine menu gets everyone warmed up for some lively dishes like Kilmore Quay fishcakes with Thai red curry oil followed by a delicious main course of seafood pie with salmon, smoked haddock, white wine, and a pureed potato and crumb crust. Almost everything seems to be sourced from suppliers in a few-square-mile radius. The place also hosts intimate gigs by some of Irelands top folk singers. ⊠ *Manor Court Lodge, Cork Rd.* ☎ *051/844–177* ⊕ *www.bodegawaterford.com* ▬ *DC, MC, V* ☾ *Closed Sun. No lunch Sat.*

$$$ ✕ **Fitzpatricks Restaurant.** The new owner of the much-loved former
FRENCH O'Grady's Restaurant and Guesthouse had a tough act to follow, but
Fodor's Choice somehow P.J. Reddy has managed to pull it off. The restaurant is in a
★ beautifully restored lodge house on the outskirts of the city, and though the interior has had a pleasing makeover, it's still traditional enough not to shock the regulars. The cuisine is firmly in the fine-dining camp with a Gallic flavor to the seafood-rich dishes on offer. Try the roulade of

lemon sole with crabmeat mousse, and served with a saffron beurre blanc or the confit of duck with buttered cabbage and Toulouse sausage. ✉ *Manor Court Lodge, Cork Rd.* ☎ *051/378–851* ⊕ *www. fitzpatricksmanorlodge.com* ⊟ *AE, MC, V* ⊗ *No lunch Sat.*

$$$$
FRENCH

✕ **Munster Dining Room.** At the heart of the noted hotel that is Waterford Castle *(⇨ below)* beats the Munster Dining Room, whose luxe— oak paneling darkened with age, and ancestral portraits spotlighted in gilt frames—hints at one of the

> **ONE WAY OR ANOTHER**
>
> Although there are several theories about the origin of the phrase, some experts credit Cromwell with coining the expression "by hook or by crook." Planning two siege routes to Waterford— one via Hook Head, the other via Crooke Village on the estuary of the River Suir—Cromwell declared that he would take the city "by Hooke or by Crooke."

most stylish menus around. The dress code is smart (jackets for the men) and the place does suggest a big night out. They only do a fixed-price, three-course menu that includes St. Tola's goat cheese parfait with spiced pear as a favorite starter; main course winners include the best of Irish steaks or the roast wild cod with pepperonata, aioli, tapenade, and Parmesan crisp. ✉ *The Island, (2 km [1 mi] south of Waterford), Ballinakill* ☎ *051/878–203* ⊟ *AE, DC, MC, V.*

WHERE TO STAY

$$$
Fodor's Choice
★

⌂ **Arlington Lodge Country House.** For a pretty, if not perfect, old-school Georgian experience take the ten-minute walk from Waterford's center to this 1760 heritage house. A somewhat simple two-story affair, the house inside has salons overflowing with ruffled drapes, thick carpets, and plush armchairs. Outside, huge windows afford great views looking down on the city. There's a really family home feel to the place that extends to the welcoming cup of tea on arrival including some melt-in-the-mouth homemade teabrack cake. Guest rooms are comfy and antiques-accented; the master suite affords a real fireplace in the winter. The restaurant, a bastion of hearty, country-house cooking, comes complete with grand piano while the William Morris bar is ideal for hot toddies on a chilly night. **Pros:** a real piece of Waterford's heritage; sumptuous breakfast included; family-run, personal feel to the service. **Cons:** popular with weddings; interior design a little too frilly; facilities limited. ✉ *John's Hill, Waterford City, Co. Waterford* ☎ *051/878–584* ⊕ *www. arlingtonlodge.com* ⌕ *20 rooms* ♿ *In-room: no a/c, Wi-Fi (some). In-hotel: restaurant, bar, Wi-Fi hotspot, parking (paid)* ⊟ *MC, V.*

$–$$

⌂ **Dooley's Hotel.** A friendly, perfect-for-families air pervades this unpretentious hotel on the banks of the River Suir right at the heart of the city and just a few minutes' walk from all the main attractions. The rooms are big, bright, and decorated in vibrant reds and yellows; some have four-poster beds. The service is excellent and the traditional-style bar is popular with locals. The New Ship restaurant serves Continental dishes and has an early-bird menu. The hotel also hosts live music shows at times. **Pros:** city center location; large guest rooms; popular bar is a good place to meet locals. **Cons:** attracts a business clientele; can get more luxury for same price elsewhere; can be a little noisy. ✉ *30 The*

CLOSE UP

Rolls-Royce of Crystal

Silica sand + potash + litharge = Waterford crystal: it reads like cold science, but something magical happens when the craftsmen of Waterford produce arguably the top crystal in the world (although France's Baccarat might have something to say about that).

When the Waterford Glass Factory opened in 1783, it provided English royalty and nobility with a regular supply of ornate handcrafted stem-ware, chandeliers, and decorative knickknacks. Since then, Waterford crystal has graced the tables of heads of state the world over, and Water-ford's earlier pieces have become priceless heirlooms.

The best Waterford glass was pro-duced from the late 18th century to the early 19th century. This early work, examples of which can be found in museums and public buildings all over the country, is characterized by a unique, slightly opaque cast that is absent from the modern product.

Crystal glass is not cheap: each piece is individually fashioned by almost two-dozen pairs of hands before it passes final inspection and receives the discreet Waterford trademark.

The first thing on the itinerary of any visitor to Waterford was for many years a tour of the glass factory, a buzzing hive of master craftspeople. But the global downturn has seen the factory close and the future of glassblowing in the area is in doubt. There is talk of a smaller specialist facility reopening soon to use some of the vast local talent going to waste, and the popular visitor center is also due to reopen in a new form and a new home.

5

Quay, Co. Waterford ☏ *051/873–531* ⊕ *www.dooleys-hotel.ie* ⤳ *113 rooms* ⟨ *In-room: no a/c, Wi-Fi. In-hotel: restaurant, bar, Wi-Fi hotspot* ⊟ *AE, DC, MC, V* ⟨○⟩ *BP.*

$$$$

Fodor's Choice

★

⌖ **Waterford Castle.** Not only does this fairy-tale castle come with an 800-year history, but it sits in the middle of a 310-acre island and allows lucky guests to be bed-and-boarded in the grandest Irish style. Back in Norman times, the Kfyeralds built a keep here and over the centuries—as their name became Fitzgerald, "Kings of Ireland in all but name"—they expanded, adding two Elizabethan-style wings in the 17th century, fitting them out with rooftop gargoyles brought from Castle Irwell in Manchester. Today, the air of exclusivity lingers as the private ferry picks you up on the shores of the River Suir, and heightens with one step inside the Great Hall, a magnificent faux-baronial room in Portland stone hung with medieval tapestries. Most guest rooms are exquisitely done in real "country-house" style, some with canopied beds, chintz armchairs, and dark mahogany furniture. Downstairs, dine in style in the luxurious Munster Dining Room. To top it all off, a highly rated 18-hole golf course adjoins the castle. Obviously, the last great Fitzgerald to occupy the house, Mary Frances (whose son, Edward Fitzgerald, translated the *Rubaiyat of Omar Khayyam* into English) would be happy to see her former domain so lovingly cared for. **Pros:** unique, historic building; great golf course on-site; the awe-inspiring

Great Hall. **Cons:** expensive for this region; books up early in summer; popular with weddings. ⊠ *The Island, Ballinakill, 2 km (1 mi) south of Waterford,Co. Waterford* ☎ *051/878–203* ⊕ *www.waterfordcastle.com* ⤳ *14 rooms, 5 suites* ⚴ *In-room: no a/c, Wi-Fi. In-hotel: restaurant, golf course, tennis courts, Wi-Fi hotspot* ⊟ *AE, DC, MC, V.*

NIGHTLIFE AND THE ARTS

The **Spraoi Festival** (☎ *051/841–808* ⊕ *www.spraoi.com*) is billed as the "biggest street carnival in Ireland"—with street theater, live music, and fireworks. This free outdoor festival, which appeals to children and adults alike, takes place annually during the August bank holiday, the first weekend of the month.The elegant **Theatre Royal** (⊠ *City Hall, The Mall* ☎ *051/874–402* ⊕ *www.theatreroyal.ie*), one of the oldest theaters in Ireland, has reopened after a major renovation and is devoted to large-scale theater and musical productions as well as live concerts. **An Emigrant's Tale** (⊠ *Dooley's Hotel, The Quays* ☎ *051/642–813* ⊕ *www.anemigrantstale.net*) is a musical/cabaret-style show featuring "trad" music and dancing with a splash of storytelling thrown in; shows are every Thursday evening.

The **Forum** (⊠ *The Glen* ☎ *051/871–111* ⊕ *www.forumwaterford.com*) is a large multipurpose entertainment venue. Here you can watch local productions or those of traveling theater companies. Two music venues host big names as well as local acts performing all kinds of music. Culture buffs shouldn't miss the **Garter Lane Arts Centre** (⊠ *22A O'Connell St.* ☎ *051/855–038* ⊕ *www.garterlane.ie*), which hosts concerts, exhibits, and theater productions. Garter Lane is home to many productions of **Red Kettle** (⊕ *www.red-kettle.com*), Waterford's most successful theater company.

Geoffs (⊠ *9 John St.* ☎ *051/874–787*) is a dimly lighted pub frequented by a mixed crowd including students and locals. Big flagstones cover the floors, and seating is on old wooden benches. An outdoor area is available for those keen to avoid Ireland's smoking ban. A wide selection of food is served until 9, every day. Known to the natives as Meade's Under the Bridge, **Jack Meades** (⊠ *Cheekpoint Rd., Halfway House, Ballycanavan* ☎ *051/873–187*) is snug under a time-stained stone bridge. In centuries past it was a stop on the coach road from Waterford to Passage East. There's a pub menu from May through September, and sing-along sessions are held throughout the year on the weekends. In winter the fireplaces roar, illuminating the wood beams and bric-a-brac.

Housed in an 800-year-old building, the **Old Ground** (⊠ *10 The Glen* ☎ *051/852–283*) is a popular pub with locals. Lunch is served daily, and traditional-music sessions sometimes break out. The circa-1700 **T&H Doolan's Bar** (⊠ *32 George's St.* ☎ *051/872–764*), reputed to be one of the oldest pubs in Ireland, hosts traditional Irish music most summer nights and Monday through Wednesday nights year-round.

SPORTS

GAELIC FOOTBALL Watch Gaelic football and hurling at the **Waterford GAA Grounds** (⊠ *Walsh Park* ☎ *51/591–5544* ⊕ *www.waterfordgaa.ie*).

GOLF **Faithlegg Golf Club** (⊠ *Faithlegg House, Checkpoint* ☎ *051/382–241* ⊕ *www.faithlegg.com*) is an 18-hole course set in mature landscape on

A faux-baronial hotel first built as a homestead for the famous Fitzgerald family, Waterford Castle can indulge "queen-for-a-stay" fantasies.

the banks of the River Suir. **Waterford Castle Golf Club** (⊠ *The Island, Ballinakill* ☎ *051/871–633* ⊕ *www.waterfordcastle.com/golf*) is an 18-hole course that claims to be Ireland's only true island course.

SHOPPING

City Square Shopping Centre (⊠ *City Sq.* ☎ *051/853–528*) has more than 40 shops, ranging from small Irish fashion boutiques to large international department stores. Fashion shows and other forms of entertainment take place on the stage area in the center of the mall.

Kellys (⊠ *75–76 The Quay* ☎ *051/873–557*) has excellent Irish souvenirs, including traditional musical instruments, dolls, Irish linen, jewelry, Waterford crystal, and CDs.

Although the famed Waterford Glass factory has sadly shut down, you can still get quality, handmade crystal at **Penrose Crystal** (⊠ *32a Johns St.* ☎ *051/876–537* ⊕ *www.penrosecrystal.com*). With a bit of notice they'll have a personally engraved piece waiting for you when you arrive.

DUNGARVAN

42 km (26 mi) southwest of Tramore on R675.

With their covering of soft grasses, the lowlands of Wexford and eastern Waterford gradually give way to heath and moorland; the wetter climate of the hillier western Waterford countryside creates and maintains the bog. The mountains responsible for the change in climate rise up behind Dungarvan, the largest coastal town in County Waterford. This bustling fishing and resort spot sits at the mouth of the River

Colligan, which empties into Dungarvan Bay here. It's a popular base for climbers and hikers.

GETTING HERE

BUS TRAVEL Bus Éireann picks up and drops off on Davitt's Quay. They have regular daily services to and from Waterford (€10.30 one-way, €13.70 round-trip; 1 hour; 11 daily); Cork (€14.90 one-way, 20.70 round-trip; 1½ hours; 13 daily); and Dublin (14.40 one-way, 16.70 round-trip; 11 daily).

Visitor Information Dungarvan Tourist Office (⊠ *The Courthouse, Co. Waterford* ☎ *058/41741* ⊕ *www.dungarvantourism.com*).

EXPLORING

In **Ring (An Rinne)**, a Gaeltacht area on Dungarvan Bay, the Irish language is still in daily use—this is unusual in the south and east of the country. At Colaiste na Rinne, a language college, courses in Irish have been taught since 1909. ⊠ *7 km (4½ mi) southeast of Dungarvan, off N674F.*

WHERE TO EAT AND STAY

$$$ ╳ **The Tannery.** Clearly, out there in Knockmealdown, the mountain air
ECLECTIC must do something to clear the brain and allow chefs to focus and
Fodor'sChoice purify. Perhaps that's why this place is besieged on weekends, when
★ Dubliners head here to taste the creations of culinary wizard Paul Flynn. He worked for almost a decade with London culinary legend Nico Ladenis and now wins raves from the likes of Sir Andrew Lloyd Webber. The dishes on offer may look slightly odd on the menu but they taste sensational on the palate. Check out the seared scallops with parsnip, fennel, and chorizo dressing. Or if that doesn't tickle your taste buds opt for the braised rabbit and bacon with sweet pickled vegetables and Riesling cream. Fanatical foodies who want to stay as close to the culinary action as possible can now overnight in the adjoining guesthouse, opened by the Flynns in 2005. Your waistline may never be the same again. ⊠ *10 Quay St.* ☎ *058/45420* ⊕ *www.tannery.ie* ▭ *AE, DC, MC, V* ⊙ *Closed Mon. and 2 wks in Jan. No dinner Sun. Sept.–May. No lunch Mon.–Thurs. and Sat.*

$–$$ ⌂ **The Gold Coast Golf Hotel.** Overlooking Dungarvan Bay, this hotel is
♺ part of a family-run and family-friendly property that also includes self-catering holiday cottages (built around the hotel) and golf villas on the edge of a woodland course on a links setting. Hotel rooms are bright, comfortable, and spacious. Guests can use the facilities of the Gold Coast's sister hotel, the Clonea Strand, just 2½ km (1½ mi) away, which include a games room, a leisure complex, and Clonea's 3-km-long (2-mi-long) sandy beach. **Pros:** great location; owners love kids; great value even in high season. **Cons:** gets a bit hectic with all those kids around; guest rooms are a little mundane; no Internet in rooms. ⊠ *Co. Waterford* ☎ *058/42249 or 058/42416* ⊕ *www.clonea.com* ⇗ *35 rooms, 2 suites, 16 cottages, 12 villas, 27 lodges* ♺ *In-hotel: a/c, restaurant, bar, golf course, tennis court, pool, gym, Internet terminal* ▭ *AE, DC, MC, V* ⦿ *BP.*

NIGHTLIFE AND THE ARTS

Several miles away from Dungarvan, a *ceilí* (Irish dance) is held nightly in summer at **Colaiste na Rinne** (✉ *Ring* ☎ *058/46104*).

ARDMORE

Fodor's Choice
★

29 km (18 mi) southwest of Dungarvan on R672.

Historic spiritual sites, white beaches, dramatic cliff walks, brawny fishermen—little Ardmore is a picture-postcard Irish town that packs a whole lot of wonder into a small peninsula at the base of a tall cliff. With a few notable exceptions—including John F. Kennedy and Gregory Peck—the cute but very real village is often overlooked by most overseas tourists.

In the 5th century, St. Declan is reputed to have disembarked here from Wales and founded a monastery, 30 years before St. Patrick arrived in Ireland. Ardmore's monastic remains are found on the top of the cliff. The ruined 12th-century **Cathedral of St. Declan** has some ogham stones inside and weathered but interesting biblical scenes carved on its west gable. The saint is said to be buried in St. Declan's Oratory, a small early Christian church that has been partially reconstructed. St. Declan's Well—a genuinely ancient place—and the ruins of his Hermitage are just on the other side of town.

On the grounds of the ruined cathedral, the 97-foot-high **Round Tower**, one of 70 round towers remaining in Ireland, is in exceptionally good condition. Round towers were built by the early Christian monks as watchtowers and belfries but came to be used as places of refuge for the monks and their valuables during Viking raids. This is the reason the doorway is 15 feet above ground level—once inside, the monks could pull the ladder into the tower with them.

WHERE TO EAT AND STAY

$$$$
ECLECTIC
★

✕ **The House Restaurant.** Celebrated Dutch chef Martjin Kajuiter presides over the compact little dining room of the new Cliff House hotel. Go in summer, when you can eat out on the expansive terrace, which winds its way down the cliffside toward the sea. The food is all locally sourced and innovatively prepared—"trad" Irish is often the base but garnishes and sauces lend a festive, nouvelle air. Dinner is a fixed-price, three-course meal with the warm Ballynatray Partridge with celeriac, foie gras, and green apple vinaigrette making the perfect starter. And you can't go wrong with the Skeaghanore duck breast seared with sweet potato dauphine morels and beetroot as your main course. ✉ *Ardmore* ☎ *024/87800* ⊕ *www.thecliffhousehotel.ie* ▬ *AE, DC, MC, V* ⊗ *No lunch weekdays.*

$$$$
Fodor's Choice
★

🛏 **Cliff House.** Sewn into the cliffs overlooking the fishing village of Ardmore at a head-turning slant, this new glass-and-grass (well, there's some grass on the roof) luxury hotel and spa is one of the most adventurous and innovative additions to Irish accommodations in years. Ageless nature here confronts modernist design, thanks to massive plate-glass windows; huge, winding public terraces that trickle down to the water; and an atrium filled with the bright blues of sea and sky. Guest rooms aren't huge, but they are neatly designed with original art and sharp, modern furniture. If you luckily land one of the 15 suites, you'll find you have a private veranda jutting right over the ocean below. In the glassed-in dining room, Irish and international influences are deftly combined. **Pros:** the sea is everywhere; great spa and pool; up the road from the wonderful Ardmore Pottery shop. **Cons:** quite pricey for the region; often have two-day minimums in summer; younger staff still learning their trade. ⊠ *Ardmore, Co. Waterford* ☎ *024/87800* ⊕ *www. thecliffhousehotel.com* ⊃ *24 rooms, 15 suites* ⚏ *In-room: refrigerator, Wi-Fi. In-hotel: a/c, restaurant, bar, pool, gym, spa, Wi-Fi hotspot* ▭ *AE, DC, MC, V.*

SHOPPING

Ardmore Pottery & Craft Gallery (⊠ *The Cliff* ☎ *024/94152* ⊕ *www. ardmorepottery.com*), home to potter Mary Lincoln, is one of the most beloved, creative, and cleverly stocked craft shops in the country, with anything from Alan Ardiff gold jewelry to Veronica Molloy's famed homemade jams. You can even watch Mary at work at the wheel and purchase some of her own beautiful, delicate but simple designs.

IN AND AROUND COUNTY TIPPERARY

"It's a long way to Tipperary . . ." So run the words of that famed song sung all over the world since World War I. Actually, Tipperary is *not* so far to go, considering that, as Ireland's biggest inland county, it's within easy striking distance of Waterford and Cork. Moving in from the coastline, you can travel through some of Ireland's most lush pasturelands and to some of its most romantic sights, such as Lismore Castle. The Blackwater Valley is renowned for its beauty, peacefulness, and excellent fishing. Some of the finest racehorses in the world are raised in the fields of Tipperary, which is also the county where you can find the Rock of Cashel—the greatest group of monastic ruins in all Ireland.

LISMORE

Fodor'sChoice
★

20 km (13 mi) northwest of Dungarvan on N72.

Lismore is one of Ireland's grandest places to get lost in. Popular with both anglers and romantics, the enchanting little town of Lismore is built on the banks of the Blackwater, a river famous for its trout and salmon. From the 7th to the 12th century it was an important monastic center, founded by St. Carthac (or Carthage), and it had one of the most renowned universities of its time. The village has two cathedrals: a soaring Roman Catholic one from the late 19th century and the Church of Ireland St. Carthage's, which dates from 1633 and incorporates fragments of an earlier church. Glamour arrived in the form of the dukes of Devonshire, who built their Irish seat here, Lismore Castle (their main house is Chatsworth in England); in the 1940s, Fred Astaire, whose sister, Adele, had married Lord Charles Cavendish, younger son of the ninth duke, would bend the elbow at the town's Madden's Pub. There were darker interludes in the town's history: Lismore was hard hit by the Great Famine of 1845 and its Famine Graveyard bears poignant witness. Other architectural jewels include a quaint library funded by Andrew Carnegie

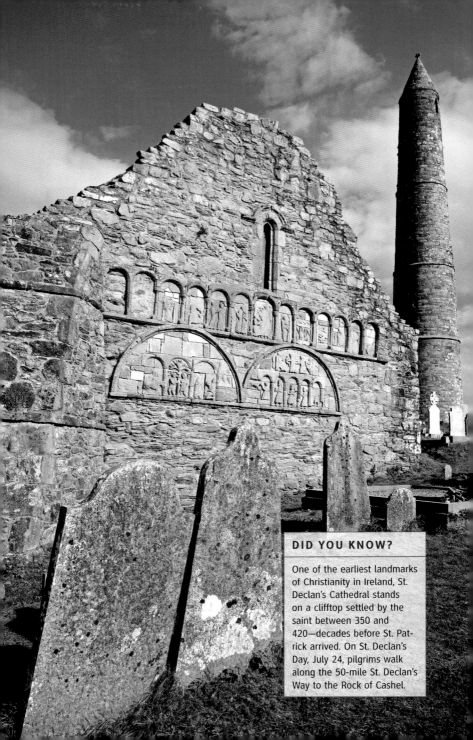

DID YOU KNOW?

One of the earliest landmarks of Christianity in Ireland, St. Declan's Cathedral stands on a clifftop settled by the saint between 350 and 420—decades before St. Patrick arrived. On St. Declan's Day, July 24, pilgrims walk along the 50-mile St. Declan's Way to the Rock of Cashel.

and the Ballysaggartmore "folly"—a Gothic-style gateway to a 19th-century house that was so costly the house itself was never erected.

Visitor Information Lismore Tourist Office (✉ *Heritage Centre, Co. Waterford* ☎ *058/54975* ⊕ *www.discoverlismore.com*).

EXPLORING

★ As you cross the bridge entering Lismore, take in the dramatic view of magnificent **Lismore Castle,** a vast, turreted, gray-stone building atop a rock that overhangs the River Blackwater. There has been a castle here since the 12th century, but the present structure, built by the sixth duke of Devonshire, dates from the mid-19th century. Today, the house remains the Irish estate of the Cavendish family and most of it is not open to the public (although you can call it your own for a very high rental fee). In 2007, however, an impressive new contemporary art gallery, designed by Cork architect Gareth O'Callaghan, opened in the west wing, perhaps a sign that the new duke, who inherited the family title in 2004, is intent on making his own mark. Happily, the upper and lower gardens, which consist of woodland walks, including an unusual yew walk said to be more than 800 years old (Edmund Spenser is said to have written parts of *The Faerie Queene* here), are open during certain months of the year. Comprising 7 acres set with 17th-century defensive walls, the gardens have an impressive display of magnolias, camellias, and shrubs, and are adorned with examples of contemporary sculpture. ☎ *058/54424* ⊕ *www.lismorecastle.com* 🎟 *€8* ⊙ *Mid-Mar.–Sept., daily 11–4:45.*

Almost the definitive example of an estate town, Lismore has in recent years taken the firm decision to project a pride of place linked with a deep sense of history. The **Lismore Heritage Center** in the former town courthouse lies at the core of the town, and its exhibits focus on the town's Celtic origins and its links to many famous people from Sir Walter Raleigh to Prince Charles to Fred Astaire. An impressive video presentation on the history of the town from its monastic 7th-century origins up to the present day is shown. ✉ *The Old Courthouse* ☎ *058/54975* ⊕ *www.discoverlismore.com* 🎟 *€6* ⊙ *May–Oct., weekdays 9:30–5:30, Sat. 10–5, Sun. noon–5; Nov.–Apr., weekdays 9:30–5:30.*

Mount Melleray Abbey was the first post-Reformation monastery, founded in 1832 by the Cistercian Order in what was then a barren mountainside wilderness. Over the years the order has transformed the site into more than 600 acres of fertile farmland. The monks maintain strict vows of silence, but you're welcome to join in services throughout the day and are permitted into most areas of the abbey. It's also possible to stay in the guest lodge by prior arrangement. If you're heading into the Knockmealdown Mountains from Lismore, you can easily stop on the way at the abbey for a visit. There's a small heritage center about the history of Irish monasticism with a few ogham stones and a short film. ✉ *South of Vee Gap, signposted off R669, 13 km (8 mi) from Lismore, Cappoquin* ☎ *058/54404* ⊕ *www.cappoquin.org/abbey.shtml* 🎟 *Free* ⊙ *Daily 8–8.*

Leaving Lismore, heading east on N72 for 6½ km (4 mi) toward Cappoquin, a well-known angling center, you can pick up R669 north into

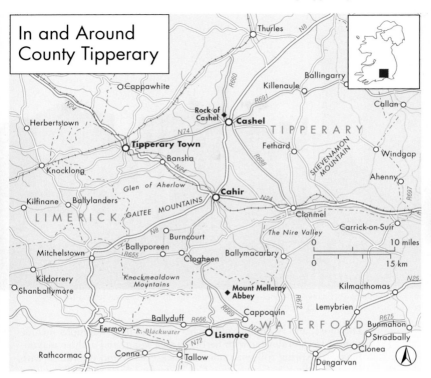

In and Around County Tipperary

the **Knockmealdown Mountains.** Your route is signposted as the Vee Gap road, the Vee Gap being its summit, from where you'll have superb views of the Tipperary plain, the Galtee Mountains in the northwest, and a peak called Slievenamon in the northeast. If the day is clear, you should be able to see the Rock of Cashel, ancient seat of the Kings of Munster, some 32 km (20 mi) away. Just before you enter the Vee Gap, look for a 6-foot-high mound of stones on the left side of the road. It marks the grave of Colonel Grubb, a local landowner who liked the view so much that he arranged to be buried here standing up so that he could look out over the scene for all eternity.

WHERE TO EAT AND STAY

$$ **Richmond House.** It's been 300 years since the Earl of Cork and Burl-
IRISH ington built this handsome country house and it still retains its imposing
★ aura of courtly elegance. Today, happily, owners Claire and Paul Deevy give it a relaxed and welcoming touch. The public rooms, with log fires and traditional rust-and-cream decor, are reminiscent of a classic country hotel, although one graced with silver plate, a tapestry, and a stuffed owl. The pièce de résistance here, however, is the restaurant (reservations essential), where Paul and his small staff wow critics and diners alike. Famous for his warm asparagus wrapped in smoked salmon, he prides himself on using local game in season and fish from Helvic,

The duke of Devonshire's Lismore Castle once sheltered Edmund Spencer when he was writing *The Fairy Queen*; today, his parklands are home to avant-garde artworks.

Dunmore, and Ardmore, adding his personal flair. Triumphs include tian of fresh crabmeat with herbs, garden salad, and a chive mayonnaise, the spring roll with smoked duck breast, and the rabbit with black pudding. ⊠ *Cappoquin, Co. Waterford* ☎ *058/54278* ⊕ *www. richmondhouse.net* ⤵ *9 rooms* ♿ *In-room: no a/c. In-hotel: restaurant, bar* ⊟ *AE, DC, MC, V* ⊗ *Closed late Dec.–mid-Jan.* ⑩ *BP.*

CAHIR

37 km (23 mi) north of Lismore, at crossroads of R668, N24, and N8.

Cahir (pronounce it "Care") is a busy but easygoing market town with a pleasant Georgian square at its heart. It is built on the river Suir at the eastern end of the Galtee mountain range. The Suir is known for its good salmon and trout fishing, as is the Aherlow river which joins it above town.

Visitor Information Cahir Tourist Office (⊠ *Castle Car Park, Co. Tipperary* ☎ *052/614–1453*).

Cahir Castle remains the unavoidable focal point of the town. Perched on a rocky island on the River Suir, it's one of Ireland's largest and best-preserved castles, retaining its dramatic keep, tower, and much of its original defensive structure. An audiovisual show and guided tour are available upon request. ☎ *052/744–1011* ⊕ *www.heritageireland. ie* ⊡ €3 ⊗ *Mid-Mar.–mid-June and Sept.–mid-Oct., daily 9:30–5:30; mid-June–Aug., daily 9–6:30; mid-Oct.–mid-Mar., daily 9:30–4:30; last entry 45 mins before closing.*

Fodor's Choice
★

If there's little storybook allure to the brute mass of Cahir Castle, fairy-tale looks grace the first earl of Glengall's 1812 **Swiss Cottage**, a dreamy relic from the days when Romanticism conquered 19th-century Ireland. A mile south of town on a particularly picturesque stretch of the River Suir, this "cottage *orné*" was probably designed by John Nash, one of the Regency period's most fashionable architects. Half thatch-roof cottage, half mansion, bordered by verandas constructed of branched trees, it was a veritable theater set that allowed the lordly couple to fantasize about being "simple folk" (down to the fact that secret doorways were constructed to allow servants to bring drinks and food without being noticed). Inside, some of the earliest Dufour wallpapers printed in Paris charm the eye. The Cottage is signposted from the R670 along the Cahir to Ardfinnan road, or you can hike from Cahir Castle on a footpath along the enchanting river. In peak season, crowds can be fierce. ☎ *052/744–1144* ⊕ *www.heritageireland.ie* ☑ *€3* ⊙ *Mid-Apr.–mid-Oct., daily 10–6.*

WHERE TO EAT AND STAY

$$$
★

Aherlow House. Built in 1928 to replace a house destroyed in Ireland's Civil War, Aherlow started life as an old Tudor hunting lodge but is now a hotel blessed by its location. Set on the slopes of Sliabh na Muc (Mountain of the Pigs), it comes with its own private forest and incredible views of the magnificent Galtee Mountains and the ancient Glen of Aherlow. Inside, the decor is a mix of modern and antiques: lots of blank walls plus slightly overdone furnishings, such as cushion-laden four-posters and heavy curtains getting in the way of those special vistas out the windows. But the really special places to stay here are the luxury (three-bedroom) family lodges, replete with wraparound sun decks and big open fireplaces. The Treetop restaurant is a bright-red showplace for tempting dishes and has the best views in the whole place. **Pros:** rooms are big; families will love the lodges; stunning natural surroundings. **Cons:** popular with local weddings and parties; gets booked up summer weekends. ⊠ *Glen of Aherlow, Co. Tipperary* ☎ *062/56153* ⊕ *www.aherlowhouse.ie* ⇨ *29 rooms* ⚏ *In-room: no a/c. In-hotel: restaurant, bar* ⊟ *MC, V* ⊙ *Closed Sun.–Thurs. during Jan.–Mar.*

$$$
★

The Old Convent. A former convent run by the Sisters of Mercy dating back over 100 years, this prim and proper country house is situated in a spectacularly scenic location close to the Vee Gap in the Knockmealdown Mountains. A wonderfully tucked-away sanctuary, overlooking rolling fields, mountains, and the famous abundance of rhododendrons in spring months, this retreat has now been tastefully restored—in all senses of the word—by Christine and Dermot Gannon. Dermot's well-established credentials as one of Ireland's most innovative chefs are lovingly displayed in the restaurant (no lunch; no dinner Monday–Wednesday; reservations essential) and his special skills in fusing Irish and Far Eastern tastes result in winners like 20-hour slow-cooked Goodherdsmen organic beef; mozzarella popover with smoked salmon; and hot-buttered-rum baked brill with a crab, pea, and pistachio risotto, all offered on eight-course tasting menus. He also prides himself on artisanal foodstuffs, so you may well find yourself munching on Keating's Baylough Cheese, Mrs. Fryday's Lettuce, and

Mrs. Houlihan's Meringues. Upstairs, Georgian-style marble titles in the hallways, living rooms in restful shades of gray and fawn, chandeliers, and bold-hue accent pillows and original artworks lend life to the Victorian manse. Bedrooms have antique furniture, silk curtains, and large bathrooms. Book in advance, as The Old Convent lies almost equidistant from Cahir and Lismore, attracting overnighters from both popular destinations. **Pros:** passionate owner/manager couple; extra-comfortable mattresses; serenity of natural surroundings. **Cons:** a trek to the nearest town; not really ideal for kids. ⊠ *Clogheen, Co. Tipperary* ☎ *052/746–5565* ⊕ *www.theoldconvent.ie* ⌁ *7 rooms* ⌂ *In-room: no a/c. In-hotel: restaurant* ☐ MC, V.

TIPPERARY TOWN

22 km (14 mi) northwest of Cahir on N24.

Tipperary Town, a dairy-farming center at the head of a fertile plain known as the Golden Vale, is a good starting point for climbing and walking in the hills around the Glen of Aherlow. The small country town, on the River Ara, is also worth visiting in its own right. In New Tipperary, a neighborhood built by local tenants during Ireland's Land War (1890–91), buildings such as Dalton's Heritage House have been restored; you can visit the Heritage House by calling the offices of Clann na Éireann. You can also visit the old Butter Market on Dillon Street; the Churchwell at the junction of Church, Emmet, and Dillon streets; and the grave of the grandfather of Robert Emmett—one of the most famous Irish patriots—in the graveyard at St. Mary's Church. A statue of Charles Kickham, whose 19th-century novel *The Homes of Tipperary* chronicled the devastation of this county through forced emigration, has a place of honor in the center of town. Adjacent to Bridewell Jail on St. Michael's Street is St. Michael's Church, with its stained-glass window depicting a soldier killed during World War I.

Visitor Information Tipperary Tourist Office (⊠ *Mitchel St., Co. Tipperary* ☎ *062/80520*).

The **Tipperary Excel** (⊠ *Mitchel St.* ☎ *062/80520* ⊕ *www.tipperary-excel. com*) arts and culture center contains the local tourist office and the Tipperary Family History research center—a top spot for all those hunting for their Irish roots.

CASHEL

17 km (11 mi) northeast of Tipperary Town on N74.

Cashel is a market town on the busy Cork–Dublin road, with a lengthy history as a center of royal and religious power. From roughly AD 370 until 1101, it was the seat of the Kings of Munster, and it was probably at one time a center of Druidic worship. Here, according to legend, St. Patrick arrived in about AD 432 and baptized King Aengus, who became Ireland's first Christian ruler. One of the many legends associated with this event is that St. Patrick plucked a shamrock to explain the mystery of the Trinity, thus giving a new emblem to Christian Ireland. By car, Cashel is on the busy N8/M8 road between Dublin and Cork. The road

Continued on page 323

TOWERING GLORY
The Rock of Cashel

Haunt of St. Patrick, Ireland's "rock of ages" is a place where history, culture, and legend collide

SOUTHEASTERN VIEW OF THE ROCK

Dormitory

Hall of Vicar's Choral
This was once the domain of the cathedral choristers

Seat of the Kings of Munster and the hallowed spot where St. Patrick first plucked a shamrock to explain the mystery of the Trinity, the Rock of Cashel is Ireland's greatest group of ecclesiastical ruins. Standing like an ominous beacon in the middle of a sloped, treeless valley, the Rock has a titanic grandeur and majesty that create what one ancient scribe called "a fingerpost to Heaven."

Historians theorize the stupendous mass was born during the Ice Age. This being Ireland, however, fulsome myths abound: There are those who believe it was created when the Devil himself took a huge bite of the Slieve Bloom Mountains only to spit it out right in the middle of the Golden Vale. Today, the great limestone mass still rises 300 feet to command a panorama over all it surveys—fittingly, the name derives from the Irish *caiseal*, meaning stone fort, and this gives a good idea of the strategic importance of Cashel in days of yore.

For centuries, Cashel was known as the "city of the kings"—from the 5th century, the lords of Munster ruled over much of southern Ireland from here. In 1101, however, they handed Cashel over to the Christian fathers, and the rock soon became the center of the reform movement that reshaped the Irish Church. Along the way, the church fathers embarked on a centuries-long building campaign that resulted in the magnificent group of chapels, round towers,

and walls you see at Cashel today. View them from afar on the N8 highway and the complex looks so complete you're surprised upon arriving to discover guides in modern dress and not knights in medieval uniform.

■ TIP→ The best approach to the rock is along the Bishop's Walk, a 10-minute hike that begins outside the drawing room of the Cashel Palace hotel on Main Street in the town of Cashel, just to the south of the rock.

Cormac's Chapel
The finest example of Hiberno-Romanesque architecture

The Choir
Look for the noted Tomb of Myler McGrath

Map labels: Bishop's Castle · Nave · South Transept · Tickets · Dormitory · St. Patrick's Cathedral

❶ HALL OF THE VICAR'S CHORAL
Built in the 15th century—though topped with a modern reconstruction of a beautifully corbeled medieval ceiling—this was once the domain of the cathedral choristers.

The Museum Located in the hall's undercroft, this collection includes the original St. Patrick's Cross and fast-forwards you to the present thanks to a striking audiovisual display on the Rock entitled the "Stronghold of the Faith."

❷ CORMAC'S CHAPEL
The real showpiece of Cashel is this chapel, built in 1127 by Cormac McCarthy, King of Desmond and Bishop of Cashel. A rare jewel in gleaming red sandstone, it is the finest example of Hiberno-Romanesque architecture. The entry archway carries a tympanum featuring a centaur in a helmet with a bow and arrow aimed at a lion, perhaps a symbol of good over evil. Such work was rare in Irish architecture and points to possible European influence. Preserved within the chapel is a splendid but broken sarcophagus, once believed to be Cormac's final resting place. At the opposite end of the chapel is the nave, where you can look for wonderful medieval paintings now showing through old plasterwork.

5

IN FOCUS TOWERING GLORY: THE ROCK OF CASHEL

ST. PATRICK'S CATHEDRAL

With thick walls that attest to its origin as a fortress, this now-roofless cathedral is the largest building on the site. Built in 1169, it was dedicated on March 17th—St. Patrick's Day. On the theory that ancient churches were oriented to the sunrise on the feast day of their dedicated saint, the cathedral points east, a direction agreeing closely with March 17th. The original cathedral, constructed in a flamboyant variation on Irish Romanesque style, was destroyed by fire in 1495. In ❸ The Choir, look for the noted Tomb of Myler McGrath. Note the tombs in the ❹ North Transept whose carvings—of the apostles, other saints, and the Beasts of the Apocalypse—are remarkably detailed. The octagonal staircase turret that ascends the cathedral's central

North Transept

tower leads to a series of defensive passages built into the thick walls—from the top of the tower, you'll have wonderful views. At the center of the cathedral is the area known as ❺ The Crossing, a magnificently detailed arch where the four sections of the building come together.

COMING OF AGE

AD 450—St. Patrick comes to Cashel, bringing the advent of Christianity when King Aengus accepts baptism from Ireland's patron saint.

990—Cashel is fortified by King Brian Boru, the legendary figure who broke the stranglehold of the Danes at the Battle of Clontarf in 1014.

1101—King Murtagh O'Brien, grandson of Brian Boru, proclaims the royal fortress "for God, St. Patrick, and St. Ailbe," making Cashel center of the Irish Church.

1317—The arrival of the Scots: Edward Bruce, brother of Robert I, is inaugurated king of Ireland, and attends Mass on the Rock where he later holds a parliament.

1749—Protestant archbishop Price earns undying infamy by pulling down the roof of the cathedral to rebuild his own church.

Detail of wooden ceiling in the Vicar's Choral, Rock of Cashel

NORTHERN VIEW OF THE ROCK

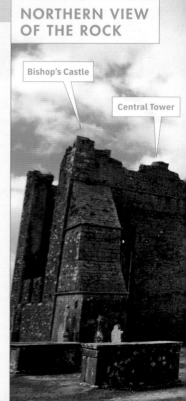

Bishop's Castle

Central Tower

❻ THE ROUND TOWER

As the oldest building on the Rock, the Round Tower rises 92 feet to command a panoramic view of the entire Vale of Tipperary. Dating back to 995, its construction followed the grim reality of the Viking invasions. A constant lookout was posted here to warn of any advancing armies, and food was always provisioned in the tower so as to outlast any prolonged siege. Note the door 10 feet from the ground, allowing ladders to be pulled up to thwart attackers, some of whom attempted to chip the rock at the base, with little effect.

❼ ST. PATRICK'S CROSS

Directly beyond the Rock's main entrance is this 7-foot-tall High Cross carved from one large block and resting upon what is said to have been the original coronation stone of the Munster kings. The cross was erected in the saint's honor to commemorate his famous visit to Cashel in 450. Upon both sides carved in high relief are two figures—the face of Christ crucified and a robed St. Patrick with his feet resting upon an ox head. Unique among High Crosses, this one has vertical supports on either side, perhaps allusions to the crosses of the good and bad thieves. A sort of early Irish bible class, these large stone crosses (which were sculpted from the 9th to the 12th centuries) were perfect teaching tools for a population that was largely illiterate. This cross is a faithfully rendered replica—the original now rests in the site museum.

The Crossing

Nave

North Transept

THE ST. PATRICK CONNECTION

While many legends surround Saint Patrick, he was an actual historical figure—his writings, a Latin text dating from the 5th century AD, yield the few undoubted facts about him. Born into a wealthy family in Roman-occupied Britain, he was kidnapped as a young man by Irish marauders and enslaved for six years as a sheepherder on the slopes of Slemish in County Antrim. He escaped, and returned to Britain, but a vision called him back to Ireland to convert the people to Christianity. Arriving in 433, he defied the pagan priests of Tara by kindling the Easter fire on Slane but went on in a peaceful conversion of Ireland to Christianity—not a drop of blood was shed—until his death in AD 460.

St. Patrick's conversion of Ireland was characterized by clever diplomacy: his missionaries were careful to combine elements of then-current druidic ritual with new Christian practice. For example, the Irish Christian church popularized the Feast of all Saints, and arranged for it to be celebrated on November 1, the same day as the great Celtic harvest festival, Samhain. Today's Halloween evolved from this linking of Celtic and Christian holidays.

Clearly a skilled negotiator as well as missionary, St. Patrick wisely preserved the social structure of Ireland, converting the people tribe by tribe. He first attempted to establish the Roman system of dioceses and bishops, but—since Ireland had never been conquered by the Romans—this arrangement did not suit a society without large cities. Instead, the Celts preferred a religious institution introduced by the desert fathers: the monastery, an idea of a "family" of monks being easy to grasp in a tribal society. Over 70 monasteries were founded in the 5th and 6th centuries, and by AD 700 abbots had replaced bishops as the leaders of the Catholic church.

In 457 St. Patrick retired to Saul, where he died. The only relic that can be tied to him is the famous 5th-century iron bell in Dublin's National Museum. Even if it was not, as is traditionally believed, used by the saint, he carried one very like it, and used it to announce his approach.

ROCK OF CASHEL INFO
⊠ *Rock of Cashel* ☎ *062/61437* ⊕ *www. cashel.ie* ⊠ *€6* ☉ *Mid-Mar.–early-June, daily 9:30–5:30; early-June–mid-Sept., daily 9–7; mid-Sept.–mid-Oct., daily 9–5:30; mid-Oct.–mid-Mar., daily 9–4:30.*

Above: Dublin, St. Patrick's Day parade

has recently been upgraded to a motorway for nearly the entire length of the trip, but at the time of writing one 20-mi section still needs to be completed. Dublin is 162 km (100 mi) or 2 hours northeast of Cashel on the N8/M8 and N7/M7. Cork City is 97 km (60 mi) or 1 hour 11 minutes south of Cashel on the N8/M8 and the N74.

GETTING HERE

BUS TRAVEL Bus Éireann runs buses between Cashel and Cork (€11.70 one-way and 19.80 round-trip; 1½ hours; eight daily) via Cahir (€3.90, 15 minutes) and Fermoy (€11.70, 1 hour 20 minutes). The bus stop for Cork is outside the Bake House on Main St. The Dublin stop (€11.70 one-way, €19.80 round-trip; 3 hours; six daily) is directly opposite. Tickets are available from the nearby Spar shop or you can buy them on the bus.

TRAIN TRAVEL **Visitor Information Cashel Tourist Office** (⊠ *Cashel Heritage Centre, Co. Tipperary* ☎ *062/62511* ⊕ *www.cashel.ie*).

Fodor's Choice The awe-inspiring, often mist-shrouded **Rock of Cashel** is one of Ireland's
★ most visited sites. *For complete information, see "Towering Glory: The Rock of Cashel" in this chapter.*

In the same building as the town TIO, the **Cashel Heritage Centre** explains the historic relationship between the town and the Rock and includes a scale model of Cashel as it looked during the 1600s. ⊠ *City Hall, Main St.* ☎ *062/62511* ⊕ *wwwcashel.ie* ☎ *Free* ☉ *Mar.–Oct., daily 9:30–5:50; Nov.–Feb., weekdays 9:30–5:30.*

The **G.P.A. Bolton Library,** on the grounds of the St. John the Baptist Church of Ireland Cathedral, has a particularly fine collection of rare books, manuscripts, and maps, some of which date from the beginning of the age of printing in Europe. ⊠ *John St.* ☎ *062/61944* ☎ *€2* ☉ *Mon.–Thurs. 10–2:30.*

WHERE TO EAT AND STAY

$$$$ ✕ **Chez Hans.** It's rather fitting that this restaurant is in a converted
MODERN IRISH church, as it's become something of a foodies' shrine. Gourmands travel
★ from Dublin and Cork to get their fix of chef Jason Matthia's cuisine, which is contemporary with a hint of nouvelle. He works wonders with fresh Irish ingredients, especially seafood. The cassoulet of seafood— half a dozen varieties of fish and shellfish with a delicate chive velouté— is legendary. Another specialty is panfried hake with prawns, lemon, coriander, and tomato. The atmosphere is wonderful, too, with dark wood and tapestries providing an elegant background for the white linen. ⊠ *Moore La.* ☎ *062/61177* ⚠ *Reservations essential* ☐ *AE, DC, MC, V* ☉ *Closed Sun. and Mon. and late Jan.–early Feb. No lunch.*

$$ ☐ **Cashel Palace.** Built in 1730 for archbishop Theophilus Bolton, this
IRISH grand house truly is a palace in every sense. It was designed by Sir Edward
Fodor's Choice Lovett Pearce, who also created the Old Parliament House in Dublin,
★ and is gorgeously offset by parkland replete with fountains and centuries-old trees. Inside, red-pine paneling, barley-sugar staircases, Corinthian columns, and a surfeit of cosseting antiques all create an air of Georgian volupté. Guest rooms on the second floor are cozier, though not small. The coach house has also been converted into 10 smaller rooms. The Bishop's Buttery restaurant relies on game in season, local lamb and beef, and fresh fish creatively prepared, and also serves simple, light meals

all day; the linguini of seared prawns and crayfish is irresistible. Don't miss the lovely gardens at the rear of the house, where you can see the descendants of the original hop plants used by Richard Guinis to brew the first "Wine of Ireland." Guinis went on, with his son, Arthur, to found the Guinness Brewery in Dublin. **Pros:** glorious period main house; great strolling gardens; good restaurant. **Cons:** expensive for this region; popular for weddings; few in-room facilities. ⊠ *Main St., Co. Tipperary* ☎ *062/62707* ⊕ *www.cashel-palace.ie* ⤴ *21 rooms* ♨ *In-room: no a/c. In-hotel: restaurant, bar, Wi-Fi hotspot* ⊟ *AE, DC, MC, V* ❘⊙❘ *BP.*

$$–$$$ ⬚ **Dundrum House Hotel.** Nestled beside the River Multeen, 12 km (7½ mi) outside busy Cashel, is this imposing, four-story 1730 Georgian house. Sixteen high-ceiling bedrooms take up the main house; the rest are in a three-story wing built during the house's previous incarnation as a convent. Opened as a hotel in 1981 by Austin and Mary Crowe, the renovation of the manor house was substantial and sensitive. Although highly renovated, many of the older rooms have accent pieces of early Victorian furniture. A big plus: lovely views of the surrounding parkland. The old convent chapel, stained-glass windows intact, is now a cocktail bar. Elaborate plaster ceilings, attractive period furniture, and open fires make the spacious dining room and lounge inviting. The latest draw is a new, award-winning health and leisure club, along with an 18-hole championship golf course designed by Ryder Cup hero Philip Walton. There are also self-catering apartments and homes available on the grounds. **Pros:** good value for Georgian comfort; wonderful parkland views; lively cocktail bar. **Cons:** main house rooms superior to others; can get a bit noisy when full; attracts flush crowd. ⊠ *Dundrum, Co. Tipperary* ☎ *062/71116* ⊕ *www.dundrumhousehotel.com* ⤴ *70 rooms, 16 holiday homes* ♨ *In-room: no a/c. In-hotel: 2 restaurants, bars, golf course, pool, gym, Wi-Fi hotspot* ⊟ *MC, V* ❘⊙❘ *BP.*

NIGHTLIFE AND THE ARTS

You can enjoy folksinging, storytelling, and dancing from mid-June through September, Tuesday through Saturday, at the **Bru Boru Centre** (☎ *062/61122*) at the foot of the Rock of Cashel. Entertainment usually begins at 7 PM and costs €20, €50 with dinner.

The Southwest

INCLUDING COUNTIES KERRY AND LIMERICK

WORD OF MOUTH

"This is kind of a Beatles or Elvis question, but which would you go to if you only had time for one: Ring of Kerry, Dingle Peninsula, or Cliffs of Moher?"

—gravysandwich

"You have three 'cute babies' here; there is no wrong answer!"

—Viajero2

WELCOME TO THE SOUTHWEST

TOP REASONS TO GO

★ **The Ring of Kerry:** The most brazenly scenic coastal drive in Ireland might have been designed with the visitor in mind—get ready to use up your entire flash card in a jiffy!

★ **Skellig Michael:** Take a wet and wonderful ride out to Ireland's most spectacular island, whose twin peaks, crowned with a medieval monastery, beckon to you along the Ring of Kerry.

★ **The Gap of Dunloe:** A half-day tour lets you walk or ride horseback through the heart of Killarney's purple mountains and cross the glittering blue lake by rowboat.

★ **Adare:** Discover Ireland's prettiest village by taking a walk past its dinky thatched cottages to the banks of the River Maigue, where the remains of priories established by medieval monks still stand.

★ **"Castle Country":** Limerick is studded with top attractions like King John's Castle on the banks of the Shannon and the fully restored Bunratty Castle and Folk Park.

1 The Iveragh Peninsula. The Ring of Kerry, one of Europe's great scenic drives, runs around the edge of this rocky peninsula, passing from the subtropical splendor of Sneem, on the sheltered Kenmare River, past Waterville, where the twin-peaked Skellig rocks hover on the horizon, to the starker views of Dingle Bay to the north.

GETTING ORIENTED

In the Southwest, five-star scenery is everywhere from the mountains and lakes of Killarney, out to Kerry's craggy western peninsulas. Brightly painted villages and small harbors encourage you to stop and linger—and when you do, you're rewarded with exceptional food, particularly in Kenmare and Dingle, towns that boast an extraordinary number of talented chefs in proportion to their size. Off the western coast, the Skelligs rank as the region's most awesome sight, though it takes an often-choppy boat ride to reach them. Adare, midway between Kerry and Limerick, is both picture-book pretty and rich in historical churches and monasteries. Limerick's historic center is the gateway to an area rich in mighty castles.

6

2 The Lakes of Killarney.
Nineteenth-century visitors founds the views of Killarney every bit as romantic and uplifting as the mountains of Switzerland; the unique combination of glacial landscape and abundant sub-tropical vegetation, studded by the bright blue waters of the lakes creates an unforgettable vista—and it smells good, too, with peat-fire smoke mingling with fresh mountain air.

3 The Dingle Peninsula.
Dingle Town is a-hopping, between the live traditional music in its numerous bars, and the sea-fresh seafood on offer in its eateries; head west to Slea Head for stunning coastal scenery, with vast sandy beaches, rocky islands, and Iron Age ruins.

4 Shannon Estuary.
Along the mouth of Ireland's greatest river is "Castle Country," an area dotted with ruined castles and abbeys, the result of Elizabeth I's 16th-century attempt to subdue the province of Munster. Limerick City, too, bears the scars of history, from a different confrontation with the English—the 1691 Siege of Limerick.

THE SOUTHWEST PLANNER

Picking a Peninsula

Two of Ireland's most scenic destinations sit side by side on the map: the Iveragh Peninsula (also known as the Ring of Kerry, for its scenic drive) and the Dingle Peninsula (also known by its Irish name, Corca Dhuibne). If you like wild, rugged scenery, archaeological remains, and Irish music, Dingle is for you. The most scenic part of the peninsula is at its tip, to the west of An Daingean/ Dingle Town. The town itself is a lively spot, with crafts shops, restaurants, and music bars. In contrast, the Ring of Kerry is a longer drive with more varied scenery, ranging from lush subtropical vegetation between Kenmare and Sneem, to rocky coves at Caherdaniel, and long sandy beaches near Glenbeigh. The scenery is punctuated by a series of small villages, all much quieter than Dingle.

Making the Most of Your Time

If you're here for a short stay—three days or fewer—you'd do well to base yourself in Killarney and devote your time to exploring the surrounding area, then heading out to the Ring of Kerry or the Dingle Peninsula.

With more time at your disposal, consider a half-day trip to Skellig Michael, a fairly tough ride in an open boat, but an unforgettable experience of a remote, rock-hewn monastery, and thousands of nesting seabirds, or Adare, one of Ireland's prettiest villages; while Limerick's historic center has a massive medieval castle and the Hunt Museum, a pocket-size museum with a world-class collection of paintings and artifacts.

Cross the Shannon to travel west to the magnificently restored Bunratty Castle, flanked by a lively Folk Village that will entertain children of all ages, and a famous old riverside pub, Durty Nelly's.

What to Bring Home

You will soon notice that parts of County Kerry have more sheep than people: sheep means wool, and in this part of Ireland wool means sweaters, socks, and wooly hats. All three will come in very useful during your stay, and make great gifts, too. **Quills Woollen Market** (⊠ Market Cross, Killarney ☎ 064/32277) has outlets in Killarney, Kenmare, Sneem, and Dingle.

Look out for "blackthorns": a traditional, craggy walking stick made from branches of the blackthorn tree, a handy accessory to have while you're here, and a great souvenir to take home. What about modern jewelry in silver or gold by **Brian de Staic** (⊠ Green St., Dingle ☎ 066/915–1298 ⊕ www.briandestaic.com)? His ancient Irish designs can be found in Killarney, Dingle, and Tralee.

Ceramics are a strong point, too, with the **Louis Mulcahy Pottery** (⊠ Clogher Strand, Dingle ☎ 066/915–6229 ⊕ www. louismulcahy.com) ceramics workshop and showrooms on Slea Head being the most western pottery in Europe.

Where to Eat

The Southwest is a great place for good food. Kenmare, Dingle, and Killarney all have a high density of restaurants and gastro-pubs serving locally reared meat, artisan cheeses, and local seafood. Kerry mountain lamb has a unique flavor imparted by the wild herbs and grasses that those sheep you see on every hillside are busy munching on.

Adare is another culinary hotspot: choose between the low-ceilinged charm of the tiny rooms in the thatched cottage restaurant, the Wild Geese, and the genuine old-world hospitality at the blissfully comfortable Dunraven Arms, an old coaching inn still with some of its original antiques, that is now one of Ireland's leading hotels.

For another kind of dining experience, check out the medieval banquets at Bunratty and Knappogue castles, near Shannon—they're an undeniably touristy good time.

Where to Stay

For accommodations, the Southwest has some of the great country houses, including Adare Manor in County Limerick; Kenmare's unique duo of the magnificent Sheen Falls Lodge and the stately Park Hotel; the Cahernane House, which recalls Killarney's Victorian heyday; and finally the rambling landmark resort, the Parknasilla Resort in Sneem, a great place for a family break.

At the other end of the spectrum is the uniquely Irish experience of a farmhouse bed-and-breakfast, such as Lakelands Farm Guesthouse in Waterville, with rowboats bobbing on Lough Currane at the bottom of the garden.

In between is a range of excellent family-owned and -run traditional hotels, such as the Loch Lein Country House in Killarney, the Butler Arms in Waterville, and the secluded Carrig Country House at Glenbeigh near Killorglin

DINING AND LODGING PRICE CATEGORIES (IN EUROS)					
	¢	$	$$	$$$	$$$$
Restaurants	under €12	€12–€18	€19–€24	€25–€32	over €32
Hotels	under €80	€80–€120	€121–€170	€171–€210	over €210

Restaurant prices are for a main course at dinner. Hotel prices are for a standard double room in high season.

When to Go

The best times to visit the Ring of Kerry, Killarney, and Dingle are mid-March to June, and September and October. In July and August it's the peak holiday period, meaning roads are more crowded, prices are higher, and the best places are booked in advance. March can be chilly, with daily temperatures in the 40s and 50s. The average high in June is 18°C (65°F), which is about as hot as it gets. May and June are the sunniest months. May and September the driest months. The farther west you go, the more likely you'll get rain. The weather is not such a crucial factor in Adare and the Limerick area, but from November to mid-March daylight hours are short, the weather is damp, and many smaller places on the Kerry coast in and Killarney are closed.

6

The Great Outdoors

Some of the most famous golf courses in Ireland are in the Southwest, including Waterville Golf Links, favored by Tiger Woods, and Bill Clinton's favorite links course, Ballybunion Golf Club. The parkland course at Adare Manor, designed by Robert Trent Jones on the ancestral estate of the Earl of Dunraven, hosts events of the highest caliber. The entire area is crisscrossed with walking trails, with the Kerry Way Trail stretching 24 km (15 mi) from Killarney to Kenmare.

GETTING AROUND

Train Travel

The region is accessible by train from Dublin Heuston Station and from Cork's Kent Station. From Dublin the region is served by two direct rail links, to Limerick Junction (where you change trains for Limerick City), and on to Tralee (via Mallow and Killarney). Journey time from Dublin to Limerick is 2½ hours; to Tralee, 3¾ hours. The rail network is mainly useful for moving from one touring base to another. There are hourly trains from Dublin to Limerick Junction, connecting with Limerick City (20 minutes), and nine trains a day from Dublin to Tralee (most of which involve one change at Mallow). There are currently five trains a day from Cork to Killarney and Tralee, but this is scheduled to improve in 2010. The journey from Cork to Tralee takes about 2 hours; from Cork to Limerick, about 1¼ hours; from Limerick to Tralee, about 3 hours.

Train Information Dublin Heuston Station
(☎ 01/836–6222). **Irish Rail– Iarnód Éireann Inquiries**
(☎ 021/450–6766 in Cork, 066/712–3522 in Tralee ⊕ www.irishrail.ie). **Kent Station, Cork** (☎ 021/450–6766 for timetable). **Limerick Rail Station** (✉ Colbert Station, Parnell St. ☎ 061/315–555). **Tralee Rail Station** (✉ Casement Station, John Joe Sheehy Rd. ☎ 066/712–3522).

Bus Travel

Bus Éireann operates express services from Dublin to Limerick City, and Tralee. Most towns in the region are served by the provincial Bus Éireann network.

The main Bus Eireann bus stations in the region are at Limerick and Tralee, and there is also a bus station in Killarney. The bus stations are located outside the railway stations.

Citylink (a private bus company) offers a reliable alternative to Bus Éireann, serving Dublin, Shannon, and Cork airports, and the city centers of Cork, Dublin, Limerick, and Galway.

Fares and Schedules

Buses tend to stop running in the early evening, which is fine if you want to stay overnight and leave the next morning, but it rules out many day trips—unless you want to spend most of the day on the bus.

As a general rule, the smaller the town, and the more remote, the less frequent its bus service: some of the smaller villages on the remote Corca Dhuibne (Dingle Peninsula) have bus service only one day a week in winter.

Bus Éireann runs a regular bus service around the Ring of Kerry between mid-June and mid-September, but there are only two buses a day, leaving Killarney at 8:45 AM or 1:45 PM.

The trip takes more than four hours. Consult with hotel concierges, tourist board staffers, or the bus line Web site for bus schedules.

Bus Information Bus Éireann (☎ 01/836–6111 in Dublin, 061/313–333 in Limerick, 066/712–3566 in Tralee ⊕ www.buseireann.ie). **Killarney Bus Station** (✉ East Avenue Rd. ☎ 064/663–0011). **Limerick Bus Station** (✉ Colbert Station, Parnell St. ☎ 061/313–333). **Tralee Bus Station** (✉ Casement Station, John Joe Sheehy Rd. ☎ 066/716–4700). **Citylink** (⊕ www.citylink.ie).

Air Travel

The Southwest can be accessed from two international airports: Cork (ORK) on the southwest coast, and Shannon (SNN) in the west. Cork Airport, 5 km (3 mi) south of Cork City on the Kinsale road, has direct flights daily to Dublin, London (Heathrow, Gatwick, and Stansted), Manchester, East Midlands, and Paris, and direct flights to many other European cities. Shannon Airport, 26 km (16 mi) west of Limerick City, is the point of arrival for many transatlantic flights, including direct flights from Boston, Chicago, Philadelphia, Toronto (summer only), and New York City (from both JFK and Newark); it also has regular flights from the United Kingdom and many European cities. Kerry County Airport (KIR) at Farranfore, 16 km (10 mi) from Killarney, has daily flights from Dublin, London (Stansted and Luton), and Frankfurt (Hahn) operated by Ryanair.

Airport Information Cork Airport (☎ 021/431–3131 ⊕ www.corkairport.com). **Kerry County Airport** (☎ 066/976–4644 ⊕ www.kerryairport.ie). **Shannon Airport** (☎ 061/471–444 ⊕ www.shannonairport.com).

Car Travel

The main driving route from Dublin is N7, which goes 192 km (120 mi) directly to Limerick City. If you land at Shannon Airport, access to the southwest is also via Limerick City; from there pick up the N21 to Killarney. An alternate, more scenic, route from Dublin leaves the N7 at Naas to join the N8 at Portlaoise, turning off the main Dublin–Cork road at Mitchelstown and following the N72 to Killarney. Both journeys from Dublin take about four hours; many people prefer to fly from Dublin to Kerry Airport (40 minutes) and pick up a rental car there. From Limerick it is about 2 hours to Killarney (111 km [69 mi]), and another half hour to Kenmare. A car is the ideal way to explore this region, packed as it is with scenic routes, attractive but remote towns, and a host of out-of-the-way restaurants and hotels that deserve a detour. Road upgrading has not kept up with the increased usage, and the result is our old friend, the peak-hour traffic jam. Killarney, and Tralee have ground-level parking lots: follow the blue P signs. In Limerick it's advisable to use a multistory parking garage, as on-street parking can be hard to find. If you do get lucky, you'll have to become familiar with "disk" parking regulations, which involve buying a ticket (or disk) for around €2 an hour from a machine or a shop and displaying it. Beware: car clamper officers are active!

Airport Transfers

A 10-minute bus route (€3.40) runs between Cork Airport and the Cork City Bus Terminal (a feeder bus run from here to the rail station) every 30 minutes.

Bus Éireann runs a 40-minute bus route (€5) between Shannon Airport and Limerick City between 8 AM and midnight.

JJ Kavanagh runs a popular bus shuttle to Shannon Airport, connecting with Limerick (45 minutes; €5 one-way).

These airport buses arrive at the tourist information office on Arthur's Quay.

Cork Airport is about two hours' drive from both Killarney and Kenmare.

Shannon Airport is 135 km (84 mi) from Killarney via Limerick, a journey that takes about 2½ hours. All buses running from Cork to Galway are routed via Limerick and Shannon Airport, giving direct connections to those cities.

For buses to Dublin, Waterford, Tralee, and Killarney, change at Limerick.

Shuttles Bus Éireann (☎ 061/47431 in Limerick ⊕ www.buseireann.ie).

JJ Kavanagh Buses (☎ 061/313333 ⊕ www.jjkavanagh.ie).

6

GETTING AROUND

Visitor Information

Bord Fáilte provides a free information service; its tourist information offices (TIOs) also sell a selection of tourist literature. For a small fee it will book accommodations anywhere in Ireland.

Seasonal TIOs in Waterville, Portmagee, Cahirciveen, and Listowelare open from May to October; the TIO in Kenmare is open April to October. All of the seasonal TIOs are generally open Monday–Saturday 9–6; in July and August they are also open Sunday 9–6.

Year-round TIOs can be found in Adare, An Daingean/Dingle, Killarney, Limerick Shannon Airport, and Tralee. These offices are usually open Monday–Saturday 9–6 and also Sunday 9–6 in July and August.

Special-Interest Tours

Country House Tours organizes self-driven or chauffeur-driven group tours with accommodations in private country houses and castles. It also conducts special-interest tours, including gardens, architecture, ghosts, and golf, while Killorglin-based Go Ireland offers comprehensive packages for walking, cycling, fishing, golfing, and equestrian holidays on the Ring of Kerry and the Dingle Peninsula with experienced local guides.

Hidden Ireland Tours has two knowledgeable Irish-based guides, Con Moriarty of Killarney and Ann Curran of Dingle, who will tailor a package to suit your interests, catering for groups of 2 to 16 people, and upwards. Consider an eight-day walking tour with bases in Killarney and Dingle, or a luxurious car tour staying in some of the region's best country-house hotels. Slow food, painting, literary tours, or antique tours can also be arranged.

Tour Companies Country House Tours (✉ 71 Waterloo Rd., Dublin ☎ 01/668–6463 ⊕ www.tourismresources. ie). **Hidden Ireland Tours** (✉ Dingle ☎ 087/258–1966 ⊕ www.hiddenirelandtours.com). **Go Ireland** (✉ Killorglin ☎ 066/976–2094 ⊕ www.govisitireland.com).

Taxi Travel

Taxis at Shannon and Cork airports connect with those cities; Shannon to Limerick City costs about €35; from Cork to Cork City Railway Station, about €12. It costs €4.10 to hire a taxi on the street (€4.45 by night); add €2 to book one by phone, and €1.03 per kilometer.

Full details of fares and conditions are on the Taxi Regulator Web site. Taxis are also found at railway stations in Tralee, Killarney, Limerick, and at Shannon and Kerry airports. Otherwise they must be prebooked by phone: ask for the number of the local company at your hotel or B&B.

Taxi Companies All Route Taxis (✉ Limerick ☎ 061/300–777). **Cork Taxi Co-Op** (✉ Cork ☎ 021/477–2222 ⊕ www.corktaxi.ie). **Killarney Cabs** (✉ Killarney ☎ 064/663–4888). **Taxi Regulator** (☎ No phone ⊕ www. taxiregulator.ie).**Tralee Radio Cabs** (✉ Tralee ☎ 066/712–5451 ⊕ www.traleeradiotaxis.com).

Boat and Ferry Travel

The Fastnet Line runs a regular car-ferry service from Swansea in Wales to Ringaskiddy on Cork Harbor, the nearest ferry port to the Southwest. The crossing takes 9 to 10 hours, and the MV *Julia* sails overnight six nights a week, with additional sailings in July and August. Swansea is on the M4 motorway, and the crossing saves about 600 km (375 mi) driving, compared to traveling to Cork from Fishguard or Port Talbot via Rosslare. If you are heading for Killarney or Kenmare, save 3 hours driving in Ireland by taking the ferry from Swansea to Cork. It departs from Cork on Tuesday, Thursday, and Saturday, and leaves Swansea for Cork on Friday and Sunday. From Rosslare Harbour by car, take N25 to Dungarvan and pick up the N72 westwards to Killarney or Kenmare, a journey of 275 km (171 mi), about 4 to 5 hours.

Boat Companies Fastnet Line (⊠ *Ferry Terminal, Ringaskiddy, Cork* ☎ *021/437–8892* ⊕ *www.fastnetline.com*.

Walking Tours

SouthWestWalks Ireland has a variety of walks on the Ring of Kerry and around Killarney; some include accommodation and evening meals. Activity Ireland organizes customized walking and climbing tours on the Ring of Kerry. Go Ireland specializes in walking and cycling excursions along the Kerry Way or the Dingle Peninsula. Hidden Ireland Tours organizes walking tours for two or more in Dingle, Killarney, and Ring of Kerry. Richard Clancy, a noted historian, offers a two-hour guided walk (€9) in Killarney National Park daily at 11 AM; departures are from O'Sullivan's Bike Shop on Lower New Street in Killarney; book early for November–April. Limerick City Tours has city walks June to September. St. Mary's Action Centre has an *Angela's Ashes* Tour daily at 11 and 2:30.

Tour Information Activity Ireland (⊠ *Caherdaniel, Co. Kerry* ☎ *066/947–5277* ⊕ *www.activityireland.com*). **Go Ireland** (⊠ *Killorglin* ☎ *066/976–2094* ⊕ *www.govisitireland.com*). **Hidden Ireland Tours** (⊠ *Dinglen* ☎ *087/258–1966* ⊕ *www.hiddenirelandtours.com*). **Limerick City Tours** (⊠ *Noel Curtin, director, Rhebogue* ☎ *061/311–935*). **Richard Clancy** (⊠ *Killarney* ☎ *064/663–3471* ⊕ *www.killarneyguidedwalks.com*). **St. Mary's Action Centre** (⊠ *44 Nicholas St., Limerick* ☎ *061/318–106* ⊕ *www.iol.ie/~smidp*). **SouthWestWalks Ireland** (⊠ *6 Church St., Tralee* ☎ *066/712–8733* ⊕ *www.southwestwalksireland.com*).

Bus Tours

Bus Éireann offers a range of daylong and half-day guided tours from June to September. You can book them at the bus station in Killarney, or at any tourist office. A full-day tour costs about €30, half-day €15.

The memorable Gap of Dunloe Tour (at €25) includes a coach or vintage bus and boat trip. Add €20 for a horse-drawn carriage ride through the Gap. There are three companies offering this tour, which can be booked through the Killarney Tourist Office.

More conventional day trips can also be made to the Ring of Kerry, An Daingean (Dingle) and Ceann Sleibne (Slea Head), and to Caragh Lake and Rossbeigh. A full-day (10:30–5) tour costs from €20 to €30 per person, excluding lunch and refreshments. These can be booked through the Killarney TIO.

Keating Coaches offers day trips and half-day tours of the Shannon region from Limerick City from June to September. Themes include "castles and gardens"; "waterways, highways, and byways"; and "flying boats, monks, and dolphins."

Bus Tour Companies
Bus Éireann (☎ *061/313–333 in Limerick, 021/450–8188 in Cork, 066/712–3566 in Tralee* ⊕ *www.buseireann.ie*). **Keating Coaches** (⊠ *Ballingarry* ☎ *069/68201* ⊕ *www.limericktours.com*). **Killarney Tourist Office** (⊠ *Beech Rd.* ☎ *064/663–4594* ⊕ *www.corkkerry.ie*).

6

Updated
by Alannah
Howard

Ever since Killarney was first "discovered" by William Thackeray and Sir Walter Scott, visitors have been searching for superlatives to describe the deep blue lakes, dark green forests, and purple mountainsides of this romantic region. Created by the rock formations that followed the retreat of the Ice Age, Killarney's magnificent sandstone mountains have always been considered as awe-inspiring as anything found in Switzerland. So perhaps it was no surprise that things couldn't remain low-key here forever. Today, the Ring of Kerry coastal drive has become a crazy and emerald green Orlando, packed with rushing tour buses. And, thronged with scurrying visitors, Killarney's town center is looking more than ever like a Celtic theme park.

But to be in a hurry in the Southwest is to be ill-mannered. It was probably a Kerryman who first remarked that when God made time, he made plenty of it. So to truly enjoy the amazing array of scenic delights found here, remember that the locals of the extreme Southwest—this region stretches from the Ring of Kerry in the south, the Dingle Peninsula in the west, through Killarney and north to Adare, Limerick, and the region's gateway, Shannon Airport—are unusually laid-back, even by Irish standards.

No matter that their day-to-day life has been elbowed out of existence by the crescendo of visitors (you'll be lucky to hear an Irish accent on the Babel-like streets of Killarney), or that the town has a ring road that goes into gridlock morning and evening, or that traffic-jams on the Ring of Kerry are common in high season. Happily, the natives still remember what attracted tourists in the first place: uncrowded roads, unpolluted beaches and rivers, easy access to golf, and unspoiled scenery. So take your cue from them and venture into the back roads. Meander along at your own pace, sampling wayside delights. Before you know it, you'll be far from Killarney's crowds and in the middle of the region's tranquil and incredibly stunning landscapes.

That is, if they are visible. To quote Cork-born writer, Frank O'Connor: "Kerry is remarkable for its scenery—when you can see it, which owning to the appalling weather the county enjoys, is very rarely." Being a Corkman, he was exaggerating. Showers of rain seldom last for long, and are seldom cold: it is the famous Irish "soft day," when the mist swirls in and out again, or a little shower falls two fields away in front of the sun, creating an unforgettable rainbow. There is no denying that if you are fortunate enough to have good weather in Kerry, your visit will be especially memorable—but even if the day is not perfect, mist-shrouded mountains can be just as beautiful as sun-lit ones.

If Mother Nature doesn't cooperate, there is always the bounty of man-made attractions. Moving northward, scenery becomes less dramatic but much cozier, with Adare's thatched cottages giving the village the reputation as one of Ireland's prettiest. Head up to Limerick and a busy four-lane highway hurls you back into the 21st century. Metropolitan hub of southwest Ireland (and the Republic's third largest city), Limerick bears the scars of history, most notably from the Siege of Limerick, a face-off with the English that took place in 1691. Its other "scars" of history—described so memorably in Frank McCourt's best seller *Angela's Ashes*—lure travelers who discover that this is a compact, vibrant city. And west of the Shannon is "Castle Country," with famed Bunratty Castle leading the pack in the Southwest's must-see stakes.

THE RING OF KERRY

Running along the perimeter of the Iveragh Peninsula, the dramatic 176 km (110 mi) Ring of Kerry is probably Ireland's single most popular tourist route. Stunning mountain and coastal views are around almost every turn. The only drawback: on a sunny day, it seems like half the nation's visitors are traveling along this two-lane road, packed into buses, riding bikes, or backpacking. The route is narrow and curvy, and the local sheep think nothing of using it for a nap; take it slowly. Tour buses tend to start in Killarney and ply the Ring counterclockwise, so consider jumping ahead and starting in Killorglin or following the route clockwise, starting in Kenmare (although this means you risk meeting tour buses head-on on narrow roads). Either way, bear in mind that most of the buses leave Killarney between 9 and 10 AM. The trip covers 176 km (110 mi) on N70 (and briefly R562) if you start and finish in Killarney; the journey will be 40 km (25 mi) shorter if you only venture between Kenmare and Killorglin. Because rain blocks views across the water to the Beara Peninsula in the east and the Dingle Peninsula in the west, hope for sunshine. It makes all the difference.

KENMARE

21 km (13 mi) north of Glengarriff on N71, 34 km (21 mi) south of Killarney

Situated slightly inland without a clear view of Kenmare Bay, Kenmare is a natural stopover for buses and travelers as it is the closest town to Killarney. Set at the head of the sheltered Kenmare River estuary, this market town makes a lively touring base for those who wish to skip hectic Killarney altogether. It's currently a matter of lively debate as to whether Kenmare has displaced Kinsale *(see the County Cork chapter)* as the culinary capital of Ireland. Kenmare offers an amazing number of stylish little restaurants for a town its size, and also boasts a top-rated Kenmare Market, with dealers in organic goods and foodstuffs (Wednesdays, 10–5, March–December). The shopping is pretty good, too, with Irish high fashion, crafts, and original art vying for your attention, along with the organic food goodies found at the Kenmare Market.

GETTING HERE

BUS TRAVEL   Kenmare is not on Bus Éireann's fast Expressway network so to venture to this region using public transportation the bus hub is the *Killarney Bus Station (see Bus Travel in Getting Around)*. There is one bus a day from Killarney to Kenmare, leaving Killarney at 7:40 AM and returning at 12:20 PM (€17.10 round-trip). The Kenmare bus stop is outside D'Arcy's Restaurant on Main Street. In July and August there is one bus a day around the Ring of Kerry (€25.50 round-trip), leaving Killarney at 12:45 PM and returning at 5:10. If you want to hop off and stay overnight (completing your journey the next day), the ticket costs €29 round-trip.

TOURS   Other than the one-a-day Bus Éireann bus that does the Ring of Kerry circuit, one can also opt to base yourself in Kenmare and take a guided tour of the Ring by minibus (€25, May–September) with the local taxi company, *Finnegan's Tours/Kenmore Coach and Cab*. Their minibuses depart from the Square for the Ring on Monday, Wednesday, and Friday at 10 AM. Other destinations include the Ring of Beara and Glengarriff. It is best to reserve by 10 PM the night before. *For bicycle hire, see the Sports and the Outdoors section below.*

ESSENTIALS

Transportation Contacts Finnegan's Tours/Kenmore Coach and Cab
(✉ *The Square, Kenmare* ☎ *064/664–1491* ⊕ *www.kenmarecoachandcab.com*).

Visitor Information Kenmare Tourist Office (✉ *The Square, Co. Kerry*
☎ *064/664–1233* ⊕ *www.kenmare.com* ⊗ *Apr.–Oct. only*).

EXPLORING

Kenmare was founded in 1670 by Sir William Petty (Oliver Cromwell's surveyor general, a multitasking entrepreneur), and most of its buildings date from the 19th century, when it was part of the enormous Lansdowne Estate—itself assembled by Petty. Perhaps the town's most notable historic sight is the nearby **Stone Circle**, a 3,000-year-old monument that dates from the early Bronze Age. Sometimes called the Druid Circle, it is within five minutes' walk of the village square down Market Street. It consists of 15 large stones arranged in a circle around a center stone (too bad industrial storage sits nearby). There's also a worthwhile walk

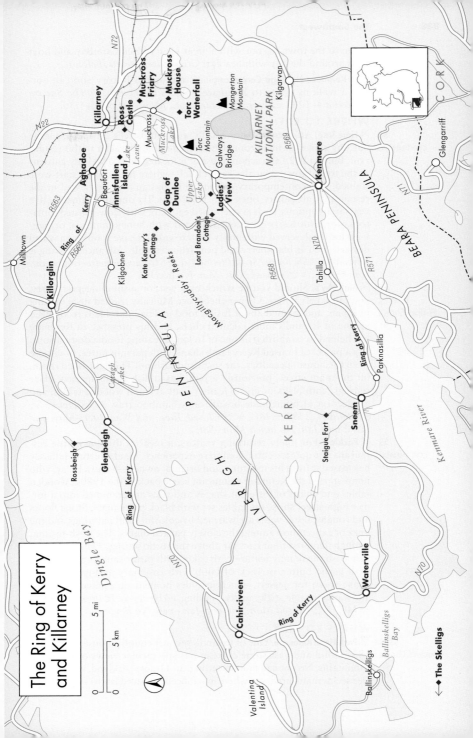

The Ring of Kerry and Killarney

Killarney National Park

CORK

Kilgarvan

Kenmare

BEARA PENINSULA

Glengarriff

Mangerton Mountain

Muckross House
Muckross Friary
Muckross Waterfall
Torc Waterfall
Torc Mountain
Ross Castle
Muckross
Muckross Lake
Galways Bridge
Ladies' View
Upper Lake
Lord Brandon's Cottage
Gap of Dunloe
Innisfallen Island
Beaufort
Aghadoe
Kate Kearny's Cottage
Kilgobnet

Lake Leane

Ring of Kerry

Milltown

Killorglin

IVERAGH PENINSULA

Macgillycuddy's Reeks

Caragh Lake

KERRY

Tahilla

Parknasilla
Ring of Kerry
Sneem

Staigue Fort

Kenmare River

Rossbeigh
Glenbeigh

Ring of Kerry

Dingle Bay

Cahirciveen

Ring of Kerry

Waterville

Valentina Island

Ballinskelligs Bay

Ballinskelligs

The Skelligs

N72
N22
R563
R562
R569
N70
R568
N71
R571

5 mi
5 km
0

down to the town harbor with a great view of Kenmare Bay and boat trips around the bay with Sea Fari Cruises *(see Sports, below).*

The **Kenmare Heritage Centre** explains the town's history and can outline a walking route to Kenmare's places of interest. ⊠ *The Square* ☎ *064/664–1233* ✆ *Free* ☉ *Easter–Sept., Mon.–Sat. 9:30–5:30.*

WHERE TO EAT

$$
CONTINENTAL

✕ **Lime Tree.** An open fire, stone walls, and a minstrel's gallery on a large balcony above the main room lend considerable character to this restaurant. Built in 1823 as a schoolhouse, it is located in its own leafy gardens at the top of town near the Park Hotel—where many of its staff were trained. The contemporary art on the walls can also be viewed in the restaurant's art gallery, open daily from 4 PM. Try one of the imaginative vegetarian options, such as deep-fried eggplant with slow-roasted tomatoes, or go for Kerry lamb oven roasted with honey-mint jus, or panfried local fish served with boxty (potato cake). Leave room for a warm dessert, such as blackberry and pear fruit crumble. Advance booking is advisable. ⊠ *Shelburne St.* ☎ *064/664–1225* ⊕ *www.limetreerestaurant. com* ▭ *MC, V* ☉ *Closed Nov.–Mar. No lunch.*

$$
ECLECTIC
Fodor's Choice
★

✕ **Mulcahy's.** Should you be struck by a yen for sushi in deepest Kerry, you can satisfy it here. Owner-chef Bruce Mulcahy studied sushi making in Japan, and learned about fusion food in Thailand. He is recognized as one of Ireland's most talented chefs, and his presence in Kenmare has helped to establish it as one of Ireland's leading foodie destinations. Try a parcel of braised Kerry lamb shank with parsnip puree, or choose from the house specialties, the sushi and sashimi. The light-filled room, on the main street, previously a pub, has stylish contemporary place settings, with black or cream leather seats at small wooden tables, and a selection of homemade breads on a bamboo tray. ⊠ *36 Henry St.* ☎ *064/664–2383* ▭ *MC, V* ☉ *Closed Tues. and Wed. Oct.–May, and last 2 wks Jan. No lunch Mon.–Sat.*

$$
CONTINENTAL

✕ **Packies.** For many returning visitors, a meal at this busy little restaurant is a quintessential Kenmare experience. Chef Martin Hallissey has leased it from his mentor—and original owner—Maura Foley, who jump-started the Kenmare restaurant scene back in the 1980s. Wooden tables and chairs of different shapes and sizes are crammed into a former high-street shop, the tables set with black place mats. Stone floors and rough-plaster walls are warmed by colorful local paintings and the buzz of expectation among the closely packed diners. The fresh-tasting, strongly flavored food rises far above the rustic setting. The contemporary Irish menu may feature crab cakes with tartar sauce, roast lobster with garlic butter, or rack of lamb with rosemary-and-garlic gravy. Leave room for dessert, which includes homemade praline ice cream and a memorable sticky toffee pudding. ⊠ *Henry St.* ☎ *064/664–1508* ▭ *MC, V* ☉ *Closed Mon. and mid-Jan.–Feb. No lunch.*

WHERE TO STAY

$$$$
Fodor's Choice
★

▦ **Park Hotel Kenmare.** One of Ireland's premier country-house hotels, this 1897 stolid and vast stone château has spectacular views of the Caha Mountains. No one can fault its setting: an 11-acre parkland, where every tree seems manicured and where magnificent terraced lawns sweep down to the bay. A welcoming fire is always burning in the lobby—a traditional setting complete with tall grandfather clock. The lobby is crammed with genuine antiques yet manages to be charmingly family-friendly. Guest rooms are tastefully furnished with Victorian antiques; suites have four-poster beds. You can watch classic movies nightly in the 12-seat cinema, take dinner in the elegant dining room or indulge in meditation walks and other goodies offered by the deluxe spa. **Pros:** amazingly friendly staff; great spa. **Cons:** a bit like living in a museum; basic room rates are quite steep. ⊠ *Shelburne Rd., Co. Kerry* ☎ *064/664–1200* ⊕ *www. parkkenmare.com* ⇨ *35 rooms, 9 suites* ⚃ *In-room: no a/c, Internet. In-hotel: restaurant, bar, golf course, tennis court, pool, spa, some pets allowed* ⊟ *AE, DC, MC, V* ⊘ *Closed Jan 2–Easter* ⵐⵔⵌ *BP*.

$$ ◫ **Sallyport House.** Across the bridge on the way into Kenmare, this 1932 family home has been enlarged to serve as a comfortable B&B. The spotless rooms, all with harbor or mountain views, are furnished with a variety of Victorian and Edwardian antiques. Owner Janey Arthur has placed family heirlooms everywhere; if you're interested in old Irish furniture, ask for a tour. A varied breakfast menu—which might include apples from Sallyport's own orchard—is served in a sunny room overlooking the garden. **Pros:** interesting antiques; impeccable house-keeping; quiet location. **Cons:** no credit cards; short opening season. ⊠ *Glengarriff Rd., Co. Kerry* ☎ *064/664–2066* ⊕ *www.sallyporthouse. com* ⇨ *5 rooms* ⚃ *In-room: no a/c, Internet. In-hotel: no kids under 13* ⊟ *No credit cards* ⊘ *Closed Nov.–Mar.* ⵐⵔⵌ *BP*.

$$ ◫ **Sea Shore Farm.** Mary Patricia O'Sullivan offers a warm but professional welcome to her spacious farmhouse on Kenmare Bay. In fair weather there are views across the sea to the hills on the Beara Peninsula, and although the place is very close to Kenmare, you can walk across her farmland to the deserted seashore and view its plentiful wildlife. You can also walk—or run—the mile into town along a scenic back road. Rooms are furnished with ornate heirlooms and have good-size bathrooms and placid views. Breakfast includes a choice of pancakes, kippers, or smoked salmon as well as the usual fry. **Pros:** quiet rural spot with views of calm estuary; personal attention from owner-manager. **Cons:** on a working cattle farm; a mile out of town; no bar or restaurant. ⊠ *Tubrid, Co. Kerry* ☎☏ *064/664–1270* ⊕ *www.seashorekenmare.com* ⇨ *6 rooms* ⚃ *In-room: no a/c, Internet* ⊟ *MC, V* ⊘ *Closed Nov.–mid-Mar.* ⵐⵔⵌ *BP*.

$$$$ ◫ **Sheen Falls Lodge.** The magnificence of this bright-yellow, slate-roof stone manor is matched only by its setting: 300 secluded acres of lawns, gardens, and forest between Kenmare Bay and the falls of the River Sheen. The public salons are painted in warm, terra-cotta tones, and the mahogany-panel library has more than 1,000 books, mainly on Ireland. Guest rooms—all modern-traditional, in bright yellows and tranquil beiges—have bay or river views. Fishing and clay pigeon shooting are available on the grounds. You can hire one of the hotel's vintage Rolls-Royces for picnics or trips into town. The Cascade Restaurant is renowned for fine dining. **Pros:** fun and informal for the price range; good sports facilities. **Cons:** modern, newly built; driving distance (2 km [1 mi]) from the village; room rates have been cut but are pricey for area. ⊠ *Sheen Falls, Co. Kerry* ☎ *064/664–1600* ⊕ *www.*

Fodor'sChoice
★

6

sheenfallslodge.ie ⟿ *55 rooms, 11 suites* ⚙ *In-room: a/c, safe, refrigerator, Internet, Wi-Fi. In-hotel: 2 restaurants, bars, tennis court, pool, gym, spa* ⊟ *AE, DC, MC, V* ⊘ *Closed Jan.* ⦿ *BP.*

SPORTS AND THE OUTDOORS

☽ **Seafari** (⊠ *Kenmare Pier* ☎ *064/664–2059* ⊕ *www.seafariireland.com*) has fun two-hour ecotours and seal-watching cruises, with complimentary tea and coffee for adults, and lollipops for the kids. Cruises cost €20 per adult, with special family rates. Reservations are essential.

Finnegan's Bike Hire (⊠ *Henry St.* ☎ *064/664–1083*) has sturdy Raleigh bikes for hire. Get a free copy of the Ring of Kerry Cycle Route brochure from the tourist information office, and explore the Ring using quiet country roads. The full trip is a blister-inducing 217 km (135 mi).

SHOPPING

Avoca Handweavers (⊠ *Moll's Gap on N71 road to Killarney* ☎ *064/663–4720*) sells wool clothing and mohair throws and rugs in remarkable palettes and a variety of weaves. **Kenmare Art Gallery** (⊠ *Bridge St.* ☎ *064/664–2999* ⊕ *www.kenmareartgallery.com*) has a good selection of works by contemporary artists, all of whom live locally but show internationally. **Kenmare Bookshop** (⊠ *Shelburne St.* ☎ *064/664–1578*) has a good selection of books of local interest, and all the bestsellers.

Noel & Holland (⊠ *3 Bridge St.* ☎ *064/664–2464*) stocks secondhand books, including Irish-interest and children's titles. At **PFK** (⊠ *18 Henry St.* ☎ *064/664–2590*), Paul Kelly makes striking, modern jewelry in gold and silver. **Sue Designer Knits** (⊠ *20 Henry St.* ☎ *064/664–8986*) sells Irish-made knitwear in lambswool and cashmere. **The White Room** (⊠ *21 Henry St.* ☎ *064/664–0600*) specializes in Irish lace and linen, both new and antique.

SNEEM

27 km (17 mi) southwest of Kenmare on N70.

The pretty village of Sneem (from the Irish for "knot") is settled around an English-style green on the Ardsheelaun River estuary, and its streets are filled with houses washed in different colors. The effect has been somewhat diminished by a cluster of developments. Beside the parish church (signposted "The Way the Fairies Went" from Quill's Sweater Shop; "fairies" are Irish-speak for the mythic wee people) are the "pyramids," as they're known locally. These 12-foot-tall, traditional stone structures with stained-glass insets look as though they've been here forever. In fact, the sculpture park was completed in 1990 to the design of the Kerry-born artist James Scanlon, who has won international awards for his work in stained glass.

Derrynane House, 30 km (18 mi) west of Sneem, makes a great excursion to a beautiful and historic country house, one of the very few on the Ring. This is famed as the home of Daniel O'Connell (1775–1847), "The Liberator," who campaigned for Catholic Emancipation (the granting of full rights of citizenship to Catholics), which became a reality in 1828. The house, with its lovely garden and 320-acre estate, now forms Derrynane National Park. The south and east wings of the house (which

O'Connell himself remodeled) are open to visitors and contain much of the furniture and other items associated with O'Connell. ⊠ *Near Caherdaniel, 30 km (18 mi) west of Sneem off N70* ☎ *066/947–5113* ⊕ *www. heritageireland.com* ☏ *€3* ⊘ *Nov.–Mar., weekends 1–5; Apr. and Oct., Tues.–Sun. 1–5; May–Sept., Mon.–Sat. 9–6, Sun. 11–7.*

The approximately 2,500-year-old, stone **Staigue Fort,** signposted 4 km (2 mi) inland at Castlecove, is almost circular and about 75 feet in diameter with a single south-side entrance. From the Iron Age (from 500 BC to the 5th century AD) and early Christian times (6th century AD), such "forts" were, in fact, the fortified homesteads for several families of one clan and their cattle. The walls at Staigue Fort are almost 13 feet wide at the base and 7 feet wide at the top; they still stand 18 feet high on the north and west sides. Within them, stairs lead to narrow platforms on which the lookouts stood. (Private land must be crossed to reach the fort, and a "compensation for trespass" of €1 is often requested by the landowner.)

WHERE TO STAY

$$$

⟳

Fodor'sChoice

★

🏨 **Parknasilla Resort.** For over a century Parknasilla, a towering, gray-stone mansion set on a stunningly beautiful inlet of the Kenmare estuary, has been synonymous with old-style resort luxury, attracting guests like George Bernard Shaw, Princess Grace, and Charles de Gaulle. In 2005 to 2009, the grand old house underwent a thorough refit to bring it into the 21st century. You can still sip your sherry beside an open fire in the Doolittle Bar and dine in the stately Pygmalion Restaurant, but you can also enjoy one of two outdoor Jacuzzis, or the sea view from the indoor infinity pool. Villas and apartment suites now stud the sylvan 500-acre grounds. Public rooms are done in an endearingly homey mix-and-match style, with large ("superior") bedrooms beautifully coordinated with fabulous inlaid antique furniture. Suites are ballroom-size, while "standard" rooms are also spacious, and all enjoy peaceful vistas. **Pros:** excellent sports facilities and spa; sheltered coastal location; great family destination. **Cons:** grounds and hotel big enough to get lost in; hugely popular with Irish families in July and August. ⊠ *Co. Kerry* ☎ *064/664–5122* ⊕ *www.parknasillahotel.ie* ⟿ *92 rooms* ⟳ *In-room: no a/c, refrigerator (some), Internet, Wi-Fi (some). In-hotel: restaurant, room service, bar, golf course, tennis court, pool, gym, spa* ⊟ *AE, DC, MC, V* ⊘ *Closed Jan.–Mar.* ⦿*BP.*

$$

🏨 **Sneem Hotel.** Meet the locals and enjoy spacious accommodation at this waterfront hotel and apartment complex opened in 2007. Goldens Cove is a rocky, sheltered spot, with views of distant mountains. The large stone portico on the long, curving three-story building leads to an airy lobby, decorated with original Irish art and cushy sofas. Beyond is a huge double-height bar and separate restaurant, both with large verandas overlooking the sea. It's worth paying a small premium for a sea-facing room with balcony to enjoy the setting sun. All rooms are decorated in tones of beige, brightened by touches of red, with light-wood furniture and black leather armchairs. **Pros:** large, modern rooms; friendly service. **Cons:** some new development detracts from the views; large bar and restaurant can be a bit eerie when not busy. ⊠ *Goldens Cove, Co. Kerry* ☎ *064/667–5100* ⊕ *www.sneemhotel.com* ⟿ *69 rooms, 25 apartments* ⟳ *In-room: a/c, safe, Internet. In-hotel: restaurant, room service, bar, gym, Wi-Fi hotspot* ⊟ *MC, V.*

Continued on page 350

6

GETTING OUTSIDE
THE RING OF KERRY

When you travel Ireland's most popular scenic route, leaving your car behind makes all the difference. Here's how to get far from the madding crowd.

The Ring of Kerry is one of Europe's great drives. The common wisdom, though, is that it suffers from its own popularity: tour buses dominate the road from sunup to sundown. There's more than a grain of truth to this reputation, but that doesn't mean you should scratch the Ring from your itinerary. Instead, plan to turn off the main road and get out of your car. You'll make a blissful

discovery: the Iveragh Peninsula—one of the most beautiful locations in all of Ireland—remains largely unspoiled. It's full of fabulous places to hike, bike, and boat—and best of all, there are views the tour-bus passengers can only dream of.

Top, Elevated coastal view from the Ring of Kerry;
Below left, on horseback in Rossbeigh Strand, Kerry;
Below right, cycling around the Ring

AROUND THE RING BY FOOT AND BY BIKE

HIKING THE RING

Option number one for getting outdoors around the Ring of Kerry is to go by foot. There are appealing walking options for every degree of fitness and experience, from gentle, paved paths to an ascent up Ireland's tallest mountain.

THE KERRY WAY

The main hiking route across the peninsula is the Kerry Way, a spectacular 133-mile footpath that's easily broken down into day-trip-size segments. The path winds from **Killarney** through the foothills of the **MacGillicuddy's Reeks** and the **Black Valley** to Glencar and **Glen-**beigh, from where it parallels the Ring through **Cahirciveen, Waterville, Caherdaniel,** and **Sneem,** before ending in **Kenmare.** The route, indicated by way markers, follows grassy old paths situated at higher elevations than the Ring—meaning better, and more tranquil, views. Hiking the entire Kerry Way can take from 10 to 12 days. Numerous outfitters organize both guided and unguided tours. For a great day trip, hike the 10 km (6 mi) section from **Waterville** to **Caherdaniel,** which has great views of small islands and rocky coves. In the **Glencar** area near

HIKING RESOURCES

A copy of the **Kerry Way Map Guide,** available from Cork Kerry Tourism, is invaluable. For organized tours of the Way, try **Activity Ireland,** based in Caherdaniel (☎ 66/9475277 ⊕ www.activity-ireland.com). Climbers should check out the website of the **Mountaineering Council of Ireland,** ⊕ www.mountaineering.ie.

Blackstones Bridge, a series of shorter signposted walks, from 3 km (2 mi) upward, put you in the shadow of **Carrauntuohill,** Ireland's highest mountain.

TAKING IT EASY: THREE GENTLE STROLLS

MUCKROSS PARK in Killarney is a car-free zone with four signposted nature trails. Try the 4 km (2½ mi) Arthur Young's Walk through old yew and oak woods frequented by sika deer. You can also take an open boat from Ross Castle to the head of the **Upper Lake,** then walk back along the lakeside to Muckross House—about 10 km (6 mi).

The trails in **DERRYNANE NATIONAL PARK,** a 320-acre estate, run through mature woodland, bordering on rocky outcrops that lead to wide sandy beaches and dunes. At low tide, you can walk to **Abbey Island** offshore.

Even in high summer, **VALENTIA ISLAND** is a peaceful spot for walking, with little traffic. Walk the road from **Knightstown** through the subtropical vegetation of the Knight of Kerry's estate, to the historic **Slate Quarry** (3 km/2 mi), 900 ft above the sea, with views of the Skelligs offshore.

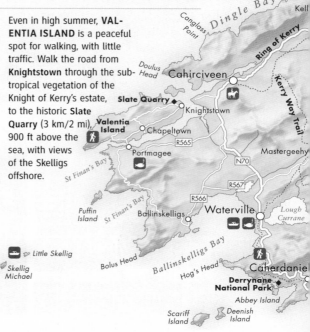

CYCLING THE RING

The Ring of Kerry Cycle Route follows the main road for about a third of its 134 miles, but the rest is on deserted roads, including a long, scenic loop through Ballinskelligs, Portmagee, and Valentia Island. There are significant climbs and strong winds along the way, so good fitness is a prerequisite.

EASY RIDES

From **Killarney,** the N71 road past **Muckross Park** and the **Upper Lake** takes you through ancient woodlands to **Ladies' View** (about 12 km/7.5 mi).

From here you have one of the area's best panoramas, with the sparkling blue lakes backed by purple mountains. The scene will be in front of you as you make the ride back.

From **Glenbeigh,** escape the traffic by riding inland to peaceful **Caragh Lake** through a bog and mountain landscape that's rich in wildlife. You might spot a herd of long-bearded wild goats, or a peregrine falcon hovering above its prey. The full circuit of the lake, returning to Glenbeigh, is about 35 km (22 mi).

BIKING RESOURCES

You can rent bikes and get route information at **O'Sullivan's Cycles** (☎ 064/31282) in Killarney. Along the Ring at Glenbeigh, bikes are for rent at **Glenross Caravan & Camping Park** (☎ 066/976-8451 ⊕ www.killarney camping.com/glenross.html).

For an organized tour, contact **Irish Cycling Safaris** (⊕ www.cyclingsafaris.com), which has trips along quiet back roads with local guides and support vans to carry luggage.

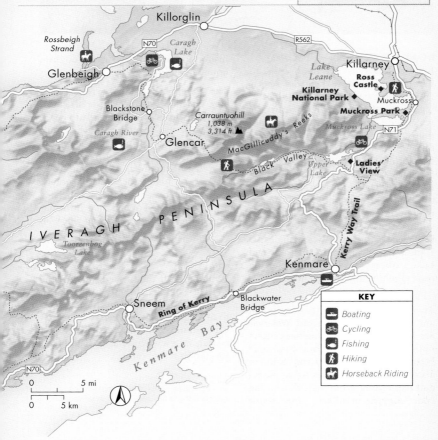

KEY	
🛶	*Boating*
🚲	*Cycling*
🎣	*Fishing*
🚶	*Hiking*
🐎	*Horseback Riding*

TESTING THE WATERS

BOATING AROUND THE RING . . .

Kenmare Bay is the best spot for boating expeditions. **Kenmare Angling** (🌐 www.kenmareanglingandisghtseeing.com) offers customized tours, on which you can see castles, seals, dolphins, and salmon farms. Boats can take up to 10 people, and cost €300 for a full day, €200 for a half day. **Seafari** (🌐 www.seafariireland.com) at Kenmare Pier has a two-hour econature and seal watching cruise and also is an outfitter for kayaking, sailing, and wind-surfing. The **Cappanalea Outdoor Education Centre** (🌐 www.cappanalea.ie), 7 mi west of Killorglin, near Caragh Lake, offers windsurfing, canoeing, rock climbing and guided hikes.

. . . AND FISHING

There's good fishing here, both inland and at sea. **Portmagee** and **Waterville** are the main deepsea angling centers; outings are generally from small open boats carrying up to 10 rods and run about €30 per person per day. Wreck and reef fishing promises pollock, ling, cod, conger, monkfish, and shark. Inshore there are bass, turbot, dogfish, flounder, and tope.

The **Caragh Lake** and the rivers **Laune, Inny, Roughty,** and **Caragh** are all excellent for wild salmon—and all are beautiful wilderness locations. **Lough Currane** near Waterville is one of the great sea trout fisheries. The season runs from March to September, and fishing permits are available locally from hotels. You'll find tackle shops in Killarney and Waterville. For detailed information before you go, check out the Web site of the South Western Regional Fisheries Board (🌐 www.swrfb.com).

. . . AND SWIMMING

Swimming off the beaches around the coast is confined to July and August, when the water temperatures reach 55 to 60 degrees. There are dive centers at Caherdaniel, Kenmare, and Valentia Island; 🌐 www.scuba.ie is a good information resource.

Top left, fishing on the bay; Right, trout fishing; Bottom left, fishing boats in the Dingle harbor

THE TWIN PEAKS OF YOUR TRIP

Above and below left, ancient monastic site on Skellig Michael with Little Skellig in the background.

The distinctive conical **Skellig Rocks** hover offshore at the western end of the Iveragh Peninsula, surrounded by swirling blue sea. They're a haunting presence that seems to follow along as you travel the mainland from Valentia to Waterville and Caherdaniel.

A venture out to the twin peaks of **Skellig Michael** (shown above, also known as Great Skellig) is a truly awesome experience. Boats leave from Waterville, Ballinskelligs, and Portmagee for a white-knuckle ride lasting about 45 minutes. Along the way you pass Michael's companion, **Little Skellig,** where people aren't allowed but gannets flourish.

Skellig Michael rises steeply for 700 feet; you reach the summit by climbing 600 steps cut into the rockface. Once there, you find, amazingly, the remains of a monastery, occupied by hermit monks from the 7th to 12th century.

Looking back to the mainland and out at the wild expanse of open sea, you get an inkling of the monks' isolation from all things worldly. A visit to Skellig Michael may not be the most comfortable outing of you trip, but it will probably be the most memorable.

BIRDS OF THE SKELLIGS

The Ring of Kerry is one of the best places in Europe for observing seabirds, and the Skelligs are a particular treasure for birders. The gannet, with a wing span of 2 yards, is Ireland's largest seabird and up to 22,000 nesting pairs reside on Little Skellig, where they dive for food from heights of up to 120 feet.

If you are lucky enough to get out to Skellig Michael in May, you'll be warned to watch out for comical-looking **puffins** (below) nesting in burrows underfoot.

Below, two puffins standing on Skellig rocks

EQUITREKKING THE RING

Horses hold a special place in the hearts of the Irish. Horsemanship and breeding are sources of national pride—it's an oft-quoted fact that the Duke of Wellington rode an Irish horse at the Battle of Waterloo, while Napoleon's horse came from County Wexford. All over the country you'll find horses grazing in the fields, being ridden down country lanes, and galloping along beaches. If you share the Irish passion for all things equine, there's no better way to see the Ring than from the back of a horse.

You can gallop along the 3 mile stretch of **Rossbeigh Strand,** or take a trek around quiet country roads, on a horse from **Burke's Horse Trekking Center** in Glenbeigh (☎ 087/237–9110). They've been in the business for years and use mainly quiet-colored cobs (black and white all-rounders). Hats and boots are included in the price, which ranges from €20 to €30.

The six-day **Reeks Trail** riding led by **Killarney Riding Stables** (☎ 064/883–1686 ⊕ www.killarney-reeks-trail.com) takes you through the mountains and woodland of MacGillicuddy's Reeks. The stables also book half- and full-day rides.

Near **Cahirciveen,** the **Final Furlong Farmhouse B & B** has a riding stable and a gorgeous location overlooking the sea. Ride as little or as much as you like during your stay, in small groups supervised by members of the proprietors, the O'Sullivan family. Contact Kathleen O'Sullivan (☎ 066/947–3300 ⊕ www.thefinalfurlong.com.)

Top: Horse racing in Rossbeigh Strand; Above left, Connemara Pony; Above right, Lakes of Killarney; Right, Bray Head, Valentia Island

WEATHER, FLORA, AND TOURING TIPS

Swimming at the Ring

THANKS TO
THE GULF STREAM . . .

The warm waters flowing from the Gulf of Mexico across the Atlantic, known as the Gulf Stream, give Ireland a mild climate, and the effects are particularly felt along the Ring of Kerry. The area is frost-free year round, with temperatures averaging 45 degrees Fahrenheit in winter and 60 in summer. But rain is a constant threat, brought in from the Atlantic by the prevailing southwesterly winds. Console yourself with this though: it may be wet, but it is never freezing.

Don't bother touring the Ring in heavy sea mist: you won't see a thing. But don't let other forms of rain deter you. Part of the attraction of the Ring is the interplay of light with sea, mountain, and distant horizons. Rain often enhances the view, and can give delightful effects. The sun is often shining before the rain has finished, so rainbows abound. Any weather, good or bad, seldom lasts more than half a day: if it's wet in the morning, it will probably be sunny in the afternoon, and vice versa.

SOCK IT TO ME

Bring a rain jacket and a warm fleece or sweater: sea winds can be chilly. Above all, wear sensible footwear. If you're venturing off-road, even in summer, you will be glad of strong, waterproof shoes. And bring plenty of socks. There's nothing more miserable than wet feet!

LAND OF EXOTIC PALMS

With no frost, Killarney and the Iveragh Peninsula are havens for subtropical vegetation. The New Zealand fern tree and the banana tree thrive. The "palm trees" you see here are usually yuccas that have been allowed to grow tall. Flax also grows to enormous size, and is often used as a shelter belt. The leaves of the gunnera can grow to the size of a compact car—look for them in Muckross Park. The lakes of Killarney are surrounded by luxuriant woods of oak, arbutus, birch, holly and mountain ash, with undergrowth of ferns, saxifrages, and mosses. Rhododendron and azaleas thrive on pockets of acid soil, and are at their best from mid-April to May.

Valentia Island

THE ICE AGE COMETH, AND GOETH

Some 60 million years ago, the great rias, or drowned rivers, that became the bays of Bantry, Kenmare, and Dingle were formed. The sea penetrated far inland, forming the peninsulas of Beara, Iveragh, and Dingle. A million years ago, these lands were gripped by the Ice Age. When the ice receded, some 10,000 years ago, it left corries (or glacial hollows) gouged out of the mountains, great rocks scattered on the landscape (giving rise to legends of giants throwing stones), and outcrops of ice-smoothed sandstone.

6

IN FOCUS GETTING OUTSIDE: THE RING OF KERRY

WATERVILLE

35 km (22 mi) west of Sneem.

Visitor Information Waterville Tourist Office (✉ *Town Center, Co. Kerry* ☎ *066/947–4646* ☾ *Open May–Oct. only*).

Waterville is famous for its sportfishing, its 18-hole championship golf course (adopted as a warm-up spot for the British Open by Tiger Woods), and for the fact that Charlie Chaplin and Charles de Gaulle spent summers here. Besides all that, the village, like many others on the Ring of Kerry, has a few restaurants and pubs, but little else. There's excellent salmon and trout fishing at nearby Lough Currane. Nearby Coomakesta Pass and Hog's Head offer challenging hikes with stunning summit views as your rewards.

Outside Waterville and 1 km (½ mi) before Ballinskelligs, an Irish-speaking fishing village, is the **Cill Rialaig,** an artistic retreat. Here, a cluster of derelict stone cottages in a deserted village were given new life as artists' studios. Cill Rialaig attracts both Irish and international artists for residencies, and their work, and ceramics, metalwork, jewelry, and other handmade crafts are exhibited and sold at the attractively designed, beehive-shaped store. There's also a coffee shop. ✉ *R566* ☎ *066/947–9277* 🎫 *Free* ☾ *Daily 11–5.*

WHERE TO STAY

$$ 🛏 **Butler Arms.** Charlie Chaplin loved it here. The rambling building—
★ with a white, castellated corner tower—is a familiar landmark on the Ring. It has been in the same family for four generations, and the clientele returns year after year for the excellent fishing and golf facilities nearby and the proximity of long, sandy, windswept beaches. Many regulars like the smallish rooms in the old part of the hotel, which are neither smart nor chic. More spacious rooms, with streamlined decor and sensational sea views, can be had in a newer wing. Everyone enjoys the rambling old lounges with open turf fires. **Pros:** charming old-world hotel, near beaches and village. **Cons:** village mainly a golfing and fishing center, dominated by all-male groups; limited nightlife, shopping, dining. ✉ *Co. Kerry* ☎ *066/947–4144* ⊕ *www.butlerarms.com* ⟿ *28 rooms, 12 suites* ⚒ *In-room: no a/c. In-hotel: restaurant, tennis court, gym, Wi-Fi hotspot* ▭ *AE, MC, V* ☾ *Closed Nov.–Mar.* ℟*BP.*

$ 🛏 **Lakelands Farm Guesthouse.** Amid rocky hills, this spacious, Dutch-gable modern house enjoys a stunning location about a mile off the Ring. Set on the shore of Lough Currane (boats for hire), Lakelands is popular with game anglers, golfers, and scenery-lovers. Exhale deeply thanks to the lounge's huge squashy leather armchairs, real turf fire, and picture windows. The exceptionally large bedrooms have great views, and some have balconies and Jacuzzis. Host Frank Donnelly is an angling/shooting guide, and his wife Ann will advise on local dining. Hikers: take note that the Kerry Way is 2 mi up the road. **Pros:** good value; great scenery; huge bedrooms. **Cons:** nearly 2 mi outside village; won't win any style kudos. ✉ *Lake Road (look for signpost on the N70 on the south side of the village)* ☎ *066/947–4303* ⊕ *www.lakelandshouse.com* ⟿ *12 rooms* ⚒ *In-room: no a/c. In-hotel: Wi-Fi hotspot* ▭ *MC, V* ☾ *Closed Oct., Feb., and Mar.*

NIGHTLIFE AND THE ARTS

Head to the **Inny Tavern** (✉ *Inny Bridge* ☎ *066/947–4512*) for live Irish music.

SPORTS AND THE OUTDOORS

Famously adopted by Tiger Woods to practice his swings for the British Open, the **Waterville Golf Links** (✉ *Co. Kerry* ☎ *066/947–4102*), an 18-hole course, remains one of the toughest and most scenic in Ireland or Britain.

THE SKELLIGS

Fodor's Choice *Islands off the coastal town of Portmagee, 21 km (13 mi) northwest*
★ *of Waterville.*

In the far northwestern corner of the Ring of Kerry, across Portmagee Channel, lies **Valentia Island,** which is reachable by a bridge erected in 1971. Visible from Valentia, and on a clear day from other points along the coast, are the **Skelligs,** one of the most spectacular sights in Ireland. Sculpted as if by the hand of God, the islands of **Little Skellig, Great Skellig,** and the **Washerwoman's Rock** are distinctively cone-shaped, surrounded by blue swirling seas. The largest island, the Great Skellig, or Skellig Michael, distinguished by its twin peaks, rises 700 feet from the Atlantic. It has the remains of a settlement of early Christian monks, reached by climbing 600 increasingly precipitous steps. In spite of a thousand years of battering by Atlantic storms, the church, oratory, and beehive-shaped living cells are surprisingly well preserved.

Visitor Information Skelligs Tourist Office (✉ *Valentia Island, Co. Kerry* ☎ *066/947–6306* ⊕ *www.corkkerry.ie*).

EXPLORING

To visit the Skelligs, you can take a half-day trip in an open boat—perfect for adventurers who pack plenty of Dramamine. The entire visit takes three to four hours, with 1½ hours on the Skellig Michael, where visitors are supervised by resident guides, and the remaining time in transit (the duration varies depending on the weather and tides). During the journey you'll pass Little Skellig, the breeding ground of more than 22,000 pairs of gannets. Puffin Island, to the north, has a large population of shearwaters and storm petrel. Puffins nest in sand burrows on the Great Skellig in the month of May. But the masterpiece is the phenomenal Skellig Michael, home to that amazing 7th- to 12th-century village of monastic beehive dwellings, and offering vertigo-inducing views. Note that the waters are choppy at the best of times, and trips are made when the weather permits. Even in fine weather, it can be a rough, white-knuckle ride (at least 45 minutes) as you cross the swell of the open sea, and it's not suitable for small children. One worthy outfitter is **Sea Quest** (✉ *Valentia Island* ☎ *066/947–6214* 💶 *€40* ⊕ *www.skelligsrock.com* ☉ *Cruises May–Aug., daily at 10 AM, weather permitting*).

Skellig Experience (✉ *Valentia Island* ☎ *066/947–6306* ⊕ *www. skelligexperience.com* 💶 *€5, cruise €27.50* ☉ *Mar.–June and Sept., daily 9:30–5; July and Aug., daily 9:30–7; Oct. and Nov., daily 10–6*), across the bridge to Valentia Island, offers an alternative for the less adventurous traveler. This center contains exhibits on local birdlife, the history of the lighthouse and keepers, and the life and work of the early Christian monks. There's also a 15-minute audiovisual show that allows you to "tour" the Skelligs without leaving dry land. The center also offers a 90-minute non-landing cruise around the islands. But if you're up for it, don't miss the boat ride from Portmagee *(see Sea Quest, above)* that lets you land on the rocks; Skellig Michael is something you won't soon forget.

WHERE TO EAT AND STAY

$ ✕ **Bridge Bar.** Hungry mariners make a beeline for this simple bar on the
IRISH windswept waterfront of the tiny fishing village of Portmagee. Overlook-
★ ing the channel between the mainland and Valentia Island, its dramatic location has led the Bridge to being featured in ads as "the quintessential Irish pub." While not overly historic in decor, the low-beam interior—fitted out with red walls, rustic pine, and an open fire—is a sweet place to enjoy the renowned seafood chowder, or opt for daily specials like grilled haddock with lemon butter or steamed mussels with garlic. In July and August the pretty, adjoining Moorings restaurant serves a more ambitious menu ($$) most evenings between May and October: call to confirm. There are also 14 en-suite rooms overhead ($) and an ace craft shop next door. ⊠ *Portmagee* ☎ *066/947–7108* ⊕ *www.moorings. ie* ⊟ *MC, V* ⊘ *Closed Mon., and Dec. 20–mid-Jan.*

$ ⊡ **Shealane Country House.** Cows graze in the adjoining field, and the
★ breakfast room at this easily reached island retreat overlooks the ocean and the mainland hills. The large, modern detached house is on Valentia Island, beside the bridge to the mainland. The Skellig Experience Visitor Centre is across the road, and a brisk five-minute walk across the bridge leads you to Portmagee and should sharpen your appetite for hearty bar food. Host Mary Lane is native to the area and can organize boat trips to the Skelligs, as well as fishing, horseback riding, and golf excursions. Her home is a delight, with bright airy rooms, polished pine floors, and large traditional wooden windows framing the peaceful views guests often dream about long after leaving. **Pros:** friendly welcome from local family; quiet rural location. **Cons:** outside the village; rooms book far in advance for July and August. ⊠ *Corha-Mor, Valentia Island* ☎ *066/947–6354* ⊕ *www.valentiaskelligs.com* ⇆ *5 rooms* ⊘ *In-room: no a/c, no phone, no TV. In-hotel: Internet terminal* ⊘ *Closed Nov.–Feb.* ⫿○⫿ *BP.*

CAHIRCIVEEN

18 km (11 mi) north of Waterville on N70.

Visitor Information Cahirciveen Tourist Office (⊠ *Church St., Co. Kerry* ☎ *066/947–2589* ⊕ *www.corkkerry.ie* ⊘ *May–Oct. only*).

Cahirciveen (pronounced cah-her-sigh-*veen*), at the foot of Bentee Mountain, is the gateway to the western side of the Ring of Kerry and the main market town for southern Kerry. Following the tradition in this part of the world, the modest, terraced houses are each painted in different colors (sometimes two or three)—the brighter the better. Head to Main Street for pubs that are perfect for downing a pint; they have live music in summer.

The **O'Connell Memorial Church**, a large, elaborate, neo-Gothic structure that dominates the main street, was built in 1888 of Newry granite and black limestone to honor the local hero Daniel O'Connell. It's the only church in Ireland named after a layman.

The **Old Barracks Heritage Centre** is in the converted former barracks of the Royal Irish Constabulary, an imposing, castle-like structure built after the Fenian Rising of 1867 to suppress further revolts. The center has well-designed displays depicting scenes from times of famine, the life of Daniel O'Connell, and the restoration of this fine building from a blackened ruin. ✉ *Barracks* ☎ *066/947–2777* 🎫 *€4* ⏲ *June–Sept., Mon.–Sat. 10–5:30, Sun. 2–5:30; Mar.–May and Oct., weekdays 9:30–5:30.*

GLENBEIGH

27 km (17 mi) northeast of Cahirciveen on N70.

The road from Cahirciveen to Glenbeigh is one of the Ring's highlights. To the north is Dingle Bay and the jagged peaks of the Dingle Peninsula, which will, in all probability, be shrouded in mist. If they aren't, the gods have indeed blessed your journey. The road runs close to the water here, and beyond the small village of Kells it climbs high above the bay, hugging the steep side of Drung Hill before descending to Glenbeigh. Note how different the stark character of this stretch of the Ring is from the gentle, woody Kenmare Bay side.

On a boggy plateau by the sea, the block-long town of Glenbeigh is a popular holiday base—there's excellent hiking in the Glenbeigh Horseshoe, as the surrounding mountains are known, and exceptionally good trout fishing in Lough Coomasaharn. The area south of Glenbeigh and west of Carrantouhill Mountain, around the shores of the Caragh River and the village of Glencar, is known as the Kerry Highlands. The scenery is wild and rough but strangely appealing. A series of circular walks have been signposted, and parts of the Kerry Way pass through here. The area attracts serious climbers who intend to scale Carrantouhill, Ireland's highest peak (3,408 feet).

Worth a quick look, the **Kerry Bog Village Museum** is a cluster of reconstructed, fully furnished cottages that vividly portray the daily life of the region's working class in the early 1800s. The adjacent pub is famous for its Irish coffee. ✉ *Beside Red Fox Bar* ☎ *066/976–9184* 🌐 *www.kerrybogvillage.ie* 🎫 *€5* ⏲ *Mar.–Nov., daily 8:30–7; Jan. and Feb. by request.*

A signpost to the right outside Glenbeigh points to **Caragh Lake,** a tempting excursion south to a beautiful expanse of water set among gorse- and heather-covered hills and majestic mountains. The road hugs the shoreline much of the way.

North of Glenbeigh, the beach at **Rossbeigh** consists of about 3 km (2 mi) of soft, sandy coast backed by high dunes. It faces Inch Strand, a similar formation across the water on the Dingle Peninsula.

WHERE TO STAY

$$$
Fodor's Choice
★
🛏 **Carrig Country House.** A rambling two-story Victorian house covered in flowering creepers and set on 4 acres of lush gardens along a secluded lakeshore, this comes pretty close to most people's dream rural retreat. The atmosphere is more grand country house than hotel, with turf fires in the main salons to encourage guests to linger in armchairs. Guest rooms are lavishly decorated with period antiques ranging from cozy cottage-style to ornate Victorian spoon-back chairs. As well as enjoying views over the gardens, the lake, and surrounding mountains, you can also *hear* the lake water lapping the shore from most rooms. Boating and fishing are available. Hosts Frank and Mary Slattery were restaurateurs and their kitchen offers a truly tempting menu (no lunch served) in their conservatory extension. **Pros:** lovely secluded location; real country-house atmosphere; affable owner-managers. **Cons:** tricky drive from Killorglin (see Web site for directions). ✉ *Caragh Lake, Killorglin, Co. Kerry* ☎ *066/976–9100* ⊕ *www.carrighouse.com* �>️ *17 rooms* ⏚ *In-room: no a/c, no TV. In-hotel: restaurant, bar, Internet terminal* ▭ *MC, V* ☉ *Closed Dec.–Feb.* ❜◯❜*BP.*

KILLORGLIN

6

14 km (9 mi) east of Glenbeigh, 22 km (14 mi) west of Killarney.

Visitor Information Killorglin Tourist Office (✉ *Iveragh Rd., Co. Kerry* ☎ *066/976–1451*).

Killorglin is on top of a hill beside the River Laune. Walk up to the "top of the town" to discover a new Continental-style piazza, with outdoor tables in good weather. (This is also the location of the tourist information office.)

Killorglin is famed as the scene of the Puck Fair, three days of merrymaking during the second weekend in August. A large billy goat with beribboned horns, installed on a high pedestal, presides over the fair. The origins of the tradition of King Puck are lost in time. Though some horse, sheep, and cattle dealing still occurs at the fair, the main attractions these days are free outdoor concerts and extended drinking hours. The crowd is predominantly young and invariably noisy, so avoid Killorglin at fair time if you've come for peace and quiet. On the other hand, if you intend to join in the festivities, be sure to book accommodations well in advance.

WHERE TO EAT

$$
IRISH
✕ **Bianconi.** This hostelry opened in the 19th century, before the days of railways, as the coaching inn for the national network of horse-drawn coaches known as Bianconis, after the Italian who set up the business. Today it's a busy pub, with guest rooms as well, at the riverside crossroads at the entrance to town. Its dark-wood Victorian interior has a rambling barroom with a tile floor, leatherette banquettes, and ancient stuffed animals above the booths. The menu includes such favorites as Dingle Bay prawns, local oak-smoked salmon, a steaming mussel pot in garlic sauce, and braised shank of Kerry lamb. Even though it's a pub,

advance booking is advisable in summer and on weekends. ⊠ *Lower Bridge St.* ☎ *066/976–1146* ▭ *AE, MC, V* ⊗ *Closed Sun.*

$$$

IRISH

✕ **Nick's Seafood and Steak.** Owner Nick Foley comes from the family that established Killarney's famous eatery, Foley's, and has made a name for himself as a chef. The restaurant consists of two old stone town houses; one has a bar–dining room with a piano, and the other contains the main dining area, where tables are set with double damask white linens and an array of tall glasses. Booking is advisable, as regular customers travel from far and near. The dark-wood furniture, wine bottles stacked on a high shelf around the wall, and piano music drifting in from the bar, make for pleasant surroundings at dinner. Foley is known for his generous portions, his wide choice of local seafood—grilled mussels, lobster thermidor—and his steaks. ⊠ *Lower Bridge St.* ☎ *066/976–1219* ▭ *MC, V* ⊗ *Closed Nov., and Mon. and Tues. Dec.–Easter.*

IN AND AROUND KILLARNEY

One of Southwest Ireland's most attractive locales, Killarney is also the most heavily visited town in the region (its proximity to the Ring of Kerry and to Shannon Airport helps to ensure this). Light rain is typical of the area, but because of the topography, it seldom lasts long. And the clouds' approach over the lakes and the subsequent showers can actually add to the scenery. The rain is often followed within minutes by brilliant sunshine and, yes, even a rainbow.

KILLARNEY AND ENVIRONS

87 km (54 mi) west of Cork City on N22, 19 km (12 mi) southeast of Killorglin, 24 km (15 mi) north of Glengarriff.

Commercialized Killarney feels like a movie set. Whether or not you find the town to be a Celtic theme park remains to be seen but no one can question its main role as gateway to the natural beauties found in Killarney National Park and the Ring of Kerry. As for the town itself, you may want to limit time spent there if discos, Irish cabarets, and singing pubs—the last of a local specialty with a strong Irish-American flavor—aren't your thing. The nightlife is at its liveliest from May to September; the Irish and Europeans pack the town in July and August. Peak season for Americans follows in September and October. At other times, particularly from November to mid-March, when many of the hotels are closed, the town is quiet to the point of being eerie. Given the choice, go to Killarney in April, May, or early October.

GETTING HERE AND AROUND

BUS TRAVEL

There are 12 Expressway (Bus Éireann) buses daily to Killarney Bus Station on East Avenue Road from Shannon Airport via Limerick (4 hours 40 minutes, €23 round-trip). From Dublin the Express bus to Killarney takes 6 hours (€32 round-trip).

JAUNTING CARS AND SIGHTSEEING

There is no local bus service in Killarney Town; the traditional way to get around, especially if you plan to visit the car-free Muckross Park, is to hire one of the famous ponies and traps, known as a "jaunting car." Offering jaunting, bus, and boat tours, the leading firm is Tangney

A Romantic Past

Such great writers as Sir Walter Scott and William Thackeray struggled to find the superlatives to describe Killarney's heather-clad peaks, subtropical vegetation, and deep-blue waters dotted with wooded isles. Indeed, the lakes and the mountains have left a lasting impression on a long stream of people, beginning in the 18th century with the English travelers Arthur Young and Bishop Berkeley.

Visitors in search of the natural beauty so beloved by the Romantic movement began to flock to the Southwest. By the mid-19th century, Killarney's scenery was considered as exhilarating as anything in Switzerland. The influx of affluent visitors that followed the 1854 arrival of the railway transformed the lives of Kerry's impoverished natives and set in motion the commercialization that continues today.

Tours. An hour's "jaunt" for four people costs about €40. Jaunting cars can be prebooked, or hired at the junction of Main Street and East Avenue. From mid-March to September you can view the National Park by taking a water-coach cruise on the Lily of Killarney boat from Ross Castle (1 hour, €10); book at the Killarney Tourist Office. *For bicycle hire, see Sports and the Outdoors below (book in advance in July and August).*

TRAIN TRAVEL Many Irish Rail trains head to Killarney Rail Station from Heuston Station Dublin, with Killarney a hub on the popular Tralee line. The journey takes 3 hours 20 minutes (€68.50 round-trip). There are nine trains a day from Dublin to Killarney. Five trains a day leave Cork for Killarney (2 hours 20 minutes, €35 round-trip). Book online (and off-peak) for great savings on ticket prices.

ESSENTIALS

Transportation Contacts Killarney Bus and Train Station (✉ *East Ave. Rd.* ☎ *064/663–0011; 064/663–1067 for trains*). **Tangney Tours** (✉ *Kinvara House, Muckross Rd., Killarney, Co. Kerry* ☎ *064/663–3358 or 087/253–2770* ⊕ *www.vacationkillarney.com/Killarney_jaunting_car_tours.htm*).

Visitor Information Killarney Tourist Office (✉ *Aras Fáilte, Beech Rd., Co. Kerry* ☎ *064/663–1633* ⊕ *www.killarney.ie*).

EXPLORING

With its glacial landscape enhanced by subtropical vegetation, the views found in and around Killarney are legendary. Yes, the lakes really are sapphire-blue (at least when the sun is out), and seen from a distance, the MacGillicuddy's Reeks really are purple. Add a scattering of large gray rocks (large, as in big as a car), and acres of lush green flowering shrubs and trees, and you're starting to get the picture.

Much of the area is part of **Killarney National Park** (⊕ *www.heritageireland. ie*), which has more than 24,000 acres and is famous for such native habitats and species as oak holly woods, yew woods, and red deer; the park itself has no hours or admission. With a **National Park Visitor Centre** found at Muckross House, the park has signposted self-guiding trails that thread these habitats. At the park's heart is Muckross Park (or Demesne);

the entrance to the Demesne area is 4 km (2½ mi) from Killarney on N71. Cars aren't allowed in Muckross Park; you can either walk, rent a bicycle, or take a traditional jaunting car—that is, a pony and a cart.

The air here smells of damp woods and heather moors. The red fruits of the Mediterranean strawberry tree (*Arbutus unedo*) are at their peak in October and November, which is also about the time when the bracken turns rust color, contrasting with the evergreens. In late April and early May, the purple flowers of the rhododendron *ponticum* put on a spectacular display.

Aghadoe (✉ *5 km [3 mi] west of Killarney on R562 [Beaufort–Killorglin Rd.]*) is an outstanding place to get a feel for what Killarney is all about: lake and mountain scenery. Stand beside Aghadoe's 12th-century ruined church and round tower, and watch the shadows creep gloriously across Lower Lake, with Innisfallen Island in the distance and the Gap of Dunloe to the west.

☾ You reach **Torc Waterfall** (✉ *Killarney National Park, Muckross Rd. [N71], 8 km [5 mi] south of Killarney*) by a footpath that begins in the parking lot outside the gates of the Muckross Park. After your first view of the roaring cascade, which will appear after about a 10 minutes' walk, it's worth the climb up a long flight of stone steps to the second, less-frequented clearing.

★ **Muckross House,** the famous 19th-century, Elizabethan-style manor, now
☾ houses the Kerry Folklife Centre, where bookbinders, potters, and weavers demonstrate their crafts. Upstairs, elegantly furnished rooms portray the lifestyle of the landed gentry in the 1800s; downstairs in the basement you can experience the conditions of servants employed in the house. Next door you'll find the Killarney National Park Visitor Centre. The informal grounds are noted for their rhododendrons and azaleas, the water garden, and the outstanding limestone rock garden. In the park beside the house, the Muckross Traditional Farms comprise reconstructed farm buildings and outbuildings, a blacksmith's forge, a carpenter's workshop, and a selection of farm animals. It's a reminder of the way things were done on the farm before electricity and the mechanization of farming. Meet and chat with the farmers and their wives as they go about their work. The visitor center has a shop and a restaurant. ✉ *Killarney National Park, Muckross Park, Muckross Rd. (N71), 6½ km (4 mi) south of Killarney* ☎ *064/663–1440* ⊕ *www.heritageireland. ie* ✆ *Visitor center free, farms €6.75, house €5.75, farms and house €10* ☉ *House and visitor center Nov.–mid-Mar., daily 9–5:30; mid-Mar.–June, Sept., and Oct., daily 9–6; July and Aug., daily 9–7. Farms mid-Mar.–Apr., weekends 1–6; May, daily 1–6; June–Sept., daily 10–7; Oct., weekends 1–6.*

The 15th-century Franciscan **Muckross Friary** is amazingly complete, although roofless. The monks were driven out by Oliver Cromwell's army in 1652. An ancient yew tree rises above the cloisters and breaks out over the abbey walls. Three flights of stone steps allow access to the upper floors and living quarters, where you can visit the cloisters and what was once the dormitory, kitchen, and refectory. ✉ *Killarney National Park, Muckross Park, Muckross Rd. (N71), 4 km (2½ mi) south of Killarney* ⊕ *www.*

heritageireland.ie 🎟 *Free* ⊘ *Mid-June–early Sept., daily 10–5.*

Ross Castle, a fully restored 14th-century stronghold, was the last place in the province of Munster to fall to Oliver Cromwell's forces in 1652. A later dwelling has 16th- and 17th-century furniture. ⊠ *Knockreer Estate, off Muckross Rd. (N71), 2 km (1 mi) south of Killarney* ☎ *064/663–5851* ⊕ *www.heritageireland.ie* 🎟 *€6* ⊘ *Mid-Mar.–May and Sept.–mid-Oct., daily 9:30–5:30; June–Aug., daily 9–6:30.*

The romantic ruins on **Innisfallen Island** date from the 6th or 7th century. Between 950 and 1350 the *Annals of Innisfallen* were compiled here by monks. (The book survives in the Bodleian Library in Oxford.) To get to the island, which is on Lough Leane, you can rent a rowboat at Ross Castle (*see above;* €5 per hour), or you can join a cruise (€10) in a covered, heated launch.

★ Massive, glacial rocks form the side of the **Gap of Dunloe,** a narrow mountain pass that stretches for 6½ km (4 mi) between MacGillicuddy's Reeks and the Purple Mountains. The rocks create strange echoes: give a shout to test it out. Five small lakes are strung out beside the road. Cars are banned from the gap, but in summer the first 3 km (2 mi) are busy with horse and foot traffic, much of which turns back at the halfway point. The entrance to the Gap is 10 km (7 mi) west of Killarney at Beaufort on the N72 Killorglin Road. So if you drive or are on a tour bus, you get off at the starting point of the car-free Gap of Dunloe and either hire your pony and trap or opt to walk. Many amble through the parkland until Lord Brandon's Cottage, where they get a boat back to Killarney town—a strong reason why many choose to do the Gap on an organized tour so they will not end up back in Killarney with their car 7 mi away at the start of the Gap.

At the entrance to the Gap of Dunloe, **Kate Kearney's Cottage** (⊠ *19 km [12 mi] west of Killarney* ☎ *064/664–4116*)> is a good place to rent a jaunting car or pony. Kate was a famous beauty who sold illegal *poteen* (moonshine) from her home, contributing greatly, one suspects, to travelers' enthusiasm for the scenery. Appropriately enough, Kearney's is now a pub and a good place to pause for an Irish coffee. The gap's southern end is marked by **Lord Brandon's Cottage** (⊠ *7 km (4½ mi) west of Killarney* ⊘ *Easter–Sept., daily 10–dusk*), a tea shop serving soup and sandwiches. From here, a path leads to the edge of Upper Lake, where you can journey onward by rowboat. It's an old tradition for the boatman to carry a bugle and illustrate the echoes. The boat passes under Brickeen Bridge and into Middle Lake, where 30 islands are steeped in legends, many of which your boatman is likely to recount. Look out for caves on the left-hand side on this narrow stretch of water.

★ If the weather is fine, head southwest 19 km (12 mi) out of Killarney on N71 to **Ladies' View,** a famed panorama of the three lakes and the surrounding mountains. The name goes back to 1905, when Queen Victoria was a guest at Muckross House. Upon seeing the view, her ladies-in-waiting were said to have been dumbfounded by its beauty.

> **TRIP TIP**
>
> While the immediate region of Killarney has a vast array of accommodations, visitors should consider staying in hotels in Glenbeigh (less than 20 minutes' drive away) if they really want to savor the region's peace and quiet.

WHERE TO EAT

$$$
CONTINENTAL

✕ **Foley's Restaurant.** A marble-top bar and an oyster tank in the reception area set the keynote for this much-loved Killarney restaurant, the venue for many a local family's special celebration. There's a touch of the old-fashioned gentleman's club about its solid wooden carver chairs, at tables formally set with white linen. Owner-chef Carol Hartnett makes use of good local ingredients, including superior Irish cream and butter, in a classically inspired menu. Try panfried John Dory with lemon butter, sirloin steak on grilled fennel with star anise and basil sauce, or rack of lamb with a hoisin glaze. A pianist entertains in summer. Inexpensive bar food can also be sampled in the bar area. ⊠ 23 High St. ☎ 064/663–1217 ⊟ AE, DC, MC, V.

$$$$
SEAFOOD

✕ **Gaby's Seafood.** Expect the best seafood in Killarney from Belgian owner-chef Gert Maes. Inside the rustic exterior is a little bar beside an open fire; steps lead up to the main dining area, where ornate wooden stick-back chairs sit atop a plush gold and navy carpet. They match a huge wooden dresser that has adorned the room since the restaurant opened in 1978. In summer you can sip an aperitif in the small garden. Try the seafood platter (seven or eight kinds of fish in a cream-and-wine sauce) or lobster Gaby (shelled, simmered in a cream-and-cognac sauce, and served back in the shell). Turbot, salmon, and sole are also regular menu items. There is also a selection of fillet and sirloin steaks, au poivre or with garlic butter, and herb-scented rack of lamb. ⊠ 27 High St. ☎ 064/663–2519 ⊟ AE, DC, MC, V ⊘ Closed Sun.–Tues. Jan.–mid-Mar. No lunch.

$$
CONTINENTAL
★

✕ **Treyvaud's.** Step behind the Victorian arched facade here and you'll discover a buzzing contemporary restaurant, masterminded by a pair of brothers, chefs Paul and Mark Treyvaud. The decor is simple—pine floorboards, wood-beam ceiling, lines of red-back chairs—so the food takes center stage (only fitting considering all those diners who have worked up a keen appetite out hiking). Winners include the shredded duck confit with beetroot carpaccio, the homemade smoked haddock fish cakes with garlic aioli, or the beef-and-Guinness pie with mashed potatoes, renowned for its flavor. In winter Treyvaud's is famous for its wide selection of game, including rabbit, wild boar, pheasant, and quail. But even its seafood plate (Dover sole, tiger prawns, and crab claws) will satisfy the hungriest hiker. ⊠ 62 High St. ☎ 064/663–3062 ⊟ AE, DC, MC, V ⊘ Closed Mon. and Tues. Apr.–Oct.

The beauty-measuring gauge flies off the scale at the Gap of Dunloe, considered by many to be the scenic star of the Lakes of Killarney region.

WHERE TO STAY

$$$$ **Aghadoe Heights.** Once inside this large, modern hotel you'll soon forget its blocklike external appearance, as the entrancing panorama of Killarney's lakes spread out before you casts its spell. It's hard to take your eyes off the view, as the famously changeable Killarney weather scuds across the skies (sunsets are not to be missed). As for the interior, standard international-hotel decor is enlivened by an impressive collection of original Irish art. Guest rooms are spacious, with plenty of luxury touches, including a fruit bowl, fluffy robes, and a booklet on hiking trails (that start right outside the hotel's door). The Lakeside Restaurant has perfect views from its outside tables; the interior is cozy with wood paneling. The Spa at Aghadoe offers a full range of treatments, or exhale in the Thermal Suite to banish any post-golfing or post-hiking aches. **Pros:** memorable views; excellent spa; super-helpful staff. **Cons:** well out of town; a big hotel by Irish standards. ⊠ *Aghadoe Heights, 4 km (2½ mi) outside Killarney, on Tralee side, signposted off N22, Co. Kerry* ☎ *064/663–1766* ⊕ *www.aghadoeheights.com* ⤳ *71 rooms, 3 suites* ⚒ *In-room: a/c, safe (some), refrigerator, Internet, Wi-Fi (some). In-hotel: restaurant, bar, tennis court, pool, gym, spa, Wi-Fi hotspot* ▭ *AE, DC, MC, V* ⦿❘ *BP.*

$$$ **Cahernane House.** Get a glimpse of the Killarney that attracted discerning 19th-century visitors at this imposing gray-stone house, which stands
Fodor's Choice
★   at the end of a long private avenue with trees that meet overhead to form a tunnel. Clearly, if you need a refuge from the touristy buzz of Killarney town, this is the place. Formerly the residence of the earls of Pembroke, the estate dates from 1877 and oozes baronial grandeur. A crackling log fire awaits you in the drawing room, which, like all the reception rooms, has highly polished mahogany furniture and wall paneling. It's worth

paying extra for a room in the original house—they have a genuine sense of history, with fine Victorian antique furniture. The newer rooms have private garden access and peaceful parkland views. For classic French cuisine, opt for the Herbert Room but some will prefer the bistro menu of the Cellar Bar. **Pros:** great old-world atmosphere; very luxe; fantastic views. **Cons:** standard rooms are disappointingly plain; lots of weddings. ⊠ *Muckross Rd., Co. Kerry* ☎ *064/663–1895* ⊕ *www.cahernane.com* ⋖ *36 rooms, 2 suites* ♿ *In-room: no a/c, Internet. In-hotel: tennis court* ⊘ *Closed Dec. 23–Feb.* ▤ *MC, V* ⦿| *BP.*

$ ⌂ **Earls Court House.** In a quiet suburb within walking distance of Killarney's center, this spacious guesthouse is furnished with interesting antiques collected by Emer Moynihan, who likes to greet her guests by offering home-baked goods in front of the open fire. The front lounge is a popular place to peruse the menus of local restaurants, read up on Kerry's attractions, or go online. Guest rooms are spacious, with large bathrooms, Victorian furniture accents, and unfussy decor with plain walls and dark colors. Older rooms have balconies, others feature four-poster beds, and some have Jacuzzi baths. **Pros:** quiet location; plenty of parking; warm welcome. **Cons:** long walk or taxi ride to town; bland suburban location. ⊠ *Woodlawn Junction, Muckross Rd., N71, Co. Kerry* ☎ *064/663–4009* ⊕ *www.killarney-earlscourt.ie* ⋖ *30 rooms* ♿ *In-room: no a/c, Internet. In-hotel: Wi-Fi hotspot* ▤ *MC, V* ⊘ *Closed mid-Nov.–mid-Mar.* ⦿| *BP.*

$ ⌂ **Friars Glen.** Set in its own 28 acres within Killarney National Park, this stone house is a dream retreat for nature lovers. The flower beds have to be protected from deer that ramble in to eat the colorful flowers. Though traditional in style, the house is new and has all the modern comforts. Owner-manager Mary Fuller keeps an eagle eye on the day-to-day running of the place, so it's spotlessly clean. A hefty pine staircase and pine-clad corridors lead to rooms with solid country pine furniture. The location is on a side road near Muckross Park's gates, a pleasant half-mile walk from the nearest pub and restaurant. **Pros:** sylvan peace; mountain air; friendly welcome. **Cons:** remote from town; limited choice of restaurants nearby; no Internet (so far). ⊠ *Mangerton Rd., Muckross, Co. Kerry* ☎ *064/663–7500* ⊕ *www.friarsglen.ie* ⋖ *10 rooms* ▤ *MC, V* ⊘ *Closed Nov.–mid-Mar.*

NIGHTLIFE AND THE ARTS

Buckley's Bar (⊠ *College St.* ☎ *064/663–1037*) in the Arbutus Hotel has traditional Irish entertainment nightly from June to September. Bars where a professional leads the songs and encourages audience participation and solos are popular in Killarney—try **The Danny Mann** (⊠ *New St.* ☎ *064/663–1640*). **Gleneagles** (⊠ *Muckross Rd.* ☎ *064/663–1870*) is the place for big-name cabaret—from Sharon Shannon to the Wolfe Tones. It also has a late-night disco. **McSorleys Nite Club** (⊠ *College St.* ☎ *064/663–9770*) is a lively late-night venue for the over-25s.

SPORTS AND THE OUTDOORS

BICYCLING A bicycle is the perfect way to enjoy Killarney's mild air, whether within the confines of Muckross Park or farther afield in the Kerry Highlands. Rent by the day or week from **O'Sullivan's Cycles** (⊠ *Bishop's La., off New St.* ☎ *064/663–1282*).

FISHING Salmon and brown trout populate Killarney's lakes and rivers. **O'Neill's** (✉ *6 Plunkett St.* ☎ *064/663–1970*) provides fishing tackle, bait, and licenses.

GOLF **Beaufort Golf Course** (✉ *Churchtown, Beaufort* ☎ *064/664–4440* ⊕ *www. beaufortgolfresort.com*) has an 18-hole course surrounded by magnificent scenery, and unlike most other Irish golf clubs, it has buggy-, trolley-, and club-rental facilities. For many, the three courses at the legendary **Killarney Golf and Fishing Club** (✉ *Mahony's Point* ☎ *064/663–1034* ⊕ *www. killarney-golf.com*) are the chief reason for coming to Killarney.

HIKING The **Kerry Way**, a long-distance walking route, passes through the Killarney National Park on its way to Glenbeigh. You can get a detailed leaflet about the route from the tourist information office. For the less adventurous, four safe and well-signposted nature trails of varying lengths are in the national park. Try the 4-km (2½-mi) Arthur Young's Walk, which passes through old yew and oak woods frequented by sika deer. You can reach the **Mangerton walking trail,** a small tarred road leading to a scenic trail that circles Mangerton Lake, by turning left off N71 midway between Muckross Friary and Muckross House (follow the signposts). The summit of **Mangerton Mountain** (2,756 feet) can be reached on foot in about two hours—less if you rent a pony. It's perfect if you want a fine, long hike with good views of woodland scenery. **Torc Mountain** (1,764 feet) can be reached off Route N71; it's a satisfying 1½-hour climb, with lake views. Don't attempt mountain climbing in the area in misty weather; visibility can quickly drop to zero.

SHOPPING

Bricín Craft Shop (✉ *26 High St.* ☎ *064/663–4902*) has interesting handicrafts, including candles, ceramics, and woolens. Visit the **Frank Lewis Gallery** (✉ *6 Bridewell La., beside General Post Office* ☎ *064/663– 4843*) for original paintings and sculptures.

The Kilkenny Shop (✉ *3 New St.* ☎ *064/663–5406*) stocks contemporary Irish pottery, ironwork, woodwork, crystal, and jewelry. **Killarney Art Gallery** (✉ *13 Main St.* ☎ *064/663–4628*) has a selection of original art and prints by living Irish artists in a wide variety of genres. The **Killarney Bookshop** (✉ *32 Main St.* ☎ *064/663–4108*) has local-interest books as well as fiction, biography, and travel titles. Bargain hunters should head for **Killarney Outlet Centre** (✉ *Fair Hill* ☎ *064/663–6744* ⊕ *www. killarneyoutletcentre.com*), adjacent to the Great Southern Hotel and the train station. The Nike Factory Store and Blarney Woollen Mills are the anchor tenants of this discount shopping center. Spórt Corrán Tuathail is the biggest outdoor clothing and sports shop in the Southwest.**MacBee's** (✉ *New St.* ☎ *064/663–3622*) is a modern boutique stocking the best of Irish high fashion. **Quills Woolen Market** (✉ *Market Cross* ☎ *064/663–2277*) has the town's largest selection of Irish knitwear. It also carries tweeds, linens, and Celtic jewelry.

6

CORCA DHUIBNE: THE DINGLE PENINSULA

The gorgeously scenic Dingle Peninsula stretches for some 48 km (30 mi) between Tralee (pronounced tra-*lee*) in the east and Ceann Sleibne (Slea Head) in the west. Often referred to by its Irish name, Corca Dhuibne (pronounced Cor-kah-guy-nay*)*, the peninsula is made up of rugged mountains, seaside cliffs, and softly molded glacial valleys and lakes. Long sandy beaches and Atlantic-pounded cliffs unravel along the coast. Drystone walls enclose small, irregular fields, and exceptional prehistoric and early Christian remains dot the countryside. As you drive over its mountain passes, looking out past prehistoric remains to the wild Atlantic sea, Dingle can be a magical destination that makes you feel like you're living in an ancient legend. Unfortunately, Dingle is notorious for its heavy rainfall and impenetrable sea mists, which can strike at any time of year. If they do, sit them out in An Daingean (Dingle Town) and enjoy the friendly bars, cafés, and crafts shops. West of Annascaul, the peninsula is Irish-speaking: English is considered a second language. A good Irish-English map can prove handy.

You can cover the peninsula in a long day trip of about 160 km (99 mi). If mist or continuous rain is forecast, postpone your trip until visibility improves. From Killarney, Killorglin, or Tralee, head for Castlemaine, and take the coast road (R561 and R559) to Dingle Town. You'll pass through the sheltered seaside resort of Inch, 19 km (12 mi) west of Castlemaine and 45 km (28 mi) northwest of Killarney, where the head of Dingle Bay is cut off by two sand spits that enclose Castlemaine Harbour. Inch has a 6½-km (4-mi) beach backed by dunes that are home to a large colony of Natterjack toads.

ANNASCAUL

47 km (30 mi) northwest of Killarney.

An important livestock center until the 1930s, this village near the junction of the Castlemaine and Tralee roads has a wide road, as cattle trading was once carried out in the streets. The town also has many pubs.

The South Pole Inn (☎ 066/915–7388) was built by local hero Tom Crean (1877–1938). Crean enlisted in the English navy at the age of 15, and served on three expeditions to Antarctica—the *Discovery* (1901–04) and the *Terra Nova* (1910–13), both under the command of Captain Robert Falcon Scott, and the *Endurance* (1914–16), where he was second officer to Ernest Shackleton. Crean himself failed to reach the South Pole on any of these expeditions, and named his pub so that in his retirement he could go to work at the South Pole every day. Memorabilia at the pub fill in the details of Crean's Antarctic adventures. Crean was famed for his amazing strength and resilience. He walked 56 km (35 mi) through an Antarctic blizzard to bring help to his colleagues, with only two bars of chocolate and three biscuits for sustenance. For this he received the Albert Medal for Bravery. On another occasion he survived a 15-day journey across 1,280 km (800 mi) of ocean in an open boat. The pub is the headquarters of

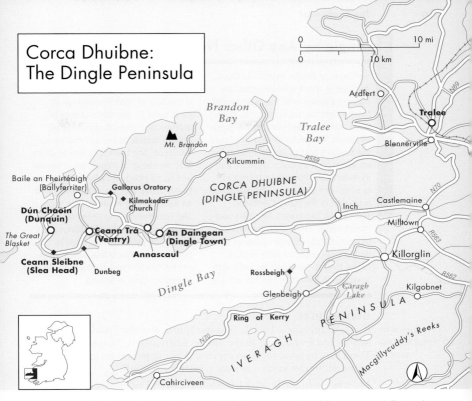

Corca Dhuibne: The Dingle Peninsula

0   10 mi

0   10 km

Brandon Bay

Mt. Brandon

Tralee Bay

Tralee

Blennerville

Ardfert

Kilcummin

R559

CORCA DHUIBNE (DINGLE PENINSULA)

Baile an Fheirtéaigh (Ballyferriter)

Gallarus Oratory

Kilmakedar Church

Inch

Castlemaine

Milltown

N70

R563

Dún Chaoin (Dunquin)

Ceann Trá (Ventry)

An Daingean (Dingle Town)

Killorglin

The Great Blasket

Ceann Sleibne (Slea Head)

Annascaul

Dunbeg

Rossbeigh

Glenbeigh

Caragh Lake

Kilgobnet

R562

Dingle Bay

Ring of Kerry

N70

IVERAGH PENINSULA

Macgillycuddy's Reeks

Cahirciveen

the Tom Crean Society, which hosts occasional lectures and festivals and has been addressed by Sir Edmund Hillary and the grandsons of both Scott and Shackleton.

AN DAINGEAN (DINGLE TOWN)

18 km (11 mi) west of Annascaul, 67 km (42 mi) west of Killarney, 45 km (28 mi) west of Killorglin on R561.

Backed by mountains and facing a sheltered harbor, An Daingean, the chief town of its eponymous peninsula, has a year-round population of 1,400 that more than doubles in summer. Although many expect Dingle (to use its English name) to be a quaint and undeveloped Gaeltacht village, it has many crafts shops, seafood restaurants, and pubs. Still, you can explore its main thoroughfares—the Mall, Main and Strand streets, and the Wood—in less than an hour. Celebrity hawks, take note: off-season Dingle is favored as a hideaway by the likes of Julia Roberts, Paul Simon, and Dolly Parton. These and others have their visits commemorated on Green Street's "path of stars."

CLOSE UP

Dingle by Any Other Name

Residents of Dingle, especially those involved in the tourist business, are fighting a battle with the government for the right to continue to call their town and their peninsula by the name of Dingle. The problem arises because the western part of Dingle Peninsula—known in Irish as Corca Dhuibne and its main town, Dingle (An Daingean, in Irish)—is officially an Irish-speaking area, part of the Kerry Gaeltacht. The Official Languages Act 2003 was introduced to strengthen the rights of Ireland's 90,000 Irish speakers to do business with the state in their native tongue—officially Ireland's first language. A side effect of this act was the necessity, under the new law, for all signposts for places where Irish is the official spoken language to be in Irish. So the name Dingle has disappeared from all signposts by official decree, to be replaced by An Daingean. The traders of Dingle claim that the name of their town is equivalent to an internationally recognized brand name, and are demanding that an exception be made in their case. The compromise suggested by the traders of Dingle, Dingle Daingean Uí Chúis, has yet to be approved by the government. Meanwhile, when heading for Dingle Town, follow signs to An Daingean. Only in Ireland.

GETTING HERE

BIKE AND SIGHTSEEING TRAVEL If you're fit, hire a bicycle *(see the Sports and the Outdoors section, below)* and spend a day in the saddle. Alternatively, Moran's Slea Head Tours runs minibus tours on demand (€20 per person for groups of four or more), or can tailor a private tour to your needs.

BOAT TRAVEL Most boats to the Blasket Islands leave from Dunquin, 21 km (13 mi) west of town, but Dingle Bay Charters has boats from the marina in Dingle Town making ecotours of the Blasket Islands daily between May and September, weather permitting (€40).

BUS TRAVEL Tralee is the transportation hub for this part of Ireland, so all buses to Dingle are routed via Tralee, which has train service from Heuston Station Dublin *(see Tralee, Getting Here).* From Tralee Bus Station, there are four buses a day to Dingle (1 hour 10 minutes, €14.20 round-trip). The best scenery is found on the 30-km (18-mi) circuit to the west of the town around Slea Head.

ESSENTIALS

Transportation Contacts Dingle Bay Charters (✉ *Dingle Marina, Co. Kerry* ☎ *066/915–1344* ⊕ *www.dinglebaycharters.com*). **Moran's Slea Head Tours** (✉ *Casement Station, Co. Kerry* ☎ *066/915–1155* ⊕ *www.dodingle.com*).

Visitor Information An Daingean (Dingle Town) Tourist Office (✉ *The Quay, Co. Kerry* ☎ *066/915–1188* ⊕ *www.dingle-peninsula.ie*).

EXPLORING

An Daingean's pubs are well known for their music, but among them **O'Flaherty's** (✉ *Bridge St., at entrance to town* ☎ *066/915–1983*), a simple, stone-floor bar, is something special and a hot spot for traditional musicians. Spontaneous sessions occur most nights in July and August,

An entry in Fodor's "Show Us Your Ireland" contest, this photo by Fodors.com member Michelle Nadal shows the coastal tip of the dramatic Dingle peninsula.

less frequently at other times. Even without music, this pub is a good place to compare notes with fellow travelers.

Since 1985, An Daingean's central attraction, apart from its "trad" music scene, has been a winsome bottle-nosed dolphin who has taken up residence in the harbor. The Dingle dolphin, or **Fungie,** as he has been named, will play for hours with swimmers (a wet suit is essential) and scuba divers, and he follows local boats in and out of the harbor. It's impossible to predict whether he will stay, but boatmen have become so confident of a sighting that they offer trippers their money back if Fungie does not appear. Boat trips (€16) leave the pier hourly in July and August between 11 and 6, weather-permitting.

WHERE TO EAT

$$$
IRISH
★

Chart House. Host Jim McCarthy is often found in the early evening leaning over the red half door of this low, cabinlike stone building. The exterior gives little hint of the spacious, cleverly lighted dining room within, nor of the beautiful pair of windows at the back that frame lovely views of Dingle Harbor's trawler fleet. Nautical artifacts, including an antique compass, complement the rusty-red walls and matching tablecloths. The atmosphere is pleasantly informal, but both food and service are polished and professional. Top choices include the phyllo parcel of Annascaul black pudding with chutney, or the roast guinea fowl in port-wine jus. Finish the meal with a selection of Irish cheeses, served with a glass of port, or a homemade apple and clove tartlet with ginger-nut crumble. ⊠ *The Mall* ☎ *066/915–2255* ═ *MC, V* ☽ *Closed Jan.–mid-Feb., and Mon. and Tues. in Oct.–May (but call to confirm hrs Oct.–May). No lunch.*

$$ ✕ **Fenton's.** Step beyond the yellow
CONTINENTAL door of this town house to find a
cozy, cottage-style restaurant with
quarry-tile floors, a stone fireplace,
and local art (for sale) on the soft-
blue walls. Rush-seat ladder-back
chairs are drawn up to wood-top
candlelighted tables. The bistro-
style menu is unfussy, allowing for
quick turnovers during Dingle's hec-
tic high season. Some dishes, such
as the *moules marinières* (steamed
mussels), are available in starter or main-course portions. Lamb and
beef come from the Fenton family farm. Sirloin steak may be served
with caramelized onions and a red-wine sauce, or try local black sole on
the bone with fresh herb butter. ⊠ *Green St.* ☎ *066/915–2172* ⊟ *MC,
V* ☉ *Closed Mon. and mid-Nov.–Easter.*

$$$ ✕ **Out of the Blue.** Every fishing port should have a simple waterfront
SEAFOOD bistro like this one, serving the best seafood (owner Tim Mason won't
open his tiny restaurant if there's no fresh-caught seafood available,
which is almost never). Lobster, scallops, and crayfish are specialties,
but also expect turbot, black sole, plaice, brill, monkfish, and even the
humble pollack on the daily blackboard menu. Scottish chef Seamus
MacDonald puts a modern twist on seafood classics, perhaps sole on
the bone with almond cream, or John Dory with a pepper sauce and
garlic eggplant. There's a short but well-chosen wine list, and a basic
dessert selection. ⊠ *Waterside beside pier* ☎ *066/915–0811* ⌨ *Reservations essential* ⊟ *MC, V* ☉ *Closed Wed. and mid-Nov.–Feb. No
lunch Mon.–Sat.*

WHERE TO STAY

$$$ ☷ **Dingle Skellig.** Rambling and modern as this building may be, its
center is occupied by a beehivelike shape that's intended to echo local
clocháns (prehistoric beehive huts). The octagonal reception area has
wood cladding, contemporary stained-glass doors, and original paint-
ings. Modern, pale-wood furniture and bold fabrics adorn the spacious
rooms, which are in separate wings, and mostly have sea views. The
Peninsula Spa offers hydrotherapy and a relaxation suite, and features
an outdoor hot tub with stunning bay views. Floor-to-ceiling windows
in the Coastguard restaurant look out over Dingle Bay. As you'd expect,
the specialty is seafood. **Pros:** waterfront location; organized entertain-
ment for children; separate floors for child-free guests. **Cons:** still shows
signs of its undistinguished 1970s architecture; edge-of-town location
a bit bleak in bad weather; food not a strong point. ⊠ *Dingle Harbour,
Co. Kerry* ☎ *066/915–0200* ⊕ *www.dingleskellig.com* ↴ *110 rooms*
△ *In-room: no a/c, refrigerator (some), Wi-Fi. In-hotel: restaurant,
room service, bar, pool, gym, spa* ⊟ *AE, DC, MC, V* ⍓ *BP.*

$$ ☷ **Emlagh House.** You'll be right on the water's edge in this spacious,
yellow, mansard-roof family home. Although many accommodations
in An Daingean are cottagelike, the Kavanagh family chose the grander
Georgian style. The marble-floor lobby, with its exquisite mahogany

side table and large vase of fresh flowers, sets a tone of quiet, unostentatious luxury—there are more than 185 pieces of original Irish art in the house from the family's private collection. Relax on the goose-down-filled velvet sofas in front of the drawing room's open fire while sipping a drink from the honor bar. Bedrooms are large, with sitting areas in the bay windows. Each one is color-themed to a local wildflower, with plush carpets, Regency-stripe drapes, and Victorian antiques. Power showers, sunken baths, and speakers in the bathroom encourage indulgence. It's a short, water's-edge walk into town to sample Dingle's famous seafood. **Pros:** spacious, romantic rooms; waterside location. **Cons:** expensive for a B&B; not the place for your rendition of Mother Macree on returning from the pub. ⊠ *An Daingean Harbour, Co. Kerry* ☎ *066/915–2345* ⊕ *www.emlaghhouse.com* ⤴ *10 rooms* ⌂ *In-room: a/c, safe, Internet, Wi-Fi (some). In-hotel: Wi-Fi hotspot* ⊟ *AE, MC, V* ⊘ *Closed Nov.– mid-Mar.* ⊖ *BP.*

$$ ▦ **Greenmount House.** Wonderful views of the town and harbor await at
Fodor's Choice this modern B&B, a short walk uphill from the town (turn right at the
★ roundabout beside the hospital before entering the town center). More like a boutique hotel than a B&B, the combination of comfort and elegance in the lobby, with its plump sofas and coffee-table books about Ireland, sets the tone. Guest rooms are spacious, with well-appointed bathrooms. Beige carpets blend in with pale oak country furniture and crisp white bed linen, and there are sofas and armchairs angled to enjoy the spectacular sunset over Dingle Harbor. Proprietor John Curran is a mine of information while wife Mary is known for her baking and excellent breakfasts. Who can resist the oatmeal topped with Irish Mist liqueur? **Pros:** plenty of private parking; wine license; nice common areas. **Cons:** new developments mar the foreground of an otherwise great view. ⊠ *Upper John St., Co. Kerry* ☎ *066/915–1414* ⊕ *www.greenmount-house.com* ⤴ *6 rooms, 6 suites* ⌂ *In-room: no a/c, Wi-Fi (some). In-hotel: Wi-Fi hotspot* ⊟ *MC, V* ⊘ *Closed Dec. 20–27* ⊖ *BP.*

$ ▦ **Heaton's Guesthouse.** This traditional-style yellow house on the water's edge was built as a guesthouse by Nuala and Cameron Heaton. The spacious lobby has a gas fire and large couches looking out to sea through the bay windows. All guest rooms are individually styled, with marble bathrooms, reproduction classic French-style antique furniture, plush carpets, flat-screen TVs, and waffle robes. Junior suites and deluxe rooms have extra space, and the best sea views. Breakfast is a major event here, with an extensive buffet preceding the traditional fry. To get here, drive through Dingle Town and out to its western fringe, following the signs for Slea Head. **Pros:** high standard of comfort and decor; ample parking; only a short walk from town. **Cons:** if it rains you'll be driving, not walking, to nearest bars and restaurants. ⊠ *The Wood, Co. Kerry* ☎ *066/915–2288* ⊕ *www.heatonsdingle.com* ⤴ *16 rooms* ⌂ *In-room: no a/c, Wi-Fi. In-hotel: Internet terminal* ⊟ *MC, V* ⊘ *Closed Dec.* ⊖ *BP.*

6

The Silence Strikes You at Once

The Great Blasket, which measures roughly 3 km by 1 km (2 mi by ½ mi), has no traffic, no pub, no hotel, and no electricity. Yet this island—centerpiece of the An Bhlaskaoid Mhóir (Blasket Islands)—is one of the most memorable places in Ireland to visit.

These days it takes only 15 minutes from Dún Chaoin (Dunquin) Pier to make the 3-km (2-mi) crossing of the Blasket Sound, but even on a calm day the swell can be considerable. In summer the island is inaccessible on about one day in five; in winter the island can be cut off for weeks. Until 1954 a small community of hardy fisherfolk and subsistence farmers eked out a living here.

Today, visitors are usually attracted by the literary heritage of the island—the Irish-language writings of Tomás Ó Criomhthain, Muiris Ó Suilleabhain, and Peig Sayers (also known in English as Tomás O Crohán and Maurice O'Sullivan)—but what makes people return is something else: a rare quality of light and an intense peace and quiet in beautiful, unspoiled surroundings.

The inadequacy of the existing piers limits visitors to the island to a maximum of about 400 per day, a figure that is reached only rarely, with the average under 200. Most visitors stay for three or four hours, walking, sketching, or taking photographs.

The silence strikes you at once. The seabirds, stone chats, and swallows sound louder than on the mainland; sheep graze silently on the steep hillside. The simple domestic ruins are very touching; you do not need to know the history to work out what happened to their owners (most departed for other places, with many settling in Springfield, Massachusetts).

When the last boat of day-trippers leaves, the foreshore teems with rabbits, and seals bask on the white strand. At the time of this writing, camping is permitted, but it may well be banned in the near future. Eat an evening meal in the island café before sitting outside to watch the stars.

Many visitors, including John Millington Synge, have warned that there's something addictive about the Great Blasket. "I have a jealousy for that Island," he wrote after his 1907 sojourn, "like the jealousy of men in love."

The **Blasket Islands Ferry** (☎ 066/ 915–4864 ⊕ www.blasketislands.ie) makes the 15-minute crossing from Dún Chaoin Pier to the island daily from April to September, weather permitting, costing €30 round-trip. The same company runs a 2½-hour ecotour around the island with the option of landing for €40. Sightings of seals are pretty well guaranteed. **Dingle Bay Charters** (☎ 066/915– 1344 ⊕ www.dinglebaycharters.com) sails from An Daingean (Dingle Town) to the island and takes about 40 minutes, costing €40 for a round-trip ticket. They also run ecotours.

Before you go, get a copy of Maurice O'Sullivan's *Twenty Years a-Growing*, which gives a fascinating account of a simple way of life that has only recently disappeared on the Blaskets. For an overview of the island's more recent history, read *Hungry for Home: Leaving the Blaskets: A Journey from the Edge of Ireland* by Cole Moreton.

NIGHTLIFE AND THE ARTS

Nearly every bar on the Corca Dhuibne (Dingle Peninsula), particularly in the town of An Daingean, offers live music nightly in July and August. For a lively night-time spot, try **An Droichead Beag (The Small Bridge)** (⊠ *Main St.* ☎ *066/915–1564*). **O'Flaherty's** (⊠ *Bridge St., at entrance to town* ☎ *066/915–1983*) is a gathering place for traditional musicians—you can hear impromptu music sessions most nights in July and August.

SPORTS AND THE OUTDOORS

You're likely to remember a bike ride around Slea Head for a long time. You can rent bicycles at **Foxy John's Hardware** (⊠ *Main St.* ☎ *066/915–1316*), which also has a great old-style bar-cum-hardware store.

SHOPPING

Don't miss An Daingean's café-bookshop, **An Cafe Liteartha** (⊠ *Bothar An Dadhgaide* ☎ *066/915–2204*), which locals insist is one of the world's first (it has been here since the 1970s). Regardless, you can find friendly conversation as well as new and secondhand books. You can watch **Brian de Staic** (⊠ *Green St.* ☎ *066/915–1298*) and his team make modern, Celtic-inspired jewelry in his studio, which is also a shop. **Greenlane Gallery** (⊠ *Holy Ground* ☎ *066/915–2018*) has shows of contemporary Irish art with an emphasis on local landscapes. **Leác a Ré** (⊠ *Strand St.* ☎ *066/915–1138*) sells handmade Irish crafts. One of Ireland's more unusual culinary success stories is **Murphys Ice Cream** (⊠ *Strand St.* ☎ *066/915–2644*), which has won international awards. Find out why at this flagship parlor. Lisbeth Mulcahy at the **Weaver's Shop** (⊠ *Green St.* ☎ *066/915–1688*) sells outstanding handwoven, vegetable-dyed woolen wraps, mufflers, and fabric for making skirts.

CEANN TRÁ (VENTRY)

8 km (5 mi) west of An Daingean (Dingle Town) on R561.

The next town after An Daingean along the coast, Ceann Trá has a small outcrop of pubs and small grocery stores (useful, since west of Dingle Town you'll find few shops of any kind), and a long sandy beach with safe swimming and ponies for rent. Between Ventry and Dún Chaoin (Dunquin) are several interesting archaeological sites on the spectacular cliff-top road along Ceann Sleibne (Slea Head).

Perched on the very edge of a Dingle Bay cliff, and set in the small district of Fagan (which is part of the larger township of Ventry), the small, well-weathered **Dunbeg Fort** was an important Iron Age defensive promontory site, inhabited from about AD 800 until around AD 1200. Its drystone mound was defended against cattle raiders by four earthen rings—note the *souterraine* (underground) escape route, by the entrance. In addition, there are a number of archaeological artifacts here to interest the time traveler. There is a 10-minute audiovisual show in the adjacent visitor center, but just as fascinating is the building itself, a modern replica of the drystone construction of the *clocháns* (pronounced cluk-*awns*), the famous prehistoric "beehive" cells first used by hermit monks in the Early Christian period. Beside it is a typical *curragh* (tarred canvas canoe), resting upside down. About half a mile farther on is another parking lot, and an interesting group of clocháns can be visited (€2 fee to resident farmer), built of drystone and set on the southern slopes of Mt. Eagle looking out directly across the sea to Skellig Michael. Far from being only prehistoric relics, as the signposts claim, clocháns were being built until a century ago; wood was scarce and stone abounded, so you'll find more than 400 of these clocháns exist between Ceann Sliebne and Dún Chaoin. ⊠ *The Stone House Restaurant, Fahan (8 km [5 mi] west of Ventry)* ☎ *066/915–9755* ⊕ *www.dunbegfort.com* ⊠ *€3.50* ⊙ *Easter–Apr., daily 9:30–7; May–Oct., 9:30–8; Nov.–Easter, phone in advance (site is open in good weather only).*

CEANN SLIEBNE (SLEA HEAD)

16 km (10 mi) west of An Daingean (Dingle Town) on R561, 8 km (5 mi) west of Ceann Trá.

From the top of the towering cliffs of Ceann Sliebne at the southwest extremity of the Dingle Peninsula, the view of the Blasket Islands and the Atlantic Ocean is guaranteed to stop you in your tracks. Alas, Slea Head—to use its English name—has become so popular that tour buses, barely able to negotiate the narrow road, are causing traffic jams, particularly in July and August. Coumenole, the long sandy strand below, looks beautiful and sheltered, but swimming here is dangerous. This treacherous stretch of coast has claimed many lives in shipwrecks—most recently in 1982, when a large cargo boat, the *Ranga,* foundered on the rocks and sank. In 1588 four ships of the Spanish Armada were driven through the Blasket Sound; two made it to shelter, and two sank. One of these, the *Santa Maria de la Rosa,* is being excavated by divers in summer.

DÚN CHAOIN (DUNQUIN)

13 km (8 mi) west of Ceann Trá on R559, 5 km (3 mi) north of Ceann Sliebne (Slea Head).

Once the mainland harbor for the Blasket islanders (when there *were* islanders, as the Blaskets are deserted now), Dún Chaoin is at the center of the Gaeltacht, and attracts many students of Irish language and folklore. David Lean shot *Ryan's Daughter* hereabouts in 1969. The movie gave the area its first major boost in tourism, though it was lambasted by critics—"Gush made respectable by millions of dollars tastefully wasted," lamented Pauline Kael—sending Lean into a dry spell he didn't come out of until 1984 with *A Passage to India.*

Kruger's Pub (☎ 066/915–6127), Dunquin's social center, has long been frequented by artists and writers, including Brendan Behan.

Dún Chaoin's **pier** (signposted from main road) is surrounded by cliffs of colored Silurian rock, more than 400 million years old and rich in fossils. Down at the pier you can see *curraghs* (open fishing boats traditionally made of animal hide stretched over wooden laths and tarred) stored upside down. Three or four men walk the curraghs out to the sea, holding them over their heads. Similar boats are used in the Aran Islands, and when properly handled they're extraordinarily seaworthy.

The Blasket Islands (An Bhlaskaoid Mhóir) are among Ireland's most
extraordinary islands. The largest visible from Ceann Sleibne is the Great
Blasket, inhabited until 1953. The Blasket islanders were great storytellers and were encouraged by Irish linguists to write their memoirs. *The
Islandman*, by Tomás O Crohán, gives a vivid picture of a hard way of
life. "Their likes will not be seen again," O Crohán poignantly observed.
The **Blasket Centre** explains the heritage of these islanders and celebrates
their use of the Irish language with videos and exhibitions. *For a run-
down on the Blasket sense of place, see the Close-Up box, "The Silence
Strikes You at Once."* ⊠ *Dún Chaoin (Dunquin)* ☎ *066/915–6444*
⊕ *www.heritageireland.ie* €4 ⊙ *Apr.–Oct., daily 10–6.*

In good weather **Blasket Islands Ferry** (⊠ *Dún Chaoin Pier* ☎ *066/915–
4864* ⊕ *www.blasketislands.ie*) vessels bring you from Dún Chaoin Pier
to Great Blasket Island, a 15-minute trip. Landing is by transfer to rub-
ber dinghy, and the island is steep and rocky, so you need to be fit and
agile. (At the time of this writing, the Irish government is in the process
of buying the island for the nation. By 2009 a new pier might be in place
on the island. Then again, it might not. Check with the Dingle Tourist
Office near your travel date.) Still, the unique experience offered by the
deserted village and old cliff paths of the island makes it well worth the
effort. The cost of the boat ride is €30 round-trip. Alternatively, you can
take a 2½-hour ecotour, with an optional landing, for €40. Boats run
from 10 to 4, weather permitting, between April and September.

**EN
ROUTE**

Clogher Strand, a dramatic, windswept stretch of rocks and sand, is not a
safe spot to swim, but it's a good place to watch the ocean dramatically
pound the rocks when a storm is approaching or a gale is blowing.

Overlooking the beach is **Louis Mulcahy's pottery studio.** One of Ireland's
leading ceramic artists, Mulcahy produces large pots and urns that are
both decorative and functional. You can watch the work in progress and
buy items at workshop prices. There is also a coffee shop. ⊠ *Clogher
Strand* ☎ *066/915–6229* ⊕ *www.louismulcahy.com* ⊙ *Daily 9:30–6.*

TRALEE

*67 km (41 mi) west of Ballyferriter, 50 km (31 mi) northeast of An
Daingean (Dingle Town) on R559.*

County Kerry's capital and its largest town, Tralee (population 21,000)
has long been associated with the popular Irish song "The Rose of
Tralee," the inspiration for the annual Rose of Tralee International
Festival. The last week of August, Irish communities worldwide send
young women to join native Irish competitors; one of them is chosen as
the Rose of Tralee. Visitors, musicians, and entertainers pack the town
then. A two-day horse-race meeting—with seven races a day—runs at
the same time, which contributes to the crowds. Modern renovations,
including concrete piazzas (which attract crowds of drinkers on weekends) have done little to ameliorate Tralee's medium-size-town-with-
little-character feel.

Almost as memorable as the boat ride to the Skellig isles is the excursion out to the unspoiled Blasket Islands, a favorite escape for poets and writers.

GETTING HERE

BUS TRAVEL Bus Éireann's Expressway buses to Kerry all stop at Tralee Bus Station, where there are onward connections to Dingle (four buses a day, 1 hour 10 minutes, €14.20 round-trip) and Killarney (40 minutes, €12.40 round-trip). Buses linking Tralee to Dublin travel via Limerick. A feeder bus from Shannon Airport also connects with the Limerick–Tralee service. There are four buses a day from Limerick to Tralee (2 hours; €17.50 round-trip). You can use scheduled services on the local bus network to visit Listowel (30 minutes, €9.50 round-trip) and Adare (2 hours, €21.50 round-trip). There are eight buses a day (€5 one-way) from Kerry Country Airport (Farranfore) to Tralee; a taxi from the airport, 16 km (10 mi) from Tralee, costs about €25.

TRAIN TRAVEL Tralee's Casement Rail Station is the main transportation hub for this part of the Southwest. Tralee is the final stop on the route run by **Irish Rail** that begins at Dublin Heuston Station. This line has at least five trains a day (3¾ hours, €72 round-trip); by booking online and traveling off-peak this can be reduced to €10 each way.

ESSENTIALS

Transportation Contacts Tralee Bus and Rail Station (✉ *Casement Station, John Joe Sheehy Rd.* ☎ *066/712–3522*).

Visitor Information Tralee Tourist Office (✉ *Ashe Memorial Hall, Denny St., Co. Kerry* ☎ *066/712–1288* ⊕ *www.tralee.ie*).

EXPLORING

A superb springboard to explore the adjoining Dingle Peninsula, Tralee is also the transportation hub of the region. As such, people used to joke that the only good things to come out of Tralee were the buses shuttling travelers elsewhere. To a certain extent, that is still the case: there are no ruins or quaint architecture. Accordingly, however, there are no tourists, so the local folk have been fashioning some worthwhile sights, including the town museum, Aquadome (a water park great for kids), and the Siamsa Tíre—the National Folk Theatre of Ireland—which stages impressive dances and plays based on Irish folklore.

Kerry County Museum, Tralee's major cultural attraction, traces the history of Kerry's people since 5000 BC, using dioramas and an entertaining audiovisual show. You can also walk through a life-size reconstruction of a Tralee street in the Middle Ages. ⊠ *Ashe Memorial Hall, Denny St.* ☎ *066/712–7777* ⊕ *www.kerrymuseum.ie* ⊠ *€8* ⊙ *Jan.–Mar., Tues.–Fri. 10–4:30; Apr. and May, Tues.–Sat. 9:30–5:30; June–Aug., daily 9:30–5:30; Sept.–Dec., Tues.–Sat. 9:30–5.*

WHERE TO STAY

$$ **Abbey Gate.** Built on the site of Tralee's old marketplace, in a quiet spot behind the main shopping street, Abbey Gate is an attractive, modern hotel. Guest rooms have country-style wood furniture and large, tile bathrooms. The Old Market Place Pub, an imaginatively designed bar, seats 500 people and has "trad" touches like wooden floors and open fireplaces (there's bar food at lunch, and music and dancing nightly from June to September and at least three nights a week at other times). **Pros:** good value; centrally located. **Cons:** Tralee town center largely rebuilt as concrete piazzas; bar can be noisy at night. ⊠ *Maine St., Co. Kerry* ☎ *066/712–9888* ⊕ *www.abbeygate-hotel.com* ⤶ *100 rooms* ♿ *In-room: no a/c. In-hotel: restaurant, bars, Wi-Fi hotspot* ⊟ *AE, DC, MC, V* ⦿ *BP.*

$ **Brook Manor Lodge.** If you're using Tralee as a touring base, it makes sense to stay out of town, avoiding its notoriously snarled-up traffic and late-night noise. Set against a dramatic backdrop of the Slieve Mish Mountain, this large double-gable country house is a nice option, found 2 km (1 mi) from the town center on the Fenit Road (R558). The young owner-managers Sandra and Jerome Lordan are a fount of touring information. Guest rooms are large and elegantly furnished, with repro-period furniture and some antiques. There really is a brook running alongside the garden, and the location is convenient for the many sandy beaches near Tralee, as well as golf. **Pros:** quiet and spacious; friendly personal welcome; delicious breakfast. **Cons:** no nearby village. ⊠ *Fenit Rd., Co. Kerry* ☎ *066/712–0406* ⊕ *www.brookmanorlodge.com* ⤶ *8 rooms* ♿ *In-room: no a/c, Wi-Fi* ⊟ *MC, V* ⦿ *BP.*

$–$$ **Meadowlands.** In a quiet suburb on the road to Listowel, a 10 minutes' walk from Tralee's city center, this lively luxury hotel is turreted like a French château and done up in exuberant, sumptuously stylish decor. Touches of nouvelle country-house style are everywhere, from the grand barrel-vaulted reception area to the two-story bar, which has a balcony library. For the full treatment, repair to the restaurant, a cozy bedazzlement of stonework, timber beams, and stone pillars.

The exceptionally comfortable guest rooms are decorated with dark-wood, Victorian-style furniture and plaster cornices on the ceilings. A festive, friendly, and stylish place, Meadowlands turns up the charm on weekends, when the bar hosts live music. **Pros:** friendly staff; good standard of comfort; ample parking. **Cons:** the faux old-time look can feel contrived; suburban location not the most exciting. ✉ *Oakpark, Co. Kerry* ☎ *066/718–0444* ⊕ *www.meadowlands-hotel.com* ⇗ *57 rooms* ☝ *In-room: a/c, safe (some), refrigerator (some), Internet (some), Wi-Fi (some). In-hotel: restaurant, room service, bar, Internet terminal, Wi-Fi hotspot* ▭ *AE, MC, V* ⦿| *BP.*

NIGHTLIFE AND THE ARTS

Ballad sessions are more popular here than traditional Irish music. **Horan's Hotel** (✉ *Clash St.* ☎ *066/712–1933*) has dance music and cabaret acts nightly during July and August and on weekends only during the off-season. Try to catch the **National Folk Theater of Ireland (Siamsa Tíre)** (✉ *Godfrey Pl.* ☎ *066/712–3055* ⊕ *www.siamsatire.com* ☉ *Shows July and Aug., Mon.–Sat. at 8:30* PM; *May, June, and Sept., Tues. and Thurs. at 8:30* PM). Language is no barrier to this colorful entertainment, which re-creates traditional rural life through music, mime, and dance.

SPORTS AND THE OUTDOORS

BICYCLING   You can rent bicycles from **Tralee Bicycle Supplies** (✉ *Strand St.* ☎ *066/712–2018*).

GOLF   Tralee is the heart of great golfing country. The **Ballybunion Golf Club** (*Old Course* ✉ *Ballybunion* ☎ *068/27146* ⊕ *www.ballybuniongolfclub. ie*) is universally regarded as one of golf's holiest grounds. The **Tralee Golf Club** (✉ *West Barrow, Ardfert* ☎ *066/713–6379* ⊕ *www.traleegolfclub. com*) is a seaside links, designed by Arnold Palmer, with cliffs, craters, and dunes.

NORTH KERRY AND SHANNONSIDE

Until several decades ago, Shannon meant little more to most people—if it meant anything at all—than the name of the longest river in Ireland and Great Britain, running for 273 km (170 mi) from County Cavan to Limerick City in County Clare. But mention Shannon nowadays and people think immediately of the airport, which has become western Ireland's principal gateway. In turn, what also comes to mind are many of the glorious sights of North Kerry and Shannonside: the storybook attractions of "Castle Country," including Bunratty and Knappogue; Adare, sometimes called "Ireland's Prettiest Village" (and the neighboring Adare Manor, a grand country-house hotel); and Limerick City, which attracts visitors tracing the memories so movingly captured in Frank McCourt's international best seller *Angela's Ashes.*

If you want to leap-frog over the Shannon Estuary and head directly into the West of Ireland, head north on N69 18 km (11 mi) from Listowel to Tarbert, the terminus for the **Shannon Ferries** (☎ *065/905–3124* ⊕ *www.shannonferries.com*) crossing to Killimer in west Clare, a convenient 20-minute shortcut to the West. The Shannon River is 273 km (170 mi) long, and its magnificent estuary stretches westward for another 96 km (60 mi) before reaching the sea.

ADARE

Fodor's Choice ★ *19 km (12 mi) southwest of Limerick City on N21, 82 km (51 mi) northeast of Tralee on N21.*

Set on the banks of the River Maigue, this once-upon-a-timefied village dotted with thatch cottages is famed as one of Ireland's prettiest spots. Perhaps it's more correct to say it's actually one of England's: the place was given a beauty makeover by a rich Anglo lord, the third earl of Dunraven, in the 1820s and 1830s, in an effort to create the "perfect rustic village." To a great extent, he succeeded.

GETTING HERE

BUS TRAVEL Adare can be reached by Bus Éireann buses to and from Limerick Bus Station and Tralee Bus Station. From Limerick take either the Killarney or the Tralee bus, one of which leaves hourly (20 minutes; €6.40 round-trip). From Tralee there is an hourly service (2 hours, €21.50 round-trip). There is no bus station in Adare; buses stop outside the Heritage Centre.

Visitor Information Adare Tourist Office (✉ *Heritage Centre* ☎ *061/396–255* ⊕ *www.adarevillage.com*).

EXPLORING

Few local feathers were ruffled since Dunraven won goodwill by restoring many villagers' houses. Playing into the mid-19th-century vogue for romantic rusticity, the earl "picturesquely" restored many of the town's historic sights, including the remains of two 13th-century abbeys, a 15th-century friary, and the keep of the 13th-century **Desmond Castle** (now the centerpiece of a private golf course). Adjacent to the Adare Heritage Centre you'll find the **Trinitarian Priory,** founded in 1230 and now a convent. From the main bridge (where you can best view the castle), head to the **Augustinian Priory** and its gracious cloister. The most fetching time-burnished allure is provided by Adare's stone-built, thatch-roof cottages, often adorned with colorful, flower-filled window boxes and built for the earl's estate tenants. Some now house boutiques selling Irish crafts and antiques, along with a fine restaurant called the Wild Geese. Adare Manor, an imposing Tudor–Gothic Revival mansion, which was once the grand house of the Dunraven peerage, is now a celebrated hotel; on its grounds you can view two 12th-century ruins, the **St. Nicholas Chapel** and the **Chantry Chapel.**

Adare Heritage Centre has an exhibition of the town's history since 1223, with a 15-minute audiovisual display. There are also a restaurant and three retail outlets: one sells sweaters, another crafts, and the third heraldry items. Guided tours of Desmond Castle (€5) depart from the center by coach from June to September. ✉ *Main St.* ☎ *061/396–666* ⊕ *www.adarevillage.com* 🖃 *Heritage center free, exhibition €5* ⊙ *Daily 9–6, historical exhibition Mar.–June, daily 9–5; July–Sept., daily 9–5:30; Oct.–Dec., weekdays 9–4, weekends 11–4.*

6

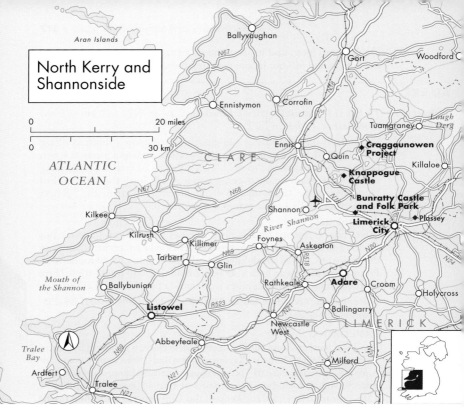

North Kerry and Shannonside

Aran Islands

ATLANTIC
OCEAN

CLARE

LIMERICK

Mouth of
the Shannon

Tralee
Bay

WHERE TO EAT AND STAY

$$$
CONTINENTAL
★

✕ **The Wild Geese.** There's a charming, old-world atmosphere in the series of small dining rooms in this low-ceiling thatch cottage, one of the prettiest in a village famed for its fairy-tale looks. Co-owner and chef David Foley uses the best local produce to create imaginative and seriously good dishes. Try roast rack of lamb with a potato and garlic gratin, or pan-seared Castletownbere scallops with a potato pancake and cauliflower puree. Lobster—grilled with snow peas and shallots and topped with a chive mayonnaise—is a popular summer option. The house dessert platter for two lets you sample all desserts, including the fantastic homemade ice cream. For a real bargain, try their Sunday lunch (€25 for three courses). The restaurant is opposite the Dunraven Arms. ✉ *Rose Cottage* ☎ *061/396–451* ☐ *AE, DC, MC, V* ☉ *Closed Mon. May–Sept; Sun.–Mon. Oct–Apr., and 3 wks Jan. No dinner Sun.*

$$$$
Fodor's Choice
★

▣ **Adare Manor Hotel and Golf Resort.** Play king or queen for a day at this spectacular (and, interestingly, American-owned) Victorian Gothic mansion, once the abode of the earls of Dunraven. The castellated mansion is enormous and set amid 840 acres of French-style gardens. Inside is a wonderland of vast stone arches and heavy wood carvings. Center stage is taken by the decorated ceiling in the baronial central hall and the 36-foot-high, 100-foot-long Minstrels' Gallery, wainscoted in oak. As for decor, the period air is sullied by some bright color schemes. The eight "staterooms" in the original house are the most sumptuous, but most rooms have super-king-size beds and all have heavy drapes and carpets. Adare's golf course, designed by Robert Trent Jones Sr., is one of Ireland's best. (Note that breakfast is a hefty €25 extra here; plan accordingly.) **Pros:** an amazing and unforgettable Gothic experience. **Cons:** dominated by golfers; even the rich find it expensive. ⊠ *Co. Limerick* ☎ *061/396–566* ⊕ *www.adaremanor.ie* ⇌ *62 rooms* ⌂ *In-room: no a/c, Internet, Wi-Fi. In-hotel: restaurant, bars, golf course, pool, Wi-Fi hotspot* ⊟ *AE, DC, MC, V.*

$$$　🏨 **Dunraven Arms.** Adare's landmark coach-stop inn, established in 1792, makes a popular first port of call if you're arriving at Shannon Airport, 40 km (25 mi) northwest—Charles Lindbergh, in fact, stayed in Room 6 while he advised on the airport's design. He might still cotton to the tranquil, antique-adorned place, even though it is somewhat over-restored and generic. Paintings and prints of horseback riders decorate the pale-yellow walls of the cozy bar and lounges; the county hunt still meets here regularly, continuing a centuries-old tradition. The comfortable guest rooms are tastefully furnished with antiques. The elegant Maigue restaurant specializes in modern Irish cuisine, or opt for dining informally in the bright, airy bar by the rose garden. **Pros:** the staff make it a memorable Irish experience; pretty village. **Cons:** decor verges on bland international; expensive for what it is. ⊠ *Main St., Co. Limerick* ☎ *061/605–900–633* ⊕ *www.dunravenhotel.com* ⇌ *76 rooms, 20 suites* ⌂ *In-room: no a/c, Internet. In-hotel: restaurant, bar, pool, gym, Wi-Fi hotspot* ⊟ *AE, DC, MC, V* ⏷❙ *BP.*

$$　　🏨 **Mustard Seed at Echo Lodge.** This is the small country hotel of your
Fodor's Choice　dreams—especially if you enjoy being off the beaten tourist trail and
　★　being pampered. It's a Victorian jewel set atop a small hill overlooking Ballingarry, the Irish equivalent of *la France profonde*—a village that time forgot, deep in rural Ireland, redolent of the days of yore, yet only 13 km (8 mi) southwest of Adare. Owner Dan Mullane has decorated what was once the parish priest's imposing house with flair and wit, placing Chinese inlaid lacquer cabinets and Georgian satinwood wardrobes in the beautifully furnished bedrooms. But for all its finery, this is a fun, down-to-earth place. Much of the food served in the restaurant is grown in the 7 acres of gardens, so the kids can have fun collecting eggs for tomorrow's breakfast. **Pros:** quirky, memorable, and extremely comfortable; acclaimed restaurant. **Cons:** in the middle of nowhere; cock crows at dawn. ⊠ *Ballingarry, Co. Limerick* ☎ *069/68508* ⊕ *www. mustardseed.ie* ⇌ *14 rooms, 2 suites* ⌂ *In-room: no a/c. In-hotel: restaurant, bar, Internet terminal, Wi-Fi hotspot* ⊟ *AE, MC, V* ⊙ *Closed 2 wks in Feb.* ⏷❙ *BP.*

SPORTS AND THE OUTDOORS

GOLF　**Adare Manor Golf Course** (☎ *061/396–204* ⊕ *www.adaremanorgolfclub. com*) is an 18-hole parkland course.

SHOPPING

Adare Cottage (⊠ *Main St.* ☎ *061/396–422*) is a gem of a craft shop in one of the village's thatched cottages.

Adare Gallery (✉ *Main St.* ☎ *061/396–898*) has Irish-made jewelry, porcelain, and woodwork, as well as original paintings. At **George Stacpoole** (✉ *Main St.* ☎ *061/396–409*) you can find antiques and books.

LIMERICK CITY

19 km (12 mi) northeast of Adare, 198 km (123 mi) southwest of Dublin.

Before you ask, there's *no* direct connection between Limerick City and the facetious five-line verse form known as a limerick, which was first popularized by the English writer Edward Lear in his 1846 *Book of Nonsense*. The city, at the head of the Shannon estuary and at the intersection of a number of major crossroads, is an industrial port and the republic's third-largest city (population 75,000). If you fly into or out of Shannon Airport, and have a few hours to spare, do take a look around. The area around the cathedral and the castle is dominated by mid-18th-century buildings with fine Georgian proportions. What's more, the city has undergone considerable revitalization since the days recounted in Frank McCourt's famed childhood memoir, *Angela's Ashes*.

GETTING HERE

BUS TRAVEL   Limerick is a major gateway to the Southwest and the West of Ireland, with frequent connections by Bus Éireann to the town's Colbert Station located here on Parnell Street. Popular routes connect with Cork, Galway, and Tralee, as well as to Dublin and Waterford. Citylink buses, bookable only online, offer a reliable alternative, serving Dublin, Shannon, and Cork airports, as well as routes connecting Limerick with Cork, Dublin, and Galway. In Limerick, Citylink buses leave from Upper Mallow Street. *See Airport Transfers in Getting Around for information on shuttle buses connecting with nearby Shannon Aiport.* As for traveling within Limerick, take the Raheen Bus from outside Brown Thomas Department store on O'Connell Street (which is one-way). The bus runs about every 15 minutes to the Georgian Quarter (a 10-minute walk) and on to the Crescent Shopping Centre at Dooradoyle (3 km [2 mi]).

TRAIN TRAVEL   There is a regular Irish Rail service from Limerick to Dublin (2 hours, €50, one-way), Waterford (2 hours, €50, one-way), Ennis (45 minutes), and Killarney (2 hours). Book online for ticket prices as little as €10 each way. That noted, bus service is usually more frequent and cheaper than trains.

ESSENTIALS

Transportation Contacts Limerick Bus and Rail Station (✉ *Colbert Station, Parnell St.* ☎ *061/315–555*).

Visitor Information Limerick City Tourist Office (✉ *Arthur's Quay, Co. Limerick* ☎ *061/317–522* ⊕ *www.visitlimerick.com*).

EXPLORING

It doesn't help that the things for which Limerick is famous—rugby football, lace, and (Catholic) religious devotion—are all so uncool. This may explain why this big city still lacks a vibrant dining scene (many people prefer to head for the country to dine out, for instance in Adare.

As cute as a Fisher-Price toy village, Adare is a thatched-roof jewel laid out with characteristics that conjure up the English rather than the Irish countryside.

In addition, Limerick is still trying hard to counter a reputation for gang warfare, confined primarily to its less privileged outer suburbs. Sadly, the city center feels like a ghost town once workers have gone home at the end of the day (until the early hours, when young revelers are released from the nightclubs), in spite of the large sums of money spent recently on revitalizing Limerick's quays.

In the Old Customs House on the banks of the Shannon in the city center, the **Hunt Museum** has the finest collection of Celtic and medieval treasures outside the National Museum in Dublin. Ancient Irish metalwork, European objets d'art, and a selection of 20th-century European and Irish paintings—including works by Jack B. Yeats—are on view. A café overlooks the river. ⊠ *Rutland St.* ☎ *061/312–833* ⊕ *www. huntmuseum.com* 🖃 *€8* ⊗ *Mon.–Sat. 10–5, Sun. 2–5.*

Limerick is a predominantly Catholic city, but the Protestant **St. Mary's Cathedral** is the city's oldest religious building. Once a 12th-century palace—pilasters and a rounded Romanesque entrance were part of the original structure—it dates mostly from the 15th century (the blackoak carvings on misericords in the choir stalls are from this period). ⊠ *Bridge St.* ☎ *061/416–238* ⊗ *Daily 9–5.*

First built by the Normans in the early 1200s, **King John's Castle** still bears traces on its north side of a 1691 bombardment. If you climb the drum towers (the oldest section), you'll have a good view of the town and the Shannon. Inside, a 22-minute audiovisual show illustrates the history of Limerick and Ireland; an archaeology center has three excavated, pre-Norman houses; and two exhibition centers display scale models of Limerick from its founding in AD 922. ✉ *Castle St.* ☎ *061/411–201* ⊕ *www.shannonheritage.com* 💰 *€9.45* ⊙ *Daily 10–5.*

⟳   The **Georgian House and Garden** will show you how people lived in Limerick's 18th-century heyday. A tall, narrow row house has been meticulously restored and filled with furnishings from the period, and the garden has been planted in a manner true to the time. The coach house at the rear of the house gives on to a Limerick lane and contains displays relating to the filming of *Angela's Ashes,* including a life-size reconstruction of the McCourt family home. ✉ *Tontine Buildings, 2 Pery Sq.* ☎ *061/314–130* ⊕ *www.limerickcivictrust.ie/georgian* 💰 *€6* ⊙ *Weekdays 10–4, weekends by appointment.*

On **O'Connell Street** you can find the main shopping area, which consists mostly of modest chain stores. However, the street lies one block inland from (east of) the Arthur's Quay Shopping Centre, a mall which, along with the futuristic tourist information center, is one of the first fruits of a civic campaign to develop the Shannonside quays. **Cruises Street,** an inviting pedestrian thoroughfare, has chic shops and occasional street entertainers. It's on the opposite side of O'Connell Street from the Arthur's Quay Shopping Centre.

WHERE TO EAT AND STAY

$$

IRISH

Fodor's Choice

★

✕ **Brasserie One.** The location—a second floor room on one of Limerick's finest Georgian houses, recently converted into a luxury hotel—is naturally elegant but the aim here is to serve robust, brasserie-style food in informal surroundings. Cream walls and gilt mirrors are lit by small crystal sconces and candelabra, while Victorian spoon-back chairs lend a raffish air, as do the lunchtime paper napkins. Fresh local produce is simply and imaginatively presented: seared foie gras with polenta to start, or a tart of onion and Cashel Blue cheese, followed by grilled rib-eye steak with fries and béarnaise sauce. Don't miss the Earl Grey sabayon with aged prunes for dessert. The bar food served in a comfortable lounge on the ground floor is also excellent. ✉ *1 Pery Square,* ☎ *061/402–402* ⊕ *www.oneperysquare.com* ▤ *AE, MC, V* ⊙ *Closed Sun. and Mon.*

$

🏩 **Jurys Inn.** Clean, airy, and in good shape (unlike some of Limerick's other inner-city lodgings), this big, well-run hotel is part of the Jurys budget chain. Rooms are good size and have light-wood furnishings. The hotel overlooks an urban stretch of the Shannon being converted from industrial to leisure use and is a short step from the main shopping and business district. **Pros:** good value for couples and families; reliable hotel chain with consistently helpful staff. **Cons:** totally bland experience; "per room" pricing policy makes it expensive for singles; hugely popular with large groups of partying Irish people. ✉ *Lower Mallow St., Mount Kennett Pl., Co. Limerick* ☎ *061/207–000* ⊕ *limerickhotels. jurysinns.com* 🛏 *151 rooms* 🛠 *In-room: no a/c, Internet. In-hotel: restaurant, bar, Wi-Fi hotspot* ▤ *AE, DC, MC, V* ⊙| *BP.*

$

🏩 **Patrick Punch's Hotel.** A striking, edgy glass-and-steel facade has been built onto a landmark Victorian pub to create a hotel where style and pizzazz are combined with a friendly Irish welcome. Located a short hop from the city ring road, midway between the town center and the

Looming over Adare's Desmond Castle is the regal Adare Manor Hotel, once home to the town's lord of the manor, the earl of Dunraven.

attractive Crescent Shopping Centre, it's a favorite with both business and leisure travelers. The spacious, modern lobby, with its funky red leather sofas and glass tables, sets the tone for a confidently stylish hotel, typical of Ireland's economic boom. Bathrooms are big and beds are huge, with porthole-like lights above pale-wood headboards. Leather tub chairs bring a note of color to the neutral tones of the uncluttered decor. Good leisure facilities, secure parking, and a lively pub and restaurant add to the appeal. **Pros:** fun and friendly; safe inner suburban location; easy access to bus and taxis. **Cons:** indoor parking is on a first-come, first-served basis; 20-minute walk or 5-minute bus or taxi ride to city center. ⊠ *Punch's Cross, Co. Limerick* ☎ *061/460–800* ⊕ *www.dghotels.com* ⬩*71 rooms* ⬥ *In-room: no a/c, Internet. In-hotel: restaurant, bar, pool, gym, Wi-Fi hotspot* ▭ *MC, V.*

NIGHTLIFE AND THE ARTS

ART GALLERIES The **Belltable Arts Center** (⊠ *69 O'Connell St.* ☎ *061/319–866* ⊕ *www. belltable.ie*) has exhibition space and a small auditorium for touring productions. The **Limerick City Gallery of Art** (⊠ *Pery Sq.* ☎ *061/310–633* ⊕ *gallery.limerick.ie*) owns a small permanent collection of Irish art and mounts exhibits of contemporary art.

PUBS, CABARET, AND DISCOS **Dolan's Pub** (⊠ *3–4 Dock Rd.* ☎ *061/314–483* ⊕ *www.dolanspub.com*) is a lively waterfront spot with traditional Irish music every night, and dancing classes from September to May. Dolan's Warehouse, under the same management and in the same location, is a live-music venue with top national and international acts. **Hogan's** (⊠ *20–24 Old Clare St.* ☎ *061/411–279*) has a traditional music session every Monday, Wednesday, and Saturday. The riverside **Locke's Bar** (⊠ *3 George's Quay*

☎ *061/413–733*) is one of Limerick's oldest bars, dating from 1724, and has Irish music Sunday, Monday, and Tuesday nights. It's also a great place for outdoor drinking in summer. There's traditional music at **Nancy Blake's Pub** (✉ *19 Denmark St.* ☎ *061/416–443*) year-round Sunday–Wednesday from 9 PM. **William G. South's Pub** (✉ *The Crescent* ☎ *061/318–850*) is an old-fashioned pub that's typical of the age of Frank McCourt's *Angela's Ashes*. There's no music, but do drop by for lunchtime bar food (Monday–Saturday 12:30–3) or a drink.

SHOPPING

DEPARTMENT STORES

Limerick has a branch of **Brown Thomas** (✉ *O'Connell St.* ☎ *061/417–222*), Ireland's upscale department store. **Debenham's** (✉ *O'Connell St.* ☎ *061/415–622*) is a large, midrange department store. **Dunnes Stores** (✉ *130 Sarsfield St.* ☎ *061/412–666*) is, perhaps, Ireland's favorite department store chain. **Penneys** (✉ *137 O'Connell St.* ☎ *061/227–244*) sells inexpensive clothing; it's a great place for low-price rain gear.

SPECIALTY SHOPS

The **Celtic Bookshop** (✉ *2 Rutland St.* ☎ *061/401–155*) specializes in books of Irish interest. **Davern & Bell** (✉ *22 Thomas St.* ☎ *061/481–967*) is a gallery of contemporary Irish crafts, mainly ceramics. **Irish Handcrafts** (✉ *Arthur's Quay* ☎ *061/415–504*) has a good selection of Irish sweaters, mohair rugs, and Irish tweed. **Seoidín** (✉ *6 Sarsfield St.* ☎ *061/318–011*) has an interesting selection of jewelry, and gifts.

BUNRATTY CASTLE AND FOLK PARK

18 km (10 mi) west of Limerick City on N18 road to Shannon Airport.

Ⓒ
★

Bunratty Castle and Folk Park are two of those rare attractions that appeal to all ages and manage to be both educational and fun. Built in 1460, the castle—a stolid, massive affair with four square keep towers—has been fully restored and decorated with 15th- to 17th-century furniture and furnishings. It gives wonderful insight into the life of those times. As you pass under the walls of Bunratty, look for the three "murder holes" that allowed defenders to pour boiling oil on attackers below.

GETTING HERE

BUS TRAVEL

Bunratty is on the route to Shannon Airport, so you can get here using this Bus Éireann route that links Shannon Airport with Limerick Bus Station. The journey takes about 15 minutes and costs €3.40 one-way. Be sure to check that the bus stops at Bunratty when you are boarding. A taxi with All Route Taxis from Limerick's city center costs around €25.

EXPLORING

Bunratty medieval banquets are world famous and held nightly at 5:45 and 8:45; the cost is €59.95. You're welcomed by Irish colleens in 15th-century dress, who bear the traditional bread of friendship. Then you're led off to a reception, where you'll quaff mead made from fermented honey, apple juice, clover, and heather. Before sitting down at long tables in the candlelighted great hall, you can don a bib. You'll need it, because you eat the four-course meal medieval-style: with your fingers. Serving "wenches" take time out to sing a few ballads or pluck harp strings. The banquets may not be authentic, but they're fun; they're also popular, so book as far in advance as possible. The Shannon Web site (⊕ *www.shannonheritage.com*) has good deals for advance booking, and includes a combination of castle visits and banquets.

On the castle grounds the quaint Bunratty Folk Park re-creates a 19th-century village street and has examples of traditional rural housing. Exhibits include a working blacksmith's forge; demonstrations of flour milling, bread making, candle making, thatching, and other skills; and a variety of farm animals. An adjacent museum of agricultural machinery can't compete with the furry and feathered live exhibits. If you can't get a reservation for the medieval banquet at the castle, a *ceilí* folk-music session known as the Traditional Irish Night, held nightly May to September at 5:45 and 9 (€49.95) at the Folk Park is the next best thing. The program features traditional Irish dance and song and a meal of Irish stew, soda bread, and apple pie. Prices for banquets and entrance to Bunratty are generously discounted if you buy online. No visit to Bunratty is complete without a drink in **Durty Nelly's** (☎ *061/364–072*), an old-world (but touristy) pub beside the Folk Park entrance. Its fanciful decor has inspired imitations around the world. ☎ *061/361–511* ⊕ *www.shannonheritage.com* 🖂 *€15.75* ⊙ *Sept.–May, daily 9–5:30, last entry at 4; June–Aug., daily 9–6, last entry at 5.*

KNAPPOGUE CASTLE

21 km (13 mi) north of Bunratty.

☺ ★ With a name that means "hill of the kiss," Knappogue is one of Ireland's most beautiful medieval tower-house castles. A 15th-century MacNamara stronghold, Knappogue Castle was renovated in the Victorian era and fitted with storybook details. Restored by a wealthy American family, the castle has now been retro-ed in 15th-century style. By day you can enjoy a castle tour, including the walled garden, which looks like something out of a medieval Book of Hours. In the evenings it hosts fun and fabulous **medieval banquets** (€57). You're first greeted at the main door by the Ladies of the Castle who escort you to the Dalcassian Hall, where you enjoy a goblet of mead (honey wine), listen to harp and fiddle, then proceed to the banqueting hall for a four-course meal, great Irish choral music, and a theatrical set-piece in which the Butler and the Earl argue the virtues of Gallantry. As an added allure, the castle looks spectacular when floodlighted. Who can resist? 🖂 *5 km (3 mi) southeast of Quin on R649* ☎ *061/368–103* ⊕ *www.shannonheritage. com* 🖂 *€8* ⊙ *May–Sept., daily 10–5.*

CRAGGAUNOWEN PROJECT

6 km (4 mi) northeast of Knappogue Castle.

☺ ★ It's a strange experience to walk across the little wooden bridge above reeds rippling in the lake into Ireland's Celtic past as a jumbo jet passes overhead on its way into Shannon Airport—1,500 years of history compressed into an instant. But if you love all things Celtic, you'll have to visit the **Craggaunowen Project.** The romantic centerpiece is Craggaunowen Castle, a 16th-century tower house restored with furnishings from the period. Huddling beneath its battlements are two replicas of early Celtic-style dwellings. On an island in the lake, reached by a narrow footbridge, is a clay-and-wattle *crannóg*, a fortified lake dwelling; it resembles what might have been built in the 6th or 7th century, when Celtic influence still predominated in Ireland. The reconstruction of a small ring fort shows how an ordinary soldier would have lived in the 5th or 6th century, at the time Christianity was being established here. Characters from the past explain their Iron Age (500 BC–AD 450) lifestyle, show you around their small holding stocked with animals, and demonstrate crafts skills from bygone ages. ⊠ *Signposted off road to Sixmilebridge, about 10 km (6 mi) east of Quin Town Sixmilebridge* ☏ *061/360–788* ⊕ *www.shannonheritage. com* ▣ *€9.40* ☉ *Mid-May–mid-Sept., daily 10–6.*

County Cork

WORD OF MOUTH

"Kissing the Blarney Stone? I do plan to make a quick swipe with a Clorox wipe before planting my lips! After reading the other posts in this Fodor's Forum, it might even have to be an 'air-kiss'!"

—abasketcase

"I doubt whether a Clorox 'wiped' stone would grant anyone the Gift of Gab."

—stokebailey

WELCOME TO COUNTY CORK

TOP REASONS TO GO

★ **Blarney Castle:** Visitors line up to kiss the Blarney Stone and acquire the gift of gab. This is an impressive 15th-century tower-house castle with unusual gardens, at their best in daffodil season— early to mid-March.

★ **Cobh:** If you have Irish roots, chances are your ancestors left from this characterful little port. The Queenstown Story commemorates the million emigrants who sailed from here.

★ **Kinsale:** This picturesque port, long a favored haven of sailors, is famed for its fine dining in tiny front-parlor eateries. It's also a chic place to see and be seen—the Irish San Tropez.

★ **The Cork Coastline:** On the drive from Kinsale to Skibbereen you'll encounter friendly locals, charming little villages, unspoiled scenery, and excellent restaurants and pubs.

★ **Bantry House:** One of Ireland's finest stately homes, packed with treasures from all over Europe, stands on a breathtaking bluff.

1 Cork City. Identifying Cork as Ireland's second-largest city is misleading— it has just one-tenth the population of Dublin, and its character is more along the lines of a college town (which it is) than a metropolis. That means lively pubs, quirky cafés, and lots of good music, trad and otherwise.

GETTING ORIENTED

After exploring the delights of Cork City, use it as a base to explore the county's famed wonders, including Blarney Castle. Get your fill of five-star scenery by traveling east to Midleton and Shanagarry—famed respectively for their whiskey and culinary traditions—then north to Fermoy and the Blackwater River, one of Ireland's prime angling locations. Due south is fashionable Kinsale while westward lies Skibbereen and picture-perfect Bantry. From here a cliff-top road with stunning views leads to ruggedly beautiful Glengarriff.

3 West Cork. The resort town of Kinsale is the gateway to an attractive rocky coastline east and west of Skibbereen, containing Roaring Water Bay. The area is known for its atmospheric pubs and cottage restaurants.

2 East and North Cork. Products of the rich farming land east of Cork city used to include whiskey: see how it was made at the Jameson Heritage Centre in Midleton, just a short drive from Ballymaloe House, pioneer of the new Irish cuisine. To the north of the city, some of the best salmon fishing in the world is to be had on the peaceful Blackwater River.

4 Bantry Bay. At the top of the long sea inlet is the imposing Georgian mansion, Bantry House, just outside Bantry Town. The road between here and subtropical Glengarriff climbs high above the water, offering sweeping views of the bay; the hills of the Beara Peninsula are a scenic highlight.

COUNTY CORK PLANNER

Transportation Basics

Scenery is the main attraction in County Cork, and unless you're a biker or hiker, the best option for taking it in is to rent a car.

Once behind the wheel, plan to adopt the local pace—slow. Covering about 100 km (60 mi) a day is ideal, with many stops along the way. Speed is dictated to some degree by the roads: most are small, with one lane in each direction and plenty of bends and hills.

Without a car, your best bet is to base yourself in Cork, accessible by train from Dublin, and take organized day trips or use the local buses.

Making the Most of Your Time

If you're here for a short stay—three days or fewer—you'd do well to base yourself in Cork City, which is easy to explore on foot. Allow a day to take in the sights of the city center, including the Crawford Gallery, the artisan food at the indoor English Market, and Patrick Street's boutiques and shopping malls. Blarney is only a short hop from town, and the half-day outing can be expanded by exploring the parkland around the castle and the village craft shops. Spend a day visiting the wildlife park at Fota and the Heritage Center in Cobh on Cork's enormous harbor near Ballymaloe House, the famous restaurant-hotel that was the fountainhead of the new Irish cuisine. Kinsale, a historic fishing port packed with restaurants and shops, is worth a day itself, and is also the gateway to the scenic coast of west Cork. Here narrow roads meander westward through attractive waterside villages to the splendid prospect of Bantry Bay, overlooked by the stately Bantry House. Still further west is another highlight, the sheltered inlet of Glengarriff, with subtropical plants and basking seals. You can drive from Kinsale to Glengarriff in under two hours, but you will want to stop and linger.

The Pick of the Ports

Lined with adorable villages and photo-friendly fishing ports, Cork's coast is one of its major attractions. The biggest port, Cobh, to the east of the Cork City, was the point of embarkation for most 19th-century Irish transatlantic passengers and it retains a strong whiff of nostalgia. Dominated by its tall-spired cathedral, the town, filled with 19th-century buildings, climbs vertiginously up and down hill and faces southwards out to sea. Kinsale is more of a village than a town, built by a hill at one end of an unspoiled fjordlike harbor. It has a buzzing, cosmopolitan air, with its yacht marinas and tempting restaurants, but also offers serious history at Charles Fort, and memorable waterside footpaths. Timoleague is a sleepy hamlet, nestled beside the romantic ruins of its abbey. Castletownshend is voted the prettiest village by many, while others prefer the sheltered waters of subtropical Glengarriff.

What to Bring Home

Locally made ceramics, knitwear, and jewelry can be found in the region's crafts shops, but it's also worth stopping to investigate signposts on the road directing you to the studios of the craftspeople themselves. The **West Cork Craft and Design Guild** (☎ 028/21890 ⊕ www.westcorkcraft. org) is an association of over 20 elite craft makers, based in the scenic west of the county, most of whom welcome visitors to their studios by appointment.

Where to Eat

The Southwest is a great place for good food. County Cork, home of Slow Food Ireland, has become Ireland's top foodie destination. Cork City has a wide choice of middle-range restaurants featuring fresh local produce.

Adventurous, well-traveled chefs make the most of the first-rate local specialties: succulent beef and lamb, game in the winter, fresh seafood, and farmhouse cheeses. The best restaurants are not all in towns: even the tiniest villages can boast a gastropub, while you need to take a ferry to dine at Island Cottage.

Where to Stay

For accommodations, County Cork has some of the great country houses, including Ballyvolane House near the Blackwater River; Ballymaloe House in east Cork, along with the guest wing at magnificent Bantry House.

At the other end of the spectrum is the uniquely Irish experience of a farmhouse bed-and-breakfast, such as the Glen Country House, where you are welcomed by the family dogs and treated as a long-lost friend. In between is a range of excellent family-owned and -run traditional hotels, such as the Blarney Castle Hotel on the village green, the riverside Innishannon House, and the Seaview in Ballylickey on Bantry Bay.

When to Go

The best times to visit County Cork are mid-March to June, and September and October. In July and August it's the peak holiday period, meaning roads are more crowded, prices are higher, and the best places are booked in advance. March can be chilly, with daily temperatures in the 40s and 50s. The average high in June is 18°C (65°F), which is about as hot as it gets. May and June are the sunniest months. May and September the driest months. The farther west you go, the more likely you'll get rain. From November to March daylight hours are short, the weather is damp, and many places close.

Best Fests

Cork is known as Ireland's festival city, the longest-running being the **Cork Film Festival** (⊕ www.corkfilmfest.org) in the second week in October, and the biggest the **Guinness Cork Jazz Festival** (⊕ www. guinnessjazzfestival.com) on the last weekend in October. The West Cork Chamber Music Festival brings internationally renowned musicians to perform in the library of Bantry House for 10 days in late June.

People come back year after year to Kinsale's **Autumn Flavours Festival** (⊕ www. kinsalerestaurants.com), which creates a party atmosphere all over town for the first weekend in October.

DINING & LODGING PRICE CATEGORIES (IN EUROS)					
	¢	$	$$	$$$	$$$$
Restaurants	under €12	€12–€18	€19–€24	€25–€32	over €32
Hotels	under €80	€80–€120	€121–€170	€171–€210	over €210

Restaurant prices are for a main course at dinner. Hotel prices are for a standard double room in high season.

GETTING AROUND

Train Travel

The direct service from Dublin Heuston Station to Cork runs hourly between 6:15 AM and 9 PM, with more trains at peak times (7 AM–9:30 AM and 5 PM–7 PM). It takes 3 hours. The best deals are to be had booking online. The regular return fare is €71 (which goes as low as €10 each way using off-peak trains booked online). There are nine trains a day from Tralee to Cork, stopping at Killarney, three of which are direct trains (on the others passengers must change at Mallow). The fare from Cork to Tralee is around €60 round-trip. The journey from Tralee takes 2 hours, and from Killarney about 1½ hours. There are nine trains a day from Limerick Junction to Cork, a journey of about an hour. Limerick Junction has connections to Ennis in the west, and to the Rosslare Ferry Port. The Rosslare-Cork journey is a cumbersome one involving changes at Waterford and Limerick, and takes at least 5 hours. A suburban rail service has 22 departures daily from Cork's Kent Station, stops at Fota Island and Cobh, and offers better Cork Harbor views than the road. The journey to Cobh takes 25 minutes. A branch line continues on to Midleton, 25 minutes from Cork.

Bus Travel

Bus Éireann operates services from Dublin, Galway, Shannon Airport, Limerick, Tralee, and Killarney to Cork City. Be warned: even their so-called Expressway services from Dublin make at least two stops en route, giving a journey time of four to five hours (depending on traffic). The good news is that they are cheap, with a standard adult round-trip fare of around €22. Most towns in the region are served by the provincial Bus Éireann network. The main bus terminal is in Cork City, where there are luggage storage facilities (manned from 9 to 6, along with the information counter). Citylink has six services a day to Cork from Galway City via Shannon Airport and Limerick, with a journey time of about four hours from Galway; these can be booked online, or consult the online timetable, and buy your ticket on the bus. Fares are about half the rail equivalent, and can be as low as €1. Aircoach has seven services a day from Dublin Airport via Dublin City Center and six towns en route to Cork City and Cork Airport at €14 each way. The first coach is at 7 AM and the last at 7 PM; travel times run from four hours upwards.

FARES AND SCHEDULES

Buses tend to stop running in the early evening, which is fine if you want to stay overnight and leave the next morning, but rules out many day trips—unless you want to spend most of the day on the bus. As a general rule, the smaller and more remote the town, the less frequent its bus service. For example, Kinsale, a well-developed resort 29 km (18 mi) from Cork, is served by at least seven buses a day, both arriving and departing. Consult with hotel concierges, tourist board staffers, or the bus line Web site for bus schedules.

Bus Information Aircoach (☎ *01/844–7118* ⊕ *www.aircoach.ie*). **Bus Éireann** (☎ *01/836–6111 in Dublin 021/450–8188 in Cork* ⊕ *www.buseireann.ie*). **Citylink** (☎ *091/564–163* ⊕ *www.citylink.ie*). **Cork Bus Station** (✉ *Parnell Pl.* ☎ *021/450–8188, 021/422–2129 recorded message off-hrs [6 PM–9 AM]*).

Air Travel

Cork (ORK) Airport has flights from European destinations, while Shannon (SNN) Airport in the West also receives transatlantic traffic.

Cork Airport, 5 km (3 mi) south of Cork City on the Kinsale road, has direct flights daily to Dublin, London (Heathrow Gatwick, and Stansted), Manchester, East Midlands, Paris, and Malaga, and direct flights to many other European cities.

Shannon Airport, 26 km (16 mi) west of Limerick City, is the point of arrival for many transatlantic flights, including direct flights from Atlanta, Chicago, Philadelphia, Toronto (summer only), and New York City (from both JFK and Newark); it also has regular flights from the United Kingdom and many European cities.

Airport Information **Cork Airport** (☎ 021/431–3131 ⊕ www.corkairport.com). **Shannon Airport** (☎ 061/471–444 ⊕ www.shannonairport.com).

Car Travel

The main driving route from Dublin is the N7/M7, connecting with the N8 in Portlaoise to continue 257 km (160 mi) on to Cork City. The journey time between Dublin and Cork is about three hours. About half of the journey is on M (motorway) roads, and most of it has two lanes in each direction. From Rosslare Harbour by car, take N25 208 km (129 mi) to Cork; allow 3½ hours for the journey.

A car is the ideal way to explore this region, packed as it is with scenic routes, attractive but remote towns, and a host of out-of-the-way restaurants and hotels that deserve a detour. Road upgrading has not kept up with the increased usage, and the result is our old friend, the peak-hour traffic jam.

As for parking, Kinsale, Clonakilty, Skibbereen, and Bantry are all amply provided with ground-level parking lots: follow the blue P signs. In Cork it's advisable to use a multistory parking garage, as on-street parking can be hard to find.

If you do get lucky, you'll have to become familiar with "disk" parking regulations, which involve buying a ticket (or disk) for around €2 an hour from a machine or a shop and displaying it. Beware: car clamper officers are active!

Airport Transfers

Skylink operate a frequent shuttle service between Cork Airport and most city center hotels from 5:20 AM to midnight. Tickets cost €5 one-way, €8 round-trip, and can be purchased online or when you board the bus. There are two routes, so state your hotel when boarding. Bus Éireann has a bus link between Cork Airport and the Cork City Bus Terminal about every 30 minutes (€3.40 one-way). Bus Éireann also runs a bus service from the airport to Kinsale, roughly every hour (€5.40 one-way, €8.80 round-trip). Tickets for both destinations can be bought on boarding the bus. Skylink also connects Cork with Shannon Airport.

Shuttles **Bus Éireann** (☎ 061/474–311 ⊕ www.buseireann.ie). **Cork City Bus Terminal** (✉ Parnell Pl., Cork ☎ 021/450–6066). **Skylink** (☎ 021/432–1020 ⊕ www.skylinkcork.com).

7

GETTING AROUND

Visitor Information

Fáilte Ireland provides a free information service; its tourist information offices (TIOs) also sell a selection of tourist literature. For a small fee it will book accommodations anywhere in Ireland. Year-round TIOs can be found in Bantry, Clonakilty, Cobh (Cork Harbour), Cork Airport (Arrivals), Cork City, and Skibbereen. Those in Blarney, Glengarriff, Kinsale, and Midleton are open May to mid-September or the end of October.

These offices are usually open Monday–Saturday 9–6; in July and August TIOs are also open Sunday 9–6.

Under a Visitor Information heading, we list the tourist office address, phone, and main Web site for the main towns that are found in this chapter.

Train Information

Irish Rail–Iarnód Éireann (☎ 01/836–6222, 021/450– 8188 for Cork train station ⊕ www.irishrail.ie). **Inquiries** (☎ 021/450–6766 in Cork). **Kent Station** (✉ Lower Glanmire Rd., Cork City ☎ 021/450–6766 for timetable).

Special-Interest Tours

Gerry Coughlan of Arrangements Unlimited can prearrange special-interest group tours of the Cork region. Half-day and full-day tours are individually planned for groups of 10 or more to satisfy each visitor's needs.

Country House Tours organizes self-driven or chauffeur-driven group tours with accommodations in private country houses and castles. It also conducts special-interest tours, including gardens, architecture, ghosts, and golf.

If you want to combine your visit to Ireland with some hands-on craft workshops, Adrian Wistreich of the Kinsale Pottery & Arts Centre will put a package together for you. Programs on offer include pottery, life drawing, drama, creative writing, jewelry making, bronze casting, and stained glass. Work as many hours a day as you like, and choose between a range of local accommodation. Adrian can also arrange for you to work with specialist craft makers, including Ben Russell, a noted wood carver, and Alison Ospina, a "green" chair maker, in their studios in West Cork.

Fees and Schedules Arrangements Unlimited (✉ 1 Woolhara Park, Douglas, Cork City, Co. Cork ☎ 021/429–3873 ⊕ www.arrangements.ie). **Country House Tours** (✉ 71 Waterloo Rd., Dublin ☎ 01/668–6463 ⊕ www.tourismresources.ie). **Kinsale Pottery & Arts Centre** (✉ Olcote, Ballinacurra, Kinsale, Co. Cork ☎ 021/477– 7758 ⊕ www.kinsaleceramics.com).

Boat and Ferry Travel

The Fastnet Line runs a regular car ferry service from Swansea in Wales to Ringaskiddy on Cork Harbour (the crossing takes 9–10 hours), while the MV *Julia* sails overnight six nights a week, with additional sailings in July and August.

Swansea is on the M4 motorway, and the crossing saves about 600 km (375 mi) driving, compared to traveling to Cork from Fishguard or Port Talbot via Rosslare *(see Getting Here in the Southeast chapter).*

The regular schedule departs from Cork on Tuesday, Thursday, and Saturday, and leaves Swansea for Cork on Friday and Sunday.

Prices and departure times vary according to season, so call to confirm.

Fastnet Line (✉ *Ferry Terminal, Ringaskiddy, Cork* ☏ *021/437–8892* ⊕ *www.fastnetline.com*).

Walking Tours

SouthWestWalks Ireland has a variety of walks along the coast of West Cork, around the Sheep's Head and Beara Peninsula in Bantry Bay; some include accommodation and evening meals.

Michael Martin's Titanic Trail is a 90-minute guided walking tour of Cobh ranging from the *Titanic* to coffin ships; it departs daily at 11 AM from the Commodore Hotel (€7.50).

Dermot Ryan, a native of Kinsale and a local history enthusiast, leads Kinsale Heritage Town Walks daily at 10:30 AM and 4:30 PM (€5). You walk the walk, he talks the talk, and children go free.

Don Herlihy's Historic Stroll in Old Kinsale departs from the town's tourist office daily at 11:15; you'll learn Kinsale's links to "Man Friday" and the truth about Kinsale Hookers pirates.

Historic Stroll in Old Kinsale (✉ *Kinsale* ☏ *021/477–2873* ⊕ *www.historicstrollkinsale.com*).

Kinsale Heritage Town Walks (✉ *Kinsale* ☏ *021/477–2729* ⊕ *www.kinsaleheritage.com*).

SouthWestWalks Ireland (✉ *6 Church St., Tralee* ☏ *066/712–8733* ⊕ *www.southwestwalksireland.com*).

Titanic Trail (✉ *Cobh* ☏ *021/481–5211* ⊕ *www.titanic-trail.com*).

Bus Tours

Bus Éireann offers a range of daylong and half-day guided tours from June to September.

You can book them at the bus station in Cork or at any tourist office.

A full-day tour costs about €32, half-day €16.

Bus Éireann also offers open-top bus tours of Cork City on Tuesday and Saturday in July and August for €6.

Bus Éireann (☏ *021/450–8188 in Cork* ⊕ *www.buseireann.ie*).

Taxi Travel

Taxis at Shannon and Cork airports connect with those cities; Shannon to Limerick City costs about €40; from Cork to Cork City Railway Station, about €15.

It costs €4.10 to hire a taxi on the street (€4.45 by night); add €2 to book one by phone, and €1.03 per kilometer or part of a kilometer for the first 15 km.

Full details of fares and conditions are on the Taxi Regulator Web site.

Taxi Companies Cork Taxi Co-Op (☏ *021/477–2222* ⊕ *www.corktaxi.ie*). **Taxi Regulator** (⊕ *taxiregulator.ie*).

Updated
by Alannah
Howard

The place names in this region have an undeniable Irish lilt: Blarney, where you can acquire the gift of the gab, famine-wracked Skibbereen, and beautiful Bantry Bay. But just as evocative is the scenery around every other turn in the road.

With its striking southwestern landscape, charming towns, mild climate, and deep-rooted history, the county of Cork is perennially popular with visitors. The county may be Ireland's largest, Cork may be Ireland's second-biggest city, and Kinsale the largest beep on the Irish foodie radar screen but nearly everything else here is small-scale and friendly. The towns are tiny, the roads narrow and twisting, with scenic views around every corner. Brightly painted villages and toy harbors encourage you to stop and linger. From Kinsale along the coast to Glengarriff you'll find miles of pretty country lanes meandering through rich farmland. Indeed, this is Ireland's picture-postcard country.

Everything seems delightfully low-key and human-scale, with plenty of isolated farmhouses and free-ranging sheep, the kind that seem to have wandered off the pages of a children's picture book. But all this scenic farmland is not just a pretty backdrop: it is the source of the raw material for a talented new generation of artisan food producers. The local chefs have used the native bounty of farms, fields, lakes, and coast to become superstars. As this chapter's special photo feature, "A Taste of Ireland," reveals, County Cork has become a little paradise of fresh, rustic Irish cuisine.

But as you look over the fuchsia-laden hedges that ring thriving dairy farms or stop at a wayside restaurant to sample locally sourced beef, it's difficult to imagine that some 150 years ago this area was decimated by famine. Thousands perished in fields and workhouses, and thousands more took "coffin ships" from Cobh in Cork Harbor to the New World. The region was battered again during both the War for Independence and the Civil War that was fought with intensity in and around "Rebel Cork" between 1919 and 1921. Economic recovery didn't pick up until the late 1960s, and tourist development did not surge until the mid-'90s.

During the Irish economic boom large sections of Cork's city center were rebuilt with an array of all-weather shopping malls. However, the landmark buildings survived and the streetscape got a much-needed face-lift in 2005, Cork's year as European Capital of Culture. The lilting up-and-down accent of Cork city's locals will immediately charm you, as will the generally festive air that prevails in its streets, making many visitors assume that some kind of festival is going on, even on those rare occasions when it is not. Cork has a reputation as Ireland's festival city, with jazz, film, and choral music festivals and the Midsummer Arts Festivals all attracting huge, good-natured crowds

The recent boom years were a mixed blessing. County Cork's main routes are no longer traffic-free, but the roads themselves are better. There's a greater choice of accommodations but many of the newer hotels are bland in decor and greeting (the once-traditional warm Irish welcome is no longer ubiquitous, so enjoy it when you get it). Although the Southwest has several country-house hotels, including the most famous of them all, Ballymaloe House, it is basically an easygoing, unpretentious region, where informality and simplicity prevail. As in the rest of Ireland, social life revolves around the pub, and a visit to any neighborhood favorite is the best way to find out what's going on. Local residents have not lost their natural curiosity about "strangers," as visitors are called. You will frequently be asked, "Are you enjoying your holiday?" "Yes" is not a good enough answer: what the locals are really after is your life story. And if you haven't got a good one you might want to make it up.

CORK CITY

The major metropolis of the South, Cork makes a great base from which to explore the whole of the southern region. It is Ireland's second-largest city—but you have to put this in perspective. It actually runs a distant second, with a population of 123,000, roughly one-tenth the size of Dublin. In the last decade, with high prices and overcrowding in Dublin, Cork became the new hot spot for urban thrills. Groups of Europeans frequently pop over for a weekend of partying, as the city is a spirited place, with a formidable pub culture, a lively traditional-music scene, a respected and progressive university, attractive art galleries, and off-beat cafés. The city received a major boost in 2005 when it was named a Capital of Culture by the European Union—the smallest city ever to receive the designation. The result was a burst in development; one of the lasting legacies is a striking but controversial redesign of the city center (Patrick Street and Grand Parade) by Barcelona-based architect Beth Galí. Next to Galway, Cork has one of the largest communities of hippies, dropouts, musicians, and poets outside Dublin. Cork can be very "Irish" (hurling, Gaelic football, locally televised plowing contests, music pubs, and peat smoke). But depending on what part of town you're in, Cork can also be distinctly un-Irish—the sort of place where hippies, gays, and conservative farmers drink at the same pub.

The city received its first charter in 1185 from Prince John of Norman England, and it takes its name from the Irish word *corcaigh,* meaning "marshy place." The original 6th-century settlement was spread over 13 small islands in the River Lee. Major development occurred during the 17th and 18th centuries with the expansion of the butter trade, and many attractive Georgian-design buildings with wide bowfront windows were constructed during this time. As late as 1770 Cork's present-day main streets—Grand Parade, Patrick Street, and the South Mall—were submerged under the Lee. Around 1800, when the Lee was partially dammed, the river divided into two streams that now flow through the city, leaving the main business and commercial center on an island, not unlike Paris's Île de la Cité. As a result, the city features a number of bridges and quays, which, although initially confusing, add greatly to the port's unique character.

In late summer and early autumn, the city hosts some of Ireland's premier festivals, including October's huge Cork Jazz Festival, which draws about 50,000 visitors from around the world, and the Cork Film Festival, also in October.

GETTING HERE AND AROUND

BUS TRAVEL Bus Éireann operates services from Dublin, Galway, Shannon Airport, Limerick, Tralee, and Killarney to Cork Bus Station, located on Parnell Place on the south side of the River Lee. As noted, Bus Éireann's Expressway services from Dublin make at least two stops en route, and the slow-but-cheap (€22, round-trip) trips can run as long as five hours. Citylink has six services a day from Galway City via Shannon Airport from €14 one-way. Bus Éireann routes connect with suburban destinations including the 30-minute ride to Blarney (€6.20) and the 40-minute ride to Kinsale (€10.50). Aircoachhas seven services a day from Dublin Airport via Dublin's city center with six stops en route, from about €12 one-way. Both Citylink and Aircoach arrive in Cork at the back entrance to the Metropole Hotel on the opposite side of the River Lee from the main Parnell Place bus station. Cork's city center is compact and walkable but if you want to bus the mile to the university campus, pick up a No. 8 outside Debenham's department store on Patrick Street (90¢ one-way). A great introductory tour is the hop-on, hop-off Cork City Tour run by Cronin's Coaches, a double-decker bus that departs daily (March-October, €14) from the Tourist Information Office on Grand Parade between 9:30 AM and 5 PM.

TRAIN TRAVEL The direct service run by Irish Rail–Iarnód Éireann from Dublin Heuston Station to Cork's Kent Station runs hourly between 6:15 AM and 9 PM, with more trains at peak times (7 AM–9:30 AM and 5 PM–7 PM). The journey takes 2 hours 55 minutes. The regular return fare is €71, which goes as low as €10 each way using off-peak trains booked online. A bus service (Route 5) leaves Kent Station every 15 minutes for Cork's city center (Patrick Street), also serving Washington Street and College Road to the west of the city.

ESSENTIALS

Transportation Contacts Cork Bus Station (✉ *Parnell Pl.* ☎ *021/450–8188, 021/422–2129 recorded message off-hrs (6 PM–9 AM)*). **Cliffs of Moher Cruises** (☎ *065/7075949* ⊕ *www.cliffs-of-moher-cruises.com*). **Cronin's Coaches** (☎ *021/430–9090* ⊕ *www.croninscoaches.com*). **Kent Rail Station** (✉ *Lower Glanmire Rd., Co. Cork* ☎ *021/450–6766 for timetable*).

Visitor Information Cork City Tourist Office (✉ *Grand Parade, Co. Cork* ☎ *021/425–5100* ⊕ *www.discoverireland.ie/southwest*).

EXPLORING

"Cork is the loveliest city in the world. Anyone who does not agree with me either was not born there or is prejudiced." Whether or not Cork merits this accolade of native poet and writer Robert Gibbings, the city does have plenty to recommend it, including several noteworthy historic sites. They're spread out a bit, but still the best way to see the city is on foot. Patrick Street is the city center's main thoroughfare. Cork may have few "don't miss" attractions, but that's not the point. It's the sum of its parts that make the city so entertaining.

You can tour the center of the city in a morning or an afternoon, depending on how much you plan to shop along the way. To really see everything, however, allow a full day, with a break for lunch at the Farmgate Café in the English Market. Also note that the Crawford Art Gallery and the English Market are closed on Sunday.

TOP ATTRACTIONS

❹ Cork Vision Centre. Located in the renovated St. Peter's Church, an 18th-century building in what was once the bustling heart of medieval Cork, this historical society provides an excellent introduction to the city's history and geography. The highlight is a detailed 1:500-scale model of the city, showing how it has changed over the ages. ✉ *Washington St., Washington Village* ☎ *021/427–2706* ⊕ *www.corkvisioncentre.com* 🎫 *Free* ♥ *Weekdays 9–5.*

❼ Crawford Art Gallery. The large redbrick building was built in 1724 as the
★ customs house and is now home to Ireland's leading provincial art gallery. An imaginative expansion has added an extra 10,000 square feet of gallery space for visiting exhibitions and adventurous shows of modern Irish artists. The permanent collection includes landscape paintings depicting Cork in the 18th and 19th centuries. Take special note of works by Irish painters William Leech (1881–1968), Daniel Maclise (1806–70), James Barry (1741–1806), and Nathaniel Grogan (1740–1807). The café, run by the Allen family of Ballymaloe, is a good place for a light lunch or a homemade sweet. ✉ *Emmet Pl., City Center South* ☎ *021/490–7855* ⊕ *www.crawfordartgallery.com* 🎫 *Free* ♥ *Mon.–Sat. 9–5.*

❶❷ English Market. Food lovers: head for one of the misleadingly small
★ entrances to this large market in an elaborate, brick-and-cast-iron Victorian building. (Its official name is the Princes Street Market, and it's also known locally as the Covered Market.) Among the 140 stalls, keep an eye out for the Alternative Bread Co., which produces more than 40 varieties of handmade bread every day. Iago, Sean Calder-Potts's deli, has fresh pasta, lots of cheeses, and charcuterie. The Olive Stall sells olive oil, olive-oil soap, and olives from Greece, Spain, France, and Italy. Kay O'Connell's Fish Stall, in the legendary fresh-fish alley, purveys local smoked salmon. O'Reilly's Tripe and Drisheen is the last existing retailer of a Cork specialty, tripe (cow's stomach), and *drisheen* (blood sausage). Upstairs is the Farmgate, an excellent café. ✉ *Entrances on Grand Parade and Princes St., City Center South* ⊕ *www.corkenglishmarket.ie* ♥ *Mon.–Sat. 9–5:30.*

7

9 **Patrick Street.** Extending from Grand Parade in the south to Patrick's Bridge in the north, Panna (as it's known locally) is Cork's main shopping thoroughfare. It has been designed as a pedestrian-priority area with wide walks and special streetlights. A mainstream mix of department stores, boutiques, pharmacies, and bookshops line the way. If you look above some of the plate-glass storefronts, you can see examples of the bowfront Georgian windows that are emblematic of old Cork. The street saw some of the city's worst fighting during the War of Independence. ⊠ *City Center South.*

10 **Patrick's Bridge.** From here you can look along the curve of Patrick Street and north across the River Lee to St. Patrick's Hill, with its tall Georgian houses. The hill is so steep that steps are cut into the pavement. Tall ships that served the butter trade used to load up beside the bridge at Merchant's Quay before heading downstream to the sea. The design of the large, redbrick shopping center on the site evokes the warehouses of old. ⊠ *Patrick St., City Center South*

8 **Paul Street.** A narrow street between the River Lee and Patrick Street and parallel to both, Paul Street is the backbone of the trendy shopping area that now occupies Cork's old French Quarter. The area was first settled by Huguenots fleeing religious persecution in France. Musicians and other street performers often entertain passersby in the Rory Gallagher Piazza, named for the rock guitarist (of the band Taste), whose family was from Cork. The shops here offer the best in modern Irish design—from local fashions to handblown glass. ⊠ *City Center South.*

5 **St. Anne's Church.** The church's pepper-pot Shandon steeple, which has a four-sided clock and is topped with a golden, salmon-shaped weather vane, is visible from throughout the city and is the chief reason why St. Anne's is so frequently visited. The Bells of Shandon were immortalized in an atrocious but popular 19th-century ballad of that name. Your reward for climbing the 120-foot-tall tower is the chance to ring the bells, with the assistance of sheet tune cards, out over Cork. Beside the church, Firkin Crane, Cork's 18th-century butter market, houses two small performing spaces. Adjacent is the Shandon Craft Market. ⊠ *Church St., Shandon* ☎ *021/450–5906* ⊕ *www.shandonbells.org* 💶 *€6* ☉ *Easter–Oct., Mon.–Sat. 9:30–5; Nov.–Easter, Mon.–Sat. 10–3.*

13 **St. Finbarre's Cathedral.** This was once the entrance to medieval Cork. According to tradition, St. Finbarre established a monastery on this site around AD 650 and is credited as being the founder of Cork. The present, compact, three-spire Gothic cathedral, which was completed in 1879, belongs to the Church of Ireland and houses a 3,000-pipe organ. ⊠ *Bishop St., Washington Village* ☎ *021/496–3387* ⊕ *www.cathedral. cork.anglican.org* 💶 *€3* ☉ *Oct.–Mar., Mon.–Sat. 10–12:45 and 2–5, Sun. 12:30–5; Apr.–Sept., Mon.–Sat. 9:30–5:30, Sun. 12:30–5.*

2 **Triskel Arts Centre.** An excellent place to get the pulse of artsy goings-on in town, Triskel Arts Centre occupies a converted pair of town houses, also home to a coffee shop and a small auditorium that hosts films and plays. Often on display are exhibitions devoted to contemporary art and crafts. ⊠ *Tobin St., Washington Village* ☎ *021/427–2022* ⊕ *www. triskelart.com* 💶 *Free* ☉ *Weekdays 11–6, Sat. 11–5.*

As the River Lee flows through Cork's center, a delightful array of bridges and quays add to the city's unique character.

⑭ University College Cork. The Doric, porticoed gates of UCC stand about 2
★ km (1 mi) from the center of the city. The college, which has a student body of roughly 10,000, is a constituent of the National University of Ireland. The main quadrangle is a fine example of 19th-century university architecture in the Tudor-Gothic style, reminiscent of many Oxford and Cambridge colleges. Several ancient ogham stones are on display in the North Quadrangle (near the visitor center), and the renovated Crawford Observatory's 1860 telescope can be visited. The Honan Collegiate Chapel, east of the quadrangle, was built in 1916 and modeled on the 12th-century, Hiberno-Romanesque style, best exemplified by the remains of Cormac's Chapel at Cashel. The UCC chapel's stained-glass windows, as well as its collection of art and crafts, altar furnishings, and textiles in the Celtic Revival style, are noteworthy. Three large, modern buildings have been successfully integrated with the old, including the Boole Library, named for mathematician George Boole (1815–64), who was a professor at the college. Both indoors and out the campus is enhanced by works of contemporary Irish art. The **Lewis Glucksman Gallery** opened in late 2004, in a striking new building in a wooded gully beside the college's entrance gates. Besides displaying works from the college's outstanding collection, it hosts cutting-edge contemporary art exhibitions. ⊠ *Western Road* ☎ *021/490–1876* ⊕ *www.ucc.ie* 🎟 *Campus free, guided tour €4* ☉ *Visitor center weekdays 9–5; guided tours May, June, Sept., and Oct., Mon., Wed., Fri., and Sat. at 3 PM; call for hrs Easter wk, July, Aug., and mid-Dec.–mid-Jan.*

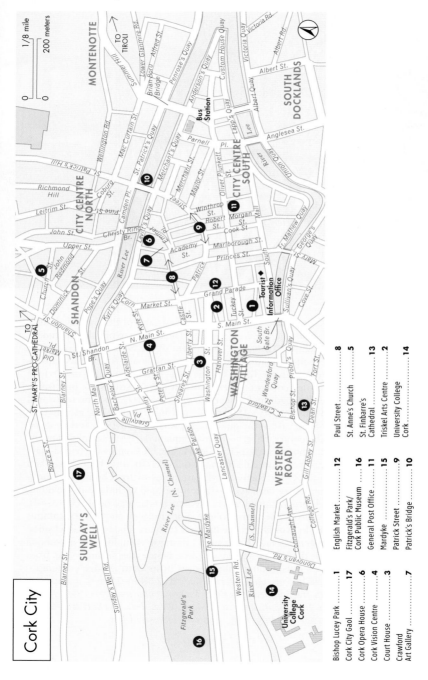

Cork City

Bishop Lucey Park **1**
Cork City Gaol **17**
Cork Opera House **6**
Cork Vision Centre **4**
Court House **3**
Crawford
Art Gallery **7**

English Market **12**
Fitzgerald's Park/
Cork Public Museum **16**
General Post Office **11**
Mardyke **15**
Patrick Street **9**
Patrick's Bridge **10**

Paul Street **8**
St. Anne's Church **5**
St. Finbarre's
Cathedral **13**
Triskel Arts Centre **2**
University College
Cork **14**

WORTH NOTING

① **Bishop Lucey Park.** This tiny green park in the heart of the city opened in 1985 in celebration of the 800th anniversary of Cork's Norman charter. During its excavation, workers unearthed portions of the city's original fortified walls, now preserved just inside the arched entrance. Sculptures by contemporary Cork artists are found throughout the park. ⊠ *Grand Parade, Washington Village.*

⑰ **Cork City Gaol.** This castle-like building contains an austere, 19th-century
☺ prison. Life-size figures occupy the cells, and sound effects illustrate the appalling conditions that prevailed here from the early 19th century through the founding of the Free State, after the 1916 Uprising. **The Radio Museum Experience** in the Governor's House tells the history of broadcasting in Cork, and features genuine artifacts from Cork's 1923 studio. ⊠ *Sunday's Well Rd., Sunday's Well* ☎ *021/430–5022* ⊕ *www.corkcitygaol.com* ⊡ *€7* ☾ *Nov.–Feb., daily 10–4; Mar.–Oct., daily 9:30–5.*

⑥ **Cork Opera House.** This is an unattractive concrete hulk that went up in 1965 to replace an ornate and much-loved opera house that was ruined in a fire. Later attempts to integrate the opera house with its neighbor, the Crawford Municipal Art Gallery, have, however, softened the grim facade. Still, it's the only show in town for opera buffs. The piazza outside has sidewalk cafés and street performers. ⊠ *Lavitt's Quay, City Center South* ☎ *021/427–0022* ⊕ *www.corkoperahouse.ie.*

③ **Court House.** A landmark in the very center of Cork, this magnificent classical building has an imposing Corinthian portico and is still used as the district's main courthouse. The exterior has been cleaned and fully restored and looks every bit as good as it did when it was built in 1835. ⊠ *Washington St., Washington Village* ☎ *021/427–2706* ⊕ *www. corkcorp.ie* ☾ *Weekdays 9–5.*

⑯ **Fitzgerald's Park.** This small, well-tended park is beside the River Lee's
☺ north channel in the west of the city. The park contains the **Cork Public Museum,** a Georgian mansion that houses a well-planned exhibit about Cork's history since ancient times, with a strong emphasis on the city's Republican history. ⊠ *Western Rd., Western Road* ☎ *021/427–0679* ⊕ *www.corkcity.ie* ⊡ *Free* ☾ *Museum weekdays 11–5, Sat. 11–1 and 2:15–4, Sun. 3–5; closed Sun. during Oct.–Mar.*

⑪ **General Post Office.** This Neoclassical building with an elegant colonnaded facade was once Cork's opera house. It dominates a street otherwise occupied by boutiques, jewelry stores, and antiques shops. ⊠ *Oliver Plunkett St., City Center South* ☎ *021/427–2000* ☾ *Weekdays 9–5:30, Sat. 9–5.*

NEED A BREAK? The friendly, old **Long Valley** café (⊠ *Winthrop St., City Center South* ☎ *021/427–2144*), popular with artists, writers, students, and eccentrics, serves tea, coffee, pints, and sandwiches. The dark, mismatched interior is

7

Cork is now one of the most happening food spots on the planet, due in no small measure to great foodie resources like the English Market.

like a time warp taking you back to early-20th-century Cork. Some of the booths are built from wood salvaged from wrecked ocean liners—ask to be told the story. The generously filled sandwiches, made to order from home-cooked meat and thickly cut bread, also seem to belong to another age.

⑮ Mardyke. This popular riverside walk links the city center with Fitzgerald's Park. Beside it is a field where cricket, very much a minority sport in Ireland, is played on summer weekends. ⊠ *Western Rd., Western Road.*

OFF THE BEATEN PATH
St. Mary's Pro-Cathedral. It's worth hiking up to St. Mary's, which dates from 1808, only if you're interested in tracing your Cork ancestors. Its presbytery has records of births and marriages dating from 1784. ⊠ *Cathedral Walk, Shandon* 🖃 *Free* ⊙ *Daily 9–6.*

WHERE TO EAT

$$$
VEGETARIAN
★

✕ **Café Paradiso.** The Mediterranean/Eastern fusion-style food here is so tasty that even dedicated meat eaters forget that it's vegetarian. Irish owner-chef Denis Cotter, who has published two acclaimed cookbooks, garners raves for his risottos with seasonal vegetables, his *gougère-choux* (cheese-flavor pastries) with savory fillings, and his homemade desserts. The simple café-style dining room is busy and colorful, with enthusiastic young waiters who love to recite the daily specials (which might include feta, pistachio, and couscous cake on citrus greens with sweet and hot pepper relish). The food is creatively arranged on massive platters or bowls, which add a sense of occasion. The restaurant is midway between the courthouse and the university. You can also stay the night here: there are three small but attractive rooms for two available for around €160

CLOSE UP

Rebel Cork

Cork City received its first charter in 1185 from Prince John of Norman England, and it takes its name from the Irish word *corcaigh,* meaning "marshy place." The original 6th-century settlement was spread over 13 small islands in the River Lee. Major development occurred during the 17th and 18th centuries with the expansion of the butter trade, and many attractive Georgian-design buildings with wide bowfront windows were constructed during this time. As late as 1770, Cork's present-day main streets—Grand Parade, Patrick Street, and the South Mall—were submerged under the Lee. Around 1800, when the Lee was partially dammed, the river

divided into two streams that now flow through the city, leaving the main business and commercial center on an island, not unlike Paris's Île de la Cité. As a result, the city features a number of bridges and quays, which, although initially confusing, add greatly to the port's unique character.

"Rebel Cork" emerged as a center of the Nationalist Fenian movement in the 19th century. The city suffered great damage during the War of Independence in 1919–21, when much of its center was burned down. Cork is now regaining some of its former glory as a result of sensitive commercial development and an ongoing program of inner-city renewal.

7

a night, or €200 including dinner. ✉ *16 Lancaster Quay, Western Road* ☎ *021/427–7939* ⊕ *www.cafeparadiso.ie* ⊟ *AE, MC, V* ☉ *Closed Sun., Mon., and last 2 wks of Aug. No lunch Sun.–Thurs.*

$
IRISH
✕ **Farmgate Café.** One of the best—and busiest—informal lunch spots in town is on a terraced gallery above the fountain at the Princes Street entrance to the atmospheric, 19th-century English Market. All ingredients used at the café are purchased in the market below. One side of the gallery opens onto the market and is self-service; the other side is glassed in and has table service (reservations advised). Tripe and *drisheen* (blood sausage) is one dish that is always on the menu; daily specials include less challenging but no less traditional dishes, such as corned beef with *colcannon* (potatoes and cabbage mashed with butter and seasonings) and loin of smoked bacon with *champ* (potatoes mashed with scallions or leeks). ✉ *English Market, City Center South* ☎ *021/427–8134* ⊟ *DC, MC, V* ☉ *Closed Sun. No dinner.*

$$$
ECLECTIC
✕ **Fenn's Quay.** This tiny city-center restaurant, on the ground floor of a 250-year-old Georgian house, is always buzzing with a faithful local clientele—legal eagles from the nearby courthouse at lunch, theater- and moviegoers at dinner. The char-grilled fillet steak with chunky chips has achieved legendary status: some regulars can't bring themselves to order anything else. But there are other good options: fish from the nearby market is given robust, unfussy treatment, and vegetarian offerings include a twice-baked goat cheese soufflé with apple and walnut salad. The ginger-and-toffee sticky pudding is a dessert specialty. Simple decor, with bright red café-style chairs and tan banquettes, gets a dose of character from striking modern paintings. If you come before 7:30 you can order from the bargain early-bird menu.

✉ *Fenn's Quay, Sheares St., Washington Village* ☎ *021/427–9527* ⊕ *www.fennsquay.ie* ▤ *AE, MC, V* ⊘ *Closed Sun.*

\$\$\$
FRENCH

✕ **Flemings.** On a hillside overlooking the river, this stately Georgian house is set in extensive grounds, which include a kitchen garden that supplies the restaurant. Classical French food is the forte of owner-chef Michael Fleming, and it's served, appropriately, in a dining room decorated in the French Empire style with plush Louis XV–

style chairs, gilt-frame mirrors, and crystal chandeliers. A blue-and-eggplant color scheme is complemented by plain white table linen on the generously sized round tables. Local ingredients are important; a starter of panfried foie gras is accompanied by black pudding from West Cork and glazed apple; it's a favorite with the regulars. Other standout items include grilled monkfish from Fleming's hometown, Courtmacsherry, served with a basil oil dressing and red wine sauce; and the fillet of beef with wild mushrooms, red onion confit, and red wine sauce. Ask about the special-value dine-and-stay package at this "restaurant with rooms." ✉ *Silver Grange House, Tivoli* ☎ *021/482–1621* ⊕ *www.flemingsrestaurant.ie* ▤ *AE, DC, MC, V.*

\$\$\$
CONTINENTAL
Fodor's Choice
★

✕ **Greenes.** Tucked away on a cobbled patio accessible only on foot, this surprising haven is part of a Victorian warehouse conversion that also contains Hotel Isaacs. The stone and redbrick walls are the backdrop for a minimalist modern interior with tall-back green rattan chairs and small tables with linen place mats. The real surprise is out back where a gigantic rock wall waterfall makes a stunning backdrop to a dining terrace. The Australian chef, Ray Clayton, has created a menu featuring both classic Continental fare and Asian- and Mediterranean-influenced fusion cuisine. Highlights include beef fillet served with horseradish mash, crispy onion rings, and bordelaise sauce, and panfried cod on homemade egg noodles with bok choy, roasted peppers, chili, honey, and soy sauce. Chocolate features prominently on the creative dessert menu. ✉ *Hotel Isaacs, 48 MacCurtain St., City Center North* ☎ *021/455–2279* ⊕ *www.greenesrestaurant.com* ▤ *AE, MC, V* ⊘ *No lunch Mon.–Sat.*

\$\$
CONTINENTAL

✕ **Isaacs.** Cross Patrick's Bridge to the River Lee's north side and turn right to reach this large, atmospheric brasserie in a converted 18th-century warehouse. Modern art, muted jazz, high ceilings, and well-spaced tables with colored wooden tops create a popular informal venue, where the food is taken seriously but the atmosphere is fun. The East-meets-Mediterranean menu features fresh local produce—which isn't so uncommon now, but was revolutionary when Isaac's came on the scene in 1992. Among the many tempting dishes are warm salads with Clonakilty black pudding, crispy duck confit with turnip and caramelized onion puree, and tempura of king prawns with eggplant, scallions, wasabi, pickled ginger, and soy dipping sauce. Service is friendly and efficient. Reservations are advisable Friday and Saturday evenings. ✉ *48 MacCurtain St., City Center North* ☎ *021/450–3805* ⊕ *www.isaacs.ie* 🍴 *AE, DC, MC, V* ☙ *No lunch Sun.*

$$$$
CONTEMPORARY
★

✗ **Ivory Tower.** Seamus O'Connell, the adventurous owner-chef here, is famous in Ireland through his television series, *Soul Food*. He describes his approach as "trans-ethnic fusion." He has cooked in Mexico and Japan, so his accomplished menu has such quirky, eclectic dishes as wild duck with vanilla, sherry, and jalapeños; pheasant tamale; and blackened shark with banana ketchup. Imaginative presentation, including a surprise taster to set the mood, compensates for the bare wooden floors and somewhat stark decor of the first-floor corner dining room. The seven-course tasting menu is a great introduction to O'Connell's inimitable style. ✉ *35 Princes St., Washington Village* ☎ *021/427–4665* 🍴 *AE, DC, MC, V* ☙ *Closed Mon. and Tues. No lunch.*

$$$
CONTINENTAL

✗ **Jacobs on the Mall.** Mercy Fenton's imaginative cooking is one attraction; the other is the location—an erstwhile Victorian-style Turkish bath. The dining room has a high ceiling, an enormous skylight, cast-iron pillars, modern art, and a tall banquette room divider. Starters include duck-liver parfait with plum chutney, and oysters with ginger-and-lime relish. For a main course, try seared John Dory with coconut rice or breast of free-range duck with roast butternut squash. Look for such desserts as date-and-butterscotch pudding with bourbon cream. ✉ *30A South Mall, City Center South* ☎ *021/425–1530* ⊕ *www.jacobsonthemall.com* 🍴 *AE, DC, MC, V* ☙ *Closed Sun.*

$$$
CONTINENTAL

✗ **Jacques.** Hidden away on a tiny side street is one of Cork's favorite restaurants. Its windowless interior, with its warm terra-cotta walls and curved art deco–style bar, is carefully lighted to soothe and make you forget the world outside. Sisters Jacque and Eithne Barry have run the place for 25 years, and know their business. Food is always sourced locally from artisan food producers, so it's as fresh and wholesome as it comes. Jacques's cooking lets the flavor shine through, whether in a starter of fresh crab and baby spinach salad, or a main course of medallions of venison with *gremolata* (finely minced parsley and garlic with lemon zest). For dessert try the fruited bread-and-butter pudding, or indulge in a chocolate-and-hazelnut torte. There's a special-value three-course dinner menu at €35. ✉ *Phoenix St., off Oliver Plunkett St. near GPO, City Center South* ☎ *021/427–7387* ⊕ *www.jacquesrestaurant. ie* 🍴 *AE, MC, V* ☙ *Closed Sun.*

$$$
FRENCH
★

✗ **Les Gourmandises.** With a Breton sommelier, Soizic, working the front of the house, and her U.K.-and-Dublin-trained Irish husband, Pat Kiely, in the kitchen, you can expect a genuinely interesting eating experience. The restaurant is small, but it has high ceilings, and natural light pours in from an overhead skylight, brightening the quarry-tile floor and red-velvet chairs. Crisp white linen and fresh flowers are typical of Soizic's attention to detail. Pat's training with Marco Pierre White, John Burton Race, and Patrick Guilbaud shows in his mastery of a robust modern French repertoire. Roasted fillet of cod is served with braised lentils and a thyme-and-balsamic dressing, while roast guinea fowl comes with caramelized chicory, roast walnuts, and sage. Desserts include vanilla crème brûlée with passion-fruit jelly and chocolate madeleine. Good-value set menus are also available before 9: 30 PM on weekdays and from 6 to 7 PM on Saturdays. ⊠ *17 Cook St., City Center South* ☎ *021/425–1959* ⊕ *www.lesgourmandises.ie* ⊟ *MC, V* ☺ *Closed Sun. and Mon., last wk in Aug., and 1st wk in Sept.*

WHERE TO STAY

$$ ⊞ **The Ambassador Hotel Best Western.** It's not the fanciest hotel in Cork, ★   nor the hippest, but it has the most character and the best view—which you pay for with a steep 10-minute walk up from the town center. It's worth visiting the bar here just to enjoy the panoramic view of Cork City and the surrounding hills. An imposing redbrick and cut-limestone Victorian-era nursing home now converted into a comfortable hotel, the Ambassador is near the army barracks in a hilly area made famous by Frank O'Connor's short stories and now favored by style-conscious academics and bohos. Guest rooms are massive, with large bathrooms, patterned wallpaper, small sitting areas, and matching floral curtains and drapes. There are three floors of bedrooms, and the higher you go, the better the view—some rooms even have splendid balconies. The Embassy Bar has dark-wood paneling and a large bay window overlooking the city, while the cocktail lounge, with book-filled shelves and chesterfields by an open fire, is a quieter venue. The Seasons restaurant is a spacious room with formal table linen and a sedate, old-fashioned air. **Pros:** strong local atmosphere; amazing views. **Cons:** steep hike up from city; some jarring notes in decor. ⊠ *Military Hill, St. Luke's, City Center North, Co. Cork* ☎ *021/455–1996* ⊕ *www.ambassadorhotel.ie* ↩ *70 rooms* ☝ *In-room: no a/c, Internet, Wi-Fi (some). In-hotel: restaurant, bars, gym, Wi-Fi hotspot* ⊟ *AE, DC, MC, V* ⦿| *BP.*

$$ ⊞ **Clarion.** Black-clad receptionists standing behind simple wooden desks at the far end of the vast, marble-floor lobby are the first indication that this place aspires to boutique-hotel chic. Occupying a corner block beside the River Lee, the Clarion is the first arrival of a huge docklands development. It's kitty-corner across the river from City Hall, and a short walk from shopping and dining. Rooms are built around a central, top-lighted atrium, and have views either of the river or the hotel's swanky main staircase. Decor is stark and hard-edged, with stylish pale-wood trim complemented by curtains and flooring in a khaki-olive theme. Kudos bar spills out onto a riverside walkway and serves Asian food from an open wok station until 8 nightly. It's a popular after-work watering hole. The more formal restaurant Sinergie serves a light Mediterranean menu amid minimalist Japanese-inspired decor. **Pros:** funky; high-luxe rooms. **Cons:** limited car parking; neighborhood deserted after dark; some rooms overlook internal atrium/staircase. ⊠ *Lapp's Quay, City Center South, Co. Cork* ☎ *021/422–4900* ⊕ *www.clarionhotelcorkcity. com* ↩ *191 rooms* ☝ *In-room: a/c, Internet, Wi-Fi (some). In-hotel: restaurant, bar, pool, gym, spa, Wi-Fi hotspot* ⊟ *AE, DC, MC, V* ⦿| *BP.*

$ ⊞ **Gabriel House.** This huge Victorian house, on a bluff high above the railway station and the docks, is located in Cork's Boho northside quarter. It's a long (10-minute) hike uphill, past fine 19th-century homes, many of which have seen better days. The guest house is under enthusiastic new management, with keen young staff, and window boxes brimming with flowers. Guest rooms vary greatly in size and orientation, with the biggest on the river side, but share a simple decor, muted colors, and a flat-screen TV. Bathrooms are small (no tubs), but have a heated towel rail and power showers. Tea and coffee are on tap all day in the breakfast room, and there is also an attractive garden. The nearest pub, Henchy's, a Victorian gem, is one of Cork's finest. **Pros:** quiet location; oodles of character; rock-bottom prices. **Cons:** verging on hostel-like; some very small rooms; taxi or bus is preferable to that long climb. ☒ *Summerhill North, St. Luke's Cross, Montenotte District* ☎ *021/450–0333* ⊕ *www.gabriel-house.ie* ⤸ *28 rooms* ⚓ *In-room: no a/c. In-hotel: Wi-Fi hotspot, parking (free)* ☰ *MC, V* ⍩*BP.*

$ ⚇ **Garnish House.** Owner-manager Johanna Lucey will be offering you
★ tea and homemade chocolate cake before you have even crossed the threshold of her home. Johanna—Hansi to her many friends—provides the kind of old-fashioned hospitality that is fast disappearing in modern Ireland. A pair of large Victorian town houses near the university, and a short walk from the town center, contain impeccably clean, well-aired rooms with net curtains, a homey assortment of furniture, well-dressed beds, and fresh fruit and flowers. The annex (the second house) is more contemporary, with light wood, original Irish art, and leather sofas in the lounge. For longer stays, self-catering suites are available. Breakfast is a highlight: porridge comes smothered in fresh cream, honey, and either Irish whiskey or Bailey's Cream liqueur, while vegetarian rissoles and light-as-a-feather soufflés offer a change from the ubiquitous "fry." **Pros:** a friendly welcome; a genuine Irish experience. **Cons:** seriously unhip; located on a busy main road; rooms book up well in advance. ☒ *Western Rd., Washington Village, Co. Cork* ☎ *021/427–5111* ⊕ *www.garnish.ie* ⤸ *14 rooms* ⚓ *In-room: no a/c, Wi-Fi. In-hotel: parking (free)* ☰ *AE, MC, V* ⍩*BP.*

$$$$ ⚇ **Hayfield Manor.** The Manor, a surprisingly soigné modern homage
Fodor'sChoice to the country-house style, is beside the UCC campus, five minutes'
★ drive from the city center. The less than scenic location in an undistinguished suburb is forgotten as soon as you cross the threshold of this deluxe establishment. Ruddy with red brick and brightened by classy white-sash windows, its exterior hints at the comfy luxury within. Beyond a splendid, carved-wood double staircase, you can find the drawing room—a symphony of gilded silk, with white-marble fireplace, 19th-century chandelier, and chic armchairs—and the wood-panel library, which overlooks a walled patio and garden. Guest rooms are spacious and elegantly furnished in a version of the Louis XV style. The Victorian-style bar serves lunch, and then bar food until 7 PM, when Orchids restaurant opens for dinner; Perrott's Garden Bistro is a casual dining alternative. **Pros:** stylish and chic. **Cons:** a taxi or car ride to city center or a dull 15-minute walk; lack of scenic views. ☒ *College Rd., Western Road, Co. Cork* ☎ *021/484–5900* ⊕ *www.hayfieldmanor.ie* ⤸ *88 rooms* ⚓ *In-room: a/c, safe, Internet (some), Wi-Fi (some). In-hotel: 2 restaurants, bar, pool, gym, spa, Wi-Fi hotspot* ☰ *AE, DC, MC, V* ⍩*BP.*

7

Thanks to streets lined with pubs and shops, a simple stroll around Cork can be a delightful way to while away the hours.

$$ 🛏 **Hotel Isaacs.** A stylish renovation transformed an old, city-center warehouse into a busy restaurant and hotel complex. The dark internal lobby has stone walls and cast-iron pillars, and a homey collection of sofas and armchairs, setting the tone of boho shabby chic that appeals to the hotel's many regular guests. Rooms vary greatly in shape and size; the most coveted ones overlook a tiny courtyard patio with a waterfall cascading down one side. Decoration is unfussy, with muted earth colors, black leatherette reclining chairs, and plain cream walls. Double-glazed windows on the street side guard against traffic noise. The restaurant, Greenes, is renowned for its talented French chef, and is a lively place at night thanks to its stunning waterfall dining terrace. **Pros:** central location near bus and train stations; memorable old-world character. **Cons:** heavy through-traffic outside; decor a bit worn at the edges; limited car parking. ⊠ *48 MacCurtain St., City Center North, Co. Cork* ☎ *021/450–0011* ⊕ *www.isaacs.ie* 🛏 *47 rooms* ⚒ *In-room: a/c, safe, refrigerator (some), Wi-Fi. In-hotel: restaurant, Wi-Fi hotspot* ⊟ *AE, MC, V* ⊚*BP.*

NIGHTLIFE AND THE ARTS

See the *Examiner* or the *Evening Echo* for details about movies, theater, and live music performances.

GALLERIES

Buckley Fine Art (⊠ *2 Fenn's Quay, Washington Village* ☎ *021/422–3577* ⊕ *www.buckleyfineart.com*) sells interesting work by contemporary Irish artists. The **Lavit Gallery** (⊠ *5 Father Mathew St., off South Mall,*

City Center South ☎ *021/427–7749*) sells work by members of the Cork Arts Society and other Irish artists. The **Lewis Glucksman Gallery** (✉ *UCC Campus, Western Rd., corner of Donovan's Rd., Western Road* ☎ *021/490–1844* ⊕ *www.glucksman.org*), part of Cork's university, has won several awards for its striking modern architecture. Offbeat exhibits can be found at the **Triskel Arts Centre** (✉ *Tobin St., off S. Main St., Washington Village* ☎ *021/427–2022* ⊕ *www.triskelart.com*).

PERFORMING ARTS AND FILM

Cork Opera House (✉ *Lavitt's Quay, City Center South* ☎ *021/427–0022* ⊕ *www.corkoperahouse.ie*) is the city's major hall for touring productions and variety acts. **Cork School of Music** (✉ *Union Quay, South Docklands* ☎ *021/427–0076* ⊕ *www.cit.ie*) is a new (2009) institute that hosts concerts in its 450-seat Curtis Auditorium and smaller Stack Auditorium. Modest-size theatrical productions are staged at the **Everyman Palace** (✉ *MacCurtain St., City Center North* ☎ *021/450–1673* ⊕ *www. everymanpalace.com*), which has an ornate Victorian interior.

PUBS AND NIGHTCLUBS

Bierhaus (✉ *Pope's Quay, Shandon* ☎ *021/455–1648*) attracts a hip young crowd, and has over 30 beers to choose from, poker on Tuesday, and a DJ every Friday. **Charlie's Bar** (✉ *Union Quay, South Docklands* ☎ *021/431–8342*) has nightly music sessions with traditional and acoustic on Sunday from 3 PM. You can hear Cajun, folk, or Irish music from Sunday to Wednesday at the **Corner House** (✉ *7 Coburg St., City Center North* ☎ *021/450–0655*).

Live music every Sunday from midday noon thanks to a classical string quartet is a feature at **Counihan's** (✉ *11 Pembroke St., City Center South* ☎ *021/427–7850*), while in the evenings you can hear a blend of traditional Irish and Latin rhythm music. **Loafers** (✉ *26 Douglas St., South Docklands* ☎ *021/431–1612*) is a friendly gay bar with a beer garden. **Long Valley** (✉ *Winthrop St., South City Center* ☎ *021/427–2144*) is a Cork institution, famous for its doorstep sandwiches (made with very thick slices of bread and lots of fillings) that are impossible to eat tidily, and its conversation, which is always lively. The bar at the **Metropole Hotel** (✉ *MacCurtain St., City Center North* ☎ *021/450–8122*) is one of Cork's best jazz spots. **The Pavilion** (✉ *Carey's Lane., City Center South* ☎ *021/427–6230* ⊕ *www.pavilioncork.com*) is a late-night bar with live entertainment and DJs Thursday to Sunday. **The Savoy** (✉ *Patrick St., City Center South* ☎ *021/425–4296*) is the major venue for night owls, operating Thursday to Saturday from 11 until late. Live acts from Ireland and elsewhere are on offer in the main room, and in the foyer there are comedy acts and DJ sets, which can vary from the Electric Dream 80s Club to Detroit techno.

SHOPPING

DEPARTMENT STORES

Brown Thomas (✉ *18 Patrick St., City Center South* ☎ *021/427–6771*), Ireland's high-end department store, carries items by Irish and international designers. The ground floor has an excellent cosmetics hall and a good selection of menswear and Irish crystal. Refuel at the coffee shop, which sells healthful open sandwiches and homemade soups. **Debenham's** (⊠ *Patrick St., City Center South* ☎ *021/427–7727*), Cork's largest department store and a branch of the U.K. chain, occupies a beautiful landmark building with a central glass dome. **Dunnes Stores** (⊠ *Merchant's Quay, City Center South* ☎ *021/427–4200*) began in Cork as a family-owned drapery store and became the place where all of Ireland buys its socks, underwear, and much more. The British retail giant **Marks & Spencer** (⊠ *6–8 Patrick St., Merchant's Quay, City Center South* ☎ *021/427–5555*) is as popular for its foods (great for picnics) and housewares as for its clothing basics. For inexpensive rain gear, T-shirts, underwear, and any other garments you forgot to pack, head for **Penney's** (⊠ *27 Patrick St., City Center South* ☎ *021/427–1935*).

MALLS

Mahon Point Shopping Centre (⊠ *Mahon Point, South Link Rd.* ☎ *021/497–2800*) is a massive out-of-town shopping center just south of the Lee Tunnel, with an emphasis on fashion. The **Merchant's Quay Shopping Centre** (⊠ *Merchant's Quay, City Center South* ☎ *021/427–5466*) is a large downtown mall.

SPECIALTY SHOPS

ANTIQUES **Diana O'Mahony** (⊠ *8 Winthrop St., City Center South* ☎ *021/427–6599*) sells antique jewelry.

Gallery 44 (⊠ *44A MacCurtain St., City Center North* ☎ *021/450–1319*) stocks antique glass, porcelain, paintings, and prints. **Stokes Fine Clocks and Watches** (⊠ *48 MacCurtain St., City Center North* ☎ *021/455–1195*) is packed with antique clocks and watches, and usually also has a barograph or two (to measure atmospheric pressure). **Victoria's** (⊠ *2 Oliver Plunkett St., City Center South* ☎ *021/427–2752*) carries interesting jewelry and Victoriana.

BOOKS **Connolly's Bookshop** (⊠ *Paul St. Piazza, City Center South* ☎ *021/427–5366*) has an extensive stock of new and secondhand books, with a good selection of Irish-interest titles. **Vibes & Scribes** (⊠ *3 Bridge St., City Center North* ☎ *021/450–5370* ⊠ *21 Lavitts Quay, City Center South* ☎ *021/427–9535*) attracts a loyal following of avid readers, with floors of new, secondhand, and discount books as well as CDs and videos; the Lavitts Quay branch has a wide selection of new bargain books, strong on art and Irish interest. **Waterstones** (⊠ *Patrick St., City Center South* ☎ *021/427–6522*) is the biggest bookshop in town, with a great choice of new fiction and nonfiction as well as a wide selection of locally published books.

CLOTHING **Cocoon** (⊠ *6 Emmet Pl., City Center South* ☎ *021/427–3393*), a little shop in a hexagonal tower, has a ravishing selection of sexy Italian boots and shoes alongside unusual jewelry and accessories. Fashion lovers adore the evening and business attire at the **Dressing Room** (⊠ *8 Emmet Pl., City Center South* ☎ *021/427–0117*), a tiny but tony boutique opposite the entrance to the Cork Opera House. **Monica John** (⊠ *French Church St., City Center South* ☎ *021/427–1399*) sells locally designed high-fashion ladies' wear as well as some imported lines. **Quills** (⊠ *107 Patrick St., City Center South* ☎ *021/427–1717*) has a good selection of Irish-made apparel for women and men. **Samui** (⊠ *17*

Drawbridge St., City Center South ☎ *021/427–8080)* stocks dramatic—often quirky, but always flattering—clothes from Ireland, France, Germany, and the United Kingdom.

JEWELRY **Designworks Ltd** (⊠ *Unit 3, Winthrop Arcade, Oliver Plunkett St., City Center South* ☎ *021/427–9420)* has imaginative, modern jewelry. **The Jewellery Boutique** (⊠ *21 Winthrop St., City Center South* ☎ *021/422– 3892)* specializes in engagement rings and custom-made gold jewelry.

MUSIC **HMV** (⊠ *Patrick St.* ☎ *021/427–4433)* has a good selection of Irish traditional music in its classical and jazz sections. **Pro Musica** (⊠ *20 Oliver Plunkett St., City Center South* ☎ *021/427–1659)* sells sheet music and instruments for classical musicians.

Vibes & Scribes (⊠ *3 Bridge St., City Center North* ☎ *021/450–5370)* has a good selection of bargain and secondhand CDs, DVDs, and videotapes.

SIDE TRIPS FROM CORK CITY

Blarney, northwest of Cork City on R617, and Cork Harbour, east of the city on N25 (follow signposts to Waterford), make perfect day trips. Blarney's attractions are Blarney Castle and the famous Blarney Stone. Cork Harbour's draws include Fota Island, with an arboretum, a wildlife park, and Fota House—a renovated hunting lodge and estate—and the fishing port of Cobh.

BLARNEY
10 km (6 mi) northwest of Cork City.

"On Galway sands they kiss your hands, they kiss your lips at Carney, but by the Lee they drink strong tea, and kiss the stone at Blarney." This famous rhyme celebrates one of Ireland's most noted icons—the Blarney Stone, which is the main reason most people journey to this small community built around a village green.

GETTING HERE

BUS TRAVEL From Cork Bus Station on Parnell Placethere are about 20 coaches a day (30 minutes, €6.20 round-trip) connecting with Blarney Village Green. Pay as you board. The bus stop is a very short walk from the castle, and the village is very small. Taxis are available from Castle Cab by phone reservation.

ESSENTIALS
Transportation Contacts Castle Cab (☎ *021/438–2222)*.

Visitor Information Blarney Tourist Office (⊠ *Co. Cork* ☎ *021/438–1624* ⊕ *www.corkkerry.ie* ☉ *June–Sept. only)*.

★ In the center of Blarney is **Blarney Castle,** or what remains of it: the ruined central keep is all that's left of this mid-15th-century stronghold. The castle contains the famed Blarney Stone; kissing the stone, it's said, endows the kisser with the fabled "gift of gab." It's 127 steep steps to the battlements. To kiss the stone, you must lie down on the battlements, hold on to a guardrail, and lean your head way back. It's good fun and not at all dangerous. Expect a line from mid-June to early September; while you wait, you can admire the views of the wooded River Lee valley and chuckle over how the word "blarney" came to mean what it does. As the story goes, Queen Elizabeth I wanted Cormac MacCarthy, Lord of Blarney, to will his castle to the Crown, but he refused her requests with eloquent excuses and soothing compliments. Exhausted by his comments, the queen reportedly exclaimed, "This is all Blarney. What he says he rarely means."

You can take pleasant walks around the castle grounds; Rock Close contains oddly shaped limestone rocks landscaped in the 18th century, and a grove of ancient yew trees that is said to have been a site of Druid worship. In early March there's a wonderful display of naturalized daffodils. ☎ 021/438–5252 ⊕ www.blarneycastle.ie ☜ €10 ⊗ May and Sept., Mon.–Sat. 9–6:30, Sun. 9–5:30; June–Aug., Mon.–Sat. 9–7, Sun. 9–5; Oct.–Apr., Mon.–Sat. 9–sunset, Sun. 9–5 or sunset.

WHERE TO EAT AND STAY

$ ✕ **Blair's Inn.** Surrounded by woods a five minutes' drive from Blarney,
CONTINENTAL   Blair's Inn—noted for its exuberant window-box displays—is the perfect retreat from Blarney's tour-bus crowds. This is a real "local," complete with genial owner-hosts John and Anne, and their son, Duncan, in the kitchen. You can opt to dine at the bar or in the quieter surroundings of the wood-panel restaurant. In summer enjoy the beer garden; in winter, warm wood fires flicker in the hearth. Freshly prepared local produce is served in generous portions all day, with special lunch and dinner menus: best bets include Irish stew with lamb, carrots, and potatoes, as well as the house special, hot corned beef with parsley sauce, and a memorable gratin of prawns, crab, and salmon, served piping hot. There's live entertainment every Monday at 9 PM from May to October. ✉ Cloghroe ☎ 021/438–1470 ▭ MC, V.

$ ▦ **Blarney Castle Hotel.** Set right on the village green only a minute's walk from the famed castle, this 1837 hotel occupies a traditional gabled building. A gas fire welcomes you into the reception area—just ring the brass bell to summon service. Ian and Una Forrest, the younger generation of this inn-keeping family, now run the business. Guest rooms are on two stories above the bar, and five of them have views of the village green. Decor is restrained and color-coordinated, with mahogany furniture and brass light fixtures. Bathrooms have a striking black-and-white color scheme, and are small but fitted with power showers. Antiques dot the corridors, and there is a quiet residents' lounge on the first floor. Locals crowd into both the bar (which has traditional music on Tuesday and Sunday and also serves food) and the Lemon Tree Restaurant. **Pros:** ideal touring base; good alternative to Cork City (5 mi); restaurant on premises; a no-smoking hotel throughout. **Cons:** bar can get busy on Sunday night; some rooms overlook car park and yard. ✉ Blarney Village Green, Co. Cork ☎ 021/438–5116 ⊕ www.blarneycastlehotel.com

🛏 *13 rooms* ⚸ *In-room: no a/c, safe, Wi-Fi (some). In-hotel: restaurant, bar, Wi-Fi hotspot* ⊟ *MC, V.*

¢ 🔲 **The Whitehouse.** A hacienda-style bungalow on an elevated site on the main road between the N20 and Blarney village (a five-minute walk from the latter), Blarney's White House has a distant view of the castle from its front door. Owners Pat and Regina Coughlan's background in hotel management provides a professional edge, combining impeccable housekeeping standards with a warm welcome—the couple are also a mine of touring information. Guest rooms are double-glazed to keep out traffic noise, and are pleasantly old-fashioned with dark mahogany furniture, some with views of the back garden. **Pros:** good value for money; quiet and comfortable; home-cooked breakfast. **Cons:** won't win any style awards. ✉ *Shean Lower* ☎ *021/438–5338* ⊕ *www. thewhitehouseblarney.com* 🛏 *6 rooms* ⚸ *In-room: no a/c, Wi-Fi. In-hotel: Internet terminal, parking (free)* ⊟ *MC, V.*

SHOPPING

Blarney has lots of crafts shops south and west of the village green, a two-minute walk from the castle. **Blarney Woollen Mills** (☎ *021/438–5280* ⊕ *www.blarney.com*) has the largest stock and the highest turnover of Blarney's crafts shops. It sells everything from Irish-made high fashion to Aran hand-knit items to leprechaun key rings.

CORK HARBOUR

16 km (10 mi) east of Cork City.

Cork City's nearby harbor district has seen a lot of history and is lined with waterside sights. Check out the pleasant harbor and then depart for some fascinating attractions nearby.

GETTING HERE

BOAT TRAVEL   If the sight of Cork harbor makes you want to take to the water, arrange an outing with Whale of a Time.

TRAIN TRAVEL   A suburban rail service has 22 departures daily from Cork's Kent Station, stops at Fota Island and Cobh, and offers better harbor views than the road. You can hop off at Fota Island, then get back on the train, and continue to Cobh using the same ticket (€6.35 round-trip). The journey to Cobh takes 25 minutes.

TOURS   If the sight of Cork harbor makes you want to take to the water, arrange an outing with Whale of a Time.

ESSENTIALS

Transportation Contacts Whale of a Time (✉ *East Ferry, Marlogue, Cobh, Co. Cork* ☎ *086/328–3250* ⊕ *www.whaleofatime.net*).

Visitor Information Cobh Tourist Office (✉ *Sirius Centre, Co. Cork* ☎ *021/481–3301* ⊕ *www.visitcobh.com*).

The 70-acre **Fota Island Wildlife Park** is 12 km (7 mi) east of Cork via N25, R624, and the main Cobh road. It's an important breeding center for cheetahs and wallabies, and also is home to monkeys, zebras, giraffes, ostriches, flamingos, emus, and kangaroos. ☎ *021/481–2678* ⊕ *www.fotawildlife.ie* 🎟 *€13.50* ⊙ *Mon.–Sat. 10–4:30, Sun. 11–4:30; last entry 1 hr before closing.*

DID YOU KNOW?

Whether or not you intend to kiss the Blarney Stone found atop Blarney Castle, the view from the 120-foot-tall square tower is most impressive. Note that the Kissing Stone is scrubbed with disinfectant several times a day so this is a completely hygenic feat.

Next to the Fota Island Wildlife Park is **Fota House,** the Smith-Barry ancestral estate: its name is derived from the Irish *Fód te,* which means "warm soil," a tribute to the unique tidal estuary microclimate here and the reason why one of Ireland's most exotic botanical gardens was established here. The original lodge house was built in the mid-18th century for the Smith-Barry family, which owned vast tracts of land in South Cork, including the whole of Fota Island. The next generation of the powerful family employed the renowned architects Richard and William Vitruvius Morrison to convert the structure into an impressive Regency-style house that has now been painstakingly restored. The symmetrical facade is relatively unadorned and stands in contrast to the resplendent Adamesque plasterwork of the formal reception rooms (somewhat denuded of furniture). The servants' quarters are almost as big as the house proper. Fota's glories continue in the gardens, which include an arboretum, a Victorian fernery, an Italian garden, an orangerie, and a special display of magnolias. You can relax over cake and scones in the tearoom after visiting the gift shop. ☎ *021/481–5543* ⊕ *www.fotahouse. com* 🖃 *€6* ☉ *Apr.–Sept., Mon.–Sat. 10–5, Sun. 11–5.*

Fodor'sChoice
★

Many of the people who left Ireland on immigrant ships for the New World departed from Cobh, a pretty fishing port and seaside resort 24 km (15 mi) southeast of Cork City on R624. The **Queenstown Story at Cobh Heritage Centre,** in the old Cobh railway station, re-creates the experience of the million emigrants who left from here between 1750 and the mid-20th century. It also tells the stories of great transatlantic liners, including the *Titanic,* whose last port of call was Cobh, and the *Lusitania,* which was sunk by a German submarine off this coast on May 7, 1915. Many of the *Lusitania*'s 1,198 victims are buried in Cobh, which has a memorial to them on the local quay. ☎ *021/481–3591* ⊕ *www.cobhheritage.com* 🖃 *€7.10* ☉ *Oct.–Apr., daily 9:30–5; May–Sept., daily 9:30–6.*

The best view of Cobh is from **St. Colman's Cathedral,** an exuberant neo-Gothic granite church designed by the eminent British architect E. W. Pugin in 1869, and completed in 1919. Inside, granite niches portray scenes of the Roman Catholic Church's history in Ireland, beginning with the arrival of St. Patrick. ☎ *021/481–3222.*

EAST CORK AND THE BLACKWATER VALLEY

Although most visitors to Cork head west out of the city for the coastal areas between Cork and Glengarriff, the east and the north of the county are also worth exploring. East Cork is popular with Irish tourists, who love the long sandy beaches here. North Cork's main attraction is the Blackwater River, which crosses the county from east to west. It's famous for its trout and salmon fishing and its scenery.

MIDLETON

12 km (8 mi) east of Cork City on N25.

Midleton is famous for its school, Midleton College, founded in 1696, and its distillery, founded in 1825 and modernized in 1975, which manufactures spirits—including Irish whiskey—for distribution worldwide.

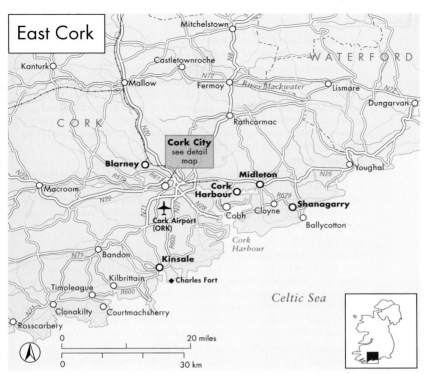

A pleasant market town set at the head of the Owenacurra River estuary, near the northeast corner of Cork Harbour, it has many gray-stone buildings dating mainly from the early 19th century.

GETTING HERE

BUS TRAVEL   Five Bus Éireann buses daily connect from the Cork Bus Station to Midleton (30 minutes, €6.35 round-trip).

TRAIN TRAVEL   Irish Rail trains from Cork's **Kent Station** (✉ *Lower Glanmire Rd., Co. Cork* ☎ *021/450–6766 for timetable*) run to Midleton (25 minutes, €6.50 round-trip), with 21 departures daily.

EXPLORING

The **Jameson Experience** has tours of the Old Midleton Distillery, to show you how Irish whiskey—*uisce beatha*, "the water of life"—was made in the old days. The old stone buildings are excellent examples of 19th-century industrial architecture, the impressively large old waterwheel still operates, and the pot still—a copper dome that can hold 32,000 imperial gallons of whiskey—is the world's largest. Early in the tour, requests are made for a volunteer "whiskey taster," so be alert if this option appeals. Tours end with a complimentary glass of Jameson's Irish whiskey (or a soft drink). A gift shop and café are also on the premises. ☎ *021/461–3594* ⊕ *www.jamesonwhiskey.com* 🎫 *€13.50* ⊙ *Apr.–Oct., daily 9–5; Nov.–Mar., tours daily 11:30, 1, 2:30, and 4.*

SHANAGARRY

15 km (8 mi) southeast of Midleton on R629, 17 km (11 mi) southeast of Cork Harbour via N25 and R632.

There are three reasons to come to Shanagarry, a farming village known chiefly for its Quaker connections: Ballymaloe House, one of Ireland's first and still most famous country-house hotels; Ballymaloe Cookery School and Gardens, a top destination for chefs-in-training; and the gallery and shop of Stephen Pearce, a leading designer of earthenware pottery. All three enterprises are run by Quaker families, testimony to the religious roots of this community.

GETTING HERE

BUS TRAVEL   There are five Bus Éireann buses daily from the Cork Bus Station to Ballycotton (1 hour, €10.20 round-trip), stopping in Shanagarry, which is just five minutes short of the last stop. These buses run from 6 AM to 6:15 PM, with the last bus returning from Ballycotton to Cork leaving at 4:45 PM.

EXPLORING

Shanagarry's most famous Quaker native son was none other than William Penn (1644–1718), the founder of the Pennsylvania colony, who grew up in **Shanagarry House,** still a private residence in the center of the village. The entry gates are across from Shanagarry Castle, now owned by the potter and entrepreneur Stephen Pearce. The house's most famous tenant since William Penn was Marlon Brando, who stayed here in the summer of 1995 while filming *Divine Rapture* in nearby Ballycotton.

The original pottery, where two styles of earthenware pottery are thrown traditionally by hand, was founded by the Pearce family in the late 1960s, and is now under new ownership by Jack O'Patsy. Ware from this factory are among many craft treasures sold at the Shanagarry Design Centre. Run by the Kilkenny Shop, the massive gallery and showroom (with scrumptious home baking in the café) is in the village center. About a dozen artists have studios in the basement, where their work is also for sale. They include a stone sculptor from Zimbabwe, an Israeli jeweler, a botanical artist, a patchwork maker, and several up-and-coming Irish artists. A tour of the pottery can be booked in advance. ⊠ *Next to Shanagarry Parish Church* ☎ *021/464–5838* 🖃 *Free* ☉ *Weekdays 10–5:30, weekends 10–5:30.*

WHERE TO EAT AND STAY

$$$$ 🍴 **Ballymaloe House.** Ballymaloe is world famous as the fountainhead
ⓒ   of the New Irish cuisine. Although masterminded by legendary Myrtle
Fodor'sChoice   Allen, the family's younger generation under head chef Jason Fahey now
★   provides marvelously inspired, this-second-fresh, and yumptious feasts, including plenty of dazzling dishes fished up from the picturesque port of Ballycotton. *(For more information on the celebrated restaurant, see "A Taste of Ireland" in this chapter.)* Originally a farmhouse and family home, albeit on a gracious scale, Ballymaloe still functions partly as a working farm, one reason why the grounds—pleasant lawns, "which way home?" paths, and vegetable gardens—don't aspire to grandeur. Inside, past the doorway's demilune window, guests like to gather in the drawing room, a symphony of whites and beiges, with fine modern Irish

Continued on page 428

A TASTE OF IRELAND

Queen scallops with aubergine caviar

Great ingredients and innovative chefs are shaping West Cork into one of the most foodie-friendly places on the planet.

The next time you wander into a time-burnished 19th-century Irish pub bent on downing a platter of steak, bland potatoes, and mushy peas, don't be surprised if you end up with a main course of skewered John Dory in Clonmel cider sauce and a dessert of Cooleeney Camembert ganache with lavender jelly. Begorra—you've encountered the much-vaunted Irish food revolution! Since the mid-1990s, the New Irish Cuisine has changed the beige, boiled, and boring food of yore into a bounty of gourmet delights. Today, haute-hungry gourmands packing chubby wallets (and the cookbooks of Margaret Johnson and Noel Cullen) are all abuzz discovering emerging culinary wizards; artisanal producers of farmhouse cheeses; organic

beef and smoked fish; and some of the best farmers' markets and provisioners around. Leading the charge of Ireland's food revolution are superstar chefs, and few have done more to transform the Irish kitchen than Myrtle Allen and her daughter-in-law, Darina Allen. The trip to bountiful Ireland begins with them.

Gubbeen Farmhouse

BALLYMALOE: A TRIP TO BOUNTIFUL

One of the dining rooms; right, Ballymaloe Cookery School

When Myrtle Allen opened a restaurant at her Georgian farm-estate, Ballymaloe (east of Cork City and pronounced Bah-lee-mal-oo), in 1964, she hadn't set out to change the way Ireland eats.

Moving to the historic Quaker stronghold of Shangarry in 1948, she and her husband, Ivan, began the restoration of an old Georgian farm estate. Before too long, their 400-acre cropland became the breeding ground for a new gastronomy as the couple reaped harvests of sea kale, parsnips, carrageen moss, rutabagas, gooseberries, globe artichokes, and other heritage veggies. Long before organic became a buzzword, Myrtle made freshness her mantra: eggs from her own hens, produce from her own garden, freshly landed fish from nearby Ballycotton. So, when she opened The Yeats Room at Ballymaloe in 1964, her refashioning of her great-grandparents, food was embraced by a generation reared on frozen pizza. In no time, food critics were raving about Myrtle's everything-old-is-new-again-but-better take.

The Herb Garden at Ballymaloe

Myrtle Allen is now retired but chef Jason Fahey has a blanced touch that is is almost Quaker-like in its subtlety. Dinners here are the real thing: fresh-picked coriander from the greenhouse for the leg of lamb, the eggs in the Carageen Pudding—a custard mixed with Cork seaweed and bittersweet Irish-coffee sauce—the gift of hens with squatters' rights, and if the plaice weren't biting that day, it won't be on the menu. Under the hosts' celebrated collection of modern Irish paintings, diners can enjoy a kaleidoscope of specialties (selections change seasonally, weekly, and daily) be it a radish-leaf soup, a Ballymaloe cheddar cheese fondue, or a roast Ballycotton cod with Ulster champ. A final testimony to Myrtle's practice of supporting small-scale, local food purveyors is the adieu offering: the amazing cheese board, which conveys local artisanship at its best. Ballymaloe House has lovely overnight accomodations ☎ 021/465-2531 ⊕ www.ballymaloe.ie ⇨ *review under Shanagarry*), just one reason why many diners enjoy a leisurely repast at night.

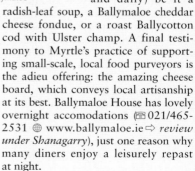

NOW WE'RE COOKING

If Myrtle Allen is the Alice Waters of Ireland, Darina Allen is its Martha Stewart. Thanks to her eight television series, her bestselling cookbooks, and the happy status of being the daughter-in-law of Myrtle, Darina's celebrity in Ireland is about on a par with U2's. She arrived in 1963 to apprentice at Ballymaloe and promptly fell in love with Myrtle's son, Tim, and her culinary dream. So, in 1983, she and Tim opened the Ballymaloe Cookery School, setting up shop two miles east on the other side of Shanagarry village at Kinoith House. The ultimate spot for a don't-just-visit, stay-and-become-an-Irish-chef experience, the school offers everything from two-hour starter lessons to the famed 12-week Certificate Course (run three times a year for 58 students), which many Irish chefs regard as a rite of passage. Half-day courses can be combined with an indulgent stay at

Darina Allen

Ballymaloe House—choose from "Sushi Made Simple," "The Magic of Phyllo," or "Discovering Tapas." A new departure is the "forgotten skills" series, day-long courses on chicken keeping, beekeeping, and organic gardening. Evidence that history repeats itself: Darina's daughter-in-law, Rachel Allen, is now making her second TV series, and publishing her second cook book.

MENU BEST BETS

Goujons of Ballycotton Haddock with Tartare Sauce

John's Rosemary, Red Wine & Garden Leek Risotto

Gubbeen Ham Braised in Chablis & Cream Served with Peperonata & Chives

Roast East Cork Beef with Roast Garlic Mayonnaise, with Fondant Potato & Vegetable Pakorash

Ballymaloe Cheddar Cheese Fondue

Grilled Ballycotton Hake with Scallops & Lobster, Herb Relish & French Beans

THE BALLYMALOE COOKERY SCHOOL is in Kinoith, just outside Shanagarry (☎ 021/464–6785 ⊕ www.cookingisfun.ie). Classes range from afternoon demonstrations (€55) to half-day classes (€70) to 1, 2½, and 5 day courses to the full 12-week Certificate (€9,995). Students can stay in charming cottages on the grounds.

7

IN FOCUS A TASTE OF IRELAND

CORK CORNUCOPIA: THE FOOD ARTISANS

Compare a traditionally made butcher's sausage with the plastic-wrapped supermarket version, and you'll understand what all the fuss is about: flavor, texture, and general deliciousness.

You'll see why Ireland's new artisanal foodstuff makers, fed up with the formulaic, tasteless foods of big industry, have stepped in to pioneer the production of farmhouse cheeses, organic beef, and organic herb cultivation and fish smoking. They got a big boost with the 1998 founding of Slow Food Ireland (⊕ www.-slowfoodireland.com), a loose collective of specialty producers and restaurateurs whose aim was to encourage careful food sourcing. West Cork has played an important role in the revival of Irish traditional foods, since incomers moving to the area seeking a change in lifestyle found that their small-business interests dovetailed with those of the traditional butchers, bakers, and farmers who had stayed put. These new artisans are now often listed on restaurant menus: Gubbeen Cheese, Ummera Smoked Salmon, Krawczyk's West Cork Salamis, Glenilen Dairy Products, and many others. Here are three of the best:

GUBBEEN FARMHOUSE PRODUCTS
Farmer Tom Ferguson tends a herd of prize cows, whose rich milk is made into creamy cheese by his wife Giana. The fresh-straw piggery allows its lucky pigs to have a view of Roaring Water Bay, one of the most scenic corners of Ireland. Tom and Giana's son, Fingal, runs the smokehouse (great smoked bacon, chorizo, and salamis), while daughter Clovisse grows organic vegetables and herbs. Products are sold at Neal's Yard in London and West Cork's farmer's markets. ⊠ *Gubbeen, Schull, near Skibbbereen, Co. Cork* ☎ *028/28231* ⊕ *www.gubbeen.com*

BELVELLY SMOKEHOUSE Frank Hederman smokes his eels, mackerel, salmon, trout, and mussels over beech rather than oak, giving them an unusually mild flavor. His smoked salmon is sold in London's Fortnum & Mason. The smokehouse is open for tastings, and his products can be bought at Cork City's English Market and Midleton's farmer's market. ⊠ *Cobh* ☎ *021/481–1089* ⊕ *www.frankhederman.com*

MACROOM OATMEAL Since the early 1800s, Donal Creedon's porridge oats have been hand-roasted on the traditional cast-iron plate at Walton's Mills before being shelled and ground, giving them a distinctive smoky, nutty flavor. Great for breadmaking, the meal is sold at many food shops. ⊠ *Kanturk, Co. Cork* ☎ *026/41800* ⊕ *macroomoatmealmills£eircom.net*

BLESSED ARE THE CHEESEMAKERS

7

IN FOCUS A TASTE OF IRELAND

Thirty years ago Irish cheese came in bright-orange blocks and tasted like salted plastic. Today, a thriving cheesemaking culture—a mix of native ingenuity and French, Swiss, German, and Dutch expertise—produces a wide range of artisanal farmhouse cheeses from the milk of goats and sheep, as well as from purebred cows. **Here are the best:**

Ardsallagh Goat's Cheese. A popular salad ingredient, this cheese can be bought from its maker, Jane Murphy, at the Midleton Farmer's Market.

Cashel Blue. The most famous Irish blue, this mild, creamy delight is made in Fethard, Co. Tipperary—it is as much used in cooking as on the cheese board.

Crozier Blue. Made from sheep's milk, this has a cult following.

Gabriel and Desmond. Using only summer-season raw milk from local herds grazed near the sea, these hard cheeses created by Americans Bill Hogan and Sean Ferry have a long maturation period, resulting in a piquant, aromatic bouquet.

Knockalara Sheep's Milk Cheese. Made by Wolfgang and Agnes Schiebitz, this is popular with chefs thanks to its soft, crumbly texture.

Milleens. This pungent, washed-rind winner is made from the milk of cows raised by Norman and Veronica Steele on their Beara Peninsula family farm.

FINDING THE FEAST

Long known as the "belly of Ireland," the West Cork region is celebrated for its rich fishing and even richer farming. These days, gourmets are busy rooting out the best Irish chorizo, sampling a new Durrus cheese and nutmeg pizza, or wolfing down Galway Bay oysters (heaven when served with Guinness!). Like a world-class picnic, this cook's tour is the tastiest recipe for a day trip through the region.

The best places to track down top temptations from Cork's gastronomic cornucopia are the area's food markets, often set in small villages and averaging only about a dozen stalls. Low overheads mean bargains for the buyers, who enjoy an amazing array of artisanal foodstuffs, from organic vegetables to sauces and relishes, Breton pancakes, handmade bread, home-cured ham, preserves, smoked salmon, and a great range of cheeses. And the markets' festive atmosphere (often livened up with a jazz trio or street performers) is complemented by the camaraderie of the stall-holders—this is often their main contact with the buying public. Darina Allen, with typical energy, can be found most Saturday mornings selling produce from her Ballymaloe Cookery School at a stall in Midleton. Check out the ever-changing market scene on its Web site (⊕ www.bordbia.ie.com) for up-to-date information. Here is a tip sheet:

COUNTY CORK

BANTRY, Main Square, Friday 9 am to 1 pm. A traditional street market, with a strong presence of growers of organic plants and veggies.

CLONAKILTY, Friday, 10 am to 2 pm. The Friday market (mainly food) is in the town car park behind the Credit Union.

KINSALE, Market Square, Tuesday 10–1. Snack on a Breton crepe while stocking up on chutneys, smoked salmon, famhouse cheeses, fresh fish, and organic veg and fruit at this cute piazza market.

MIDLETON, Saturday 10 am–2 pm. One of the liveliest farmers' markets, it's held in a small car park, with buskers creating a festive vibe.

SCHULL, Sunday 11–3. At its best in summer and at Christmas, this foodie's market showcases superb products from local bakers, fish smokers and cheesemakers, and Gubbeen smoked pork products, all sold by their makers.

COUNTY KERRY

KENMARE, Wednesday 10 am–5 pm, closed Jan. and Feb. About 15 outdoor stalls offer local organic produce and a few exotic imports to an appreciative local clientele. Look out for Knockatee cheese from Tuosist down the road, Olivier's smoked trout from Killorglin, organic vegs, homemade pâtés, fresh fish, and French soaps and sweets.

KILLARNEY, Parochial Hall, Country Market, Friday 11:30 am–1:30 pm. Famed for cakes, bread, savory tarts, jams, and farm-fresh eggs, the produce is all genuinely homemade, much of it from local farms, and sold at bargain prices.

MILLTOWN, Old Church Market, Saturday 10 am–2pm. Organic producers converge on this church, on the main road (N70) between Killorglin and Castlemaine—specialist bakers, organic growers, a wheatgrass stall, and an herbalist are highlights.

OTHER FOODIE FAVES

THE ENGLISH MARKET Today, this famous city-center covered market is a thriving hub of artisanal butchers, fishmongers, and greengrocers. Organic fruits and vegs, top-quality meat and fresh fish, imported coffees and teas, locally made charcuterie, farmhouse cheeses—even a champagne from a local wine merchant, Bubble Brothers. ⊠ *Grand Parade, Cork City* ⊕ *www.corkcity.ie*

THE LETTERCOLLUM SHOP Founders of the Lettercollum Kitchen Project, Con McLaughlin and Karen Austin are masters of the vegetarian and ethnic repertory (and also offer cooking classes). Their shop/bakery sells specialist breads, cooks'

ingredients, sandwiches, and savory herb tarts. Pick up a picnic. ⊠ *22 Connolly St., Clonakilty* ☎ *023/883–6938* ⊕ *www.lettercollum.ie*

URRU Once Ruth Healy took the Ballymaloe Certificate Cookery Course she left the corporate treadmill to open the ultimate cook's shop, which aims to bring urban chic to rural Ireland. Sip a latte while browsing among local artisanal foods, including home-made pâtés and patisserie, and a tempting range of cookbooks, cookwares, and chocolates. ⊠ *The Mill, MacSwiney Quay, Bandon, Co. Cork* ☎ *023/885–4731* ⊕ *www.urru.ie*

paintings on the walls. A bigger dose of country charm can be found in some guest rooms cocooned in floral wallpapers. Nearly every corner of the Georgian manor is used, down to the charming "stable" bedrooms on the first floor and the tiny, ivy-covered gatekeeper's cottage—perhaps the cutest accommodation in all Ireland. Newer, more spacious rooms downstairs have direct access to the pool and tennis court, and to

views of the river and the garden's abundant birdlife. This arcadia has been overseen by three generations of the Allen family (in point of fact, Darina Allen, Myrtle's daughter, now only runs the cookery school at a separate location and has nothing to do with this place) and their loyal staff. **Pros:** top restaurant; child-friendly family atmosphere; great wholesome food; quiet rural location near sandy beach. **Cons:** advance booking essential; village and beach driving, not walking, distance. ⊠ Co. Cork 🖀 021/465–2531 ⊕ www.ballymaloe.ie ⤴ 33 rooms ♿ In-room: no a/c, no TV (some). In-hotel: restaurant, bar, golf course, tennis court, pool, Internet terminal, some pets allowed ⊟ AE, DC, MC, V ⊠ BP.

KINSALE TO GLENGARRIFF

The historic old port—and now booming seaside town—of Kinsale is the perfect place to begin the 136-km (85-mi) trip, via Bantry Bay and through a variety of seascapes, to the lush vegetation of Glengarriff. If you tackle this scenic West Cork coastal route nonstop, the drive takes less than two hours, but the whole point of this journey is to linger in places that tickle your fancy. Must-sees include the famed 18th-century manse of Bantry House and the romantic island gardens of Ilnacullin.

KINSALE

29 km (18 mi) southwest of Cork City on R600.

Foodies flock to Kinsale, a picturesque port that pioneered the Irish small-town tradition of fine dining in unbelievably small restaurants. Back in the early '80s, Kinsale had a village-size population of 2,000 and at least a dozen top-grade restaurants, mostly run by enthusiastic owner-chefs. Things have leveled out since then—the town has grown, while the number of restaurants has remained nearly the same, and most of the original chefs have moved on—but there is still a great buzz during the annual **Kinsale Food Festival** (⊕ *www.kinsalerestaurants.com*) held in October. Year-round, head to Market Square (Tuesday 10–1) to find Kinsale Market, a cute piazza market where you can snack on a Breton crepe while stocking up on chutneys, smoked salmon, farmhouse cheeses, fresh fish, and an array of organic goodies.

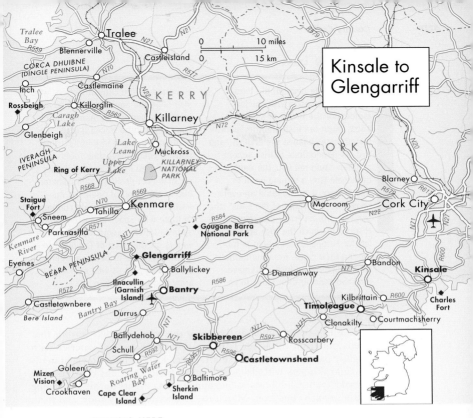

Kinsale to Glengarriff

GETTING HERE

BUS TRAVEL
Bus Éireann runs up to 15 buses a day from to Kinsale (50 minutes, €10.50 round-trip) from the Cork Bus Station via Cork Airport. The bus winds up in Kinsale's town center. There is no public transport in the Kinsale area but taxis can be booked from Kinsale Cabs.

TOURS
For an overview of Kinsale's great natural harbor, take an hour-long cruise on the *Spirit of Kinsale* offered by Kinsale Harbour Cruises. You can situate yourself on its covered lower deck, which has a bar and a coffee station, or wrap up and sit on the open deck. You'll get informative commentary and views of wildlife, including herons, seals, and otters.

ESSENTIALS

Transportation Contacts Kinsale Cabs (✉ Market Sq. ☎ 021/477–2642 ⊕ www.kinsalecabs.com). **Kinsale Harbour Cruises** (✉ Pier Rd. ☎ 021/477–8946 ⊕ www.kinsaleharbourcruises.com ⛴ €12.50 ⊙ May–Sept., daily, weather permitting).

Visitor Information Kinsale Tourist Office (✉ Pier Rd. ☎ 021/477–2234 ⊕ www.kinsale.ie/kinsnew.htm).

CLOSE UP

A Battle Lost

Before Kinsale became the foodie capital of Ireland, it was chiefly famous for the Battle of Kinsale in 1601, when the Irish and the Spanish joined forces against the English—and lost. As generations of Irish school-children could tell you, the Battle of Kinsale was a turning point in Irish history. It precipitated an event known as "the Flight of the Earls" (the subject of Brian Friels' play *Making History*), in which the Irish aristocracy left for Europe, to seek help in fur-thering their cause from the Catholic king of Spain. The Irish earls never returned, leaving their lands to be colonized by the English settlers, who also filled the power vacuum created by their absence. The Spanish influ-ence that can be traced back to this battle can be seen in Kinsale's older houses, which have slate roofs and unusual slate fronts. Because of its geographical position (approximately 800 km [500 mi] of open sea due north of La Coruna) Kinsale continued to trade with Spain, and even today, Spanish trawlers regularly fish in the waters off the coast of County Cork. Kinsale went on to become an impor-tant fishing port as well as a British army and naval base.

EXPLORING

In Kinsale's town center, at the tip of the wide, fjordlike harbor that opens out from the River Bandon, upscale shops and eateries with brightly painted facades line small streets. Kinsale has two yacht mari-nas, and skippers with deep-sea angling boats offer day charters. The Kinsale Yacht Club hosts racing and cruising events during the sailing season, which runs from March to October for hardy souls and from June to August for everyone else. This town is also where you can find Ireland's largest bareboat charter

The **Desmond Castle and the International Museum of Wine** are in a 15th-century fortified town house—originally a custom house—that has a dark history. It was used as a prison for French and American seamen in the 1700s, and was subsequently a jail and then a workhouse. Now it contains displays that tell the story of the wine trade and its importance to the Irish diaspora in France, America, Australia, and New Zealand. ⊠ *Cork St.* ☎ *021/477-4855* ⊕ *www.winegeese.ie* ⊠ *€3* ☿ *Mid-Apr.–Oct., daily 10–6.*

Memorabilia from the wreck of the *Lusitania* are among the best arti-facts in the **Kinsale Museum,** which is in a 17th-century, Dutch-style courthouse. The 1915 inquest into that ship's sinking took place in the courtroom, briefly making it the focus of the world's attention; it has been preserved as a memorial. Because the staff consists of volunteers, it's best to call to confirm opening times. ⊠ *Old Courthouse, Market Pl.* ☎ *021/477-7930* ⊠ *€2.50* ☿ *Mon.–Sat. 11–5, Sun. 3–5.*

★ The British built **Charles Fort** on the east side of the Bandon River estuary in the late 17th century, after their defeat of the Spanish and Irish forces. One of Europe's best-preserved "star forts" encloses some 12 cliff-top acres and is similar to Fort Ticonderoga in New York State. If the sun is shining, take the footpath signposted Scilly Walk; it winds along the har-bor's edge under tall trees and then through the village of Summer Cove.

✉ *3 km (2 mi) east of town* ☎ *021/477–2263* ⊕ *www.heritageireland.ie* 🚗*€4* ☉ *Mid-Mar.–Oct., daily 10–6; Nov.–mid-Mar., daily 10–5.*

The **Spaniard Inn** looks over the town and harbor from a hairpin bend on the road to Charles Fort. Inside, sawdust-covered floors and a big open fireplace make this onetime fishermen's bar a cozy spot in winter. In summer you can take a pint to the restaurant's veranda and watch the world go by on land and sea. ✉ *Scilly* ☎ *021/477–2436.*

WHERE TO EAT

$$
SEAFOOD
Fodor's Choice
★

✕ **Fishy Fishy Café.** Originally a café in a fish shop, Fishy Fishy has moved up in the world, and now occupies sumptuous indoor-outdoor premises in the town park. Previously an art gallery, the renovated quarters were remade by yacht designers, and the eatery's nautical style, with classy wooden furniture and massive parasols, is modern and clean-lined. Chef Martin Shanahan and his wife, Marie, do not take reservations for lunch (but they do for dinner, and booking is advisable) with limited dinner service: they stay open until 9, Tuesday through Friday, from April to October. Still, the crowds flock to stand in line for a table at peak times (1–2:30). Martin, who learned his craft in San Francisco, brings California pizzazz to his dishes. Look for wok-fried clams with spring onions, coriander, and ginger; "fishy fish" pie (white fish, salmon, and shellfish in a hot cream sauce and mash, au gratin); and seafood salad with a sweet chili dressing. It's all served by stylish young staff who give the impression they are thrilled to be part of the show. Some 18 wines are available by the glass. The café is open until 9 PM Easter to September, then only until 8 PM October to Easter; on Sundays and Mondays they close at 4:30 PM. If here for dinner, reservations are imperative. ✉ *Crowley's Quay* ☎ *021/470–0415* 🍴 *Reservations essential at dinner* 🟰 *MC, V.*

$$$
CONTINENTAL
★

✕ **Jim Edwards.** One of Ireland's original bar-restaurants, this is a famous Kinsale institution known for its generous portions of local steak, lamb, and duck, and fresh seafood, all prepared under the careful eye of the owner and his wife, Paula. Choose from the inexpensive daily specials in the busy bar ($), or have a more leisurely meal among the mahogany tables and dark-red decor of the somewhat baronial restaurant. With seafood this fresh, the preparation is kept simple: Kinsale oysters au naturel or crab claws tossed in garlic butter to start, followed by 10 ounces of prime fillet steak or medallions of monkfish (caught this morning) in a spring onion, ginger, and lime sauce. Fresh lobster from the tank is always available. The classic homemade desserts (profiteroles, crème brûlée) are substantial, and the Irish coffee is renowned. ✉ *Market Quay* ☎ *021/477–2541* ⊕ *www. jimedwardskinsale.com* 🟰 *AE, DC, MC, V.*

$$$
CONTINENTAL
★

✕ **Man Friday.** Yes, the name refers to Kinsale's alleged connection with the original Robinson Crusoe, Alexander Selkirk, for the town was reputedly his last port of call before shipwreck. Set about 1 km (½ mi) outside town, next to the Spaniard Inn on a hilltop overlooking the harbor, the restaurant focuses on steaks and seafood, prepared in an unpretentious Continental style. A rustic downhill walkway leads to a series of interconnected rooms and a terrace where diners enjoy drinks in fine weather. The generous portions and the warm atmosphere make it the sort of place you'll want to revisit. ✉ *Scilly* ☎ *021/477–2260* 🟰 *AE, MC, V* ☉ *Closed Sun. No lunch.*

Thanks to locals painting their houses with bright colors the historic seaside village of Kinsale has become one of Ireland's most picturesque photo-ops.

$$$ ✕ **Max's Wine Bar and Restaurant.** Polished antique tables, a large stone
FRENCH chimney, and bay windows facing the street lend this tiny town house
(more a restaurant than a wine bar) considerable charm. Lunches are
light; it's a good place if you're keen on salads. At dinner, owner-chef
Olivier Queva's classical French background is evident in his treatment
of the daily catch, which includes fresh grilled lobster in the summer,
and in his clever ways with such unusual cuts of meat as oxtail, trotters,
and a wide range of offal. In winter, the catch of the day is replaced
by game: quail, pheasant, wild duck, or venison. Olivier's Irish wife,
Anne-Marie, ably tends the front of the house. The wine list is long and
includes a good selection of French and New World wines, ranging in
price from about €15 to €85. ⊠ *Main St.* ☎ *021/477–2443* ▭ *AE, MC,*
V ☺ *Closed Tues. and Dec.–mid-Mar.*

WHERE TO STAY

$ ⌂ **Friar's Lodge.** A large Georgian town house has been tastefully con-
★ verted into a cheerful guesthouse, with an array of facilities (but no
bar or restaurant) that would do a hotel proud. The quiet residential
location is only a short walk from the town center, and adjacent to
the town's three churches, the bells of which merrily ring the hours.
Guest rooms are large, pleasantly decorated in the Georgian style,
with mustard-yellow spreads and drapes, wing armchairs, and good-
size bathrooms. The warm welcome and friendly touring advice from
owner-manager Maureen Tierney and her team, good parking facilities
(in a town where spaces can be hard to find), and excellent value make
this a popular spot with regular visitors (many of whom are golfers).
Pros: private parking; quiet location; amazingly attentive service. **Cons:**

no restaurant; no bar. ✉ *Friar's St., Co. Cork* ☎ *021/477–7384* ⊕ *www. friars-lodge.com* ⤶ *18 rooms* ♺ *In-room: no a/c, Wi-Fi. In-hotel: Wi-Fi hotspot* ⊟ *AE, MC, V* ☉ *Closed Christmas wk* ⊙| *BP.*

$$ ⊡ **Innishannon House.** A pretty country house built in 1720 in the châteaux style on the banks of the Bandon, Innishannon retains plenty of casual character. The bar and dining room are hung with contemporary Irish art, and have a busy local trade. Guest rooms vary greatly in shape and size—as do their windows—but have a variety of interesting antiques and strong color schemes. The hotel is surrounded by gardens and woods, with an attractive stretch of the Bandon River running through it, bordering the grounds. It's in a quiet rural location just off N7, about 6 km (4 mi) from Kinsale; it's quite perfect both as a retreat and as a base for touring the area. **Pros:** scenic riverside location; highly romantic; private car parking. **Cons:** a mile from nearest village; sometimes hosts wedding parties. ✉ *Innishannon, Co. Cork* ☎ *021/477–5121* ⊕ *www.innishannon-hotel.ie* ⤶ *12 rooms* ♺ *In-room: no a/c. In-hotel: restaurant, bar* ⊟ *AE, DC, MC, V* ⊙| *BP.*

$$ ⊡ **Trident.** The modern three-story building may lack old-world charm, but the waterfront location more than compensates. Built around three sides of a former dockyard on the very edge of Kinsale's magnificent harbor, the Trident features large rooms that all showcase fabulous sea views. The hotel is adjacent to a working pier where rusty coasters tie up overnight, adding to the authentic harbor atmosphere and providing a conversation topic as you breakfast in the first-floor restaurant within feet of a ship's stern. The Wharf Tavern and its bar-food menu are popular with locals who range from stevedores to owners of the million-dollar yachts moored at the neighboring marina. **Pros:** great sea views; plenty of parking. **Cons:** bland decor; pool and spa at sister hotel a five-minute walk away. ✉ *World's End, Co. Cork* ☎ *021/477–9300* ⊕ *www.tridenthotel.com* ⤶ *75 rooms* ♺ *In-room: no a/c, Wi-Fi. In-hotel: restaurant, bar, pool, gym* ⊟ *AE, MC, V* ⊙| *BP.*

NIGHTLIFE

The **Shanakee** (✉ *Market St.* ☎ *021/477–4472*) is renowned for live music—both rock and Irish traditional. Check out the **Spaniard Inn** (✉ *Scilly* ☎ *021/477–2436*) for rock and folk groups. There's a traditional Irish session on Wednesday from 10 PM year-round.

THE OUTDOORS

BICYCLING Rent a bike from **Myley Murphy's** (✉ *Pearse St.* ☎ *021/477–2703*) to explore the picturesque hinterland of Kinsale.

SHOPPING

Giles Norman Photography Gallery (✉ *44 Main St.* ☎ *021/477–4373*) sells black-and-white photographs of Irish scenes. **Granny's Bottom Drawer** (✉ *53 Main St.* ☎ *021/477–4839*) has fine linen and lace in classic and contemporary styles.

The **Keane on Ceramics** (✉ *Pier Rd.* ☎ *021/477–2085*) gallery represents the best of Ireland's ceramics artists.

You can spend quite a bit of time browsing through the excellent selection of Irish poetry and books on local history at the **Kinsale Bookshop** (✉ *8 Main St.* ☎ *021/477–4244*).

Kinsale Crystal (⊠ *Market St.* ☎ *021/477–4463*) is a studio that sells 100% Irish, handblown, hand-cut crystal.

Hilary Hale (⊠ *Rincurran Hall, Summercove* ☎ *021/477–2010* ⊕ *www.hilaryhale.com*) is a wood turner who uses storm-felled locally grown timber to make lamps, bowls, and platters. **The Trading House** (⊠ *54 Main St.* ☎ *021/477–7497*) has exclusive housewares from France, Spain, and Scandinavia alongside Irish and French antiques.

Victoria Murphy (⊠ *Market Quay* ☎ *021/477–4317*) sells small antiques and antique jewelry.

TIMOLEAGUE

19 km (12 mi) west of Kinsale on R600.

The romantic silhouette of its ruined abbey dominates the view when you're approaching Timoleague, a village of multicolor houses on the Argideen River estuary. The town marks the eastern end of the Seven Heads Peninsula, which stretches around to Clonakilty. There is no visitor-friendly public transport to Timoleague and Courtmacsherry. However, there is one bus a day to Cork leaving Timoleague at 8:05 AM and returning at 5:45 PM.

You can glimpse **Courtmacsherry,** the postcard village of multicolor cottages, just across the water. It has a sandy beach that makes it a favorite for vacationers. To reach it, follow the signposts from Timoleague.

Farther on you'll find that many storefronts in **Clonakilty,** a small market town 9½ km (6 mi) west of Timoleague on R600/N71, have charmingly traditional, hand-painted signs and wooden facades. The town has an indoor market with foods sold on Thursday and crafts for sale on Saturday. **Inchydoney,** 3 km (2 mi) outside Clonakilty, is one of the area's finest sandy beaches, backed by sheltered sand dunes.

WHERE TO EAT AND STAY

$$ ✕ **Casino House.** Stop midway between Kinsale and Timoleague, on coastal
CONTINENTAL route R600, for a meal at this farmhouse, which has been renovated in
Fodor'sChoice a cool, minimalist style and converted into a restaurant by the owner-
★ chef Michael Relja and his wife, Kerrin, who gives a warm welcome and tends front-of-house. You can take an aperitif outside in summer, or in the uncluttered sitting room, which, like the dining areas, are decorated in a light and Continental style, with plain whitewashed walls and wooden floors, all retaining a simple, farmhouse charm. Seasonal menus feature the finest local ingredients, including Ummera smoked salmon and fresh seafood landed nearby. Menu highlights from talented Croatian owner-chef Michael Relja include garlic prawn salad, lobster risotto, a fine roast loin of lamb served with Roman gnocchi, and, as one of the top seasonal desserts, summer fruits with sabayon. ⊠ *Coolmaine, Kilbrittain, Co. Cork* ☎ *023/884–9944* ⊕ *casinohouse.ie* ⊟ *MC, V* ☺ *Closed Wed. and mid-Jan.–mid-Mar. No dinner Sun. No lunch Mon.–Sat.*

$$ ☷ **The Glen Country House.** Located midway between Kinsale and Clonak-
Fodor'sChoice ilty (9 mi from both) on the scenic R600, this elegant country hideaway
★ makes an excellent touring base, though many guests just love to nestle down to enjoy the sheltered sea estuary and good walks. Guy and Diana

Monks and Wine

A mid-13th-century Franciscan abbey at the water's edge is Timoleague's most striking monument. (Walk around the back to find the entrance gate.) The view of the sea framed by its ruined Gothic windows is an unmissable photo-op.

The abbey was built before the estuary silted up, and its main business was the importing of wine from Spain.

A tower and walls with Gothic-arch windows still stand, and you can trace the ground plan of the old friary—chapel, refectory, cloisters, and the extensive wine cellar.

It was sacked by the English in 1642 but like many other ruins of its kind was used as a burial place until the late 20th century, hence the modern gravestones.

Scott have renovated this creeper-clad Victorian house (on a 300-acre farm) to the highest standards, combining family heirlooms with stylish contemporary touches: the grandfather clock in the hall sits opposite an abstract painting by Guy's distinguished uncle, artist and architect Patrick Scott. The family spaniels are usually on hand to offer a friendly welcome in the sitting room, where you can enjoy an open fire (in season) and an honesty bar. Guest rooms are spacious and all have views across rolling country to the sea. Babysitting, cots, and children's "high tea" can be arranged, as can grown-ups' dinner from Monday to Wednesday, when the excellent local restaurants are closed. **Pros:** family atmosphere; gracious surroundings; great value. **Cons:** must drive, not walk, to nearest shops and eateries. ⊠ *Kilbrittain, Co. Cork* ☎ *023/884–9862* ⊕ *www. glencountryhouse.com* ➷ *5 rooms* ☖ *In-room: no a/c, Wi-Fi. In-hotel: some pets allowed* ⊟ *MC, V* ☺ *Closed Nov.–Mar.* ⫶◉⫶ *BP.*

SHOPPING

Peter and Fran Wolstenholme's hand-thrown and slab-made tableware is eagerly collected, and sold only from their studio home and shop, **Court-macsherry Ceramics** (⊠ *Main St.* ☎ *023/884–6239*).

Edward Twomey (⊠ *16 Pearse St., Clonakilty* ☎ *023/883–3365*) is a traditional butcher's shop famed for its Clonakilty Black Pudding, a breakfast product that's prominently featured on the shop's nifty T-shirts—the ultimate West Cork souvenirs. Etain is one of Ireland's leading ceramic artists, and her shop, **Etain Hickey Collections** (⊠ *40 Ashe St.* ☎ *023/882–1479*), stocks the best of contemporary crafts from local artists and Fair Trade sources.

Assemble a superior picnic at the **Lettercollum Kitchen Shop** (⊠ *22 Connolly St., Clonakilty* ☎ *023/883–6938*), a bakery and deli selling tasty breads and local organic produce. **Spiller's Lane Gallery** (⊠ *Spiller's La., Clonakilty* ☎ *023/883–8416*), in a converted grain store at a pretty mews, sells Irish-made jewelry, cutlery, pottery, and paintings.

SKIBBEREEN

35 km (22 mi) west of Timoleague. Skibbereen is the main market town in this neck of southwest Cork. The Saturday country market and the plethora of pubs punctuated by bustling shops and coffeehouses keep the place jumping year-round.

GETTING HERE

BIKE TRAVEL   Skibbereen is also a designated hub of the National Cycle Network, with three signposted routes of one-day and half-day cycles. Book a bike in advance from Roycroft Cycles.

BUS TRAVEL   There are seven Bus Éireann buses a day from Cork's Parnell Place bus station to Skibbereen (which is on the same line as Clonakilty), three of which continue to Schull and Goleen. The journey to Skibbereen (€20.70 round-trip) takes 1½ hours. If visiting the area by bus, it makes sense to stay overnight, or you will only have a few hours to look around. For local excursions check the rates at West Cork Cabs.

ESSENTIALS

Transportation Contacts Roycroft Cycles (✉ *Heron Court, Town Carpark* ☎ *028/21766*). **West Cork Cabs** (✉ *Market Sq.* ☎ *087/840–8808*).

Visitor Information Skibbereen Tourist Office (✉ *North St., Co. Cork* ☎ *028/21766* ⊕ *www.discoverireland.ie/skibbereen*).

EXPLORING

A thoughtful renovation of a stone gasworks building has created an attractive, architecturally appropriate home for the **Skibbereen Heritage Center.** An elaborate audiovisual exhibit on the Great Famine presents dramatized firsthand accounts of what it was like to live in this community when it was hit hard by hunger. Other attractions include displays on area marine life, walking tours, access to local census information, and a varying schedule of special programs. ✉ *Upper Bridge St.* ☎ *028/40900* ⊕ *www.skibbheritage.com* ✉ *€6* ⊙ *Mid-Mar.–mid-May and mid-Sept.–Oct., Tues.–Sat. 10–6; late May–mid-Sept., daily 9:30–6; mid-Nov.–mid-Mar., by appointment.*

The **Mizen Vision Visitor Centre,** which occupies a lighthouse at the tip of the Mizen Head (follow the R591 through Goleen to the end of the road), is the Irish mainland's most southerly point. The lighthouse itself is on a rock at the tip of the headland; to reach it, you must cross a dramatic 99-step suspension footbridge. The lighthouse was completed in 1910; the Engine Room and Keepers' House have been restored by the local community. The exhilaration of massive Atlantic seas swirling 164 feet below the footbridge and the great coastal views guarantee a memorable outing. ✉ *Harbour Rd., Goleen* ☎ *028/35115* ⊕ *www.mizenhead.ie* ✉ *€6* ⊙ *Mid-Mar.–May and Oct., daily 10:30–5; June–Sept., daily 10–6; Nov.–mid-Mar., weekends 11–4.*

THE ARTS

The **West Cork Arts Center** (⊠ *North St., Skibbereen* ☎ *028/22090*) has regular exhibits of work by local artists and an on-site crafts shop.

CASTLETOWNSHEND

8 km (5 mi) southeast of Skibbereen.

This town has an unusual number of large, gracious stone houses, most of them dating from the mid-18th century, when it was an important trading center. The main street runs steeply downhill to the 17th-century castle (built by the noted regional family of the Townshends) and the sea. The sleepy town awakens in July and August, when its sheltered harbor bustles. Sparkling views await from cliff-top St. Barrahane's Church, which has a medieval oak altarpiece and three stained-glass windows by early-20th-century Irish artist Harry Clarke. There is no bus service to Castletownshend *(see Skibbereen for taxi contact, West Cork Cabs).*

WHERE TO EAT

$$$

CONTINENTAL

★

✕**Mary Ann's.** Writer Edna O'Brien calls this her favorite pub in the world. Low-beamed, and one of Ireland's oldest, Mary Ann's attracts wealthy visitors from the United Kingdom and from other parts of Ireland, who mingle happily with the few locals left in the village in the front barroom, the quieter back room, or the large garden beyond. Energetic owner-manager Fergus O'Mahony is a brilliant host, and is always on the spot, supervising operations and contributing to the *craic* (lively conversation). The bar-food menu ($) is served all day in the main bar area. Upstairs, the 32-seat restaurant nearly always buzzes, so reservations are a good idea. Try the trademark baked avocado stuffed with crabmeat, the massively generous platter of Castlehaven Bay shellfish and seafood, or the succulent T-bone steak. This is a good place to sample a platter of the local farmhouse cheeses, such as Durrus, Milleens, Gabriel, and Gubbeen. ⊠ *Main St.* ☎ *028/36146* ▭ *MC, V* ⊘ *Closed Nov.–Mar. No bar food Mon. in Nov.–Mar.*

BANTRY

Fodor's Choice

★

33 km (21 mi) northwest of Castletownshend, 25 km (16 mi) northwest of Skibbereen on N71.

As the road nears the head of Bantry Bay, it divides into two. The right fork takes you to Glengariff, the left to Bantry, lying at the end of Bantry Bay itself, at between 6 and 8 mi wide one of the largest natural harbors in the world. It was here that the French attempted to land a force of some 14,000 men in 1796, during the Napoleonic Wars. A combination of foul winds and naval incompetence proved their undoing. Some French "spoils," however, are on view in the town's famed country estate manor, Bantry House.

GETTING HERE

BUS TRAVEL

There are 11 Bus Éireann buses a day from the Cork Bus Station to Bantry (2 hours, €20.70 round-trip), starting from 9:15 AM. Some continue to Glengariff, another half-hour. It is possible to do a day trip to Bantry by bus—returning to Cork from Bantry, say, at 6:30 PM—but an overnight stay is recommended if you also want to explore Glengarriff.

Visitor Information Bantry Tourist Office (✉ *New Bantry St.* ☎ *027/50229* ⊕ *www.west-cork.com/bantry-tourism*).

EXPLORING

As you enter Bantry from the east—a somewhat unprepossessing town topped out with a large square that attracts artisans, craftspeople, and musicians to its Friday morning market in summer—on the right-hand side of the road, just before a gigantic new hotel, you'll see the parking lot and entrance to **Bantry House and Gardens.** One of Ireland's most famed manors, it's noted for its picture-perfect perch: on a hillock above the south shore of Bantry Bay, it's surrounded by a series of stepped gardens and parterres that make up "the stairway to the sky." Spreading out below the Georgian mansion lies the bay and, in the far distance, the spectacular range of the Caha Mountains—one of the great vistas of Ireland. Built in the early 1700s and altered and expanded later that century, the manor was the ancestral seat of the White family. The house is largely the vision of Richard White, the first earl of Bantry, who traveled extensively through Europe and brought a lot of it back with him: fabulous Aubusson tapestries said to have been commissioned by Louis XV adorn the Rose Drawing Room, while state portraits of King George III and Queen Charlotte glitter in floridly Rococo gilt frames in the hypertheatrical, Wedgwood-blue and gold dining room. An antique or two is thought to have belonged to Marie-Antoinette.

Outside, the drama continues in the stepped garden terraces, set with marble statues, framed by stone balustrades, and showcasing such delights as an embroidered parterre of dwarf box. The tearoom serves light lunches, and features local artisan foods. In summer the house hosts concerts in the grand library room, notably the West Cork Chamber Music Festival (held during the first week of July). ☎ *027/50047* ⊕ *www.bantryhouse.ie* ✉ *House and gardens €10, gardens €5* ☉ *Mar.–Oct., daily 10–6.*

WHERE TO STAY

$$$ ⬚ **Bantry House.** When the day-trippers leave, you can play lord and lady
★   of this celebrated manor for the night, thanks to 12 guest bedrooms. Set in a self-contained wing off a long corridor with sea views, these are not the biggest nor the stateliest of stately-home guest bedrooms, but the ambience is truly memorable. The rooms overlook the south-facing garden and its famous stone terraces, linked by the Hundred Steps, so the vistas across Bantry Bay as the sun goes down over the water will be long remembered (especially if you are blessed with a moonlit night). The smallish rooms are luxuriously appointed, with embroidered silk curtains and under-floor heating in the recently renovated bathrooms. The real lord of the manor, Egerton Shelswell-White, will probably be on hand to book you into a local restaurant for dinner. Breakfast is taken in a large basement room, prettily decked out in gingham. **Pros:** a genuine heritage experience; unique location; friendly, helpful hosts; not as pricey as you'd think. **Cons:** a longish walk (or a short drive) into town; worth the premium only if you are into history and heritage.

Divided by the Hundred Steps, the gardens of Bantry House are adorned with exotic plants due to the micro-climate of its bay setting.

✉ Co. Cork ☎ 027/50047 ⊕ www.bantryhouse.ie ➲ 12 rooms ⌂ In-room: no a/c, Internet ⊟ MC, V ⊘ Closed Nov.–mid-Mar.

$$$ ⊞ **Seaview House.** Among private, wooded grounds overlooking Bantry Bay, you'll find this large, three-story, 19th-century country house. Owner-manager Kathleen O'Sullivan keeps an eagle eye on what was, until 1980, her private home and today remains an oasis of calm, nestled in its own gardens well away from the main road. Antique furniture, plump sofas, polished brass, and ornate curtains provide comfort and elegance. In the dining room, polished tables are set with crocheted mats and linen napkins; service is friendly and informal. **Pros:** unostentatious comfort; good food; low-key, friendly service. **Cons:** make your own entertainment; "village" is more a suburb of Bantry, with only one pub. ✉ Ballylickey, Co. Cork ☎ 027/50073 ⊕ www.seaviewhousehotel.com ➲ 25 rooms ⌂ In-room: no a/c. In-hotel: restaurant, bar, Internet terminal ⊟ AE, MC, V ⊘ Closed mid-Nov.–mid-Mar. ⍾ BP.

SHOPPING

Manning's Emporium (✉ Ballylickey ☎ 027/51049) is a showcase for locally made farmhouse cheeses, pâtés, and salamis—an excellent place to put together a picnic or just to browse.

GLENGARRIFF

★ *14 km (8 mi) northwest of Bantry on N71, 21 km (13 mi) south of Kenmare.*

One of the jewels of Bantry Bay is Glengarriff, the "rugged glen" much loved by Thackeray and Sir Walter Scott *(for public transport options see*

Bantry, above). The descent into wooded, sheltered Glengarriff reveals yet another landscape: thanks to the Gulf Stream, it's mild enough down here for subtropical plants to thrive. Trails along the shore are covered with rhododendrons and offer beautiful views of the nearby inlets, loughs, and lounging seals. You're very much on the beaten path, however, with crafts shops, tour buses, and boatmen soliciting your business by the roadside. Many are heading this way because of that Irish Eden, **Ilnacullin.** On Garnish Island, about 10 minutes offshore from Glengarriff and beyond islets populated by comical-looking basking seals, you can find one of the country's horticultural wonders. In 1910 a Belfast businessman, John Annan Bryce, purchased this rocky isle, and, with the help of famed English architect Howard Peto and Scottish plantsman Murdo Mackenzie, transformed it into a botanical Disneyland. The main showpiece is a wisteria-covered "Casita"—a rather strange-looking half-shed, half-mansion Peto cooked up—which overlooks a sunken Italian garden. A touch of Japan is supplied by the bonsai specimens lining the terrace. In fact, Ilnacullin has a little bit of everything, from a Grecian temple to a Martello tower (from which the British watched for attempted landings by Napoleonic forces) to a Happy Valley, all bedded with extraordinary shrubs, trees, and many unusual subtropical flowers. You get to Ilnacullin by taking a Blue Pool ferry, which departs for the island from Glengarriff. George Bernard Shaw found Ilnacullin peaceful enough to allow him to begin his *St. Joan* here; maybe you'll find Garnish inspiring, too. ✉ *Garnish Island* ☏ *027/63040* 🌐 *www.heritageireland.ie* 🎫 *Gardens €3.70, ferry €12 round-trip* ⏲ *July and Aug., Mon.–Sat. 9:30–6:30, Sun. 11–6:30; Apr.–June and Sept., Mon.–Sat. 10–6:30, Sun. noon–6:30; Oct.–Mar., Mon.–Sat. 10–4:30, Sun. 1–5.*

WHERE TO STAY

$ 🏨 **Glengarriff Eccles.** This landmark hotel has stood at the entrance to Glengarriff since before the Victorian novelist William Thackeray passed through. Fronted by a massive wrought-iron balcony, the stately building looks out over the calm water of the harbor and it is worth paying a small supplement for a harbor view. Guest rooms have plain walls, large mahogany headboards, tartan blankets on white comforters, and flat TV screens, the one concession to the modern age. The public salons are also traditional in style, with lots of dark woods and dark red upholstery. A busy passing trade and child-friendly staff bring the place alive. **Pros:** water's edge location; great sense of history; locals use the bar. **Cons:** 5-minute walk from village; a bit eerie when not busy. ✉ *Glengarriff Harbor* ☏ *027/63003* 🌐 *www.eccleshotel.com* 🛏 *66 rooms* 👍 *In-room: no a/c. In-hotel: restaurant, bar, Wi-Fi hotspot* 💳 *MC, V* ⏲ *Closed Jan.*

County Clare, Galway, and the Aran Islands

WORD OF MOUTH

"The famous Cliffs of Moher now have a nice, wide paved path with a trail up to O'Brien's Tower. In the opposite direction, the trail only goes to the first bend in the cliffs, with signage barring visitors from continuing along the cliffs that are private property. It's disappointing that Shannon Heritage didn't purchase more of that pathway for the public."

—wojazz

WELCOME TO COUNTY CLARE, GALWAY, AND THE ARAN ISLANDS

TOP REASONS TO GO

★ **Ancient Aran:** Spend at least one night on one of the Oileáin Árainn (Aran Islands), three outposts of Gaelic civilization, which still have a strong whiff of the "old ways"—and not just the whiff of turf smoke.

★ **Foot-Tapping in Doolin and Ennis:** Tap your foot in time to "trad" Irish music— those heavenly strains of traditional Irish folk music— and sip your pint as you while away an afternoon and maybe an evening as well, in one of Doolin's or Ennis's noted music bars.

★ **High-Style Galway:** A university town and booming, buzzing hive of activity, with great theaters, bars, nightlife, shopping, and restaurants, Galway is the city that loves to celebrate and, as one of Europe's fastest-growing townships, has much to offer.

★ **The Mighty Cliffs of Moher:** Rising straight out of the sea to a height of 700 feet, these cliffs—standing in silence as they look out over the wild Atlantic—give you a new understanding of the word "awesome."

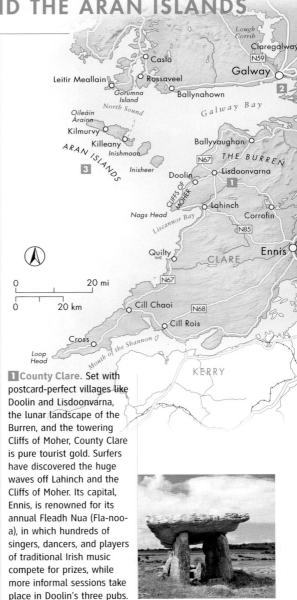

1 County Clare. Set with postcard-perfect villages like Doolin and Lisdoonvarna, the lunar landscape of the Burren, and the towering Cliffs of Moher, County Clare is pure tourist gold. Surfers have discovered the huge waves off Lahinch and the Cliffs of Moher. Its capital, Ennis, is renowned for its annual Fleadh Nua (Fla-noo-a), in which hundreds of singers, dancers, and players of traditional Irish music compete for prizes, while more informal sessions take place in Doolin's three pubs.

GETTING ORIENTED

Once you cross the Shannon in Limerick City you are officially in the West of Ireland. The rocky limestone plateau known as the Burren, dotted with megalithic remains, overlooks Galway Bay, lined with characterful villages like Ballyvaughan and Kinvara, and cradling the Aran Islands that lie across its entrance. Galway City is one of Ireland's liveliest, with a compact historic center bursting with artistic energy and a lively pub culture. This is the place to organize your trip to the Aran Islands, three windswept rocky islands where Irish is still spoken, with an almost total absence of traffic.

8

2 Galway City. This is easily the liveliest city in Ireland after Dublin. You've got to get your fill of its buzz when visiting, best done by checking out its eye-popping "g" hotel, stylish new boutiques and crafts shops, and dazzling weekend festivals.

3 Aran Islands. An hour or less away via ferry are the ageless Aran Islands. Once famed for their isolation, they are now disturbed a bit by 200,000-plus curious annual visitors, but even so they retain a distinctive identity, with traditional communities where Irish is still the daily language.

COUNTY CLARE, GALWAY, AND ARAN PLANNER

Transportation Basics

Public transport is not a strong point in the West. Trains arrive from Dublin on separate lines to Ennis and Galway, but do not run between these towns. The bus network is more flexible, but there are not many services a day, so plan accordingly. Ferries and flights to the Aran Islands can all be reached by shuttle services from Galway City and also from the piers near Doolin. But to do full justice to the region, you really need a car—and a good map. *For details, see the Getting Around section.*

When to Go

It will most likely rain, but the locals just call it "soft" weather. Average rainfall in the rest of Ireland is between 31 inches and 47 inches, but here on the west coast, it can exceed 79 inches. It is said to rain in the west on at least 300 of the 365 days in the year. Take comfort from the thought that it may be damp, but it is never really cold, with a mean daily temperature around 6°C (43°F) in January and February, the coldest months. In the warmest months, July and August, average temperatures are around 15°C (60°F).

Destination: Aran Islands

The spell of the Aran Islands is such that many travelers can't resist their siren call and make for the first ferry leaving from Doolin. However, locals will tell you that it may be best to wait until you are in Galway City before you make arrangements to travel to the famed Oileáin Árainn (Aran Islands). That way you can postpone your trip if the weather looks bad, and shop around for the best deals from the various ferry firms.

You can do a day trip, leaving the city at 9:30 or noon and returning by 6:30, but staying overnight is more rewarding.

Everyone wants to go to the islands, and it is made as easy as possible to organize by the various transport companies. They are all genuine and licensed: no one is going to rip you off. Book at the Galway Tourist Information Office in Forster Place, where the ferry companies and Aer Arran have concessions.

The standard ferry deal is €25 round-trip and €6 for bus transfer to the ferry port at Rossaveal. Look out for money-saving offers that may include bed-and-breakfast accommodation, free transfers to Rossaveal, or Connemara Airport (both 40 minutes away), bicycle rental on the islands, or a ferry-out, flight-back plan.

There are three different ferry operators, and tickets are not transferable, so check the return sailing times of your operator when you get on board.

If you opt for the five-minute flight, for safety reasons, you (yes, you, not your bags!) will be weighed at check-in, and allocated an appropriate seat. *For more information, see Boat and Ferry Travel in the Getting Around section of this chapter.*

When Ireland Celebrates

For visitors and locals alike, festivals provide both free entertainment and a chance to meet people from all backgrounds who share a common interest.

Some festivals are traditional events, now tarted up with entertaining sideshows. For instance, Kinvara's **Criuinniú na mBád** (⊕ www.kinvara.com/cruinniu/index/html) on the third Thursday in August centers around turf-laden "hookers" (heavy wooden sailing boats) racing across Galway Bay.

The Willie Clancy Summer School at Miltown Malbay on the Clare coast is Ireland's largest summer school for traditional musicians and dancers, with 135 daily workshops. The **Fleadh Nua** (⊕ www.fleadhnua.com) in Ennis in late May is one of the country's biggest traditional music festivals, and a great place to make friends.

There is plenty of free entertainment here, and also at the Lisdoonvarna Matchmaking Festival held in late September, an outing that may well change your life—stranger things have happened!

In contrast, the **Galway Arts Festival** (⊕ www. galwayartsfestival.com), in the middle two weeks of July, hosts an international array of the best of contemporary theater, film, rock, jazz, traditional music, poetry readings, comedy acts, and visual arts exhibitions.

The festival's open-air parade by the street theater company Macnas, one of several local troupes to gain international recognition, is always a big draw.

This is followed immediately by the Galway Races, the "only place" for Irish socialites to be seen in late July. These Thoroughbred horse races now feature a new sport: the game of Spot the Celebrity (usually arriving by helicopter).

Both Galway and neighboring Clarinbridge have oyster festivals in September, celebrating the local product with oyster-opening competitions and lots of free entertainment.

WHAT IT COSTS IN EUROS

	¢	$	$$	$$$	$$$$
Restaurants	under €12	€12–€18	€19–€24	€25–€32	over €32
Hotels	under €80	€80–€120	€121–€170	€171–€210	over €210

Restaurant prices are for a main course at dinner. Hotel prices are for a standard double room in high season.

Finding a Place to Stay

Some of Ireland's finest country-house and castle hotels are in this area. Dromoland Castle, between Shannon Airport and Ennis, provides a standard of luxury that you should experience at least once, if you can stretch your budget.

Star country-house destinations include the creeper-clad Georgian house, known as Gregan's Castle Hotel, a tranquil retreat with views of the Burren and Galway Bay, and Glenlo Abbey, a rural hideaway just a 10-minute drive from Galway City. Try to sample some of the smaller B&Bs as well: the home cooking at Kilmurvey House on the Aran Islands is renowned. Other memorable destinations include the cliff-top Moy House at Lahinch, and Ballinalacken Castle, a shooting lodge set in 100 acres of wildflower meadows next to the ruins of an O'Brien castle. Among the newer, mid-range hotels, Vaughan Lodge in Lahinch and the Park House Hotel in Galway's city center offer exceptional standards of comfort and design. Indoor pools and tennis courts are the exception rather than the rule in this region, where business is largely seasonal, and the emphasis is on outdoor pursuits. *Note: During peak events, such as the Galway Race Week, hotel rates in Galway do shoot up.* Assume that all hotel rooms *in this chapter* have in-room phones, TVs, and private bathrooms, unless otherwise indicated.

8

GETTING AROUND

Car, Train, or Bus?

A car can be very helpful in the West region, especially from September through June. Although the main cities are easily reached from the rest of Ireland by rail or bus, transport within the region can be sparse. If a rental car is out of the question, one option is to make Galway your base and take day tours south to the Cliffs of Moher and the Burren, and a day or overnight trip to the Aran Islands. Of course, there are local and intercity bus services, but have no illusions that buses run every hour.

Car Travel

The 219-km (136-mi) Dublin–Galway trip takes about three hours. From Cork City take N20 through Mallow and N21 to Limerick City, picking up the N18 Ennis–Galway road in Limerick. The 209-km (130-mi) drive from Cork to Galway takes about three hours. From Killarney the shortest route to cover the 193 km (120 mi) to Galway (three hours) is to take N22 to Tralee, then N69 through Listowel to Tarbert and ferry across the Shannon Estuary to Killimer. From here, join N68 in Kilrush, and then pick up N18 in Ennis.

Road Conditions

The West has good, wide main roads (National Primary Routes) and better-than-average local roads (National Secondary Routes), both known as "N" routes. If you stray off the beaten track on the smaller Regional ("R") routes, particularly in west Clare, you may encounter some challenging roads.

Narrow and twisty, they are also used by hikers and cyclists from Easter to October, as well as local traffic (which can take the form of huge trucks serving the local agricultural co-ops, and school buses, both full-size and mini).

The speed limits on these Regional routes is a whacking great 80 km per hour (50 MPH), even for trucks and buses, but use your common sense and adjust your speed accordingly. If traffic builds up behind you, it is customary to signal to the left, and slow down (or pull off the road if there is space) to let the locals whiz past. Your kind gesture will usually be acknowledged with a smile and a wave.

Train Travel

The region's main rail stations are in Galway City, Ennis, and Limerick City. Trains for Galway and Limerick leave from Dublin's Heuston Station (but they are on different lines).

Trains run direct to Galway via Athlone, taking about three hours, while for Limerick City (which is on the Cork and Tralees line) you must change to a branch line at Limerick Junction, and change again at Limerick City on to the newly opened (2010) local link between Limerick City and Galway City, which travels via Ennis, Gort, and Athenry.

Journey time from Limerick to Ennis is 40 minutes (€11.80 round trip), while Limerick City to Galway takes about two hours (prices not yet available at this writing).

Train Information Irish Rail–Iarnod Éireann (⊕ *www. irishrail.ie*). **Ennis Station** (☎ *065/684–0444*). **Dublin Heuston Station** (☎ *01/836–6222*). **Galway Station–Ceannt Railway Station** (☎ *091/564–222*). **Limerick City Station** (☎ *061/315–555*).

Bus Travel

Bus Éireann runs several Expressway buses into the region from Dublin, Cork City, and Limerick City to Ennis, and Galway City, the principal depots in the region. All buses mentioned are Bus Éireann (which includes Expressway) unless specified otherwise. Expect bus rides to last about one hour longer than the time it would take you to travel the distance by car. In July and August, the provincial bus service is augmented by daily services to most resort towns. Outside these months, many coastal towns receive only one or two buses per week. Bus routes are often slow and circuitous, and service can be erratic. The Cliffs of Moher, Lisdoonvarna, Doolin, Liscannor, and Lahinch have two scheduled services a day (in each direction) from Galway, and only one from Ennis. Using a scheduled bus service costs about €10 less than a guided tour, which will also take in other attractions in the Burren area. Guided tours of the Cliffs of Moher and the Burren leave from the bus stations in Galway City and Ennis.A copy of the Bus Éireann timetable (local information free from Tourist Information Offices or the bus station) is essential.Citylink operates frequent buses, with up to 17 departures daily, between Galway City and Dublin and Dublin Airport. The trip costs €15 one-way. Citylink also makes six daily trips in each direction between Shannon Airport and Galway City, costing €16 one-way, with onward connections to Cork City and Airport from Shannon.

Bus Depots Ennis Station (✉ *Station Rd. Ennis* ☎ *065/682–4177*). **Galway Bus Station** (*Ceannt Railway Station* ☎ *091/562–000*).

Bus Lines Bus Éireann (☎ *01/836–6111 in Dublin* ⊕ *www.buseireann.ie*). **Citylink** (☎ *091/564–163* ⊕ *www. citylink.ie*).

Taxi Travel

Taxis operate on the meter for journeys of up to 30 km (22 mi). For longer journeys, agree on the fare in advance. Sample fares include Galway to Moycullen €50, to Salthill €7; Shannon Airport to Galway City €120; Knock Airport to Galway City €120.

AAA Taxis (✉ *Ennis* ☎ *065/689–2999*). **Big O Taxis** (✉ *Galway City* ☎ *091/585–858* ⊕ *www.bigotaxis.com*). **Burren Taxi** (✉ *Ennis* ☎ *065/682–3456*). **Galway Taxis** (✉ *Galway* ☎ *091/561–111* ⊕ *www.galwaytaxis.com*).

Airport Transfers

From Shannon Airport you can pick up a rental car to drive into the West, or you can take a bus to Galway or Ennis.

Galway Airport is 6½ km (4 mi) from Galway City.

No regular bus service is available from the airport to Galway, but most flight arrivals are taken to Galway Rail Station in the city center by an airline courtesy coach. Inquire when you book.

A taxi from the airport to the city center costs about €15. Connemara Airport is 27 km (16 mi) from Galway City, and is accessible by shuttle bus.

This is usually included in your ticket price.

Information Please

If you're traveling extensively by public transportation, be sure to load up on information (the best taxi-for-call companies, rail and bus schedules, etc.) upon arriving at the ticket counter or help desk of the bigger train and bus stations in the area, such as Ennis and Galway City.

Those places also have the biggest and most useful Tourist Information Offices.

GETTING AROUND

Boat and Ferry Information

Aran Doolin Ferries
(✉ Doolin Pier ☎ 065/707–4455 ⊕ www.doolinferries.com).

Aran Link
(✉ Victoria Pl., 29 Forster St., Galway City ☎ 091/506–786 ⊕ www.arandirect.com).

Island Ferries
(✉ Tourist Information Office, Forster St., Eyre Sq., Galway City ☎ 091/568–903 or 091/537–700 ⊕ www.aranislandferries.com).

Tarbert–Killimer Ferry
(✉ 065/905–3124 ⊕ www.shannonferries.com).

Word of Mouth

"You might not have found the Bus Éireann tour from Galway to the Cliffs of Moher online, because it's a regular Expressway service of Bus Éireann, so technically spoken not a 'tour.' It's listed as service #50 when you go to the page with the 'long distance services' at ⊕ www.buseireann.ie. While Bus Éireann's buses do not have toilets, there is a 'service break' every two hours or so."
—Cowboy1968

Boat and Ferry Travel

The Tarbert–Killimer Ferry leaves every hour on the half hour and takes 20 minutes to cross the Shannon Estuary from North County Kerry to West County Clare; this saves you a 137-km (85-mi) drive through Limerick City. The ferry runs every day of the year except Christmas and costs €18 one-way, €28 round-trip. (Ferries return from Killimer every hour on the hour.)

There are several options for traveling to the Oileáin Árainn (Aran Islands). Island Ferries runs a boat to the islands from Ros an Mhíl (Rossaveal), 32 km (20 mi) west of Galway City, which makes the crossing in 20 minutes and costs about €30 round-trip (or, weather-permitting, you can opt for a boat that takes an hour, costing about €25), and an extra €7 for the shuttle bus from Galway; they also offer a ferry route between Doolin and the Aran Islands. Note that there's a handy ticket office in the TIO (Tourist Information Office) in Galway City.

If you're heading for Inis Oírr (Inisheer), the smallest island, the shortest crossing is from Doolin in County Clare on Aran Doolin Ferries. Aran Doolin Ferries offers service from Doolin Pier, with up to 12 sailings daily, from June through the end of September. The crossing takes about 20 minutes and costs €30 round-trip.

Aran Link goes from Doolin and Rossaveal and does inter-island hops. Bicycles are transported free off-season, but there may be a charge in July and August: inquire when booking.

There's lively competition between the ferry companies, so shop around for the best deal. Discounts are available for families, students, and groups of four or more. If you want to stay a night or two on the islands, ask about accommodations when booking your ferry, as there are some very good deals.

For travel between the Aran Islands, frequent interisland ferries (run by Island Ferries) are available in summer, but tickets are nontransferable, so ask the captain of your ferry about the interisland schedule if you plan to visit more than one island. You can purchase ferry tickets on the island or at the TIO in Galway. *For more information, see "Destination: Aran Islands," above.*

Air Travel

Aer Arann has seven flights a day from London's Luton Airport and five a day from Dublin to Galway Airport (GWY). Aer Arann also flies to Edinburgh, Manchester, Lorient, and Waterford from Galway. Ryanair flies to Knock daily from London's Stansted Airport and Luton Airport; flying time is 80 minutes. BmiBaby has several flights to Knock from Manchester daily. Aer Arann flies hourly in July and August to the Oileáin Árainn (Aran Islands) from Connemara Airport in Inverin. Off-peak there are half a dozen flights a day, fewer in December and January. These flights call at all three Aran Islands.

The journey takes about six minutes and costs about €45 round-trip. The airline will book a B&B for you when you book your flight. Ask about other special offers, including scenic routes, at the time of booking.

Carriers Aer Arann (☎ 091/593–034 ⊕ www.aerarann. ie). **Aer Lingus** (☎ 0818/365–022 ⊕ www.aerlingus.com). **BmiBaby** (☎ 1890/340–122 ⊕ www.bmibaby.com). **Ryanair** (☎ 0818/303–030 ⊕ www.ryanair.com).

Airports

The West's most convenient international airport is Shannon, 25 km (16 mi) east of Ennis *(see Chapter 7, The Southwest)*. Galway Airport, 8 km (5 mi) from Galway City, is used mainly for internal flights, and some U.K. traffic.

Flying time from Dublin is 25 to 30 minutes to all airports. No scheduled flights run from the United States to Galway; use Shannon Airport. Connemara Airport at Inverin, which is 29 km (18 mi) west of Galway on R336, services the Aran Islands.

Ask about transport to the airport when buying your ticket: there is usually a courtesy bus from the center of Galway City.

Airport Information Connemara Airport (☎ 091/593–034). **Galway Airport** (☎ 091/752–874 ⊕ www. galwayairport.com). **Shannon Airport** (☎ 061/471–444 ⊕ www.shannonairport.com).

Visitor Information

Bord Fáilte provides free information service, tourist literature, and an accommodations booking service at its TIOs (Tourist Information Offices).

The following offices are open all year, generally weekdays 9–6, daily during the high season: Aran Islands (Inis Mór), Ennis, and Galway City.

Other TIOs that operate seasonally, generally weekdays 9–6 and Saturday 9–1, are open as follows:

Cliffs of Moher (April–October), Salthill (May–September), Thoor Ballylee (April–mid-October).

Tourist Information

Information on the areas of County Galway covered in this chapter (Kinvara, Galway City, Aran Islands) can be found on the Web site ⊕ www. discoverireland.ie/west.

Information on the main sights in County Clare—Coole Park, Thoor Ballylee, the Burren and the Cliffs of Moher, and Ennis—can be found at ⊕ www. discoverireland.ie/shannon.

In addition to these main Web sites, we sometimes also list a town Web site (which is occasionally not official but an ad-supported—though often helpful—Web site).

8

Updated
by Alannah
Hopkin

With some of the most westerly seaboard in Europe, the old Irish province of Connaught remains a place apart. Today comprising much of counties Clare and Galway, this is the region where the Irish go to reconnect with their heritage, whether by practicing their jigs at the Fleadh Nua folk festival or trading news with a Gaeltacht (Irish-speaking) resident. Wherever you go in the West, you'll not only see, but more importantly *hear*, how the best of traditional Ireland survives.

Memories of West Clare, Galway City, and the Aran Islands make even a streetwise Dubliner get misty-eyed. With its dramatic coast of cliffs and sandy beaches, a vibrant compact city with history in every stone, and remote islands, these places draw you in, bidding you to leave 21st-century angst behind when you head westward across the Shannon River.

Even a Jackeen (Dubliner) will tell you that this area is distinctly different from the rest of Ireland and is bent on retaining its unspoiled, rugged way of life. With much of nature's magnificence on display—the majestic Cliffs of Moher, the rocky Burren, and the sublime Aran Islands—it's easy to see why. Visitors continue to relish the unique thrill of standing high above the pounding Atlantic, watching seabirds reel below, as the numerous Cliffs of Moher posts on YouTube demonstrate.

This area lies at the far western extremity of Europe, facing its nearest North American neighbors across thousands of miles of the Atlantic Ocean. Although other areas of Ireland were influenced by Norman, Scots, or English settlers, the West largely escaped systematic resettlement and, with the exception of the walled town of Galway, remained purely Irish in outlook. No wonder these western regions have the highest concentration of Irish-speaking communities and the best traditional musicians in the Republic.

West Clare, in fact, is the guardian of Ireland's musical traditions, where people still flock to learn new dance steps and fiddle riffs. The hub of the area remains Galway, the city that loves to celebrate. Saunter through its naturally festive, pedestrianized center and the city's many pubs prove Galway's reputation for good times. Not far away are villages like Ennis, Doolin, and Kinvara that are also noted as "trad"-music hotspots.

Visitors will find, particularly in western County Galway, the highest concentration of Gaeltacht (Irish-speaking) communities in Ireland, with roughly 40,000 native Irish speakers and the country's first Irish-language TV station based in tiny An Spidéal (Spiddle). Everywhere you'll see plenty of signs printed in Irish only. This is especially the case out on the isolated Oileáin Árainn (Aran Islands), which do constant battle with the fury of the Atlantic. Many Irish schoolchildren have their first experience of a place where Irish is the main language during summer camps on these isles, which have never been easier to visit than today (thanks to comfortable modern ferries).

These limestone islands are actually geological extensions of the mainland expanse known as the Burren, rich in megalithic remains and unique geological formations. This spectacular natural scenery has been behind the region's economic development. Just look at the highly successful €30 million visitor center at the Cliffs of Moher. Effortlessly absorbing hundreds of thousands of visitors a year, it was built to ensure its grass-roofed, semi-subterranean center did not intrude on the landscape. With improved paths, safer access points, and buildings constructed of local Liscannor stone, the center brings in countless visitors, most of whom *fly* through their digital-camera flash cards here.

8

COUNTY CLARE: THE BURREN AND BEYOND

County Clare claims two of Ireland's unique natural sights: the awesome Cliffs of Moher and the stark, mournful landscape of the Burren, which hugs the coast from Black Head in the north to Doolin and the Cliffs of Moher in the south. Yet western County Clare (West Clare for short) is widely beloved among native Irish for a natural phenomenon significantly less unique than these: its sandy beaches. Recently the surf that rolls in on these beaches, and on the rocky shores of the Aran Islands, has been attracting big-wave enthusiasts from all over the world. So whether you're looking for inimitable scenery, the perfect wave, or just a lovely beach to plunk down on to relax in the sun (if you're lucky!) for a few hours, you can delightfully find it in West Clare.

This journey begins at Newmarket-on-Fergus, within minutes of Shannon Airport, a good jumping-off point for a trip through the West if you've just arrived in Ireland and are planning to head for Galway. *This route also follows directly from the end of Chapter 7, which concludes 10 km (6 mi) down the road, at Bunratty Castle and Folk Park (and the Knappogue Castle and Craggaunowen Project, also nearby), so be sure to take a moment to glance at those sights to decide whether to include them as you get under way.* The Shannon region is also the connecting

CLOSE UP

Tour Guide Options

Galway City's TIO (Tourist Information Office) has details of walking tours of Galway, including the City River two-hour guided walk along the River Corrib led by Mike Lynch daily (contact him to confirm times), departing from Galway City Museum.

Barratt Tours offer a day trip by coach visiting the Cliffs of Moher, the Burren, and Galway Bay (€27). Book at Ennis Tourist Information Office, which is also the departure point. The tour runs on Saturdays only from March 21 to early May, and Saturday–Thursday from early May to mid-September.

Burren Wild runs a daily bus tour from Galway Bus Station that travels through Kinvara and along the coast of Galway Bay to a farm (with shop and café) in the village of Oughtmama in the Burren (€25). Here you stop for a one-hour guided walk of this unique landscape (included in tour price) before returning to the bus and continuing to the Cliffs of Moher. Burren Wild also has daily guided walks starting from their farm at 10:40 AM (see Web site for directions) lasting 1½ hours (€10). Longer afternoon walks with qualified guide John A. Connolly, starting at 12:15 and lasting 2½ hours (€25), can be booked by appointment. Bus Éireann has a daily tour to the Cliffs of Moher and the Burren (each €25). Tours run from early May to late September only. Depart from and book in advance at the Galway City TIO, Ceannt Railway Station on Eyre Square.

Heart of Burren Walks has guided walks leaving the Burren Display Center in Kilfenora between June and August on Tuesday, Thursday, Saturday, and Sunday at 2:30 and lasting over 2 hours (€20), visiting local antiquities and exploring the region's geology, including the Burren's biggest *turlough* (seasonal lake). Lally Tours runs a day tour to the Burren. It also operates a vintage double-decker bus, departing from Eyre Square, which runs hourly tours of Galway City from 10:30 AM until 4:30 PM from mid-March to October; tickets cost €12. O'Neachtain Day Tours operates full-day tours of the Burren. Tickets, €25 each, can be purchased from the Galway City TIO; tours depart across the street. Healy Tours offers historical sightseeing tours with professional guides, including the Cliffs of Moher and the Burren. Tickets, €25 each, can be purchased from the Galway Tourist Information Offices or on the tour bus.

Tours **Barratt Tours** (✉ *Silvermine View, Pallasbeg, Cappamore, Co. Limerick* ☎ *087/237–5986* ⊕ *www.4tours. biz*). **Burren Wild** (✉ *Oughtmama, Bellharbour, Co. Clare* ☎ *087/877– 9565* ⊕ *www.burrenwalks.com*). **Bus Éireann** (☎ *091/562–000* ⊕ *www. buseireann.ie*). **Ennis Tourist Information Office** (✉ *Arthur's Row, Ennis, Co. Clare* ☎ *065/682–8366* ⊕ *www. discoverireland.ie/shannon*). **Galway City Museum** (☎ *091/562–000*). **Galway City Tourist Information Office** (✉ *Forster Pl., Center* ☎ *091/537–700* ⊕ *www.irelandwest. ie*). **Healy Tours** (☎ *091/770–066* ⊕ *www.healytours.ie*). **Heart of Burren Walks** (✉ *Kilnaboy, Co. Clare* ☎ *065/682–7707* ⊕ *www. heartofburrenwalks.com*). **Lally Tours** (☎ *091/562–905* ⊕ *www.lallytours. com*). **Mike Lynch** (☎ *086/382–6425*). **O'Neachtain Day Tours** (☎ *091/553– 188* ⊕ *www.ontours.biz*). **Salthill TIO** (☎ *091/520–500*).

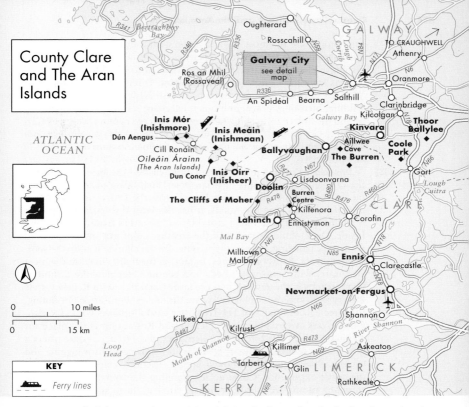

County Clare
and The Aran
Islands

ATLANTIC
OCEAN

KEY

Ferry lines

link between County Limerick (and other points in the Southwest) and Galway City. If you're approaching it from County Kerry to the south and you're not going into Limerick City, it makes sense to begin exploring the region from Killimer, reached via the ferry from Tarbert.

NEWMARKET-ON-FERGUS

13 km (8 mi) north of Shannon Airport on N18.

A small town in County Clare, Newmarket-on-Fergus is chiefly remarkable as the village nearest the famed hotel of Dromoland Castle, formerly the home of Lord Inchiquin, chief of the O'Brien clan.

WHERE TO EAT AND STAY

$$ **Carrygerry Country House.** Modest and gabled, this 1793 country house is only 8 km (5 mi) from Shannon Airport, but a world apart, with views across the plains where horses calmly graze, as they have done for centuries, to the distant Shannon estuary. It's a popular first- and last-night stopover with transatlantic passengers: you can see the airport's control tower, but are not on the flight path. Young owners Niall and Gillian Ennis have decorated the lounge and bar with a homey assortment of Victorian antiques and hunting prints, and books of local interest, with an open fire in the bar. The six bedrooms in the

main house are the most elegant, some with four-poster beds, all with modest antiques. Simpler, less expensive rooms in the converted stables also have plenty of character. Most guests opt to watch the sensational sunsets from the Conservatory Restaurant. Directions are on the hotel Web site. **Pros:** proximity to airport; real Irish character; abundant wildlife, birdsong, peace, and quiet; excellent restaurant. **Cons:** tricky to find the first time; nothing to do nearby except country walks. ⊠ *Carrygerry, Co. Limerick* 🕾 *061/360–500* ⊕ *www.carrygerryhouse.com* ➲ *11 rooms* � *In-room: no a/c, Internet. In-hotel: restaurant, bar, Wi-Fi hotspot* ⊟ *AE, MC, V.*

$$$$

Fodor'sChoice

★

🍴 **Dromoland Castle.** A massive neo-Gothic castle—the ancestral home of the O'Briens, descendants of Brian Bórú, High King of Ireland—Dromoland certainly looks the part. Dating from the 19th century and now one of Ireland's grandest hotels, it bristles with towers rising up over a picture-perfect lake like a storybook illustration from King Arthur. Inside, Dromoland provides all the creature comforts any king would want: oak paneling, ancestral portraits, crystal chandeliers, Irish-Georgian antiques. Bedrooms (suites, in fact) in the main wing are the most elaborate, with four-poster beds and genuine Hepplewhite armoires. Guest rooms in the newer wings are more hotel-like, with Regency-style furniture. Rooms with a lake view are the most sought-after. For dining, the Green Room Bar and Fig Tree offer casual options while the neo-Gothic, oak-wainscoted Earl of Thomond Restaurant is the place for a chandeliered French feast. For activities, the 440-acre estate offers a golf course, tennis, fishing, spa, and woodlands perfect for jogging and cycling. **Pros:** real old-fashioned luxury; friendly, helpful staff; genuine castle experience. **Cons:** golfers spoiling the romantic idyll; some standard rooms are a little ordinary; you'll want to stay much longer than you can afford. ⊠ *5 km (3 mi) west of Newmarket-on-Fergus, signposted from N18, Co. Clare* 🕾 *061/368–144* ⊕ *www.dromoland. ie* ➲ *99 rooms* � *In-room: no a/c, Internet. In-hotel: 2 restaurants, bar, golf course, tennis courts, pool, spa, bicycles, Wi-Fi hotspot* ⊟ *AE, DC, MC, V.*

SPORTS AND THE OUTDOORS

Dromoland Golf Course (🕾 *061/368–144*) is one of the most scenic in the country, set in a 700-acre estate of rich woodland on the grounds of Dromoland Castle. The 18-hole, par-71 course has a natural lake that leaves little room for error on a number of holes. Improvers take note: a state-of-the-art golf academy can help you to improve your swing.

ENNIS

9½ km (6 mi) north of Newmarket-on-Fergus on N18, 37 km (23 mi) northwest of Limerick, 142 km (88 mi) north of Tralee.

A major crossroads and a convenient stop between the West and the Southwest, Ennis is the main town of County Clare. The pleasant market town has an attractively renovated, pedestrian-friendly center, bisected by the fast-flowing River Fergus.

GETTING HERE

BUS TRAVEL   Ennis is a major bus hub, with hourly Bus Éireann Expressway connections to Cork, Limerick/Shannon Airport, and Galway, plus helpful buses to the popular Cliffs of Moher. Journey time from Cork is three hours (€13.50 one-way, €20.70 round-trip), and from Limerick it is 1 hour 15 minutes (€8.10 one-way, €12.60 round-trip), and about the same time and fare from Ennis to Galway City. From Ennis there are two Bus Éireann buses a day to the Cliffs of Moher Visitor Centre, at 10:25 AM and 6:25 PM (€14 round-trip; 50 minutes); the same bus also calls at Lisdoonvarna and Doolin.

TOURS   Local bus company Barratt Tours offers a guided tour of the Cliffs of Moher and the Burren leaving from the Tourist Information Office in Ennis (€27; Saturdays only from March 21 to early May, then Saturday–Thursday from early May to mid-September). Or opt for taxis whose rates for long trips can be affordable if shared by four people.

TRAIN TRAVEL   Ennis Railway Station can be accessed from Limerick City and Galway on the big new Irish Rail commuter route linking Limerick and Galway. The hourly service connecting Limerick with Ennis takes 40 minutes (€9.50 one-way, €17.80 round-trip). Galway is 1 hour 20 minutes by train from Ennis. From Limerick City, to reach Dublin or Cork, take a 20-minute train ride and change at Limerick Junction. Trains run almost hourly.

ESSENTIALS

Transportation Contacts Barratt Tours (✉ *Silvermine View, Pallasbeg, Cappamore, Co. Limerick* ☎ *087/237–5986* ⊕ *www.4tours.biz*).

Visitor Information Ennis Tourist Office (✉ *Arthur's Row, Town Center, Co. Clare* ☎ *065/682–8366* ⊕ *www.ennis.ie*).

Ennis is famed for fostered Irish traditional arts, especially fiddle-playing and step-dancing (a kind of square dance). The town is also one of the West's most popular "trad"-music hot spots, with a wide and tempting array of concerts and folk sessions. The **Fleadh Nua** (pronounced fla-*noo*-a) festival at the end of May attracts both performers and students of Irish music and serves as the venue for the National Dancing Championships. *For the full scoop on this Ennis event and other folk music festivals in the region, see our special photo feature, "Gael Force: The Boom in Irish Music and Dance" in this chapter.* Offering a striking contrast to the interest in Irish folk arts here is the fact that Ennis's town center has become pleasantly multicultural, as many emigrants arriving at Shannon Airport from faraway locations—including Brazil and West Africa—have settled here.

Two Members of Parliament for Ennis have been national leaders at times of great significance for Irish democracy, and each is commemorated by a memorial in Ennis. On a tall limestone column above a massive pediment in the town center stands a statue of Daniel O'Connell (1775–1847), "The Liberator" who was instrumental in bringing about Catholic Emancipation. Outside the courthouse (in the town park) stands a giant statue of Eamon De Valera (1882–1975), the dominant figure in Irish politics during the 20th century, serving as prime minister for most of the years from 1937 until 1959.

While the opulent interiors of Dromoland Castle will wow all guests, the hotel's parklands are even more enticing thanks to a vast array of sporting facilities.

WHERE TO STAY

$ **Lynch West County**. You will meet both leisure and business travelers CONTINENTAL   from all walks of life at this popular stopping point on the Limerick–Galway road (N18), a lively, modern hostelry affiliated with Best Western. It's a five-minute walk from Ennis's town center. Rooms are ample, with modern pale-wood furniture—most overlook the parking lot but are at least quiet. Service is helpful and friendly, despite the hotel's relatively large size. In July and August there's nightly Irish cabaret-style entertainment in the large bar, Boru's Porterhouse, which also serves bar food. **Pros:** well-located, functional hotel; good choice for first-time visitors; good sports facilities; child-friendly. **Cons:** lots of tour bus and conference business; lobby can get chaotically busy; rooms overlook the parking lot. ⊠ *Clare Rd., Co. Clare* ☎ *065/682–3000* ⊕ *www.lynchotels.com* ⤵ *152 rooms* ⌂ *In-room: no a/c, Wi-Fi (some). In-hotel: 3 restaurants, bar, pool, gym, Wi-Fi hotspot* ☱ *AE, MC, V* ¶⊚¶ *BP.*

$ **Temple Gate**. Before its conversion, this lodging was a Gothic-style convent, and remnants of its previous existence (including the chapel, which is now a banquet hall) give character to this bright, modern hotel in the town center. Coordinated drapes and bedspreads in warm, earthy colors decorate the compact, well-equipped rooms, which have unusual views of pretty corners of Ennis's historic center. Preachers Pub is popular with locals, while the guest lounge is a country-house-style library. The entrance is via a cobblestone courtyard adorned with Victorian street lamps. **Pros:** more character than most modern hotels; good town center location. **Cons:** can get very busy with local functions at weekends; standard rooms a bit small; worth upgrading to executive if you need space. ⊠ *The Square, Co. Clare* ☎ *065/682–3300* ⊕ *www.*

templegatehotel.com ⚓ *70 rooms* ⬠ *In-room: no a/c, Internet, Wi-Fi (some). In-hotel: restaurant, bar, Wi-Fi hotspot* ▭ *AE, MC, V* ⦿ *BP.*

NIGHTLIFE AND THE ARTS

Glór–Irish Music Centre (✉ *Friar's Walk* ☎ *065/684–3103* ⊕ *www.glor. ie*) is Ennis's venue for large concerts, hosting competitions of Irish music, song, and dance—including May's wildly popular **Fleadh Nua** (⊕ *fleadhnua.com*)—and big-name touring acts on the Irish music scene, including Mary Black, Paul Brady, and Aslan. There's also a crafts gallery and coffee shop, and free parking.

Although Ennis is not as fashionable as, say, Galway, it's one of the West's traditional-music hot spots. You're likely to hear sessions at the following pubs, but keep in mind that sessions don't necessarily take place every night and that the scene is constantly changing. Phone ahead to check whether a session is happening.

Cruise's (✉ *Abbey St.* ☎ *065/684–1800*). **Fawl's** (✉ *The Railway Bar, 69 O'Connell St.* ☎ *065/682–4463*). **Kerins'** (✉ *Lifford* ☎ *065/682–0582*). **Knox's** (✉ *Abbey St.* ☎ *065/682–9264*). **Poet's Corner Bar** (✉ *Old Ground Hotel, Main St.* ☎ *065/682–8155*). **Preachers Pub** (✉ *Temple Gate Hotel, the Square* ☎ *065/682–3300*).

SPORTS AND THE OUTDOORS

BICYCLING   You can follow the scenic Burren Cycleway (69 km [43 mi]) to the famous Cliffs of Moher on a bike rented from **Tierney Cycles & Fishing** (✉ *17 Abbey St.* ☎ *065/682–9433*).

SHOPPING

Stop in at the **Antique Loft** (✉ *Clarecastle* ☎ *065/684–1969*) for collectibles and pine and mahogany antiques. **Carraig Donn** (✉ *29 O'Connell Sq.* ☎ *065/682–8188*) sells its own line of knitwear. The long-established **Ennis Bookshop** (✉ *13 Abbey St.* ☎ *065/682–9000* ⊕ *www. ennisbookshop.ie*) carries a big range of local history and Irish-interest titles. **Giftvenue** (✉ *34–36 Abbey St.* ☎ *065/686–7891*) carries Belleek china, Waterford crystal, Newbridge silverware, and Donegal Parian china, as well as Lladró, Hummel, and other collectible china. **Seodin** (✉ *52 O'Connell St.* ☎ *065/682–3510*) has a good selection of gold and silver jewelry and Irish-made gifts.

LAHINCH

30 km (18 mi) west of Ennis on N85.

Noted for hotels packed with people touring the nearby Cliffs of Moher, Lahinch (also spelled Lehinch, at least on in-car sat-nav systems) is a busy resort village beside a long, sandy beach backed by dunes. It is best known for its links golf courses and—believe it or not—its surfing. In 1972 the European Surfing Finals were held here, putting Lahinch on the world surfing map, where it has stayed ever since. But the center ring here is occupied by golf—with three world-class courses and a dazzling bay-view backdrop, Lahinch is often called the "St. Andrews of Ireland." Between golfers, surfers, and vacationers in general, the permanent winter population of 650 swells to 7,000 in the summer. Other Moher-bound people prefer to stay in Doolin *(see below)*.

WHERE TO EAT AND STAY

$$
SEAFOOD
★

✕**Morrissey's Seafood Bar and Grill.** Sporting distinctive colorful window boxes, this pretty family-run village pub has been transformed into an enormously popular seafood and steak restaurant. Burgundy leather banquettes line the walls, bentwood chairs sit at plain wooden tables beneath brass ceiling fans, while the cream walls are

enlivened by a collection of paintings and photos of local scenes. There are no reservations, but you can take a drink at the bar while waiting your turn, or in summer, retreat to the wide deck overlooking the river. Happily, it's worth waiting for the fresh, simply prepared local food: Atlantic jumbo prawns with garlic and herb butter served with homemade breads, or smoked and barbecued salmon with capers, red onion, and crème fraîche. Angus sirloin steak is served with homemade onion rings, and kids love the Morrissey beef burger. There are also seven bedrooms overhead. ⊠ *Doonbeg, Co. Clare* ☎ *065/905–5304* ▭ *MC, V* ⊗ *Closed Jan. and Feb., Mon. mid-May–Sept., and Mon. and Tues. in Oct., Nov., and Mar.–mid-May.*

$$$$
Fodor'sChoice
★

⊡ **Moy House.** Built for Sir Augustine Fitzgerald, this enchanting, 18th-century Italianate-style lodge sits amid 15 private acres on an exhilarating, Wuthering Heights–like windswept cliff top that's a three-minute drive from Lahinch. It's a world away from the bustling seaside resort—a peaceful haven, where you are made to feel like you're a guest in a privately owned country house. The decor is most alluring, with period velvet sofas, marble fireplaces, and gilt-frame paintings. Upstairs, brocade curtains and Oriental rugs complement the guest rooms' Georgian and Victorian polished-mahogany antiques. Some rooms have open fires, some have freestanding cast-iron bathtubs, six have stunning sea views, and two overlook the pretty, sheltered garden. Once you settle in, enjoy a drink at the honesty bar in the elegant drawing room (help yourself, and write it down); in bad weather, curl up with a book in the peaceful library. The cozy dining room (guests only) serves an imaginative four-course dinner (€55) of contemporary cuisine. The real dessert is the vista from the veranda over Lahinch Bay. **Pros:** romantic cliff-top location. **Cons:** Lahinch itself feels a bit downmarket in comparison. ⊠ *Milltown Malbay Rd., Co. Clare* ☎ *065/708–2800* ⊕ *www. moyhouse.com* ↻ *9 rooms* ⌂ *In-room: no a/c. In-hotel: restaurant, Internet terminal* ▭ *AE, MC, V* ⊗ *Closed Jan.–mid-Feb.* ⫯⊙ *BP.*

$$$

⊡ **Vaughan Lodge.** Michael Vaughan is a fourth-generation Lahinch hotelier, and he and his wife, Maria, uphold the tradition splendidly in their Edwardian-style lodge. Set at the quiet end of Lahinch, only a short walk from the busy village, it combines the facilities of a top hotel with the charm of a country house. The bar is table service only, and has a clublike atmosphere with plump leather and suede sofas in calming shades of gray and buff, and a corner library. Half of the bedrooms have views of the Atlantic, just across the road, and the rest look out onto green gardens. Rooms are large, with 6 foot, 3 inch square beds, with white linen comforters, dark-red throws and cushions, and effective reading lamps. Michael's own photographs decorate the walls, and he and his staff are a fount of local information. In addition, the seafood restaurant is one of the best in town. **Pros:** quiet location; high standard of comfort; excellent restaurant on-site. **Cons:** location lacks the full scenic wham-bam; bedrooms may recall big-city hotels to those who travel for business. ⊠ *Road to Ennistymon, Co. Clark* ☎ *065/708–1111* ⊕ *www.vaughanlodge.ie* ⤵ *22 rooms* ⌂ *In-room: no a/c, Internet. In-hotel: restaurant, bar, Wi-Fi hotspot* ⊟ *AE, DC, MC, V* ⊗ *Closed Nov.–Mar.*

NIGHTLIFE AND THE ARTS

For traditional music try the **19th Bar** (⊠ *Main St.* ☎ *065/708–1440*). **O'Looney's** (⊠ *The Promenade* ☎ *065/708–1414*) is known as Lahinch's surfers' pub; there's music every night in summer and on Saturday night in winter.

THE CLIFFS OF MOHER

10 km (6 mi) northwest of Lahinch on R478, 9 km (11 mi) north of Liscannor.

One of Ireland's most breathtaking natural sights, the majestic Cliffs of Moher rise vertically out of the sea in a wall that stretches over a long, 8-km (5-mi) swath and in places reaches a height of 710 feet. On a clear day you can see the Aran Islands and the mountains of Connemara to the north, as well as the lighthouse on Loop Head and the mountains of Kerry to the south. Get up close and you can study the stratified deposits of five different rock layers visible in the cliff face. But most visitors prefer to take in the grand distant vistas, especially as they open up every turn of the trail along the famous Burren Way that runs from Doolin to the Cliffs.

GETTING HERE

BUS TRAVEL There is a bus service to the Cliffs of Moher Visitor Centre from both Ennis and Galway. The Ennis bus leaves at 10:25 AM, and returns at 6:25 PM (€14 round-trip), traveling via Corofin and Lahinch, and continuing to Lisdoonvarna and Doolin. The journey to the cliffs takes about 50 minutes. From Galway city there are five buses a day between 8:40 AM and 6 PM, traveling via Kinvara and Ballyvaughan, and continuing to Lisdoonvarna and Doolin, the journey to the cliffs taking 1 hour 50 minutes (€14 one-way, €18.90 round-trip).

> ### SEA FOR YOURSELF
>
> To get a new perspective, why not try one of the sightseeing boat cruises that sail up and down the coast along the Cliffs of Moher? A sea voyage under the command of **Captain P. J. Garrihy** (⊠ *Doolin Pier* ☎ *065/707–5949* ⊕ *www. cliffs-of-moher-cruises.com* ☒ *€10 for 1 hr*) will allow you to view the awesome Cliffs of Moher from beneath, and get a better view of more than 20 species of seabirds that nest on its ledges. April through October there are three sailings per day, at noon and 3 PM; advance booking is highly recommended.

TOURS   You'd never know if you just headed to the main car park for the Cliffs of Moher but one of the most popular ways of viewing these natural wonders is by heading to Doolin (alternative port: Liscannor) to pick up one of the famous Cliffs of Moher cruises. Two of the biggest outfitters heading out from Doolin Pier are Cliffs of Moher Cruises and the O'Brien Line. Cliffs of Moher Cruises has one-hour cruises departing every day, weather permitting, from April to October at noon and 3 PM; tickets go for €20. O'Brien Lines operates mid-March to mid-November, with sailings usually at noon, 3, and 4 PM; tickets go for €10.

ESSENTIALS

Transportation Contacts Cliffs of Moher Cruises (☎ 065/7075949 ⊕ www. cliffs-of-moher-cruises.com). **Ennis Bus Station** (✉ Station Rd. ☎ 065/682–4177). **O'Brien Cruises** (☎ 065/7075555 ⊕ www.obrienline.com).

Visitor Information Cliffs of Moher Tourist Office. (✉ Near Liscannor, on road heading north to Lisdoonvarna, Co. Clare ☎ 065/708–1171 ⊕ www. discoverireland.ie/shannon ☽ Apr.–Oct. only).

EXPLORING

Fodor's Choice   The preferred way to see the magnificent natural wonder that are the
★   Cliffs of Moher is to hike the 4-km (2½ mi) Burren Way from Doolin.
☾   Known also as the "Old Road," this rugged dirt trail (walk past the Doolin Hostel, cross the riverbed, and continue straight) keeps entirely to the coast, providing great views of the sea and the occasional village of run-down thatched cottages. But hikers have to be careful as the trail can get perilously close to the cliff edge at places. If you wish to enjoy the Cliffs far from the putter of tour buses, read more about the Burren Way under our entry for the Burren, below.

The Cliffs of Moher have a long and nearly hallowed history. They were sacred in the Celtic era and were a favorite hunting retreat of Brian Boru, the High King of Ireland. Numerous seabirds, including a large colony of puffins, make their homes in the shelves of rock on the cliffs. Built in 1835 by Cornelius O'Brien—of Bunratty Castle fame and a descendant of the Kings of Thomond—**O'Brien's Tower** is a defiant, broody sentinel on the Cliffs' highest point, built to encourage tourism (yes, there were tourists even back then). Cornelius also erected here a wall of Liscannor flagstones (noted for their imprints of prehistoric eels).

Found on the road from Liscannor to Lisdoonvarna, the grass-roof, subterranean **visitor center** (and adjacent car-park) is built into the cliff face and is a good refuge from passing rain squalls. Note that there is no specific address for the Cliffs, which go on for miles, but you cannot miss the only road that gives access to the Cliffs, which is found on the main road from Liscannor to the north, a road which is heavily signposted. The visitor center interior imitates the limestone caves of County Clare and contains a gift shop, public toilets, and a tearoom. The Atlantic Edge exhibition is an optional extra, with information panels and interactive consoles for children—the highlight is the Ledge, a vertiginous virtual reality tour of the Cliffs from a bird's-eye point of view. Outside the center extensive hiking paths (some with elevated viewing platforms) gives access to the real thing, including O'Brien's

Tower at the northern extremity. ⊠ *Cliffs of Moher Visitor Centre (signposted on the road north from Liscannor)* ☎ *065/708–1171* ⊕ *www. cliffsofmoher.ie* 🅿 *Parking €8 (includes access to visitor center, cliffedge paths, and viewing platforms), Atlantic Edge €4* ⊙ *Cliffs daily 24 hrs. Visitor center Nov.–Feb., daily 9–5:30; Mar., Apr., and Oct., daily 9–6; May–Sept., daily 8:30 AM–9 PM. O'Brien's Tower May–Sept., daily 9:30–5:30, weather permitting.*

DOOLIN

★ *6 km (4 mi) north of the Cliffs of Moher on R479.*

Once an enchanting, multihue-housed backwater, this tiny village—set at the point where the Cliffs of Moher flatten out and disappear into the sea as limestone plateaus—now seems to consist almost entirely of B&Bs, hostels, hotels, holiday homes, pubs, and restaurants. The reason for all this development (much of it newly built during Ireland's Celtic Tiger economic boom) is that Doolin is reputed to have three of the best pubs for traditional music in Ireland: McGann's, McDermott's, and O'Connor's. With the worldwide surge of interest in Irish music since the mid-1990s, the village has become more of a magnet for European musicians than it is for young, or even established, Irish artists. Amazingly, there is no tourist board office in Doolin but a sponsored Web site does offer plenty of listings for the town (⊕ *www.doolin-tourism. com*).

Popularity, of course, brings its own price: when every other person is toting a video cam at a packed evening session, the magic can disappear quickly. However, if the music is disappointing in one pub, there are two more to try.

Aran Doolin Ferries (☎ *065/707–4455* ⊕ *www.doolinferries.com*) makes the 30-minute trip from Doolin Pier to Inis Oírr (Inisheer), the smallest of the Aran Islands, from spring until early fall (weather permitting, €15 round-trip). There are at least three round-trip sailings a day, and up to eight in July and August, but inquire on the day you plan to embark, as schedules vary according to weather and demand. There is also a day trip to the Aran Islands which includes a cruise under the Cliffs of Moher (€20). Usually more than one ferry company operates out of Doolin; your return ticket will be valid only with the company that took you out, so when boarding the outbound ferry, be sure to check the return schedule.

WHERE TO EAT AND STAY

$$$
SEAFOOD
✕**Cullinan's Seafood Restaurant and Guesthouse.** The small 25-seat restaurant, set in the back of an attractively renovated traditional farmhouse, is famed for its fresh, simply prepared seafood, but vegetarian and meat dishes are also served. Owner-chef James Cullinan uses fresh local ingredients—Inagh goat cheese, Burren smoked salmon, Doolin crabmeat, and Aran scallops—to form the basis of a light, imaginative menu. Try oven-roasted fillet of Clare lamb, with spiced couscous and garlic aioli. Desserts are all homemade; or try a plate of farmhouse cheeses. A €30 early-bird set menu is served from 6 to 6:45.

8

The floor-to-ceiling windows on two sides of the restaurant overlook the Aille River. The eight (€90 double occupancy) cottage-style rooms have simple pine furniture, fresh cotton comforters, pleasant country views, Wi-Fi, and room TVs on request. ⊠ *Coast Rd.* ☎ *065/707–4183* ⊕ *www.cullinansdoolin.com* ▭ *MC, V* ☺ *Guesthouse closed mid-Dec.– mid-Feb.; no dinner Wed.; restaurant closed Sun. and Oct.–Easter.*

$$ 🖥 **Aran View House.** This extensively modernized 1736 house on 100 acres of farmland offers magnificent views in nearly every direction: the Aran Islands to the west, the Cliffs of Moher to the south, and the gray limestone rocks of the Burren to the north. The interior is decorated with antique touches; some rooms have four-poster beds and all have Georgian reproduction furniture. You can savor the view from the bar or the residents' lounge. Don't miss the sunset over the Aran Islands, which can be spectacular. It's on the coast road in the Fanore direction, about a 10-minute walk north from Doolin village. **Pros:** well-located; amazing views; bar and restaurant on-site. **Cons:** a rather sprawling development, painted in an odd shade of pink; the exterior is less attractive than the interior. ⊠ *Coast Rd., Co. Clare* ☎ *065/707–4061* ⊕ *www. aranview.com* ⤳ *19 rooms* ᴥ *In-room: no a/c. In-hotel: restaurant, bar, Internet terminal* ▭ *MC, V* ☺ *Closed Nov.–Easter* ⦿ *BP.*

$$ 🖥 **Ballinalacken Castle.** One hundred acres of wildflower meadows surround this restored, low-slung Victorian lodge, which was built alongside the 16th-century ruins of an O'Brien castle (hence its somewhat bogus name). It's one of the most memorably sited of Ireland's coastal inns, with panoramic views of the Atlantic, the Aran Islands, and distant Connemara. The sense of spaciousness is exhilarating, and manager Declan O'Callaghan reports that many guests regularly oversleep due to the quietness. The public rooms display a mix of comfy old armchairs and antique, baronial-style Irish oak, amid floral wallpaper and rampant pots of aspidistra. Guest rooms in the older house have massive four-poster beds, marble fireplaces, and high ceilings. Some large, sunny rooms have bay windows to frame that stunning view; nice but plainer rooms in the new wing, with antique-style decor, are equally sought after. The restaurant has an imaginative and sophisticated Continental menu ($$$$) where you can sometimes snag its roast loin of Burren lamb only with a reservation. **Pros:** fabulous location; warm old-fashioned welcome from the O'Callaghan family. **Cons:** not in walking distance of other hostelries; not in fact a "castle." ⊠ *Coast Rd., about 1 km (½ mi) outside Doolin on the Lisdoonvarna Rd., Co. Clare* ☎ *065/707–4025* ⊕ *www.ballinalackencastle.com* ⤳ *10 rooms, 2 suites* ᴥ *In-room: no a/c. In-hotel: restaurant, bar, Internet terminal* ▭ *MC, V* ☺ *Closed Nov.–mid-Apr.* ⦿ *BP.*

NIGHTLIFE AND THE ARTS

Famous for their traditional-music sessions, Doolin's three traditional pubs are designed to hold big crowds, which means you should expect minimal comfort: hard benches or bar stools if you're lucky, and spit-and-sawdust flooring. The theory is that the music will be so good, you won't notice anything else. However, interesting music-related memorabilia hang on the walls, and O'Connor's and McGann's serve simple bar food from midday until 9 (Irish stew is a good bet). As you

might imagine, the word is out about Doolin's "trad" scene—some nights the pubs overflow with crowds (and the video cams can get really annoying).

Gus O'Connor's (⊠ *Fisher St.* ☎ *065/707–4168*) sits midway between the village center and the pier and has tables outside near a stream. **McDermott's** (⊠ *Lisdoonvarna Rd.* ☎ *065/707–4700*) is popular with locals. Autumn through spring it's sometimes closed during the daytime. **McGann's** (⊠ *Lisdoonvarna Rd.* ☎ *065/707–4133*), across the road from McDermott's, is the smallest of Doolin's three famous pubs and has been run by the same family for 70 years.

THE BURREN

Extending throughout western County Clare from Cliffs of Moher in south to Black Head in north, and as far southeast as Corofin.

★ As you travel north toward Ballyvaughan, the landscape becomes rockier and stranger. Instead of the seemingly ubiquitous Irish green, gray becomes the prevailing color. You're now in the heart of the Burren, a 300-square-km (116-square-mi) expanse that is one of Ireland's strangest landscapes. The Burren is aptly named: it's an Anglicization of the Irish word *bhoireann* (a rocky place). Stretching off in all directions, as far as the eye can see, are vast, irregular slabs of fissured limestone, known as karst, with deep cracks between them. From a distance, it looks like a lunar landscape, so dry that nothing could possibly grow on it. But in spring (especially from mid-May to mid-June), the Burren becomes a wild rock garden, as an astonishing variety of wildflowers blooms in the cracks between the rocks, among them at least 23 native species of orchid. The Burren also supports an incredible diversity of wildlife, including frogs, newts, lizards, badgers, stoats, sparrow hawks, kestrels, and dozens of other birds and animals. The wildflowers and other plants are given life from the spectacular caves, streams, and potholes that lie beneath the rough, scarred pavements. With the advent of spring, *turloughs* (seasonal lakes that disappear in dry weather) appear on the plateau's surface. Botanists are particularly intrigued by the cohabitation of Arctic and Mediterranean plants, many so tiny (and so rare, so please do not pick any) you can't see them from your car window; make a point of exploring some of this rocky terrain on foot. Numerous signposted walks run through both coastal and inland areas.

The **Burren Way** is a way-marked hiking trail from Lahinch to Ballyvaughan on the shores of Galway Bay, a distance of 35 km (22 mi). The most spectacular part of the trail runs along the top of the Cliffs of Moher from Doolin to the coast near Lisdoonvarna, a distance of about 5 km (3 mi). The trail continues through the heart of the Burren's gray, rocky limestone landscape, with ever-changing views offshore of the Aran Islands and Galway Bay. You'll need to buy a map locally.

The tiny **Burren Display Centre** has a modest audiovisual display and other exhibits that explain the Burren's geology, flora, and archaeology. Also here are a café and a crafts shop with good maps and locally published guides. ⊠ *8 km (5 mi) southeast of Lisdoonvarna on R476, Kilfenora*

☎ *065/708–8030* ⊕ *www.theburrencentre.ie* ✉ *€6* ☉ *Mid-Mar.–May, Sept., and Oct., daily 10–5; June–Aug., daily 9:30–6.*

For the personal touch, join a **guided walk** offered by a number of outfitters who are experts about the Burren's extraordinary landscape. May and June are peak months for flora, but a tour is worthwhile at any time of year. **Heart of Burren Walks** (☎ *065/682–7707* ⊕ *www. heartofburrenwalks.com* ✉ *€20*) has guided walks leaving the Burren Display Centre in Kilfenora between June and August on Tuesday, Thursday, Saturday, and Sunday at 2:30 and lasting over two hours, visiting local antiquities and exploring the region's geology, including the Burren's biggest turlough. Guide Tony Kirby can also lead walks by appointment year-round. A well-known guide is John A. Connolly of **Burren Wild** (✉ *Oughtmama, Bellharbour* ☎ *087/877–9565* ⊕ *www. burrenwalks.com* ✉ *€10*), who is a graduate in archaeology and offers 1½-hour hikes starting at 10:40 daily on the family farm. Shane Connolly of **Burren Hill Walks** (☎ *065/707–7168* ⊕ *homepage.eircom. net/~burrenhillwalks* ✉ *€15*) is a guide who has been conducting tours for many years.

Beside the Burren Centre in Kilfenora, the ruins of a small 12th-century church, once the **Cathedral of St. Fachtna,** have been partially restored as a parish church. There are some interesting carvings in the roofless choir, including an unusual, life-size human skeleton. In a field about 165 feet west of the ruins is an elaborately sculpted high cross that is worth examining, though parts of it are badly weathered.

NIGHTLIFE AND THE ARTS
Vaughan's Pub (✉ *Main St., Kilfenora* ☎ *065/708–8004*) is known for its traditional-music sessions.

SPORTS AND THE OUTDOORS
You can book a self-guided cycle tour of the Burren through **Irish Cycle Hire** (✉ *Enterprise Centre, Ardee* ☎ *041/685–3772* ⊕ *www. irishcyclehire.com*), which rents bikes and provides luggage transfers.

BALLYVAUGHAN

16 km (10 mi) north of Lisdoonvarna on N67.

A pretty little waterside village and a good base for exploring the Burren, Ballyvaughan attracts walkers and artists who enjoy the views of Galway Bay and access to the Burren.

Aillwee Cave is the only such chamber in the region accessible to those who aren't spelunkers. This vast 2-million-year-old cave is illuminated for about 3,300 feet and contains an underground river and waterfall. Aboveground, there are a big crafts shop, cheese-making demonstrations, and the **Burren Birds of Prey Centre,** which puts on flying displays from eagles, falcons, hawks, and owls daily at noon and 3 PM (weather permitting). ✉ *5 km (3 mi) south of Ballyvaughan on R480* ☎ *065/707–7036* ⊕ *www.aillweecave.ie* ✉ *Cave €10, joint ticket for cave and birds €17, birds alone €8* ☉ *Sept.–June, daily 10–5:30, July and Aug., daily 10–6:30.*

WHERE TO STAY

$ ⊞ **Drumcreehy House.** The pretty gabled facade with dormer windows is traditional in style, but, in fact, Bernadette Moloney and her German husband, Armin Grefkes, designed and built this house specifically as a B&B. It's just across the road from the sea, about 2 km (1 mi) north of the village, just beyond the Whitethorn Craft Shop. The interior has character and style, thanks to a mix of imposing 19th-century German antiques, stripped-pine floors, and comfortable sofas and armchairs. Each guest room is individually styled on a wildflower theme, with plain walls, color-coordinated quilts and curtains, brass bedsteads, and attractive small antiques. The delicious breakfast menu offers an unusually wide choice. Your hosts are knowledgeable about the area, and have a good supply of books and maps. **Pros:** big bedrooms for a B&B; nice waterfront location; peaceful nights. **Cons:** a long (1 mi-plus) walk down a narrow busy road to village; no morning newspaper. ⊠ *Co. Clare* ☎ *065/707–7377* ⊕ *www.drumcreehyhouse.com* ⇨ *12 rooms* ⚛ *In-room: no a/c. In-hotel: Wi-Fi hotspot* ═ *MC, V* ⊗ *Closed Nov.–Feb. (but call to confirm)* ⊙| *BP.*

$$$$
★ ⊞ **Gregan's Castle Hotel.** One of Ireland's best-loved country-house hotels, this quiet, low-key retreat is a romantic, creeper-covered Georgian house, set amid pretty gardens with a splendid view of the rocky Burren hills and Galway Bay beyond. A row of purple Wellington boots in ascending sizes in the entrance porch is there to spare guests' footwear in the perennially damp garden: a detail typical of Simon Haden and his interior-designer wife, Freddie. The whiff of open turf fires pervades the air, while a charming and stylish mix of fine antiques, luxurious furnishings (including hand-tufted Connemara wool carpets and a Waterford crystal chandelier), and a collection of modern Irish art create an atmosphere of effortless, sophisticated elegance. Guest rooms are bright, airy, and uncluttered; choose between a magical view of stony hills and sparkling sea, or a ground-floor room with private patio garden. The Corkscrew Bar (after the approach road, the aptly named Corkscrew Hill, N67) is a peaceful haven for a predinner drink, and the restaurant is renowned. Little wonder this is the hideout of choice for many discerning celebrities. **Pros:** perfectly judged decor; birdsong morning and evening; excellent restaurant. **Cons:** 5 km (3 mi) from nearest village; almost a TV-free zone, and no satellite channels; no elevator. ⊠ *Base of Corkscrew Hill, Co. Clare* ☎ *065/707–7005* ⊕ *www.gregans.ie* ⇨ *15 rooms, 6 suites* ⚛ *In-room: no a/c, no TV. In-hotel: restaurant, bar, bicycles, Wi-Fi hotspot* ═ *AE, MC, V* ⊗ *Closed Dec.–mid-Feb.* ⊙| *BP.*

$ ⊞ **Hyland's Burren Hotel.** A turf fire greets you in the lobby of the village-center hotel, a cheerful, welcoming spot with a reputation for friendliness and good entertainment. This unpretentious coaching inn, in the heart of the Burren, dates from the early 18th century, and has been much expanded. Guest rooms vary in size and shape, but all have modern pine furniture and color-coordinated drapes and spreads. Ask for a room overlooking the Burren, and check out the amazingly clear night sky. There's a spacious residents' lounge on the first floor, with an outdoor deck, for further stargazing. The bar hosts live music most nights from June to mid-September, and Irish storytelling once a week. Ask about special midweek rates. **Pros:** central location; bar and restaurant on-site; pleasant staff. **Cons:** won't win any style contests; bar and restaurant very busy July and August. ⊠ *Main St., Co. Clare* ☎ *065/707–7037* ⊕ *www.hylandsburren.com* ⇌ *30 rooms* ♿ *In-room: no a/c. In-hotel: restaurant, bar, Wi-Fi hotspot* ⊟ *AE, MC, V* ⊙ *Closed Jan. 5–Feb. 5.* ℐ⊙ℐ *BP.*

NIGHTLIFE AND THE ARTS

Fodor's Choice
★
The friendly **Monk's Pub** (⊠ *Main St.* ☎ *065/707–7059*), near the waterfront, hosts sessions of traditional and folk music on Sunday from 4 to 6 PM. The bar food is excellent.

COOLE PARK

24 km (15 mi) northeast of Corofin on N18.

Coole Park, north of the little town of Gort, was once the home of Lady Augusta Gregory (1859–1932), patron of W. B. Yeats and cofounder with the poet of Dublin's Abbey Theatre. Yeats visited here often, as did almost all the other writers who contributed to the Irish literary revival in the first half of the 20th century, including George Bernard Shaw (1856–1950) and Sean O'Casey (1880–1964). Douglas Hyde (1860–1949), the first president of Ireland, was also a visitor. The house became derelict after Lady Gregory's death and was demolished in 1941; the grounds are now a national forest and wildlife park. Picnic tables make this a lovely alfresco lunch spot. The only reminder of its literary past is the Autograph Tree, a copper beech on which many of Lady Gregory's famous guests carved their initials. There's also a visitor center with displays on Lady Gregory and Yeats. ⊠ *Galway Rd.* ☎ *091/631–804* 🎫 *Park free, visitor center €3* ⊙ *Park daily 8:30–7:30; visitor center Apr.–mid-June and Sept. Tues.–Sun. 10–5; mid-June–Aug., daily 9:30–6:30.*

8

THOOR BALLYLEE

5 km (3 mi) north of Coole Park, signposted from N66.

Thoor Ballylee is a sight Yeats fans won't want to miss. (It's one of the few major Yeats-related sights in the West that's not in County Sligo.) In his 50s and newly married, Yeats bought this 14th-century Norman "thoor," or tower, as a ruin in 1916 for the equivalent of about €45 in today's currency. The tower stands beside a whitewashed, thatch-roof cottage with a tranquil stream running alongside it. Its proximity to Lady Gregory's house at Coole Park made this a desirable location, though it required significant work on Yeats's part to make the ruin livable. He stayed here intermittently until 1929 and penned some of his more mystical works here, including *The Tower* and *The Winding Stair.* It's now fully restored and some rooms showcase the poet's original furnishings. The audiovisual display is a useful introduction to Yeats and his times. High up on the tower's parapet you can get some great views of Coole's Seven Woods. ⊠ *N66, 3 km (2 mi) north of Gort* ☎ *091/631–436* ⊕ *www.irelandwest.ie* ✉ *€6* ⊙ *June–Sept., Mon.–Sat. 9:30–5.*

KINVARA

★ *13½ km (8 mi) east of Ballyvaughan, 15 km (9 mi) northwest of Gort on N67, 25 km (15½ mi) south of Galway City.*

The picture-perfect village of Kinvara is a growing holiday base, thanks to its gorgeous bay-side locale, great walking and sea angling, and numerous pubs. It's well worth a visit, whether you're coming from Ballyvaughan or Gort. Kinvara is best known for its longstanding early August sailing event, **Cruinniú na mBád** (Festival of the Gathering of the Boats), in which traditional brown-sail Galway hookers laden with turf race across the bay. Hookers were used until the early part of this century to carry turf, provisions, and cattle across Galway Bay and out to the Aran Islands. A sculpture in Galway's Eyre Square honors their local significance.

GETTING HERE

BUS TRAVEL From Galway City, Bus Éireann runs five buses a day to Kinvara between 8:40 AM and 6 PM. Tickets cost €6.90 one-way, €9.50 round-trip, and the journey takes about 30 minutes. The same bus continues to the Cliffs of Moher, Lisdoonvarna, and Doolin.

EXPLORING

★ On a rock north of Kinvara Bay, the 16th-century **Dunguaire Castle** spectacularly commands all the approaches to Galway Bay. It's said to stand on the site of a 7th-century castle built by the King of Connaught. Built in 1520 by the O'Hynes clan, the tiny storybook castle takes its name from the fabled king of Connaught, Guaire. In 1929 it was purchased by Oliver St. John Gogarty, the noted surgeon, man of letters, and model for Buck Mulligan, a character in James Joyce's *Ulysses*. To his outpost came many of the leading figures of the 19th-century Celtic revival in Irish literature. Today Dunguaire is used for a Middle Ages–style banquet that honors local writers and others with ties to the West, including Lady Gregory, W. B. Yeats, Sean O'Casey, and Pádraic O'Conaire (book on-line for banquet tickets to get substantial discounts). ✉ *West Village* ☎ *091/637–108* ⊕ *www.shannonheritage.com* ✉ *Castle €7, banquet €59.95* ⊙ *Castle mid-Apr.–mid-Sept., daily 10–5; last entry 4:30. Banquet Apr.–Oct. at 5:30 and 8:30.*

WHERE TO EAT AND STAY

$ ✕ **Moran's Oyster Cottage.** Signposted off the main road on the south side of Clarinbridge, this waterside thatch cottage, the home of the Moran family since 1760, houses at its rear a simply furnished restaurant that serves only seafood: Gigas oysters, chowder, smoked salmon, seafood cocktail, lobster with boiled potatoes and garlic butter, and fresh crab salad. It's *the* place to sample the local oysters, grown on a nearby bed owned by the Moran family, who have had the pub for six generations. Hope for good weather, so that you can eat outside overlooking the weir and watch the swans float by. The front bar has been preserved in the "old style," which means it's small and cramped, but very interesting if you want to get an idea of what most pubs around here were like 50 years ago. ⊠ *The Weir, Kilcolgan* ☎ *091/796–113* ⊕ *www.moran-soysterscottage.com* ⊟ *AE, MC, V.*

¢ ▦ **Burren View Farm.** A million-dollar view awaits you at this modest, yellow, two-story B&B on the edge of Galway Bay, 5 km (3 mi) west of Kinvara. Set on a working sheep and cattle farm, it's relatively isolated amid stone-walled fields dotted with sheep. The breakfast room, sun lounge, and front bedrooms look out across a wide sea inlet to the gray expanse of the Burren. Rooms are plain and homey but clean and well maintained. Spare some time for a chat with your hostess, Bridget O'Connor, a mature farmer's wife, imbued with folk wisdom. You can get an evening meal at the local pub, a five-minute walk away, or drive into Kinvara. Alternatively, Bridget will cook you an evening meal. **Pros:** great scenic location; a slice of genuine Irish life. **Cons:** very simple accommodation in a small, architecturally undistinguished farmhouse; rainy days could be a problem: bring a good book. ⊠ *Doorus, Co. Galway* ☎ *091/637–142* ⊕ *homepage.eircom.net/~burrenviewfarm/* ⋧4 rooms ⌂ In-room: no a/c, no phone, no TV ⊙ Closed Nov.–Apr. ⎮◯⎮ BP.

$ ▦ **Merriman Inn.** Don't let its traditional looks deceive you: this white-washed, thatch inn on the shores of Galway Bay is, in fact, a mid-size hotel, decorated with locally made, well-designed furniture, and original crafts, paintings, and sculpture. Guest rooms are medium-size with smallish, cottage-style windows at head height, and modern pine furniture; small paintings of local scenes provide the principal color. If you're lucky you could get a room with a breathtaking view of Galway Bay; less than half have one, so if it matters, ask when booking. The Quilty Room is a large, airy restaurant hung with interesting land-scapes by a painter named Quilty. Its menu is French-influenced—try the outstanding tournedos of salmon. **Pros:** center of village; secure car parking; decent restaurant; choice of other restaurants and bars nearby. **Cons:** bar gets very busy at weekends; bigger windows would be nice, to get more of the view. ⊠ *Main St., Co. Galway* ☎ *091/638–222* ⊕ *www.merrimanhotel.com* ⋧32 rooms ⌂ In-room: no a/c. In-hotel: restaurant, bar, Wi-Fi hotspot ⊟ AE, DC, MC, V ⊙ Closed Jan. and Feb. ⎮◯⎮ BP.

NIGHTLIFE AND THE ARTS

The first weekend in May, Kinvara hosts the annual **Cuckoo Fleadh** (⊠ *Main St.* ☎ *091/637–145*), a traditional-music festival. Traditional music is played most nights at the **Winkles Hotel bar** (⊠ *The Square* ☎ *91/637–137*), where Sharon Shannon got her start in the music business.

GALWAY CITY

Galway is often said to be a state of mind as much as it is a specific place. The largest city in the West today and the ancient capital of the province of Connaught, Galway, with a current population of 72,700, is also one of the fastest-growing cities in Europe. It's an astonishing fact, and you have to wonder where this city can possibly grow. For despite

Galway's size, its commercially busy ring road, and its ever-spreading suburbs, its heart is *tiny*—a warren of streets so compact that if you spend more than a few hours here, you'll soon be strolling along with the sort of easy familiarity you'd feel in any small town.

For many Irish people, Galway is a favorite weekend getaway: known as the city of festivals, it's the liveliest place in the republic. It's also a university town: University College Galway (or UCG as it's locally known) is a center for Gaelic culture (Galway marks the eastern gateway to the West's large Gaeltacht). A fair share of UCG's 9,000 students pursue their studies in the Irish language. Galway is, in fact, permeated by youth culture. On festival weekends, you'll see as many pierced and tattooed teenagers and twentysomethings here as you'd find at a rock concert. (If you're looking for the quiet, quaint side of Ireland depicted on travel posters, have a quick look at Galway and push on to Clifden or Westport, where you can still savor the atmosphere of a small old-world town.) But Galway's students aren't its only avant-garde, as Galway has long attracted writers, artists, and musicians. The latter whip up brand-new jigs while also keeping the traditional-music pubs lively year-round. And the city's two small but internationally acclaimed theater companies draw a steady stream of theater people.

Although you're not conscious of it when you're in the center of town, Galway is spectacularly situated, on the north shore of Galway Bay, where the River Corrib flows from Lough Corrib to the sea. The seaside suburb of Salthill, on the south-facing shore of Galway Bay, has spectacular vistas across the vividly blue bay to Black Head and the Burren on the opposite shore.

Galway's growth and popularity mean that at its busiest moments, its narrow, one-way streets are jam-packed with pedestrians, while cars are gridlocked. If there's a city in Ireland that never sleeps, this must be it. In fact, if you want to be guaranteed a quiet night's sleep, ask either for a room in the back of your center-city hotel or simply stay outside of town.

GETTING HERE

AIR TRAVEL   Aer Arann (see Getting Around section) has seven flights a day from London's Luton Airport and five a day from Dublin to Galway Airport (GWY). Aer Arann also flies to Edinburgh, Manchester, Lorient, and Waterford from Galway. Taxis to the city center cost around €15 but most passengers use the courtesy coach; Bus Éireann has three buses a day to the airport at 6:10 AM, 1 PM, and 11 PM and two buses back to the city at 2:10 PM and 11:40 PM (€3 one-way, €5 round-trip).

BUS TRAVEL   Bus Éireann Expressway bus services to Galway from Dublin are available from both Bus Éireann and Citylink. Citylink has up to 17 buses a day linking Dublin Airport, Dublin, and Galway City, for €15 one-way (Citylink), €13.50 one way (Bus Eireann), with better rates online. Both take about 3 hours 40 minutes from Dublin City Center. Bus services to Galway from Cork call at Limerick and Shannon Airport. Journey time from Cork is 4½ hours (€16.20 one-way). There are also daily buses from Galway to Westport (1½ hours), Ballina (2½ hours), Sligo

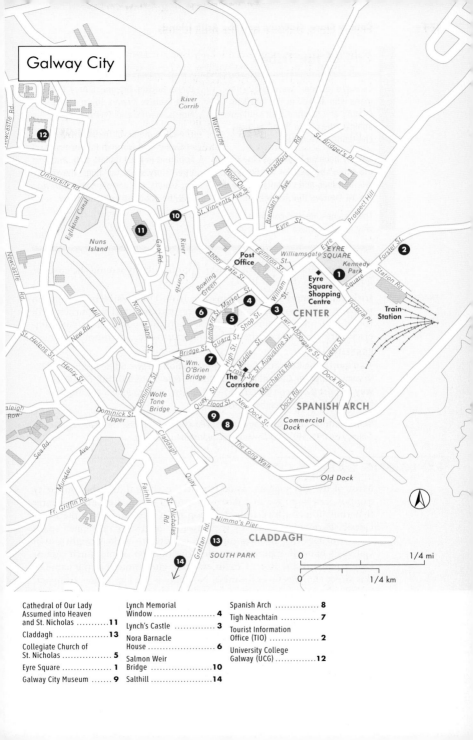

Galway City

CLOSE UP

City of the Tribes

Galway's founders were Anglo-Normans who arrived in the mid-13th century and fortified their settlement against "the native Irish," as local chieftains were called.

Galway became known as "the City of the Tribes" because of the dominant role in public and commercial life of the 14 families that founded it.

Their names are still common in Galway and elsewhere in Ireland: Athy, Blake, Bodkin, Browne, D'Arcy, Dean, Font, French, Kirwan, Joyce, Lynch, Morris, Martin, and Skerret.

The city's medieval heritage, a fusion of Gaelic and Norman influences, is apparent in the intimate two- and three-story stone buildings, the winding streets, the narrow passageways, and the cobblestones underfoot.

(2½ hours) and Belfast (6½ hours). For quick hops around the city, use a taxi, such as those of Big O.

TRAIN TRAVEL Irish Rail–Iarnod Éireann trains run from Dublin's Heuston Station to Galway City via Athlone about every two hours. The journey (€48 round-trip) takes 2 hours 10 minutes. There are hourly trains from Limerick City via Ennis on the new commuter route, a two-hour journey.

ESSENTIALS

Transportation Contacts Ceannt (Rail) Station (⊠ Eyre Sq. ☎ 091/564–222 ⊕ www.irishrail.ie). **Ceannt (Bus) Station** (⊠ Eyre Sq. ☎ 091/562–000).**Galway Airport** (⊠ Inverin ☎ 091/755–569 ⊕ www.galwayairport.com).**Big O** (☎ 091/585–858 ⊕ www.bigotaxis.com).

Visitor Information Galway City Tourist Office (⊠ Forster St., Eyre Sq., Co. Galway ☎ 091/537–700 ⊕ www.discoverireland.ie/west).

EXPLORING GALWAY CITY

Most of the city's sights, aside from the cathedral and the university campus, can be found in a narrow sector of the medieval town center that runs in a southwesterly direction from Eyre Square to the River Corrib. Eyre Square is easily recognizable, as it's the only open space in central Galway. It takes only five minutes to walk straight down Galway's main shopping street, the continuation of the north side of Eyre Square, to the River Corrib, where it ends (note that the name of this street changes several times). Not only is the city center compact, but it's also largely pedestrian-friendly, so the best way to explore it is on foot. Even the farthest point, the university campus, is less than a 15-minute walk from Eyre Square. A walk (or drive, for that matter) to Galway's seaside suburb, Salthill, 3 km (2 mi) west of Galway, with its long seaside promenade, is a favorite local occupation, traditionally undertaken on a Sunday afternoon.

While Galway's historic center is compact and can be explored on foot, many visitors enjoy a quick orientation hop aboard Lally Tours' vintage double-decker bus for an hour-long **Old Galway City Tour.** Five buses a day leave from the tourist office in Forster Place on the corner of Eyre Square. ✉ *Lally Tours* ☎ *091/562–905* ⊕ *www.lallytours.com* ✉ *€10* ⊙ *Daily 10:30* AM–*4:15* PM.

TRAVEL TIP

If you have postcards to mail, you may want to stop at the General Post Office at the start of your walking exploration of Galway. It's on the left side of Eglinton Street, the first right off Williamsgate Street as you head toward the river from Eyre Square.

TOP ATTRACTIONS

① **Eyre Square.** The largest open space in central Galway and the heart of the city, on the east side of the River Corrib, Eyre Square incorporates a sculpture garden and children's play area on its east side, while its west side is bound by a heavily traveled road. A controversial renovation saw the removal of several well-loved landmarks, including most of the trees in the square (they were diseased). They were replaced by 95 new trees that will take time to mature. In the center is **Kennedy Park,** a patch of lawn named in honor of John F. Kennedy, who spoke here when he visited the city in June 1963. At the north end of the park, a 20-foot-high steel sculpture standing in the pool of a fountain represents the brown sails seen on Galway hookers, the area's traditional sailing boats. Now the entrance to Kennedy Park, the **Browne Doorway** was taken in 1905 from the Browne family's town house on Upper Abbeygate Street; it has the 17th-century coats of arms of both the Browne and Lynch families (two of Galway's 14 founding families), called a "marriage stone" because when the families were joined in marriage their coats of arms were, too. Keep an eye out for similar if less elaborate Browne doorways as you walk around the old part of town.

⑥ **Nora Barnacle House.** On June 16, 1904, James Joyce (1882–1941) had his first date with Nora Barnacle, who would later become his wife. He subsequently chose to set *Ulysses* on this day, now known universally as Bloomsday—"a recognition of the determining effect upon his life of his attachment to her," as Joyce's biographer Richard Ellman has said. Nora, the daughter of a poor baker, was born here. Today it has a modest collection of photographs, letters, and memorabilia, and a small gift shop. ✉ *4 Bowling Green, Center* ☎ *091/564–743* ✉ *€2.50* ⊙ *Mid-May–Aug., Mon.–Sat. 10–5; Sept.–mid-May, by appointment.*

⑭ **Salthill.** A lively, hugely popular seaside resort, Salthill is beloved for its seaside promenade—the traditional place "to sit and watch the moon rise over Claddagh, and see the sun go down on Galway Bay," as Bing Crosby used to croon in the most famous song about the city. The main attraction of the village, set 3 km (2 mi) west of Galway, is the long sandy beach along the edge of Galway Bay and the promenade above it. The building of big new hotels along the seafront has nevertheless left plenty of room for the traditional amusement arcades (full of slot machines), seasonal cafés, and a fairground.

⑧ **Spanish Arch.** Built in 1584 to protect the quays where Spanish ships unloaded cargoes of wines and brandies, the arch now stands in the parking lot opposite Jurys Inn Galway. It's easily (and often) mistaken

8

A Shopping Tour of Galway

There's no question about it: they have a different look in Galway. People have always dressed differently, because they dress for the Galway weather, which can be wet and windy at any time of year. But ever since Galway was transformed by Ireland's "Celtic Tiger" economic boom, they have also dressed—and decorated—with a real sense of style. Want proof? Just join the locals on the following walk.

Pick up a free map of Galway from the **Tourist Information Office** on Forster Place. Turn left out the front door to reach the **Hotel Meyrick** (formerly the Great Southern), a monumental 19th-century grande dame in cut stone (its lobby is just the place for "scene-iors" to take their coffee or tea). Turn left beyond the hotel and right into Merchants Road to find the lively **Bold Art Gallery.**

Then turn left into **Flood Street,** the heart of medieval Galway, a tiny area where all the cutest shops are jam-packed together, including **Cobwebs,** abrim with offbeat antique jewelry, old binoculars, and bronze model airplanes. For a feel of the essential Galway, cross the road to the banks of the **River Corrib** and walk to your left to the **Spanish Arch.** When natives feel homesick, this is the view they think of: white water breaking on the dark surface of the swift-flowing Corrib, the fishing boats of the Claddagh, and as many as a hundred swans floating by, while a heron perches on top of parked cars.

Staying on this side of the Corrib, cross over the bridge and take the riverside footpath past the contempo Jurys Inn and some old warehouses. Turn left over O'Brien's Bridge for the historic **Bridge Mills,** now outfitted with a designer swap shop, a fun florist-cum-café, and **Sam Beardon, Sculptor and Jeweller.** Continue along Bridge Street, turning right into Cross Street and right into Kirwan's Lane. Here, **Design Concourse Ireland/Judy Greene Pottery** has locally made turned-wood objects, basketware, and perfumery.

Medieval Kirwan's Lane leads you on to Quay Street and **Twice as Nice,** a vintage and antique clothing boutique with old Irish linen. Continue up High Street to **Faller's Sweaters and Tweeds,** just the place to buy an Aran sweater, and **The Kilkenny Shop,** Galway's largest emporium of Irish-designed products, with a dazzling selection of chic John Rocha crystal, Newbridge Silver, and Nicholas Mosse pottery.

Farther up on the right, **Maille** has some great mohair wraps and *the* essential Galway fashion item, a Jack Murphy raincoat. Choose between a short version or a caped version (for those really wet days)—top one off with a rainproof Stetson with a feather in it and you'll pass for a local.

High Street leads into William Street, where you'll find **The Treasure Chest,** a three-story shop selling upmarket Irish goods. Its exterior, painted in Wedgwood blue with white swags, just like the famous china, is a favorite with photographers. **Brown Thomas,** on William at the corner of Eglinton, has long been Galway's most upscale department store. The post office is on Eglinton Street. A few steps up Williamsgate Street brings us back to Eyre Square and your starting point at the TIO.

Pedestrian alleys and high-style boutiques help make Galway into a stroller's paradise—keep your eye out for the many 19th-century footscrapers.

for a pile of weathered stones, yet it's another reminder of Galway's—and Ireland's—past links with Spain. ⊠ *The Long Walk, Spanish Arch*.

❼ Tigh Neachtain *(Naughton's Pub)*. Galway City's most famous pub, **Fodor's Choice** which stands at a busy little crossroads in the heart of the old town, ★ is treasured for its unrenovated interior. Grab a spot at one of its old-fashioned partitioned snugs at lunchtime for an inexpensive selection of imaginative bar food. It's a good place to mingle with local actors, writers, artists, musicians, and students, although it can become sardine-can crowded. ⊠ *17 Cross St., Spanish Arch* ☎ *091/568–820*.

❷ Tourist Information Office *(TIO)*. Just off Eyre Square, east of the bus and train station and the Great Southern Hotel, this is the place to make reservations for events around town and find out about the latest happenings. You can also book tickets to the Aran Islands here. ⊠ *Forster Pl., Center* ☎ *091/537–700* ⊕ *www.discoverireland.ie/west* ⊙ *Weekdays 9–6, Sat. 9–1*.

WORTH NOTING

⓫ Cathedral of Our Lady Assumed into Heaven and St. Nicholas. On Nun's Island, which forms the west bank of the River Corrib beside the Salmon Weir Bridge, stands Galway's largest Catholic church, dedicated by Cardinal Cushing of Boston in 1965. The cathedral was built on the site of the old Galway jail; a white cross embedded in the pavement of the adjacent parking lot marks the site of the cemetery that stood beside the prison. ⊠ *Nun's Island* ☎ *No phone* ⊠ *Free*.

⓭ Claddagh. On the west bank of the Corrib estuary, this district was once an Irish-speaking fishing village outside the walls of the old town. The

The Galway Saturday Market

CLOSE UP

Locals get up very early on Saturday in Galway in order to get the pick of the goods on offer at the Saturday food market. About 90 colorful stall-holders, many of whom follow an alternative lifestyle, set out their wares in the area behind the Collegiate Church of St. Nicholas in the city center. Take your pick of the Mediterranean goods on offer at the Real Olive Company, or sample some Aran Smoked Salmon, or treat yourself to an outdoor lunch at the Madras Curry Stall, or sushi from the Japanese-run Da Kappa-ya Sushi, followed by dessert from Yummy Crêpes. Organic-vegetable sellers, plant sellers, herbalists, cheese mongers, and bakers are joined by hat sellers, wood carvers, and knitwear stalls. A selection of Galway's famously wacky buskers entertain with music, juggling, and dance. Who could resist? Have a preview at ⊕ www.galwaymarket.net.

name is an Anglicization of the Irish *cladach*, which means "marshy ground." It retained a strong, separate identity until the 1930s, when its traditional thatch cottages were replaced by a conventional housing plan and its unique character and traditions were largely lost. One thing has survived: the Claddagh ring, composed of two hands clasped around a heart with a crown above it (symbolizing love, friendship, and loyalty), is still used by many Irish people as a wedding ring. Reproductions in gold or silver are favorite Galway souvenirs.

⑤ Collegiate Church of St. Nicholas. Built by the Anglo-Normans in 1320 and enlarged in 1486 and again in the 16th century, the church contains many fine carvings and gargoyles dating from the late Middle Ages, and it's one of the best-preserved medieval churches in Ireland. Legend has it that Columbus prayed here on his last stop before setting off on his voyage to the New World. On Saturday mornings, a street market, held in the pedestrian way beside the church, attracts two dozen or so vendors and hundreds of shoppers. ⊠ *Lombard St., Center* ☎ *No phone* 🎫 *Free* ☉ *Daily 8–dusk.*

⑨ Galway City Museum. The city's civic museum, housed in a modern building behind the Spanish Arch, contains materials relating to local history: old photographs, antiquities (the oldest is a stone ax head carbon-dated to 3500 BC), and other historical gewgaws. ⊠ *Fishmarket, Spanish Arch* ☎ *091/567–641* ⊕ *www.galwaycitymuseum.ie* 🎫 *Free* ☉ *June–Sept., daily 10–5; Oct.–May, Tues.–Sat. 10–5.*

④ Lynch Memorial Window. Embedded in a stone wall above a built-up Gothic doorway off Market Street, the window marks the spot where, according to legend, James Lynch FitzStephen, mayor of Galway in the early 16th century, condemned his son to death after the young man confessed to murdering a Spanish sailor who had romanced his girlfriend. When no one could be found to carry out the execution, Judge Lynch hanged his son himself, ensuring that justice prevailed, before retiring into seclusion. ⊠ *Market St., Center.*

❸ Lynch's Castle. Now a branch of the Allied Irish Banks, this is the finest remaining example in Galway of a 16th-century fortified house—fortified because neighboring Irish tribes persistently raided the village, whose commercial life excluded them. The decorative details on its stone lintels are of a type usually found only in southern Spain. Like the Spanish Arch, it serves as a reminder of the close trading links that once existed between Galway and Spain. ⊠ *Shop St., Center.*

❿ Salmon Weir Bridge. The bridge itself is nothing special, but in season—
★ from mid-April to early July—shoals of salmon are visible from its deck as they lie in the clear river water before making their way upstream to the spawning grounds of Lough Corrib. ⊠ *West end of St. Vincent's Ave., Center.*

⓬ University College Galway *(UCG).* Opened in 1846 to promote the development of local industry and agriculture, the UCG today is a center for Irish-language and Celtic studies. The Tudor Gothic–style quadrangle, completed in 1848, is worth a visit, though much of the rest of the campus is architecturally undistinguished. The library here has an important archive of Celtic-language materials, and in July and August the university hosts courses in Irish studies for overseas students. The campus is across the River Corrib, in the northwestern corner of the city. ⊠ *Newcastle Rd., University.*

WHERE TO EAT

$ ✕**K.C. Blake's.** K.C. stands for Casey, as in owner-chef John Casey, a
CONTINENTAL larger-than-life character, who turned a medieval stone town house once associated with the Blake family—one of the families that founded Galway—into an ultramodern eatery. The hard-edge, minimalist interior, with sleek black walls, provides a strong contrast with the old stone building. Dishes range from traditional beef-and-Guinness stew, or sole meunière, to funky starter combinations like black pudding croquettes with pear and cranberry sauce. ⊠ *10 Quay St., Spanish Arch* ☎ *091/561–826* ▭ *AE, MC, V.*

$$ ✕**Kirwan's Lane.** Look for Mike O'Grady's stylish modern restaurant in
CONTINENTAL a revamped alley at the river end of Quay Street. Tables clad in white damask (covered with paper tablecloths at lunchtime), narrow floor-to-ceiling windows, and a quarry-tile floor set the stage for an informal, bistro-style menu. Fresh prawn cocktail is served with sauce Marie-Rose and a passion-fruit mayonnaise; A great starter of crisp julienne of ox-tongue and pancetta is partnered with a fennel and orange cream. Main courses have similarly unpredictable twists—oven-roasted ham hock comes with colcannon, broad beans, garlic cream, and apricots, and monkfish tails are served with a simple lemon and coriander dressing. ⊠ *Kirwan's La., Spanish Arch* ☎ *091/568–266* ▭ *AE, MC, V* ☾ *No lunch Sun.*

$$$ ✕**Malt House.** Hidden away in a flower-filled courtyard off High Street
CONTINENTAL in the center of old Galway is the lunch and dinner venue of choice for Galway's movers and shakers. A cool, contemporary space with leather tub chairs, small but with well-spaced wooden-top tables and a wooden floor, the specialty here is seasonal local seafood, with daily specials

on the blackboard. Oysters come from Clarinbridge, fresh crab from Miltown Malbay, and smoked salmon from the Burren Smokehouse, Lisdoonvarna. Cooking is cool and contemporary, too: start with sushi rolls, or Galway Bay Oysters with bacon and cabbage and béarnaise sauce; Clare Island salmon is served with udon noodles, lemongrass, and chili broth, while roast saddle of rabbit is stuffed with spinach, apricots, and pine nuts. Vegetarians can sample fresh pasta with local asparagus, arugula, and Parmesan. Desserts include chocolate and chili tart, rhubarb trifle, or an Irish farmhouse cheese board. ⊠ *Old Malte Arcade, High St., Center* ☎ *091/567–866* ▭ *AE, DC, MC, V* ⊗ *Closed Sun.*

$$$ ╳ **McDonagh's Seafood House.** This longtime Galway landmark is partly
SEAFOOD a self-service fish-and-chips bar and partly a "real" fish restaurant. If
★ you haven't yet tried fish-and-chips, this is the place to start: cod, whiting, mackerel, haddock, or hake is deep-fried in a light batter while you watch. The gently priced fish is served with a heap of fabulous freshly cooked chips (which recently won a nationwide competition for the best french fries in Ireland), and eaten at communal tables—a great way to meet the locals. Or go for the more sophisticated (and expensive) Seafood Restaurant menu: Galway oysters au naturel, perhaps, or scallops sautéed in creamed garlic butter, followed by flame-grilled turbot. The McDonaghs are one of Galway's biggest entrepreneurial families, in charge of several hotels in addition to this spot. ⊠ *22 Quay St., Spanish Arch* ☎ *091/565–001* ▭ *DC, MC, V* ⊗ *Restaurant closed Sun.*

$$ ╳ **Nimmo's.** Good food and the friendly, enthusiastic staff make this
CONTINENTAL bustling bistro one of Galway's most popular restaurants. The central location in an old stone building overlooking the Corrib River adds to the pleasure. Downstairs is a one of Galway's busiest wine bar and luncheon spots, Ard Bia, which serves casual meals ($), while upstairs is a more sophisticated restaurant. The long, spacious, second-floor room has brightly colored paintings on the off-white walls, wooden floors, and well-spaced tables, with an eclectic mix of quirky white-painted stick or spoon-back chairs. The menu is short but well balanced, and while presentation is flamboyant, the food also tastes good. Try the west coast scallops with citrus salsa to start, then belly of pork with potato and celeriac, or grilled fillet of sea bass with spring-onion mashed potatoes, dill aioli, and organic leaves. Lobster and black sole are available in season. ⊠ *The Long Walk, Spanish Arch* ☎ *091/561–114* ▭ *MC, V* ⊗ *Closed Mon.*

$$$ ╳ **Sheridan's.** Nab a window seat for waterside views at this upstairs
IRISH restaurant down on the docks. Just a two-minute walk from the busy
★ Quay Street area, this is a new showcase for adventurous, edgy food that sometime comes with wild accents (edible seaweed, anyone?). The owners are known as top cheesemongers, and great cheeses are found on both bar and restaurant menus. Exposed stone walls, solid wood tables and chairs, and white tableware on black mats provide a neutral backdrop for locally sourced dishes such as wild rabbit *rillettes* (coarse pâté) with piccalilli, the cured duck breast with watercress, or the skate wing with celeriac, cockles, and pickled dillisk (seaweed). An excellent value menu (€25 for 3 courses) is on offer from 6 to 7. ⊠ *Lower Dock Rd., Spanish Arch* ☎ *091/546905* ▭ *MC, V* ⊗ *Closed Sun. and Mon.*

WHERE TO STAY

$ ⊞ **Adare Guest House.** A five-minute walk from the city center, across the River Coribb, this family-run guesthouse, managed by the son of the original owners, makes a handy base for exploring Galway. There's ample space to park your car, and there's none of the nighttime noise of the city center. Rooms are relatively spacious for the price, extremely well equipped, and plainly decorated in browns and creams. The multi-choice breakfast is served in a sunny room with country-pine furniture and floors overlooking a flower-filled patio. **Pros:** convenient, quiet location; free parking; walking distance of pub-restaurant area. **Cons:** exterior of building very plain; bedrooms vary in size; hugely popular: book early. ⊠ *9 Father Griffin Pl., Spanish Arch, Co. Galway* ☎ *091/582–638* ⊕ *www.adareguesthouse.ie* ⤵ *11 rooms* ♿ *In-room: no a/c. In-hotel: parking (free)* ⊟ *AE, MC, V* ⍧| *BP.*

$$$$ ⊞ **the g.** "G" is for glamour—or good grief (depending on your taste)—at this flamboyant player at the top end of Galway's hotel scene. The g opened in 2006 beside a busy roundabout, about 15 minutes' walk from Eyre Square in the Wellpark neighborhood—an oddly unhip location for a style icon. The architects worked with superstar hat designer Philip Treacy (a native of Galway) to create an interior that is every bit as extreme as Treacy's hats. The reception area is in black glass and marble, lighted by a tank of sedately bobbing, Connemara-bred sea horses. Yes, sea horses. Black-and-white op-art whorls feature on the aptly named Vertigo carpet in the vivid Pink Room, where afternoon tea (€59 with a glass of pink champagne) is popular with the ladies. Dimly lighted corridors with pink carpet lead to rooms where the decor is thankfully more restrained. Massive, extremely comfortable beds are dressed in white linen, and graceful custom-made furniture has an Art Deco air. Windows look onto pebbled areas with greenery that distract from the mundane views. Seashell-theme bathrooms are luxurious havens of marble and fine porcelain. Perched on scallop-shaped purple velvet banquettes or gumdrop-bright chairs in the ordinary but expensive Matz at the g, you can order from a contemporary Irish menu. The ESPA spa takes pampering to serious extremes. **Pros:** a must for design lovers; it may be OTT, but it's fun and an icon of Celtic Tiger Ireland. **Cons:** will eat deep into your budget; weird location 1 km (½ mi) from town center. ⊠ *Wellpark, Co. Galway* ☎ *091/865–200* ⊕ *www.theghotel.ie* ⤵ *98 rooms* ♿ *In-room: a/c, refrigerator, Wi-Fi. In-hotel: restaurant, bars, gym, spa, Internet terminal* ⊟ *AE, DC, MC, V* ⍧| *BP.*

$$$$ ⊞ **Glenlo Abbey.** With distant views of Lough Corrib and a golf course on its 138-acre estate, Glenlo Abbey is a rural hideaway just 5 km (2½ mi) from Galway. Built as a private home in 1740, it takes its name from the vast church built next door for the owner's ailing wife, who died before it was consecrated. Today, the church is used as a conference center and banquet room. The Abbey's lobby resembles a gentlemen's club, with parquet floors, chesterfields, and leather-bound books. Upstairs, official and correct Georgian-style furniture, brass lamps, and king-size beds fill the spacious bedrooms. Warming everything up, happily, is the genuinely friendly service. The delightfully unstuffy atmosphere is especially apparent in the Pullman Restaurant, Glenlo's most

8

popular feature. This is set in two *Orient Express* carriages installed on the grounds (and used in the famous Agatha Christie film of that name), offering a fun dining experience, complete with background click-clacks and train whistles. For more formal surroundings, repair to the classical River Room restaurant. Chandeliers hang from high stucco ceilings and tall windows framed by peach-color curtains overlook the river. The food, beautifully served, includes delights like marinated venison on a bed of braised red cabbage. **Pros:** exceptionally pleasant and friendly staff; pleasant views of distant lake. **Cons:** 2½ mi out of town; often hosts large weddings. ⊠ *Bushy Park, Co. Galway* ☎ *091/526–666* ⊕ *www.glenlo.com* 🛏 *38 rooms, 6 suites* ♿ *In-room: a/c, refrigerator, Wi-Fi. In-hotel: 2 restaurants, bar, golf course, Internet terminal, Wi-Fi hotspot* ⊟ *AE, DC, MC, V.*

$ 🏨 **Jurys Inn Galway.** Expect good-quality budget accommodations at this four-story hotel set beside the historic Spanish Arch and the river. Each room is big enough for three adults, or two adults and two children, and the rates are the same regardless of how many guests stay in each unit. The light, airy rooms have modern pine fittings, plain carpets and walls, double-glaze windows, and fully equipped bathrooms. Those overlooking the river are quieter than those in front. The atmosphere runs toward anonymous international, but the inn is central—at the foot of Galway's busy Quay Street, right on the bank of the Corrib—and the level of comfort is high for the price (note that rates shoot up at peak times, such as during the Galway Races). **Pros:** reliable Irish budget hotel chain; great location for pubs, clubs, and river views. **Cons:** rates subject to demand, so book early; favorite hotel chain for large groups of partying Irish. ⊠ *Quay St., Spanish Arch, Co. Galway* ☎ *091/566–444* ⊕ *www.jurysinn.com* 🛏 *130 rooms* ♿ *In-room: no a/c, Wi-Fi. In-hotel: restaurant, bar, Internet terminal, parking (paid)* ⊟ *AE, DC, MC, V.*

$$ 🏨 **Park House Hotel.** Even though this is a large, luxury hotel in central Galway, it feels like a home-away-from-home, thanks to attentive owner-managers. From the porter who organizes the valet parking of your car to the friendly reception and bar staff, everyone seems to want to help. Converted from a 200-year-old warehouse, the Park House only reveals its origins in its exterior; inside, a modern wing has been cleverly incorporated. Furnished with sofas and coffee tables, the lobby area is a quiet rendezvous for morning coffee. The lively bar has a big local clientele, and serves food until 9:30 PM; there is also a large formal restaurant. Guest rooms are triple-glazed—in some cases twice (against the noise of late-night revelers). The very quietest ones overlook an interior roof garden. The fanciest have high ceilings and antiques, combined with striking modern prints in warm colors. All are spacious, with good quality art deco–style furniture, and have generous-size bathrooms. **Pros:** friendly, professional staff; a haven of quiet. **Cons:** tricky to find vehicle entrance first time. ⊠ *Forster St., Center, Co. Galway* ☎ *091/564–924* ⊕ *www.parkhousehotel.ie* 🛏 *84 rooms* ♿ *In-room: a/c, safe, refrigerator, Wi-Fi. In-hotel: restaurant, bar, parking (free)* ⊟ *MC, V* ⊠⊡ *BP.*

$$$$ 🖫 **Radisson Blu SAS.** The striking contemporary design of the Radisson
Fodor's Choice   has revived a run-down area a stone's throw from Eyre Square and
★   overlooking a landlocked inflow of Galway Bay, Lough Atalia. Against
several newcomers, the hotel has successfully defended its reputation as
Galway's hippest hotel. Potted 20-foot bamboo sways at the entrance,
while four palm trees grow in the spacious reception area. Two glass-
wall elevators divide the lobby from the bar and waft you upstairs while
delivering breathtaking views of Galway Bay. Rooms are spacious, with
fully tiled bathrooms, restful, unfussy color schemes, Scandinavian-
design contemporary furniture, and comfortable sitting areas. Double-
glazing and altitude (starting on the third story) insulate the rooms
from noise even on the loudest Galway night. The Atrium lounge and
bar, its triple-height windows framing views of the water, is a popular
lunch spot and buzzes with life from early to late. A pianist entertains
on weekends, and in summer the large terrace with its views of the sea
and the distant hills is a lively spot. Also overlooking the Lough, the
spacious blue-and-white Marinas restaurant offers a wide selection of
seafood. **Pros:** stylish venue right at the heart of the social scene; sea
views in the city center. **Cons:** very busy during Galway's many festivals;
arriving by car can be a slow business in peak periods. ⊠ *Lough Atalia
Rd., Center, Co. Galway* ☎ *091/538–300* ⊕ *www.radissonhotelgalway.
com* ⇆ *261 rooms* ♻ *In-room: a/c, refrigerator, Internet, Wi-Fi (some).
In-hotel: restaurant, bars, pool, spa, Wi-Fi hotspot, parking (paid)*
⊟ *AE, DC, MC, V* ⊙ *BP.*

NIGHTLIFE AND THE ARTS

8

Because of its small size and concentration of pubs and restaurants,
Galway can seem even livelier at 11 PM than it does at 11 AM. On weekends, when there are lots of students and other revelers in town, Eyre
Square and environs can be rowdy after pub-closing time—which is 2
AM on Friday and Saturday. On the plus side, if you've been staying
out in the country and you're ready for a little nightlife, you're certain
to find plenty of it here.

CLUBS AND PUBS

The best spot for traditional music is the area between Eyre Square and
the Spanish Arch. There's a big post-nightclub (open until 1 or 2) scene
here: although there are some clubs in town, most everyone heads to
Salthill, the small suburban community 3 km (2 mi) west of Galway.
The main road, Upper Salthill, is lined with clubs.

CLUBS   **The Cellar** (⊠ *Eglinton St., Center* ☎ *091/563–966*) has live entertainment seven nights, including DJs, and acoustic two-pieces, electro,
techno, and house. Best of all, there's no cover charge. **Cuba** (⊠ *Eyre Sq.,
Center* ☎ *091/565–991*), in the heart of Galway City, with three floors,
draws diners and salsa lovers for Cuban cocktails and cigars to the beat
of Latin music from DJs and live bands. Busy with students from the
university, **GPO** (⊠ *Eglinton St., Center* ☎ *091/563–073*) is perhaps the
most popular dance club in the city center. For many people the quintessential Galway bar is **The Quays** (⊠ *Quay St., Center* ☎ *091/568–347*), a
tall, narrow pub on three stories with live music upstairs. For late-night

Continued on page 492

Gael Force

THE BOOM IN IRISH MUSIC & DANCE

Traditional Irish music and dance have taken the world by storm—but you need to journey to the West of Ireland to really get in step.

Folkloric music and dance may have faded in countries around the globe, but don't tell that to the thousands of young Irish who are learning to play hornpipes and concertinas, sing the old shanties, and dance the old jigs. Once languishing, these "old-fashioned" arts have taken on a modern chic here at home and the reason why can be summed up in one word: Riverdance.

When this eye-popping spectacular first "tapped" its way into the Irish psyche in 1995 by jazzing up traditional step dancing and moving it from the local parish hall to the stages of Dublin's Point Theatre, it immediately sent its audiences reeling—in more ways than one. The first troupe to introduce the Irish jig to world theaters, it has since performed before 18 million people and, having taken in more than $1 billion at the box office, has danced all the way to the bank.

A GAELIC REBIRTH

Hand in hand with the fiddle-fueled rise of traditional Irish music—the wistful drone of an Irish tin whistle helped make 1997's *Titanic* the best-selling film soundtrack of all time—Riverdance has resulted in the spectacular rebirth of old Gaelic culture over the past decade. And today, the world has fallen in step—literally. Riverdance's most fervent audiences are now found in far-off lands like Japan and Estonia; there's practically an Irish Step Dancing *Feis* (Irish for festival) every week somewhere in the U.S., and the sensational success of Celtic Woman—their Eire-savvy fusion of new-age pop, Celtic music, and classical crossover has catapulted their CDs to the top of the

charts—are all signs that the tree of Irish music has deep roots around the globe.

GOING "TRAD"

What acccounts for Irish music's enormous crossover success? Does it appeal because it offers a return to a simpler time? Or allows us to enjoy a dazzling slice of national culture in an age that has grown blandly homogeneous? Or is it because songs such as "Oh, Danny Boy, the Pipes, the Pipes Are Calling" offer deep and universal resonances of love and loss, distance and memory? Whatever the answer, you'll find that Ireland's "trad" musicians and dancers are seeking to bring Gaelic culture into the realm of world music.

HARPING ON

Ireland is the only country to have a musical instrument as its national emblem. The harp appears on *garda* (police) caps, Irish Euro coins, and government stationery. The original Irish harp was a small, triangular instrument designed to be held on the knee (not the large version of today's concert halls). The harp was first used as a logo for Guiness stout in 1850. The Guinness harp faces right, while the national emblem faces left.

COME AND MEET THOSE DANCING FEET

Ireland was swept off its feet, and its collective feet onto the boards, by the spectacular success of Riverdance. Thanks to that phenomenon, the thunderous dancing, stomping, clacking feet of today's Irish youth have once again taken up the trigger-quick step dances of old and the traditional music of the past.

Before Riverdance, Irish dancing was something schoolchildren performed chiefly for competitions, and sometimes on civic occasions, with their arms rigidly held by their sides (only the legs would move—a holdover from religious teachings that felt that dancing was sinful), and an expression of grave concentration on their faces. Today, it's a big thing for young people and also, due to those glitzy costumes and contests, a very expensive hobby.

Riverdance was a conscious attempt to project a more modern image of Ireland, and central to its roaring success were two American step dancers, Michael Flatley and Jean Butler. Their dazzling innovations reflected their origin in the more flexible American step dance competition world. Before Riverdance, the only options for prize-winning Irish step-dancers were to teach or to retire—now hundreds of dancers are employed worldwide in touring shows inspired by Riverdance, such as Flatley's Celtic Tiger and Butler's Dancing on Dangerous Ground.

SET DANCING

Set dancing is also the name given to social dancing in which four couples face one another in a square in dances based on the French cotillion and the quadrilles. Nearly every town in Ireland once again has dancing at least one evening a week.

STEPS & SETS

Ireland has a long tradition of solo dancing, first introduced by the jigs, reels, and hornpipes that traveling dancing masters taught in the 18th century. Some are performed in hard shoes, with the dancer beating out rhythms on the floor to complement the music, while others are danced with soft shoes to emphasize their graceful, airborne nature. In both cases, the main interest of the dance is in the foot and lower leg. Some solo dances have specific patterns of steps and are only danced to one tune and are known as "set dances"—in some places, set dances are known as table dances because the dancer often jumped up on the table to display his or her skills.

FANCY FOOTWORK

Because there were no accompanying drums, the sound of the feet on wooden floors has always been an important element in Irish dancing. When dancing really took off in the 18th century, many cabins only had earth floors, so the custom was to remove the top half of the half-door, and dance on that. Dancing masters used to display their prowess on fair days by dancing on soapy barrel lids, so they developed the ability to vary their steps in a confined space. From this came the tradition of dancing solos on one spot.

The main interest of the dance is in the foot and lower leg

JUST FOLLOW THE SOUND OF THE MUSIC . . .

If you're interested in "Trad" music, the beat of a bodhrán or the tap of a shoe will likely lead you to Galway and County Clare's great folk *fleadhs* (festivals) and pub *seisiuns* (sessions).

THE BIGGEST FLEADH

The biggest festival of all is a three-day event called the All-Ireland finals at Fleadh Cheoil na hÉireann (pronounced flah-kwoil—"festival of music"). The 2010 event was held in Cavan, County Cavan, August 16–22, and was attended by nearly 10,000 musicians and 200,000 visitors, many of them second-generation Irish from overseas. This noncommercial festival of traditional music takes over a whole town, whose pubs become centers for casual music making. The All-Ireland rotates to different towns every year, much to the delight of the pub owners in the chosen town (⊕ www.fleadh2010.ie).

THE ENNIS BLOW-OUT

During the last week in May, the pleasant county town of Ennis hosts the **Fleadh Nua** (⊕ http://fleadhnua.com/), a massive eight-day-long celebration of dancing and song, with concerts, workshops, competitions, and *céilis*. Many of the events are open-air and free, and there is a great festive buzz. Ennis is home to a growing cadre of musicians:

the Custys, Siobhán and Tommy Peoples, flute player Kevin Crawford, and accordion whiz kid Murty Ryan. Check out **Knox's Pub** (✉ Abbey St. ☎ 065/682–9264) and **Cruise's Bar** (✉ Abbey St. ☎ 065/684–1800) for lively evening sessions.

TOE-TAPPING IN MILTOWN

Held during the first week in July, the **Willie Clancy Summer School** (⊕ http://www.setdancingnews.net/wcss) is Ireland's biggest traditional music summer school. Classes, lectures, and recitals attract around 1,500 students from 42 countries to this tiny village on the west coast of Clare near Spanish Point. Set dancing is a big draw here, and a surefire way to make friends.

CEOL AGUS RINCE

Ceol (pronounced coil) is the Irish for music. And what always goes with the Irish for music? *Rince* (pronounced rincha), the Irish for dance: Music and Dance: you often see *Ceol agus Rince* on a poster advertising a traditional session or a céili.

A Trad seisiun, Sligo, Co. Sligo, Ireland

Taafe's, Galway

DARLIN' DOOLIN

Doolin, County Clare, is little more than a dot on the map on the west coast of Clare. To traditional musicians its three main pubs— **O'Connor's** (✉ Fisher St. ☎ 065/707–4168 🌐 www.oconnorspubdoolin.com), **McDermott's** (✉ Lisdoonvarna Rd. ☎ 065/707–4700 🌐 www.mcdermottspubdoolin.com), and **McGann's** (✉ Lidoonvarna Rd. ☎ 065/707–4133 🌐 www.esatclear.ie/mcgannsdoolin) are an irresistible magnet, as is the village's legendary charm.

CUCKOOS AND WINKLES

Kinvara, County Galway, is a pretty waterside village with a strong traditional music tradition. During the first weekend in May Kinvara hosts the annual **Cuckoo Fleadh** (✉ Main St. ☎ 091/637–145), a traditional music festival. Resident musicians like De Danann alumni Jackie Daly and Charlie Piggott play regularly at the town's **Winkles Hotel** (✉ The Square ☎ 091/637–137). Back in 1989, a young accordion player got together with her friends for a casual recording session. The resulting album, *Sharon Shannon*, became the most successful Trad-music recording ever released.

GIGGING IN GALWAY

Galway has nurtured some of the most durable names in Irish music: Dé Danann, Arcady, singers Dolores and Seán Keane, and the mercurial accordion genius, Mairtín O'Connor. Seán Ryan, master of the tin whistle, has been playing every Sunday at

Crane's (✉ 2 Sea Rd. ☎ 091/587–419) since the 1980s. **Tigh Coili** (✉ Mainguard St. ☎ 091/561–294) has traditional Irish music sessions every day at 5:30 and 10 PM. **Monroe's Tavern** (✉ Dominick St. ☎ 091/583–397) has traditional music every night from 9:30 PM, and invites you to join the locals in set dancing. There is also plenty of music to be found at old favorites in the city center like **Tigh Neachtain** (✉ 17 Cross St. ☎ 091/568–820), **Taaffe's** (✉ 19 Shop St. ☎ 091/564–066), and **An Pucan** (✉ 11 Forster St. ☎ 091/561–528). **The Bard's Den** (✉ Main St. ☎ 091/41042) in Letterfrack, Co. Galway, is noted for its Trad sessions. **Molloy's Bar** (✉ Bridge St. ☎ 098/26655) in Westport, Co. Mayo, is owned by Matt Molloy, flute player of the Chieftains, and is renowned for its great sessions.

■ TIP➜ For details, log on to www.comhaltas.com or get a copy of the "trad" bible, Walton's Guide to Irish Music (www.walton-music.com).

GOOD BEHAVIOR

If you happen on a pub session there are a few ground rules. Don't talk during the solo, and don't stare at the singer; most people look at the floor. Buy the musicians a drink if it's a small session, and if at all possible, have a party piece to contribute yourself. the gesture that counts.

FIDDLING AROUND

Irish Traditional music is very much the music of the people, played on relatively simple, portable instruments: fiddle, flute, tin whistle, accordion, handheld drum, and, recent additions, guitar or banjo.

UILLEANN PIPES

The uilleann (pronounced "illun") pipes, literally "elbow" pipes, are a quieter indoor version of bagpipes. The player sits while playing with a bag under one arm, the bellows under the other, and the "chanter," which plays the melody, on the thigh. A temperamental instrument, it can be heartrenderingly beautiful in the hands of a master like Liam O'Flynn or Paddy Keenan of the Bothy Band.

FIDDLE

The classical violin all but in name, this is the most popular instrument in Trad music for its singing, swooping versatility, its portability, and its relative affordability. Local fiddle styles still persist, especially in Donegal, Sligo, and the Sliabh Luachra region of Cork and Kerry and virtuosos such as Frankie Gavin of Dé Dannan, Martin Hayes, Tommy Peoples, and Liz Doherty are famed for their rhythm, color, and ornamentation.

SQUEEZE-BOXES & ACCORDIONS

Squeeze-box is a generic term for a variety of melodeons, accordions, and concertinas. The concertina is a small, hexagonal-shaped button-key instrument. The simplest accordion is the one-row button accordion, usually called a melodeon. Styles of playing can vary enormously. Sharon Shannon is rooted in the highly rhythmic East Clare style but can veer into swing and Cajun styles as she plays her wildly energetic dance music.

FLUTES & WHISTLE

The tin whistle is the ideal beginner's instrument, but be sure to buy one in the key of D. It is still called the penny whistle because it costs so little to buy. But the flute used in Irish music is usually a simple wooden flute—hear it at its best in the hands of Matt Molloy and Paddy Moloney of the Chieftains, Mary Bergin, and Olean Masterson.

BODHRÁN

The Bodhrán (pronounced "bow-rawn") is a simple goat's skin drum played with the back of the hand or a small wooden stick. When played well, by Mel Mercier, John Joe Kelly, or Tommy Hayes, it makes an exciting addition to the running rhythms of Trad music. They make it look easy, but in the hands of an untrained amateur, a badly played bodhrán can wreck a session.

HAPPY LISTENING!

Olcan Masterson, on the whistle

SEÁN Ó RIADA The father of "modern" Trad music, this composer and visionary Irish language enthusiast (1931–71)—noted for his film score *Míse Éire* and his Irish language *Mass Cúil Aodha*—established the prototype traditional Irish group, Ceoltóiríc Chualann, in 1963, who evolved into the Chieftains.

DÉ DANNAN This famed group grew from regular sessions in Hughe's bar in Spiddal, Co. Galway, in 1974. Brilliant fiddle and flute player Frankie Gavin, bouzouki whiz Alec Finn, banjo master Carlie Piggot, and Johnny "Ringo" McDonagh on bodhrán were joined by singers Dolores Keane, Mary Black, and Maura O'Connell (all now solo artists). *Dé Dannan* (1975) and *Mist-Covered Mountain* (1980) are their timeless evocations of the West of Ireland.

THE CHIEFTAINS If you've seen a poster of Irish musicians wearing unhip cardigans, baggy trousers, and bad haircuts, it was probably the Chieftains, who went professional in 1975. Outstanding musicians, they include uilleann-piper Paddy Moloney, flute player Matt Molloy, harper Derek Bell (recently deceased), and Seán Keane and Martin Fay (fiddlers). Any of their famous 35 albums are worth owning.

PLANXTY The word *planxty* means a lively tune (without words) written to honor a patron, but it is now forever associated with a "super-group" formed in 1972 by singer Christy Moore, with Dónal Lunny, Andy Irvine, and Liam O'Flynn. Their haunting debut album, *Planxty* (1972), is a must. Reincarnated in the later '70s as The Bothy Band, their 1975 debut album remains a classic.

ALTAN Donegal-born husband-and-wife duo, Frankie Kennedy on flute and Máiréead Mhaonaight (fiddle and vocals), showcase the special Donegal way with fiddle and flute.

ANÚNA This vocal and instrumental ensemble, founded in the 1990s, represents the mys-tical, spiritual aspect of Celtic music, and is widely known through performances with the original Riverdance production. *Anúna* (1993), their first album, is still their best.

KILA Touted by the under-30s to be the future of Irish music, this group shows African percussion, Andean flute, and Eastern European folk music among the influences on their debut album, *Tóg É Go Bog É*—roughly translated as "The Living is Easy.

Altan

8

IN FOCUS GAEL FORCE

sounds heard from the comfort of your own table, try **Sally Longs** (⊠ *Upper Abbeygate St., Center* ☎ *091/565–756*), Galway's hard-rock pub, much loved by bikers.

PUBS Master of the tin whistle Seán Ryan plays every Sunday at **Crane's** (⊠ *2 Sea Rd.* ☎ *091/587–419*). **The Dáil Bar** (⊠ *42–44 Middle St., Center*

☎ *091/563–777*), looks traditional with its dark-wood decor but is a new arrival on the pub scene, and very popular with a younger crowd. **The Front Door** (⊠ *3 High St., Center* ☎ *091/563–757*) is a lively spot for the twentysomethings, with five bars spread over three floors, and a late bar until 2 AM Wednesday to Sunday. You can usually find a session after about 9 PM at **King's Head** (⊠ *15 High St., Center* ☎ *091/566–630*). **McSwiggan's** (⊠ *3 Eyre St., Wood Quay, Center* ☎ *091/568–917*) is a huge Galway City place, with everything from church pews to ancient carriage lamps contributing to its eclectic character. **Monroe's** (⊠ *20 Dominick St., Center* ☎ *091/583–397*) is a large, sociable pub with traditional music nightly and set dancing on Tuesday. **Roisin Dubh** (⊠ *Dominick St., Spanish Arch* ☎ *091/586–540*) is a serious venue for emerging rock and traditional bands—it often showcases big, if still-struggling, talents. **Taaffe's** (⊠ *19 Shop St., Center* ☎ *091/564–066*), in the midst of the shopping district, is very busy on afternoons. Up-and-coming young musicians play at the cozy **Tigh Coili Bar** (⊠ *Mainguard St., Center* ☎ *091/561–294*) in traditional sessions daily at 5:30 and 10 PM. **Tigh Neachtain** (⊠ *17 Cross St., Spanish Arch* ☎ *091/568–820*) is *the* place to check out the Galway vibe, and each visit will be an experience.

THEATER

An Taibhdhearc (⊠ *Middle St., Center* ☎ *091/562–024* ⊕ *www.antaibhdhearc.com*), pronounced *on tie*-vark, was founded in 1928 by Hilton Edwards and Mícheál Macliammóir as the national Irish-language theater. It continues to produce first-class shows, mainly of Irish works in both the English and the Irish languages and hosts touring productions.

The **Druid Theatre Company** (⊠ *Chapel La., Center* ☎ *091/568–617* ⊕ *www.druidtheatre.com*) is esteemed for its adventurous and accomplished productions, mainly of 20th-century Irish and European plays. The players perform at the Royal Court's small stage in London. When they're home, they usually appear at the Town Hall, and they host many productions during the Galway Arts Festival in late July.

Macnas (⊠ *Center* ☎ *091/561–462* ⊕ *www.macnas.com*) is an internationally renowned, roving Galway-based troupe of performance artists who have raised street theater to new levels. Their participation in the Galway Arts Festival's annual parade is always much anticipated.

VISUAL ARTS AND GALLERIES

Bold (⊠ *Merchants Rd. and Augustine St., Center* ☎ *091/539–900* ⊕ *www.boldartgallery.com*) shows work by big-name and up-and-coming Irish artists.

Reflecting a passion for modern Irish art, **Norman Villa Gallery** (⊠ *86 Lower Salthill, Salthill* ☎ *091/521–131* ⊕ *www.normanvillagallery.com*) shows work in the gallery owner's home and garden. The art gallery at **University College Galway** (⊠ *Newcastle Rd., University* ☎ *091/524–411*) has a number of exhibits each year.

SPORTS AND THE OUTDOORS

BICYCLING

Set off to explore the Galway area, especially its coast, by renting a bike from **Mountain Trail Bike Shop** (⊠ *The Cornstore, Middle St., Center* ☎ *091/569–888* ⊕ *www.mountaintrailbikeshop.com*.

FISHING

Galway City is the gateway to Connemara, and Connemara is the place to fish. You can get fishing licenses, tackle, and bait, and arrange to hire a traditional fly-fishing guide or book a sea-angling trip at **Freeny's Sports** (⊠ *19–23 High St., Center* ☎ *091/562–609*).

GOLF

Galway Bay Golf and Country Club (⊠ *Renville, Oranmore* ☎ *091/790–500*) is an 18-hole parkland course, designed by Christy O'Connor Jr., on the shores of Galway Bay. The **Galway Golf Club** (⊠ *Blackrock, Salthill* ☎ *091/522–033*) is an 18-hole course with excellent views of Galway Bay, the Burren, and the Aran Islands. Some of the fairways run close to the ocean.

RIVER CRUISING

A **Corrib Cruise** (☎ *091/592–447* ⊕ *www.corribprincess.ie*) from Wood Quay, behind the Town Hall Theatre at the Rowing Club, is a lovely way to spend a fine afternoon; it lasts 1½ hours and travels 8 km (5 mi) up the River Corrib and about 6 km (4 mi) around Lough Corrib. There's a bar on board, tea and coffee, and a commentary. The trip costs €14, and boats depart daily at 2:30 and 4:30 from May through September, with an additional departure at 12:30 July through August. You can also rent the boat for an evening.

SHOPPING

ANTIQUES

Tempo Antiques (⊠ *9 Cross St., Center* ☎ *091/562–282* ⊕ *www.tempo-antiques.com*) has an interesting collection of small antiques, including jewelry, porcelain, and other small collectibles.

BOOKS

Charlie Byrne's Bookshop (⊠ *Middle St., Center* ☎ *091/561–766*) sells a large, varied selection of new and used books and remainders.

CLOTHING

Faller's Sweater Shop (✉ *25 High St., Center* ☎ *091/564–833* ✉ *35 Eyre Sq., Center* ☎ *091/561–255*) has the choicest selection of Irish-made sweaters, competitively priced. **O'Máille's** (✉ *16 High St., Center* ☎ *091/562–696*) carries Aran sweaters, handwoven tweeds, and classically tailored clothing.

CRAFTS AND GIFTS

★ Don't miss **Judy Greene/Design Concourse** (✉ *Kirwan's La., Center* ☎ *091/561–753*), a spectacular one-stop shop for the best in Irish handcrafted design. Ceramics by Judy Greene and others, small pieces of furniture, contemporary basketware, handmade jewelry, wood turnings, handblown glass—in fact just about anything for the home that can be handmade—will be found in this two-story treasure trove.

Galway Irish Crystal (✉ *Dublin Rd., Merlin Park* ☎ *091/757–311* ⊕ *www.galwaycrystal.ie*), a factory outlet on the city's ring road, sells hand-cut Irish glass, Belleek Pottery, and other fine porcelain.

The **Kilkenny Shop** (✉ *6 High St., Center* ☎ *091/566–110*) is synonymous with good modern design in Ireland. This shop stocks the best ceramics, crystal, leatherware, clothing, and other craft items from around the country.

Meadows & Byrne (✉ *Castle St., Center* ☎ *091/567–776*) sells the best in modern household items.

Browse in **Treasure Chest** (✉ *William St., Center* ☎ *091/563–862*) for china, crystal, gifts, and classic clothing.

FOOD

Sheridan's Cheesemongers (✉ *16 Churchyard St.* ☎ *091/564–829* ⊕ *www.sheridanscheesemongers.com*) is run by Seamus and Kevin Sheridan. Together, they know all of Ireland's artisan cheese makers personally and stock the widest possible range of delectable cheeses, complemented by charcuterie (mainly Italian). The wineshop upstairs will complete your picnic.

JEWELRY

Phyllis MacNamara's cute two-story boutique, **Cobwebs** (✉ *7 Quay St., Spanish Arch* ☎ *091/564–388* ⊕ *www.cobwebs.ie*), is filled with an irresistible selection of antique jewelry (real and costume) and collectibles for men and women, all with a witty twist. Dating from 1750, **Thomas Dillon's** (✉ *1 Quay St., Spanish Arch* ☎ *091/566–365* ⊕ *www.claddaghring.ie*) claims to be the original maker of Galway's famous Claddagh ring. In the back of the shop there's a small but interesting display of antique Claddagh rings and old Galway memorabilia.

MALLS

The spacious indoor **Galway Shopping Centre** (✉ *Headford Rd.*) is a mall with more than 60 outlets, 10 minutes' walk from Eyre Square with ample car parking. On the southwest side of Eyre Square and imaginatively designed to incorporate parts of the old town walls, the **Eyre Square Shopping Centre** is a good spot to pick up moderately priced clothing and household goods.

MUSIC

Back2Music (✉ *30 Upper Abbeygate St., Center* ☎ *091/565–272*) specializes in traditional Irish musical instruments, including the handheld drum, the *bodhrán* (pronounced bau-*rawn*). **Mulligan** (✉ *5 Middle St. Ct., Center* ☎ *091/564–961*) carries thousands of CDs, records, and cassettes, with a large collection of traditional Irish music. **P. Powell and Sons** (✉ *The Four Corners, William St., Center* ☎ *091/562–295*) sells traditional Irish musical instruments and CDs, and has a knowledgeable staff.

THE OILEÁIN ÁRAINN (ARAN ISLANDS)

No one knows for certain when the Aran Islands—Inis Mór (Inishmore), Inis Meáin (Inishmaan), and Inis Oirr (Inisheer)—were first inhabited, but judging from the number of Bronze Age and Iron Age forts found here (especially on Inis Mór), 3000 BC is a safe guess. Why wandering nomads in deerskin jerkins would be attracted to these barren islets remains a greater mystery, not least because fresh water and farmable land were (and still are) scarce commodities. Remote western outposts of the ancient province of Connaught (though they are not the country's westernmost points; that honor belongs to the Blasket Islands), these three islands were once as barren as the limestone pavements of the Burren, of which they are a continuation. Today, the land is parceled into small, human-made fields surrounded by stone walls: centuries of erosion, generations of backbreaking labor, sheep, horses, and their attendant tons of manure have finally transformed this rocky wasteland into reasonably productive cropland.

While traditional Irish culture fights a rear-guard battle on the mainland, the islanders continue to preserve as best as they can a culture going back generations. Still, the Irish-speaking inhabitants enjoy a daily air service to Galway (subsidized by the government), motorized curraghs, satellite TV, and all the usual modern home conveniences. Yet they have retained a distinctness from mainlanders, preferring simple home decor, very plain food, and tightly knit communities, like the hardy fishing and farming folk from whom they are descended. Crime is virtually unknown in these parts; at your B&B, you'll likely find no locks on the guest-room doors, and the front-door latch will be left open. Many islanders have sampled life in Dublin or cities abroad but have returned to raise families, keeping the population stable at around 1,500. Tourists now flock here to see the ancient sights and savor the spectacular

8

ISLAND NIGHTS

To appreciate the fierce loneliness of the Aran Islands you must spend the night on one. Because all the islands, especially Inishmore, crawl with day-trippers, it's difficult to let their rugged beauty sink into your soul until 10 PM, when the sky is dark and the pubs fill with the acrid smell of peat smoke and Guinness. Once the day-trippers clear out, the islands' stunningly fierce and brooding beauty is disturbed only by the "baa" of the sheep and the incessant rush of the wind.

CLOSE UP

Aran Rediscovered

During the 1800s, the islands, wracked by famine and mass emigration, were virtually forgotten by mainland Ireland. At the turn of the 20th century, however, the books of J.M. Synge (1871–1909)—who learned Irish on Inishmaan and wrote about its people in his famous play *Riders to the Sea*—prompted Gaelic revivalists to study and document this isolated bastion of Irish culture. To this day, Synge's travel book *The Aran Islands,* first published in 1907, and reissued by Penguin with a brilliant introduction by artist and mapmaker Tim Robinson in 1992, remains the best book ever written about the islands. Liam O'Flaherty

became one of the most famous sons of Inishmore through his novels, such as *Famine.* And in 1934, American director Robert Flaherty filmed his classic documentary *Man of Aran* on Inishmore, recording the islanders' dramatic battles with sea and storm, and bringing the islands into the world spotlight. The film is shown in the *Ionad Árainn* (Aran Heritage Center) in Cill Rónáin (Kilronan) on Inishmore daily during July, August, and early September. Flaherty, incidentally, continues to be a common surname on the islands; it is hard to visit the islands *without* meeting a Flaherty.

views: the uninterrupted expanse of the Atlantic on the western horizon; the Connemara coast and its Twelve Bens to the northeast; and County Clare's Burren and the Cliffs of Moher to the southeast.

There's a small hotel on Inisheer and one on Inishmore, but there's no shortage of guesthouses and B&Bs, mostly in simple family homes. The best way to book is through the Galway City TIO. Each island has at least one wine-licensed restaurant serving plain home cooking. Most B&Bs will provide a packed lunch and an evening meal (called high tea) on request. For general information about visiting the Aran Islands and useful links, try the islands' official Web site (⊕ *www. visitaranislands.ie*).

GETTING HERE

AIR TRAVEL Aer Arran offers 10-minute flights. Their standard flights to the Aran Islands are €45 round-trip, leaving from Connemara Airport near Inverin, 30 km (19 mi) west of Galway.

BOAT TRAVEL The best place to book your trip to the Aran Islands is at the Galway Tourist Information Office (*see Galway, above*). The ferry companies and Aer Arran have concessions here. Decide between a short flight, a 20-minute boat ride on a high-speed catamaran, or an hour-long trip on comfortable ferries. The majority of boats for the Aran Islands leave from Rossaveale, 37 km (23 mi) west of Galway City, and charge €25 round-trip. (You

WORD OF MOUTH

"In my opinion, the visit to Dún Aengus made the trip to Ireland worthwhile. It is a stunningly beautiful fort situated on cliffs that drop off dramatically into the Atlantic Ocean. The views are exhilarating. I can't begin to imagine how beautiful it would be on a sunny day?"   —Desiderado

can also reach the islands from Doolin in County Clare; *see Doolin, above*). Park at Rossaveale, or book a shuttle bus from the city (€7 round-trip) when buying your ticket. There are at least two sailings a day, and four or more in high season, timed to facilitate day trips. Ask when boarding about inter-island ferries if you intend to visit more than one island. Inishmore, the biggest island, is the only one with organized transport. Book a tour or taxi in advance (through the TIO in Galway), or hire a bicycle (€12 per day) or pony and trap on landing. Galway-based Lally Tours sell a package of bus and ferry for €32.

ESSENTIALS

Transportation Contacts Aer Arran (☎ *091/593–034* ⊕ *www.aerarannislands. ie*). **Aran Bike Hire** (✉ *Kilronan Pier, Inishmore* ☎ *099/61132*). **Galway City Tourist Office** (✉ *Forster St., Eyre Sq., Co. Galway* ☎ *091/537–700* ⊕ *www.discoverireland. ie/west*) for ferry tickets to Aran Islands. **Noel Mahon Luxury Tours** (✉ *Killeany, Kilronan, Inishmore* ☎ *087/788–2775* ⊕ *www.tourbusaranislands.com*).

INIS MÓR (INISHMORE)

★ *31 km (18 mi) southwest of Salthill docks, 48 km (30 mi) west of Galway Docks.*

With a population of 900, Inis Mór is the largest of the islands and the closest to the Connemara coast. It's also the most commercialized, its appeal slightly diminished by road traffic. In summer, ferries arriving at Cill Ronáin (Kilronan), Inis Mór's main village and port, are met by minibuses and pony-and-cart drivers, all eager to show visitors "the sights." More than 8 km (5 mi) long and about 3 km (2 mi) wide at most points, with an area of 7,640 acres, the island is just a little too large to explore comfortably on foot in a day. The best way to see it is really by bicycle; bring your own or rent one from one of the vendors operating near the quay.

Visitor Information Oileáin Árainn (Aran Islands)–Inis Mór (Inishmore) Tourist Office (✉ *Aran Heritage Centre, Cill Ronáin [Kilronan], Co. Galway* ⊕ *www.aranislands.ie*).

EXPLORING

If you are lucky enough to stay overnight on Inishmore island, try to get away from the crowds of day-trippers in the daytime, who clog up the road between Kilronan and Dún Aengus from 11 AM to about 6 PM. Head for the less frequented west of the island, visiting Dún Dúchathair, a dramatically sited promontory fort (freely accessible), only slightly less impressive than Dún Aengus, or walk the secluded east coast.

The **Ionad Árainn (Aran Heritage Centre)** explains the history and culture of the islanders, who for many years lived in virtual isolation from the mainland. ✉ *Cill Ronáin (Kilronan)* ☎ *099/61355* ⊕ *www. visitaranislands.ie* 💶 *€3* ⊙ *Apr., May, Sept., and Oct., daily 11–5; June–Aug., daily 10–7; Nov.–Mar., by appointment.*

Even if you have only a few hours to explore Inis Mór, rent a bike (next to the pier) and head straight for **Dún Aengus,** one of the finest prehistoric monuments in Europe, dating from about 2000 BC. Spectacularly set on the edge of a 300-foot-tall cliff overlooking a sheer drop, the fort

As you arrive by plane over the Aran Islands, their famous stone-wall fences—built by medieval farmers to clear lands for farms—come into view.

has defenses consisting of three rows of concentric circles. Whom the builders were defending themselves against is a matter of conjecture. From the innermost rampart there's a great view of the island and the Connemara coast. In order to protect this fragile monument from erosion, you should approach it only through the visitor center, which gives access to a 1-km (½-mi) uphill walk over uneven terrain—wear sturdy footwear. ⊠ 7 km (4 mi) west of Cill Ronáin (Kilronan), Kilmurvey ☎ 099/61010 ⊕ www.heritageireland.ie/en/West/DunAonghasa ☜ €3 ☉ Mar.–Oct., daily 10–6; Nov.–Feb., daily 10–4.

WHERE TO STAY

$ 🏨 **Ard Einne Guesthouse.** Almost every window at this B&B on Inishmore looks out to the sea, making it the perfect place to de-stress. The rambling 80-year-old house, with its distinctive dormer windows, is close to both the beach and the town; many guests base themselves here for two or three nights, to make a thorough exploration of the island. The public rooms and guest rooms are relaxed, with modern decor including light-color linens and walls paneled with blond wood. **Pros:** great location for getting away from it all; walking distance to pubs (half a mile) and restaurants (a mile and a half). **Cons:** no Internet access; one of the island's biggest guesthouses, thoroughly modernized; no elevator. ⊠ Cill Ronáin (Kilronan), Co. Galway ☎ 099/61126 ⊕ www.ardeinne. com ➘ 8 rooms ♿ In-room: no a/c, no phone, no TV. In-hotel: restaurant ☰ MC, V ☉ Closed Nov.–Jan. ⦿l BP.

$ 🏨 **Kilmurvey House.** This rambling 200-year-old stone farmhouse, run
★ by the warm, chatty owner, Treasa Joyce, is the first choice of many visitors to the island. It's at the foot of Dún Aengus fort, a three-minute

walk from the beach, and about 6½ km (4 mi) from the quay and the airport (accessible by minibus). The old stone house has been cleverly extended to provide extra guest rooms. The neatly kept front garden leads to a large, high-ceiling hall and wide stairs, giving a pleasant sense of space. The walls are hung with portraits of the house's previous owners, the warrior clan of O'Flahertys—one of whom was Oscar Wilde's godfather—whose descendants include the famed writers Liam and Robert. Rooms are spacious and comfortable, with views of the fort, or distant sea views. It's worth paying a small supplement for one of the four larger rooms with king-size beds. **Pros:** lovely warm welcome; home-cooked evening meal served five nights a week; memorable location adjacent to historic fort. **Cons:** 4 mi from village, pubs, and restaurants; minibus costs €5 each way; no elevator. ⊠ *Cill Ronáin (Kilronan), Co. Galway* ☎ *099/61218* ⊕ *www.kilmurveyhouse.com* ⤴ *12 rooms* ⟁ *In-room: no a/c, no TV. In-hotel: restaurant, Wi-Fi hotspot* ⊟ *MC, V* ⊘ *Closed Nov.–Mar.*

NIGHTLIFE AND THE ARTS

The place to go for traditional music is **Ostán Oileáin Árainn** (⊠ *Cill Ronáin [Kilronan]* ☎ *099/61104*).

Joe Mac's (⊠ *Cill Ronáin [Kilronan]* ☎ *099/61248*), right off the pier, is a good place for a pint while waiting for the ferry home. **Joe Watty's** (⊠ *Main Rd., Cill Ronáin [Kilronan]* ☎ *099/61155*) is a good bet for traditional music virtually every night in summer.

INIS MEÁIN (INISHMAAN)

3 km (2 mi) east of Inis Mór (Inishmore).

EXPLORING

The middle island in both size and location, Inis Meáin has a population of about 300 and can be comfortably explored on foot. In fact, you have no alternative if you want to reach the island's major antiquities: **Dún Conor (Conor Fort)**, a smaller version of Dún Aengus; the ruins of two **early Christian churches**; and a chamber tomb known as the **Bed of Diarmuid and Grainne**, dating from about 2000 BC. You can also take wonderful cliff walks above secluded coves. It's on Inishmaan that the traditional Aran lifestyle is most evident. Most islanders still don hand-knitted Aran sweaters, though nowadays they wear them with jeans and sneakers.

SHOPPING

Inis Meáin Knitting (⊠ *Carrown Lisheen* ☎ *099/73009*) is a young company producing quality knitwear in luxury fibers for the international market—including Liberty of London, Barneys New York, and Bergdorf Goodman—while providing much-needed local employment. The factory showroom has an extensive selection of garments at discount prices. To get here from the pier, walk five minutes due west.

8

INIS OIRR (INISHEER)

4 km (2½ mi) east of Inis Meáin (Inishmaan), 8 km (5 mi) northwest of Doolin docks.

EXPLORING

The smallest and flattest of the islands, Inis Oirr can be explored on foot in an afternoon, though if the weather is fine you may be tempted to linger on the long, sandy

beach between the quay and the airfield. Only one stretch of road, about 500 yards long, links the airfield and the sole village. "The back of the island," as Inis Oirr's uninhabited side facing the Atlantic is called, has no beaches, but people swim off the rocks.

It's worth making a circuit of the island to get a sense of its utter tranquility. A maze of footpaths runs between the high stone walls that divide the fields, which are so small that they can support only one cow each, or two to three sheep. Those that are not cultivated or grazed turn into natural wildflower meadows between June and August, overrun with harebells, scabious, red clover, oxeye daisies, saxifrage, and tall grasses. It seems almost a crime to walk here—but how can you resist taking a rest in the corner of a sweet-smelling meadow on a sunny afternoon, sheltered by high stone walls with no sound but the larks above and the wind as it sifts through the stones?

The **Church of Kevin,** signposted to the southeast of the quay, is a small, early Christian church that gets buried in sand by storms every winter. Each year the islanders dig it out of the sand for the celebration of St. Kevin's Day on June 14.

A pleasant walk through the village takes you up to **O'Brien's Castle,** a ruined 15th-century tower on top of a rocky hill—the only hill on the island.

WHERE TO STAY

$$ **Hotel Inisheer.** A pleasant, modern low-rise in the middle of the island's only village, a few minutes' walk from the quay and the airstrip, this simple, whitewashed building with a slate roof and half-slate walls has bright, plainly furnished rooms, with pine-frame beds, pine floors, and white bed linen. The social life of the island centers on "the hotel," as it is called, and there are nightly sessions of traditional music. **Pros:** island's only all-in-one destination, with pub and restaurant; good location between pier and airstrip; very clean. **Cons:** basic standard of comfort: certainly no frills; very busy July and August. ⊠ *Lurgan Village, Co. Galway* ☎ *099/75020* ⟵ *14 rooms* ⌂ *In-room: no a/c, no phone, no TV. In-hotel: restaurant, bar* ⊟ *AE, DC, MC, V* ☯ *Closed Oct.–Mar.* ⎮⊙⎮ *BP.*

Connemara and County Mayo

INCLUDING COUNTIES GALWAY AND MAYO

WORD OF MOUTH

"We loved the Connemara area. It was maybe our favorite landscape of the entire trip. Hills, lakes, misty fields with sheep and horses, wildflowers and stone bridges crossing peaceful streams. Connemara is picture-postcard Ireland. With not a giant tour bus in sight, we could really experience some Irish culture and interact with the natives."

—erin74

WELCOME TO CONNEMARA AND COUNTY MAYO

TOP REASONS TO GO

★ **Captivating Connemara:** An almost uninhabited landscape of misty bogland, studded with deep blue lakes under huge Atlantic skies: painters have strived for generations to capture the ever-changing light.

★ **Cong à la Hollywood:** Fetching ivy-covered thatched cottages—including one commemorating the making of the archetypal "Irish" movie *The Quiet Man*—beside a ruined medieval monastery contrast with the baronial splendor of Ashford Castle, one of Ireland's most luxurious hotels.

★ **Clifden and the Sky Road:** Walk the Sky Road to take in its breathtaking scenery—sea views on one side, the Twelve Bens Mountains on the other—to the compact village of Clifden, the liveliest spot for miles around.

★ **Wordly Westport:** An engagingly old-fashioned country town, Westport has an octagonal market square that dates from the 18th century and a quayside (on Clew Bay) that offers spectacular Atlantic sunsets.

1 Lough Corrib and Environs. As soon as you leave Galway City you will have glimpses of Lough Corrib, Ireland's second largest lake, some 40 km (25 mi) long and 11 km (7 mi) across, edged with reeds and rolling hills. Oughterard is a peaceful village beloved of game anglers, while Cong to the north is picture-book pretty and rich in heritage. Both are havens of away-from-it-all peace and quiet. A boat service joins the two, and allows you to enjoy some memorable scenery, or you can take a long scenic drive to Cong via Maam Cross.

2 **Connemara National Park.** The area west of Maam Cross and out to the rocky coast is the famed Connemara, and consists mainly of rugged, sparsely-inhabited hills, enhanced by the ever-changing light of the Atlantic weather, with rainbows every time a shower crosses the sun. Get up close to a bog among the displays at the Visitor Center in Letterfrack, the heart of the 5,000-acre National Park, to understand the fragile ecology of the peatlands. Then take a hike to explore the territory.

GETTING ORIENTED

With the most westerly seaboard in Europe, this region remains a place apart—the most Irish part of Ireland. While just to the west and north of hip Galway City, this area is famed for its wild and rural character. Connemara sits in the northwest corner of County Galway. County Mayo is Ireland's third largest county, with coast on three of its four sides, and the River Moy and the huge expanse of Lough Conn and Lough Cullin on the fourth. Bright lights are to be found in Clifden and Westport, both lively small towns of great charm.

9

3 **County Mayo.** Outside the main towns—Castlebar and Westport—the rest of the county has long empty roads leading to isolated shorelines, stunning vistas from remote peaks, and silent ghostly valleys that stretch along for miles. Apart from Achill Island and Westport, this is a relatively undeveloped destination, where the natives still provide a glimpse of the Ireland of old, and there is always time for a long chat.

CONNEMARA AND COUNTY MAYO PLANNER

Transportation Basics

Public transport is not a strong point in the West. Trains arrive from Dublin on separate lines to Westport and Ballina, but there is no service between these towns. The bus network is more flexible, but there are not many services each day and the entire bus system goes into semi-hibernation during the winter months, so plan accordingly. In fact, your main transportation hub for this region could lie to the south in Galway City (see the County Clare, Galway, and the Aran Islands chapter). To do full justice to the regions in this chapter, you really need a car—and a good map.

When to Go

There is a local saying in the Westport area: if you can't see the summit of Croaghpatrick, then it is raining; if you can see it, it is about to rain. Try not to visit between November and February, when many places close for the winter and the days are short and overcast. In fact, you could have your umbrellas out constantly during all times but the warmest months, July and August, when the average temperatures are around 15°C (60°F).

Mayo Contrasts

Long beloved by traditional anglers, who still pack hotels and B&Bs when the May fly rises, County Mayo has also been discovered by the Millennium generation, with couples flocking from Dublin to Westport on weekends, where the Celtic Tiger made a huge investment in boutique-style hotels and spas.

And yet, just down the road, on the third weekend in July, barefoot pilgrims still climb Croaghpatrick, in the footsteps of their parents and grandparents.

Clare Island in Clew Bay has long been a haven for bird watchers, archaeologists, and natural historians; now it is also the venue for highly successful singles weekends—a novel way to meet your match.

Boomtown Westport has stolen the spotlight from historic Castlebar, the largely Georgian county town of Mayo.

Nearby is the only branch of the National Museum of Ireland outside Dublin, the Museum of Country Life at Turlough.

The museum has collaborated with the National Folklore Commission to commemorate a way of life that is fast disappearing.

Even as the museum opened in 1991, Turlough's school, shop, and one of its pubs closed, and its population shrank to 300, mainly commuters working in Castlebar.

Quo vadis, County Mayo?

WHAT IT COSTS IN EUROS

	¢	$	$$	$$$	$$$$
Restaurants	under €12	€12–€18	€19–€24	€25–€32	over €32
Hotels	under €80	€80–€120	€121–€170	€171–€210	over €210

Restaurant prices are for a main course at dinner. Hotel prices are for a standard double room in high season.

Making the Most of Your Time

If you're a city lover, and tend to fade without daily doses of caffeine and retail therapy, then base yourself in Clifden for the first night, where there is coffee-aplenty, and the shopping is surprisingly good for a very small town (Irish designer wear, locally made tweed, traditional hand-knits, and wackier hand-crafted knitwear).

Then move on to Westport, another highspot for shoppers; the mood here is set by its weekly market which has stalls selling agricultural overalls and boots to the local farmers, as well as nicely designed locally made crafts.

The shops are laid out in a triangle, and you will find antiques and a second-hand bookshop as well as knitwear and designer fashion among the hardware and souvenir shops.

If you love the outdoors, dramatic scenery, empty roads, and deserted coves, then you'll be in heaven in Connemara and Mayo.

Allow a full day to meander slowly from Galway City to Clifden, either exploring the jagged rocks of the coastline, or climbing the slopes of the heather-clad mountains.

Next morning, hire a Connemara pony, or take a stroll along the Sky Road before heading to the Connemara National Park Visitor Centre in Letterfrack.

A side trip to Renvyle to enjoy the view is worth it in clear weather. Spend the night in the Letterfrack area, then take in Kylemore Abbey next day, and push on to Killary Harbour where you can take a boat trip on Ireland's only fjord. Drive the scenic Doolough Valley to Westport for your third night.

Next day, climb Croaghpatrick, or take a walk on the big sandy beach at its base, or a day trip to Clare Island.

After a second night in Westport head up towards Ballina, stopping at the Museum of Country Life (allow two hours), taking the scenic road through Pontoon, for a grand finale.

Fishing Around?

Connemara is a major center for anglers keen to test their skills on Lough Corrib, particularly during the mayfly period (mid-May to mid-June). "Dapping" is the best method of catching them, an activity in which the line is given gentle tugs, enabling the bait to hop lightly on the water. An experienced boatman (vital for the uninitiated) plus his boat can be hired for the day; your hotel or tourist office can help arrange this.

Where to Stay

Accommodation in the area tends to the traditional; outside Westport there are few indoor pools and gyms: instead there are informal, friendly places where you will probably end up comparing notes with other travelers over a huge cooked breakfast.

Add variety by alternating rural isolation with the lively towns. Both Clifden in Connemara and Westport in Mayo have lively pub scenes.

Clifden attracts a younger, mainly single, crowd, especially in July and August, so be warned: the music might be rock rather than Irish.

Lakeside Cong is a tiny village, but is a magnet for visitors. It is often pointed out that Ashford Castle, one of the most sumptuous of Ireland's castle hotels, is bigger than the village.

All is perfectly manicured at this mock-Gothic baronial showpiece, built in 1870 as a country retreat for the Guinness family.

Rosleague Manor, a pink-washed Georgian house on the waterside near Letterfrack, is among the prettiest Irish country house hotels.

The lake, sea, and mountain views from its 30 acres, its excellent restaurant, and elegant lounges means you need not leave the estate at all.

9

GETTING AROUND

Car, Train, Bus, or Bike?

A car can be very helpful in the West region, especially from September through June. Although the main cities are easily reached from the rest of Ireland by rail or bus, transport within the region is sparse. If a rental car is out of the question, one option is to make Westport your base, and take a day trip to Connemara and Kylemore Abbey. There is no direct bus connection between Clifden and Westport, the two most attractive touring bases in the area. And the hardy can always consider making a biking trip through the region, even though it does get periods of strong rain.

Taxi Travel

Within Westport taxis operate on the meter. Outside the town, agree on the fare in advance.

Westport Taxis (📞 087/222–6227 ⊕ www.westporttaxis. com).

Road Conditions

Connemara and Mayo have good, wide main roads (National Primary Routes) and better-than-average local roads (National Secondary Routes), both known as "N" routes. If you stray off the beaten track on the smaller Regional ("R") or Local ("L") routes you may encounter some hazardous mountain roads. Narrow, steep, and twisty, they are also frequented by untended sheep, cows, and ponies grazing "the long acre" (as the strip of grass beside the road is called) or simply straying in search of greener pastures. If you find a sheep in your path, just sound the horn, and it should scramble away. A good maxim for these roads is: "you never know what's around the next corner." Bear this in mind, and adjust your speed accordingly. Hikers and cyclists constitute an additional hazard on narrow roads.

Within the Connemara Irish-speaking area, signs are in Irish only. The main signs to recognize are Gaillimh (Galway), Ros an Mhil (Rossaveal), An Teach Doite (Maam Cross), and Sraith Salach (Recess).

Train Travel

The region's main rail stations are in Galway City, Westport, and Ballina. Trains for Galway, Westport, and Ballina leave from Dublin's Heuston Station. The journey time to Galway is 3 hours; to Ballina, 3¾ hours; and to Westport, 3½ hours.

Rail service within the region is limited. The major destinations of Galway City and Westport/Ballina are on different branch lines. Connections can be made only between Galway and the other two cities by traveling inland for about an hour to Athlone.

Train Information Irish Rail–Iarnod Éireann (📞 098/25253 in Westport ⊕ www.irishrail.ie/home). **Ballina Station** (📞 096/20229). **Dublin Heuston Station** (📞 01/836–6222). **Galway Station** (📞 091/564–222). **Westport Station** (📞 098/25253).

Bus Travel

Bus Éireann runs several expressway buses into the region from Dublin, Cork City, and Limerick City to Galway City, Westport, and Ballina, the principal depots in the region.

Citylink operates frequent buses, with up to 17 departures daily, between Clifden, Galway City, and Dublin and Dublin Airport. The trip costs €15 one-way.

Citylink also makes five daily trips in each direction between Shannon Airport and Galway City, costing €16 one-way.

Within Connemara and Mayo, bus routes are often slow and circuitous, and service can be erratic. A copy of the Bus Éireann Expressway timetable (€3 from any station) is useful for long trips. If possible use the Web site or phone the bus station (they are always very helpful) to plan local bus journeys.

Bus Eireann local buses travel from Galway City to Cong, Clifden, and Westport, and from Westport to Ballina. There are no buses between (linking) Cong, Clifden, and Westport: you must return to Galway City and take a different bus line out again to visit each place.

Bus Depots Ballina Station (☎ 096/71800). **Galway City Station** (*Ceannt Station* ☎ 091/562–000). **Westport Station** (☎ 098/25711).

Bus Lines Bus Éireann (☎ 091/562000 in Galway, 096/71800 in Ballina, 01/836–6111 in Dublin, 021/508–188 in Cork ⊕ www.buseireann.ie). **Citylink** (✉ Unit 1, Forster Ct., Galway City ☎ 091/564–163 ⊕ www.citylink.ie).

Car Travel

If you're lucky enough to travel by car, here are some main routes to keep in mind. The 219-km (136-mi) Dublin–Galway trip takes about three hours.

From Cork City take N20 through Mallow and N21 to Limerick City, picking up the N18 Ennis–Galway road in Limerick. The 209-km (130-mi) drive from Cork to Galway takes about three hours, and another 45 minutes to Oughterard, where the Connemara scenery begins.

From Killarney the shortest route to cover the 193 km (120 mi) to Galway (three hours) is to take N22 to Tralee, then N69 through Listowel to Tarbert and ferry across the Shannon Estuary to Killimer. From here, join N68 in Kilrush, and then pick up N18 in Ennis.

Airport Transfers

From Shannon Airport you can pick up a rental car to drive into the West, or you can take a bus to Limerick, from which there are bus connections into the West.

Galway Airport is 6½ km (4 mi) from Galway City. No regular bus service is available from the airport to Galway, but most flight arrivals are taken to Galway Rail Station in the city center by an airline courtesy coach. Inquire when you book.

A taxi from the airport to the city center costs about €15.

If you're flying to Knock International Airport, you can pick up your rental car at the airport.

Otherwise, inquire at the time of booking about transport to your final destination.

There's a bus link to Charlestown where you can connect with Bus Éireann's national network.

Information, Please

If you're traveling extensively by public transportation, be sure to load up on information (the best taxi-for-call companies, rail and bus schedules, etc.) upon arriving at the ticket counter or help desk of the bigger train and bus stations in the area, such as Westport.

GETTING AROUND

Only in the West

As you drive through Connemara, you will not only see sheep roaming the hillsides (lots of sheep: more sheep than people) but also herds of wild ponies, usually gray (the proper term for white horses) or dun (buckskin) in color.

Connemara ponies are strong, hardy, and companionable, highly intelligent, and also surprisingly elegant: averaging around 13 to 14 hands, they are much sought after for riding and show jumping. They are assumed to be a cross between a native Irish breed and Spanish-bred Arab horses imported in the Middle Ages.

The breed was only recognized in the early 20th century, and is celebrated on the third weekend in August at the Connemara Pony Show in Clifden.

The whole town takes on a festive air and parties long into the night as breeders and competitors from all over Ireland enjoy their annual get-together. The show-jumping competitions are pretty nifty, too.

Boat and Ferry Travel

The Tarbert–Killimer Ferry leaves every hour on the half hour and takes 20 minutes to cross the Shannon Estuary from North County Kerry to West County Clare; this saves you a 137-km (85-mi) drive through Limerick City. It is very handy if you are heading from the Ring of Kerry or Dingle area to the Cliffs of Moher. The ferry runs every day of the year except Christmas and costs €18 one-way, €28 round-trip. (Ferries return from Killimer every hour on the hour.)

Corrib Cruises run daily cruises on Lough Corrib from April to October, with great views of Ashford Castle and the Connemara mountains, and an optional visit to the monastic ruins on Inchagoill Island. The boat has indoor and outdoor seating and a licensed bar. Board either at Cong or at Oughterard, on the opposite side of the lake. You can use the cruise as a ferry service from one village to the other, or opt for a historic cruise with guide (both options €20). Their 6 PM traditional music cruise from Cong (June–September) is always popular.

Clare Island in Clew Bay and its smaller neighbor, Inishturk Island, are increasingly popular day-trip destinations with hikers and natural historians. Clare Island Ferry Company sails to Clare Island and Inishturk between May and September leaving the mainland at 10:45 AM and returning at 4:45 PM (€15 round-trip). O'Malley Ferries is a year-round operator serving Clare Island. Both leave from Roonagh Pier at Louisburgh, a 35-minute drive from Westport. Tickets can be bought at the Westport Tourist Office.

From April through October Killary Cruises runs 90-minute trips around Killary Harbour (€21), Ireland's only fjord, in an enclosed catamaran launch with seating for 150 passengers, plus a bar and restaurant. They offer a "no seasickness money-back guarantee."

Clare Island Ferry Company (☎ 098/28288 ⊕ www.clareislandferry.com). **Corrib Cruises** (☎ 094/954–6029 ⊕ www.corribcruises.com). **Killary Cruises** (✉ Nancy's Point, 2 km [1 mi] west of Leenane on N59 Clifden Rd. ☎ 091/566–736 ⊕ www.killarycruises.com). **O'Malley Ferries Clare Island** (☎ 098/25045 ⊕ www.omalleyferries.com). **Tarbert–Killimer Ferry** (☎ 065/905–3124 ⊕ www.shannonferries.com).

Air Travel

Aer Arann has seven flights a day from London's Luton Airport and five a day from Dublin to Galway Airport (GWY). Aer Arann also flies to Edinburgh, Manchester, Lorient, and Waterford from Galway.

Ryanair flies to Knock daily from London's Stansted Airport and Luton Airport; flying time is 80 minutes. BmiBaby has several flights to Knock from Manchester daily. Aer Arann flies hourly in July and August to the Oileáin Árainn (Aran Islands) from Connemara Airport in Inverin. Off-peak there are half a dozen flights a day, fewer in December and January.

These flights call at all three Aran Islands. The journey takes about six minutes and costs about €45 round-trip. The airline will book a B&B for you when you book your flight. Ask about other special offers, including scenic routes, at the time of booking.

Carriers Aer Arann (☎ 091/593–034 ⊕ www.aerarann. ie). **Aer Lingus** (☎ 0818/365–022 ⊕ www.aerlingus.com). **BmiBaby** (☎ 1890/340122 ⊕ www.bmibaby.com). **Ryanair** (☎ 0818/303–030 ⊕ www.ryanair.com).

Airports

The West's most convenient international airport is Shannon, 25 km (16 mi) east of Ennis *(see the County Clare, Galway City, and the Aran Islands chapter)*. Galway Airport, 8 km (5 mi) from Galway City, is used mainly for internal flights, with some U.K. traffic.

Knock International Airport, at Charlestown—near Knock, in County Mayo—has direct daily service to London's Stansted, Luton, and Gatwick, and to Manchester and Birmingham.

A small airport for internal traffic only is at Knockrowen, Castlebar, in County Mayo.

Flying time from Dublin is 25 to 30 minutes to all airports. No scheduled flights run from the United States to Galway or Knock; use Shannon Airport.

Airport Information Galway Airport (☎ 091/752–874 ⊕ www.galwayairport.com). **Knock International Airport** (☎ 094/936–7222 ⊕ www.knockairport.com). **Shannon Airport** (☎ 061/471–444 ⊕ www.shannonairport.com).

Visitor Information

Bord Fáilte provides free information service, tourist literature, and an accommodations booking service at its TIOs (Tourist Information Offices).

Oughterard and Wesport TIOs are open all year, generally weekdays 9–6, daily during the high season.

Other TIOs that operate seasonally, generally weekdays 9–6 and Saturday 9–1, are open as follows:

Castlebar (May–mid-September), Clifden (March–October), and Cong (May–mid-September).

Information on Connemara and Mayo can be found at ⊕ www.discoverireland.ie/west. In addition to this main Web site, we sometimes also list a town Web site in individual town sections; this is occasionally an ad-supported site that is unofficial, but still helpful).

Generally speaking, tourism has been carefully nurtured in this region. Ferry services to the islands and on Lough Corrib have been upgraded, while walking and cycling holidays are a big growth area. The traditional attractions of sea and game angling, rough shooting, and golf have been augmented by investment in existing heritage attractions, including the magnificently located Kylemore Abbey in Connemara, Westport House and Country Park, and the endlessly entertaining Museum of Country Life near Castlebar.

HIKING THE WEST

More and more travelers are discovering that Ireland's Western regions are hiking heaven. In fact, hikes or guided walks through Connemara or County Mayo are the best ways to get to know these territories at first hand, or rather, foot.

(above) Eco-hiking in spectacular Connemara National Park; (right, top) Many "way-marked" hikes go past beautiful lakes like Lough Corrib; (right, bottom) Stop and smell the heather.

Why hike the West? It has some of the finest rugged scenery and dramatic indented coastline in all Ireland. In Connemara serried ranks of heather-clad mountains, interspersed with bright blue lakes, beckon to the walker as dramatic cloud formations scud across huge Atlantic skies. In County Mayo, the huge conical bulk of Croaghpatrick spectacularly looms above Clew Bar. Or what about earning some blisters along the black waters of Killary Fjord, set in the shadow of Mweelrea Mountain? The attraction lies in the terrific views nearly everywhere you look. Coastal views alternate with mountain vistas, often topped by a perfect rainbow. A daily highlight is the spectacular sunset over the Atlantic, at its biggest and best in late August.

BUY IN IRELAND

Walkers on way-marked trails are advised to buy an Ordnance Survey map of the area, which are sold locally. Most tourist offices also have free maps of less ambitious walks on roads and local footpaths. Because of the wind, most Irish walkers wear knitted or fleece hats, often decorated with a Guinness logo or a wooly sheep: shop around locally.

Hiking buffs will be glad to know that the last decade has seen the completion of various "way-marked" (signposted) walking routes, which can be sampled in easy one or two hour "loops," or, for more serious walkers, made the focus of a visit.

TOP HIKING DESTINATIONS

The Western Way's County Galway section extends from Oughterard on Lough Corrib through the mountains of Connemara to Leenane on Killary Harbor, a distance of 50 km (30 mi). Its 177-km (110-mi) County Mayo section, known as the Western Way (Mayo), continues past Killary Harbor to Westport on Clew Bay to the Ox Mountains east of Ballina. This trail should be the first choice of serious walkers, as it includes some of the finest mountain and coastal scenery in Ireland. A new, 224-km (140-mi) hiking route, slí Chonamara, through Irish-speaking Connemara, stretches along the shores of Galway Bay from An Spidéal to Carraroe, Carna, Letterfrack, and Recess.

Another perfect hiking destination is Connemara National Park, which consists of some 5,000 acres of untamed mountain wilderness in and around the Twelve Bens peaks. Allow two to three hours to hike the Diamond Hill Loop, along 7 km (4 mi) of gravel tracks and paved mountain paths, to a 1,493 foot peak, with a 360-degree vista taking in

the distant sea, the turrets of Kylemore Abbey, and the higher peaks in the south. The nearby visitor center (March–October, free) has displays on the flora, fauna, and geology of Connemara.

WALKING IN COMPANY

Walking festivals are becoming increasingly popular, with organized guided walks in the day and free entertainment by night. Achill Island in Country Mayo hosts the **Achill Walks Festival** (⊕ *www.achilltourism.com*) in March, to tempt people out again after the long dark winter, while Castlebar, in inland Mayo, has an **International Four Days Walks Festival** (⊕ *www.castlebar4dayswalks.com*) in early July. Meet walkers from over 21 different countries.

BRING WITH YOU

You cannot hike Connemara and Mayo in sneakers, due to the combination of bog, rocky terrain and frequent showers. Bring a pair of waterproof hiking boots, a lightweight waterproof rain-suit (preferably breathable), or at the very least waterproof boots, and a day pack to carry them in. A lightweight fleece over a T-shirt gives enough protection from the wind in summer; in autumn and spring you'll probably also need a light weatherproof jacket.

9

Updated
by Alannah
Hopkin

There's something special about Connemara and County Mayo. With its remote islands that proclaim themselves "the last parish before America," hidden lakes dripping in history, and its empty, wide-open spaces, these regions are places that will haunt your memory long after you have left. This most distinct area of Ireland has always been one of contrasts—ancient history, sacred and savage; culture and literature, illuminating and unique; yesteryear and today, all in one memorable package. While the bustling town of Westport has assumed the identity of the ultrahip destination of a younger, newer, more confident Ireland, the surrounding countryside still provides endless fodder for the "rugged and rural" Irish stereotype.

A land where melancholic antiquity sits comfortably with modern progress, these regions possess a spirit that has always spoken to the hidden poet within all who travel here. The philosopher Wittgenstein, who lived alone here for a time, called Connemara "one of the last pools of darkness in Europe." But you don't have to travel too far within the northwest corner of County Galway and also County Mayo to find happy pub crowds, elegant county-house hotels (like Ashford Castle), and characterful towns such as Clifden and Leenane, rife with good restaurants and pubs.

It is the countryside, however, that takes center stage. This is a landscape where the thundering Atlantic forms the pounding backbeat to the most westerly seaboard in Europe, one richly endowed with magnificent vistas: Connemara's combination of rugged coastline, mountains, moorland, and lakes; the distinctive conelike shape of Croaghpatrick, towering over the 365 islands of Clew Bay, and the rippling waters of

Lough Corrib, Lough Conn, and many smaller lakes. The Irish people are well aware of what a jewel they have in the largely unspoiled wilderness, grazed by sheep and herds of wild ponies, that is the 5,000-acre Connemara National Park, the result of a successful lobby for landscape preservation. Peatlands, or bogs as they are called around here, are at last being valued for their unique botanical character.

It is little wonder that time seems to have a different value out here, as if the 21st century had never begun. It is still not unusual to be stuck behind two cars parked either side of the white line, drivers' windows open while local news (or perhaps family trees names going back to the 12th century) is exchanged, oblivious to your revving engine behind them. Visitors are often geared to a faster pace but they should allow at least two days for exploring the region, four to six days if you intend to do some serious hiking or cycling, take a boat trip on Lough Corrib, visit Clare Island, and enjoy the village (and pub) life of Clifden and Westport. Although distances between sights are not great, you may want to take scenic—meaning slower—national secondary routes. Covering 80 km to 112 km (50 mi to 70 mi) per day on these roads is a comfortable target.

Unlike most of Ireland where the marks of Viking, Norman, and English invaders blotted out much of the rich heritage of the ancient Irish kingdoms, these western counties retained, by virtue of their remoteness, those essential Celtic characteristics of rebellion and individuality, and the accompanying graces of unstinting hospitality and courtly good manners. These traits survive, despite the purges of Cromwell's English armies and the all-pervasive trauma of the Great Famine (1845–49). That era started a tradition of emigration that continued to deprive the area of the majority of its youth well into the 1960s. Those that remained worked hard to eke a living from the produce of the rocky seashore and the harsh mountain territory. Where today's visitor, fleeing the stress and constant chatter of urban living, finds solace and romantic peacefulness in the emptiness of the area, its low population is also a reminder of how hard it is to make a living out in rocky territory.

But it will still most likely be an outdoor memory that stays with you after spending time in these unspoiled hills and boglands: a spectacular red sunset lingering over the Atlantic perhaps, the shocking lapis-lazuli blue of your first Connemara lough, or the fleeting moment when the way ahead is framed by a completely semi-circular rainbow. Here is where the magic lies.

CONNEMARA

Bordered by the long expanse of Lough Corrib on the east and the jagged coast of the Atlantic on the west is the rugged, desolate region of western County Galway known as Connemara. Like the American West, it's an area of spectacular, almost myth-making geography—of glacial lakes; gorgeous, silent mountains; lonely roads; and hushed, uninhabited boglands. To quote Tim Robinson in his exceptional book *Connemara: Listening to the Wind*, this is a place of "huge, luminous

CLOSE UP

Tour Guide Options

All TIOs in the West provide lists of suggested cycling tours. The only guided bus tours in the region, which take in the main sights of Connemara (€25), start from Galway and Westport and run only between June and September. Book at the bus station or tourist office.

Lally Tours runs a day tour through Connemara and County Mayo. O'Neachtain Day Tours operates full-day tours of Connemara. Tickets, €25, can be purchased from the Galway City TIO; tours depart across the street.

Galway-based Healy Tours offers historical sightseeing tours (€25) with professional guides, including Kylemore Abbey and Connemara. Tickets can be purchased from the Galway and Salthill tourist information offices *(see the County Clare, Galway City, and the Aran Islands chapter)* or on the tour bus.

Michael Gibbons in Clifden organizes everything from daylong mountain treks to weeklong holidays. Also based in Clifden, Connemara Safari Walking Holidays offers five- and seven-day residential walking holidays starting in either Clifden or Westport. They specialize in "island-hopping" and remote island hikes.

Croagh Patrick Walking Holidays runs weeklong walking holidays between April and September, based in B&B accommodations near Westport; contact Gerry Greensmyth. Killary Tours offers a range of self-guided or customized tours for walkers, cyclists, golfers, and horseback riders. Groups of 8 to 16 people participate in three-, four-, or seven-day programs, staying in a comfortable B&B near Westport, or traveling to a new destination each night with luggage transfer. Walk Clare

Biking Connemara

Island, climb Diamond Hill, or gallop along a sandy beach on Clew Bay.

Tours Connemara Safari Walking Holidays (✉ *Sky Rd., Clifden, Co. Galway* ☎ *095/21071* ⊕ *www.walkingconnemara.com*).

Croagh Patrick Walking Holidays (✉ *Belclare, Westport, Co. Mayo* ☎ *098/26090* ⊕ *www.walkingguideireland.com*).

Healy Tours (☎ *091/770–066* ⊕ *www.healytours.ie*).

Galway City Museum (☎ *091/562–000*).

Galway City TIO (✉ *Forster Pl., Center* ☎ *091/537–700* ⊕ *www.discoverireland.ie/west*).

Killary Tours (✉ *Leenane, Co. Galway* ☎ *095/42276* ⊕ *www.killary.com*).

Lally Tours (☎ *091/562–905* ⊕ *www.lallytours.com*).

Michael Gibbons (✉ *Market St., Clifden, Co. Galway* ☎ *095/21379* ⊕ *www.walkingireland.com*).

Mike Lynch (☎ *086/382–6425*).

O'Neachtain Day Tours (☎ *091/553–188* ⊕ *www.ontours.biz*).

Salthill TIO (☎ *091/520–500*).

spaces." The glacially carved Twelve Bens mountain range, together with the Maamturk Mountains to their north, lord proudly over the area's sepia boglands. In the midst of this wilderness there are few people, since Connemara's population is sparse even by Irish standards. Especially in the off-season, you're far more likely to come across sheep strolling its roads than another car.

Two main routes—one inland, the other coastal—lead through Connemara. To take the inland route described below, leave Galway City on the well-signposted outer-ring road and follow signs for N59, the road that goes west through Moycullen, Oughterard, and Clifden (names that are also prominently signposted if you head out from Galway). If you choose to go the coastal route, you can travel due west from Galway City to Ros an Mhil (Rossaveal) on R336 through Salthill, Bearna, and An Spidéal—all in the heart of the West's strong Gaeltacht, home to roughly 40,000 Irish speakers (note that most place signage hereabouts will be in Irish, so a map with both English and Irish names will prove handy). You can continue north on R336 from Ros an Mhil (Rossaveal) to Maam Cross and then head for coastal points west, or pick up R340 and putter along the coast.

OUGHTERARD

27 km (17 mi) northwest of Galway City on N59.

Bustling Oughterard (pronounced *ook*-ter-ard) is the main village on the western shores of Lough Corrib and one of Ireland's leading angling resorts. Boats can be hired for excursions to the many wooded islands studding the lakes. It is known as a fine center for exploring the beauty spots of the Twelve Bens, and other mountain ranges hereabouts, such as the Maamturk and Cloosh.

GETTING HERE

BOAT TRAVEL Explore Lough Corrib with **Corrib Cruises** (☎ 094/954–6029 ⊕ *www. corribcruises.com*), which runs daily boat trips from Oughterard Pier from April to October. Take a day trip to Cong on the opposite side of the lake, or opt for a historic cruise with guide (both options €20).

BUS TRAVEL Buses traveling from Galway to Clifden stop at Oughterard, a 40-minute journey. Bus Éireann (*see Planner*) has only two services a day during school holidays (Easter, July and August) at 7:15 and 10 am (€7.60 one-way); up to six at other times of the year. Citylink has four services daily leaving Galway at 9 AM, noon, 4 PM, and 5:30 PM (€7 one-way).

Visitor Information Oughterard Tourist Office (✉ *Main St., Co. Galway* ☎ *091/552–808* ⊕ *www.oughterardtourism.com*).

EXPLORING

The prettiest part of the village is on the far (Clifden) side, beyond the busy commercial center, beside a wooded section of the River Corrib. The lough is signposted to the right in the village center, less than 1½ km (1 mi) up the road. From mid-June to early September, local boatmen offer trips on the lough, which has several islands. It's also possible to take a boat trip to the village of Cong, at the north shore of the lough.

Midway between Oughterard and Cong, Inchagoill Island (the Island of the Stranger), a popular destination for a half-day trip, has several early Christian church remains.

WHERE TO STAY

$$ ⛅ **Ross Lake House.** Well off the beaten path, this surprisingly stylish
★ country hideaway sits near a stream and is surrounded by 5 acres of colorful gardens. Built by James Edward Jackson, land agent for Lord Iveagh at Ashford Castle, the white-trim Georgian house, managed by the enthusiastic Henry and Elaine Reid, has a suavely furnished interior, with 19th-century antiques and welcoming open fires. Guest rooms in the converted stables are simpler and a little smaller than those in the house, but all have peaceful garden views, and 20-inch flat-screen TVs, should you feel the need. **Pros:** country quiet—silence, in fact—with style; good restaurant on the premises. **Cons:** 3 mi out of town; no pubs nearby. ⊠ *Rosscahill (5 km [3 mi] from Oughterard), Co. Galway* ☎📠 *091/550-109* ⊕ *www.rosslakehotel.com* ⇲ *11 rooms, 2 suites* ⚷ *In-room: no a/c. In-hotel: restaurant, bar, tennis court, Internet terminal, Wi-Fi hotspot* ⊟ *AE, MC, V* ⊘ *Closed Nov.–mid-Mar.* ⌾ *BP.*

NIGHTLIFE

For good traditional music, drop in at **Flaherty's** (⊠ *Main St.* ☎ *091/552-194*).

EN
ROUTE As you continue northwest from Oughterard on N59, you'll soon pass a string of small lakes on your left; their shining blue waters reflecting the blue sky are a typical Connemara sight on a sunny day. About 16 km (10 mi) northwest of Oughterard, the continuation of the coast road (R336) meets N59 at Maam Cross in the shadow of Leckavrea Mountain. Once an important meeting place for the people of north and south Connemara, it's still the location of a large monthly cattle fair. Walkers will find wonderful views of Connemara by heading for any of the local peaks visible from the road.

Beyond Maam Cross, some of the best scenery in Connemara awaits on the road to Recess, 16 km (10 mi) west of Maam Cross on N59. At many points on this drive, a short walk away from either side of the main road will lead you to the shores of one of the area's many small loughs. Stop and linger if the sun is out—even intermittently—for the light filtering through the clouds gives splendor to the distant, dark-gray mountains and creates patterns on the brown-green moorland below. In June and July, it stays light until 11 PM or so, and it's worth taking a late-evening stroll to see the sun's reluctance to set.

In Recess, **Joyce's** (☎ *095/34604*) is a crafts shop owned by a family that is famed for its traditional Connemara tweeds. The emporium has a good selection of tweed, and also carries an enticing selection of contemporary ceramics, handwoven shawls, books of Irish interest, original paintings, and small sculptures.

CONG

Fodor's Choice *23 km (14 mi) northeast of Maam Cross on N59.*

★ Set on a narrow isthmus between Lough Corrib and Lough Mask on the County Mayo border near Maam Cross, the pretty, old-fashioned village of Cong is still as camera-ready as it was when John Ford's *The Quiet Man* was filmed here. Dotted with ivy-covered thatch cottages and lorded over by one immensely posh hotel, Ashford Castle, this tiny village continues to have a world-wide fan base.

GETTING HERE

BUS TRAVEL There is a limited service from Galway Bus Station to Cong, with at least one Bus Éireann bus a day in each direction Monday to Saturday. Be sure to get a bus that goes to Ryan's, the bus stop in the village center. The journey takes just over an hour (€11.40 one-way, €17.50 round-trip). You can also take a delightful day-trip to Cong by Corrib Cruises boat from Oughterard *(see above)* between April and October.

Visitor Information Cong Tourist Office (✉ *Abbey St., Co. Galway* ☎ *092/46542* ⊕ *www.congtourism.com* ☉ *May–mid-Sept. only*).

EXPLORING

Just two blocks long, and bisected by the chocolate-brown River Cong, the village is surrounded on all sides by thickly forested hills. Cong is famed for its luxury Ashford Castle hotel (note: it also has a hostel and the new Lisloughrey Lodge Country House, which was not open at press time) and rumor has it that you can explore the castle grounds if you pay a fee (inquire at the hotel to get a peek at the aristocratic lobby; better, opt for a fancy lunch or dinner there). A more romantic way to see the castle is on a boat trip run by the local Corrib Cruises. To get an overview of the stupendous natural beauty surrounding the town, head past Cong Abbey toward the banks of Lough Corrib, about a mile south—along the way you may pass some of the many caves, stone circles, and burial mounds around the village. Ask at the village tourist office for information on walks in the region.

Cong's 15 minutes of fame came in 1952, when John Ford filmed *The Quiet Man,* one of his most popular films, here; John Wayne plays a prizefighter who goes home to Ireland to court the fiery Maureen O'Hara. (Film critic Pauline Kael called the movie "fearfully Irish and green and hearty.") The **Quiet Man Heritage Cottage,** in the village center, is an exact replica of the cottage used in the film, with reproductions of the furniture and costumes, a few original artifacts, and pictures of actors Barry Fitzgerald and Maureen O'Hara on location. For much of the year, Margaret and Gerry Collins host Quiet Man tours, originating at the cottage and exploring such Cong village sites as the river fight scene, the "hats in the air" scene, and Pat Cohan's Bar. ✉ *Circular Rd., Cong Village Center* ☎ *094/954–6089* ⊕ *www.quietman-cong.com* 🎫 *€5* ☉ *Daily 10–5.*

Cong is surrounded by many stone circles and burial mounds, but its most notable ruins are those of the **Augustine Abbey** (✉ *Abbey St.*), dating from the early 13th century and still exhibiting some finely carved

The village of Cong is world-famous as the setting for John Wayne's *Quiet Man* Oscar-winner and the Quiet Man Heritage Cottage takes you behind the scenes.

details. It can be seen overlooking a river near fabulous Ashford Castle, now a hotel.

WHERE TO STAY

$$$$
★

Ashford Castle. Nearly bigger than the neighboring village of Cong, this famed mock-Gothic baronial showpiece was built in 1870 for the Guinness family and has been wowing visitors like Prince Rainier, John Travolta, and Jack Nicholson ever since. Massive, flamboyantly turreted, Ashford is the very picture of a romantic Irish castle. It remains strong on luxury and good service, but light on authenticity: time-stained charm has given way to too many creature comforts. Deluxe guest rooms have generous sitting areas, heavily carved antique furniture, open fireplaces, and extra-large bathrooms. Standard bedrooms in the discreetly added new wing are smaller, with marble bathroom fittings and Victorian-style antiques. The suites in the original castle building are vast, with double-height windows and Georgian antiques, and are blissfully comfortable. The Prince of Wales Cocktail Bar (named for the one who visited in the 1890s) is the venue for elegant pre-dinner drinks. The cuisine, by distinguished Swiss chef Stefan Matz, is stylish and unfussy. The hotel makes the most of its superb location at the head of Lough Corrib, and the surrounding formal gardens are possibly the most neatly manicured outdoor space in Ireland. The riverbank has been landscaped to facilitate angling while there has also been massive investment in the hotel's spa facilities. **Pros:** baronial flamboyance; no-expense-spared facilities; regal grounds. **Cons:** so luxurious you are in a world apart, nearly divorced from the normal hubbub of Irish life. ⊠ *Co. Mayo* ☎ *094/954–6003* ⊕ *www.ashford.ie* ↝ *72 rooms, 11 suites*

♿ *In-room: no a/c, Internet, Wi-Fi. In-hotel: 2 restaurants, bars, golf course, tennis courts, gym, spa* 🖃 *AE, DC, MC, V.*

CLIFDEN

★ *46 km (29 mi) southwest of Cong on N59, 79 km (49 mi) northwest of Galway City on N59.*

With roughly 1,100 residents, Clifden would be called a village by most, but in these parts it's looked on as something of a metropolis. It's far and away the prettiest town in Connemara, as well as its unrivaled "capital." Clifden's first attraction is its location—perched high above Clifden Bay on a forested plateau, its back to the spectacular Twelve Ben Mountains. The tapering spires of the town's two churches add to its alpine look.

GETTING HERE

BUS TRAVEL Bus Éireann has at least three services a day from Galway Bus Station, and Citylink runs at least four services a day to Clifden. Bus Éireann charges €12.50 one-way, €18 round-trip and takes 2 hours (at least half of that through great scenery). Citylink's service takes 1½ hours (€13 one-way), and continues from Galway to Dublin and Dublin Airport. Some of these services continue to Letterfrack (about 20 minutes) and Leenane (about an hour). Check with Galway Bus Station on day of travel.

Visitor Information Clifden Tourist Office (🖃 *Galway Rd., Co. Galway* ☎ *095/21163* 🌐 *www.clifdenconnemara.com* ⊘ *Mar.–Oct. only*).

EXPLORING

Clifden is a popular base thanks to its selection of small restaurants, lively bars with music most summer nights, pleasant accommodations, and excellent walks. It's quiet out of season, but in July and August crowds flock here, especially for August's world-famous Connemara Pony Show. Year-round, unfortunately, Clifden's popularity necessitates a chaotic one-way traffic system and on summer Sunday afternoons loud techno music blasts out of certain bars. So if you're looking for a sleepy country town that time forgot, push on to Westport.

A 2-km (1-mi) walk along the beach road through the grounds of the ruined **Clifden Castle** is the best way to explore the seashore. The castle was built in 1815 by John D'Arcy, the town's founder, who laid out the town's wide main street on a long ridge with a parallel street below it. D'Arcy was High Sheriff of Galway, and his greatest wish was to establish a center of law and order in what he saw as the lawless wilderness of Connemara. Before the founding of Clifden, the interior of Connemara was largely uninhabited, with most of its population clinging to the seashore.

Take the aptly named **Sky Road** to really appreciate Clifden's breathtaking scenery. Signposted at the west end of town, this high, narrow circuit of about 5 km (3 mi) heads west to Kingstown, skirting Clifden Bay's precipitous shores.

9

Prince Rainier, John Travolta, Jack Nicholson…and now you? Lucky travelers call Ashford Castle their Cong home-away-from-home.

WHERE TO EAT AND STAY

$
SEAFOOD

✕ **Mitchell's Seafood.** A town-center shop has been cleverly converted into a stylish, two-story eatery. On the first floor, beyond the plate-glass windows, there's a welcoming open fire, and you can eat at the bar or at one of the polished wood tables. Exposed stone walls and wooden floors are alluring accents on the quieter second level. Braised whole sea bass with fennel butter typifies the simple treatment given to seafood. The all-day menu also features lighter options like homemade spicy fish cakes and fresh crab salad. There are several meat options, including traditional Irish stew of Connemara lamb and fresh vegetables. ✉ *Market St.* ☎ *095/21867* ☰ *AE, MC, V* ☙ *Closed Nov.–Feb.*

$$$
Fodor's Choice
★

🏨 **Abbeyglen Castle Hotel.** Creeper covered, as if under a Sleeping Beauty spell, gorgeous Abbeyglen sits framed by towering trees at the foot of the glorious Twelve Bens Mountains. If time hasn't completely stopped here, it has certainly slowed down—but that's just the way the relaxed guests want it. Surrounded by gardens with waterfalls and streams, the Victorian castle-manor was built in 1832 by John D'Arcy, the founder of Clifden. Inside, each guest room is uniquely decorated, some with wooden floors, some with gas open fires, some with four-poster beds. Insist on a front room when booking if you enjoy great views. Even though it's a castle, it is also a fun place to stay, owned by the famously hospitable Hughes brothers, Paul and Brian. Complimentary afternoon tea is served in the bar, effortlessly giving way to evening drinks, as the piano player strikes up. Beware Gilbert the parrot, who has the run of reception: he wolf-whistles, but he also bites. **Pros:** laid-back, easygoing atmosphere; pleasantly homey for all its grandeur; friendly hosts and staff. **Cons:** uphill walk back from Clifden. ⊠ *Sky Rd., Co. Galway* ☎ *095/22832* ⊕ *www.abbeyglen.ie* ↪ *45 rooms* ⅏ *In-room: no a/c. In-hotel: restaurant, bar, tennis court, pool, Internet terminal* ☰ *AE, DC, MC, V* ☺ *Closed Jan.* ⦿ *BP.*

$ ⛭ **Dún Rí.** An old town house in the lower, quieter part of Clifden has been extended and converted into a comfortable guesthouse with private parking. The town's bars and restaurants are only two minutes' walk away, yet there can be sheep grazing on a vacant lot across the road. Rooms are a good size, with hotel-like features including adjustable radiators, swagged floral curtains, and efficient showers. Help yourself to tea and coffee in the residents' lounge, a good place to compare notes with fellow travelers. The breakfast room has a pine floor and white damask cloths, and the toast is accompanied by homemade jams. **Pros:** hotel-grade rooms at B&B prices; quiet central location. **Cons:** bland style of decor; parking lot is effectively on-street, not secured. ⊠ *Hulk St., Co. Galway* ☎ *095/21625* ⊕ *www.dunri.et* ↪ *13 rooms* ⅏ *In-room: no a/c. In-hotel: bar* ☰ *MC, V* ⦿ *BP.*

$$ ⛭ **Quay House.** Nineteenth-century time travelers would feel right at
★ home walking into this three-story Georgian house, Clifden's oldest (1820). Ancestral portraits, mounted fish, Victorian engravings, and cosseting fabrics all lend a frozen-in-amber allure, made all the more homey by such touches as model boats (a few too many animal-skin rugs, though). A roaring turf fire in the sitting room greets you as you enter the burnished breakfast room, while the nearby terrace has been gloriously sheathed in glass to give it a gorgeous "conservatory" feel. This oasis of calm beside the harbor quay (just a short walk from the town center) contains guest rooms that are unusually spacious; those in the main house are imaginatively decorated with deep-color walls and wonderful period accents; all but two have sea views. There's also a new wing with seven studio rooms with balconies overlooking the harbor. **Pros:** fetching decor; harbor views. **Cons:** uphill walk into town. ⊠ *The Quay, Connemara, Co. Galway* ☎ *095/21369* ⊕ *www.thequayhouse. com* ↪ *14 rooms* ⅏ *In-room: no a/c, kitchen (some). In-hotel: Internet terminal, Wi-Fi* ☰ *MC, V* ☺ *Closed Nov.–mid-Mar.* ⦿ *BP.*

9

THE ARTS

Clifden Arts Week (⊕ *www.clifdenartsweek.ie*), in mid-September, has a great selection of music, arts, and poetry in a friendly informal atmosphere, making it an excellent time to tune in to local culture.

SPORTS AND THE OUTDOORS

BICYCLING Explore Connemara by renting a bike from **John Mannion & Son** (⊠ *Railway View* ☎ *095/21160*).

GOLF On a dramatic stretch of Atlantic coastline, the 18-hole course at the **Connemara Golf Club** (⊠ *South of Clifden, Ballyconneely* ☎ *095/23502*) measures 7,174 yards.

SHOPPING

The Connemara Hamper (⊠ *Market St.* ☎ *095/21054*), a small but well-stocked specialty food shop, is an ideal place to pick up picnic fare, with its excellent Irish farmhouse cheeses, pâtés, smoked Connemara salmon, and handmade Irish chocolates. **Millar's Connemara Tweeds** (✉ *Main St.* ☎ *095/21038*), an arts-and-crafts gallery, carries a good selection of traditional tweeds and hand knits. The **Station House Courtyard** (✉ *Old Railway Station, Bridge St.* ☎ *095/21699*) is a cobbled courtyard with crafts studios and designer-wear outlets.

LETTERFRACK

14 km (9 mi) north of Clifden on N59.

This is one of the main gateway villages to the famous Connemara National Park. It also makes a handy base for those visiting spectacular Kylemore Abbey, one of Ireland's grandest ancestral estates.

GETTING HERE

BUS TRAVEL
Bus Éireann has three services a day between 8:45 AM and 6 PM linking Letterfrack and Clifden. The fare for the 20-minute journey is €7. The non-express service originates in Galway, and takes about 2 hours 30 minutes (€14 one-way) to reach Letterfrack. There are also three services a day in each direction by Citylink between Letterfrack and Clifden (continuing to Galway), leaving Letterfrack at 8:45, 10:55, and 5:55 for the same fare.

EXPLORING

The 5,000-acre **Connemara National Park** lies southeast of the village of Letterfrack. Its visitor center covers the area's history and ecology, particularly the origins and growth of peat—and presents the depressing statistic that more than 80% of Ireland's peat, 5,000 years in the making, has been destroyed in the last 90 years. You can also get details on the many excellent walks and beaches in the area. The misleadingly named "park" is, in fact, just rocky or wooded wilderness territory, albeit with some helpful trails marked out to aid your exploration. It includes part of the famous **Twelve Bens** mountain range, which is for experienced hill walkers only. An easier hike is the Lower Diamond Hill Walk, at about 3 km (5 mi). Ask for advice on a hike suited to your abilities and interests at the Park and Visitor Centre, which is on the N59 as you arrive in Letterfrack from Clifden, on your right, clearly signposted, not too far southeast of the center of Letterfrack. ✉ *Park and Visitor Centre, on the N59 near Letterfrack* ☎ *095/41054* ⊕ *www. connemaranationalpark.ie* 🖾 *Free* ⊙ *Park daily, dawn–dusk; visitor center Mar.–May and Sept.–mid-Oct., daily 9–5:30.*

WHERE TO EAT AND STAY

$$ ✕ **The Bards Den.** Many visitors to Connemara share a memory of the IRISH Den's huge stove, where weary travelers have dried their soaking clothes and warmed frozen hands while sipping restorative glasses of stout. While the low-ceilinged, warrenlike pub has long served food—and great traditional Irish music at night, it now has a restaurant with blackboard menu. The food is described as "fresh, local, and Irish," including smoked salmon, Connemara lamb stew, and prime Irish beef T-bone steaks. ✉ *Main St.* ☎ *095/41042* ⊕ *www.bardsden.com* 🖃 *MC, V.*

$ 🔳 **Renvyle House.** A lake at its front door, the Atlantic Ocean at its
★ back door, and the mountains of Connemara as a backdrop form the

Few landscapes are as quintessentially Irish as the ravishing and rugged ones found in Connemara National Park.

enthralling setting for this hotel 8 km (5 mi) north of Letterfrack. Once the retreat of that noted Irish man of letters Oliver St. John Gogarty of Dublin (on whom James Joyce modeled Buck Mulligan in *Ulysses*), Renvyle is rustic and informal; it has exposed beams and brickwork, and numerous open turf fires. The main salon, called the Long Room, is one of the most eminently civilized rooms in Ireland—all tranquil beige, endless chairs, and pretty pictures. The comfortable guest rooms, plainly decorated in an uncluttered style, in shades of beige and cream, all have breathtaking views. **Pros:** amazing views; secluded end-of-the-world location; recommended for artists and photographers; cheerful, unpretentious version of the country-house hotel experience. **Cons:** driving distance to anywhere else; bar and restaurant very busy at peak times. ⊠ *Renvyle, Co. Galway* ☎ *095/43511* ⊕ *www.renvyle.com* ⤳ *68 rooms* ⌂ *In-room: no a/c. In-hotel: restaurant, bar, golf course, tennis courts, pool, Wi-Fi hotspot* ➾ *AE, DC, MC, V* ⊙ *Closed Dec. 1–24 and Jan. 7–mid-Feb.* ⫿⊙⫿ *BP.*

$$$ **Rosleague Manor.** This pink, creeper-clad, two-story Georgian house
★ occupies 30 lovely acres and has an eye-knocking view: a gorgeous lawn backdropped by Ballinakill Bay and the dreamy mountains of Connemara. Inside, the grandfather clock in the hall flanked by framed family portraits and hunting prints sets the informal, country-house tone. The Conservatory Bar is an elegant, light-filled spot with rattan bucket chairs and octagonal marble and cast-iron tables, while the drawing room is decorated in low-key shades. Well-used antiques, four-poster or large brass bedsteads, and sumptuous drapes decorate the solidly comfortable and impeccably kept bedrooms. The best rooms are at the

front on the first floor, overlooking the bay. At dinner in the superb restaurant, baked monkfish with crispy capers and balsamic vinegar is one of the tastiest entrées. **Pros:** quiet and elegant; mesmerizing views; excellent restaurant. **Cons:** can be very quiet off-season. ⊠ *Rosleague Bay, Co. Galway* ☎ *095/41101* ⊕ *www.rosleague.com* ⤙ *20 rooms* ⚒ *In-room: no a/c, Wi-Fi. In-hotel: restaurant, bar, tennis court* ⊟ *AE, MC, V* ⊙ *Closed mid-Nov.–mid-Mar.* ⵏ⃝*BP.*

NIGHTLIFE

For traditional music, the best option in this region is the **Bards Den** (⊠ *Main St.* ☎ *095/41042* ⊕ *www.bardsden.com*).

SHOPPING

Connemara Handcrafts (⊠ *N59, village center* ☎ *095/41058*) carries an extensive selection of crafts and women's fashions made by the stellar Avoca Handweavers; there's also a quaint coffee shop.

KYLEMORE VALLEY

Runs for 6½ km (4 mi) between Letterfrack and intersection of N59 and R344.

One of the more conventionally beautiful stretches of road in Connemara passes through Kylemore Valley, which is between the Twelve Bens to the south and the naturally forested Dorruagh Mountains to the north. Kylemore (the name is derived from *Coill Mór,* Irish for "big wood") looks "as though some colossal giant had slashed it out with a couple of strokes from his mammoth sword," as artist and author John FitzMaurice Mills has written.

Fodor's Choice ★ **Kylemore Abbey,** one of the most photographed castles in all of Ireland, is visible across a reedy lake with a backdrop of wooded hillside. The vast Gothic Revival, turreted, gray-stone castle was built as a private home between 1861 and 1868 by Mitchell Henry, a member of parliament for County Galway, and his wife, Margaret, who had fallen in love with the spot during a carriage ride while on their honeymoon. The Henrys spared no expense—the final bill for their house is said to have come to 1.5 million—and employed mostly local laborers, thereby abetting the famine relief effort (this area was among the worst hit in all of Ireland). Adjacent to the house is a spectacular neo-Gothic chapel, which, sadly, became the burial place for Margaret, who died after contracting "Nile fever" on a trip to Egypt. In 1920, nuns from the Irish Abbey of the Nuns of St. Benedict, who fled their abbey in Belgium during World War I, eventually sought refuge in Kylemore, which had gone through a number of owners and decades of decline after the Henrys died. Still in residence, the Benedictine nuns run a girls' boarding school here. Three reception rooms and the main hall are open to the public, as are a crafts center and cafeteria. There's also a 6-acre walled Victorian garden; a shuttle bus from the abbey to the garden departs every 15 minutes during opening hours. An exhibition and video explaining the history of the house can be viewed year-round at the abbey, and the grounds are freely accessible most of the year. Ask at the excellent crafts shop for directions to the **Gothic Chapel** (a five-minute walk from the abbey), a tiny replica of Norwich Cathedral built by the Henrys. ✉ *About ¾ km (½ mi) back from Kylemore Valley Rd.* ☎ *095/41146* ⊕ *www.kylemoreabbey.com* 🖾 *€12, including shuttle bus to garden* ☺ *Mar.–Oct., daily 10–7; Nov.–Feb., daily 10–4:30.*

Fodor's Choice
★

Beyond Kylemore, N59 travels for some miles along **Killary Harbour,** a narrow fjord (the only one in Ireland) that runs for 16 km (10 mi) between County Mayo's Mweelrea Mountain to the north and County Galway's Maamturk Mountains to the south. The dark, deep water of the fjord reflects the magnificent steep-sided hills that border it, creating a haunting scene of natural grandeur. The harbor has an extremely safe anchorage, 13 fathoms (78 feet) deep for almost its entire length, and is sheltered from storms by mountain walls. The rafts floating in Killary Harbour belong to fish-farming consortia that raise salmon and trout in cages beneath the water. This is a matter of some controversy all over the West. Although some people welcome the employment opportunities, others bemoan the visual blight of the rafts. For cruises around the harbor, see Killary Cruises listed under Leenane, below.

LEENANE

18 km (11 mi) east of Letterfrack on N59.

Nestled idyllically at the foot of the Maamturk Mountains and overlooking the tranquil waters of Killary Harbour, Leenane is a tiny village noted for its role as the setting for the film *The Field,* which starred Richard Harris.

GETTING HERE

BUS TRAVEL
Leenane has at least one Bus Éireann bus a day, traveling to Galway via Clifden, taking about 1 hour 15 minutes to Clifden, and another 2 hours to Galway (€17). In summer there is also a bus once a day to Westport, a 45-minute journey costing €7 one-way.

TOURS
Take a 90-minute trip around Killary Harbour in an enclosed Killary Cruises catamaran launch with seating for 150 passengers, bar, and restaurant.

ESSENTIALS

Transportation Contacts Killary Cruises (✉ *Nancy's Point, 2 km [1 mi] west of Leenane on N59 [Clifden Rd.]* ☎ *091/566–736* ⊕ *www.killarycruises.com*).

EXPLORING

The **Sheep and Wool Centre,** in the center of Leenane, focuses on the traditional industry of North Connemara and West Mayo. Several breeds of sheep graze around the house, and there are demonstrations of carding, spinning, weaving, and the dyeing of wool with natural plant dyes. ☎ *095/42323* ⊕ *www.sheepandwoolcentre.com* 🖾 *€3* ☺ *Apr.–June, Sept., and Oct., daily 9:30–7; July and Aug., daily 9–7.*

EN
ROUTE

You have two options for traveling onward to Westport. The first is to take the direct route on N59. The second is to detour through the **Doolough Valley** between the Mweelrea Mountains (to the west) and the Sheeffry Hills (to the east) and on to Westport via Louisburgh (on the southern shore of Clew Bay). The latter route adds about 24 km (15 mi) to the trip, but devotees of this part of the West claim that it

will take you through the region's most impressive, unspoiled stretch of scenery. If you opt for the longer route, turn left onto R335 1½ km (1 mi) beyond Leenane. Just after this turn, you can hear the powerful rush of the Aasleagh Falls. You can park over the bridge, stroll along the river's shore, and soak in the splendor of the surrounding mountains.

Look out as you travel north for the great bulk of 2,500-foot-high **Croagh Patrick**; its size and conical shape make it one of the West's most distinctive landmarks. On

clear days a small white building is visible at its summit (it stands on a ½-acre plateau), as is the wide path that ascends to it. The latter is the Pilgrim's Path. Each year about 25,000 people, many of them barefoot, follow the path to pray to St. Patrick in the oratory on its peak. St. Patrick spent the 40 days and nights of Lent here in 441, during the period in which he was converting Ireland to Christianity. The traditional date for the pilgrimage is the last Sunday in July; in the past, the walk was made at night, with pilgrims carrying burning torches, but that practice has been discontinued. The climb involves a gentle uphill slope, but you need to be fit and agile to complete the last half hour, over scree (small loose rocks with no trail). This is why most climbers carry a stick or staff (traditionally made of ash, and called an ash plant), which helps you to stop sliding backward. These can sometimes be bought in the parking area. The hike can be made in about three hours (round-trip) on any fine day and is well worth the effort for the magnificent views of the islands of Clew Bay, the Sheeffry Hills to the south (with the Bens visible behind them), and the peaks of Mayo to the north. The climb starts at Murrisk, a village about 8 km (5 mi) before Westport on the R335 Louisburgh road.

COUNTY MAYO

County Mayo has long empty roads that stretch along for miles. The Museum of Country Life, the only branch of the National Museum outside Dublin, commemorates a disappearing way of life, and is fittingly located here in Torlough. Castlebar has been overshadowed by its neighbor Westport, which boasts an elegantly laid-out 18th-century town and quays on the shore of island-studded Clew Bay, under the towering conical peak of St Patrick's holy mountain, Croagh Patrick. Not only does Westport have scenery, it also has some excellent hotels and bars, some a legacy of the boom years that brought metropolitan chic to the heart of the west.

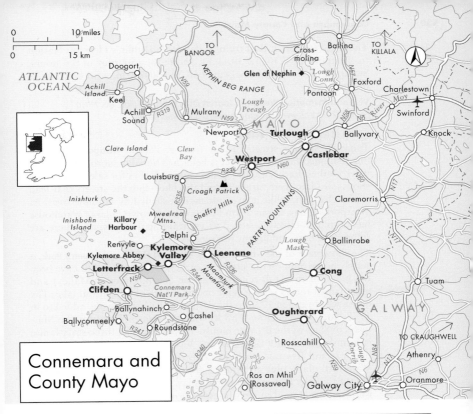

WESTPORT

★ *32 km (20 mi) north of Leenane on R335.*

By far the most attractive town in County Mayo, Westport is on an inlet of Clew Bay, a wide expanse of sea dotted with islands and framed by mountain ranges. It's one of the most gentrified and Anglo-Irish heritage towns in Ireland, its Georgian origins clearly defined by the broad streets skirting the gently flowing river and, particularly, by the lime-fringed central avenue called the Mall. Built as an O'Malley stronghold, the entire town received a face-lift when the Brownes, who had come from Sussex in the reign of Elizabeth I, constructed Westport House and much of the modern town, which was laid out by architect James Wyatt when he was employed to finish the grand estate of Westport House.

GETTING HERE

BUS TRAVEL   There are four Bus Éireann buses daily from Westport (the Octagon monument) to Galway, traveling on the non-scenic N17 via Claremorris. The express takes 1 hour 50 minutes, while the non-express bus takes over 2 hours. Both cost about €17 one-way. There are three buses a day direct from Westport to Ballina, a journey of about an hour (€12.70 one-way, €17 round-trip). There is no bus station in Westport.

There are four Irish Rail trains a day from Dublin's Heuston Station to Westport, at 7:50, 12:30, 3:30, and 6:30, a journey of 3½ hours. Standard fares are €35 one-way, €48.50 round-trip, with better rates online.

Visitor Information Westport Tourist Office (✉ *The Mall, Co. Mayo* ☎ *098/25711* ⊕ *www.westporttourism.com/index.html*).

EXPLORING

Today Westport's streets radiate from its central **Octagon,** where an old-fashioned farmers' market is held on Thursday morning; look for work clothes, harnesses, tools, and children's toys for sale. Traditional shops—ironmongers, drapers, and the like—line the streets that lead to the Octagon, while a riverside mall is shaded by tall lime trees. At Westport's Quay, about 2 km (1 mi) outside town, a large warehouse has been attractively restored as vacation apartments, and there are some good bars and decent restaurants.

The showpiece of the town remains **Westport House and Country Park,** a stately home built on the site of an earlier castle (believed to have been the home of the 16th-century warrior queen, Grace O'Malley) and most famed for its setting right on the shores of a beautiful lake. The house was begun in 1730 to the designs of Richard Castle, added to in 1778, and completed in 1788 by architect James Wyatt for the Marquess of Sligo of the Browne family. The rectangular, three-story house is furnished with late-Georgian and Victorian pieces. Family portraits by Opie and Reynolds, a huge collection of old Irish silver and old Waterford glass, plus an opulent group of paintings—including *The Holy Family* by Rubens—are on display. A word of caution: Westport isn't your usual staid country house. The old dungeons now house video games and the grounds have given way to a small amusement park for children and a children's zoo. In fact, the lake is now littered with swan-shaped "pedaloes," boats that may be fun for families but help destroy the perfect Georgian grace of the setting. If these elements don't sound like a draw, arrive early when it's less likely to be busy. The Farmyard area has garden-plant sales, an indoor soft-play area, a gift shop, and a coffee shop. ✉ *Off N59, south of Westport turnoff, clearly signposted from Octagon* ☎ *098/25430* ⊕ *www.westporthouse.ie* 🎫 *House €12, attractions €22, family day-ticket for house and attractions €75* ☉ *House, gardens, and attractions, Apr.–Sept., daily 11:30–5:30.*

Clew Bay is said to have 365 islands, one for every day of the year. The biggest and most interesting to visit is **Clare Island,** at the mouth of the bay. In fine weather the rocky, hilly island, which is 8 km (5 mi) long and 5 km (3 mi) wide, affords beautiful views south toward Connemara, east across Clew Bay, and north to Achill Island. About 150 people live on the island today, but before the 1845–47 famine it had a population of about 1,700. A 15th-century tower overlooking the harbor was once the stronghold of Granuaile, the pirate queen, who ruled the area until her death in 1603. She is buried on the island, in its 12th-century Cistercian abbey. Today most visitors seek out the island for its unusual peace and quiet, golden beaches, and unspoiled landscape. A Singles Weekend (over 30s) held annually on the second weekend in June has proved a great success (⊕ *www.irelandsislands.com*). Ferries depart from Roonagh Pier, near Louisburgh, a scenic 19-km (12-mi) drive from Westport on R335 past several long sandy beaches. The crossing takes about 15 minutes. Dolphins often accompany the boats on the trip, and there are large populations of seals under the island's cliffs. Bird-watchers, hikers, cyclists, and sea anglers may want to stay for longer than a day trip; inquire at the Westport TIO or call the **Clare Island Development Office** (☎ *098/25087*) or go to ⊕ *www.clare-island.org* for information about accommodations on the island. ☎ *098/25045 O'Malley's Ferries, 098/25212 Pirate Queen boat* ☏ *Ferry €15 round-trip* ⊙ *May–mid-Sept., sailings usually twice daily, weather permitting.*

WHERE TO EAT AND STAY

$$$
SEAFOOD ✕ **The Tavern Bar and Restaurant.** An outing to this traditional pub in the tiny village of Murrisk—at the foot of Croagh Patrick, just across the road from the seashore—is a popular excursion from Westport. Its distinctive, fuchsia-pink facade leads into a simple, family-run tavern where the emphasis is firmly on food. Carefully sourced local produce including Clew Bay seafood, Connemara lamb, and farmhouse cheese from the nearby village of Carrowholly are served in hearty portions. Connemara lamb sausages with spring-onion mash, or the house-special beef braised in Guinness with carrots, onions, and parsnips are two winners. Fishermen arrive regularly with freshly landed langoustine, which are then poached and served in garlic butter. Upstairs is the more formal restaurant, with a quieter, candlelit atmosphere, and more elaborate cooking: warm scallops and smoked bacon salad, followed perhaps by pan-roasted medallion of monkfish with a light thyme mousse. The fillet steaks are also renowned. ⊠ *Murrisk, 5 km (3 mi) from Westport* ☎ *098/64060* ⊟ *AE, MC, V* ⊙ *Closed Mon.–Thurs. in Nov. and Jan.–mid-Mar., but call to confirm.*

$ ⛫ **Clew Bay.** Set in Westport's town center, this hotel welcomes guests with a warmly traditional wooden facade. Once inside, however, a contemporary glass-roofed lobby comprises the centerpiece of a stylish modern interior decorated with original art works. The current owners' parents opened the hotel in 1959, and it has been a well-loved Westport institution ever since. The Riverside Restaurant offers formal dining, while Madden's Bistro is a popular value-for-money eatery, with a busy local trade. Guest rooms are strikingly decorated with cherrywood headboards backed by striking patterned fabrics. The back rooms are the quietest and have views of parkland and the river. Residents have free use of the nearby public pool and reception can arrange special rates for Westport House: ask when booking. **Pros:** central location; friendly owner-managers; good value. **Cons:** risk of late-night noise in front rooms; no private parking; bathrooms a bit old-fashioned. ⊠ *James St., Co. Mayo* ☎ *098/28088* ⊕ *www. www.clewbayhotel.com* ⛱ *40 rooms* ⬦ *In-room: no a/c. In-hotel: 2 restaurants, bar, Internet terminal* ⊟ *MC, V.*

$$$ ⛫ **Westport Plaza Hotel.** Walk in off the street of this small Irish town, past topiary balls in square wicker holders, to the vast marble lobby with its double-sided gas fire, some 16 giant sofas, and New Age mood music, and you could be in the heart of metropolitan anywhere. A product of Ireland's economic boom, this swish and stylish boutique hotel may not be what you've come to the West of Ireland to experience, but here it is: enjoy! It's part of a large new complex in the town center, and shares leisure facilities with its more traditional sister hotel, the Castlecourt. The best bedrooms overlook a Zen-like inner roof garden, while others have balconies overlooking the fountain and ground-floor courtyard. Guest rooms are huge, with large, veneered Art Deco–style furniture; bathrooms have Jacuzzi baths and walk-in showers. **Pros:** all the creature comforts; best of modern design; quiet and central. **Cons:** avoid few bedrooms with street views; you might forget you're in Ireland. ⊠ *Castlebar St., Co. Mayo* ☎ *098/51166* ⊕ *www. westportplazahotel.ie* ⚲ *85 rooms, 3 suites* ⌂ *In-room: a/c, safe, refrigerator, Internet. In-hotel: restaurant, bar, pool, gym, spa, Wi-Fi hotspot* ⊟ *AE, DC, MC, V.*

NIGHTLIFE

In Westport's town center try **Matt Molloy's** (⊠ *Bridge St.* ☎ *098/26655*) ; Matt Malloy is not only the owner but also a member of the musical group the Chieftains. Traditional music is, naturally, the main attraction. A good spot to try for traditional music and good pub grub is the **Towers Pub and Restaurant** (⊠ *The Quay* ☎ *098/26534*). In summer there are outdoor tables set up here beside the bay.

SPORTS AND THE OUTDOORS

BICYCLING   Enjoy the spectacular scenery of Clew Bay at a leisurely pace on a rented bike from **J. P. Breheny & Sons** (⊠ *Castlebar St.* ☎ *098/25020*).

GOLF   The Fred Hawtree–designed **Westport Golf Club** (⊠ *Carrowholly* ☎ *098/28262*), beneath Croagh Patrick, overlooks Clew Bay. The 18-hole course has twice been the venue for the Irish Amateur Championship.

SHOPPING

Carraig Donn (⊠ *Bridge St.* ☎ *098/26287*) carries its own line of knitwear and a good selection of crystal, jewelry, and ceramics. **Hewetson Bros** (⊠ *Bridge St.* ☎ *098/26018*) is an old-fashioned fishing tackle shop that also stocks gear for surfing, climbing, and hiking. **McCormack's** (⊠ *Bridge St.* ☎ *098/25619*) has a traditional butcher shop downstairs, but upstairs it's an attractive gallery and café with work by local artists for sale. **O'Reilly/Turpin** (⊠ *Bridge St.* ☎ *098/28151*) sells the best of contemporary Irish design in knitwear, ceramics, and other decorative items. **Thomas Moran's** (⊠ *Bridge St.* ☎ *098/25562*) stocks locally made blackthorn sticks, bargain umbrellas, and some offbeat souvenirs. **Treasure Trove** (⊠ *Bridge St.* ☎ *098/25118*) has a good stock of antiques and curios, including linen and local memorabilia.

CASTLEBAR

18 km (11 mi) east of Westport on N5.

The administrative capital of Mayo, Castlebar is a tidy little town with an attractive, tree-bordered green. Hatred of landlords ran high in the area, due to the ruthless, battering-ram evictions ordered by the Earl of Lucan during the mid-19th-century famine. The disappearance in the 1960s of his high-living successor, the seventh earl, after the violent death in London of his children's nanny, is said to have given the few tenants who remain a perfect pretext for withholding their rents.

In 1879 Michael Davitt founded the Land League, which fought for land reform, in the **Imperial Hotel** (⊠ *The Green* ☎ *094/902–1961*). It's worth a visit to take in the splendor of the decor in the Gothic-style dining room, which was used for many historic meetings in the 19th century.

At the **Linen Hall Arts Centre** (⊠ *Linenhall St.* ☎ *094/902–3733* ⊕ *www. thelinenhall.com*), exhibitions and performances are often scheduled.

TURLOUGH

24 km (15 mi) east of Castlebar on N5.

Before the opening of the Museum of Country Life, Turlough was chiefly visited for its round tower (freely accessible), which marks the site of an early monastery, traditionally associated with St. Patrick, and the nearby ruins of a 17th-century church. Nowadays, it's one of many Irish villages whose empty streets bear witness to dramatic changes in the rural way of life. Once a thriving hub, with a village school, two pubs, and a busy shop, Turlough now has a population of about 300, one pub with a small shop attached, and no school. Rather than working on the land, most of the locals commute to jobs in nearby Castlebar.

GETTING HERE

BUS TRAVEL Bus Éireann buses from Westport to Ballina via Castlebar will stop at the Museum of Country Life on request (ask the driver as you board). There are at least three buses a day, with a fare of about €12 round-trip; confirm times by ringing the Ballina Bus Station.

EXPLORING

Fodor's Choice ★ To understand the forces that have led to such dramatic changes in Turlough, pay a visit to the **Museum of Country Life**, which focuses on rural Ireland between 1860 and 1960—a way of life that remained unchanged for many years, then suddenly came to an end within living memory. At this highly acclaimed museum, the only branch of the National Museum of Ireland outside Dublin, you're invited to imagine yourself back in a vanished world, before the internal combustion engine, rural electrification, indoor plumbing, television, and increased education transformed people's lives and expectations. For many, this is a journey into a strange place, where water had to be carried from a well, turf had to be brought home from the bog, fires had to be lighted daily for heat and cooking, and clothes had to be made painstakingly by hand in the long winter evenings. Among the displayed items are authentic furniture and utensils; hunting, fishing, and agricultural implements; clothing; and objects relating to games, pastimes, religion, and education.

The museum experience starts in Turlough Park House, built in the High Victorian Gothic style in 1865 and set in pretty lakeside gardens. Just three rooms have been restored to illustrate the way the landowners lived. A sensational modern four-story, curved building houses the

9

main exhibit. Cleverly placed windows afford panoramic views of the surrounding park and the distant round tower, allowing you to reflect on the reality beyond the museum's walls. Temporary exhibitions, such as one called "Romanticism and Reality," help illustrate the divide between the dreamy image of old rural life and its actual hardships. The shop sells museum-branded and handcrafted gift items as well as a good selection of books on related topics. A café with indoor and outdoor tables is in the stable yard, and you can take scenic lakeside walks in the park. Crafts demonstrations and workshops take place on Wednesday and Sunday afternoons. ⊠ *Turlough Park on the N4 (7 km [4 mi] east of Castlebar)* ☎ *094/903–1755* ⊕ *www.museum.ie* ✉ *Free* ⊙ *Tues.–Sat. 10–5, Sun. 2–5.*

The Northwest

INCLUDING COUNTIES DONEGAL,
LEITRIM, AND SLIGO

WORD OF MOUTH

"Walking is always uphill both ways—the parking lot is on the top
of one hill and whatever you want to see is three miles over on the
next hill. Really, an 'Irish' 5-minute walk translates to an 'American'
20 and if there is a way to add steps they've added them. Like a
carrot at the end of a stick we took to chanting 'Guinness and a
nap' over and over as we climbed our way through Ireland!"
—12perfectdays

WELCOME TO THE NORTHWEST

TOP REASONS TO GO

★ **Gaeltacht Country:** Venture to the seaside village of Ard an Ratha to listen to the seductive rhythms of locals conversing in full Irish (Gaelic) flight. Don't worry: everyone has English at the ready for lost visitors.

★ **The Yeats Trail:** From Sligo Town's museums head out to the majestic Ben Bulben peak to follow in the footsteps of the famous brother duo, W. B. Yeats, the great poet, and Jack B. Yeats, one of Ireland's finest 20th-century painters.

★ **Garbo's Castle:** The legendary screen actress was just one of the many notables who enjoyed a stay at Glenveagh Castle.

★ **Hiking the Slieve League cliffs:** To truly humble yourself before ocean, cliff, and sky, hike these fabled headlands, the highest sea cliffs in Europe. The views will set your heart racing and the Atlantic sea winds are sure to blow away the cobwebs.

1 Yeats Country. What the poet William Butler Yeats would say about his native Sligo Town—a once picturesque spot now overrun with modern shopping malls—can only be imagined, but it makes a great jumping-off point for exploring Yeats Country: the lake isle at Innisfree, the cairn-crowned Knocknarea (a peak often painted by brother Jack), and Drumcliff, where W. B. lies buried under the shadow of Ben Bulben.

2 Around Donegal Bay. Donegal Town, with its fine medieval castle and abbey, is the gateway to County Donegal, regarded by many as the runner-up to Kerry as Ireland's most scenic region. This is the ever-shrinking heart of the Donegal Gaeltacht (Irish-speaking region), where the moody hamlet of Gleann Cholm Cille and the majestic Slieve League Mountains beckon, as does the Belleek china of Ballyshannon.

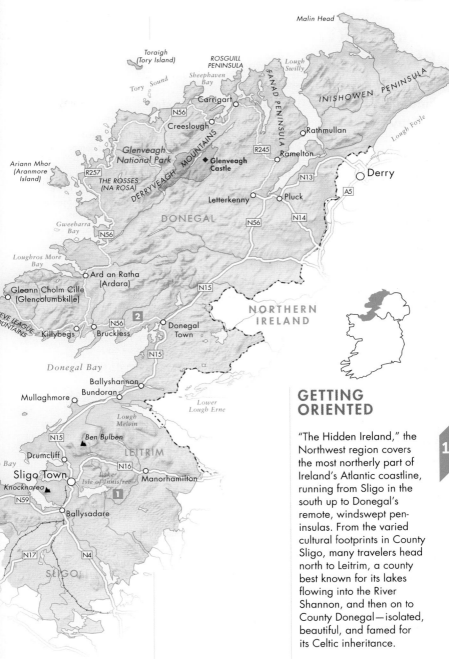

Malin Head

Toraigh
(Tory Island)

ROSGUILL
PENINSULA

Lough
Swilly

Sheephaven
Bay

Tory Sound

INISHOWEN PENINSULA

Carrigart

N56

Creeslough

FANAD PENINSULA

Lough Foyle

Rathmullan

Glenveagh
National Park

DERRYVEAGH MOUNTAINS

R245

Ramelton

Ariann Mhor
(Aranmore
Island)

R257

THE ROSSES
(NA ROSA)

◆ Glenveagh
Castle

N13

Derry

Letterkenny

Pluck

A5

DONEGAL

N56

N14

Gweebarra
Bay

N56

Loughros More
Bay

Ard an Ratha
(Ardara)

N15

Gleann Cholm Cille
(Glencolumbkille)

NORTHERN
IRELAND

SLIEVE LEAGUE
MOUNTAINS

N56

2

Killybegs

Bruckless

Donegal
Town

N15

Donegal Bay

Ballyshannon

Mullaghmore

Bundoran

Lower
Lough Erne

Lough
Melvin

N15

Ben Bulben

LEITRIM

Drumcliff

N16

Lake
Isle of Innisfree

Manorhamilton

Sligo Town

Knocknarea

1

N59

Ballysadare

N17

N4

SLIGO

GETTING
ORIENTED

10

"The Hidden Ireland," the Northwest region covers the most northerly part of Ireland's Atlantic coastline, running from Sligo in the south up to Donegal's remote, windswept peninsulas. From the varied cultural footprints in County Sligo, many travelers head north to Leitrim, a county best known for its lakes flowing into the River Shannon, and then on to County Donegal—isolated, beautiful, and famed for its Celtic inheritance.

THE NORTHWEST PLANNER

Finding a Place to Stay

True, it's the farthest-flung corner of Ireland, but thanks to the area's popularity, good bed-and-breakfasts and small hotels are abundant.

In the two major towns—Sligo Town and Donegal Town—and the small coastal resorts in between, many traditional provincial hotels have been modernized (albeit not always elegantly). Yet most manage to retain some of the charm that comes with older buildings and personalized service.

Away from these areas, your best overnight choice is usually a modest guesthouse that includes bed, breakfast, and an evening meal, though you can also find first-class country-house hotels with a gracious professionalism found elsewhere in Ireland.

Consider staying in an Irish-speaking home to get to know members of the area's Gaeltacht population; the local Tourist Information Office (TIO) can be helpful in making a booking with an Irish-speaking family.

Assume that all hotel rooms reviewed *in this chapter* have in-room phones, TVs, and private bathrooms unless otherwise noted.

Transportation Basics

Getting around by bus is easy enough if you plan to visit only the larger towns. Ireland's principal bus company is Bus Éireann.

The routes are regular and reliable and you'll find route planners and schedules on ⊕ *www.buseireann.ie*. There are also several privately run local bus companies operating in the northwest, including McGeehan Coaches.

As for train travel, Sligo Town is the northernmost direct rail link to Dublin. From Dublin, eight trains a day make the three-hour-and-five-minute journey (prices vary and can be higher on weekends, but it's cheaper booking online).

If you want to get to Sligo Town by rail from other provincial towns, you're forced to make some inconvenient connections and take roundabout routes. Sadly, the rest of the region has no railway service.

In all honesty, there is only one way to fully explore the rural Northwest of Ireland and that's by car.

Once here, you can always rent a car at Ireland West Airport Knock or Sligo Town.

But if coming from Dublin, many opt to rent from one of the bigger companies at the larger airports.

If arriving from Northern Ireland, there are rental agencies aplenty in Derry or Belfast, but be sure to tell your agency if you are planning to cross the border.

Cars are invariably compact—no SUVs—and stick shift is the norm (you will have to specially request an automatic).

The roads between the larger towns are fairly well maintained and signposted, but go slightly off the beaten track and conditions can vary from bad to dirt track.

As long as you're not in a mad rush, this can add to the delight of your journey.

This is rural Ireland and if the scenery doesn't make this blissfully clear, then the suspension on your rented car certainly will!

Do You Read Irish?

County Donegal was part of the ancient kingdom of Ulster not conquered by the English until the 17th century.

When the English withdrew in the 1920s, they had still not eradicated rural Donegal's Celtic inheritance.

It thus shouldn't come as a surprise that it contains Ireland's largest Gaeltacht (Irish-speaking) area.

Driving in this part of the country, you may either be frustrated or amused when you come to a crossroads whose signposts show only the Irish place-names, often so unlike the English versions as to be completely incomprehensible.

To make things more confusing, some shop and hotel owners have opted to go with the English, not Irish, variant for their establishment's name.

All is not lost, however, as maps generally give both the Irish and English names.

And locals are usually more than happy to help out with directions (in English)—often with a colorful yarn thrown in.

Tour Options

Bus Éireann has budget-price, guided, one-day bus tours of the Donegal Highlands and to Glenveagh National Park; they start from Bundoran, Sligo Town, Ballyshannon, and Donegal Town.

For a friendly, relaxed minibus tour of the area in July and August, call John Houze. He's a knowledgeable guide who leads popular tours to the Lake Isle of Innisfree, the Holy Well, and Parke's Castle; and north of Sligo Town to W. B. Yeats's grave and Glencar Lake and waterfall.

Bus Tours Bus Éireann (☏ *01/836–6111* ⊕ *www. buseireann.ie*). **John Houze** (☏ *071/914–2747*).

DINING AND LODGING PRICE CATEGORIES (IN EUROS)					
	¢	$	$$	$$$	$$$$
Restaurants	Under €12	€12–€18	€19–€24	€25–€32	over €32
Hotels	under €80	€80–€120	€121–€170	€171–€210	over €210

Restaurant prices are for a main course at dinner. Hotel prices are for a standard double room in high season.

When to Go

When it rains, it really pours. Forget about the winter months, when inclement weather and a heavy fog swing in from the Atlantic and settle in until spring, masking much of the beautiful scenery. But in all seasons remember to pack a warm and waterproof coat (especially if you're headed to the coast) and bring a good pair of walking shoes.

It's not all doom and gloom: the weather can be glorious in the summer months—just don't bet your house on it.

Féiles and Festivals

In the Northwest, each village tends to have its own *féile* (festival) during the summer months and it's often worth making the effort to attend. Music festivals are tops, from the traditional Irish Sligo Feis Ceoil in mid-April to the country-and-western Bundoran Music Festival in June, and the jazz and blues weekend féile in Gortahork, Donegal County, in April.

But being an Irish-speaking stronghold, the emphasis is on Irish traditional music. Every summer weekend you are guaranteed a bit of *craic* (fun) with lively sessions in most pubs. Sligo Town, Ard an Ratha (Ardara), and Letterkenny are all hot spots. There are village festivals dedicated to hill-walking, fishing, poetry, art, and food.

10

GETTING AROUND

Train Travel

Sligo Town is the northernmost direct rail link to Dublin. From Dublin, eight trains a day make the journey (3 hours and 5 minutes) for €27 one-way, €32 round-trip (prices are a bit higher on weekends but cheaper if you book online).

If you want to get to Sligo Town by rail from other provincial towns, you must make some inconvenient connections and take roundabout routes. The rest of the region has no railway service.

Train Information Irish Rail (☎ 01/836–6222, 071/916– 9888 Sligo train station ⊕ www.irishrail.ie).

HITCH A RIDE?

Normally, we would say a hearty "No." But in a region of such limited train and practically no bus service, there's no denying that the Northwest can be a very hard region to navigate.

As it turns out, a lot of the locals go in for hitching. Even if you get stuck in what seems like the middle of nowhere, odds are some farmer with a thick accent with eventually offer you a lift to the next pub. Of course, be sure to be street-smart (or should we say, village-smart) about any offers.

Bus Travel

Bus Éireann can get you from Dublin to Sligo Town in four hours for €19 one-way and round-trip. Seven buses a day from Dublin are available. Another bus route, six times a day from Dublin (five on Sunday), goes to Letterkenny, in the heart of County Donegal, in 4¼ hours, via a short trip across the Northern Ireland border; it's €18 one-way, €20 round-trip. Other Bus Éireann services connect Sligo to towns all over Ireland. From Sligo Town, you can reach almost any point in the region for less than €18.

Bus Éireann helpfully offers a flexible Open Road bus passes ideally suited for travelers in the Northwest. A three-day pass costs €54 and each additional day's travel is €15. You can go anywhere in the republic on the nationwide network of services with this pass but it is not valid across the border in Northern Ireland.

Bus Information Bus Éireann (☎ 01/836–6111 in Dublin, 071/916–0066 in Sligo, 074/912–1309 in Letterkenny ⊕ www.buseireann.ie). **Feda O'Donnell Coaches** (☎ 074/954–8114 ⊕ www.fedaodonnell.com). **Lough Swilly Bus Company** (☎ 074/912–2873 ⊕ loughswillybusco.com). **McGeehan Coaches** (☎ 074/954–6150 ⊕ www.mcgeehancoaches.com). **North West Busways** (☎ 074/938–2619 ⊕ www.foylecoaches.com).

Car Travel

Sligo, the largest town in Northwest Ireland, is relatively accessible on the main routes. The N4 travels the 224 km (140 mi) directly from Dublin to Sligo. Allow at least four hours for this journey.

The N15 continues from Sligo Town to Donegal Town and proceeds from Donegal Town to Derry City, just over the border in Northern Ireland. The fastest approach for anyone driving up from the west and the southwest is on N17, connecting Sligo to Galway, though the landscape is undistinguished. For more on car travel, see Transportation Basics.

Air Travel

The principal international air-arrival point to Northwest Ireland is Ireland West Airport Knock, 55 km (34 mi) south of Sligo Town.

City of Derry Airport, a few miles over the border, receives flights from Manchester and Glasgow. City of Derry (also called Eglinton) is a particularly convenient airport for reaching northern County Donegal. Donegal Airport, in Carrickfinn, typically receives flights from Dublin. Sligo Airport at Strandhill, 8 km (5 mi) west of Sligo Town, is the other area airport.

Aer Arann has flights from Ireland West Airport Knock daily to Dublin. It also flies twice daily between Sligo and Dublin. BmiBaby flies from Knock to Manchester daily and to Birmingham six days a week. Ryanair has daily flights to Ireland West Airport Knock from London Stansted and London Gatwick, and also serves City of Derry Airport daily from London and Dublin. British Airways flies to City of Derry Airport from Glasgow and Dublin.

Airport Information City of Derry Airport (☎ 028/7181–0784 ⊕ www.derryairport.com). **Donegal Airport** (☎ 074/954–8232 ⊕ www.donegalairport.ie). **Ireland West Airport Knock** (☎ 094/936–7222 ⊕ www. irelandwestairport.com). **Sligo Airport** (☎ 071/916–8280 or 071/916–8318 ⊕ www.sligoairport.com).

Carriers Aer Arann (☎ 091/541–900 or 0870/876–7676 ⊕ www.aerarann.com). **British Airways City Express** (☎ 0844/493–0787 ⊕ www.britishairways.com). **BmiBaby** (☎ 0844/848–4888 ⊕ www.bmibaby.com). **Ryanair** (☎ 0818/830–3030 or 0871/246–000 ⊕ www.ryanair.com).

Airport Transfers

If you aren't driving, Ireland West Airport Knock becomes less attractive; there are no easy public transportation links, except the once-a-day (in season) local bus to Charlestown, 11 km (7 mi) away. Nor can you rely on catching a bus at the smaller airports, except at Sligo Airport, where buses run from Sligo Town to meet all flights.

You can get taxis—both cars and minibuses—right outside Ireland West Airport Knock. The average rate is around €1.50 per kilometer. If you're not flying into Knock, you may have to phone a taxi company. Phone numbers of taxi companies are available from airport information desks and are also displayed beside pay phones.

Visitor Information

The Tourist Information Office (TIO) in Sligo Town provides a walking map of Sligo, information about bus tours of Yeats Country as well as Yeats Trail leaflets, and details of boat tours of Lough Gill. It's also the main visitor information center for Northwest Ireland. Open hours are September to mid-March, weekdays 9–5; mid-March to August, weekdays 9–6, Saturday 10–4, and Sunday 11–3. If you're traveling in County Donegal in the north, try the TIO at Letterkenny, about 1½ km (1 mi) south of town. It's open September to May, weekdays 9–5; June to August, Monday–Saturday 9–6 and Sunday noon–3. The office at Bundoran is open only in summer (usually the first week in June to the second week in September). Important tourist offices are listed under the main towns in this chapter.

Road Conditions

Roads are not congested, but in some places they are in a poor state of repair. (French bus drivers refused to take their buses into County Donegal some summers back, as a gesture of protest about the state of the roads.) In the Irish-speaking areas, signposts are written only in the Irish (Gaelic) language, which can be confusing. Make sure that your map lists both English and Irish place-names.

10

Updated by
Paul Clements

Comprising counties Mayo, Sligo, Leitrim, and Donegal, this most inaccessible and isolated corner of Ireland provides rich rewards for intrepid travelers willing to overcome vast distances and spotty transportation. While the rest of the Emerald Isle has been fully explored, the Northwest can still proclaim itself "the hidden Ireland"—and that's no blarney.

Glance at a map of Ireland that has scenic roads printed in green and chances are your eye will be drawn to the far-flung peninsulas of Northwest Ireland. At virtually every bend in the roads there will be something to justify all those green markings. On an island with no shortage of majestic scenery, the Northwest claims its full share. Cool, clean waters from the roaring Atlantic have carved the terrain into long peninsulas—creating a raw, sensual landscape that makes it seem as if the earth is still under construction.

But what you see *this moment* may not be what you will see an hour hence. Clouds and rain linger over mountains, glens, cliffs, beaches, and bogs, to be chased minutes later by sunshine and rainbows. The air, light, and colors of the countryside change as though viewed under a kaleidoscope. The writer William Butler Yeats and his brother Jack Butler Yeats, a painter, immortalized this splendidly lush and rugged countryside in their work.

Northwest Ireland is overwhelmingly rural and underpopulated. That's not to say there isn't a bit of action here. Sligo Town, for instance, has gone through a major renaissance. On a typical weekday, the little winding streets are as busy as those of Galway, and when it comes to stylish restaurants and trendy people, it seems to be giving Dublin's Temple Bar a run for its money—an amazing feat for a town of only 18,000. Sligo Town pulses not only in the present but also with the charge of history, for it was the childhood home of W. B. and Jack B. Yeats, the place that, more than any other, gave rise to their particular geniuses—or, as Jack B. put it: "Sligo was my school and the sky above it."

YEATS COUNTRY: SLIGO TO DRUMCLIFF

Just as James Joyce made Dublin his own through his novels and stories, Sligo and environs are bound to the work of W. B. Yeats (1865–1939), Ireland's first of four Nobel laureates, and to the work of his brother Jack B. (1871–1957), one of Ireland's most important 20th-century painters, whose expressionistic landscapes and portraits are as emotionally fraught as his brother's poems are lyrical and plangent. The brothers intimately knew and eloquently celebrated in their art not only Sligo Town itself but the surrounding countryside, with its lakes, farms, woodland, and dramatic mountains that rise up not far from the center of town. On this route, you will often see glimpses of Ben Bulben Mountain, which looms over the western end of the Dartry range. The areas covered here are the most accessible parts of Northwest Ireland, easily reached from Galway.

SLIGO TOWN

60 km (37 mi) northeast of Ballina, 138 km (86 mi) northeast of Galway, 217 km (135 mi) northwest of Dublin.

Sligo, the only sizable town in the whole of Northwest Ireland, is the best place to begin a tour of Yeats Country. Since the early 2000s, the streets have been ringing with the bite of buzz saws, as apartments, shopping malls, and cinema complexes have been erected behind tasteful, traditional facades, although with the demise of the Celtic Tiger building development has now tapered off. By day Sligo is as lively and crowded as its considerably larger neighbor to the southwest, Galway, with locals, students from the town's college, and tourists bustling past its historic buildings and along its narrow sidewalks and winding streets, and crowding its one-of-a-kind shops, restaurants, and traditional pubs. More than any other town in Northwest Ireland, the Sligo of today has an energy that would surprise anyone who hasn't been here in the past few years.

GETTING HERE

BUS TRAVEL If trains are in short supply in the Northwest region, then buses are plentiful. From Sligo Town buses spider out frequently in all directions serving rural towns and villages in counties Sligo and Leitrim and much farther afield. The main service is operated by Bus Éireann, which has 47 departures daily from its McDiarmada Station at Lord Edward Street to many points of the Irish geographical compass. Seven daily express services link Sligo with Dublin Airport (€19 round-trip) and Dublin city center's Busaras Station (€22 round-trip; 4 hours). There are daily services south to Ballina and Westport in County Mayo. Galway City is a 2½-hour journey (€22 round-trip). Main bus corridors north of Sligo run to Bundoran, Donegal Town, Letterkenny, and Derry. There are also four daily services between Sligo and Belfast, a trip which takes about three hours and costs €23.50 one-way, €35.50 round-trip.

TRAIN TRAVEL Iarnród Éireann, the Irish Rail company, operates efficient intercity train connections from Sligo to Dublin. However, other towns in County Donegal are not served by trains, nor are other nearby cities in Ireland:

10

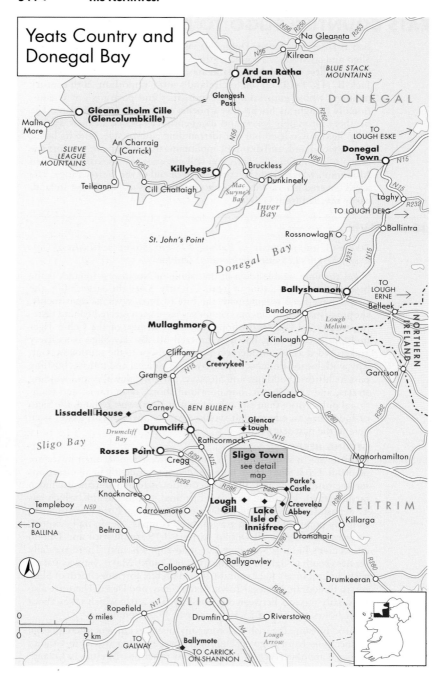

Yeats Country and Donegal Bay

even if you're traveling to nearby Galway or Belfast, you must transfer in Dublin first. Eight daily services run to and from Dublin's Connolly station taking three hours and five minutes to reach Sligo. Standard class round-trip fares are €32 but are considerably cheaper if booked online. Sligo's McDiarmada Station is located on Lord Edward Street, a 10-minute walk to the city center (walk downhill and turn left).

Visitor Information Sligo Tourist Office (✉ *Temple St., Co. Sligo* ☎ *071/916–1201* ⊕ *www.discoverireland.ie/northwest* ⊕ *www.sligotourism.ie*).

EXPLORING

Squeezed onto a patch of land between Sligo Bay and Lough Gill, Sligo Town is clustered on the south shore between two bridges that span the River Garavogue, just east of where the river opens into the bay. Thanks to the pedestrian zone along the south shore of the river (between the two bridges), you can enjoy vistas of the river while right in the center of town. All along High Street and Church and Charles streets, Sligo has churches of almost every denomination. Presbyterians, Methodists, and even Plymouth Brethren are represented, as are Anglicans (Church of Ireland) and, of course, Roman Catholics. According to the Irish writer Sean O'Faolain, "The best Protestant stock in all Ireland is in Sligo." The Yeats family was part of that stock.

Sligo was often a battleground in its earlier days. It was attacked by Viking invaders in 807; later, it was invaded by a succession of rival Irish and Anglo-Norman conquerors. In 1642 the British soldiers of Sir Frederick Hamilton fell upon Sligo, killing every visible inhabitant, burning the town, and destroying the interior of the beautiful medieval abbey. Between 1845 and 1849, more than a million inhabitants of Sligo County died in the potato famine or fled to escape it—an event poignantly captured in a letter written in 1850 by a local father, Owen Larkin, to his son in America. Its words are inscribed on a brass plaque down by the river: "I am now I may say alone in the world all my brothers and sisters are dead and children but yourself. We are all ejected out of Lord Ardilaun's ground, the times was so bad and all Ireland in such a state of poverty that no person could pay rent. My only hope now rests with you, as I am without one shilling and I must either beg or go to the poorhouse." Stand here a moment by the river, then turn again to the bustling heart of Sligo, and marvel at humanity's capacity to rise above adversity.

In the summer a good way to get your bearings is to join one of the guided walking tours of Sligo that leave from the tourist office on Temple Street. During June, July, and August (Tuesday–Friday 11 AM–1 PM) these free two-hour tours are led by a knowledgeable guide and cover cultural history as well as stopping at many of the architectural highlights featured in the historic sites listed below.

TOP ATTRACTIONS

1 Yeats Memorial Building. Set atop the stone Hyde Bridge, this structure makes for a suitably imposing address for the Yeats Society and Sligo Art Gallery. On the first floor, the **Sligo Art Gallery** (⊕ *www. sligoartgallery.com*) lends itself well to the host of rotating exhibitions of contemporary art. In addition, the Yeats International Summer

School is conducted here every August and in 2009 celebrated its 50th School. On the ground floor, drop in to the delightful Sligo Tea Room, serving brown bread, scones, soda bread, and cakes, plus a delicious selection of salads, open sandwiches, and vegetarian options. Across the street is Rowan Gillespie's photo-worthy sculpture of the poet, draped in a flowing coat overlaid with excerpts from his work. It was unveiled in 1989 by Michael Yeats, W. B.'s son, in commemoration of the 50th anniversary of his father's death. ⊠ *Hyde Bridge* ☎ *071/914–5847 gallery; 074/914–2693 summer school* ⊕ *www.yeats-sligo.com* ✉ *Free* ⊙ *Mon.–Sat. 10:30–5:30.*

Yeatsian aficionados will want to follow **The Yeats Trail,** a tourist trail established jointly by Fáilte Ireland and the Yeats Society in January 2009 to mark the 70th anniversary of the poet's death. The trail takes in places strongly linked with W. B. Yeats, predominantly in Sligo, but also in County Galway and Dublin. It was launched by the Nobel Prize–winning poet Seamus Heaney, who proclaimed Yeats the greatest poet in the English language in the 20th century and one inextricably linked with Sligo. Amusingly, a local tourism official described Yeats as "the first public relations officer for the northwest of Ireland." A leaflet on the trail, with a detailed map, is available from the tourist office; once you have visited at least five of the locations—"the places of silence and solitude" to which W. B. Yeats retreated—you receive passport stamps and a personalized Yeats Trail certificate.

❷ **The Model, Home of the Niland Collection.** Since its reopening in 2010, after a two-year €6 million renovation, this arts center has put Sligo well and truly on the international cultural map as a multi-disciplinary arts center. Housed in a beautifully renovated school built in 1862 the Model, now a third bigger in size, is one of Ireland's premier arts venues with an extensive calendar devoted to the visual and performing arts. The main attraction is one of Ireland's largest collections of works by 20th-century artists from Ireland and abroad. The gallery displays more than 60 works by famed Irish painter Jack B. Yeats, including a wide variety from the earliest watercolors and pencil drawings to his later-period abstract oils. He once said, "I never did a painting without putting a thought of Sligo in it." (Beckett wrote that Yeats painted "desperately immediate images.") Paintings by John Yeats (father of Jack B. and W. B.), who had a considerable reputation as a portraitist, also hang here, as do portraits by Sean Keating and Paul Henry. As part of the renovation, new performance and workshop spaces were built, a new gallery was opened to increase and complete the circuit on the first floor, and seven artists' studios were added. A revamped main entrance and new restaurant complete the ambitious and dynamic makeover. Check the Web site for the latest details as the collection on view rotates several times a year. ⊠ *The Mall* ☎ *071/914–1405* ⊕ *www.themodel.ie* ✉ *Free* ⊙ *Tues.–Sat. 10:30–5:30, Sun., noon–4.*

❻ **Sligo County Museum.** The showpiece of this museum is its Yeats Hall, which houses a comprehensive collection of W. B. Yeats's writings from 1889 to 1936, various editions of his plays and prose, the Nobel prize medal awarded to him in 1923, and the Irish tricolor (flag) that draped his coffin when he was buried at nearby Drumcliff. W. B. Yeats's

Sligo's most famous native son, poet W. B. Yeats, is honored by many memorials and statues found throughout the town.

letters to James Stephens and Oliver St. John Gogarty offer insight into Yeats's obsessive love for Sligo. The museum also has small sections on local society, history, and archaeology. ⊠ *Stephen St.* ☎ *071/911–1850* ⊕ *www.sligolibrary.ie* ✉ *Free* ⊘ *June–Sept., Tues.–Sat. 9:30–12:30 and 2–4:50; Oct.–May, Tues.–Sat. 2–4:50.*

WORTH NOTING

❸ **Sligo Abbey.** A massive stone complex that is still redolent of "auld grandeur" and famed for its medieval tomb sculptures, Sligo Abbey is the town's only existing relic of the Middle Ages. Maurice FitzGerald erected the structure for the Dominicans in 1253. After a fire in 1414, it was extensively rebuilt, only to be destroyed again by Cromwell's Puritans under the command of Sir Frederick Hamilton, in 1642. Today the abbey consists of a ruined nave, aisle, transept, and tower. Some fine stonework remains, especially in the 15th-century cloisters. The visitor center is the base for guided tours, which are included with admission. The site is accessible to the disabled, though some parts of the grounds are quite rocky. ⊠ *Abbey St.* ☎ *071/914–6406* ⊕ *www.heritageireland. ie* ✉ *€3* ⊘ *Apr.–Oct., daily 10–6.*

❹ **Courthouse.** Built in 1878, Sligo Town's courtyard is built in the Victorian Gothic style with a suitably flamboyant and turreted sandstone exterior. After it was constructed, it became a symbol of English power. The Courthouse takes its inspiration from the much larger Law Courts in London. Unfortunately, the structure is not open to tourists. In 2001 a major €7 million refurbishment was completed. During 2009 additional renovations costing €300,000 were carried out returning one of Ireland's major architectural monuments to pristine condition. Just

north of the Courthouse on the east side of Teeling Street, look for the window designating the law firm Argue and Phibbs, one of Sligo's most popular photo-ops. ⊠ *Teeling St.* ☎ *No phone*

❺ **St. John's Cathedral.** Designed in 1730 by Richard Castle, who designed Powerscourt and Russborough houses in County Wicklow, this *(Church of Ireland) cathedral* has a handsome square tower and fortifications. In the north transept is a memorial to Susan Mary Yeats, mother of W. B. and Jack B. A beautiful stained-glass window commemorates William and Elizabeth Pollexfen, Yeats's maternal grandparents and a memorial plaque has been erected in memory of the Yeats family. Next door is the larger and newer Roman Catholic Cathedral of the Immaculate Conception (with an entrance on Temple Street), consecrated in 1874. ⊠ *John St.* ☎ *No phone.*

WHERE TO EAT AND STAY

$ ✕ **Bistro Bianconi.** With blond-wood furniture and white-tile floors, Bianconi lives up to its name in the dining room's design, but it serves Italian food that's full of color. Peruse the long list of fancy pizzas that are baked in a wood-burning oven. Chicken *bocconcini* is the famed signature dish; lasagna is also popular. ⊠ *44 O'Connell St.* ☎ *071/914–1744* ⊕ *www.bistrobianconi.ie* ⊟ *MC, V.*

ITALIAN

$$$$
Fodor's Choice
★

Coopershill. Seven generations of the O'Hara family have lived in this three-story Georgian farmhouse since it was built in 1774. Beyond the elegant, symmetrical stone facade, with its central Palladian window, an appealing mix of antique bureaus, marble busts, mounted deer heads, and 19th-century paintings fill the large reception rooms—especially the main emerald-hue salon. Spacious, beautifully furnished guest rooms have floral wallpaper and most have four-poster or canopy beds. Dine by candlelight (at 8:15 PM sharp), on meals such as pot-roast venison (they have their own farm with a herd of 300 fallow deer) made with fresh Irish ingredients. **Pros:** cross the door, enter a delightful haven of peace, sink into the roll-top bath, and lose yourself in luxury; wander around the croquet lawn, admire the strutting peacocks or feed the wild barn owls. **Cons:** rooms can be chilly on cold days; quite a trek to the nearest pub or shops. ✉ *Off N4, 17 km (11 mi) southeast of Sligo, Riverstown, Co. Sligo* ☎ *071/916–5108* ⊕ *www.coopershill.com* ⤴ *8 rooms* ♿ *In-room: no a/c, no TV, Wi-Fi. In-hotel: restaurant, tennis court* 🚬 *AE, DC, MC, V* ☺ *Closed Nov.–Mar.* ⦿ *BP.*

$
Fodor's Choice
★

The Glasshouse. Cosmopolitan modernists will love this funky, shiny six-story riverside hotel—it elevates accommodation in Sligo to a brash new level. The towering exterior is designed to resemble a ship docked at the harbor. Inside, each of the floors has an alternating color scheme that may not be to everyone's taste: three floors bright orange, three floors lime green (with color-coordinated linens), and in the corridors a swirling-pattern gaudy carpet design that some find a little disconcerting. Candlelighted meals in the stylish Kitchen restaurant include spicy Toulouse sausages and Thai chicken curry. It's worth a visit to breathe in the cutting-edge architecture and enhance your color senses. **Pros:** excellent location: Sligo's bustling heart is around the corner; underground car parking is included. **Cons:** bring your shades, as colors will dazzle until you adjust; lacks leisure facilities such as gym or pool. ✉ *Swan Point, Sligo, Co. Sligo* ☎ *071/919–4300* ⊕ *www.theglasshouse. ie* ⤴ *116 rooms, 4 suites* ♿ *In-room: a/c, Wi-Fi. In-hotel: restaurant, bars* 🚬 *AE, MC, V* ⦿ *BP.*

$$–$$$
Fodor's Choice
★

Markree Castle. One of the most beautiful fortress fronts in Ireland greets you on arrival at Markree, Sligo's oldest inhabited castle and the home of the Cooper family for 350 years. Today, Charles and Mary Cooper preside over this lush and lavish 1,000-acre estate. Renovated in 1802, the castle was given the full storybook treatment, complete with a vast, oak-panel entry hall and skylight atrium. Atop the grand oak staircase is a glorious stained-glass window depicting the Cooper family tree. Upstairs, guest bedrooms are super-spacious, many adorned with cozy-sumptuous pieces of 19th-century-style furniture; bathrooms are modern. The Knockmuldowney restaurant dining room has ornate Louis XIV plasterwork—ask about the three-course prix-fixe menu (€35) that includes Markree venison and woodcock caught on the estate. **Pros:** nature lovers will be at home with walks across parkland and down to the Unsin River; alternatively, get cozy with all the gilt cherubs and Rococo plasterwork. **Cons:** rooms above the kitchen can be noisy at night; check out on time (11:30 AM) or you'll be liable for a hefty surcharge of €50 per hour. ✉ *11 km (7 mi) south of Sligo Town,*

10

*off N4, Collooney, Co. Sligo ☏ 071/916–7800 ⊕ www.markreecastle.ie
🛏 30 rooms ♿ In-room: no a/c, Wi-Fi. In-hotel: restaurant, bar ▭ AE,
MC, V ⧫ BP, MAP.*

$ 🖾 **Sligo Park Hotel & Leisure Club.** Expect a modern establishment designed
for a contemporary traveler: a first-rate fitness center, dancing and piano
entertainment some evenings, and the Hazelwood restaurant as well
as the popular Rathana bar. It's a reasonable base of operations for
touring Yeats Country. The staff is quite friendly. Rooms are tastefully
decorated and some, such as those on the second floor, were refurbished
and upgraded in 2008. They all have crisp white duvets and most come
with added extras such as DVD players. Ask for a room with a view
looking across to Sligo Bay in the distance. **Pros:** functional rooms;
good facilities include a modern leisure center and ample car parking. **Cons:** as it's a suburban hotel, it's a 30-minute walk into town if
you're feeling energetic; the dining focus is on pub grub rather than
restaurant meals. ✉ *Pearse Rd. off N4, Co. Sligo ☏ 071/ 919–0400
⊕ www.sligoparkhotel.com 🛏 138 rooms ♿ In-room: no a/c. In-hotel:
restaurant, bar, tennis court, pool, gym, Internet terminal ▭ AE, MC,
V ⧫ BP, MAP.*

NIGHTLIFE AND THE ARTS

PUBS A few miles south of town is a popular spot with the locals, the **Thatch
pub** (✉ *Thatch, Ballysadare ☏ 071/916–7288*), which has traditional
music sessions in the summer from Thursday to Sunday.

A sizable dance floor at **Toffs** (✉ *Kennedy Parade ☏ 071/916–1250*)
teems with Sligo's younger set moving to a mix of contemporary dance
music and older favorites. It stays open later than most places.

Part of the social fabric of Sligo since it opened over 150 years ago, **Hargadons Bar** (✉ *4–5 O'Connell St. ☏ 071/915–3709 ⊕ www.hargadons.
com*) closed in 2007, but luckily this was only a temporary blip as a
rejuvenated bar—thankfully preserving its unique historic character—
reopened in the fall of 2008. Full of wood paneling, cozy snugs (small
booths) for a private powwow, marble-top counters, little glass doors
on hinges make this place especially conducive to that intangible Irish
element, the craic. Check out the walls, covered with historical black-
and-white photos as well as fading invoices from the bar's early days.
Walk through the bar and in separate premises at the back you will find
the well-stocked Hargadons Wine Shop.

THEATER With a jam-packed calendar year-round, **Hawk's Well Theatre** (✉ *Temple
St. ☏ 071/916–1526 ⊕ www.hawkswell.com*) hosts amateur and professional companies from all over Ireland (and occasionally from Britain) in an eclectic mix of shows. Shows run €15–€30; the box office is
open weekdays 10–6, Saturday 1–4, and on Sunday 3–6 when there is
a performance.

If you're visiting in the fall, don't miss the **Sligo Live Music and Arts Festival**
(⊕ *www.sligolive.ie*), held at various venues around town. Established
in 2005, the festival runs over the bank-holiday weekend at the end of
October. It is elbow-room only as hotels, pubs, and cafés are crammed
with scores of live sessions while fiddlers, dancers, jugglers, and pup-
peteers fill the streets. A Brooklyn native, Tony DeMarco, recognized

Famed as a Sligo landmark since it opened its doors 150 years ago, Hargadon's Bar has a time-burnished interior and also some of the freshest muscles around.

as one of America's finest fiddlers and one of the world's leading exponents of Sligo-style fiddling, set the festival alight in 2009. For dates and details of gigs, check the program at the Web site, where you can buy tickets.

SHOPPING

Sligo Town has Northwest Ireland's most thriving shopping scene, with lots of food-related, crafts, and hand-knits shops.

In addition to stylish sweaters, **Carraig Donn** (⌧ *41 O'Connell St.* ☎ *071/914–4158* ⊕ *www.carraigdonn.com*) carries pottery, glassware, linens, and Aran knits for children.

The Cat & the Moon (⌧ *4 Castle St.* ☎ *071/914–3686* ⊕ *www.thecat-andthemoon.com*) specializes in eclectic and stylish Irish-made crafts, jewelry, pottery, ironwork, and scarves; it's named after the play by W.B. Yeats.

The upscale deli **Cosgrove and Son** (⌧ *32 Market St.* ☎ *071/914–2809*) sells everything from Parma ham to carrageen moss boiled in milk (a local cure for upset stomachs). Stock up here for a picnic.

Cross Sections (⌧ *2 Grattan St.* ☎ *071/914–2265*) sells lovely tableware, glassware, and kitchenware.

Tír na nóg (⌧ *Grattan St.* ☎ *071/916–2752*), Irish for "Land of the Ever-young," sells organic foods, including local cheeses and honeys, and other health-oriented items. A sister store across the street sells cards and posters.

LOUGH GILL

★   *1½ km (1 mi) east of Sligo Town on R286.*

Lough Gill means simply "Lake Beauty." In fine weather the beautiful river-fed lough and its surroundings are serenity itself: sunlight on the meadows all around, lough-side cottages, the gentle sound of water, salmon leaping, a yacht sailing by. To get to the lake from Sligo Town, take Stephen Street, which turns into N16 (signposted to Manorhamilton and Enniskillen). Turn right almost at once onto R286. Within minutes you can see gorgeous views of the lake so adored by the young W. B. Yeats.

In the 17th century an English Planter (a Protestant colonist settling on Irish lands confiscated from Catholic owners) built the fortified house of **Parke's Castle** on the eastern shore of Lough Gill. He needed the strong fortifications to defend himself against a hostile populace. His relations with the people were made worse by the fact that he obtained his building materials mainly by dismantling a historic fortress on the site that had belonged to the clan leaders, the O'Rourkes of Breffni (once the name of the district). The entrance fee includes a short video show on the castle and local history, and a guided tour every hour. In summer, boat tours of the lough leave from here. There's also a snack bar. ⊠ *R288, Fivemile Bourne* ☎ *071/916–4149* ⊕ *www.heritageireland.ie* ⌨ *€3* ⊙ *May–Oct., daily 10–6; last entry at 5:15.*

A few minutes' walk along a footpath south of Parke's Castle lie the handsome ruins of **Creevelea Abbey.** In fact not an abbey but a friary, Creevelea was founded for the Franciscans in 1508 by a later generation of O'Rourkes. It was the last Franciscan community to be founded before the suppression of the monasteries by England's King Henry VIII. Like many other decrepit abbeys, the place still holds religious significance for the locals, who revere it. One curiosity here is the especially large south transept; notice, too, its endearing little cloisters, with well-executed carvings on the pillars of St. Francis of Assisi. ⊠ *R288, Dromahair.*

WHERE TO EAT AND STAY

¢   ⛉ **Stanford Village Inn.** With a 200-year-old pedigree and in the same family for six generations this rustic stone-front inn is one of the few stops for sustenance near Lough Gill. The inn was renovated and extended in 2010 with three new self-catering apartments added while the existing six rooms were refurbished. A hearty meal of traditional, homey food ($–$$), an open fire, and, if your timing is good, an impromptu session of traditional Irish music await you. **Pros:** blissful, pastoral location; lunch here will sustain you through the rest of the day. **Cons:** hard-to-find location; service can be hit or miss on busy days. ⊠ *7 km (5 mi) from Parke's Castle, 19 km (12 mi) from Sligo Town, off R288, Dromahair, Co. Leitrim* ☎ *071/916–4140* ⊕ *www.stanfordinn.ie* ⇨ *9 rooms* ⚖ *In-room: no a/c, Internet. In-hotel: restaurant, bar* ⊟ *MC, V* ⊙⊙ *BP.*

Continued on page 557

SHOPPING FOR A PIECE OF THE SHAMROCK

Prepping dishes for Spongeware patterns

With its Belleek porcelains and Waterford crystals, Ireland has always been a treasured island for shoppers. Today, its traditional crafts—centuries old yet very much alive—are enjoying a revival of the fittest.

A CRAFT REVIVAL

Remember all those traditional lepre-chaun figurines with "Made in China" stickers on their bottoms? Today, how-ever, Irish traditional crafts are flourish-ing as never before. In a land where many villages are still redolent of a preindus-trial age, "trad" culture has become commerce—big commerce. Claddagh friendship rings, spongeware pottery, heir-loom Aran sweaters, Bel-leek china wedding plates, Carrickmacross lace, and Waterford crystal (so finely cut you'll need to don anti-bril-liance eye goggles) are all objects endowed with vibrant personality. If Ireland has never been a country of great artists it has always been one of great artistry.

Above: Claddagh ring.
Below: Louis Mulcahey at work on his pottery.
Dingle Peninsula, Southwest Ireland

WHERE TO BUY
While the entire country is bloom-ing with craftsworkers, the Northwest region offers some seventh-level shop-ping, thanks to hand-knit Aran sweat-ers, fine Parian china, and handwoven tweeds. Those who want to make brows-ing—and buying—easy will find the famous multidealer town cooperatives (such as Midleton's Courtyard Crafts or Doolin's Celtic Waves) tempting. But, in general, the more interesting craftspeople are found outside the main cities, and intrepid consumers should head for smaller towns where overheads are lower (and the scenery is better). Don't buy the first blackthorn walking stick you see. Take a good look around and visit any number of crafts shops— you'll probably end up with a bogwood paperweight and basketweave china tureen as well!

CHERISHED COLLECTIBLES

WATERFORD CRYSTAL

Founded in 1783, Waterford crystal is noted for its sparkle, clarity, and heft. Thicker glass means that each piece can be wedge-cut on a diamond wheel to dramatic effect (as you can see during the famous factory tour held at the Waterford factory in Southeast Ireland). Waterford artisans apprentice for *eight* years.

BELLEEK CHINA

China has been made in Belleek, a village just on the border with County Fermanagh, Northern Ireland, since 1857. This local product is a lustrous fine-bone china with a delicate green or yellow-on-white design and often incorporates weave-effect pottery. Americans love it. Old Belleek is an expensive collector's item, but modern Belleek is more reasonably priced and very likely to appreciate in value over the years (according to some experts).

TRADITIONAL LACEMAKING

Traditional Irish crochet and lace-making use a fine cotton and date back to the 1840s when they originated in the cottage homes and lace schools of Carrickmacross.

SPONGEWARE POTTERY

One of Ireland's most beautiful collectibles, Irish Spongeware first appeared in 18th-century potteries. With the use of a cut sponge, patterns and images—often "rural" in flavor, like plants and sheep—are applied to the lovely cream-colored surface.

CLADDAGH RINGS

Born in the Claddagh area of Galway during the 17th century, the Claddagh ring incorporates three symbols: a heart (for love), a pair of hands (for friendship), and a crown (for loyalty). Worn on the right hand, with crown and heart facing out, it symbolizes the wearer is still "free"; worn on the left, with symbols tucked under, indicates marriage.

ARAN: FROM FLEECE TO FASHION

Made of plain, undyed wool and knit with distinctive crisscross patterns, sometimes referred to as *bainin* sweaters or "ganseys," the Aran sweater is a combination of folklore and fashion.

Since harsh weather made warmth and protection vital out in the Atlantic Ocean, the women of Aran long ago discovered the solution to this problem in this strong, comfortable, hand-knit sweater. Indeed, these Arans can hold 30 percent of their weight in water before they even start to feel wet. The reason? Traditionally, the wool used was unwashed and retained its water-repellent natural sheep's lanolin.

LOOK FOR THE PATTERN

Not so long ago, these pullovers were worn by every County Donegal fisherman, usually made to a design belonging exclusively to his own family. It's said that a native can tell which family the knitter belongs to from the patterns used in a genuine Aran sweater. Often the patterns used religious symbols and folk motifs, such as the Tree of Life, the Honeycomb (standing for thrift and thought to be lucky), the SeaHorse, the Blackberry—all are patterns in the almost sculptured, deeply knitted work that characterizes the Aran method. Their famous basket stitch represents the fisherman's basket, a hope for a *curragh* (fisherboat) heavy with catch. A colorful belt called a *crios* (pronounced "criss")

is handcrafted in many traditional designs as a useful accessory.

MAKING YOUR PURCHASE

Most of the Aran sweaters you'll see throughout Ireland are made far north of the islands themselves, in County Donegal, an area most associated with high-quality, handwoven textiles. The best are painstakingly knitted by hand, a process that can take weeks. As a result, prices are not cheap, and if you think you've found a bargain, check the label before buying—it's more likely a factory copy. Still, the less expensive, lighter-weight, hand-loomed sweaters (knitted on a mechanical loom, not with needles) are less than half the price, and more practical for most lifestyles. But the real McCoy is still coveted: some of the finest examples woven by Inis Meáin are sold at luxury stores like Bergdorf Goodman and Wilkes Bashford. And young Irish designers like Liadain De Buitlear are giving the traditional Aran a newer-than-now spin, highly popular in Dublin boutiques.

Above Left: A large selection of styles and sizes; Above right: Spun yarns ready to be knit into Aran sweaters

LAKE ISLE OF INNISFREE

15 km (9 mi) south of Sligo Town via Dromahair on N4 and R287.

In 1890 W.B. Yeats was walking through the West End of London when, seeing in a shop window a ball dancing on a jet of water, he was suddenly overcome with nostalgia for the lakes of his Sligo home. It was the moment, and the feeling, that shaped itself into his most famous poem, "The Lake Isle of Innisfree":

I will arise and go now, and go to Innisfree,

And a small cabin build there, of clay and wattles made:

Nine bean-rows will I have there, a hive for the honey-bee,

And live alone in the bee-loud glade.

And I shall have some peace there, for peace comes dropping slow.

Though there's nothing visually exceptional about Innisfree (pronounced *in-nish*-free), the "Lake Isle" is a must-see if you're a W.B. Yeats fan. To reach Innisfree from Dromahair, take R287, the minor road that heads back along the south side of Lough Gill, toward Sligo Town. Turn right at a small crossroads, after 4 or 5 km (2 or 3 mi), where signposts point to Innisfree. A little road leads another couple of miles down to the lakeside, where you can see the island just offshore.

ROSSES POINT

8 km (5 mi) northwest of Sligo Town on R291.

It's obvious why W.B. and Jack B. Yeats often stayed at Rosses Point during their summer vacations: glorious pink-and-gold summer sunsets over a seemingly endless stretch of sandy beach. Coney Island lies just off Rosses Point. Local lore has it that the captain of the ship *Arathusa* christened Brooklyn's Coney Island after this one, but there's probably more legend than truth to this, as it's widely agreed that New York's Coney Island was named after the Dutch word *konijn* (wild rabbits, which abounded there during the 17th century).

GETTING HERE

BUS TRAVEL Bus Éireann operates seven services Monday through Saturday from Sligo bus station to Rosses Point and drops you off at the Roman Catholic Church. The bus serves Rosses Point beach only in July and August.

EXPLORING

The popular **County Sligo Golf Club** (☎ *071/917–7134* ⊕ *www.county-sligogolfclub.ie*) is one of Ireland's grand old venues; it's more than a century old, and has hosted most of the country's major championships. Established in 1894 on land leased from Henry Middleton, an uncle of the famous Yeats brothers, the course offers magnificent views of the sea and Ben Bulben.

The **Sligo Yacht Club** (☎ *071/917–7168* ⊕ *www.sligoyachtclub.org*), with a fleet of some 90 boats, has sailing and social programs, and regularly hosts races.

DRUMCLIFF

15 km (9 mi) northeast of Rosses Point, 7 km (4½ mi) north of Sligo Town on N15.

W.B. Yeats lies buried with his wife, Georgie, in an unpretentious grave in the cemetery of Drumcliff's simple Protestant church, where his grandfather was rector for many years. W.B. died on the French Riviera in 1939; it took almost a decade for his body to be brought back to the place that more than any other might be called his soul-land. In the poem "Under Ben Bulben," he spelled out not only where he was to be buried but also what should be written on the tombstone: "Cast a cold eye / On life, on death. / Horseman, pass by!" It is easy to see why the majestic Ben Bulben (1,730 feet), with its sawed-off peak (not unlike Yosemite's Half-Dome), made such an impression on the poet: the mountain gazes calmly down upon the small church, as it does on all of the surrounding landscape—and at the same time stands as a sentinel facing the mighty Atlantic. The Sligo–Donegal Town bus (six services Monday through Saturday) stops at Drumcliff and sets down passengers at the post office from where it's a five-minute walk to the grave of W.B. Yeats. Journey time is 15 minutes and a round-trip costs €6.20.

Drumcliff is where St. Columba, a recluse and missionary who established Christian churches and religious communities in Northwest Ireland, is thought to have founded a monastic settlement around AD 575. The monastery that he founded before sailing off to the Scottish isle of Iona flourished for many centuries, but all that is left of it now is the base of a round tower and a carved high cross (both across N15 from the church) dating from around AD 1000, with scenes from the Old and New Testaments, including Adam and Eve with the serpent, and Cain slaying Abel.

Drumcliff Tea House and Craft Shop is a good place to buy local crafts, books of W.B. Yeats's poetry, and books about the poet's life. You can also get light lunches and snacks here including soup, sandwiches, and paninis. ⊠ *Next to Protestant church* ☎ *071/914–4956* ☉ *Mon.–Sun. 9–6.*

LISSADELL HOUSE

3 km (2 mi) west of Drumcliff, 15 km (9 mi) northwest of Sligo Town off N15.

Fodor'sChoice
★
Beside the Atlantic waters of Drumcliff Bay, on the peninsula that juts out between Donegal and Sligo bays, Lissadell—"That old Georgian mansion," as W.B. Yeats called it—is an austere but classic residence built in 1834 by Sir Robert Gore-Booth. An enlightened landlord, he

mortgaged the house to help his poverty-stricken tenants during the famine years. His descendants still own Lissadell, which is filled with all manner of artifacts brought back from every corner of the globe by members of the family, who were avid travelers. W.B. became a good friend of the family. On a visit to the house in 1894 he met the two Gore-Booth daughters, Eva and Constance, and subsequently recalled the meeting in verse: "The light of evening, Lissadell, / Great windows open to the south, / Two girls in silk kimonos." Eva became a poet, while sister Constance Markievicz led a dramatic political life as a fiery Irish nationalist, taking a leading role in the 1916 Easter Uprising against the British. She survived the uprising, later becoming the first female member of the Dáil (Irish Parliament).

Lissadell was designed by the London architect Francis Goodwin. Its two most notable features are a dramatic 33-foot-high gallery, with 24-foot-tall Doric columns, clerestory windows, and skylights; and the dining room, where Constance's husband, Count Markievicz, painted portraits of members of the family and household employees on the pilasters. A copy of W.B.'s poem "In Memory of Eva Gore-Booth and Con Markievicz" is displayed in the house. A guided tour lasts 45 minutes. In 2007, to mark the 80th anniversary of the death of Constance Markievicz, a permanent exhibition featuring her paintings and letters was opened. This is the most definitive collection of material open to the public and features rarely seen memorabilia.

Both the house and gardens have undergone extensive renovation since being taken over in 2003 by a Dublin barrister and his wife. Many rooms, including the china room, butler's pantry, billiard room, and reception rooms have been restored; so, too, has the Coach House and tearoom. The garden shop sells plants, chutneys, and jams. There is also an extensive crafts shop. The walled Victorian kitchen garden, created in 1841, now showcases heritage vegetables and fruit similar to that grown in the heyday of the garden when the estate employed more than 200 people. The woods of the Lissadell estate have become a forestry and wildlife reserve; they house Ireland's largest colony of barnacle geese, along with representatives of several other species of wildfowl. Please check the Web site to confirm opening hours. There is no bus service to Lissadell House. Taxis operate from Sligo center and charge €40 round-trip. ☎ 071/916–3150 ⊕ *www.lissadellhouse.com* ☜ *House €6, Alpine garden €5, kitchen garden €5* ۩ *Daily 10:30–6:30.*

10

AROUND DONEGAL BAY

As you drive north to Donegal Town, the glens of the Dartry Mountains (to which Ben Bulben belongs) gloriously roll by to the east. Look across coastal fields for views of the waters of Donegal Bay to the west. In the distant horizon the Donegal hills beckon. This stretch, dotted with numerous prehistoric sites, has become Northwest Ireland's most popular vacation area. There are a few small and unremarkable seashore resorts, and in some places you may find examples of haphazard and fairly tasteless construction that detracts from the scenery. In between these minor resort developments, wide-open spaces are free of traffic.

The Yeats brothers were often visitors to regal Lissadell House, whose antiques-filled salons are now open to the public.

The most intriguing area lies on the north side of the bay—all that rocky indented coastline due west of Donegal Town. Here you enter the heart of away-from-it-all: County Donegal.

MULLAGHMORE

37 km (24 mi) north of Sligo Town off N15.

In July and August, the sleepy fishing village of Mullaghmore becomes congested with tourists. Its main attractions: a 3-km-long (2-mi-long) sandy beach; and the turreted, fairy-tale Classie Bawn—the late Lord Louis Mountbatten's home (he, his grandson, and a local boy were killed when the IRA blew up his boat in the bay in 1979; the castle is still privately owned and not open to the public). A short drive along the headland is punctuated by unobstructed views beyond the rocky coastline out over Donegal Bay. When the weather is fair, you can see all the way across to St. John's Point and Drumanoo Head in Donegal.

Creevykeel is one of Ireland's best megalithic court-tombs. There's a burial area and an enclosed open-air court where rituals were performed around 3000 BC. Bronze artifacts found here are now in the National Museum in Dublin. The site (signposted from N15) lies off the road, just beyond the edge of the village of Cliffony. ⊠ *3 km (2 mi) southeast of Mullaghmore off N15.*

WHERE TO STAY

$$ ⌂ **Beach Hotel.** If there's a chill in the air, you can warm up at the roaring fires in the restaurant and residents' lounge of this large harborside Victorian hotel. The exterior of the simple, three-story building wears a

dashing coat of red. Inside, nautical accents tout the history of the bay (it seems three galleons of the Spanish Armada went aground here in September 1588). Enjoy wonderful views of the pier and the bay from the hotel bars, or tuck into the de'Cuellar restaurant's acclaimed seafood menu. Try the favorites: hot crab claws, lobster, and the house seafood platter. Save room for the homemade apple-and-rhubarb crumble. In the Boatman's bar you can snack on chicken burritos or enjoy fish chowders. **Pros:** well managed and professionally run with a friendly staff; the themed murder-mystery weekends are fun. **Cons:** no Internet in the rooms; extra charge of €10 per night for a sea-view room; the single beds are pretty tight. ⊠ *The Harbour, Co. Sligo* ☎ *071/916–6103* ⊕ *www.beachhotelmullaghmore.com* ⤳ *28 rooms* ⌂ *In-room: no a/c. In-hotel: restaurant, bars, pool, gym* ▭ *AE, MC, V* ⏺ *BP, MAP.*

BALLYSHANNON

23 km (15 mi) north of Mullaghmore, 42 km (26 mi) northeast of Sligo Town on N15.

The former garrison town of Ballyshannon rises gently from the banks of the River Erne and has good views of Donegal Bay and the surrounding mountains. Come early August, this quiet village springs to life with a grand fest of traditional music, the **Ballyshannon Folk Festival** (☎ *086/252–7400* ⊕ *www.ballyshannonfolkfestival.com*), Ireland's longest-running music gathering. The town is a hodgepodge of shops, arcades, and hotels. Its triangular central area has several bars and places to grab a snack. The town was also the birthplace of the prolific poet William Allingham.

A few kilometers down the road are several factories where, for generations, master craftsmen have made eggshell-thin Irish porcelain. It's said that if a newlywed couple receives a piece of this china, their marriage will be blessed with everlasting happiness.

The name Belleek has become synonymous with much of Ireland's delicate ivory porcelain figurines and woven china baskets (sometimes painted with shamrocks). **Belleek Pottery Ltd.** is the best known of the producers, in operation since 1857. The main factories are just down the road from Ballyshannon in Northern Ireland (which is why their prices are quoted in pounds sterling, not euros). Watch the introductory film, take the 30-minute tour, stop by for refreshment in the tearoom, or just head to the on-site shop. The factory-museum-store is near the border with Northern Ireland. Company products can also be found in the shops of Donegal and Sligo. ⊠ *6 km (4 mi) east of Ballyshannon, Belleek, Northern Ireland* ☎ *028/6865–9300 in Northern Ireland* ⊕ *www.belleek.ie* ⤳ *£4* ⏲ *Jan. and Feb., weekdays 9–5:30; Mar.–June, weekdays 9–6, Sat. 10–6, Sun. 2–6; July–Oct., weekdays 9–6, Sat. 10–6, Sun. noon–6; Nov. and Dec., weekdays 9–5:30, Sat. 10–5:30.*

The fourth generation (since 1866) of the Daly family hand crafts and paints the elaborate floral and basket-weave designs at **Celtic Weave China.** Because it's a small, personal operation, they can make a single piece of china to your specifications. They also carry out design work for Tiffany Jewelers of New York. Prices start at €10, and most pieces

10

cost less than €125, although you can spend up to €3,000 on a double photo frame. ⊠ *R230, 5 km (3 mi) east of Ballyshannon, Cloghore* ☎ *071/985–1844* ⊕ *www.celticweavechina.com* ✉ *Free* ⊙ *Weekdays 8–6, Sat. 9–5.*

**OFF THE
BEATEN
PATH**

Lough Derg. From Whitsunday to the Feast of the Assumption (June to mid-August), tens of thousands beat a path to the shores of Lough Derg, ringed by heather-clad slopes. In the center of the lake, Station Island—known as St. Patrick's Purgatory (the saint is said to have fasted here for 40 days and nights)—is one of Ireland's most popular pilgrimage sites. It's also the most rigorous and austere of such sites in the country. Pilgrims stay on the island for three days without sleeping, and ingest only black tea and dry toast. They walk barefoot around the island, on its flinty stones, to pray at a succession of shrines. Non-pilgrims may not visit the island from June to mid-August. To find out how to become a pilgrim, write to the Reverend Prior. To reach the shores of Lough Derg, turn off the main N15 Sligo–Donegal road in the village of Laghy onto the minor R232 Pettigo road, which hauls itself over the Black Gap and descends sharply into the border village of Pettigo, about 21 km (13 mi) from N15. From here, take the Lough Derg access road for 8 km (5 mi). During pilgrim season, buses connect Pettigo with Ballyshannon and Enniskillen from Thursday to Monday. There are no services on Tuesday or Wednesday. It's a 30-minute journey from both towns and the return fare is €15. ⊠ *Pettigo* ☎ *071/986–1518* ⊕ *www.loughderg.org.*

NIGHTLIFE

The biggest and most popular pub, **Seán Óg's** (⊠ *Market St.* ☎ *071/985–8964*), has live music on Friday, Saturday, and Sunday evenings.

DONEGAL TOWN

21 km (13 mi) north of Ballyshannon, 66 km (41 mi) northeast of Sligo Town on N15.

With a population of about 3,000, Donegal is Northwest Ireland's largest small village—marking the entry into the back-of-the-beyond of the wilds of County Donegal. The town is centered on the triangular Diamond, where three roads converge (N56 to the west, N15 to the south and the northeast) and the mouth of the River Eske pours gently into Donegal Bay. You should have your bearings in five minutes, and seeing the historical sights takes less than an hour; if you stick around any longer, it'll probably be to do some shopping—arguably Donegal's top attraction.

GETTING HERE

BUS TRAVEL   Public transport throughout Donegal is limited to buses. Bus Éireann operates nine year-round direct daily services from Donegal Town to Dublin airport and the city center, which also stop in the nearby towns of Ballyshannon and Belleek. They run regular services between the bigger towns linking Donegal Town with Bundoran, Letterkenny, and west to Killybegs, Glencolumbkille, Glenties, and Dungloe. There is no bus station but buses stop outside the Abbey Hotel in the Diamond. A raft of smaller independently-run buses crisscrosses Donegal's roads—including McGeehan Coaches, Patrick Gallagher Coaches,

Devout pilgrims head to the beautiful shores of Lough Derg and set sail for Station Island to pray in the footsteps of St. Patrick every summer.

Feda O'Donnell Coaches, John McGinley Coach Travel, and Donegal Coaches—and these companies pick up and drop off in Quay Street.

Visitor Information Discover Ireland Centre, Donegal Town (✉ *The Quay, Co. Donegal* ☎ *074/972–1148* ⊕ *www.discoverireland.ie*).

EXPLORING

The town of Donegal was previously known in Irish as *Dun na nGall*, "Fort of the Foreigners." The foreigners were Vikings, who set up camp here in the 9th century to facilitate their pillaging and looting. They were driven out by the powerful O'Donnell clan (originally Cinel Conail), who made it the capital of Tyrconail, their extensive Ulster territories. Donegal was rebuilt in the early 17th century, during the Plantation period, when Protestant colonists were planted on Irish property confiscated from its Catholic owners. The **Diamond**, like that of many other Irish villages, dates from this period. Once a marketplace, it has a 20-foot-tall obelisk monument (1937), which honors the town monks who, before being driven out by the English in the 17th century, took the time to copy down a series of Old Irish legends in what they called *The Annals of the Four Masters*.

Donegal Castle was built by clan leader Hugh O'Donnell in the 1470s. More than a century later, this structure was the home of his descendant Hugh Roe O'Donnell, who faced the might of the invading English and was the last clan chief of Tyrconail. In 1602 he died on a trip to Spain while trying to rally reinforcements from his allies. In 1610 its new English owner, Sir Basil Brooke, modified the little castle, fitting Jacobean towers and turrets to the main fort and adding a Jacobean mansion (which is now a ruin). Inside, you can peer into the garderobe (the restroom) and the storeroom, and survey a great banqueting hall with an exceptional vaulted wood-beam roof. Also of note is the gargantuan sandstone fireplace nicely wrought with minute details. Mind your head on the low doorways and be careful on the narrow trip stairwell. The small, enclosed grounds are pleasant. ⊠ *Tirchonaill St., near north corner of Diamond* ☎ *074/972–2405* ⚅ *€4* ☉ *Mar.–Oct., daily 9:30–5:15; Nov.–Feb., Thurs.–Mon. 9:30–3:45.*

The ruins of the **Franciscan Abbey,** founded in 1474 by Hugh O'Donnell, are a five-minute walk south of town at a spectacular site perched above the Eske River, where it begins to open up into Donegal Bay. The complex was burned to the ground in 1593, razed by the English in 1601, and ransacked again in 1607; the ruins include the choir, south transept, and two sides of the cloisters, between which lie hundreds of graves dating to the 18th century. The abbey was probably where *The Annals of the Four Masters,* which chronicles the whole of Celtic history and mythology of Ireland from earliest times up to the year 1618, was written from 1632 to 1636. The Four Masters were monks who believed (correctly, as it turned out) that Celtic culture was doomed by the English conquest, and they wanted to preserve as much of it as they could. At the National Library in Dublin, you can see copies of the monks' work; the original is kept under lock and key. ⊠ *Off N15 behind Central Hotel* ⚅ *Free* ☉ *Freely accessible.*

WHERE TO EAT AND STAY

¢

CAFÉ

★

✕ **Blueberry Tea Room and Restaurant.** Proprietors Brian and Ruperta Gallagher serve breakfast, lunch, afternoon tea, and a light evening meal—always using homegrown herbs. Daily specials—Irish lamb stew, pasta dishes, and quiche—are served from 8 AM to 7 PM. Soups, sandwiches, salads, and fruit are on the regular menu, along with homemade desserts, breads, scones, and jams. Upstairs is an Internet café but check in downstairs first. It's across the street from Donegal Castle. Get there early for lunch, as the lines stretch out onto the street on busy days. ⊠ *Castle St.* ☎ *074/972–2933* ▭ *V* ☉ *Closed Sun.*

$–$$

Fodor'sChoice

★

⌂ **Central Hotel.** With its bright white shutters and boldly red facade, this pretty-as-an-Irish-picture inn sits smack on Donegal's central square, more correctly called the "Diamond." While family-run, it is affiliated with the big Irish firm of White's Hotels. Huge picture windows in the back reveal lovely views of Donegal Bay and the River Eske. The suites have queen beds and spacious lounge areas. The efficient staff serve good, filling food in the Just Williams carvery, or opt for the Thai restaurant. In 2008 the hotel opened Rick's Café Bar with a Casablanca theme, which has proved a big hit with both locals and visitors. **Pros:** top marks for convenience for exploring the town and its history; friendly and knowledgeable staff. **Cons:** no frills; relentless surge of taxis and motorbikes circling the Diamond. ⊠ *The Diamond, Co. Donegal* ☎ *074/972–1027* ⊕ *www.centralhoteldonegal.com* ➪ *112 rooms, 10 apartments* ⚅ *In-room: no a/c, Wi-Fi. In-hotel: 2 restaurants, bar, pool, gym* ▭ *AE, DC, MC, V* ⊙*BP, MAP.*

$$$$

Fodor'sChoice

★

⌂ **Harvey's Point Country Hotel.** Set in a remote and breathtaking location in landscaped gardens on the shores of Lough Eske at the foot of the Blue Stack Mountains, Harvey's Point has, for 22 years, been a spirit-lifting escape. The drive to the Gysling family's hotel is awe-inspiring in itself and your surprise is complete when the elegant edifice looms up along the shores of the lake. Reception areas gleam with cherrywood and polished stone and flaunt great views. A major extension, with 42 additional guest rooms, was completed in 2005, with huge suites and bathrooms the size of most Irish hotel rooms. The Irish-with-a-French-flair restaurant has winning dishes like the roast Emyvale duckling with butternut squash and passion-fruit puree. Even if your itinerary prevents you from overnighting, it is well worth dropping in for the Sunday carvery lunch, a buffet that has become justly famous and costs €32. **Pros:** luxury and style in timeless grandeur; peaceful surroundings; great concierge Brendan Brien. **Cons:** older rooms lack the opulence of new ones; long walk to ATM. ⊠ *6 km (4 mi) northwest of Donegal Town, off N15, Lough Eske, Co. Donegal* ☎ *074/972–2208* ⊕ *www. harveyspoint.com* ⊠ *70 rooms, 4 suites* ⅃ *In-room: no a/c, Wi-Fi. In-hotel: 2 restaurants, bar, bicycles* ⊟ *AE, DC, MC, V* ❘⊙❘ *MAP.*

NIGHTLIFE

The **Abbey Hotel** (⊠ *The Diamond* ☎ *074/972–1014* ⊕ *www. abbeyhoteldonegal.com*) has music every night in July and August and a disco every Saturday and Sunday night throughout the year. In summer, people pack **O'Donnell's Bar** (⊠ *The Diamond* ☎ *074/972–1049*) to hear traditional music Thursday night and contemporary music on weekends.

SPORTS AND THE OUTDOORS

Donegal Golf Club (⊠ *8 km [5 mi] south on the Sligo Road from Donegal Town, Laghy, Co. Donegal* ☎ *074/973–4054* ⊕ *www.donegalgolfclub. ie*) is one of Ireland's great 18-hole championship courses.

SHOPPING

Long the principal marketplace for the region's wool products, Donegal Town has several smaller shops with local hand weaving, knits, and crafts. Explore **Donegal Craft Village** (⊠ *N15, 1½ km [1 mi] south of town* ☎ *074/972–3222*), a complex of workshops where you can buy pottery, handwoven goods, jewelry, and ceramics from young, local craftspeople. You can even watch the items being made Monday to Saturday 9–6, and Sunday 11–6. The Aroma Café in the Craft Village is a top-class spot for homemade cakes and breads, and also serves dishes with an Italian twist. For the best selection of local history books on Donegal and Ireland in general, Ordnance Survey maps, and travel guides, as well as CDs, DVDs, and Celtic jewelry, the **Four Masters Book-shop** (⊠ *The Diamond* ☎ *074/972–1526*) is a great place to browse.

The main hand-weaving store in town, **Magee's** (⊠ *The Diamond* ☎ *074/972–2660* ⊕ *www.mageeireland.com*) carries renowned private-label tweeds for both men and women (jackets, hats, scarves, suits, and more), as well as pottery, linen, and crystal. **Simple Simon's** (⊠ *The Diamond* ☎ *074/972–2687*), the only fresh-food shop here, sells organic vegetables, essential oils, and other whole-earth items, as well as breads and cakes from the kitchen on the premises. They also stock a lot of local Irish cheeses.

10

To make the Slieve League mountains—Ireland's highest—more accessible a viewing station now allows access to one of Europe's grandest sea vistas.

EN ROUTE

As you travel west on N56, which runs slightly inland from a magnificent shoreline of rocky inlets with great sea views, it's worthwhile to turn off the road from time to time to catch a better view of the coast. About 6 km (4 mi) out of Donegal Town, N56 skirts Mountcharles, a bleak hillside village that looks back across the bay.

KILLYBEGS

28 km (17 mi) west of Donegal Town.

Trawlers from Spain and France are moored in the harbor at Killybegs, one of Ireland's busiest fishing ports. Though it's one of the most industrialized places along this coast, it's not without some charm, thanks to its waterfront location. Killybegs once served as a center for the manufacture of Donegal hand-tufted carpets, examples of which are in the White House and the Vatican.

The **Maritime and Heritage Centre** factory produces high-quality hand-knotted and hand-tufted carpets to order: a square meter costs around €2,000. Visitors are welcome to commission a piece, but examples of the carpets are not sold off the peg. ⊠ *Kilcar Rd.* ☎ *074/974–1944* ⊕ *www.visitkillybegs.com* 🖥 *€5* ⊘ *Sept.–June, weekdays 10–6; July and Aug., weekdays 10–6, weekends 1–5.*

EN ROUTE

The narrows, climbs, and twists of R263 afford terrific views of Donegal Bay before descending into pretty Cill Chartaigh (Kilcar), a traditional center of tweed making. Signposted by its Irish name, the next village, An Charraig (Carrick), clings to the foot of the **Slieve League Mountains**, whose dramatic, color-streaked ocean cliffs are, at 2,000 feet, the highest in Ireland and among the most spectacular. Slieve League (Sliah Liec, or Mountain of the Pillars) is a ragged, razor-back rise bordered by the River Glen. To see the cliffs, take the little road to the Irish-speaking village of Teileann, 1½ km (1 mi) south from Carrick. Then take the narrow lane (signposted to the Bunglass Cliffs) that climbs steeply to the top of the cliffs. The mountain looks deceptively climbable from the back (the inaccessible point borders the Atlantic), but once the fog rolls in, the footing can be perilous. If you want to take in this thrilling perspective—presuming you're hardy and careful—walk along the difficult coastal path from Teileann: not for the dizzily squeamish. In 2009 Donegal County Council and the tourist board made the cliffs more accessible by widening the road to the top and enhancing it with parking lots, turnouts, fencing, and an information panel as part of the Donegal Interpretative Project, the first of its kind anywhere in Ireland. A newly erected viewing point over the sea cliffs ensures visitors can appreciate one of the finest panoramas in Europe in safety.

Stop off at Tí Linn, the **Slieve League Cultural Centre** (✉ *Cliffs Rd., Teileann, Carrick* ☎ *074/973–9077* ⊕ *www.sliabhleague.com* ⊗ *Daily 10:30–5*), where they serve Italian Illy coffee; sample their delectable traditional home-baked cakes that include carrot, banana and date, coconut, and Victoria sponge. At the same time you can stock up on information about the cultural history of the region. Paddy Clarke runs the center and is a rich source of information about the area, especially the archaeological heritage.

WHERE TO STAY

$–$$

Fodor's Choice

★

Bay View Hotel & Leisure Centre. Across from Killybegs's harbor, the Bay View is a bustling spot. The hotel lobby, done in light wood, offers a modern take on classic designs, and the functional bedrooms are decorated in pale colors; many rooms offer bay-side views. The hotel is well placed for seeing the glorious north shore of Donegal Bay. Special rates include golf greens fees for Portnoo (outside Ard an Ratha) and Murvagh (outside Donegal). The hotel's proud claim is that it has been in business for three centuries. Famous Bay View residents of days gone by include Eamon de Valera and the soldier and statesman Michael Collins. As for dining, head to the informal Wheelhouse Bar and Bistro for an array of meals and snacks, with seafood selections headlining the menu. **Pros:** plain and unadorned, but the rooms are comfortable; convenient location for a wider exploration of south Donegal. **Cons:** room furnishings showing wear and tear with carpet stains in some rooms; the smell of fish emanating from the harbor can be overpowering. (✉ *Main St., Co. Donegal* ☎ *074/973–1950* ⊕ *www.bayviewhotel.ie* 🛏 *40 rooms* ⚓ *In-room: no a/c, Wi-Fi. In-hotel: restaurant, bar, pool, gym* ⊟ *AE, MC, V* ⫶⫶⫶ *BP, MAP*).

SHOPPING

The **Harbour Store** (✉ *Main St.* ☎ *074/973–2122*), right on the wharf, has plenty to make both fisherfolk and landlubbers happy, including boots and rain gear, competitively priced sweaters, and unusual bright-yellow or orange fiberglass-covered gloves (made in Taiwan).

10

To step back in time just head to Gleann Cholm Cille—if you're lucky you'll catch the locals rethatching their roofs.

GLEANN CHOLM CILLE (GLENCOLUMBKILLE)

27 km (17 mi) west of Killybegs on R263, 54 km (27 mi) west of Donegal Town.

Fodor's Choice
★

"The Back of Beyond," at the far end of a stretch of barren moorland, the tiny hamlet of Gleann Cholm Cille clings dramatically to the rock-bound harbor of Glen Bay. Known alternatively as Glencolumbkille (pronounced glen-colm-*kill*), it remains the heart of County Donegal's shrinking Gaeltacht region and retains a strong rural Irish flavor, as do its pubs and brightly painted row houses. The name means St. Columba's Glen; the legend goes that St. Columba, the Christian missionary, lived here during the 6th century with a group of followers before many of them moved on to find greater glory by settling Scotland's Isle of Iona. Some 40 prehistoric cairns, scattered around the village, have become connected locally with the St. Columba myths. The village has a Web site (⊕ *www.gleanncholmcille.ie*) where hopeful overnighters can track down one of the village B&Bs. There are no hotels in town, but walking lodges, friendly inns that cater to hikers, that opened in 2007 are worth checking out.

GETTING HERE

BUS TRAVEL The main Donegal Town to Dungloe Bus Éireann service does not go to Glencolumbkille, but there is a morning Bus Éireann bus service (Tuesday, Thursday, and Saturday only) that leaves Donegal Town for Glencolumbkille year-round. There is also a Monday–Saturday bus from Glencolumbkille to Donegal Town at 7:30 AM. From July 7 to August 22, a Hills of Donegal Bus Éireann scheduled service runs

Set at the "Back of Beyond," the seaside hamlet of Gleann Cholm Cille welcomes travelers at its beachfront Folk Village Museum.

Tuesday–Saturday from Donegal Town to top attractions like Glencolumbkille, Teelin Village (for the Slieve League cliffs), and Glenveagh National Park. The route is stunningly scenic but not high-speed (Donegal to Glencolumbkille alone takes 90 minutes; €25 round-trip). The main bus station in these parts is the Stranorlar Bus Station; Stranorlar is Ballybofey's "twin" town and is found 80 km (55 mi) east of Glencolumbkille, in east Donegal, near the border with Northern Ireland.

ESSENTIALS
Transportation Contacts Stranorlar Bus Station (☎ *074/913–1008*).

EXPLORING
The **House of St. Columba,** on the cliff top rising north of the village, is a small oratory said to have been used by the saint himself. Inside, stone constructions are thought to have been his bed and chair. Every year on June 9, starting at midnight, local people make a 3-km (2-mi) barefoot procession called An Turas (the journey) around 15 medieval crosses and ancient cairns, collectively called the stations of the cross.

★ Walk through the beachfront **Folk Village Museum** to explore rural life. This *clachan,* or tiny village, comprises a mere six cottages, all of which are whitewashed, thatch-roofed, and extremely modest in appearance. Three showcase particular years in Irish culture: 1720, 1820, and 1920; pride of place goes to the 1881 schoolhouse and the re-created *shebeen* (pub). The complex was built after local priest Father McDyer started a cooperative to help combat rural depopulation. You'll also find an interpretive center, teashop (don't dare miss out on the Guinness cakes), and crafts shop selling local handmade products. In summer the museum hosts traditional music evenings. Three small cottages, with bare-earth

Dream-Weavers

Most of the Aran sweaters you'll see throughout Ireland are made in County Donegal, the area most associated with high-quality, handwoven tweeds and hand-knit items. Made of plain, undyed wool and knit with distinctive crisscross patterns, Aran sweaters are durable, soft, often weatherproof, and can be astonishingly warm. They once provided essential protection against the wild, stormy Atlantic Ocean. Indeed, these Arans can hold 30% of their weight in water before they even start to feel wet.

Not so long ago, these pullovers were worn by every County Donegal fisherman, usually made to a design belonging exclusively to his own family. It's said that a native can tell which family the knitter belongs to from the patterns used in a genuine Aran sweater. Produced for centuries in the fishing communities of north and west Ireland, they are painstakingly knitted by hand, a process that can take weeks. As a result, prices are not cheap, and if you think you've found a bargain, check the label before buying—it's more likely a factory copy.

When it comes to Donegal tweed, weavers—inspired by the soft greens, red rusts, and dove grays of the famed Donegal landscape—have been producing it for centuries. In long-gone days, crofters' wives concocted the dyes to give Donegal tweed its distinctive flecks, and their husbands wove the cloth into tweed. Traditional Donegal tweed was a salt-and-pepper mix, but gradually, weavers began adding dyes distilled from yellow gorse, purple blackberries, orange lichen, and green moss. Today most tweed comes from factories. However, there are still about 25 local craftsmen working from their cottages. Chic fashion designers like Armani, Ralph Lauren, and Burberry all use handwoven Donegal tweed—obviously, more fashionable than ever.

The sweaters are enjoying a revival thanks partly to the traditional music group the High Kings, who toured the United States in 2008, impressing critics and audiences not only with their tunes and *bodhráns,* but also their Aran jumpers. There is a huge amount of romance and folklore attached to the sweaters and many regard them as a badge of iconic chic—a 21st-century symbol of Irish folk art.

floors, represent the very basic living conditions of the 1720s, 1820s, and 1920s. ⊠ *Near beach* ☎ *074/973–0017* ⊕ *www.glenfolkvillage.com* ⌦ *€3.50* ☉ *Easter–Sept., Mon.–Sat. 10–6, Sun. noon–6.*

Cliffs surrounding Gleann Cholm Cille rise up to more than 700 feet, including Glen Head; many cliffs are studded with ancient hermit cells. Also of note is a squat **Martello tower**, built by the British in 1804 to protect against an anticipated French invasion that never happened. Another good walk is the 8-km (5-mi) trek to Malinbeg, reached by the coast road running past Doon Point. Look for the ruins of no less than five burial cairns, a ring fort, a second Martello tower, and one of the best beaches in Ireland, famed for its calm waters, dramatic scenery, and lovely golden sand.

WHERE TO STAY

¢ ⌂ **Ionad Siúl Walking Lodge.** Lovely Gleann Cholm Cille has enough charms to entice loads of travelers but amazingly suffers from an acute shortage of accommodations. Happily, this walking lodge has now stepped into the breach. Not a hotel per se—there is no bar, pool, or meal plan—Ionad Siúl does have clean, comfortable, and spacious rooms, all en suite (bathroom included), with a handy kitchen for those who can whip up their own breakfasts. Before long, most guests want to pull on their walking boots and they can count on owners Charlie McGuire and his sisters to fill them in on the best guided tours of the region—a great way to explore the area's rich heritage and stunning landscape (prebooking is essential). **Pros:** set in spectacular countryside; friendly service; good value. **Cons:** rooms are basic; local facilities are limited. ⌂ *Gleann Cholm Cille, Co. Donegal* ☎ *074/973–0302* ⊕ *www.ionadsiul.ie* ⤵ *11 rooms* ☰ *MC, V.*

ARD AN RATHA (ARDARA)

★ *28 km (17 mi) northeast of Gleann Cholm Cille, 40 km (25 mi) northwest of Donegal Town on N56.*

At the head of a lovely ocean inlet, the unpretentious, old-fashioned hamlet of Ard an Ratha (Ardara) is built around the L-shaped intersection of its two main streets. (If you come from Gleann Cholm Cille, expect a scenic drive full of hairpin curves and steep hills as you cross over Glengesh Pass.) For centuries, great cloth fairs were held on the first of every month; cottage workers in the surrounding countryside still provide Ard an Ratha (and County Donegal) with high-quality, handwoven cloths and hand knits.

WHERE TO EAT AND STAY

$$$ ✕ **Nesbitt Arms Hotel.** Offering casual pub grub and more substantial fare, this old-fashioned inn gets understandably busy in summer. Decor harks back to the days when Ard an Ratha was Donegal's foremost weaving and wool center, which explains the wooden loom in the corner of the dining room. And what about the weaver depicted on the menu? He's the grandfather of the owner, Marie Gallagher, who runs the business, which has a long pedigree stretching back to 1838. If you want a quick bite, check out the daily specials in the Weavers Bistro—the beef-and-Guinness pie is particularly tasty. Upstairs in the dining room, a standout is the Hangman's Steak Kebab with onions and peppers served on a breadboard (replete with hanging spike). There's music in the bar every Friday and Saturday night. The hotel also rents simple rooms. ⌂ *Main St.* ☎ *074/954–1103* ⊕ *www.nesbittarms.com* ☰ *MC, V.*

IRISH

¢ ⌂ **Green Gate.** For an alternative to country estates and village hotels, make a beeline for Frenchman Paul Chatenoud's remote cottage B&B overlooking Ard an Ratha, the Atlantic, and some spectacular Donegal scenery—it's one of Ireland's most beautiful little guesthouses. Apart from the cozy hideaway main house, the four spare guest rooms are set in a converted stone outbuilding with a thatch roof. Oozing charm like his premises, the owner loves his guests and eagerly directs them to Donegal's best-kept secrets (he also serves 20 different types of jams

Fodor's Choice
★

10

and marmalade at breakfast; try the Irish whiskey one to kick-start your day). To reach the hotel from Ard an Ratha, follow the sign for Donegal and turn right after 200 yards. **Pros:** tons of local information; great camaraderie with fellow travelers. **Cons:** cottages have few extras; hard to find on a dark drunken night. ⊠ *Ardvally, Co. Donegal* ☎ *074/954– 1546* ⊕ *www.thegreengate.eu* ⤳ *4 rooms* ♿ *In-room: no a/c, no phone, no TV. In-hotel: Internet terminal* ⊟ *No credit cards* ⭐ *BP.*

$–$$

Fodor's Choice

★

🏠 **Woodhill House.** The cream-color exterior of John and Nancy Yates's spacious manor house is Victorian, but parts of the interior and the coach house date from the 17th century. High ceilings, marble fireplaces, and stained glass are part of the public spaces. Bedrooms have superb views of the Donegal highlands and the new guest rooms completed in 2008 overlook the gardens. The 40-seat restaurant (where prices are usually in the $$$ range) uses local ingredients in dishes on its French-Irish €40 prix-fixe menus; don't miss the wild Donegal salmon with Provençal tomatoes and basmati rice, or duck confit with orange sauce, or wonderfully concocted desserts, such as whiskey ice cream. Frequent Irish folk-music sessions take place in the bar. **Pros:** quiet location; beautifully maintained house where visitors fall in love with the gardens. **Cons:** some don't like the library-like breakfast-time silences; complaints about poor TV reception. ⊠ *Wood Rd.,Co. Donegal* ☎ *074/954–1112* ⊕ *www.woodhillhouse.com* ⤳ *13 rooms* ♿ *In-room: no a/c, Wi-Fi. In-hotel: restaurant, bar* ⊟ *AE, DC, MC, V* ☾ *Closed Christmas wk* ⭐ *BP.*

NIGHTLIFE

For a small, old-fashioned village, Ard an Ratha has a surprising number of pubs, many of which have traditional music in the evening. **The Corner Bar** (⊠ *Main St.* ☎ *074/954–1736*) has music almost every night in July and August and on weekends the rest of the year. One of the smallest bars in the republic, **Nancy's Pub** (⊠ *Front St.* ☎ *074/954–1187*), makes you wonder if you've wandered into the owner's sitting room, but it occasionally finds space for a folk group.

SHOPPING

Many handwoven and locally made knitwear items are on sale in Ard an Ratha. Some stores commission goods directly from knitters, and prices are about as low as anywhere. Handsome, chunky Aran hand-knit sweaters (€80–€130), cardigans (similar prices), and scarves (€25) are all widely available. Stores such as **Campbells Tweed Shop** (⊠ *Front St.* ☎ *074/954–1128*) carry ready-to-wear tweeds—sports jackets can run up to €120. **C. Bonner and Son** (⊠ *Front St.* ☎ *074/954–1303*) stocks factory knitwear from €30 to €120, as well as pottery, tweeds, jewelry, and gifts. There's also a good selection of hand-knit Aran sweaters and cardigans available. **E. Doherty (Ardara) Ltd** (⊠ *Front St.* ☎ *074/954–1304*) sells handwoven tweeds, from scarves for €25 to capes for €195, as well as traditional Irish products, such as glassware and linen, from Ard an Ratha and other parts of the country. At **John Molloy** (⊠ *Main St.* ☎ *074/954–1133*) you will find a factory shop offering high-quality, handwoven Donegal tweed, and hand-knit Aran sweaters.

Northern Ireland

INCLUDING COUNTIES OF ANTRIM, ARMAGH, DERRY, DOWN, FERMANAGH, AND TYRONE

WORD OF MOUTH

"A Belfast Black Taxi Tour was a highlight but I was shocked to find that in the Shankhill Rd./Falls Road area most of the political murals have been replaced with 'positive' ones depicting historic events. I understand wanting to move beyond 'the Troubles'—but it felt wrong to erase history. Even so, I found the tour profoundly moving and was close to tears at the sites of the bombings."

—chevre

WELCOME TO NORTHERN IRELAND

TOP REASONS TO GO

★ **Belfast, Gateway City:** As the locals put it, "Despite what you've probably heard, Belfast is not what you expect"—so get ready to love this bustling city that bristles with Victorian shop fronts and hip restaurants.

★ **The Giant's Causeway:** This spectacular remnant of Ireland's volcanic period will steal you away from your 21st-century existence and transport you to a time when the giant Finn McCool roamed the land.

★ **Nine Glens of Antrim:** Fabled haunt of "the wee folk," the glacier-carved valleys have a beauty that has become synonymous with Irishness. Don't miss Glenariff, dubbed "Little Switzerland" by Thackeray.

★ **Ulster-American Folk Park:** A tale of two countries joined by a common people is told at this impressive open-air museum, which re-creates a 19th-century Tyrone village and boasts the Centre for Migration Studies.

1 The Giant's Causeway Coast. North of the famously beautiful Glens of Antrim—still considered "gentle" (supernatural) in spirit—the coast continues up to Northern Ireland's premier attraction, the Giant's Causeway. Farther along the North Antrim coast are Bushmills, the oldest distillery in the world; Dunluce Castle, spectacularly perched over its "Mermaid's Cave"; and the heart-stopping Carrick-a-Rede rope bridge.

2 Derry. A walk through Ireland's only walled city provides a unique way to view the layout of the 17th-century inner town, particularly noticeable in the streets and alleys that fan outward from the Diamond, where fine examples of Georgian and Victorian architecture rub shoulders with old-style pubs and museums.

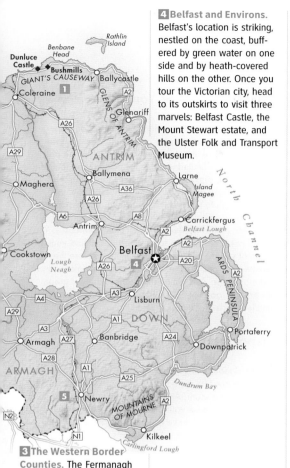

4 Belfast and Environs. Belfast's location is striking, nestled on the coast, buffered by green water on one side and by heath-covered hills on the other. Once you tour the Victorian city, head to its outskirts to visit three marvels: Belfast Castle, the Mount Stewart estate, and the Ulster Folk and Transport Museum.

GETTING ORIENTED

With peace—precious peace—abiding, Northern Ireland can finally go about the business of charming visitors full-time. While July 2010 saw violent protests mounted by Irish nationalists, the country is greatly intent on welcoming tourists. North of the vibrant Victorian city of Belfast, you'll find the ageless wonders of the Causeway Coast while south of the inspiring skyline of Derry lie the Border Counties, where tiny "Ulster" towns dot the scenic landscapes around the Lakes of Fermanagh and Mountains of Mourne.

3 The Western Border Counties. The Fermanagh Lakeland is an intricate patchwork quilt of undulating hillsides and some of the most uncongested lakes in Europe. A paradise of open horizons and opportunities for those who love the outdoor life, it is also home to stately mansions such as Florence Court and Castle Coole, the Ulster-American Folk Park, and the famous porcelain town of Belleek.

5 The Eastern Border Counties. South of Belfast past the Ards Peninsula is St. Patrick Country: Downpatrick, reputed to be the burial place of the saint; Armagh's two St. Patrick cathedrals; and the seaside Mountains of Mourne.

NORTHERN IRELAND PLANNER

Talking About It

Although "The Troubles" are now ideally a thing of the past, Northern Ireland is a political entity that draws its mandate from religion and history—a country where God and politics are tightly interwoven and where ancient quarrels can sometimes still affect the tone of everyday life. So if you find yourself in a pub, it often helps to play a little dumb about facts and events, as the residents seem to be even more willing to explain the history to visitors with no preconceived notions of how things should be. Take any questions of politics gently at first, smell the air of the company you're in, then play the gee-this-is-all-new-to-me card, and things should roll along fine. And certainly stay away from any deep political discussion after four pints of beer!

Making the Most of Your Time

Though Northern Ireland may not look that big on paper, tackling a fair share of its many attractions in less than a week isn't possible without exhausting yourself in the process. If your time is limited, choose the eastern half (Belfast, the Antrim Coast, and the Mountains of Mourne) or the western half (Derry and the Border Counties). The cities are small enough to tackle in a day or two. But remember that the rural wonders—the Antrim Coast, the Fermanagh lakes, the Mountains of Mourne—cast their spell easily. You may head out to enjoy them for a day trip and find yourself wishing that you'd factored in more time to explore the endless string of postcard-worthy villages, misty glens, and rugged mountains. And although distances are not great, neither are the roads—you'll spend most of your time traveling smaller roads, not major express highways.

Transportation Basics

Northern Ireland is small—about half the size of Delaware and less than one-fifth the size of the Republic of Ireland, its neighbor to the south. And because it's so small, one option is to simply base yourself in the two main cities, Belfast and Derry, and make day trips out. However, one of the real glories of Ulster is its endless supply of spectacular rural scenery, so much so that you may find yourself ho-humming at your umpteenth view of emerald-green glens. The good news is that bus travel is both quick and fairly priced. The extensive network of the state-owned Ulsterbus (⊕ www.translink.co.uk) means it's easy to reach many towns. The bad news is that Northern Ireland Railways (NIR) is sorely limited, with only three main routes: Belfast–Derry, Belfast–Bangor, and Belfast–Dublin. In the past decade, however, more runs have been scheduled by Translink (⊕ www.translink.co.uk), the company that runs the buses and trains; Translink Goldline refers to superior express buses that run only run on high-demand routes. That noted, in many areas, including the wildly popular Causeway Coast, you'll definitely end up on smaller bus routes as the Causeway Coast Express if you don't drive a car.

Finding a Place to Stay

Major hotel chains based both in the republic and abroad have invested in Northern Ireland's cities. In Belfast's environs you can also choose from the humblest terraced town houses or farm cottages to the grandest country houses. Dining rooms of country-house lodgings frequently match the standard of top-quality restaurants. All accommodations in the province are inspected and categorized by the Northern Ireland Tourist Board Information Centre, which publishes hostelry names, addresses, and ratings in the free guidebooks *Hotel and Guest House Guide* and *Bed & Breakfast Guide,* also available online. Hundreds of excellent-value specials—single nights to weekend deals, the most intimate bed-and-breakfasts to Belfast's finest hotels—become available in the low season, October to March. Assume that all hotel rooms reviewed have in-room phones and TVs, along with private bathrooms, unless otherwise indicated.

Feeling Festive in Belfast?

Northern Ireland is a great place for festivals and almost every town has its own theme festival of some sort. The **Belfast Festival** (⊕ *www.belfastfestival.com*) at Queen's University is one of the biggest with a packed program of arts, music, and literature held in October. Belfast's **Cathedral Arts Quarter Festival** (⊕ *www.cqaf.com*), held late April–early May, uses established, new, and unusual venues throughout the oldest part of the city center for two weeks of music, theater, and visual arts. **Féile an Phobail,** the West Belfast Festival (⊕ *www.feilebelfast.com*), held in early August, is a 10-day schedule of events with a political and international theme. **Hillsborough International Oyster Festival** (⊕ *www.hillsboroughoysterfestival.com*), held in September, is three days of good food and entertainment. For a rundown on many other festivals, contact the Northern Ireland Tourist Board.

When to Go

If the weather is good—and most of the year it isn't—touring Northern Ireland can be a real pleasure. But the place is so green for a reason: lots of rain, which means you should certainly pack your Burberry. Because you're on the coast, even on bright summer days you can feel the chill from the sea, so it's best to travel layered-up. Needless to say, the weather is a little friendlier to tourists May to September.

Pounds, Not Euros

Northern Ireland uses British currency. Euros are accepted in some shops along the border areas and in some shopping centers in Belfast. You may sometimes be given bank notes, drawn on Ulster banks. Be sure not to get stuck with a lot of these when you leave, because they're accepted with reluctance, if at all, in the rest of the United Kingdom and will be difficult to change at banks back home.

DINING AND LODGING PRICE CATEGORIES (IN POUNDS STERLING)

	¢	$	$$	$$$	$$$$
Restaurants	under £7	£7–£13	£14–£18	£19–£22	over £22
Hotels	under £50	£50–£80	£81–£115	£116–£160	over £160

Restaurant prices are for a main course at dinner. Hotel prices are for a standard double room in high season.

GETTING AROUND

Car Travel

Many roads from the Irish Republic into Northern Ireland were once closed for security reasons, but all are now reinstated, leaving you with a choice of legitimate crossing points. The army checkpoints at approved frontier posts have all been removed, and few customs formalities are observed.

The fast N1/A1 road connects Belfast to Dublin in 160 km (100 mi) with an average driving time of just over two hours.

When in Belfast, if you don't avail yourself of the many parking garages, you'll have to opt for street meter-ticket parking. Before parking on the street, check the posted regulations: during rush hours many spots become no-parking.

Parking

In Northern Ireland there are plenty of parking lots in the towns (usually free except in Belfast), and you should use them. In Belfast, you can't park your car in some parts of the city center, more because of congestion than security problems.

Bus Travel

Northern Ireland's main bus company, Ulsterbus, runs direct service between Dublin and Belfast. Queries about Ulsterbus service, or any other bus and rail transportation in Northern Ireland, can be answered by the company that runs Ulsterbus, the national central reservation center called Translink. The Translink Goldline service (these are superior express buses with more modern comfortable seats that are operated only on some high-demand routes) between the two cities is a 24-hour service operating daily and departing from Belfast's Europa Buscentre on the hour.

The republic's Bus Éireann runs direct services to Belfast from Dublin, calling at Dublin Airport. Buses arrive at and depart from the Buscentre; the ride takes three hours. The efficient Air Coach operates hourly between Belfast and Dublin (change buses at Dublin Airport for central Dublin) from 6:30 AM to 8:30 PM. Buses arrive and depart Belfast from outside Jurys Inn, Fisherwick Place. These Air Coach buses to Belfast also run from London and from Birmingham, making the Stranraer ferry crossing. You can take advantage of frequent and inexpensive Ulsterbus links between all Northern Ireland towns. In Belfast, the Europa Buscentre is just behind the Europa Hotel.

Within Belfast the city bus service is comprehensive (there is no subway). All routes start from Donegall Square, where the Metro Kiosk, on Donegall Square West, has timetables. The Metro service operates on most suburban routes to and from the city center. A one-day ticket, Monday to Saturday, costs £3.50 (£2.70 after 9:30 AM).

If you want to tour the north by bus and train, contact Translink: an iLink ticket allows unlimited travel on bus or train (£15 per day, or £55 per week; it costs £1.50 to buy the card).

Bus Depot Europa Buscentre (⊠ *Great Victoria St., Golden Mile, Belfast* ☎ *028/9066–6630*).

Bus Lines Air Coach (☎ *028/9033–0655* ⊕ *www. aircoach.ie*). **Belfast Metro Service** (⊠ *Donegall Square West, Belfast* ☎ *028/9066–6630* ⊕ *www.translink. co.uk*). **Bus Éireann** (☎ *01/836–6111 in Dublin* ⊕ *www. buseireann.ie*). **Translink** (☎ *028/9066–6630* ⊕ *www. translink.co.uk*).

11

Train Travel

The Dublin–Belfast Express train, run jointly by Northern Ireland Railways (a company operated by Translink) and Irish Rail–Iarnród Éireann (which only services the Republic of Ireland), travels between the two cities in about two hours. Eight trains (check timetables, as some trains are much slower) run daily in each direction (five on Sunday) between Dublin and Belfast's misnamed Central Station—it's not, in fact, that central. A single journey costs £25; a day return is £30. You can change trains at Central Station for the city-center Great Victoria Street Station, which is adjacent to the Europa Buscentre and the Europa Hotel.

Northern Ireland Railways (NIR) runs only four rail routes from Belfast's Central Station: northwest to Derry via Coleraine; east to Bangor along the shore of Belfast Lough; northeast to Larne (for the P&O European ferry to Scotland); and south to Dublin.

There are frequent connections to Central Station from the city-center Great Victoria Street Station and from Botanic Station in the university area. A Freedom of Northern Ireland ticket allows unlimited travel on trains (£15 per day, £36 for three days, and £53 per week). If you want to tour the north by train, contact Translink: an iLink ticket allows unlimited travel on bus or train (£15 per day, or £55 per week; it costs £1.50 to buy the card).

Train Lines **Iarnród Éireann** (☎ 1850/366–222 timetables ⊕ www.irishrail.ie). **Northern Ireland Railways** (✉ Central Station, E. Bridge St., Belfast ☎ 028/9066–6630 ⊕ www. translink.co.uk). **Translink** (☎ 028/9066–6630 ⊕ www. translink.co.uk).

Train Stations **Botanic Station** (✉ Botanic Ave., University Area, Belfast ☎ 028/9089–9400). **Central Station** (✉ E. Bridge St., Belfast ☎ 028/9089–9400).

Taxi Travel

Most taxis operate on the meter; ask for a price for longer journeys. You can order in advance. Belfast International Airport to Belfast city center is around £25; Belfast City Airport to the city center is around £6; Derry City Airport to Derry city center is around £12. The minimum fare is usually £2.50 and £1.05 per mile thereafter.

Taxi Companies **FonACAB** (✉ Belfast ☎ 028/9033–3333 ⊕ www.fonacab.com). **Foyle Taxis** (✉ Derry ☎ 028/7126–3905). **Value Cabs** (✉ Belfast ☎ 028/9080–9080 ⊕ www. valuecabs.co.uk).

Boat and Ferry Travel

Norfolkline has 12 eight-hour daytime or overnight car ferries that connect Belfast with the English west-coast port of Liverpool every day.

P&O European Ferries has a one-hour sailing to Larne from Cairnryan, Scotland.

In addition, infrequent trains take passengers on to Belfast. Stena Line operates a fast catamaran (1½ hours) between Belfast and Stranraer, Scotland.

Boat and Ferry Information
Port of Belfast (✉ Belfast Harbour Commissioners, Corporation Sq., Belfast ☎ 028/9055–4422 ⊕ www. belfast-harbour.co.uk).

Norfolkline (✉ Victoria Terminal 2, W. Bank Rd., Belfast ☎ 028/9077–9090 ⊕ www. norfolkline.com).

P&O European Ferries (☎ 0871/664–4777 ⊕ www. poirishsea.com).

Stena Line (☎ 028/9074–7747 ⊕ www.stenaline.com).

GETTING AROUND

Airports

Belfast International Airport at Aldergove is the north's principal air arrival point, 30½ km (19 mi) north of town. George Best Belfast City Airport is the secondary airport, 6½ km (4 mi) east of the city. It receives flights from U.K. provincial airports, from London's Gatwick and Heathrow, and from Stansted and Luton (both near London). City of Derry Airport is 8 km (5 mi) from Derry and receives flights from Dublin, Glasgow, London, and Manchester.

Airport Information George Best Belfast City Airport (☎ 028/9093–9093 ⊕ www.belfastcityairport.com). **Belfast International Airport at Aldergove** (☎ 028/9448–4848 ⊕ www.belfastairport.com). **City of Derry Airport** (☎ 028/7181–0784 ⊕ www.cityofderryairport.com).

Word of Mouth

"I really didn't feel like walking all the way down to the Giant's Causeway. And the thought of walking back up was even less fun. So it's a good thing that they have the Causeway Coaster bus and goes every tenth minute. Cost 1 pound for a single ticket, 2 pounds for a return ticket."   —anyegr

Air Travel

Scheduled services from the United States and Canada are mostly routed through Dublin, Glasgow, London, or Manchester.

A considerable number of new routes have been introduced to Belfast International to great fanfare in the past 10 years.

Frequent services to Belfast's two airports are scheduled throughout the day from London Heathrow, London Gatwick, and Luton (all of which have fast coordinated subway or rail connections to central London) and from 17 other U.K. airports.

Flights from London take about one hour. Aer Arann flies twice daily from Cork to Belfast on weekdays.

Ryanair flies from Derry to Luton, Stansted, Birmingham, Bristol, East Midlands, Glasgow, and Liverpool.

British Midland, through its low-cost carrier BmiBaby, flies from Birmingham, Cardiff, Manchester, and Nottingham to Belfast International.

British Midland flies between George Best Belfast City Airport and Heathrow.

Jet2.com flies from Belfast International to Blackpool, Ibiza, Jersey, Leeds, Majorca, Pisa, Tenerife, and Toulouse.

EasyJet flies from Belfast International to 19 European airports, including Alicante, Amsterdam, Barcelona, Bristol, Edinburgh, Glasgow, Liverpool, Luton, Nice, Paris, and London Stansted.

Flybe, also known as British European Airways, flies from Belfast City to Aberdeen, Birmingham, Edinburgh, Glasgow, Leeds, London Gatwick, Norwich, and Southampton, among others.

Aer Lingus operates 10 routes to Amsterdam, Barcelona, Faro, Lanzarote, London, Málaga, Milan, Munich, Paris, and Rome.

Airport Bus and Taxi Transfers

A branch of Translink, Ulsterbus operates an Airbus service every 10 minutes (one-way £7, round-trip £10) between Belfast International Airport and Belfast city center (6:50 AM–6:15 PM), as well as between George Best Belfast City Airport and the city center (one-way £2, round-trip £3; weekdays every 20 minutes, 6 AM–10:05 PM). Contact Translink for information on all buses.

From the City Airport, you can also travel into Belfast by train from Sydenham Halt to Central Station or catch a taxi from the airport to your hotel.

If you arrive at the City of Derry Airport, you may need to call a taxi to get to your destination. A direct bus service, the Airporter, links Derry with both Belfast International and George Best Belfast City airports (one-way £17.50, round-trip £27.50).

Airport Transfer Contacts Airporter (☎ 028/7126–9996 ⊕ www.airporter.co.uk). **Delta Cabs** (☎ 028/7127–9999). **Eglinton Taxis** (☎ 028/7181–1231). **Foyle Taxis** (☎ 028/7126–3905). **Translink** (☎ 028/9066–6630 ⊕ www.translink.co.uk).

Guided Bus Tours

Ulsterbus operates half-day or full-day trips June through September from Belfast to the Glens of Antrim, the Giant's Causeway, the Fermanagh lakes, Lough Neagh, the Mountains of Mourne, and the Ards Peninsula.

Ulsterbus has also teamed up with the Old Bushmills Distillery to run an open-top tour bus running from Coleraine (via Bushmills to observe whiskey making) to the Giant's Causeway and the coastal resorts in summer. Contact Ulsterbus through Translink.

Allens Tours (from £15) and Mini-Coach Tours operate day tours of Belfast (£8–£16), and to the Giant's Causeway, Bushmills Distillery, and Carrickfergus (£17.50). A top guided tour bus company is Belfast City Sightseeing.

Bus Tour Contacts Allens Tours (☎ 028/9091–5613 ⊕ www.allenstours.co.uk). **Belfast City Sightseeing** (☎ 028/9045–9035 ⊕ www.belfastcitysightseeing.com). **Mini-Coach** (✉ 22 Donegall Rd., Central District, Belfast ☎ 028/9031–5333 ⊕ www.minicoachni.co.uk). **Translink** (☎ 028/9066–6630 ⊕ www.translink.co.uk).

Guided Bike Tours

11

Irish Cycle Tours organizes four- and eight-day tours of the Mournes, Glens of Antrim, and Causeway Coast, and the Sperrin Mountains and Donegal. The company closed its Belfast office in 2004 and is based in County Kerry in the Republic, hence the southern Irish phone number. Mourne Cycle Tours runs bike tours complete with hotel accommodations (bikes are delivered to the hotel), with rates for a two-night booking costing between £90 and £110.

Irish Cycle Tours (☎ 066/712–8733 in Republic ⊕ www.irishcycletours.com). **Mourne Cycle Tours** (☎ 028/4372–4348 ⊕ www.mournecycletours.com).

Main Airlines

Aer Arann (☎ 081/821–0210 or 0800/587–2324 ⊕ www.aerarann.com). **Aer Lingus** (☎ 0871/718–5000 ⊕ www.aerlingus.com). **British Airways** (☎ 0844/493–0787 ⊕ www.britishairways.com). **British Midland Airways** (☎ 0870/607–0555 ⊕ www.bmibaby.com). **Continental** (☎ 0845/607–6760 ⊕ www.continental.com). **Easy-Jet** (☎ 0871/244–2366 ⊕ www.easyjet.com). **Flybe** (☎ 0871/700–2000 ⊕ www.flybe.com). **Jet2** (☎ 0871/226–1737 ⊕ www.jet2.com). **Ryanair** (☎ 081/830–3030 ⊕ www.ryanair.com).

ALL ABOUT IRISH WHISKEYS

Located on the Antrim coast, the small town of Bushmills lays claim to the world's oldest distillery. Today, its name is synonymous with the best in whiskey. Taste one drop and you may never drink Tennessee whiskey or Jack Daniels again.

(above): Liquid history on view at Bushmills Distillery; (right, top) Learn how malted barley and yeasts are alchemized into whiskey; (right, bottom): Drink Bushmills neat.

OLD BUSHMILLS

✉ *2 Distillery Rd., Bushmills, Co. Antrim*
☎ *028/2073–3218*
⊕ *www.bushmills.com*
🎫 *£6* ⏱ *Tours Apr.–Oct., Mon.–Sat. 9:15–5, Sun. noon–5; Nov.–Mar., weekdays 9:30–3:30, weekends 12:30–3:30. For more information on the Distillery tours, see our listing under Bushmills, below.*

Some 125 years ago, Ireland had 28 whiskey distilleries in what was a great industry. Today, only four working ones remain: Bushmills in Antrim, Midleton in Cork, Kilbeggan in Westmeath, and Cooley in Louth. For some, Bushmills is the best, literally: at the 2009 San Francisco Wine and Spirit Awards, it won the Best Irish Whiskey title. And to celebrate its 400th anniversary in 2008, it was selected as the icon of Northern Ireland, and was featured on Bank of Ireland notes. Where does the whiskey drinker start? Some prefer the classic melt-in-the-mouth Black Bush (drunk neat) to the more expensive malt. Other delights include the limited-edition 1608, the Original, and four single malts: aged 10 years, 12 years, 16 years, and 21 years.

THE "WATER OF LIFE"

Whiskey is a word that comes from the Irish *uisce beatha*, meaning "water of life." Water is a major factor influencing the flavor of any whiskey.

For Bushmills, it flows from the crystal clear St. Columb's Rill, taking its character from the basalt and turf bed of the River Bush. Another key ingredient is malted barley, which is here ground into grist in the mash house and added to boiling water in vats to become wort. Yeast is then added to the mix, and the fermentation turns the sugars to alcohol. The wash goes into a copper pot and is distilled three times, each distillation making the alcohol purer.

By comparison, American whisky is distilled only once. The spirit is diluted then matured in oak casks and seasoned by sherry, bourbon, or port. A small portion, about 2% of the distillate, evaporates and is affectionately known as the Angels' Share.

Remember to first try Bushmills neat and then add water in teaspoonful increments, as a soupçon of water unlocks the flavor while knocking a little fire out of the whiskey—there's a crucial tipping point so don't dilute too much!

WHAT'S IRISH ABOUT WHISKEY?

First off, it is spelled with an "e," to distinguish it from Scotch whisky. "Irish" has a characteristic flavor which distinguishes it from Scotch, bourbon, or rye;

try it straight or with water as it is best without a mixer. And don't go chasing after Poteen (pronounced "potcheen"), the famed Irish moonshine. Any attempts by a "stranger" to procure it will result either in meeting a brick wall or a wild goose chase. Just as well: it produces one of the worst hangovers known to man or woman.

TOURING THE DISTILLERY

Set in an area of natural beauty a short distance from the Giant's Causeway, Bushmills was granted its first license in 1608, although records refer as far back as 1276.

Visitors to the distillery are shown around a higgledy-piggledy collection of redbrick and whitewashed buildings that include eleven warehouses brimming with 187,000 barrels of whiskey. Look out for the long rows of Oloroso sherry casks, where the drink is aged in some instances, for more than 25 years (they favor a generous gestation here).

Tours run every half hour and cost £6. If you're in the mood to splurge, take the two-hour deluxe Bush Experience tour, which offers eight varieties of whiskey and costs £60 (reservations required, with a minimum of six). Tasting sessions all take place in the 1608 pub where American troops were once billeted during World War II.

Updated by
Paul Clements

Legend has it that a millennium ago a seafaring chieftain caught sight of the green shores of Northern Ireland, and offered the land to whichever of his two sons would be first to lay a hand upon it. As the two rivals rowed toward shore in separate boats, one began to draw ahead, whereupon the other drew his sword, cut off his own hand, and hurled it onto the beach—and so, by blood and sacrifice, gained the province. To this day the coat of arms of Northern Ireland bears the severed limb: the celebrated "Red Hand of Ulster."

From this ancient bardic tale to the recent Troubles—lasting from 1969 to 1994—Northern Ireland has had a long and often ferocious history. But all such thoughts vanish in the face of the country's natural beauty, magnificent stately houses, and the warm hospitality of its people. The Six Counties, or Ulster (as Northern Ireland is often called), cover less than 14,245 square km (5,500 square mi). These boundaries contain some of the most unspoiled scenery you could ever hope to find on this earth: the granite Mountains of Mourne; the Giant's Causeway, made of extraordinary volcanic rock; more than 320 km (200 mi) of coastline beaches and hidden coves; and rivers and leaf-sheltered lakes, including Europe's largest freshwater lake, Lough Neagh, that provide fabled fishing grounds. Ancient castles and Palladian-perfect 18th-century houses are as numerous here as almost anywhere else in Europe, and each has its own tale of heroic feats, dastardly deeds, and lovelorn ghosts.

Northern Ireland not only houses this heritage within its native stone, but has also given the world perhaps an even greater legacy: its roster of celebrated descendants. Nearly one in six of the more than 4.5 million Irish who journeyed across the Atlantic in search of fortune in the New World came from Ulster, and of this group (and from their family stock), more than a few left their mark in America: Davy Crockett, President

Andrew Jackson, General Ulysses S. Grant, President Woodrow Wilson, General Stonewall Jackson, financier Thomas Mellon, merchant J. Paul Getty, writers Edgar Allan Poe and Mark Twain, and astronaut Neil Armstrong.

Present-day Northern Ireland, a province under the rule of the United Kingdom, includes six of the old Ulster's nine counties and retains its sense of separation, both in the vernacular of the landscape and, some would say, in the character of the people. The hardheaded and industrious Scots-Presbyterians, imported to make Ulster a bulwark against Ireland's Catholicism, have had a profound and ineradicable effect on the place. For all that, the border between north and south is of little consequence if you're just here to see the country.

On the political front, peace reigns in Northern Ireland today. There are no checkpoints anymore—not security-related ones anyway. As far as border issues go (with the Republic of Ireland to the south), the border is there in name only. No one is stopped or questioned, no passports are checked, and there isn't even a sign announcing you are passing into the republic. Visitors—even ones with English accents—are not hassled in any way, and Americans are more than warmly welcomed. The "peace dividend" has led to massive investment in places like Belfast and Derry. Every year, Derry gets dolled up for its annual Halloween fancy-dress party and Northern Ireland's vivacious spirit truly takes center stage. Naysayers may remind you that Belfast is no utopia and there is still a ways to go, but just come during Féile an Phobail (the West Belfast Festival held in August) and you'll see just how wholeheartedly the city celebrates Northern Ireland's newfound peace.

BELFAST

The city of Belfast was a great Victorian success story, an industrial boomtown whose prosperity was built on trade—especially linen and shipbuilding. Famously (or infamously), the *Titanic* was built here, giving Belfast, for a time, the nickname "Titanic Town." Huge plans are afoot, on the eve of the 100th anniversary of the sinking on April 14, 1912, to commemorate the liner.

For two decades, news about Belfast meant news about the Troubles—until the 1994 cease-fire. Since then, Northern Ireland's capital city has benefited from major hotel investment, gentrified quaysides (or strands), a heralded performing arts center, and strenuous efforts on the part of the tourist board to claim a share of the visitors pouring into the Emerald Isle. Although the 1996 bombing of offices at the Canary Wharf in London disrupted the 1994 peace agreement, the cease-fire was officially reestablished on July 20, 1997, and this embattled city began its quest for a newfound identity.

Belfast is a fairly compact city, 167 km (104 mi) north of Dublin. The city center is made up of three roughly contiguous areas that are easy to navigate on foot; from the south end to the north it's about an hour's leisurely walk. The main tourist office is the Belfast Welcome Centre on Donegall Place, which also provides information for all of

Northern Ireland and includes an accommodation reservation service, ticket sales for tours and events, an Internet café, and a crafts shop. Ask for the Belfast Regional voucher booklet, which gives discounts on visitor attractions, hotels, cafés, and restaurants as well as shops. Also pick up a free copy of *What About,* a bimonthly listing of what's on and what's hot in the entertainment world. It's also worth reading *Belfast in Your Pocket* (⊕ *www.belfast.inyourpocket.com*), a bimonthly booklet with up-to-date listings of all the major events.

GETTING HERE AND AROUND

BUS TRAVEL   In Belfast, the pink-and-white Metro buses, with 12 high-frequency suburban routes, are the best way to get around. Fares range from £1.30 to £1.90, depending on the zone. If you're staying a few days, buy a Smartlink Travel Card for more than five journeys, which is a 30% saving; a weekly card is £14.50, plus £1.50 to initially buy the card. A Metro day ticket costs £3.50 (£2.70 after 9:30) and takes you anywhere on the network Monday–Saturday. Check for details at the Metro Kiosk at Donegall Square West, beside City Hall.

In and out of Belfast, buses have a much more extensive network than trains. Belfast International Airport has regular services to and from the Europa Buscentre (£10 round-trip), as does George Best Belfast City Airport (£3 round-trip). Daily service operates from Belfast to Dublin with both Translink, and its rival, the Aircoach. Both stop at Dublin Airport. The larger Northern Ireland cities, like Derry and Armagh have frequent Translink Goldline connections to Belfast. Goldline is the network's flagship, offering a high-quality coach service with comfy seats. Typical fares from Belfast to most large towns range between £10 to £15 and include regular daily services to Enniskillen, Omagh, Bangor, and Downpatrick. Best buy: the Sunday Rambler Ticket for £8 for unlimited travel on all scheduled Ulsterbus services within Northern Ireland.

TRAIN TRAVEL   As the capital city of Northern Ireland, Belfast is well served by an efficient train network. Most trains arrive and leave from Central Station, a 15-minute walk from the city center. The high-speed, two-hour Enterprise cross-border service links Belfast with Dublin and has eight trains per day running from 6:50 AM until late evening. Some trains are slower and make more stops, and there are fewer on weekends. Fares vary, and at certain times—notably in the fall—deals are available; it is up to 50% cheaper to book online (but do so three days prior to your trip). From Belfast south you can also take a train to Lisburn, Portadown, and Newry, or east to Holywood and Bangor. Nine daily weekday services, starting from 6:20 AM to 9:25 PM, operate between Belfast and Derry with seven trains on Saturday and five on Sunday. The journey time is about two hours, and a round-trip ticket costs £15. If you travel after 9:30 AM you'll get a third off the standard fare. Best buy: the £6 Sunday Day Tracker gives you unlimited travel on all scheduled train services within Northern Ireland.

11

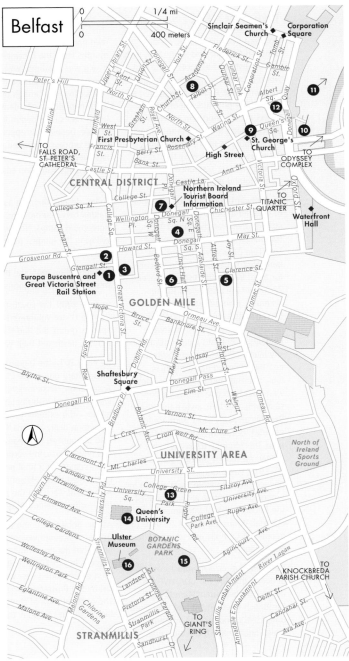

THE TROUBLES

Northern Ireland's historic conflict between Catholic and Protestant, Irish and English, had its roots in the first Norman incursions in the 12th century, when the English endeavored to subdue the potential enemy they saw as Ireland. The northern province of Ulster proved the hardest to conquer, but in 1607, its Irish nobility fled, their lands then given by the English to "the Planters"—staunch Protestants from England and Scotland.

Fast-forward through three centuries of smoldering tensions and religious strife to the overwhelming 1918 Nationalist vote across Ireland for Sinn Féin ("Ourselves Alone"), the party that believed in independence for all of Ireland. In Ulster, however, 22 (out of 29) seats went to the Unionists, who believed in maintaining British rule. After 50 years of living with a Unionist majority, students in Belfast's Queen's University launched a civil rights protest in 1968, claiming equal rights in jobs, housing, and opportunity. They were met by brutal British suppression, which, in turn, awoke the Irish Republican Army (IRA), dormant for decades. Britain then imposed Direct Rule. This struggle tragically came to a head on Bloody Sunday, January 30, 1972, when British paratroopers opened fire on people participating in a nonviolent protest in Derry against the British policy of internment without trial. When the smoke cleared, 13 people, all Catholic and unarmed, had been killed.

Decades of guerrilla conflict ensued between the IRA, the UDA/UVF (Protestant/Loyalist paramilitaries), and the British government and continued until 1998's Good Friday Agreement, which finally gave the province its own parliament. But a mere two months later, the province's fragile peace was shattered when a massive car bomb exploded in the quiet market town of Omagh on August 15. A minority of dissident Republicans had succeeded in killing 31 people. Despite this appalling act, the peace process continued and Unionists eventually entered government proceedings with Sinn Féin at the end of 1999.

Today, despite ongoing assembly battles between pro- and anti-agreement camps, Northern Ireland is enjoying the longest period of peace in its history.

In September 2005, the IRA decommissioned all its weapons.

In June 2009, the Loyalist paramilitaries, the Ulster Volunteer Force and its splinter group, the Red Hand Commando, destroyed their weapons.

By early 2010 the biggest Loyalist paramilitary group, the Ulster Defence Association, decommissioned all weapons. Two Irish Republican terror groups—the extreme Irish National Liberation Army and the Official IRA—also announced they had put weapons beyond use. In February 2010 the endorsement of a final political deal culminated in the Hillsborough Castle Agreement, securing the stability of the Northern Ireland Assembly.

As this book was going to press, Belfast saw some violent protests break out during demonstrations held in early July 2010 by Irish nationalists on a day presided over by marches led by the Protestant Orange order. The political saga of Northern Ireland continues to draw the world's attention.

ESSENTIALS

Transportation Contacts Belfast Metro Service (✉ *Donegall Square West, Belfast* ☎ *028/9066–6630* ⊕ *www.translink.co.uk*). **Botanic Rail Station** (✉ *Botanic Ave., University Area, Belfast* ☎ *028/9089–9400*). **Central Rail Station** (✉ *E. Bridge St., Belfast* ☎ *028/9089–9400*). **Europa Buscentre** (✉ *Great Victoria St., Golden Mile, Belfast* ☎ *028/9066–6630*).

Visitor Information Belfast Welcome Centre (✉ *47 Donegall Pl., Central District, Belfast* ☎ *028/9024–6609* ⊕ *www.gotobelfast.com* ☉ *Oct.–May, Mon.–Sat. 9–5:30; June–Sept., Mon.–Sat. 9–7, Sun. 11–4*).

EXPLORING

Magnificent Victorian structures still line the streets of the city center, but instead of housing linen mills or cigarette factories, they are home to chic new hotels and fashionable bars. Smart restaurants abound, and the people of Belfast, who for years would not venture out of their districts, appear to be making up for lost time. Each area of the city has changed considerably in the new peaceful era, but perhaps none more than the docklands around the Harland and Wolff shipyards, whose historic and enormous cranes, known to the locals as Samson and Goliath, still dominate the city's skyline. New developments—such as the Titanic Quarter—are springing up all around the now-deserted shipyards, ranging from luxury hotels to modern office blocks. And in the center of the city, Victoria Square is a gigantic new shopping and residential complex, replete with geodesic dome, floors of glossy shops, and renovated Victorian row houses. In the west of the city, the physical scars of the Troubles are still evident, from the peace line that divides Catholic and Protestant West Belfast to the murals on every gable wall. Visitors are discovering that it's safe to venture beyond the city center; indeed, backpackers are becoming a regular sight on the Falls Road, and taxi tours of these once troubled areas are more popular than ever.

Before English and Scottish settlers arrived in the 1600s, Belfast was a tiny village called Béal Feirste ("sandbank ford") belonging to Ulster's ancient O'Neill clan. With the advent of the Plantation period (when settlers arrived in the 1600s), Sir Arthur Chichester, from Devon in southwest England, received the city from the English Crown, and his son was made Earl of Donegall. Huguenots fleeing persecution from France settled near here, bringing their valuable linen-work skills. In the 18th century Belfast underwent a phenomenal expansion—its population doubled in size every 10 years, despite an ever-present sectarian divide. Although the Anglican gentry despised the Presbyterian artisans—who, in turn, distrusted the native Catholics—Belfast's growth continued at a dizzying speed. Having laid the foundation stone of the city's university in 1845, Queen Victoria returned to Belfast in 1849 (she is recalled in the names of buildings, streets, bars, monuments, and other places around the city), and in the same year, the university opened under the name Queen's College. Nearly 40 years later, in 1888, Victoria granted Belfast its city charter. Today its population is nearly 300,000—one-quarter of Northern Ireland's citizens.

GOLDEN MILE

This arrowhead-shaped area extending from Howard Street in the north to Shaftesbury Square at the southern tip, and bordered on the west by Great Victoria Street and on the east by Bedford Street and Dublin Road, is a great area from which to begin an exploration of Belfast. Although it doesn't glow quite the way the name suggests, bustling Golden Mile and its immediate environs harbor some of Belfast's most noteworthy historic buildings. In addition, the area is filled with hotels and major civic and office buildings, as well as some restaurants, cafés, and shops. Even if you don't end up staying here, you're likely to pass through it often.

TOP ATTRACTIONS

❹ City Hall. The marble has been freshly cleaned, the massive dome ★ repainted, the chandeliers polished, and the floors repaired, and in 2009 the exuberant Renaissance Revival City Hall reopened its doors after an £11 million two-year interior restoration and refurbishment program. Built of Portland stone between 1898 and 1906 and modeled on St. Paul's Cathedral in London, it was designed by Brumwell Thomas, who was knighted but had to sue to get his fee. Before you enter, take a stroll around Donegall Square, to see statues of Queen Victoria; a monument commemorating the *Titanic*, which was built in Belfast; and a column honoring the U.S. Expeditionary Force, which landed in the city on January 26, 1942—the first contingent of the U.S. Army to land in Europe during World War II. Enter under the porte cochere at the front of the building. From the entrance hall (the base of which is a whispering gallery), the view up to the heights of the 173-foot-high Great Dome is a feast for the eyes. With its complicated series of arches and openings, stained-glass windows, Italian-marble inlays, decorative plasterwork, and paintings, this is Belfast's most ornate public space—homage to the might of the British Empire. Now the modernized building has been brought into the 21st century. It comes replete with the Bobbin coffee shop and the Waking a Giant exhibition, in which historic photographs tell the story of Belfast's industrial development. Another exhibition, No Mean City, an interactive and photographic display, celebrates 68 inspirational people of the last 100 years, including Thomas Andrews (the designer of the *Titanic)*, singer Van Morrison, and footballer George Best. In the courtyard a 60-jet fountain has been dedicated to Belfast City Council members killed during the Troubles. Free, guided one-hour tours are given. ✉ *Donegall Sq., Golden Mile* ☎ *028/9032–0202, 028/9027–0456 tours* ⊕ *www.belfastcity.gov.uk* ✉ *Tours free* ☉ *Tours weekdays at 11, 2, and 3; Sat. at 2 and 3.*

❸ Crown Liquor Saloon. Opposite the Europa Hotel on Great Victoria Street
Fodor's Choice and owned by the National Trust (the United Kingdom's official con-
★ servation organization), the Crown is one of Belfast's glories. It began life in 1826 as the Railway Tavern; in 1885 the owner asked Italian craftsmen working on churches in Ireland to moonlight on rebuilding it, and its place in Irish architectural pub history was assured. The bar has richly carved woodwork around cozy snugs (cubicles—known to regulars as "confessional boxes"), leather seats, color tile work, and an

A monument of the High Victorian style, Belfast's City Hall towers over Donegall Place in the heart of the city center.

abundance of mirrors. The Crown entered a new phase in its history in 2007 when the Trust spent £500,000 on a major restoration project. An ostentatious box of delights, it has been immaculately preserved— it is still lighted by gas. The pièce de résistance is the embossed ceiling with its swirling arabesques and rosettes of burnished primrose, amber, and gold, as dazzling again now as the day it was installed. The Crown claims to serve the perfect pint of Guinness—so no need to ask what anyone's drinking—and you can order a great plateful of warming Irish stew. When you settle down in your snug, note the little gunmetal plates used by the Victorians for lighting their matches as well as the newly restored antique push-button bells for ordering another round. Ageless, timeless, and classless—some would say the Crown is even priceless. ⊠ *46 Great Victoria St., Golden Mile* ☎ *028/9024–3187* ⊕ *www. crownbar.com* ☾ *Mon.–Sat. 11:30.*

❷ Grand Opera House. The Grand Opera House exemplifies the Victorians' ★ fascination with ornamentation, opulent gilt moldings, and intricate plasterwork. The renowned theater architect Frank Matcham beautifully designed the building in 1894. In the past six years, the theater has undergone a massive extension program that has almost doubled its size, thanks to a new foyer bar, café, and party room. Contemporary Irish artist Cherith McKinstry's exquisite angel-and-cherub-laden fresco floats over the auditorium ceiling. You can take a behind-the-scenes Sunday tour of the opera house, but by far the best way to see and enjoy the place is to attend a show. The theater regularly hosts musicals, operas, plays, and concerts. ⊠ *Great Victoria St., Central*

CLOSE UP

Belfast Guided Walks

The Historic Belfast tour provides the chance to explore Belfast on foot. En route you will find out about the city's origins and its Victorian architecture. The tour lasts 90 minutes and the cost is £6. It departs from the Belfast Welcome Centre on Wednesday, Friday, Saturday, and Sunday at 2 PM. The Centre also offers a variety of brochures and digital tours about exploring the city's *Titanic* past.

On the Blackstaff Way tour you will find out how Belfast developed between three rivers: the Blackstaff, the Farset, and the Lagan; you will see the Boyne Bridge, the oldest bridge in Belfast, and discover the significance of the Mystery Stone from Belfast Castle. The tour lasts 90 minutes and costs £6. It departs from the Belfast Welcome Centre on Saturday at 11 AM.

Historical Pub Tours of Belfast walking tours of the city's pubs leave from the Crown Liquor Saloon on Thursday at 7 PM and Saturday at 4 PM (May–October). The cost is £7.

Belfast Ghost Walks leave from City Hall's front gates Sunday–Thursday (March–October) at 4 PM and 7 PM. The cost is £7.

Belfast Welcome Centre (✉ *47 Donegall Pl., Central District, Belfast* ☎ *028/9024–6609* ⊕ *www.gotobelfast.com*).

Belfast Ghost Walks (✉ *Departs from City Hall front gates, Donegall Sq., Central District, Belfast* ☎ *028/9127–1793* ⊕ *www.ghostwalkbelfast.com*).

Historical Pub Tours of Belfast (✉ *Depart from Crown Liquor Saloon, 46 Great Victoria St., Golden Mile, Belfast* ☎ *028/9268–3665* ⊕ *www.belfastpubtours.com*).

District ☎ *028/9024–1919* ⊕ *www.goh.co.uk* 🎫 *£4* ⊙ *Tours Sun. at 11, noon, and 1.*

❺ St. Malachy's Church. In 2009 the wrappers came off the new-look St. Malachy's Church and, after a 15-month, £3.5 million restoration program, one of the most impressive redbrick Tudor Revival churches in Ireland was unveiled to the public. Opened in 1844 at a cost of £5,679, St. Malachy's was designed by Thomas Jackson of Waterford. The extensive makeover included replacing brickwork and rebuilding the stone-dressed castellated towers and the slender octagonal corner turrets. One of the interior highlights is the densely patterned fan-vaulted ceiling, a delightfully swirling masterpiece of plasterwork—whose inspiration was taken from the chapel of Henry VII at Westminster Abbey in London—tastefully repainted in cream. The high altarpiece featuring Pugin's *Journey to Calvary* was originally carried out by the portraitist Felix Piccioni whose family were refugees to Belfast from Austrian Italy. In 1868 the largest bell in Belfast was added to the church but after complaints that its deafening noise was interfering with the maturing of whiskey in the nearby Dunville distillery, it was wrapped in felt to soften its peal and vibration. Today, along the southeast wall of the church gazing out in contemplative mood with his brown eyes and torn chocolate brown coat, the delicate Statue of the Ragged Saint has also been cleaned. St. Benedict Joseph Labre, the patron saint of the unemployed, once again welcomes visitors into the ethereal elegance of one of Belfast's most architecturally romantic buildings. ⌧ *Alfred St., Golden Mile* ☎ *028/9032–1713* ⊕ *www. saintmalachys.org* 💬 *Free.*

❻ Ulster Hall. It has hosted Charles Dickens, the Rolling Stones, and Rachmaninov as well as a diverse range of Irish politicians from Charles Stewart Parnell to Ian Paisley. The Ulster Hall, affectionately known as the Grand Dame of Bedford Street, reopened in 2009 after an £8.5 million renovation. Built in 1862 as a ballroom, it has been part of the cultural lifeblood of the city for 150 years. Much of W.J. Barrie's original decor has now been restored and 13 historic oil paintings (worth in total nearly £900,000) reflecting the history and mythology of Belfast by local artist Joseph Carey are newly on display in their original magnificence in the Carey Gallery. Another highlight of the restoration is an interpretative display featuring poetry, pictures, and sound telling the history of the hall through personal reminiscences. During World War II the building was used as a dance hall by U.S. troops based in Northern Ireland. The hall is also the permanent home of the Ulster Orchestra. Stop by the Café Grand Dame, drink in some of Belfast's colorful history, and reflect on the fact that it was here in March 1971 that Led Zeppelin performed their stage debut of "Stairway to Heaven." At the box office you can buy tickets for all upcoming events at both Ulster Hall and Waterfront Hall. ⌧ *Bedford St., Golden Mile* ☎ *028/9033–4400* ⊕ *www.ulsterhall.co.uk* ⊙ *Guided tours by appointment.*

WORTH NOTING

❶ Europa Hotel. A landmark in Belfast, the Europa is a monument to the resilience of the city in the face of the Troubles. The most bombed hotel in Western Europe, it was targeted 11 times by the IRA starting in the early 1970s and was refurbished every time; today it shows no signs of its explosive history. Indeed, even with this track record, President Bill Clinton and his wife, Hillary, chose the hotel for an overnight visit during their 1995 visit—for 24 hours the phones were answered with "White House Belfast, can I help you?" The president's room is now called the Clinton Suite and contains memorabilia from the presidential stay. In 2008 the Europa was outfitted with an Italian marble lobby and expanded to 272 rooms, including six suites. It is owned by affable Ulster millionaire and hotel magnate Billy Hastings. ⌧ *Great*

VICTORIAN GRISLY

Most of Belfast's landmarks were built during the reign of Queen Victoria. Once considered unappealing—"Victorian Grisly" was the epithet used by more than one critic—today they are marvelous remnants of an age that considered show, pomp, and circumstance paramount. Most of these buildings are found within 20 blocks of each other and a time-travel walk can hit many of them, including City Hall, Linen Hall Library, the Grand Opera House, Crown Liquor Saloon, Ulster Hall, St. Malachy's Church, Albert Memorial Clock Tower, and St. Anne's Cathedral.

CLOSE UP

Belfast Tour Options

With a fleet of eight new buses introduced in 2010, Belfast City Sightseeing runs the most comprehensive open-top tour through Belfast. The Belfast city tour (£12.50) covers the City Hall, Albert Clock, Shipyard, Titanic Quarter, Stormont, Shankill Road, peace line, and Falls Road, and goes past the Grand Opera House on Great Victoria Street. Tours leave High Street until May 2011 and thereafter from Castle Place (opposite McDonald's) daily on the hour 10–4 October–February, and every 30 minutes March–September, and tickets are valid all day on a hop-on, hop-off basis. The entire route, without stops, takes about 1 hour and 40 minutes.

CONTACTS
Allens Tours (☎ 028/9091–5613 ⊕ www.allenstours.co.uk). **Belfast City Sightseeing** (☎ 028/9032–1321 ⊕ www.belfastcitysightseeing.co.uk).

Mini-Coach (✉ 22 Donegall Rd., Central District, Belfast ☎ 028/9031–5333 ⊕ www.minicoachni.co.uk).

Translink (☎ 028/9066–6630 ⊕ www.translink.co.uk).

More than 10 companies operate taxi tours of Belfast. Belfast City Black Taxi Tours does 75-minute tours in a London-style black taxi visiting both Loyalist and Nationalist sights. The cost is £25 for up to two people, £30 for three people, and £33 for four people. Black Taxi Tours provides a similar itinerary at £25 per taxi for one or two people and £8 per person after that. For all companies, including popular Taxi Traks, the Loyalist tours leave from North Street or Bridge Street and prices can vary depending on pick-up point; the Nationalist tours pick you up at your hotel.

Contacts Belfast City Black Taxi Tours (☎ 028/9030–1832 ⊕ www.allirelandtours.com). **Black Taxi Tours** (☎ 028/9064–2264 ⊕ www.belfasttours.com). **Taxi Traks** (☎ 028/9031–5777 ⊕ www.taxitrax.com).

Victoria St. at Glengall St., Golden Mile ☎ 028/9027–1066 ⊕ www.hastingshotels.com.

CENTRAL DISTRICT

Belfast's Central District, immediately north of the Golden Mile, extends from Donegall Square north to St. Anne's Cathedral. It's not geographically the center of the city, but it's the old heart of Belfast. It's a frenetic place—the equivalent of Dublin's Grafton and Henry streets in one—where both locals and visitors shop. Cafés, pubs, offices, and shops of all kinds, from department stores to the Gap and Waterstone's (there's even a Disney store), occupy the redbrick, white Portland-stone, and modern buildings that line its narrow streets. Many of the streets are pedestrian-only, so it's a good place to take a leisurely stroll, browse, and see some sights to boot. It's easy to get waylaid shopping and investigating sights along the river when taking this walk, so give yourself at least two hours to cover the area comfortably.

TOP ATTRACTIONS

9 Albert Memorial Clock Tower. Tilting a little to one side, not unlike Pisa's more notorious leaning landmark, is the clock tower that was named for Queen Victoria's husband, Prince Albert. The once-dilapidated square on which it stands has undergone a face-lift and a restoration has brought the clock back to its original glory. The tower itself is not open to the public. ✉ *Victoria Sq., Central District.*

★ **High Street.** Off High Street, especially down to Ann Street (parallel to the south), run narrow lanes and alleyways called entries. Though mostly cleaned up and turned into chic shopping lanes, they still hang on to something of their raffish character, and have distinctive pubs with little-altered Victorian interiors. Among the most notable are the Morning Star (Pottinger's Entry off High Street), with its large windows and fine curving bar; White's Tavern (entry off High Street), Belfast's oldest pub, founded in 1630, which, although considerably updated, is still warm and comfortable, with plush seats and a big, open fire; Ronnie Drew's (on May Street), in splendid counterpoint to the Waterfront's space-age style; and McHugh's (in Queen's Square), in what is reckoned to be the city's oldest extant building, dating from 1710.

10 Lagan Boat Company. A 75-minute *Titanic* tour takes in this shipyard where the famous liner was built. Scheduled *Titanic* tours are offered April–October, daily at 12:30 PM, 2, and 3:30; and November–March, weekends at 12:30 and 3:30. The boat departure point is from Donegall Quay near the Big Fish sculpture, a gigantic salmon covered in tiles and printed with text and imagery about Belfast. ✉ *48 St. John's Close, at Laganbank Rd., Central District* ☎ *028/9033–0844* ⊕ *www.titanicboattours.com* 🖃 *Tours £10.*

11 Titanic's Dock and Pump-House. Historic centerpiece of Belfast's spectacular new Titanic Quarter waterfront regeneration scheme, this has long been the city's outstanding relic of the doomed ship's history. Officially known as the Thompson Dock and Pump-House, or the Thompson dry dock, this is the only original part of the ship's legacy open to the public and represents *Titanic's* physical footprint. Built by 500 men over a period of seven years, it was the biggest dry dock in the world and was the beating heart of the shipyard's operation during the construction of the great White Star Liners—*Britannic, Olympic,* and RMS *Titanic.* The dock is nearly 900 feet long, could hold 21 million gallons of water, and the *Titanic* just about fit in. The original steel-casing gate (now showing some signs of rust) that enclosed the dock and kept ships watertight, weighs a staggering 1,000 tons. Visitors can take an audiovisual guide in the Pump House, which also houses a visitor center located in the Northern Ireland Science Park at Queen's Island.

Fodor'sChoice
★

The *Titanic's* **Dock and Pump-House tour** (☎ *028/9073–7813* ⊕ *www.titanicsdock.com* 🖃 *£6* ☉ *Mar.–Oct., daily at 11, 12:30, and 2*) is a fascinating, fact-filled walk run by Colin Cobb that helps visitors—through visual aids of the Titanic—imagine, relive, and reflect on the importance of shipbuilding in Belfast's heritage as well as taking in a masterpiece of engineering.

CLOSE UP

TITANIC 2012

BELFAST HONORS THE 100th ANNIVERSARY

"ICEBERG, STRAIGHT AHEAD!"
Tragically touted as "unsinkable," the *Titanic* set sail from Belfast's famed Harland & Wolff shipyards on April 2, 1912. Five miles of decks, twenty-nine boilers, sixteen-ton forward anchor... and just 62 seconds to launch. But four days into her maiden voyage to New York—at precisely 11:40 PM on the night of April 14th—lookouts Fredrick Fleet and Reginald Lee alarmingly sounded the ship's bell to ring out three times to warn "Iceberg, Straight Ahead!"

Too late: even though the Marconi wireless service on-board had received iceberg warnings from other ships—disregarded in favor of messages for first-class passengers—the huge iceberg sliced open five watertight compartments (only four and the ship would have stayed afloat). With a 300-foot gash in her hull, the doomed liner sank two hours and forty minutes later—at 2:20 AM—the next morning. Of the 2,201 passengers and crew, only 711 survived... because there were not enough lifeboats provided for the "ship of dreams."

Around the world that day the *Titanic* passed from history into legend. Now, to commemorate the 100th anniversary of her birth, and death, *Titanic's* hometown will be paying homage with "Titanic 2012," a year-long array of special events, concerts, tours, museums, with many to be held in Belfast's spectacular new Titanic Quarter waterfront redevelopment project. Everything from a new Titanic Signature Building museum to a giant new Titanic restaurant (we won't mention the Thai-tanic eaterie on Eglantine

Avenue), and a Titanic Heritage Trail will honor the anniversary.

WHERE IT'S ALL HAPPENING: TITANIC QUARTER
Billed as the largest waterfront development in Europe, the eponymously named Titanic Quarter is budgeted at an estimated £1 billion and will remake the former shipyard region in the Queen's Island sector (set across the River Lagan and accessed by the Queen Elizabeth or Queen's bridges), northeast of the city center, with an array of new projects. The heart will comprise the extant Victorian and Edwardian harbor buildings that have now been imaginatively re-purposed into 21st century visitor attractions, centered around the refurbished Titanic's Dock and Pump-House attraction. Once complete—and it could take 15 years—this mini-city on a 185-acre site will house new hotels, restaurants, and residential towers alongside a gleaming new marina in Abercorn basin.

THE TITANIC TRAIL: TOURING THE HISTORIC WATERFRONT
Running along along Queen's Road the new Titanic Heritage Trail passes the main landmarks of the giant Harland & Wolff shipyards, the actual birthplace of the Titanic. Some historians have gone so far as to point fingers at the shoddy quality of Harland's steel and their overly hasty production schedule—others state the evidence is totally inconclusive—but, these dour historical findings notwithstanding, this trail will be a sacred pilgrimage for many visitors. Note that several of these attractions are only open to the public on a reservations-only basis, usually as part of one of the organized tours run by the big sightseeing

The Titanic under construction (Collection Ulster Folk and Transportation Museum)

outfits (listed below). For others you can only view the exteriors—the interiors are still privately owned. Here is a run-down of the main landmarks:

Titanic Signature Building: Set for completion in 2012 this world-class attraction showcases a Titanic Experience Exhibition, with five linked interpretative galleries outlining the dramatic story as well as the wider theme of Belfast's seafaring and industrial heritage. There'll also be a Flying Theater with a suspended simulation experience, café, and restaurant. Service data (such as hours and prices) was not available at press time.

Titanic's Dock and Pump-House: Located at the Thompson Graving Dock, these attractions represent the liner's physical footprint and the last place she rested on dry ground. The giant ship just fit into this dock with a few feet to spare, giving you a sense of her amazing size. Listen to the powerful pumps in action and watch a two-hour drama-documentary, "Titanic:

Birth of a Legend". Now operational, see our full write-up of this museum in the Belfast Exploring section.

Titanic and Olympic Slipways: Set in the Titanic Quarter, these massive twin slipways at Queen's Yard, where RMS Titanic and Olympic were built, are part of the walking trail. Note that they can best be studied on one of the harbor boat tours.

Harland & Wolff Drawing Office: This long and elegant three-story former drawing office block in sandstone and brick is where the concept design and detailed construction drawings for Titanic were laid out. Nearby is the Paint Hall, where the parts of the ship were painted under climate control. Interiors are closed to the public.

SS *Nomadic*, Hamilton Dock: The sister ship to Titanic and last White Star Line ship in existence, SS Nomadic operated as a shuttle ship and delivered 142 first class passengers—including John Jacob

CLOSE UP

The Titanic Lives On

Astor and Benjamin Guggenheim—to Titanic in Cherbourg (whose harbor was too small for the big liners to berth) before its departure for New York. In 2006 it returned to Belfast for restoration and is now open to visitors, by tour only, and arranged through the Belfast Welcome Centre (✉ *47 Donegall Pl., Central District, Belfast* ☎ *028/9024–6609* ⊕ *www. nomadicbelfast.com* 🕙 *Oct.–May, Mon.–Sat. 9–5:30; June–Sept., Mon.– Sat. 9–7, Sun. 11–4*). This ship is berthed at the Hamilton Graving Dock.

Samson and Goliath: Towering over everything, the giant yet noble yellow gantry cranes used in *Titanic*'s construction provide a top photo-op for tourists; sadly you can't climb them as there is no public access.

TOP TITANIC TOURS
In addition to the new Titanic Heritage Trail (above), Belfast has already lined up a bevy of top "Titanic Tours."

At the **Belfast Welcome Centre** (✉ *47 Donegall Pl., Central District, Belfast* ☎ *028/9024–6609* ⊕ *www. gotobelfast.com*) you can hire a Node Explorer, a hand-held multimedia device, which leads you on a self-guided walking tour of the Titanic Trail. This Titanic Interactive Trail "Global Positioning System" digital tour can be rented for three-hour sessions at £8.

The **Lagan Boat Company** (⊕ *www. titanicboattours.com*) operates tours of *Titanic* sites. A 75-minute *Titanic* tour takes in the Harland & Wolff shipyard. Scheduled *Titanic* tours are offered April–October, daily at 12:30 PM, 2, and 3:30; and November–March, weekends at 12:30 and 3:30. The departure point is from Donegall Quay. Savor a walk

through Sir Thomas Andrews's Belfast (he was the designer of the boat) with a **Blue Badge Guide** (⊕ *www. bluebadgeireland.org*).

You can stroll the **Thompson Titanic Trail,** which sets out from the centerpiece of the city's link with the ship, the Thompson dry dock (⊕ *www. titanicsdock.com*). Two walking tours, both run by the affable and knowledgeable Colin Cobb, are well worth taking to help you capture your own slice of maritime magic.

Titanic Walking Tours (☎ *028/9073– 7813* ⊕ *www.titanicwalk.com* 💷 *£12* 🕙 *Mar.–Oct., daily at 11 and 2*) depart from the Odyssey Arena and last 2½ hours. This tour includes a 30-minute coffee/tea break and takes in Titanic's dock and pump house as well as the SS Nomadic, the slipways, and the former shipyard drawing office. He also runs tours at the Titanic's Dock and Pump-House (see our listing).

For a more in-depth tour—one that also takes in Nomadic, Titanic's Dock and Pump House, as well as several other locations—consider **Titanic Tours Belfast** (☎ *028/9065–9971* ⊕ *www.titanictours-belfast.co.uk*), which is run by Susie Millar, the great-granddaughter of a crew member who sailed on the ill-fated liner. The tours, which are by appointment are chauffeured in a luxury Mercedes. These cost £30 and last two hours.

Belfast City Sightseeing (✉ *Castle Place, Central District, Belfast* ☎ *028/9045–9035* ⊕ *www. belfastcitysightseeing.com*) has a regular open top bus trip with an informative commentary, stopping at selected Titanic Quarter locations. Tours leave from Castle Place in the city center and cost £12.50.

The Thompson Graving Dock, home to Titanic's Dock and Pump-House

The tours last one hour 40 minutes. **Allen's** (✉ *High St., Central District, Belfast* ☎ *028/9091–5613* ⊕ *www.allenstours.co.uk*) offers similar tours to Belfast City Sightseeing, with open top buses manned by tour guides stopping at an array of Titanic Quarter landmarks. These tours leave from High Street and cost £9. The tours last approximately 90 minutes.

100TH ANNIVERSARY EVENTS

One hundred years on from the exact date of the tragedy: April 14, 2012, Belfast Titanic Society will hold a civic service at the City Hall Memorial to mark the occasion. But the calendar kicks off in May 2011 when Belfast hosts an international convention sponsored by the hyper-active Belfast Titanic Society with a gala dinner at City Hall to commemorate the launch anniversary.

During April 2012 the "Titanic: Made in Belfast" festival will take over the city. Parallel with this a galaxy of musical events is scheduled, including "Titanic: The Musical," a Titanic opera, a Titanic requiem, and even a good old-style Titanic ceili (music festival) in Ulster Hall. For the curious visitor wanting to discover the liner's legacy a century later this is a jam-packed line-up.

AND FOR YOUR OWN TOUR . . .

Robinson's Bar: one of the largest private collections of *Titanic* memorabilia in Ireland is on display in Robinson's Bar in Great Victoria St. (opposite Europa Hotel). It includes letters and postcards written on board the ship and poignant items such as "Philomena," the doll recovered floating at the wreck site.

Titanic Restaurant: a 60-seater *Titanic* themed café on Newtownards Rd., in East Belfast, newly renovated for 2011-12 selling "titanic" portions and *Titanic* steamer drinks. Framed newspaper articles, photographs, and postcards decorate the walls along with the rigging plan, cartoons, and lifeboat models.

There is no individual access to the pump house: all visitors must be on an accompanied tour. Hot snacks and sandwiches are available in the pump-house café and visitor center (open March–October, daily 10:30–4), where you can buy Titanic postcards and other souvenirs, including a deck-plan poster. The Metro Bus Route No. 26 from City Hall is the easiest way to get to the pump house, or opt for a 20-minute walk to Queen's Road from the Odyssey complex (home to the Odyssey Arena and W5 science center). ⊠ *Queen's Rd., Titanic Quarter* ☎ *028/9073–7813* ⊕ ⊙ *Tours Wed., Sat., and Sun. at 2.*

NEED A BREAK? At the start of Royal Avenue, turn left onto Bank Street to find Kelly's Cellars (⊠ *30–32 Bank St., Central District* ☎ *028/9024–6058*), a circa-1720 pub with loads of character. Try the specialty: Irish stew. Two centuries ago, Kelly's Cellars was the regular meeting place of a militant Nationalist group, the Society of United Irishmen, whose leader, Wolfe Tone (who was a Protestant), is remembered as the founder of Irish Republicanism. Traditional music and plenty of local banter make the pub particularly lively on weekends.

⟳ **W5: Whowhatwherewhywhen.** Part of the Odyssey complex in Belfast's docks, this science discovery center takes a high-tech, hands-on approach to interpreting science and creativity for adults and children. Video displays and flashing lights complement the futuristic feel, and you can do everything from explore the weather to build bridges and robots. There are more than 180 interactive exhibits in four areas and constantly changing exhibitions as well as new schedules of events on a regular basis. ⊠ *2 Queen's Quay, Central District* ☎ *028/9046–7700* ⊕ *www.w5online.co.uk* ▨ *£7* ⊙ *Mon.–Thurs. 10–5, Fri. and Sat. 10–6, Sun. noon–6; last entry 1 hr before closing.*

WORTH NOTING

⑫ **Custom House.** The 19th-century architect Charles Lanyon designed the Custom House. This building, along with many others in Belfast, including the main building of Queen's University and the unusual Sinclair Seaman's Church, bear the hallmarks of his skill. It's not open to the public, but it's worth circling the house to view the lofty pediment of Britannia, Mercury, and Neptune on the front, carved by acclaimed stonemason Thomas Fitzpatrick. Custom House Square has been refurbished for use for open-air concerts and performances during the autumn festival season. ⊠ *Donegall Quay, Central District.*

❼ **Linen Hall Library.** This gray building on Donegall Square's northwest ⟳ corner is in fact a comfortable private library, founded in 1788 and designed by Charles Lanyon. The library has an unparalleled collection of 80,000 documents relating to the Troubles. One early librarian, Thomas Russell, was hanged in 1803 for supporting an Irish uprising. On the walls are paintings and prints depicting Belfast views and landmarks. Much of this artwork is for sale. It's an ideal hideaway for relaxing with a newspaper and enjoying the library's café. ⊠ *17 Donegall Sq. N, Central District* ☎ *028/9032–1707* ⊕ *www.linenhall.com* ▨ *Free* ⊙ *Weekdays 9:30–5:30, Sat. 9:30–1.*

8 **St. Anne's Cathedral.** A somber heaviness—a hallmark of the Irish neo-Romanesque style—marks this large edifice, which is basilican in plan and was built at the turn of the 20th century. Lord Carson (1854–1935), who was largely responsible for keeping the six counties inside the United Kingdom, is buried here beneath a suitably austere gray slab. His is the only tomb; he was buried here by virtue of a special Act of Parliament. New landscaping around the Anglican cathedral provides a perch to rest your feet in good weather. The guides on duty show you around for no charge. In April 2007, the 175-foot stainless steel Spire of Hope was erected atop the cathedral's roof, adding a new feature to the city's skyline and shining brightly as a beacon of the newfound optimism for the future. ⊠ *Donegall St., Cathedral Quarter* ☎ *028/9032–8332* ⊕ *www.belfastcathedral.org* 🎫 *Free* ☉ *Mon.–Sat. 10–4.*

UNIVERSITY AREA

At Belfast's southern end, the part of the city around Queen's University is dotted with parks, botanical gardens, and leafy streets with fine, intact, two- and three-story 19th-century buildings. The area evokes an older, more leisurely pace of life. The many pubs and excellent restaurants make this area the hub of the city's nightlife. However, remember that Belfast is a student town and this is the main university area—the pace of life here can be fast (and sometimes a little furious) during school-term weekends.

TOP ATTRACTIONS

15 **Botanic Gardens.** In the Victorian heyday, it was not unusual to find ★ 10,000 of Belfast's citizens strolling about here on a Saturday afternoon. These gardens are a glorious haven of grass, trees, flowers, curving walks, and wrought-iron benches, all laid out in 1827 on land that slopes down to the River Lagan. The curved-iron and glass Palm House is a conservatory marvel designed in 1839 by Charles Lanyon. The Tropical Ravine House, though not architecturally distinguished, has an outstanding collection of tropical flora, in addition to some indigenous plants (it was famously said that it once held more Killarney ferns than could be found in Killarney itself). Once known as "the Glen," the Ravine House is unusually and exotically built over a faux-ravine that you walk around. ⊠ *Stranmillis Rd., University Area* ☎ *028/9031–4762* 🎫 *Free* ☉ *Gardens daily dawn–dusk; Palm House and Tropical Ravine House Apr.–Sept., weekdays 10–5, weekends 1–5; Oct.–Mar., weekdays 10–4, weekends 1–4.*

14 **Queen's University.** Dominating University Road is Queen's University. The main buildings, modeled on Oxford's Magdalen College and designed by the ubiquitous Charles Lanyon, were built in 1849 in the Tudor Revival style. The long, handsome redbrick-and-sandstone facade of the main building features large lead-glass windows, and is topped with three square towers and crenellations galore. University Square, really a terrace, is from the same era. The Seamus Heaney Library is named after the Ulster-born 1997 Nobel Prize–winning poet. In 2009 the Library at Queen's in College Park opened at a cost of £50 million.

Belfast's Wall Murals

In Northern Ireland they say the Protestants make the money and the Catholics make the art, and as with all clichés, there is some truth in it. It's a truth that will become clear as you look up at the gable walls of blue-collar areas of Belfast on which the two communities—Catholic and Protestant—have expressed themselves in colorful murals that have given rise to one of the more quirky tours of the city.

Although the wildly romantic Catholic murals often aspire to the heights of Sistine Chapel–lite, those in Protestant areas (like the tough, no-nonsense Shankill and the Newtownards Road) are more workmanlike efforts that sometimes resemble war comics without the humor. It was not always this way.

In Protestant areas, murals were once painted by skilled coachbuilders to mark the July 12 celebrations of the defeat of the Catholic King James by King William at the Battle of the Boyne. As such, they typically depicted William resplendent in freshly laundered scarlet tunic and plumed cap, sitting on a white stallion that has mastered the art of walking on water. On the banks of the Boyne sits a mildly disheveled James, the expression on his face making him look as if he has just eaten an overdose of anchovies. Other popular themes in Protestant areas are the Red Hand of Ulster, symbolizing the founding of the province, and, on Carnmore Street, the 13 Protestant apprentice boys shutting the gates of Derry against King James in 1688, leading to the famous siege.

More recently, though, Protestant murals have taken on a grimmer air, and typical subjects include walleyed paramilitaries perpetually standing firm against increasing liberalism, nationalism, and all the other isms that Protestants see eroding their stern, Bible-driven way of life. Nationalist murals, on the other hand, first sprang up in areas like the Falls Road in 1981, when IRA inmates of the Maze prison began a hunger strike in an unsuccessful bid to be recognized by the British government as political prisoners rather than common criminals. Ten died, and the face of the most famous, Bobby Sands, looks down now from a gable wall on the Falls Road alongside the words "Our revenge will be the laughter of our children."

Since then, themes of freedom from oppression and a rising Nationalist confidence have expressed themselves in murals that romantically and surreally mix and match images from the *Book of Kells*, the Celtic Mist mock-heroic posters of Irish artist Jim Fitzpatrick, assorted phoenixes rising from ashes, and revolutionaries clad in splendidly idiosyncratic sombreros and bandannas from ideological battlegrounds in Mexico and South America. Irish words and phrases that you will see springing up regularly include the much-used slogan *Tiocfaidh ár lá* (pronounced *chuck-y ohr law* and meaning "Our day will come") and the simple cry *Saoirse* (pronounced *seer-she*), meaning "Freedom."

The murals in both Protestant and Catholic areas are safe to view in daylight and outside the sensitive week of the July 12 marches by Protestant Orangemen. However, the most sensible way to view them would be to take a guided tour with Belfast City Sightseeing or one of the other bus tour companies.

Anchoring Freedom Corner are loyalist murals found on Lower Newtownards Road, near the center of Protestant East Belfast

Designed by Boston-based architects Shepley, Bulfinch, Richardson & Abbot (SBRA)—who also worked on libraries at Yale, Cornell, and Harvard—the library features a multistory open atrium, 1.5 million volumes, and the Brian Friel Theatre, named in honor of one of Ireland's most illustrious playwrights. The C. S. Lewis reading room on the first floor has a replica of the wardrobe door used in the film, *The Lion, the Witch, and the Wardrobe.* The Queen's Welcome Centre hosts a regular program of exhibitions and serves as an information point for visitors and tourists, as well as offering a varied selection of souvenirs and gifts. Guided tours can be arranged by prior reservation. ✉ *University Rd., University Area* ☎ *028/9097–5252* ⊕ *www.qub.ac.uk* 🚌 *Tours £5* ⊙ *Welcome Centre Mar.–Nov., Mon.–Sat. 9:30–4:30; Dec.–Feb., weekdays 10–4.*

16 **Ulster Museum.** Set in an impressive edifice at the southwest corner of the Botanic Gardens, the Ulster Museum reopened in fall 2009 following a £17 million redevelopment project and has been an instant hit with visitors. The rejuvenated museum with its spacious light-filled atrium and polished steel is a world away from the tenebrous galleries of old. The museum's forte is the history and prehistory of Ireland using exhibitions to colorfully trace the rise of Belfast's crafts, trade, and industry, and offering a reflective photographic archive of the Troubles. In addition, the museum has a large natural history section, with famed skeleton of the extinct Irish giant deer, and a trove of jewelry and gold ornaments recovered from the Spanish Armada vessel *Girona* sunk off the Antrim coast in 1588. Take time to seek out the *Girona*'s stunning gold salamander studded with rubies and still dazzling after 400 years in the Atlantic. The museum includes a first-rate collection of 19th- and 20th-century art from Europe, Britain, and America. The new art, history, and nature discovery zones are jam-packed with hands-on activities for children. Kids also enjoy Peter the polar bear exhibit, and the famed Egyptian mummy, Takabuti. There's also an innovative 360-degree light-and-sound immersive experience, museum shop, café, and restaurant. ✉ *Stranmillis Rd., University Area* ☎ *028/9044–0000* ⊕ *www.nmni.com/um* ✉ *Free* ☉ *Tues.–Sun. 10–5.*

⓭ **Union Theological College.** Like Queen's University on the opposite side of the street, the Union Theological College, with its colonnaded Doric facade, owes the charm of its appearance to architect Charles Lanyon. The building's other claim to fame is that, before the completion of the parliament buildings at Stormont, Northern Ireland's House of Commons was convened in its library, and the college's chapel played host to the Senate. The college completed a major renovation in 2002 and offers tours to visitors. ✉ *108 Botanic Ave., University Area* ☎ *028/9020–5080* ⊕ *www.union.ac.uk* ✉ *Free.*

WORTH NOTING

Stranmillis. Once its own village, Stranmillis is now an off-campus quarter—an appealing neighborhood with tree-lined residential streets and a wide choice of ethnic eateries. You can get here via Stranmillis Road (near the Ulster Museum). The stretch of shops and cafés extends down to the riverside towpath along the Lagan. Malone Road joins the river farther south, close to the out-of-town Giant's Ring (off Ballylesson Road), a large, Neolithic earthwork focused on a dolmen. To get this far, unless you're a vigorous walker (it's possible to come all the way on the Lagan towpath), you may be happier driving or taking a bus. Ulsterbus 13 passes close to the site, and on the return journey it will take you back to Donegall Square.

BELFAST ENVIRONS

However, none of the sights along the Ards Peninsula and the north coast are more than an hours' drive from Belfast—perfect for day trips.

TOP ATTRACTIONS

★ **Belfast Castle.** In 1934 this spectacularly baronial castle, built for the Marquis of Donegall in 1865, was passed to Belfast Corporation. Although the castle functions primarily as a restaurant, it also houses the Cave Hill Visitor Centre, which provides information about the castle's history and its natural surroundings in Cave Hill Country Park. Guided tours (by reservation) of the reception rooms built by the Earls of Shaftesbury are sometimes offered on weekends in May, June, and December. The best reason to visit is to take a stroll in the lovely ornamental gardens and then make the ascent to McArt's Fort. This promontory, at the top of sheer cliffs 1,200 feet above the city, affords an excellent view across Belfast. Take the path uphill from the parking lot, turn right at the next intersection of pathways, and then keep left as you journey up the sometimes-steep hill to the fort. ✉ *4 km (2½ mi) north*

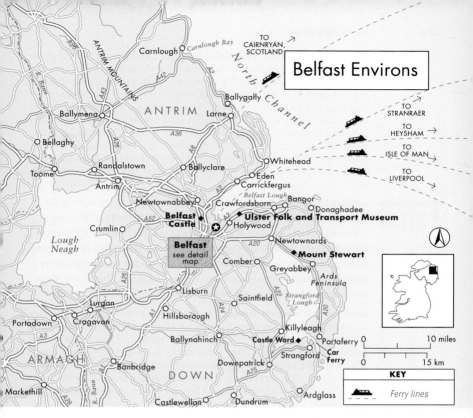

Belfast Environs

Carnlough
Carnlough Bay
TO CAIRNRYAN, SCOTLAND
North Channel
Ballygally
ANTRIM MOUNTAINS
Ballymena
Larne
Ballygalty
ANTRIM
TO STRANRAER
TO HEYSHAM
TO ISLE OF MAN
TO LIVERPOOL
Bellaghy
R. Bann
Randalstown
Ballyclare
Whitehead
Toome
Antrim
Eden
Carrickfergus
Newtownabbey
Crawfordsborn
Belfast Lough Bangor
Donaghadee
Belfast Castle
Ulster Folk and Transport Museum
Holywood
Crumlin
Lough Neagh
Belfast see detail map
Newtownards
Mount Stewart
Comber
Greyabbey
Ards Peninsula
Lisburn
Saintfield
Strangford Lough
Lurgan
Portadown
Craigavon
Hillsborough
Killyleagh
ARMAGH
Ballynahinch
Castle Ward
Portaferry
Strangford Car Ferry
Banbridge
DOWN
Downpatrick
Markethill
R. Bann
Castlewellan
Dundrum
Ardglass

10 miles
15 km

KEY
Ferry lines

of Belfast on Antrim Rd. ☎ *028/9077–6925* ⊕ *www.belfastcastle.co.uk*
🎟 *Free* ☉ *Visitor center Mon.–Sat. 9 AM–10 PM, Sun. 9–6.*

★ **Mount Stewart.** The grandest stately house near Belfast, this was the country estate of the Marquesses of Londonderry, whose fame, or infamy, became known around the world thanks to the historical role played by the second Marquess. Known as Castlereagh, this Secretary of Ireland put down the Rising of 1798, helped forge the Act of Union, and killed himself by cutting his own throat. Mount Stewart was constructed in two stages where an earlier house had stood: George Dance designed the west facade (1804–05), and William Vitruvius Morrison designed the Neoclassical main part of the building (1845–49), complete with an awe-inspiring Grecian portico facade. The seventh Marchioness, Edith, managed to wave her wand over the interior—after a fashion: Chinese vases, Louis-Philippe tables, and Spanish oak chairs do their worst to clutter up the rooms here. Still, the house does have some noted 18th-century interiors, including the Central Hall and the grand staircase hung with one of George Stubbs's most famous portraits, that of the celebrated racehorse Hambletonian, after he won one of the most prominent contests of the 18th century—this is perhaps the greatest in situ setting for a painting in Ireland. On the grounds, don't miss the octagonal Temple of the Winds—a copy of a similar structure in

Athens—and there's a remarkable bathhouse and pool at the end of the wooded peninsula just before the entrance to the grounds. Ask for a free copy of the *Mount Stewart Garden Guide*, with a folding map showing the scale and diversity of the 18 named garden walks—you'll need more than one day to explore them all. Opening times often change here—it's prudent to phone ahead or log on to the Web site for the complete schedule. ⊠ *Portaferry Rd., Newtownards* ☎ *028/4278–8387* ⊕ *www. nationaltrust.org.uk* 🎫 *£7.80* ⊙ *Gardens Apr. and Oct., daily 11–6; May–Sept., daily 10–6; Nov.–Mar., daily 10–4. House by guided tour Mar.–June and Oct., weekends 11–6; July and Aug., daily 11–6; Sept., Wed.–Mon. noon–6.*

NEED A BREAK?

Reputed to be the oldest pub in Ireland, **Grace Neill's** (⊠ **33 High St., 22 km [13 mi] from Mount Stewart, Donaghadee** ☎ **028/9188–4595** ⊕ **www. graceneills.com**) served its first pint in 1611 and has hosted such luminaries as Peter the Great, Franz Liszt, and John Keats. Behind the original pub, a cubby under the stairs with bar stools, is a larger bar where you can try a simple peppered beef sandwich with a pint of Guinness. There's live music on Friday and Saturday nights and on Sunday afternoon.

Fodor's Choice ★

Ulster Folk and Transport Museum. Devoted to the province's social history, the excellent Ulster Folk and Transport Museum vividly brings Northern Ireland's past to life. First, the Folk Museum invites you to visit Ballycultra—a typical Ulster town of the early 1900s—which comes alive thanks to costumed guides who practice such regional skills as lace making, sampler making, spinning, weaving, wood turning, forgework, printing, open-hearth cooking, carpentry, basket making, and needlework. The setting is evocative: a score of reconstructed buildings moved here from around the region, including a traditional weaver's dwelling, terraces of Victorian town houses, an 18th-century country church, a village flax mill, a farmhouse, and a rural school. Across the main road (by footbridge) is the beautifully designed Transport Museum, where exhibits include locally built airplanes and motorcycles, as well as the iconoclastic car produced by former General Motors whiz kid John DeLorean in his Belfast factory in 1982. The museum is on the 70 acres of Cultra Manor, encircled by a larger park and recreation area. ⊠ *163 Bangor Rd., 16 km (10 mi) northeast of Belfast on A2, Cultra* ☎ *028/9042–8428* ⊕ *www.nmni.com* 🎫 *£7.50* ⊙ *Mar.–June, Tues.–Fri. 10–4, Sat. 10–6, Sun. 11–6; July–Sept., Tues.– Sat. 10–6, Sun. 11–6; Oct.–Feb., Tues.–Sat. 10–4, Sun. 11–4; last entry 1½ hrs before closing.*

WHERE TO EAT

$$
ASIAN
★

✕ **Aldens.** East Belfast was a gastronomic wilderness until this cool modernist restaurant opened. Now city-center folk regularly make the pilgrimage to take advantage of an opulent menu and wine list at comparably reasonable prices. The fixed-price dinner menus on weekdays (and Saturday 5:30–6:30) are particularly good value—£20 for three courses or £17.50 for two courses. Lunch is an informal affair— sea bass, pork-and-leek sausages, or minute steak—but dinner tarts up with such tasty treats as roast baby chicken with tabbouleh and broad beans, or roast fillet of cod with shrimp. With its great atmosphere, gentle prices, perpetually friendly staff, and fine food, it's little wonder that Aldens has scooped several top awards, including the prestigious Bridgestone accolade. This is a good time-out if visiting the Parliament buildings at Stormont. ✉ *229 Upper Newtownards Rd., East Belfast* ☎ *028/9065–0079* ⊕ *www.aldensrestaurant.com* ▭ *AE, DC, MC, V.*

> **DORMANT ED ISN'T DEAD**
>
> The Ulster Museum's showstopper, Edmontosaurus, is the most complete dinosaur fossil on display in Ireland. "Ed," as he's affectionately known, roamed America about 70 million years ago and would have looked a bit like a plucked turkey. At 20 feet long, Ed has settled into his 21st-century home and is now a big attraction.

$$
CONTINENTAL
Fodor's Choice
★

✕ **Cayenne.** One of Belfast's most exciting restaurants, Cayenne explodes with culinary fireworks. To wit, the salt-and-chili squid, crispy-duck salad, and seared Korean beef salad, all worthy starters—and let's not forget the passion-fruit pavlova or chocolate crepe soufflé with Grand Marnier ice cream. These are just a few of the creations of celebrity TV chefs Paul and Jeanne Rankin. The cutting-edge fusion cuisine, always with an Asian twist, comes up a winner with such mains as seared diver scallops, soy-glazed halibut, and Szechuan-peppered Finnebrogue venison. A favorite with theatergoers, they also offer a two-course pre-theater menu for £14.50 or £16.50 for three courses. Cayenne accepts orders until 11:15 on Friday and Saturday evenings. ✉ *7 Ascot House, Shaftesbury Sq. at Great Victoria St., Golden Mile* ☎ *028/9033–1532* ⊕ *www.cayenne-restaurant.co.uk* ▭ *AE, DC, MC, V* ⊗ *No lunch Sat.–Wed.*

$
CONTINENTAL
★

✕ **Deanes Deli.** Half take-out deli, half comfort-food eatery, this is another great addition to the Michael Deane kingdom. Close to historic Ulster Hall, it's an all-day affair and, at that, you'll rarely find an empty seat. Try the old-fashioned beer-battered fish-and-chips or one of the ever-changing daily specials. Next door is the gourmet deli, where the shelves groan with homemade cheeses, breads, chocolates, and chutneys, many of them from the local farmers' market. They make great take-away sandwiches. ✉ *42–44 Bedford St., Central District* ☎ *028/9024–8800* ▭ *AE, MC, V* ⊗ *Closed Sun.*

$$$
CONTINENTAL
Fodor's Choice
★

✕ **Deanes Restaurant.** After burst water pipes forced a temporary closure early in 2010, the newly redecorated Deanes re-emerged triumphant, continuing to draw the crowds to its tables for both lunch and dinner. For 13 consecutive years the restaurant has picked up a Michelin star (it's the only one in Northern Ireland with a star). It's reinvented itself as a high-end brasserie complete with an informal seafood bar. Head chef Derek Creagh leads a talented team and watches over the open kitchen turning out innovative dishes including foie gras and chicken liver parfait, breast of wood pigeon, and local smoked eel with glazed beetroot for starters. Main courses include the tender and flavor-filled Finnebrogue venison and breast of Silver Hill duck. If you want a light and inexpensive lunch, the seafood bar serves a filling bowl of chowder or mussels with bread for £7. So sit back and enjoy the sleek and elegant interior alongside the company of Belfast's dining elite. ⊠ *36–40 Howard St., Golden Mile* ☎ *028/9033–1134* ⊕ *www.michaeldeane.co.uk* ☱ *AE, MC, V* ☉ *Closed Sun. and Mon.*

$ **Drennans Restaurant.** A magnificently
IRISH   restored stained-glass window featuring St. Cecilia (the patron saint of musicians) playing her pipes and looking down on diners sets the mood in this classy restaurant run by Lawrence Delaney, who has years of experience pleasing hungry customers. Since opening in 2007, Drennans has established itself as a

busy dining spot near Queen's University. The owner is interested in Irish history and named his restaurant after Dr. William Drennan, who coined the sobriquet the "Emerald Isle." Reminiscent of a Parisian-style bistro, it offers an early-bird menu (£12.95 for two courses) laden with sirloin steak, buttered chicken, pork belly, lamb, and fish. Options from the regular dinner menu include sea bass over tagliatelle with asparagus and Parmesan shavings. Be assured the warm sticky toffee pudding in butterscotch sauce will linger long on the taste buds. The restaurant is BYOB. As befits a restaurant with a musical saint, each night a live pianist switches effortlessly between blues, pop, and jazz. ⊠ *43 University Rd., University Area* ☎ *028/9020–4556* ⊕ *www.drennans.co.uk* ⌂ *Reservations essential* ☱ *No credit cards.*

$ ✕ **The Ginger Bistro.** Chef-owner Simon McCance's modern Irish classics
CONTINENTAL   with an international twist attract foodies to this gem just off Great
Fodor'sChoice   Victoria Street. A short but perfectly balanced menu emphasizes locally
★   sourced seafood and lean meats. Fishy dinner highlights include fillet of hake, brill, or sea bass; pan-roast breast of duck or roasted loin of rare-breed pork are also highly recommended, but the flavorsome fried spiced squid far outsells anything else on the menu. For lunchgoers in a hurry there is an excellent-value menu offering such delights as haddock and chips, fish pie, or rib-eye steak. The wine list is outstanding, or try malt-flavored handcrafted Belfast ales or lagers from the Mourne Mountains. Chalked-up blackboards warn: "Can't have any pudding if you don't eat your greens." For those who do, the dessert menu represents a tyranny of choice: delectable crème brûlée with raspberry compote, the soft-centered chocolate cake with berries, or the sticky toffee pudding for an unforgettable coup de grâce? ⊠ *7–8 Hope St., Golden Mile* ☎ *028/9024–4421* ⊕ *www.gingerbistro.com* ☱ *MC, V* ☉ *Closed Sun.*

In the early 20th century, the marchioness of Londonderry remade her Mount Stewart estate into the horticultural showplace of Northern Ireland.

$$$$
CONTINENTAL

✕ **The Great Room.** Inside the swank and lavish Merchant Hotel, beneath the grand dome of this former bank's great hall and Ireland's biggest chandelier, you'll find the perfect setting for a memorable dinner of adventurous European fare. Exceptional offerings from the kitchen include Dover sole *niçoise*, rib of Kettyle beef, or for vegetarians, *pappardelle* (broad-noodle) pasta with black truffles and olive oil. The wonderful extravaganza of profiterole swans swimming delicately in a small lake of chocolate sauce is just one delight found on the dessert trolley. First-class service in truly opulent surroundings makes this restaurant worth a detour. The set £25 per person dinner menu, Monday–Thursday, is great value, while at weekends it increases to between £80 and £100 for two with a bottle of wine. ⊠ *35 Waring St., Central District* ☎ *028/9023–4888* ⊕ *www.themerchanthotel.com* ▭ *AE, MC, V.*

¢
IRISH
★

✕ **Long's.** For more than 95 years, Long's has been serving fish-and-chips in its tiny, completely basic Athol Street premises. Garbage collectors, millionaires, and every sector in between flock here for the secret-batter-recipe fish, served with chips, bread and butter, and a mug of tea. ⊠ *39 Athol St., Golden Mile* ☎ *028/9032–1848* ▭ *No credit cards* ☉ *Closed Sun.*

$
IRISH

✕ **The Morning Star.** Halfway down a narrow lane is the 19th-century Morning Star, one of the city's most historic pubs, first built as a coaching stop for the Belfast to Dublin post. There's a traditional bar downstairs and a cozy velvet and wood-panel restaurant upstairs. On the menu you might find venison and game in winter, lamb in spring, and grilled haddock with dark rum or roast Antrim pork in summer. Also notable is the steak menu; you'd be hard-pressed to find a larger assortment of aged-beef cuts. Sizzling steaks arrive at the table in red-hot cast-iron skillets and are served with a flourish by the friendly staff. ✉ *17–19 Pottinger's Entry, Central District* ☎ *028/9023–5986* ⊟ *MC, V.*

$$
CONTINENTAL
Fodor's Choice
★

✕ **Nick's Warehouse.** Ever since 1989, the energetic Nick Price has presided over a cozy wine bar and buzz-filled restaurant on a narrow cobbled street in the fashionable Cathedral Quarter. The informal ground-floor Anix restaurant is frequented by legal, financial, and media types for lunch. Using local ingredients and produce, the menu draws on a wide range of influences in dishes ranging from fillet of sea bass with fennel to rump of lamb with Boulangère potatoes.

> **CARBING UP**
>
> When it comes to food, Northern Ireland is most famed (or notorious) for its Ulster Fry, a fried-up, carbohydrate blowout of a breakfast that is a cardiologist's nightmare. Sausage, bacon, eggs, black pudding, fried soda bread, and potato bread (perhaps a grilled tomato or fried mushrooms) all make a meal that sounds as dangerous to your health as bungee jumping without a rope. After a night on the Guinness, however, you'll understand why this breakfast is so popular: it makes a great cure for a hangover.

The upstairs restaurant, which serves dinner on Saturday night, has a different persona and a more expensive menu to go with it. Even the bread is made on the premises: a pastry chef bakes wonderful soda, wheaten, and whole-grain breads. ✉ *35–39 Hill St., Cathedral Quartert* ☎ *028/9043–9690* ⊕ *www.nickswarehouse.co.uk* ⌛ *Reservations essential* ⊟ *AE, MC, V* ⊗ *Closed Sun. and Mon.*

$
CONTINENTAL

✕ **The Northern Whig.** Housed in an elegant former newspaper building, the Northern Whig is spacious and stylish. Three 30-foot-high statues of Soviet heroes that once topped Communist Party headquarters in Prague dominate the wood-and-leather interior. In the evenings, one wall slides away so you can watch classic movies, a jazz band, or a DJ playing laid-back blues, soul, or retro music. The food is brasserie style—not astonishing, but good. It's the environment, the thoughtful wine list, and the cocktail bar—which specializes in rare vodkas such as Finlandia mango vodka (dynamite in "Storm in a Glass")—that are the main draws. ✉ *2 Bridge St., Central District* ☎ *028/9050–9888* ⊕ *www.thenorthernwhig.com* ⊟ *MC, V.*

$$
CHINESE

✕ **Red Panda.** It comes as a surprise to visitors to learn that Belfast has a large Chinese community, a sizable portion of which seems to favor this bustling spot (making reservations always a good way to go). Both venues—in Belfast city center and in the Odyssey Arena complex—are large, spacious, and modern with plenty going on to tempt the taste buds. A five-course set dinner can include such delights as crispy aromatic duck pancakes or sizzling king prawns with ginger. More adventurous diners will want to spring for the stir-fried squid with bok choy. ✉ *60 Great Victoria St., Central District* ☎ *028/9080–8700* ✉ *Odyssey Arena 2, Queen's Quay* ☎ *028/9046–6644* ⊕ *www.theredpanda.co.uk* ⊟ *AE, DC, MC, V* ⊗ *No lunch Sat.*

$$
JAPANESE

✕ **Zen.** Entrepreneur Eddie Fung has miraculously transformed a red-brick 19th-century Belfast mill into an Asian oasis housing the city's finest Japanese restaurant. Upstairs you traverse a 30-foot-long mirrored catwalk with a glass walkway to get to the seating area. Choose between wooden booths, or, if you're prepared to hunker down on the floor, Japanese-style, opt for the traditional dining area. Downstairs, handpick your meal at the sushi bar, or choose a discreet table for two under the serene gaze of (reputedly) Ireland's largest Buddha. Zen has a reputation for authentic fresh sushi and sashimi. Purists may be bemused at the crispy prawns but everyone declares them delicious. Finish your meal with a Japanese malt whiskey: Nikka Black is smoky and mellow and will round off the perfect dinner. ⊠ *Behind City Hall, 55–59 Adelaide St., Central District* ☎ *028/9023–2244* ⊕ *www. zenbelfast.co.uk* ⊟ *AE, MC, V* ⊙ *No lunch Sat.*

WHERE TO STAY

CENTRAL DISTRICT

$ ☒ **Benedict's of Belfast.** Friendly, lively, and convenient, Benedict's looms large on Shaftesbury Square. Guest rooms on the second floor are bright and colorful, and have wooden floors; rooms on the third floor are darker, with an Asian influence—dark wood and light walls, simple but comfortable. If you don't feel like straying too far from your home base for some nightlife, Benedict's has a buzzing bar and restaurant serving finely done Continental food. They have a "beat the clock" promotion on their menu: a rib-eye steak with champ potatoes and brandy sauce, for instance, is usually £14, but order it up between 5:30 and 7 PM and it's only £5.50. **Pros:** rooms are plain but functional and clean; great value dining. **Cons:** guests have experienced late check-in due to rooms not being ready; some parts of hotel show wear and tear. ⊠ *7–21 Bradbury Pl., Golden Mile, Co. Down* ☎ *028/9059–1999* ⊕ *www.benedictshotel.co.uk* ⬐ *32 rooms* ⌂ *In-room: no a/c, Wi-Fi. In-hotel: restaurant, bar* ⊟ *AE, MC, V* ⦿ *BP.*

$$–$$$ ☒ **Holiday Inn Belfast.** Expect outstanding facilities at a reasonable price. Furnishings are modernist blond wood and leather, and rooms are best described as Japan-meets-Sweden: they have strong, simple colors and sliding wooden screens (a lovely touch) instead of curtains. The funky menu at the Junction bar includes goat cheese penne, scampi, and a selection of deli sandwiches. They have a great-value Discover Belfast deal offering two nights' bed-and-breakfast with dinner, and a city-sightseeing bus tour thrown in for £99 per person. The hotel is superbly located, only a 10-minute walk to the city center and five minutes to the Golden Mile. **Pros:** good value deals on offer; health club and facilities are top-notch; the hotel is directly opposite the BBC studios so you may spot TV celebrities. **Cons:** queues at busy times at check-in and checkout; no car-parking spaces available. ⊠ *22 Ormeau Ave., Golden Mile, Co. Down* ☎ *028/9032–8511* ⊕ *www.holidayinn.com/Belfast* ⬐ *170 rooms* ⌂ *In-room: no a/c, Wi-Fi. In-hotel: restaurant, bar, pool, gym, spa* ⊟ *AE, DC, MC, V* ⦿ *BP, MAP.*

$–$$ ☒ **Jurys Inn Belfast.** The first Jurys north of the border brings the chain's flat-rate formula—a single price for up to three adults or two adults and two children—to the Golden Mile. Once you get past the forbidding warehouselike exterior, a spacious, marble-tile foyer with warm green and salmon hues awaits. Room decor is pretty standard. Some rooms overlook College Square, the cricket lawn of the 1814 Royal Belfast Academical Institution. The Innfusion restaurant serves well-prepared hotel food. Dark wood decorates the Inntro Bar, which serves pub grub all day. **Pros:** prime central location; staff helpful and friendly; spacious rooms. **Cons:** some guests have complained of bedrooms not being properly cleaned; lack of car parking is a problem. ⊠ *Fisherwick Pl. at Great Victoria St., Golden Mile, Co. Down* ☎ *028/9053–3500* ⊕ *www.jurysinns.com* ⤳ *190 rooms* ⌂ *In-room: no a/c, Wi-Fi. In-hotel: restaurant, bar* ⊟ *AE, DC, MC, V* ⊺⊙⊺ *CP.*

$$$$
Fodor's Choice
★

⊺⊺⊺ **The Merchant Hotel.** Four years after its 2006 opening in central Belfast, the Merchant added a breathtaking £16 million extension that's been a huge success among the indulgent set. The sleek and sumptuous new addition is a modern, streamlined building that borrows from the art-deco spirit of the 1920s. It's a startling contrast to the architecturally opulent main hotel, made of formidable Giffnock sandstone and built for the headquarters of Ulster Bank in the mid-19th century. Set with grand columns and crowned with a dramatic group of sculptures depicting Britannia, Justice, and Commerce, the exterior is exuberantly Italianate in style. Inside, a riot of tall urns, fruit, foliage designs, and plump ebullient cherubs are on show, climaxing in the Great Room restaurant (the former banking hall), so magnificent it puts most of England's stately halls to shame. The ornate guest rooms come with antique furnishings, works of art, rich fabrics, and enormous plasma-screen TVs. New are 37 bedrooms with a lighter, brighter color scheme and spacious Carrara marble bathrooms. There's now an underground spa with five treatment rooms, a rooftop gym with hot tub, and—should you feel the need—a champagne nail bar after which you can repair to the cool Bert's Jazz Bar. **Pros:** an opulent place with attentive reception and bar staff; the deep King Koil mattresses leave a mellow afterglow; history and architecture buffs will love it. **Cons:** revelers from pubs and clubs in the surrounding streets detract from the internal serenity; at £15, breakfast room service is for high rollers only. ⊠ *35–39 Waring St., Central District, Co. Down* ☎ *028/9023–4888* ⊕ *www.themerchanthotel.com* ⤳ *63 rooms, 5 suites* ⌂ *In-room: a/c, refrigerator, Wi-Fi. In-hotel: restaurant, bars gym, spa, parking (paid)* ⊟ *AE, MC, V.*

$$$–$$$$
★

⊺⊺⊺ **Ten Square.** You don't get much more downtown or contemporary than this fashionable boutique hotel right behind City Hall. The Neoclassical facade of this former post office hides a serene interior that houses a fashionable bar and a Grill Room, which serves breakfast, lunch, and dinner. The bedrooms are minimalist-Asian in style—with king-size beds in all rooms topped with white duvets and soft armchairs to sink into. Lovers will opt for the Romance Package that offers a rose-petal turndown, chilled champagne, and chocolate truffles—all for £195 in a superior guest room. All rooms were refurbished in 2009. **Pros:** luxurious surroundings with attention to detail in the attractive rooms; super-king beds make it a memorable place to stay; convivial feel to the Grill Room. **Cons:** the noisy bar can be sweaty; sit outside, but only if you don't mind the fumes from taxis, cars, and buses. ⊠ *10 Donegall Sq. S, Golden Mile, Co. Down* ☎ *028/9024–1001* ⊕ *www. tensquare.co.uk* ⤶ *23 rooms* ⅃ *Inroom: a/c, Wi-Fi. In-hotel: restaurant, bars, parking (free)* ⊟ *AE, MC, V* ⏃⏃⏃ *BP, MAP.*

> ### HIDEOUT HISTORY
>
> If you're lucky enough to stay in the oldest parts of the Old Inn, you still may be able to uncover a secret hiding place for contraband, as smugglers, like the famous highwayman Dick Turpin, made this one of their favored homes-away-from-home.

OUTSIDE THE CITY CENTER

$$$$
★
Culloden Estate and Spa. Built in 1876, this imposingly grand vision in Belfast stone presides over the forested slopes of the Holywood hills and the busy waters of Belfast Lough. Topped off with a storybook turret and crenellated tower, the Scottish Baronial mansion was greatly enlarged in the early 20th century when it was given as a residence to the Bishops of Down, then transformed in the 1960s into a hotel. Inside, Neoclassical salons warmed by lime-green walls, gilded coffered ceilings, 19th-century paintings, stained-glass accents, and overstuffed Louis XV–style chairs make you feel like you're a member of the Robinson family. Antiques and silk-and-velvet fabrics grace guest rooms both in the original section and in a newer wing; all rooms have fine views. At mealtime choose from the posh Mitre restaurant and the Cultra Inn, which serves snacks and full meals. The hotel is close to both the village of Holywood (temptingly filled with boutiques) and the Ulster Folk and Transport Museum. Or spend the afternoon at the hotel's Spa, a glamorous Beverly Hills–type affair. **Pros:** building oozing character and personality; top class service. **Cons:** suites are just big rooms and don't measure up; the restaurant can be stuffy; massages, manicures, and vintage champagne don't come cheap. ⊠ *142 Bangor Rd., Holywood (8 km [5 mi] east of Belfast on A2), Co. Down* ☎ *028/9042–1066* ⊕ *www.hastingshotels.com* ⤶ *105 rooms, 22 suites* ⅃ *In-room: no a/c, Wi-Fi. In-hotel: 2 restaurants, bar, tennis court, pool, spa* ⊟ *AE, DC, MC, V* ⏃⏃⏃ *BP, MAP.*

$–$$
Fodor's Choice
★
The Old Inn. Set in the village of Crawfordsburn, this 1614 coach inn, reputedly Ireland's oldest, certainly looks the part: it's pure 17th-century England, with a sculpted thatch roof, half doors, and leaded-glass windows. As it was near one of the leading cross-channel ports linking Ireland and England, the coach always stopped here, often bearing visitors with names like Swift, Tennyson, Thackeray, Dickens, and Trollope. Some of the finest bedrooms have 17th-century-style woodwork, sitting rooms, and faux-Jacobean beds, while public salons offer beam ceilings and roaring log fires. During 2010 the inn underwent a £2.5 million restoration to repair the 1614 Restaurant and bar area. The food is as reliable as ever and you can tuck into Finnebrogue venison with sweet-potato puree, Portavogie scallops, and Irish lamb. Also savor the delicious setting of flocked curtains, English wood panels, sculpted portrait medallions, and a soaring coved ceiling. Over the centuries, large portions of the inn were rebuilt, and the East Wing is a completely modern take on Irish Georgian style. **Pros:** a proverbial step back in

time. **Cons:** slow service; breakfasts not always up to snuff; some areas need redecoration. ✉ *15 Main St., Crawfordsburn (16 km [10 mi] east of Belfast on A2), Co. Down* ☎ *028/9185–3255* ⊕ *www.theoldinn.com* ⇱ *31 rooms, 4 suites* ⚷ *In-room: no a/c, Wi-Fi. In-hotel: restaurant, bars* ⊟ *AE, MC, V* ⏐◯⏐ *BP.*

UNIVERSITY AREA

¢   🖾 **All Seasons.** Enjoying a superb location on the fashionable Lisburn Road in the south of the city, this spot is steps from some of the city's most stylish boutiques and trendiest bars. Friendly owner Theodore McLaughlin has created a cozy home with a comfortable lounge, spacious dining room, and spotlessly clean rooms. Cranmore Park, a popular venue during the summer for sunbathers, is two minutes away on foot. **Pros:** top-notch location for exploring the cafés and bars on Lisburn Road; warm, welcoming, and inviting owner. **Cons:** family rooms can be a tight squeeze; few toiletries and no hair dryers. ✉ *356 Lisburn Rd., University Area, Co. Down* ☎ *028/9068–2814* ⊕ *www.allseasonsbelfast.com* ⇱ *7 rooms* ⚷ *In-room: no a/c, Wi-Fi* ⊟ *MC, V* ⏐◯⏐ *BP.*

$ 🖾 **Dukes at Queens.** The handsomely transformed hotel reopened in
★   2009, bringing a whiff of trendiness to an area that's about as bohemian as Belfast gets. Although it has retained its distinguished redbrick Victorian facade, the inside has been revamped in a cool contemporary style. Handsomely appointed guest rooms come in varying sizes and now focus on chic modern, making this a fave for weekenders, and during the week, the smart business set. Villeroy & Boch bathrooms with their drench shower bring bliss while swank and comfy Rolf Benz swivel armchairs in burgundy and red are added bonuses. The restaurant with its authentic wood-fired oven specializes in pizzas and monkfish. The location is perfect: Queen's University and Botanic Gardens are a five-minute stroll away, and if you want to eat out you can wander the leafy streets and choose from a range of restaurants serving Chinese, Indian, Japanese, Italian, as well as Irish cuisine. **Pros:** stylish hotel offering excellent service; good value for the money. **Cons:** area is thronged at lunchtime with office workers and even busier at night—noise is an ever-present reality. ✉ *65–67 University St., University Area, Co. Down* ☎ *028/9023–6666* ⊕ *www.dukesatqueens.com* ⇱ *32 rooms* ⚷ *In-room: a/c, Wi-Fi. In-hotel: restaurant, bar, laundry service* ⊟ *DC, MC, V* ⏐◯⏐ *BP.*

NIGHTLIFE AND THE ARTS

NIGHTLIFE

Belfast has dozens of pubs packed with relics of the Victorian and Edwardian periods. Although pubs typically close around 11:30 PM, many city-center–Golden Mile nightclubs stay open until 1 AM.

CENTRAL   **Bittles Bar** (✉ *70 Upper Church La., Central District* ☎ *028/9031–1088*),
DISTRICT   on Victoria Square, serves pub grub. Gilded shamrocks bedeck this interesting triangular Victorian pub on the fringes of the Cathedral Quarter. Paintings of literary characters and local landmarks adorn the walls, while a high, wood-panel ceiling gives an illusion of spaciousness.

Get your perfect pint of Guinness at the Crown Liquor Saloon, a Victorian extravaganza of embossed ceilings, gilded arabesques, and carved woodwork.

Café Vaudeville (✉ *25 Arthur St., Central District* ☎ *028/9043–9160*) is a glamorous and ornate setting whose upstairs Bolli Bar attracts local celebrities and the beautiful people. A must for every traveler's hit list, **The John Hewitt** (✉ *51 Donegall St., Central District* ☎ *028/9023–3768* ⊕ *www.thejohnhewitt.com*) bar, named after one of Ulster's most famous poets, is traditional in style with a marble counter, waist-high wooden paneling, high ceilings, and open fire. It channels Hewitt's socialist sensibility, as it's owned by the Belfast Unemployed Centre (which it helps fund with its profits)—top pub grub is on tap at lunch while live music is featured most nights, including the excellent Panama Jazz Band on Friday (except the first Friday of each month). **Kelly's Cellars** (✉ *30–32 Bank St., Central District* ☎ *028/9024–6058*), open since 1720, has blues bands on Saturday night. The **Kremlin** (✉ *96 Donegall St., Central District* ☎ *028/9031–6060* ⊕ *www.kremlin-belfast.com*) nightclub is the city's oldest and most outrageous gay-oriented club. A massive statue of Lenin above the front door greets customers, and the over-the-top Soviet theme continues inside. Superstar DJs regularly fly in to perform.

Regulars prop up the horseshoe-shaped bar in the Victorian showpiece, the **Morning Star** (✉ *17–19 Pottinger's Entry, Central District* ☎ *028/9023–5968*), from noon until night. Strike up a conversation with some of the locals and you're guaranteed a bit of craic. **McHugh's** (✉ *29–30 Queen's Sq., Central District* ☎ *028/9050–9999* ⊕ *www.mchughsbar.com*), in Belfast's oldest building, dating from 1711, has three floors of bars and restaurants, and live music on weekends. **Union Street** (✉ *8–14 Union St., Central District* ☎ *028/9031–6060*) is a gay-friendly bar near the Cathedral Quarter housed in a converted 19th-century shoe factory. The three-story redbrick Victorian is one of the city's few "gastro-pubs," with a more formal upstairs restaurant that's popular with local foodies. **White's Tavern** (⊠ *2–12 Winecellar Entry, Central District* ☎ *028/9024–3080* ⊕ *www.whitestavern.co.uk*) claims to be the oldest public house in Belfast. In winter a roaring fire greets you as soon as you enter the bar. Friendly staff serve good pub grub, including the famous creamy, buttery, cholesterol-laden potato champ. Enjoy the traditional Irish sessions on Friday and Saturday nights.

GOLDEN MILE AREA The glorious Crown Liquor Saloon is far from being the only old pub in the Golden Mile area—some, but by no means all, of Belfast's evening life takes place in bars and restaurants here. There are a number of replicated Victorian bars where more locals and fewer visitors gather.

Benedict's (⊠ *7–21 Bradbury Pl., Golden Mile* ☎ *028/9059–1999*) is a bar, music venue, disco, 150-seat restaurant, and hotel. The faux-Gothic exterior of the hotel belies its modern origins. Straying from the model of the Victorian-style public house, the **Limelight** (⊠ *17 Ormeau Ave., Golden Mile* ☎ *028/9032–5968*) is a disco-nightclub with cabaret on Tuesday, Friday, and Saturday, and recorded music on other nights. It's extremely popular with students, and books musicians as well as DJs.

Morrisons (⊠ *21 Bedford St., Golden Mile* ☎ *028/9032–0030*) is a haunt of media types. It has a music lounge upstairs with weekend gigs. **Robinsons** (⊠ *38–42 Great Victoria St., Golden Mile* ☎ *028/9024–7447* ⊕ *www.robinsonsbar.co.uk*), two doors from the Crown, is a popular pub that draws a young crowd with folk music in its Fibber Magee's bar on Sunday and funk in the trendy BT1 wine and cocktail bar on weekends.

UNIVERSITY AREA The stylish and modern **Bar Twelve** (⊠ *Crescent Town House, 13 Lower Crescent, University Area* ☎ *028/9032–3349*) is an excellent venue for some fashionable wine-sipping. On weekends, DJs spin 1960s and '70s soul and funk tunes.

On the increasingly fashionable Lisburn Road, **Monzu** (⊠ *701 Lisburn Rd., University Area* ☎ *028/9066–4422*) is a spacious, chic bar filled with a cool, under-30 crowd. The restaurant serves good casual food for lunch and dinner.

The **M-Club** (⊠ *23 Bradbury Pl., University Area* ☎ *028/9023–3131*) is Belfast's hottest place for dedicated clubbers, with soap-opera celebrities flown in weekly to mix with the local nighthawks.

THE ARTS

The **Northern Ireland Arts Council** (☎ *028/9038–5200* ⊕ *www.arts-council-ni.org*) is the main development agency for the arts in Northern Ireland and supports a range of cultural and artistic events. **Culture Northern Ireland** (☎ *028/9087–2217* ⊕ *www.culturenorthernireland.org*) is an Internet initiative and a useful resource for visitors. It provides information on music, film, and multimedia, literature, heritage, sports, the visual and performing arts, as well as a "What's On" listing that includes blogs and podcasts of latest events. The **Ulster Orchestra Concerts** (☎ *028/9023–9955* ⊕ *www.ulsterorchestra.com*) are performed throughout the year by the Ulster Orchestra.

Belfast has seen a phenomenal growth in **festivals** in recent years with a spectrum of different types covering music, drama, dance, film, and history. The long-established **Belfast Festival at Queen's University** (*Festival office:* ✉ *8 Fitzwilliam St., University Area* ☎ *028/9097–1034* ⊕ *www.belfastfestival.com*) lasts for three weeks (usually late October into early November) and is the city's major arts festival. The **Cathedral Quarter Arts Festival** (✉ *Cathedral Quarter* ☎ *028/9024–6609* ⊕ *www.cqaf.com*), held in early May, is full of energy and attracts top-class local, national and international acts. The **Festival of Fools** (✉ *Cathedral Quarter 028/9023–6007* ⊕ *www.foolsfestival.com*), held as part of the Cathedral Quarter festival, is a vibrant five-day event taking place on streets and public spaces across the city.

ART GALLERIES Central Belfast is awash with small, quirky art galleries that have sprung up along red-brick back streets—especially in Cathedral Quarter—in the past few years, featuring an eclectic mix of painting, sculpture, photography, and printmaking, as well as installation artists with digital and video work. Check ⊕ *www.belfastgalleries.com* for a more detailed listing.

One of the best galleries is the **Golden Thread Gallery** (✉ *84–94 Great Patrick St., Cathedral Quarter* ☎ *028/9096–0920* ⊕ *www.gtgallery.org.uk*), internationally renowned with links to the Venice Biennale and running the International Symposium for Electronic Art. Opposite the Merchant Hotel, the **Northern Ireland Print Gallery** (✉ *42 Waring St., Central District* ☎ *028/9032–3059* ⊕ *www.craftnidirectory.org*) is a hotbed of crafts where street performers at Cotton Court regularly entertain crowds on summer Sundays. **Ormeau Baths Gallery** (✉ *18a Ormeau Ave., Central District* ☎ *028/9032–1402* ⊕ *www.ormeaubaths.co.uk*) is in a delightful Queen Anne–style building, formerly the public baths, that now displays contemporary Irish and touring art and photographic exhibitions.

MAJOR VENUES **Belfast Waterfront.** Everyone in Belfast sings the praises of this striking civic structure. From the looks of it, the hall is an odd marriage of *Close Encounters* modern and Castel Sant'Angelo antique. It houses a major 2,235-seat concert hall (for ballet and classical, rock, and Irish music) and a 500-seat studio space (for modern dance, jazz, and experimental theater). The Arc Brasserie and two bars make the Waterfront a convenient place to eat, have a pint, and enjoy the river views before or after your culture fix. ✉ *Lanyon Pl., Central District* ☎ *028/9033–4455* ⊕ *www.waterfront.co.uk*.

Crescent Arts Centre. After a £7.2 million renovation program in 2009, the Crescent moved back into its huge rambling stone building—a former girls' high—in the University area in spring 2010. It offers experimental dance and theater, concerts, workshops, and evening classes. ✉ *2 University Rd.* ☎ *028/9024–2338* ⊕ *www.crescentarts.org*.

Cultúrlann McAdam Ó Fiaich. A cosmopolitan arts center celebrating Irish language and culture, it hosts an array of exhibitions, book launches, concerts, drama, and poetry readings. The shop sells a range of Irish-language books as well as gifts and crafts. There is a tourist information point and a café. ✉ *216 Falls Rd., West Belfast* ☎ *028/9096–4180* ⊕ *www.culturlann.ie* ⊙ *Daily 9–9.*

Grand Opera House. Shows from all over the British Isles—and sometimes farther afield—play at this beautifully restored Victorian theater. Though it has no company of its own, there's a constant stream of West End musicals and plays of widely differing kinds, plus occasional operas and ballets. It's worth going to a show if only to enjoy the opera house itself. The Baby Grand—a theater within a theater—hosts comedy, live music, and education workshops as well as film and special events. Luciano's Café Bar (named after the opera giant Pavarotti) serves a satisfying selection of meals from 10 AM to curtain time. ⊠ *2 Great Victoria St., Golden Mile* ☎ *028/9024–1919* ⊕ *www.goh.co.uk.*

Lyric Theatre. Slated to open in spring 2011 after a three-year closure and £18 million rebuild, the original Lyric is where Liam Neeson made his 1976 stage debut in Brian Friel's *Philadelphia, Here I Come!* The sparkling new theater, on the banks of the Lagan beside King's Bridge, specializes in traditional and contemporary Irish drama. The 390-seat venue contains an additional auditorium that can hold up to 150 people. The new entrance stone features an engraved verse from a Seamus Heaney poem, "Peter Street at Bankside," about a carpenter Peter Street who helped build the Globe Theatre in London. ⊠ *55 Ridgeway St., University Area* ☎ *028/9038–5685* ⊕ *www.lyrictheatre.co.uk.*

Odyssey Arena. Built to mark the millennium and now home to the Belfast Giants—the city's first ice-hockey team (most of whom hail from North America)—the Odyssey complex also features the interactive science and technology center known as W5, an indoor bowling alley, and the Odyssey Pavilion complex (⊕ *www.odysseypavilion.com*), replete with bars, restaurants, shops, and nightclubs. The center ring is the 10,000-seat Arena, Ireland's biggest indoor venue, which often hosts rock, pop, and classical troupes. Situated on Queen's Island, the Odyssey is close to the old Harland and Wolff shipyard and set along the banks of the River Lagan. ⊠ *2 Queen's Quay, Central District* ☎ *028/9076–6000* ⊕ *www.odysseyarena.com.*

Ulster Hall. In 2009 the historic Ulster Hall became the permanent home to the Ulster Orchestra shortly after the building reopened following a multimillion-pound refit. At the gala civic ceremony on the reopening night the Orchestra played "Rhapsody on a Theme of Paganini" by Sergei Rachmaninov who himself once played in the hall. The classical music season runs from September through April. Concerts are mostly held on Friday but you can call in to catch free open rehearsals and look out for the 50-minute lunchtime concerts. Apart from classical, a range of musical tastes covering rock, folk, traditional Irish, blues, and jazz are on offer year-round along with comedy and cabaret acts. The reopening of the hall marks another chapter in the economic regeneration of the city and has considerably enriched the cultural landscape. With superb acoustics it is, in short, the perfect listening and foot-tapping experience. ⊠ *Bedford St., Golden Mile* ☎ *028/9033–4400* ⊕ *www.ulsterhall.co.uk.*

SHOPPING

Belfast's main shopping streets include High Street, Donegall Place, Royal Avenue, and several of the smaller streets connecting them. The area is mostly traffic-free (except for buses and delivery vehicles). The long thoroughfare of Donegall Pass, running from Shaftesbury Square at the point of the Golden Mile east to Ormeau Road, is a unique mix of biker shops and antiques arcades.

MARKETS AND MALLS

Castle Court (✉ *10 Royal Ave., Central District* ☎ *028/9023–4591* ⊕ *www.westfield.com/castlecourt*) is the city's second-largest shopping mall. Debenhams department store can fill many of your shopping needs, from cosmetics to kitchenware. Trendy stores such as the Gap can be found under Castle Court's glass roof, alongside British clothing chains such as Miss Selfridge and Warehouse. Boys who like their toys will be in their element in the G4 shop. Plenty of parking makes shopping easy in the mall. Castle Court is euro-friendly and shops accept both sterling and euros.

If you've an interest in bric-a-brac, visit the enormous, renovated **St. George's Market** (✉ *May St., Central District* ☎ *028/9043–5704* ⊕ *www. stgeorgesmarket.com*), an indoor market that takes place Friday and Saturday morning. Originally opened in the 1890s, this historic market sold butter, eggs, poultry, and fruit. In those days Belfast was known as the "City of Seven Smells": these came from such fixtures as gasworks, slaughterhouse, and soap factory. Today it is a vibrant place with 100 traders selling everything from apples to zippers and antiques to shark meat. Get there early on Saturday for an award-winning farmers' market, featuring organically grown fruit and vegetables, as well as treats such as homemade cakes and bread. Stop by Piece of Cake Bakery, run by Darko Marjanovic, and choose from a terrific range of 20 breads, including rye, spelt, ciabatta, olive, whole wheat, walnut, focaccia, and banana, or sample the delicious baklava. Next door is S.D. Bell's coffee stand; the company is older than the market, as it was set up in 1887 and has been brewing nonstop ever since.

Occupying an eight-block site in central Belfast, **Victoria Square** (✉ *Chichester, Montgomery, and Ann Sts., and Victoria Square, Central District* ☎ *028/9032–2277* ⊕ *www.victoriasquare.com* ☉ *Mon. and Tues. 9:30– 6, Wed.–Fri. 9:30–9, Sat. 9–6, Sun. 1–6*) has changed the Belfast skyline with a Disneyland-like complex of shopping malls and residences adding a fresh dimension to the retail world as well as a huge contribution to the city's regeneration. Opened in 2008 with a pyrotechnic display, a ticker-tape party, and to an accompanying fanfare of gushing superlatives from the marketing pros, the much-hyped £400 million flagship Victoria Square complex is one of the largest construction projects in Ireland. All glittering steel, it is presided over by a vast geodesic glass dome eight stories high complete with viewing platforms over the city (you need a ticket to get into the viewing gallery but admission is free). The center covers 800,000 square feet and has attracted leading London brand names to Northern Ireland for the first time. The House of Fraser department store is the main anchor tenant and a portfolio of designer shops such as Cruise, Hugo Boss, Reiss, and All Saints have brought thousands of people into the city for some retail therapy and a fix of happiness. Other internationally known names are Agent Provocateur, French Connection, and River Island, as well as a raft of coffee shops and fast-food restaurants. There is also an eight-screen cinema. Offering a delightful contrast, however, the complex also incorporates noted Victorian landmarks such as the McErvel's Seed Warehouse and the Royal Belfast Ginger Ale Manufactury. With the opening of the complex, many commentators feel that consumerism has at last trumped terrorism in Northern Ireland. The **Q-Park** (⊕ *www.q-park.co.uk*) provides 1,000 parking spaces and is open 24/7.

SPECIALTY SHOPS

Clark and Dawe (✉ *485 Lisburn Rd., University Area* ☎ *028/9066–8228*) makes and sells men's and women's suits and shirts. This clothes shop is one of more than 200 independent businesses on the retail-haven of Lisburn Road, jam-packed with trendy designer shops, lifestyle emporia, galleries, and antiques stores. There's also a diverse range of coffee shops, wine bars, delis, and restaurants that come and go with dizzying speed. The Lisburn Road Business Association (LRBA) has special offers on its Web site (⊕ *www.visitlisburnroad.com*).

The Church of Ireland Bookshop (✉ *61/67 Donegall St., Cathedral Quarter* ☎ *028/9024–4825*) stocks new Christian and secular books.

Just the way a bookstore should be, **No Alibis** (✉ *83 Botanic Ave., University Area* ☎ *028/9031–9601* ⊕ *www.noalibis.com*) specializes in British and American crime thrillers, as well as general fiction and nonfiction, plus a smattering of local books—all in all, a bibliophile's delight.

Smyth and Gibson (✉ *Bedford House, Bedford St., Golden Mile* ☎ *028/ 9023–0388*) makes and sells beautiful, luxurious linen and cotton shirts and accessories.

Looking for linen souvenirs? **Smyth's Irish Linens** (✉ *65 Royal Ave., Central District* ☎ *028/9024–2232*) carries a large selection of handkerchiefs, tablecloths, napkins, and other traditional goods. It's opposite Castle Court Mall.

The Steensons (✉ *Bedford House, Bedford St., Golden Mile* ☎ *028/9024–8269* ⊕ *www.thesteensons.com*) sells superb, locally designed jewelry. **Utopia** (✉ *Fountain Centre, College St., Central District* ☎ *028/9024–1342*) stocks intricate silver pendants and earrings made by up-and-coming local jewelry designer Alpha Zed. Also worth a look are the hand-carved wooden and marble chess sets.

THE GIANT'S CAUSEWAY COAST

Starting in Belfast, stretching for 80 km (50 mi) along Northern Ireland's Atlantic shore, the Causeway Coast holds many of the province's "don't miss" attractions. The man-made brilliance of the castle at Dunluce, the endless string of whitewashed fishing villages along the sea, and the world-famous natural wonder that is the Giant's Causeway are just

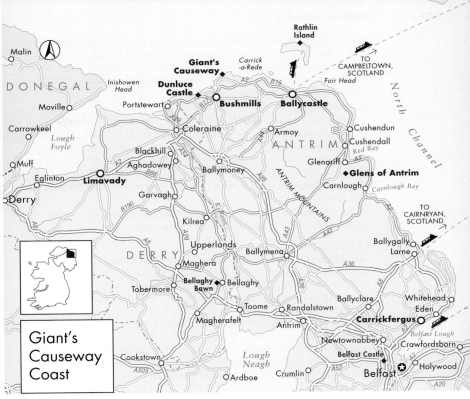

Giant's Causeway Coast

some of the delights to be discovered here. Once your car or mountain bike (ideal for the Causeway's flat terrain) makes its way past some fair-size towns, you'll enter the splendid Glens area—one of the more "gentle" (an Irish turn-of-phrase for supernatural) places in all Ireland. Here, ageless villages—still inhabited by descendants of the ancient Irish and the Hebridean Scots who hailed from across the narrow Sea of Moyle—are set in peaceful, old-growth forests that have become synonymous with Irishness. But once past the Giant's Causeway you'll find more cosmopolitan pleasures, including Bushmills—the oldest licensed distillery in the world—and the old walled city of Derry.

CARRICKFERGUS

16 km (10 mi) northeast of Belfast on A2.

Carrickfergus, on the shore of Belfast Lough, grew up around its ancient castle. When the town was enclosed by ramparts at the start of the 17th century, it was the only English-speaking town in Ulster. Not surprisingly, this was the loyal port where William of Orange chose to land on his way to fight the Catholic forces at the Battle of the Boyne in 1690. However, the English did have one or two small setbacks, including the improbable victory in 1778 of John Paul Jones, the American naval hero, over the British warship HMS *Drake*. Although a long way from home, this stands as the first naval victory of America's fledgling navy fleet. After this battle, which was waged in Belfast Lough, the inhabitants of Carrickfergus stood on the waterfront and cheered Jones when his ship passed the town castle, demonstrating their support for the American Revolution.

GETTING HERE

TRAIN TRAVEL   Trains run by Northern Ireland Railways from Belfast on this section of the Antrim coast go only as far as the 40 km (25 mi) to Larne. Daily service stops at a number of towns, including Carrickfergus, Whitehead, and Glynn. A round-trip ticket from Belfast's Yorkgate or Central Station to Carrickfergus costs £5.50; from Belfast to Larne, it's £9.30. There are frequent services with up to six trains operating per hour at peak times.

Visitor Information Carrickfergus Tourist Office & Museum (⊠ *11 Antrim St., Co. Antrim* ☎ *028/9335–8049* ⊕ *www.carrickfergus.org*).

EXPLORING

Carrickfergus Castle, one of the first and one of the largest of Irish castles, is still in good shape. It was built atop a rock ledge in 1180 by John de Courcy, provincial Ulster's first Anglo-Norman invader. Apart from being captured briefly by the French in 1760, the castle stood as a bastion of British rule right up until 1928, at which time it still functioned as an English garrison. Walk through the castle's 13th-century gatehouse into the Outer Ward. Continue into the Inner Ward, the heart of the fortress, where the five-story keep stands, a massive, sturdy building with walls almost 8 feet thick. If you're here at the end of July, you can enjoy the annual Lughnasa festival, a lively medieval-costume entertainment. ⊠ *Off A2* ☎ *028/9335–1273* 🖃 *£3* ☉ *Apr.–Sept., daily 10–6; Oct.–Mar., daily 10–4.*

Old buildings that remain from Carrickfergus's past include St. Nicholas's Church, built by John de Courcy in 1205 (remodeled in 1614) and the handsomely restored North Gate in the town's medieval walls. Dobbins Inn on High Street, which has been a hotel for more than three centuries, is a watering hole that's popular with locals.

The **Andrew Jackson Cottage and U.S. Rangers Centre** tells the tale of the U.S. president whose parents emigrated from here in 1765. This thatch cottage just outside of town is a reconstruction of an 18th-century structure thought to resemble their home. The cottage is open year-round, but access is by arrangement through Carrickfergus tourist office. ⊠ *1½ km (1 mi) northeast of Carrickfergus, Larne Rd., Boneybefore* ☎ *028/9335–8049* ⊕ *www.carrickfergus.org/tourism/museum/andrew-jackson-cottage* 🖃 *Free.*

GLENS OF ANTRIM

★   *Beginning 24 km (15 mi) north of Carrickfergus at Larne.*

BUS TRAVEL   The only way of taking in the Glens of Antrim and the north coast on public transport is by bus. The Antrim Coaster Goldline ranks as one of Europe's most scenic routes. The service operates from Belfast along the complete stretch of the famed narrow and twisting County Antrim coastline all the way to Coleraine—a 160-km (100-mi) journey that takes about four hours, as there are 30 stops en route. The complete journey costs £15 round-trip, and it's worth every penny. The Monday–Saturday service operates year-round, while a Sunday service runs only early July–mid-September. Be warned: there is no advance booking on the Antrim Coaster, and in the height of the summer it's an extremely popular service—arrive early to be assured a window seat. Departures are from the Europa Buscentre in Belfast, and round-trip cost to the Giant's Causeway is £15.

> **WATCH YOUR BACK**
>
> In the beautiful Glens of Antrim, locals often talk of "the wee folk," said to reside in and around the "gentle" (i.e., supernatural) places of Lurigethan Mountain and Tiveragh Hill. The fairies inhabiting these places are mischievous creatures who mostly mind their own business, but woe betide anyone rash enough to cut off a fairy thorn (a type of bush).

Soon after Larne, the coast of County Antrim becomes spectacular—wave upon wave of high green hills that curve down to the hazy sea are dotted with lush glens, or valleys, first carved out by glaciers at the end of the last ice age. Nine wooded river valleys occupy the 86 km (54 mi) between Larne and Ballycastle. A narrow, winding, two-lane road (A2, which splits from the coastal at Cushendall) hugs the slim strip of land between the hills and the sea, bringing you to the magnificent Glens of Antrim running down from the escarpment of the Antrim Plateau to the eastern shore. Until the building of this road in 1834, the Glens were home to isolated farming communities—people who adhered to the romantic, mystical Celtic legends and the everyday use of the Irish language. Steeped in Irish mythology, the Glens were first inhabited by small bands of Irish monks as early as AD 700. Some residents proudly note that Ossian, the greatest of the Celtic poets, is supposedly buried near Glenaan. Given the original remoteness of the area, a great tradition of storytelling still exists.

The Glens are worth several days of serious exploration. Even narrower B-roads curl west off A2, up each of the beautiful glens, where trails await hikers. You'll need a full week and a rainproof tent to complete the nine-glen circuit (working from south to north, Glenarm, Glencloy, Glenariff, Glenballyeamon, Glenaan, Glencorp, Glendun, Glenshesk, and Glentasie); or you could just head for Glenariff Park, the most accessible of Antrim's glens. Tourist offices in the area, such as the one in Cushendall, sell a *Guide to the Glens*.

A little resort made of white limestone, **Carnlough** overlooks a charming harbor that's surrounded by stone walls. The harbor can be reached by crossing over the limestone bridge from Main Street, built especially for the Marquis of Londonderry. The small harbor, once a port of call for fishermen, now shelters pleasure yachts. Carnlough is surrounded on three sides by hills that rise 1,000 feet from the sea. There's a small tourist office inside McKillop's shop, which is useful if you need information on exploring the scenic Glens of Antrim and the coast road. ✉ *24 km (15 mi) north of Larne on A2.*

★ In **Glenariff Forest Park** you can explore the most beautiful and unsettled of Antrim's glens. Glenariff was christened "Little Switzerland" by Thackeray for its spectacular combination of rugged hills and lush vales. The main valley opens onto Red Bay at the village of Glenariff (also known as Waterfoot). Inside the park are picnic facilities and dozens of good hikes. The 5½-km (3½-mi) Waterfall Trail, marked with blue arrows, passes outstanding views of Glenariff River, its waterfalls, and small but swimmable loughs. Escape from the summer crowds by taking one of the longest trails, such as the Scenic Hike. Pick up a detailed trail map at the park visitor center, which also has a small cafeteria. ⊠ 98 Glenariff Rd. (7 km [5 mi] north of Carnlough, off A2), Glenariff ☎ 028/2175–8232 ☞ Vehicles £4, pedestrians £2 ⊗ Apr.–Sept., daily 8–8; Oct.–Mar., daily 10–dusk.

> **ELIXIR OF YOUTH?**
>
> The coastal caves of Cushendall have been used for various purposes, including housing. One of the more colorful residents was a lady called Nun Marry who lived in one cave for 50 years, supplementing her income as one of the region's best potion brewers. The damp and windy conditions obviously agreed with her—as did perhaps a taste of her own brew?—for she lived to the ripe old age of 100.

Turnley's Tower—a curious, fortified square tower of red stone, built in 1820 as a curfew tower and jail for "idlers and rioters"—stands in **Cushendall,** at a crossroads in the middle of the village. Cushendall is called the capital of the Glens due to having a few more streets than the other villages hereabouts. The road from Waterfoot to Cushendall is barely a mile long and worth the walk or cycle out to see the coastal caves (one of which had a resident called Nun Marry) that line the route. ⊠ 3 km (2 mi) north of Glenariff on A2.

★ Off the main A2 route, the road between Cushendall and Cushendun turns into one of a Tour-de-France hilliness, so cyclists beware. Your reward, however, will be the tiny jewel of a village, **Cushendun,** which was designed by Clough Williams-Ellis, who also designed the famous Italianate village of Portmeirion in Wales. From this part of the coast you can see the Mull of Kintyre on the Scottish mainland. ⊠ 2 km (1½ mi) north of Cushendall on Coast Rd.

EN ROUTE   The narrow and precipitous Antrim Coast Road cuts off from A2 and heads north from Cushendun past dramatically beautiful Murlough Bay to Fair Head and on to Ballycastle. In this area is Drumnakill, a renowned pagan site; Torr Head, a jutting peninsula; and three state parks that allow for some fabulous hikes, fine hill-walking, and great views of Scotland from Fair Head. Or you can rejoin A2 at Cushendun via B92 (a left turn). After a few miles the road descends—passing ruins of the Franciscans' 16th-century Bonamargy Friary—into Ballycastle.

WHERE TO STAY

$$$ ▦ **Ballygally Castle.** A baronial castle, built by a Scottish lord in 1625, rises dramatically beside Ballygally Bay. Attached to it is a modern extension that provides room for facilities but clashes a bit with the

original. Bedrooms in the castle have retained beamed ceilings but have bland-if-comfortable furnishings throughout. Ask for a room in a turret—they are named after four of the nine Antrim Glens—and one comes complete with milady's ghost. The four guest rooms are attractively furnished. On Saturday in the dining room, a decent set-menu dinner is served to musical accompaniment; a Sunday bistro meal is also available. A sign over the check-in desk captures the friendly nature of the hotel: "There are no strangers here, only friends you haven't met." **Pros:** their stock-in-trade is looking after their guests; handy stopover en route to the Giant's Causeway. **Cons:** can fill up quickly, leading to delays particularly at peak holiday times; the room heating system seems to have a mind of its own. ⊠ *274 Coast Rd., Ballygally, Co. Antrim* ☎ *028/2858–1066* ⊕ *www.hastingshotels.com* ⌖ *44 rooms* ⌂ *In-room: no a/c, Wi-Fi. In-hotel: restaurant, bar* ⊟ *AE, DC, MC, V* ❘⊙❘ *BP.*

$$$ **Galgorm Resort & Spa.** The manor house itself is photogenic, and the

Fodor'sChoice   160 acres of estate grounds—where you may go riding, practice archery,

★   and shoot clay pigeons—cinematic. Full privileges at an 18-hole golf course, a mere five minutes from the hotel, are an added treat. The River Maine (good for brown trout) flows within view of many of the large rooms, which have wood beams on the ceilings above substantial dark-wood beds. Gillies bar is decidedly Irish; the River Room restaurant serves hearty portions of traditional Irish food ($–$$). A spa contains 12 treatment rooms, five climate rooms, heated loungers, and an out-door hot tub. The hotel hosts private dinners in its Titanic room, where guests sit at a table commissioned originally for the *Titanic* liner. Built in Belfast, it wasn't completed in time and was used in the first Parliament in Belfast and later owned by Arthur Conan Doyle. Galgorm is off A42, 3 km (2 mi) west of Ballymena, 32 km (20 mi) inland of Larne, 40 km (25 mi) north of Belfast. **Pros:** an elegant mix of the cozy and luxurious that ticks all the right boxes; the perfect place for pamper potential. **Cons:** if you're not a golfer, swimmer, or spa fan, there's not a lot to do apart from relaxing; hovers on the edge of remoteness and a long walk to shops. ⊠ *136 Fenaghy Rd., Ballymena (40 km [25 mi] east of Larne on A36), Co. Antrim* ☎ *028/2588–1001* ⊕ *www.galgorm. com* ⌖ *75 rooms* ⌂ *In-room: no a/c, Wi-Fi. In-hotel: restaurant, bar, pool, gym, spa* ⊟ *AE, MC, V* ❘⊙❘ *BP, MAP*

$$ **Londonderry Arms Hotel.** What awaits at Londonderry Arms are lovely

★   seaside gardens, ivy-clad walls, gorgeous antiques, regional paintings and maps, and lots of fresh flowers. This ivy-covered traditional inn on Carnlough Harbour was built as a coach stop in 1848. In 1921 Sir Winston Churchill inherited it from his great-grandmother; since 1947 it has been owned and run by the hospitable O'Neill family. Both the original and the newer rooms have Georgian furnishings and luxurious fabrics, and are immaculately kept. The restaurant serves substantial, traditional Irish meals that emphasize fresh, local seafood as well as rib eye of prime Irish beef, all simply prepared. The Coach House bistro offers a more informal and cheaper alternative with welcoming open fires. In 2010 the hotel began offering a series of creative workshops—including painting, lace making, and digital photography—and started a treasure trail around the area. **Pros:** fine historic vibe; cheerful staff; free newspapers. **Cons:** guests have complained of cold bedrooms; old-fashioned hotels (and creaky floor-boards) aren't everyone's taste. ✉ *20 Harbor Rd., Carnlough, Co. Antrim* ☎ *028/2888–5255* ⊕ *www.glensofantrim.com* ↩ *35 rooms* ⚐ *In-room: no a/c, Wi-Fi. In-hotel: restaurant, bar* ▭ *AE, DC, MC, V* ⊚| *BP, MAP.*

> ### SHOOT THE CHUTE
>
> If you summon up the nerve to cross the famous 60-foot-long Carrick-a-Rede rope bridge, which sways over a rocky outcrop and the turbulent sea, be mindful that you have to do it again to get back to the mainland.

BALLYCASTLE

86 km (54 mi) northeast of Larne, 37½ km (23 mi) north of Carnlough.

Ballycastle is the main resort at the northern end of the Glens of Antrim. People from all over the province flock here in summer. The town is shaped like an hourglass—with its strand and dock on one end, its pubs and chippers on the other, and the 1-km (½-mi) Quay Road in between. Beautifully aged shops and pubs line its Castle, Diamond, and Main streets.

Visitor Information Ballycastle Tourist Office (✉ *7 Mary St., Co. Antrim* ☎ *028/2076–2024* ⊕ *www.moyle-council.org*).

EXPLORING

Every year since 1606, on the last Monday and Tuesday in August, Ballycastle has hosted the **Oul' Lammas Fair,** a modern version of the ancient Celtic harvest festival of Lughnasa (Irish for "August"). Ireland's oldest fair, this is a very popular two-day event at which sheep and wool are still sold alongside the wares of more modern shopping stalls. Treat yourself to the fair's traditional snacks, dulse (sun-dried seaweed), and yellowman (rock-hard yellow toffee).

★ Off the coast at Ballintoy in Larrybane adrenalin junkies love the **Carrick-a-Rede** rope bridge, which spans a 60-foot gap between the mainland and tiny Carrick-a-Rede Island. The island's name means "rock in the road" and refers to how it stands in the path of the salmon that follow the coast as they migrate to their home rivers to spawn. The bridge is open to the public daily, weather-permitting. More than 227,000 visitors cross it (or at least take a look at it) each year and it has some heart-stopping views of the crashing waves 100 feet below. For an exhilarating cliff-top experience the rope bridge walk takes some beating. ✉ *119a White Park Rd. (8 km [5 mi] west of Ballycastle on B15), Ballintoy* ☎ *028/2076–9839* ⊕ *www.nationaltrust.org.uk* ☂ *£5.40* ⊗ *Nov.–Jan., daily 10:30–3:30; Feb.–May and Sept.–Oct., daily 10–6; June–Aug., daily 10–7; last entry 45 mins before closing.*

Grand Prize winner of Fodor's "Show Us Your Ireland" contest, this entry by Fodors.com member Traveling shows the famed Carrick-a-Rede rope bridge.

GIANT'S CAUSEWAY

Fodor'sChoice *19½ km (12 mi) west of Ballycastle.*

★   "When the world was moulded and fashioned out of formless chaos, this must have been a bit over—a remnant of chaos," said the great Thackeray about Northern Ireland's premier tourist draw, the Giant's Causeway. Imagine a mass of 37,000 mostly hexagonal pillars of volcanic basalt, clustered like a giant honeycomb and extending hundreds of yards into the sea. Legend has it this "causeway" was created 60 million years ago, when boiling lava, erupting from an underground fissure that stretched from Northern Ireland to the Scottish coast, crystallized as it burst into the sea, and formed according to the same natural principle that structures a honeycomb. As all Ulster folk know, though, the truth is that the columns were created as stepping-stones by the giant Finn McCool in a bid to reach a giantess he'd fallen in love with on the Scottish island of Staffa (where the causeway resurfaces). Unfortunately, the giantess's boyfriend found out, and in the ensuing battle, Finn pulled out a huge chunk of earth and flung it toward Scotland. The resulting hole became Lough Neagh, and the sod landed to create the Isle of Man.

BUS TRAVEL   The Antrim Coaster 252 Translink Goldline bus is one of the best ways to take in the dramatic coastline. Round-trip from Belfast (departure at 9:05 from the Europa Buscentre) to the Giant's Causeway costs £15. The Coaster stops on the Nook Main Road, where you can catch a shuttle bus (£2 round-trip) down to the Causeway itself. If coming from Coleraine, a fun way to make the trip to the Causeway is to board the Translink North Coast Open Topper Service, a double-decker bus

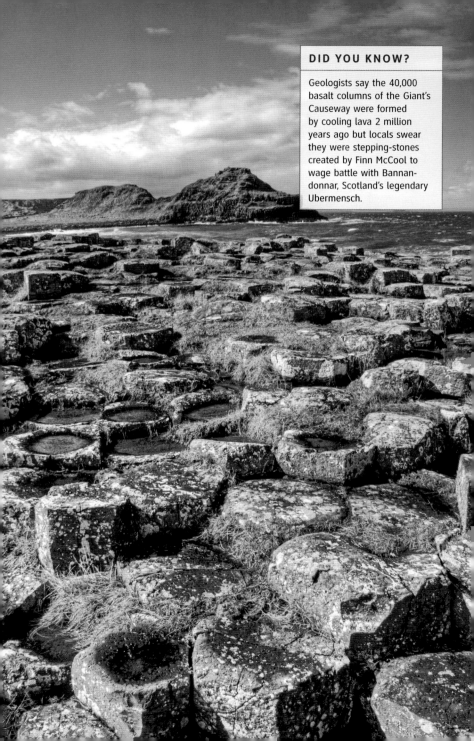

DID YOU KNOW?

Geologists say the 40,000 basalt columns of the Giant's Causeway were formed by cooling lava 2 million years ago but locals swear they were stepping-stones created by Finn McCool to wage battle with Bannan-donnar, Scotland's legendary Ubermensch.

(£5.20), running July and August (weather permitting)—it's great for the kids. This bus also links with the Translink Causeway Rambler high-frequency service (June–mid-September), from which you can tick off all the main visitor attractions, including Bushmills Distillery, Giant's Causeway, and the Carrick-a-Rede rope bridge. An all-day Rambler ticket allows you to hop on and off as many times as you like. It costs £4.50 and is valid only the day of purchase (buy at main Europa Buscentre in Belfast or at any nearby Translink staions). For a more direct bus between Belfast and Coleraine, catch the Translink Goldline Express service for £15.

TOURS Several private tour companies also operate trips to the Giant's Causeway from Belfast, including McComb's Causeway Express and Allen's Tours.

TRAIN TRAVEL Although there are no regular public trains serving the Giant's Causeway, a fun passenger link is provided on a narrow-gauge train running from Bushmills. The Giant's Causeway and Bushmills Railway leaves Runkerry Road, Bushmills, for the 3-km (2-mi) journey along the track bed of the former causeway tram. The train operates from Easter, every weekend, until the end of June, and daily July–August. The nearest Translink train stations are 21 km (14 mi) away in Portrush or 18 km (11 mi) west in Coleraine, where the main Belfast-Derry train stops (£15 round-trip). If you buy a one-day iLink ticket you can mix and match your journey plan by using buses and trains to get to and from the Giant's Causeway.

ESSENTIALS

Transportation Contacts Allen's Tours (☎ 028/9091–5613 ⊕ www. allenstours.co.uk). **Giant's Causeway and Bushmills Railway** (☎ 028/2073–2844 ⊕ www.giantscausewayrailway.webs.com). **McComb's Causeway Express** (☎ 028/9031–5333 ⊕ www.minicoachni.co.uk).

Visitor InformationGiant's Causeway Tourist Office (⊠ Visitor Centre, Causeway Hotel, Causeway Rd., Co. Antrim ☎ 028/2073–1855 ⊕ www. giantscausewaycentre.com). **Causeway Coast and Glens Tourism Partnership** (⊠ 11 Lodge Rd., Coleraine, Derry ☎ 028/7032–7720 ⊕ www. causewaycoastandglens.com).

To reach the causeway, you can either walk 1½ km (1 mi) down a long, scenic hill or take the Causeway Coaster minibus. A popular option with many visitors is to take the 20-minute walk downhill to the main causeway rock formation and catch the shuttle bus back uphill. The Causeway is Northern Ireland's only UNESCO World Heritage Site. In the peak summer months it can be very busy—get there early before the crowds or leave your visit until late afternoon when it's generally quieter. Be sure to take a seat in the Wishing Chair and look out for the Giant's Boot, Camel, Harp, and the Giant's Organ pipes.

West of the causeway, Port-na-Spania is the spot where the 16th-century Spanish Armada galleon *Girona* went down on the rocks. The ship was carrying an astonishing cargo of gold and jewelry, some of which was recovered in 1967. Beyond this, Chimney Point is the name given to one of the causeway structures on which the Spanish fired, thinking that it was Dunluce Castle, which is 8 km (5 mi) west.

The nearby Causeway Hotel is a good place to stop off for lunch after any hunger-inducing walk. During 2011, part of the hotel dining room will be the temporary home of the National Trust shop and Giant's Causeway visitor center. A new £18.8 million center, which includes improved facilities and interpretation, is scheduled to open in 2012. Work, which started in 2010, will continue throughout 2011 to upgrade and expand trail paths (the Causeway remains open during this entire process). Word of warning: dress appropriately by taking a warm jacket and wear sensible walking shoes, as the causeway can be slippery on wet days. Small children will need to be properly supervised. ⊠ *44 Causeway Rd., Bushmills* ☎ *028/2073–1582* ⊕ *www.nationaltrust.org. uk* 🚗 *Parking £6* ☉ *Visitor center Mar.–June, Sept., and Oct., daily 10–5; July and Aug., daily 10–6; Nov.–Feb., daily 10–4:30.*

BUSHMILLS

3 km (2 mi) west of Giant's Causeway.

Reputedly the oldest licensed distillery in the world, Bushmills was first granted a charter by King James I in 1608, though historical records refer to a distillery here as early as 1276. Bushmills produces the most famous of Irish whiskeys—its namesake—and what is widely regarded as the best, the rarer black-label version known to aficionados as Black Bush. On the guided tour you will discover the secrets of the special water from St. Columb's Rill, the story behind malted Irish barley, and learn about triple distillation in copper stills and aging (which happens for long years in oak casks). You begin in the mashing and fermentation room, proceed to the maturing and bottling warehouse, and conclude, yes, with the much anticipated, complimentary shot of *uisce beatha,* the "water of life." You can also have a light lunch in the Distillery Kitchen or buy souvenirs in the distillery gift shop. To mark its 400th anniversary, the company produced Bushmills 1608, a limited edition whiskey distilled with crystal malt, a special type of malted barley with an alluring aroma and sweet toffeelike smoothness. It's a buy at £45 (£5 off if you take the tour). Bushmills Master Distiller, Colum Egan, describes it with the following colorful personification: "It is a very approachable whiskey with great depth of character, and in true Irish style, it has plenty of personality and a gentle touch." Children under 8 are not permitted on the tour. For more on Bushmills, see our Spotlight feature, "All About Irish Whiskeys" in this chapter. ⊠ *2 Distillery Rd. off A2, Bushmills, Co. Antrim* ☎ *028/2073–3218* ⊕ *www.bushmills. com* 🚗 *£6* ☉ *Tours Apr.–Oct., Mon.–Sat. 9:15–5, Sun. noon–5; Nov.– Mar., weekdays 9:30–3:30, weekends 12:30–3:30.*

WHERE TO STAY

★
$$$–$$$$
🛏 **Bushmills Inn.** Owner Alan Dunlop oversees this cozy old coach inn. Stripped pine, peat fires, and gaslights warm the public rooms. The Inn was revamped in 2009, adding an extra nine bedrooms with four-poster beds. The hotel is a warren of corridors with a timbered wood burner in the sitting room, and a turret with a false bookcase. The

livery stables house the informal restaurant, which serves fresh and hearty food, and the bar. Meals are satisfyingly filling with the dinner menu offering prime sirloin steak, Donegal salmon, and stuffed pork. With its soft illumination and intimate snugs, the Gas Bar is the ideal place to appreciate the music of the seven-piece Scad the Beggars complete with harp, hammered dulcimer, and songsters. You can also sample the 25-year-old Bushmills malt whiskey from the hotel's own private cask. The staff can provide a baby-listening service—you leave the tot in the room with a baby

monitor, and they alert you to cries. The distillery is a stroll away from the main square and the inn, as is the salmon-filled River Bush. **Pros:** the proximity to the distillery—never mind the Giant's Causeway— helps ensure it's a choice location with comfortable rooms; tourists and chatty locals cross paths in the bar. **Cons:** if you're tall, look out for the low timber beams; it's hard to leave—even with the distractions of the surrounding area. ⊠ *9 Dunluce Rd., Bushmills, Co. Antrim* ☎ *028/2073–3000 or 028/2073–2339* ⊕ *www.bushmillsinn.com* ⤴ *41 rooms, 5 suites* ♨ *In-room: no a/c, Wi-Fi. In-hotel: restaurant, bar* ⊟ *AE, MC, V* ⧄ *BP.*

¢ ⊞ **Causeway Hotel.** Owned by England's National Trust and flaunting a stunning location overlooking the Atlantic Ocean, this hotel is only a half-mile from the celebrated Giant's Causeway. The hotel was founded in the 1840s and in 1890 it became the first Irish hotel to be completely lighted by electricity. Alas and alack, they should bring back some of the candles. Nearly all the historic patina has long disappeared—both the exterior and the interior are largely made up of white-on-white walls. Granted, the bar is welcoming and the "high tea" a winner, and prices here are downright budget, even more of a bargain considering the beautiful coastline right at your doorstep. **Pros:** bracing coastal walks (often chilly even in summer) but you'll feel the warmth when you enter. **Cons:** too many family parties; some rooms are dated. ⊠ *40 Causeway Rd., Bushmills, Co. Antrim* ☎ *028/2073–1210 or 028/2073– 1226* ⊕ *www.giants-causeway-hotel.com* ⤴ *28 rooms* ♨ *In-room: no a/c, Wi-Fi. In-hotel: restaurant, bar* ⊟ *MC, V* ⧄ *MAP.*

DUNLUCE CASTLE

★ *3 km (2 mi) west of Bushmills.*

Halfway between Portrush and the Giant's Causeway, dramatically perched on a cliff at land's end, Dunluce Castle is one of the north's most evocative ruins. Even roofless, this shattered bulk conjures up a strength and aura that is quintessentially Antrim. Its long-storied

While cliff erosion has played havoc with what's left of its battlements, Dunluce Castle still remains one of Northern Ireland's most intensely beautiful sights.

history is filled with marvels, beginning with the fact that it stands on a 100-foot-high basalt rock that contains the "Mermaid's Cave" (accessible by both land and sea). Originally a 13th-century Norman fortress, it was captured in the 16th century by the local MacDonnell clan chiefs—the so-called Lords of the Isles. They enlarged the castle, paying for some of the work with their profits from salvaging the Spanish galleon *Girona*—note the two openings in the old gatehouse wall made for cannons that Sorely Boy MacDonnell rescued from the wreck—and made it an important base for ruling northeastern Ulster. Perhaps they expanded the castle a little too much, for in 1639 faulty construction caused the kitchens (with all the cooks) to plummet into the sea during a storm. You can watch the story come alive by watching the 10-minute video in the building beside the gift shop. ⊠ *87 Dunluce Rd., Bushmills* ☎ *028/2073–1938* ⊕ *www.ni-environment.gov.uk* 💷 *£2* ⊗ *Apr.–Sept., Mon.–Sun. 10–6; Oct.–Mar., Mon.–Sun. 10–4; last entry 30 mins before closing.*

Dunluce Center is an entertainment complex with three floors of interactive play zones, shops, a café and a tourist information center in Portrush. ⊠ *10 Sandhill Dr., Portrush* ☎ *028/7082–4444* ⊕ *www. dunlucecentre.co.uk* 💷 *£4.50* ⊗ *Easter week, July, and Aug., daily 10–6; end of Apr.–June, Sept., and Oct., weekends noon–5.*

WHERE TO EAT

$

CONTINENTAL

★

✕ **Ramore Wine Bar.** On Portrush's attractive harbor, this spot has panoramic views, with daily offerings posted on a blackboard. ⊠ *The Harbor, Portrush* ☎ *028/7082–4313* ⊕ *www.ramorerestaurant.com* 🖃 *MC, V.*

SPORTS AND THE OUTDOORS

In a poll of legendary Irish courses, the **Royal Portrush Golf Club** (✉ *Dunluce Rd., Portrush* 📞 *028/7082–2311* ⊕ *www.royalportrushgolfclub. com*) came out tops. The championship Dunluce is a sea of sand hills and curving fairways (£120 weekdays, £135 weekends). The valley course is a less-exposed, tamer track (£35 weekdays, £40 weekends). Both are typically open to visitors on weekdays, but it's best to call ahead. *For more details, see chapter 10, Irish Greens.*

Portstewart Strand (✉ *118 Strand Rd., Portstewart* 📞 *028/7083–6396* 🚗*£4.50 per car* ⊙ *Facilities Mar., Oct., and Nov., daily 10–4; Apr. and Sept., daily 10–5; May, daily 10–6; June–Aug., daily 10–7*) is signposted as "The Strand" on all major junctions in the town. The magnificent 2 mi of golden sand is one of the north coast's finest beaches suitable for all ages. It is the ideal spot for picnics, swimming, or long walks into the sand dunes that are a haven for wildflowers and butterflies. On-site facilities include changing rooms and toilets, as well as a shop and café.

LIMAVADY

27 km (17 mi) east of Derry.

In 1851, at No. 51 on Limavady's Georgian main street, Jane Ross wrote down the tune played by a traveling fiddler and called it "Londonderry Air," better known now as "Danny Boy." While staying at an inn on Ballyclose Street, William Thackeray (1811–63) wrote his rather lustful poem "Peg of Limavaddy" about a barmaid. Among the many Americans descended from Ulster emigrants was President James Monroe, whose relatives came from the Limavady area.

Visitor Information Limavady Tourist Office (✉ *Connell St., Co. Derry* 📞 *028/7776–0307* ⊕ *www.limavady.gov.uk/visiting*).

WHERE TO STAY

$$$ 🏨 **Radisson Blu Roe Park Resort.** A country estate serves as the model for the deluxe modern resort on 155 acres on the banks of the River Roe. The place is relatively large and impersonal, although the lobby is a feast of welcoming ruby-hue carpets and gilt lanterns. Regular guest rooms have simple, clean-line beds in woods and rich earth tones. Suite furnishings move a bit up the ornate scale with canopy beds and velvet armchairs. Green's restaurant is formal and international; the Coach House brasserie is a relaxed place where golfers congregate; and O'Cahan's bar takes its name from a local chieftain besieged on a riverside promontory, whose Irish wolfhound leaped an impossible chasm to bring relief—doubtless an inspiration to golfers flagging at the ninth. For those who need pointers, there's an on-site golfing academy. **Pros:** the hotel is an ideal location for pampering and relaxation; lively bars good for post-golf analysis and comparison of strokes. **Cons:** can be noisy with evening wedding parties; older rooms have a somewhat tired appearance. ✉ *Roe Park, Co. Derry* 📞 *028/7772–2222* ⊕ *www. radissonroepark.com* 🛏 *118 rooms, 7 suites* ⚲ *In-room: no a/c, Inter-*

CLOSE UP

Derry's Tour Options

Walking tours of Derry's city walls leave from the **Derry Visitor and Convention Bureau** and last just over one hour. The bureau overflows with a huge range of local guides, books, leaflets, and brochures as well as information about all parts of Ireland. ⊠ *44 Foyle St., West Bank* ☎ *028/7126–7284 or 028/7137–7577* ⊕ *www.derryvisitor.com* ⊂ *Center free, tour £5* ⊙ *Tours Sept.–June weekdays at 2:30; July and Aug., weekdays at 11:15, 2:30, and 3:15. Office hours Oct.–June, weekdays 9–5, Sat. 10–5; July–Sept., weekdays 9–7, Sat. 10–6, Sun. 10–5.*

Thanks to **Top Tours Ireland**, you can tour Derry on a double-decker bus. Departing from the visitor bureau and Guildhall, the bus ride lasts an hour, hits all the sightseeing spots,

and has a guide with onboard commentary. ⊠ *44 Foyle St., West Bank* ☎ *077/6318–1239* ⊕ *www.derryvisitor.com* ⊂ *£8* ⊙ *Tours Mon.–Sat. on the hr 10–5.*

For 18 years Martin McCrossan has been sharing his detailed knowledge of Derry with visitors through **City Tours.** Recounting both the recent troubled history and centuries-old stories, Martin brings alive his passion for his city. His tour, which departs from both the visitor bureau and from 11 Carlisle Road, lasts one hour and incorporates not only history but also architecture as well as an engaging sprinkling of local lore and humor. ⊠ *11 Carlisle Rd., West Bank* ☎ *028/7127–1996* ⊕ *www.irishtourguides.com* ⊂ *£4* ⊙ *Tours daily at 10, noon, and 2.*

---

net. In-hotel: 2 restaurants, bars, golf course, pool, gym, spa, Wi-Fi hotspot ⊟ *AE, DC, MC, V* ⊙| *BP, MAP.*

DERRY

If Belfast were the Beethoven of Northern Ireland, Derry would be the Mozart—fey, witty, and a touch surreal. Every Halloween, for example, the entire populace of Derry—the second-largest city in Northern Ireland—turns out in wild homemade costumes, and pubs have been known to refuse a drink to anyone who hasn't made the effort to dress up. Despite the derelict factories along the banks of the River Foyle and a reputation marred by Troubles-related violence, the city has worked hard to move forward. Such efforts show in the quaint, bustling city center, encircled by 20-foot-tall 17th-century walls. The city's winding streets slope down to the Foyle, radiating from the Diamond—Derry's historic center—where St. Columba founded his first monastery in 546. Fine Georgian and Victorian buildings sit side by side with gaily painted Victorian-front shops, cafés, and pubs.

GETTING HERE

BUS TRAVEL Fast Translink Goldline Express buses link Derry and Belfast on a trip over the mighty Glenshane Pass. Journey time is one hour and 40 minutes (£15 round-trip). Weekend services, especially Sunday, are less frequent. An alternative, slightly longer route, operated by Translink

Goldline between Belfast and Derry goes along the M1 motorway and through County Tyrone—it takes about two hours. Translink buses run from Derry to neighboring towns, with fares averaging about £12.50 round-trip. You can also catch a bus from City of Derry Airport into the Foyle Street bus station in the city center (£6 round-trip). The Airporter Coach operates between Derry and Belfast International Airport and George Best Belfast City Airport. Tickets to both airports cost £27.50 round-trip. If you're traveling across the border from Derry into Donegal, then you have a choice of using Bus Éireann or the Lough Swilly Bus Company.

TRAIN TRAVEL One of the most relaxing ways to arrive in Derry is by train. Frequent daily services on Northern Ireland Railways link it with Coleraine, Ballymena, Antrim, and Belfast. For the final 20-minute section of the journey—along the County Derry coastline—the track runs parallel with the sea and is one of Ireland's most stunning routes. The journey time from Belfast to is about two hours (£15 round-trip). The main station is in the Waterside area of the city—catch a free 10-minute shuttle bus across Craigavon Bridge to get to the west bank, where most attractions are concentrated.

ESSENTIALS

Transportation Contacts Airporter Coach (☎ 028/7126–9996 ⊕ www. airporter.co.uk). **Lough Swilly** (☎ 074/912–2873).

Visitor Information Derry Visitor and Convention Bureau (✉ 44 Foyle St., West Bank, Co. Derry ☎ 028/7126–7284 or 028/7137–7577 ⊕ www.derryvisitor. com).

EXPLORING

Derry's name shadows its history. Those in favor of British rule call the city Londonderry, its old Plantation-period name: the "London" part was tacked on in 1613 after the Flight of the Earls, when the city and county were handed over to the Corporation of London, which represented London's merchants. The corporation brought in a large population of English and Scottish Protestant settlers, built towns for them, and reconstructed Derry within the city walls, which survive almost unchanged to this day. Both before then and after, Derry's sturdy ramparts withstood many fierce attacks—they have never been breached, which explains the city's coy sobriquet, "The Maiden City." The most famous attack was the siege of 1688–89, begun after 13 apprentice boys slammed the city gates in the face of the Catholic king, James II. Inhabitants, who held out for 105 days and were reduced to eating dogs, cats, and laundry starch, nevertheless helped to secure the British throne for the Protestant king, William III. Whatever you choose to call it, Derry is one of Northern Ireland's most underrated towns. The city, incidentally, has links to Boston that date as far back as the 17th and 18th centuries, when many Derry residents escaped their hardships at home by emigrating to that U.S. city and beyond.

TOP ATTRACTIONS

❶ Derry City Walls. To really experience Derry's history, stroll along the parapet walkway atop the ramparts of the city walls (⊕ *www.derryswalls. com*), built between 1614 and 1618 and one of the few intact sets of city walls in Europe. Pierced by eight gates (originally four) and as much as 30 feet thick, the gray-stone ramparts are only 1½ km (1 mi) all around. Today most of the life of the town takes place outside of them. You can join one of the guided tours given by the visitor bureau.

Derry Wall Murals. Throughout the city there are a large number of dramatic wall murals showing the power of art as historical document and serving as a reminder of painful pasts. Symbolic of the different communities, the murals have attracted considerable curiosity from tourists in recent years. The Bogside Gallery of Murals, painted by William Kelly, Kevin Hasson, and Tom Kelly, are made up of 12 wall paintings known collectively as "The Peoples Gallery." They include the *Bloody Sunday Commemoration, The Death of Innocence, Civil Rights, The Hunger Strikes*, and a poignant one unveiled in 2008 featuring the Nobel Peace Prize–winning Derry politician John Hume along with Martin Luther King Jr., Nelson Mandela, and Mother Teresa—all beside Brooklyn Bridge. The paintings span the length of Rossville Street in the heart of the Bogside where the artists have their studios. In 2009 the Bogside artists opened an indoor gallery on William Street, showcasing local, national and international artists' work. Visitors can pick up prints and posters of their favorite mural images a well as books and T-shirts. The 90-minute walking tours of the murals are held three times daily at 11, 2, and 4 (£5). On the other side of the political divide, close to the city walls, the Protestant Fountain estate is home to one of the oldest King Billy murals along with other colorful ones linked to the siege of Derry. ⊠ *46 William St., Bogside* ☎ *028/7137–3842* ⊕ *www. bogsideartists.com.*

❷ Guildhall. Derry city council meets monthly at Guildhall, an ornate Victorian stone and sandstone building dating from 1890. Some of the most beautiful glass creations in Ireland, the hall's stained-glass windows were shattered by two IRA bombs in June 1977 and rebuilt by the Campbell's firm in Belfast, which had installed the original windows in 1890 and still had the plans (now *that's* a filing system). Elsewhere, the eye is delighted by neo-Gothic strutwork, ornate ceilings, baronial wood paneling, a magnificent organ, and the fourth-largest clock (modeled on Big Ben) in Ireland. The Guildhall also hosts occasional musical recitals. Short tours are available July–September, daily 11–3. ⊠ *Guildhall Sq., West Bank* ☎ *028/7137–7335* ⊕ *www.derrycity.gov. uk* ☐ *Free* ☉ *Weekdays 8:30–5.*

❻ Museum of Free Derry. At Free Derry Corner stands the white gable wall where Catholics defiantly painted the slogan "You are now entering Free Derry" as a declaration of a zone from which police and the British Army were banned until 1972, when the army broke down the barricades. That year, 13 civil rights marchers were shot and killed by British soldiers in an event that rankles Catholics to this day. Bloody Sunday, as it became known, is commemorated by a mural of the civil rights march. Now, historical homage is paid thanks to the new Museum of Free

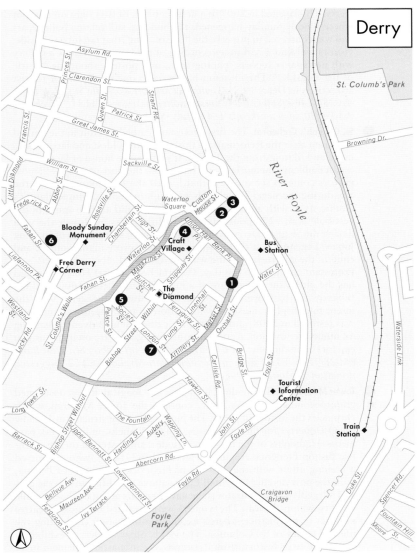

Derry

11

Derry. This opened in 2007 in a derelict block of flats right on the spot where Bloody Sunday happened; the building still retains bullet scars and was conserved to preserve the "line of sight" that fateful day. Inside, visitors will find a real-time recording of the event as well as a gallery with newspaper reports, photographs, and posters about the "Battle of the Bogside." The museum has become one of the major tourist attractions in Derry. ⊠ *55 Glenfada Park, off Rossville St., West Bank* ☎ *028/7136–0880* ⊕ *www.museumoffreederry.org* ✉ *£3* ⊙ *Weekdays 9:30–4:30; also weekends 1–4 in July–Sept.*

❼ St. Columb's Cathedral. The first Protestant cathedral built in the United Kingdom after the Reformation, this houses the oldest and largest bells in Ireland (dating from the 1620s). It's a treasure house of Derry Protestant emblems, memorials, and relics from the siege of 1688–89; most visitors come to see the keys that locked the four main gates of the city during the siege. The church was built in 1633 in simple Planter's Gothic style, with an intricate corbeled roof and austere spire. In the vestibule is the 270-pound mortar ball that was fired over the wall during the Siege of Derry, with an invitation to surrender sent by King James. Legend has it that when it was read, every man, woman, and child in the city rushed to the walls and shouted, "No surrender!"—a Protestant battle cry to this day. The attached Chapter House Museum has the oldest surviving copy of a map of Derry (from 1600) and the Bible owned by Governor George Walker during the siege. View the interesting display cases and information panels. The tower and spire was restored in 2008, and in 2010 the cathedral underwent a yearlong £2 million renovation. Knowledgeable tour guides are on hand, or you can hire an audio tour for £3. ⊠ *London St., off Bishop St., West Bank* ☎ *028/7126–7313* ⊕ *www.stcolumbscathedral.org* ✉ *£2 suggested donation* ⊙ *Mon.–Sat. 9–5.*

❹ ★ Tower Museum. Tall, brooding, medieval, and magical, the reconstructed granite-stone O'Dohertys Tower contains the Tower Museum, which chronicles the history of Derry. The building was constructed in 1615 by the O'Dohertys for their overlords, the O'Donnells, in lieu of tax payments. Highlights of the museum include a small section on the eccentric Bishop Frederick Augustus Hervey (1763–1803), who conducted a lifelong affair with the mistress of Frederick William II of Prussia, built the now derelict Downhill Castle above the cliffs outside the city, and allegedly had his curates stage naked sprints along the beach while he horsewhipped them. The winners were awarded the most lucrative parishes in the district. There's excellent information celebrating the life and legacy of St. Columba. The vivid "Story of Derry" exhibition covers the city's history, from its origins as a monastic settlement in an oak grove up to the Troubles, beginning in 1969 after years of institutionalized discrimination in jobs and public housing. (A well-known Derry joke is that the skeleton in the city's coat of arms was actually a Catholic waiting for a house.) There's also an exhibition, spread over four floors, on the Spanish Armada, thanks to the fact that its fourth-largest ship, *La Trinidad Valencera*, foundered in Kinnagoe Bay, in County Donegal, in 1588. ⊠ *Union Hall Pl., West Bank* ☎ *028/7137–2411* ⊕ *www.derrycity.gov.uk/museums* ✉ *£4* ⊙ *Sept.–June, Tues.–Sat.*

10–5; July and Aug., Mon.–Sat. 10–5, Sun. 11–3; last entry 45 mins before closing.

NEED A
BREAK? Derry is packed with agreeable pubs, but Badgers (⊠ *16 Orchard St., West Bank* ☎ *028/7136–0763*) has the best choice of wholesome food. It's also the watering hole for local media types, artists, writers, and musicians.

WORTH NOTING

⑤ **Apprentice Boys' Memorial Hall.** Imposing in its Scottish Baronial fortified grandeur, this is a meeting place for the exclusively Protestant organization set up in 1715 to honor 13 apprentice boys who slammed the city gate in the face of the Catholic King James in 1688 and sparked the Siege of Derry, and it has remained a symbol of Protestant stubbornness ever since. Inside there's an initiation room in which 20,000 have pledged to uphold Protestant values, and a magnificently chaotic museum filled to the brim with furniture, firearms, books, bombs, swords, and sculpture. It's a fascinating glimpse into a mostly closed world. An upstairs bar and dance hall—now used for meetings, initiations, and social events organized by the Apprentice Boys—has walls lined with 12 banners representing the lost tribes of Israel. (Some Protestants believe the lost tribes of Israel ended up in Northern Ireland and are their forebears.) More recent exhibitions showcase the story of the siege and show a scale model of how the city walls looked at the time of the siege. ⊠ *Society St., West Bank* ☎ *028/7126–3571* ☎ *£2* ⊘ *June–Oct., weekdays 10–4:30; tours by appointment.*

Walker Memorial, a statue of the governor of Derry during the siege, is a symbol of Derry's divided nature. It was blown up by the IRA in 1973, and the story goes that the statue's head rolled down the hill into the Catholic Bogside, where it was captured by a local youth. He ransomed it back to the Protestants for a small fortune, and today it sits on the shoulders of a replica of the original statue beside the Apprentice Boys' Memorial Hall. ⊠ *Apprentice Boys' Memorial Hall, Society St., West Bank.*

③ **Harbour Museum.** Next door to the Guildhall stands this noted museum, today housed in the former harbor commissioners' office, an Italianate block of boulder-faced sandstone built in 1882. Designed as a traditional Victorian-style museum, it deals with the city's maritime heritage. In the ground floor exhibition room the largest currach (Irish traditional boat) ever built is on display. It was made in 1963 for a party of Church of Ireland clerics and re-creates the voyage 1,400 years earlier of St. Colmcille from Derry to the Scottish island of Iona where in 563 he founded one of the most famous monasteries in Christendom. Look out also for the exquisite paintings of John Noah Gosset who captured Ulster scenes covering the period 1841–46. They include a fascinating glimpse of Derry and its hinterland shortly before dramatic changes came about. ⊠ *Harbour Sq., West Bank* ☎ *028/7137–7331* ⊕ *www.derrycity.gov.uk/museums* ☎ *Free* ⊘ *Weekdays 10–1 and 2–4:30.*

EN
ROUTE For a delightfully rustic alternative to driving back to Belfast on A6, drive along the minor road B48, which skirts the foot of the Sperrin Mountains and reaches all the way to Omagh. Or, you may want to

head north from Derry to explore the Inishowen Peninsula, the northernmost point of Ireland.

WHERE TO EAT

$$
IRISH

✕ **The Exchange.** Overdressed twentysomethings lounge by the circular and ultramodern bar in this chic restaurant-cum-wine bar. It's become *the* place to be seen in Derry, so weekend evenings can be extremely busy. Unfortunately, reservations are not taken, so be prepared to wait at the bar—with a chilled glass of sauvignon blanc

from the excellent wine list, it's no hardship. Locally caught seafood is delicious, and the standout dish is medallions of monkfish with tiger prawns. Service is super-efficient but can be a touch brisk. ⊠ *Exchange House, Queen's Quay, Central District* ☎ *028/7127–3990* ⊕ *www.exchangerestaurant.com* ⊟ *AE, MC, V.*

$
AMERICAN

✕ **Fitzroy's.** This popular city-center brasserie gives "quare packin" (Derry-speak for good value for money), with belt-busting portions of old favorites like burgers, steaks, and Caesar salads in the evening. Lunchtimes are busy, with weary shoppers and office staff stopping by for seafood chowder or the popular chicken melter, made up of cheese, tobacco onions, and bacon with Mexican spices. ⊠ *2–4 Bridge St., Central District* ☎ *028/7126–6211* ⊕ *www.fitzroysrestaurant.com* ⊟ *MC, V.*

$$
ASIAN

✕ **Spice.** It's worth the walk up the hill from town to this cozy restaurant with food that draws heavily on Pan-Asian influences. ⊠ *162 Spencer Rd., East Bank* ☎ *028/7134–4875* ⊕ *www.spicerestaurantderry.com* ⊟ *MC, V.*

$$
IRISH
Fodor's Choice
★

✕ **Thompsons on the River.** This spot takes its name from the old Thompsons Mill that once occupied this historic building on the banks of the Foyle and is based in the City Hotel. Decor is airy and cool while the cuisine is stylish and hot: best bets include honey loin of pork or the salmon or sea bass dishes. Thanks to its popularity, reservations are recommended (and practically essential on weekends). The Two's Company menu, based on two people sharing two courses, is good value at £11.95 per person—it includes a glass of house wine. Throw in an impressive but not expensive wine list and it all adds up to a fine place to chill with great views of the river. ⊠ *City Hotel on Queen's Quay, Central District* ☎ *028/7136–5800* ⊕ *www.cityhotelderry.com* ⊟ *AE, MC, V.*

WHERE TO STAY

¢
Fodor's Choice
★

🏠 **The Merchant's House.** No. 16 Queen Street was originally a Victorian merchant's family town home built to Georgian proportions, then a rectory and bank, before Joan Pyne turned it into the city's grandest B&B. Garnet-color walls, elaborate plasterwork, and a fireplace make the parlor warm and welcoming to such famed guests as the late Hurd Hatfield. In 2009 the cellars were renovated to include three en suite modern bedrooms. Joan also owns a similar but smaller building three minutes' walk away called the Saddler's House. Charming and cozy, this Victorian jewel of a home (who can resist its picture-gallery red living room?) is packed with interesting antiques and family portraits. **Pros:** graceful and elegant, and great value; for the discriminating traveler; resident pooche Bertie. **Cons:** rooms next to kitchen noisy in morning; small bathrooms. ☒ *16 Queen St., West Bank, Co. Derry* ☏ *028/7126–9691* ⊕ *www.thesaddlershouse.com* ⇌ *10 rooms in Merchant's House; 7 rooms with shared bath in Saddler's House* ⇧ *In-room: no a/c, Wi-Fi. In-hotel: Wi-Fi hotspot* ▭ *MC, V* �‖ *BP.*

$$ ⊞ **Tower Hotel.** The only hotel within Derry city's historic walls, this modern building has more to offer than its unequaled location. Guest rooms are decorated in vibrant shades of red and green, with pine furnishings and well-stocked bathrooms, while the Walls Restaurant has delights like Irish salmon with horseradish and parsnips. But it is the primo location that's the draw—a one-minute walk to Austin's of the Diamond (world's oldest department store), the view of the Bogside and the "Free Derry" corner from the upper bedrooms, and window vistas that take in rooftops of rows of neat terraced houses and the city's famous murals (when booking, do request a room with a view). **Pros:** top-notch location for exploring Derry's walls, sights, shops, and idiosyncrasies; practical, clean, and tastefully decorated rooms with modern facilities. **Cons:** limited parking available; wedding guests and conference delegates spill over into the sometimes noisy crowded lobby. ☒ *Butcher St., Central District, Co. Derry* ☏ *028/7137–1000* ⊕ *www.towerhotelderry.com* ⇌ *90 rooms, 3 suites* ⇧ *In-room: no a/c. In-hotel: restaurant, bar, gym, Wi-Fi hotspot* ▭ *AE, DC, MC, V* �‖ *BP, MAP.*

NIGHTLIFE AND THE ARTS

ART GALLERIES The **Context Gallery** (☒ *5–7 Artillery St., West Bank* ☏ *028/7137–3538*) shows works by up-and-coming Irish and international artists. The **McGilloway Gallery** (☒ *6 Shipquay St., West Bank* ☏ *028/7136–6011* ⊕ *www.themcgillowaygallery.com*) stocks a broad selection of representational modern Irish art. Owner Ken McGilloway serves wine on Friday evening until 9 PM during selected exhibitions.

PUBS AND The **Gweedore Bar** (☒ *59–63 Waterloo St., West Bank* ☏ *028/7137–*
CLUBS *2318*) is a favorite for hip-hop and house music. Listen to traditional Irish music at **Peadar O'Donnell's** (☒ *63 Waterloo St., West Bank* ☏ *028/7137–2318*). **Sugar Nightclub** (☒ *33 Shipquay St., West Bank* ☏ *028/7126–6017*) is the place for dance music.

THEATER The catch-all **Millennium Forum Theatre and Conference Centre** (☒ *New-*
AND OPERA *market St., West Bank* ☏ *028/7126–4455* ⊕ *www.millenniumforum. co.uk*) presents everything and anything—from comedians to musicians to plays—on stage. The **Playhouse** (☒ *5–7 Artillery St., West Bank* ☏ *028/7126–8027* ⊕ *www.derryplayhouse.co.uk*) with an impressive auditorium and workshop spaces, stages traditional and contemporary plays and also holds contemporary music concerts. The **Verbal Arts Centre** (☒ *Bishop St., Stable La., and Mall Wall, West Bank* ☏ *028/7126–6946* ⊕ *www.verbalartscentre.co.uk*) celebrates literature through performances and classes. It re-creates the great old Irish tradition of fireside

tales at regular storytelling events. The Arts Centre also produces *Verbal,* a monthly literary magazine packed with book reviews, author profiles, and forthcoming reading events (distributed free across Northern Ireland with daily newspapers). The center also houses Blooms Café, a delightful spot looking out over Derry's walls.

SHOPPING

Shopping in town is generally low-key and unpretentious, but there are some upscale gems of Irish craftsmanship. Stroll up Shipquay Street to find small arts-and-crafts stores and an indoor shopping center.

Occasions (⊠ *48 Spencer Rd., East Bank* ☏ *028/7132–9595*) sells Irish crafts and gifts.

Stop at the gift shop **Pauline's Patch** (⊠ *32 Shipquay St., West Bank* ☏ *028/7127–9794*) for knickknacks.

Thomas the Goldsmith (⊠ *7 Pump St., West Bank* ☏ *028/7137–4549* ⊕ *www.thomasgoldsmiths.com*) stocks exquisite work by international jewelry designers.

Off Shipquay Street, the **Trip** (⊠ *29 Ferryquay St., West Bank* ☏ *028/7137–2382*) is a teenage-clothing shop that specializes in knitwear.

Book lovers should visit **Foyle Books** (⊠ *12 Magazine St., West Bank* ☏ *028/7137–2530*) for the largest selection of secondhand and antiquarian titles to be found in the city. Major sections cover English literature, Irish language books, criticism, poetry, biography, travel, music, and sport.

THE WESTERN BORDER COUNTIES

While blissfully off the beaten track, this region contains some dazzling sights: the Ulster-American Folk Park; the great stately houses of Castle Coole and Florence Court; and the pottery town of Belleek. During the worst of the Troubles, the counties of Tyrone, Fermanagh, Armagh, and Down, which border the republic, were known as "bandit country," but now you can enjoy a worry-free trip through the calm countryside and stop in at some very "Ulster" towns, delightfully distinct from the rest of Ireland.

OMAGH

55 km (34 mi) south of Derry on A5.

Omagh, the county town of Tyrone, lies close to the Sperrin Mountains, with the River Strule to the north. Playwright Brian Friel was born here. Sadly, it's better known as the scene of the worst atrocity of the Troubles, when an IRA bomb killed 31 people in 1998. On the 10th anniversary of the bombing, a touching memorial, the Garden of Light, by artist Sean Hillen and landscape architect Desmond Fitzgerald, was opened. A heliostatic mirror in the memorial park tracks the sun and directs a beam of light onto 31 small mirrors, each etched with the name of a victim. They in turn bounce the light via another hidden mirror onto a heart-shaped crystal in an obelisk at the bomb site.

CLOSE UP

Beautiful Belleek

A Belleek artisan at work

The origins of Belleek china are every bit as romantic as the Belleek blessing plates traditionally given to brides and grooms on their wedding day—that is, if you believe the legends.

The story goes that in the mid-1800s, John Caldwell Bloomfield, the man behind the world-famous porcelain, accidentally discovered the raw ingredients necessary to produce china. After inheriting his father's estate in the Fermanagh Lakelands on the shore of the Erne River, he whitewashed his cottage using a flaky white powder dug up in his backyard. A passerby, struck by the luminescent sheen of the freshly painted cottage, commented on the unusual brightness of the walls to Bloomfield, who promptly ordered a survey of the land, which duly uncovered all the minerals needed to make porcelain. The venture was complete when Bloomfield met his business partners—London architect Robert Armstrong and the wealthy Dublin merchant David McBirney. They decided to first produce earthenware, and then porcelain. And the rest, as they say, is history.

The delicate, flawless porcelain (Bloomfield declared that any piece with even the slightest blemish should be destroyed) soon attracted the attention of Queen Victoria and many other aristos. Other companies tried to mimic the china's delicate beauty, but genuine Belleek porcelain is recognizable by its seashell designs, basket weaves, and marine themes.

The company is now owned by an Irish-born American businessman, Dr. George Moore, and continues to flourish. It has become a favored tradition in Ireland to give a piece of Belleek china at weddings, giving rise to a saying: "If a newly married couple receives a piece of Belleek, their marriage will be blessed with lasting happiness."

GETTING HERE

BUS TRAVEL   The Translink Goldline service operates buses aplenty between Derry and Belfast and traverses a delightful incantation of mellifluous-sounding Tyrone towns, from Strabane to Ballygawley, and thence along the M1 into Belfast. Journey time is just under two hours (£15 roundtrip). Services in both directions stop on request at the popular Ulster-American Folk Park.

EXPLORING

Fodor's Choice   Several miles north of Omagh is the big attraction of the region: the
★   excellent **Ulster-American Folk Park** re-creates a Tyrone village of two centuries ago, a log-built American settlement of the same period, and the docks and ships that the emigrants to America would have used. The centerpiece of the park is an old whitewashed cottage, now a museum, which is the ancestral home of Thomas Mellon (1855–1937), the U.S. banker and philanthropist. Another thatch cottage is a reconstruction of the boyhood home of Archbishop John Hughes, founder of New York's St. Patrick's Cathedral. There are also full-scale replicas of Irish peasant cottages, Pennsylvania farmhouses, a New York tenement room, immigrant transport ship holders, plus a 19th-century Ulster village, complete with staff dressed in 19th-century costumes. Other exhibitions trace the contribution of the Northern Irish people to American history, and there is a center for migration studies with an excellent research library containing 12,000 books and periodicals, and an Irish emigration database including passenger lists from 1800 to 1860 and emigrant letters. The park also has a currency exchange, crafts shop, and café, as well as a 38-bed residential center. ⊠ *Mellon Rd., Castletown, Omagh (10 km [6 mi] north of town on A5)* ☎ *028/8224–3292* ⊕ *www.nmni. com* ✏ *£6* ♥ *Apr.–Sept., Tues.–Sun. 10:30–6; Oct.–Mar., Tues.–Sun. 10:30–4; last entry 1½ hrs before closing.*

BELLEEK

42 km (25 mi) southwest of Omagh off A46.

World-famous Belleek Pottery is made in the old town of Belleek on the northwestern edge of Lower Lough Erne, at the border with northwest Ireland. Other porcelain-ware makers are a few kilometers across the border.

On the riverbank stands the visitor center of **Belleek Pottery Ltd.**, producers of Parian china, a fine, eggshell-thin, ivory porcelain shaped into dishes, figurines, vases, and baskets. There's a factory, showroom, exhibition, museum, and café. On tours of the factory you can get up close and talk to craftspeople—there's hardly any noise coming from machinery in the workshops. Everything here is made by hand just as they did back in 1857. The showroom is filled with beautiful but pricey gifts: a shamrock cup-and-saucer set costs about £42, and a bowl in a basket-weave style (typical of Belleek) runs £95 and up. In 2009 the company launched a jewelry portfolio called Belleek Living, comprising designs inspired by the Irish landscape. ⊠ *3 Main St., Co. Fermanagh* ☎ *028/6865–8501* ⊕ *www.belleek.ie* ✏ *£4* ♥ *Mar.–Oct., weekdays*

An annual Bluegrass music festival at the Ulster-American Folk Park reaffirms the strong links between Northern Ireland and the United States.

9–6, Sat. 10–6, Sun. noon–6; Nov. and Dec., weekdays 9–5:30, Sat. 10–5:30; Jan. and Feb., weekdays 9–5:30.

WHERE TO EAT

$ CAFÉ ✕ **The Thatch.** Housed in a lovely building dating to the 18th century, this simple café is well worth a visit—not just for the excellent soups, sandwiches, baked potatoes, and similarly light fare—but also because it's the only thatch-roof establishment in the entire county. Full of locals and rife with the sounds of easy banter, it's the perfect place to glean local knowledge and gossip about the surrounding area. ⌂ *Main St., Belleek* ☎ *028/6865–8181* ═ *MC, V* ◷ *Closed Sun.*

ENNISKILLEN

5 km (3 mi) south of Devenish Island, Lower Lough Erne, on A32.

Enniskillen is the pleasant, smart-looking capital of County Fermanagh and the only place of any size in the county. The town center is, strikingly, on an island in the River Erne between Lower and Upper Lough Erne. The principal thoroughfares, Townhall and High streets, are crowded with old-style pubs and rows of redbrick Georgian flats. The tall, dark spires of the 19th-century St. Michael's and St. Macartin's cathedrals, both on Church Street, tower over the leafy town center.

GETTING HERE

BUS TRAVEL Translink's Goldline Express buses connect Enniskillen with Belfast, 145 km (90 mi) east. Regular daily services run from early morning to late evening, with a two-hour journey time (£15 round-trip). Local service operates from the bus depot on Wellington Road, beside the

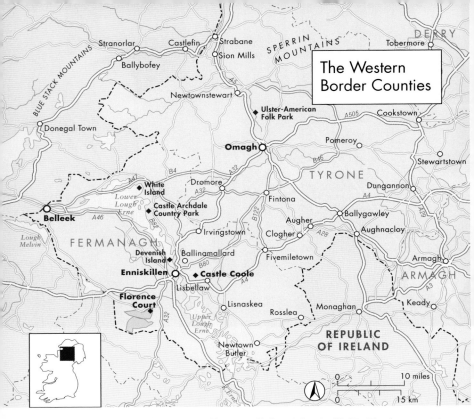

The Western
Border Counties

tourist information office; an all-day ticket is £2.30. The bus to visit some of Fermanagh's attractions, such as Castle Coole historic house, costs £1.30 and drops you off on request at the entrance gates. Enniskillen also has a slew of cross-border services in many directions. Bus Éireann operates Expressway routes west to Sligo.

Visitor Information Enniskillen Tourist Office (⊠ *Lakeland Visitor Centre, Wellington Rd., Co. Fermanagh* ☎ *028/6632–3110* ⊕ *www.findfermanagh.com*).

EXPLORING

Among the several relaxed and welcoming old pubs in Enniskillen's town center, the one with the most appeal is **Blake's of the Hollow** on the main street, a place hardly altered since it opened in 1887. Its name derives from the fact that the heart of the town lies in a slight hollow and the pub's landlord is named William Blake. (Don't ask: he's not related to the English poet, painter, and engraver.) ⊠ *6 Church St.* ☎ *028/6632–2143.*

A wonderful collection of 16 arts and crafts shops selling pottery, jewelry, and paintings are gathered at the **Buttermarket.** This restored dairy market built in 1835 also has a café. ⊠ *Down St.* ☎ *028/6632–3117.*

Enniskillen's main sight is the waterfront **Enniskillen Castle,** one of the best-preserved monuments in the north. Built by the Maguire clan in 1670, this stronghold houses the local history collection of the Fermanagh County Museum and the polished paraphernalia of the Royal Inniskilling Fusiliers Regimental Museum. A Heritage Centre—Fermanagh County Museum, with displays of pottery and lace—also stands within the curtilage of the castle. In 2009 the castle keep was redeveloped with new exhibitions and interactive displays, and the following year a Roll of Honor containing the names of the 9,100 people from all over Ireland who died in World War II was presented to the Regimental Museum. ⊠ *Castlebarracks* ☎ *028/6632–5000* ⊕ *www.enniskillen-castle.co.uk* ☐ *£ 3.50* ☉ *May, June, and Sept., Mon. and Sat. 2–5, Tues.–Fri. 10–5; July and Aug., Mon. and weekends 2–5, Tues.–Fri. 10–5; Oct.–Apr., Mon. 2–5, Tues.–Fri. 10–5.*

> ### BEAUTY IS NOT SKIN DEEP
>
> If it's raining in Fermanagh, an ideal half-day activity is to go underground to visit the **Marble Arch Caves Global Geopark** (☎ *028/6634–8855* ⊕ *www.marblearchcavesgeopark.com* ☐ *£8*), one of Europe's finest show caves and open daily March–September, 10–4:30. Stalactites glisten above streams as you admire fragile mineral veils and cascades of calcite-coated walls and waterfalls. Guided tours last 75 minutes; bring walking shoes and a warm sweater. Tours begin at Marlbank Scenic Loop Centre, Florencecourt. In 2009 the Geopark expanded south to Co. Cavan.

At the Erne riverside, the 16th-century **Water Gate,** between two handsome turrets, protected the town from invading armies.

Beyond the West Bridge is **Portora Royal School,** established in 1608 by King James I. On the grounds are some ruins of Portora Castle. Among writers educated here are Samuel Beckett and Oscar Wilde, the pride of the school (until his trial for homosexuality).

On Lower Lough Erne, **Erne Tours** operates approximately 90-minute boat tours aboard the *Kestrel,* a 56-seat water bus, that leave from Round O Pier at Enniskillen. Weekdays the boat stops for 45 minutes at Devenish Island. From early May to the end of September the company also has a Saturday evening dinner cruise departing at 6:30. The three-course meal costs £25, and the cruise, which leaves from the Killyhevlin Hotel near Enniskillen, lasts two hours. ⊠ *Round O Pier, Enniskillen* ☎ *028/6632–2882* ⊕ *www.ernetoursltd.com* ☐ *90-min tours £10* ☉ *90-min tours May and Sept., Tues., Sat., and Sun. at 2:15 and 4:15; June, daily at 2:15 and 4:15; July and Aug., daily at 10:30, 12:15, 2:15, and 4:15.*

WHERE TO EAT AND STAY

★

$$$$ ⊞ **Lough Erne Resort.** Flickering beech log fires greet you on arrival in the lobby of this sparkling and sumptuous five-star hotel, a resort set between two of Fermanagh's lakes on the small island of Ely. The headliner is the 18-hole Faldo Course, designed by legendary touring pro Nick Faldo, but other elements are winners here, too. From the outside the building exudes a country-house feel in a mix of reconstituted sandstone and Danish timber. Lodges come with kitchenettes and guarantee

Fabled haunt of "the little people," the stately abode of Florence Court sits in a vale reputedly populated by leprechauns and fairies.

privacy, while the handsome guest rooms have appealing warmth. Diners can enjoy loin of Fermanagh lamb with Dauphinoise potatoes as done by one of Ireland's most celebrated chefs, Noel McMeel, at the elegant Catalina restaurant, or head for the Seafood Experience, secreted in a log cabin behind the 9th green. If you don't opt for the two 18-hole championship golf courses, an affable gillie, Packie Trotter, is happy to show you the tricks of casting with flies. Weary golfers can repair to the hotel's Thai spa but this entire resort is rejuvenating in many wonderful ways. **Pros:** binoculars in rooms for bird-watching; velour slippers and bathrobe; luxury Irish bed linen and Egyptian cotton towels. **Cons:** luxury comes at a steep price; queues at busy breakfast times. ⊠ *5 km (3 mi) north of Enniskillen, Belleek Rd., Co. Fermanagh* ☎ *028/6632-3230* ⊕ *www.lougherneresort.com* ⊅ *120 rooms, 6 suites, 25 lodges* ᗄ *In-room: a/c, refrigerator, Wi-Fi. In-hotel: 4 restaurants, bars, golf courses, pool, spa* ▭ *AE, D, MC, V* ⊺⊙⊺ *BP.*

FLORENCE COURT

11 km (7 mi) south of Enniskillen on A4 and A32.

Fodor's Choice
★

When it comes to Early Irish Georgian houses, there are few as magical as Florence Court. Less known than some showier estates, this three-story Anglo-Irish mansion was built around 1730 for John Cole, father of the first earl of Enniskillen. Topped off about 1760 with its distinctive two flanking colonnaded wings, the central house is adorably adorned with a positive surfeit of Palladian windows, keystones, and balustrades thanks to, as one architectural historian put it, "the vaingloriousness of a provincial hand." Even more impressive is its bucolically baroque setting, as the Cuilcagh Mountains form a wonderful contrast to the shimmering white-stone facade. Up until a few years ago, the house was barely furnished but a magnificent National Trust restoration have returned many family heirlooms to these interiors. Showstoppers in terms of decor are the Rococo plasterwork ceilings in the dining room; the Venetian Room; and the famous staircase, all ascribed to Robert West, one of Dublin's most famous

stuccadores (plaster workers). For a peek at the "downstairs" world, check out the restored kitchen and other service quarters. In 2009 a shop, reception area, and secondhand bookstore were added, and hte Men's Way and South Yard were converted into a holiday apartment. ⊠ *11 km (7 mi) south of Enniskillen on A4 and A32* ☎ *028/6634–8249* ⊕ *www.nationaltrust.org.uk* 🖃 *£5* ☉ *Grounds £3.25 Nov.–Apr., daily 10–4; May–Oct., daily 10–7. Mansion Mar. and Oct., weekends 11–5, Apr., daily 11–5; May–June and Sept., Wed.–Mon. 11–5; July and Aug., daily 11–5.*

CASTLE COOLE

★ *3 km (2 mi) east of Enniskillen on A4.*

In the 18th century and through most of the 19th, the Loughs of Erne and their environs were remote places far from Ireland's bustling cities. But it was just this isolated green and watery countryside that attracted the Anglo-Irish gentry, who built grand houses. This "uncommonly perfect" mansion (to quote the eminent architectural historian Desmond Guinness) is on its own landscaped oak woods and gardens at the end of a long tree-lined driveway. Although the Irish architect Richard Johnston made the original drawings in the 1790s, and was responsible for the foundation, the castle was, for all intents and purposes, the work of James Wyatt, commissioned by the first Earl of Belmore. One of the best-known architects of his time, Wyatt was based in London but visited Ireland only once, so Alexander Stewart was drafted as the resident builder-architect. The designer wasn't the only imported element; in fact, much of Castle Coole came from England, including the main facade, which is clad in Portland stone and hauled here by bullock carts. And what a facade it is—in perfect symmetry, white colonnaded wings extend from either side of the mansion's three-story, nine-bay center block, with a Palladian central portico and pediment. It is perhaps the apotheosis of the 18th century's reverence for the Greeks.

Inside, the house is remarkably preserved; most of the lavish plasterwork and original furnishings are in place. On its completion in September 1798, the construction had cost £70,000 and the furnishings another £22,000, compared with the £6 million cost of a restoration in 1995–96. The saloon is one of the finest rooms in the house, with a vast expanse of oak flooring, gilded Regency furniture, and gray scagliola pilasters with Corinthian capitals. The Life Below Stairs exhibition features tours of the servants' rooms and service quarters; above stairs, so to speak, is the present Earl of Belmore, who still lives on the estate and often attends the public concerts held here in the summer. ⊠ *Dublin Rd., A4* ☎ *028/6632–2690* ⊕ *www.nationaltrust.org.uk* 🖭 *Grounds free, parking £3.50, mansion £5.50* ⊙ *Grounds Nov.–Feb., daily 10–4; Mar.–Oct., daily 10–7. Mansion Mar.–May and Sept., weekends 11–5 (excluding Easter week, when it's open daily 11–5); June, Wed.–Mon. 11–5; July and Aug., daily 11–5.*

THE EASTERN BORDER COUNTIES

Home to St. Patrick's shrines of Armagh and Downpatrick and one of Ireland's best-known ranges—the Mountains of Mourne—Counties Armagh and Down make a fittingly moving finale to any tour of Northern Ireland.

ARMAGH

74 km (42 mi) east of Castle Coole.

The spiritual capital of Ireland for 5,000 years, and the seat of both Protestant and Catholic archbishops, Armagh is the most venerated of Irish cities. St. Patrick called it "my sweet hill" and built his stone church on the hill where the Anglican cathedral now stands. On the opposite hill, the twin-spire Catholic cathedral is flanked by two large marble statues of archbishops who look across the land. Despite the pleasing Georgian terraces around the elegant Mall east of the town center, Armagh can seem drab. Having suffered as a trouble spot in the sectarian conflict, though, it's now the scene of some spirited and sympathetic renovation.

GETTING HERE

BUS TRAVEL Buses link the historic city of Armagh with neighboring towns as well as Belfast, an 80-minute journey. You can catch a Translink Goldline Express from the Buscentre on the Lonsdale Road in Armagh (£14.50 round-trip). Cross-border buses also operate out of Armagh—you can hop aboard the Belfast–Galway Bus Éireann service that runs via Cavan town and Athlone. Round-trip to Galway is £33.15. Bus Éireann Expressway connections run from Dublin to Portrush on the north coast and stop in Armagh. The Armagh–Dublin bus journey is 2¾ hours and costs £22.15 round-trip.

Visitor Information Armagh Tourist Office (⊠ *40 English St., Co. Armagh* ☎ *028/3752–1800* ⊕ *www.armagh.co.uk*).

EXPLORING

The centerpiece of **Armagh Planetarium** is the Digital Theater, with each star show offering a fascinating tour of the night sky or an adventure into space projected in 3-D color onto the theater's dome. Take a break from all the dizziness by stopping off in the Voyager café or browse in the Astrosales shop through astronomical equipment that will intrigue

Thackeray admired the Church of Ireland's St. Patrick's Cathedral which, with St. Patrick's Roman Catholic Cathedral, jointly presides over Armagh.

stargazers of all ages. The outdoor 30-acre AstroPark has a model solar system. ✉ *College Hill* ☎ *028/3752–3689* ⊕ *www.armaghplanet.com* 🎫 *£6, includes Digital Theater* ⊙ *Weekdays 1–5, Sat. 11:30–5.*

The pale limestone, Gothic **St. Patrick's Roman Catholic Cathedral,** the seat of a Roman Catholic archdiocese, rises above a hill to dominate the north end of Armagh. Inside, the rather gloomy interior is enlivened by a magnificent organ, the potential of which is fully realized at services. Construction of the twin-spire cathedral started in 1840 in the neo-Gothic style, but the Great Famine brought work to a halt until 1854. It was finally completed in 1873. An arcade of statues over the main doorway on the exterior is one of the cathedral's most interesting features. The altar is solid Irish granite and the woodwork is Austrian oak. ✉ *Cathedral Rd.* ☎ *028/3752–2638* ⊕ *www.armagharchdiocese.org.*

Near the town center, a squat battlement tower identifies **St. Patrick's Anglican Cathedral,** in simple, early-19th-century, low-Gothic style. It stands on the site of much older churches and contains several relics of Armagh's long history, including sculpted, pre-Christian idols. Brian Boru, the High King (King of All Ireland) who visited Armagh in 1004—and was received with great ceremony—is buried here. In 1014, at the Battle of Clontarf, he drove the Vikings out of Ireland—but was killed after the battle was won. Inside are memorials and tombs by important 18th-century sculptors such as Roubilliac and Rysbrack. ✉ *Abbey St.* ☎ *028/3752–3142* ⊕ *www.stpatricks-cathedral.org* 🎫 *£3* ⊙ *Nov.–Mar., weekdays 9–4; Apr.–Oct., weekdays 9:30–5.*

A former church behind the tourist office has been reinvented as a visitor complex called **St. Patrick's Trian.** It contains three main exhibitions:

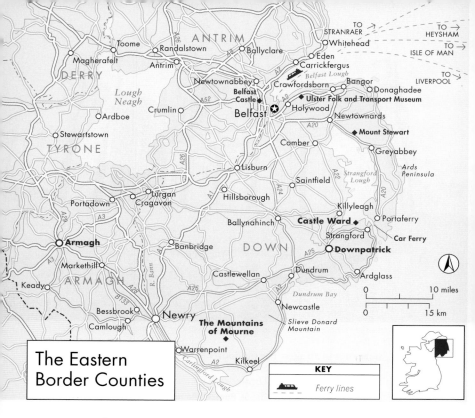

The Eastern
Border Counties

the Armagh Story, which explores the city's rich history and Pagan monuments; the Book of Armagh, which considers the writings of St. Patrick found in the ancient manuscript (with touch-screen language translations in English, French, and German); and the Land of Lilliput, the story of Jonathan Swift's most famous book *Gulliver's Travels*, as told by one of the book's "giants"—a big hit with children. ✉ 40 English St., Co. Armagh ☎ 028/3752–1801 ⊕ www.visitarmagh.co.uk 💷 £5 ⊘ Mon.–Sat. 10–5, Sun. 2–5

Just outside Armagh, **Navan Centre and Fort** is Ulster's Camelot—the region's ancient capital. Excavations date evidence of activity to 700 BC. The fort has strong associations with figures of Irish history. Legend has it that thousands of years ago this was the site of the palace of Queen Macha; subsequent tales call it the barracks of the legendary Ulster warrior Cuchulainn and his Red Branch Knights. Remains dating from 94 BC are particularly intriguing: a great conical structure, 120 feet in diameter, was formed from five concentric circles made of 275 wooden posts, with a 276th, about 12 yards high, situated in the center. In a ritual whose meaning is not known, it was filled with brushwood and set on fire. ✉ 81 Killyleagh Rd., 3 km (2 mi) west of Armagh on A28 ☎ 028/3752–9644 ⊕ www.armagh.co.uk 💷 £5 ⊘ July–Sept., daily 10–7; Oct.–Dec., daily 10–4. Closed Jan.–June.

THE MOUNTAINS OF MOURNE

52½ km (32½ mi) southeast of Armagh on A28, 51 km (32 mi) south of Belfast.

Subjects of a song that is sung on every Irish occasion from baptisms to funerals, the Mountains of Mourne must surely qualify as one of Ireland's best-known ranges. According to those lyrics by Percy French, the Mountains of Mourne "sweep down to the sea," from 2,000-foot summits. East of the

WORD OF MOUTH

"If you like hiking, consider the Mountains of Mourne—wonderful scenery and very few other people other than walkers and locals know about their beauty. It is also the area where the Brontë family originated. The Silent Valley drive is wonderful."   —Cambe

unprepossessing border city of Newry, this area was long considered ungovernable, its hardy inhabitants living from smuggling contraband into the numerous rocky coves on the seashore. Much of the Mourne range is still inaccessible except on foot. The countryside is gorgeous: high, windswept pasture and moorland threaded with bright streams, bound by a tracery of drystone walls, and dotted with sheep and white-washed farmhouses snuggled in stands of sycamore. It's the perfect landscape for away-from-it-all walkers, cyclists, and serious climbers. Climbers should inform their hotel when and where they're going before setting off.

GETTING HERE

BUS TRAVEL   Newcastle bus station on Railway Street is the arrival and departure point for all routes to one of the most scenic parts of Northern Ireland. Ulsterbus service leaves Belfast regularly for the 48-km (30-mi) trip to Newcastle (70 mins, £12.50 round-trip). Stops are made at the market towns of Dundrum, Castlewellan, Annsborough, Clough, and Ballynahinch. If you wish to appreciate the panoramic glory of the Mountains of Mourne, take a bus from Newcastle along the coast to the foothill towns of Annalong and Kilkeel (£6.80 round-trip). To truly get an up-close feel for the mountains, board the Mourne Rambler (info found on Rambler Services on the Translink site), a 23-seat rural transport bus that brings you right into the heart of Mourne country, with its network of small fields bounded by hedges and stone walls. A complete circuit on the Rambler, which runs only in July and August, takes 90 minutes (£5.80). You can also catch a bus from Newcastle to Dublin. This service starts from Downpatrick and runs from Newcastle to Castlewellan, Newry, and across the border to Dublin (£19.15 round-trip).

EXPLORING

The road to the **Silent Valley** reservoir park leads to mountain views and excellent photo-ops. There is a coffee shop and visitor center with an informative exhibition explaining the history of Silent Valley. ✉ 6 km (4 mi) north of Kilkeel off B27, right turn ☎ 028/9074–6581 ⊕ www.niwater.com/thesilentvalley.asp 🚗 Vehicles £4.50, pedestrians £1.60 ⊙ June–Aug., daily 10–6:30; Sept.–May, daily 10–4.

A four-hour ascent of the Slieve Donard peak—queen of the magnificent Mountains of Mourne—offers vistas that reach as far as Scotland and the Isle of Man.

Newcastle, a bracing Victorian cold-water bathing station, is the main center for visitors to the hills.

Looming above Newcastle is **Slieve Donard,** its panoramic, 2,796-foot-high summit grandly claiming views into England, Wales, and Scotland "when it's clear enough"—in other words, "rarely," say the pessimists. It's not possible to drive up the mountain, so leave your car in the Donard parking lot. It should take roughly three hours to climb to the summit and no longer than two hours to descend. Experienced hikers should not find it difficult, but if you prefer an easier trek, follow the trails signposted in Tollymore Forest Park. Hiking boots are essential and, as the weather can be unpredictable, it's advisable to take an extra layer of clothing, even in summer.

Covering 1,200 acres and entered through picturesque Gothic gateways, **Tollymore Forest Park** extends up the valley of the River Shimna. Many pretty stone bridges cross over the sparkling waters here. ⊠ *Tullybrannigan Rd., Newcastle* ☎ *028/4372–2428* ⊕ *www.forestserviceni.gov.uk* 🚗 *Vehicles £4.20, pedestrians £2* ☉ *Daily 10–dusk.*

A huge maze, grown to symbolize the convoluted path to peace, is the latest addition to **Castlewellan Forest Park,** which comprises 1,150 acres of forested hills running between the Mourne Mountains and Slieve Croob. With the maze, lake, secluded arbors, and arboretum, the park makes an excellent introduction to the area. ⊠ *Castlewellan* ☎ *028/4377–8664* ⊕ *www.forestserviceni.gov.uk* 🚗 *Vehicles £4.20, pedestrians free* ☉ *Daily 10* AM*–dusk.*

WHERE TO STAY

$$–$$$

Fodor's Choice

★

🏠 **Glassdrumman Lodge.** For those who wish to be pampered as well as immersed in the ancient Kingdom of Mourne, Graeme and Joan Hall's eclectically simple and stylish lodge is the place. The outside of the house is less than spectacular, but the busy estate has more than enough drama to compensate, for the family grows their own crops, raises their own farm animals, and bakes their own bread. Guest rooms are decorated in bright colors and have large windows with glorious views. **Pros:** stunning location in the heart of the mountains with the sea on your doorstep; rooms well appointed with pleasant en suite bathrooms. **Cons:** some say the restaurant is overrated; pity they've stopped churning their own butter. ✉ *Mill Rd., Annalong, Co. Down* ☎ *028/4376–8451* ⊕ *www.glassdrummanlodge.com* 🛏 *10 rooms, 2 suites* ⟁ *In-room: no a/c, Wi-Fi. In-hotel: restaurant* ⊟ *AE, DC, MC, V* ⦿ *BP.*

$$$$

Fodor's Choice

★

🏠 **Slieve Donard Resort & Spa.** A lavish redbrick monument to Victoriana, this turreted hotel, built in 1898, stands like a palace on green lawns at one end of Newcastle's 6½-km (4-mi) sandy beach. The traditional furnishings may make you feel as if you're stepping back in time to the town's turn-of-the-20th-century heyday as an elegant seaside resort, though the guest rooms have modern comforts and are bright and airy. Ask for a room overlooking the water; the views of the mountains and sea are striking. Amenities include a stylishly designed 16-room spa complete with saunas, amethyst steam rooms, and vitality pools. Dinner—classified as a grand buffet—is served in the Oak Restaurant. Chaplin's Bar is named after a visit to the hotel by Charlie Chaplin, who enjoyed the comforts for a weekend in 1921. The Royal County Down Golf Club is next door. **Pros:** appealing mix of luxury, history, and style; renovations brought hotel into the 21st century; fireplaces in lobby welcome on chilly days. **Cons:** housekeeping slow with requests; occasional cacophony from wedding receptions. ✉ *Downs Rd., Newcastle, Co. Down* ☎ *028/4372–1066* ⊕ *www.hastingshotels.com* 🛏 *178 rooms, 6 suites* ⟁ *In-room: no a/c (some), Wi-Fi. In-hotel: 3 restaurants, bar, tennis courts, pool, gym, spa* ⊟ *AE, DC, MC, V* ⦿ *BP, MAP.*

SPORTS AND THE OUTDOORS

Tollymore Mountain Centre (✉ *Bryansford, Newcastle* ☎ *028/4372–2158*) provides advice on mountain climbing and trails. The **Royal County Down** (✉ *Off A2, Newcastle* ☎ *028/4372–3314* ⊕ *www.royalcountydown. org*) is considered by many golfers to be one of the finest courses in the world. Between April and October, a game on the Championship Links can run up to £155; the Annesley Links top out at £40.

DOWNPATRICK

21 km (18 mi) east of Newcastle on A2 and A25.

Downpatrick once was called "Plain and Simple Down" but had its name changed by John de Courcy, a Norman knight who moved to the town in 1176. De Courcy set about promoting St. Patrick, the 5th-century Briton who was captured by the Irish and served as a slave in the Down area before he escaped to France, where he learned about

Christianity and bravely returned to try to convert the local chiefs. Although it's not true that Patrick brought a new faith to Ireland—there was already a bishop of Ireland before Patrick got here—he must have been a better missionary than most because he did indeed win influential converts. The clan chief of the Down area gave him land at the village of Saul, near Downpatrick, to build a monastery.

GETTING HERE

BUS TRAVEL   Buses arrive at the main station in Downpatrick from many points of County Down and beyond. Frequent Translink Goldline Express services run to and from Belfast. The journey time is one hour (£9.10 round-trip). Some services link up with the Belfast Metro network of suburban routes. To visit Strangford, there are daily services from Downpatrick (£5.40 round-trip); to visit Castle Ward ask the driver to stop by the roadside. Buses also leave Downpatrick for Dublin; the journey takes just over three hours (£19.15 round-trip).

Visitor Information Downpatrick Tourist Office (⊠ 53A Market St., Co. Down ☎ 028/4461–2233 ⊕ www.downdc.gov.uk).

EXPLORING

Down Cathedral is one of the disputed burial places of St. Patrick. In the churchyard, a somber slab inscribed "Patric" is supposedly the saint's tomb, but no one knows where he's actually buried. It might be here, at Saul, or, some scholars argue, more likely at Armagh. The church, which lay ruined from 1538 to 1790 (it reopened in 1818), preserves parts of some of the earlier churches and monasteries that have stood on this site, the oldest of which dates to the 6th century. Even by then, the cathedral site had long been an important fortified settlement: Down takes its name from the Celtic word *dun,* or fort. ⊠ *35 English St.* ⊕ *www.downcathedral.org* 🖺 *£1.*

★   For some hard facts concerning the patron saint of Ireland, visit the
☾   interactive exhibits of **St. Patrick Centre,** where the ancient myths and stories of early Christian Ireland are brought to life; you can explore how St. Patrick's legacy developed in Early Christian times and examine the art and metalwork that was produced during this golden age. The Grove art gallery exhibits jewelry, textiles, photographs, sculpture, and paintings by local artists and craftsmen. After lunch at Daisy's Café, browse through the gift shop and buy your own crock of shamrock. The center also includes an art gallery, terraced gardens, and a tourist information kiosk. ⊠ *53A Lower Market St.* ☎ *028/4461–9000* ⊕ *www.saintpatrickcentre.com* 🖺 *£4.95* ☉ *Oct.–Mar., Mon.–Sat. 10–5; Apr., May, and Sept., Mon.–Sat. 9:30–5:30, Sun. 1–5:30; June–Aug., Mon.–Sat. 9:30–6, Sun. 10–6.*

After returning to Ireland in the year AD 432, Ireland's patron saint popped up everywhere on his peregrinations. You can explore some places associated with him along the **St. Patrick's Trail** (⊕ *www. saintpatrickscountry.com*), an automobile route linking 15 historic and ecclesiastical sites across the beautiful drumlin hills of counties Down and Armagh.

Housed in an elegantly restored 18th-century jail between the cathedral and the courthouse, **Down County Museum** is brimful of living history.

The museum tells the story of Down from the prehistoric hunters, through the Norman Conquest, to the 18th-century landlords who left their imprint on the area. Behind the museum, a short signposted trail leads to the Mound of Down, an example of a Norman motte and bailey. ⊠ *The Mall, English St.* ☎ *028/4461–5218* ⊕ *www. downcountymuseum.com* ✉ *Free* ☉ *Weekdays 10–5, weekends 1–5.*

WHERE TO EAT AND STAY

$

IRISH

✕ **Denvir's Hotel.** In this wonderfully atmospheric pub and hotel—an old coaching inn dating to 1642—oak beams, stone floors, meat hooks hanging from the ceiling, and a large open fireplace testify to the antiquity. The bar top was crafted from the timbers of ships wrecked in Lough Foyle. Back in the mists of time, it was a member of the same Denvir family who gave the family name to a small settlement in Colorado, its name later modified to Denver. Six guest rooms have been sympathetically refurbished to retain the character of the old inn and come with original wooden floors and period wooden beds. Solid traditional dishes dominate the menu—steak, roast chicken, spring lamb, duck, and the daily fresh fish. Live music in the bar features traditional Irish as well as old classics, Thursday to Sunday night. ⊠ *14–16 English St.* ☎ *028/4461–2012* ⊕ *www.denvirshotel. com* ⊟ *MC, V.*

$

Fodor'sChoice

★

▭ **Dufferin Coaching Inn.** Leontine Haines presides over this 1803 inn next to picture-perfect, grandly gracious Killyleagh Castle (reputedly the longest-inhabited castle in Ireland and most probably the country's prettiest). Rooms in the low-slung, yellow building are quaint, lush, and cozy, with four-poster beds. The bar next door has a rustic feel to it with friendly snugs (cubicles) and Cajun and jazz music keeping things lively on Saturday afternoons and evenings. **Pros:** ideally located for exploring Strangford Lough and its many attractions; good value for the money. **Cons:** with the proximity to the pub, noise can be a problem; long way to go if you want the bright city lights; no elevator. ⊠ *33 High St. (10 km [6 mi] north of Downpatrick), Killyleagh, Co. Down* ☎ *028/4482–1134* ⊕ *www.dufferincoachinginn.com* ▭ *7 rooms* △ *In-room: no a/c, Internet. In-hotel: restaurant, bars, Internet terminal* ⊟ *AE, MC, V* ⦿ *BP.*

CASTLE WARD

★ *11 km (7 mi) northeast of Downpatrick, 3 km (2 mi) west of Strangford village on A25; on southern shore of Strangford Lough, entrance by Ballyculter Lodge.*

With a 500-acre park, an artificial lake, a Neoclassical temple, and a vast house in Bath stone magically set on the slopes running down to the Narrows of the southern shore of Strangford Lough, Castle Ward must have been some place to call home. About 3 km (2 mi) from the village of Strangford, off the road to Downpatrick, this regal stately home was designed around 1760 in, rather famously, two differing styles. Bernard Ward, 1st Viscount Bangor, could rarely see eye to eye (gossip had it) with his wife, Lady Anne, and the result was that he decided to make the entrance front and salons elegant exercises in Palladian Neoclassicism, while milady transformed the garden facade and

her own rooms using the most fashionable style of the day, Strawberry Hill Gothic. His white-and-beige Music Room is picked out in exquisite plasterwork (note how craftsmen decided to save a little money by taking objects, such as a tricorn hat and basket, and simply covering them in plaster), while her Boudoir has an undulating fan-vaulted ceiling that conjures up the "gothick" medievalisms of King Henry VII's chapel at Westminster. In point of fact, the couple's contretemps were dinner-table hearsay: they actually got along famously and the Gothic style was primarily used to beef up the ancestral image of a "Castle" Ward. Be sure to walk through the park (which has its own Wildlife Center) to enjoy the wonderful vistas overlooking the waters to the town of Portaferry and the Ards Peninsula. ⊠ *1½ km (1 mi) west of Strangford on Downpatrick Rd. (A25)* ☎ *028/4488–1204* ⊕ *www.nationaltrust. org.uk* ⊑ *£5.80* ☉ *Castle July and Aug., daily 11–5; Feb.–June, Sept., and Oct., weekends 1–6. Grounds Apr.–Aug., daily 10–8; Sept.–Mar., daily 10–4.*

The Best Irish Greens

WORD OF MOUTH

"For great golf, Ireland is a pilgrimage that no golfer should miss. If I had only two days I would choose between Ballybunion and Lahinch. The natural dunes along the sea is links golf at its finest. Not only is the golf great, the west coast of Ireland is the best scenery that the Emerald Isle has to offer. Bring your raingear and a thirst for Guinness."

—39Steps

Updated by
Anto Howard

The wonderfully alive, challenging natural terrain is one of the things that makes Irish golf so remarkable. Of the estimated 150 top-quality links courses in the world, 39 of them are in Ireland. Most of these leading courses were designed by celebrated golf architects, such as Tom Morris, James Braid, Harry Colt, and Alister MacKenzie, who capitalized on spectacular landscapes. Others—such as Jack Nicklaus, with his new course at Killeen Castle in County Meath—will continue in their steps.

The Weather Factor. You see all kinds of weather in Ireland—driving winds, rain, sleet, and sunshine—and you may see it all in one round. There are no rain checks here. You play unless there's lightning, so pack your sweaters and rain gear, especially if you're planning your trip between fall and spring.

The Sunday Bag Factor. If you don't have a golf bag that's light enough for you to carry for 18 holes, invest in one before your trip. Electric carts are generally available only at the leading venues, so you usually have the option of using a caddy or caddy car (pull cart)—or of carrying your own bag. Many courses have caddies but don't guarantee their availability because they're not employed by the course, so you may have to tote your bag yourself. Be prepared with a carryall or a Sunday bag.

The Northern Ireland Factor. Some of the best and most beautiful courses are in Northern Ireland, where the leading venues—like Royal County Down and Royal Portrush—are less remote than in the republic. Remember that this part of the island is under British rule, so all currency is in U.K. pounds, although many clubs and businesses will accept the euro. There are no restrictions when traveling from one part of the country to the other.

The Private Club Factor. Unlike those in America, most private golf clubs in Ireland are happy to let visitors play their courses and use their facilities.

12

It's important to remember, however, that such clubs place members first; guests come second. In some, you'll need a letter of introduction from your club in America to secure your playing privilege. There are often preferred days for visitors; call in advance to be sure that a club can make time for you.

The Downturn Factor. The recent rapid economic downturn in Ireland has seen a few courses close and a slew of them—mostly in the republic—start to drop their highly inflated prices to a much more reasonable rate for 2010 and 2011. Ireland is now packed with newer premium courses all competing to undercut each other pricewise—the "perfect storm" for the price-conscious visitors who still want to test themselves against the best golf courses the country has to offer.

NORTH OF DUBLIN

Carton House Golf Club. This just-outside-of-Dublin estate has quickly become one of the brightest stars in the Irish golfing universe. It's in a majestic 1,100-acre park that was the ancestral home of the earls of Kildare, presided over by an enormous and very grand 18th-century stately house. Two of the biggest names in golf designed the championship courses here. The parkland Mark O'Meara course makes use of the estate's rolling hills, specimen trees, and the River Rye. The highlight comprises the 14th, 15th, and 16th stretch: a pair of classy par-3s wrapped around a heroic par-5. The second 18 holes, created by Colin Montgomerie, make up an inland links-style course, which is flatter and virtually treeless. There's a good mix of long par-4s backed up with tricky short ones. Recessed pot bunkers lie in wait to pick up off-line shots. ⊠ *Maynooth, Co. Kildare* ☎ *01/628–6271* ⊕ *www.carton.ie* ↑ *36 holes. Yardage: 7,006 (O'Meara), 7,301 (Montgomerie). Both courses: Par 72. Practice area, caddies, caddy carts, buggies, club rental, shoe rental, catering* ⊟ *Fees: May–Oct., Mon.–Thur. €75, Fri.–Sun. €85; Nov.–Apr., Mon.–Thurs. €60, Fri.–Sun. €70* ☉ *Visitors: daily.*

Killeen Castle. The great Jack Nicklaus had a hands-on involvement in the design and construction of this championship-level course and golf school set in the serene woodlands of Norman Killeen Castle in Meath. Covering twice the acreage of an average championship course—you might need a buggy to get around—Nicklaus really had room to let his imagination run free and the natural water features and stonework are a special treat. The course is due to host the Solheim Cup in 2011. Check out the wonderful Paul Ferriter sculpture of the great man himself near the first tee box. ⊠ *Killeen Castle, Co. Meath* ☎ *01/689–3000* ⊕ *www.killeencastle.com* ↑ *18 holes. Yardage: 7,650. Par 72. Practice area, driving range, caddies, caddy carts, buggies, club rental, shoe rental, catering, golf school* ⊟ *Fees: Apr.–Oct., Mon.–Thurs. and Sun. €100, Fri. and Sat. €125; Nov.–Mar., daily €75* ☉ *Visitors: weekdays.*

Fodor's Choice
★

Portmarnock Golf Club. The hoo-ha and court battles over Portmarnock's refusal to admit women members often overshadows the club's position as the most famous of Ireland's "Big Four" (Ballybunion, Royal County Down, and Royal Portrush are the others). This links course, on a sandy peninsula north of Dublin, has hosted numerous major championships and Tom Watson often used it as a preparation for the Open. Known for its flat fairways and greens and its 100-plus bunkers, it provides a fair test for any golfer who can keep it out of the heavy rough. Greens fees include lunch. ⊠ *Portmarnock, Co. Dublin* ☎ *01/846–2968* ⊕ *www.portmarnockgolfclub.ie* 🏌 *27 holes. Yardage: 7,382, 3,449. Par 72, 37. Practice area, driving range, caddies (reserve in advance), caddy carts, club rental, catering* ☒ *Fees: €180 (includes light lunch)* ☉ *Visitors: daily.*

SOUTH OF DUBLIN

Druids Glen Golf Club. The beautiful Druids Glen course, 40 km (25 mi) south of Dublin in County Wicklow, has hosted the Irish Open on four occasions since it opened in 1995 and is known in golfing circles as the "Augusta of Europe." The wonderful landscaping and the extensive use of water in the layout explain the comparisons to the home of the Masters. It's essentially an American-style target course incorporating some delightful changes in elevation, and its forbidding, par-3 17th has an island green, like the corresponding hole at TPC Sawgrass. A second course, Druids Heath, is a marvelous attempt to combine the best of links, heathland, and parkland golf. ⊠ *Newtownmountkennedy, Co. Wicklow* ☎ *01/287–3600* ⊕ *www.druidsglen.ie* 🏌 *36 holes. Yardage: 6,560 (Glen), 6,629 (Heath). Both courses: Par 71. Practice area, caddies, caddy carts, buggies, club rental, shoe rental, catering* ☒ *Fees: €150 (Glen), €90 (Heath)* ☉ *Visitors: daily.*

★ **Heritage Golf and Country Club.** Millions of dollars have been spent on developing this recent arrival to the Irish golf scene—and it shows. This 18-hole championship course is a challenge for the pros but somehow manages to be forgiving to the amateur at the same time. Heritage has second-to-none facilities including a 38,000-square-foot clubhouse. A life-size bronze of Seve Ballesteros (by the renowned sports sculptor Paul Ferriter) greets you at the entrance to the course he designed here, which is noted for its mix of challenging doglegs and water traps (including five on-course lakes). Add four demanding par-5s to the mix and the result is a truly world-class parkland course. The development of luxury on-site accommodation has also increased the club's attractiveness to the visiting golfer. ⊠ *Killenard, Co. Laois* ☎ *057/865–5500* ⊕ *www. theheritage.com* 🏌 *18 holes. Yardage: 7,319. Par 72. Practice area, driving range, caddies, caddy carts, buggies, club rental, shoe rental, catering* ☒ *Fees: May–Oct., weekdays €70, weekends €80; Nov.–Apr., daily €60* ☉ *Visitors: daily.*

The K Club. "Home to the 2006 Ryder Cup" says all a golfer needs to know about the pedigree of the K Club. It remains Ireland's premier luxury golf resort, with two full championship parkland courses. The Palmer course is named after its designer, the legendary Arnold Palmer, and offers a round of golf in lush, wooded surroundings bordered by the River Liffey. The generous fairways and immaculate greens are offset by formidable length, which makes it one of the most demanding courses in the Dublin vicinity. Additional stress is presented by negotiating the numerous doglegs, water obstacles, and sand bunkers. The Smurfitt

12

course is essentially an "inland links" course. The signature 7th hole wows visitors with its water cascades and man-made rock-quarry feature. The on-site facilities are terrific and include a 95-room resort with three restaurants, a health club, tennis and squash courts, a pool, and massage and other spa treatments. ⊠ *Kildare Country Club, Straffan, Co. Kildare* ☎ *01/601–7321* ⊕ *www.kclub.com* ⌿ *36 holes. Yardage: 7,350 (Palmer), 7,277 (Smurfitt). Both courses: Par 72. Practice area, driving range, caddies, caddy carts, club rental, shoe rental, catering* ⊠ *Fees: €150–€305* ⊘ *Visitors: daily.*

Fodor'sChoice
★

Mount Juliet Golf Course. Attached to a magisterial country-house hotel, this Jack Nicklaus–designed championship parkland course, 19 km (11 mi) from Kilkenny Town, includes practice greens, a driving range, and, for those who feel a little rusty, a David Leadbetter golf academy. The heavily forested course has eight holes that play over water, including the wonderful 3rd hole—a par-3 over a stream from an elevated tee. The back 9 presents a series of difficult bunker shots. A sporting day out comes to a welcome end in the Hunter's Yard or Rose Garden lodge, which cater to both the thirsty and the hungry. Greens fees are above average, and although visitors are always welcome, a weekday round is best, since it's often crowded with members on weekends. ⊠ *Mount Juliet Estate, Thomastown, Co. Kilkenny* ☎ *056/777–3064* ⊕ *www.mountjuliet.ie* ⌿ *18 holes. Yardage: 7,264. Par 72. Practice area, driving range, caddy carts, club rental, catering* ⊠ *Fees: Apr.–Oct., weekdays €100, weekends €120; Nov.–Mar., weekdays €80, weekends €100* ⊘ *Visitors: daily.*

Powerscourt Golf Club. Set on the most spectacular estate in Ireland (once presided over by the Slazenger family), these two recently built courses are nestled in the foothills of the Wicklow Mountains on the ancient Powerscourt lands, home to a legendary 18th-century stately home and garden. Panoramic views to the sea and Sugarloaf Mountain—and all those 200-year-old trees—give the impression that the course has been here for years. The older East course is a largely parkland course, but some holes have certain links characteristics. The course's tiered greens will test even the best golfers. The more recently built West course is even more challenging and is designed with top-class tournament golf in mind. ⊠ *Enniskerry, Co. Wicklow* ☎ *01/204–6033* ⊕ *www.powerscourt. ie* ⌿ *36 holes. Yardage: 7,022 (East), 6,938 (West). Both courses: Par 72. Practice area, driving range, caddies, caddy carts, club rental, catering* ⊠ *Fees: Apr.–Sept. €120, Oct.–Mar. €65* ⊘ *Visitors: daily.*

SOUTHWEST

Adare Manor Golf Course. This parkland stretch is on the ancestral estate of the Earl of Dunraven. Its immediate success was virtually guaranteed by the international profile of its designer, Robert Trent Jones Sr. The grand old man of golf-course architects seemed far more comfortable with the wooded terrain here than he was when designing the second links at Ballybunion. As a result, he delivered a course with the potential to host events of the highest caliber. The front 9 is dominated by an artificial 14-acre lake with a $500,000 polyethylene base. It's in play at the

3rd, 5th, 6th, and 7th holes. The dominant hazards on the homeward journey are the River Mague and the majestic trees, which combine to make the par-5 18th one of the most challenging finishing holes imaginable. ⊠ *Adare, Co. Limerick* ☎ *061/395–044* ⊕ *www.adaremanor.com* ⚑ *18 holes. Yardage: 7,453. Par 72. Practice area, caddies, caddy carts, club rental, catering* 🍽 *Fees: May–Sept. €125, Oct. and Apr. €95, Nov. €90, Dec.–Mar. €80* ◔ *Visitors: daily.*

Fodor's Choice
★

Ballybunion Golf Club. President Bill Clinton will be eternally associated in Irish golfers' minds with this revered course. In fact, there's even a brass statue of him teeing off in the nearby village, to commemorate his visit here in 1999. On the shore of the Atlantic next to the southern entrance of the Shannon, Ballybunion has the huge dunes of Lahinch without the blind shots. It's no pushover, but every hole is pleasurable. Watch out for "Mrs. Simpson," a double fairway bunker on the 1st hole, named after the wife of Tom Simpson, the architect who remodeled the course in 1937. (Tom Watson did the same in 1995.) The Cashen Course, which opened in 1985, was designed by Robert Trent Jones Sr. and currently is free to play if you've paid for a round on the Old Course. ⊠ *Sandhill Rd., Ballybunion, Co. Kerry* ☎ *068/27611* ⊕ *www.ballybuniongolfclub.ie* ⚑ *36 holes. Yardage: 6,568 (Old), 6,306 (Cashen). Par 72 (Old), 70 (Cashen). Practice area, driving range, caddies, caddy carts, club rental, catering* 🍽 *Fees: May–Sept. €180 (Old), €110 (Cashen), €265 to play both on same day; Oct.–Apr. €140 (Old), €90 (Cashen)* ◔ *Visitors: weekdays.*

Fodor's Choice
★

Killarney Golf and Fishing Club. Freshwater fishing is the sport here, for this club is among a stunning mixture of mountains, lakes, and forests. There are three courses: Mahony's Point, along the shores of Lough Leane; the Lackabane, on the far side of the road from the main entrance; and the jewel in the crown, water-feature-packed Killeen (which hosts the Irish Open in 2010 and so is currently having extra rough and bunkers added). Despite the abundance of seaside links, many well-traveled golfers name Killarney their favorite place to play in Ireland. ⊠ *Mahony's Point, Killarney, Co. Kerry* ☎ *064/31034* ⊕ *www.killarney-golf.com* ⚑ *54 holes. Yardage: 6,780 (Mahony's Point), 7,050 (Lackabane), 7,178 (Killeen). All courses: Par 72. Practice area, caddies, caddy carts, club rental, catering* 🍽 *Fees: mid-Apr.–mid-Oct. €70 (Mahony's Point), €50 (Lackabane), €100 (Killeen); mid-Oct.–mid-Apr. €50 (Mahony's Point), €40 (Lackabane), €60 (Killeen)* ◔ *Visitors: Mon.–Sat.*

Old Head Golf Links. Golf doesn't get much more spectacular than this. On a celebrated 215-acre County Cork peninsula, which juts out into the wild Atlantic nearly 300 feet below, you can find an awe-inspiring spectacle that defies comparison. The only golfing stretches that could be likened to it are the 16th and 17th holes at Cypress Point and small, Pacific sections of Pebble Beach, from the 7th to the 10th, and the long 18th. Even if your golf is moderate, expect your pulse to race at the stunning views and wildlife. They've recently added 15 suites so you can now stay at the course for a few days. ⊠ *Kinsale, Co. Cork* ☎ *021/477–8444* ⊕ *www.oldhead.com* ⚑ *18 holes. Yardage: 7,215. Par 72. Practice area, caddies (reserve in advance), caddy carts, club rental, catering* 🍽 *Fees: €200* ◔ *Visitors: daily. Course is closed Nov.–mid-Apr.*

WEST

Doonbeg Golf Club. Despite being held up for a time (due to government legislation to protect a rare local snail), Greg Norman–designed Doonbeg has arrived with a major splash on the Irish links scene. Physically stunning, this tough, unforgiving course stretches along nearly 2 mi of pristine Atlantic beach and dunes. The magnificent par-4 15th—with funnel-shaped green surrounded by huge dunes—is at the center of the whole course. Gamblers beware: anything long could easily run off the green and never be seen again. If you make it to the tricky 18th, you'll be rewarded with breathtaking views of the ocean. ⊠ *Doonbeg, Co. Clare* ☎ *065/905–5602* ⊕ *www.doonbeggolfclub.com* ⌘ *18 holes. Yardage: 6,885. Par 72. Practice area, caddies, caddy carts, catering* ▧ *Fees: May–Oct., Mon.–Thurs. €160, Fri.–Sun. €190; Nov.–Apr., Mon.–Thurs. €85, Fri.–Sun. €95* ☉ *Visitors: daily.*

Westport Golf Club. Twice this inland course hosted the Irish Amateur Championship. It lies in the shadows of religious history: rising 2,500 feet above Clew Bay, with its hundreds of islands, is Croagh Patrick, a mountain that legend connects with St. Patrick. The mountain is considered sacred, and it attracts multitudes of worshippers to its summit every year. All the prayers might pay off at the 15th, where your drive has to carry the ball over 200 yards of ocean. ⊠ *Westport, Co. Mayo* ☎ *098/28262* ⊕ *www.golfwestport.com* ⌘ *18 holes. Yardage: 7,000. Par 73. Practice area, driving range, caddies, caddy carts, buggies, catering* ▧ *Fees: weekdays €35, weekends €45* ☉ *Visitors: daily.*

NORTHWEST

Donegal Golf Club. Famously named by *Golf World* as one of Ireland's top 10 clubs, this is a course that has always rated high in the estimation of local golfers. On the shores of Donegal Bay and approached through a forest, the windswept links are shadowed by the Blue Stack Mountains, with the Atlantic as a backdrop. The greens are large, but the rough is deep and penal, and there's a constant battle against erosion by the sea. The par-3 5th, fittingly called the "Valley of Tears," begins a run of four of the course's biggest challenges, which could have you discreetly hiding your scorecard by the time you reach the 18th. ⊠ *Murvagh, Laghey, Co. Donegal* ☎ *074/973–4054* ⊕ *www.donegalgolfclub. ie* ⌘ *18 holes. Yardage: 6,753. Par 73. Practice area, caddy carts, buggies, club rental, catering* ▧ *Fees: Mar.–Oct., weekdays €50, weekends €65; Nov.–Feb., weekdays €35, weekends €40* ☉ *Visitors: daily.*

NORTHERN IRELAND

Castlerock Golf Club. Where else in the world can you play a hole called "Leg o' Mutton"? It's a 200-yard par-3 with railway tracks to the right and a burn to the left—just one of several unusual holes at the Missenden course, which claims to have the best greens in Ireland. The finish is spectacular: from the elevated 17th tee, where you can see the shores of Scotland, to the majestic 18th, which plays uphill to a plateau green. The club also boasts the equally scenic 9-hole Bann course.

✉ *65 Circular Rd., Castlerock, Co. Derry* ☎ *048/7084–8314* ⊕ *www. castlerockgc.co.uk* ⛳ *27 holes. Yardage: 6,747 (Missenden), 4,892 (Bann). Par 73 (Missenden), 68 (Bann). Practice area, caddies (reserve in advance), caddy carts, catering* ☕ *Fees: weekdays £65 (Missenden), £12 (Bann); weekends £80 (Missenden), £15 (Bann)* ☉ *Visitors: daily.*

Fodor's Choice   **Royal County Down.** Recently ousting the Old Course at St. Andrews as
★   the best course outside the United States in *Golf Digest*'s annual survey, Royal County Down is a links course with a sea of craterlike bunkers and small dunes; catch it on the right day at the right time and you may think you're on the moon. And for better players, every day is the right one. Back in his day, Harry Vardon labeled it the toughest course on the Emerald Isle, and if you can't hit your drive long and straight, you might find it the toughest course in the world. ✉ *Golf Links Rd., Newcastle, Co. Down* ☎ *048/4372–2419* ⊕ *www.royalcountydown. org* ⛳ *36 holes. Yardage: 7,204 (Championship), 4,617 (Annesley). Par 71 (Championship), 66 (Annesley). Practice area, caddies, caddy carts, catering* ☕ *Fees: weekdays £120–£160 (Championship), £50 (Annesley); weekends £180 (Championship), £40 (Annesley)* ☉ *Visitors: Sun.– Tues., Thurs., and Fri. (Championship); daily (Annesley).*

Fodor's Choice   **Royal Portrush.** In addition to Royal County Down, Portrush also makes
★   *Golf Digest*'s top 10 non-U.S. courses. A legend in Irish golfing circles, Portrush is the only Irish club to have hosted a British Open. The championship Dunluce course is named for the ruins of a nearby castle and is a sea of sand hills and curving fairways. Despite its understated appearance it poses many and varied challenges. "White Rocks," the par-5 5th hole, is quite literally a cliff-hanger. It's a wicked dogleg with the green perched on the edge of a cliff. The Valley course is a less-exposed, tamer track. Both are conspicuous for their lack of bunkers. In a poll of Irish golf legends, Dunluce was voted the best in Ireland. ✉ *Dunluce Rd., Portrush, Co. Antrim* ☎ *048/7082–2311* ⊕ *www. royalportrushgolfclub.com* ⛳ *36 holes. Yardage: 7,143 (Dunluce), 6,304 (Valley). Par 72 (Dunluce), 70 (Valley). Practice area, caddies, caddy carts, buggies, catering* ☕ *Fees: Apr.–Oct. weekdays £125 (Dunluce), £35 (Valley); weekends £140 (Dunluce), £40 (Valley). Nov.–Mar. £60 (Dunluce), £35 (Valley)* ☉ *Visitors: daily (some restrictions).*

Travel Smart
Ireland

WORD OF MOUTH

"Be very aware of driving on the 'wrong side'—it is particularly important in Ireland on those very narrow, curvy, sheep-filled roads. I've had some anxious moments each time . . . especially on the two-lane country roads (one-and-a-half lanes!). Tip: Stop at a pub or ask directions from a bystander . . . the golden brogue will bring a smile to yer face . . . and don't hesitate to ask him/her to repeat!"

—tower

"The Irish Republic's public transport system is mediocre at best by the standards of small European countries. You can interrogate all of it pretty well from www.buseireann.ie (buses) and www.irishrail.ie (trains); the Northern Irish system's a lot better (www.translink.co.uk)."

—flanneruk

GETTING HERE AND AROUND

▮ BY AIR

Flying time to Ireland is 6½ hours from New York, 7½ hours from Chicago, 10 hours from Los Angeles, and 1 hour from London.

Flying into Ireland involves few hassles, although an increase in traffic in the last decade has caused a slight increase in flight delays and time spent waiting for baggage to clear customs. Flights within Ireland tend to be filled with business travelers. Increased competition on internal routes has led internal flights to be competitive with rail travel if you can travel outside peak business hours. However, given problems with passenger numbers and long lines for security clearance at Dublin Airport, rail is often preferable.

Checking in and boarding an outbound plane tends to be civilized. Security is professional but not overbearing, and airport staffers are usually helpful and patient. In the busy summer season lines can get long, and you should play it safe and arrive a couple of hours before your flight.

Airlines and Airports Airline and Airport Links.com (⊕ www.airlineandairportlinks.com) has links to many of the world's airlines and airports.

Airline Security Issues Transportation Security Administration (⊕ www.tsa.gov) has answers for almost every question that might come up.

AIRPORTS

The major gateways to Ireland are Dublin Airport (DUB) on the east coast, 10 km (6 mi) north of the city center, and Shannon Airport (SNN) on the west coast, 25 km (16 mi) west of Limerick. Two airports serve Belfast: Belfast International Airport (BFS) at Aldergrove, 24 km (15 mi) from the city, handles local and U.K. flights, as well as all other international traffic; Belfast City Airport (BHD), 6½ km (4 mi) from the city, handles local and

U.K. flights only. In addition, the City of Derry Airport (LDY) receives flights from Dublin and Manchester, Liverpool, East Midlands, and Glasgow in the United Kingdom. If you plan to visit mainly the Southwest of Ireland, use Cork Airport (ORK), which handles flights from Dublin and the U.K., and has daily direct flights from Paris, Malaga, and Rome.

Airport Information City of Derry Airport (☎ 028/7181–0784 ⊕ www.cityofderryairport. com). **Cork Airport** (☎ 021/431–3131 ⊕ www. corkairport.com). **Dublin Airport** (☎ 01/814–1111 ⊕ www.dublinairport.com). **George Best Belfast City Airport** (☎ 028/9093–9093 ⊕ www.belfastcityairport.com). **Belfast International Airport at Aldergrove** (☎ 028/9448–4848 ⊕ www.belfastairport.com). **Shannon Airport** (☎ 061/712–000 ⊕ www. shannonairport.com).

FLIGHTS

From North America and the United Kingdom, Aer Lingus, the national flag carrier, has the greatest number of direct flights to Ireland.

Aer Lingus operates regularly scheduled flights to Shannon and/or Dublin from New York's JFK (John F. Kennedy Airport), Chicago's O'Hare, Boston, Washington D.C., San Francisco, and Orlando. Delta has a daily departure from New York's JFK that flies first to Shannon and then to Dublin. Continental flies daily direct to Dublin, Shannon and Belfast, departing from Newark Liberty International Airport in New Jersey. With the exception of special offers, the prices of the three airlines tend to be similar. London to Dublin is one of the world's busiest international air routes. Aer Lingus, British Airways, British Midlands, and CityJet all have several daily flights. Ryanair—famous for its cheap, no-frills service—offers several daily flights from London Gatwick, Luton, and Stansted airports, while its low-cost rival, EasyJet, flies to many of these same destinations.

With such healthy competition, bargains abound. British Airways, BMI, andEasy-Jet offer regularly scheduled flights to Belfast from London Gatwick, Luton, and Stansted airports.

Within Ireland, Aer Lingus provides service to Dublin, Cork, Galway, Kerry, and Shannon. Aer Arann Express flies from Dublin to Cork, Derry, Donegal, Galway, Knock, and Sligo. British Airways has daily service between Dublin and Derry.

As for telephoning these carriers, keep in mind: if you are dialing the Aer Arann number (for instance) within the Republic of Ireland you must put a zero before the 1844, making it 01/844–7700, a Dublin number; if you are dialing from outside Ireland it is country code +353, then drop the zero and dial 1844, etc.; in the Republic of Ireland, you do not, of course, dial the 353.

Airline Contacts Aer Arann (☎ *0800/587–2324, 353/1844–7700 in Republic of Ireland* ⊕ *www.aerarann.com*). **Aer Lingus** (☎ *800/474–7424* ⊕ *www.aerlingus.com*). **American Airlines** (☎ *800/433–7300* ⊕ *www.aa.com*). **BMI** (☎ *0870/607–0555* ⊕ *www.flybmi.com*). **British Airways** (☎ *800/147–9297* ⊕ *www.ba.com*). **Continental Airlines** (☎ *800/231–0856* ⊕ *www.continental.com*). **Delta Airlines** (☎ *800/221–1212* ⊕ *www.delta.com*). **EasyJet** (⊕ *www.easyjet.com*). **Ryanair** (⊕ *www.ryanair.com*).

▌BY BOAT

TO AND FROM IRELAND

The ferry is a convenient way to travel between Ireland and elsewhere in Europe, particularly the United Kingdom. There are five main ferry ports to Ireland; four in the republic at Dublin Port, Dun Laoghaire, Rosslare and Cork, and two in Northern Ireland at Belfast and Larne. The cost of your trip can vary substantially, so spend time with a travel agent and compare prices carefully. Bear in mind, too, that flying can be cheaper, so look into all types of transportation before booking.

Irish Ferries operates the *Ulysses*, the world's largest car ferry, on its Dublin to Holyhead, Wales, route (3 hrs, 15 mins); there's also a swift service (1 hr, 50 mins) between these two ports. There are several trips daily. The company also runs between Rosslare and Pembroke, Wales (3 hrs, 45 mins), and has service to France. Stena Line sails several times a day between Dublin and Holyhead (3 hrs, 15 mins) and has swift service to Dun Laoghaire (2 hrs). The company also runs a fast craft (2 hrs) and a superferry (3 hrs) between Belfast and Stranraer, Scotland, as well as a fast craft (2 hrs) between Rosslare and Fishguard, Wales. There are several trips daily on both routes. The Fastnet Line sails a cruise ferry between Cork and Swansea (10 hrs) with at least five sailings a week. Swansea is on the M4 motorway, and the crossing saves about 600 km (375 mi) driving, compared to traveling to Cork from Fishguard or Pembroke Dock via Rosslare.

Norfolk Line offers a Dublin and Belfast to Liverpool service (8 hrs). P&O Irish Sea vessels run between Larne and Troon, Scotland (2 hrs), a couple of times a day. The company also sails from Dublin to Liverpool twice daily (8 hrs) with a choice of daytime or overnight sailings.

WITHIN IRELAND

There are regular services to the Aran Islands from Rossaveal in County Galway, and Doolin in County Clare. Ferries also sail to Inishbofin off the Galway coast and Arranmore off the Donegal coast, and to Bere, Whiddy, Sherkin, and Cape Clear Islands off the coast of County Cork. Bere and Whiddy have a car ferry, but the other islands are all small enough to explore on foot, so the ferries are for foot passengers and bicycles only. Other islands—the Blaskets and the Skelligs in Kerry, Rathlin in Antrim, and Tory, off the Donegal coast—have seasonal ferry services running daily between May and September, less frequently outside these months. Fáilte Ireland publishes a free guide and map with ferry details, *Ireland's Islands*, or see

⊕ *www.irelandsislands.com*. Alternatively, check with the nearest Tourist Information Office near the time of your visit, or see ⊕ *www.discoverireland.ie*. Boating the Shannon River system is an appealing alternative to traveling overland. In some places bicycles can be rented so you can drop anchor and explore. See the Getting Here sections in the various regional towns and cities for other ferry routes.

FARES AND SCHEDULES

You can get schedules and purchase tickets, with a credit card if you like, directly from the ferry lines. You can also pick up tickets at Dublin tourism offices and at any major travel agent in Ireland or the United Kingdom. Payment must be made in the currency of the country of the port of departure. Bad weather can delay or cancel ferry sailings so it's always a good idea to call before departing for the port.

Information Fastnet Line (☎ 0844/544–3323 in Ireland, 0844/544–3323 in U.K. ⊕ www. fastnetline.com). **Irish Ferries** (☎ 1890/313–131 in Ireland, 08705/171–717 in U.K., 0143/944–694 in France ⊕ www.irishferries. com). **Norfolk Line** (☎ 01/819–2999 in Ireland, 0844/499–0007 in U.K. ⊕ www. norfolkline.com). **P&O Irish Sea** (☎ 1800/409–049 in Ireland, 0871/664–4999 in U.K. ⊕ www. poirishsea.com). **Stena Line** (☎ 01/204–7777 in Ireland, 028/9074–7747 in Northern Ireland, 08705/707–070 in U.K. ⊕ www.stenaline.co.uk).

Boat Travel on the Shannon Carrickcraft (✉ Lurgan ☎ 028/3834–4993 ⊕ www.cruise-ireland.com). **Emerald Star** (✉ Connaught Harbor, Portumna ☎ 071/962–7633 ⊕ www. emeraldstar.ie). **Riversdale Barge Holidays** (✉ Ballinamore ☎ 071/964–4122 ⊕ www. riversdalebargeholidays.com). **Shannon Castle Line** (✉ Williamstown Harbor, Whitegate ☎ 061/927–042 ⊕ www.shannoncruisers.com). **Silver Line Cruisers** (✉ The Marina, Banagher ☎ 0509/51112 ⊕ www.silverlinecruisers.com). **Waveline Cruisers** (✉ Quigley's Marina, Killinure Point, Glassan ☎ 0906/485–711 ⊕ www. waveline.ie).

∎ BY BUS

In the Republic of Ireland, long-distance bus services are operated by Bus Éireann, which also provides local service in Cork, Galway, Limerick, and Waterford. There's only one class, and prices are similar for all seats. Note, though, that outside of the peak season, services are limited; some routes (e.g., Ring of Kerry) disappear altogether.

A new chapter in Bus Éireann service opened several years ago with the addition of their Expressway service. Expressway buses go directly, in the straightest available line, from one biggish town to another, and stop at a limited number of designated places only. There's sometimes only one trip a day on express routes. Their other divisions comprised commuter buses, as in the rest of the world, and then a kind of community service bus that rambles around the countryside passing through as many villages as possible, and stopping whereever anyone wants to get on or off, allowing as many people as possible to get to the nearest big town at least once a week. This used to be the *only* kind of bus service 30 years ago, which is why Bus Éireann so proudly trumpets their Expressway network.

Rural bus services shut down at around 7 or 8 PM. To ensure that a bus journey is feasible, buy a copy of Bus Éireann's timetable—€3 from any bus terminal—or check online. Many of the destination indicators are in Irish (Gaelic), so make sure you get on the right bus.

Numerous bus companies run between Britain and the Irish Republic, but be ready for long hours on the road and possible delays. All use either the Holyhead–Dublin or Fishguard/Pembroke–Rosslare ferry routes. Eurolines, a subsidiary of National Express, the British bus company, has services from all major British cities to more than 90 Irish destinations. Buses are cheap but slow: the journey from London to Galway takes around 17 hours.

In Northern Ireland, all buses are operated by the state-owned Ulsterbus. Service is generally good, with particularly useful links to those towns not served by train. Ulsterbus also offers tours. Buses to Belfast run from London and from Birmingham, making the Stranraer–Port of Belfast crossing. Contact National Express for that specific route.

Check with the bus office to see if reservations are accepted for your route; if not, show up early to get a seat. Note: prepaid tickets don't apply to a particular bus time, just a route, so if one vehicle is full you can try another. You can buy tickets online, or at the main tourist offices, at the bus station, or on the bus (though it's cash only for the latter option). A round-trip from Dublin to Cork costs €22 and Dublin to Galway return is €19.

You can save money by buying a multi-day pass, some of which can be combined with rail service. There are also cost-cutting passes that will give access to travel in both Northern Ireland and the Republic of Ireland. An iLink Card costs £55 for seven days' unlimited bus and rail travel in all parts of Northern Ireland—a really good deal when you consider that a one-day ticket costs £15. In the republic, passes include the Irish Explorer Rail and Bus Pass, which gives you eight days' bus travel out of 15 consecutive days for €245. The bus-only Irish Rover Card costs €190 for eight days' travel out of 15 consecutive days across both Northern Ireland and the republic. Contact Bus Éireann or Ulsterbus for details.

An Irish Rover bus ticket from Ulsterbus covers Ireland, north and south, and costs £56 for 3 days, £127 for 8, and £188 for 15. It also includes city center bus travel in Cork, Waterford, Limerick, Galway, and on the Metro services in Belfast—but not Dublin.

Bus Information Bus Éireann (☎ *01/836–6111 in Republic of Ireland* ⊕ *www.buseireann.ie*). **Eurolines** (☎ *08717/818–181 in U.K.* ⊕ *www.eurolines.co.uk*). **Ulsterbus**

(☎ *028/9033–3000 in Northern Ireland* ⊕ *www.ulsterbus.co.uk*).

▌ BY CAR

U.S. driver's licenses are recognized in Ireland.

Roads in the Irish Republic are generally good, though four-lane highways, or motorways, are the exception rather than the rule. In addition, many roads twist and wind their way up and down hills and through towns, which can slow you down. On small, rural roads, watch out for cattle and sheep; they may be just around the next bend. Reckless drivers (surveys says that Irish drivers are among the worst) are also a problem in the countryside, so remain cautious and alert. Road signs in the republic are generally in both Irish (Gaelic) and English; destinations in which Irish is the spoken language are signposted only in Irish. The most important one to know is An Daingean, which is now the official name of Dingle Town. It is best to get a good, bilingual road map. Knowing the name of the next town on your itinerary is more important than knowing the route number: neither the small local signposts nor the local people refer to roads by official numbers. Traffic signs are the same as in the rest of Europe, and roadway markings are standard. On the new green signposts in the republic distances are in kilometers; on some of the old white signposts they're still miles, but the majority of signposts are in kilometers. Most importantly, remember that speed limits are signposted in the republic (but not in Northern Ireland) in kilometers.

There are no border checkpoints between the republic and Northern Ireland, where the road network is excellent and, outside Belfast, uncrowded. Road signs and traffic regulations conform to the British system.

All ferries on both principal routes to the Irish Republic take cars. Fishguard and Pembroke are relatively easy to reach by road. The car trip to Holyhead, on the other hand, is sometimes difficult: delays on the A55 North Wales coastal road aren't unusual. Car ferries to Belfast leave from the Scottish port of Stranraer and the English city of Liverpool; those to Larne leave from Stranraer and Cairnryan. Speed limits are generally 95 to 100 KPH (roughly 60 to 70 MPH) on the motorways, 80 KPH (50 MPH) on other roads, and 50 KPH (30 MPH) in towns.

GASOLINE

You can find gas stations along most roads. Self-service is the norm. Major credit cards and traveler's checks are usually accepted. Prices are near the lower end for Europe, with unleaded gas priced around €1.25 in Ireland and £1.12 a liter in Northern Ireland—gasoline prices in the United States are a bit more than half the price in Ireland. Prices vary significantly from station to station, so it's worth driving around the block.

ROAD CONDITIONS

Most roads are paved and make for easy travel. Roads are classified as *M, N,* or *R*: those designated with an *M* for "motorway" are double-lane divided highways with paved shoulders; *N,* or national, routes are generally undivided highways with shoulders; and *R,* or regional, roads tend to be narrow and twisty.

Rush hour traffic in Dublin, Cork, Limerick, Belfast, and Galway can be intense. Rush hours in Dublin run 7 AM to 9:30 AM and 5 PM to 7 PM; special events such as football (soccer) games will also tie up traffic in and around the city as will heavy rain.

ROADSIDE EMERGENCIES

Membership in an emergency car service is a good idea if you're using your own vehicle in Ireland. The Automobile Association of Ireland is a sister organization of its English counterpart and is highly recommended. Note that the AA can help you or your vehicle only if you are a member of the association. If not, contact your car-rental company for assistance. If involved in an accident you should note the details of the vehicle and the driver and witnesses and report the incident to a member of the Garda Síochána (the Irish Police) or the Police Service of Northern Ireland (PSNI) as soon as possible. Since traffic congestion is chronic in Dublin, emergency services are more likely to be dispatched quickly to help you and to clear the road. If your car does break down, if at all possible try to stop it in a well-lighted area near a public phone. If you're on a secondary or minor road, remain in your car with the doors locked after you call for assistance. If you break down on the motorway, you should pull onto the hard shoulder and stay out of your car with the passenger side door open and the other doors locked. This will allow you to jump into the car quickly if you sense any trouble. Make sure you check credentials of anyone who offers assistance—note the license-plate number and color of the assisting vehicle before you step out of the car.

Emergency Services An Garda Síochána (Police) (☎ *112 or 999* ⊕ *www.garda. ie*). **Automobile Association of Ireland** (☎ *01/617–9999 in Ireland, 0800/887–766 in Northern Ireland, 08457/887–766 from cell phone in Northern Ireland* ⊕ *www.aaireland.ie; www.theaa.com for Northern Ireland*). **Police Service of Northern Ireland** (☎ *999* ⊕ *www. psni.police.uk*).

RULES OF THE ROAD

The Irish, like the British, drive on the left-hand side of the road in whatever direction they are headed (not, as in America, on the right-hand side). Safety belts must be worn by the driver and all passengers, and children under 12 must travel in the back unless riding in a car seat. It's compulsory for motorcyclists and their passengers to wear helmets. Speed limits in Ireland are posted in kilometers per hour and in Northern Ireland in miles per hour, so if crossing the border be sure to make the adjustment. In towns and cities the speed limit is 50 KPH (31 MPH). On Regional (R) and Local (L) roads, the speed limit is 80 KPH (50 MPH), indicated by white signs. On National (N) roads, the speed limit is 100 KPH (62 MPH), indicated by green signs. On Motorways (M), the speed limit is 120 KPH (74 MPH), indicated by blue signs.

Drunk-driving laws are strict. The legal limit is 80 mg of alcohol per 100 ml of blood. Ireland has a Breathalyzer test, which the police can administer anytime. If you refuse to take it, the odds are you'll be prosecuted anyway. As always, the best advice is don't drink if you plan to drive.

Speed cameras and radar are used throughout Ireland. Speeding carries an on-the-spot fine of €80 and if the Gardaí (police) charges you with excessive speeding you could be summoned to court. This carries a much higher fine and you will be summoned within six months (meaning you could be required to return to Ireland).

Note that a continuous white line down the center of the road prohibits passing. Barred markings on the road and flashing yellow beacons indicate a crossing, where pedestrians have right of way. At a junction of two roads of equal importance, the driver to the right has right of way. On a roundabout, vehicles approaching from the right have right of way. Also, remember there are no left turns permitted on a red light. If another motorist flashes their headlights at you, they are not warning of a speed trap ahead, they are giving you right of way.

Despite the relatively light traffic, parking in towns can be a problem. Signs with the letter *P* indicate that parking is permitted; a stroke through the *P* warns you to stay away or you'll be liable for a fine of €20–€65; however, if your car gets towed away or clamped, the fine is around €180. In Dublin and Cork, parking lots are your best bet, but check the rate first in Dublin; they vary wildly.

In Northern Ireland there are plenty of parking lots in the towns (usually free except in Belfast), and you should use them. In Belfast, you can't park your car in some parts of the city center, more because of congestion than security problems.

▌ BY TRAIN

The republic's Irish Rail trains are generally reliable, reasonably priced, and comfortable. You can easily reach all the principal towns from Dublin, though services between provincial cities are roundabout. To get to Cork City from Wexford, for example, you have to go via Limerick Junction. It's often quicker, though perhaps less comfortable, to take a bus. Most mainline trains have one standard class. Round-trip tickets are usually cheapest. Visitors aged 66 and over are entitled to free rail travel on all rail routes, including intercity, Dublin Area Rapid Transport (Dart), and commuter trains. You can access the scheme on the Fáitle Ireland Web site before arriving to arrange for a Golden Trekker reservation, or once in Ireland, by visiting any Fáilte Ireland Tourist Information Office. Tickets are issued in blocks of four days, giving unlimited rail travel during that time, a saving on the normal rate of about €100. These tickets are not valid in Northern Ireland.

Northern Ireland Railways has three main rail routes, all operating out of Belfast's Central Station. These are north to Derry, via Ballymena and Coleraine; east to Bangor along the shores of Belfast Lough; and south to Dublin and the Irish Republic. Note that Eurail Passes aren't valid in Northern Ireland.

You should plan to be at the train station at least 30 minutes before your train departs to ensure you'll get a seat. It's not uncommon on busier routes to find that you have to stand since all seats have been sold and taken.

Ireland (excluding Northern Ireland) is one of 17 countries in which you can use an **InterRail Pass,** which provides unlimited rail travel in all of the participating countries for the duration of the pass. If you plan to rack up the miles, get a standard pass. These are available from

Rail Europe (the company that services many of the passes listed here), for 15 days (£373), 21 days (£439), and one month (£560). In addition to standard Eurail Passes, ask about special rail-pass plans. Among these are the **Eurail Youth Pass** (for those under age 26), the **Eurail Saver Pass** (which gives a discount for two or more people traveling together), the **EurailDrive Pass** and the **Eurail Select Pass 'n Drive** (which combines travel by train and rental car). Whichever pass you choose, you must purchase your pass before you leave for Europe. For these passes, buy online from www.Eurail.com or through your travel agent.

The **Irish Explorer Rail & Bus Pass** covers all the state-run and national railways and bus lines throughout the republic. It does not apply to the North or to transportation within cities. An eight-day ticket for use on buses *and* trains during a 15-day period is €245. Irish Rail provides details on both (bus and rail) passes.

In Northern Ireland, the iLink Card entitling you to up to seven days' unlimited travel on scheduled bus and rail services throughout Northern Ireland is available from main Northern Ireland Railways stations. It costs about £55 for adults (half price for children under 12 and senior citizens). InterRail tickets are also valid in Northern Ireland.

Train schedules are easy to obtain and available in a variety of formats. Irish Rail and Northern Ireland Railways have Web sites that produce a schedule in response to your input of an itinerary. Alternatively you can visit any train station to obtain a printed schedule or call either company's customer service line.

Sample fares? A return ticket from Dublin to Cork will cost around €60; Dublin to Belfast is approximately €55. Considerable savings can be made by booking online where off-peak tickets are sold for as little as €10 each way on most long journeys.

Tickets can be purchased online or at the train station. Cash, traveler's checks, and credit-card payments are accepted. You must pay in the local currency. Dublin, Connolly, and Heuston stations have automated ticket machines that take either cash or credit-card payments, offering a convenient way to avoid long lines at ticket windows.

Many travelers assume that rail passes guarantee them seats on the trains they wish to ride. Not so. You need to book seats ahead even if you're using a rail pass. Seat reservations are required on some European trains, particularly high-speed trains, and are a good idea on trains that may be crowded—particularly in summer on popular routes. You'll also need a reservation if you purchase sleeping accommodations.

There's only one class of train travel in Ireland (with the exception of the Enterprise, the express train that travels from Dublin to Belfast, for which you can purchase a First Class or Standard Class ticket, and the Dublin to Cork train). All tickets bought online on the Cork–Dublin train include a seat reservation. Otherwise, specific seat reservations can be made only for trains deemed to be busy (ask when buying your ticket if they're taking reservations for your route). For example, the train traveling from Dublin to Cork on a Friday evening is considered a peak time, thanks to all the students and business travelers heading home for the weekend, and it would be advisable to have a seat reservation, and to board the train early. At peak hours and for popular routes, it's advisable to arrive early at the station to purchase your ticket (or buy it online) or you may find yourself standing for a significant portion of your journey.

Information and Passes Eurail (⊕ *www. eurail.com*). **Fáilte Ireland** (⊕ *www. discoverireland.com*).

Train Information Irish Rail (*Iarnrod Éireann* ☎ *01/836–6222* ⊕ *www.irishrail.ie*). **Northern**

Ireland Railways (☎ 028/9089–9411 ⊕ www.translink.co.uk).

Train Station Information Belfast Central Station (✉ East Bridge St., Belfast ☎ 028/9089–9400 ⊕ www.translink.co.uk). **Connolly Station** (✉ Amiens St., Dublin ☎ 01/703–2358 ⊕ www.irishrail.ie). **Galway Station** (✉ Station Rd., Galway ☎ 091/564–222 ⊕ www.irishrail.ie). **Heuston Station** (✉ Dublin ☎ 01/703–3299 ⊕ www.irishrail.ie). **Kent Station** (✉ Lower Glanmire Rd., Cork ☎ 021/450–6766 ⊕ www.irishrail.ie).

ESSENTIALS

■ ACCOMMODATIONS

From cottages to castles, Ireland has a vast range of accommodations. And while some of them rank among Europe's prettiest and priciest, the recent economic downturn has meant one thing: bargains galore. One minute of research will uncover deals like two nights and a B&B with two dinners, all for about half of the full price, sometimes with a third night free. Many hotels have halved their prices since 2008, the height of the Celtic Tiger boom years. So remember to ask for a discount and see what they offer.

In Dublin and other cities, boutique hotels combine luxury with contemporary (and often truly Irish) design. Manors and castles offer a unique combination of luxury and history. Less impressive, but equally charming, are the provincial inns and country hotels with simple but adequate facilities.

You can meet a wide cross section of Irish people by hopping from one bed-and-breakfast to the next, or you can keep to yourself for a week or two in a thatched cottage. B&Bs approved by Tourism Ireland display a green shamrock outside and are usually considered more reputable than unregistered ones. Hotels and other accommodations in Northern Ireland are similar to those in the Republic of Ireland.

Fáilte Ireland has a grading system and maintains a list of registered hotels, guesthouses, B&Bs, farmhouses, hostels, and campgrounds. For each accommodation, the list gives a maximum charge that can't be exceeded without special authorization. Prices must be displayed in every room; if the hotel oversteps its limit, don't hesitate to complain to the hotel manager and/or Fáilte Ireland.

The lodgings we list are the cream of the crop in each price category. We always list the facilities that are available, but we don't specify whether they cost extra; when pricing accommodations, always ask what's included and what costs extra. Lodgings are assigned price categories based on the range from their least-expensive standard double room at high season (excluding holidays) to the most expensive.

Most hotels and other lodgings require you to give your credit-card details before they will confirm your reservation. If you don't feel comfortable e-mailing this information, ask if you can fax it (some places even prefer faxes). However you book, get confirmation in writing and have a copy of it handy when you check in.

Be sure you understand the hotel's cancellation policy. Some places allow you to cancel without any kind of penalty—even if you prepaid to secure a discounted rate—if you cancel at least 24 hours in advance. Others require you to cancel a week in advance or penalize you the cost of one night. Small inns and B&Bs are most likely to require you to cancel far in advance. Most hotels allow children under a certain age to stay in their parents' room at no extra charge, but others charge for them as extra adults; find out the cutoff age for discounts.

■TIP➔ Assume that hotels operate on the European Plan (**EP**, no meals) unless we specify that they use the Breakfast Plan (**BP**, with full breakfast), Continental Plan (**CP**, Continental breakfast), Full American Plan (**FAP**, all meals), Modified American Plan (**MAP**, breakfast and dinner) or are all-inclusive (**AI**, all meals and most activities).

APARTMENT AND HOUSE RENTALS

Local Agents Bord Fáilte (☎ *01/602–4000* ⊕ *www.discoverireland.ie*).

Days Serviced Apartments (☎ *01/639–1100* ⊕ *www.apartments-dublin.com*).

ONLINE BOOKING RESOURCES

Contacts At Home Abroad (☏ 212/421–9165 ⊕ www.athomeabroadinc.com). **Barclay International Group** (☏ 516/364–0064 or 800/845–6636 ⊕ www.barclayweb.com). **Drawbridge to Europe** (☏ 541/482–7778 or 888/268–1148 ⊕ www.drawbridgetoeurope. com). **Hosted Villas** (☏ 416/920–1873 or 800/374–6637 ⊕ www.hostedvillas.com). **Interhome** (☏ 954/791–8282 or 800/882–6864 ⊕ www.interhomeusa.com). **Suzanne B. Cohen & Associates** (☏ 207/622–0743 ⊕ www.villaeurope.com). **Villanet** (☏ 206/417–3444 or 800/964–1891 ⊕ www. rentavilla.com). **Villas & Apartments Abroad** (☏ 212/213–6435 or 800/433–3020 ⊕ www. vaanyc.com).**Villas International** (☏ 415/499–9490 or 800/221–2260 ⊕ www.villasintl.com). **Villas of Distinction** (☏ 707/778–1800 or 800/289–0900 ⊕ www.villasofdistinction.com). **Wimco** (☏ 800/449–1553 ⊕ www.wimco.com).

BED AND BREAKFASTS

B&Bs are classified as either town homes, country homes, or farmhouses. Many B&Bs now have at least one bedroom with a bathroom, but don't expect this as a matter of course. The Irish farms that offer rooms by the week with partial or full board are more likely to be modern bungalows or undistinguished two-story houses than creeper-clad Georgian mansions. Room and part board—breakfast and an evening meal—starts at around €60 per person per night. Many travelers don't bother booking a B&B in advance. They are so plentiful in rural areas that it's often more fun to leave the decision open, allowing yourself a choice of final destinations for the night. However, if you have discerning taste and enjoy meeting a variety of pleasant characters, check out the places listed by Friendly Homes of Ireland. Long weekends are the exception to this rule, with B&Bs often getting booked up far in advance, so keep an eye on the calendar of local holidays.

To qualify as a guesthouse, establishments must have at least five bedrooms. Some guesthouses are above a bar or restaurant; others are part of a home. As a rule, they're cheaper (some include an optional evening meal) and offer fewer amenities than hotels. But often that's where the differences end. Most have high standards of cleanliness and hospitality, and most have a bathroom, a TV, and a direct-dial phone in each room. Premier Guesthouses are generally small inns, run by the owner, and hard to distinguish from hotels.

Local Services Bed & Breakfast Association of Northern Ireland (☏ 28/4461–5542). **Friendly Homes of Ireland** (☏ 01/660–7975 ⊕ www.tourismresources.ie). **Irish Farm Holidays** (☏ 061/400–700 ⊕ www. irishfarmholidays.com). **Town, Farm and Country Homes (B&B Ireland)** (☏ 071/982–2222 ⊕ www.bandbireland.com). **Premier Guesthouses** (☏ 01/205–2826 ⊕ www. premierguesthouses.com).

CASTLES AND MANORS

Among the most magical experiences on an Irish vacation are stays at some of the country's spectacular castle-hotels, such as Dromoland (Newmarket-on-Fergus), Ashford (Cong), and Castle Leslie (Glaslough). For directories to help you get to know the wide array of manor house and castle accommodations, including a goodly number of private country estates and castles, contact Ireland's Blue Book of Country Houses & Restaurants, or Hidden Ireland.

Reservations Services Hidden Ireland (☏ 98/66650 ⊕ www.hiddenireland.com). **Ireland's Blue Book** (☏ 01/676–9914 ⊕ www. irelandsbluebook.com).

COTTAGES

Vacation cottages, which are usually in clusters, are rented by the week. Although often built in the traditional style, most have central heating and all the other modern conveniences. It's essential to reserve in advance.

Reservations Services Irish Cottage Holiday Homes Association (✉ Bracken Court, Bracken Rd., Sandyford, Dublin ☏ 01/205-2777 ⊕ www.irishcottageholidays.com). **Northern Ireland Self-Catering Holidays Association**

(✉ *63 Somerton Rd., North Belfast, Belfast*
☎ *28/9077–6174* ⊕ *www.nischa.com*).

HOME EXCHANGES

With a direct home exchange you stay in someone else's home while they stay in yours. Some outfits also deal with vacation homes, so you're not actually staying in someone's full-time residence, just their vacant weekend place.

Exchange Clubs Home Exchange.com
(☎ *800/877–8723* ⊕ *www.homeexchange. com*) ; $59.95 for a 1-year online listing. **HomeLink International** (☎ *800/638–3841* ⊕ *www.homelink.org*) ; $80 yearly for Web-only membership; $125 includes Web access and two catalogs. **Intervac U.S.** (☎ *800/756–4663* ⊕ *www.intervacus.com*) ; $78.88 for Web-only membership; $126 includes Web access and a catalog.

HOSTELS

Hostels offer bare-bones lodging at low, low prices—often in shared dorm rooms with shared baths—to people of all ages, though the primary market is young travelers, especially students. Most hostels serve breakfast; dinner and/or shared cooking facilities may also be available. In some hostels you aren't allowed to be in your room during the day, and there may be a curfew at night. Nevertheless, hostels provide a sense of community, with public rooms where travelers often gather to share stories. Many hostels are affiliated with Hostelling International (HI), an umbrella group of hostel associations with some 4,500 member properties in more than 70 countries. Other hostels are completely independent and may be nothing more than a really cheap hotel.

Membership in any HI association, open to travelers of all ages, allows you to stay in HI-affiliated hostels at member rates. One-year membership is about $28 for adults; hostels charge about $10–$30 per night. Members have priority if the hostel is full; they're also eligible for discounts around the world, even on rail and bus travel in some countries.

Information Hostelling International—USA (☎ *301/495–1240* ⊕ *www.hiusa.org*). **Independent Holiday Hostels** (☎ *01/836–4700* ⊕ *www.hostels-ireland.com*). **Irish Youth Hostel Association** (*An Óige* ✉ *67 Mountjoy St., North City Centre, Dublin* ☎ *01/830–4555* ⊕ *www.anoige.ie*). **Northern Ireland Hostelling International** (✉ *22–32 Donegal Rd., University Area, Belfast* ☎ *28/9032–4733* ⊕ *www. hini.org.uk*).

HOTELS

Standard features in most hotels include private bath, two twin beds (you can usually ask for a king-size instead), TV (often with DVD), free parking, and no-smoking rooms. There's usually no extra charge for these services. All hotels listed have private bath unless otherwise noted.

Information Ireland Hotels Federation (☎ *01/808–4419* ⊕ *www.irelandhotels. com*). **Northern Ireland Hotels Federation** (☎ *28/9077–6635–0* ⊕ *www.nihf.co.uk*). **Tourism Ireland** (⊕ *www.tourismireland.com*).

▮ COMMUNICATIONS

INTERNET

If you're traveling with a laptop, carry a spare battery and adapter. Most laptops will work at both 120V and 220V, but you will need an adapter so the plug will fit in the socket. In the countryside, a surge protector is a good idea.

Going online is becoming routine in Dublin, thanks, in part, to the Wi-Fi hot spots—which allow you to make a wireless connection from your laptop onto a network—popping up across the city. Net House, an Internet café chain, has the most locations in the country, with nine in Dublin and one in Cork.

There are also many independent Internet cafés across the country. Prices vary from the low end in Dublin of €2.60 per hour to €5 per hour in smaller cities. There are also many Wi-Fi hot spots (not just focused on Internet users) throughout the country, such as the Insomnia Coffee/ Sandwich Bar chain in Galway. Dublin

Airport and Dun Laoghaire Harbor have facilities to access wireless connection to the Internet. Most hotels in cities and large towns now offer a Wi-Fi hotspot in the lobby or lounge. A Wi-Fi connection can cost about €9 for an hour or €22 for unlimited access within a 24-hour period. In most cases, however, Wi-Fi access is free if you are using the facilities of the hotel or café.

Contacts Cybercafes (⊕ www.cybercafes. com) lists over 4,000 Internet cafés worldwide.

PHONES

The good news is that you can now make a direct-dial telephone call from virtually any point on earth. The bad news? You can't always do so cheaply. Calling from a hotel is almost always the most expensive option; hotels usually add huge surcharges to all calls, particularly international ones. In some countries you can phone from call centers or even the post office. Calling cards usually keep costs to a minimum, but only if you purchase them locally. And then there are mobile phones (⇨ below), which are sometimes more prevalent—particularly in the developing world—than land lines; as expensive as mobile phone calls can be, they are still usually a much cheaper option than calling from your hotel.

Ireland's telephone system is up to the standards of the United Kingdom and the United States. Direct-dialing is common; local phone numbers have five to eight digits. You can make international calls from most phones, and some cell phones also work here, depending on the carrier.

Do not make calls from your hotel room unless it's absolutely necessary. Practically all hotels add 200% to 300% to the cost.

The country code for Ireland is 353; for Northern Ireland, which is part of the United Kingdom telephone system, it's 44. The local area code for Northern Ireland is 028. However, when dialing Northern Ireland from the republic you can simply dial 048 without using the U.K. country code. When dialing an Irish number from abroad, drop the initial 0 from the local area code. The country code is 1 for the United States and Canada, 61 for Australia, 64 for New Zealand, and 44 for the United Kingdom.

Public pay phones can be found in street booths and in restaurants, hotels, bars, and shops, some of which display a sign saying YOU CAN PHONE FROM HERE. There are at least three models of pay phones; read the instructions or ask for assistance.

CALLING WITHIN IRELAND

If the operator has to connect your call, it will cost at least one-third more than direct dial.

Directory Information Republic of Ireland (☎ 11811 for directory inquiries in the republic and Northern Ireland, 11818 for U.K. and international numbers, 114 for operator assistance with international calls, 10 for operator assistance for calls in Ireland, Northern Ireland, and U.K.). **Northern Ireland and the U.K.** (☎ 192 for directory inquiries in Northern Ireland and U.K., 153 for international directory inquiries, which includes the republic, 155 for the international operator, 100 for operator assistance for calls in U.K. and Northern Ireland).

Public phones take either coins or cards, but not both. Card phones are rapidly replacing coin-operated phones, and are also cheaper. Phone cards can be bought at newsagents, convenience stores, and post offices in units of €5 upwards. It's worth carrying one, especially in rural areas where coin-operated phones are a rarity. In the republic, €0.40 will buy you a three-minute local call; around €1.50 is needed for a three-minute long-distance call within the republic. In Northern Ireland, a local call costs 20p.

To make a local call, just dial the number direct. To make a long-distance call, dial the area code, then the number. The local code for Northern Ireland is 028, unless you're dialing from the republic, in which case you dial 048 or 004428, followed by the eight-digit number.

CALLING OUTSIDE IRELAND

The country code for the United States is 1.

The international prefix from Ireland is 00. For calls to Great Britain (except Northern Ireland), dial 0044 before the exchange code, and drop the initial zero of the local code. For the United States and Canada dial 001, for Australia 0061, and for New Zealand 0064.

Access Codes AT&T Direct (☎ 1800/550–000 from Republic of Ireland, 0500/890–011 from Northern Ireland). MCI WorldPhone (☎ 1800/551–001 from Republic of Ireland, 0800/890–222 from Northern Ireland using British Telecom [BT], 0500/890–222 using Cable & Wireless [C&W]). Sprint International Access (☎ 1800/552–001 from Republic of Ireland, 0800/890–877 from Northern Ireland using BT, 0500/890–877 using C&W).

CALLING CARDS

"Callcards" are sold in post offices and newsagents. These range in price from €5 to €30.

MOBILE PHONES

If you have a multiband phone (some countries use different frequencies than what's used in the United States) and your service provider uses the world-standard GSM network (as do T-Mobile, Cingular, and Verizon), you can probably use your phone abroad. Roaming fees can be steep, however: 99¢ a minute is considered reasonable. And overseas you normally pay the toll charges for incoming calls. It's almost always cheaper to send a text message than to make a call, since text messages have a very low set fee (often less than 5¢).

If you just want to make local calls, consider buying a new SIM card (note that your provider may have to unlock your phone for you to use a different SIM card) and a prepaid service plan in the destination. You'll then have a local number and can make local calls at local rates. If your trip is extensive, you could also simply buy a new cell phone in your des-

tination, as the initial cost will be offset over time.

■TIP➜ If you travel internationally frequently, save one of your old mobile phones or buy a cheap one on the Internet; ask your cell phone company to unlock it for you, and take it with you as a travel phone, buying a new SIM card with pay-as-you-go service in each destination.

Contacts Cellular Abroad (☎ 800/287–5072 ⊕ www.cellularabroad.com) rents and sells GMS phones and sells SIM cards that work in many countries. Mobal (☎ 888/888–9162 ⊕ www.mobalrental.com) rents mobiles and sells GSM phones (starting at $49) that will operate in 140 countries. Per-call rates vary throughout the world. Planet Fone (☎ 888/988–4777 ⊕ www.planetfone.com) rents cell phones, but the per-minute rates are expensive.

∎ CUSTOMS AND DUTIES

You're always allowed to bring goods of a certain value back home without having to pay any duty or import tax. But there's a limit on the amount of tobacco and liquor you can bring back duty-free, and some countries have separate limits for perfumes; for exact figures, check with your customs department. The values of so-called "duty-free" goods are included in these amounts. When you shop abroad, save all your receipts, as customs inspectors may ask to see them as well as the items you purchased. If the total value of your goods is more than the duty-free limit, you'll have to pay a tax (most often a flat percentage) on the value of everything beyond that limit.

Duty-free allowances have been abolished for those traveling between countries in the EU. For goods purchased outside the EU, you may import duty-free: (1) 200 cigarettes or 100 cigarillos or 50 cigars or 250 grams of smoking tobacco; (2) 2 liters of wine, and either 1 liter of alcoholic drink over 22% volume or 2 liters of alcoholic drink under 22% volume (sparkling or fortified wine included); (3)

50 grams (60 ml) of perfume and ¼ liter of eau de toilette; and (4) other goods (including beer) to a value of €175 per person (€90 per person for travelers under 15 years of age).

Goods that cannot be freely imported to the Irish Republic include firearms, ammunition, explosives, indecent or obscene books and pictures, oral smokeless tobacco products, meat and meat products, poultry and poultry products. Plants and plant products (including shrubs, vegetables, fruit, bulbs, and seeds) can be imported from other countries within the EU only, provided they are eligible under the EU's plant passport scheme. Domestic cats and dogs from outside the United Kingdom and live animals from outside Northern Ireland must be quarantined for six months, unless they are traveling under the EU's Pet Travel Scheme.

Information in Ireland Customs and Excise (✉ *Irish Life Building, 2nd fl., Middle Abbey St., Dublin* ☎ *01/878-8811* ⊕ *www.revenue.ie*). **HM Customs and Excise** (✉ *Portcullis House, 21 Cowbridge Rd. E, Cardiff* ☎ *0845/010-9000, 0208/929-0152, 0208/929-6731, 0208/910-3602 complaints* ⊕ *www.hmce.gov.uk*).

For details of the **Pet Travel Scheme** see (⊕ *www.agriculture.gov.ie*).

U.S. Information U.S. Customs and Border Protection (⊕ *www.cbp.gov*).

▌ EATING OUT

MEALS AND MEALTIMES
Unless otherwise noted, the restaurants listed in this guide are open daily for lunch and dinner.

No longer will you "enjoy" your favorite tipple in the blue haze of a smoke-filled pub. The Republic of Ireland became the first European country to ban smoking in all pubs and restaurants in March 2004. A smoking ban was introduced in Northern Ireland in 2007.

Breakfast is served from 7 to 10, lunch runs from 12:30 to 2:30, and dinners are usually mid-evening occasions.

Pubs are generally open Monday and Tuesday 10:30 AM–11:30 PM and Wednesday–Saturday 10:30 AM–12:30 AM. On Sunday, pubs are open 12:30 PM–11 PM or later on certain Sundays. All pubs close on Christmas Day and Good Friday, but hotel bars are open for guests.

Pubs in Northern Ireland are open 11:30 AM–11 PM Monday–Saturday and 12:30 PM–2:30 PM and 7 PM–10 PM on Sunday (note that Sunday openings are at the owner's or manager's discretion).

PAYING
Traveler's checks and credit cards are widely accepted, although it's cash-only at smaller pubs and takeout restaurants. Note that in Dublin, Southeast, and Southwest chapters prices are a few euros higher.

For guidelines on tipping see Tipping, below.

RESERVATIONS AND DRESS
Regardless of where you are, it's a good idea to make a reservation if you can. In some places, it's expected. We mention them specifically only when reservations are essential (there's no other way you'll ever get a table) or when they are not accepted. For popular restaurants, book as far ahead as you can (often 30 days), and reconfirm as soon as you arrive. (Large parties should always call ahead to check the reservations policy.) We mention dress only when men are required to wear a jacket or a jacket and tie.

WINES, BEER, AND SPIRITS
All types of alcoholic beverages are available in Ireland. Beer and wine are sold in shops and supermarkets, and you can get drinks "to go" at some bars, although at inflated prices. Stout (Guinness, Murphy's, Beamish) is the Irish beer; whiskey comes in many brands, the most notable being Bushmills and Jameson, and is smoother and more blended than Scotch.

LANGUAGE DOS AND TABOOS

In the old days, Ireland's native language was called Gaelic and some people chuckled that it was the world's most perfect medium for prayers, curses, and lovemaking.

These days, Gaelic is called Irish and no one is joking any longer.

In March 2005, legislation was passed to restore the sovereignty of Irish, originally a Celtic language related to Scots Gaelic, Breton, and Welsh, as Ireland's official national language.

English is technically the second language of the country but it is, in fact, the everyday tongue of 95% of the population.

However, the western coastlands of Ireland are still home to the Gaeltacht (pronounced *gale*-taukt).

These Irish-speaking communities are found mainly in sparsely populated rural areas along the western seaboard, on some islands, and in pockets in West Cork and County Waterford.

Travelers to these western seaboard regions in counties Donegal and Galway should note that new laws have mandated Irish as the sole language for signage.

In these Gaeltacht areas, English is now outlawed in road signs and official maps.

As the Associated Press reported, "Locals concede the switch will confuse foreigners in an area that depends heavily on tourism, but they say it's the price of patriotism."

The Gaeltacht includes some big tourist destinations.

For instance, if travelers are in Killarney and now wish to go to Dingle, they will have to follow signposts that say AN DAINGEAN, which is Dingle in Irish. Other instances include: Oileáin Árainn (Aran Islands); Corca Dhuibne (Dingle Peninsula); and Arainn Mhor (Aranmore Island).

As this changeover affects more than 2,000 other place-names, have an updated or Irish-friendly map if touring these Gaeltacht regions. Don't rely on official Ordnance Survey maps, which can now print only Irish place-names in these areas.

This is even in cases where the English versions remain popular in local parlance (many hotels will retain their English names, such as the Dingle Bay Hotel).

Main place-names are given in both Irish and English in this guidebook for the affected regions.

Outside these Gaeltacht areas, Ireland remains officially bilingual in its road signs.

"This will allow you to get lost in both Irish and English," as Mr. O'Reilly pointed out on Fodor's Talk Forums on their Web site.

With just 55,000 native Irish speakers in a population of 4 million, a major national debate has sprung up, with local councils and tourist authorities beginning to protest the new laws. (You can follow the debate by searching online for "Official Languages Act 2003". Of course, some basic Irish vocabulary certainly wouldn't hurt: *fir* (men) and *mná* (women) should prove useful when inquiring about public restrooms.

■ ELECTRICITY

The current in Ireland is 220 volts, 50 cycles alternating current (AC); wall outlets take plugs with three prongs.

Consider making a small investment in a universal adapter, which has several types of plugs in one lightweight, compact unit. Most laptops and mobile phone chargers are dual voltage (i.e., they operate equally well on 110 and 220 volts), so require only an adapter. These days the same is true of small appliances such as hair dryers. Always check labels and manufacturer instructions to be sure. Don't use 110-volt outlets marked FOR SHAVERS ONLY for high-wattage appliances such as hair dryers.

Contacts Steve Kropla's Help for World Travelers (⊕ *www.kropla.com*) has information on electrical and telephone plugs around the world.

■ EMERGENCIES

The police force in the Republic of Ireland is called the Garda Síochána ("Guardians of the Peace," in English), usually referred to as the Gardaí (pronounced gar-*dee*). The force is unarmed and is headed by a government-appointed commissioner, who is answerable to the Minister for Justice, who in turn is accountable to the Dáil (the Irish legislature). Easily identified by their fluorescent yellow blazers in winter, or, if weather permits in summer, by a dark blue shirt and peaked cap, the Gardaí are generally very helpful. They, and all other emergency forces, can be contacted by dialing 999 (in the Republic of Ireland, 112, the European standard, is also in use). These numbers will connect you with local police, ambulance, and fire services. You can expect a prompt response to your call. The Garda Síochána Web site provides contact information for local stations. In Northern Ireland the police force is the Police Service of Northern Ireland (PSNI). They are distinguished by their dark blue coats and white shirts.

They can be contacted by dialing 999 in Northern Ireland.

United States Embassy (⊠ *42 Elgin Rd., Ballsbridge, Dublin* ☎ *01/668–7122* ⊠ **United States Consulate General** ⊠ *Danesfort House, 223 Stranmills Rd., Belfast* ☎ *028/9038–61009*).

General Emergency Contacts Ambulance, fire, police (☎). **An Garda Síochána** (⊕ *www.garda.ie*). **Police Service of Northern Ireland** (⊕ *www.psni.police.uk*).

■ GUIDED TOURS

Guided tours are a good option when you don't want to do it all yourself. The companies below all offer tours to Ireland on a "land-only" basis. A "land-only" tour includes all your travel (by bus, in most cases) once you arrive in the destination country, but not necessarily your flights to your destination. And remember that you'll be expected to tip your guide (in cash) at the end of the tour.

GENERAL TOURS

CIE Tours International is one of the biggest and longest-established (75 years) tour operators in the Irish market. They offer a selection of fully inclusive, escorted bus tours, or independent fly-drive vacations. An eight-day itinerary with car rental and confirmed hotel bookings starts at $607 per person, with two people traveling. The Heritage Tour is an eight-day bus tour, starting with two nights in Dublin, and taking in Bunratty Castle and Folk Park, Blarney Castle, the Cliffs of Moher, the Skellig

Experience, and the lakes of Killarney, among other attractions, with accommodation in top hotels.

Myguideireland, a young company set up by three friends on their return to Ireland from living and working in Philadelphia, aims to create the best holiday experience by using enthusiastic local guides. A customized seven-day self-drive tour across Ireland starts from $478 per person, with two people traveling. The price includes six nights at a B&B, car rental, and toll-free calls to your vacation specialist. Escorted bus tours include the Irish Jaunt, which includes one day in Dublin, a drive to Blarney Castle via the Rock of Cashel, Killarney, the Ring of Kerry, and the Cliffs of Moher, and offers five days, four nights, five meals, and accommodation in superior hotels, and costs from $640 per person.

Contacts CIE Tours International (☎ *1800/243–8687* ⊕ *www.cietours.com*). **myguideireland** (☎ *1800/255–9302* ⊕ *www. myguideireland.com*).

SPECIAL-INTEREST TOURS
BIKING
Irish Cycling Safaris pioneered cycling holidays in Ireland, and offer easygoing to moderate cycling trips along rural back roads with luggage transfer and accommodation in small family-run hotels and guesthouses. A weeklong tour of the Beara Peninsula in County Cork costs €670 per person sharing. Tour groups are accompanied by a local guide who drives the support van. Alternatively, you can opt for a self-led tour that includes bike rental, itinerary, and prebooked accommodation, also €670 per person sharing.

Iron Donkey gets raves from Fodor's readers. Offering something for everyone from novices to hammerheads, their mainstay are guided group tours: for instance, the Clare and Burren itinerary sets out from Ennis and includes Kilkee, Loop Head, Spanish Point, the Cliffs of Moher, the Burren coastline, and Bunratty Castle (cost is about €900 per person sharing). But others swear by the super-thorough and well-run custom tours, where they meet you at the first lodging (all great options, incidentally) with your bikes and size them to you, go over your route, and beautifully prep you for the ride.

■TIP→ Most airlines accommodate bikes as luggage, provided they're dismantled and boxed.

Contacts Irish Cycling Safaris (☎ *01/260– 0749* ⊕ *www.cyclingsafaris.com*). **Iron Donkey** (☎ *028/908–13200* ⊕ *www.irondonkey.com*).

CULTURE
Adams & Butler is Ireland's leading purveyor of customized vacations, with an unbeatable range of contacts in the upper end of the market. Most of their tours are customized for small groups in chauffeur-driven cars or on small luxury buses. They can offer you a week in Ireland with a self-drive car, with and itinerary and B&B in 4-star luxury hotels from $599; up that price to $4,000 per person for a luxury hotel with driver guide and 5-star accommodation. Should you prefer to travel by helicopter and stay in the presidential suites of Ireland's top hotels your week could run to $48,000. Charter a whole country house hotel for the family, or stay in a smaller historic or haunted house: whatever your whim, Adams & Butler will be able to indulge it—or so they say.

Contacts Adams & Butler (☎ *1800/894– 5712 or 3531/288–9355* ⊕ *www. adamsandbutler.com*).

GOLF
Executive Golf and Leisure, Scotland-based golf specialists, offer customized golf breaks or packages, such as a six-day golf tour of Ireland for $6,540 with luxury accommodation, transfers, and rounds on some of the finest courses: the K Club, Old Portmarnock, Royal Dublin, Waterville, Tralee, and the Old Head of Kinsale.

Golfbreaks.com will customize a golf tour for you, and also have tours of different regions of Ireland. Their Northern Ireland and the Northwest package includes rounds at the legendary Royal County Down and Royal Portrush courses.

Contacts Executive Golf and Leisure (☎ 1877/295–2247 or 044/1786/832–244 ⊕ www.execgolf-leisure.com). **Golfbreaks.com** (☎ 0800/279–7988 ⊕ www.golfbreaks.com).

HIKING

Isle Inn offers self-drive holidays and escorted tours, and has an interesting range of activity holidays and escorted hiking holidays averaging 10 to 12 mi a day, staying in family-run guesthouses and characterful small hotels, while walking through scenic areas, including Donegal coast, the Glens of Antrim, and Achill island and Mayo. The Yoga Trek starts at $1,405, while escorted hiking holidays start from $1,320 and cycling from $855. Savor the Journey (from $1,539) combines culture and cuisine, offering six nights at top hotels with three gourmet dinners and a driver to escort you.

Contacts Isle Inn (☎ 1800/237–9376 ⊕ www.isleinntours.com).

RAIL

Railtours Ireland uses the Irish railway network for major transfers, and coaches for sightseeing at the destination, avoiding long, leg-numbing stretches of coach travel. The five-day tour starts with a train ride from Dublin to Cork (2 hours, 45 minutes) including breakfast, and continues with a bus tour to Blarney, train to Killarney, bus tour of the Ring of Kerry, and also visits Galway, the Cliffs of Moher, and Connemara, starting at €599 per person, with accommodation in B&Bs and modest hotels.

Contacts Railtours Ireland (☎ 3531/856–0045 ⊕ www.railtoursireland.com).

■ HOURS OF OPERATION

Business hours are 9–5, sometimes later in the larger towns. In smaller towns, stores often close from 1 to 2 for lunch. If a holiday falls on a weekend, most businesses are closed on Monday.

Banks are open 10–4 weekdays. In small towns banks may close from 12:30 to 1:30. They remain open until 5 one afternoon per week; the day varies but it's usually Thursday. Post offices are open weekdays 9–5 and Saturday 9–1; some of the smaller branches close for lunch.

In Northern Ireland bank hours are weekdays 9:30–4:30. Post offices are open weekdays 9–5:30, Saturday 9–1. Some close for an hour at lunch (1–2).

There are some 24-hour gas stations along the highways; otherwise, hours vary from morning rush hour to late evenings.

Museums and sights are generally open Tuesday–Saturday 10–5 and Sunday 2–5.

Most pharmacies are open Monday–Saturday 9–5:30 or 6. Larger towns and cities often have 24-hour establishments.

Most shops are open Monday–Saturday 9–5:30 or 6. Once a week—normally Wednesday, Thursday, or Saturday—shops close at 1 PM. These times do *not* apply to Dublin, where stores generally stay open later, and they can vary from region to region, so it's best to check locally. Larger malls usually stay open late once a week—generally until 9 on Thursday or Friday. Convenience stores, supermarkets, and gas stations in both Dublin and rural Ireland are generally open until 8 or 9 PM.

Shops in Belfast are open weekdays 9–5:30, with a late closing on Thursday, usually at 9. Elsewhere in Northern Ireland, shops close for the afternoon once a week, usually Wednesday or Thursday. In addition, most smaller shops close for an hour or so at lunch.

HOLIDAYS

Irish national holidays in 2011 are as follows: January 3 (New Year's Day); March 17 (St. Patrick's Day); April 22 (Good Friday); April 25 (Easter Monday); May 2 (May Day); June 6 and August 2 (summer bank holidays); October 31 (autumn bank holiday); and December 25, 26, and 27 (Christmas and St. Stephen's Day). If you plan to visit at Easter, remember that theaters and cinemas are closed for the last three days of the preceding week.

In Northern Ireland the following are holidays: January 3 (New Year's Day); March 17 (St. Patrick's Day); April 22 (Good Friday); April 25 (Easter Monday); May 2 (early May bank holiday); May 30 (spring bank holiday); July 12 (Battle of the Boyne); August 29 (summer bank holiday); and December 25, 26, and 27 (Christmas and Boxing Day).

▌ MAIL

Outside of Dublin and Northern Ireland, postal codes aren't used; what's more important here is the county, so be sure to include it when addressing an envelope.

Letters by standard post take a week to 10 days to reach the United States and Canada, 3 to 5 days to reach the United Kingdom.

Airmail rates to the United States and Canada from the Irish Republic are €0.82 for letters and postcards. Rates are also €0.82 for letters and postcards to Europe. Mail to overseas can be sent economy or airmail. Letters and postcards within the Irish Republic cost €0.55.

Rates from Northern Ireland are 56p for letters and postcards (not over 10 grams) to continental Europe, and 62p to the United States and Canada, Australia, and New Zealand. To the rest of the United Kingdom and the Irish Republic, rates are 39p for first-class letters and 30p for second-class.

Mail can be held for collection at any post office for free for up to three months. It should be addressed to the recipient "c/o Poste Restante." In Dublin, use the General Post Office. The postal service in the Reuplic of Ireland, known as An Post, has a Web site with a branch locator and loads of other postal information. In Northern Ireland mail service is run by the Royal Mail.

Contact **An Post** (⊕ *www.anpost.ie*). **General Post Office** (✉ *O'Connell St., Dublin* ☎ *01/705–8833*).

▌ MONEY

A modest hotel in Dublin costs about €140 a night for two; this figure can be reduced to under €90 by staying in a registered guesthouse or inn, and reduced to about €70 by staying in a suburban B&B. Lunch, consisting of a good one-dish plate of bar food at a pub, costs around €10–€14; a sandwich at the same pub costs about €5. In Dublin's better restaurants, dinner will run €45–€60 (dinner being a three-course meal) per person, excluding drinks and tip.

Theater and entertainment in most places are inexpensive—about €18 for a good seat, and double or triple that for a bigname, pop-music concert. For the price of a few drinks and (in Dublin and Killarney) a small entrance fee of about €2, you can spend a memorable evening at a *seisun* (pronounced say-*shoon* when referring to this folk music session), in a music pub. Entrance to most public galleries is free, but stately homes and similar attractions charge anywhere from €4 to a whopping €12 per person.

Just about everything is more expensive in Dublin, so add at least 10% to these sample prices: cup of coffee, €2; pint of beer, €5; soda, €2.40; and 2-km (1-mi) taxi ride, €8. Due to the exchange rate, Canadians, Australians, New Zealanders, Americans, and U.K. residents will find Ireland a little pricey when they convert costs to their home currency.

Hotels and meals in Northern Ireland are less expensive than in the United Kingdom and the Republic of Ireland. Also, the lower level of taxation makes taxable goods such as gasoline, alcoholic drinks, and tobacco cheaper.

Prices throughout this guide are given for adults. Substantially reduced fees are almost always available for children, students, and senior citizens.

■TIP➜ Banks never have every foreign currency on hand, and it may take as long as a week to order. If you're planning to exchange funds before leaving home, don't wait till the last minute.

ATMS AND BANKS

Your own bank will probably charge a fee for using ATMs abroad; the foreign bank you use may also charge a fee. Nevertheless, you'll usually get a better rate of exchange at an ATM than you will at a currency-exchange office or even when changing money in a bank. And extracting funds as you need them is a safer option than carrying around a large amount of cash.

■TIP➜ PINs with more than four digits are not recognized at ATMs in many countries. If yours has five or more, remember to change it before you leave.

ATMs are found in all major towns and are, by far, the easiest way to keep yourself stocked with euros and pounds. Most major banks are connected to Cirrus or PLUS systems; there's a four-digit maximum for your PIN.

CREDIT CARDS

Throughout this guide, the following abbreviations are used: **AE,** American Express; **DC,** Diners Club; **MC,** Master-Card; and **V,** Visa.

It's a good idea to inform your credit-card company before you travel, especially if you're going abroad and don't travel internationally very often. Otherwise, the credit-card company might put a hold on your card owing to unusual activity—not a good thing halfway through your trip. Record all your credit-card numbers—as well as the phone numbers to call if your cards are lost or stolen—in a safe place, so you're prepared should something go wrong. Both MasterCard and Visa have general numbers you can call (collect if you're abroad) if your card is lost, but you're better off calling the number of your issuing bank, since MasterCard and

Visa usually just transfer you to your bank; your bank's number is usually printed on your card.

If you plan to use your credit card for cash advances, you'll need to apply for a PIN at least two weeks before your trip. Although it's usually cheaper (and safer) to use a credit card abroad for large purchases (so you can cancel payments or be reimbursed if there's a problem), note that some credit-card companies *and* the banks that issue them add substantial percentages to all foreign transactions, whether they're in a foreign currency or not. Check on these fees before leaving home, so there won't be any surprises when you get the bill.

When using your credit card, check that the merchant is putting the transaction through in euros or pounds sterling. If he or she puts it through in the currency of your home country—a transaction called a dynamic currency conversion—the exchange rate might be less favorable and the service charges higher than if you allow the credit-card company to do the conversion for you. Be sure to ask at the time, and insist on being billed in euros to get the most advantageous rate and avoid the service charge.

Reporting Lost Cards American Express (☎ 800/992–3404 in U.S. or 336/393–1111 collect from abroad ⊕ www.americanexpress. com). **Diners Club** (☎ 800/234–6377 in U.S. or 303/799–1504 collect from abroad ⊕ www. dinersclub.com). **MasterCard** (☎ 800/622–7747 in U.S. or 636/722-7111 collect from abroad ⊕ www.mastercard.com). **Visa** (☎ 800/847–2911 in U.S. or 410/581–9994 collect from abroad ⊕ www.visa.com).

CURRENCY AND EXCHANGE

The Irish Republic is a member of the European Monetary Union (EMU). Euro notes come in denominations of €500, €200, €100, €50, €20, €10, and €5. The euro is divided into 100 cents, and coins are available as €2 and €1 and 50, 20, 10, 5, 2, and 1 cent.

The unit of currency in Northern Ireland is the pound sterling (£), divided into 100 pence (p). The bills (called notes) are 50, 20, 10, and 5 pounds. Coins are £2, £1, 50p, 20p, 10p, 5p, 2p, and 1p. The bank of Northern Ireland prints its own notes, which look different from the English or Scottish Sterling.

Check out today's rates at ⊕ *www.oanda. com.*

At this writing, €1 is equal to U.S. $1.35. One pound sterling is equal to U.S. $1.5. Rates fluctuate regularly, though, particularly for the euro, so monitor them closely.

■TIP➔ **Even if a currency-exchange booth has a sign promising no commission, rest assured that there's some kind of huge, hidden fee. (Oh . . . that's right. The sign didn't say no *fee*.) And as for rates, you're almost always better off getting foreign currency at an ATM or exchanging money at a bank.**

TRAVELER'S CHECKS AND CARDS

Some consider this the currency of the cave man, and it's true that fewer establishments accept traveler's checks these days. Nevertheless, they're a cheap and secure way to carry extra money, particularly on trips to urban areas. Both Citibank (under the Visa brand) and American Express issue traveler's checks in the United States, but Amex is better known and more widely accepted; you can also avoid hefty surcharges by cashing Amex checks at Amex offices. Whatever you do, keep track of all the serial numbers in case the checks are lost or stolen.

Contacts American Express (✆ *888/412– 6945 in U.S., 801/945–9450 collect outside of U.S. to add value or speak to customer service ⊕ www.americanexpress.com).*

▌PACKING

In Ireland you can experience all four seasons in a day. There can be damp chilly stretches even in July and August, the warmest months of the year. Layers are the best way to go. Pack several long- and short-sleeve T-shirts (in winter, some should be thermal or silk), a sweatshirt, a lightweight sweater, a heavyweight sweater, and a hooded, waterproof windbreaker that's large enough to go over several layers if necessary. A portable umbrella is absolutely essential, and the smaller and lighter it is, the better, as you'll want it with you every second. You should bring at least two pairs of walking shoes; footwear can get soaked in minutes and then take hours to dry.

The Irish are generally informal about clothes. In the more expensive hotels and restaurants people dress formally for dinner, and a jacket and tie may be required in bars after 7 PM, but very few places operate a strict dress policy. Old or tattered blue jeans and running shoes are forbidden in certain bars and dance clubs.

If you're used to packing things or stowing dirty clothes in plastic shopping or drawstring bags, bring your own. About the only place you can find the latter here is in the closets of better hotel rooms (for on-site dry cleaning and laundry). Plastic bags carry a 22¢ government levy and can be sold by supermarkets, but it's illegal to give them away. Most stores use paper bags or recycle boxes.

▌PASSPORTS

All U.S. citizens, even infants, need a valid passport to enter Ireland for stays of up to 90 days. Citizens of the United Kingdom, when traveling on flights departing from Great Britain, do not need a passport to enter Ireland but it's advisable to carry some form of photo ID. Passport requirements for Northern Ireland are the same as for the republic.

We're always surprised at how few Americans have passports—only 25% at this writing. This number is expected to grow in coming years, now that it is impossible to reenter the United States from trips to neighboring Canada or Mexico without one.

U.S. passports are valid for 10 years. You must apply in person if you're getting a passport for the first time; if your previous passport was lost, stolen, or damaged; or if your previous passport has expired and was issued more than 15 years ago or when you were under 16. All children under 18 must appear in person to apply for or renew a passport. Both parents must accompany any child under 14 (or send a notarized statement with their permission) and provide proof of their relationship to the child.

■TIP→ Before your trip, make two copies of your passport's data page (one for someone at home and another for you to carry separately). Or scan the page and e-mail it to someone at home and/or yourself.

There are 13 regional passport offices, as well as 7,000 passport acceptance facilities in post offices, public libraries, and other governmental offices. If you're renewing a passport, you can do so by mail. Forms are available at passport acceptance facilities and online.

The cost to apply for a new passport is $100 for adults, $85 for children under 16; renewals are $75. Allow six weeks for processing, both for first-time passports and renewals. For an expediting fee of $60 you can reduce this time to about two weeks. If your trip is less than two weeks away, you can get a passport even more rapidly by going to a passport office with the necessary documentation. Private expediters can get things done in as little as 48 hours, but charge hefty fees for their services.

U.S. Passport Information U.S. Department of State (☎ 877/487-2778 ⊕ http://travel. state.gov/passport).

U.S. Passport and Visa Expediters A. Briggs Passport & Visa Expeditors (☎ 800/806-0581 or 202/464-3000 ⊕ www. abriggs.com). American Passport Express (☎ 800/455-5166 or 603/559-9888 ⊕ www. americanpassport.com). Passport Express (☎ 800/362-8196 or 401/272-4612 ⊕ www. passportexpress.com). Travel Document

Systems (☎ 800/874-5100 or 202/638-3800 ⊕ www.traveldocs.com). Travel the World Visas (☎ 866/886-8472 or 301/495-7700 ⊕ www.world-visa.com).

■ RENTAL CARS

When you reserve a car, ask about cancellation penalties, taxes, drop-off charges (if you're planning to pick up the car in one city and leave it in another), and surcharges (for being under or over a certain age, for additional drivers, or for driving across state or country borders or beyond a specific distance from your point of rental). All these things can add substantially to your costs. Request car seats and extras such as GPS when you book.

Rates are sometimes—but not always—better if you book in advance or reserve through a rental agency's Web site. There are other reasons to book ahead, though: for popular destinations, during busy times of the year, or to ensure that you get certain types of cars (vans, SUVs, exotic sports cars).

■TIP→ Make sure that a confirmed reservation guarantees you a car. Agencies sometimes overbook, particularly for busy weekends and holiday periods.

If you're renting a car in the Irish Republic and intend to visit Northern Ireland (or vice versa), make this clear when you get your car, and check that the rental insurance applies when you cross the border.

Renting a car in Ireland is far more expensive than organizing a rental before you leave home. Rates in Dublin for an economy car with a manual transmission and unlimited mileage are from €35 a day and €160 a week to €50 a day and €190 a week, depending on the season. This includes the republic's 12.5% tax on car rentals. Rates in Belfast begin at £25 a day and £130 a week, including the 17.5% tax on car rentals in the North.

Both manual and automatic transmissions are readily available, though automatics cost extra. Typical economy car models include Volkswagen Lupo, Ford Focus, Fiat Panda, and Nissan Micra. Minivans, luxury cars (Mercedes or Alfa Romeos), and four-wheel-drive vehicles (say, a Jeep Cherokee) are also options, but the daily rates are high. Argus Rent A Car and Dan Dooley have convenient locations at Dublin, Shannon, Belfast, and Belfast City airports as well as at ferry ports.

Most rental companies require you to be over 24 to rent a car in Ireland (a few will rent to those over 21) and to have had a license for more than a year. Some companies refuse to rent to visitors over 70, or in some cases, 74. Children under 12 years of age aren't allowed to ride in the front seat unless they're in a properly fitted child seat.

Drivers between the ages of 21 and 26, and 70 and 76 will probably be subject to an insurance surcharge—if they're allowed to drive a rental car at all. An additional driver will add about €5 a day to your car rental, and a child seat costs about €20 for the rental and will require 24-hour advance notice.

Your driver's license may not be recognized outside your home country. You may not be able to rent a car without an International Driving Permit (IDP), which can be used only in conjunction with a valid driver's license and which translates your license into 10 languages. Check the AAA Web site for more info as well as for IDPs ($10) themselves. Happily, U.S. driver's licenses are recognized in Ireland.

CAR RENTAL RESOURCES

Local Agencies Local and international car hire companies in both the Republic and Northern Ireland are listed on ⊕ *www. carhireireland.com.* **Argus Rent A Car** (☏ *499–9608 in Dublin, 048/9442–3444 in Belfast* ⊕ *www.argus-rentacar.com).* **Dan Dooley Car Rentals** (☏ *800/331–9301 in U.S., 0800/282–189 in U.K., 062/53103 in Ireland* ⊕ *www.dan-dooley.ie).*

Major Agencies Alamo (☏ *800/522–9696, 1800/301–401 in Ireland, 01/260–3771 in Dublin* ⊕ *www.alamo.com).* **Avis**

(☏ *800/331–1084, 1890/405–060 in Ireland, 01/605–7500 in Dublin* ⊕ *www.avis.com).* **Budget** (☏ *800/472–3325, 1850/575–767 in Ireland* ⊕ *www.budget.com).* **Dollar** (☏ *800/800–6000 in U.S., 01/670–7890 in Dublin* ⊕ *www.dollar.com).* **Hertz** (☏ *800/654– 3001, 01/676–7476 in Ireland* ⊕ *www.hertz. com).* **National Car Rental** (☏ *800/227–7368, 01/844–4162 in Dublin, 1800/301–401 in Ireland* ⊕ *www.nationalcar.com).*

Wholesalers Auto Europe (☏ *888/223–5555* ⊕ *www.autoeurope.com).* **Europe by Car** (☏ *800/223–1516, 212/581–3040 in New York* ⊕ *www.europebycar.com).* **Eurovacations** (☏ *877/471–3876* ⊕ *www.eurovacations.com).* **Kemwel** (☏ *877/820–0668* ⊕ *www.kemwel. com).*

▌ RESTROOMS

Public restrooms are in short supply in Ireland. They'll be easy enough to find in public places such as airports, train stations, and shopping malls, but if you don't find yourself in one of these locations your best bet is to look for the nearest pub (never more than a few minutes away in Ireland!). Restrooms are often labeled in Irish—FIR (men) and MNÁ (women). Pubs are increasingly putting up signs saying that restrooms are for customers only— but this is difficult to enforce. If it's outside of shopping or pub hours your last option may be the nearest hotel. Most gas stations will have toilets available. Only toilets in hotels or shopping centers will be up to a polished North American standard. Although many toilets look well-worn they are generally clean. Unfortunately, few toilets are heated and an open window is typically used for ventilation, making for uncomfortably cold restrooms in the colder months.

Find a Loo The Bathroom Diaries (⊕ *www. thebathroomdiaries.com*) is flush with unsanitized info on restrooms the world over—each one located, reviewed, and rated.

▌TAXES

When leaving the Irish Republic, U.S. and Canadian visitors get a refund of the value-added tax (V.A.T.), which currently accounts for a hefty 21% of the purchase price of many goods and 13.5% of those that fall outside the luxury category. Apart from clothing, most items of interest to visitors, right down to ordinary toilet soap, are rated at 21%. V.A.T. is not refundable on accommodation, car rental, meals, or any other form of personal services received on vacation.

Many crafts outlets and department stores operate a system that enables U.S. and Canadian visitors to collect V.A.T. rebates in the currency of their choice at Dublin or Shannon Airport on departure. Some stores give you the rebate at the register; with others you claim your refund after you've returned home. Refund forms, known as a Tax-Free Shopping Cheque, must be picked up at the time of purchase, and they must be stamped by customs, and mailed back to the store before you leave for home. It may take months for your refund to be processed. Many merchants work with a service such as Global Refund, which has offices at major ports and airports, and will refund your money immediately in return for a 4% fee. If a store gives you a refund at the register, you'll also be given papers to have stamped by customs; you'll then put the papers in an envelope (also provided by the store) and mail it before you leave. Most major stores deduct V.A.T. at the time of sale if goods are to be shipped overseas; however, there's a shipping charge.

When leaving Northern Ireland, U.S. and Canadian visitors can also get a refund of the 17.5% V.A.T. by the over-the-counter and the direct-export methods. Most larger stores provide these services on request and will handle the paperwork. For the over-the-counter method, you must spend more than £75 in one store. Ask the store for Form V.A.T. 407 (you must have identification—passports are best), to be given to customs when you leave the country. The refund will be forwarded to you in about eight weeks (minus a small service charge) either in the form of a sterling check or as a credit to your charge card. The direct-export method, where the goods are shipped directly to your home, is more cumbersome. V.A.T. Form 407/1/93 must be certified by customs, police, or a notary public when you get home and then sent back to the store, which will refund your money.

When making a purchase, ask for a V.A.T. refund form and find out whether the merchant gives refunds—not all stores do, nor are they required to. Have the form stamped like any customs form by customs officials when you leave the country or, if you're visiting several European Union countries, when you leave the EU. After you're through passport control, take the form to a refund-service counter for an on-the-spot refund (which is usually the quickest and easiest option), or mail it to the address on the form (or the envelope with it) after you arrive home. You receive the total refund stated on the form, but the processing time can be long, especially if you request a credit-card adjustment.

Global Refund is a Europe-wide service with 225,000 affiliated stores and more than 700 refund counters at major airports and border crossings. Its refund form, called a Tax Free Check, is the most common across the European continent. The service issues refunds in the form of cash, check, or credit-card adjustment.

V.A.T. Refunds Global Refund (☎ *800/566–9828* ⊕ *www.globalrefund.com*).

▌TIME

Dublin is five hours ahead of New York and eight hours ahead of Los Angeles.

▌ TIPPING

In some hotels and restaurants a service charge of around 10%—rising to 15% in plush spots—is added to the bill. If in doubt, ask whether service is included. In places where it's included, tipping isn't necessary unless you have received particularly good service. If there's no service charge, add a minimum of 10% to the total. Taxi drivers or hackney cab drivers, who make the trip for a prearranged sum, don't expect tips. There are few porters and plenty of baggage trolleys at airports, so tipping is usually not an issue; if you use a porter, €1 is the minimum. Tip hotel porters at least €1 per suitcase. Hairdressers normally expect about 10% of the total spent. You don't tip in pubs, but for waiter service in a bar, a hotel lounge, or a Dublin lounge bar, leave about €1. It's not customary to tip for regular concierge service.

TIPPING GUIDELINES FOR IRELAND	
Bellhop	€1 to €2, depending on the level of the hotel
Hotel Concierge	€5 or more, if he or she performs a special service for you
Hotel Doorman	€1–€2 if he helps you get a cab
Hotel Maid	€1–€3 a day (either daily or at the end of your stay, in cash)
Hotel Room-Service Waiter	€1 to €2 per delivery, even if a service charge has been added
Taxi Driver	10%, or just round up the fare to the next euro amount
Tour Guide	10% of the cost of the tour
Valet Parking Attendant	€1–€2, but only when you get your car
Waiter	Just small change (up to a euro or two) to round out your bill if service is included
Restroom Attendant	Restroom attendants in more expensive restaurants expect some small change or €1.

▌ VISITOR INFORMATION

For information on travel in the Irish Republic, contact Tourism Ireland, the international marketing authority for Fáilte Ireland (pronounced *fal*-cha), as the tourist information network is called within the Republic of Ireland. They have two Web sites, one for people logging on internationally (⊕ *www.discoverireland. com*) and one for people logging on domestically (⊕ *www.discoverireland. com*). Information on travel in the north is available from the Northern Ireland Tourist Board.

Information Fáilte Ireland (✉ *88–95 Amiens St., Dublin* ☎ *01/884–7700, 1890/525–525 toll-free within Ireland* ⊕ *www.failteireland.ie*). **Northern Ireland Tourist Board** (NITB✉ *59 North St., Belfast* ☎ *028/9023–1221* ⊕ *www. discovernorthernireland.com*). **Tourism Ireland** (⊕ *www.discoverireland.com, www. discoverireland.ie*). **Tourism Ireland, Canada office** (✉ *2 Bloor St. W, Suite 1501, Toronto, Ontario* ☎ *416/925–6368 or 1800/223–6470*). **Tourism Ireland, U.K. office** (✉ *Nation House, 103 Wigmore St., London* ☎ *020/7518–0800 or 0800/039–7000* ⊕ *www.discoverireland.com*). **Tourism Ireland, U.S. office** (✉ *345 Park Ave., 17th fl., New York, NY* ☎ *212/418–0800 or 1800/223–6470* ⊕ *www.discoverireland.com*).

ONLINE TRAVEL TOOLS

The main Web site for the Irish tourist board, Tourism Ireland is ⊕ *www. discoverireland.com*; this is meant for people logging on internationally. Fáilte Ireland (the National Tourism Development Authority) sponsors Discover Ireland, at ⊕ *www.discoverireland.ie.*, which is geared for people logging on domestically. For lots of entertaining bits—Irish and otherwise—visit ⊕ *www.irishabroad.*

com. Some of the most popular sites are ⊕ *www.browseireland.com* and ⊕ *www. heritageireland.ie.* The Web site ⊕ *www. ireland-information.com* is dedicated to providing as many free resources and as much free information about Ireland as possible on an array of topics from genealogy to shopping. For a central directory of links to all things Irish, log on to ⊕ *www. finditireland.com.* Comhaltas Ceoltóirí Eireann is an association that promotes the music, culture, and art of Ireland, and its Web site ⊕ *www.comhaltas.ie* has helpful news about the Irish traditional music scene. For listings of all music, film, and theater events, see ⊕ *www.entertainment. ie.* For general information on Irish current affairs, sport, entertainment, and more log on to ⊕ *www.ireland.com.* Keep in mind that many of the leading newspapers of Ireland have Web sites, which can be gold mines of timely information. See, for example, the *Irish Times*' Web site, ⊕ *www.irishtimes.com.* For a weekly newsletter to keep Irish people abroad up-to-date on events at home, log on to ⊕ *www.emigrant.ie.*

Officially designated Heritage Towns are featured on ⊕ *www.heritagetowns. com.* A range of heritage attractions are flagged on ⊕ *www.heritageisland.com.* For information on arts events of all kinds, try ⊕ *www.art.ie,* which is affiliated with the arts councils of both the Irish Republic and Northern Ireland. For more information on counties in the west of Ireland, try ⊕ *www.discoverireland. com/west.* A handy regional site for the area near Shannon Airport is ⊕ *www. shannonregiontourism.com,* while ⊕ *www. visitdublin.com* has all you need to know about the capital. Portions of the Tourism Ireland's eloquent magazine, *Ireland of the Welcomes,* are available online at ⊕ *www.irelandofthewelcomes.com.* For an eloquent site devoted to some of Ireland's most historic houses, castles, and gardens see   ⊕ *www.castlesgardensireland.com,* while the castle lover will enjoy ⊕ *www.*

celticcastles.com. Food lovers should check out ⊕ *www.bordbia.ie.*

ALL ABOUT IRELAND

Currency Conversion Google (⊕ *www. google.com*) does currency conversion. Just type in the amount you want to convert and an explanation of how you want it converted (e.g., "14 Swiss francs in dollars"), and then voilà. **Oanda.com** (⊕ *www.oanda.com*) also allows you to print out a handy table with the current day's conversion rates. **XE.com** (⊕ *www.xe.com*) is a good currency conversion Web site.

Safety Transportation Security Administration (*TSA;* ⊕ *www.tsa.gov*).

Time Zones Timeanddate.com (⊕ *www. timeanddate.com/worldclock*) can help you figure out the correct time anywhere.

Weather Accuweather.com (⊕ *www. accuweather.com*) is an independent weather-forecasting service. **Weather.com** (⊕ *www. weather.com*) is the Web site for the Weather Channel.

Other Resources CIA World Factbook (⊕ *www.odci.gov/cia/library/publications/the-world-factbook*) has profiles of every country in the world. It's a good source if you need some quick facts and figures.

INDEX

PHOTO CREDITS

328, Loimere/Flickr. 330, AGITA LEIMANE/iStockphoto. 332, Eoghan Kavanagh/Tourism Ireland. 334, Ivica Drusany/Shutterstock. 342-43, Joe Gough/iStockphoto. 343 (left), Jonathan Hession/Tourism Ireland. 343 (right), John Brennan/iStockphoto. 344, Rambling Traveler/Flickr. 346 (top left), Tim Connor/iStockphoto. 346 (bottom left), Insuratelu Gabriela Gianina/Shutterstock. 346 (right), Giovanni Rinaldi/iStockphoto. 347 (top), Stephan Hoerold/iStockphoto. 347 (bottom left), ingmar wesemann/iStockphoto. 347 (bottom right), Ariel Cione/iStockphoto. 348 (top), Jonathan Hession/Tourism Ireland. 348 (middle left), Michael Steden/Shutterstock. 348 (middle right), Cork Kerry Tourism. 348 (bottom), Bertrand Collet/Shutterstock. 349 (top), Jonathan Hession/Tourism Ireland. 349 (bottom), nagelestock.com / Alamy. 353, ARCO / Ludaescher / age fotostock. 361, walshphotos/Shutterstock. 367, Michelle Nadal, Fodors.com member. 374, Justin James Wilson/Shutterstock. 381, David Mason/iStockphoto. 383, Patryk Kosmider/iStockphoto. **Chapter 7: County Cork:** 387, The Irish Image Colle / age fotostock. 388, Holger Leue/Tourism Ireland. 389, Andrew Bradley/Tourism Ireland. 390, walshphotos/Shutterstock. 393, Guilhem D./wikipedia.org. 394, mozzercork/Flickr. 396, John Woodworth/iStockphoto. 401, Richard Cummins / age fotostock. 404, RIEGER Bertrand / age fotostock. 410, IIC / age fotostock. 416-17, walshphotos/Shutterstock. 421 (top), Marco Cristofori/age fotostock. 421 (bottom), Gubbeen Farmhouse Products. 422-23 (all), Ballymaloe Cooking School. 424 (left), Belvelly Smoke House. 424 (right), Gubbeen Farmhouse Products. 425 (top left), John Minehan. 425 (bottom), Gubbeen Farmhouse Products. 425 (top right), Urru Culinary Store. 426 (left), RIEGER Bertrand / age fotostock. 426 (top right), Jaroslaw Grudzinski/Shutterstock. 426 (bottom left), Rick Senley / age fotostock. 432, IIC / age fotostock. 439, Christian Handl / age fotostock. **Chapter 8: County Clare, Galway, and the Aran Islands:** 441, IIC / age fotostock. 442, Alan Tobey/iStockphoto. 443 (bottom), Jonathan Hession/Tourism Ireland. 443 (top), Stephen Bonk/Shutterstock. 444, foodandwinephotography/iStockphoto. 450, boocal/Flickr. 456, Shannon Development/Tourism Ireland. 460-61, Patryk Kosmider/Shutterstock. 465, Nutan/Tourism Ireland. 477, rejflinger/Flickr. 484 (top left), Daniel P. Acevedo / age fotostock. 484 (bottom), The Irish Image Colle / age fotostock. 484 (bottom), Martin Bobrovsky / age fotostock. 485 (top), Andrew Fox / Alamy. 485 (bottom), Photodisc/Punchstock. 487, Chris Coe / age fotostock. 488, Jon Arnold/Agency Jon Arnold Images. 489, MATTES René / age fotostock. 490 (top left and top right), Photodisc/Punchstock. 490 (bottom left), Brand X Pictures/Punchstock. 490 (center right), ARCO / Krieger C / age fotostock. 490 (bottom right), Photodisc/Punchstock. 491 (top), Chris Coe / age fotostock. 491 (bottom), Kerry Garratt/Flickr. 498, Chris Hill/Tourism Ireland. **Chapter 9: Connemara and County Mayo:** 501, IIC / age fotostock. 502, Holger Leue/Tourism Ireland. 503, Kellie Diane Stewart/Shutterstock. 510, Ivica Drusany/Shutterstock. 511 (top), Holger Leue/Tourism Ireland. 511 (bottom), @ LaRsNoW @/Flickr. 512, James Fennell/Tourism Ireland. 514, Holger Leue/Tourism Ireland. 518, The Irish Image Colle / age fotostock. 520, Patryk Kosmider/Shutterstock. 523, Roger Kinkead/Tourism Ireland. 526-27, Holger Leue/Tourism Ireland. **Chapter 10: The Northwest:** 535, Holger Leue/Tourism Ireland. 536 (top left), Duby Tal/Tourism Ireland. 536 (bottom left), rejflinger/Flickr. 536 (top right), Chris Hill/Tourism Ireland. 536 (bottom right), Geray Sweeney/Tourism Ireland. 542, Chris Hill/Tourism Ireland. 547, Ken Welsh / age fotostock. 551, www.studioseventyseven.com. 553, Jonathan Hession/Tourism Ireland. 554 (bottom), Barry Lewis / Alamy. 554 (top), CLM/Shutterstock. 555 (top left), Cameron Swinton/Shutterstock. 555 (bottom left) Photography/Flickr. 555 (top right), June Marie Sobrito/Shutterstock. 555 (bottom right), Nicholas Mosse Pottery. 556 (left), Shannon Development. 556 (right), ideeone/iStockphoto. 560, IIC / age fotostock. 563, Marie Cloke/Shutterstock. 566, Holger Leue/Tourism Ireland. 568-69, The Irish Image Colle / age fotostock. **Chapter 11: Northern Ireland:** 573, Brian Morrison/Northern Ireland Tourist Board. 574 (top), Nutan/Tourism Ireland. 574 (bottom), Northern Ireland Tourist Board. 575, Tony Pleavin/Northern Ireland Tourist Board. 576, Brian Morrison/Tourism Ireland. 577, Brian Morrison/Northern Ireland Tourist Board. 582, Martin Bobrovsky / age fotostock. 583 (left), David Cordner/Northern Ireland Tourist Board. 583 (right), yvescosentino/Flickr. 584, Chris Hill/Tourism Ireland. 591, Geray Sweeney/Tourism Ireland. 597, giulio andreini / age fotostock. 599, Andy Barker / age fotostock. 603, Joe Fox / age fotostock. 609, Brian Morrison/Tourism Ireland. 615, IIC / age fotostock. 627, traveling, Fodors.com member. 628, Josemaria Toscano/Shutterstock. 632, Brian Kelly/iStockphoto. 643, Northern Ireland Tourist Board. 645, Geray Sweeney/Tourism Ireland. 648, Brian Morrison/Northern Ireland Tourist Board. 651 and 654, Tony Pleavin/Northern Ireland Tourist Board. **Chapter 12: The Best Irish Greens:** 659, The Irish Image Colle / age fotostock. 660, Chris Hill/Tourism Ireland.

NOTES

ABOUT OUR WRITERS

Paul Clements was born in County Tyrone and is based in Belfast where he is a writer and tutor. For 25 years he worked for BBC-TV and radio news as a journalist and assistant editor in Belfast and London. He now writes for a range of newspapers and magazines including the *Irish Times, Irish Examiner,* and *Escape* travel magazine. His writing is grounded in a passion for, and knowledge of, the Irish landscape, of the layers of history within it, and of the location of many of the best pubs—interests he found highly apropos when he began updating the Midlands, Northwest, and Northern Ireland chapters of this book (for this edition, he also wrote our new Close-Up box on the 2012 Titanic Anniversary commemorations in Belfast and our Cruising on the Shannon feature). In addition, Paul has written two travel books about Ireland: *Irish Shores, A Journey Round the Rim of Ireland*— based on a hitchhiking trip around the coast—and the best-selling *The Height of Nonsense: The Ultimate Irish Road Trip,* which tells the story of a quirky quest for the highest geographic point in each of Ireland's 32 counties. He has also written and edited two books on the famed travel writer Jan Morris. When he's not on the road, he tutors travel writing at Queen's University in Belfast and at the Irish Writers' Centre in Dublin.

Alannah Hopkin grew up in London but spent most of her childhood summers on her uncle's farm near Kinsale, where she learned two of the most important things in life: how to ride a horse and how to sail a boat. After graduate studies in Irish literature she worked as a writer in London, but ancestral voices were calling her home, and she spent more and more time in County Cork, where horses and boats were easier to find. After publishing her first novel, she made the big leap, and moved to Kinsale for a trial six months . . . and is still there 20 years later. Another novel was followed by a travel book about the places associated with St. Patrick, and an acclaimed guide to the pleasures of County Cork. She has written on travel and the arts for the *Sunday Times,* the *Guardian,* and the *Financial Times* in London, and contributes regularly to the *Irish Examiner* and the *Irish Times.* In 2008 she published *Eating Scenery: West Cork, the People and the Place* (The Collins Press, Cork), a travel book rich in humor and anecdote, focusing on the great social and economic changes that have taken place in the scenic southwest over the past 30 years. She has worked on *Fodor's Ireland* since 1985, and this year she updated our Southwest and Travel Smart chapters in addition to newly expanding and greatly rewriting three new chapters in the book: County Cork; County Clare, Galway, and the Aran Islands; and Connemara and County Mayo.

For our coverage of Dublin, Anto Howard has checked every fact, burnished every metaphor to the fine gleam of ancient brogues, and has so lovingly described the towns and villages found in the Dublin Environs and Southeast chapters that even their natives will leave for the pleasure of coming back (he also did the updating honors for the Irish Greens chapter). For this edition he also wrote our Great Outdoors, Dublin's Seafood Bounty, and Ireland's Historic Heart sections. Six post-graduate years of living in New York City recently convinced Anto of the charms of his native Ireland and he duly returned to take up residence in Dublin. He was written and edited books and articles about such far-flung places as Costa Rica, Las Vegas, and Russia, and has contributed to such publications as *National Geographic Traveler* and *Budget Travel.* Anto (christened Anthony— Dubliners have a habit of abbreviating perfectly good names) is also a playwright, and his shows have been produced in Dublin and in New York.